Volume II Chapters 12–25

Fundamental Accounting Principles

18 edition

John J. Wild
University of Wisconsin at Madison

Kermit D. Larson
University of Texas at Austin

Barbara Chiappetta
Nassau Community College

 McGraw-Hill Irwin

Boston   Burr Ridge, IL   Dubuque, IA   Madison, WI   New York
San Francisco   St. Louis   Bangkok   Bogotá   Caracas   Kuala Lumpur
Lisbon   London   Madrid   Mexico City   Milan   Montreal   New Delhi
Santiago   Seoul   Singapore   Sydney   Taipei   Toronto

To my wife **Gail** and children, **Kimberly, Jonathan, Stephanie,** and **Trevor.**
To my wife **Nancy.**
To my husband **Bob,** my sons **Michael** and **David,** and my **mother.**

McGraw-Hill
Irwin

FUNDAMENTAL ACCOUNTING PRINCIPLES
Published by McGraw-Hill/Irwin, a business unit of The McGraw-Hill Companies, Inc., 1221 Avenue of the Americas, New York, NY, 10020. Copyright © 2007 by The McGraw-Hill Companies, Inc. All rights reserved. No part of this publication may be reproduced or distributed in any form or by any means, or stored in a database or retrieval system, without the prior written consent of The McGraw-Hill Companies, Inc., including, but not limited to, in any network or other electronic storage or transmission, or broadcast for distance learning.

Some ancillaries, including electronic and print components, may not be available to customers outside the United States.

This book is printed on acid-free paper.

1 2 3 4 5 6 7 8 9 0 DOW/DOW 0 9 8 7 6

ISBN-13: 978-0-07-299653-1 (combined edition)
ISBN-10: 0-07-299653-6 (combined edition)
ISBN-13: 978-0-07-299656-2 (volume 1, chapters 1–12)
ISBN-10: 0-07-299656-0 (volume 1, chapters 1–12)
ISBN-13: 978-0-07-299655-5 (volume 2, chapters 12–25)
ISBN-10: 0-07-299655-2 (volume 2, chapters 12–25)
ISBN-13: 978-0-07-326631-2 (with working papers volume 1, chapters 1–12)
ISBN-10: 0-07-326631-0 (with working papers volume 1, chapters 1–12)
ISBN-13: 978-0-07-326632-9 (with working papers volume 2, chapters 12–25)
ISBN-10: 0-07-326632-9 (with working papers volume 2, chapters 12–25)
ISBN-13: 978-0-07-299654-8 (principles, chapters 1–17)
ISBN-10: 0-07-299654-4 (principles, chapters 1–17)

Editorial director: *Stewart Mattson*
Senior sponsoring editor: *Steve Schuetz*
Developmental editor I: *Kelly Odom*
Executive marketing manager: *Krista Bettino*
Senior media producer: *Elizabeth Mavetz*
Lead project manager: *Lori Koetters*
Lead production supervisor: *Michael R. McCormick*
Lead designer: *Matthew Baldwin*
Photo research coordinator: *Kathy Shive*

Photo researcher: *Sarah Evertson*
Lead media project manager: *Becky Szura*
Cover design: *Matthew Baldwin*
Interior design: *Kay Fulton*
Cover image: © *Corbis Images*
Typeface: *10.5/12 Times Roman*
Compositor: *Techbooks*
Printer: *R. R. Donnelley*

The Library of Congress has cataloged the one-volume edition as follows
Wild, John J.
    Fundamental accounting principles / John J. Wild, Kermit D. Larson, Barbara Chiappetta.—18th ed.
      p. cm.
    Kermit D. Larson's name appears first on the 17th edition.
    Includes index.
    ISBN-13: 978-0-07-299653-1 (alk. paper)
    ISBN-10: 0-07-299653-6 (alk. paper)
    1. Accounting. I. Larson, Kermit D. II. Chiappetta, Barbara. III. Title.
HF5635.P975 2007
657—dc22
                2006041956

www.mhhe.com

Clear. Concise. Cutting Edge.

Dear Colleagues/Friends,

As we roll out the 18th edition of *Fundamental Accounting Principles*, we wish to thank each of you who adopted the prior edition. As teachers, we appreciate the importance of selecting the best textbook. We are humbled that you have helped make our book the fastest growing accounting principles textbook on the market—with the number of users growing by 45% over the past two editions. Our publisher, McGraw-Hill/Irwin, recognized this remarkable growth by selecting this book for its "Outstanding Revision of the Year" award.

Our goal in this edition is to further that success. In the past couple years, we again listened closely to you, to our own students, and to our colleagues across the country. As a result, this edition addresses the needs of you and your students better than any previous edition. Above all, we enhanced aspects of the book that contribute to its current success: cutting-edge technology, engaging and accurate content, and clear and concise writing.

Instructors and students tell us this edition's technology package caters to different learning styles and helps students better learn accounting. For example, Homework Manager Plus offers new features to enhance student learning and assist instructor grading. iPod Content lets students study on the go, and the new Algorithmic Test Bank provides an infinite number of exam problems. We believe you and your students will find these technology learning tools both easy to use and highly valuable.

We owe a huge debt of gratitude to the hundreds of colleagues like you who took time to discuss with us the needs of today's instructors and students. We feel fortunate to witness our profession's extraordinary devotion to teaching and helping students learn accounting. Your feedback and suggestions are reflected in everything we write. Please accept our heartfelt thanks for your dedication in helping today's students understand and appreciate accounting.

With kindest regards,

John J. Wild   *Kermit D. Larson*   *Barbara Chiappetta*

Fundamental Accounting Principles is #1

For the second consecutive edition, *Fundamental Accounting Principles* rates #1 in both Instructor and Student satisfaction. Both independent research and development reviews confirm that *Fundamental Accounting Principles* is #1 in the following categories…

#1 in Accuracy

#1 in Readability

#1 in Organization

#1 in Topic Coverage

#1 in Problems and Exercises

#1 in Instructor Supplements

#1 in Overall Textbook Satisfaction

With ratings such as these, it is no surprise that *Fundamental Accounting Principles* is the fastest growing textbook in the accounting principles market.

Take a **look at what instructors are saying** about *Fundamental Accounting Principles*.

Linda Mallory, Central Virginia Community College
"This is an excellent book and one of the best on the market. The topical coverage and the sequence of coverage surpass anything on the market."

Patricia Walczak, Lansing Community College
"Better coverage of the accounting cycle (Chapters 1-4) and the quality of the quick study exercises and exercises at the end of the chapter."

Shirly Kleiner, Johnson County Community College
"Well-written, organized, and covers the main concepts necessary for fundamental accounting courses."

Lynette Yerbury, Salt Lake Community College
"Readable, readable, readable! I love the book. It's easy to read. There are tons of homework problems available."

Larry Swisher, Muskegon Community College
"A good textbook with good homework assignments and supplements backed by an organization that really cares about what instructors want in a textbook."

Janice Stoudemire, Midlands Technical College
"I am impressed with the overall clarity of the managerial chapters. Not only is the readability excellent, but also the authors have an ability to clearly explain both the simple and complex concepts. These chapters are excellent- far better than my current textbook."

Janet Adeyiga, Hampton University
"Demonstration Problems and application to real life cases and problems included in each chapter."

John J. Wild is a professor of accounting and the Robert and Monica Beyer Distinguished Professor at the University of Wisconsin at Madison. He previously held appointments at Michigan State University and the University of Manchester in England. He received his BBA, MS, and PhD from the University of Wisconsin.

Professor Wild teaches accounting courses at both the undergraduate and graduate levels. He has received the Mabel W. Chipman Excellence-in-Teaching Award, the departmental Excellence-in-Teaching Award, and the Teaching Excellence Award from the 2003 and 2005 business graduates at the University of Wisconsin. He also received the Beta Alpha Psi and Roland F. Salmonson Excellence-in-Teaching Award from Michigan State University. Professor Wild is a past KPMG Peat Marwick National Fellow and is a recipient of fellowships from the American Accounting Association and the Ernst and Young Foundation.

Professor Wild is an active member of the American Accounting Association and its sections. He has served on several committees of these organizations, including the Outstanding Accounting Educator Award, Wildman Award, National Program Advisory, Publications, and Research Committees. Professor Wild is author of *Financial Accounting* and *Financial Statement Analysis*, both published by McGraw-Hill/Irwin. His research appears in The Accounting Review, Journal of Accounting Research, Journal of Accounting and Economics, Contemporary Accounting Research, Journal of Accounting, Auditing and Finance, Journal of Accounting and Public Policy, and other journals. He is past associate editor of Contemporary Accounting Research and has served on several editorial boards including The Accounting Review.

Professor Wild, his wife, and four children enjoy travel, music, sports, and community activities.

Kermit D. Larson is the Arthur Andersen & Co. Alumni Professor of Accounting Emeritus at the University of Texas at Austin. He served as chairman of the University of Texas Department of Accounting and was visiting professor at Tulane University. His scholarly articles have been published in a variety of journals, including The Accounting Review, Journal of Accountancy, and Abacus. He is the author of several books, including *Financial Accounting* and *Fundamentals of Financial and Managerial Accounting*, both published by McGraw-Hill/Irwin.

Professor Larson is a member of the American Accounting Association, the Texas Society of CPAs, and the American Institute of CPAs. His positions with the AAA have included vice president, southwest regional vice president, and chairperson of several committees, including the Committee of Concepts and Standards. He was a member of the committee that planned the first AAA doctoral consortium and served as its director.

Professor Larson served as president of the Richard D. Irwin Foundation. He also served on the Accounting Accreditation Committee and on the Accounting Standards Committee of the AACSB. He was a member of the Constitutional Drafting Committee of the Federation of Schools of Accountancy and a member of the Commission on Professional Accounting Education. He has been an expert witness on cases involving mergers, antitrust litigation, consolidation criteria, franchise taxes, and expropriation of assets by foreign governments. Professor Larson served on the Board of Directors and Executive Committee of Tekcon, Inc., and on the National Accountants Advisory Board of Safe-Guard Business Systems. In his leisure time, he enjoys skiing and is an avid sailor and golfer.

Barbara Chiappetta received her BBA in Accountancy and MS in Education from Hofstra University and is a tenured full professor at Nassau Community College. For the past 17 years, she has been an active executive board member of the Teachers of Accounting at Two-Year Colleges (TACTYC), serving 10 years as vice president and as president from 1993 through 1999. As an active member of the American Accounting Association, she has served on the Northeast Regional Steering Committee, chaired the Curriculum Revision Committee of the Two-Year Section, and participated in numerous national committees.

In 1998, Professor Chiappetta was inducted into the American Accounting Association Hall of Fame for the Northeast Region. She received the Nassau Community College dean of instruction's Faculty Distinguished Achievement Award in 1995. Professor Chiappetta was honored with the State University of New York Chancellor's Award for Teaching Excellence in 1997. As a confirmed believer in the benefits of the active learning pedagogy, Professor Chiappetta has authored *Student Learning Tools*, an active learning workbook for a first-year accounting course, published by McGraw-Hill/Irwin.

In her leisure time, Professor Chiappetta enjoys tennis and participates on a U.S.T.A. team. She also enjoys the challenge of bridge. Her husband, Robert, is an entrepreneur in the leisure sport industry. She has two sons—Michael, a lawyer, specializing in intellectual property law in New York, and David, a composer, pursuing a career in music for film in Los Angeles.

Give your students an Edge!

Fundamental Accounting Principles 18e

Help your students ride the wave of Success by giving them the Edge they need to succeed in today's accounting principles course.

Fundamental Accounting Principles (FAP) has helped a generation of students succeed by **giving them an edge** with leading-edge accounting content that engages students, and with state-of-the-art technology.

One of the greatest challenges students confront in a principles course is seeing the relevance of materials. *FAP* tackles this issue head on with **engaging content** and a **motivating style**. Students are motivated when reading materials that are **clear and relevant**. *FAP* stands apart in engaging students. Its chapter-opening vignettes showcase dynamic, successful, entrepreneurial individuals and companies guaranteed to **interest and excite readers**. This edition's featured companies—Best Buy, Circuit City, and Apple—engage students with their annual reports, which are great vehicles for **learning** financial statements. Further, this book's coverage of the accounting cycle fundamentals is widely praised for its **clarity and effectiveness**.

FAP also delivers **cutting-edge technology** to help students succeed. **Homework Manager** provides students with instant grading and feedback for assignments that are completed online. **Homework Manager Plus** integrates an online version of the textbook with our popular Homework Manager system and provides unlimited access to an Online Tutor. A new **Algorithmic Test Bank** in Homework Manager offers infinite variations of numerical test bank questions. *FAP* is also the first book to offer accounting students portable **iPod-ready content**.

We're confident you'll agree that *FAP* **gives your students the edge to succeed**.

Cutting-Edge Content

FAP content continues to set the standard in the principles market. Take a look at Chapter 1 and you'll see how *FAP* leads the market with the best coverage of the accounting cycle. We are the first book to cover equity transactions the way most instructors teach it and students learn it—by introducing the separate equity accounts upfront and not waiting until a chapter or two later. *FAP* also motivates students with engaging chapter openers. Students identify with them and can even picture themselves as future entrepreneurs. Also, each book includes the financial statements of Circuit City, Best Buy, and Apple to further engage students.

Cutting-Edge Technology

FAP offers the most advanced and comprehensive technology on the market in a seamless, easy-to-use platform. As students learn in different ways, *FAP* provides a technology smorgasbord that helps students learn more effectively and efficiently. Homework Manager, eBook options, iPod content, and Topic Tackler are some of the options available. Homework Manager Plus takes learning to another level by integrating an online version of the textbook with all the power of Homework Manager and our online NetTutor service. Technology offerings include the following:

- Homework Manager
- Homework Manager Plus
- iPod content
- Algorithmic Test Bank
- Online Learning Center

- Topic Tackler
- Carol Yacht's General Ledger and Peachtree Complete
- ALEKS for the Accounting Cycle
- ALEKS for Financial Accounting

Cutting-Edge Support

McGraw-Hill/Irwin has mobilized a new force of product specialists committed to training and supporting the technology we offer. Our commitment to instructor service and support is top notch and leads the industry. Our new "McGraw-Hill Cares" program provides you with the fastest answers to your questions or solutions to your training needs. Ask your McGraw-Hill sales rep about our Key Media Support Plan and the McGraw-Hill Cares Program.

Through current and motivating content, cutting-edge technology, and committed service and support programs... *FAP* provides you and your students the edge to succeed in today's principles course.

What Can McGraw-Hill Technology Offer You?

Whether you are just getting started with technology in your course, or you are ready to embrace the latest advances in electronic content delivery and course management, McGraw-Hill/Irwin has the technology you need, and provides training and support that will help you every step of the way.

Our most popular technologies, Homework Manager and Homework Manager Plus, are optional online Homework Management systems that will allow you to assign problems and exercises from the text for your students to work out in an online format. Student results are automatically graded, and the students receive instant feedback on their work. Homework Manager Plus adds an online version of the text and an online tutorial service called NetTutor for direct access while completing homework within Homework Manager.

Students can also use the Online Learning Center associated with this text on their own to enhance their knowledge of accounting. Plus we now offer iPod content for students who want to study on the go with their iPod.

For instructors, we provide all of the crucial instructor supplements on one easy to use Instructor CD-ROM; we can help build a custom class Website for your course using PageOut; we can deliver a fully developed online course for you to conduct through Blackboard, WebCT, or eCollege; and we have a technical support team that will provide training and support for our key technology products.

How Can Students Study on the Go Using Their iPod?

iPod Content
Harness the power of one of the most popular technology tools students use today–the Apple iPod. Our innovative approach allows students to download audio and video presentations right into their iPod and take learning materials with them wherever they go. It makes review and study time as easy as putting in headphones. Visit the *FAP* Online Learning Center (www.mhhe.com/wildFAP18e) to learn more details on available iPod content–and enhance your learning experience today.

How Can My Students Use the Web to Complete Their Homework?

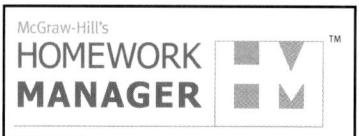

McGraw-Hill's Homework Manager
is a Web-based supplement that duplicates problem structures directly from the end-of-chapter material in your textbook, using algorithms to provide a limitless supply of online self-graded assignments that can be used for student practice, homework, or testing. Each assignment has a unique solution. Say goodbye to cheating in your classroom; say hello to the power and flexibility you've been waiting for in creating assignments. All Quick Studies, Exercises, and Problems are available with Homework Manager.

McGraw-Hill's Homework Manager is also a useful grading tool. All assignments can be delivered over the Web and are graded automatically, with the results stored in your private grade book. Detailed results let you see at a glance how each student does on an assignment or an individual problem—you can even see how many tries it took them to solve it.

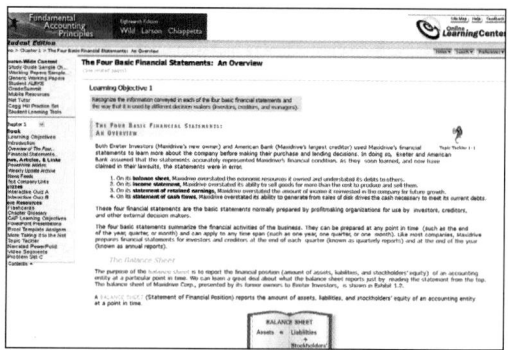

Jim Shelton, Freed-Hardeman University
"Homework Manager is working out really well, and I believe it is significantly contributing to increased performance on exams."

Homework Manager Plus
is an extension of McGraw-Hill's popular Homework Manager System. With Homework Manager Plus you get all of the power of Homework Manager plus an integrated online version of the text, and unlimited access to our NetTutor service. Students simply receive one single access code which provides access to all of the resources available through Homework Manager Plus.

Paula Ratliff, Arkansas State University
"I like the idea that there are online assignments that change algorithmically so that students can practice with them."

When students find themselves needing to reference the textbook in order to complete their homework, now they can simply click on hints and link directly to the most relevant materials associated with the problem or exercise they are working on. If they cannot figure out the problem from referencing the online version of the text, then they can link over to access the NetTutor service. Through NetTutor the student can chat with a live tutor who can provide help and advice towards completing their homework.

How Can Busy Students Get Text-Specific Help at Their Convenience?

NetTutor™

Many students work or have other commitments outside of class, making it difficult for them to get help with their questions during regular school hours. NetTutor is a breakthrough program that connects your students with qualified tutors online so they can get help at their convenience.

Students can communicate with tutors in a variety of ways:

- The Live Tutor Center, where students can view tutor-created spreadsheets, T-accounts, and instant responses to their questions.
- The Q&A Center, which allows students to submit questions anytime and receive answers within 24 hours.
- The Archive Center that lets students browse for answers to previously asked questions. They can also search for questions pertinent to a particular topic.

With Homework Manager Plus, students receive unlimited access to NetTutor for the length of the course. Otherwise, you can package a NetTutor Access Card with your text.

How Can Text-Related Web Resources Enhance My Course?

Online Learning Center (OLC)

We offer an Online Learning Center (OLC) that follows *Fundamental Accounting Principles* chapter by chapter. It doesn't require any building or maintenance on your part. It's ready to go the moment you and your students type in the URL: www.mhhe.com/wildFAP18e.

As students study and learn from *Fundamental Accounting Principles*, they can visit the Student Edition of the OLC Website to work with a multitude of helpful tools:

- Generic Template Working Papers
- Cogg Hill Practice Set
- Chapter Learning Objectives
- Chapter Glossaries
- Key Term Flashcards
- Interactive Chapter Quizzes A & B
- PowerPoint® Presentations
- Narrated PowerPoint® Presentations

- Topic Tackler Plus Tutorial
- Video Segments
- Excel Template Assignments
- Animated Demonstration Problems
- Problem Set C
- More Taking It To The Net Exercises
- *BusinessWeek* articles
- NetTutor

A secured Instructor Edition stores essential course materials to save you prep time before class. Everything you need to run a lively classroom and an efficient course is included. All resources available to students, plus . . .

- Sample Syllabi
- Transition Notes
- Cogg Hill Practice Set Solutions Manual
- General Ledger and Peachtree Solution Files
- Instructor's Manual

- Solutions Manual
- Solutions to Excel Template Assignments
- Solutions to Problem Set C
- Solutions to More Taking It To The Net Exercises

The OLC Website also serves as a doorway to other technology solutions, like course management systems.

Try One of Our New e-Books Options!

For budget-conscious students, every dollar makes a difference. That's why we offer FAP in two convenient, cost-effective digital formats.

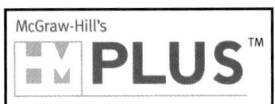

McGraw-Hill's Homework Manager Plus

If you use Homework Manager in your course, your students can purchase McGraw-Hill's Homework Manager Plus for *FAP* 18e. Homework Manager Plus gives students direct access to an online edition of the text while working assignments within Homework Manager. If you get stuck working a problem, simply click the "Hint" link and jump directly to relevant content in the online edition of the text.

Visit the Online Learning Center at www.mhhe.com/wildFAP18e to purchase McGraw-Hill's Homework Manager Plus.

Zinio Digital Edition

A leader in digital media, Zinio offers students using *Fundamental Accounting Principles* 18e the full benefit of its powerful, flexible digital reading system. Using the Zinio reader, you can search your digital textbook, highlight important passages, or jot down electronic notes. Navigating a textbook has never been easier. You can even print pages to study from off line.

To order your Zinio Digital Edition of *Fundamental Accounting Principles* 18e visit www.textbooks.zinio.com.

With either option you choose you'll be blown away by what you can do and how much you'll save.

Roy Carson, Anne Arundel Community College

"I am certain I will make good use of the (Zinio) e-Book, and I suspect students will like it."

McGraw-Hill/Irwin CARES

At McGraw-Hill/Irwin, we understand that getting the most from new technology can be challenging. That's why our services don't stop after you purchase our product. Each professor will receive a customer McGraw-Hill Cares support card that is your complete guide to McGraw-Hill/Irwin technology product support. You can e-mail our Product Specialists 24 hours a day, get product training online, or search our knowledge bank of Frequently Asked Questions on our support Website.

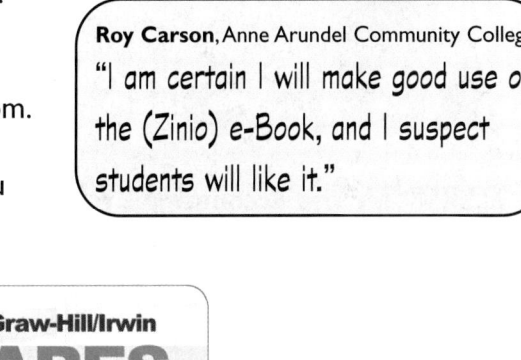

McGraw-Hill/Irwin Customer Care Contact Information

For all Customer Support call **(800) 331-5094**,
Email **hmsupport@mcgraw-hill.com**,
or visit **www.mhhe.com/support**.
One of our Technical Support Analysts will be able to assist you in a timely fashion.

Scott Barhight, Northampton Community College

"McGraw-Hill gives some of the best customer support, including personal support from John Wild the author of the text."

How Can I Make My Classroom Discussions More Interactive?

CPS Classroom Performance System

This is a revolutionary system that brings ultimate interactivity to the classroom. CPS is a wireless response system that gives you immediate feedback from every student in the class. CPS units include easy-to-use software for creating and delivering questions and assessments to your class. With CPS you can ask subjective and objective questions. Then every student simply responds with their individual, wireless response pad, providing instant results. CPS is the perfect tool for engaging students while gathering important assessment data.

eInstruction

> **Janice Stoudemire**, Midlands Technical College
>
> "The supplemental material that this principles accounting text provides is impressive: homework manager, the extensive online learning center, general ledger application software, the topic tackler, net tutor, as well as ALEKS."

How Can McGraw-Hill Help Me Teach My Course Online?

ALEKS®

ALEKS® for the Accounting Cycle and ALEKS® for Financial Accounting

Available from McGraw-Hill over the World Wide Web, ALEKS (Assessment and LEarning in Knowledge Spaces) provides precise assessment and individualized instruction in the fundamental skills your students need to succeed in accounting.

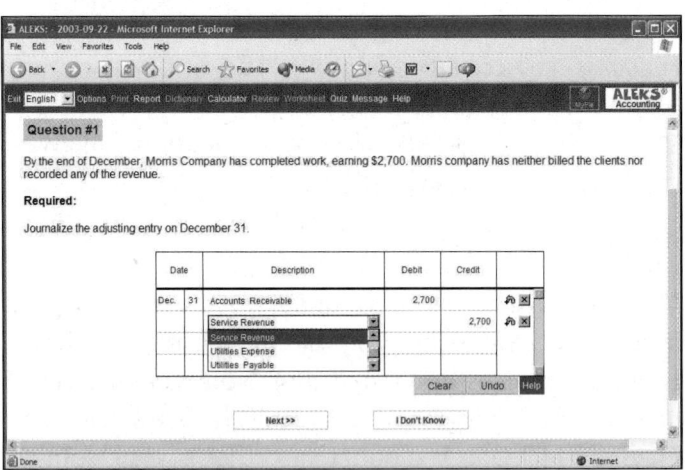

ALEKS motivates your students because ALEKS can tell what a student knows, doesn't know, and is most ready to learn next. ALEKS does this using the ALEKS Assessment and Knowledge Space Theory as an artificial intelligence engine to exactly identify a student's knowledge of accounting. When students focus on precisely what they are ready to learn, they build the confidence and learning momentum that fuel success.

To learn more about adding ALEKS to your principles course, visit www.business.aleks.com.

> **Liz Ott**, Casper College
>
> "I originally adopted the book because of the tools that accompanied it: Homework Manager, ALEKS, CPS."

Online Course Management

No matter what online course management system you use (WebCT, BlackBoard, or eCollege), we have a course content ePack available for *FAP* 18e. Our new ePacks are specifically designed to make it easy for students to navigate and access content online. They are easier than ever to install on the latest version of the course management system available today.

Don't forget that you can count on the highest level of service from McGraw-Hill. Our online course management specialists are ready to assist you with your online course needs. They provide training and will answer any questions you have throughout the life of your adoption. So try our new ePack for *FAP* 18e and make online course content delivery easy and fun.

PageOut: McGraw-Hill's Course Management System

PageOut is the easiest way to create a Website for your accounting course. There is no need for HTML coding, graphic design, or a thick how-to book. Just fill in a series of boxes with simple English and click on one of our professional designs. In no time, your course is online with a Website that contains your syllabus!

Should you need assistance in preparing your Website, we can help. Our team of product specialists is ready to take your course materials and build a custom Website to your specifications. You simply need to call a McGraw-Hill/Irwin PageOut specialist to start the process. To learn more, please visit www.pageout.net and see "PageOut & Service" below.

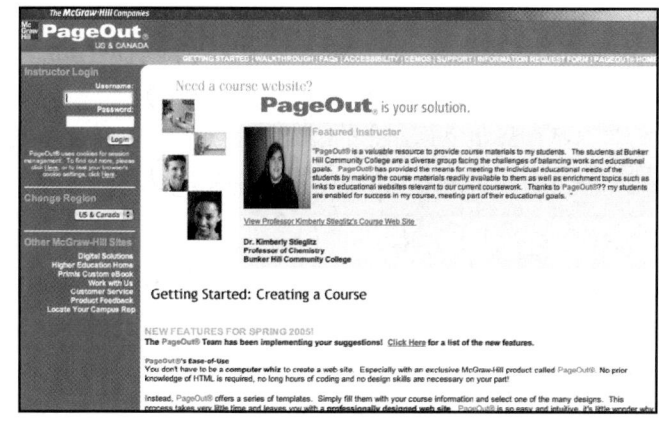

Best of all, PageOut is free when you adopt *Fundamental Accounting Principles*!

PageOut Service

Our team of product specialists is happy to help you design your own course Website. Just call 1-800-634-3963, press 0, and ask to speak with a PageOut specialist. You will be asked to send in your course materials and then participate in a brief telephone consultation. Once we have your information, we build your Website for you, from scratch.

What tools bring Accounting to life

Decision Center

Whether we prepare, analyze, or apply accounting information, one skill remains essential: decision-making. To help develop good decision-making habits and to illustrate the relevance of accounting, *Fundamental Accounting Principles* 18e uses a unique pedagogical framework called the Decision Center. This framework is comprised of a variety of approaches and subject areas, giving students insight into every aspect of business decision-making. Answers to Decision Maker and Ethics boxes are at the end of each chapter.

"This text has the best introductions of any text that I have reviewed or used. Some texts simply summarize the chapter, which is boring to students. Research indicates that material needs to be written in an 'engaging manner.' That's what these vignettes do—they get the students interested."
Clarice McCoy, Brookhaven College

CAP Model

The Conceptual/Analytical/Procedural (CAP) Model allows courses to be specially designed to meet your teaching needs or those of a diverse faculty. This model identifies learning objectives, textual materials, assignments, and test items by C, A, or P, allowing different instructors to teach from the same materials, yet easily customize their courses toward a conceptual, analytical, or procedural approach (or a combination thereof) based on personal preferences.

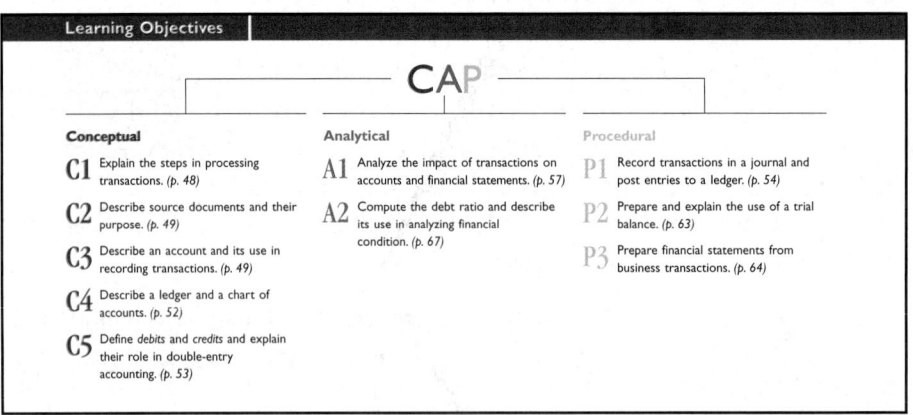

and engage your students?

XV

Chapter Preview with Flow Chart

This feature provides a handy textual/visual guide at the start of every chapter. Students can now begin their reading with a clear understanding of what they will learn and when, allowing them to stay more focused and organized along the way.

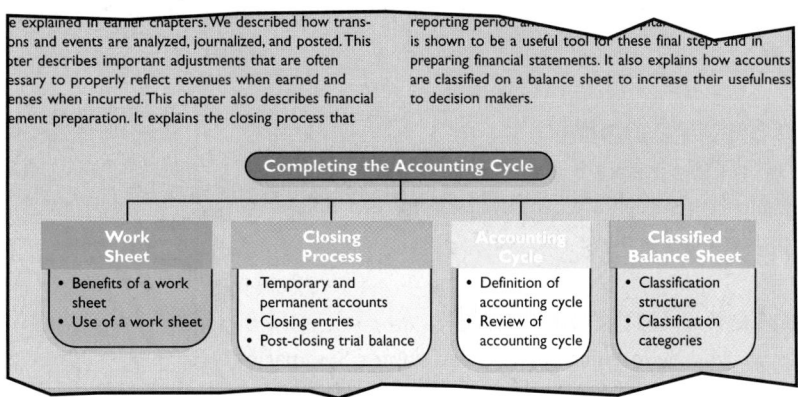

...e explained in earlier chapters. We described how trans-...ons and events are analyzed, journalized, and posted. This ...ter describes important adjustments that are often ...essary to properly reflect revenues when earned and ...enses when incurred. This chapter also describes financial ...ement preparation. It explains the closing process that

reporting period ... is shown to be a useful tool for these final steps and in preparing financial statements. It also explains how accounts are classified on a balance sheet to increase their usefulness to decision makers.

Completing the Accounting Cycle

Work Sheet	Closing Process	Accounting Cycle	Classified Balance Sheet
• Benefits of a work sheet • Use of a work sheet	• Temporary and permanent accounts • Closing entries • Post-closing trial balance	• Definition of accounting cycle • Review of accounting cycle	• Classification structure • Classification categories

Quick Check

These short question/answer features reinforce the material immediately preceding them. They allow the reader to pause and reflect on the topics described, then receive immediate feedback before going on to new topics. Answers are provided at the end of each chapter.

Quick Check   Answers—p. 112

1. Describe a company's annual reporting period.
2. Why do companies prepare interim financial statements?
3. What two accounting principles most directly drive the adjusting process?
4. Is cash basis accounting consistent with the matching principle? Why or why not?
5. If your company pays a $4,800 premium on April 1, 2007, for two years' insurance coverage, how much insurance expense is reported in 2008 using cash basis accounting?

> "(This book is) visually friendly with many illustrations. Good balance sheet presentation in margin."
>
> **Joan Cook,** Milwaukee Area Technical College

Marginal Student Annotations

These annotations provide students with additional hints, tips, and examples to help them more fully understand the concepts and retain what they have learned. The annotations also include notes on global implications of accounting and further examples.

...luding depreciation) and unearned rev-...ceived *before* a related expense or rev-...use the recognition of an expense (or ...or received). The right side of this ex-...hich reflect transactions when cash is ...cognized. Adjusting entries are neces-..., and liabilities are correctly reported. ...cts one or more income statement ac-...t the Cash account).

Point: Adjusting is a 3-step process: (1) Determine current account balance, (2) Determine what current account balance should be, and (3) Record entry to get from step 1 to step 2.

FastForward

FastForward is a case that takes students through the Accounting Cycle, chapters 1-4. The FastForward icon is placed in the margin whenever this case is discussed.

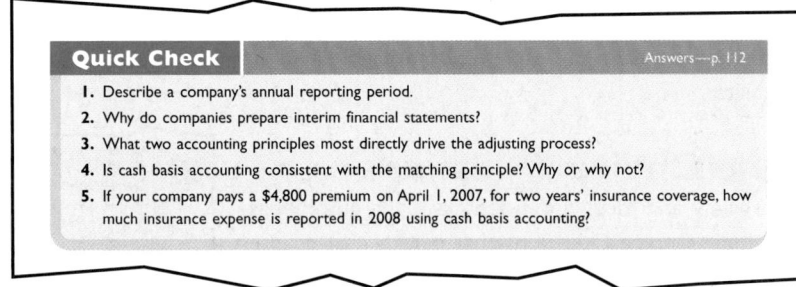

...huck Taylor invests $30,000 cash in FastForward.

Assets	=	Liabilities	+	Equity
Cash				**C. Taylor, Capital**
+30,000	=	0	+	30,000

(1)	Cash	101	30,000	
	C. Taylor, Capital	301		30,000

How are chapter concepts

Once a student has finished reading the chapter, how well he or she retains the material can depend greatly on the questions, exercises, and problems that reinforce it. This book leads the way in comprehensive, accurate end-of-chapter assignments.

Demonstration Problems
present both a problem and a complete solution, allowing students to review the entire problem-solving process and achieve success.

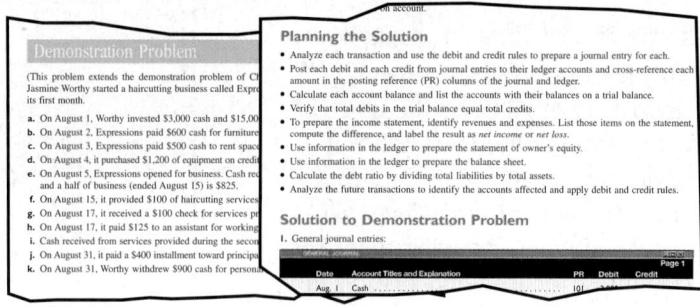

Chapter Summaries
provide students with a review organized by learning objectives. Chapter Summaries are a component of the CAP model (see page xiv), which recaps each conceptual, analytical, and procedural objective.

Key Terms
are bolded in the text and repeated at the end of the chapter with page numbers indicating their location. The book also includes a complete Glossary of Key Terms. Key Terms are also available as online flash cards at the book's Website.

Multiple Choice Questions
In response to review and focus group feedback, the author has created Multiple Choice Questions that quickly test chapter knowledge before a student moves on to complete Quick Studies, Exercises, and Problems.

Quick Study
assignments are short exercises that often focus on one learning objective. All are included in Homework Manager. There are usually 8-10 Quick Study assignments per chapter.

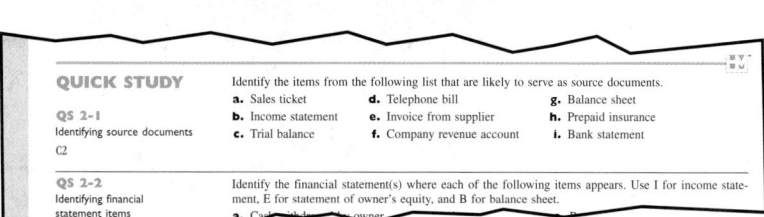

Exercises
are one of this book's many strengths and a competitive advantage. There are about 10-15 per chapter and all are included in Homework Manager.

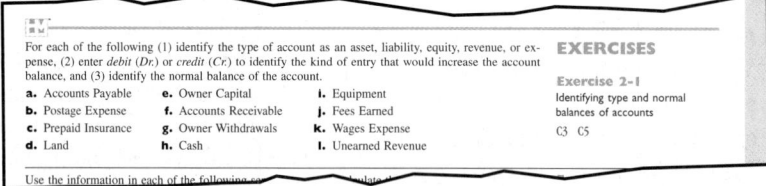

Problem Sets A & B
are proven problems that can be assigned as homework or for in-class projects. Problem Set C is available on the book's Website. All problems are coded according to the CAP model (see page xiv), and all are included in Homework Manager.

"One of the best features in FAP is the Serial Problem. I find the continuation of a company from a service to a merchandiser, to a manufacturing, and from a sole proprietorship form or business to a corporation, provides the student a real picture of a company's development. It also provides a consistency from one lesson to another."

Barbara Marotta, Northern Virginia Community College, Woodbridge

Beyond the Numbers

Beyond the Numbers exercises ask students to use accounting figures and understand their meaning. Students also learn how accounting applies to a variety of business situations. These creative and fun exercises are all new or updated, and are divided into 10 sections:

- Reporting in Action
- Comparative Analysis
- Ethics Challenge
- Communicating in Practice
- Taking It To The Net
- Teamwork in Action
- Hitting the Road
- *BusinessWeek* Activity
- Entrepreneurial Decision
- Global Decision

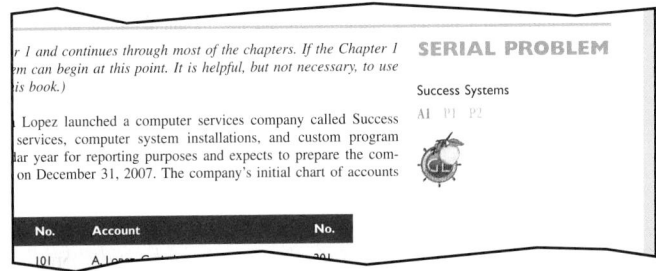

Serial Problems

Serial Problems use a continuous running case study to illustrate chapter concepts in a familiar context. Serial Problems can be followed continuously from the first chapter or picked up at any later point in the book; enough information is provided to ensure students can get right to work.

> "The best feature of this book is the use of real (financial) information in the Beyond the Numbers section. This is something that I do on my own, which can be very time consuming. I also like the Entrepreneurial questions, which are not even addressed in most textbooks."
>
> **Cindy Navaroli,** Chaffey Community College

The End of the Chapter Is Only the Beginning

Our valuable and proven assignments aren't just confined to the book. From problems that require technological solutions to materials found exclusively online, this book's end-of-chapter material is fully integrated with its technology package.

- Quick Studies, Exercises, and Problems available on Homework Manager (see page ix) are marked with an icon.

- Problems supported by the General Ledger Application Software or Peachtree are marked with an icon.

- The Online Learning Center (OLC) includes more Taking It To The Net exercises, Personal Interactive Quizzes, Excel template assignments, and Problem Set C.

mhhe.com/wildFAP18e

- Problems supported with Microsoft Excel template assignments are marked with an icon.

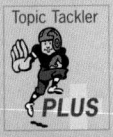

- Material that receives additional coverage (slide shows, videos, audio, etc.) in Topic Tackler is marked with an icon.

Put Away Your Red Pen

We pride ourselves on the accuracy of this book's assignment materials. Independent research reports that instructors and reviewers point to the accuracy of this book's assignment materials as one of its key competitive advantages.

The authors extend a special thanks to accuracy checkers Barbara Schnathorst, The Write Solution, Inc.; Helen Roybark, Radford University; Beth Woods, CPA, Accuracy Counts; Alice Sineath, Forsyth Technical Community College; Teressa Farough, CPA, and Marilyn Sagrillo, University of Wisconsin - Green Bay.

Content Changes for FAP 18e

FAP's revisions are in response to feedback from both instructors and students. Many of these revisions are summarized below. Feedback suggests that *FAP* is the book instructors want to teach from and students want to learn from. Some overall revisions include:

- New multiple choice questions at each chapter-end
- Revised assignments throughout
- New chapter-opening layout
- Updated ratio analyses
- New and revised entrepreneurial elements
- New assignments using chapter openers

- Revised serial problem running through nearly all chapters
- New Circuit City annual report with comparisons to Best Buy, Dixons (UK), and the industry–including new assignments
- New Apple financial statements and assignments

Chapter 1

LoveSac NEW opener with new entrepreneurial assignment

Revised, early introduction to financial statements

Enhanced transaction analysis using expanded accounting equation

New material on frauds such as Tyco and WorldCom

Revised illustration and assignments on ethical decisions

New insight on principles-based accounting

New evidence on small businesses

Enhanced materials on Sarbanes-Oxley

New multiple choice questions

Chapter 2

Cake Love NEW opener with new entrepreneurial assignment

Enhanced introduction to asset accounts

Streamlined introduction to double-entry accounting

New color layout for transaction analysis

New insight on women entrepreneurs

Revised insight on unearned revenues

New insight on manager pay under Sarbanes-Oxley

Chapter 3

Alienware NEW opener with new entrepreneurial assignment

New graphics for prepaid expenses

New graphic for unearned revenues

New insight on gift card sales as unearned revenues

New illustration of accrued revenues

Revised exhibit on accounting adjustments

Enhanced assignments for adjusting entries and ethics

Chapter 4

Betty Rides NEW opener with new entrepreneurial assignment

Streamlined exhibit for closing entries

New assignment on aggressive estimates

Streamlined discussion of work sheet

New visual from closing entries to accounts

Chapter 5

CoCaLo NEW opener with new entrepreneurial assignment

Enhanced illustration on operating cycle

Revised exhibit on merchandisers' closing entries

Streamlined multi-step income statement

Merchandiser work sheet in appendix

Chapter 6

Surf Diva NEW opener with new entrepreneurial assignment

Improved exhibit on cost flow assumptions

Updated exhibit on inventory methods

Enhanced illustration on lower of cost or market

Revised serial problem to add LCM

Chapter 7

Ring Masters NEW opener with new entrepreneurial assignment

Enhanced diagrams on special journals and ledgers

New assignments on identifying the special journal of entry

Updated enterprise resource planning (ERP)

New insights on Internet frauds and controls

Chapter 8

Raising Cane's Chicken Fingers NEW opener with new entrepreneurial assignment

New material on e-commerce, its risks, its controls, and identity theft

New insight on credit card fraud

New illustration on "Hacker" risks

New diagram on controls for over-the-counter cash receipts

Updated data on Internet frauds

New information on check fraud

New data on fees for bank services

Chapter 9

Linditas' NEW opener with new entrepreneurial assignment

New explanation of credit and debit cards

Simplified estimation of uncollectibles

New data on PayPal and credit card growth

Enhanced exhibit on aging of receivables

New data on bad debt percentages

Enhanced exhibit on computing maturity date

Chapter 10

Fairytale Brownies NEW opener with new entrepreneurial assignment

Revised exhibit on plant asset disposals

Updated data on depreciation methods used

Moved plant asset exchanges to appendix

Updated book for new standard on asset exchanges

New assignments on asset disposals, goodwill, and intangibles

Chapter 11

Wildflower Linen NEW opener with new entrepreneurial assignment

New insight on gift card liabilities

Updated IRS tax forms

Updated IRS withholding table

New insight on guaranteed salary liabilities

New insight on extended-warranty contracts

Applied 2006 payroll tax rates throughout

New diagram for contingent liabilities

Chapter 12

Rookie Skateboards NEW opener with new entrepreneurial assignment

Enhanced explanation and accounting for limited liability companies

New assignment on limited partnerships

New insight on Broadway partnerships

Chapter 13

Medsite NEW opener with new entrepreneurial assignment

Enhanced graphic on equity composition

'Paid-in capital' used in lieu of 'contributed capital'

Moved section on dividends before preferred stock

Streamlined computation of weighted-average shares

Updated and streamlined stock options

New assignments on stock, EPS, and ethics

Moved discontinued and extraordinary items to Chapter 17

Chapter 14

Melton Franchise Systems NEW opener with new entrepreneurial assignment

Enhanced exhibit on bond interest computation and entry

Moved debt features to decision analysis section

Streamlined bond-issuing procedures

Moved 'issuing bonds between interest dates' to appendix

Streamlined installment notes

New ratio analysis on debt-to-equity

Chapter 15

TOKYOPOP NEW opener with new entrepreneurial assignment

Streamlined and enhanced explanation of investments

New illustration on purchases listed in a foreign currency

New return on assets analysis of Gap

Chapter 16

Ashtae Products NEW opener with new entrepreneurial assignment

New diagram on cash effects of changes in current assets and liabilities

Enhanced exhibit on summary adjustments for indirect method

New insight on measuring free cash flow

New assignments on computing operating cash flows, and financing and investing cash flows

Chapter 17

The Motley Fool REVISED opener with new entrepreneurial assignment

New horizontal and vertical analysis using Best Buy

Enhanced common-size analysis of Circuit City and Best Buy

New ratio analysis of Best Buy and Circuit City

New debt-to-equity analysis

New appendix on 'sustainable income,' including new requirements for accounting changes

Streamlined intro to comprehensive income

Chapter 18

Garrison Guitars NEW opener with new entrepreneurial assignment

New discussion and assignments on manufacturing cycle time and efficiency

Moved unit contribution margin to Chapter 22

New assignments on direct and indirect costs

New assignments on lean manufacturing and operating efficiencies

Enhanced graphics and streamlined discussion of cost flows

Expanded discussion of service businesses and cost controls

Chapter 19

Antelope Valley Medical College NEW opener with new entrepreneurial assignment

New insight on target costing

New illustrations and entries for cost flows in a job order system

Enhanced discussion for service businesses

New assignment on Ikea's costing strategy and success

Chapter 20

Duwop NEW opener with new entrepreneurial assignment

New discussion on tracking costs in a process operation

New focus on weighted average costing

Moved FIFO costing to appendix

Streamlined process costing illustrations and exhibits

Simplified computation of equivalent units

Streamlined the cost reconciliation and process cost summary

Chapter 21

Jungle Jim's International Market NEW opener with new entrepreneurial assignment

Streamlined activity-based costing illustration

Enhanced illustration of performance measurement

New assignment on costing and control of off-site employees

Chapter 22

Chinasprout NEW opener with new entrepreneurial assignment

Enhanced illustration and computations for measuring cost behaviors

Expanded explanation and illustration of high-low costing method

New illustration of unit contribution margin

Enhanced illustration of contribution margin income statement

New assignments on cost behavior estimation, and on cost, profits, and product giveaways

Chapter 23

Cloudveil NEW opener with new entrepreneurial assignment

Enhanced section on budgeted financial reports

New assignment on benefits of budgeting for startups

Chapter 24

Under Armour NEW opener with new entrepreneurial assignment

Enhanced explanation of flexible budgets

Streamlined overhead cost variance analysis

Enhanced budgeting for service businesses

Chapter 25

Progressive Telecom NEW opener with new entrepreneurial assignment

Enhanced explanation of depreciation and cash flow

Simplified selected present value calculations

Expanded applications to service businesses

Instructor's Resource CD-ROM

Vol. 1, Chapters 1-12
ISBN13: 9780073266558
ISBN10: 0073266558

FAP 18e, Chapters 1-25
ISBN13: 9780073266374
ISBN10: 007326637X

This is your all-in-one resource. It allows you to create custom presentations from your own materials or from the following text-specific materials provided in the CD's asset library:

- Instructor's Resource Manual
- Solutions Manual
- Test Bank, Computerized Test Bank
- PowerPoint® Presentations *Prepared by Domenico A. Tavella and Tim Samolis, Pittsburgh Technical Institute* Presentations allow for revision of lecture slides, and includes a viewer, allowing screens to be shown with or without the software.
- Excel Template Assignments
- Link to PageOut
- Video Clips

Test Bank

Vol. 1, Chapters 1-12
ISBN13: 9780073266442
ISBN10: 0073266442

Vol. 2, Chapters 13-25
ISBN13: 9780073266398
ISBN10: 0073266396

Revised by Gregory Prescott, Univeristy of South Alabama–Mobile and Gloria Worthy, Southwest Tennessee Community College–Macon Campus.

Instructor's Resource Manual, *FAP* 18e, Chapters 1-25

ISBN13: 9780073266527
ISBN10: 0073266523

Written by Barbara Chiappetta, Nassau Community College, and Patricia Walczak, Lansing Community College.

This manual contains (for each chapter) a Lecture Outline, a chart linking all assignment materials to Learning Objectives, a list of relevant active learning activities, and additional visuals with transparency masters. An electronic version is available on the Website and on the Instructor's Resource CD-ROM.

Algorithmic Test Bank

ISBN13: 9780073266612
ISBN10: 0073266619

Solutions Manual

Vol. 1, Chapters 1-12
ISBN13: 9780073266428
ISBN10: 0073266426

Vol. 2, Chapters 13-25
ISBN13: 9780073266510
ISBN10: 0073266515

Written by John J. Wild and Marilyn Sagrillo.

Solutions Acetates

Vol. 1, Chapters 1-12
ISBN13: 9780073266572
ISBN10: 0073266574

Vol. 2, Chapters 13-25
ISBN13: 9780073266589
ISBN10: 0073266582

Geoffrey Heriot, Greenville Technical College
"The text is well presented and has excellent materials for both students and instructors. It is certainly one of the top texts in an entry level principles of accounting marketplace."

Excel Working Papers CD

Vol. 1, Chapters 1-12
ISBN13: 9780073266411
ISBN10: 0073266418

Vol. 2, Chapters 12-25
ISBN13: 9780073266503
ISBN10: 0073266507

PFA, Chapters 1-17
ISBN13: 9780073266350
ISBN10: 0073266353

Written by John J. Wild.

Working Papers delivered in Excel spreadsheets. Excel Working Papers are available on CD-ROM and can be bundled with the printed Working Papers; see your representative for information.

Working Papers

Vol. 1, Chapters 1-12
ISBN13: 9780073266565
ISBN10: 0073266566

Vol. 2, Chapters 12-25
ISBN13: 9780073266404
ISBN10: 007326640X

PFA, Chapters 1-17
ISBN13: 9780073266367
ISBN10: 0073266361

Written by John J. Wild.

Study Guide

Vol. 1, Chapters 1-12
ISBN13: 9780073266435
ISBN10: 0073266434

Vol. 2, Chapters 12-25
ISBN13: 9780073266381
ISBN10: 0073266388

PFA, Chapters 1-17
ISBN13: 9780073266497
ISBN10: 0073266493

Written by Barbara Chiappetta, Nassau Community College, and Patricia Walczak, Lansing Community College.

Covers each chapter and appendix with reviews of the learning objectives, outlines of the chapters, summaries of chapter materials, and additional problems with solutions.

Carol Yacht's General Ledger & Peachtree Complete 2006 CD-ROM

ISBN 13: 9780073266336
ISBN 10: 0073266337

GL Software developed by Jack E. Terry, ComSource Associates, Inc.

Peachtree templates prepared by Carol Yacht.

The CD-ROM includes fully functioning versions of McGraw-Hill's own General Ledger Application software as well as Peachtree Complete 2006. Problem templates are included that allow you to assign text problems for working in either Yacht's General Ledger or Peachtree Complete 2006.

Zinio eBook

ISBN13: 9780073266473
ISBN10: 0073266477

Topic Tackler Plus DVD

ISBN13: 9780073266534
ISBN10: 0073266531

Prepared by Jeannie Folk, College of DuPage.

See page xvii for complete description.

Contributing Author
The authors and book team wish to thank Marilyn Sagrillo for her excellent contributions.

Marilyn Sagrillo is an associate professor at the University of Wisconsin at Green Bay. She received her BA and MS from Northern Illinois University and her PhD from the University of Wisconsin at Madison. Her scholarly articles are published in *Accounting Enquiries, Journal of Accounting Case Research*, and the *Missouri Society of CPAs Casebook*. She is a member of the American Accounting Association and the Institute of Management Accountants. She previously received the UWGB Founder's Association Faculty Award for Excellence in Teaching. Professor Sagrillo is an active volunteer for the Midwest Renewable Energy Association. She also enjoys reading, traveling, and hiking.

Acknowledgments

John J. Wild, Kermit D. Larson, Barbara Chiappetta, and McGraw-Hill/Irwin would like to recognize the following instructors for their valuable feedback and involvement in the development of *Fundamental Accounting Principles* 18e. We are thankful for their suggestions, counsel, and encouragement.

Matilda Abavana, Essex County College

Janet Adeyiga, Hampton University

Lelia Austin, Lake City Community College

Mazen Badra, Sanford-Brown College

Thomas Badley, Baker College of Port Huron

Joyce Barden, DeVry University

Scott Barhight, Northampton Community College

Richard Barnhart, Grand Rapids Community College

Mary Barnum, Grand Rapids Community College

Cheryl Baron, Ridgewater College

Dan Bayak, Northampton Community College

Allen Bealle, Delgado Community College

Irene Bembenista, Davenport University

James Benedum, Milwaukee Area Technical College

Joe Berlinski, Prairie State College

Michelle Berube, Florida Metropolitan University

William Black, Raritan Valley CC

Mike Blackett, National American University

Linda Bolduc, Mount Wachusett Community College

Rick Bowden, Oakland CC - Auburn Hills

Deborah Boyce, Mohawk Valley Community College

Nancy Boyd, Middle Tennessee State University

Sarah Brown, University of North Alabama

Mary Burnell, Fairmont State College

Earl Butler, Broward Community College North

Paula Campbell, United Education Institute

Ronald L. Campbell, North Carolina A&T State University

Sharon Campbell, University of North Alabama

Gary Carlson, Kirkwood Community College

Lloyd Carroll, Borough of Manhattan Community College

Roy Carson, Anne Arundel Community College

Al Case, Southern Oregon University

Fatma Cebenoyan, Hunter College

Amy Chataginer, Mississippi Gulf Coast Community College

Sandra Check, Texas School of Business

Bea Chiang, College of New Jersey

Marilyn G. Ciolino, Delgado Community College

Joan Cook, Milwaukee Area Technical College

Ken Couvillion, San Joaquin Delta College

Jim Crowther, Kirkwood Community College

Patricia Davis, Keystone College

Lee Daugherty, Lorain County Community College

Thomas W. DeBerry, North Georgia College and State University

Andrea Deebach, Lake Washington Technical College

Joan H. Demko, Wor-Wic Community College

Linda Dening, Jefferson Community College

Mike Deschamps, Chaffey College

Jack Dodds, Des Moines Area Community College

Patricia Doherty, Old Dominion University

Alex Dontoh, New York University

Ron Douglas, Southwest Minnesota State University

Andy Dressler, Walla Walla College

Michael Farina, Cerritos College

Tim Farmer, University of Missouri-St. Louis

Charles Fazzi, Saint Vincent College

Patricia Feller, Nashville State Community College

Albert Fisher, Community College of Southern Nevada

Carolyn Fitzmorris, Hutchinson Community College

Jim Formosa, Nashville State Technical College

Jayne Fuglister, Cleveland State University

John Gabelman, Columbus State Community College

Dennis Gaffney, Cleveland State University

Dan Galvin, Diablo Valley College

Tesfa G. Gebremedhin, West Virginia University

Harold Gellis, York College

Barbara Gershowitz, Nashville State Community College

Natalie Gillard, Mesalands Community College

Marie Gould, Springfield College

Harry E. Gray, Ivy Tech State College

Ann Gregory, South Plains College

Curtis Gustafson, South Dakota State University

Bill Guthrie, DeVry University - Westminster

Betty Habershon, Prince Georges Community College

Patricia Halliday, Santa Monica College

Fred Hampel, Frontrange Community College

John Hancock, University of California Davis

Mark Handley, Delaware Technical and Community College

Heidi Hansel, Kirkwood Community College

James Hansen, Minnesota State University

Jeannie Harrington, Middle Tennessee State University

William Harvey, Henry Ford Community College

Yvonne Hatami, Boro of Manhattan Community College

Laurie Hays, Western Michigan University

Ken Heaslip, Kean State University

Dianne Henline, Texarkana College

Geoffrey Heriot, Greenville Technical Community College

Bernie Hill, Spokane Community College

Kathy Hill, Leeward Community College

Ted Hopple, Columbus State Community College

Richard Hudanick, Sanford Brown College

Regina C. Ivory, Fort Valley State University

Beverly Jenkins, Phoenix College

Cathy Jeppson, California State University

Bill Johnstone, Montgomery College - Rockville

Jeffery Jones, Community College of Southern Nevada

John Karayan, Occidental College

Naomi Karolinski, Monroe Community College

Sushila Kedia, Grambling University

Howard Keller, Indiana University/Purdue University Indiana

Miriam Keller-Perkins, Berkeley College

Chris Kelly, Community College of Southern Nevada

Chula King, University of West Florida

Debra Kiss, Davenport University

Jay Klein, Florida Metropolitan University

Mary Kline, Blackhawk College

Shirly Kleiner, Johnson County Community College

Christy Kloezeman, Glendale Community College

Susan R. Koch, Austin Peay State University

Jerry Kreuze, Western Michigan University

Tara Laken, Joliet Junior College

Michael Landers, Middlesex County Community College

Sam Lanzafame, Bryant and Stratton

Deborah Leitsch, Goldey-Beacom College

Denise Leggett, Middle Tennessee State University

Natasha Librizzi, Milwaukee Area Technical College

Danny Litt, University of California - Los Angeles

William P. Logan, Middle Georgia College

Dorinda Lynn, Pensacola Junior College

Linda Mallory, Central Virginia Community College

Maria Mari, Miami Dade College

Barbara Marotta, North Virginia Community College, Woodbridge

Mary Maury, St. John's University

Linda McAnally, Sul Ross State University

Larry C. McCabe, Muhlenberg College

Dorothy McCaden, Gibbs College

Cynthia McCall, Des Moines Area Community College

Irene McCarthy, St. John's University

Clarice McCoy, Brookhaven College

Florence McGovern, Bergen Community College

Andrew W. McKee, North Country Community College

Teri Meta, Seminole Community College - Sanford

James E. Miller, Gannon University

Shea Mears, Des Moines Area Community College

Andy Morgret, University of Memphis

David E. Morris, North Georgia College & State University

Audrey Morrison, Pensacola Junior College

Richard Murdock, Ohio State University

Andrea Murowski, Brookdale Community College

Charles Murphy, Bunker Hill Community College

Cindy Navaroli, Chaffey College

Bruce R. Neumann, University of Colorado at Denver

Joe Nicassio, Westmoreland County CC

Dave Nichols, University of Mississippi

Deborah Niemer, Oakland Community College

Jon Nitschke, Montana State University - Great Falls

Eugene O'Donnell, Harcum College

Liz Ott, Casper College

Lydia Parham, Baker College of Flint

Jane Park, California State University

Robert D. Patterson, Penn State Erie

Deborah Pavelka, Roosevelt University

Dennis Pelzek, Waukesha County Technical College

Shirley Powell, Arkansas State University

Greg Prescott, University of Southern Alabama

Lisa Rackley, Rich Mountain Community College

Lavonda Ramey, Schoolcraft College

Nova Randolph, Shawnee Community College

Paula Ratliff, Arkansas State University

Kathie Reeslund, Normandale Community College

Robert Ricketts, Texas Tech University

Paul Rivers, Bunker Hill Community College

Frank Rodjius, Northwestern University

Harold Royer, Miami Dade Community College

Al Ruggiero, Suffolk Community College

John A. Rude, Bloomsburg University

Jerry Scott, Ivy Tech State College

Gary Schader, Kean University

Angela Seidel, Cambria-Rowe Business College

Joe Shambley, Sullivan County Community College

Lynn Shuster, Central Penn College

Lois Slutsky, Broward Community College - South Pembroke Pines

Judy Smith, American InterContinental University

Horace Stearman, Remington College

Stacey Stewart, Colorado Northwestern Community College

Verlindsey Stewart, J.F. Drake State Technical

Bill Stibrany, Allentown Business School

Undine Stinnette, Roosevelt University

Janice Stoudemire, Midlands Technical College

Scott Stroher, Glendale Community College

Pamela Strysick, Broward Community College South

Linda Stuckey, Virginia Western Community College

Ron Summers, Oklahoma City Community College

David R. Swarts, Clinton Community College

Larry Swisher, Muskegon Community College

Domenico A. Tavella, Pittsburgh Technical Institute

Steve Teeter, Utah Valley State University

Katherene Terrell, University of Central Oklahoma

Ronald R. Tidd, Central Washington University

Christine N. Todd, William Woods University

Shafi Ullah, Broward Community College South

Bob Urell, Irvine Valley College

Peter Vander Weyst, Edmonds Community College

Patricia Walczak, Lansing Community College

Kenton Walker, University of Wyoming

Debra A. Warren, Chadron State College

John Weber, DeVry University

Terry Wegner, Casper College

Keith Weidkamp, Sierra College

Christian Widmer, Tidewater Community College

Jack Wiehler, San Joaquin Delta College

Denise N. Wooten, Erie Community College

Patricia Worsham, Riverside Community College-Norco

Gloria Worthy, Southwest Tennessee Community College

Nancy L. Wyant, International College - Fort Myers

Lynette Yerbury, Salt Lake City Community College

Judy Zander, Grossmont College

Charlie Zaruba, Florida Metropolitan University

In addition to the helpful and generous colleagues listed above, we thank the entire McGraw-Hill/Irwin *Fundamental Accounting Principles* 18e team, including Stewart Mattson, Steve Schuetz, Kelly Odom, Lori Koetters, Matthew Baldwin, Michael McCormick, Becky Szura, and Elizabeth Mavetz. We also thank the great marketing and sales support staff, including Krista Bettino, Dan Silverburg, and Liz Farina. Many talented educators and professionals worked hard to create the supplements for this book, and for their efforts we're grateful. Finally, many more people we either did not meet or whose efforts we did not personally witness nevertheless helped to make this book everything that it is, and we thank them all.

John J. Wild   Kermit D. Larson   Barbara Chiappetta

Brief Contents

Contents

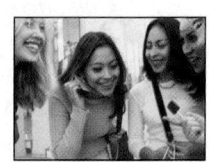

Fundamental Accounting Principles

12 Accounting for Partnerships

A Look Back

Chapter 11 focused on how current liabilities are identified, computed, recorded, and reported. Attention was directed at notes, payroll, sales taxes, warranties, employee benefits, and contingencies.

A Look at This Chapter

This chapter explains the partnership form of organization. Important partnership characteristics are described along with the accounting concepts and procedures for its most fundamental transactions.

A Look Ahead

Chapter 13 extends our discussion to the corporate form of organization. We describe the accounting and reporting for stock issuances, dividends, and other equity transactions.

Learning Objectives

CAP

Conceptual

C1 Identify characteristics of partnerships and similar organizations. (p. 472)

Analytical

A1 Compute partner return on equity and use it to evaluate partnership performance. (p. 484)

Procedural

P1 Prepare entries for partnership formation. (p. 475)

P2 Allocate and record income and loss among partners. (p. 475)

P3 Account for the admission and withdrawal of partners. (p. 478)

P4 Prepare entries for partnership liquidation. (p. 482)

ROOKIE ROOKIE ROOKIE ROOKIE ROOKIE ROOKIE

"We're just really happy that we can still do what we enjoy doing . . . we're lucky as hell"
—Catharine Lyons (on right; Elska Sandor on left)

Skating Partners

NEW YORK, NY—In a Chinatown loft just off New York's Canal Street, **Rookie Skateboards** (**RookieSkateboards.com**) creates skateboard decks and apparel. But founders Catharine Lyons and Elska Sandor run a different sort of business. "Although we are women and happen to be the first women owned and operated skateboard company," says Catharine, "we run a company that simply celebrates the art and spirit of skate boarding." Adds Elska, "Tomboy can be chic—although skating is perhaps more difficult in a knee-length skirt."

The partners quickly learned there is more to the skate business than skating. Knowledge of partnerships and their financial implications became important to Rookie's success. "It's been hard for us to catch up with the business side of it," says Catharine. "We don't have much enthusiasm for the unpleasant details of running a business." Yet she stresses the importance of attending to partnership formation, agreements, and financials to stay afloat.

Success is causing their partnership to evolve. "We want to offer a unique route for all skateboarders and especially girls, but at the same time we want to be considered a legitimate skateboard company, not

a novelty," says Catharine. "I don't feel the need to make a point of being a woman. What I'm doing is—in the end—about skating." As their skateboards and apparel evolve, the partners have not sold out. "I don't have to have daisies on my board," says Elska. "I can play with the same toys and still be a girl in the end. We are certainly not women trying to be men."

Still, the partners are gaining business savvy. "We're trying to get ourselves as streamlined and efficient as possible," says Catharine. "Rookie embodies an enthusiasm and positive outlook for the future while keeping a 'scrappy' edge."

The partners also know to ask for help. When starting a partnership "it's good to be honest about what you are good at and what you are not, and align yourself with good professionals, like accountants, to fill in the gaps," says Catharine. "Don't take yourself too seriously. Laugh a lot, and at yourself. Know how to enjoy yourself. That helps make it work."

[Sources: *Rookie Skateboards Website*, January 2006; *Koch Entertainment Website*, January 2004; *Entrepreneur*, May 2003; *Newsday*, April 2003; *Billboard*, June 2002]

The three basic types of business organizations are proprietorships, partnerships, and corporations. Partnerships are similar to proprietorships, except they have more than one owner. This chapter explains partnerships and looks at several variations of them such as limited partnerships, limited liability partnerships, S corporations, and limited liability companies. Understanding the advantages and disadvantages of the partnership form of business organization is important for making informed business decisions.

Accounting for Partnerships

Partnership Organization
- Characteristics
- Organizations with partnership characteristics
- Choice of a business form

Basic Partnership Accounting
- Organizing a partnership
- Dividing income or loss
- Partnership financial statements

Partner Admission and Withdrawal
- Admission of partner
- Withdrawal of partner
- Death of partner

Partnership Liquidation
- No capital deficiency
- Capital deficiency

Partnership Form of Organization

C1 Identify characteristics of partnerships and similar organizations.

A **partnership** is an unincorporated association of two or more people to pursue a business for profit as co-owners. Many businesses are organized as partnerships. They are especially common in small retail and service businesses. Many professional practitioners, including physicians, lawyers, investors, and accountants, also organize their practices as partnerships.

Characteristics of Partnerships

Partnerships are an important type of organization because they offer certain advantages with their unique characteristics. We describe these characteristics in this section.

Voluntary Association A partnership is a voluntary association between partners. Joining a partnership increases the risk to one's personal financial position. Some courts have ruled that partnerships are created by the actions of individuals even when there is no *express agreement* to form one.

Point: When a new partner is admitted, all parties usually must agree to the admission.

Partnership Agreement Forming a partnership requires that two or more legally competent people (who are of age and of sound mental capacity) agree to be partners. Their agreement becomes a **partnership contract,** also called *articles of copartnership*. Although it should be in writing, the contract is binding even if it is only expressed verbally. Partnership agreements normally include details of the partners' (1) names and contributions, (2) rights and duties, (3) sharing of income and losses, (4) withdrawal arrangement, (5) dispute procedures, (6) admission and withdrawal of partners, and (7) rights and duties in the event a partner dies.

Point: The end of a partnership is referred to as its *dissolution*.

Limited Life The life of a partnership is limited. Death, bankruptcy, or any event taking away the ability of a partner to enter into or fulfill a contract ends a partnership. Any one of the partners can also terminate a partnership at will.

Point: Partners are taxed on their share of partnership income, not on their withdrawals.

Taxation A partnership is not subject to taxes on its income. The income or loss of a partnership is allocated to the partners according to the partnership agreement, and it is included in determining the taxable income for each partner's tax return. Partnership income or loss is allocated each year whether or not cash is distributed to partners.

Mutual Agency   **Mutual agency** implies that each partner is a fully authorized agent of the partnership. As its agent, a partner can commit or bind the partnership to any contract within the scope of the partnership business. For instance, a partner in a merchandising business can sign contracts binding the partnership to buy merchandise, lease a store building, borrow money, or hire employees. These activities are all within the scope of a merchandising firm. A partner in a law firm, acting alone, however, cannot bind the other partners to a contract to buy snowboards for resale or rent an apartment for parties. These actions are outside the normal scope of a law firm's business. Partners also can agree to limit the power of any one or more of the partners to negotiate contracts for the partnership. This agreement is binding on the partners and on outsiders who know it exists. It is not binding on outsiders who do not know it exists. Outsiders unaware of the agreement have the right to assume each partner has normal agency powers for the partnership. Mutual agency exposes partners to the risk of unwise actions by any one partner.

Point: The majority of states adhere to the Uniform Partnership Act for the basic rules of partnership formation, operation, and dissolution.

Unlimited Liability   **Unlimited liability** implies that each partner can be called on to pay a partnership's debts. When a partnership cannot pay its debts, creditors usually can apply their claims to partners' *personal* assets. If a partner does not have enough assets to meet his or her share of the partnership debt, the creditors can apply their claims to the assets of the other partners. A partnership in which all partners have *mutual agency* and *unlimited liability* is called a **general partnership.** Mutual agency and unlimited liability are two main reasons that most general partnerships have only a few members.

Point: Limited life, mutual agency, and unlimited liability are disadvantages of a partnership.

Co-Ownership of Property   Partnership assets are owned jointly by all partners. Any investment by a partner becomes the joint property of all partners. Partners have a claim on partnership assets based on their capital account and the partnership contract.

Organizations with Partnership Characteristics

Organizations exist that combine certain characteristics of partnerships with other forms of organizations. We discuss several of these forms in this section.

Limited Partnerships   Some individuals who want to invest in a partnership are unwilling to accept the risk of unlimited liability. Their needs can be met with a **limited partnership.** This type of organization is identified in its name with the words "Limited Partnership," or "Ltd.," or "LP." A limited partnership has two classes of partners, general and limited. At least one partner must be a **general partner,** who assumes management duties and unlimited liability for the debts of the partnership. The **limited partners** have no personal liability beyond the amounts they invest in the partnership. Limited partners have no active role except as specified in the partnership agreement. A limited partnership agreement often specifies unique procedures for allocating income and losses between general and limited partners. The accounting procedures are similar for both limited and general partnerships.

Decision Insight

Nutty Partners   The Hawaii-based **ML Macadamia Orchards LP** is one of the world's largest growers of macadamia nuts. It reported the following partners' capital balances ($ 000s) in its balance sheet:

| General Partner | . . . . | $ 505 |
| Limited Partners | . . . . | $50,037 |

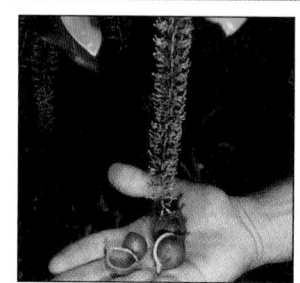

Limited Liability Partnerships   Most states allow individuals to form a **limited liability partnership.** This is identified in its name with the words "Limited Liability Partnership" or by "LLP." This type of partnership is designed to protect innocent partners from malpractice or negligence claims resulting from the acts of another partner. When a partner provides service resulting in a malpractice claim, that partner has personal liability for the claim. The remaining partners who were not responsible for the actions resulting in the claim are not personally liable for it. However, most states hold all partners personally liable for other partnership debts. Accounting for a limited liability partnership is the same as for a general partnership.

Point: Many accounting services firms are set up as LLPs.

S Corporations   Certain corporations with 75 or fewer stockholders can elect to be treated as a partnership for income tax purposes. These corporations are called *Sub-Chapter S* or simply **S corporations.** This distinguishes them from other corporations, called *Sub-Chapter C* or simply **C corporations.** S corporations provide stockholders the same limited liability feature that C corporations do. The advantage of an S corporation is that it does not pay income taxes. If stockholders work for an S corporation, their salaries are treated as expenses of the corporation. The remaining income or loss of the corporation is allocated to stockholders for inclusion on their personal tax returns. Except for C corporations having to account for income tax expenses and liabilities, the accounting procedures are the same for both S and C corporations.

Limited Liability Companies   A relatively new form of business organization is the **limited liability company.** The names of these businesses usually include the words "Limited Liability Company" or an abbreviation such as "LLC" or "LC." This form of business has certain features similar to a corporation and others similar to a limited partnership. The owners, who are called *members,* are protected with the same limited liability feature as owners of corporations. While limited partners cannot actively participate in the management of a limited partnership, the members of a limited liability company can assume an active management role. A limited liability company usually has a limited life. For income tax purposes, a limited liability company is typically treated as a partnership. This treatment depends on factors such as whether the members' equity interests are freely transferable and whether the company has continuity of life. A limited liability company's accounting system is designed to help management comply with the dictates of the articles of organization and company regulations adopted by its members. The accounting system also must provide information to support the company's compliance with state and federal laws, including taxation.

Choosing a Business Form

Choosing the proper business form is crucial. Many factors should be considered, including taxes, liability risk, tax and fiscal year-end, ownership structure, estate planning, business risks, and earnings and property distributions. The following table summarizes several important characteristics of business organizations:

	Proprietorship	Partnership	LLP	LLC	S Corp.	Corporation
Business entity	yes	yes	yes	yes	yes	yes
Legal entity	no	no	no	yes	yes	yes
Limited liability	no	no	limited*	yes	yes	yes
Business taxed	no	no	no	no	no	yes
One owner allowed	yes	no	no	yes	yes	yes

* A partner's personal liability for LLP debts is limited. Most LLPs carry insurance to protect against malpractice.

We must remember that this table is a summary, not a detailed list. Many details underlie each of these business forms, and several details differ across states. Also, state and federal laws change, and a body of law is still developing around LLCs. Business owners should look at these details and consider unique business arrangements such as organizing various parts of their businesses in different forms.

Quick Check   Answers—p. 487

1. A partnership is terminated in the event (a) a partnership agreement is not in writing, (b) a partner dies, (c) a partner exercises mutual agency.
2. What does the term *unlimited liability* mean when applied to a general partnership?
3. Which of the following forms of organization do not provide limited liability to *all* of its owners: (a) S corporation, (b) limited liability company, (c) limited partnership?

Basic Partnership Accounting

Since ownership rights in a partnership are divided among partners, partnership accounting

- Uses a capital account for each partner.
- Uses a withdrawals account for each partner.
- Allocates net income or loss to partners according to the partnership agreement.

This section describes partnership accounting for organizing a partnership, distributing income and loss, and preparing financial statements.

Organizing a Partnership

When partners invest in a partnership, their capital accounts are credited for the invested amounts. Partners can invest both assets and liabilities. Each partner's investment is recorded at an agreed-on value, normally the market values of the contributed assets and liabilities at the date of contribution. To illustrate, Kayla Zayn and Hector Perez organize a partnership on January 11 called BOARDS that offers year-round facilities for skateboarding and snowboarding. Zayn's initial net investment in BOARDS is $30,000, made up of cash ($7,000), boarding facilities ($33,000), and a note payable reflecting a bank loan for the new business ($10,000). Perez's initial investment is cash of $10,000. These amounts are the values agreed on by both partners. The entries to record these investments follow.

P1   Prepare entries for partnership formation.

Zayn's Investment

Jan. 11	Cash	7,000	
	Boarding facilities	33,000	
	Note payable		10,000
	K. Zayn, Capital		30,000
	To record the investment of Zayn.		

Assets   = Liabilities + Equity
+7,000   +10,000   +30,000
+33,000

Perez's Investment

Jan. 11	Cash	10,000	
	H. Perez, Capital		10,000
	To record the investment of Perez.		

Assets   = Liabilities + Equity
+10,000   +10,000

In accounting for a partnership, the following additional relations hold true: (1) Partners' withdrawals are debited to their own separate withdrawals accounts. (2) Partners' capital accounts are credited (or debited) for their shares of net income (or net loss) when closing the accounts at the end of a period. (3) Each partner's withdrawals account is closed to that partner's capital account. Separate capital and withdrawals accounts are kept for each partner.

Point: Both equity and cash are reduced when a partner withdraws cash from a partnership.

Dividing Income or Loss

Partners are not employees of the partnership but are its owners. If partners devote their time and services to their partnership, they are understood to do so for profit, not for salary. This means there are no salaries to partners that are reported as expenses on the partnership income statement. However, when net income or loss of a partnership is allocated among partners, the partners can agree to allocate "salary allowances" reflecting the relative value of services provided. Partners also can agree to allocate "interest allowances" based on the amount invested. For instance, since Zayn contributes three times the investment of Perez, it is only fair that this be considered when allocating income between them. Like salary allowances, these interest allowances are not expenses on the income statement.

P2   Allocate and record income and loss among partners.

Partners can agree to any method of dividing income or loss. In the absence of an agreement, the law says that the partners share income or loss of a partnership equally. If partners agree on how to share income but say nothing about losses, they share losses the same way they share income. Three common methods to divide income or loss use (1) a stated ratio basis, (2) the ratio of capital balances, or (3) salary and interest allowances and any remainder according to a fixed ratio. We explain each of these methods in this section.

Allocation on Stated Ratios   The *stated ratio* (also called the *income-and-loss-sharing ratio,* the *profit and loss ratio,* or the *P&L ratio*) method of allocating partnership income or loss gives each partner a fraction of the total. Partners must agree on the fractional share each receives. To illustrate, assume the partnership agreement of K. Zayn and H. Perez says Zayn receives two-thirds and Perez one-third of partnership income and loss. If their partnership's net income is $60,000, it is allocated to the partners when the Income Summary account is closed as follows.

Dec. 31	Income Summary	60,000	
	K. Zayn, Capital		40,000
	H. Perez, Capital		20,000
	To allocate income and close Income Summary.		

Allocation on Capital Balances   The *capital balances* method of allocating partnership income or loss assigns an amount based on the ratio of each partner's relative capital balance. If Zayn and Perez agree to share income and loss on the ratio of their beginning capital balances—Zayn's $30,000 and Perez's $10,000—Zayn receives three-fourths of any income or loss ($30,000/$40,000) and Perez receives one-fourth ($10,000/$40,000). The journal entry follows the same format as that using stated ratios (see preceding entries).

Allocation on Services, Capital, and Stated Ratios   The *services, capital, and stated ratio* method of allocating partnership income or loss recognizes that service and capital contributions of partners often are not equal. Salary allowances can make up for differences in service contributions. Interest allowances can make up for unequal capital contributions. Also, the allocation of income and loss can include *both* salary and interest allowances. To illustrate, assume that the partnership agreement of K. Zayn and H. Perez reflects differences in service and capital contributions as follows: (1) annual salary allowances of $36,000 to Zayn and $24,000 to Perez, (2) annual interest allowances of 10% of a partner's beginning-year capital balance, and (3) equal share of any remaining balance of income or loss. These salaries and interest allowances are *not* reported as expenses on the income statement. They are simply a means of dividing partnership income or loss. The remainder of this section provides two illustrations using this three-point allocation agreement.

Illustration when income exceeds allowance.   If BOARDS has first-year net income of $70,000, and Zayn and Perez apply the three-point partnership agreement described in the prior paragraph, income is allocated as shown in Exhibit 12.1. Zayn gets $42,000 and Perez gets $28,000 of the $70,000 total.

Illustration when allowances exceed income.   The sharing agreement between Zayn and Perez must be followed even if net income is less than the total of the allowances. For example, if BOARDS' first-year net income is $50,000 instead of $70,000, it is allocated to the partners as shown in Exhibit 12.2. Computations for salaries and interest are identical to those in Exhibit 12.1. However, when we apply the total allowances against income, the balance of income is negative. This $(14,000) negative balance is allocated equally to the partners per their sharing agreement. This means that a negative $(7,000) is allocated to each partner. In this case, Zayn ends up with $32,000 and Perez with $18,000. If BOARDS had experienced a net loss, Zayn and Perez would share it in the same manner as the $50,000 income. The only difference is that they would have begun with a negative amount because of the loss. Specifically, the partners would still have been allocated their salary and interest allowances, further adding

---

Point: Partners can agree on one ratio to divide income and another ratio to divide a loss.

Point: The fractional basis can be stated as a proportion, ratio, or percent. For example, a 3:2 basis is the same as ⅗ and ⅖, or 60% and 40%.

Assets = Liabilities + Equity
    −60,000
    +40,000
    +20,000

Point: To determine the percent of income received by each partner, divide an individual partner's share by total net income.

Topic Tackler

PLUS

12-1

Point: When allowances exceed income, the amount of this negative balance often is referred to as a *sharing agreement loss* or *deficit.*

Point: Check to make sure the sum of the dollar amounts allocated to each partner equals net income or loss.

	Zayn	Perez	Total
Net income			**$70,000**
Salary allowances			
Zayn	$ 36,000		
Perez		$ 24,000	
Interest allowances			
Zayn (10% × $30,000)	3,000		
Perez (10% × $10,000)		1,000	
Total salaries and interest	39,000	25,000	64,000
Balance of income			⌐ 6,000
Balance allocated equally			
Zayn	3,000 ←		
Perez		3,000 ←	
Total allocated			6,000
Balance of income			$ 0
Income of each partner	**$42,000**	**$28,000**	

Exhibit 12.1

Dividing Income When Income Exceeds Allowances

	Zayn	Perez	Total
Net income			**$50,000**
Salary allowances			
Zayn	$ 36,000		
Perez		$ 24,000	
Interest allowances			
Zayn (10% × $30,000)	3,000		
Perez (10% × $10,000)		1,000	
Total salaries and interest	39,000	25,000	64,000
Balance of income			⌐(14,000)
Balance allocated equally			
Zayn	(7,000) ←		
Perez		(7,000) ←	
Total allocated			(14,000)
Balance of income			$ 0
Income of each partner	**$32,000**	**$18,000**	

Exhibit 12.2

Dividing Income When Allowances Exceed Income

to the negative balance of the loss. This *total* negative balance *after* salary and interest allowances would have been allocated equally between the partners. These allocations would have been applied against the positive numbers from any allowances to determine each partner's share of the loss.

Point: When a loss occurs, it is possible for a specific partner's capital to increase (when closing income summary) if that partner's allowance is in excess of his or her share of the negative balance. This implies that decreases to the capital balances of other partners exceed the partnership's loss amount.

Quick Check
Answers—p. 487

4. Denzel and Shantell form a partnership by contributing $70,000 and $35,000, respectively. They agree to an interest allowance equal to 10% of each partner's capital balance at the beginning of the year, with the remaining income shared equally. Allocate first-year income of $40,000 to each partner.

Partnership Financial Statements

Partnership financial statements are similar to those of other organizations. The **statement of partners' equity,** also called *statement of partners' capital,* is one exception. It shows *each* partner's beginning capital balance, additional investments, allocated income or loss, withdrawals, and ending capital balance. To illustrate, Exhibit 12.3 shows the statement of partners'

Beach Buddies   The **Casa Munras Hotel Partners LP** operates the Casa Munras Garden Hotel and several leased retail stores in Monterey, California. Its recent statement of partners' equity reports zero in partners' withdrawals and a total deficit of $2.5 million in partners' capital balances.

equity for BOARDS prepared using the sharing agreement of Exhibit 12.1. Recall that BOARDS' income was $70,000; also, assume that Zayn withdrew $20,000 and Perez $12,000 at year-end.

The equity section of the balance sheet of a partnership usually shows the separate capital account balance of each partner. In the case of BOARDS, both K. Zayn, Capital, and H. Perez, Capital, are listed in the equity section along with their balances of $52,000 and $26,000, respectively.

Exhibit 12.3
Statement of Partners' Equity

BOARDS **Statement of Partners' Equity** **For Year Ended December 31, 2008**			
	Zayn	**Perez**	**Total**
Beginning capital balances	$ 0	$ 0	$ 0
Plus			
Investments by owners	30,000	10,000	40,000
Net income			
Salary allowances	$36,000	$24,000	
Interest allowances	3,000	1,000	
Balance allocated	3,000	3,000	
Total net income	42,000	28,000	70,000
	72,000	38,000	110,000
Less partners' withdrawals	(20,000)	(12,000)	(32,000)
Ending capital balances	**$52,000**	**$26,000**	**$78,000**

Admission and Withdrawal of Partners

P3   Account for the admission and withdrawal of partners.

A partnership is based on a contract between individuals. When a partner is admitted or withdraws, the present partnership ends. Still, the business can continue to operate as a new partnership consisting of the remaining partners. This section considers how to account for the admission and withdrawal of partners.

Admission of a Partner

A new partner is admitted in one of two ways: by purchasing an interest from one or more current partners or by investing cash or other assets in the partnership.

Topic Tackler

PLUS

12-2

Purchase of Partnership Interest   The purchase of partnership interest is a *personal transaction between one or more current partners and the new partner.* To become a partner, the current partners must accept the purchaser. Accounting for the purchase of partnership interest involves reallocating current partners' capital to reflect the transaction. To illustrate, at the end of BOARDS' first year, H. Perez sells one-half of his partnership interest to Tyrell Rasheed for $18,000. This means that Perez gives up a $13,000 recorded interest ($26,000 × 1/2) in the partnership (see the ending capital balance in Exhibit 12.3). The partnership records this January 4 transaction as follows.

Assets = Liabilities + Equity	Jan. 4	H. Perez, Capital.	13,000	
−13,000		T. Rasheed, Capital.		13,000
+13,000		*To record admission of Rasheed by purchase.*		

After this entry is posted, BOARDS' equity shows K. Zayn, Capital; H. Perez, Capital; and T. Rasheed, Capital, and their respective balances of $52,000, $13,000, and $13,000.

Two aspects of this transaction are important. First, the partnership, does *not* record the $18,000 Rasheed paid Perez. The partnership's assets, liabilities, and *total equity* are unaffected by this transaction among partners. Second, Zayn and Perez must agree that Rasheed is to become a partner. If they agree to accept Rasheed, a new partnership is formed and a new contract with a new income-and-loss-sharing agreement is prepared. If Zayn or Perez refuses to accept Rasheed as a partner, then (under the Uniform Partnership Act) Rasheed gets Perez's sold share of partnership income and loss. If the partnership is liquidated, Rasheed gets Perez's sold share of partnership assets. Rasheed gets no voice in managing the company unless Rasheed is admitted as a partner.

Point: Partners' withdrawals are not constrained by the partnership's annual income or loss.

Investing Assets in a Partnership   Admitting a partner by accepting assets is a *transaction between the new partner and the partnership*. The invested assets become partnership property. To illustrate, if Zayn (with a $52,000 interest) and Perez (with a $26,000 interest) agree to accept Rasheed as a partner in BOARDS after an investment of $22,000 cash, this is recorded as follows.

Jan. 4	Cash...................................	22,000	
	T. Rasheed, Capital......................		22,000
	To record admission of Rasheed by investment.		

Assets = Liabilities + Equity
+22,000 +22,000

After this entry is posted, both assets (cash) and equity (T. Rasheed, Capital) increase by $22,000. Rasheed now has a 22% equity in the assets of the business, computed as $22,000 divided by the entire partnership equity ($52,000 + $26,000 + $22,000). Rasheed does not necessarily have a right to 22% of income. Dividing income and loss is a separate matter on which partners must agree.

Bonus to old partners.   When the current value of a partnership is greater than the recorded amounts of equity, the partners usually require a new partner to pay a bonus for the privilege of joining. To illustrate, assume that Zayn and Perez agree to accept Rasheed as a partner with a 25% interest in BOARDS if Rasheed invests $42,000. Recall the partnership's accounting records show Zayn's recorded equity in the business is $52,000 and Perez's recorded equity is $26,000 (see Exhibit 12.3). Rasheed's equity is determined as follows.

Equities of existing partners ($52,000 + $26,000)	$ 78,000
Investment of new partner	42,000
Total partnership equity	$120,000
Equity of Rasheed (25% × $120,000)	$ 30,000

Although Rasheed invests $42,000, the equity attributed to Rasheed in the new partnership is only $30,000. The $12,000 difference is called a *bonus* and is allocated to existing partners (Zayn and Perez) according to their income-and-loss-sharing agreement. A bonus is shared in this way because it is viewed as reflecting a higher value of the partnership that is not yet reflected in income. The entry to record this transaction follows.

Jan. 4	Cash...................................	42,000	
	T. Rasheed, Capital......................		30,000
	K. Zayn, Capital ($12,000 × ½).............		6,000
	H. Perez, Capital ($12,000 × ½)............		6,000
	To record admission of Rasheed and bonus.		

Assets = Liabilities + Equity
+42,000 +30,000
+6,000
+6,000

Bonus to new partner.   Alternatively, existing partners can grant a bonus to a new partner. This usually occurs when they need additional cash or the new partner has exceptional talents. The bonus to the new partner is in the form of a larger share of equity than the amount invested. To illustrate, assume that Zayn and Perez agree to accept Rasheed as a partner with a 25% interest in the partnership, but they require Rasheed to invest only $18,000. Rasheed's equity is determined as follows.

Equities of existing partners ($52,000 + $26,000)	$78,000
Investment of new partner	18,000
Total partnership equity	$96,000
Equity of Rasheed (25% × $96,000)	$24,000

The old partners contribute the $6,000 bonus (computed as $24,000 minus $18,000) to Rasheed according to their income-and-loss-sharing ratio. Moreover, Rasheed's 25% equity does not necessarily entitle Rasheed to 25% of future income or loss. This is a separate matter for agreement by the partners. The entry to record the admission and investment of Rasheed is

Assets	= Liabilities +	Equity
+18,000		−3,000
		−3,000
		+24,000

Jan. 4	Cash	18,000	
	K. Zayn, Capital ($6,000 × ½)	3,000	
	H. Perez, Capital ($6,000 × ½)	3,000	
	T. Rasheed, Capital.		24,000
	To record Rasheed's admission and bonus.		

Withdrawal of a Partner

A partner generally withdraws from a partnership in one of two ways. (1) First, the withdrawing partner can sell his or her interest to another person who pays for it in cash or other assets. For this, we need only debit the withdrawing partner's capital account and credit the new partner's capital account. (2) The second case is when cash or other assets of the partnership are distributed to the withdrawing partner in settlement of his or her interest. To illustrate these cases, assume that Perez withdraws from the partnership of BOARDS in some future period. The partnership shows the following capital balances at the date of Perez's withdrawal: K. Zayn, $84,000; H. Perez, $38,000; and T. Rasheed, $38,000. The partners (Zayn, Perez, and Rasheed) share income and loss equally. Accounting for Perez's withdrawal depends on whether a bonus is paid. We describe three possibilities.

No Bonus   If Perez withdraws and takes cash equal to Perez's capital balance, the entry is

Assets	= Liabilities +	Equity
−38,000		−38,000

Oct. 31	H. Perez, Capital.	38,000	
	Cash		38,000
	To record withdrawal of Perez from partnership		
	with no bonus.		

Perez can take any combination of assets to which the partners agree to settle Perez's equity. Perez's withdrawal creates a new partnership between the remaining partners. A new partnership contract and a new income-and-loss-sharing agreement are required.

Bonus to Remaining Partners   A withdrawing partner is sometimes willing to take less than the recorded value of his or her equity to get out of the partnership or because the recorded value is overstated. Whatever the reason, when this occurs, the withdrawing partner in effect gives the remaining partners a bonus equal to the equity left behind. The remaining partners share this unwithdrawn equity according to their income-and-loss-sharing ratio. To illustrate, if Perez withdraws and agrees to take $34,000 cash in settlement of Perez's

capital balance, the entry is

Oct. 31	H. Perez, Capital..............................	38,000		Assets = Liabilities + Equity
	Cash		34,000	−34,000 −38,000
	K. Zayn, Capital..........................		2,000	+2,000
	T. Rasheed, Capital......................		2,000	+2,000
	To record withdrawal of Perez and bonus to remaining partners.			

Perez withdrew $4,000 less than Perez's recorded equity of $38,000. This $4,000 is divided between Zayn and Rasheed according to their income-and-loss-sharing ratio.

Bonus to Withdrawing Partner A withdrawing partner may be able to receive more than his or her recorded equity for at least two reasons. First, the recorded equity may be understated. Second, the remaining partners may agree to remove this partner by giving assets of greater value than this partner's recorded equity. In either case, the withdrawing partner receives a bonus. The remaining partners reduce their equity by the amount of this bonus according to their income-and-loss-sharing ratio. To illustrate, if Perez withdraws and receives $40,000 cash in settlement of Perez's capital balance, the entry is

Oct. 31	H. Perez, Capital..............................	38,000		Assets = Liabilities + Equity
	K. Zayn, Capital	1,000		−40,000 −38,000
	T. Rasheed, Capital	1,000		−1,000
	Cash		40,000	−1,000
	To record Perez's withdrawal from partnership with a bonus to Perez.			

Falcon Cable Communications LLC set up a partnership withdrawal agreement. Falcon owns and operates cable television systems and had two managing general partners. The partnership agreement stated that either partner "can offer to sell to the other partner the offering partner's entire partnership interest . . . for a negotiated price. If the partner receiving such an offer rejects it, the offering partner may elect to cause [the partnership] . . . to be liquidated and dissolved."

Death of a Partner

A partner's death dissolves a partnership. A deceased partner's estate is entitled to receive his or her equity. The partnership contract should contain provisions for settlement in this case. These provisions usually require (1) closing the books to determine income or loss since the end of the previous period and (2) determining and recording current market values for both assets and liabilities. The remaining partners and the deceased partner's estate then must agree to a settlement of the deceased partner's equity. This can involve selling the equity to remaining partners or to an outsider, or it can involve withdrawing assets.

Liquidation of a Partnership

When a partnership is liquidated, its business ends and four concluding steps are required.

1. Record the sale of noncash assets for cash and any gain or loss from their liquidation.
2. Allocate any gain or loss from liquidation of the assets in step 1 to the partners using their income-and-loss-sharing ratio.

3. Pay or settle all partner liabilities.

4. Distribute any remaining cash to partners based on their capital balances.

Partnership liquidation usually falls into one of two cases, as described in this section.

No Capital Deficiency

P4   Prepare entries for partnership liquidation.

No capital deficiency means that all partners have a zero or credit balance in their capital accounts for final distribution of cash. To illustrate, assume that Zayn, Perez, and Rasheed operate their partnership in BOARDS for several years, sharing income and loss equally. The partners then decide to liquidate. On the liquidation date, the current period's income or loss is transferred to the partners' capital accounts according to the sharing agreement. After that transfer, assume the partners' recorded equity balances (immediately prior to liquidation) are Zayn, $70,000; Perez, $66,000; and Rasheed, $62,000.

Next, assume that BOARDS sells its noncash assets for a net gain of $6,000. In a liquidation, gains or losses usually result from the sale of noncash assets, which are called *losses and gains from liquidation*. Partners share losses and gains from liquidation according to their income-and-loss-sharing agreement (equal for these partners) yielding the partners' revised equity balances of Zayn, $72,000; Perez, $68,000; and Rasheed, $64,000.[1] Then, after partnership assets are sold and any gain or loss is allocated, the liabilities must be paid. After creditors are paid, any remaining cash is divided among the partners according to their capital account balances. BOARDS' only liability at liquidation is $20,000 in accounts payable. The entries to record the payment to creditors and the final distribution of cash to partners follow.

Assets = Liabilities + Equity
−20,000   −20,000

Assets = Liabilities + Equity
−204,000   −72,000
                      −68,000
                      −64,000

Jan. 15	Accounts Payable	20,000	
	Cash		20,000
	To pay claims of creditors.		
Jan. 15	K. Zayn, Capital	72,000	
	H. Perez, Capital.	68,000	
	T. Rasheed, Capital	64,000	
	Cash		204,000
	To distribute remaining cash to partners.		

It is important to remember that the final cash payment is distributed to partners according to their capital account balances, whereas gains and losses from liquidation are allocated according to the income-and-loss-sharing ratio.

---

[1] The concepts behind these entries are not new. For example, assume that BOARDS has two noncash assets recorded as boarding facilities, $15,000, and land, $25,000. The entry to sell these assets for $46,000 is

Jan. 15	Cash	46,000	
	Boarding facilities		15,000
	Land		25,000
	Gain from Liquidation.		6,000
	Sold noncash assets at a gain.		

We then record the allocation of any loss or gain (a gain in this case) from liquidation according to the partners' income-and-loss-sharing agreement as follows.

Jan. 15	Gain from Liquidation	6,000	
	K. Zayn, Capital		2,000
	H. Perez, Capital		2,000
	T. Rasheed, Capital		2,000
	To allocate liquidation gain to partners.		

Capital Deficiency

Capital deficiency means that at least one partner has a debit balance in his or her capital account at the point of final cash distribution. This can arise from liquidation losses, excessive withdrawals before liquidation, or recurring losses in prior periods. A partner with a capital deficiency must, if possible, cover the deficit by paying cash into the partnership.

To illustrate, assume that Zayn, Perez, and Rasheed operate their partnership in BOARDS for several years, sharing income and losses equally. The partners then decide to liquidate. Immediately prior to the final distribution of cash, the partners' recorded capital balances are Zayn, $19,000; Perez, $8,000; and Rasheed, $(3,000). Rasheed's capital deficiency means that Rasheed owes the partnership $3,000. Both Zayn and Perez have a legal claim against Rasheed's personal assets. The final distribution of cash in this case depends on how this capital deficiency is handled. Two possibilities exist.

Partner Pays Deficiency   Rasheed is obligated to pay $3,000 into the partnership to cover the deficiency. If Rasheed is willing and able to pay, the entry to record receipt of payment from Rasheed follows.

				Assets	= Liabilities +	Equity
Jan. 15	Cash...............................	3,000		+3,000		+3,000
	T. Rasheed, Capital.....................		3,000			
	To record payment of deficiency by Rasheed.					

After the $3,000 payment, the partners' capital balances are Zayn, $19,000; Perez, $8,000; and Rasheed, $0. The entry to record the final cash distributions to partners is

				Assets	= Liabilities +	Equity
Jan. 15	K. Zayn, Capital..........................	19,000		−27,000		−19,000
	H. Perez, Capital.........................	8,000				−8,000
	Cash..............................		27,000			
	To distribute remaining cash to partners.					

Partner Cannot Pay Deficiency   The remaining partners with credit balances absorb any partner's unpaid deficiency according to their income-and-loss-sharing ratio. To illustrate, if Rasheed is unable to pay the $3,000 deficiency, Zayn and Perez absorb it. Since they share income and loss equally, Zayn and Perez each absorb $1,500 of the deficiency. This is recorded as follows.

				Assets	= Liabilities +	Equity
Jan. 15	K. Zayn, Capital..........................	1,500				−1,500
	H. Perez, Capital.........................	1,500				−1,500
	T. Rasheed, Capital.....................		3,000			+3,000
	To transfer Rasheed deficiency to Zayn and Perez.					

After Zayn and Perez absorb Rasheed's deficiency, the capital accounts of the partners are Zayn, $17,500; Perez, $6,500; and Rasheed, $0. The entry to record the final cash distribution to the partners is

				Assets	= Liabilities +	Equity
Jan. 15	K. Zayn, Capital..........................	17,500		−24,000		−17,500
	H. Perez, Capital.........................	6,500				−6,500
	Cash..............................		24,000			
	To distribute remaining cash to partners.					

Rasheed's inability to cover this deficiency does not relieve Rasheed of the liability. If Rasheed becomes able to pay at a future date, Zayn and Perez can each collect $1,500 from Rasheed.

Decision Analysis | **Partner Return on Equity**

A1 Compute partner return on equity and use it to evaluate partnership performance.

An important role of partnership financial statements is to aid current and potential partners in evaluating partnership success compared with other opportunities. One measure of this success is the **partner return on equity** ratio:

$$\text{Partner return on equity} = \frac{\text{Partner net income}}{\text{Average partner equity}}$$

This measure is separately computed for each partner. To illustrate, Exhibit 12.4 reports selected data from the **Boston Celtics LP**. The return on equity for the *total* partnership is computed as $216/[(\$84 + \$252)/2] = 128.6\%$. However, return on equity is quite different across the partners. For example, the **Boston Celtics LP I** partner return on equity is computed as $44/[(\$122 + \$166)/2] = 30.6\%$, whereas the **Celtics LP** partner return on equity is computed as $111/[(\$270 + \$333)/2] = 36.8\%$. Partner return on equity provides *each* partner an assessment of its return on its equity invested in the partnership. A specific partner often uses this return to decide whether additional investment or withdrawal of resources is best for that partner. Exhibit 12.4 reveals that the year shown produced good returns for all partners (the Boston Celtics LP II return is not computed because its average equity is negative due to an unusual and large distribution in the prior year).

Exhibit 12.4

Selected Data from Boston Celtics LP

($ thousands)	Total*	Boston Celtics LP I	Boston Celtics LP II	Celtics LP
Beginning-year balance	$ 84	$122	$(307)	$270
Net income (loss) for year	216	44	61	111
Cash distribution	(48)	—	—	(48)
Ending-year balance	$252	$166	$(246)	$333
Partner return on equity	128.6%	30.6%	n.a.	36.8%

* Totals may not add up due to rounding.

Demonstration Problem

The following transactions and events affect the partners' capital accounts in several successive partnerships. Prepare a table with six columns, one for each of the five partners along with a total column to show the effects of the following events on the five partners' capital accounts.

Part 1

4/13/2007   Ries and Bax create R&B Company. Each invests $10,000, and they agree to share income and losses equally.

12/31/2007   R&B Co. earns $15,000 in income for its first year. Ries withdraws $4,000 from the partnership, and Bax withdraws $7,000.

1/1/2008   Royce is made a partner in RB&R Company after contributing $12,000 cash. The partners agree that a 10% interest allowance will be given on each partner's beginning-year capital balance. In addition, Bax and Royce are to receive $5,000 salary allowances. The remainder of the income or loss is to be divided evenly.

12/31/2008   The partnership's income for the year is $40,000, and withdrawals at year-end are Ries, $5,000; Bax, $12,500; and Royce, $11,000.

1/1/2009   Ries sells her interest for $20,000 to Murdock, whom Bax and Royce accept as a partner in the new BR&M Co. Income or loss is to be shared equally after Bax and Royce each receives $25,000 salary allowances.

12/31/2009   The partnership's income for the year is $35,000, and year-end withdrawals are Bax, $2,500, and Royce, $2,000.

1/1/2010   Elway is admitted as a partner after investing $60,000 cash in the new Elway & Associates partnership. He is given a 50% interest in capital after the other partners transfer $3,000 to his account from each of theirs. A 20% interest allowance (on the beginning-year capital balances) will be used in sharing any income or loss, there will be no salary allowances, and Elway will receive 40% of the remaining balance—the other three partners will each get 20%.

12/31/2010   Elway & Associates earns $127,600 in income for the year, and year-end withdrawals are Bax, $25,000; Royce, $27,000; Murdock, $15,000; and Elway, $40,000.

1/1/2011   Elway buys out Bax and Royce for the balances of their capital accounts after a revaluation of the partnership assets. The revaluation gain is $50,000, which is divided in using a 1:1:1:2 ratio (Bax:Royce:Murdock:Elway). Elway pays the others from personal funds. Murdock and Elway will share income on a 1:9 ratio.

2/29/2011   The partnership earns $10,000 of income since the beginning of the year. Murdock retires and receives partnership cash equal to her capital balance. Elway takes possession of the partnership assets in his own name, and the company is dissolved.

Part 2

Journalize the events affecting the partnership for the year ended December 31, 2008.

Planning the Solution

- Evaluate each transaction's effects on the capital accounts of the partners.
- Each time a new partner is admitted or a partner withdraws, allocate any bonus based on the income-or-loss-sharing agreement.
- Each time a new partner is admitted or a partner withdraws, allocate subsequent net income or loss in accordance with the new partnership agreement.
- Prepare entries to (1) record Royce's initial investment; (2) record the allocation of interest, salaries, and remainder; (3) show the cash withdrawals from the partnership; and (4) close the withdrawal accounts on December 31, 2008.

Solution to Demonstration Problem

Part 1

Event	Ries	Bax	Royce	Murdock	Elway	Total
4/13/2007						
Initial Investment	$10,000	$10,000				$ 20,000
12/31/2007						
Income (equal)	7,500	7,500				15,000
Withdrawals	(4,000)	(7,000)				(11,000)
Ending balance	$13,500	$10,500				$ 24,000
1/1/2008						
New investment			$12,000			$ 12,000
12/31/2008						
10% interest	1,350	1,050	1,200			3,600
Salaries		5,000	5,000			10,000
Remainder (equal)	8,800	8,800	8,800			26,400
Withdrawals	(5,000)	(12,500)	(11,000)			(28,500)
Ending balance	$18,650	$12,850	$16,000			$ 47,500
1/1/2009						
Transfer interest	(18,650)			$18,650		$ 0
12/31/2009						
Salaries		25,000	25,000			50,000
Remainder (equal)		(5,000)	(5,000)	(5,000)		(15,000)
Withdrawals		(2,500)	(2,000)			(4,500)
Ending balance	$ 0	$30,350	$34,000	$13,650		$ 78,000
1/1/2010						
New investment					$ 60,000	60,000
Bonuses to Elway		(3,000)	(3,000)	(3,000)	9,000	0
Adjusted balance		$27,350	$31,000	$10,650	$ 69,000	$138,000

[continued on next page]

[continued from previous page]

Event	Ries	Bax	Royce	Murdock	Elway	Total
12/31/2010						
20% interest		5,470	6,200	2,130	13,800	27,600
Remainder (1:1:1:2)		20,000	20,000	20,000	40,000	100,000
Withdrawals		(25,000)	(27,000)	(15,000)	(40,000)	(107,000)
Ending Balance		$27,820	$30,200	$17,780	$ 82,800	$158,600
1/1/2011						
Gain (1:1:1:2)		10,000	10,000	10,000	20,000	50,000
Adjusted balance		$37,820	$40,200	$27,780	$102,800	$208,600
Transfer interests		(37,820)	(40,200)		78,020	0
Adjusted balance		$ 0	$ 0	$27,780	$180,820	$208,600
2/29/2011						
Income (1:9)				1,000	9,000	10,000
Adjusted balance				$28,780	$189,820	$218,600
Settlements				(28,780)	(189,820)	(218,600)
Final balance				$ 0	$ 0	$ 0

Part 2

2008			
Jan. 1	Cash	12,000	
	Royce, Capital		12,000
	To record investment of Royce.		
Dec. 31	Income Summary	40,000	
	Ries, Capital		10,150
	Bax, Capital		14,850
	Royce, Capital		15,000
	To allocate interest, salaries, and remainders.		
Dec. 31	Ries, Withdrawals	5,000	
	Bax, Withdrawals	12,500	
	Royce, Withdrawals	11,000	
	Cash		28,500
	To record cash withdrawals by partners.		
Dec. 31	Ries, Capital	5,000	
	Bax, Capital	12,500	
	Royce, Capital	11,000	
	Ries, Withdrawals		5,000
	Bax, Withdrawals		12,500
	Royce, Withdrawals		11,000
	To close withdrawal accounts.		

Summary

C1   **Identify characteristics of partnerships and similar organizations.** Partnerships are voluntary associations, involve partnership agreements, have limited life, are not subject to income tax, include mutual agency, and have unlimited liability. Organizations that combine selected characteristics of partnerships and corporations include limited partnerships, limited liability partnerships, S corporations, and limited liability companies.

A1   **Compute partner return on equity and use it to evaluate partnership performance.** Partner return on equity provides each partner an assessment of his or her return on equity invested in the partnership.

P1   **Prepare entries for partnership formation.** A partner's initial investment is recorded at the market value of the assets contributed to the partnership.

P2   **Allocate and record income and loss among partners.** A partnership agreement should specify how to allocate partnership income or loss among partners. Allocation can be based on a stated ratio, capital balances, or salary and interest allowances to compensate partners for differences in their service and capital contributions.

P3   **Account for the admission and withdrawal of partners.** When a new partner buys a partnership interest directly from one or more existing partners, the amount of cash paid from one partner to another does not affect the partnership total recorded equity. When a new partner purchases equity by investing additional assets in the partnership, the new partner's investment can yield a bonus either to existing partners or to the new partner. The entry to record a withdrawal can involve payment from either (1) the existing partners' personal assets or (2) partnership assets. The latter can yield a bonus to either the withdrawing or remaining partners.

P4 **Prepare entries for partnership liquidation.** When a partnership is liquidated, losses and gains from selling partnership assets are allocated to the partners according to their income-and-loss-sharing ratio. If a partner's capital account has a deficiency that the partner cannot pay, the other partners share the deficit according to their relative income-and-loss-sharing ratio.

Guidance Answer to **Decision Ethics**

Financial Planner The partnership agreement apparently fails to mention liabilities or use the term *net assets*. To give the estate one-third of total assets is not fair to the remaining partners because if the partner had lived and the partners had decided to liquidate, the liabilities would need to be paid out of assets before any liquidation. Also, a settlement based on the deceased partner's recorded equity would fail to recognize excess of current value over book value. This value increase would be realized if the partnership were liquidated. A fair settlement would seem to be a payment to the estate for the balance of the deceased partner's equity based on the *current value of net assets.*

Guidance Answers to **Quick Checks**

1. (*b*)

2. *Unlimited liability* means that the creditors of a partnership require each partner to be personally responsible for all partnership debts.

3. (*c*)

4.

	Denzel	Shantell	Total
Net Income			$40,000
Interest allowance (10%)	$ 7,000	$ 3,500	10,500
Balance of income			$29,500
Balance allocated equally	14,750	14,750	29,500
Balance of income			$ 0
Income of partners	$21,750	$18,250	

Key Terms are available at the book's Website for learning and testing in an online Flashcard Format.

C corporation (p. 474)
General partner (p. 473)
General partnership (p. 473)
Limited liability company (LLC) (p. 474)
Limited liability partnership (p. 473)

Limited partners (p. 473)
Limited partnership (p. 473)
Mutual agency (p. 473)
Partner return on equity (p. 484)
Partnership (p. 472)

Partnership contract (p. 472)
Partnership liquidation (p. 482)
S corporation (p. 474)
Statement of partners' equity (p. 477)
Unlimited liability (p. 473)

Multiple Choice Quiz   Answers on p. 497   mhhe.com/wildFAP18e

Multiple Choice Quizzes A and B are available at the book's Website.

1. Stokely and Leder are forming a partnership. Stokely invests a building that has a market value of $250,000; and the partnership assumes responsibility for a $50,000 note secured by a mortgage on that building. Leder invests $100,000 cash. For the partnership, the amounts recorded for the building and for Stokely's Capital account are:

a. Building, $250,000; Stokely, Capital, $250,000.
b. Building, $200,000; Stokely, Capital, $200,000.
c. Building, $200,000; Stokely, Capital, $100,000.
d. Building, $200,000; Stokely, Capital, $250,000.
e. Building, $250,000; Stokely, Capital, $200,000.

2. Katherine, Alliah, and Paulina form a partnership. Katherine contributes $150,000, Alliah contributes $150,000, and Paulina contributes $100,000. Their partnership agreement calls for the income or loss division to be based on the ratio of capital invested. If the partnership reports income of $90,000 for its first year of operations, what amount of income is credited to Paulina's capital account?
   a. $22,500
   b. $25,000
   c. $45,000
   d. $30,000
   e. $90,000

3. Jamison and Blue form a partnership with capital contributions of $600,000 and $800,000, respectively. Their partnership agreement calls for Jamison to receive $120,000 per year in salary. Also, each partner is to receive an interest allowance equal to 10% of the partner's beginning capital contributions, with any remaining income or loss divided equally. If net income for its initial year is $270,000, then Jamison and Blue's respective shares are:
   a. $135,000; $135,000
   b. $154,286; $115,714
   c. $120,000; $150,000

d. $185,000; $85,000
e. $85,000; $185,000

4. Hansen and Fleming are partners and share equally in income or loss. Hansen's current capital balance in the partnership is $125,000 and Fleming's is $124,000. Hansen and Fleming agree to accept Black with a 20% interest. Black invests $75,000 in the partnership. The bonus granted to Hansen and Fleming equals:
   a. $13,000 each.
   b. $5,100 each.
   c. $4,000 each.
   d. $5,285 to Jamison; $4,915 to Blue.
   e. $0; Jamison and Blue grant a bonus to Black.

5. Mee Su is a partner in Hartford Partners, LLC. Her partnership capital balance at the beginning of the current year was $110,000, and her ending balance was $124,000. Her share of the partnership income is $10,500. What is her partner return on equity?
   a. 8.97%
   b. 1060.00%
   c. 9.54%
   d. 1047.00%
   e. 8.47%

Discussion Questions

1. If a partnership contract does not state the period of time the partnership is to exist, when does the partnership end?

2. What does the term *mutual agency* mean when applied to a partnership?

3. Can partners limit the right of a partner to commit their partnership to contracts? Would such an agreement be binding (*a*) on the partners and (*b*) on outsiders?

4. Assume that Amey and Lacey are partners. Lacey dies, and her son claims the right to take his mother's place in the partnership. Does he have this right? Why or why not?

5. Assume that the Barnes and Ardmore partnership agreement provides for a two-third/one-third sharing of income but says nothing about losses. The first year of partnership operation resulted in a loss, and Barnes argues that the loss should be shared equally because the partnership agreement said nothing about sharing losses. Is Barnes correct? Explain.

6. Allocation of partnership income among the partners appears on what financial statement?

7. What does the term *unlimited liability* mean when it is applied to partnership members?

8. How does a general partnership differ from a limited partnership?

9. George, Burton, and Dillman have been partners for three years. The partnership is being dissolved. George is leaving the firm, but Burton and Dillman plan to carry on the business. In the final settlement, George places a $75,000 salary claim against the partnership. He contends that he has a claim for a salary of $25,000 for each year because he devoted all of his time for three years to the affairs of the partnership. Is his claim valid? Why or why not?

10. Kay, Kat, and Kim are partners. In a liquidation, Kay's share of partnership losses exceeds her capital account balance. Moreover, she is unable to meet the deficit from her personal assets, and her partners shared the excess losses. Does this relieve Kay of liability?

11. After all partnership assets have been converted to cash and all liabilities paid, the remaining cash should equal the sum of the balances of the partners' capital accounts. Why?

12. Assume a partner withdraws from a partnership and receives assets of greater value than the book value of his equity. Should the remaining partners share the resulting reduction in their equities in the ratio of their relative capital balances or according to their income-and-loss-sharing ratio?

 Red numbers denote Discussion Questions that involve decision-making.

QUICK STUDY

Amaya and Leon are partners in operating a store. Without consulting Amaya, Leon enters into a contract to purchase merchandise for the store. Amaya contends that she did not authorize the order and refuses to pay for it. The vendor sues the partners for the contract price of the merchandise. (*a*) Must the partnership pay for the merchandise? Why? (*b*) Does your answer differ if Amaya and Leon are partners in a public accounting firm? Explain.

QS 12-1
Partnership liability

C1

Ann Stolton and Susie Bright are partners in a business they started two years ago. The partnership agreement states that Stolton should receive a salary allowance of $15,000 and that Bright should receive a $20,000 salary allowance. Any remaining income or loss is to be shared equally. Determine each partner's share of the current year's net income of $52,000.

QS 12-2
Partnership income allocation

P2

Blake and Matthai are partners who agree that Blake will receive a $100,000 salary allowance and that any remaining income or loss will be shared equally. If Matthai's capital account is credited for $2,000 as her share of the net income in a given period, how much net income did the partnership earn in that period?

QS 12-3
Partnership income allocation

P2

Frain organized a limited partnership and is the only general partner. Mourlan invested $20,000 in the partnership and was admitted as a limited partner with the understanding that he would receive 10% of the profits. After two unprofitable years, the partnership ceased doing business. At that point, partnership liabilities were $85,000 larger than partnership assets. How much money can the partnership's creditors obtain from Mourlan personal assets to satisfy the unpaid partnership debts?

QS 12-4
Liability in limited partnerships

P1

Stein agrees to pay Choi and Amal $10,000 each for a one-third (33⅓%) interest in the Choi and Amal partnership. Immediately prior to Stein's admission, each partner had a $30,000 capital balance. Make the journal entry to record Stein's purchase of the partners' interest.

QS 12-5
Partner admission
through purchase of interest   P3

Jules and Johnson are partners, each with $40,000 in their partnership capital accounts. Kwon is admitted to the partnership by investing $40,000 cash. Make the entry to show Kwon's admission to the partnership.

QS 12-6
Admission of a partner   P3

Howe and Duley's company is organized as a partnership. At the prior year-end, partnership equity totaled $150,000 ($100,000 from Howe and $50,000 from Duley). For the current year, partnership net income is $25,000 ($20,000 allocated to Howe and $5,000 allocated to Duley), and year-end total partnership equity is $200,000 ($140,000 from Howe and $60,000 from Duley). Compute the total partnership return on equity *and* the individual partner return on equity ratios.

QS 12-7
Partner return on equity

A1

EXERCISES

Next to the following list of eight characteristics of business organizations, write a brief description of how each characteristic applies to general partnerships.

Exercise 12-1
Characteristics of partnerships

C1

Characteristic	Application to General Partnerships
1. Life	
2. Owners' liability	
3. Legal status	
4. Tax status of income	
5. Owners' authority	
6. Ease of formation	
7. Transferability of ownership	
8. Ability to raise large amounts of capital	

Exercise 12-2
Forms of organization

C1

For each of the following separate cases, recommend a form of business organization. With each recommendation, explain how business income would be taxed if the owners adopt the form of organization recommended. Also list several advantages that the owners will enjoy from the form of business organization that you recommend.

a. Sharif, Henry, and Korb are recent college graduates in computer science. They want to start a Website development company. They all have college debts and currently do not own any substantial computer equipment needed to get the company started.

b. Dr. Ward and Dr. Liu are recent graduates from medical residency programs. Both are family practice physicians and would like to open a clinic in an underserved rural area. Although neither has any funds to bring to the new venture, a banker has expressed interest in making a loan to provide start-up funds for their practice.

c. Munson has been out of school for about five years and has become quite knowledgeable about the commercial real estate market. He would like to organize a company that buys and sells real estate. Munson believes he has the expertise to manage the company but needs funds to invest in commercial property.

Exercise 12-3
Journalizing partnership transactions

P2

On March 1, 2008, Eckert and Kelley formed a partnership. Eckert contributed $82,500 cash and Kelley contributed land valued at $60,000 and a building valued at $100,000. The partnership also assumed responsibility for Kelley's $92,500 long-term note payable associated with the land and building. The partners agreed to share income as follows: Eckert is to receive an annual salary allowance of $25,000, both are to receive an annual interest allowance of 10% of their beginning-year capital investment, and any remaining income or loss is to be shared equally. On October 20, 2008, Eckert withdrew $34,000 cash and Kelley withdrew $20,000 cash. After the adjusting and closing entries are made to the revenue and expense accounts at December 31, 2008, the Income Summary account had a credit balance of $90,000.

1. Prepare journal entries to record (*a*) the partners' initial capital investments, (*b*) their cash withdrawals, and (*c*) the December 31 closing of both the Withdrawals and Income Summary accounts.

Check (2) Kelley, $79,250

2. Determine the balances of the partners' capital accounts as of December 31, 2008.

Exercise 12-4
Income allocation in a partnership

P2

Kramer and Knox began a partnership by investing $60,000 and $80,000, respectively. During its first year, the partnership earned $160,000. Prepare calculations showing how the $160,000 income should be allocated to the partners under each of the following three separate plans for sharing income and loss: (1) the partners failed to agree on a method to share income; (2) the partners agreed to share income and loss in proportion to their initial investments (round amounts to the nearest dollar); and (3) the partners agreed to share income by granting a $50,000 per year salary allowance to Kramer, a $40,000 per year salary allowance to Knox, 10% interest on their initial capital investments, and the remaining balance shared equally.

Check Plan 3, Kramer, $84,000

Exercise 12-5
Income allocation in a partnership

P2

Check (2) Kramer, $(4,400)

Assume that the partners of Exercise 12-4 agreed to share net income and loss by granting annual salary allowances of $50,000 to Kramer and $40,000 to Knox, 10% interest allowances on their investments, and any remaining balance shared equally.

1. Determine the partners' shares of Kramer and Knox given a first-year net income of $98,800.

2. Determine the partners' shares of Kramer and Knox given a first-year net loss of $16,800.

Exercise 12-6
Sale of partnership interest   P3

The partners in the Biz Partnership have agreed that partner Mandy may sell her $100,000 equity in the partnership to Brittney, for which Brittney will pay Mandy $85,000. Present the partnership's journal entry to record the sale of Mandy's interest to Brittney on September 30.

Exercise 12-7
Admission of new partner

P3

The Struter Partnership has total partners' equity of $510,000, which is made up of Main, Capital, $400,000, and Frist, Capital, $110,000. The partners share net income and loss in a ratio of 80% to Main and 20% to Frist. On November 1, Madison is admitted to the partnership and given a 15% interest in equity and a 15% share in any income and loss. Prepare the journal entry to record the admission of Madison under each of the following separate assumptions: Madison invests cash of (1) $90,000; (2) $120,000; and (3) $80,000.

Holland, Flowers, and Tulip have been partners while sharing net income and loss in a 5:3:2 ratio. On January 31, the date Tulip retires from the partnership, the equities of the partners are Holland, $150,000; Flowers, $90,000; and Tulip, $60,000. Present journal entries to record Tulip's retirement under each of the following separate assumptions: Tulip is paid for her equity using partnership cash of (1) $60,000; (2) $80,000; and (3) $30,000.

Exercise 12-8
Retirement of partner
P3

The Red, White & Blue partnership was begun with investments by the partners as follows: Red, $180,000; White, $240,000; and Blue, $210,000. The operations did not go well, and the partners eventually decided to liquidate the partnership, sharing all losses equally. On August 31, after all assets were converted to cash and all creditors were paid, only $60,000 in partnership cash remained.

1. Compute the capital account balance of each partner after the liquidation of assets and the payment of creditors.

2. Assume that any partner with a deficit agrees to pay cash to the partnership to cover the deficit. Present the journal entries on August 31 to record (*a*) the cash receipt from the deficient partner(s) and (*b*) the final disbursement of cash to the partners.

3. Assume that any partner with a deficit is not able to reimburse the partnership. Present journal entries (*a*) to transfer the deficit of any deficient partners to the other partners and (*b*) to record the final disbursement of cash to the partners.

Exercise 12-9
Liquidation of partnership
P4

Check (1) Red, $(10,000)

Turner, Roth, and Lowe are partners who share income and loss in a 1:4:5 ratio. After lengthy disagreements among the partners and several unprofitable periods, the partners decided to liquidate the partnership. Immediately before liquidation, the partnership balance sheet shows: total assets, $126,000; total liabilities, $78,000; Turner, Capital, $2,500; Roth, Capital, $14,000; and Lowe, Capital, $31,500. The cash proceeds from selling the assets were sufficient to repay all but $28,000 to the creditors. (*a*) Calculate the loss from selling the assets. (*b*) Allocate the loss to the partners. (*c*) Determine how much of the remaining liability should be paid by each partner.

Exercise 12-10
Liquidation of partnership P4

Check (b) Lowe, Capital after allocation, $(6,500)

Assume that the Turner, Roth, and Lowe partnership of Exercise 12-10 is a limited partnership. Turner and Roth are general partners and Lowe is a limited partner. How much of the remaining $28,000 liability should be paid by each partner?

Exercise 12-11
Liquidation of limited partnership
P4

Hunt Sports Enterprises LP is organized as a limited partnership consisting of two individual partners: Soccer LP and Football LP. Both partners separately operate a minor league soccer team and a semipro football team. Compute partner return on equity for each limited partnership (and the total) for the year ended June 30, 2008, using the following selected data on partner capital balances from Hunt Sports Enterprises LP.

Exercise 12-12
Partner return on equity
A1

	Soccer LP	Football LP	Total
Balance at 6/30/2007	$189,000	$ 758,000	$ 947,000
Annual net income	22,134	445,898	468,032
Cash distribution	—	(50,000)	(50,000)
Balance at 6/30/2008	$211,134	$1,153,898	$1,365,032

Kim Ries, Tere Bax, and Josh Thomas invested $80,000, $112,000, and $128,000, respectively, in a partnership. During its first calendar-year, the firm earned $249,000.

PROBLEM SET A

Problem 12-1A
Allocating partnership income
P2

Required

Prepare the entry to close the firm's Income Summary account as of its December 31 year-end and to allocate the $249,000 net income to the partners under each of the following separate assumptions: The partners (1) have no agreement on the method of sharing income and loss; (2) agreed to share income and loss in the ratio of their beginning capital investments; and (3) agreed to share income and loss by providing annual salary allowances of $66,000 to Ries, $56,000 to Bax, and $80,000 to Thomas; granting 10% interest on the partners' beginning capital investments; and sharing the remainder equally.

Check (3) Thomas, Capital, $97,800

Problem 12-2A

Allocating partnership income and loss; sequential years

P2

mhhe.com/wildFAP18e

Irma Watts and John Lyon are forming a partnership to which Watts will devote one-half time and Lyon will devote full time. They have discussed the following alternative plans for sharing income and loss: (*a*) in the ratio of their initial capital investments, which they have agreed will be $42,000 for Watts and $63,000 for Lyon; (*b*) in proportion to the time devoted to the business; (*c*) a salary allowance of $6,000 per month to Lyon and the balance in accordance with the ratio of their initial capital investments; or (*d*) a salary allowance of $6,000 per month to Lyon, 10% interest on their initial capital investments, and the balance shared equally. The partners expect the business to perform as follows: Year 1, $36,000 net loss; Year 2, $90,000 net income; and Year 3, $150,000 net income.

Required

Prepare three tables with the following column headings.

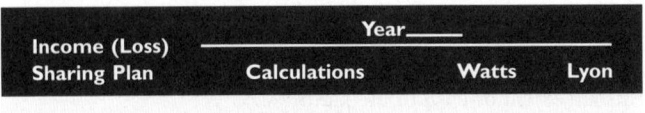

Income (Loss) Sharing Plan	Year_____		
	Calculations	Watts	Lyon

Check Plan d, Year 1, Lyon's share, $19,050

Complete the tables, one for each of the first three years, by showing how to allocate partnership income or loss to the partners under each of the four plans being considered. (Round answers to the nearest whole dollar.)

Problem 12-3A

Partnership income allocation, statement of partners' equity, and closing entries

P2

mhhe.com/wildFAP18e

Bill Beck, Bruce Beck, and Barb Beck formed the BBB Partnership by making capital contributions of $67,500, $262,500, and $420,000, respectively. They predict annual partnership net income of $450,000 and are considering the following alternative plans of sharing income and loss: (*a*) equally; (*b*) in the ratio of their initial capital investments; or (*c*) salary allowances of $80,000 to Bill, $60,000 to Bruce, and $90,000 to Barb; interest allowances of 10% on their initial capital investments; and the balance shared equally.

Required

1. Prepare a table with the following column headings.

Income (Loss) Sharing Plan	Calculations	Bill	Bruce	Barb	Total

Check (2) Barb, Ending Capital, $456,000

Use the table to show how to distribute net income of $450,000 for the calendar year under each of the alternative plans being considered. (Round answers to the nearest whole dollar.)

2. Prepare a statement of partners' equity showing the allocation of income to the partners assuming they agree to use plan (*c*), that income earned is $209,000, and that Bill, Bruce, and Barb withdraw $34,000, $48,000, and $64,000, respectively, at year-end.

3. Prepare the December 31 journal entry to close Income Summary assuming they agree to use plan (*c*) and that net income is $209,000. Also close the withdrawals accounts.

Problem 12-4A

Partner withdrawal and admission

P3

Check (1e) Cr. Lau, Capital, $38,250

Part 1. Meir, Benson, and Lau are partners and share income and loss in a 3:2:5 ratio. The partnership's capital balances are as follows: Meir, $168,000; Benson, $138,000; and Lau, $294,000. Benson decides to withdraw from the partnership, and the partners agree to not have the assets revalued upon Benson's retirement. Prepare journal entries to record Benson's February 1 withdrawal from the partnership under each of the following separate assumptions: Benson (*a*) sells his interest to North for $160,000 after Meir and Lau approve the entry of North as a partner; (*b*) gives his interest to a son-in-law, Schmidt, and thereafter Meir and Lau accept Schmidt as a partner; (*c*) is paid $138,000 in partnership cash for his equity; (*d*) is paid $214,000 in partnership cash for his equity; and (*e*) is paid $30,000 in partnership cash plus equipment recorded on the partnership books at $70,000 less its accumulated depreciation of $23,200.

Part 2. Assume that Benson does not retire from the partnership described in Part 1. Instead, Rhodes is admitted to the partnership on February 1 with a 25% equity. Prepare journal entries to record Rhodes's entry into the partnership under each of the following separate assumptions: Rhodes invests (*a*) $200,000; (*b*) $145,000; and (*c*) $262,000.

(2c) Cr. Benson, Capital, $9,300

Kendra, Cogley, and Mei share income and loss in a 3:2:1 ratio. The partners have decided to liquidate their partnership. On the day of liquidation their balance sheet appears as follows.

Problem 12-5A
Liquidation of a partnership

P4

KENDRA, COGLEY, AND MEI			
Balance Sheet			
May 31			
Assets		**Liabilities and Equity**	
Cash	$180,800	Accounts payable	$245,500
Inventory	537,200	Kendra, Capital	93,000
		Cogley, Capital	212,500
		Mei, Capital	167,000
Total assets	$718,000	Total liabilities and equity	$718,000

Required

Prepare journal entries for (*a*) the sale of inventory, (*b*) the allocation of its gain or loss, (*c*) the payment of liabilities at book value, and (*d*) the distribution of cash in each of the following separate cases: Inventory is sold for (1) $600,000; (2) $500,000; (3) $320,000 and any partners with capital deficits pay in the amount of their deficits; and (4) $250,000 and the partners have no assets other than those invested in the partnership. (Round to the nearest dollar.)

Check   (4) Cash distribution, Mei, $102,266

Matt Albin, Ryan Peters, and Seth Ramsey invested $164,000, $98,400, and $65,600, respectively, in a partnership. During its first calendar-year, the firm earned $270,000.

PROBLEM SET B

Problem 12-1B
Allocating partnership income

P2

Required

Prepare the entry to close the firm's Income Summary account as of its December 31 year-end and to allocate the $270,000 net income to the partners under each of the following separate assumptions. (Round answers to whole dollars.) The partners (1) have no agreement on the method of sharing income and loss; (2) agreed to share income and loss in the ratio of their beginning capital investments; and (3) agreed to share income and loss by providing annual salary allowances of $96,000 to Albin, $72,000 to Peters, and $50,000 to Ramsey; granting 10% interest on the partners' beginning capital investments; and sharing the remainder equally.

Check   (3) Ramsey, Capital, $62,960

Maria Bell and J. R. Green are forming a partnership to which Bell will devote one-third time and Green will devote full time. They have discussed the following alternative plans for sharing income and loss: (*a*) in the ratio of their initial capital investments, which they have agreed will be $104,000 for Bell and $156,000 for Green; (*b*) in proportion to the time devoted to the business; (*c*) a salary allowance of $4,000 per month to Green and the balance in accordance with the ratio of their initial capital investments; or (*d*) a salary allowance of $4,000 per month to Green, 10% interest on their initial capital investments, and the balance shared equally. The partners expect the business to perform as follows: Year 1, $36,000 net loss; Year 2, $76,000 net income; and Year 3, $188,000 net income.

Problem 12-2B
Allocating partnership income and loss; sequential years

P2

Required

Prepare three tables with the following column headings.

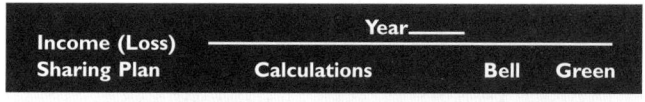

Income (Loss) Sharing Plan	Year_____		
	Calculations	Bell	Green

Complete the tables, one for each of the first three years, by showing how to allocate partnership income or loss to the partners under each of the four plans being considered. (Round answers to the nearest whole dollar.)

Problem 12-3B

Partnership income allocation, statement of partners' equity, and closing entries

P2

Sally Cook, Lin Xi, and Ken Schwartz formed the CXS Partnership by making capital contributions of $144,000, $216,000, and $120,000, respectively. They predict annual partnership net income of $240,000 and are considering the following alternative plans of sharing income and loss: (*a*) equally; (*b*) in the ratio of their initial capital investments; or (*c*) salary allowances of $40,000 to Cook, $30,000 to Xi, and $80,000 to Schwartz; interest allowances of 12% on their initial capital investments; and the balance shared equally.

Required

1. Prepare a table with the following column headings.

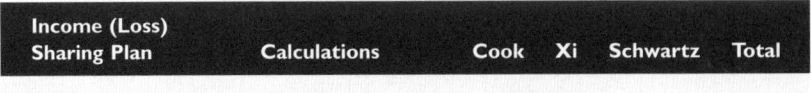

Income (Loss) Sharing Plan	Calculations	Cook	Xi	Schwartz	Total

Use the table to show how to distribute net income of $240,000 for the calendar year under each of the alternative plans being considered. (Round answers to the nearest whole dollar.)

2. Prepare a statement of partners' equity showing the allocation of income to the partners assuming they agree to use plan (*c*), that income earned is $87,600, and that Cook, Xi, and Schwartz withdraw $18,000, $38,000, and $24,000, respectively, at year-end.

3. Prepare the December 31 journal entry to close Income Summary assuming they agree to use plan *c* and that net income is $87,600. Also close the withdrawals accounts.

Problem 12-4B

Partner withdrawal and admission

P3

Part 1. Craig, Cook, and Chan are partners and share income and loss in a 5:1:4 ratio. The partnership's capital balances are as follows: Craig, $606,000; Cook, $148,000; and Chan, $446,000. Craig decides to withdraw from the partnership, and the partners agree not to have the assets revalued upon Craig's retirement. Prepare journal entries to record Craig's April 30 withdrawal from the partnership under each of the following separate assumptions: Craig (*a*) sells her interest to Collin for $250,000 after Cook and Chan approve the entry of Collin as a partner; (*b*) gives her interest to a daughter-in-law, Cam, and thereafter Cook and Chan accept Cam as a partner; (*c*) is paid $606,000 in partnership cash for her equity; (*d*) is paid $350,000 in partnership cash for her equity; and (*e*) is paid $200,000 in partnership cash plus manufacturing equipment recorded on the partnership books at $538,000 less its accumulated depreciation of $336,000.

Part 2. Assume that Craig does not retire from the partnership described in Part 1. Instead, Chip is admitted to the partnership on April 30 with a 20% equity. Prepare journal entries to record the entry of Chip under each of the following separate assumptions: Chip invests (*a*) $300,000; (*b*) $196,000; and (*c*) $426,000.

Problem 12-5B

Liquidation of a partnership

P4

Lasure, Ramirez, and Toney, who share income and loss in a 2:1:2 ratio, plan to liquidate their partnership. At liquidation, their balance sheet appears as follows.

LASURE, RAMIREZ, AND TONEY
Balance Sheet
January 18

Assets		Liabilities and Equity	
Cash	$348,600	Accounts payable	$342,600
Equipment	617,200	Lasure, Capital	300,400
		Ramirez, Capital	195,800
		Toney, Capital	127,000
Total assets	$965,800	Total liabilities and equity	$965,800

Required

Prepare journal entries for (*a*) the sale of equipment, (*b*) the allocation of its gain or loss, (*c*) the payment of liabilities at book value, and (*d*) the distribution of cash in each of the following separate cases: Equipment is sold for (1) $650,000; (2) $530,000; (3) $200,000 and any partners with capital deficits pay in the amount of their deficits; and (4) $150,000 and the partners have no assets other than those invested in the partnership.

Check (4) Cash distribution, Lasure, $73,600

 Problem Set C is available at the book's Website to further reinforce and assess your learning.

PROBLEM SET C

(This serial problem began in Chapter 1 and continues through most of the book. If previous chapter segments were not completed, the serial problem can begin at this point. It is helpful, but not necessary, for you to use the Working Papers that accompany the book.)

SERIAL PROBLEM

Success Systems

SP 12 At the start of 2008, Adriana Lopez is considering adding a partner to her business. She envisions the new partner taking the lead in generating sales of both services and merchandise for Success Systems. Lopez's equity in Success Systems as of January 1, 2008, is reflected in the following capital balance.

A. Lopez, Capital $117,435

Required

1. Lopez is evaluating whether the prospective partner should be an equal partner with respect to capital investment and profit sharing (1:1) or whether the agreement should be 3:1 with Lopez retaining three-fourths interest with rights to three-fourths of the net income or loss. What factors should she consider in deciding which partnership agreement to offer?

2. Prepare the January 1, 2008, journal entry(ies) necessary to admit a new partner to Success Systems through the purchase of a partnership interest for each of the following two separate cases (*a*) 1:1 sharing agreement and (*b*) 3:1 sharing agreement.

3. Prepare the January 1, 2008, journal entry(ies) required to admit a new partner if the new partner invests cash of $39,145.

4. After posting the entry in part 3, what would be the new partner's equity percentage?

BEYOND THE NUMBERS

BTN 12-1 Take a step back in time and imagine **Best Buy** in its infancy as a company. The year is 1966.

REPORTING IN ACTION

C1

Required

1. Read the history of Best Buy at **BestBuymedia.tekgroup.com**. Can you determine from the history whether Best Buy was originally organized as a sole proprietorship, partnership, or corporation?

2. Assume that Best Buy was originally organized as a partnership. Best Buy's income statement in Appendix A varies in several key ways from what it would look like for a partnership. Explain how a corporate income statement differs from a partnership income statement.

3. Compare the Best Buy balance sheet in Appendix A to what a partnership balance sheet would have shown. Identify and explain any account differences you would anticipate.

BTN 12-2 Over the years **Best Buy** and **Circuit City** have evolved into large corporations. Today it is difficult to imagine them as fledgling start-ups. Research each company's history online.

COMPARATIVE ANALYSIS

C1

Required

1. Which company is older?

2. Which company started as a partnership?

3. In what years did each company first achieve $1,000,000 in sales?

4. In what years did each company have its first public offering of stock?

**ETHICS
CHALLENGE**

P2

BTN 12-3   Doctors Maben, Orlando, and Clark have been in a group practice for several years. Maben and Orlando are family practice physicians, and Clark is a general surgeon. Clark receives many referrals for surgery from his family practice partners. Upon the partnership's original formation, the three doctors agreed to a two-part formula to share income. Every month each doctor receives a salary allowance of $3,000. Additional income is divided according to a percent of patient charges the doctors generate for the month. In the current month, Maben generated 10% of the billings, Orlando 30%, and Clark 60%. The group's income for this month is $50,000. Clark has expressed dissatisfaction with the income-sharing formula and asks that income be split entirely on patient charge percents.

Required

1. Compute the income allocation for the current month using the original agreement.

2. Compute the income allocation for the current month using Clark's proposed agreement.

3. Identify the ethical components of this partnership decision for the doctors.

**COMMUNICATING
IN PRACTICE**

C1

BTN 12-4   Assume that you are studying for an upcoming accounting exam with a good friend. Your friend says that she has a solid understanding of general partnerships but is less sure that she understands organizations that combine certain characteristics of partnerships with other forms of business organization. You offer to make some study notes for your friend to help her learn about limited partnerships, limited liability partnerships, S Corporations, and limited liability companies. Prepare a one-page set of well-organized, complete study notes on these four forms of business organization.

**TAKING IT TO
THE NET**

P1   P2

BTN 12-5   Access the February 8, 2005, filing of the December 31, 2004, 10-K of **America First Tax Exempt Investors LP**. This company deals with tax-exempt mortgage revenue bonds that, among other things, finance student housing properties.

1. Locate its December 31, 2004, balance sheet and list the account titles reported in the equity section of the balance sheet.

2. Locate its statement of partners' capital and comprehensive income (loss). How many units of limited partnership (known as "beneficial unit certificate holders") are outstanding at December 31, 2004?

3. What is the partnership's largest asset and its amount at December 31, 2004?

**TEAMWORK IN
ACTION**

P2

BTN 12-6   This activity requires teamwork to reinforce understanding of accounting for partnerships.

Required

1. Assume that Baker, Warner, and Rice form the BWR Partnership by making capital contributions of $200,000, $300,000, and $500,000, respectively. BWR predicts annual partnership net income of $600,000. The partners are considering various plans for sharing income and loss. Assign a different team member to compute how the projected $600,000 income would be shared under each of the following separate plans:

   a. Shared equally.

   b. In the ratio of the partners' initial capital investments.

   c. Salary allowances of $50,000 to Baker, $60,000 to Warner, and $70,000 to Rice, with the remaining balance shared equally.

   d. Interest allowances of 10% on the partners' initial capital investments, with the remaining balance shared equally.

2. In sequence, each member is to present his or her income-sharing calculations with the team.

3. As a team, identify and discuss at least one other possible way that income could be shared.

BTN 12-7 Read the article "A Partnership That's Really Limited" in the May 25, 2005, issue of *BusinessWeek*. (This book's Website provides a free link.)

1. Who does the author contend are the winners in a limited partnership such as **Williams Partners**?
2. Why does the author say that the general partner will be better off in Williams Partners than the limited partners?
3. Why do investors invest in limited partnerships if the general partners seem to do better than the limited partners?

BusinessWeek ACTIVITY

C1

BTN 12-8 Revisit the chapter's opening feature involving Catharine Lyons and Elska Sandor and their company **Rookie Skateboards**. Assume that Lyons and Sandor have decided to expand with the help of general partners.

ENTREPRENEURIAL DECISION

C1

Required

1. What details should Lyons, Sandor, and their future partners specify in their general partnership agreements?
2. What advantages should Lyons, Sandor, and their future partners be aware of with respect to organizing as general partnerships?
3. What disadvantages should Lyons, Sandor, and their future partners be aware of with respect to organizing as general partnerships?

BTN 12-9 Access **Dixons**'s Website (**Dixons-Group.com**) and research the company's history.

1. When was the company founded, and what was its original form of ownership?
2. Why did the company use the name Dixons?
3. What were some of the acquisitions that caused Dixons to become "Dixons Group?"

GLOBAL DECISION

C1

Dixons

ANSWERS TO MULTIPLE CHOICE QUIZ

1. e; Capital = $250,000 − $50,000
2. a; $90,000 × [$100,000/($150,000 + $150,000 + $100,000)] = $22,500
3. d;

	Jamison	Blue	Total
Net income			$ 270,000
Salary allowance	$120,000		(120,000)
Interest allowance.	60,000	$80,000	(140,000)
Balance of income.			10,000
Balance divided equally	5,000	5,000	(10,000)
Totals.	$185,000	$85,000	$ 0

4. b; Total partnership equity = $125,000 + $124,000 + $75,000 = $324,000
   Equity of Black = $324,000 × 20% = $64,800
   Bonus to old partners = $75,000 − $64,800 = $10,200, split equally
5. a; $10,500/[($110,000 + $124,000)/2] = 8.97%

13 Accounting for Corporations

A Look Back

Chapter 12 focused on the partnership form of organization. We described crucial characteristics of partnerships and the accounting and reporting of their important transactions.

A Look at This Chapter

This chapter emphasizes details of the corporate form of organization. The accounting concepts and procedures for equity transactions are explained. We also describe how to report and analyze income, earnings per share, and retained earnings.

A Look Ahead

Chapter 14 focuses on long-term liabilities. We explain how to value, record, amortize, and report these liabilities in financial statements.

Learning Objectives

CAP

Conceptual

C1 Identify characteristics of corporations and their organization. (p. 500)

C2 Describe the components of stockholders' equity. (p. 503)

C3 Explain characteristics of common and preferred stock. (p. 511)

C4 Explain the items reported in retained earnings. (p. 516)

Analytical

A1 Compute earnings per share and describe its use. (p. 518)

A2 Compute price-earnings ratio and describe its use in analysis. (p. 519)

A3 Compute dividend yield and explain its use in analysis. (p. 519)

A4 Compute book value and explain its use in analysis. (p. 520)

Procedural

P1 Record the issuance of corporate stock. (p. 504)

P2 Record transactions involving cash dividends. (p. 507)

P3 Account for stock dividends and stock splits. (p. 508)

P4 Distribute dividends between common stock and preferred stock. (p. 511)

P5 Record purchases and sales of treasury stock and the retirement of stock. (p. 514)

"Keep your eye on the big picture of where you want to be five years from now; don't get lost in the day to day"
—Sundeep Bhan
(Top; Sanjay Pingle and Sameer Shariff, middle, left to right; and Rajnish Kapoor, bottom)

Genesis of a Life-Saving Business

NEW YORK, NY—Sundeep Bhan, Sanjay Pingle, Sameer Shariff, and Rajnish Kapoor are immigrant success stories. Together, they launched **Medsite, Inc. (Medsite.com)**, a healthcare marketing and pharmaceutical services company. The genesis for Medsite was Sundeep's frustration with a lack of spell-checking software in the medical field—and the birthplace of their startup was a cramped Manhattan loft. Sundeep says, "I had some furniture, a computer, and together we had about $5,000." But by the time they had sold their first product, the spell-checker, to Mosby, the entrepreneurial spirit had overcome them.

Cofounder, Sanjay Pingle, says they then "set up a few Websites for products... and people started calling in. That's when we realized we were onto something bigger." The friends began providing promotional and educational help to physicians, including continuing education. "We really started out with the physician in mind, and have been able to keep that as a core part of our vision," adds Sundeep.

With limited capital, the four entrepreneurs struggled to get financial backing. Investors wanted to see success, but without cash it was an uphill battle. "We once had to leave a restaurant because they would take only cash, no credit cards," recalls co-founder Sameer Shariff. The four also faced serious accounting-related corporate issues, including corporate formation, organization form, capital stock, and stock issuance. Yet the friends persisted. "We wanted something of our own," says Sanjay. "We all had the crazy [entrepreneurial] drive."

The four also shared a sense of community and a commitment to helping others. Our educational service "is a great tool to get information to physicians, and a great way for pharmaceuticals to sponsor medical education," says Sundeep. He also credits Medsite's success to an online database of drug products and its online continuing-education courses for physicians. Those services are free for doctors and paid for by Medsite's pharmaceutical clients.

Medsite's success in the business of saving lives has helped it secure financing. Although the company still confronts the realities of a corporate world—such as stock distributions, dividends, and equity reporting—it seems to be worth the effort. Sundeep proudly exclaims, "We want a [company]... where people come in to work looking forward to the day, and leave work in the evening looking forward to coming back the next morning."

[Sources: *Medsite Website*, January 2006; *Rediff.com*, May 1999; *Siliconindia*, July 1999; *Indus Business Journal*, September 2002; *Frost and Sullivan Market Insight*, April 2004]

This chapter focuses on equity transactions. The first part of the chapter describes the basics of the corporate form of organization and explains the accounting for common and preferred stock. We then focus on several special financing transactions, including cash and stock dividends, stock splits, and treasury stock. The final section considers accounting for retained earnings, including prior period adjustments, retained earnings restrictions, and reporting guidelines.

Accounting for Corporations

Corporations	Common Stock	Dividends	Preferred Stock	Treasury Stock	Reporting on Equity
• Characteristics • Organization and management • Stockholders • Stock basics	• Par value • No-par value • Stated value • Stock for noncash assets	• Cash dividends • Stock dividends • Stock splits	• Issuance of preferred • Dividend preferences • Convertible preferred • Callable preferred	• Purchasing treasury stock • Reissuing treasury stock • Retiring stock	• Statement of retained earnings • Statement of stockholders' equity • Stock options

Corporate Form of Organization

A **corporation** is an entity created by law that is separate from its owners. It has most of the rights and privileges granted to individuals. Owners of corporations are called *stockholders* or *shareholders*. Corporations can be separated into two types. A *privately held* (or *closely held*) corporation does not offer its stock for public sale and usually has few stockholders. A *publicly held* corporation offers its stock for public sale and can have thousands of stockholders. *Public sale* usually refers to issuance and trading on an organized stock market.

Characteristics of Corporations

C1 Identify characteristics of corporations and their organization.

Corporations represent an important type of organization. Their unique characteristics offer advantages and disadvantages.

Advantages of Corporate Characteristics

■ **Separate legal entity:** A corporation conducts its affairs with the same rights, duties, and responsibilities of a person. It takes actions through its agents, who are its officers and managers.

■ **Limited liability of stockholders:** Stockholders are neither liable for corporate acts nor corporate debt.

■ **Transferable ownership rights:** The transfer of shares from one stockholder to another usually has no effect on the corporation or its operations except when this causes a change in the directors who control or manage the corporation.

■ **Continuous life:** A corporation's life continues indefinitely because it is not tied to the physical lives of its owners.

■ **Lack of mutual agency for stockholders:** A corporation acts through its agents, who are its officers and managers. Stockholders, who are not its officers and managers, do not have the power to bind the corporation to contracts—referred to as *lack of mutual agency*.

Point: The *business entity principle* requires a corporation to be accounted for separately from its owners (shareholders).

Global: U.S., U.K., and Canadian corporations finance much of their operations with stock issuances, but companies in countries such as France, Germany, and Japan finance mainly with note and bond issuances.

■ **Ease of capital accumulation:** Buying stock is attractive to investors because (1) stockholders are not liable for the corporation's acts and debts, (2) stocks usually are transferred easily, (3) the life of the corporation is unlimited, and (4) stockholders are not corporate agents. These advantages enable corporations to accumulate large amounts of capital from the combined investments of many stockholders.

Disadvantages of Corporate Characteristics

■ **Government regulation:** A corporation must meet requirements of a state's incorporation laws, which subject the corporation to state regulation and control. Proprietorships and partnerships avoid many of these regulations and governmental reports.

■ **Corporate taxation:** Corporations are subject to the same property and payroll taxes as proprietorships and partnerships plus *additional* taxes. The most burdensome of these are federal and state income taxes that together can take 40% or more of corporate pretax income. Moreover, corporate income is usually taxed a second time as part of stockholders' personal income when they receive cash distributed as dividends. This is called *double taxation.* (The usual dividend tax is 15%; however, it is less than 15% for lower income taxpayers, and in some cases zero.)

Point: Proprietorships and partnerships are not subject to income taxes. Their income is taxed as the personal income of their owners.

Point: Double taxation is less severe when a corporation's owner-manager collects a salary that is taxed only once as part of his or her personal income.

Corporate Organization and Management

This section describes the incorporation, costs, and management of corporate organizations.

Incorporation   A corporation is created by obtaining a charter from a state government. A charter application usually must be signed by the prospective stockholders called *incorporators* or *promoters* and then filed with the proper state official. When the application process is complete and fees paid, the charter is issued and the corporation is formed. Investors then purchase the corporation's stock, meet as stockholders, and elect a board of directors. Directors oversee a corporation's affairs.

Point: A corporation is not required to have an office in its state of incorporation.

Organization Expenses   **Organization expenses** (also called *organization costs*) are the costs to organize a corporation; they include legal fees, promoters' fees, and amounts paid to obtain a charter. The corporation records (debits) these costs to an expense account called *Organization Expenses.* Organization costs are expensed as incurred because it is difficult to determine the amount and timing of their future benefits.

Management of a Corporation   The ultimate control of a corporation rests with stockholders who control a corporation by electing its *board of directors,* or simply, *directors.* Each stockholder usually has one vote for each share of stock owned. This control relation is shown in Exhibit 13.1. Directors are responsible for and have final authority for managing corporate activities. A board can act only as a collective body and usually limits its actions to setting general policy.

A corporation usually holds a stockholder meeting at least once a year to elect directors and transact

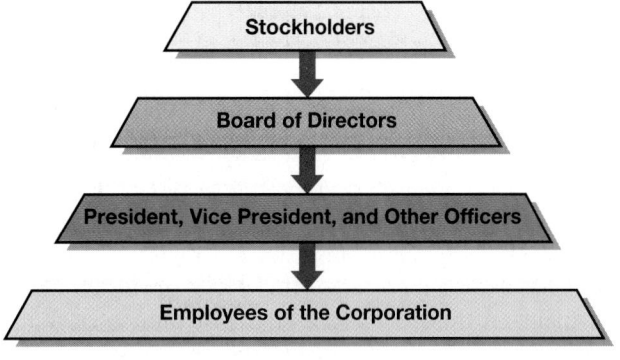

Exhibit 13.1

Corporate Structure

Point: *Bylaws* are guidelines that govern the behavior of individuals employed by and managing the corporation.

Global: Some corporate labels are:

Country	Label
United States	Inc.
France	SA
United Kingdom	
Public	PLC
Private	LTD
Germany	
Public	AG
Private	GmbH
Sweden	AB
Italy	SpA

business as its bylaws require. A group of stockholders owning or controlling votes of more than a 50% share of a corporation's stock can elect the board and control the corporation. Stockholders who do not attend stockholders' meetings must have an opportunity to delegate their voting rights to an agent by signing a **proxy,** a document that gives a designated agent the right to vote the stock.

Day-to-day direction of corporate business is delegated to executive officers appointed by the board. A corporation's chief executive officer (CEO) is often its president. Several vice presidents, who report to the president, are commonly assigned specific areas of management responsibility such as finance, production, and marketing. One person often has the dual role of chairperson of the board of directors and CEO. In this case, the president is usually designated the chief operating officer (COO).

Stockholders of Corporations

This section explains stockholder rights, stock purchases and sales, and the role of registrar and transfer agents.

Rights of Stockholders   When investors buy stock, they acquire all *specific* rights the corporation's charter grants to stockholders. They also acquire *general* rights granted stockholders by the laws of the state in which the company is incorporated. When a corporation has only one class of stock, it is identified as **common stock.** State laws vary, but common stockholders usually have the general right to

1. Vote at stockholders' meetings.
2. Sell or otherwise dispose of their stock.
3. Purchase their proportional share of any common stock later issued by the corporation. This **preemptive right** protects stockholders' proportionate interest in the corporation. For example, a stockholder who owns 25% of a corporation's common stock has the first opportunity to buy 25% of any new common stock issued.
4. Receive the same dividend, if any, on each common share of the corporation.
5. Share in any assets remaining after creditors are paid when, and if, the corporation is liquidated. Each share receives the same amount of remaining liquidated assets.

Stockholders also have the right to receive timely financial reports.

Global: Stockholders' access to financial information varies across countries both in scope and by level of ownership. For instance, stockholders of Mexican companies holding small percent ownership often have difficulty obtaining quality financial information.

Stock Certificates and Transfer   Investors who buy a corporation's stock, sometimes receive a *stock certificate* as proof of share ownership. Many corporations issue only one

Exhibit 13.2

Stock Certificate

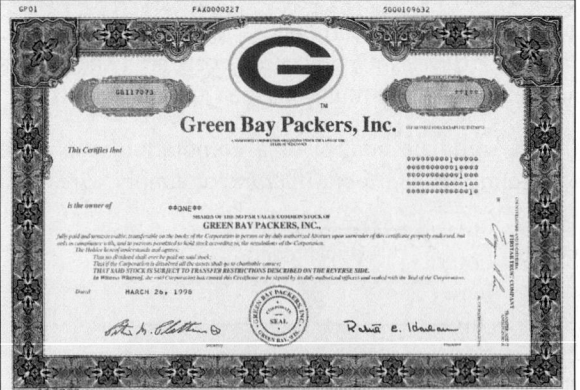

certificate for each block of stock purchased. A certificate can be for any number of shares. Exhibit 13.2 shows a stock certificate of the **Green Bay Packers**. A certificate shows the company name, stockholder name, number of shares, and other crucial information. Issuance of certificates is becoming less common. Instead, many stockholders maintain accounts with the corporation or their stockbrokers and never receive actual certificates.

Registrar and Transfer Agents   If a corporation's stock is traded on a major stock exchange, the corporation must have a registrar and a transfer agent. A *registrar* keeps stockholder records and prepares official lists of stockholders for stockholder meetings and dividend payments. A *transfer agent* assists with purchases and sales of shares by receiving and issuing certificates as necessary. Registrars and transfer agents are usually large banks or trust companies with computer facilities and staff to do this work.

Basics of Capital Stock

Capital stock is a general term that refers to any shares issued to obtain capital (owner financing). This section introduces terminology and accounting for capital stock.

Authorized Stock **Authorized stock** is the number of shares that a corporation's charter allows it to sell. The number of authorized shares usually exceeds the number of shares issued (and outstanding), often by a large amount. (*Outstanding stock* refers to issued stock held by stockholders.) No formal journal entry is required for stock authorization. A corporation must apply to the state for a change in its charter if it wishes to issue more shares than previously authorized. A corporation discloses the number of shares authorized in the equity section of its balance sheet or notes. **Best Buy**'s balance sheet in Appendix A reports 1 billion shares authorized as of 2005.

C2 Describe the components of stockholders' equity.

Selling (Issuing) Stock A corporation can sell stock directly or indirectly. To *sell directly*, it advertises its stock issuance to potential buyers. This type of issuance is most common with privately held corporations. To *sell indirectly*, a corporation pays a brokerage house (investment banker) to issue its stock. Some brokerage houses *underwrite* an indirect issuance of stock; that is, they buy the stock from the corporation and take all gains or losses from its resale.

> **Decision Insight**
>
> **Pricing Stock** A prospectus accompanies a stock's initial public offering (IPO), giving financial information about the company issuing the stock. A prospectus should help answer these questions to price an IPO: (1) Is the underwriter reliable? (2) Is there growth in revenues, profits, and cash flows? (3) What is management's view of operations? (4) Are current owners selling? (5) What are the risks?

Market Value of Stock **Market value per share** is the price at which a stock is bought and sold. Expected future earnings, dividends, growth, and other company and economic factors influence market value. Traded stocks' market values are available daily in newspapers such as *The Wall Street Journal* and online. The current market value of previously issued shares (for example, the price of stock in trades between investors) does not impact the issuing corporation's stockholders' equity.

Classes of Stock When all authorized shares have the same rights and characteristics, the stock is called *common stock*. A corporation is sometimes authorized to issue more than one class of stock, including preferred stock and different classes of common stock. **American Greetings**, for instance, has two types of common stock: Class A stock has 1 vote per share and Class B stock has 10 votes per share.

> **Decision Insight**
>
> **Stock Quote** The **Best Buy** stock quote is
>
> | 52 Weeks | | | Yld | | Vol | | | | Net |
> |---|---|---|---|---|---|---|---|---|---|
> | Hi | Lo | Sym | Div | % | PE | 100s | Hi | Lo | Close | Chg |
> | 53.17 | 31.85 | BBY | 0.32 | 0.7 | 22 | 220 | 47.26 | 46.48 | 46.61 | −0.37 |
>
> interpreted as (left to right): **Hi,** highest price in past 52 weeks; **Lo,** lowest price in past 52 weeks; **Sym,** company exchange symbol; **Div,** dividends paid per share in past year; **Yld %,** dividend divided by closing price; **PE,** stock price per share divided by earnings per share; **Vol 100s,** number (in 100s) of shares traded; **Hi,** highest price for the day; **Lo,** lowest price for the day; **Close,** closing price for the day; **Net Chg,** change in closing price from prior day.

Par Value Stock **Par value stock** is a class of stock assigned a **par value,** which is an amount assigned per share by the corporation in its charter. For example, Best Buy's common stock has a par value of $0.10. Other commonly assigned par values are $10, $5, $1 and $0.01. There is no restriction on the assigned par value. In many states, the par value of a stock establishes **minimum legal capital,** which refers to the least amount that the buyers of stock must contribute to the corporation or be subject to paying at a future date. For example, if a corporation issues 1,000 shares of $10 par value stock, the corporation's minimum legal capital in these states would be $10,000. Minimum legal capital is intended to protect a corporation's creditors. Since creditors cannot demand payment from stockholders' personal assets, their claims are limited to the corporation's assets and any minimum legal capital. At liquidation, creditor claims are paid before any amounts are distributed to stockholders.

Point: Managers are motivated to set a low par value when minimum legal capital or state issuance taxes are based on par value.

Point: Minimum legal capital was intended to protect creditors by requiring a minimum amount of net assets in the corporation. However, such net assets can be lost by unprofitable operations.

No-Par Value Stock **No-par value stock,** or simply *no-par stock,* is stock *not* assigned a value per share by the corporate charter. Its advantage is that it can be issued at any price without the possibility of a minimum legal capital deficiency.

Point: Par, no-par, and stated value do *not* set the stock's market value.

Exhibit 13.3

Equity Composition

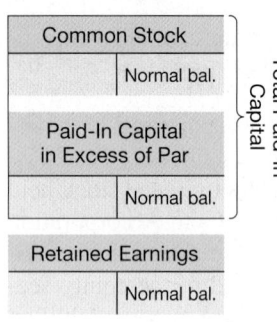

Corporation

Common Stock
	Normal bal.

Paid-In Capital in Excess of Par
	Normal bal.

Retained Earnings
	Normal bal.

Total Paid-In Capital

Point: Paid-in capital comes from stock-related transactions, whereas retained earnings comes from operations.

Stated Value Stock **Stated value stock** is no-par stock to which the directors assign a "stated" value per share. Stated value per share becomes the minimum legal capital per share in this case.

Stockholders' Equity A corporation's equity is known as **stockholders' equity,** also called *shareholders' equity* or *corporate capital.* Stockholders' equity consists of (1) paid-in (or contributed) capital and (2) retained earnings; see Exhibit 13.3. **Paid-in capital** is the total amount of cash and other assets the corporation receives from its stockholders in exchange for common stock. **Retained earnings** is the cumulative net income (and loss) retained by a corporation.

Quick Check

Answers—p. 525

1. Which of the following is *not* a characteristic of the corporate form of business? (*a*) Ease of capital accumulation, (*b*) Stockholder responsibility for corporate debts, (*c*) Ease in transferability of ownership rights, or (*d*) Double taxation.

2. Why is a corporation's income said to be taxed twice?

3. What is a proxy?

Common Stock

P1 Record the issuance of corporate stock.

Topic Tackler
PLUS

13-1

Accounting for the issuance of common stock affects only paid-in (contributed) capital accounts; no retained earnings accounts are affected.

Issuing Par Value Stock

Par value stock can be issued at par, at a premium (above par), or at a discount (below par). In each case, stock can be exchanged for either cash or noncash assets.

Issuing Par Value Stock at Par   When common stock is issued at par value, we record amounts for both the asset(s) received and the par value stock issued. To illustrate, the entry to record Dillon Snowboards' issuance of 30,000 shares of $10 par value stock for $300,000 cash on June 5, 2008, follows.

Assets = Liabilities + Equity
+300,000   +300,000

June 5	Cash	300,000	
	Common Stock, $10 Par Value		300,000
	Issued 30,000 shares of $10 par value common stock at par.		

Exhibit 13.4 shows the stockholders' equity of Dillon Snowboards at year-end 2008 (its first year of operations) after income of $65,000 and no dividend payments.

Exhibit 13.4

Stockholders' Equity for Stock Issued at Par

Stockholders' Equity	
Common Stock—$10 par value; 50,000 shares authorized;	
30,000 shares issued and outstanding	$300,000
Retained earnings	65,000
Total stockholders' equity	$365,000

Issuing Par Value Stock at a Premium   A **premium on stock** occurs when a corporation sells its stock for more than par (or stated) value. To illustrate, if Dillon Snowboards issues its $10 par value common stock at $12 per share, its stock is sold at a $2 per share premium. The premium, known as **paid-in capital in excess of par value,** is reported as part of equity; it is not revenue and is not listed on the income statement. The entry to record Dillon Snowboards' issuance of 30,000 shares of $10 par value stock for $12 per share on June 5, 2008, follows

Point: The "Paid-In Capital in Excess of Par Value, Common Stock" account is also called "Additional Paid-In Capital, Common Stock."

June 5	Cash	360,000	
	Common Stock, $10 Par Value		300,000
	Paid-In Capital in Excess of		
	Par Value, Common Stock		60,000
	Sold and issued 30,000 shares of $10 par value common stock at $12 per share.		

Assets = Liabilities + Equity
+360,000   +300,000
           +60,000

The Paid-In Capital in Excess of Par Value account is added to the par value of the stock in the equity section of the balance sheet as shown in Exhibit 13.5.

Point: The *Paid-In Capital* terminology is interchangeable with *Contributed Capital.*

Exhibit 13.5

Stockholders' Equity for Stock Issued at a Premium

Stockholders' Equity	
Common Stock—$10 par value; 50,000 shares authorized; 30,000 shares issued and outstanding	$300,000
Paid-in capital in excess of par value, common stock	60,000
Retained earnings	65,000
Total stockholders' equity	$425,000

Issuing Par Value Stock at a Discount   A **discount on stock** occurs when a corporation sells its stock for less than par (or stated) value. Most states prohibit the issuance of stock at a discount. In states that allow stock to be issued at a discount, its buyers usually become contingently liable to creditors for the discount. If stock is issued at a discount, the amount by which issue price is less than par is debited to a *Discount on Common Stock* account, a contra to the common stock account, and its balance is subtracted from the par value of stock in the equity section of the balance sheet. This discount is not an expense and does not appear on the income statement.

Point: Retained earnings can be negative, reflecting accumulated losses. Amazon.com had an accumulated deficit of $2.4 billion at the start of 2005.

Issuing No-Par Value Stock

When no-par stock is issued and is not assigned a stated value, the amount the corporation receives becomes legal capital and is recorded as Common Stock. This means that the entire proceeds are credited to a no-par stock account. To illustrate, a corporation records its October 20 issuance of 1,000 shares of no-par stock for $40 cash per share as follows.

Oct. 20	Cash	40,000	
	Common Stock, No-Par Value		40,000
	Issued 1,000 shares of no-par value common stock at $40 per share.		

Assets = Liabilities + Equity
+40,000   +40,000

Issuing Stated Value Stock

When no-par stock is issued and assigned a stated value, its stated value becomes legal capital and is credited to a stated value stock account. Assuming that stated value stock is issued at an amount in excess of stated value (the usual case), the excess is credited to Paid-In Capital

Frequency of Stock Types

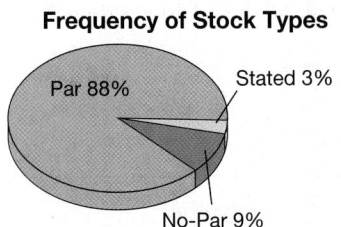

Par 88%   Stated 3%   No-Par 9%

Point: A *premium* is the amount by which issue price exceeds par (or stated) value. It is recorded in a separate equity account.

in Excess of Stated Value, Common Stock, which is reported in the stockholders' equity section. To illustrate, a corporation that issues 1,000 shares of no-par common stock having a stated value of $40 per share in return for $50 cash per share records this as follows.

Assets = Liabilities + Equity
+50,000   +40,000
                         +10,000

Oct. 20	Cash	50,000	
	Common Stock, $40 Stated Value		40,000
	Paid-In Capital in Excess of Stated		
	Value, Common Stock		10,000
	Issued 1,000 shares of $40 per share stated		
	value stock at $50 per share.		

Issuing Stock for Noncash Assets

Point: Stock issued for noncash assets should be recorded at the market value of either the stock or the noncash asset, whichever is more clearly determinable.

A corporation can receive assets other than cash in exchange for its stock. (It can also assume liabilities on the assets received such as a mortgage on property received.) The corporation records the assets received at their market values as of the date of the transaction. The stock given in exchange is recorded at its par (or stated) value with any excess recorded in the Paid-In Capital in Excess of Par (or Stated) Value account. (If no-par stock is issued, the stock is recorded at the assets' market value.) To illustrate, the entry to record receipt of land valued at $105,000 in return for issuance of 4,000 shares of $20 par value common stock on June 10 is

Assets = Liabilities + Equity
+105,000   +80,000
                        +25,000

June 10	Land	105,000	
	Common Stock, $20 Par Value		80,000
	Paid-In Capital in Excess of Par Value,		
	Common Stock		25,000
	Exchanged 4,000 shares of $20 par value		
	common stock for land.		

Point: Any type of stock can be issued for noncash assets.

   A corporation sometimes gives shares of its stock to promoters in exchange for their services in organizing the corporation, which the corporation records as **Organization Expenses.** The entry to record receipt of services valued at $12,000 in organizing the corporation in return for 600 shares of $15 par value common stock on June 5 is

Assets = Liabilities + Equity
                        −12,000
                        +9,000
                        +3,000

June 5	Organization Expenses	12,000	
	Common Stock, $15 Par Value		9,000
	Paid-In Capital in Excess of Par Value,		
	Common Stock		3,000
	Gave promoters 600 shares of $15 par value		
	common stock in exchange for their services.		

Quick Check
Answers—p. 525

4. A company issues 7,000 shares of its $10 par value common stock in exchange for equipment valued at $105,000. The entry to record this transaction includes a credit to (*a*) Paid-In Capital in Excess of Par Value, Common Stock, for $35,000. (*b*) Retained Earnings for $35,000. (*c*) Common Stock, $10 Par Value, for $105,000.

5. What is a premium on stock?

6. Who is intended to be protected by minimum legal capital?

Dividends

This section describes both cash and stock dividend transactions.

P2 Record transactions involving cash dividends.

Cash Dividends

The decision to pay cash dividends rests with the board of directors and involves more than evaluating the amounts of retained earnings and cash. The directors, for instance, may decide to keep the cash to invest in the corporation's growth, to meet emergencies, to take advantage of unexpected opportunities, or to pay off debt. Alternatively, many corporations pay cash dividends to their stockholders at regular dates. These cash flows provide a return to investors and almost always affect the stock's market value.

Accounting for Cash Dividends Dividend payment involves three important dates: declaration, record, and payment. **Date of declaration** is the date the directors vote to declare and pay a dividend. This creates a legal liability of the corporation to its stockholders. **Date of record** is the future date specified by the directors for identifying those stockholders listed in the corporation's records to receive dividends. The date of record usually follows the date of declaration by at least two weeks. Persons who own stock on the date of record receive dividends. **Date of payment** is the date when the corporation makes payment; it follows the date of record by enough time to allow the corporation to arrange checks, money transfers, or other means to pay dividends.

Percent of Corporations Paying Dividends

Point: A cash dividend reduces a company's assets (and its working capital).

To illustrate, the entry to record a January 9 declaration of a $1 per share cash dividend by the directors of Z-Tech, Inc., with 5,000 outstanding shares is

Date of Declaration

Jan. 9	Retained Earnings............................	5,000	
	Common Dividend Payable		5,000
	Declared $1 per common share cash dividend.[1]		

Assets = Liabilities + Equity
+5,000   −5,000

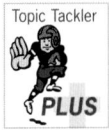

Topic Tackler
PLUS

13-2

Common Dividend Payable is a current liability. The date of record for the Z-Tech dividend is January 22. *No formal journal entry is needed on the date of record.* The February 1 date of payment requires an entry to record both the settlement of the liability and the reduction of the cash balance, as follows:

Date of Payment

Feb. 1	Common Dividend Payable....................	5,000	
	Cash		5,000
	Paid $1 per common share cash dividend.		

Assets = Liabilities + Equity
−5,000   −5,000

Deficits and Cash Dividends A corporation with a debit (abnormal) balance for retained earnings is said to have a **retained earnings deficit,** which arises when a company incurs cumulative losses and/or pays more dividends than total earnings from current and prior years. A deficit is reported as a deduction on the balance sheet, as shown in Exhibit 13.6. Most states prohibit a corporation with a deficit from paying a cash dividend to its stockholders. This legal restriction is designed to protect creditors by preventing distribution of assets to stockholders when the company may be in financial difficulty.

Point: It is often said a dividend is a distribution of retained earnings, but it is more precise to describe a dividend as a distribution of assets to satisfy stockholder claims.

Point: The Retained Earnings Deficit account is also called *Accumulated Deficit.*

---

[1] An alternative entry is to debit Dividends instead of Retained Earnings. The balance in Dividends is then closed to Retained Earnings at the end of the reporting period. The effect is the same: Retained Earnings is decreased and a Dividend Payable is increased. For simplicity, all assignments in this chapter use the Retained Earnings account to record dividend declarations.

Exhibit 13.6

Stockholders' Equity with a Deficit

Common stock—$10 par value, 5,000 shares authorized, issued, and outstanding	$50,000
Retained earnings deficit	**(6,000)**
Total stockholders' equity	$44,000

Some state laws allow cash dividends to be paid by returning a portion of the capital contributed by stockholders. This type of dividend is called a **liquidating cash dividend,** or simply *liquidating dividend,* because it returns a part of the original investment back to the stockholders. This requires a debit entry to one of the contributed capital accounts instead of Retained Earnings at the declaration date.

Quick Check

Answers—p. 525

7. What type of an account is the Common Dividend Payable account?
8. What three crucial dates are involved in the process of paying a cash dividend?
9. When does a dividend become a company's legal obligation?

Stock Dividends

P3 Account for stock dividends and stock splits.

A **stock dividend,** declared by a corporation's directors, is a distribution of additional shares of the corporation's own stock to its stockholders without the receipt of any payment in return. Stock dividends and cash dividends are different. A stock dividend does not reduce assets and equity but instead transfers a portion of equity from retained earnings to contributed capital.

Reasons for Stock Dividends   Stock dividends exist for at least two reasons. First, directors are said to use stock dividends to keep the market price of the stock affordable. For example, if a corporation continues to earn income but does not issue cash dividends, the price of its common stock likely increases. The price of such a stock may become so high that it discourages some investors from buying the stock (especially in lots of 100 and 1,000). When a corporation has a stock dividend, it increases the number of outstanding shares and lowers the per share stock price. Another reason for a stock dividend is to provide evidence of management's confidence that the company is doing well and will continue to do well.

Point: Berkshire Hathaway has not declared a cash dividend since 1967. Its recent stock price was about $85,000 per share.

Accounting for Stock Dividends   A stock dividend affects the components of equity by transferring part of retained earnings to contributed capital accounts, sometimes described as *capitalizing* retained earnings. Accounting for a stock dividend depends on whether it is a small or large stock dividend. A **small stock dividend** is a distribution of 25% or less of previously outstanding shares. It is recorded by capitalizing retained earnings for an amount equal to the market value of the shares to be distributed. A **large stock dividend** is a distribution of more than 25% of previously outstanding shares. A large stock dividend is recorded by capitalizing retained earnings for the minimum amount required by state law governing the corporation. Most states require capitalizing retained earnings equal to the par or stated value of the stock.

To illustrate stock dividends, we use the equity section of X-Quest's balance sheet shown in Exhibit 13.7 just *before* its declaration of a stock dividend on December 31.

Exhibit 13.7

Stockholders' Equity *before* Declaring a Stock Dividend

Stockholders' Equity (before dividend)	
Common stock—$10 par value, 15,000 shares authorized, 10,000 shares issued and outstanding	$100,000
Paid-in capital in excess of par value, common stock	8,000
Retained earnings	35,000
Total stockholders' equity	$143,000

Recording a small stock dividend.   Assume that X-Quest's directors declare a 10% stock dividend on December 31. This stock dividend of 1,000 shares, computed as 10% of its 10,000 issued and outstanding shares, is to be distributed on January 20 to the stockholders of record on January 15. Since the market price of X-Quest's stock on December 31 is $15 per share, this small stock dividend declaration is recorded as follows:

Point: Small stock dividends are recorded at market value.

Date of Declaration

Dec. 31	Retained Earnings............................	15,000	
	Common Stock Dividend Distributable........		10,000
	Paid-In Capital in Excess of Par Value,		
	Common Stock......................		5,000
	Declared a 1,000-share (10%) stock dividend.		

Assets = Liabilities + Equity
−15,000
+10,000
+5,000

The $10,000 credit in the declaration entry equals the par value of the shares and is recorded in *Common Stock Dividend Distributable*. Its balance exists only until the shares are issued. The $5,000 credit equals the amount by which market value exceeds par value. This amount increases the Paid-In Capital in Excess of Par Value account in anticipation of the issue of shares. In general, the balance sheet changes in three ways when a stock dividend is declared. First, the amount of equity attributed to common stock increases; for X-Quest, from $100,000 to $110,000 for 1,000 additional declared shares. Second, paid-in capital in excess of par increases by the excess of market value over par value for the declared shares. Third, retained earnings decreases, reflecting the transfer of amounts to both common stock and contributed capital in excess of par. The stockholders' equity of X-Quest is shown in Exhibit 13.8 *after* its 10% stock dividend is declared on December 31.

Point: The term *Distributable* (not *Payable*) is used for stock dividends.

Point: The credit to Paid-In Capital in Excess of Par Value is recorded when the stock dividend is declared. This account is not affected when stock is later distributed.

Point: A stock dividend is never a liability on a balance sheet because it never reduces assets.

Stockholders' Equity (after dividend)

Common stock—$10 par value, 15,000 shares authorized, 10,000 shares issued and outstanding	$100,000
Common stock dividend distributable—1,000 shares	**10,000**
Paid-in capital in excess of par value, common stock	**13,000**
Retained earnings	**20,000**
Total stockholders' equity	$143,000

Exhibit 13.8

Stockholders' Equity *after* Declaring a Stock Dividend

No entry is made on the date of record for a stock dividend. On January 20, the date of payment, X-Quest distributes the new shares to stockholders and records this entry:

Point: A stock dividend does not affect assets (or working capital).

Date of Payment

Jan. 20	Common Stock Dividend Distributable	10,000	
	Common Stock, $10 Par Value.............		10,000
	To record issuance of common stock dividend.		

Assets = Liabilities + Equity
−10,000
+10,000

The combined effect of these stock dividend entries is to transfer (or capitalize) $15,000 of retained earnings to paid-in capital accounts. The amount of capitalized retained earnings equals the market value of the 1,000 issued shares ($15 × 1,000 shares). A stock dividend has no effect on the ownership percent of individual stockholders.

Decision Maker   Answer—p. 525

Entrepreneur A company you cofounded and own stock in announces a 50% stock dividend. Has the value of your stock investment increased, decreased, or remained the same?

Recording a large stock dividend.   A corporation capitalizes retained earnings equal to the minimum amount required by state law for a large stock dividend. For most states, this amount is the par or stated value of the newly issued shares. To illustrate, suppose X-Quest's board declares a stock dividend of 30% instead of 10% on December 31. Since this dividend is more

Point: Large stock dividends are recorded at par or stated value.

than 25%, it is treated as a large stock dividend. Thus, the par value of the 3,000 dividend shares is capitalized at the date of declaration with this entry:

Date of Declaration

Dec. 31	Retained Earnings............................	30,000	
	Common Stock Dividend Distributable........		30,000

Declared a 3,000-share (30%) stock dividend.

This transaction decreases retained earnings and increases contributed capital by $30,000. On the date of payment the company debits Common Stock Dividend Distributable and credits Common Stock for $30,000. The effects from a large stock dividend on balance sheet accounts are similar to those for a small stock dividend except for the absence of any effect on contributed capital in excess of par.

Stock Splits

A **stock split** is the distribution of additional shares to stockholders according to their percent ownership. When a stock split occurs, the corporation "calls in" its outstanding shares and issues more than one new share in exchange for each old share. Splits can be done in any ratio, including 2-for-1, 3-for-1, or higher. Stock splits reduce the par or stated value per share.

To illustrate, CompTec has 100,000 outstanding shares of $20 par value common stock with a current market value of $88 per share. A 2-for-1 stock split cuts par value in half as it replaces 100,000 shares of $20 par value stock with 200,000 shares of $10 par value stock. Market value is reduced from $88 per share to about $44 per share. The split does not affect any equity amounts reported on the balance sheet or any individual stockholder's percent ownership. Both the Paid-In Capital and Retained Earnings accounts are unchanged by a split, and *no journal entry is made*. The only effect on the accounts is a change in the stock account description. CompTec's 2-for-1 split on its $20 par value stock means that after the split, it changes its stock account title to Common Stock, $10 Par Value. This stock's description on the balance sheet also changes to reflect the additional authorized, issued, and outstanding shares and the new par value.

The difference between stock splits and large stock dividends is often blurred. Many companies report stock splits in their financial statements without calling in the original shares by simply changing their par value. This type of "split" is really a large stock dividend and results in additional shares issued to stockholders by capitalizing retained earnings or transferring other paid-in capital to Common Stock. This approach avoids administrative costs of splitting the stock. **Harley-Davidson** recently declared a 2-for-1 stock split executed in the form of a 100% stock dividend.

Point: A reverse stock split is the opposite of a stock split. It increases both the market value per share and the par or stated value per share by specifying the split ratio to be less than 1-for-1, such as 1-for-2. A reverse stock split results in fewer shares.

Assets = Liabilities + Equity
−30,000
+30,000

Quick Check   Answers—p. 525

10. How does a stock dividend impact assets and retained earnings?

11. What distinguishes a large stock dividend from a small stock dividend?

12. What amount of retained earnings is capitalized for a small stock dividend?

Preferred Stock

A corporation can issue two basic kinds of stock, common and preferred. **Preferred stock** has special rights that give it priority (or senior status) over common stock in one or more areas. Special rights typically include a preference for receiving dividends and for the distribution of assets if the corporation is liquidated. Preferred stock carries all rights of common stock unless the corporate charter nullifies them. Most preferred stock, for instance, does not confer the right to vote. Exhibit 13.9 shows that preferred stock is issued by about one-fourth of large corporations. All corporations issue common stock.

No Preferred Stock 73%

Issued Preferred Stock 27%

Exhibit 13.9

Corporations and Preferred Stock

Issuance of Preferred Stock

Preferred stock usually has a par value. Like common stock, it can be sold at a price different from par. Preferred stock is recorded in its own separate capital accounts. To illustrate, if Dillon Snowboards issues 50 shares of $100 par value preferred stock for $6,000 cash on July 1, 2008, the entry is

C3 Explain characteristics of common and preferred stock.

July 1	Cash	6,000	
	Preferred Stock, $100 Par Value		5,000
	Paid-In Capital in Excess of Par Value, Preferred Stock		1,000
	Issued preferred stock for cash.		

Assets = Liabilities + Equity
+6,000   +5,000
                          +1,000

The equity section of the year-end balance sheet for Dillon Snowboards, including preferred stock, is shown in Exhibit 13.10. (This exhibit assumes that common stock was issued at par.) Issuing no-par preferred stock is similar to issuing no-par common stock. Also, the entries for issuing preferred stock for noncash assets are similar to those for common stock.

Stockholders' Equity

Common stock—$10 par value; 50,000 shares authorized; 30,000 shares issued and outstanding	$300,000
Preferred stock—$100 par value; 1,000 shares authorized; 50 shares issued and outstanding	5,000
Paid-in capital in excess of par value, preferred stock	1,000
Retained earnings	65,000
Total stockholders' equity	$371,000

Exhibit 13.10

Stockholders' Equity with Common and Preferred Stock

Dividend Preference of Preferred Stock

Preferred stock usually carries a preference for dividends, meaning that preferred stockholders are allocated their dividends before any dividends are allocated to common stockholders. The dividends allocated to preferred stockholders are usually expressed as a dollar amount per share or a percent applied to par value. A preference for dividends does *not* ensure dividends. If the directors do not declare a dividend, neither the preferred nor the common stockholders receive one.

P4 Distribute dividends between common stock and preferred stock.

Cumulative or Noncumulative Dividend Most preferred stocks carry a cumulative dividend right. **Cumulative preferred stock** has a right to be paid both the current and all prior periods' unpaid dividends before any dividend is paid to common stockholders. When preferred stock is cumulative and the directors either do not declare a dividend to preferred stockholders or declare one that does not cover the total amount of cumulative dividend, the unpaid dividend amount is called **dividend in arrears.** Accumulation of dividends in arrears on cumulative preferred stock does not guarantee they will be paid. **Noncumulative preferred stock** confers no right to prior periods' unpaid dividends if they were not declared in those prior periods.

Point: Dividend preference does not imply that preferred stockholders receive more dividends than common stockholders, nor does it guarantee a dividend.

To illustrate the difference between cumulative and noncumulative preferred stock, assume that a corporation's outstanding stock includes (1) 1,000 shares of $100 par, 9% preferred stock—yielding $9,000 per year in potential dividends, and (2) 4,000 shares of $50 par value common stock. During 2007, the first year of operations, the directors declare cash dividends of $5,000. In year 2008, they declare cash dividends of $42,000. See Exhibit 13.11 for the allocation of dividends for these two years. Allocation of year 2008 dividends depends on whether the preferred stock is noncumulative or cumulative. With noncumulative preferred, the preferred stockholders never receive the $4,000 skipped in 2007. If the preferred stock is cumulative, the $4,000 in arrears is paid in 2008 before any other dividends are paid.

Exhibit 13.11

Allocation of Dividends (noncumulative vs. cumulative preferred stock)

	Preferred	Common
Preferred Stock Is Noncumulative		
Year 2007	$ 5,000	$ 0
Year 2008		
Step 1: Current year's preferred dividend	$ 9,000	
Step 2: Remainder to common		$33,000
Preferred Stock Is Cumulative		
Year 2007	$ 5,000	$ 0
Year 2008		
Step 1: Dividend in arrears	$ 4,000	
Step 2: Current year's preferred dividend	9,000	
Step 3: Remainder to common		$29,000
Totals for year 2008	$13,000	$29,000

A liability for a dividend does not exist until the directors declare a dividend. If a preferred dividend date passes and the corporation's board fails to declare the dividend on its cumulative preferred stock, the dividend in arrears is not a liability. The *full-disclosure principle* requires a corporation to report (usually in a note) the amount of preferred dividends in arrears as of the balance sheet date.

Participating or Nonparticipating Dividend   **Nonparticipating preferred stock** has a feature that limits dividends to a maximum amount each year. This maximum is often stated as a percent of the stock's par value or as a specific dollar amount per share. Once preferred stockholders receive this amount, the common stockholders receive any and all additional dividends. **Participating preferred stock** has a feature allowing preferred stockholders to share with common stockholders in any dividends paid in excess of the percent or dollar amount stated on the preferred stock. This participation feature does not apply until common stockholders receive dividends equal to the preferred stock's dividend percent. Many corporations are authorized to issue participating preferred stock but rarely do, and most managers never expect to issue it.[2]

---

[2] Participating preferred stock is usually authorized as a defense against a possible corporate *takeover* by an "unfriendly" investor (or a group of investors) who intends to buy enough voting common stock to gain control. Taking a term from spy novels, the financial world refers to this type of plan as a *poison pill* that a company swallows if enemy investors threaten its capture. A poison pill usually works as follows: A corporation's common stockholders on a given date are granted the right to purchase a large amount of participating preferred stock at a very low price. This right to purchase preferred shares is *not* transferable. If an unfriendly investor buys a large block of common shares (whose right to purchase participating preferred shares does *not* transfer to this buyer), the board can issue preferred shares at a low price to the remaining common shareholders who retained the right to purchase. Future dividends are then divided between the newly issued participating preferred shares and the common shares. This usually transfers value from common shares to preferred shares, causing the unfriendly investor's common stock to lose much of its value and reduces the potential benefit of a hostile takeover.

Convertible Preferred Stock

Preferred stock is more attractive to investors if it carries a right to exchange preferred shares for a fixed number of common shares. **Convertible preferred stock** gives holders the option to exchange their preferred shares for common shares at a specified rate. When a company prospers and its common stock increases in value, convertible preferred stockholders can share in this success by converting their preferred stock into more valuable common stock.

Callable Preferred Stock

Callable preferred stock gives the issuing corporation the right to purchase (retire) this stock from its holders at specified future prices and dates. Many issues of preferred stock are callable. The amount paid to call and retire a preferred share is its **call price,** or *redemption value,* and is set when the stock is issued. The call price normally includes the stock's par value plus a premium giving holders additional return on their investment. When the issuing corporation calls and retires a preferred stock, the terms of the agreement often require it to pay the call price *and* any dividends in arrears.

Point: The issuing corporation has the right, or option, to retire its callable preferred stock.

Reasons for Issuing Preferred Stock

Corporations issue preferred stock for several reasons. One is to raise capital without sacrificing control. For example, suppose a company's organizers have $100,000 cash to invest and organize a corporation that needs $200,000 of capital to start. If they sell $200,000 worth of common stock (with $100,000 to the organizers), they would have only 50% control and would need to negotiate extensively with other stockholders in making policy. However, if they issue $100,000 worth of common stock to themselves and sell outsiders $100,000 of 8%, cumulative preferred stock with no voting rights, they retain control.

A second reason to issue preferred stock is to boost the return earned by common stockholders. To illustrate, suppose a corporation's organizers expect to earn an annual after-tax income of $24,000 on an investment of $200,000. If they sell and issue $200,000 worth of common stock, the $24,000 income produces a 12% return on the $200,000 of common stockholders' equity. However, if they issue $100,000 of 8% preferred stock to outsiders and $100,000 of common stock to themselves, their own return increases to 16% per year, as shown in Exhibit 13.12.

Net (after-tax) income	$24,000
Less preferred dividends at 8%	(8,000)
Balance to common stockholders	$16,000
Return to common stockholders ($16,000/$100,000)	16%

Exhibit 13.12

Return to Common Stockholders When Preferred Stock Is Issued

Common stockholders earn 16% instead of 12% because assets contributed by preferred stockholders are invested to earn $12,000 while the preferred dividend is only $8,000. Use of preferred stock to increase return to common stockholders is an example of **financial leverage** (also called *trading on the equity*). As a general rule, when the dividend rate on preferred stock is less than the rate the corporation earns on its assets, the effect of issuing preferred stock is to increase (or *lever*) the rate earned by common stockholders.

Other reasons for issuing preferred stock include its appeal to some investors who believe that the corporation's common stock is too risky or that the expected return on common stock is too low.

Point: Financial leverage also occurs when debt is issued and the interest rate paid on it is less than the rate earned from using the assets the creditors lend the company.

Decision Maker   Answer—p. 525

Concert Organizer   Assume that you alter your business strategy from organizing concerts targeted at under 1,000 people to those targeted at between 5,000 to 20,000 people. You also incorporate because of increased risk of lawsuits and a desire to issue stock for financing. It is important that you control the company for decisions on whom to schedule. What types of stock do you offer?

Treasury Stock

P5 Record purchases and sales of treasury stock and the retirement of stock.

Corporations acquire shares of their own stock for several reasons: (1) to use their shares to acquire another corporation, (2) to purchase shares to avoid a hostile takeover of the company, (3) to reissue them to employees as compensation, and (4) to maintain a strong market for their stock or to show management confidence in the current price.

A corporation's reacquired shares are called **treasury stock,** which is similar to unissued stock in several ways: (1) neither treasury stock nor unissued stock is an asset, (2) neither receives cash dividends or stock dividends, and (3) neither allows the exercise of voting rights. However, treasury stock does differ from unissued stock in one major way: The corporation can resell treasury stock at less than par without having the buyers incur a liability, provided it was originally issued at par value or higher. Treasury stock purchases also require management to exercise ethical sensitivity because funds are being paid to specific stockholders instead of all stockholders. Managers must be sure the purchase is in the best interest of all stockholders. These concerns cause companies to fully disclose treasury stock transactions.

Corporations and Treasury Stock

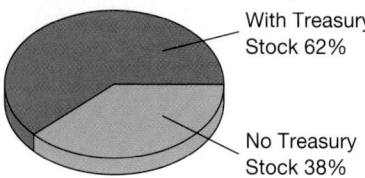

With Treasury Stock 62%

No Treasury Stock 38%

Purchasing Treasury Stock

Purchasing treasury stock reduces the corporation's assets and equity by equal amounts. (We describe the *cost method* of accounting for treasury stock, which is the most widely used method. The *par value* method is another method explained in advanced courses.) To illustrate, Exhibit 13.13 shows Cyber Corporation's account balances *before* any treasury stock purchase (Cyber has no liabilities).

Exhibit 13.13

Account Balances *before* Purchasing Treasury Stock

Assets		Stockholders' Equity	
Cash	$ 30,000	Common stock—$10 par; 10,000 shares	
Other assets	95,000	authorized, issued, and outstanding	$100,000
		Retained earnings	25,000
Total assets	$125,000	Total stockholders' equity	$125,000

Global: Many countries, such as China, Japan, and Singapore, do not permit purchase of treasury stock.

Cyber then purchases 1,000 of its own shares for $11,500 on May 1, which is recorded as follows.

Assets = Liabilities + Equity
−11,500   −11,500

May 1	Treasury Stock, Common	11,500	
	Cash		11,500
	Purchased 1,000 treasury shares at $11.50 per share.		

This entry reduces equity through the debit to the Treasury Stock account, which is a contra equity account. Exhibit 13.14 shows account balances *after* this transaction.

Point: Treasury stock does not carry voting or dividend rights.

Assets		Stockholders' Equity	
Cash	$ 18,500	Common stock—$10 par; 10,000 shares authorized and issued; 1,000 shares in treasury	$100,000
Other assets	95,000	Retained earnings, $11,500 restricted by treasury stock purchase	25,000
		Less cost of treasury stock	(11,500)
Total assets	$113,500	Total stockholders' equity	$113,500

Exhibit 13.14

Account Balances *after* Purchasing Treasury Stock

The treasury stock purchase reduces Cyber's cash, total assets, and total equity by $11,500 but does not reduce the balance of either the Common Stock or the Retained Earnings account. The equity reduction is reported by deducting the cost of treasury stock in the equity section. Also, two disclosures are evident. First, the stock description reveals that 1,000 issued shares are in treasury, leaving only 9,000 shares still outstanding. Second, the description for retained earnings reveals that it is partly restricted.

Point: The Treasury Stock account is *not* an asset. This contra equity account is a subtraction in the equity section.

Point: A treasury stock purchase is also called a *stock buyback*.

Reissuing Treasury Stock

Treasury stock can be reissued by selling it at cost, above cost, or below cost.

Selling Treasury Stock at Cost   If treasury stock is reissued at cost, the entry is the reverse of the one made to record the purchase. For instance, if on May 21 Cyber reissues 100 of the treasury shares purchased on May 1 at the same $11.50 per share cost, the entry is

May 21	Cash	1,150	
	Treasury Stock, Common.		1,150
	Received $11.50 per share for 100 treasury shares costing $11.50 per share.		

Assets = Liabilities + Equity
+1,150   +1,150

Selling Treasury Stock *above* Cost   If treasury stock is sold for more than cost, the amount received in excess of cost is credited to the Paid-In Capital, Treasury Stock account. This account is reported as a separate item in the stockholders' equity section. No gain is ever reported from the sale of treasury stock. To illustrate, if Cyber receives $12 cash per share for 400 treasury shares costing $11.50 per share on June 3, the entry is

Point: Treasury stock does not represent ownership. A company cannot own a part of itself.

June 3	Cash	4,800	
	Treasury Stock, Common.		4,600
	Paid-In Capital, Treasury Stock.		**200**
	Received $12 per share for 400 treasury shares costing $11.50 per share.		

Assets = Liabilities + Equity
+4,800   +4,600
                        +200

Selling Treasury Stock *below* Cost   When treasury stock is sold below cost, the entry to record the sale depends on whether the Paid-In Capital, Treasury Stock account has a credit balance. If it has a zero balance, the excess of cost over the sales price is debited to Retained Earnings. If the Paid-In Capital, Treasury Stock account has a credit balance, it is debited for the excess of the cost over the selling price but not to exceed the balance in this account. When the credit balance in this paid-in capital account is eliminated, any remaining difference between the cost and selling price is debited to Retained Earnings. To illustrate, if Cyber sells its remaining 500 shares of treasury stock at $10 per share on July 10,

Point: The term *treasury stock* is believed to arise from the fact that reacquired stock is held in a corporation's treasury.

Point: The Paid-In Capital, Treasury Stock account can have a zero or credit balance but never a debit balance.

equity is reduced by $750 (500 shares × $1.50 per share excess of cost over selling price), as shown in this entry:

Assets = Liabilities + Equity
+5,000   −200
                        −550
                        +5,750

July 10	Cash....................................	5,000	
	Paid-In Capital, Treasury Stock..............	**200**	
	Retained Earnings	**550**	
	Treasury Stock, Common..................		5,750
	Received $10 per share for 500 treasury shares costing $11.50 per share.		

This entry eliminates the $200 credit balance in the paid-in capital account created on June 3 and then reduces the Retained Earnings balance by the remaining $550 excess of cost over selling price. A company never reports a loss (or gain) from the sale of treasury stock.

Retiring Stock

Point: Wrigley Company reported that its "Directors adopted a resolution retiring the entire balance of shares of Common Stock held in the corporate treasury."

Point: Recording stock retirement results in canceling the equity from the original issuance of the shares.

A corporation can purchase its own stock and retire it. Retiring stock reduces the number of issued shares. Retired stock is the same as authorized and unissued shares. Purchases and retirements of stock are permissible under state law only if they do not jeopardize the interests of creditors and stockholders. When stock is purchased for retirement, we remove all capital amounts related to the retired shares. If the purchase price exceeds the net amount removed, this excess is debited to Retained Earnings. If the net amount removed from all capital accounts exceeds the purchase price, this excess is credited to the Paid-In Capital from Retirement of Stock account. A company's assets and equity are always reduced by the amount paid for the retiring stock.

Quick Check   Answers—p. 526

16. Purchase of treasury stock (*a*) has no effect on assets; (*b*) reduces total assets and total equity by equal amounts; or (*c*) is recorded with a debit to Retained Earnings.

17. Southern Co. purchases shares of Northern Corp. Should either company classify these shares as treasury stock?

18. How does treasury stock affect the authorized, issued, and outstanding shares?

19. When a company purchases treasury stock, (*a*) retained earnings are restricted by the amount paid; (*b*) Retained Earnings is credited; or (*c*) it is retired.

Reporting of Equity

Statement of Retained Earnings

C4   Explain the items reported in retained earnings.

Retained earnings generally consist of a company's cumulative net income less any net losses and dividends declared since its inception. Retained earnings are part of stockholders' claims on the company's net assets, but this does *not* imply that a certain amount of cash or other assets is available to pay stockholders. For example, **Circuit City** has $1,247 million in retained earnings, but only $880 million in cash. This section describes events and transactions affecting retained earnings and how retained earnings are reported.

Global: Some countries, such as Japan, require companies to set up reserves at specified rates for the protection of creditors.

Restrictions and Appropriations   The term **restricted retained earnings** refers to both statutory and contractual restrictions. A common *statutory* (or *legal*) *restriction* is to limit treasury stock purchases to the amount of retained earnings. The balance sheet in Exhibit 13.14 provides an example. A common *contractual restriction* involves loan agreements that restrict paying dividends beyond a specified amount or percent of retained earnings. Restrictions are usually described in the notes. The term **appropriated retained earnings** refers to a voluntary transfer of amounts from the Retained Earnings account to the Appropriated Retained Earnings account to inform users of special activities that require funds.

Prior Period Adjustments   **Prior period adjustments** are corrections of material errors in prior period financial statements. These errors include arithmetic mistakes, unacceptable accounting, and missed facts. Prior period adjustments are reported in the *statement of retained earnings* (or the statement of stockholders' equity), net of any income tax effects. Prior period adjustments result in changing the beginning balance of retained earnings for events occurring prior to the earliest period reported in the current set of financial statements. To illustrate, assume that ComUS makes an error in a 2006 journal entry for the purchase of land by incorrectly debiting an expense account. When this is discovered in 2008, the statement of retained earnings includes a prior period adjustment, as shown in Exhibit 13.15. This exhibit also shows the usual format of the statement of retained earnings.

Many items reported in financial statements are based on estimates. Future events are certain to reveal that some of these estimates were inaccurate even when based on the best data avail-

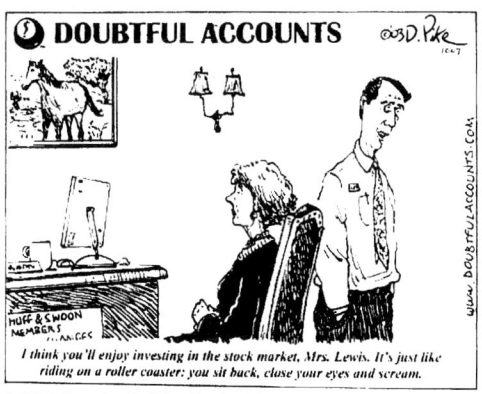

DOUBTFUL ACCOUNTS

I think you'll enjoy investing in the stock market, Mrs. Lewis. It's just like riding on a roller coaster: you sit back, close your eyes and scream.

© 2005 Douglas E. Pike. Used with permission.

Point: If a year 2006 error is discovered in 2007, the company records the adjustment in 2007. But if the financial statements include 2006 and 2007 figures, the statements report the correct amounts for 2006, and a note describes the correction.

ComUS Statement of Retained Earnings For Year Ended December 31, 2008	
Retained earnings, Dec. 31, 2007, as previously reported	$4,745,000
Prior period adjustment	
Cost of land incorrectly expensed (net of $63,000 income taxes)	**147,000**
Retained earnings, Dec. 31, 2007, as adjusted	4,892,000
Plus net income	1,224,300
Less cash dividends declared	(301,800)
Retained earnings, Dec. 31, 2008	$5,814,500

Exhibit 13.15

Statement of Retained Earnings with a Prior Period Adjustment

Point: Accounting for changes in estimates is sometimes criticized as two wrongs to make a right. Consider a change in an asset's life. Depreciation neither before nor after the change is the amount computed if the revised estimate were originally selected. Regulators chose this approach to avoid restating prior period numbers.

able at the time. These inaccuracies are *not* considered errors and are *not* reported as prior period adjustments. Instead, they are identified as **changes in accounting estimates** and are accounted for in current and future periods. To illustrate, we know that depreciation is based on estimated useful lives and salvage values. As time passes and new information becomes available, managers may need to change these estimates and the resulting depreciation expense for current and future periods.

Statement of Stockholders' Equity

Instead of a separate statement of retained earnings, companies commonly report a statement of stockholders' equity that includes changes in retained earnings. A **statement of stockholders' equity** lists the beginning and ending balances of each equity account and describes the changes that occur during the period. The companies in Appendix A report such a statement. The usual format is to provide a column for each component of equity and use the rows to describe events occurring in the period. Exhibit 13.16 shows a condensed statement for **Apple Computer**.

Reporting Stock Options

The majority of corporations whose shares are publicly traded issue **stock options,** which are

Decision Insight

Future Fortunes   Some managers have fortunes to reap from unexercised stock options. Four of the larger treasures are:

Lawrence Ellison (**Oracle**)	$425 million
Terry Semel (**Yahoo!**)	396 million
John Chambers (**Cisco**)	225 million
John Thompson (**Symantec**) ...	193 million

Exhibit 13.16

Statement of Stockholders' Equity

APPLE COMPUTER Statement of Stockholders' Equity					
($ millions, shares in thousands)	Common Stock Shares	Common Stock Amount	Retained Earnings	Other	Total Equity
Balance, Sept. 27, 2003	366,727	$1,926	$2,394	$ (97)	$4,223
Net income	—	—	276	—	276
Issuance of Common Stock	24,717	588	—	—	588
Other	—	—	—	(11)	(11)
Cash Dividends ($0.00 per share)	—	—	—	—	—
Balance, Sept. 25, 2004	391,444	$2,514	$2,670	$(108)	$5,076

rights to purchase common stock at a fixed price over a specified period. As the stock's price rises above the fixed price, the option's value increases. **Starbucks** and **Home Depot** offer stock options to both full- and part-time employees. Stock options are said to motivate managers and employees to (1) focus on company performance, (2) take a long-run perspective, and (3) remain with the company. A stock option is like having an investment with no risk ("a carrot with no stick").

To illustrate, Quantum grants each of its employees the option to purchase 100 shares of its $1 par value common stock at its current market price of $50 per share anytime within the next 10 years. If the stock price rises to $70 per share, an employee can exercise the option at a gain of $20 per share (acquire a $70 stock at the $50 option price). With 100 shares, a single employee would have a total gain of $2,000, computed as $20 × 100 shares. Companies report the cost of stock options in the income statement. Measurement of this cost is explained in advanced courses.

Decision Ethics
Answer—p. 525

Director The board of Intex is planning its stockholders' meeting. The first item is whether to disclose a contract just signed that will increase future income. One officer argues, "The meeting should focus on actual results." After agreeing not to disclose the contract, the next item is a motion for stockholders to approve a two-year option for managers to buy shares at a price equal to the average stock price over the next 2 weeks. What action (if any) do you take?

Decision Analysis
Earnings per Share, Price-Earnings Ratio, Dividend Yield, and Book Value per Share

Earnings per Share

A1 Compute earnings per share and describe its use.

The income statement reports **earnings per share,** also called *EPS* or *net income per share,* which is the amount of income earned per each share of a company's outstanding common stock. The **basic earnings per share** formula is shown in Exhibit 13.17. When a company has no preferred stock, then preferred dividends are zero. The weighted-average common shares outstanding is measured over the income reporting period; its computation is explained in advanced courses.

Exhibit 13.17

Basic Earnings per Share

$$\text{Basic earnings per share} = \frac{\text{Net income} - \text{Preferred dividends}}{\text{Weighted-average common shares outstanding}}$$

To illustrate, assume that Quantum Co. earns $40,000 net income in 2008 and declares dividends of $7,500 on its noncumulative preferred stock. (If preferred stock is *non*cumulative, the income available [numerator] is the current period net income less any preferred dividends *declared* in that same period. If preferred stock is cumulative, the income available [numerator] is the current period net

income less the preferred dividends whether declared or not.) Quantum has 5,000 weighted-average common shares outstanding during 2008. Its basic EPS[3] is

Global: Some countries, such as Japan and Australia, use the number of shares outstanding at the end of the period when computing EPS.

$$\text{Basic earnings per share} = \frac{\$40,000 - \$7,500}{5,000 \text{ shares}} = \$6.50$$

Price-Earnings Ratio

A stock's market value is determined by its *expected* future cash flows. A comparison of a company's EPS and its market value per share reveals information about market expectations. This comparison is traditionally made using a **price-earnings (or PE) ratio,** expressed also as *price earnings, price to earnings,* or *PE.* Some analysts interpret this ratio as what price the market is willing to pay for a company's current earnings stream. Price-earnings ratios can differ across companies that have similar earnings because of either higher or lower expectations of future earnings. The price-earnings ratio is defined in Exhibit 13.18.

A2 Compute price-earnings ratio and describe its use in analysis.

Point: The average PE ratio of stocks in the 1950–2005 period is about 14.

$$\text{Price-earnings ratio} = \frac{\text{Market value (price) per share}}{\text{Earnings per share}}$$

Exhibit 13.18

Price-Earnings Ratio

Point: Average PE ratios for U.S. stocks increased over the past two decades. Some analysts interpret this as a signal the market is overpriced. But higher ratios can at least partly reflect accounting changes that have reduced reported earnings.

This ratio is often computed using EPS from the most recent period (for Amazon, its PE is 31; for Altria, its PE is 13). However, many users compute this ratio using *expected* EPS for the next period.

Some analysts view stocks with high PE ratios (higher than 20 to 25) as more likely to be overpriced and stocks with low PE ratios (less than 5 to 8) as more likely to be underpriced. These investors prefer to sell or avoid buying stocks with high PE ratios and to buy or hold stocks with low PE ratios. However, investment decision making is rarely so simple as to rely on a single ratio. For instance, a stock with a high PE ratio can prove to be a good investment if its earnings continue to increase beyond current expectations. Similarly, a stock with a low PE ratio can prove to be a poor investment if its earnings decline below expectations.

Decision Maker

Answer—p. 525

Money Manager You plan to invest in one of two companies identified as having identical future prospects. One has a PE of 19 and the other a PE of 25. Which do you invest in? Does it matter if your *estimate* of PE for these two companies is 29 as opposed to 22?

Dividend Yield

Investors buy shares of a company's stock in anticipation of receiving a return from either or both cash dividends and stock price increases. Stocks that pay large dividends on a regular basis, called *income stocks,* are attractive to investors who want recurring cash flows from their investments. In contrast, some stocks pay little or no dividends but are still attractive to investors because of their expected stock price increases. The stocks of companies that distribute little or no cash but use their cash to finance expansion are called *growth stocks.* One way to help identify whether a stock is an income stock or a growth stock is to analyze its dividend yield. **Dividend yield,** defined in Exhibit 13.19, shows the annual amount of cash dividends distributed to common shares relative to their market value.

A3 Compute dividend yield and explain its use in analysis.

$$\text{Dividend yield} = \frac{\text{Annual cash dividends per share}}{\text{Market value per share}}$$

Exhibit 13.19

Dividend Yield

---

[3] A corporation can be classified as having either a simple or complex capital structure. The term **simple capital structure** refers to a company with only common stock and nonconvertible preferred stock outstanding. The term **complex capital structure** refers to companies with dilutive securities. **Dilutive securities** include options, rights to purchase common stock, and any bonds or preferred stock that are convertible into common stock. A company with a complex capital structure must often report two EPS figures: basic and diluted. **Diluted earnings per share** is computed by adding all dilutive securities to the denominator of the basic EPS computation. It reflects the decrease in basic EPS *assuming* that all dilutive securities are converted into common shares.

Dividend yield can be computed for current and prior periods using actual dividends and stock prices and for future periods using expected values. Exhibit 13.20 shows recent dividend and stock price data for **Amazon** and **Altria Group** to compute dividend yield.

Exhibit 13.20

Dividend and Stock
Price Information

Company	Cash Dividends per Share	Market Value per Share	Dividend Yield
Amazon	$0.00	$45	0.0%
Altria Group	2.82	55	5.1

Dividend yield is zero for Amazon, implying it is a growth stock. An investor in Amazon would look for increases in stock prices (and eventual cash from the sale of stock). Altria has a dividend yield of 5.1%, implying it is an income stock for which dividends are important in assessing its value.

Book Value per Share

Point: The *payout ratio* equals cash dividends declared on common stock divided by net income. A low payout ratio suggests that a company is retaining earnings for future growth.

Case 1: Common Stock (Only) Outstanding. **Book value per common share,** defined in Exhibit 13.21, is the recorded amount of stockholders' equity applicable to *common* shares on a per share basis. To illustrate, we use Dillon Snowboards' data from Exhibit 13.4. Dillon has 30,000 outstanding common shares, and the stockholders' equity applicable to common shares is $365,000. Dillon's book value per common share is $12.17, computed as $365,000 divided by 30,000 shares.

A4   Compute book value and explain its use in analysis.

Exhibit 13.21

Book Value per Common Share

$$\text{Book value per common share} = \frac{\text{Stockholders' equity applicable to common shares}}{\text{Number of common shares outstanding}}$$

Point: Book value per share is also referred to as *stockholders' claim to assets on a per share basis.*

Case 2: Common and Preferred Stock Outstanding. To compute book value when both common and preferred shares are outstanding, we allocate total stockholders' equity between the two types of shares. The **book value per preferred share** is computed first; its computation is shown in Exhibit 13.22.

Exhibit 13.22

Book Value per Preferred Share

$$\text{Book value per preferred share} = \frac{\text{Stockholders' equity applicable to preferred shares}}{\text{Number of preferred shares outstanding}}$$

The stockholders' equity applicable to preferred shares equals the preferred share's call price (or par value if the preferred is not callable) plus any cumulative dividends in arrears. The remaining stockholders' equity is the portion applicable to common shares. To illustrate, consider LTD's stockholders' equity in Exhibit 13.23. Its preferred stock is callable at $108 per share, and two years of cumulative preferred dividends are in arrears.

Exhibit 13.23

Stockholders' Equity with
Preferred and Common Stock

Stockholders' Equity	
Preferred stock—$100 par value, 7% cumulative, 2,000 shares authorized, 1,000 shares issued and outstanding	$100,000
Common stock—$25 par value, 12,000 shares authorized, 10,000 shares issued and outstanding	250,000
Paid-in capital in excess of par value, common stock	15,000
Retained earnings	82,000
Total stockholders' equity	$447,000

The book value computations are in Exhibit 13.24. Equity is first allocated to preferred shares before the book value of common shares is computed.

Exhibit 13.24

Computing Book Value per Preferred
and Common Share

Total stockholders' equity		$447,000
Less equity applicable to preferred shares		
Call price (1,000 shares × $108)	$108,000	
Dividends in arrears ($100,000 × 7% × 2 years)	14,000	(122,000)
Equity applicable to common shares		$325,000
Book value per preferred share ($122,000/1,000 shares)		**$122.00**
Book value per common share ($325,000/10,000 shares)		**$ 32.50**

Book value per share reflects the value per share if a company is liquidated at balance sheet amounts. Book value is also the starting point in many stock valuation models, merger negotiations, price setting for public utilities, and loan contracts. The main limitation in using book value is the potential difference between recorded value and market value for assets and liabilities. Investors often adjust their analysis for estimates of these differences.

Decision Maker   Answer—p. 525

Investor You are considering investing in **BMX**, whose book value per common share is $4 and price per common share on the stock exchange is $7. From this information, are BMX's net assets priced higher or lower than its recorded values?

Demonstration Problem 1

Barton Corporation began operations on January 1, 2008. The following transactions relating to stockholders' equity occurred in the first two years of the company's operations.

2008

Jan. 1 Authorized the issuance of 2 million shares of $5 par value common stock and 100,000 shares of $100 par value, 10% cumulative, preferred stock.

Jan. 2 Issued 200,000 shares of common stock for $12 cash per share.

Jan. 3 Issued 100,000 shares of common stock in exchange for a building valued at $820,000 and merchandise inventory valued at $380,000.

Jan. 4 Paid $10,000 cash to the company's founders for organization activities.

Jan. 5 Issued 12,000 shares of preferred stock for $110 cash per share.

2009

June 4 Issued 100,000 shares of common stock for $15 cash per share.

Required

1. Prepare journal entries to record these transactions.

2. Prepare the stockholders' equity section of the balance sheet as of December 31, 2008, and December 31, 2009, based on these transactions.

3. Prepare a table showing dividend allocations and dividends per share for 2008 and 2009 assuming Barton declares the following cash dividends: 2008, $50,000, and 2009, $300,000.

4. Prepare the January 2, 2008, journal entry for Barton's issuance of 200,000 shares of common stock for $12 cash per share assuming

   a. Common stock is no-par stock without a stated value.

   b. Common stock is no-par stock with a stated value of $10 per share.

Planning the Solution

- Record journal entries for the transactions for 2008 and 2009.
- Determine the balances for the 2008 and 2009 equity accounts for the balance sheet.
- Prepare the contributed capital portion of the 2008 and 2009 balance sheets.
- Prepare a table similar to Exhibit 13.11 showing dividend allocations for 2008 and 2009.
- Record the issuance of common stock under both specifications of no-par stock.

Solution to Demonstration Problem 1

1. Journal entries.

2008			
Jan. 2	Cash	2,400,000	
	Common Stock, $5 Par Value		1,000,000
	Paid-In Capital in Excess of Par Value, Common Stock		1,400,000
	Issued 200,000 shares of common stock.		

[continued on next page]

[continued from previous page]

Jan. 3	Building....................................	820,000	
	Merchandise Inventory	380,000	
	Common Stock, $5 Par Value..............		500,000
	Paid-In Capital in Excess of Par Value,		
	Common Stock......................		700,000
	Issued 100,000 shares of common stock.		
Jan. 4	Organization Expenses	10,000	
	Cash		10,000
	Paid founders for organization costs.		
Jan. 5	Cash..	1,320,000	
	Preferred Stock, $100 Par Value		1,200,000
	Paid-In Capital in Excess of Par Value,		
	Preferred Stock......................		120,000
	Issued 12,000 shares of preferred stock.		
2009			
June 4	Cash..	1,500,000	
	Common Stock, $5 Par Value..............		500,000
	Paid-In Capital in Excess of Par Value,		
	Common Stock......................		1,000,000
	Issued 100,000 shares of common stock.		

2. Balance sheet presentations (at December 31 year-end).

	2008	2009
Stockholders' Equity		
Preferred stock—$100 par value, 10% cumulative, 100,000 shares authorized, 12,000 shares issued and outstanding	$1,200,000	$1,200,000
Paid-in capital in excess of par value, preferred stock	120,000	120,000
Total paid-in capital by preferred stockholders	1,320,000	1,320,000
Common stock—$5 par value, 2,000,000 shares authorized, 300,000 shares issued and outstanding in 2008, and 400,000 shares issued and outstanding in 2009	1,500,000	2,000,000
Paid-in capital in excess of par value, common stock	2,100,000	3,100,000
Total paid-in capital by common stockholders	3,600,000	5,100,000
Total paid-in capital	$4,920,000	$6,420,000

3. Dividend allocation table.

	Common	Preferred
2008 ($50,000)		
Preferred—current year (12,000 shares × $10 = $120,000)	$ 0	$ 50,000
Common—remainder (300,000 shares outstanding)	0	0
Total for the year	$ 0	$ 50,000
2009 ($300,000)		
Preferred—dividend in arrears from 2008 ($120,000 − $50,000)	$ 0	$ 70,000
Preferred—current year	0	120,000
Common—remainder (400,000 shares outstanding)	110,000	0
Total for the year	$110,000	$190,000
Dividends per share		
2008	$ 0.00	$ 4.17
2009	$ 0.28	$ 15.83

4. Journal entries.

   a. For 2008:

Jan. 2	Cash	2,400,000	
	Common Stock, No-Par Value		2,400,000
	Issued 200,000 shares of no-par common		
	stock at $12 per share.		

   b. For 2008:

Jan. 2	Cash	2,400,000	
	Common Stock, $10 Stated Value		2,000,000
	Paid-In Capital in Excess of		
	Stated Value, Common Stock		400,000
	Issued 200,000 shares of $10 stated value		
	common stock at $12 per share.		

Demonstration Problem 2

Precision Company began year 2008 with the following balances in its stockholders' equity accounts.

Common stock—$10 par, 500,000 shares authorized,	
200,000 shares issued and outstanding	$2,000,000
Paid-in capital in excess of par, common stock	1,000,000
Retained earnings	5,000,000
Total	$8,000,000

All outstanding common stock was issued for $15 per share when the company was created. Prepare journal entries to account for the following transactions during year 2008.

Jan. 10   The board declared a $0.10 cash dividend per share to shareholders of record Jan. 28.
Feb. 15   Paid the cash dividend declared on January 10.
Mar. 31   Declared a 20% stock dividend. The market value of the stock is $18 per share.
May 1   Distributed the stock dividend declared on March 31.
July 1   Purchased 30,000 shares of treasury stock at $20 per share.
Sept. 1   Sold 20,000 treasury shares at $26 cash per share.
Dec. 1   Sold the remaining 10,000 shares of treasury stock at $7 cash per share.

Planning the Solution

- Calculate the total cash dividend to record by multiplying the cash dividend declared by the number of shares as of the date of record.
- Decide whether the stock dividend is a small or large dividend. Then analyze each event to determine the accounts affected and the appropriate amounts to be recorded.

Solution to Demonstration Problem 2

Jan. 10	Retained Earnings	20,000	
	Common Dividend Payable		20,000
	Declared a $0.10 per share cash dividend.		
Feb. 15	Common Dividend Payable	20,000	
	Cash		20,000
	Paid $0.10 per share cash dividend.		

   [continued on next page]

[continued from previous page]

Mar. 31	Retained Earnings............................	720,000	
	Common Stock Dividend Distributable.........		400,000
	Paid-In Capital in Excess of		
	Par Value, Common Stock		320,000
	Declared a small stock dividend of 20% or		
	40,000 shares; market value is $18 per share.		
May 1	Common Stock Dividend Distributable	400,000	
	Common Stock...........................		400,000
	Distributed 40,000 shares of common stock.		
July 1	Treasury Stock, Common	600,000	
	Cash		600,000
	Purchased 30,000 common shares at $20 per		
	share.		
Sept. 1	Cash......................................	520,000	
	Treasury Stock, Common.................		400,000
	Paid-In Capital, Treasury Stock		120,000
	Sold 20,000 treasury shares at $26 per share.		
Dec. 1	Cash......................................	70,000	
	Paid-In Capital, Treasury Stock.................	120,000	
	Retained Earnings...........................	10,000	
	Treasury Stock, Common.................		200,000
	Sold 10,000 treasury shares at $7 per share.		

Summary

C1 **Identify characteristics of corporations and their organization.** Corporations are legal entities whose stockholders are not liable for its debts. Stock is easily transferred, and the life of a corporation does not end with the incapacity of a stockholder. A corporation acts through its agents, who are its officers and managers. Corporations are regulated and subject to income taxes.

C2 **Describe the components of stockholders' equity.** Authorized stock is the stock that a corporation's charter authorizes it to sell. Issued stock is the portion of authorized shares sold. Par value stock is a value per share assigned by the charter. No-par value stock is stock *not* assigned a value per share by the charter. Stated value stock is no-par stock to which the directors assign a value per share. Stockholders' equity is made up of (1) paid-in capital and (2) retained earnings. Paid-in capital consists of funds raised by stock issuances. Retained earnings consists of cumulative net income (losses) not distributed.

C3 **Explain characteristics of common and preferred stock.** Preferred stock has a priority (or senior status) relative to common stock in one or more areas, usually (1) dividends and (2) assets in case of liquidation. Preferred stock usually does not carry voting rights and can be convertible or callable. Convertibility permits the holder to convert preferred to common. Callability permits the issuer to buy back preferred stock under specified conditions.

C4 **Explain the items reported in retained earnings.** Many companies face statutory and contractual restrictions on retained earnings. Corporations can voluntarily appropriate retained earnings to inform others about their disposition. Prior period adjustments are corrections of errors in prior financial statements.

A1 **Compute earnings per share and describe its use.** A company with a simple capital structure computes basic EPS by dividing net income less any preferred dividends by the weighted-average number of outstanding common shares. A company with a complex capital structure must usually report both basic and diluted EPS.

A2 **Compute price-earnings ratio and describe its use in analysis.** A common stock's price-earnings (PE) ratio is computed by dividing the stock's market value (price) per share by its EPS. A stock's PE is based on expectations that can prove to be better or worse than eventual performance.

A3 **Compute dividend yield and explain its use in analysis.** Dividend yield is the ratio of a stock's annual cash dividends per share to its market value (price) per share. Dividend yield can be compared with the yield of other companies to determine whether the stock is expected to be an income or growth stock.

A4 **Compute book value and explain its use in analysis.** Book value per common share is equity applicable to common shares divided by the number of outstanding common shares. Book value per preferred share is equity applicable to preferred shares divided by the number of outstanding preferred shares.

P1 **Record the issuance of corporate stock.** When stock is issued, its par or stated value is credited to the stock account and any excess is credited to a separate contributed capital account. If a stock has neither par nor stated value, the entire proceeds are credited to the stock account. Stockholders must contribute assets equal to minimum legal capital or be potentially liable for the deficiency.

P2 **Record transactions involving cash dividends.** Cash dividends involve three events. On the date of declaration, the directors bind the company to pay the dividend. A dividend declaration reduces retained earnings and creates a current liability. On the date of record, recipients of the dividend are identified. On the date of payment, cash is paid to stockholders and the current liability is removed.

P3 **Account for stock dividends and stock splits.** Neither a stock dividend nor a stock split alters the value of the company. However, the value of each share is less due to the distribution of additional shares. The distribution of additional shares is according to individual stockholders' ownership percent. Small stock dividends (≤25%) are recorded by capitalizing retained earnings equal to the market value of distributed shares. Large stock dividends (>25%) are recorded by capitalizing retained earnings equal to the par or stated value of distributed shares. Stock splits do not yield journal entries but do yield changes in the description of stock.

P4 **Distribute dividends between common stock and preferred stock.** Preferred stockholders usually hold the right to dividend distributions before common stockholders. When preferred stock is cumulative and in arrears, the amount in arrears must be distributed to preferred before any dividends are distributed to common.

P5 **Record purchases and sales of treasury stock and the retirement of stock.** When a corporation purchases its own previously issued stock, it debits the cost of these shares to Treasury Stock. Treasury stock is subtracted from equity in the balance sheet. If treasury stock is reissued, any proceeds in excess of cost are credited to Paid-In Capital, Treasury Stock. If the proceeds are less than cost, they are debited to Paid-In Capital, Treasury Stock to the extent a credit balance exists. Any remaining amount is debited to Retained Earnings. When stock is retired, all accounts related to the stock are removed.

Guidance Answers to **Decision Maker** and **Decision Ethics**

Entrepreneur The 50% stock dividend provides you no direct income. A stock dividend often reveals management's optimistic expectations about the future and can improve a stock's marketability by making it affordable to more investors. Accordingly, a stock dividend usually reveals "good news" and because of this, it likely increases (slightly) the market value for your stock.

Concert Organizer You have two basic options: (1) different classes of common stock or (2) common and preferred stock. Your objective is to issue to yourself stock that has all or a majority of the voting power. The other class of stock would carry limited or no voting rights. In this way, you maintain control and are able to raise the necessary funds.

Director This case deals with insider trading in a company's stock. The ethical conflict is between your director responsibilities to stockholders (and the public) and your interest in increasing personal wealth from the options. If information about the new contract is kept private until after the option plan is approved and the options are priced, you are likely to make more money. (*Note:* Insider trading laws may make nondisclosure in this case a crime.) You should raise ethical and legal concerns to the board. You might also consider whether staying on the board of this company is proper since it appears there was some intent to deceive outsiders.

Money Manager Since one company requires a payment of $19 for each $1 of earnings, and the other requires $25, you would prefer the stock with the PE of 19; it is a better deal given identical prospects. You should make sure these companies' earnings computations are roughly the same, for example, no extraordinary items, unusual events, and so forth. Also, your PE estimates for these companies do matter. If you are willing to pay $29 for each $1 of earnings for these companies, you obviously expect both to exceed current market expectations.

Investor Book value reflects recorded values. BMX's book value is $4 per common share. Stock price reflects the market's expectation of net asset value (both tangible and intangible items). BMX's market value is $7 per common share. Comparing these figures suggests BMX's market value of net assets is higher than its recorded values (by an amount of $7 versus $4 per share).

Guidance Answers to **Quick Checks**

1. (*b*)

2. A corporation pays taxes on its income, and its stockholders normally pay personal income taxes (at the 15% rate or lower) on any cash dividends received from the corporation.

3. A proxy is a legal document used to transfer a stockholder's right to vote to another person.

4. (*a*)

5. A stock premium is an amount in excess of par (or stated) value paid by purchasers of newly issued stock.

6. Minimum legal capital intends to protect creditors of a corporation by obligating stockholders to some minimum level of equity financing and by constraining a corporation from excessive payments to stockholders.

7. Common Dividend Payable is a current liability account.

8. The date of declaration, date of record, and date of payment.

9. A dividend is a legal liability at the date of declaration, on which date it is recorded as a liability.

10. A stock dividend does not transfer assets to stockholders, but it does require an amount of retained earnings to be transferred to a contributed capital account(s).

11. A small stock dividend is 25% or less of the previous outstanding shares. A large stock dividend is more than 25%.

12. Retained earnings equal to the distributable shares' market value should be capitalized for a small stock dividend.

13. Typically, preferred stock has a preference in receipt of dividends and in distribution of assets.

14. (*a*)

15. (*b*)

Total cash dividend	$288,000
To preferred shareholders	135,000*
Remainder to common shareholders	$153,000

* 9,000 × $50 × 10% × 3 years = $135,000.

16. (*b*)

17. No. The shares are an investment for Southern Co. and are issued and outstanding shares for Northern Corp.

18. Treasury stock does not affect the number of authorized or issued shares, but it reduces the outstanding shares.

19. (*a*)

Key Terms

Key Terms are available at the book's Website for learning and testing in an online Flashcard Format.

Appropriated retained earnings (p. 517)
Authorized stock (p. 503)
Basic earnings per share (p. 518)
Book value per common share (p. 520)
Book value per preferred share (p. 520)
Call price (p. 513)
Callable preferred stock (p. 513)
Capital stock (p. 503)
Changes in accounting estimates (p. 517)
Common stock (p. 502)
Complex capital structure (p. 519)
Convertible preferred stock (p. 513)
Corporation (p. 500)
Cumulative preferred stock (p. 511)
Date of declaration (p. 507)
Date of payment (p. 507)
Date of record (p. 507)
Diluted earnings per share (p. 519)
Dilutive securities (p. 519)

Discount on stock (p. 505)
Dividend in arrears (p. 511)
Dividend yield (p. 519)
Earnings per share (EPS) (p. 518)
Financial leverage (p. 513)
Large stock dividend (p. 508)
Liquidating cash dividend (p. 508)
Market value per share (p. 503)
Minimum legal capital (p. 503)
Noncumulative preferred stock (p. 511)
Nonparticipating preferred stock (p. 512)
No-par value stock (p. 503)
Organization expenses (p. 501)
Paid-in capital (p. 504)
Paid-in capital in excess of par value (p. 505)
Participating preferred stock (p. 512)
Par value (p. 503)
Par value stock (p. 503)

Preemptive right (p. 502)
Preferred stock (p. 510)
Premium on stock (p. 505)
Price-earnings (PE) ratio (p. 519)
Prior period adjustment (p. 517)
Proxy (p. 502)
Restricted retained earnings (p. 516)
Retained earnings (p. 504)
Retained earnings deficit (p. 507)
Reverse stock split (p. 510)
Simple capital structure (p. 519)
Small stock dividend (p. 508)
Stated value stock (p. 504)
Statement of stockholders' equity (p. 517)
Stock dividend (p. 508)
Stock options (p. 517)
Stock split (p. 510)
Stockholders' equity (p. 504)
Treasury stock (p. 514)

Multiple Choice Quiz

Multiple Choice Quizzes A and B are available at the book's Website.

1. A corporation issues 6,000 shares of $5 par value common stock for $8 cash per share. The entry to record this transaction includes:
 a. A debit to Paid-In Capital in Excess of Par Value for $18,000.
 b. A credit to Common Stock for $48,000.
 c. A credit to Paid-In Capital in Excess of Par Value for $30,000.
 d. A credit to Cash for $48,000.
 e. A credit to Common Stock for $30,000.

2. A company reports net income of $75,000. Its weighted-average common shares outstanding is 19,000. It has no other stock outstanding. Its earnings per share is:
 a. $4.69
 b. $3.95

 c. $3.75
 d. $2.08
 e. $4.41

3. A company has 5,000 shares of $100 par preferred stock and 50,000 shares of $10 par common stock outstanding. Its total stockholders' equity is $2,000,000. Its book value per common share is:
 a. $100.00
 b. $ 10.00
 c. $ 40.00
 d. $ 30.00
 e. $ 36.36

4. A company paid cash dividends of $0.81 per share. Its earnings per share is $6.95 and its market price per share is $45.00. Its dividend yield is:
   a. 1.8%
   b. 11.7%
   c. 15.4%
   d. 55.6%
   e. 8.6%

5. A company's shares have a market value of $85 per share. Its net income is $3,500,000, and its weighted-average common shares outstanding is 700,000. Its price-earnings ratio is:
   a. 5.9
   b. 425.0
   c. 17.0
   d. 10.4
   e. 41.2

Discussion Questions

1. What are organization expenses? Provide examples.

2. How are organization expenses reported?

3. Who is responsible for directing a corporation's affairs?

4. What is the preemptive right of common stockholders?

5. List the general rights of common stockholders.

6. What is the difference between authorized shares and outstanding shares?

7. Why would an investor find convertible preferred stock attractive?

8. What is the difference between the market value per share and the par value per share?

9. What is the difference between the par value and the call price of a share of preferred stock?

10. Identify and explain the importance of the three dates relevant to corporate dividends.

11. Why is the term *liquidating dividend* used to describe cash dividends debited against paid-in capital accounts?

12. How does declaring a stock dividend affect the corporation's assets, liabilities, and total equity? What are the effects of the eventual distribution of that stock?

13. What is the difference between a stock dividend and a stock split?

14. Courts have ruled that a stock dividend is not taxable income to stockholders. What justifies this decision?

15. How does the purchase of treasury stock affect the purchaser's assets and total equity?

16. Why do laws place limits on treasury stock purchases?

17. How are EPS results computed for a corporation with a simple capital structure?

18. What is a stock option?

19. How is book value per share computed for a corporation with no preferred stock? What is the main limitation of using book value per share to value a corporation?

20. Review the balance sheet for **Best Buy** in Appendix A and list the classes of stock that it has issued.

21. Refer to the balance sheet for **Circuit City** in Appendix A. What is the par value per share of its common stock? Suggest a rationale for the amount of par value it assigned.

22. Refer to the financial statements for **Apple** in Appendix A. Did it issue or repurchase any common stock for the year ended September 25, 2004? Explain.

 Red numbers denote Discussion Questions that involve decision-making.

Of the following statements, which are true for the corporate form of organization?
1. Ownership rights cannot be easily transferred.
2. Owners have unlimited liability for corporate debts.
3. Capital is more easily accumulated than with most other forms of organization.
4. Corporate income that is distributed to shareholders is usually taxed twice.
5. It is a separate legal entity.
6. It has a limited life.
7. Owners are not agents of the corporation.

QUICK STUDY

QS 13-1
Characteristics of corporations
C1

Prepare the journal entry to record Zende Company's issuance of 75,000 shares of $5 par value common stock assuming the shares sell for:
a. $5 cash per share.
b. $6 cash per share.

QS 13-2
Issuance of common stock
P1

QS 13-3

Issuance of par and stated value common stock

P1

Prepare the journal entry to record Jevonte Company's issuance of 36,000 shares of its common stock assuming the shares have a:

a. $2 par value and sell for $18 cash per share.

b. $2 stated value and sell for $18 cash per share.

QS 13-4

Issuance of no-par common stock

P1

Prepare the journal entry to record Autumn Company's issuance of 63,000 shares of no-par value common stock assuming the shares:

a. Sell for $29 cash per share.

b. Are exchanged for land valued at $1,827,000.

QS 13-5

Issuance of common stock

P1

Prepare the issuer's journal entry for each separate transaction. (*a*) On March 1, Atlantic Co. issues 42,500 shares of $4 par value common stock for $297,500 cash. (*b*) On April 1, OP Co. issues no-par value common stock for $70,000 cash. (*c*) On April 6, MPG issues 2,000 shares of $25 par value common stock for $45,000 of inventory, $145,000 of machinery, and acceptance of a $94,000 note payable.

QS 13-6

Issuance of preferred stock

C3

a. Prepare the journal entry to record Tamasine Company's issuance of 5,000 shares of $100 par value 7% cumulative preferred stock for $102 cash per share.

b. Assuming the facts in part 1, if Tamasine declares a year-end cash dividend, what is the amount of dividend paid to preferred shareholders? (Assume no dividends in arrears.)

QS 13-7

Accounting for cash dividends

P2

Prepare journal entries to record the following transactions for Fletcher Corporation.

May 15 Declared a $54,000 cash dividend payable to common stockholders.

June 31 Paid the dividend declared on May 15.

QS 13-8

Accounting for small stock dividend

C2 P3

The stockholders' equity section of Jun Company's balance sheet as of April 1 follows. On April 2, Jun declares and distributes a 10% stock dividend. The stock's per share market value on April 2 is $20 (prior to the dividend). Prepare the stockholders' equity section immediately after the stock dividend.

Common stock—$5 par value, 375,000 shares authorized, 200,000 shares issued and outstanding	$1,000,000
Paid-in capital in excess of par value, common stock	600,000
Retained earnings	833,000
Total stockholders' equity	$2,433,000

QS 13-9

Dividend allocation between classes of shareholders

P4

Stockholders' equity of Ernst Company consists of 80,000 shares of $5 par value, 8% cumulative preferred stock and 250,000 shares of $1 par value common stock. Both classes of stock have been outstanding since the company's inception. Ernst did not declare any dividends in the prior year, but it now declares and pays a $110,000 cash dividend at the current year-end. Determine the amount distributed to each class of stockholders for this two-year-old company.

QS 13-10

Purchase and sale of treasury stock P5

On May 3, Zirbal Corporation purchased 4,000 shares of its own stock for $36,000 cash. On November 4, Zirbal reissued 850 shares of this treasury stock for $8,500. Prepare the May 3 and November 4 journal entries to record Zirbal's purchase and reissuance of treasury stock.

QS 13-11

Accounting for changes in estimates; error adjustments

C4

Answer the following questions related to a company's activities for the current year:

1. A review of the notes payable files discovers that three years ago the company reported the entire amount of a payment (principal and interest) on an installment note payable as interest expense. This mistake had a material effect on the amount of income in that year. How should the correction be reported in the current year financial statements?

2. After using an expected useful life of seven years and no salvage value to depreciate its office equipment over the preceding three years, the company decided early this year that the equipment will last only two more years. How should the effects of this decision be reported in the current year financial statements?

Murray Company reports net income of $770,000 for the year. It has no preferred stock, and its weighted-average common shares outstanding is 280,000 shares. Compute its basic earnings per share.

QS 13-12
Basic earnings per share A1

Epic Company earned net income of $900,000 this year. The number of common shares outstanding during the entire year was 400,000, and preferred shareholders received a $20,000 cash dividend. Compute Epic Company's basic earnings per share.

QS 13-13
Basic earnings per share A1

Compute Topp Company's price-earnings ratio if its common stock has a market value of $32.60 per share and its EPS is $3.95. Would an analyst likely consider this stock potentially over- or underpriced? Explain.

QS 13-14
Price-earnings ratio A2

Foxboro Company expects to pay a $2.30 per share cash dividend this year on its common stock. The current market value of Foxboro stock is $32.50 per share. Compute the expected dividend yield on the Foxboro stock. Would you classify the Foxboro stock as a growth or an income stock? Explain.

QS 13-15
Dividend yield

A3

The stockholders' equity section of Montaigne Company's balance sheet follows. The preferred stock's call price is $40. Determine the book value per share of the common stock.

QS 13-16
Book value per common share

A4

Preferred stock—5% cumulative, $10 par value, 20,000 shares authorized, issued and outstanding	$ 200,000
Common stock—$5 par value, 200,000 shares authorized, 150,000 shares issued and outstanding	750,000
Retained earnings	890,000
Total stockholders' equity	$1,840,000

Describe how each of the following characteristics of organizations applies to corporations.

EXERCISES

1. Owner authority and control
2. Ease of formation
3. Transferability of ownership
4. Ability to raise large capital amounts
5. Duration of life
6. Owner liability
7. Legal status
8. Tax status of income

Exercise 13-1
Characteristics of corporations

C1

Rodriguez Corporation issues 19,000 shares of its common stock for $152,000 cash on February 20. Prepare journal entries to record this event under each of the following separate situations.
1. The stock has neither par nor stated value.
2. The stock has a $2 par value.
3. The stock has a $5 stated value.

Exercise 13-2
Accounting for par, stated, and no-par stock issuances

P1

Prepare journal entries to record the following four separate issuances of stock.
1. Two thousand shares of no-par common stock are issued to the corporation's promoters in exchange for their efforts, estimated to be worth $40,000. The stock has no stated value.
2. Two thousand shares of no-par common stock are issued to the corporation's promoters in exchange for their efforts, estimated to be worth $40,000. The stock has a $1 per share stated value.
3. Four thousand shares of $5 par value common stock are issued for $35,000 cash.
4. One thousand shares of $50 par value preferred stock are issued for $60,000 cash.

Exercise 13-3
Recording stock issuances

P1

Sudoku Company issues 7,000 shares of $7 par value common stock in exchange for land and a building. The land is valued at $45,000 and the building at $85,000. Prepare the journal entry to record issuance of the stock in exchange for the land and building.

Exercise 13-4
Stock issuance for noncash assets

P1

Exercise 13-5

Identifying characteristics of preferred stock

C2 C3

Match each description 1 through 6 with the characteristic of preferred stock that it best describes by writing the letter of the characteristic in the blank next to each description.

A. Callable   **B.** Convertible   **C.** Cumulative

D. Noncumulative   **E.** Nonparticipating   **F.** Participating

_____ **1.** Holders of the stock are entitled to receive current and all past dividends before common stockholders receive any dividends.

_____ **2.** The issuing corporation can retire the stock by paying a prespecified price.

_____ **3.** Holders of the stock can receive dividends exceeding the stated rate under certain conditions.

_____ **4.** Holders of the stock are not entitled to receive dividends in excess of the stated rate.

_____ **5.** Holders of this stock can exchange it for shares of common stock.

_____ **6.** Holders of the stock lose any dividends that are not declared in the current year.

Exercise 13-6

Stock dividends and splits

P3

On June 30, 2008, Sharper Corporation's common stock is priced at $62 per share before any stock dividend or split, and the stockholders' equity section of its balance sheet appears as follows.

Common stock—$10 par value, 120,000 shares authorized, 50,000 shares issued and outstanding	$ 500,000
Paid-in capital in excess of par value, common stock	200,000
Retained earnings	660,000
Total stockholders' equity	$1,360,000

1. Assume that the company declares and immediately distributes a 50% stock dividend. This event is recorded by capitalizing retained earnings equal to the stock's par value. Answer these questions about stockholders' equity as it exists *after* issuing the new shares.

a. What is the retained earnings balance?

Check (1b) $1,360,000

b. What is the amount of total stockholders' equity?

c. How many shares are outstanding?

2. Assume that the company implements a 3-for-2 stock split instead of the stock dividend in part 1. Answer these questions about stockholders' equity as it exists *after* issuing the new shares.

(2a) $660,000

a. What is the retained earnings balance?

b. What is the amount of total stockholders' equity?

c. How many shares are outstanding?

3. Explain the difference, if any, to a stockholder from receiving new shares distributed under a large stock dividend versus a stock split.

Exercise 13-7

Stock dividends and per share book values

P3

The stockholders' equity of TVX Company at the beginning of the day on February 5 follows.

Common stock—$10 par value, 150,000 shares authorized, 60,000 shares issued and outstanding	$ 600,000
Paid-in capital in excess of par value, common stock	425,000
Retained earnings	550,000
Total stockholders' equity	$1,575,000

On February 5, the directors declare a 20% stock dividend distributable on February 28 to the February 15 stockholders of record. The stock's market value is $40 per share on February 5 before the stock dividend. The stock's market value is $33.40 per share on February 28.

1. Prepare entries to record both the dividend declaration and its distribution.

Check (2) Book value per share: before, $26.250; after, $21.875

2. One stockholder owned 800 shares on February 5 before the dividend. Compute the book value per share and total book value of this stockholder's shares immediately before and after the stock dividend of February 5.

3. Compute the total market value of the investor's shares in part 2 as of February 5 and February 28.

York's outstanding stock consists of (*a*) 80,000 shares of noncumulative 7.5% preferred stock with a $5 par value and (*b*) 200,000 shares of common stock with a $1 par value. During its first four years of operation, the corporation declared and paid the following total cash dividends.

2006	$ 20,000
2007	28,000
2008	200,000
2009	350,000

Determine the amount of dividends paid each year to each of the two classes of stockholders. Also compute the total dividends paid to each class for the four years combined.

Exercise 13-8
Dividends on common and noncumulative preferred stock
P4

Check Total paid to preferred, $108,000

Use the data in Exercise 13-8 to determine the amount of dividends paid each year to each of the two classes of stockholders assuming that the preferred stock is cumulative. Also determine the total dividends paid to each class for the four years combined.

Exercise 13-9
Dividends on common and cumulative preferred stock P4

On October 10, the stockholders' equity of Sherman Systems appears as follows.

Common stock—$10 par value, 72,000 shares authorized, issued, and outstanding	$ 720,000
Paid-in capital in excess of par value, common stock	216,000
Retained earnings	864,000
Total stockholders' equity	$1,800,000

Exercise 13-10
Recording and reporting treasury stock transactions
P5

1. Prepare journal entries to record the following transactions for Sherman Systems.
   a. Purchased 5,000 shares of its own common stock at $25 per share on October 11.
   b. Sold 1,000 treasury shares on November 1 for $31 cash per share.
   c. Sold all remaining treasury shares on November 25 for $20 cash per share.
2. Explain how Sherman's equity section changes after the October 11 treasury stock purchase, and prepare the revised equity section of its balance sheet at that date.

Check (1c) Dr. Retained Earnings, $14,000

The following information is available for Amos Company for the year ended December 31, 2008.
a. Balance of retained earnings, December 31, 2007, prior to discovery of error, $1,375,000.
b. Cash dividends declared and paid during 2008, $43,000.
c. It neglected to record 2006 depreciation expense of $55,500, which is net of $4,500 in income taxes.
d. Amos earned $126,000 in 2008 net income.
Prepare a 2008 statement of retained earnings for Amos Company.

Exercise 13-11
Preparing a statement of retained earnings
C4

Ecker Company reports $2,700,000 of net income for 2008 and declares $390,000 of cash dividends on its preferred stock for 2008. At the end of 2008, the company had 678,000 weighted-average shares of common stock.
1. What amount of net income is available to common stockholders for 2008?
2. What is the company's basic EPS for 2008?

Exercise 13-12
Earnings per share
A1

Check (2) $3.41

Kelley Company reports $960,000 of net income for 2008 and declares $130,000 of cash dividends on its preferred stock for 2008. At the end of 2008, the company had 379,000 weighted-average shares of common stock.
1. What amount of net income is available to common stockholders for 2008?
2. What is the company's basic EPS for 2008?

Exercise 13-13
Earnings per share
A1

Exercise 13-14

Price-earnings ratio computation and interpretation

A2

Compute the price-earnings ratio for each of these four separate companies. Which stock might an analyst likely investigate as being potentially undervalued by the market? Explain.

Company	Earnings per Share	Market Value per Share
1	$12.00	$176.00
2	10.00	96.00
3	7.50	94.00
4	50.00	250.00

Exercise 13-15

Dividend yield computation and interpretation

A3

Compute the dividend yield for each of these four separate companies. Which company's stock would probably *not* be classified as an income stock? Explain.

Company	Annual Cash Dividend per Share	Market Value per Share
1	$16.00	$220.00
2	14.00	136.00
3	4.00	72.00
4	1.00	80.00

Exercise 13-16

Book value per share

A4

The equity section of Cyril Corporation's balance sheet shows the following.

Preferred stock—6% cumulative, $25 par value, $30 call price, 10,000 shares issued and outstanding	$ 250,000
Common stock—$10 par value, 80,000 shares issued and outstanding	800,000
Retained earnings	535,000
Total stockholders' equity	$1,585,000

Determine the book value per share of the preferred and common stock under two separate situations.

Check (1) Book value of common, $16.06

1. No preferred dividends are in arrears.

2. Three years of preferred dividends are in arrears.

PROBLEM SET A

Problem 13-1A

Stockholders' equity transactions and analysis

C2   C3   P1

Kinkaid Co. is incorporated at the beginning of this year and engages in a number of transactions. The following journal entries impacted its stockholders' equity during its first year of operations.

a.	Cash	300,000	
	Common Stock, $25 Par Value		250,000
	Paid-In Capital in Excess of Par Value, Common Stock		50,000
b.	Organization Expenses	150,000	
	Common Stock, $25 Par Value		125,000
	Paid-In Capital in Excess of Par Value, Common Stock		25,000

[continued on next page]

[continued from previous page]

c.	Cash	43,000	
	Accounts Receivable.	15,000	
	Building	81,500	
	Notes Payable.		59,500
	Common Stock, $25 Par Value		50,000
	Paid-In Capital in Excess of		
	Par Value, Common Stock		30,000
d.	Cash	120,000	
	Common Stock, $25 Par Value		75,000
	Paid-In Capital in Excess of		
	Par Value, Common Stock		45,000

Required

1. Explain each journal entry (*a*) through (*d*).

2. How many shares of common stock are outstanding at year-end?

3. What is the amount of minimum legal capital (based on par value) at year-end?

4. What is the total paid-in capital at year-end?

5. What is the book value per share of the common stock at year-end if total paid-in capital plus retained earnings equals $695,000?

Check (2) 20,000 shares

(3) $500,000

(4) $650,000

Kohler Corporation reports the following components of stockholders' equity on December 31, 2008.

Common stock—$10 par value, 100,000 shares authorized,		
40,000 shares issued and outstanding	$400,000	
Paid-in capital in excess of par value, common stock	60,000	
Retained earnings	270,000	
Total stockholders' equity	$730,000	

Problem 13-2A
Cash dividends, treasury stock, and statement of retained earnings

C2 C4 P2 P5

In year 2009, the following transactions affected its stockholders' equity accounts.

Jan.   1   Purchased 4,000 shares of its own stock at $20 cash per share.

Jan.   5   Directors declared a $2 per share cash dividend payable on Feb. 28 to the Feb. 5 stockholders of record.

Feb. 28   Paid the dividend declared on January 5.

July   6   Sold 1,500 of its treasury shares at $24 cash per share.

Aug. 22   Sold 2,500 of its treasury shares at $17 cash per share.

Sept. 5   Directors declared a $2 per share cash dividend payable on October 28 to the September 25 stockholders of record.

Oct. 28   Paid the dividend declared on September 5.

Dec. 31   Closed the $388,000 credit balance (from net income) in the Income Summary account to Retained Earnings.

Required

1. Prepare journal entries to record each of these transactions for 2009.

2. Prepare a statement of retained earnings for the year ended December 31, 2009.

3. Prepare the stockholders' equity section of the company's balance sheet as of December 31, 2009.

Check (2) Retained earnings, Dec. 31, 2009, $504,500.

At September 30, the end of Beijing Company's third quarter, the following stockholders' equity accounts are reported.

Common stock, $12 par value	$360,000
Paid-in capital in excess of par value, common stock	90,000
Retained earnings	320,000

Problem 13-3A
Equity analysis—journal entries and account balances

P2 P3

In the fourth quarter, the following entries related to its equity accounts are recorded.

Oct. 2	Retained Earnings...........................	60,000	
	Common Dividend Payable		60,000
Oct. 25	Common Dividend Payable	60,000	
	Cash		60,000
Oct. 31	Retained Earnings	75,000	
	Common Stock Dividend Distributable		36,000
	Paid-In Capital in Excess of Par Value, Common Stock		39,000
Nov. 5	Common Stock Dividend Distributable	36,000	
	Common Stock, $12 Par Value		36,000
Dec. 1	Memo—Change the title of the common stock account to reflect the new par value of $4.		
Dec. 31	Income Summary	210,000	
	Retained Earnings		210,000

Required

1. Explain each journal entry.

2. Complete the following table showing the equity account balances at each indicated date.

	Oct. 2	Oct. 25	Oct. 31	Nov. 5	Dec. 1	Dec. 31
Common stock	$_____	$_____	$_____	$_____	$_____	$_____
Common stock dividend distributable	_____	_____	_____	_____	_____	_____
Paid-in capital in excess of par, common stock	_____	_____	_____	_____	_____	_____
Retained earnings	_____	_____	_____	_____	_____	_____
Total equity	$_____	$_____	$_____	$_____	$_____	$_____

Check   Total equity: Oct. 2, $710,000; Dec. 31, $920,000

Problem 13-4A

Analysis of changes in stockholders' equity accounts

C4   P2   P3   P5

The equity sections from Atticus Group's 2008 and 2009 year-end balance sheets follow.

Stockholders' Equity (December 31, 2008)

Common stock—$4 par value, 100,000 shares authorized, 40,000 shares issued and outstanding	$160,000
Paid-in capital in excess of par value, common stock	120,000
Retained earnings	320,000
Total stockholders' equity	$600,000

Stockholders' Equity (December 31, 2009)

Common stock—$4 par value, 100,000 shares authorized, 47,400 shares issued, 3,000 shares in treasury	$189,600
Paid-in capital in excess of par value, common stock	179,200
Retained earnings ($30,000 restricted by treasury stock)	400,000
	768,800
Less cost of treasury stock	(30,000)
Total stockholders' equity	$738,800

The following transactions and events affected its equity accounts during year 2009.

Jan.	5	Declared a $0.50 per share cash dividend, date of record January 10.
Mar.	20	Purchased treasury stock for cash.
Apr.	5	Declared a $0.50 per share cash dividend, date of record April 10.
July	5	Declared a $0.50 per share cash dividend, date of record July 10.
July	31	Declared a 20% stock dividend when the stock's market value is $12 per share.

Aug. 14 Issued the stock dividend that was declared on July 31.
Oct.   5 Declared a $0.50 per share cash dividend, date of record October 10.

Required

1. How many common shares are outstanding on each cash dividend date?
2. What is the total dollar amount for each of the four cash dividends?
3. What is the amount of the capitalization of retained earnings for the stock dividend?
4. What is the per share cost of the treasury stock purchased?
5. How much net income did the company earn during year 2009?

Check (3) $88,800

(4) $10

(5) $248,000

Raphael Corporation's common stock is currently selling on a stock exchange at $85 per share, and its current balance sheet shows the following stockholders' equity section.

Problem 13-5A
Computation of book values and dividend allocations

C3 A4 P4

Preferred stock—5% cumulative, $___ par value, 1,000 shares authorized, issued, and outstanding	$ 50,000
Common stock—$___ par value, 4,000 shares authorized, issued, and outstanding	80,000
Retained earnings	150,000
Total stockholders' equity	$280,000

Required

1. What is the current market value (price) of this corporation's common stock?
2. What are the par values of the corporation's preferred stock and its common stock?
3. If no dividends are in arrears, what are the book values per share of the preferred stock and the common stock?
4. If two years' preferred dividends are in arrears, what are the book values per share of the preferred stock and the common stock?
5. If two years' preferred dividends are in arrears and the preferred stock is callable at $55 per share, what are the book values per share of the preferred stock and the common stock?
6. If two years' preferred dividends are in arrears and the board of directors declares cash dividends of $11,500, what total amount will be paid to the preferred and to the common shareholders? What is the amount of dividends per share for the common stock?

Check (4) Book value of common, $56.25

(5) Book value of common, $55

(6) Dividends per common share, $1.00

Analysis Component

7. What are some factors that can contribute to a difference between the book value of common stock and its market value (price)?

Weiss Company is incorporated at the beginning of this year and engages in a number of transactions. The following journal entries impacted its stockholders' equity during its first year of operations.

PROBLEM SET B

Problem 13-1B
Stockholders' equity transactions and analysis

C2 C3 P1

a.	Cash	120,000	
	Common Stock, $1 Par Value		3,000
	Paid-In Capital in Excess of Par Value, Common Stock		117,000
b.	Organization Expenses	40,000	
	Common Stock, $1 Par Value		1,000
	Paid-In Capital in Excess of Par Value, Common Stock		39,000
c.	Cash	13,300	
	Accounts Receivable	8,000	
	Building	37,000	
	Notes Payable		18,300
	Common Stock, $1 Par Value		800
	Paid-In Capital in Excess of Par Value, Common Stock		39,200

[continued on next page]

[continued from previous page]

d.			
	Cash	60,000	
	Common Stock, $1 Par Value		1,200
	Paid-In Capital in Excess of		
	Par Value, Common Stock		58,800

Required

1. Explain each journal entry (*a*) through (*d*).

Check (2) 6,000 shares

(3) $6,000

(4) $260,000

2. How many shares of common stock are outstanding at year-end?

3. What is the amount of minimum legal capital (based on par value) at year-end?

4. What is the total paid-in capital at year-end?

5. What is the book value per share of the common stock at year-end if total paid-in capital plus retained earnings equals $283,000?

Problem 13-2B

Cash dividends, treasury stock, and statement of retained earnings

C2 C4 P2 P5

Balthus Corp. reports the following components of stockholders' equity on December 31, 2008.

Common stock—$1 par value, 320,000 shares authorized,	
200,000 shares issued and outstanding	$ 200,000
Paid-in capital in excess of par value, common stock	1,400,000
Retained earnings	2,160,000
Total stockholders' equity	$3,760,000

It completed the following transactions related to stockholders' equity in year 2009.

Jan. 10 Purchased 40,000 shares of its own stock at $12 cash per share.
Mar. 2 Directors declared a $1.50 per share cash dividend payable on March 31 to the March 15 stock-holders of record.
Mar. 31 Paid the dividend declared on March 2.
Nov. 11 Sold 24,000 of its treasury shares at $13 cash per share.
Nov. 25 Sold 16,000 of its treasury shares at $9.50 cash per share.
Dec. 1 Directors declared a $2.50 per share cash dividend payable on January 2 to the December 10 stockholders of record.
Dec. 31 Closed the $1,072,000 credit balance (from net income) in the Income Summary account to Retained Earnings.

Required

1. Prepare journal entries to record each of these transactions for 2009.

Check (2) Retained earnings, Dec. 31, 2009, $2,476,000

2. Prepare a statement of retained earnings for the year ended December 31, 2009.

3. Prepare the stockholders' equity section of the company's balance sheet as of December 31, 2009.

Problem 13-3B

Equity analysis—journal entries and account balances

P2 P3

At December 31, the end of Chilton Communication's third quarter, the following stockholders' equity accounts are reported.

Common stock, $10 par value	$ 960,000
Paid-in capital in excess of par value, common stock	384,000
Retained earnings	1,600,000

In the fourth quarter, the following entries related to its equity accounts are recorded.

Jan. 17	Retained Earnings	96,000	
	Common Dividend Payable		96,000
Feb. 5	Common Dividend Payable	96,000	
	Cash		96,000

[continued on next page]

[continued from previous page]

Feb. 28	Retained Earnings..........................	252,000	
	Common Stock Dividend Distributable........		120,000
	Paid-In Capital in Excess of Par Value, Common Stock		132,000
Mar. 14	Common Stock Dividend Distributable	120,000	
	Common Stock, $10 Par Value		120,000
Mar. 25	Memo—Change the title of the common stock account to reflect the new par value of $5.		
Mar. 31	Income Summary	720,000	
	Retained Earnings		720,000

Required

1. Explain each journal entry.

2. Complete the following table showing the equity account balances at each indicated date.

	Jan. 17	Feb. 5	Feb. 28	Mar. 14	Mar. 25	Mar. 31
Common stock	$_____	$_____	$_____	$_____	$_____	$_____
Common stock dividend distributable	_____	_____	_____	_____	_____	_____
Paid-in capital in excess of par, common stock	_____	_____	_____	_____	_____	_____
Retained earnings	_____	_____	_____	_____	_____	_____
Total equity	$_____	$_____	$_____	$_____	$_____	$_____

Check Total equity: Jan. 17, $2,848,000; Mar. 31, $3,568,000

The equity sections from Hovo Corporation's 2008 and 2009 balance sheets follow.

Problem 13-4B
Analysis of changes in
stockholders' equity accounts

C4 P2 P3 P5

Stockholders' Equity (December 31, 2008)

Common stock—$20 par value, 30,000 shares authorized, 17,000 shares issued and outstanding	$340,000
Paid-in capital in excess of par value, common stock	60,000
Retained earnings	270,000
Total stockholders' equity	$670,000

Stockholders' Equity (December 31, 2009)

Common stock—$20 par value, 30,000 shares authorized, 19,000 shares issued, 1,000 shares in treasury	$380,000
Paid-in capital in excess of par value, common stock	104,000
Retained earnings ($40,000 restricted by treasury stock)	295,200
	779,200
Less cost of treasury stock	(40,000)
Total stockholders' equity	$739,200

The following transactions and events affected its equity accounts during year 2009.

Feb.	15	Declared a $0.40 per share cash dividend, date of record five days later.
Mar.	2	Purchased treasury stock for cash.
May	15	Declared a $0.40 per share cash dividend, date of record five days later.
Aug.	15	Declared a $0.40 per share cash dividend, date of record five days later.
Oct.	4	Declared a 12.5% stock dividend when the stock's market value is $42 per share.
Oct.	20	Issued the stock dividend that was declared on October 4.
Nov.	15	Declared a $0.40 per share cash dividend, date of record five days later.

Required

1. How many common shares are outstanding on each cash dividend date?

2. What is the total dollar amount for each of the four cash dividends?

3. What is the amount of the capitalization of retained earnings for the stock dividend?

4. What is the per share cost of the treasury stock purchased?

5. How much net income did the company earn during year 2009?

Problem 13-5B

Computation of book values and dividend allocations

C3 A4 P4

Soltech Company's common stock is currently selling on a stock exchange at $90 per share, and its current balance sheet shows the following stockholders' equity section.

Preferred stock—8% cumulative, $___ par value, 1,500 shares authorized, issued, and outstanding	$ 375,000
Common stock—$___ par value, 18,000 shares authorized, issued, and outstanding	900,000
Retained earnings	1,125,000
Total stockholders' equity	$2,400,000

Required

1. What is the current market value (price) of this corporation's common stock?

2. What are the par values of the corporation's preferred stock and its common stock?

3. If no dividends are in arrears, what are the book values per share of the preferred stock and the common stock?

4. If two years' preferred dividends are in arrears, what are the book values per share of the preferred stock and the common stock?

5. If two years' preferred dividends are in arrears and the preferred stock is callable at $280 per share, what are the book values per share of the preferred stock and the common stock?

6. If two years' preferred dividends are in arrears and the board of directors declares cash dividends of $100,000, what total amount will be paid to the preferred and to the common shareholders? What is the amount of dividends per share for the common stock?

Analysis Component

7. Discuss why the book value of common stock is not always a good estimate of its market value.

PROBLEM SET C

  Problem Set C is available at the book's Website to further reinforce and assess your learning.

SERIAL PROBLEM

Success Systems

(This serial problem began in Chapter 1 and continues through most of the book. If previous chapter segments were not completed, the serial problem can begin at this point. It is helpful, but not necessary, for you to use the Working Papers that accompany the book.)

SP 13   Adriana Lopez created Success Systems on October 1, 2007. The company has been successful, and Adriana plans to expand her business. She believes that an additional $100,000 is needed and is investigating three funding sources.

a. Adriana's sister Cicely is willing to invest $100,000 in the business as a common shareholder. Since Adriana currently has $120,000 invested in the business, Cicely's investment will mean that Adriana will maintain about 55% ownership, and Cicely will have 45% ownership of Success Systems.

b. Adriana's uncle Marcello is willing to invest $100,000 in the business as a preferred shareholder. Marcello would purchase 1,000 shares of $100 par value, 7% preferred stock.

c. Adriana's banker is willing to lend her $100,000 on a 7%, 10-year note payable. Adriana would make monthly payments of $1,160.00 per month for 10 years.

Required

1. Prepare the journal entry to reflect the initial $100,000 investment under each of the options (a), (b), and (c).
2. Evaluate the three proposals for expansion, providing the pros and cons of each option.
3. Which option do you recommend Adriana adopt? Explain.

BTN 13-1   Refer to **Best Buy**'s financial statements in Appendix A to answer the following.

1. How many shares of common stock are issued and outstanding at February 26, 2005, and February 28, 2004? How do these numbers compare with the weighted-average common shares outstanding at February 26, 2005 and February 28, 2004?
2. What is the book value of its entire common stock at February 26, 2005?
3. What is the total amount of cash dividends paid to common stockholders for the years ended February 26, 2005, and February 28, 2004?
4. Identify and compare basic EPS amounts across years 2005, 2004, and 2003. Identify and comment on any marked changes.
5. Does Best Buy hold any treasury stock as of February 26, 2005? As of February 28, 2004?

REPORTING IN ACTION

C2 C3 A1 A4

Fast Forward

6. Access Best Buy's financial statements for fiscal years ending after February 26, 2005, from its Website (**BestBuy.com**) or the SEC's EDGAR database (**www.sec.gov**). Has the number of common shares outstanding increased since February 26, 2005? Has Best Buy increased the total amount of cash dividends paid compared to the total amount for fiscal year 2005?

BTN 13-2   Key comparative figures for both **Best Buy** and **Circuit City** follow.

COMPARATIVE ANALYSIS

A1 A2 A3 A4

Key Figures	Best Buy	Circuit City
Net income (in millions)	$ 984	$ 62
Cash dividends declared per common share	$ 0.42	$ 0.07
Common shares outstanding (in millions)	328	188
Weighted-average common shares outstanding (in mil.)	326	193
Market value (price) per share	$51.69	$15.63
Equity applicable to common shares (in millions)	$4,449	$2,087

Required

1. Compute the book value per common share for each company using these data.
2. Compute the basic EPS for each company using these data.
3. Compute the dividend yield for each company using these data. Does the dividend yield of either company characterize it as an income or growth stock? Explain.
4. Compute, compare, and interpret the price-earnings ratio for each company using these data.

BTN 13-3   Harriet Moore is an accountant for New World Pharmaceuticals. Her duties include tracking research and development spending in the new product development division. Over the course of the past six months, Harriet notices that a great deal of funds have been spent on a particular project for a new drug. She hears "through the grapevine" that the company is about to patent the drug and expects it to be a major advance in antibiotics. Harriet believes that this new drug will greatly improve company performance and will cause the company's stock to increase in value. Harriet decides to purchase shares of New World in order to benefit from this expected increase.

ETHICS CHALLENGE

C4

Required

What are Harriet's ethical responsibilities, if any, with respect to the information she has learned through her duties as an accountant for New World Pharmaceuticals? What are the implications to her planned purchase of New World shares?

**COMMUNICATING
IN PRACTICE**

A1   A2

Hint: Make a transparency of each team's memo for a class discussion.

BTN 13-4   Teams are to select an industry, and each team member is to select a different company in that industry. Each team member then is to acquire the selected company's financial statements (or Form 10-K) from the SEC EDGAR site (www.sec.gov). Use these data to identify basic EPS. Use the financial press (or finance.yahoo.com) to determine the market price of this stock, and then compute the price-earnings ratio. Communicate with teammates via a meeting, e-mail, or telephone to discuss the meaning of this ratio, how companies compare, and the industry norm. The team must prepare a single memorandum reporting the ratio for each company and identifying the team conclusions or consensus of opinion. The memorandum is to be duplicated and distributed to the instructor and teammates.

**TAKING IT TO
THE NET**

C2

BTN 13-5   Access the March 4, 2005, filing of the 2004 calendar-year 10-K report of **McDonald's,** (ticker MCD) from www.sec.gov.

Required

1. How many classes of stock has McDonald's issued?
2. What are the par values, number of authorized shares, and issued shares of the classes of stock you identified in part 1?
3. What total amount of cash did McDonald's pay in 2004 to purchase treasury stock?
4. What amount did McDonald's pay out in cash dividends for 2004?

**TEAMWORK IN
ACTION**

P5

Hint: Instructor should be sure each team accurately completes part 1 before proceeding.

BTN 13-6   This activity requires teamwork to reinforce understanding of accounting for treasury stock.

1. Write a brief team statement (*a*) generalizing what happens to a corporation's financial position when it engages in a stock "buyback" and (*b*) identifying reasons that a corporation would engage in this activity.
2. Assume that an entity acquires 100 shares of its $100 par value common stock at a cost of $134 cash per share. Discuss the entry to record this acquisition. Next, assign *each* team member to prepare *one* of the following entries (assume each entry applies to all shares):
   a. Reissue treasury shares at cost.
   b. Reissue treasury shares at $150 per share.
   c. Reissue treasury shares at $120 per share; assume the contributed capital account from treasury shares has a $1,500 balance.
   d. Reissue treasury shares at $120 per share; assume the contributed capital account from treasury shares has a $1,000 balance.
   e. Reissue treasury shares at $120 per share; assume the contributed capital account from treasury shares has a zero balance.
3. In sequence, each member is to present his/her entry to the team and explain the *similarities* and *differences* between that entry and the previous entry.

**BusinessWeek
ACTIVITY**

A1   C4

BTN 13-7   Read the commentary "How Tax Reform Drives Growth and Investment" by Robert J. Barro in the January 24, 2005, issue of *BusinessWeek*.

Required

1. How did the 2003 tax cuts related to dividend taxation affect companies' decisions to pay cash dividends? Explain.
2. What kinds of companies increased their dividends following those tax cuts? Why?
3. Why do you believe managers of these companies acted as they did?

BTN 13-8 Assume that Sundeep Bhan's launch of **Medsite, Inc.** requires $500,000 of start-up capital. Bhan contributes $375,000 of personal assets in return for 15,000 shares of common stock but needs to raise another $125,000 in cash. There are two alternative plans for raising the additional cash. Plan A is to sell 3,750 shares of common stock to one or more investors for $125,000 cash. Plan B is to sell 1,250 shares of cumulative preferred stock to one or more investors for $125,000 cash (this preferred stock would have a $100 par value, an annual 8% dividend rate, and be issued at par).

1. If the business is expected to earn $72,000 of after-tax net income in the first year, what rate of return on beginning equity will Bhan personally earn under each alternative? Which plan will provide the higher expected return to Bhan?

2. If the business is expected to earn $16,800 of after-tax net income in the first year, what rate of return on beginning equity will Bhan personally earn under each alternative? Which plan will provide the higher expected return to Bhan?

3. Analyze and interpret the differences between the results for parts 1 and 2.

ENTREPRENEURIAL DECISION

C2 C3 P2

BTN 13-9 Watch 30 to 60 minutes of financial news on the **CNBC** television channel. Take notes on companies that are catching analysts' attention. You might hear reference to over- and undervaluation of firm and to reports about PE ratios, dividend yields, and earnings per share. Be prepared to give a brief description to the class of your observations of CNBC.

HITTING THE ROAD

A1 A2 A3

BTN 13-10 Financial information for **Dixons** (**Dixons-Group.com**) follows.

Net income (in millions)	£ 283
Cash dividends declared per share	£ 0.07
Number of shares outstanding (in millions)*	1,945
Equity applicable to shares (in millions)	£1,428

GLOBAL DECISION

A1 C4

Dixons

* Assume that the year-end number of shares outstanding approximates the weighted-average shares outstanding.

Required

1. Compute book value per share for Dixons.

2. Compute EPS for Dixons.

3. Compare Dixons' dividends per share with its EPS. Is Dixons paying out a large or small amount of its income as dividends? Explain.

ANSWERS TO MULTIPLE CHOICE QUIZ

1. e; Entry to record this stock issuance is:

Cash (6,000 × $8)	48,000	
Common Stock (6,000 × $5)		30,000
Paid-In Capital in Excess of Par Value, Common Stock		18,000

2. b; $75,000/19,000 shares = $3.95 per share

3. d; Preferred stock = 5,000 × $100 = $500,000
Book value per share = ($2,000,000 − $500,000)/50,000 shares = $30 per common share

4. a; $0.81/$45.00 = 1.8%

5. c; Earnings per share = $3,500,000/700,000 shares = $5 per share
PE ratio = $85/$5 = 17.0

14

Long-Term Liabilities

A Look Back

Chapter 13 focused on corporate equity transactions, including stock issuances and dividends. We also explained how to report and analyze income, earnings per share, and retained earnings.

A Look at This Chapter

This chapter describes the accounting for and analysis of bonds and notes. We explain their characteristics, payment patterns, interest computations, retirement, and reporting requirements. An appendix to this chapter introduces leases and pensions.

A Look Ahead

Chapter 15 focuses on how to classify, account for, and report investments in both debt and equity securities. We also describe accounting for transactions listed in a foreign currency.

Learning Objectives

CAP

Conceptual

C1 Explain the types and payment patterns of notes. (p. 554)

C2 Appendix 14A—Explain and compute the present value of an amount(s) to be paid at a future date(s). (p. 561)

C3 Appendix 14C—Describe the accrual of bond interest when bond payments do not align with accounting periods. (p. 565)

C4 Appendix 14D—Describe accounting for leases and pensions. (p. 567)

Analytical

A1 Compare bond financing with stock financing. (p. 544)

A2 Assess debt features and their implications. (p. 557)

A3 Compute the debt-to-equity ratio and explain its use. (p. 558)

Procedural

P1 Prepare entries to record bond issuance and bond interest expense. (p. 546)

P2 Compute and record amortization of bond discount. (p. 547)

P3 Compute and record amortization of bond premium. (p. 550)

P4 Record the retirement of bonds. (p. 553)

P5 Prepare entries to account for notes. (p. 555)

"We offer individuals the opportunity to realize their dreams of owning their own business"
—Mark Melton
(Holly Melton on left)

Cleaning Up in Business

CARPINTERIA, CA—Mark and Holly Melton always wanted to be entrepreneurs, and a special idea made it happen. The Meltons identified a growing demand for high-quality cleaning services. "Cleaning offices is not glamorous," says Mark. "But it's stable, year-round, and highly sought after [work]. And, no technology is going to make the industry obsolete."

Mark and Holly quickly developed a business plan, partnered with Coverall Cleaning Concepts (**Coverall.com/Locations**), and launched **Melton Franchise Systems**. Their company operates as a "master franchisor," which means it recruits and organizes smaller, individual franchise owners. It also provides their franchisees with equipment, training, and marketing and billing services in return for royalty fees. The Meltons currently serve over 300 franchise owners—many of whom are immigrants. "[Our company] provides local residents with an opportunity to own or manage their own business, where they might not have had the chance otherwise," Mark says proudly. "We offer individuals the opportunity to realize their dreams."

A key to their success, say the Meltons, is providing long-term financing for each individual franchise owner. Franchise owners typically provide only one-half of their financing up front, and the rest becomes a long-term liability. Mark and Holly must also manage their own company's long-term financing needs. The Meltons took on an SBA loan of over $600,000 in liabilities. Consequently, they are like their franchise owners in that they confront the realities of debt, interest payments, and collateral agreements.

Inc. magazine named the Meltons as heading one of the fastest-growing privately held U.S. companies. Mark humbly recognizes the company's dedicated employees. "Instead of the high turnover associated with low wage and marginally trained employees . . . we are able to offer our janitorial customers the services of a highly trained franchise owner who brings the consistency and caring of an owner," says Mark.

The Meltons say they are "thrilled" to continue expanding. Mark adds, "Our rapid growth is evidence that more and more companies are counting on [us]." With continued smart financing and sound management of liabilities, expect them to clean up the competition.

[Sources: *Coverall Website*, January 2006; *Inc.*, April 2005; *SBA.gov Website*, January 2005; *BizJournals*, April 2005; *Franchise News*, May 2004; *Building Services Management*, November 2004]

Individuals, companies, and governments issue bonds to finance their activities. In return for financing, bonds promise to repay the lender with interest. This chapter explains the basics of bonds and the accounting for their issuance and retirement. The chapter also describes long-term notes as another financ-ing source. We explain how present value concepts impact both the accounting for and reporting of bonds and notes. Appendixes to this chapter discuss present value concepts applicable to liabilities, effective interest amortization, and the accounting for leases and pensions.

Long-Term Liabilities

Bond Basics	Bond Issuances	Bond Retirement	Long-Term Notes
• Bond financing • Bond trading • Issuance procedures	• Issuance at par • Issuance at a discount • Issuance at a premium • Bond pricing	• At maturity • Before maturity • By conversion	• Installment notes • Mortgage terms

Basics of Bonds

This section explains the basics of bonds and a company's motivation for issuing them.

Bond Financing

Projects that demand large amounts of money often are funded from bond issuances. (Both for-profit and nonprofit companies, as well as governmental units, such as nations, states, cities, and school districts, issue bonds.) A **bond** is its issuer's written promise to pay an amount identified as the par value of the bond with interest. The **par value of a bond,** also called the *face amount* or *face value,* is paid at a specified future date known as the bond's *maturity date.* Most bonds also require the issuer to make semiannual interest payments. The amount of interest paid each period is determined by multiplying the par value of the bond by the bond's contract rate of interest. This section explains both advantages and disadvantages of bond financing.

A1 Compare bond financing with stock financing.

Advantages of Bonds There are three main advantages of bond financing:

1. *Bonds do not affect owner control.* Equity financing reflects ownership in a company, whereas bond financing does not. A person who contributes $1,000 of a company's $10,000 equity financing typically controls one-tenth of all owner decisions. A person who owns a $1,000, 11%, 20-year bond has no ownership right. This person, or bond-holder, is to receive from the bond issuer 11% interest, or $110, each year the bond is outstanding and $1,000 when it matures in 20 years.

2. *Interest on bonds is tax deductible.* Bond interest payments are tax deductible for the issuer, but equity payments (distributions) to owners are not. To illustrate, assume that a corporation with no bond financing earns $15,000 in income *before* paying taxes at a 40% tax rate, which amounts to $6,000 ($15,000 × 40%) in taxes. If a portion of its financing is in bonds, however, the resulting bond interest is deducted in computing taxable income. That is, if bond interest expense is $10,000, the taxes owed would be $2,000 ([$15,000 − $10,000] × 40%), which is less than the $6,000 owed with no bond financing.
3. *Bonds can increase return on equity.* A company that earns a higher return with borrowed funds than it pays in interest on those funds increases its return on equity. This process is called *financial leverage* or *trading on the equity.*

To illustrate the third point, consider Magnum Co., which has $1 million in equity and is planning a $500,000 expansion to meet increasing demand for its product. Magnum predicts the $500,000 expansion will yield $125,000 in additional income before paying any interest. It currently earns $100,000 per year and has no interest expense. Magnum is considering three plans. Plan A is to not expand. Plan B is to expand and raise $500,000 from equity financing. Plan C is to expand and issue $500,000 of bonds that pay 10% annual interest ($50,000). Exhibit 14.1 shows how these three plans affect Magnum's net income, equity, and return on equity (net income/equity). The owner(s) will earn a higher return on equity if expansion occurs. Moreover, the preferred expansion plan is to issue bonds. Projected net income under Plan C ($175,000) is smaller than under Plan B ($225,000), but the return on equity is larger because of less equity investment. Plan C has another advantage if income is taxable. This illustration reflects a general rule: *Return on equity increases when the expected rate of return from the new assets is higher than the rate of interest expense on the debt financing.*

Point: Financial leverage can be achieved by issuing either bonds, notes, or preferred stock.

Example: Compute return on equity for all three plans if Magnum currently earns $150,000 instead of $100,000.
Answer ($ 000s):
Plan A = 15%   ($150/$1,000)
Plan B = 18.3%   ($275/$1,500)
Plan C = 22.5%   ($225/$1,000)

	Plan A Do Not Expand	Plan B Equity Financing	Plan C Bond Financing
Income before interest expense	$ 100,000	$ 225,000	$ 225,000
Interest expense	—	—	(50,000)
Net income	**$ 100,000**	**$ 225,000**	**$ 175,000**
Equity	$1,000,000	$1,500,000	$1,000,000
Return on equity	**10.0%**	**15.0%**	**17.5%**

Exhibit 14.1

Financing with Bonds versus Equity

Disadvantages of Bonds   The two main disadvantages of bond financing are:

1. *Bonds can decrease return on equity.* When a company earns a lower return with the borrowed funds than it pays in interest, it decreases its return on equity. This downside risk of financial leverage is more likely to arise when a company has periods of low income or net losses.

2. *Bonds require payment of both periodic interest and the par value at maturity.* Bond payments can be especially burdensome when income and cash flow are low. Equity financing, in contrast, does not require any payments because cash withdrawals (dividends) are paid at the discretion of the owner (or board).

Point: Debt financing is desirable when interest is tax deductible, when owner control is preferred, and when return on equity is higher than interest rate on debt.

A company must weigh the risks and returns of the disadvantages and advantages of bond financing when deciding whether to issue bonds to finance operations.

Bond Trading

Bonds are securities that can be readily bought and sold. A large number of bonds trade on both the New York Exchange and the American Exchange. A bond *issue* consists of a number of bonds, usually in denominations of $1,000 or $5,000, and is sold to many different lenders.

After bonds are issued, they often are bought and sold by investors, meaning that any particular bond probably has a number of owners before it matures. Since bonds are exchanged (bought and sold) in the market, they have a market value (price). For convenience, bond market values are expressed as a percent of their par (face) value. For example, a company's bonds might be trading at 103½, meaning they can be bought or sold for 103.5% of their par value. Bonds can also trade below par value. For instance, if a company's bonds are trading at 95, they can be bought or sold at 95% of their par value.

Decision Insight

Quotes The bond quote here is interpreted (left to right) as **Bonds,** issuer name; **Rate,** contract interest rate (7%); **Mat,** matures in year 2025 when principal is paid; **Yld,** yield rate (5.9%) of bond at current price; **Vol,** daily dollar worth ($130,000) of trades (in 1,000s); **Close,** closing price (119.25) for the day as percent of par value; **Chg,** change (+1.25) in closing price from prior day's close.

Bonds	Rate	Mat	Yld	Vol	Close	Chg
IBM	7	25	5.9	130	119¼	+1¼

Bond-Issuing Procedures

State and federal laws govern bond issuances. Bond issuers also want to ensure that they do not violate any of their existing contractual agreements when issuing bonds. Authorization of bond issuances includes the number of bonds authorized, their par value, and the contract interest rate.

Exhibit 14.2

Bond Certificate

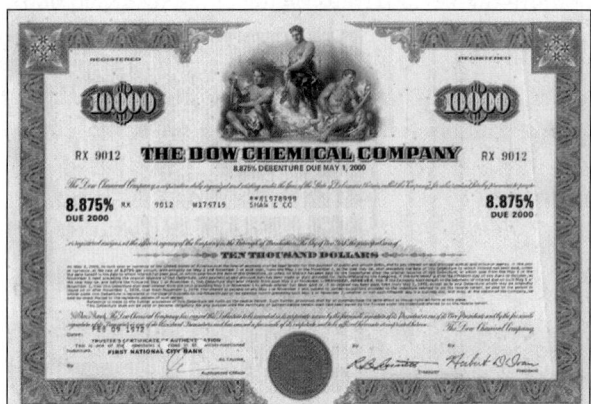

The legal document identifying the rights and obligations of both the bond-holders and the issuer is called the **bond indenture,** which is the legal contract between the issuer and the bond-holders. A bondholder may also receive a bond certificate as evidence of the company's debt. A **bond certificate,** such as that shown in Exhibit 14.2, includes specifics such as the issuer's name, the par value, the contract interest rate, and the maturity date. Many companies reduce costs by not issuing paper certificates to bondholders.[1]

Bond Issuances

Topic Tackler

PLUS

14-1

P1   Prepare entries to record bond issuance and bond interest expense.

This section explains accounting for bond issuances at par, below par (discount), and above par (premium). It also describes how to amortize a discount or premium and record bonds issued between interest payment dates.

Issuing Bonds at Par

To illustrate an issuance of bonds at par value, suppose a company receives authorization to issue $800,000 of 9%, 20-year bonds dated January 1, 2008, that mature on December 31, 2027, and pay interest semiannually on each June 30 and December 31. After accepting the bond indenture on behalf of the bondholders, the trustee can sell all or a portion of the bonds to an underwriter. If all bonds are sold at par value, the issuer records the sale as:

Assets   = Liabilities + Equity
+800,000   +800,000

2008			
Jan. 1	Cash.....................................	800,000	
	Bonds Payable..........................		800,000
	Sold bonds at par.		

This entry reflects increases in the issuer's cash *and* long-term liabilities.

The issuer records the first semiannual interest payment as follows.

Assets   = Liabilities + Equity
−36,000   −36,000

2008			
June 30	Bond Interest Expense	36,000	
	Cash		36,000
	Paid semiannual interest (9% × $800,000 × ½ year).		

---

[1] The issuing company normally sells its bonds to an investment firm called an *underwriter,* which resells them to the public. An issuing company can also sell bonds directly to investors. When an underwriter sells bonds to a large number of investors, a *trustee* represents and protects the bondholders' interests. The trustee monitors the issuer to ensure that it complies with the obligations in the bond indenture. Most trustees are large banks or trust companies. The trustee writes and accepts the terms of a bond indenture before it is issued. When bonds are offered to the public, called *floating an issue,* they must be registered with the Securities and Exchange Commission (SEC). SEC registration requires the issuer to file certain financial information. Most company bonds are issued in par value units of $1,000 or $5,000. *A baby bond* has a par value of less than $1,000, such as $100.

The issuer pays and records its semiannual interest obligation every six months until the bonds mature. When they mature, the issuer records its payment of principal as:

2027				
Dec. 31	Bonds Payable	800,000		Assets = Liabilities + Equity
	Cash		800,000	−800,000 −800,000
	Paid bond principal at maturity.			

Bond Discount or Premium

The bond issuer pays the interest rate specified in the indenture, the **contract rate,** also referred to as the *coupon rate, stated rate,* or *nominal rate.* The annual interest paid is determined by multiplying the bond par value by the contract rate. The contract rate is usually stated on an annual basis, even if interest is paid semiannually. For example, if a company issues a $1,000, 8% bond paying interest semiannually, it pays annual interest of $80 (8% × $1,000) in two semiannual payments of $40 each.

The contract rate sets the amount of interest the issuer pays in *cash,* which is not necessarily the *bond interest expense* actually incurred by the issuer. Bond interest expense depends on the bond's market value at issuance, which is determined by market expectations of the risk of lending to the issuer. The bond's **market rate** of interest is the rate that borrowers are willing to pay and lenders are willing to accept for a particular bond and its risk level. As the risk level increases, the rate increases to compensate purchasers for the bonds' increased risk. Also, the market rate is generally higher when the time period until the bond matures is longer due to the risk of adverse events occurring over a longer time period.

Many bond issuers try to set a contract rate of interest equal to the market rate they expect as of the bond issuance date. When the contract rate and market rate are equal, a bond sells at par value, but when they are not equal, a bond does not sell at par value. Instead, it is sold at a *premium* above par value or at a *discount* below par value. Exhibit 14.3 shows the relation between the contract rate, market rate, and a bond's issue price.

> **Decision Insight**
>
> **Ratings Game** Many bond buyers rely on rating services to assess bond risk. The best known are **Standard & Poor's** and **Moody's.** These services focus on the issuer's financial statements and other factors in setting ratings. Standard & Poor's ratings, from best quality to default, are AAA, AA, A, BBB, BB, B, CCC, CC, C, and D. Ratings can include a plus (+) or minus (−) to show relative standing within a category.

Point: Business acquisitions are sometimes financed by issuing "junk bonds" that carry high market rates of interest but offer little security. Bondholders can suffer huge losses if the bond issuers do not generate adequate cash flows to pay interest and principal.

Exhibit 14.3

Relation between Bond Issue Price, Contract Rate, and Market Rate

> **Quick Check** Answers—p. 570
>
> 1. Unsecured bonds backed only by the issuer's general credit standing are called (*a*) serial bonds, (*b*) debentures, (*c*) registered bonds, or (*d*) convertible bonds.
> 2. How do you compute the amount of interest a bond issuer pays in cash each year?
> 3. When the contract rate is above the market rate, do bonds sell at a premium or a discount? Do purchasers pay more or less than the par value of the bonds?

Issuing Bonds at a Discount

A **discount on bonds payable** occurs when a company issues bonds with a contract rate less than the market rate. This means that the issue price is less than par value. To illustrate, assume that **Fila** announces an offer to issue bonds with a $100,000 par value, an 8% annual

P2 Compute and record amortization of bond discount.

contract rate (paid semiannually), and a five-year life. Also assume that the market rate for Fila bonds is 10%. These bonds then will sell at a discount since the contract rate is less than the market rate. The exact issue price for these bonds is 92.277 (or 92.277% of par value); we show how to compute this issue price later in the chapter. These bonds obligate the issuer to pay two separate types of future cash flows.

1. Par value of $100,000 cash at the end of the bonds' five-year life.
2. Cash interest payments of $4,000 (4% × $100,000) at the end of each semiannual period during the bonds' five-year life.

The exact pattern of cash flows for the Fila bonds is shown in Exhibit 14.4.

Exhibit 14.4

Cash Flows for Fila Bonds

								$100,000
$4,000	$4,000	$4,000	$4,000	$4,000		$4,000	$4,000	$4,000
0	6 mo.	12 mo.	18 mo.	24 mo.	...	48 mo.	54 mo.	60 mo.

When Fila accepts $92,277 cash for its bonds on the issue date of December 31, 2008, it records the sale as follows.

Assets = Liabilities + Equity				
+92,277 +100,000	**Dec. 31**	Cash	92,277	
−7,723		Discount on Bonds Payable	7,723	
		Bonds Payable		100,000
		Sold bonds at a discount on their issue date.		

These bonds are reported in the long-term liability section of the issuer's December 31, 2008, balance sheet as shown in Exhibit 14.5. A discount is deducted from the par value of bonds to yield the **carrying (book) value of bonds.** Discount on Bonds Payable is a contra liability account.

Exhibit 14.5

Balance Sheet Presentation of Bond Discount

Long-term liabilities		
Bonds payable, 8%, due December 31, 2013	$100,000	
Less discount on bonds payable	**7,723**	**$92,277**

Amortizing a Bond Discount Fila receives $92,277 for its bonds; in return it must pay bondholders $100,000 after five years (plus semiannual interest payments). The $7,723 discount is paid to bondholders at maturity and is part of the cost of using the $92,277 for five years. The upper portion of panel A in Exhibit 14.6 shows that total bond interest expense of $47,723 is the difference between the total amount repaid to bondholders ($140,000) and the amount borrowed from bondholders ($92,277). Alternatively, we can compute total bond interest expense as the sum of the 10 interest payments and the bond discount. This alternative computation is shown in the lower portion of panel A.

The total $47,723 bond interest expense must be allocated across the 10 semiannual periods in the bonds' life, and the bonds' carrying value must be updated at each balance sheet date. This is accomplished using the straight-line method (or the effective interest method in Appendix 14B). Both methods systematically reduce the bond discount to zero over the five-year life. This process is called *amortizing a bond discount*.

Straight-Line Method The **straight-line bond amortization** method allocates an equal portion of the total bond interest expense to each interest period. To apply the straight-line method to Fila's bonds, we divide the total bond interest expense of $47,723 by 10 (the number

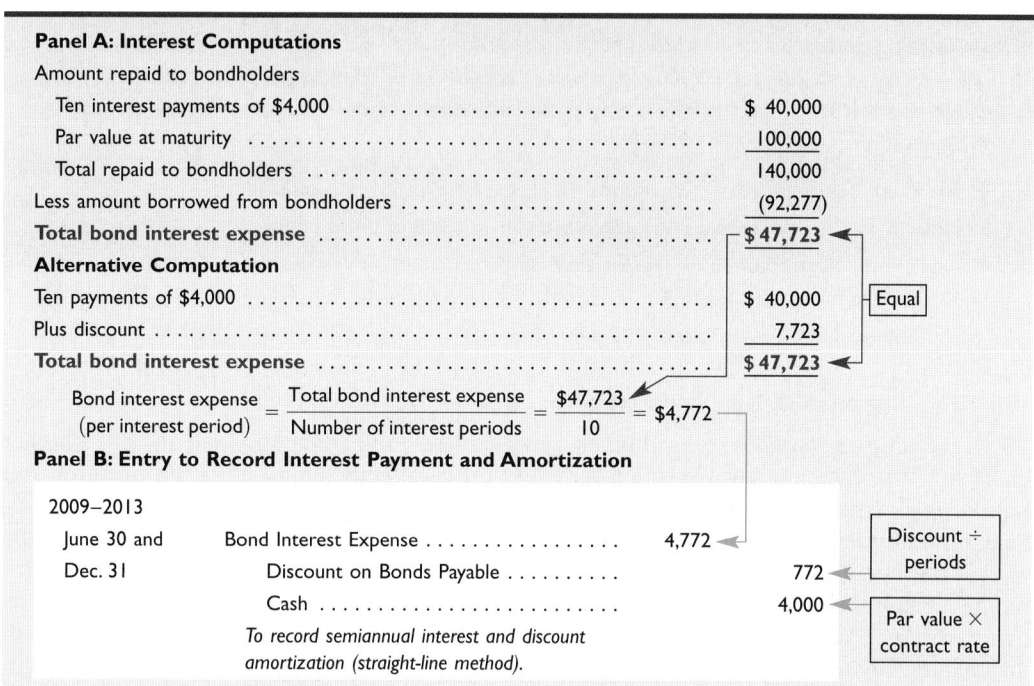

Exhibit 14.6

Interest Computation and Entry for Bonds Issued at a Discount

of semiannual periods in the bonds' life). This gives a bond interest expense of $4,772 per period (all computations, including those for assignments, are rounded to the nearest whole dollar). Alternatively, we can find this number by first dividing the $7,723 discount by 10, which yields the $772 amount of discount to be amortized each interest period. When the $772 is added to the $4,000 cash payment, the bond interest expense for each period is $4,772. Panel B of Exhibit 14.6 shows how the issuer records bond interest expense and updates the balance of the bond liability account at the end of *each* of the 10 semiannual interest periods (June 30, 2009, through December 31, 2013).

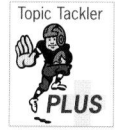

Topic Tackler

PLUS

14-2

Exhibit 14.7 shows the pattern of decreases in the Discount on Bonds Payable account and the pattern of increases in the bonds' carrying value. The following points summarize the discount bonds' straight-line amortization.

1. At issuance, the $100,000 par value consists of the $92,277 cash received by the issuer plus the $7,723 discount.

2. During the bonds' life, the (unamortized) discount decreases each period by the $772 amortization ($7,723/10), and the carrying value (par value less unamortized discount) increases each period by $772.

3. At maturity, the unamortized discount equals zero, and the carrying value equals the $100,000 par value that the issuer pays the holder.

Semiannual Period-End		Unamortized Discount*	Carrying Value†
(0)	12/31/2008	$7,723	$ 92,277
(1)	6/30/2009	6,951	93,049
(2)	12/31/2009	6,179	93,821
(3)	6/30/2010	5,407	94,593
(4)	12/31/2010	4,635	95,365
(5)	6/30/2011	3,863	96,137
(6)	12/31/2011	3,091	96,909
(7)	6/30/2012	2,319	97,681
(8)	12/31/2012	1,547	98,453
(9)	6/30/2013	775	99,225
(10)	**12/31/2013**	0‡	100,000

Exhibit 14.7

Straight-Line Amortization of Bond Discount

The two columns always sum to par value for a discount bond.

* Total bond discount (of $7,723) less accumulated periodic amortization ($772 per semiannual interest period).

† Bond par value (of $100,000) less unamortized discount.

‡ Adjusted for rounding.

Notice that the issuer incurs a $4,772 bond interest expense each period but pays only $4,000 cash. The $772 unpaid portion of this expense is added to the bonds' carrying value. (The total $7,723 unamortized discount is "paid" when the bonds mature; $100,000 is paid at maturity but only $92,277 was received at issuance.)

Answers—p. 570

Quick Check

Five-year, 6% bonds with a $100,000 par value are issued at a price of $91,893. Interest is paid semiannually, and the bonds' market rate is 8% on the issue date. Use this information to answer the following questions:

4. Are these bonds issued at a discount or a premium? Explain your answer.
5. What is the issuer's journal entry to record the issuance of these bonds?
6. What is the amount of bond interest expense recorded at the first semiannual period using the straight-line method?

Issuing Bonds at a Premium

P3 Compute and record amortization of bond premium.

When the contract rate of bonds is higher than the market rate, the bonds sell at a price higher than par value. The amount by which the bond price exceeds par value is the **premium on bonds.** To illustrate, assume that **Adidas** issues bonds with a $100,000 par value, a 12% annual contract rate, semiannual interest payments, and a five-year life. Also assume that the market rate for Adidas bonds is 10% on the issue date. The Adidas bonds will sell at a premium because the contract rate is higher than the market rate. The exact issue price for these bonds is 107.72 (or 107.72% of par value); we show how to compute this issue price later in the chapter. These bonds obligate the issuer to pay out two separate future cash flows.

1. Par value of $100,000 cash at the end of the bonds' five-year life.
2. Cash interest payments of $6,000 (6% × $100,000) at the end of each semiannual period during the bonds' five-year life.

The exact pattern of cash flows for the Adidas bonds is shown in Exhibit 14.8.

Exhibit 14.8

Cash Flows for Adidas Bonds

								$100,000
	$6,000	$6,000	$6,000	$6,000		$6,000	$6,000	$6,000
0	6 mo.	12 mo.	18 mo.	24 mo.	...	48 mo.	54 mo.	60 mo.

When Adidas accepts $107,720 cash for its bonds on the issue date of December 31, 2008, it records this transaction as follows.

Assets = Liabilities + Equity
+107,720   +100,000
            +7,720

Dec. 31	Cash.......................................	107,720	
	Premium on Bonds Payable		7,720
	Bonds Payable...........................		100,000
	Sold bonds at a premium on their issue date.		

These bonds are reported in the long-term liability section of the issuer's December 31, 2008, balance sheet as shown in Exhibit 14.9. A premium is added to par value to yield the carrying (book) value of bonds. Premium on Bonds Payable is an adjunct (also called *accretion*) liability account.

Exhibit 14.9

Balance Sheet Presentation of Bond Premium

Long-term liabilities		
Bonds payable, 12%, due December 31, 2013	$100,000	
Plus premium on bonds payable	**7,720**	$107,720

Amortizing a Bond Premium Adidas receives $107,720 for its bonds; in return, it pays bondholders $100,000 after five years (plus semiannual interest payments). The $7,720 premium not repaid to issuer's bondholders at maturity goes to reduce the issuer's expense of using the $107,720 for five years. The upper portion of panel A of Exhibit 14.10 shows that total bond interest expense of $52,280 is the difference between the total amount repaid to bondholders ($160,000) and the amount borrowed from bondholders ($107,720). Alternatively, we can compute total bond interest expense as the sum of the 10 interest payments less the bond premium. The premium is subtracted because it will not be paid to bondholders when the bonds mature; see the lower portion of panel A. Total bond interest expense must be allocated over the 10 semiannual periods using the straight-line method (or the effective interest method in Appendix 14B).

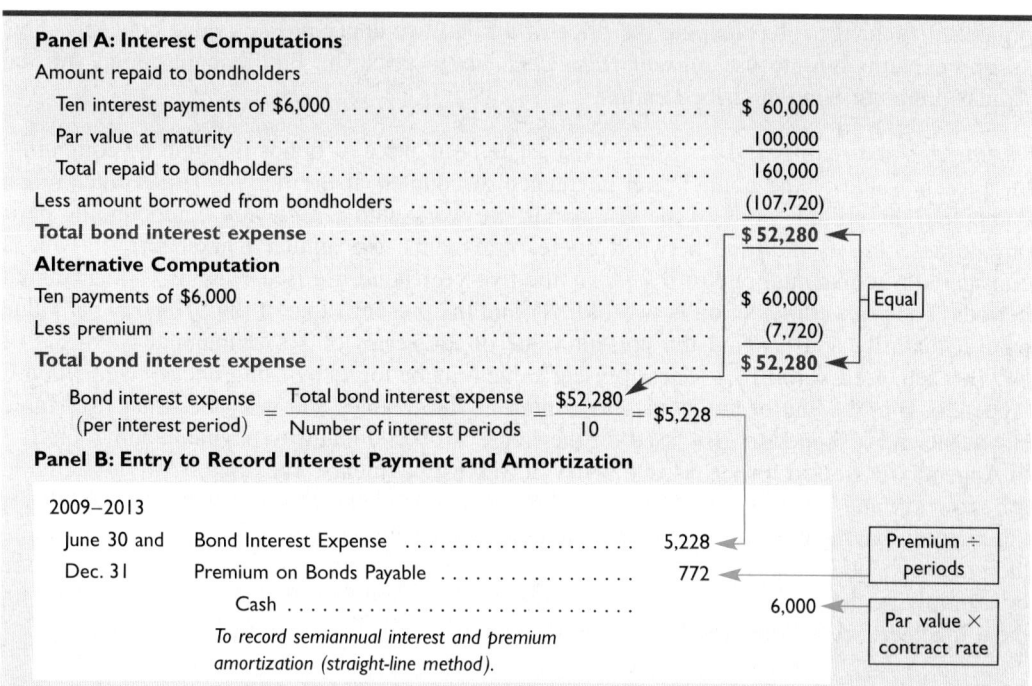

Exhibit 14.10

Interest Computation and Entry for Bonds Issued at a Premium

Straight-Line Method The straight-line method allocates an equal portion of total bond interest expense to each of the bonds' semiannual interest periods. To apply this method to Adidas bonds, we divide the five years' total bond interest expense of $52,280 by 10 (the number of semiannual periods in the bonds' life).

Point: A premium decreases Bond Interest Expense while a discount increases it.

This gives a total bond interest expense of $5,228 per period. Panel B of Exhibit 14.10 shows how the issuer records bond interest expense and updates the balance of the bond liability account for *each* semiannual period (June 30, 2009, through December 31, 2013).

Exhibit 14.11 shows the pattern of decreases in the unamortized Premium on Bonds Payable account and in the bonds' carrying value. The following points summarize straight-line amortization of the premium bonds.

Exhibit 14.11

Straight-Line Amortization of Bond Premium

Semiannual Period-End	Unamortized Premium*	Carrying Value†
(0) 12/31/2008	$7,720	$107,720
(1) 6/30/2009	6,948	106,948
(2) 12/31/2009	6,176	106,176
(3) 6/30/2010	5,404	105,404
(4) 12/31/2010	4,632	104,632
(5) 6/30/2011	3,860	103,860
(6) 12/31/2011	3,088	103,088
(7) 6/30/2012	2,316	102,316
(8) 12/31/2012	1,544	101,544
(9) 6/30/2013	772	100,772
(10) 12/31/2013	**0**	**100,000**

During the bond life, carrying value is adjusted to par and the amortized premium to zero.

1. At issuance, the $100,000 par value plus the $7,720 premium equals the $107,720 cash received by the issuer.

* Total bond premium (of $7,720) less accumulated periodic amortization ($772 per semiannual interest period).

† Bond par value (of $100,000) plus unamortized premium.

2. During the bonds' life, the (unamortized) premium decreases each period by the $772 amortization ($7,720/10), and the carrying value decreases each period by the same $772.

3. At maturity, the unamortized premium equals zero, and the carrying value equals the $100,000 par value that the issuer pays the holder.

The next section describes bond pricing. An instructor can choose to cover bond pricing or not. Assignments requiring the next section are: Quick Study 14-4, Exercises 14-6 & 14-7, Problems 14-1A & 14-1B and 14-4A & 14-4B.

Bond Pricing

Point: InvestingInBonds.com is an excellent bond research and learning source.

Prices for bonds traded on an organized exchange are often published in newspapers and through online services. This information normally includes the bond price (called *quote*), its contract rate, and its current market (called *yield*) rate. However, only a fraction of bonds are traded on organized exchanges. To compute the price of a bond, we apply present value concepts. This section explains how to use *present value concepts* to price the Fila discount bond and the Adidas premium bond described earlier.

Present Value of a Discount Bond   The issue price of bonds is found by computing the present value of the bonds' cash payments, discounted at the bonds' market rate. When computing the present value of the Fila bonds, we work with *semiannual* compounding periods because this is the time between interest payments; the annual market rate of 10% is considered a semiannual rate of 5%. Also, the five-year bond life is viewed as 10 semiannual periods. The price computation is twofold: (1) find the present value of the $100,000 par value paid at maturity and (2) find the present value of the series of 10 semiannual payments of $4,000 each; see Exhibit 14.4. These present values can be found by using *present value tables*. Appendix B at the end of this book shows present value tables and describes their use. Table B.1 at the end of Appendix B is used for the single $100,000 maturity payment, and Table B.3 in Appendix B is used for the $4,000 series of interest payments. Specifically, we go to Table B.1, row 10, and across to the 5% column to identify the present value factor of 0.6139 for the maturity payment. Next, we go to Table B.3, row 10, and across to the 5% column, where the present value factor is 7.7217 for the series of interest payments. We compute bond price by multiplying the cash flow payments by their corresponding present value factors and adding them together; see Exhibit 14.12.

Point: A bond's market value (price) at issuance equals the present value of all its future cash payments (the interest [discount] rate used is the bond's market rate).

Point: Many calculators provide present value functions for computation of bond prices.

Point: The general approach to bond pricing is identical for discount bonds and premium bonds.

Exhibit 14.12

Computing Issue Price for the Fila Discount Bonds

Cash Flow	Table	Present Value Factor	Amount	Present Value
$100,000 par (maturity) value	B.1	0.6139	× $100,000 =	$ 61,390
$4,000 interest payments	B.3	7.7217	× 4,000 =	30,887
Price of bond				$92,277

Present Value of a Premium Bond   We find the issue price of the Adidas bonds by using the market rate to compute the present value of the bonds' future cash flows. When computing the present value of these bonds, we again work with *semiannual* compounding periods because this is the time between interest payments. The annual 10% market rate is applied as a semiannual rate of 5%, and the five-year bond life is viewed as 10 semiannual periods. The computation is twofold: (1) find the present value of the $100,000 par value paid at maturity and (2) find the present value of the series of 10 payments of $6,000 each; see Exhibit 14.8. These present values can be found by using present value tables. First, go to Table B.1, row 10, and across to the 5% column where the present value factor is 0.6139 for the maturity payment. Second, go to Table B.3, row 10, and across to the 5% column, where the present value factor is 7.7217 for the series of interest payments. The bonds' price is computed by multiplying the cash flow payments by their corresponding present value factors and adding them together; see Exhibit 14.13.

Point: There are nearly 5 million individual U.S. bond issues, ranging from huge treasuries to tiny municipalities. This compares to about 12,000 individual U.S. stocks that are traded.

Exhibit 14.13

Computing Issue Price for the Adidas Premium Bonds

Cash Flow	Table	Present Value Factor	Amount	Present Value
$100,000 par (maturity) value	B.1	0.6139	× $100,000 =	$ 61,390
$6,000 interest payments	B.3	7.7217	× 6,000 =	46,330
Price of bond				$107,720

Quick Check   Answers—p. 570

On December 31, 2007, a company issues 16%, 10-year bonds with a par value of $100,000. Interest is paid on June 30 and December 31. The bonds are sold to yield a 14% annual market rate at an issue price of $110,592. Use this information to answer questions 7 through 9:

7. Are these bonds issued at a discount or a premium? Explain your answer.

8. Using the straight-line method to allocate bond interest expense, the issuer records the second interest payment (on December 31, 2008) with a debit to Premium on Bonds Payable in the amount of (a) $7,470, (b) $530, (c) $8,000, or (d) $400.

9. How are these bonds reported in the long-term liability section of the issuer's balance sheet as of December 31, 2008?

Bond Retirement

This section describes the retirement of bonds (1) at maturity, (2) before maturity, and (3) by conversion to stock.

Bond Retirement at Maturity

The carrying value of bonds at maturity always equals par value. For example, both Exhibits 14.7 (a discount) and 14.11 (a premium) show that the carrying value of bonds at the end of their lives equals par value ($100,000). The retirement of these bonds at maturity, assuming interest is already paid and entered, is recorded as follows:

P4 Record the retirement of bonds.

2013			
Dec. 31	Bonds Payable	100,000	
	Cash		100,000
	To record retirement of bonds at maturity.		

Assets = Liabilities + Equity
−100,000   −100,000

Bond Retirement before Maturity

Issuers sometimes wish to retire some or all of their bonds prior to maturity. For instance, if interest rates decline significantly, an issuer may wish to replace high-interest-paying bonds with new low-interest bonds. Two common ways to retire bonds before maturity are to (1) exercise a call option or (2) purchase them on the open market. In the first instance, an issuer can reserve the right to retire bonds early by issuing callable bonds. The bond indenture can give the issuer an option to *call* the bonds before they mature by paying the par value plus a *call premium* to bondholders. In the second case, the issuer retires bonds by repurchasing them on the open market at their current price. Whether bonds are called or repurchased, the issuer is unlikely to pay a price that exactly equals their carrying value. When a difference exists between the bonds' carrying value and the amount paid, the issuer records a gain or loss equal to the difference.

To illustrate the accounting for retiring callable bonds, assume that a company issued callable bonds with a par value of $100,000. The call option requires the issuer to pay a call premium of $3,000 to bondholders in addition to the par value. Next, assume that after the June 30, 2008, interest payment, the bonds have a carrying value of $104,500. Then on July 1, 2008, the issuer calls these bonds and pays $103,000 to bondholders. The issuer recognizes a $1,500 gain from the difference between the bonds' carrying value of $104,500 and the retirement price of $103,000. The issuer records this bond retirement as:

Point: Bond retirement is also referred to as *bond redemption.*

Point: Gains and losses from retiring bonds were *previously* reported as extraordinary items. New standards require that they now be judged by the "unusual and infrequent" criteria for reporting purposes.

July 1	Bonds Payable	100,000	
	Premium on Bonds Payable.	4,500	
	Gain on Bond Retirement		1,500
	Cash		103,000
	To record retirement of bonds before maturity.		

Assets = Liabilities + Equity
−103,000   −100,000   +1,500
                −4,500

An issuer usually must call all bonds when it exercises a call option. However, to retire as many or as few bonds as it desires, an issuer can purchase them on the open market. If it retires less than the entire class of bonds, it recognizes a gain or loss for the difference between the carrying value of those bonds retired and the amount paid to acquire them.

Bond Retirement by Conversion

Convertible Bond

We describe convertible bonds in the Decision Analysis section of this chapter. Holders of convertible bonds have the right to convert their bonds to stock. When conversion occurs, the bonds' carrying value is transferred to equity accounts and no gain or loss is recorded. (The market prices of the bonds and stock are *not* relevant to this entry; the material in Chapter 13 is helpful in understanding this transaction.) To illustrate, assume that on January 1 the $100,000 par value bonds of **Converse**, with a carrying value of $100,000, are converted to 15,000 shares of $2 par value common stock. The entry to record this conversion is:

Assets = Liabilities + Equity
−100,000   +30,000
           +70,000

Jan. 1	Bonds Payable	100,000	
	Common Stock		30,000
	Paid-In Capital in Excess of Par Value		70,000
	To record retirement of bonds by conversion.		

Quick Check
Answer—p. 570

10. Six years ago, a company issued $500,000 of 6%, eight-year bonds at a price of 95. The current carrying value is $493,750. The company decides to retire 50% of these bonds by buying them on the open market at a price of 102½. What is the amount of gain or loss on retirement of these bonds?

Long-Term Notes Payable

Like bonds, notes are issued to obtain assets such as cash. Unlike bonds, notes are typically transacted with a *single* lender such as a bank. An issuer initially records a note at its selling price; that is, the note's face value minus any discount or plus any premium. Over the note's life, the amount of interest expense allocated to each period is computed by multiplying the market rate (at issuance of the note) by the beginning-of-period note balance. The note's carrying (book) value at any time equals its face value minus any unamortized discount or plus any unamortized premium; carrying value is also computed as the present value of all remaining payments, discounted using the market rate at issuance.

Installment Notes

C1 Explain the types and payment patterns of notes.

An **installment note** is an obligation requiring a series of payments to the lender. Installment notes are common for franchises and other businesses when lenders and borrowers agree to spread payments over several periods. To illustrate, assume that Foghog borrows $60,000 from a bank to purchase equipment. It signs an 8% installment note requiring six annual payments of principal plus interest and it records the note's issuance at January 1, 2008, as follows.

Assets = Liabilities + Equity
+60,000   +60,000

Jan. 1	Cash	60,000	
	Notes Payable		60,000
	Borrowed $60,000 by signing an 8%, six-year		
	installment note.		

Payments on an installment note normally include the accrued interest expense plus a portion of the amount borrowed (the *principal*). This section describes an installment note with equal payments.

The equal total payments pattern consists of changing amounts of both interest and principal. To illustrate, assume that Foghog borrows $60,000 by signing a $60,000 note that requires six *equal payments* of $12,979 at the end of each year. (The present value of an annuity of six annual payments of $12,979, discounted at 8%, equals $60,000; we show this computation in footnote 2 on the next page.) The $12,979 includes both interest and principal, the amounts of which change with each payment. Exhibit 14.14 shows the pattern of equal total payments and its two parts, interest and principal. Column A shows the note's beginning balance. Column B shows accrued interest for each year at 8% of the beginning note balance. Column C shows the impact on the note's principal, which equals the difference between the total payment in column D and the interest expense in column B. Column E shows the note's year-end balance.

P5   Prepare entries to account for notes.

Point: Most consumer notes are installment notes that require equal total payments.

Exhibit 14.14

Installment Note: Equal Total Payments

			Payments			
Period Ending Date	(A) Beginning Balance	(B) Debit Interest Expense 8% × (A)	+	(C) Debit Notes Payable (D) − (B)	= (D) Credit Cash (computed)	(E) Ending Balance (A) − (C)
(1) 12/31/2008	$60,000	$ 4,800		$ 8,179	$12,979	$51,821
(2) 12/31/2009	51,821	4,146		8,833	12,979	42,988
(3) 12/31/2010	42,988	3,439		9,540	12,979	33,448
(4) 12/31/2011	33,448	2,676		10,303	12,979	23,145
(5) 12/31/2012	23,145	1,852		11,127	12,979	12,018
(6) 12/31/2013	12,018	961		12,018	12,979	0
		$17,874		$60,000	$77,874	

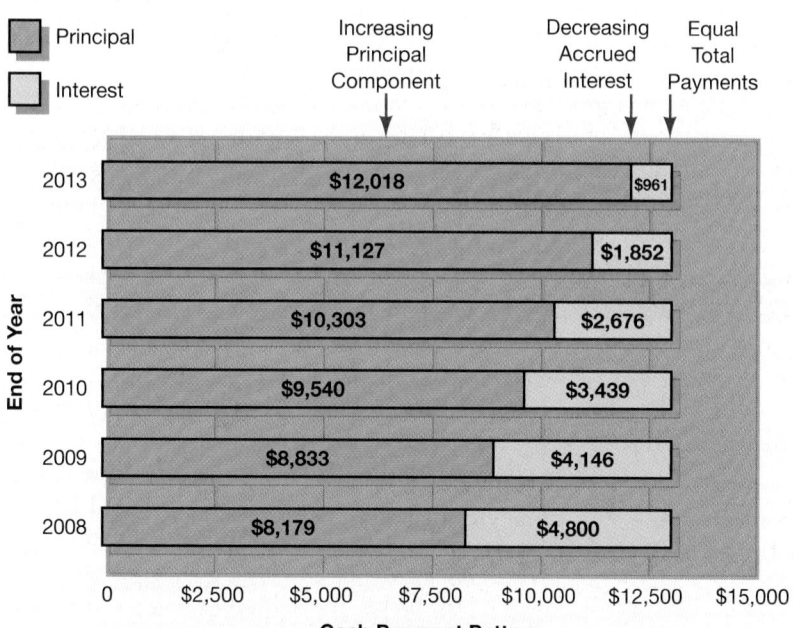

Although the six cash payments are equal, accrued interest decreases each year because the principal balance of the note declines. As the amount of interest decreases each year, the portion of each payment applied to principal increases. This pattern is graphed in the lower part

Point: The Truth-in-Lending Act requires lenders to provide information about loan costs including finance charges and interest rate.

of Exhibit 14.14. Foghog uses the amounts in Exhibit 14.14 to record its first two payments (for years 2008 and 2009) as follows:

2008				
Dec. 31	Interest Expense	4,800	
	Notes Payable	8,179	
	Cash		12,979
	To record first installment payment.		

Assets = Liabilities + Equity
−12,979   −8,179   −4,800

2009				
Dec. 31	Interest Expense	4,146	
	Notes Payable	8,833	
	Cash		12,979
	To record second installment payment.		

Assets = Liabilities + Equity
−12,979   −8,833   −4,146

Decision Maker

Answer—p. 570

Entrepreneur You are an electronics retailer planning a holiday sale on a custom stereo system that requires no payments for two years. At the end of two years, buyers must pay the full amount. The system's suggested retail price is $4,100, but you are willing to sell it today for $3,000 cash. What is your holiday sale price if payment will not occur for two years and the market interest rate is 10%?

Foghog records similar entries but with different amounts for each of the remaining four payments. After six years, the Notes Payable account balance is zero.[2]

Mortgage Notes and Bonds

A **mortgage** is a legal agreement that helps protect a lender if a borrower fails to make required payments on notes or bonds. A mortgage gives the lender a right to be paid from the cash proceeds of the sale of a borrower's assets identified in the mortgage. A legal document, called a *mortgage contract,* describes the mortgage terms.

Mortgage notes carry a mortgage contract pledging title to specific assets as security for the note. Mortgage notes are especially popular in the purchase of homes and the acquisition of plant assets. Less common *mortgage bonds* are backed by the issuer's assets. Accounting for mortgage notes and bonds is similar to that for unsecured notes and bonds, except that the mortgage agreement must be disclosed. For example, **Musicland** reports that its "mortgage note payable is collateralized by land, buildings and certain fixtures."

Global: Countries vary in the preference given to debtholders vs. stockholders when a company is in financial distress. Some countries such as Germany, France, and Japan give preference to stockholders over debtholders.

Quick Check

Answers—p. 570

11. Which of the following is true for an installment note requiring a series of equal total cash payments? (a) Payments consist of increasing interest and decreasing principal; (b) Payments consist of changing amounts of principal but constant interest; or (c) Payments consist of decreasing interest and increasing principal.

12. How is the interest portion of an installment note payment computed?

13. When a borrower records an interest payment on an installment note, how are the balance sheet and income statement affected?

Example: Suppose the $60,000 installment loan has an 8% interest rate with eight equal annual payments. What is the annual payment? *Answer* (using Table B.3): $60,000/5.7466 = $10,441

---

[2] Table B.3 in Appendix B is used to compute the dollar amount of the six payments that equal the initial note balance of $60,000 at 8% interest. We go to Table B.3, row 6, and across to the 8% column, where the present value factor is 4.6229. The dollar amount is then computed by solving this relation:

Table	Present Value Factor		Dollar Amount		Present Value
B.3	4.6229	×	?	=	$60,000

The dollar amount is computed by dividing $60,000 by 4.6229, yielding $12,979.

Debt Features and the Debt-to-Equity Ratio

Decision Analysis

Collateral agreements can reduce the risk of loss for both bonds and notes. Unsecured bonds and notes are riskier because the issuer's obligation to pay interest and principal has the same priority as all other unsecured liabilities in the event of bankruptcy. If a company is unable to pay its debts in full, the unsecured creditors (including the holders of debentures) lose all or a portion of their balances. These types of legal agreements and other characteristics of long-term liabilities are crucial for effective business decisions. The first part of this section describes the different types of features sometimes included with bonds and notes. The second part explains and applies the debt-to-equity ratio.

Features of Bonds and Notes

This section describes common features of debt securities.

A2 Assess debt features and their implications.

Secured or Unsecured   **Secured bonds** (and notes) have specific assets of the issuer pledged (or *mortgaged*) as collateral. This arrangement gives holders added protection against the issuer's default. If the issuer fails to pay interest or par value, the secured holders can demand that the collateral be sold and the proceeds used to pay the obligation. **Unsecured bonds** (and notes), also called *debentures,* are backed by the issuer's general credit standing. Unsecured debt is riskier than secured debt. *Subordinated debentures* are liabilities that are not repaid until the claims of the more senior, unsecured (and secured) liabilities are settled.

Secured Debt   **Unsecured Debt**

Term or Serial   **Term bonds** (and notes) are scheduled for maturity on one specified date. **Serial bonds** (and notes) mature at more than one date (often in series) and thus are usually repaid over a number of periods. For instance, $100,000 of serial bonds might mature at the rate of $10,000 each year from 6 to 15 years after they are issued. Many bonds are **sinking fund bonds,** which to reduce the holder's risk, require the issuer to create a *sinking fund* of assets set aside at specified amounts and dates to repay the bonds.

Registered or Bearer   Bonds issued in the names and addresses of their holders are **registered bonds.** The issuer makes bond payments by sending checks (or cash transfers) to registered holders. A registered holder must notify the issuer of any ownership change. Registered bonds offer the issuer the practical advantage of not having to actually issue bond certificates, which protects holders against loss of bonds. Bonds payable to whoever holds them (the *bearer*) are called **bearer bonds** or *unregistered bonds.* Sales or exchanges might not be recorded, so the holder of a bearer bond is presumed to be its rightful owner. As a result, lost bearer bonds are difficult to replace. Many bearer bonds are also **coupon bonds.** This term reflects inter-

est coupons that are attached to the bonds. When each coupon matures, the holder presents it to a bank or broker for collection. At maturity, the holder follows the same process and presents the bond certificate for collection. Issuers of coupon bonds cannot deduct the related interest expense for taxable income. This is to prevent abuse by taxpayers who own coupon bonds but fail to report interest income on their tax returns.

Convertible Debt   **Callable Debt**

Convertible and/or Callable   **Convertible bonds** (and notes) can be exchanged for a fixed number of shares of the issuing corporation's common stock. Convertible debt offers holders the potential to participate in future increases in stock price. Holders still receive periodic interest while the debt is held and the par value if they hold the debt to maturity. In most cases, the holders decide whether and when to convert debt to stock. **Callable bonds** (and notes) have an option exercisable by the issuer to retire them at a stated dollar amount before maturity.

Debt-to-Equity Ratio

A3 Compute the debt-to-equity ratio and explain its use.

Beyond assessing different characteristics of debt as described above, we want to know the level of debt, especially in relation to total equity. Such knowledge helps us assess the risk of a company's financing structure. A company financed mainly with debt is more risky because liabilities must be repaid—usually with periodic interest—whereas equity financing does not. A measure to assess the risk of a company's financing structure is the **debt-to-equity ratio** (see Exhibit 14.15).

Exhibit 14.15

Debt-to-Equity Ratio

$$\text{Debt-to-equity} = \frac{\text{Total liabilities}}{\text{Total equity}}$$

The debt-to-equity ratio varies across companies and industries. Industries that are more variable tend to have lower ratios, while more stable industries are less risky and tend to have higher ratios. To apply the debt-to-equity ratio, let's look at this measure for **Six Flags** in Exhibit 14.16.

Exhibit 14.16

Debt-to-Equity Ratio for Six Flags

($ millions)	2004	2003	2002
Total liabilities	$2,816	3,321	3,011
Total equity	826	1,362	1,360
Debt-to-equity	3.4	2.4	2.2
Industry debt-to-equity	0.9	0.8	0.7

Decision Maker

Answer—p. 570

Bond Investor   You plan to purchase debenture bonds from one of two companies in the same industry that are similar in size and performance. The first company has $350,000 in total liabilities, and $1,750,000 in equity. The second company has $1,200,000 in total liabilities, and $1,000,000 in equity. Which company's debenture bonds are less risky based on the debt-to-equity ratio?

Six Flags' 2004 debt-to-equity ratio is 3.4, meaning that debtholders contributed $3.4 for each $1 contributed by equityholders. This implies a fairly risky financing structure for Six Flags. A similar concern is drawn from a comparison of Six Flags with its competitors, where the 2004 industry ratio is 0.9. Analysis across the years also shows that Six Flags' financing structure has grown increasingly risky over the past few years. Given its declining revenues and increasing costs over the past few years (see its annual report), Six Flags is increasingly at risk of financial distress.

Demonstration Problem

Water Sports Company (WSC) patented and successfully test-marketed a new product. To expand its ability to produce and market the new product, WSC needs to raise $800,000 of financing. On January 1, 2007, the company obtained the money in two ways:

a. WSC signed a $400,000, 10% installment note to be repaid with five equal annual installments to be made on December 31 of 2007 through 2011.

b. WSC issued five-year bonds with a par value of $400,000. The bonds have a 12% annual contract rate and pay interest on June 30 and December 31. The bonds' annual market rate is 10% as of January 1, 2007.

Required

1. For the installment note, (*a*) compute the size of each annual payment, (*b*) prepare an amortization table such as Exhibit 14.14, and (*c*) prepare the journal entry for the first payment.

2. For the bonds, (*a*) compute their issue price; (*b*) prepare the January 1, 2007, journal entry to record their issuance; (*c*) prepare an amortization table using the straight-line method; (*d*) prepare the June 30, 2007, journal entry to record the first interest payment; and (*e*) prepare a journal entry to record retiring the bonds at a $416,000 call price on January 1, 2009.

3.ᴮRedo parts 2(*c*), 2(*d*), and 2(*e*) assuming the bonds are amortized using the effective interest method.

Planning the Solution

- For the installment note, divide the borrowed amount by the annuity factor (from Table B.3) using the 10% rate and five payments to compute the amount of each payment. Prepare a table similar to Exhibit 14.14 and use the numbers in the table's first line for the journal entry.
- Compute the bonds' issue price by using the market rate to find the present value of their cash flows (use tables found in Appendix B). Then use this result to record the bonds' issuance. Next, prepare an amortization table like Exhibit 14.11 (and Exhibit 14B.2) and use it to get the numbers needed for the journal entry. Also use the table to find the carrying value as of the date of the bonds' retirement that you need for the journal entry.

Solution to Demonstration Problem

Part 1: Installment Note

a. Annual payment = Note balance/Annuity factor = $400,000/3.7908 = $105,519 (Note: Annuity factor is for five payments and a rate of 10%.)

b. Amortization table follows.

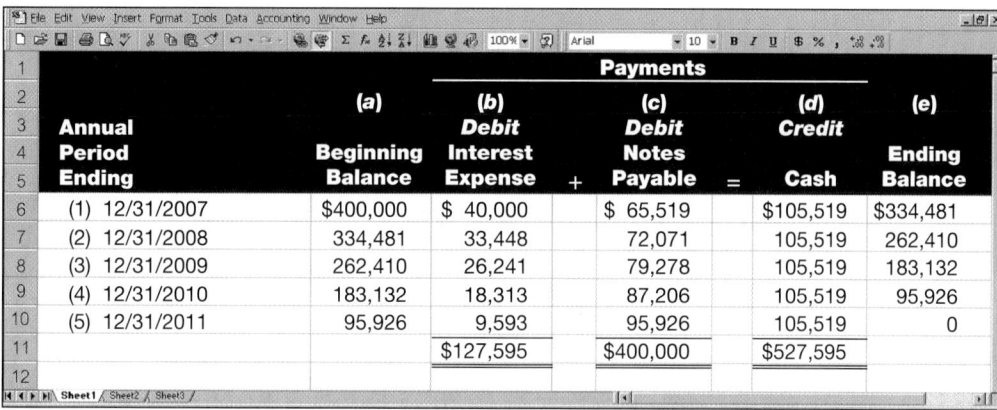

Annual Period Ending	(a) Beginning Balance	(b) Debit Interest Expense	(c) Debit Notes Payable	(d) Credit Cash	(e) Ending Balance
(1) 12/31/2007	$400,000	$ 40,000	$ 65,519	$105,519	$334,481
(2) 12/31/2008	334,481	33,448	72,071	105,519	262,410
(3) 12/31/2009	262,410	26,241	79,278	105,519	183,132
(4) 12/31/2010	183,132	18,313	87,206	105,519	95,926
(5) 12/31/2011	95,926	9,593	95,926	105,519	0
		$127,595	$400,000	$527,595	

c. Journal entry for December 31, 2007, payment.

Dec. 31	Interest Expense	40,000	
	Notes Payable	65,519	
	Cash		105,519
	To record first installment payment.		

Part 2: Bonds (straight-line amortization)

a. Compute the bonds' issue price.

Cash Flow	Table	Present Value Factor*	Amount	Present Value
Par (maturity) value	B.1 in App. B (PV of 1)	0.6139	× 400,000 =	$245,560
Interest payments	B.3 in App. B (PV of annuity)	7.7217	× 24,000 =	185,321
Price of bond				$430,881

* Present value factors are for 10 payments using a semiannual market rate of 5%.

b. Journal entry for January 1, 2007, issuance.

Jan. 1	Cash	430,881	
	Premium on Bonds Payable		30,881
	Bonds Payable		400,000
	Sold bonds at a premium.		

c. Straight-line amortization table for premium bonds.

	Semiannual Period-End	Unamortized Premium	Carrying Value
(0)	1/1/2007	$30,881	$430,881
(1)	6/30/2007	27,793	427,793
(2)	12/31/2007	24,705	424,705
(3)	6/30/2008	21,617	421,617
(4)	12/31/2008	18,529	418,529
(5)	6/30/2009	15,441	415,441
(6)	12/31/2009	12,353	412,353
(7)	6/30/2010	9,265	409,265
(8)	12/31/2010	6,177	406,177
(9)	6/30/2011	3,089	403,089
(10)	12/31/2011	0*	400,000

* Adjusted for rounding.

d. Journal entry for June 30, 2007, bond payment.

June 30	Bond Interest Expense	20,912	
	Premium on Bonds Payable	3,088	
	Cash		24,000
	Paid semiannual interest on bonds.		

e. Journal entry for January 1, 2009, bond retirement.

Jan. 1	Bonds Payable	400,000	
	Premium on Bonds Payable	18,529	
	Cash		416,000
	Gain on Retirement of Bonds		2,529
	To record bond retirement (carrying value as of Dec. 31, 2008).		

Part 3: Bonds (effective interest amortization)[B]

c. Effective interest amortization table for premium bonds.

	Semiannual Interest Period	(A) Cash Interest Paid 6% × $400,000	(B) Interest Expense 5% × Prior (E)	(C) Premium Amortization (A) − (B)	(D) Unamortized Premium Prior (D) − (C)	(E) Carrying Value $400,000 + (D)
(0)	1/1/2007				$30,881	$430,881
(1)	6/30/2007	$ 24,000	$ 21,544	$ 2,456	28,425	428,425
(2)	12/31/2007	24,000	21,421	2,579	25,846	425,846
(3)	6/30/2008	24,000	21,292	2,708	23,138	423,138
(4)	12/31/2008	24,000	21,157	2,843	20,295	420,295
(5)	6/30/2009	24,000	21,015	2,985	17,310	417,310
(6)	12/31/2009	24,000	20,866	3,134	14,176	414,176
(7)	6/30/2010	24,000	20,709	3,291	10,885	410,885
(8)	12/31/2010	24,000	20,544	3,456	7,429	407,429
(9)	6/30/2011	24,000	20,371	3,629	3,800	403,800
(10)	12/31/2011	24,000	20,200	3,800	0	400,000
		$240,000	$209,119	$30,881		

* Adjusted for rounding.

d. Journal entry for June 30, 2007, bond payment.

June 30	Bond Interest Expense	21,544	
	Premium on Bonds Payable.	2,456	
	Cash		24,000
	Paid semiannual interest on bonds.		

e. Journal entry for January 1, 2009, bond retirement.

Jan. 1	Bonds Payable	400,000	
	Premium on Bonds Payable.	20,295	
	Cash		416,000
	Gain on Retirement of Bonds		4,295
	To record bond retirement (carrying value as of December 31, 2008).		

APPENDIX

Present Values of Bonds and Notes

14A

This appendix explains how to apply present value techniques to measure a long-term liability when it is created and to assign interest expense to the periods until it is settled. Appendix B at the end of the book provides additional discussion of present value concepts.

Present Value Concepts

The basic present value concept is that cash paid (or received) in the future has less value now than the same amount of cash paid (or received) today. To illustrate, if we must pay $1 one year from now, its present value is less than $1. To see this, assume that we borrow $0.9259 today that must be paid back in one year with 8% interest. Our interest expense for this loan is computed as $0.9259 \times 8\%$, or $0.0741.

C2 Explain and compute the present value of an amount(s) to be paid at a future date(s).

When the $0.0741 interest is added to the $0.9259 borrowed, we get the $1 payment necessary to repay our loan with interest. This is formally computed in Exhibit 14A.1. The $0.9259 borrowed is the present value of the $1 future payment. More generally, an amount borrowed equals the present value of the

Amount borrowed	$0.9259
Interest for one year at 8%	0.0741
Amount owed after 1 year	$ 1.0000

Exhibit 14A.1

Components of a One-Year Loan

future payment. (This same interpretation applies to an investment. If $0.9259 is invested at 8%, it yields $0.0741 in revenue after one year. This amounts to $1, made up of principal and interest.)

To extend this example, assume that we owe $1 two years from now instead of one year, and the 8% interest is compounded annually. *Compounded* means that interest during the second period is based on the total of the amount borrowed plus the interest accrued from the first period. The second period's interest is then computed as 8% multiplied by the sum of the amount borrowed plus interest earned in the first period. Exhibit 14A.2 shows how we compute the present value of $1 to be paid in two years. This amount is $0.8573. The first year's interest of $0.0686 is added to the principal so that the second year's interest is based on $0.9259. Total interest for this two-year period is $0.1427, computed as $0.0686 plus $0.0741.

Point: Benjamin Franklin is said to have described compounding as "the money, money makes, makes more money."

Amount borrowed	$0.8573
Interest for first year ($0.8573 $\times$ 8%)	0.0686
Amount owed after 1 year	0.9259
Interest for second year ($0.9259 $\times$ 8%)	0.0741
Amount owed after 2 years	$ 1.0000

Exhibit 14A.2

Components of a Two-Year Loan

Present Value Tables

The present value of $1 that we must repay at some future date can be computed by using this formula: $1/(1 + i)^n$. The symbol i is the interest rate per period and n is the number of periods until the future payment must be made. Applying this formula to our two-year loan, we get $1/(1.08)^2$, or $0.8573. This is the same value shown in Exhibit 14A.2. We can use this formula to find any present value. However, a simpler method is to use a *present value table*, which lists present values computed with this formula for various interest rates and time periods. Many people find it helpful in learning present value concepts to first work with the table and then move to using a calculator.

Exhibit 14A.3 shows a present value table for a future payment of 1 for up to 10 periods at three different interest rates. Present values in this table are rounded to four decimal places. This table is drawn from the larger and more complete Table B.1 in Appendix B at the end of the book. Notice that the first value in the 8% column is 0.9259, the value we computed earlier for the present value of a $1 loan for one year at 8% (see Exhibit 14A.1). Go to the second row in the same 8% column and find the present value of 1 discounted at 8% for two years, or 0.8573. This $0.8573 is the present value of our obligation to repay $1 after two periods at 8% interest (see Exhibit 14A.2).

Exhibit 14A.3

Present Value of 1

Periods	Rate 6%	Rate 8%	Rate 10%
1	0.9434	**0.9259**	0.9091
2	0.8900	**0.8573**	0.8264
3	0.8396	0.7938	0.7513
4	0.7921	0.7350	0.6830
5	0.7473	0.6806	0.6209
6	0.7050	0.6302	0.5645
7	0.6651	0.5835	0.5132
8	0.6274	0.5403	0.4665
9	0.5919	0.5002	0.4241
10	0.5584	0.4632	0.3855

Example: Use Exhibit 14A.3 to find the present value of $1 discounted for 2 years at 6%. *Answer:* Present value = $0.8900

Applying a Present Value Table

To illustrate how to measure a liability using a present value table, assume that a company plans to borrow cash and repay it as follows: $2,000 after one year, $3,000 after two years, and $5,000 after three years. How much does this company receive today if the interest rate on this loan is 10%? To answer, we need to compute the present value of the three future payments, discounted at 10%. This computation is shown in Exhibit 14A.4 using present values from Exhibit 14A.3. The company can borrow $8,054 today at 10% interest in exchange for its promise to make these three payments at the scheduled dates.

Exhibit 14A.4

Present Value of a Series of Unequal Payments

Periods	Payments	Present Value of 1 at 10%	Present Value of Payments
1	$2,000	0.9091	$ 1,818
2	3,000	0.8264	2,479
3	5,000	0.7513	3,757
Present value of all payments			**$8,054**

Present Value of an Annuity

The $8,054 present value for the loan in Exhibit 14A.4 equals the sum of the present values of the three payments. When payments are not equal, their combined present value is best computed by adding the individual present values as shown in Exhibit 14A.4. Sometimes payments follow an **annuity,** which is a series of *equal* payments at equal time intervals. The present value of an annuity is readily computed.

To illustrate, assume that a company must repay a 6% loan with a $5,000 payment at each year-end for the next four years. This loan amount equals the present value of the four payments discounted at 6%. Exhibit 14A.5 shows how to compute this loan's present value of $17,326 by multiplying each payment by its matching present value factor taken from Exhibit 14A.3.

However, the series of $5,000 payments is an annuity, so we can compute its present value with either of two shortcuts. First, the third column of Exhibit 14A.5 shows that the sum of the present values of 1 at 6% for periods 1 through 4 equals 3.4651. One shortcut is to multiply this total of 3.4651 by the $5,000 annual payment to get the combined present value of $17,326. It requires one multiplication instead of four.

Exhibit 14A.5

Present Value of a Series of Equal Payments (Annuity) by Discounting Each Payment

Periods	Payments	Present Value of 1 at 6%	Present Value of Payments
1	$5,000	0.9434	$ 4,717
2	5,000	0.8900	4,450
3	5,000	0.8396	4,198
4	5,000	0.7921	3,961
Present value of all payments		**3.4651**	**$17,326**

The second shortcut uses an *annuity table* such as the one shown in Exhibit 14A.6, which is drawn from the more complete Table B.3 in Appendix B. We go directly to the annuity table to get the present value factor for a specific number of payments and interest rate. We then multiply this factor by the amount of the payment to find the present value of the annuity. Specifically, find the row for four periods and go across to the 6% column, where the factor is 3.4651. This factor equals the present value of an annuity with four payments of 1, discounted at 6%. We then multiply 3.4651 by $5,000 to get the $17,326 present value of the annuity.

Periods	Rate		
	6%	8%	10%
1	0.9434	0.9259	0.9091
2	1.8334	1.7833	1.7355
3	2.6730	2.5771	2.4869
4	**3.4651**	3.3121	3.1699
5	4.2124	3.9927	3.7908
6	4.9173	4.6229	4.3553
7	5.5824	5.2064	4.8684
8	6.2098	5.7466	5.3349
9	6.8017	6.2469	5.7590
10	7.3601	6.7101	6.1446

Exhibit 14A.6

Present Value of an Annuity of 1

Example: Use Exhibit 14A.6 to find the present value of an annuity of eight $15,000 payments with an 8% interest rate. *Answer:* Present value = $15,000 × 5.7466 = $86,199

Compounding Periods Shorter than a Year

The present value examples all involved periods of one year. In many situations, however, interest is compounded over shorter periods. For example, the interest rate on bonds is usually stated as an annual rate but interest is often paid every six months (semiannually). This means that the present value of interest payments from such bonds must be computed using interest periods of six months.

Assume that a borrower wants to know the present value of a series of 10 *semiannual payments* of $4,000 made over five years at an *annual interest rate* of 12%. The interest rate is stated as an annual rate of 12%, but it is actually a rate of 6% per semiannual interest period. To compute the present value of this series of $4,000 payments, go to row 10 of Exhibit 14A.6 and across to the 6% column to find the factor 7.3601. The present value of this annuity is $29,440 (7.3601 × $4,000).

Example: If this borrower makes five semiannual payments of $8,000, what is the present value of this annuity at a 12% annual rate? *Answer:* 4.2124 × $8,000 = $33,699

Appendix B further describes present value concepts and includes more complete present value tables and assignments.

Quick Check	Answers—p. 570

14. A company enters into an agreement to make four annual year-end payments of $1,000 each, starting one year from now. The annual interest rate is 8%. The present value of these four payments is (*a*) $2,923, (*b*) $2,940, or (*c*) $3,312.

15. Suppose a company has an option to pay either (*a*) $10,000 after one year or (*b*) $5,000 after six months and another $5,000 after one year. Which choice has the lower present value?

APPENDIX

Effective Interest Amortization

14B

Effective Interest Amortization of a Discount Bond

The straight-line method yields changes in the bonds' carrying value while the amount for bond interest expense remains constant. This gives the impression of a changing interest rate when users divide a constant bond interest expense over a changing carrying value. As a result, accounting standards allow use of the straight-line method only when its results do not differ materially from those obtained using the effective interest method. The **effective interest method,** or simply *interest method,* allocates total bond interest expense over the bonds' life in a way that yields a constant rate of interest. This constant rate of interest is the market rate at the issue date. Thus, bond interest expense for a period equals the carrying value of the bond at the beginning of that period multiplied by the market rate when issued.

Point: The effective interest method consistently computes bond interest expense using the market rate at issuance. This rate is applied to a changing carrying value.

Exhibit 14B.1 shows an effective interest amortization table for the Fila bonds (as described in Exhibit 14.4). The key difference between the effective interest and straight-line methods lies in computing bond interest expense. Instead of assigning an equal amount of bond interest expense to each period, the effective interest method assigns a bond interest expense amount that increases over the life of a discount bond. **Both methods allocate the *same* $47,723 of total bond interest expense to the bonds' life, but in different patterns.** Specifically, the amortization table in Exhibit 10B.1 shows that the balance of the discount (column D) is amortized until it reaches zero. Also, the bonds' carrying value (column E) changes each period until it equals par value at maturity. Compare columns D and E to the corresponding columns in Exhibit 14.7 to see the amortization patterns. Total bond interest expense is $47,723, consisting of $40,000 of semiannual cash payments and $7,723 of the original bond discount, the same for both methods.

Exhibit 14B.1

Effective Interest Amortization of Bond Discount

		(A) Cash Interest Paid	(B) Bond Interest Expense	(C) Discount Amortization	(D) Unamortized Discount	(E) Carrying Value
Semiannual Interest Period-End						
(0)	12/31/2008				$7,723	$ 92,277
(1)	6/30/2009	$4,000	$4,614	$ 614	7,109	92,891
(2)	12/31/2009	4,000	4,645	645	6,464	93,536
(3)	6/30/2010	4,000	4,677	677	5,787	94,213
(4)	12/31/2010	4,000	4,711	711	5,076	94,924
(5)	6/30/2011	4,000	4,746	746	4,330	95,670
(6)	12/31/2011	4,000	4,784	784	3,546	96,454
(7)	6/30/2012	4,000	4,823	823	2,723	97,277
(8)	12/31/2012	4,000	4,864	864	1,859	98,141
(9)	6/30/2013	4,000	4,907	907	952	99,048
(10)	12/31/2013	4,000	4,952	952	0	100,000
		$40,000	$47,723	$7,723		

Bonds: $100,000 Par Value, Semiannual Interest Payments, Five-Year Life, 4% Semiannual Contract Rate, 5% Semiannual Market Rate

Column (A) is par value ($100,000) multiplied by the semiannual contract rate (4%).
Column (B) is prior period's carrying value multiplied by the semiannual market rate (5%).
Column (C) is the difference between interest paid and bond interest expense, or [(B) − (A)].
Column (D) is the prior period's unamortized discount less the current period's discount amortization.
Column (E) is par value less unamortized discount, or [$100,000 − (D)].

Except for differences in amounts, journal entries recording the expense and updating the liability balance are the same under the effective interest method and the straight-line method. We can use the numbers in Exhibit 14B.1 to record each semiannual entry during the bonds' five-year life (June 30, 2009, through December 31, 2013). For instance, we record the interest payment at the end of the first semiannual period as:

Assets = Liabilities + Equity
−4,000   +614   −4,614

2009			
June 30	Bond Interest Expense	4,614	
	Discount on Bonds Payable		614
	Cash		4,000
	To record semiannual interest and discount *amortization (effective interest method).*		

Effective Interest Amortization of a Premium Bond

Exhibit 14B.2 shows the amortization table using the effective interest method for the Adidas bonds (as described in Exhibit 14.8). Column A lists the semiannual cash payments. Column B shows the amount of bond interest expense, computed as the 5% semiannual market rate at issuance multiplied by the beginning-of-period carrying value. The amount of cash paid in column A is larger than the bond interest expense because the cash payment is based on the higher 6% semiannual contract rate. The excess cash payment over the interest expense reduces the principal. These amounts are shown in column C. Column E

565

Exhibit 14B.2

Effective Interest Amortization
of Bond Premium

	Bonds: $100,000 Par Value, Semiannual Interest Payments, Five-Year Life, 6% Semiannual Contract Rate, 5% Semiannual Market Rate					
	Semiannual Interest Period-End	(A) Cash Interest Paid	(B) Bond Interest Expense	(C) Premium Amortization	(D) Unamortized Premium	(E) Carrying Value
(0) 12/31/2008					$7,720	$107,720
(1) 6/30/2009	$6,000	$5,386	$ 614	7,106	107,106
(2) 12/31/2009	6,000	5,355	645	6,461	106,461
(3) 6/30/2010	6,000	5,323	677	5,784	105,784
(4) 12/31/2010	6,000	5,289	711	5,073	105,073
(5) 6/30/2011	6,000	5,254	746	4,327	104,327
(6) 12/31/2011	6,000	5,216	784	3,543	103,543
(7) 6/30/2012	6,000	5,177	823	2,720	102,720
(8) 12/31/2012	6,000	5,136	864	1,856	101,856
(9) 6/30/2013	6,000	5,093	907	949	100,949
(10) 12/31/2013	6,000	5,051*	949	0	100,000
	$60,000	$52,280	$7,720		

Column (A) is par value ($100,000) multiplied by the semiannual contract rate (6%).
Column (B) is prior period's carrying value multiplied by the semiannual market rate (5%).
Column (C) is the difference between interest paid and bond interest expense, or [(A) − (B)].
Column (D) is the prior period's unamortized premium less the current period's premium amortization.
Column (E) is par value plus unamortized premium, or [$100,000 + (D)].
* Adjusted for rounding.

shows the carrying value after deducting the amortized premium in column C from the prior period's carrying value. Column D shows the premium's reduction by periodic amortization. When the issuer makes the first semiannual interest payment, the effect of premium amortization on bond interest expense and bond liability is recorded as follows:

2009			
June 30	Bond Interest Expense	5,386	
	Premium on Bonds Payable	614	
	Cash		6,000
	To record semiannual interest and premium amortization (effective interest method).		

Assets = Liabilities + Equity
−6,000   −614   −5,386

Similar entries with different amounts are recorded at each payment date until the bond matures at the end of 2013. The effective interest method yields decreasing amounts of bond interest expense and increasing amounts of premium amortization over the bonds' life.

APPENDIX

Issuing Bonds between Interest Dates

14C

An issuer can sell bonds at a date other than an interest payment date. When this occurs, the buyers normally pay the issuer the purchase price plus any interest accrued since the prior interest payment date. This accrued interest is then repaid to these buyers on the next interest payment date. To illustrate, suppose **Avia** sells $100,000 of its 9% bonds at par on March 1, 2008, sixty days after the stated issue date.

C3 Describe the accrual of bond interest when bond payments do not align with accounting periods.

The interest on Avia bonds is payable semiannually on each June 30 and December 31. Since 60 days have passed, the issuer collects accrued interest from the buyers at the time of issuance. This amount is $1,500 ($100,000 × 9% × $^{60}/_{360}$ year). This case is reflected in Exhibit 14C.1.

Exhibit 14C.1

Accruing Interest between Interest Payment Dates

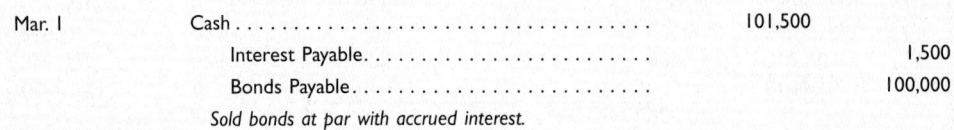

Avia records the issuance of these bonds on March 1, 2008, as follows:

Mar. 1	Cash	101,500	
	Interest Payable.		1,500
	Bonds Payable.		100,000
	Sold bonds at par with accrued interest.		

Assets = Liabilities + Equity
+101,500   +100,000
           +1,500

Note that liabilities for interest payable and bonds payable are recorded in separate accounts. When the June 30, 2008, semiannual interest date arrives, Avia pays the full semiannual interest of $4,500 ($100,000 × 9% × ½ year) to the bondholders. This payment includes the four months' interest of $3,000 earned by the bondholders from March 1 to June 30 *plus* the repayment of the 60 days' accrued interest collected by Avia when the bonds were sold. Avia records this first semiannual interest payment as follows:

Example: How much interest is collected from a buyer of $50,000 of Avia bonds sold at par 150 days after the contract issue date? *Answer:* $1,875 (computed as $50,000 × 9% × $^{150}/_{360}$ year)

June 30	Interest Payable	1,500	
	Bond Interest Expense	3,000	
	Cash		4,500
	Paid semiannual interest on the bonds.		

Assets = Liabilities + Equity
−4,500   −1,500   −3,000

Global: In some countries such as Kuwait, Saudi Arabia, and Iran, charging explicit interest for use of money is rare due to Islamic law.

The practice of collecting and then repaying accrued interest with the next interest payment is to simplify the issuer's administrative efforts. To explain, suppose an issuer sells bonds on 15 or 20 different dates between the stated issue date and the first interest payment date. If the issuer does not collect accrued interest from buyers, it needs to pay different amounts of cash to each of them according to the time that passed after purchasing the bonds. The issuer needs to keep detailed records of buyers and the dates they bought bonds. Issuers avoid this recordkeeping by having each buyer pay accrued interest at purchase. Issuers then pay the full semiannual interest to all buyers, regardless of when they bought bonds.

Decision Maker

Answer—p. 570

Bond Rater   You must assign a rating to a bond that reflects its risk to bondholders. Identify factors you consider in assessing bond risk. Indicate the likely levels (relative to the norm) for the factors you identify for a bond that sells at a discount.

Accruing Bond Interest Expense

If a bond's interest period does not coincide with the issuer's accounting period, an adjusting entry is needed to recognize bond interest expense accrued since the most recent interest payment. To illustrate, assume that the Adidas bonds described in Exhibit 14.10 are sold on the stated issue date of September 1, 2008, instead of December 31, 2008. As a result, four months' interest (and premium amortization) accrue before the end of the 2008 calendar year. Interest for this period equals $3,485, or ⅘ of the first six months' interest of $5,228. Also, the premium amortization is $515, or ⅘ of the first six months' amortization of $772. The sum of the bond interest expense and the amortization is $4,000 ($3,485 + $515), which equals ⅘ of the $6,000 cash payment due on February 28, 2009. Adidas records these effects with an adjusting entry at December 31, 2008:

Point: Computation of accrued bond interest may use months instead of days for simplicity purposes. For example, the accrued interest computation for the Adidas bonds is based on months.

Dec. 31	Bond Interest Expense	3,485	
	Premium on Bonds Payable.	515	
	Interest Payable.		4,000
	To record four months' accrued interest and		
	premium amortization.		

Assets = Liabilities + Equity
          −515   −3,485
          +4,000

Similar entries are made on each December 31 throughout the bonds' five-year life. When the $6,000 cash payment occurs on each February 28 interest payment date, Adidas must recognize bond interest expense and amortization for January and February. It must also eliminate the interest payable liability created by the December 31 adjusting entry. For example, Adidas records its payment on February 28, 2009, as:

Feb. 28	Interest Payable	4,000	
	Bond Interest Expense ($5,228 × ⅔)	1,743	
	Premium on Bonds Payable ($772 × ⅔)	257	
	Cash		6,000
	To record 2 months' interest and amortization and		
	eliminate accrued interest liability.		

Assets = Liabilities + Equity
−6,000   −4,000   −1,743
          −257

The interest payments made each August 31 are recorded as usual because the entire six-month interest period is included within this company's calendar-year reporting period.

Quick Check   Answer—p. 570

16. On May 1, a company sells 9% bonds with a $500,000 par value that pay semiannual interest on each January 1 and July 1. The bonds are sold at par plus interest accrued since January 1. The issuer records the first semiannual interest payment on July 1 with (*a*) a debit to Interest Payable for $15,000, (*b*) a debit to Bond Interest Expense for $22,500, or (*c*) a credit to Interest Payable for $7,500.

APPENDIX

Leases and Pensions

14D

This appendix briefly explains the accounting and analysis for both leases and pensions.

Lease Liabilities

A **lease** is a contractual agreement between a *lessor* (asset owner) and a *lessee* (asset renter or tenant) that grants the lessee the right to use the asset for a period of time in return for cash (rent) payments. Nearly one-fourth of all equipment purchases is financed with leases. The advantages of lease financing include the lack of an immediate large cash payment and the potential to deduct rental payments in computing taxable income. From an accounting perspective, leases can be classified as either operating or capital leases.

C4 Describe accounting for leases and pensions.

Operating Leases   **Operating leases** are short-term (or cancelable) leases in which the lessor retains the risks and rewards of ownership. Examples include most car and apartment rental agreements. The lessee records such lease payments as expenses; the lessor records them as revenue. The lessee does not report the leased item as an asset or a liability (it is the lessor's asset). To illustrate, if an employee of Amazon leases a car for $300 at an airport while on company business, Amazon (lessee) records this cost as:

Point: Home Depot's annual report indicates that its rental expenses from operating leases total more than $600 million.

July 4	Rental Expense	300	
	Cash		300
	To record lease rental payment.		

Assets = Liabilities + Equity
−300   −300

Capital Leases **Capital leases** are long-term (or noncancelable) leases by which the lessor transfers substantially all risks and rewards of ownership to the lessee.[3] Examples include most leases of airplanes and department store buildings. The lessee records the leased item as its own asset along with a lease liability at the start of the lease term; the amount recorded equals the present value of all lease payments. To illustrate, assume that K2 Co. enters into a six-year lease of a building in which it will sell sporting equipment. The lease transfers all building ownership risks and rewards to K2 (the present value of its $12,979 annual lease payments is $60,000). K2 records this transaction as follows:

Assets = Liabilities + Equity
+60,000   +60,000

2008			
Jan. 1	Leased Asset—Building.	60,000	
	Lease Liability		60,000
	To record leased asset and lease liability.		

Point: Home Depot reports *"certain retail locations are leased under capital leases."* The net present value of its Lease Liability is about $350 million.

K2 reports the leased asset as a plant asset and the lease liability as a long-term liability. The portion of the lease liability expected to be paid in the next year is reported as a current liability.[4] At each year-end, K2 records depreciation on the leased asset (assume straight-line depreciation, six-year lease term, and no salvage value) as follows:

Assets = Liabilities + Equity
−10,000   −10,000

Dec. 31	Depreciation Expense—Building	10,000	
	Accumulated Depreciation—Building		10,000
	To record depreciation on leased asset.		

K2 also accrues interest on the lease liability at each year-end. Interest expense is computed by multiplying the remaining lease liability by the interest rate on the lease. Specifically, K2 records its annual interest expense as part of its annual lease payment ($12,979) as follows (for its first year):

Assets = Liabilities + Equity
−12,979   −8,179   −4,800

2008			
Dec. 31	Interest Expense	4,800	
	Lease Liability.	8,179	
	Cash		12,979
	To record first annual lease payment.*		

* These numbers are computed from a *lease payment schedule*. For simplicity, we use the same numbers from Exhibit 14.14 for this lease payment schedule—with different headings as follows:

	(A)	(B) Debit	(C) Debit	(D) Credit	(E)
Period Ending Date	Beginning Balance of Lease Liability	Interest on Lease + Liability 8% × (A)	Lease = Liability (D) − (B)	Cash Lease Payment	Ending Balance of Lease Liability (A) − (C)
12/31/2008	$60,000	$ 4,800	$ 8,179	$12,979	$51,821
12/31/2009	51,821	4,146	8,833	12,979	42,988
12/31/2010	42,988	3,439	9,540	12,979	33,448
12/31/2011	33,448	2,676	10,303	12,979	23,145
12/31/2012	23,145	1,852	11,127	12,979	12,018
12/31/2013	12,018	961	12,018	12,979	0
		$17,874	$60,000	$77,874	

[3] A *capital lease* meets any one or more of four criteria: (1) transfers title of leased asset to lessee, (2) contains a bargain purchase option, (3) has a lease term that is 75% or more of the leased asset's useful life, or (4) has a present value of lease payments that is 90% or more of the leased asset's market value.

[4] Most lessees try to keep leased assets and lease liabilities off their balance sheets by failing to meet any one of the four criteria of a capital lease. This is because a lease liability increases a company's total liabilities, making it more difficult to obtain additional financing. The acquisition of assets without reporting any related liabilities (or other asset outflows) on the balance sheet is called **off-balance-sheet financing.**

Pension Liabilities

A **pension plan** is a contractual agreement between an employer and its employees for the employer to provide benefits (payments) to employees after they retire. Most employers pay the full cost of the pension, but sometimes employees pay part of the cost. An employer records its payment into a pension plan with a debit to Pension Expense and a credit to Cash. A *plan administrator* receives payments from the employer, invests them in pension assets, and makes benefit payments to *pension recipients* (retired employees). Insurance and trust companies often serve as pension plan administrators.

Many pensions are known as *defined benefit plans* that define future benefits; the employer's contributions vary, depending on assumptions about future pension assets and liabilities. Several disclosures are necessary in this case. Specifically, a pension liability is reported when the accumulated benefit obligation is *more than* the plan assets, a so-called *underfunded plan*. The accumulated benefit obligation is the present value of promised future pension payments to retirees. *Plan assets* refer to the market value of assets the plan administrator holds. A pension asset is reported when the accumulated benefit obligation is *less than* the plan assets, a so-called *overfunded plan*. An employer reports pension expense when it receives the benefits from the employees' services, which is sometimes decades before it pays pension benefits to employees. (*Other Postretirement Benefits* refer to nonpension benefits such as health care and life insurance benefits. Similar to a pension, costs of these benefits are estimated and liabilities accrued when the employees earn them.)

Point: Fringe benefits are often 40% or more of salaries and wages, and pension benefits make up nearly 15% of fringe benefits.

Point: Two types of pension plans are (1) *defined benefit plan*—the retirement benefit is defined and the employer estimates the contribution necessary to pay these benefits and (2) *defined contribution plan*—the pension contribution is defined and the employer and/or employee contributes amounts specified in the pension agreement.

Summary

C1 Explain the types and payment patterns of notes. Notes repaid over a period of time are called *installment notes* and usually follow one of two payment patterns: (1) decreasing payments of interest plus equal amounts of principal or (2) equal total payments. Mortgage notes also are common.

C2^A Explain and compute the present value of an amount(s) to be paid at a future date(s). The basic concept of present value is that an amount of cash to be paid or received in the future is worth less than the same amount of cash to be paid or received today. Another important present value concept is that interest is compounded, meaning interest is added to the balance and used to determine interest for succeeding periods. An annuity is a series of equal payments occurring at equal time intervals. An annuity's present value can be computed using the present value table for an annuity (or a calculator).

C3^C Describe the accrual of bond interest when bond payments do not align with accounting periods. Issuers and buyers of debt record the interest accrued when issue dates or accounting periods do not coincide with debt payment dates.

C4^D Describe accounting for leases and pensions. A lease is a rental agreement between the lessor and the lessee. When the lessor retains the risks and rewards of asset ownership (an *operating lease*), the lessee debits Rent Expense and credits Cash for its lease payments. When the lessor substantially transfers the risks and rewards of asset ownership to the lessee (a *capital lease*), the lessee capitalizes the leased asset and records a lease liability. Pension agreements can result in either pension assets or pension liabilities.

A1 Compare bond financing with stock financing. Bond financing is used to fund business activities. Advantages of bond financing versus stock include (1) no effect on owner control, (2) tax savings, and (3) increased earnings due to financial leverage. Disadvantages include (1) interest and principal payments and (2) amplification of poor performance.

A2 Assess debt features and their implications. Certain bonds are secured by the issuer's assets; other bonds, called *debentures,* are unsecured. Serial bonds mature at different points in time;

term bonds mature at one time. Registered bonds have each bondholder's name recorded by the issuer; bearer bonds are payable to the holder. Convertible bonds are exchangeable for shares of the issuer's stock. Callable bonds can be retired by the issuer at a set price. Debt features alter the risk of loss for creditors.

A3 Compute the debt-to-equity ratio and explain its use. Both creditors and equity holders are concerned about the relation between the amount of liabilities and the amount of equity. A company's financing structure is at less risk when the debt-to-equity ratio is lower, as liabilities must be paid and usually with periodic interest.

P1 Prepare entries to record bond issuance and bond interest expense. When bonds are issued at par, Cash is debited and Bonds Payable is credited for the bonds' par value. At bond interest payment dates (usually semiannual), Bond Interest Expense is debited and Cash credited; the latter for an amount equal to the bond par value multiplied by the bond contract rate.

P2 Compute and record amortization of bond discount. Bonds are issued at a discount when the contract rate is less than the market rate, making the issue (selling) price less than par. When this occurs, the issuer records a credit to Bonds Payable (at par) and debits both Discount on Bonds Payable and Cash. The amount of bond interest expense assigned to each period is computed using either the straight-line or effective interest method.

P3 Compute and record amortization of bond premium. Bonds are issued at a premium when the contract rate is higher than the market rate, making the issue (selling) price greater than par. When this occurs, the issuer records a debit to Cash and credits both Premium on Bonds Payable and Bonds Payable (at par). The amount of bond interest expense assigned to each period is computed using either the straight-line or effective interest method. The Premium on Bonds Payable is allocated to reduce bond interest expense over the life of the bonds.

P4 Record the retirement of bonds. Bonds are retired at maturity with a debit to Bonds Payable and a credit to Cash at par value. The issuer can retire the bonds early by exercising a call option or purchasing them in the market. Bondholders can also retire bonds early by exercising a conversion feature on convertible bonds. The issuer recognizes a gain or loss for the difference between the amount paid and the bond carrying value.

P5 **Prepare entries to account for notes.** Interest is allocated to each period in a note's life by multiplying its beginning-

period carrying value by its market rate at issuance. If a note is repaid with equal payments, the payment amount is computed by dividing the borrowed amount by the present value of an annuity factor (taken from a present value table) using the market rate and the number of payments.

Guidance Answers to **Decision Maker**

Entrepreneur   This is a "present value" question. The market interest rate (10%) and present value ($3,000) are known, but the payment required two years later is unknown. This amount ($3,630) can be computed as $3,000 × 1.10 × 1.10. Thus, the sale price is $3,630 when no payments are received for two years. Note that the $3,630 received two years from today is equivalent to $3,000 cash today.

Bond Investor   The debt-to-equity ratio for the first company is 0.2 ($350,000/$1,750,000) and for the second company is 1.2 ($1,200,000/$1,000,000), suggesting that the financing structure of

the second company is more risky than that of the first company. Consequently, as a buyer of unsecured debenture bonds, you prefer the first company (all else equal).

Bond Rater   Bonds with longer repayment periods (life) have higher risk. Also, bonds issued by companies in financial difficulties or facing higher than normal uncertainties have higher risk. Moreover, companies with higher than normal debt and large fluctuations in earnings are considered of higher risk. Discount bonds are more risky on one or more of these factors.

Guidance Answers to **Quick Checks**

1. (b)

2. Multiply the bond's par value by its contract rate of interest.

3. Bonds sell at a premium when the contract rate exceeds the market rate and the purchasers pay more than their par value.

4. The bonds are issued at a discount, meaning that issue price is less than par value. A discount occurs because the bond contract rate (6%) is less than the market rate (8%).

5.

Cash	91,893
Discount on Bonds Payable	8,107
Bonds Payable	100,000

6. $3,811 (Total bond interest expense of $38,107 divided by 10 periods; or the $3,000 semiannual cash payment plus the $8,107 discount divided by 10 periods.)

7. The bonds are issued at a premium, meaning issue price is higher than par value. A premium occurs because the bonds' contract rate (16%) is higher than the market rate (14%).

8. (b) For each semiannual period: $10,592/20 periods = $530 premium amortization.

9.

Bonds payable, 16%, due 12/31/2017	$100,000
Plus premium on bonds payable	9,532* $109,532

* Original premium balance of $10,592 less $530 and $530 amortized on 6/30/2008 and 12/31/2008, respectively.

10. $9,375 loss. Computed as the difference between the repurchase price of $256,250 [50% of ($500,000 × 102.5%)] and the carrying value of $246,875 (50% of $493,750).

11. (c)

12. The interest portion of an installment payment equals the period's beginning loan balance multiplied by the market interest rate at the time of the note's issuance.

13. On the balance sheet, the account balances of the related liability (note payable) and asset (cash) accounts are decreased. On the income statement, interest expense is recorded.

14. (c) Computed as 3.3121 × $1,000 = $3,312.

15. The option of paying $10,000 after one year has a lower present value. It postpones paying the first $5,000 by six months. More generally, the present value of a further delayed payment is always lower than a less delayed payment.

16. (a) Reflects payment of accrued interest recorded back on May 1; $500,000 × 9% × 4/12 = $15,000.

Key Terms   mhhe.com/wildFAP18e

Key Terms are available at the book's Website for learning and testing in an online Flashcard Format.

Annuity (p. 562)
Bearer bonds (p. 557)
Bond (p. 544)
Bond certificate (p. 546)
Bond indenture (p. 546)

Callable bonds (p. 557)
Capital leases (p. 568)
Carrying (book) value of bonds (p. 548)
Contract rate (p. 547)
Convertible bonds (p. 557)

Coupon bonds (p. 557)
Debt-to-equity ratio (p 558)
Discount on bonds payable (p. 547)
Effective interest method (p. 563)
Installment note (p. 554)

Lease (p. 567)	**Par value of a bond** (p. 544)	**Serial bonds** (p. 557)
Market rate (p. 547)	**Pension plan** (p. 569)	**Sinking fund bonds** (p. 557)
Mortgage (p. 556)	**Premium on bonds** (p. 550)	**Straight-line bond amortization** (p. 548)
Off-balance-sheet financing (p. 568)	**Registered bonds** (p. 557)	**Term bonds** (p. 557)
Operating leases (p. 567)	**Secured bonds** (p. 557)	**Unsecured bonds** (p. 557)

Multiple Choice Quiz   Answers on p. 583   mhhe.com/wildFAP18e

Multiple Choice Quizzes A and B are available at the book's Website.

1. A bond traded at 97½ means that:
  a. The bond pays 97½% interest.
  b. The bond trades at $975 per $1,000 bond.
  c. The market rate of interest is below the contract rate of interest for the bond.
  d. The bonds can be retired at $975 each.
  e. The bond's interest rate is 2½%.

2. A bondholder that owns a $1,000, 6%, 15-year bond has:
  a. The right to receive $1,000 at maturity.
  b. Ownership rights in the bond issuing entity.
  c. The right to receive $60 per month until maturity.
  d. The right to receive $1,900 at maturity.
  e. The right to receive $600 per year until maturity.

3. A company issues 8%, 20-year bonds with a par value of $500,000. The current market rate for the bonds is 8%. The amount of interest owed to the bondholders for each semiannual interest payment is:
  a. $40,000.
  b. $0.
  c. $20,000.

  d. $800,000.
  e. $400,000.

4. A company issued 5-year, 5% bonds with a par value of $100,000. The company received $95,735 for the bonds. Using the straight-line method, the company's interest expense for the first semiannual interest period is:
  a. $2,926.50.
  b. $5,853.00.
  c. $2,500.00.
  d. $5,000.00.
  e. $9,573.50.

5. A company issued 8-year, 5% bonds with a par value of $350,000. The company received proceeds of $373,745. Interest is payable semiannually. The amount of premium amortized for the first semiannual interest period, assuming straight-line bond amortization, is:
  a. $2,698.
  b. $23,745.
  c. $8,750.
  d. $9,344.
  e. $1,484.

Superscript letter ^{B} $(^{C,\,D})$ denotes assignments based on Appendix 14B (14C, 14D).

Discussion Questions

1. What is the main difference between a bond and a share of stock?

2. What is the main difference between notes payable and bonds payable?

3. What is the advantage of issuing bonds instead of obtaining financing from the company's owners?

4. What are the duties of a trustee for bondholders?

5. What is a bond indenture? What provisions are usually included in it?

6. What are the *contract* rate and the *market* rate for bonds?

7. What factors affect the market rates for bonds?

8.^{B}Does the straight-line or effective interest method produce an interest expense allocation that yields a constant rate of interest over a bond's life? Explain.

9.^{C}Why does a company that issues bonds between interest dates collect accrued interest from the bonds' purchasers?

10. If you know the par value of bonds, the contract rate, and the market rate, how do you compute the bonds' price?

11. What is the issue price of a $2,000 bond sold at 98¼? What is the issue price of a $6,000 bond sold at 101½?

12. Describe the debt-to-equity ratio and explain how creditors and owners would use this ratio to evaluate a company's risk.

13. What obligation does an entrepreneur (owner) have to investors that purchase bonds to finance the business?

14. Refer to **Best Buy**'s annual report in Appendix A. Is there any indication that Best Buy has issued bonds?

15. Refer to the statement of cash flows for **Circuit City** in Appendix A. For the year ended February 28, 2005, what was the amount of principal payments on long-term debt?

16. Refer to the annual report for **Apple** in Appendix A. For the year ended September 25, 2004, did it raise more cash by issuing stock or debt?

17.^{D}When can a lease create both an asset and a liability for the lessee?

18.^{D}Compare and contrast an operating lease with a capital lease.

19.^{D}Describe the two basic types of pension plans.

 Red numbers denote Discussion Questions that involve decision-making.

QUICK STUDY

QS 14-1
Bond computations—
straight-line   P1 P2

Enviro Company issues 8%, 10-year bonds with a par value of $250,000 and semiannual interest payments. On the issue date, the annual market rate for these bonds is 10%, which implies a selling price of 87½. The straight-line method is used to allocate interest expense.

1. What are the issuer's cash proceeds from issuance of these bonds?
2. What total amount of bond interest expense will be recognized over the life of these bonds?
3. What is the amount of bond interest expense recorded on the first interest payment date?

QS 14-2^B
Bond computations—
effective interest

P1 P3

Garcia Company issues 10%, 15-year bonds with a par value of $240,000 and semiannual interest payments. On the issue date, the annual market rate for these bonds is 8%, which implies a selling price of 117¼. The effective interest method is used to allocate interest expense.

1. What are the issuer's cash proceeds from issuance of these bonds?
2. What total amount of bond interest expense will be recognized over the life of these bonds?
3. What amount of bond interest expense is recorded on the first interest payment date?

QS 14-3
Journalize bond issuance   P1

Prepare the journal entry for the issuance of the bonds in both QS 14-1 and QS 14-2. Assume that both bonds are issued for cash on January 1, 2008.

QS 14-4
Computing bond price   P2 P3

Using the bond details in both QS 14-1 and QS 14-2, confirm that the bonds' selling prices given in each problem are approximately correct. Use the present value tables B.1 and B.3 in Appendix B.

QS 14-5
Bond retirement by call option

P4

On July 1, 2008, Advocate Company exercises an $8,000 call option (plus par value) on its outstanding bonds that have a carrying value of $416,000 and par value of $400,000. The company exercises the call option after the semiannual interest is paid on June 30, 2008. Record the entry to retire the bonds.

QS 14-6
Bond retirement by stock
conversion   P4

On January 1, 2008, the $2,000,000 par value bonds of Spitz Company with a carrying value of $2,000,000 are converted to 1,000,000 shares of $1.00 par value common stock. Record the entry for the conversion of the bonds.

QS 14-7
Computing payments for
an installment note   C1

Murray Company borrows $340,000 cash from a bank and in return signs an installment note for five annual payments of equal amount, with the first payment due one year after the note is signed. Use Table B.3 in Appendix B to compute the amount of the annual payment for each of the following annual market rates: (a) 4%, (b) 8%, and (c) 12%.

QS 14-8
Bond features and terminology

A2

Enter the letter of the description A through H that best fits each term or phrase 1 through 8.

A. Records and tracks the bondholders' names.
B. Is unsecured; backed only by the issuer's credit standing.
C. Has varying maturity dates for amounts owed.
D. Identifies rights and responsibilities of the issuer and the bondholders.
E. Can be exchanged for shares of the issuer's stock.
F. Is unregistered; interest is paid to whoever possesses them.
G. Maintains a separate asset account from which bondholders are paid at maturity.
H. Pledges specific assets of the issuer as collateral.

1. _____ Registered bond		**5.** _____ Convertible bond
2. _____ Serial bond		**6.** _____ Bond indenture
3. _____ Secured bond		**7.** _____ Sinking fund bond
4. _____ Bearer bond		**8.** _____ Debenture

Compute the debt-to-equity ratio for each of the following companies. Which company appears to have a riskier financing structure? Explain.

QS 14-9
Debt-to-equity ratio

A2

	Atlanta Company	Spokane Company
Total liabilities	$429,000	$ 548,000
Total equity	572,000	1,827,000

Madrid Company plans to issue 8% bonds on January 1, 2008, with a par value of $4,000,000. The company sells $3,600,000 of the bonds on January 1, 2008. The remaining $400,000 sells at par on March 1, 2008. The bonds pay interest semiannually as of June 30 and December 31. Record the entry for the March 1 cash sale of bonds.

QS 14-10^C
Issuing bonds between
interest dates

P1

Jin Li, an employee of ETrain.com, leases a car at O'Hare airport for a three-day business trip. The rental cost is $250. Prepare the entry by ETrain.com to record Jin Li's short-term car lease cost.

QS 14-11^D
Recording operating leases   C4

Algoma, Inc., signs a five-year lease for office equipment with Office Solutions. The present value of the lease payments is $15,499. Prepare the journal entry that Algoma records at the inception of this capital lease.

QS 14-12^D
Recording capital leases   C4

Round dollar amounts to the nearest whole dollar. Assume no reversing entries are used.

EXERCISES

On January 1, 2008, Boston Enterprises issues bonds that have a $3,400,000 par value, mature in 20 years, and pay 9% interest semiannually on June 30 and December 31. The bonds are sold at par.

1. How much interest will Boston pay (in cash) to the bondholders every six months?

2. Prepare journal entries to record (*a*) the issuance of bonds on January 1, 2008; (*b*) the first interest payment on June 30, 2008; and (*c*) the second interest payment on December 31, 2008.

3. Prepare the journal entry for issuance assuming the bonds are issued at (*a*) 98 and (*b*) 102.

Exercise 14-1
Recording bond issuance and
interest

P1

Tano issues bonds with a par value of $180,000 on January 1, 2008. The bonds' annual contract rate is 8%, and interest is paid semiannually on June 30 and December 31. The bonds mature in three years. The annual market rate at the date of issuance is 10%, and the bonds are sold for $170,862.

1. What is the amount of the discount on these bonds at issuance?

2. How much total bond interest expense will be recognized over the life of these bonds?

3. Prepare an amortization table like the one in Exhibit 14.7 for these bonds; use the straight-line method to amortize the discount.

Exercise 14-2
Straight-line amortization of
bond discount

P2

Stanford issues bonds dated January 1, 2008, with a par value of $500,000. The bonds' annual contract rate is 9%, and interest is paid semiannually on June 30 and December 31. The bonds mature in three years. The annual market rate at the date of issuance is 12%, and the bonds are sold for $463,140.

1. What is the amount of the discount on these bonds at issuance?

2. How much total bond interest expense will be recognized over the life of these bonds?

3. Prepare an amortization table like the one in Exhibit 14B.1 for these bonds; use the effective interest method to amortize the discount.

Exercise 14-3^B
Effective interest amortization
of bond discount

P2

Quatro Co. issues bonds dated January 1, 2008, with a par value of $400,000. The bonds' annual contract rate is 13%, and interest is paid semiannually on June 30 and December 31. The bonds mature in three years. The annual market rate at the date of issuance is 12%, and the bonds are sold for $409,850.

1. What is the amount of the premium on these bonds at issuance?

2. How much total bond interest expense will be recognized over the life of these bonds?

3. Prepare an amortization table like the one in Exhibit 14.11 for these bonds; use the straight-line method to amortize the premium.

Exercise 14-4
Straight-line amortization of
bond premium

P3

Exercise 14-5^B

Effective interest amortization of bond premium P3

Refer to the bond details in Exercise 14-4 and prepare an amortization table like the one in Exhibit 14B.2 for these bonds using the effective interest method to amortize the premium.

Exercise 14-6

Computing bond interest and price; recording bond issuance

P2

Brigham Company issues bonds with a par value of $800,000 on their stated issue date. The bonds mature in 10 years and pay 6% annual interest in semiannual payments. On the issue date, the annual market rate for the bonds is 8%.

1. What is the amount of each semiannual interest payment for these bonds?

2. How many semiannual interest payments will be made on these bonds over their life?

3. Use the interest rates given to determine whether the bonds are issued at par, at a discount, or at a premium.

Check (4) $691,287

4. Compute the price of the bonds as of their issue date.

5. Prepare the journal entry to record the bonds' issuance.

Exercise 14-7

Computing bond interest and price; recording bond issuance

P3

Citywide Company issues bonds with a par value of $150,000 on their stated issue date. The bonds mature in five years and pay 10% annual interest in semiannual payments. On the issue date, the annual market rate for the bonds is 8%.

1. What is the amount of each semiannual interest payment for these bonds?

2. How many semiannual interest payments will be made on these bonds over their life?

3. Use the interest rates given to determine whether the bonds are issued at par, at a discount, or at a premium.

Check (4) $162,172

4. Compute the price of the bonds as of their issue date.

5. Prepare the journal entry to record the bonds' issuance.

Exercise 14-8

Bond computations, straight-line amortization, and bond retirement

P2 P4

On January 1, 2007, Shay issues $700,000 of 10%, 15-year bonds at a price of 97¾. Six years later, on January 1, 2013, Shay retires 20% of these bonds by buying them on the open market at 104½. All interest is accounted for and paid through December 31, 2012, the day before the purchase. The straight-line method is used to amortize any bond discount.

1. How much does the company receive when it issues the bonds on January 1, 2007?

2. What is the amount of the discount on the bonds at January 1, 2007?

3. How much amortization of the discount is recorded on the bonds for the entire period from January 1, 2007, through December 31, 2012?

4. What is the carrying (book) value of the bonds as of the close of business on December 31, 2012? What is the carrying value of the 20% soon-to-be-retired bonds on this same date?

5. How much did the company pay on January 1, 2013, to purchase the bonds that it retired?

Check (6) $8,190 loss

6. What is the amount of the recorded gain or loss from retiring the bonds?

7. Prepare the journal entry to record the bond retirement at January 1, 2013.

Exercise 14-9^C

Recording bond issuance with accrued interest

C4 P1

On May 1, 2008, Brussels Enterprises issues bonds dated January 1, 2008, that have a $3,400,000 par value, mature in 20 years, and pay 9% interest semiannually on June 30 and December 31. The bonds are sold at par plus four months' accrued interest.

1. How much accrued interest do the bond purchasers pay Brussels on May 1, 2008?

Check (1) $102,000

2. Prepare Brussels' journal entries to record (a) the issuance of bonds on May 1, 2008; (b) the first interest payment on June 30, 2008; and (c) the second interest payment on December 31, 2008.

Exercise 14-10

Straight-line amortization and accrued bond interest expense

P1 P2

Duval Co. issues four-year bonds with a $100,000 par value on June 1, 2007, at a price of $95,948. The annual contract rate is 7%, and interest is paid semiannually on November 30 and May 31.

1. Prepare an amortization table like the one in Exhibit 14.7 for these bonds. Use the straight-line method of interest amortization.

2. Prepare journal entries to record the first two interest payments and to accrue interest as of December 31, 2007.

On January 1, 2008, Eagle borrows $100,000 cash by signing a four-year, 7% installment note. The note requires four equal total payments of accrued interest and principal on December 31 of each year from 2008 through 2011.

1. Compute the amount of each of the four equal total payments.

2. Prepare an amortization table for this installment note like the one in Exhibit 14.14.

Exercise 14-11
Installment note with equal total payments C1 P5
Check (1) $29,523

Use the information in Exercise 14-11 to prepare the journal entries for Eagle to record the loan on January 1, 2008, and the four payments from December 31, 2008, through December 31, 2011.

Exercise 14-12
Installment note entries P5

Montclair Company is considering a project that will require a $500,000 loan. It presently has total liabilities of $220,000, and total assets of $610,000.

1. Compute Montclair's (a) present debt-to-equity ratio and (b) the debt-to-equity ratio assuming it borrows $500,000 to fund the project.

2. Evaluate and discuss the level of risk involved if Montclair borrows the funds to pursue the project.

Exercise 14-13
Applying debt-to-equity ratio
A3

Indicate whether the company in each separate case 1 through 3 has entered into an operating lease or a capital lease.

1. The lessor retains title to the asset, and the lease term is three years on an asset that has a five-year useful life.

2. The title is transferred to the lessee, the lessee can purchase the asset for $1 at the end of the lease, and the lease term is five years. The leased asset has an expected useful life of six years.

3. The present value of the lease payments is 95% of the leased asset's market value, and the lease term is 70% of the leased asset's useful life.

Exercise 14-14^D
Identifying capital and operating leases
C4

Harbor (lessee) signs a five-year capital lease for office equipment with a $10,000 annual lease payment. The present value of the five annual lease payments is $41,000, based on a 7% interest rate.

1. Prepare the journal entry Harbor will record at inception of the lease.

2. If the leased asset has a 5-year useful life with no salvage value, prepare the journal entry Harbor will record each year to recognize depreciation expense related to the leased asset.

Exercise 14-15^D
Accounting for capital lease
C4

General Motors advertised three alternatives for a 25-month lease on a new Blazer: (1) zero dollars down and a lease payment of $1,750 per month for 25 months, (2) $5,000 down and $1,500 per month for 25 months, or (3) $38,500 down and no payments for 25 months. Use the present value Table B.3 in Appendix B to determine which is the best alternative (assume you have enough cash to accept any alternative and the annual interest rate is 12% compounded monthly).

Exercise 14-16^D
Analyzing lease options
C2 C3 C4

Round dollar amounts to the nearest whole dollar. Assume no reversing entries are used.

Hartford Research issues bonds dated January 1, 2008, that pay interest semiannually on June 30 and December 31. The bonds have a $40,000 par value, an annual contract rate of 10%, and mature in 10 years.

Required

For each of the following three separate situations, (a) determine the bonds' issue price on January 1, 2008, and (b) prepare the journal entry to record their issuance.

1. Market rate at the date of issuance is 8%.

2. Market rate at the date of issuance is 10%.

3. Market rate at the date of issuance is 12%.

PROBLEM SET A

Problem 14-1A
Computing bond price and recording issuance
P1 P2 P3

Check (1) Premium, $4,537

(3) Discount, $4,588

Problem 14-2A
Straight-line amortization of bond discount and bond premium

P1 P2 P3

mhhe.com/wildFAP18e

Check (3) $4,143,552

(4) 12/31/2008 carrying value, $3,528,920

Hillside issues $4,000,000 of 6%, 15-year bonds dated January 1, 2007, that pay interest semiannually on June 30 and December 31. The bonds are issued at a price of $3,456,448.

Required

1. Prepare the January 1, 2007, journal entry to record the bonds' issuance.
2. For each semiannual period, compute (*a*) the cash payment, (*b*) the straight-line discount amortization, and (*c*) the bond interest expense.
3. Determine the total bond interest expense to be recognized over the bonds' life.
4. Prepare the first two years of an amortization table like Exhibit 14.7 using the straight-line method.
5. Prepare the journal entries to record the first two interest payments.
6. Assume that the bonds are issued at a price of $4,895,980. Repeat parts 1 through 5.

Problem 14-3A
Straight-line amortization of bond premium; computing bond price

P1 P3

mhhe.com/wildFAP18e

Check (2) 6/30/2009 carrying value, $252,668

Ellis issues 6.5%, five-year bonds dated January 1, 2007, with a $250,000 par value. The bonds pay interest on June 30 and December 31 and are issued at a price of $255,333. The annual market rate is 6% on the issue date.

Required

1. Calculate the total bond interest expense over the bonds' life.
2. Prepare a straight-line amortization table like Exhibit 14.11 for the bonds' life.
3. Prepare the journal entries to record the first two interest payments.

Problem 14-4A[B]
Effective interest amortization of bond premium; computing bond price   P1 P3

Check (2) 6/30/2009 carrying value, $252,865

(4) $252,326

Refer to the bond details in Problem 14-3A.

Required

1. Compute the total bond interest expense over the bonds' life.
2. Prepare an effective interest amortization table like the one in Exhibit 14B.2 for the bonds' life.
3. Prepare the journal entries to record the first two interest payments.
4. Use the market rate at issuance to compute the present value of the remaining cash flows for these bonds as of December 31, 2009. Compare your answer with the amount shown on the amortization table as the balance for that date (from part 2) and explain your findings.

Problem 14-5A
Straight-line amortization of bond discount

P1 P2

Check (2) $97,819

(3) 12/31/2008 carrying value, $308,589

Legacy issues $325,000 of 5%, four-year bonds dated January 1, 2007, that pay interest semiannually on June 30 and December 31. They are issued at $292,181 and their market rate is 8% at the issue date.

Required

1. Prepare the January 1, 2007, journal entry to record the bonds' issuance.
2. Determine the total bond interest expense to be recognized over the bonds' life.
3. Prepare a straight-line amortization table like the one in Exhibit 14.7 for the bonds' first two years.
4. Prepare the journal entries to record the first two interest payments.

Analysis Component

5. Assume the market rate on January 1, 2007, is 4% instead of 8%. Without providing numbers, describe how this change affects the amounts reported on Legacy's financial statements.

Problem 14-6A[B]
Effective interest amortization of bond discount   P1 P2

Check (2) $97,819

(3) 12/31/2008 carrying value, $307,308

mhhe.com/wildFAP18e

Refer to the bond details in Problem 14-5A.

Required

1. Prepare the January 1, 2007, journal entry to record the bonds' issuance.
2. Determine the total bond interest expense to be recognized over the bonds' life.
3. Prepare an effective interest amortization table like the one in Exhibit 14B.1 for the bonds' first two years.
4. Prepare the journal entries to record the first two interest payments.

Ike issues $180,000 of 11%, three-year bonds dated January 1, 2007, that pay interest semiannually on June 30 and December 31. They are issued at $184,566. Their market rate is 10% at the issue date.

Required

1. Prepare the January 1, 2007, journal entry to record the bonds' issuance.
2. Determine the total bond interest expense to be recognized over the bonds' life.
3. Prepare an effective interest amortization table like Exhibit 14B.2 for the bonds' first two years.
4. Prepare the journal entries to record the first two interest payments.
5. Prepare the journal entry to record the bonds' retirement on January 1, 2009, at 98.

Analysis Component

6. Assume that the market rate on January 1, 2007, is 12% instead of 10%. Without presenting numbers, describe how this change affects amounts reported on Ike's financial statements.

Problem 14-7A[B]
Effective interest amortization of bond premium; retiring bonds

P1   P3   P4

Check   (3) 6/30/2008 carrying value, $182,448

(5) $5,270 gain

mhhe.com/wildFAP18e

On November 1, 2007, Norwood borrows $200,000 cash from a bank by signing a five-year installment note bearing 8% interest. The note requires equal total payments each year on October 31.

Required

1. Compute the total amount of each installment payment.
2. Complete an amortization table for this installment note similar to the one in Exhibit 14.14.
3. Prepare the journal entries in which Norwood (*a*) records accrued interest as of December 31, 2007 (the end of its annual reporting period), and (*b*) the first annual payment on the note.

Problem 14-8A
Installment notes

C1   P5

Check   (2) 10/31/2011 ending balance, $46,382

At the end of the current year, the following information is available for both the Pulaski Company and the Scott Company:

	Pulaski Company	Scott Company
Total assets	$900,000	$450,000
Total liabilities	360,000	240,000
Total equity	540,000	210,000

Required

1. Compute the debt-to-equity ratio for both companies.
2. Comment on your results and discuss the riskiness of each company's financing structure.

Problem 14-9A
Applying the debt-to-equity ratio

A3

Rogers Company signs a five-year capital lease with Packer Company for office equipment. The annual lease payment is $10,000, and the interest rate is 8%.

Required

1. Compute the present value of Rogers' five-year lease payments.
2. Prepare the journal entry to record Rogers' capital lease at its inception.
3. Complete a lease payment schedule for the five years of the lease with the following headings. Assume that the beginning balance of the lease liability (present value of lease payments) is $39,927. (*Hint:* To find the amount allocated to interest in year 1, multiply the interest rate by the beginning-of-year lease liability. The amount of the annual lease payment not allocated to interest is allocated to principal. Reduce the lease liability by the amount allocated to principal to update the lease liability at each year-end.)

Problem 14-10A[D]
Capital lease accounting

C4

Check   (1) $39,927

(3) Year 3 ending balance, $17,833

Period Ending Date	Beginning Balance of Lease Liability	Interest on Lease Liability	Reduction of Lease Liability	Cash Lease Payment	Ending Balance of Lease Liability

4. Use straight-line depreciation and prepare the journal entry to depreciate the leased asset at the end of year 1. Assume zero salvage value and a five-year life for the office equipment.

PROBLEM SET B

Problem 14-1B
Computing bond price and recording issuance

P1   P2   P3

Check   (1) Premium, $6,948

(3) Discount, $6,326

Flagstaff Systems issues bonds dated January 1, 2008, that pay interest semiannually on June 30 and December 31. The bonds have a $90,000 par value, an annual contract rate of 12%, and mature in five years.

Required

For each of the following three separate situations, (a) determine the bonds' issue price on January 1, 2008, and (b) prepare the journal entry to record their issuance.

1. Market rate at the date of issuance is 10%.
2. Market rate at the date of issuance is 12%.
3. Market rate at the date of issuance is 14%.

Problem 14-2B
Straight-line amortization of bond discount and bond premium

P1   P2   P3

Check   (3) $3,790,000

(4) 6/30/2008 carrying value, $3,068,500

Romero issues $3,400,000 of 10%, 10-year bonds dated January 1, 2007, that pay interest semiannually on June 30 and December 31. The bonds are issued at a price of $3,010,000.

Required

1. Prepare the January 1, 2007, journal entry to record the bonds' issuance.
2. For each semiannual period, compute (a) the cash payment, (b) the straight-line discount amortization, and (c) the bond interest expense.
3. Determine the total bond interest expense to be recognized over the bonds' life.
4. Prepare the first two years of an amortization table like Exhibit 14.7 using the straight-line method.
5. Prepare the journal entries to record the first two interest payments.
6. Assume that the bonds are issued at a price of $4,192,932. Repeat parts 1 through 5.

Problem 14-3B
Straight-line amortization of bond premium; computing bond price

P1   P3

Check   (2) 6/30/2009 carrying value, $326,493

Ripkin Company issues 9%, five-year bonds dated January 1, 2007, with a $320,000 par value. The bonds pay interest on June 30 and December 31 and are issued at a price of $332,988. Their annual market rate is 8% on the issue date.

Required

1. Calculate the total bond interest expense over the bonds' life.
2. Prepare a straight-line amortization table like Exhibit 14.11 for the bonds' life.
3. Prepare the journal entries to record the first two interest payments.

Problem 14-4B[B]
Effective interest amortization of bond premium; computing bond price   P1   P3

Check   (2) 6/30/2009 carrying value, $327,136

(4) $325,807

Refer to the bond details in Problem 14-3B.

Required

1. Compute the total bond interest expense over the bonds' life.
2. Prepare an effective interest amortization table like the one in Exhibit 14B.2 for the bonds' life.
3. Prepare the journal entries to record the first two interest payments.
4. Use the market rate at issuance to compute the present value of the remaining cash flows for these bonds as of December 31, 2009. Compare your answer with the amount shown on the amortization table as the balance for that date (from part 2) and explain your findings.

Problem 14-5B
Straight-line amortization of bond discount

P1   P2

Check   (2) $257,506

(3) 6/30/2008 carrying value, $202,646

Gomez issues $240,000 of 6%, 15-year bonds dated January 1, 2007, that pay interest semiannually on June 30 and December 31. They are issued at $198,494, and their market rate is 8% at the issue date.

Required

1. Prepare the January 1, 2007, journal entry to record the bonds' issuance.
2. Determine the total bond interest expense to be recognized over the life of the bonds.
3. Prepare a straight-line amortization table like the one in Exhibit 14.7 for the bonds' first two years.
4. Prepare the journal entries to record the first two interest payments.

Refer to the bond details in Problem 14-5B.

Problem 14-6B[B]

Effective interest amortization of bond discount

Required

1. Prepare the January 1, 2007, journal entry to record the bonds' issuance.

2. Determine the total bond interest expense to be recognized over the bonds' life.

3. Prepare an effective interest amortization table like the one in Exhibit 14B.1 for the bonds' first two years.

4. Prepare the journal entries to record the first two interest payments.

P1   P2

Check   (2) $257,506;
(3) 6/30/2008 carrying value, $200,803

Valdez issues $450,000 of 13%, four-year bonds dated January 1, 2007, that pay interest semiannually on June 30 and December 31. They are issued at $493,608, and their market rate is 10% at the issue date.

Problem 14-7B[B]

Effective interest amortization of bond premium; retiring bonds

P1   P3   P4

Required

1. Prepare the January 1, 2007, journal entry to record the bonds' issuance.

2. Determine the total bond interest expense to be recognized over the bonds' life.

3. Prepare an effective interest amortization table like the one in Exhibit 14B.2 for the bonds' first two years.

4. Prepare the journal entries to record the first two interest payments.

5. Prepare the journal entry to record the bonds' retirement on January 1, 2009, at 106.

Check   (3) 6/30/2008 carrying value, $479,202

(5) $3,088 loss

Analysis Component

6. Assume that the market rate on January 1, 2007, is 14% instead of 10%. Without presenting numbers, describe how this change affects amounts reported on Valdez's financial statements.

On October 1, 2007, Gordon Enterprises borrows $150,000 cash from a bank by signing a three-year installment note bearing 10% interest. The note requires equal total payments each year on September 30.

Problem 14-8B

Installment notes

C1   P5

Required

1. Compute the total amount of each installment payment.

2. Complete an amortization table for this installment note similar to the one in Exhibit 14.14.

3. Prepare the journal entries in which Gordon records (*a*) accrued interest as of December 31, 2007 (the end of its annual reporting period) and (*b*) the first annual payment on the note.

Check   (2) 9/30/2009 ending balance, $54,836

At the end of the current year, the following information is available for both Atlas Company and Bryan Company.

Problem 14-9B

Applying the debt-to-equity ratio

A3

	Atlas Company	Bryan Company
Total assets	$180,000	$750,000
Total liabilities	81,000	562,500
Total equity	99,000	187,500

Required

1. Compute the debt-to-equity ratio for both companies.

2. Comment on your results and discuss what they imply about the relative riskiness of these companies.

Braun Company signs a five-year capital lease with Verdi Company for office equipment. The annual lease payment is $20,000, and the interest rate is 10%.

Problem 14-10B[D]

Capital lease accounting

C4

Required

1. Compute the present value of Braun's lease payments.

2. Prepare the journal entry to record Braun's capital lease at its inception.

Check   (1) $75,816

(3) Year 3 ending balance,
$34,712

3. Complete a lease payment schedule for the five years of the lease with the following headings. Assume that the beginning balance of the lease liability (present value of lease payments) is $75,816. (*Hint:* To find the amount allocated to interest in year 1, multiply the interest rate by the beginning-of-year lease liability. The amount of the annual lease payment not allocated to interest is allocated to principal. Reduce the lease liability by the amount allocated to principal to update the lease liability at each year-end.)

Period Ending Date	Beginning Balance of Lease Liability	Interest on Lease Liability	Reduction of Lease Liability	Cash Lease Payment	Ending Balance of Lease Liability

4. Use straight-line depreciation and prepare the journal entry to depreciate the leased asset at the end of year 1. Assume zero salvage value and a five-year life for the office equipment.

PROBLEM SET C

Problem Set C is available at the book's Website to further reinforce and assess your learning.

SERIAL PROBLEM

Success Systems

(This serial problem began in Chapter 1 and continues through most of the book. If previous chapter segments were not completed, the serial problem can begin at this point. It is helpful, but not necessary, for you to use the Working Papers that accompany the book.)

SP 14   Adriana Lopez has consulted with her local banker and is considering financing an expansion of her business by obtaining a long-term bank loan. Selected account balances at March 31, 2008, for Success Systems follow.

Total assets	$147,529	Total liabilities	$1,050	Total equity	$146,479

Required

1. The bank has offered a long-term secured note to Success Systems. The bank's loan procedures require that a client's debt-to-equity ratio not exceed 0.8. As of March 31, 2008, what is the maximum amount that Success Systems could borrow from this bank (rounded to nearest dollar)?

2. If Success Systems borrows the maximum amount allowed from the bank, what percentage of assets would be financed (*a*) by debt, and (*b*) by equity?

3. What are some factors Lopez should consider before borrowing the funds?

BEYOND THE NUMBERS

REPORTING IN ACTION

A1 A2

BTN 14-1   Refer to **Best Buy**'s financial statements in Appendix A to answer the following.

1. Identify the items that make up Best Buy's long-term debt at February 26, 2005? (Hint: See note 4.)

2. How much annual cash interest must Best Buy pay on the 2.25% convertible subordinated debt?

3. Did it have any additions to long-term debt that provided cash for the year-end February 26, 2005?

Fast Forward

4. Access Best Buy's financial statements for the years ending after February 26, 2005, from its Website (**BestBuy.com**) or the SEC's EDGAR database (**www.sec.gov**). Has it issued additional long-term debt since the year-end February 26, 2005? If yes, indentify the amount(s).

BTN 14-2 Key comparative figures ($ millions) for both **Best Buy** and **Circuit City** follow.

COMPARATIVE
ANALYSIS
A3

Key Figures	Best Buy Current Year	Best Buy Prior Year	Circuit City Current Year	Circuit City Prior Year
Total Assets	$10,294	$8,652	$3,789	$3,731
Total Liabilities	5,845	5,230	1,702	1,507
Total Equity	4,449	3,422	2,087	2,224

Required

1. Compute the debt-to-equity ratio for Best Buy and Circuit City for both the current year and the prior year.
2. Use the ratio you computed in part 1 to determine which company's financing structure is less risky. Assume an industry average of 1.1 for debt-to-equity.

BTN 14-3 Brevard County needs a new county government building that would cost $24 million. The politicians feel that voters will not approve a municipal bond issue to fund the building since it would increase taxes. They opt to have a state bank issue $24 million of tax-exempt securities to pay for the building construction. The county then will make yearly lease payments (of principal and interest) to repay the obligation. Unlike conventional municipal bonds, the lease payments are not binding obligations on the county and, therefore, require no voter approval.

ETHICS
CHALLENGE
C4 A1

Required

1. Do you think the actions of the politicians and the bankers in this situation are ethical?
2. How do the tax-exempt securities used to pay for the building compare in risk to a conventional municipal bond issued by Brevard County?

BTN 14-4 Your business associate mentions that she is considering investing in corporate bonds currently selling at a premium. She says that since the bonds are selling at a premium, they are highly valued and her investment will yield more than the going rate of return for the risk involved. Reply with a memorandum to confirm or correct your associate's interpretation of premium bonds.

COMMUNICATING
IN PRACTICE
P3

BTN 14-5 Access the April 11, 2005, filing of the 10-K report of **Home Depot** for the year ended January 30, 2005, from www.sec.gov (Ticker: HD). Refer to Home Depot's balance sheet, including its Note 2 (on long-term debt).

TAKING IT TO
THE NET
A2

Required

1. Identify Home Depot's long-term liabilities and the amounts for those liabilities from Home Depot's balance sheet at January 30, 2005.
2. Review Home Depot's Note 2. The note reports that it "issued $1.0 billion of 3¾% senior notes due September 15, 2009, at a discount of $5 million with interest payable semiannually on March 15 and September 15 each year."
   a. Why would Home Depot issue $1 billion of its notes for only $995 million?
   b. How much cash interest must Home Depot pay each March 15 and September 15 on these notes?

BTN 14-6[B] Break into teams and complete the following requirements related to effective interest amortization for a premium bond.

TEAMWORK IN
ACTION
P2 P3

1. Each team member is to independently prepare a blank table with proper headings for amortization of a bond premium. When all have finished, compare tables and ensure all are in agreement.

Parts 2 and 3 require use of these facts: On January 1, 2008, BC issues $100,000, 9%, five-year bonds at 104.1. The market rate at issuance is 8%. BC pays interest semiannually on June 30 and December 31.

2. In rotation, *each* team member must explain how to complete *one* line of the bond amortization table, including all computations for his or her line. (Round amounts to the nearest dollar.) All members are to fill in their tables during this process. You need not finish the table; stop after all members have explained a line.

3. In rotation, *each* team member is to identify a separate column of the table and indicate what the final number in that column will be and explain the reasoning.

Hint: Rotate teams to report on parts 4 and 5. Consider requiring entries for issuance and interest payments.

4. Reach a team consensus as to what the total bond interest expense on this bond issue will be if the bond is not retired before maturity.

5. As a team, prepare a list of similarities and differences between the amortization table just prepared and the amortization table if the bond had been issued at a discount.

BusinessWeek ACTIVITY

A2

BTN 14-7   Read the article "A Growing Tide of Risky Mortgages" in the May 18, 2005, issue of *BusinessWeek*. (The book's Website provides a free link.)

Required

1. What is an interest-only mortgage? How is this different from a conventional mortgage? Why would a borrower seek an interest-only mortgage?

2. Refer to the article's example of a conventional $400,000 mortgage with a fixed rate of 4.875% for the first five years yielding monthly payments of $2,120. Determine the monthly payment if this loan were an interest-only loan. What would be the loan balance after the second payment?

3. What would be the loan balance after the second payment if the loan were a conventional mortgage?

4. What are the risks involved in interest-only mortgages?

ENTREPRENEURIAL DECISION

A1

BTN 14-8   Mark and Holly Melton are entrepreneurs and owners of **Melton Franchise Systems**. Assume that Meltons' franchise program currently has $250,000 in equity; and they are considering a $100,000 expansion to meet increased demand. The $100,000 expansion would yield $16,000 in additional annual income before interest expense. Assume that Meltons' franchise program currently earns $40,000 annual income before interest expense of $10,000, yielding a return on equity of 12% ($30,000/$250,000). To fund the expansion, the Meltons are considering the issuance of a 10-year, $100,000 note with annual interest payments (the principal due at the end of 10 years).

Required

1. Using return on equity as the decision criterion, show computations to support or reject Meltons' expansion if interest on the $100,000 note is (*a*) 10%, (*b*) 15%, (*c*) 16%, (*d*) 17%, and (*e*) 20%.

2. What general rule do the results in part 1 illustrate?

HITTING THE ROAD

A1

BTN 14-9   Visit your city or county library. Ask the librarian to help you locate the recent financial records of your city or county government. Examine the records.

Required

1. Determine the amount of long-term bonds and notes currently outstanding.

2. Read the supporting information to your municipality's financial statements and record:

     a. Market interest rate(s) when the bonds and/or notes were issued.

     b. Date(s) when the bonds and/or notes will mature.

     c. Any rating(s) on the bonds and/or notes received from **Moody's**, **Standard & Poor's**, or another rating agency.

BTN 14-10   **Dixons** (<u>Dixons-Group.com</u>), **Best Buy**, and **Circuit City** are competitors in the global marketplace. Selected results from these companies follow.

Key Figures	Dixons (£ millions)		Best Buy ($ millions)		Circuit City ($ millions)	
	Current Year	Prior Year	Current Year	Prior Year	Current Year	Prior Year
Total assets	£3,874	£4,158	$10,294	$8,652	$3,789	$3,731
Total liabilities	2,406	2,782	5,845	5,230	1,702	1,507
Total equity	1,468	1,376	4,449	3,422	2,087	2,224
Debt-to-equity ratio	?	?	1.3	1.5	0.8	0.7

Required

1. Compute Dixons' debt-to-equity ratio for the current year and the prior year.

2. Use the data provided and the ratios you computed in part 1 to determine which company's financing structure is least risky.

ANSWERS TO MULTIPLE CHOICE QUIZ

1. b

2. a

3. c; $500,000 \times 0.08 \times \frac{1}{2}$ year = $20,000

4. a; Cash interest paid = $100,000 \times 5\% \times \frac{1}{2}$ year = $2,500
Discount amortization = ($100,000 - $95,735)/10 periods = $426.50
Interest expense = $2,500.00 + $426.50 = $2,926.50

5. e; ($373,745 - $350,000)/16 periods = $1,484

15

Investments and International Operations

A Look Back

Chapter 14 focused on long-term liabilities—a main part of most companies' financing. We explained how to value, record, amortize, and report these liabilities in financial statements.

A Look at This Chapter

This chapter focuses on investments in securities. We explain how to identify, account for, and report investments in both debt and equity securities. We also explain accounting for transactions listed in a foreign currency.

A Look Ahead

Chapter 16 focuses on reporting and analyzing a company's cash flows. Special emphasis is directed at the statement of cash flows—reported under the indirect method.

Learning Objectives

CAP

Conceptual

C1 Distinguish between debt and equity securities and between short-term and long-term investments. (p. 586)

C2 Identify and describe the different classes of investments in securities. (p. 587)

C3 Describe how to report equity securities with controlling influence. (p. 593)

C4 *Appendix 15A*—Explain foreign exchange rates between currencies. (p. 599)

Analytical

A1 Compute and analyze the components of return on total assets. (p. 594)

Procedural

P1 Account for trading securities. (p. 589)

P2 Account for held-to-maturity securities. (p. 590)

P3 Account for available-for-sale securities. (p. 590)

P4 Account for equity securities with significant influence. (p. 591)

P5 *Appendix 15A*—Record transactions listed in a foreign currency. (p. 600)

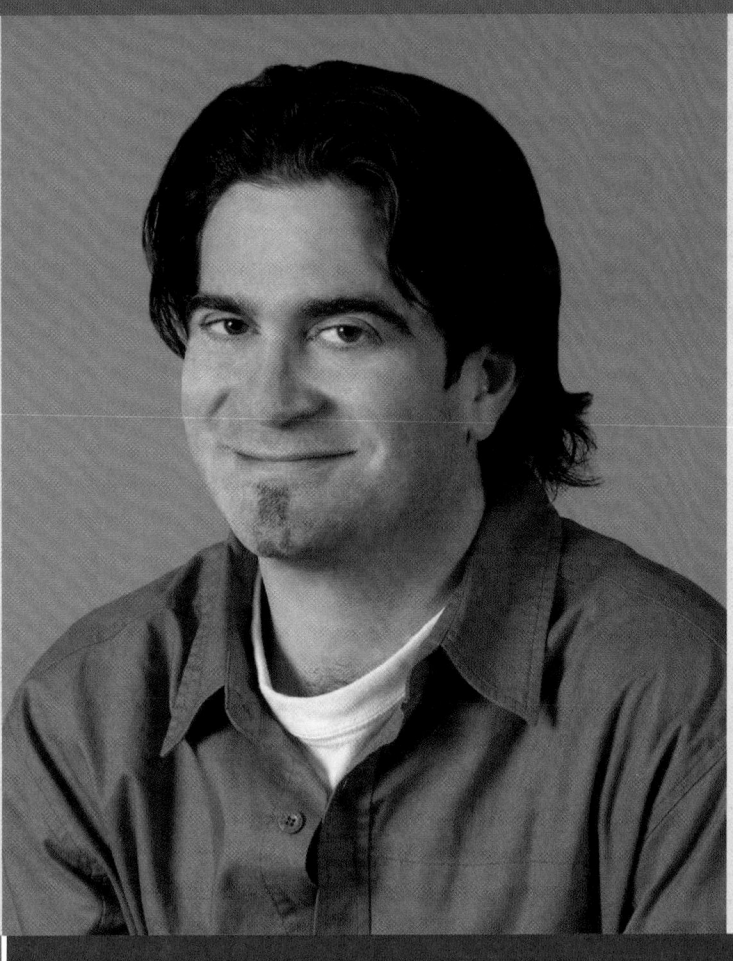

Manga-nificent Entertainment

LOS ANGELES, CA—"I fell in love with the combination of old and new, East and West—sort of a neo-Buddhist modernism—that hooked me the most," says Stu Levy, founder of **TOKYOPOP (Tokyopop.com).** The object of Stu's desire is manga (pronounced MAHN-gah), a form of graphic entertainment native to Japan. TOKYOPOP is a leading multimedia company that specializes in publishing manga in English. Manga is described as the Japanese counterpart to comic books, though quicker to read and with a wider range of genres, characters, and layouts.

"The art [of manga] really resonates with this generation of young people, teenagers, and children," explains Stu. "We are putting a lot of time and energy into getting it out there into the hands of the potential audience. I love the ability to merge the visual medium with lyrical storytelling."

The art of running a company that publishes manga involves the business of acquiring and developing material. Stu likens himself to a producer. As he puts it, "A producer gets the team together, handles the finances, but is also totally involved in the creative side. [Yet] acquisitions and development is probably my most enjoyable and largest job. I also handle our capital-raising activities," adds Stu.

TOKYOPOP's acquisition and development activities involve considerable investment in manga. This often means investing in the Japanese rights to material that the company then translates for its U.S. audience. Accordingly, Stu's job requires conducting international transactions and performing currency translations. These tasks demand that he know the accounting and reporting requirements for investments. This chapter focuses on how to account for investments, particularly those in the debt and equity securities of other companies.

"The publishing part of our business is kind of like a platform. . . we are a delivering mechanism," says Stu. "Most people who read manga. . . get hooked. It's addictive," he adds. Revenues should continue to look *manga-nificent* for years to come because the more people experience manga, the larger the market grows. "Our goal at TOKYOPOP is to deliver the most exciting entertainment possible and merging the best cultures in the world to do so," says Stu. "I dove into the Japanese culture and Asian culture. . . but I fell in love with manga."

[Sources: *TOKYOPOP Website*, January 2006, *Entrepreneur*, November 2004; *Japan Today*, February 2004; *License!*, May 2005; *Comic Book Resources*, February 2002; *FSB Magazine*, June 2004]

This chapter's main focus is investments in securities. Many companies have investments, and many of these are in the form of debt and equity securities issued by other companies. We describe investments in these securities and how to account for them. An increasing number of companies also invest in international operations. We explain how to account for and report international transactions listed in foreign currencies.

Investments and International Operations

Basics of Investments
- Motivation for investments
- Short-term versus long-term
- Classification and reporting
- Accounting basics

Noninfluential Investments
- Trading securities
- Held-to-maturity securities
- Available-for-sale securities

Influential Investments
- Securities with significant influence
- Securities with controlling influence
- Accounting summary

Basics of Investments

C1 Distinguish between debt and equity securities and between short-term and long-term investments.

Point: Reporting securities at market value is referred to as *mark-to-market* accounting.

This section describes the motivation for investments, the distinction between short- and long-term investments, and the different classes of investments.

Motivation for Investments

Companies make investments for at least three reasons. First, companies transfer *excess cash* into investments to produce higher income. Second, some entities, such as mutual funds and pension funds, are set up to produce income from investments. Third, companies make investments for strategic reasons. Examples are investments in competitors, suppliers, and even customers.

Exhibit 15.1 shows short-term (S-T) and long-term (L-T) investments as a percent of total assets for several companies.

Exhibit 15.1

Investments of Selected Companies

Gap S-T 8% L-T 1%
Pfizer S-T 15% L-T 3%
Starbucks S-T 11% L-T 9%
Dell S-T 22% L-T 19%

0%   25%   50%
Percent of total assets

Short-Term versus Long-Term

Cash equivalents are investments that are both readily converted to known amounts of cash and mature within three months. Many investments, however, mature between 3 and 12 months. These investments are **short-term investments,** also called *temporary investments* and *marketable securities*. Specifically, short-term investments are securities that (1) management intends to convert to cash within one year or the operating cycle, whichever is longer, and (2) are readily convertible to cash. Short-term investments are reported under current assets and serve a purpose similar to cash equivalents.

Long-term investments in securities are defined as those securities that are not readily convertible to cash or are not intended to be converted into cash in the short term. Long-term investments can also include funds earmarked for a special purpose, such as bond sinking funds and investments in land or other assets not used in the company's operations. Long-term investments are reported in the noncurrent section of the balance sheet, often in its own separate line titled *Long-Term Investments*.

Investments in securities can include both debt and equity securities. *Debt securities* reflect a creditor relationship such as investments in notes, bonds, and certificates of deposit; they are

Topic Tackler

PLUS

issued by governments, companies, and individuals. *Equity securities* reflect an owner relationship such as shares of stock issued by companies.

Classification and Reporting

Accounting for investments in securities depends on three factors: (1) security type, either debt or equity, (2) the company's intent to hold the security either short term or long term, and (3) the company's (investor's) percent ownership in the other company's (investee's) equity securities. Exhibit 15.2 identifies five classes of securities using these three factors. It describes each of these five classes of securities and the reporting required under each class.

C2 Identify and describe the different classes of investments in securities.

Exhibit 15.2

Investments in Securities

ᵃ Holding less than 20% of voting stock (equity securities only).   ᵇ Holding 20% or more, but not more than 50%, of voting stock.
ᶜ Holding more than 50% of voting stock.
* Unrealized gains and losses reported on the income statement.
** Unrealized gains and losses reported in the equity section of the balance sheet and in comprehensive income.

Accounting Basics for <u>Debt Securities</u>

This section explains the accounting basics for debt securities, including that for acquisition, disposition, and any interest.

Acquisition.   Debt securities are recorded at cost when purchased. Assume that Music City paid $29,500 plus a $500 brokerage fee on September 1, 2008, to buy Dell's 7%, two-year bonds payable with a $30,000 par value. The bonds pay interest semiannually on August 31 and February 28. Music City intends to hold the bonds until they mature on August 31, 2010; consequently, they are classified as held-to-maturity (HTM) securities. The entry to record this purchase follows. (If the maturity of the securities was short term, and management's intent was to hold them until they mature, then they would be classified as Short-Term Investments—HTM.)

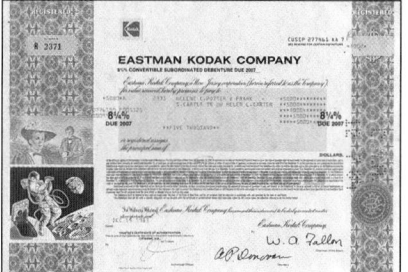

2008			
Sept. 1	Long-Term Investments—HTM (Dell)	30,000	
	Cash		30,000
	Purchased bonds to be held to maturity.		

Assets = Liabilities + Equity
+30,000
−30,000

Interest earned.   Interest revenue for investments in debt securities is recorded when earned. On December 31, 2008, at the end of its accounting period, Music City accrues interest receivable as follows.

Dec. 31	Interest Receivable.	700	
	Interest Revenue.		700
	Accrued interest earned ($30,000 × 7% × ¹⁄₁₂).		

Assets = Liabilities + Equity
+700   +700

The $700 reflects 4/6 of the semiannual cash receipt of interest—the portion Music City earned as of December 31. Relevant sections of Music City's financial statements at December 31, 2008, are shown in Exhibit 15.3.

Exhibit 15.3

Financial Statement Presentation
of Debt Securities

On the income statement for year 2008:	
Interest revenue	**$ 700**
On the December 31, 2008, balance sheet:	
Long-term investments—Held-to-maturity securities (at amortized cost)	**$30,000**

On February 28, 2009, Music City records receipt of semiannual interest.

Assets = Liabilities + Equity
+1,050   +350
 −700

Feb. 28	Cash	1,050	
	Interest Receivable		700
	Interest Revenue		350
	Received six months' interest on Dell bonds.		

Disposition. When the bonds mature, the proceeds (not including the interest entry) are
recorded as:

Assets = Liabilities + Equity
+30,000
−30,000

2010			
Aug. 31	Cash	30,000	
	Long-Term Investments—HTM (Dell)		30,000
	Received cash from matured bonds.		

Example: What is cost per share?
Answer: Cost per share is the total cost
of acquisition, including broker fees,
divided by number of shares acquired.

The cost of a debt security can be either higher or lower than its maturity value. When the
investment is long term, the difference between cost and maturity value is amortized over the
remaining life of the security. We assume for ease of computations that the cost of a long-term
debt security equals its maturity value.

Accounting Basics for Equity Securities

This section explains the accounting basics for equity securities, including that for acquisition,
dividends, and disposition.

Acquisition.   Equity securities are recorded at cost when acquired, including commissions or
brokerage fees paid. Assume that Music City purchases 1,000 shares of Intex common stock
at par value for $86,000 on October 10, 2008. It records this purchase of available-for-sale
(AFS) securities as follows.

Assets = Liabilities + Equity
+86,000
−86,000

Oct. 10	Long-Term Investments—AFS (Intex)	86,000	
	Cash		86,000
	Purchased 1,000 shares of Intex.		

Dividend earned.   Any cash dividends received are credited to Dividend Revenue and reported
in the income statement. On November 2, Music City receives a $1,720 quarterly cash divi-
dend on the Intex shares, which it records as:

Assets = Liabilities + Equity
+1,720   +1,720

Nov. 2	Cash	1,720	
	Dividend Revenue		1,720
	Received dividend of $1.72 per share.		

Disposition.   When the securities are sold, sale proceeds are compared with the cost, and any
gain or loss is recorded. On December 20, Music City sells 500 of the Intex shares for $45,000
cash and records this sale as:

Assets = Liabilities + Equity
+45,000   +2,000
−43,000

Dec. 20	Cash	45,000	
	Long-Term Investments—AFS (Intex)		43,000
	Gain on Sale of Long-Term Investments		2,000
	Sold 500 Intex shares ($86,000 × 500/1,000).		

Reporting of *Non*influential Investments

Companies must value and report most noninfluential investments at *fair market value,* or simply *market value.* The exact reporting requirements depend on whether the investments are classified as (1) trading, (2) held-to-maturity, or (3) available-for-sale.

P1 Account for trading securities.

Trading Securities

Trading securities are *debt and equity securities* that the company intends to actively manage and trade for profit. Frequent purchases and sales are expected and are made to earn profits on short-term price changes.

Point: Trading securities are *always* reported under current assets.

Valuing and reporting trading securities. The entire portfolio of trading securities is reported at its market value; this requires a "market adjustment" from the cost of the portfolio. The term *portfolio* refers to a group of securities. Any **unrealized gain (or loss)** from a change in the market value of the portfolio of trading securities is reported on the income statement. Most users believe accounting reports are more useful when changes in market value for trading securities are reported in income.

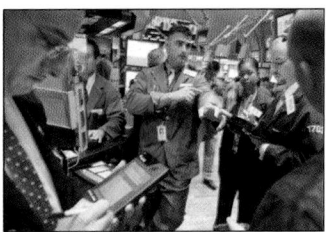

Point: The phrase *unrealized gain (or loss)* refers to a change in market value that is not yet realized through an actual sale.

To illustrate, TechCom's portfolio of trading securities had a total cost of $11,500 and a market value of $13,000 on December 31, 2008, the first year it held trading securities. The difference between the $11,500 cost and the $13,000 market value reflects a $1,500 gain. It is an unrealized gain because it is not yet confirmed by actual sales. The market adjustment for trading securities is recorded with an adjusting entry at the end of each period to equal the difference between the portfolio's cost and its market value. TechCom records this gain as follows.

Point: Market Adjustment—Trading is a *permanent account,* shown as a deduction or addition to Short-Term Investments—Trading.

Dec. 31	Market Adjustment—Trading.	1,500	
	Unrealized Gain—Income		1,500
	To reflect an unrealized gain in market values of trading securities.		

Assets = Liabilities + Equity
+1,500   +1,500

The Unrealized Gain (or Loss) is reported in the Other Revenues and Gains (or Expenses and Losses) section on the income statement. Unrealized Gain (or Loss)—Income is a *temporary* account that is closed to Income Summary at the end of each period. Market Adjustment—Trading is a *permanent* account, which adjusts the reported value of the trading securities portfolio from its prior period market value to the current period market value. The total cost of the trading securities portfolio is maintained in one account, and the market adjustment is recorded in a separate account. For example, TechCom's investment in trading securities is reported in the current assets section of its balance sheet as follows.

Example: If TechCom's trading securities have a cost of $14,800 and a market of $16,100 at Dec. 31, 2009, its adjusting entry is
Unrealized Loss—Income 200
  Market Adj.—Trading 200
This is computed as: $1,500 Beg. Dr. bal. + $200 Cr. = $1,300 End. Dr. bal.

Current Assets		
Short-term investments—Trading (at cost)	$11,500	
Market adjustment—Trading	1,500	
Short-term investments—Trading (at market)		$13,000
	or simply	
Short-term investments—Trading (at market; cost is $11,500)		$13,000

Selling trading securities. When individual trading securities are sold, the difference between the net proceeds (sale price less fees) and the cost of the individual trading securities that are sold is recognized as a gain or a loss. Any prior period market adjustment to the portfolio is *not* used to compute the gain or loss from sale of individual trading securities. For example, if TechCom sold some of its trading securities that had cost $1,000 for $1,200 cash on January 9, 2009, it would record the following.

Assets = Liabilities + Equity
+1,200   +200
−1,000

Jan. 9	Cash	1,200	
	Short-Term Investments—Trading		1,000
	Gain on Sale of Short-Term Investments.......		200
	Sold trading securities costing $1,000 for $1,200 cash.		

A gain is reported in the Other Revenues and Gains section on the income statement, whereas a loss is shown in Other Expenses and Losses. When the period-end market adjustment for the portfolio of trading securities is computed, it excludes the cost and market value of any securities sold.

Held-to-Maturity Securities

P2   Account for held-to-maturity securities.

Point: Only debt securities can be classified as *held-to-maturity*; equity securities have no maturity date.

Held-to-maturity (HTM) securities are *debt* securities a company intends and is able to hold until maturity. They are reported in current assets if their maturity dates are within one year or the operating cycle, whichever is longer. HTM securities are reported in long-term assets when the maturity dates extend beyond one year or the operating cycle, whichever is longer. All HTM securities are recorded at cost when purchased, and interest revenue is recorded when earned.

The portfolio of HTM securities is reported at (amortized) cost, which is explained in advanced courses. There is no market adjustment to the portfolio of HTM securities—neither to the short-term nor long-term portfolios. The basics of accounting for HTM securities were described earlier in this chapter.

Decision Maker   Answer—p. 602

Money Manager   You expect interest rates to sharply fall within a few weeks and remain at this lower rate. What is your strategy for holding investments in fixed-rate bonds and notes?

Available-for-Sale Securities

P3   Account for available-for-sale securities.

Available-for-sale (AFS) securities are *debt and equity securities* not classified as trading or held-to-maturity securities. AFS securities are purchased to yield interest, dividends, or increases in market value. They are not actively managed like trading securities. If the intent is to sell AFS securities within the longer of one year or operating cycle, they are classified as short-term investments. Otherwise, they are classified as long-term.

Valuing and reporting available-for-sale securities.   As with trading securities, companies adjust the cost of the portfolio of AFS securities to reflect changes in market value. This is done with a market adjustment to its total portfolio cost. However, any unrealized gain or loss for the portfolio of AFS securities is *not* reported on the income statement. Instead, it is reported in the equity section of the balance sheet (and is part of *comprehensive income,* explained later). To illustrate, assume that Music City had no prior period investments in available-for-sale securities other than those purchased in the current period. Exhibit 15.4 shows both the cost and market value of those investments on December 31, 2008, the end of its reporting period.

Example: If market value in Exhibit 15.4 is $70,000 (instead of $74,550), what entry is made? *Answer:*
Unreal. Loss—Equity ... 3,000
    Market Adj.—AFS 3,000

Exhibit 15.4

Cost and Market Value of Available-for-Sale Securities

	Cost	Market Value	Unrealized Gain (Loss)
Improv bonds	$30,000	$29,050	$ (950)
Intex common stock, 500 shares	43,000	45,500	2,500
Total	$73,000	$74,550	**$1,550**

The year-end adjusting entry to record the market value of these investments follows.

Assets = Liabilities + Equity
+1,550   +1,550

Dec. 31	Market Adjustment—Available-for-Sale (LT)	1,550	
	Unrealized Gain—Equity		1,550
	To record adjustment to market value of available-for-sale securities.		

Point: Unrealized Loss—Equity and Unrealized Gain—Equity are *permanent* (balance sheet) *accounts* reported in the equity section.

Exhibit 15.5 shows the December 31, 2008, balance sheet presentation—it assumes these investments are long term, but they can also be short term. It is also common to combine the cost of investments with the balance in the Market Adjustment account and report the net as a single amount.

Assets

Long-term investments—Available-for-sale (at cost)	$73,000	
Market adjustment— Available-for-sale	1,550	
Long-term investments—Available-for-sale (at market)		$74,550

or simply

Long-term investments—Available-for-sale (at market; cost is $73,000)	$74,550

Equity

... consists of usual equity accounts ...

Add unrealized gain on available-for-sale securities*	$ 1,550

Reconciled

Exhibit 15.5

Balance Sheet Presentation of Available-for-Sale Securities

* Often included under the caption Accumulated Other Comprehensive Income.

Let's extend this illustration and assume that at the end of its next calendar year (December 31, 2009), Music City's portfolio of long-term AFS securities has an $81,000 cost and an $82,000 market value. It records the adjustment to market value as follows.

Dec. 31	Unrealized Gain—Equity......................	550	
	Market Adjustment—Available-for-Sale (LT).		550
	To record adjustment to market value of available-for-sale securities.		

Point: Income can be window-dressed upward by selling AFS securities with unrealized gains; income is reduced by selling those with unrealized losses.

Assets = Liabilities + Equity
−550   −550

The effects of the 2008 and 2009 securities transactions are reflected in the following T-accounts.

Market Adjustment—Available-for-Sale (LT)			
Bal. 12/31/08	1,550	Adj. 12/31/09	550
Bal. 12/31/09	1,000		

Unrealized Gain—Equity			
Adj. 12/31/09	550	Bal. 12/31/08	1,550
		Bal. 12/31/09	1,000

Amounts reconcile.

Example: If cost is $83,000 and market is $82,000 at Dec. 31, 2009, it records the following adjustment:
Unreal. Gain—Equity . . . 1,550
Unreal. Loss—Equity . . . 1,000
    Mkt. Adj.—AFS   2,550

Selling available-for-sale securities.   Accounting for the sale of individual AFS securities is identical to that described for the sale of trading securities. When individual AFS securities are sold, the difference between the cost of the individual securities sold and the net proceeds (sale price less fees) is recognized as a gain or loss.

Point: Market Adjustment— Available-for-Sale is a permanent account, shown as a deduction or addition to the Investment account.

Quick Check   Answers—p. 602

1. How are short-term held-to-maturity securities reported (valued) on the balance sheet?
2. How are trading securities reported (valued) on the balance sheet?
3. Where are unrealized gains and losses on available-for-sale securities reported?
4. Where are unrealized gains and losses on trading securities reported?

Alert   The FASB released a 2006 Exposure Draft that would permit companies to use market value in reporting financial assets (referred to as the fair value option). This option would allow companies to report any financial asset at fair market value and recognize value changes in income. This method was previously reserved only for trading securities, but would now be an option for available-for-sale and held-to-maturity securities. It is unclear whether many companies will choose that option—stay tuned...

Reporting of Influential Investments

Investment in Securities with Significant Influence

A long-term investment classified as **equity securities with significant influence** implies that the investor can exert significant influence over the investee. An investor that owns 20% or more (but not more than 50%) of a company's voting stock is usually presumed to have

P4   Account for equity securities with significant influence.

a significant influence over the investee. In some cases, however, the 20% test of significant influence is overruled by other, more persuasive, evidence. This evidence can either lower the 20% requirement or increase it. The **equity method** of accounting and reporting is used for long-term investments in equity securities with significant influence, which is explained in this section.

Long-term investments in equity securities with significant influence are recorded at cost when acquired. To illustrate, Micron Co. records the purchase of 3,000 shares (30%) of Star Co. common stock at a total cost of $70,650 on January 1, 2008, as follows.

Assets = Liabilities + Equity
+70,650
−70,650

Jan. 1	Long-Term Investments—Star..................	70,650	
	Cash		70,650
	To record purchase of 3,000 Star shares.		

The investee's (Star) earnings increase both its net assets and the claim of the investor (Micron) on the investee's net assets. Thus, when the investee reports its earnings, the investor records its share of those earnings in its investment account. To illustrate, assume that Star reports net income of $20,000 for 2008. Micron then records its 30% share of those earnings as follows.

Assets = Liabilities + Equity
+6,000   +6,000

Dec. 31	Long-Term Investments—Star..................	6,000	
	Earnings from Long-Term Investment		6,000
	To record 30% equity in investee earnings.		

The debit reflects the increase in Micron's equity in Star. The credit reflects 30% of Star's net income. Earnings from Long-Term Investment is a *temporary* account (closed to Income Summary at each period-end) and is reported on the investor's (Micron's) income statement. If the investee incurs a net loss instead of a net income, the investor records its share of the loss and reduces (credits) its investment account. The investor closes this earnings or loss account to Income Summary.

The receipt of cash dividends is not revenue under the equity method because the investor has already recorded its share of the investee's earnings. Instead, cash dividends received by an investor from an investee are viewed as a conversion of one asset to another; that is, dividends reduce the balance of the investment account. To illustrate, Star declares and pays $10,000 in cash dividends on its common stock. Micron records its 30% share of these dividends received on January 9, 2009, as:

Point: Insider trading usually refers to officers and employees who buy or sell shares in their firm based on information unavailable to the public. Generally, insider trading is illegal in the U.S., but some countries permit it.

Assets = Liabilities + Equity
+3,000
−3,000

Jan. 9	Cash.....................................	3,000	
	Long-Term Investments—Star...............		3,000
	To record share of dividend paid by Star.		

The book value of an investment under the equity method equals the cost of the investment plus (minus) the investor's equity in the *undistributed* (*distributed*) earnings of the investee. Once Micron records these transactions, its Long-Term Investments account appears as in Exhibit 15.6.

Exhibit 15.6

Investment in Star Common Stock (Ledger Account)

Date	Explanation	Debit	Credit	Balance
2008				
Jan. 1	Investment acquisition	70,650		70,650
Dec. 31	Share of earnings	6,000		76,650
2009				
Jan. 9	Share of dividend		3,000	73,650

Point: Security prices are sometimes listed in fractions. For example, a debt security with a price of $22\frac{1}{4}$, is the same as $22.25.

Micron's account balance on January 9, 2009, for its investment in Star is $73,650. This is the investment's cost *plus* Micron's equity in Star's earnings since its purchase *less* Micron's equity in Star's cash dividends since its purchase. When an investment in equity securities is sold, the gain or loss is computed by comparing proceeds from the sale with the book value of the investment on the date of sale. If Micron sells its Star stock for $80,000 on January 10, 2009, it records the sale as:

Jan. 10	Cash	80,000		Assets = Liabilities + Equity
	Long-Term Investments—Star		73,650	+80,000 +6,350
	Gain on Sale of Investment		6,350	−73,650
	Sold 3,000 shares of stock for $80,000.			

Investment in Securities with Controlling Influence

A long-term investment classified as **equity securities with controlling influence** implies that the investor can exert a controlling influence over the investee. An investor who owns more than 50% of a company's voting stock has control over the investee. This investor can dominate all other shareholders in electing the corporation's board of directors and has control over the investee's management. In some cases, controlling influence can extend to situations of less than 50% ownership. Exhibit 15.7 summarizes the accounting for investments in equity securities based on an investor's ownership in the stock.

C3 Describe how to report equity securities with controlling influence.

Exhibit 15.7

Accounting for Equity Investments by Percent of Ownership

The *equity method with consolidation* is used to account for long-term investments in equity securities with controlling influence. The investor reports *consolidated financial statements* when owning such securities. The controlling investor is called the **parent,** and the investee is called the **subsidiary.** Many companies are parents with subsidiaries. Examples are (1) **McGraw-Hill,** the parent of *Business Week,* Standard & Poor's, and Compustat; (2) **Gap, Inc.,** the parent of Gap, Old Navy, and Banana Republic; and (3) **Brunswick,** the parent of Mercury Marine, Sea Ray, and U.S. Marine. A company owning all the outstanding stock of a subsidiary can, if it desires, take over the subsidiary's assets, retire the subsidiary's stock, and merge the subsidiary into the parent. However, there often are financial, legal, and tax advantages if a business operates as a parent controlling one or more subsidiaries. When a company operates as a parent with subsidiaries, each entity maintains separate accounting records. From a legal viewpoint, the parent and each subsidiary are separate entities with all rights, duties, and responsibilities of individual companies.

Consolidated financial statements show the financial position, results of operations, and cash flows of all entities under the parent's control, including all subsidiaries. These statements are prepared as if the business were organized as one entity. The parent uses the equity method in its accounts, but the investment account is *not* reported on the parent's financial statements. Instead, the individual assets and liabilities of the parent and its subsidiaries are combined on one balance sheet. Their revenues and expenses also are combined on one income statement, and their cash flows are combined on one statement of cash flows. The procedures for preparing consolidated financial statements are in advanced courses.

Accounting Summary for Investments in Securities

Exhibit 15.8 summarizes the accounting for investments in securities. Recall that many investment securities are classified as either short term or long term depending on management's intent and ability to convert them in the future. Understanding the accounting for these investments enables us to draw better conclusions from financial statements in making business decisions.

Comprehensive Income The term **comprehensive income** refers to all changes in equity for a period except those due to investments and distributions to owners. This means that it includes (1) the revenues, gains, expenses, and losses reported in net income *and* (2) the gains and losses that bypass net income but affect equity. An example of an item that bypasses net income is unrealized gains and losses on available-for-sale securities. These items make up *other*

Exhibit 15.8
Accounting for Investments in Securities

Classification	Accounting
Short-Term Investment in Securities	
Held-to-maturity (debt) securities	Cost (without any discount or premium amortization)
Trading (debt and equity) securities	Market value (with market adjustment to income)
Available-for-sale (debt and equity) securities	Market value (with market adjustment to equity)
Long-Term Investment in Securities	
Held-to-maturity (debt) securities	Cost (with any discount or premium amortization)
Available-for-sale (debt and equity) securities	Market value (with market adjustment to equity)
Equity securities with significant influence	Equity method
Equity securities with controlling influence	Equity method (with consolidation)

comprehensive income and are usually reported as a part of the statement of stockholders' equity. (Two other options are as a second separate income statement or as a combined income statement of comprehensive income; these less common options are described in advanced courses.) Most often this simply requires one additional column for Other Comprehensive Income in the usual columnar form of the statement of stockholders' equity (the details of this are left for advanced courses). The FASB encourages, but does *not* require, other comprehensive income items to be grouped under the caption *Accumulated Other Comprehensive Income* in the equity section of the balance sheet, which would include unrealized gains and losses on available-for-sale securities. For instructional benefits, we use actual account titles for these items in the equity section instead of this general, less precise caption.

Point: Many users believe that since AFS securities are not actively traded, reporting market value changes in income would unnecessarily increase income variability and decrease usefulness.

Quick Check
Answers—p. 602

5. Give at least two examples of assets classified as long-term investments.
6. What are the requirements for an equity security to be listed as a long-term investment?
7. Identify similarities and differences in accounting for long-term investments in debt securities that are held-to-maturity versus those available-for-sale.
8. What are the three possible classifications of long-term equity investments? Describe the criteria for each class and the method used to account for each.

Decision Analysis

Components of Return on Total Assets

A1 Compute and analyze the components of return on total assets.

A company's **return on total assets** (or simply *return on assets*) is important in assessing financial performance. The return on total assets can be separated into two components, profit margin and total asset turnover, for additional analyses. Exhibit 15.9 shows how these two components determine return on total assets.

Exhibit 15.9
Components of Return on Total Assets

$$\text{Return on total assets} = \text{Profit margin} \times \text{Total asset turnover}$$
$$\frac{\text{Net income}}{\text{Average total assets}} = \frac{\text{Net income}}{\text{Net sales}} \times \frac{\text{Net sales}}{\text{Average total assets}}$$

Profit margin reflects the percent of net income in each dollar of net sales. Total asset turnover reflects a company's ability to produce net sales from total assets. All companies desire a high return on total assets. By considering these two components, we can often discover strengths and weaknesses not revealed by return on total assets alone. This improves our ability to assess future performance and company strategy.

To illustrate, consider return on total assets and its components for **Gap Inc.** in Exhibit 15.10.

Fiscal Year	Return on Total Assets	=	Profit Margin	×	Total Asset Turnover
2005	11.1%	=	7.1%	×	1.57
2004	9.8%	=	6.5%	×	1.51
2003	5.2%	=	3.3%	×	1.57

Exhibit 15.10

Gap's Components of Return on Total Assets

At least three findings emerge. First, Gap's return on total assets steadily improved from 2003 through 2005. Second, total asset turnover has remained steady at 1.5 to 1.6. Third, Gap's profit margin sharply rose between 2003 and 2005. These components reveal the dual role of profit margin and total asset turnover in determining return on total assets. They also reveal that the driver of Gap's rebound is not total asset turnover but profit margin.

Generally, if a company is to maintain or improve its return on total assets, it must meet any decline in either profit margin or total asset turnover with an increase in the other. If not, return on assets will decline. Companies consider these components in planning strategies. A component analysis can also reveal where a company is weak and where changes are needed, especially in a competitor analysis. If asset turnover is lower than the industry norm, for instance, a company should focus on raising asset turnover at least to the norm. The same applies to profit margin.

Decision Maker

Answer—p. 602

Retailer You are an entrepreneur and owner of a retail sporting goods store. The store's recent annual performance reveals (industry norms in parentheses): return on total assets = 11% (11.2%); profit margin = 4.4% (3.5%); and total asset turnover = 2.5 (3.2). What does your analysis of these figures reveal?

Demonstration Problem—1

Garden Company completes the following selected transactions related to its short-term investments during 2008.

May 8   Purchased 300 shares of FedEx stock as a short-term investment in available-for-sale securities at $40 per share plus $975 in broker fees.
Sept. 2   Sold 100 shares of its investment in FedEx stock at $47 per share and held the remaining 200 shares; broker's commission was $225.
Oct. 2   Purchased 400 shares of Ajay stock for $60 per share plus $1,600 in commissions. The stock is held as a short-term investment in available-for-sale securities.

Required

1. Prepare journal entries for the above transactions of Garden Company for 2008.
2. Prepare an adjusting journal entry as of December 31, 2008, if the market prices of the equity securities held by Garden Company are $48 per share for FedEx and $55 per share for Ajay. (Year 2008 is the first year Garden Company acquired short-term investments.)

Solution to Demonstration Problem—1

1.

May 8	Short-Term Investments—AFS (FedEx)	12,975	
	Cash		12,975
	Purchased 300 shares of FedEx stock		
	(300 × $40) + $975.		

[continued on next page]

[continued from previous page]

Sept. 2	Cash	4,475	
	Gain on Sale of Short-Term Investment		150
	Short-Term Investments—AFS (FedEx)		4,325
	Sold 100 shares of FedEx for $47 per share less		
	a $225 commission. The original cost is		
	($12,975 × 100/300).		
Oct. 2	Short-Term Investments—AFS (Ajay)............	25,600	
	Cash		25,600
	Purchased 400 shares of Ajay for $60 per share		
	plus $1,600 in commissions.		

2. Computation of unrealized gain or loss follows.

Short-Term Investments in Available-for-Sale Securities	Shares	Cost per Share	Total Cost	Market Value per Share	Total Market Value	Unrealized Gain (Loss)
FedEx	200	$43.25	$ 8,650	$48.00	$ 9,600	
Ajay	400	64.00	25,600	55.00	22,000	
Totals			$34,250		$31,600	$(2,650)

The adjusting entry follows.

Dec. 31	Unrealized Loss—Equity......................	2,650	
	Market Adjustment—Available-for-Sale (ST)		2,650
	To reflect an unrealized loss in market values		
	of available-for-sale securities.		

Demonstration Problem—2

The following transactions relate to Brown Company's long-term investments during 2008 and 2009. Brown did not own any long-term investments prior to 2008. Show (1) the appropriate journal entries and (2) the relevant portions of each year's balance sheet and income statement that reflect these transactions for both 2008 and 2009.

2008

Sept. 9 Purchased 1,000 shares of Packard, Inc., common stock for $80,000 cash. These shares represent 30% of Packard's outstanding shares.

Oct. 2 Purchased 2,000 shares of AT&T common stock for $60,000 cash. These shares represent less than a 1% ownership in AT&T.

17 Purchased as a long-term investment 1,000 shares of Apple Computer common stock for $40,000 cash. These shares are less than 1% of Apple's outstanding shares.

Nov. 1 Received $5,000 cash dividend from Packard.

30 Received $3,000 cash dividend from AT&T.

Dec. 15 Received $1,400 cash dividend from Apple.

31 Packard's net income for this year is $70,000.

31 Market values for the investments in equity securities are Packard, $84,000; AT&T, $48,000; and Apple Computer, $45,000.

31 For preparing financial statements, note the following post-closing account balances: Common Stock, $500,000, and Retained Earnings, $350,000.

2009

Jan. 1 Sold Packard, Inc., shares for $108,000 cash.

May 30 Received $3,100 cash dividend from AT&T.

June 15 Received $1,600 cash dividend from Apple.

Aug. 17   Sold the AT&T stock for $52,000 cash.
    19   Purchased 2,000 shares of Coca-Cola common stock for $50,000 cash as a long-term investment. The stock represents less than a 5% ownership in Coca-Cola.
Dec. 15   Received $1,800 cash dividend from Apple.
    31   Market values of the investments in equity securities are Apple, $39,000, and Coca-Cola, $48,000.
    31   For preparing financial statements, note the following post-closing account balances: Common Stock, $500,000, and Retained Earnings, $410,000.

Planning the Solution

- Account for the investment in Packard under the equity method.
- Account for the investments in AT&T, Apple, and Coca-Cola as long-term investments in available-for-sale securities.
- Prepare the information for the two years' balance sheets by including the appropriate asset and equity accounts.

Solution to Demonstration Problem—2

1. Journal entries for 2008.

Sept. 9	Long-Term Investments—Packard	80,000	
	Cash		80,000
	Acquired 1,000 shares, representing a 30% equity in Packard.		
Oct. 2	Long-Term Investments—AFS (AT&T)	60,000	
	Cash		60,000
	Acquired 2,000 shares as a long-term investment in available-for-sale securities.		
Oct. 17	Long-Term Investments—AFS (Apple)	40,000	
	Cash		40,000
	Acquired 1,000 shares as a long-term investment in available-for-sale securities.		
Nov. 1	Cash	5,000	
	Long-Term Investments—Packard.		5,000
	Received dividend from Packard.		
Nov. 30	Cash	3,000	
	Dividend Revenue		3,000
	Received dividend from AT&T.		
Dec. 15	Cash	1,400	
	Dividend Revenue		1,400
	Received dividend from Apple.		
Dec. 31	Long-Term Investments—Packard	21,000	
	Earnings from Investment (Packard)		21,000
	To record 30% share of Packard's annual earnings of $70,000.		
Dec. 31	Unrealized Loss—Equity.	7,000	
	Market Adjustment—Available-for-Sale (LT)*		7,000
	To record change in market value of long-term available-for-sale securities.		

* Market adjustment computations:

	Cost	Market Value	Unrealized Gain (Loss)
AT&T	$ 60,000	$48,000	$(12,000)
Apple	40,000	45,000	5,000
Total	$100,000	$93,000	$ (7,000)

Required balance of the Market Adjustment—Available-for-Sale
(LT) account (credit) . . . . $(7,000)
Existing balance 0
Necessary adjustment (credit) . . . . . $(7,000)

2. The December 31, 2008, selected balance sheet items appear as follows.

Assets	
Long-term investments	
Available-for-sale securities (at market; cost is $100,000)	$ 93,000
Investment in equity securities	96,000
Total long-term investments	189,000
Stockholders' Equity	
Common stock	500,000
Retained earnings	350,000
Unrealized loss—Equity	(7,000)

The relevant income statement items for the year ended December 31, 2008, follow.

Dividend revenue	$ 4,400
Earnings from investment	21,000

1. Journal entries for 2009.

Jan. 1	Cash	108,000	
	Long-Term Investments—Packard.		96,000
	Gain on Sale of Long-Term Investments		12,000
	Sold 1,000 shares for cash.		
May 30	Cash	3,100	
	Dividend Revenue		3,100
	Received dividend from AT&T.		
June 15	Cash	1,600	
	Dividend Revenue		1,600
	Received dividend from Apple.		
Aug. 17	Cash	52,000	
	Loss on Sale of Long-Term Investments	8,000	
	Long-Term Investments—AFS (AT&T).		60,000
	Sold 2,000 shares for cash.		
Aug. 19	Long-Term Investments—AFS (Coca-Cola)	50,000	
	Cash		50,000
	Acquired 2,000 shares as a long-term		
	investment in available-for-sale securities.		
Dec. 15	Cash	1,800	
	Dividend Revenue		1,800
	Received dividend from Apple.		
Dec. 31	Market Adjustment—Available-for-Sale (LT)*.	4,000	
	Unrealized Loss—Equity		4,000
	To record change in market value of long-term		
	available-for-sale securities.		

* Market adjustment computations:

	Cost	Market Value	Unrealized Gain (Loss)
Apple	$40,000	$39,000	$(1,000)
Coca-Cola	50,000	48,000	(2,000)
Total	$90,000	$87,000	$(3,000)

Required balance of the Market Adjustment—Available-for-Sale (LT) account (credit)	$(3,000)
Existing balance (credit)	(7,000)
Necessary adjustment (debit)	$ 4,000

2. The December 31, 2009, balance sheet items appear as follows.

Assets	
Long-term investments	
Available-for-sale securities (at market; cost is $90,000)	$ 87,000
Stockholders' Equity	
Common stock	500,000
Retained earnings	410,000
Unrealized loss—Equity	(3,000)

The relevant income statement items for the year ended December 31, 2009, follow.

Dividend revenue	$ 6,500
Gain on sale of long-term investments	12,000
Loss on sale of long-term investments	(8,000)

APPENDIX

Investments in International Operations

15A

Many entities from small entrepreneurs to large corporations conduct business internationally. Some entities' operations occur in so many different countries that the companies are called **multinationals.** Many of us think of **Coca-Cola** and **McDonald's**, for example, as primarily U.S. companies, but most of their sales occur outside the United States. Exhibit 15A.1 shows the percent of international sales and income for selected U.S. companies. Managing and accounting for multinationals present challenges. This section describes some of these challenges and how to account for and report these activities.

Two major accounting challenges that arise when companies have international operations relate to transactions that involve more than one currency. The first is to account for sales and purchases listed in a foreign currency. The second is to prepare consolidated financial statements with international subsidiaries. For ease in this discussion, we use companies with a U.S. base of operations and assume the need to prepare financial statements in U.S. dollars. This means the *reporting currency* of these companies is the U.S. dollar.

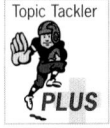

Exhibit 15A.1

International Sales and Income as a Percent of Their Totals

Topic Tackler

PLUS

15-2

Point: Transactions *listed* or *stated* in a foreign currency are said to be *denominated* in that currency.

Exchange Rates between Currencies

Markets for the purchase and sale of foreign currencies exist all over the world. In these markets, U.S. dollars can be exchanged for Canadian dollars, British pounds, Japanese yen, Euros, or any other legal currencies. The price of one currency stated in terms of another currency is called a **foreign exchange rate.** Exhibit 15A.2 lists recent exchange rates for selected currencies. The exchange rate for British pounds and U.S. dollars is $1.8054, meaning 1 British pound could be purchased for $1.8054. On that same day, the exchange rate between Mexican pesos and U.S. dollars is $0.0925, or 1 Mexican peso can be purchased for

C4 Explain foreign exchange rates between currencies.

Decision Insight

Rush to Russia Investors are still eager to buy Russian equities even in the face of rampant crime, corruption, and slow economic growth. Why? Many argue Russia remains a bargain-priced, if risky, bet on future growth. Some analysts argue that natural-resource-rich Russia is one of the least expensive emerging markets.

Exhibit 15A.2

Foreign Exchange Rates for
Selected Currencies*

Source (unit)	Price in $U.S.	Source (unit)	Price in $U.S.
Britain (pound)	$1.8054	Canada (dollar)	$0.8439
Mexico (peso)	0.0925	Japan (yen)	0.0090
Taiwan (dollar)	0.0305	Europe (Euro)	1.2219

* Rates will vary over time based on economic, political, and other changes.

Point: For currency conversion, see XE.com

$0.0925. Exchange rates fluctuate due to changing economic and political conditions, including the supply and demand for currencies and expectations about future events.

Sales and Purchases Listed in a Foreign Currency

P5 Record transactions listed in a foreign currency.

When a U.S. company makes a credit sale to an international customer, accounting for the sale and the account receivable is straightforward if sales terms require the international customer's payment in U.S. dollars. If sale terms require (or allow) payment in a foreign currency, however, the U.S. company must account for the sale and the account receivable in a different manner.

> **Decision Insight**
>
> **Global Greenback** What do changes in foreign exchange rates mean? A decline in the price of the U.S. dollar against other currencies usually yields increased international sales for U.S. companies, without hiking prices or cutting costs, and puts them on a stronger competitive footing abroad. At home, they can raise prices without fear that foreign rivals will undercut them.

To illustrate, consider the case of the U.S.-based manufacturer Boston Company, which makes credit sales to London Outfitters, a British retail company. A sale occurs on December 12, 2008, for a price of £10,000 with payment due on February 10, 2009. Boston Company keeps its accounting records in U.S. dollars. To record the sale, Boston Company must translate the sales price from pounds to dollars. This is done using the exchange rate on the date of the sale. Assuming the exchange rate on December 12, 2008, is $1.80, Boston records this sale as follows.

Assets = Liabilities + Equity
+18,000   +18,000

Dec. 12	Accounts Receivable—London Outfitters	18,000	
	Sales*		18,000
	*To record a sale at £10,000, when the exchange rate equals $1.80. * (£10,000 × $1.80)*		

When Boston Company prepares its annual financial statements on December 31, 2008, the current exchange rate is $1.84. Thus, the current dollar value of Boston Company's receivable is $18,400 (10,000 × $1.84). This amount is $400 higher than the amount recorded on December 12. Accounting principles require a receivable to be reported in the balance sheet at its current dollar value. Thus, Boston Company must make the following entry to record the increase in the dollar value of this receivable at year-end.

Assets = Liabilities + Equity
+400   +400

Dec. 31	Accounts Receivable—London Outfitters	400	
	Foreign Exchange Gain		400
	To record the increased value of the British pound for the receivable.		

Point: Foreign exchange gains are credits, and foreign exchange losses are debits.

On February 10, 2009, Boston Company receives London Outfitters' payment of £10,000. It immediately exchanges the pounds for U.S. dollars. On this date, the exchange rate for pounds is $1.78. Thus, Boston Company receives only $17,800 (£10,000 × $1.78). It records the cash receipt and the loss associated with the decline in the exchange rate as follows.

Assets = Liabilities + Equity
+17,800   −600
−18,400

Feb. 10	Cash.....................................	17,800	
	Foreign Exchange Loss	600	
	Accounts Receivable—London Outfitters......		18,400
	Received foreign currency payment of an account and converted it into dollars.		

Gains and losses from foreign exchange transactions are accumulated in the Foreign Exchange Gain (or Loss) account. After year-end adjustments, the balance in the Foreign Exchange Gain (or Loss) account is reported on the income statement and closed to the Income Summary account.

Accounting for credit purchases from an international seller is similar to the case of a credit sale to an international customer. In particular, if the U.S. company is required to make payment in a foreign currency, the account payable must be translated into dollars before the U.S. company can record it. If the exchange rate is different when preparing financial statements and when paying for the purchase, the U.S. company must recognize a foreign exchange gain or loss at those dates. To illustrate, assume NC Imports, a U.S. company, purchases products costing €20,000 (euros) from Hamburg Brewing on January 15, when the exchange rate is $1.20 per euro. NC records this transaction as follows.

Example: Assume that a U.S. company makes a credit purchase from a British company for £10,000 when the exchange rate is $1.62. At the balance sheet date, this rate is $1.72. Does this imply a gain or loss for the U.S. company? *Answer:* A loss.

Jan. 15	Inventory.	24,000		Assets = Liabilities + Equity
	Accounts Payable—Hamburg Brewing.		24,000	+24,000 +24,000
	To record a €20,000 purchase when exchange rate is $1.20 (€20,000 × $1.20)			

NC Imports makes payment in full on February 14 when the exchange rate is $1.25 per euro, which is recorded as follows.

Feb. 14	Accounts Payable—Hamburg Brewing	24,000		Assets = Liabilities + Equity
	Foreign Exchange Loss	1,000		−25,000 −24,000 −1,000
	Cash		25,000	
	To record cash payment towards €20,000 account when exchange rate is $1.25 (€20.000 × $1.25).			

Consolidated Statements with International Subsidiaries

A second challenge in accounting for international operations involves preparing consolidated financial statements when the parent company has one or more international subsidiaries. Consider a U.S.-based company that owns a controlling interest in a French subsidiary. The reporting currency of the U.S. parent is the dollar. The French subsidiary maintains its financial records in euros. Before preparing consolidated statements, the parent must translate financial statements of the French company into U.S. dollars. After this translation is complete (including that for accounting differences), it prepares consolidated statements the same as for domestic subsidiaries. Procedures for translating an international subsidiary's account balances depend on the nature of the subsidiary's operations. The process requires the parent company to select appropriate foreign exchange rates and to apply those rates to the foreign subsidiary's account balances. This is described in advanced courses.

Global: A weaker U.S. dollar often increases global sales for U.S. companies.

Decision Maker   Answer—p. 602

Entrepreneur   You are a U.S. home builder that purchases lumber from mills in both the U.S. and Canada. The price of the Canadian dollar in terms of the U.S. dollar jumps from US$0.70 to US$0.80. Are you now more or less likely to buy lumber from Canadian or U.S. mills?

Summary

C1   Distinguish between debt and equity securities and between short-term and long-term investments. *Debt securities* reflect a creditor relationship and include investments in notes, bonds, and certificates of deposit. *Equity securities* reflect an owner relationship and include shares of stock issued by other companies. Short-term investments in securities are current assets that meet two criteria: (1) They are expected to be converted into cash within one year or the current operating cycle of the business, whichever is longer and (2) they are readily convertible to cash, or *marketable*. All other investments in securities are long-term. Long-term investments also include assets not used in operations and those held for special purposes, such as land for expansion.

C2   Identify and describe the different classes of investments in securities. Investments in securities are classified into

one of five groups: (1) trading securities, which are always short-term, (2) debt securities held-to-maturity, (3) debt and equity securities available-for-sale, (4) equity securities in which an investor has a significant influence over the investee, and (5) equity securities in which an investor has a controlling influence over the investee.

C3   Describe how to report equity securities with controlling influence. If an investor owns more than 50% of another company's voting stock and controls the investee, the investor's financial reports are prepared on a consolidated basis. These reports are prepared as if the company were organized as one entity.

C4^A   Explain foreign exchange rates between currencies. A foreign exchange rate is the price of one currency stated in terms of another. An entity with transactions in a foreign currency when the exchange rate changes between the transaction dates and their settlement will experience exchange gains or losses.

A1 **Compute and analyze the components of return on total assets.** Return on total assets has two components: profit margin and total asset turnover. A decline in one component must be met with an increase in another if return on assets is to be maintained. Component analysis is helpful in assessing company performance compared to that of competitors and its own past.

P1 **Account for trading securities.** Investments are initially recorded at cost, and any dividend or interest from these investments is recorded in the income statement. Investments classified as trading securities are reported at market value. Unrealized gains and losses on trading securities are reported in income. When investments are sold, the difference between the net proceeds from the sale and the cost of the securities is recognized as a gain or loss.

P2 **Account for held-to-maturity securities.** Debt securities held-to-maturity are reported at cost when purchased. Interest revenue is recorded as it accrues. The cost of long-term held-to-maturity securities is adjusted for the amortization of any difference between cost and maturity value.

P3 **Account for available-for-sale securities.** Debt and equity securities available-for-sale are recorded at cost when pur-

chased. Available-for-sale securities are reported at their market values on the balance sheet with unrealized gains or losses shown in the equity section. Gains and losses realized on the sale of these investments are reported in the income statement.

P4 **Account for equity securities with significant influence.** The equity method is used when an investor has a significant influence over an investee. This usually exists when an investor owns 20% or more of the investee's voting stock but not more than 50%. The equity method means an investor records its share of investee earnings with a debit to the investment account and a credit to a revenue account. Dividends received reduce the investment account balance.

P5^A **Record transactions listed in a foreign currency.** When a company makes a credit sale to a foreign customer and sales terms call for payment in a foreign currency, the company must translate the foreign currency into dollars to record the receivable. If the exchange rate changes before payment is received, exchange gains or losses are recognized in the year they occur. The same treatment is used when a company makes a credit purchase from a foreign supplier and is required to make payment in a foreign currency.

Guidance Answers to **Decision Maker**

Money Manager   If you have investments in fixed-rate bonds and notes when interest rates fall, the value of your investments increases. This is so because the bonds and notes you hold continue to pay the same (high) rate while the market is demanding a new lower interest rate. Your strategy is to continue holding your investments in bonds and notes, and, potentially, to increase these holdings through additional purchases.

Retailer   Your store's return on assets is 11%, which is similar to the industry norm of 11.2%. However, disaggregation of return on assets reveals that your store's profit margin of 4.4% is much higher than the norm of 3.5%, but your total asset turnover of 2.5 is much lower than the norm of 3.2. These results suggest that, as compared with competitors, you are less efficient in using assets. You need to focus on increasing sales or reducing as-

sets. You might consider reducing prices to increase sales, provided such a strategy does not reduce your return on assets. For instance, you could reduce your profit margin to 4% to increase sales. If total asset turnover increases to more than 2.75 when profit margin is lowered to 4%, your overall return on assets is improved.

Entrepreneur   You are now less likely to buy Canadian lumber because it takes more U.S. money to buy a Canadian dollar (and lumber). For instance, the purchase of lumber from a Canadian mill with a $1,000 (Canadian dollars) price would have cost the U.S. builder $700 (U.S. dollars, computed as C$1,000 × US$0.70) before the rate change, and $800 (US dollars, computed as C$1,000 × US$0.80) after the rate change.

Guidance Answers to **Quick Checks**

1. Short-term held-to-maturity securities are reported at cost.

2. Trading securities are reported at market value.

3. The equity section of the balance sheet (and in comprehensive income).

4. The income statement.

5. Long-term investments include (1) long-term funds earmarked for a special purpose, (2) debt and equity securities that do not meet current asset requirements, and (3) long-term assets not used in the regular operations of the business.

6. An equity investment is classified as long term if it is not marketable or, if marketable, it is not held as an available source of cash to meet the needs of current operations.

7. Debt securities held-to-maturity and debt securities available-for-sale are both recorded at cost. Also, interest on both is accrued as earned. However, only long-term securities held-to-maturity require amortization of the difference between cost and maturity value. In addition, only securities available-for-sale require a period-end adjustment to market value.

8. Long-term equity investments are placed in one of three categories and accounted for as follows: (a) **available-for-sale** (noninfluential, less than 20% of outstanding stock)—market value; (b) **significant influence** (20% to 50% of outstanding stock)—equity method; and (c) **controlling influence** (holding more than 50% of outstanding stock)—equity method with consolidation.

Key Terms   mhhe.com/wildFAP18e

Key Terms are available at the book's Website for learning and testing in an online Flashcard Format.

Available-for-sale (AFS) securities (p. 590)

Comprehensive income (p. 593)

Consolidated financial statements (p. 593)

Equity method (p. 592)

Equity securities with controlling influence (p. 593)

Equity securities with significant influence (p. 591)

Foreign exchange rate (p. 599)

Held-to-maturity (HTM) securities (p. 590)

Long-term investments (p. 586)

Multinational (p. 599)

Parent (p. 593)

Return on total assets (p. 594)

Short-term investments (p. 586)

Subsidiary (p. 593)

Trading securities (p. 589)

Unrealized gain (loss) (p. 589)

Multiple Choice Quiz   Answers on p. 619   mhhe.com/wildFAP18e

Multiple Choice Quizzes A and B are available at the book's Website.

1. A company purchased $30,000 of 5% bonds for investment purposes on May 1. The bonds pay interest on February 1 and August 1. The amount of interest revenue accrued at December 31 (the company's year-end) is:
   a. $1,500
   b. $1,375
   c. $1,000
   d. $625
   e. $300

2. Earlier this period, Amadeus Co. purchased its only available-for-sale investment in the stock of Bach Co. for $83,000. The period-end market value of this stock is $84,500. Amadeus records a:
   a. Credit to Unrealized Gain—Equity for $1,500
   b. Debit to Unrealized Loss—Equity for $1,500
   c. Debit to Investment Revenue for $1,500
   d. Credit to Market Adjustment—Available-for-Sale for $3,500
   e. Credit to Cash for $1,500

3. Mozart Co. owns 35% of Melody Inc. Melody pays $50,000 in cash dividends to its shareholders for the period. Mozart's entry to record the Melody dividend includes a:
   a. Credit to Investment Revenue for $50,000.
   b. Credit to Long-Term Investments for $17,500.
   c. Credit to Cash for $17,500.

   d. Debit to Long-Term Investments for $17,500.
   e. Debit to Cash for $50,000.

4. A company has net income of $300,000, net sales of $2,500,000, and total assets of $2,000,000. Its return on total assets equals:
   a. 6.7%
   b. 12.0%
   c. 8.3%
   d. 80.0%
   e. 15.0%

5. A company had net income of $80,000, net sales of $600,000, and total assets of $400,000. Its profit margin and total asset turnover are:

	Profit Margin	Total Asset Turnover
a.	1.5%	13.3
b.	13.3%	1.5
c.	13.3%	0.7
d.	7.0%	13.3
e.	10.0%	26.7

Superscript ᴬ denotes assignments based on Appendix 15A.

Discussion Questions

1. Under what two conditions should investments be classified as current assets?

2. On a balance sheet, what valuation must be reported for short-term investments in trading securities?

3. If a short-term investment in available-for-sale securities costs $6,780 and is sold for $7,500, how should the difference between these two amounts be recorded?

4. Identify the three classes of noninfluential and two classes of influential investments in securities.

5. Under what conditions should investments be classified as current assets? As long-term assets?

6. If a company purchases its only long-term investments in available-for-sale debt securities this period and their market value is below cost at the balance sheet date, what entry is required to recognize this unrealized loss?

7. On a balance sheet, what valuation must be reported for debt securities classified as available-for-sale?

8. Under what circumstances are long-term investments in debt securities reported at cost and adjusted for amortization of any difference between cost and maturity value?

9. For investments in available-for-sale securities, how are unrealized (holding) gains and losses reported?

10. In accounting for investments in equity securities, when should the equity method be used?

11. Under what circumstances does a company prepare consolidated financial statements?

12.^A What are two major challenges in accounting for international operations?

13.^A Assume a U.S. company makes a credit sale to a foreign customer that is required to make payment in its foreign currency. In the current period, the exchange rate is $1.40 on

the date of the sale and is $1.30 on the date the customer pays the receivable. Will the U.S. company record an exchange gain or loss?

14.^A If a U.S. company makes a credit sale to a foreign customer required to make payment in U.S. dollars, can the U.S. company have an exchange gain or loss on this sale?

15. Refer to **Best Buy**'s statement of changes in stockholders' equity in Appendix A. What is the amount of foreign currency translation adjustment for the year ended February 26, 2005? Is this adjustment an unrealized gain or an unrealized loss?

16. Refer to the balance sheet of **Circuit City** in Appendix A. How can you tell that Circuit City uses the consolidated method of accounting?

17. Refer to the financial statements of **Apple** in Appendix A. Compute its return on total assets for the year ended September 25, 2004.

 Red numbers denote Discussion Questions that involve decision-making.

QUICK STUDY

QS 15-1

Short-term equity investments C2 P1

On April 18, Riley Co. made a short-term investment in 300 common shares of XLT Co. The purchase price is $42 per share and the broker's fee is $250. The intent is to actively manage these shares for profit. On May 30, Riley Co. receives $1 per share from XLT in dividends. Prepare the April 18 and May 30 journal entries to record these transactions.

QS 15-2

Available-for-sale securities

C2 P3

Journ Co. purchased short-term investments in available-for-sale securities at a cost of $50,000 on November 25, 2008. At December 31, 2008, these securities had a market value of $47,000. This is the first and only time the company has purchased such securities.

1. Prepare the December 31, 2008, year-end adjusting entry for the securities' portfolio.

2. For each account in the entry for part 1, explain how it is reported in financial statements.

3. Prepare the April 6, 2009, entry when Journ sells one-half of these securities for $26,000.

QS 15-3

Available-for-sale securities

C2 P3

Prepare Hertog Company's journal entries to reflect the following transactions for the current year.

May 7	Purchases 200 shares of Kraft stock as a short-term investment in available-for-sale securities at a cost of $50 per share plus $300 in broker fees.
June 6	Sells 200 shares of its investment in Kraft stock at $56 per share. The broker's commission on this sale is $150.

QS 15-4

Available-for-sale securities

C2 P3

Hiker Company completes the following transactions during the current year.

May 9	Purchases 200 shares of Higo stock as a short-term investment in available-for-sale securities at a cost of $25 per share plus $150 in broker fees.
June 2	Sells 100 shares of its investment in Higo stock at $28 per share. The broker's commission on this sale is $90.
Dec. 31	The closing market price of the Higo stock is $23 per share.

Prepare the May 9 and June 2 journal entries and the December 31 adjusting entry. This is the first and only time the company purchased such securities.

QS 15-5

Identifying long-term investments

C1

Which of the following statements are true of long-term investments?

a. They are held as an investment of cash available for current operations.

b. They can include funds earmarked for a special purpose, such as bond sinking funds.

c. They can include investments in trading securities.

d. They can include debt securities held-to-maturity.

e. They are always easily sold and therefore qualify as being marketable.

f. They can include debt and equity securities available-for-sale.

g. They can include bonds and stocks not intended to serve as a ready source of cash.

Complete the following descriptions by filling in the blanks.

1. Accrual of interest on bonds held as long-term investments requires a credit to ____ ____.

2. Equity securities giving an investor significant influence are accounted for using the ____ ____.

3. Available-for-sale debt securities are reported on the balance sheet at ____ ____.

4. Trading securities are classified as ____ assets.

5. The controlling investor (more than 50% ownership) is called the ____, and the investee company is called the ____.

QS 15-6
Describing investments in securities

C1   C2   C3

On February 1, 2008, Garzon purchased 6% bonds issued by PBS Utilities at a cost of $40,000, which is their par value. The bonds pay interest semiannually on July 31 and January 31. For 2008, prepare entries to record Garzon's July 31 receipt of interest and its December 31 year-end interest accrual.

QS 15-7
Debt securities transactions

C2   P2

On May 20, 2008, Montero Co. paid $1,000,000 to acquire 25,000 common shares (10%) of ORD Corp. as a long-term investment. On August 5, 2009, Montero sold one-half of these shares for $625,000. What valuation method should be used to account for this stock investment? Prepare entries to record both the acquisition and the sale of these shares.

QS 15-8
Recording equity securities

C2   P3

Assume the same facts as in QS 15-8 except that the stock acquired represents 40% of ORD Corp.'s outstanding stock. Also assume that ORD Corp. paid a $100,000 dividend on November 1, 2008, and reported a net income of $700,000 for 2008. Prepare the entries to record (a) the receipt of the dividend and (b) the December 31, 2008, year-end adjustment required for the investment account.

QS 15-9
Equity method transactions

C2   P4

During the current year, Reed Consulting Group acquired long-term available-for-sale securities at a $70,000 cost. At its December 31 year-end, these securities had a market value of $58,000. This is the first and only time the company purchased such securities.

1. Prepare the necessary year-end adjusting entry related to these securities.

2. Explain how each account used in part 1 is reported in the financial statements.

QS 15-10
Recording market adjustment for securities

P3

How is the return on total assets computed? What does this important ratio reflect?

QS 15-11
Return on total assets   A1

Write the formula to separate the return on total assets into its two basic components. Explain how these components of the return on total assets are helpful to financial statement users for business decisions.

QS 15-12
Component return on total assets   A1

A U.S. company sells a product to a British company with the transaction listed in British pounds. On the date of the sale, the transaction total of $14,500 is billed as £10,000, reflecting an exchange rate of 1.45 (that is, $1.45 per pound). Prepare the entry to record (1) the sale and (2) the receipt of payment in pounds when the exchange rate is 1.35.

QS 15-13^A
Foreign currency transactions

P5

On March 1, 2008, a U.S. company made a credit sale requiring payment in 30 days from a Malaysian company, Hamac Sdn. Bhd., in 20,000 Malaysian ringgits. Assuming the exchange rate between Malaysian ringgits and U.S. dollars is $0.4538 on March 1 and $0.4899 on March 31, prepare the entries to record the sale on March 1 and the cash receipt on March 31.

QS 15-14^A
Foreign currency transactions

P5

EXERCISES

Exercise 15-1
Accounting for transactions in short-term securities

C2 P1 P2 P3

Check (c) Dr. Cash $122,400

(f) Dr. Cash $11,760

Prepare journal entries to record the following transactions involving the short-term securities investments of Blake Co., all of which occurred during year 2008.

a. On February 15, paid $120,000 cash to purchase RTF's 90-day short-term debt securities ($120,000 principal), dated February 15, that pay 8% interest (categorized as held-to-maturity securities).

b. On March 22, purchased 700 shares of XIF Company stock at $27.50 per share plus a $150 brokerage fee. These shares are categorized as trading securities.

c. On May 16, received a check from RTF in payment of the principal and 90 days' interest on the debt securities purchased in transaction *a*.

d. On August 1, paid $80,000 cash to purchase Flash Co.'s 10% debt securities ($80,000 principal), dated July 30, 2008, and maturing January 30, 2009 (categorized as available-for-sale securities).

e. On September 1, received a $1.00 per share cash dividend on the XIF Company stock purchased in transaction *b*.

f. On October 8, sold 350 shares of XIF Co. stock for $34 per share, less a $140 brokerage fee.

g. On October 30, received a check from Flash Co. for 90 days' interest on the debt securities purchased in transaction *d*.

Exercise 15-2
Accounting for trading securities

C1 P1

Check (3) Gain, $2,000

Brooks Co. purchases various investments in trading securities at a cost of $66,000 on December 27, 2008. (This is its first and only purchase of such securities.) At December 31, 2008, these securities had a market value of $72,000.

1. Prepare the December 31, 2008, year-end adjusting entry for the trading securities' portfolio.

2. Explain how each account in the entry of part 1 is reported in financial statements.

3. Prepare the January 3, 2009, entry when Brooks sells a portion of its trading securities (that had originally cost $33,000) for $35,000.

Exercise 15-3
Adjusting available-for-sale securities to market

C2 P3

Check Unrealized loss, $9,100

On December 31, 2008, Reggit Company held the following short-term investments in its portfolio of available-for-sale securities. Reggit had no short-term investments in its prior accounting periods. Prepare the December 31, 2008, adjusting entry to report these investments at market value.

	Cost	Market Value
Verrizano Corporation bonds payable	$89,600	$91,600
Preble Corporation notes payable	70,600	62,900
Lucerne Company common stock	86,500	83,100

Exercise 15-4
Transactions in short-term and long-term investments

C1 C2

Prepare journal entries to record the following transactions involving both the short-term and long-term investments of Cancun Corp., all of which occurred during calendar year 2008. Use the account Short-Term Investments for any transactions that you determine are short term.

a. On February 15, paid $160,000 cash to purchase American General's 90-day short-term notes at par, which are dated February 15 and pay 10% interest (classified as held-to-maturity).

b. On March 22, bought 700 shares of Fran Industries common stock at $51 cash per share plus a $150 brokerage fee (classified as long-term available-for-sale securities).

c. On May 15, received a check from American General in payment of the principal and 90 days' interest on the notes purchased in transaction *a*.

d. On July 30, paid $100,000 cash to purchase MP3 Electronics' 8% notes at par, dated July 30, 2008, and maturing on January 30, 2009 (classified as trading securities).

e. On September 1, received a $1 per share cash dividend on the Fran Industries common stock purchased in transaction *b*.

f. On October 8, sold 350 shares of Fran Industries common stock for $64 cash per share, less a $125 brokerage fee.

g. On October 30, received a check from MP3 Electronics for three months' interest on the notes purchased in transaction *d*.

On December 31, 2008, Lujack Co. held the following short-term available-for-sale securities.

Exercise 15-5
Market adjustment to available-for-sale securities

P3

	Cost	Market Value
Nintendo Co. common stock	$44,450	$48,900
Atlantic Richfield Co. bonds payable	49,000	47,000
Kellogg Co. notes payable	25,000	23,200
McDonald's Corp. common stock	46,300	44,800

Lujack had no short-term investments prior to the current period. Prepare the December 31, 2008, year-end adjusting entry to record the market adjustment for these securities.

Pilsen Co. began operations in 2007. The cost and market values for its long-term investments portfolio in available-for-sale securities are shown below. Prepare Pilsen's December 31, 2008, adjusting entry to reflect any necessary market adjustment for these investments.

Exercise 15-6
Market adjustment to available-for-sale securities

P3

	Cost	Market Value
December 31, 2007	$87,855	$80,293
December 31, 2008	89,980	90,980

Ticker Services began operations in 2006 and maintains long-term investments in available-for-sale securities. The year-end cost and market values for its portfolio of these investments follow. Prepare journal entries to record each year-end market adjustment for these securities.

Exercise 15-7
Multi-year market adjustments to available-for-sale securities

P3

	Cost	Market Value
December 31, 2006	$372,000	$360,860
December 31, 2007	428,500	455,800
December 31, 2008	600,200	700,500
December 31, 2009	876,900	780,200

Information regarding Central Company's individual investments in securities during its calendar-year 2008, along with the December 31, 2008, market values, follows.

Exercise 15-8
Classifying investments in securities; recording market values

C1 C2 P2 P3 P4

a. Investment in Beeman Company bonds: $420,500 cost, $457,000 market value. Central intends to hold these bonds until they mature in 2011.

b. Investment in Baybridge common stock: 29,500 shares; $362,450 cost; $391,375 market value. Central owns 32% of Baybridge's voting stock and has a significant influence over Baybridge.

c. Investment in Carroll common stock: 12,000 shares; $165,500 cost; $178,000 market value. This investment amounts to 3% of Carroll's outstanding shares, and Central's goal with this investment is to earn dividends over the next few years.

d. Investment in Newtech common stock: 3,500 shares; $90,300 cost; $88,625 market value. Central's goal with this investment is to reap an increase in market value of the stock over the next three to five years. Newtech has 30,000 common shares outstanding.

e. Investment in Flock common stock: 16,300 shares; $100,860 cost; $111,210 market value. This stock is marketable and is held as an investment of cash available for operations.

Required

1. Identify whether each investment should be classified as a short-term or long-term investment. For each long-term investment, indicate in which of the long-term investment classifications it should be placed.

2. Prepare a journal entry dated December 31, 2008, to record the market value adjustment of the long-term investments in available-for-sale securities. Central had no long-term investments prior to year 2008.

Check   Unrealized gain, $10,825

Exercise 15-9
Securities transactions;
equity method

P4   C2

Prepare journal entries to record the following transactions and events of Kodan Company.

2008

Jan.   2   Purchased 30,000 shares of Goreten Co. common stock for $408,000 cash plus a broker's fee of $3,000 cash. Goreten has 90,000 shares of common stock outstanding and its policies will be significantly influenced by Kodan.
Sept. 1   Goreten declared and paid a cash dividend of $1.50 per share.
Dec. 31   Goreten announced that net income for the year is $486,900.

2009

June   1   Goreten declared and paid a cash dividend of $2.10 per share.
Dec. 31   Goreten announced that net income for the year is $702,750.
Dec. 31   Kodan sold 10,000 shares of Goreten for $320,000 cash.

Exercise 15-10
Return on total assets

A1

The following information is available from the financial statements of Regae Industries. Compute Regae's return on total assets for 2008 and 2009. (Round returns to one-tenth of a percent.) Comment on the company's efficiency in using its assets in 2008 and 2009.

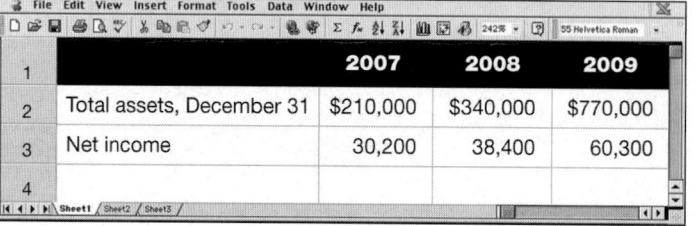

	2007	2008	2009
Total assets, December 31	$210,000	$340,000	$770,000
Net income	30,200	38,400	60,300

Exercise 15-11ᴬ
Foreign currency transactions

P5

Leigh of New York sells its products to customers in the United States and the United Kingdom. On December 16, 2008, Leigh sold merchandise on credit to Bronson Ltd. of London at a price of 17,000 pounds. The exchange rate on that day for £1 was $1.4583. On December 31, 2008, when Leigh prepared its financial statements, the rate was £1 for $1.4382. Bronson paid its bill in full on January 15, 2009, at which time the exchange rate was £1 for $1.4482. Leigh immediately exchanged the 17,000 pounds for U.S. dollars. Prepare Leigh's journal entries on December 16, December 31, and January 15 (round to the nearest dollar).

Exercise 15-12ᴬ
Computing foreign exchange
gains and losses on receivables

C4   P5

On May 8, 2008, Jett Company (a U.S. company) made a credit sale to Lopez (a Mexican company). The terms of the sale required Lopez to pay 800,000 pesos on February 10, 2009. Jett prepares quarterly financial statements on March 31, June 30, September 30, and December 31. The exchange rates for pesos during the time the receivable is outstanding follow.

May 8, 2008 . . . . $0.1323
June 30, 2008 . . . .   0.1352
September 30, 2008 . . . .   0.1368
December 31, 2008 . . . .   0.1335
February 10, 2009 . . . .   0.1386

Compute the foreign exchange gain or loss that Jett should report on each of its quarterly income statements for the last three quarters of 2008 and the first quarter of 2009. Also compute the amount reported on Jett's balance sheets at the end of each of its last three quarters of 2008.

PROBLEM SET A

Problem 15-1A
Recording transactions and
market adjustments for
trading securities

C2   P1

Carlsville Company, which began operations in 2008, invests its idle cash in trading securities. The following transactions are from its short-term investments in its trading securities.

2008

Jan. 20   Purchased 800 shares of Ford Motor Co. at $26 per share plus a $125 commission.
Feb.   9   Purchased 2,200 shares of Lucent at $44.25 per share plus a $578 commission.
Oct. 12   Purchased 750 shares of Z-Seven at $7.50 per share plus a $200 commission.

2009

Apr. 15   Sold 800 shares of Ford Motor Co. at $29 per share less a $285 commission.
July   5   Sold 750 shares of Z-Seven at $10.25 per share less a $102.50 commission.
July 22   Purchased 1,600 shares of Hunt Corp. at $30 per share plus a $444 commission.
Aug. 19   Purchased 1,800 shares of Donna Karan at $18.25 per share plus a $290 commission.

2010

Feb. 27   Purchased 3,400 shares of HCA at $34 per share plus a $420 commission.
Mar. 3   Sold 1,600 shares of Hunt at $25 per share less a $250 commission.
June 21   Sold 2,200 shares of Lucent at $42 per share less a $420 commission.
June 30   Purchased 1,200 shares of Black & Decker at $47.50 per share plus a $595 commission.
Nov. 1   Sold 1,800 shares of Donna Karan at $18.25 per share less a $309 commission.

Required

1. Prepare journal entries to record these short-term investment activities for the years shown. (Ignore any year-end adjusting entries.)

2. On December 31, 2010, prepare the adjusting entry to record any necessary market adjustment for the portfolio of trading securities when HCA's share price is $36 and Black & Decker's share price is $43.50. (Assume the Market Adjustment—Trading account had an unadjusted balance of zero.)

Check (2) Dr. Market
Adjustment—Trading $985

Rose Company had no short-term investments prior to year 2008. It had the following transactions involving short-term investments in available-for-sale securities during 2008.

Apr. 16   Purchased 4,000 shares of Gem Co. stock at $24.25 per share plus a $180 brokerage fee.
May   1   Paid $100,000 to buy 90-day U.S. Treasury bills (debt securities): $100,000 principal amount, 6% interest, securities dated May 1.
July   7   Purchased 2,000 shares of PepsiCo stock at $49.25 per share plus a $175 brokerage fee.
      20   Purchased 1,000 shares of Xerox stock at $16.75 per share plus a $205 brokerage fee.
Aug. 3   Received a check for principal and accrued interest on the U.S. Treasury bills that matured on July 29.
      15   Received an $0.85 per share cash dividend on the Gem Co. stock.
      28   Sold 2,000 shares of Gem Co. stock at $30 per share less a $225 brokerage fee.
Oct.   1   Received a $1.90 per share cash dividend on the PepsiCo shares.
Dec. 15   Received a $1.05 per share cash dividend on the remaining Gem Co. shares.
      31   Received a $1.30 per share cash dividend on the PepsiCo shares.

Problem 15-2A
Recording, adjusting, and reporting short-term available-for-sale securities

C2 P3

Required

1. Prepare journal entries to record the preceding transactions and events.

2. Prepare a table to compare the year-end cost and market values of Rose's short-term investments in available-for-sale securities. The year-end market values per share are: Gem Co., $26.50; PepsiCo, $46.50; and Xerox, $13.75.

3. Prepare an adjusting entry, if necessary, to record the year-end market adjustment for the portfolio of short-term investments in available-for-sale securities.

Check (2) Cost = $164,220

(3) Dr. Unrealized Loss—
Equity $4,470

Analysis Component

4. Explain the balance sheet presentation of the market adjustment for Rose's short-term investments.

5. How do these short-term investments affect Rose's (a) income statement for year 2008 and (b) the equity section of its balance sheet at year-end 2008?

Grass Security, which began operations in 2008, invests in long-term available-for-sale securities. Following is a series of transactions and events determining its long-term investment activity.

2008

Jan. 20   Purchased 1,000 shares of Johnson & Johnson at $20.50 per share plus a $240 commission.
Feb. 9   Purchased 1,200 shares of Sony at $46.20 per share plus a $225 commission.
June 12   Purchased 1,500 shares of Mattel at $27.00 per share plus a $195 commission.
Dec. 31   Per share market values for stocks in the portfolio are Johnson & Johnson, $21.50; Mattel, $30.90; Sony, $38.00.

Problem 15-3A
Recording, adjusting, and reporting long-term available-for-sale securities

C2 P3

2009

Apr. 15   Sold 1,000 shares of Johnson & Johnson at $23.50 per share less a $525 commission.
July   5   Sold 1,500 shares of Mattel at $23.90 per share less a $235 commission.
July 22   Purchased 600 shares of Sara Lee at $22.50 per share plus a $480 commission.
Aug. 19   Purchased 900 shares of Eastman Kodak at $17.00 per share plus a $198 commission.
Dec. 31   Per share market values for stocks in the portfolio are: Kodak, $19.25; Sara Lee, $20.00; Sony, $35.00.

2010

Feb. 27   Purchased 2,400 shares of Microsoft at $67.00 per share plus a $525 commission.
June 21   Sold 1,200 shares of Sony at $48.00 per share less an $880 commission.
June 30   Purchased 1,400 shares of Black & Decker at $36.00 per share plus a $435 commission.
Aug.   3   Sold 600 shares of Sara Lee at $16.25 per share less a $435 commission.
Nov.   1   Sold 900 shares of Eastman Kodak at $22.75 per share less a $625 commission.
Dec. 31   Per share market values for stocks in the portfolio are: Black & Decker, $39.00; Microsoft, $69.00.

Required

1. Prepare journal entries to record these transactions and events and any year-end market adjustments to the portfolio of long-term available-for-sale securities.

Check (2b) Market adjustment bal.: 12/31/08, $(3,650); 12/31/09; $(13,818)

2. Prepare a table that summarizes the (*a*) total cost, (*b*) total market adjustment, and (*c*) total market value of the portfolio of long-term available-for-sale securities at each year-end.

(3b) Unrealized Gain at 12/31/2010, $8,040

3. Prepare a table that summarizes (*a*) the realized gains and losses and (*b*) the unrealized gains or losses for the portfolio of long-term available-for-sale securities at each year-end.

Problem 15-4A

Long-term investment transactions; unrealized and realized gains and losses

C2 C3 P3 P4

Stoll Co.'s long-term available-for-sale portfolio at December 31, 2007, consists of the following.

Available-for-Sale Securities	Cost	Market Value
40,000 shares of Company A common stock	$535,300	$490,000
7,000 shares of Company B common stock	159,380	154,000
17,500 shares of Company C common stock	662,750	640,938

Stoll enters into the following long-term investment transactions during year 2008.

Jan. 29   Sold 3,500 shares of Company B common stock for $79,188 less a brokerage fee of $1,500.
Apr. 17   Purchased 10,000 shares of Company W common stock for $197,500 plus a brokerage fee of $2,400. The shares represent a 30% ownership in Company W.
July   6   Purchased 4,500 shares of Company X common stock for $126,562 plus a brokerage fee of $1,750. The shares represent a 10% ownership in Company X.
Aug. 22   Purchased 50,000 shares of Company Y common stock for $375,000 plus a brokerage fee of $1,200. The shares represent a 51% ownership in Company Y.
Nov. 13   Purchased 8,500 shares of Company Z common stock for $267,900 plus a brokerage fee of $2,450. The shares represent a 5% ownership in Company Z.
Dec.   9   Sold 40,000 shares of Company A common stock for $515,000 less a brokerage fee of $4,100.

The market values of its investments at December 31, 2008, are: B, $81,375; C, $610,312; W, $191,250; X, $118,125; Y, $531,250; and Z, $278,800.

Required

1. Determine the amount Stoll should report on its December 31, 2008, balance sheet for its long-term investments in available-for-sale securities.

Check (2) Cr. Unrealized Loss— Equity, $20,002

2. Prepare any necessary December 31, 2008, adjusting entry to record the market value adjustment for the long-term investments in available-for-sale securities.

3. What amount of gains or losses on transactions relating to long-term investments in available-for-sale securities should Stoll report on its December 31, 2008, income statement?

Selk Steel Co., which began operations on January 4, 2008, had the following subsequent transactions and events in its long-term investments.

Problem 15-5A
Accounting for long-term investments in securities; with and without significant influence

C2 P3 P4

2008

Jan. 5   Selk purchased 60,000 shares (20% of total) of Kildaire's common stock for $1,560,000.
Oct. 23   Kildaire declared and paid a cash dividend of $3.20 per share.
Dec. 31   Kildaire's net income for 2008 is $1,164,000, and the market value of its stock at December 31 is $30.00 per share.

2009

Oct. 15   Kildaire declared and paid a cash dividend of $2.60 per share.
Dec. 31   Kildaire's net income for 2009 is $1,476,000, and the market value of its stock at December 31 is $32.00 per share.

2010

Jan. 2   Selk sold all of its investment in Kildaire for $1,894,000 cash.

Part 1

Assume that Selk has a significant influence over Kildaire with its 20% share of stock.

Required

1. Prepare journal entries to record these transactions and events for Selk.
2. Compute the carrying (book) value per share of Selk's investment in Kildaire common stock as reflected in the investment account on January 1, 2010.
3. Compute the net increase or decrease in Selk's equity from January 5, 2008, through January 2, 2010, resulting from its investment in Kildaire.

Check (2) Carrying value per share, $29

Part 2

Assume that although Selk owns 20% of Kildaire's outstanding stock, circumstances indicate that it does not have a significant influence over the investee and that it is classified as an available-for-sale security investment.

Required

1. Prepare journal entries to record the preceding transactions and events for Selk. Also prepare an entry dated January 2, 2010, to remove any balance related to the market adjustment.
2. Compute the cost per share of Selk's investment in Kildaire common stock as reflected in the investment account on January 1, 2010.
3. Compute the net increase or decrease in Selk's equity from January 5, 2008, through January 2, 2010, resulting from its investment in Kildaire.

(1) 1/2/10 Dr. Unrealized Gain—Equity $360,000

(3) Net increase, $682,000

Doering Company, a U.S. corporation with customers in several foreign countries, had the following selected transactions for 2008 and 2009.

Problem 15-6A
Foreign currency transactions

C4 P5

2008

Apr. 8   Sold merchandise to Salinas & Sons of Mexico for $5,938 cash. The exchange rate for pesos is $0.1043 on this day.
July 21   Sold merchandise on credit to Sumito Corp. in Japan. The price of 1.5 million yen is to be paid 120 days from the date of sale. The exchange rate for yen is $0.0094 on this day.
Oct. 14   Sold merchandise for 19,000 pounds to Smithers Ltd. of Great Britain, payment in full to be received in 90 days. The exchange rate for pounds is $1.4566 on this day.
Nov. 18   Received Sumito's payment in yen for its July 21 purchase and immediately exchanged the yen for dollars. The exchange rate for yen is $0.0092 on this day.
Dec. 20   Sold merchandise for 17,000 ringgits to Hamid Albar of Malaysia, payment in full to be received in 30 days. On this day, the exchange rate for ringgits is $0.4501.

Dec. 31   Recorded adjusting entries to recognize exchange gains or losses on Doering's annual financial statements. Rates for exchanging foreign currencies on this day follow.

Pesos (Mexico)	$0.1055
Yen (Japan)	0.0093
Pounds (Britain)	1.4620
Ringgits (Malaysia)	0.4456

2009

Jan. 12   Received full payment in pounds from Smithers for the October 14 sale and immediately exchanged the pounds for dollars. The exchange rate for pounds is $1.4699 on this day.

Jan. 19   Received Hamid Albar's full payment in ringgits for the December 20 sale and immediately exchanged the ringgits for dollars. The exchange rate for ringgits is $0.4420 on this day.

Required

1. Prepare journal entries for the Doering transactions and adjusting entries (round amounts to the nearest dollar).

Check   (2) 2008 total foreign exchange loss, $274

2. Compute the foreign exchange gain or loss to be reported on Doering's 2008 income statement.

Analysis Component

3. What actions might Doering consider to reduce its risk of foreign exchange gains or losses?

PROBLEM SET B

Problem 15-1B

Recording transactions and market adjustments for trading securities

C2 P1

Harris Company, which began operations in 2008, invests its idle cash in trading securities. The following transactions relate to its short-term investments in its trading securities.

2008

Mar. 10   Purchased 2,400 shares of AOL at $59.15 per share plus a $1,545 commission.
May 7   Purchased 5,000 shares of MTV at $36.25 per share plus a $2,855 commission.
Sept. 1   Purchased 1,200 shares of UPS at $57.25 per share plus a $1,250 commission.

2009

Apr. 26   Sold 5,000 shares of MTV at $34.50 per share less a $2,050 commission.
Apr. 27   Sold 1,200 shares of UPS at $60.50 per share less a $1,788 commission.
June 2   Purchased 3,600 shares of SPW at $172 per share plus a $3,250 commission.
June 14   Purchased 900 shares of Wal-Mart at $50.25 per share plus a $1,082 commission.

2010

Jan. 28   Purchased 2,000 shares of PepsiCo at $43 per share plus a $2,890 commission.
Jan. 31   Sold 3,600 shares of SPW at $168 per share less a $2,040 commission.
Aug. 22   Sold 2,400 shares of AOL at $56.75 per share less a $2,480 commission.
Sept. 3   Purchased 1,500 shares of Vodaphone at $40.50 per share plus a $1,680 commission.
Oct. 9   Sold 900 shares of Wal-Mart at $53.75 per share less a $1,220 commission.

Required

1. Prepare journal entries to record these short-term investment activities for the years shown. (Ignore any year-end adjusting entries.)

Check   (2) Cr. Market Adjustment—Trading $13,820

2. On December 31, 2010, prepare the adjusting entry to record any necessary market adjustment for the portfolio of trading securities when PepsiCo's share price is $41 and Vodaphone's share price is $37. (Assume the Market Adjustment—Trading account had an unadjusted balance of zero.)

Slip Systems had no short-term investments prior to 2008. It had the following transactions involving short-term investments in available-for-sale securities during 2008.

Feb.   6   Purchased 3,400 shares of Nokia stock at $41.25 per share plus a $3,000 brokerage fee.

      15   Paid $20,000 to buy six-month U.S. Treasury bills (debt securities): $20,000 principal amount, 6% interest, securities dated February 15.

Apr.   7   Purchased 1,200 shares of Dell Co. stock at $39.50 per share plus a $1,255 brokerage fee.

June   2   Purchased 2,500 shares of Merck stock at $72.50 per share plus a $2,890 brokerage fee.

      30   Received a $0.19 per share cash dividend on the Nokia shares.

Aug. 11   Sold 850 shares of Nokia stock at $46 per share less a $1,050 brokerage fee.

      16   Received a check for principal and accrued interest on the U.S. Treasury bills purchased February 15.

      24   Received a $0.10 per share cash dividend on the Dell shares.

Nov.   9   Received a $0.20 per share cash dividend on the remaining Nokia shares.

Dec. 18   Received a $0.15 per share cash dividend on the Dell shares.

Problem 15-2B

Recording, adjusting, and reporting short-term available-for-sale securities

C2   P3

Required

1. Prepare journal entries to record the preceding transactions and events.

2. Prepare a table to compare the year-end cost and market values of the short-term investments in available-for-sale securities. The year-end market values per share are: Nokia, $40.25; Dell, $40.50; and Merck, $59.

3. Prepare an adjusting entry, if necessary, to record the year-end market adjustment for the portfolio of short-term investments in available-for-sale securities.

Check   (2) Cost = $340,232

(3) Dr. Unrealized
Loss—Equity, $41,494

Analysis Component

4. Explain the balance sheet presentation of the market adjustment to Slip's short-term investments.

5. How do these short-term investments affect (*a*) its income statement for year 2008 and (*b*) the equity section of its balance sheet at the 2008 year-end?

Paris Enterprises, which began operations in 2008, invests in long-term available-for-sale securities. Following is a series of transactions and events involving its long-term investment activity.

Problem 15-3B

Recording, adjusting, and reporting long-term available-for-sale securities

C2   P3

2008

Mar. 10   Purchased 1,200 shares of Apple Computer at $25.50 per share plus $800 commission.

Apr.   7   Purchased 2,500 shares of Ford at $22.50 per share plus $1,033 commission.

Sept.   1   Purchased 600 shares of Polaroid at $47.00 per share plus $890 commission.

Dec. 31   Per share market values for stocks in the portfolio are: Apple, $27.50; Ford, $21.00; Polaroid, $49.00.

2009

Apr. 26   Sold 2,500 shares of Ford at $20.50 per share less a $1,207 commission.

June   2   Purchased 1,800 shares of Duracell at $19.25 per share plus a $1,050 commission.

June 14   Purchased 1,200 shares of Sears at $21.00 per share plus a $280 commission.

Nov. 27   Sold 600 shares of Polaroid at $51 per share less an $845 commission.

Dec. 31   Per share market values for stocks in the portfolio are: Apple, $29.00; Duracell, $18.00; Sears, $23.00.

2010

Jan. 28   Purchased 1,000 shares of Coca-Cola Co. at $40 per share plus a $1,480 commission.

Aug. 22   Sold 1,200 shares of Apple at $21.50 per share less a $1,850 commission.

Sept.   3   Purchased 3,000 shares of Motorola at $28.00 per share plus a $780 commission.

Oct.   9   Sold 1,200 shares of Sears at $24.00 per share less a $599 commission.

Oct. 31   Sold 1,800 shares of Duracell at $15.00 per share less an $898 commission.

Dec. 31   Per share market values for stocks in the portfolio are: Coca-Cola, $48.00; Motorola, $24.00.

Required

1. Prepare journal entries to record these transactions and events and any year-end market adjustments to the portfolio of long-term available-for-sale securities.

Check   (2b) Market adjustment bal.:
12/31/08, $(2,873); 12/31/09, $2,220

        (3b) Unrealized loss at
12/31/2010, $6,260

2. Prepare a table that summarizes the (a) total cost, (b) total market adjustment, and (c) total market value for the portfolio of long-term available-for-sale securities at each year-end.

3. Prepare a table that summarizes (a) the realized gains and losses and (b) the unrealized gains or losses for the portfolio of long-term available-for-sale securities at each year-end.

Problem 15-4B

Long-term investment
transactions; unrealized and
realized gains and losses

C2   C3   P3   P4

Troyer's long-term available-for-sale portfolio at December 31, 2007, consists of the following.

Available-for-Sale Securities	Cost	Market Value
27,500 shares of Company R common stock	$559,125	$599,063
8,500 shares of Company S common stock	308,380	293,250
11,000 shares of Company T common stock	147,295	151,800

Troyer enters into the following long-term investment transactions during year 2008.

Jan. 13 Sold 2,125 shares of Company S common stock for $72,250 less a brokerage fee of $1,195.
Mar. 24 Purchased 15,500 shares of Company U common stock for $282,875 plus a brokerage fee of $1,980. The shares represent a 62% ownership in Company U.
Apr. 5 Purchased 42,500 shares of Company V common stock for $133,875 plus a brokerage fee of $1,125. The shares represent a 10% ownership in Company V.
Sept. 2 Sold 11,000 shares of Company T common stock for $156,750 less a brokerage fee of $2,700.
Sept. 27 Purchased 2,500 shares of Company W common stock for $50,500 plus a brokerage fee of $1,050. The shares represent a 25% ownership in Company W.
Oct. 30 Purchased 5,000 shares of Company X common stock for $48,750 plus a brokerage fee of $1,170. The shares represent a 13% ownership in Company X.

The market values of its investments at December 31, 2008, are: R, $568,125; S, $210,375; U, $272,800; V, $134,938; W, $54,689; and X, $45,625.

Required

1. Determine the amount Troyer should report on its December 31, 2008, balance sheet for its long-term investments in available-for-sale securities.

Check   (2) Dr. Unrealized Loss—
Equity, $16,267; Cr. Market Adjustment,
$45,580

2. Prepare any necessary December 31, 2008, adjusting entry to record the market value adjustment of the long-term investments in available-for-sale securities.

3. What amount of gains or losses on transactions relating to long-term investments in available-for-sale securities should Troyer report on its December 31, 2008, income statement?

Problem 15-5B

Accounting for long-term
investments in securities; with
and without significant influence

C2   P3   P4

Brinkley Company, which began operations on January 3, 2008, had the following subsequent transactions and events in its long-term investments.

2008

Jan. 5 Brinkley purchased 20,000 shares (25% of total) of Bloch's common stock for $200,500.
Aug. 1 Bloch declared and paid a cash dividend of $1.05 per share.
Dec. 31 Bloch's net income for 2008 is $82,000, and the market value of its stock is $11.90 per share.

2009

Aug. 1 Bloch declared and paid a cash dividend of $1.35 per share.
Dec. 31 Bloch's net income for 2009 is $78,000, and the market value of its stock is $13.65 per share.

2010

Jan. 8 Brinkley sold all of its investment in Bloch for $375,000 cash.

Part 1

Assume that Brinkley has a significant influence over Bloch with its 25% share.

Required

1. Prepare journal entries to record these transactions and events for Brinkley.

2. Compute the carrying (book) value per share of Brinkley's investment in Bloch common stock as reflected in the investment account on January 7, 2010.

Check (2) Carrying value per share, $9.63

3. Compute the net increase or decrease in Brinkley's equity from January 5, 2008, through January 8, 2010, resulting from its investment in Bloch.

Part 2

Assume that although Brinkley owns 25% of Bloch's outstanding stock, circumstances indicate that it does not have a significant influence over the investee and that it is classified as an available-for-sale security investment.

Required

1. Prepare journal entries to record these transactions and events for Brinkley. Also prepare an entry dated January 8, 2010, to remove any balance related to the market adjustment.

(1) 1/8/10 Dr. Unrealized Gain—Equity $72,500

2. Compute the cost per share of Brinkley's investment in Bloch common stock as reflected in the investment account on January 7, 2010.

3. Compute the net increase or decrease in Brinkley's equity from January 5, 2008, through January 8, 2010, resulting from its investment in Bloch.

(3) Net increase, $222,500

Datamix, a U.S. corporation with customers in several foreign countries, had the following selected transactions for 2008 and 2009.

Problem 15-6B[A]
Foreign currency transactions

C4 P5

2008

May 26   Sold merchandise for 6.5 million yen to Fuji Company of Japan, payment in full to be received in 60 days. On this day, the exchange rate for yen is $0.0093.

June   1   Sold merchandise to Fordham Ltd. of Great Britain for $64,800 cash. The exchange rate for pounds is $1.4498 on this day.

July 25   Received Fuji's payment in yen for its May 26 purchase and immediately exchanged the yen for dollars. The exchange rate for yen is $0.0092 on this day.

Oct. 15   Sold merchandise on credit to Martinez Brothers of Mexico. The price of 378,000 pesos is to be paid 90 days from the date of sale. On this day, the exchange rate for pesos is $0.1020.

Dec.   6   Sold merchandise for 250,000 yuans to Chi-Ying Company of China, payment in full to be received in 30 days. The exchange rate for yuans is $0.1439 on this day.

Dec. 31   Recorded adjusting entries to recognize exchange gains or losses on Datamix's annual financial statements. Rates of exchanging foreign currencies on this day follow.

Yen (Japan)	$0.0094
Pounds (Britain)	1.4580
Pesos (Mexico)	0.1060
Yuans (China)	0.1450

2009

Jan.   5   Received Chi-Ying's full payment in yuans for the December 6 sale and immediately exchanged the yuans for dollars. The exchange rate for yuans is $0.1580 on this day.

Jan. 13   Received full payment in pesos from Martinez for the October 15 sale and immediately exchanged the pesos for dollars. The exchange rate for pesos is $0.1039 on this day.

Required

1. Prepare journal entries for the Datamix transactions and adjusting entries.

2. Compute the foreign exchange gain or loss to be reported on Datamix's 2008 income statement.

Check 2008 total foreign exchange gain, $1,137

Analysis Component

3. What actions might Datamix consider to reduce its risk of foreign exchange gains or losses?

   Problem Set C is available at the book's Website to reinforce and assess your learning.   **PROBLEM SET C**

SERIAL PROBLEM

Success Systems

(This serial problem began in Chapter 1 and continues through most of the book. If previous chapter segments were not completed, the serial problem can begin at this point. It is helpful, but not necessary, for you to use the Working Papers that accompany the book.)

SP 15   While reviewing the March 31, 2008, balance sheet of Success Systems, Adriana Lopez notes that the business has built a large cash balance of $87,171. Its most recent bank money market statement shows that the funds are earning an annualized return of 0.75%. Lopez decides to make several investments with the desire to earn a higher return on the idle cash balance. Accordingly, in April 2008, Success Systems makes the following investments in trading securities:

April 16   Purchases 400 shares of Johnson & Johnson stock at $55 per share plus $300 commission.
April 30   Purchases 200 shares of Starbucks Corporation at $27 per share plus $250 commission.

On June 30, 2008, the per share market price of the Johnson & Johnson shares is $60 and the Starbucks shares is $24.

Required

1. Prepare journal entries to record the April purchases of trading securities by Success Systems.
2. On June 30, 2008, prepare the adjusting entry to record any necessary market adjustment to its portfolio of trading securities.

BEYOND THE NUMBERS

REPORTING IN ACTION

C3 C4 A1

BTN 15-1   Refer to **Best Buy**'s financial statements in Appendix A to answer the following.

1. Are Best Buy's financial statements consolidated? How can you tell?
2. What is Best Buy's *comprehensive income* for the year ended February 26, 2005?
3. Does Best Buy have any foreign operations? How can you tell?
4. Compute Best Buy's return on total assets for the year ended February 26, 2005.

Fast Forward

5. Access Best Buy's annual report for a fiscal year ending after February 26, 2005, from either its Website (**BestBuy.com**) or the SEC's EDGAR database (**www.sec.gov**). Recompute Best Buy's return on total assets for the years subsequent to February 26, 2005.

COMPARATIVE ANALYSIS

A1

BTN 15-2   Key comparative figures ($ millions) for **Best Buy** and **Circuit City** follow.

Key Figures	Best Buy			Circuit City		
	Current Year	1 Year Prior	2 Years Prior	Current Year	1 Year Prior	2 Years Prior
Net income	$ 984	$ 705	$ 99	$ 62	$ (89)	$ 82
Net sales	27,433	24,548	20,943	10,472	9,857	10,055
Total assets	10,294	8,652	7,694	3,789	3,731	3,841

Required

1. Compute return on total assets for Best Buy and Circuit City for the two most recent years.
2. Separate the return on total assets computed in part 1 into its components for both companies and both years according to the formula in Exhibit 15.9.
3. Which company has the higher total return on assets? The higher profit margin? The higher total asset turnover? What does this comparative analysis reveal? (Assume an industry average of 6.5% for return on assets.)

BTN 15-3   Kendra Wecker is the controller for Wildcat Company, which has numerous long-term investments in debt securities. Wildcat's investments are mainly in 10-year bonds. Wecker is preparing its year-end financial statements. In accounting for long-term debt securities, she knows that each long-term investment must be designated as a held-to-maturity or an available-for-sale security. Interest rates rose sharply this past year causing the portfolio's market value to substantially decline. The company does not intend to hold the bonds for the entire 10 years. Wecker also earns a bonus each year, which is computed as a percent of net income.

ETHICS CHALLENGE

C2   P2   P3

Required

1. Will Wecker's bonus depend in any way on the classification of the debt securities? Explain.
2. What criteria must Wecker use to classify the securities as held-to-maturity or available-for-sale?
3. Is there likely any company oversight of Wecker's classification of the securities? Explain.

BTN 15-4   Assume that you are Jackson Company's accountant. Company owner Abel Terrio has reviewed the 2009 financial statements you prepared and questions the $6,000 loss reported on the sale of its investment in Blackhawk Co. common stock. Jackson acquired 50,000 shares of Blackhawk's common stock on December 31, 2007, at a cost of $500,000. This stock purchase represented a 40% interest in Blackhawk. The 2008 income statement reported that earnings from all investments were $126,000. On January 3, 2009, Jackson Company sold the Blackhawk stock for $575,000. Blackhawk did not pay any dividends during 2008 but reported a net income of $202,500 for that year. Terrio believes that because the Blackhawk stock purchase price was $500,000 and was sold for $575,000, the 2009 income statement should report a $75,000 gain on the sale.

COMMUNICATING IN PRACTICE

C2   P4

Required

Draft a one-half page memorandum to Terrio explaining why the $6,000 loss on sale of Blackhawk stock is correctly reported.

BTN 15-5   Access the August 26, 2005, 10-K filing (for year-end June 30, 2005) of **Microsoft** (MSFT) at www.sec.gov. Review its footnote 3, "Investments."

TAKING IT TO THE NET

C1   C2

Required

1. How does the cost-basis total for cash and securities as of June 30, 2005, compare to the prior year–end amount?
2. Identify at least eight types of short-term investments held by Microsoft as of June 30, 2005.
3. What were Microsoft's unrealized gains and its unrealized losses from cash and securities for 2005?
4. Was the cost or market (recorded) value of the investments higher as of June 30, 2005?

BTN 15-6   Each team member is to become an expert on a specific classification of long-term investments. This expertise will be used to facilitate other teammates' understanding of the concepts and procedures relevent to the classification chosen.

TEAMWORK IN ACTION

C1   C2   C3   P1   P2   P3   P4

1. Each team member must select an area for expertise by choosing one of the following classifications of long-term investments.
   a. Held-to-maturity debt securities
   b. Available-for-sale debt and equity securities
   c. Equity securities with significant influence
   d. Equity securities with controlling influence
2. Learning teams are to disburse and expert teams are to be formed. Expert teams are made up of those who select the same area of expertise. The instructor will identify the location where each expert team will meet.
3. Expert teams will collaborate to develop a presentation based on the following requirements. Students must write the presentation in a format they can show to their learning teams in part (4).

Requirements for Expert Presentation

  a. Write a transaction for the acquisition of this type of investment security. The transaction description is to include all necessary data to reflect the chosen classification.

  b. Prepare the journal entry to record the acquisition.

    [*Note:* The expert team on equity securities with controlling influence will substitute requirements (*d*) and (*e*) with a discussion of the reporting of these investments.]

  c. Identify information necessary to complete the end-of-period adjustment for this investment.

  d. Assuming that this is the only investment owned, prepare any necessary year-end entries.

  e. Present the relevant balance sheet section(s).

4. Re-form learning teams. In rotation, experts are to present to their teams the presentations they developed in part 3. Experts are to encourage and respond to questions.

BusinessWeek ACTIVITY

C2

BTN 15-7 Read the article "Accounting: Bringing the Future into Play" in the March 11, 2002, issue of *BusinessWeek*. (This book's Website provides a free link.)

Required

1. On what types of data do accountants focus? How does this compare with the data desired by investors?

2. Explain the phrase "marking to market."

3. What ideas have been proposed to allow marking to market that will also limit fraud by insiders?

4. How do accountants respond to the economists' argument that mark-to-market accounting will result in "asymmetrical" information for investors?

5. What is the best argument for mark-to-market accounting?

ENTREPRENEURIAL DECISION

C4 P5

BTN 15-8ᴬ Refer to the opening feature in this chapter about Stu Levy and **TOKYOPOP**. Stu must acquire the Japanese rights to material that is then translated for the U.S. audience. Assume that on January 1, 2008, Stu acquires the rights to manga material from a Japanese distributor and agrees to pay 12,000,000 yen per year for those rights. Quarterly payments are due March 31, June 30, September 30, and December 31 each year. On January 1, 2008, the yen is worth $0.00891.

Required

1. Prepare the journal entry to record the publishing rights purchased on January 1, 2008.

2. Prepare the journal entries to record the payments on March 31, June 30, September 30, and December 31, 2008. The value of the yen on those dates follows.

March 31	$0.00893
June 30	0.00901
September 30	0.00902
December 31	0.00897

3. How can Stu protect himself from unanticipated gains and losses from currency translation if all of his payments are specified to be paid in yen?

HITTING THE ROAD C4

BTN 15-9ᴬ Assume that you are planning a spring break trip to Europe. Identify three locations where you can find exchange rates for the dollar relative to the Euro or other currencies.

BTN 15-10 **Dixons**, **Best Buy**, and **Circuit City** are competitors in the global marketplace. Following are selected data from each company.

| Key Figure | Dixons (£ millions) | | | Best Buy | | Circuit City | |
	Current Year	One Year Prior	Two Years Prior	Current Year	Prior Year	Current Year	Prior Year
Net income	£ 284	£ 209	£ 211	—	—	—	—
Total assets	3,874	4,158	3,577	—	—	—	—
Net sales	6,492	5,758	4,868	—	—	—	—
Profit margin	?	?	—	3.6%	2.9%	0.6%	(0.9)%
Total asset turnover	?	?	—	2.9	3.0	2.8	2.6

Required

1. Compute Dixons' return on total assets for the most recent two years using the data provided.

2. Which of these three companies has the highest return on total assets? Highest profit margin? Highest total asset turnover?

ANSWERS TO MULTIPLE CHOICE QUIZ

1. d; $30,000 × 5% × 5/12 = $625
2. a; Unrealized gain = $84,500 − $83,000 = $1,500
3. b; $50,000 × 35% = $17,500

4. e; $300,000/$2,000,000 = 15%
5. b; Profit margin = $80,000/$600,000 = 13.3%
   Total asset turnover = $600,000/$400,000 = 1.5

16

Reporting the Statement of Cash Flows

A Look Back

Chapter 15 focused on how to identify, account for, and report investments in securities. We also accounted for transactions listed in a foreign currency.

A Look at This Chapter

This chapter focuses on reporting and analyzing cash inflows and cash outflows. We emphasize how to prepare and interpret the statement of cash flows.

A Look Ahead

Chapter 17 focuses on tools to help us analyze financial statements. We also describe comparative analysis and the application of ratios for financial analysis.

Learning Objectives

CAP

Conceptual

C1 Explain the purpose and importance of cash flow information. (p. 622)

C2 Distinguish between operating, investing, and financing activities. (p. 623)

C3 Identify and disclose noncash investing and financing activities. (p. 625)

C4 Describe the format of the statement of cash flows. (p. 625)

Analytical

A1 Analyze the statement of cash flows. (p. 639)

A2 Compute and apply the cash flow on total assets ratio. (p. 640)

Procedural

P1 Prepare a statement of cash flows. (p. 626)

P2 Compute cash flows from operating activities using the indirect method. (p. 629)

P3 Determine cash flows from both investing and financing activities. (p. 635)

P4 Appendix 16A—Illustrate use of a spreadsheet to prepare a statement of cash flows. (p. 643)

P5 Appendix 16B—Compute cash flows from operating activities using the direct method. (p. 646)

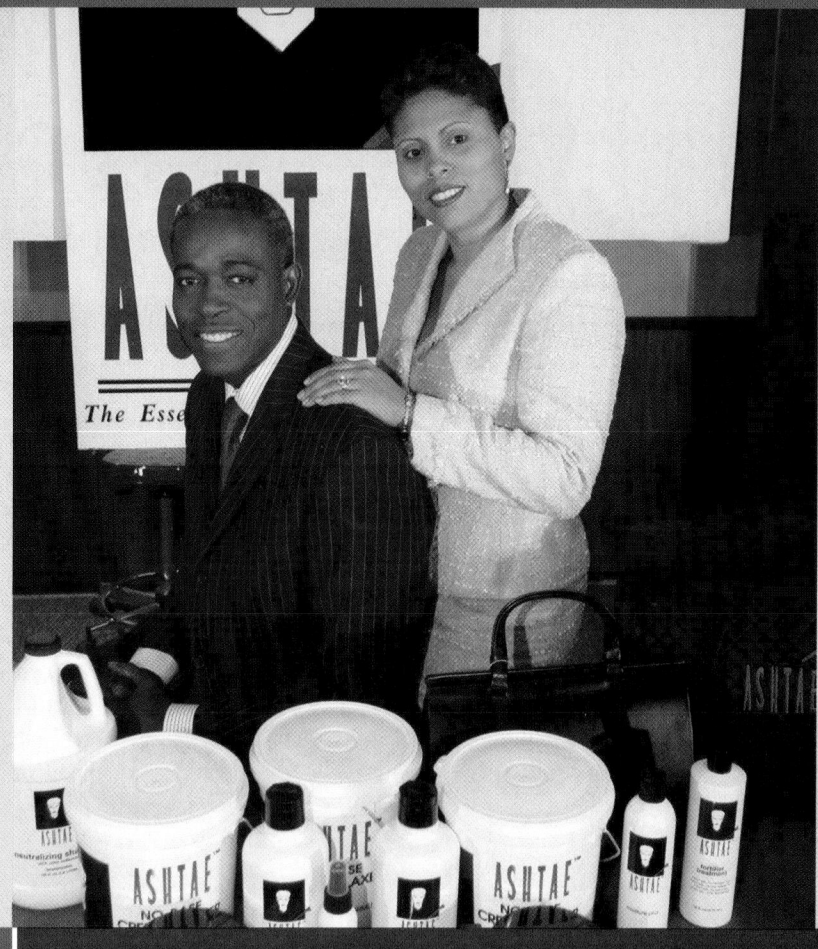

"We don't sell products. . . we sell relationships" —Michael Woods (Ramona Woods on right)

Hair-Raising Cash Flows

GREENSBORO, NC—Although cash may not *be* king, it certainly improves the King's health. Just ask Michael and Ramona Woods, entrepreneurial cofounders of **Ashtae Products (ASHTAE.com),** a multicultural hair-care products and services company. The husband-and-wife team opened Ashtae, named after daughters Ashley and Taylore, in 1995—and revenues now exceed $5 million per year.

But early on, all was not well in the kingdom. "We did everything wrong when we started our business," says Ramona. Cash flow was a constant battle for fledgling Ashtae, as cash flows ran short despite growing profits. "Our mortgage went into foreclosure. Our cars were repossessed," recalls Ramona. "I had to take the bus with two little kids. Sometimes I didn't have the money for the bus. . . we did so much wrong."

Michael and Ramona learned the importance of cash flows the hard way. "We failed to realize that knowing how to sell and make money doesn't mean you know how to keep it," says Michael. Cash outflows for inventory and asset growth yielded negative cash flows for Ashtae in spite of growing sales and profits.

Managing cash was a constant struggle. The couple eventually learned how to monitor and control cash flows associated with each of its operating, investing, and financing activities. They discovered, says Michael, how "to plan for the various stages of growth" and to manage cash flows.

This chapter focuses on cash flows—its measurement, presentation, analysis, and interpretation. It describes how to analyze separately the cash flows related to operating, investing, and financing activities. Michael and Ramona know first-hand the importance of scrutinizing and overseeing cash flows. Says Ramona, "We had to learn to draw the line. . . [to achieve] a profitable business." With healthy cash flows today, the outlook for King Michael and Queen Ramona is good. As Michael puts it, "WOW! That is the only word that can describe our performance."

[Sources: *Ashtae Website,* May 2006; *The Business Journal,* July 2005, January 2005, and December 2004; *SCORE.org Website,* September 2005; *Age Venture News,* February 2003]

Profitability is a main goal of most managers, but not the only goal. A company cannot achieve or maintain profits without carefully managing cash. Managers and other users of information pay close attention to a company's cash position and the events and transactions affecting cash. This chapter explains how we prepare, analyze, and interpret a statement of cash flows. It also discusses the importance of cash flow information for predicting future performance and making managerial decisions. More generally, effectively using the statement of cash flows is crucial for managing and analyzing the operating, investing, and financing activities of businesses.

Reporting the Statement of Cash Flows

Basics of Cash Flow Reporting
- Purpose
- Importance
- Measurement
- Classification
- Noncash activities
- Format
- Preparation

Cash Flows from Operating
- Indirect and direct methods of reporting
- Application of indirect method of reporting
- Summary of indirect method adjustments

Cash Flows from Investing
- Three-stage process of analysis
- Analysis of noncurrent assets
- Analysis of other assets

Cash Flows from Financing
- Three-stage process of analysis
- Analysis of noncurrent liabilities
- Analysis of equity

Basics of Cash Flow Reporting

This section describes the basics of cash flow reporting, including its purpose, measurement, classification, format, and preparation.

Purpose of the Statement of Cash Flows

C1 Explain the purpose and importance of cash flow information.

The purpose of the **statement of cash flows** is to report all major cash receipts (inflows) and cash payments (outflows) during a period. This includes separately identifying the cash flows related to operating, investing, and financing activities. The statement of cash flows does more than simply report changes in cash. It is the detailed disclosure of individual cash flows that makes this statement useful to users. Information in this statement helps users answer questions such as these:

■ How does a company obtain its cash?
■ Where does a company spend its cash?
■ What explains the change in the cash balance?

The statement of cash flows addresses important questions such as these by summarizing, classifying, and reporting a company's cash inflows and cash outflows for each period.

Point: Internal users rely on the statement of cash flows to make investing and financing decisions. External users rely on this statement to assess the amount and timing of a company's cash flows.

Topic Tackler PLUS

Importance of Cash Flows

Information about cash flows can influence decision makers in important ways. For instance, we look more favorably at a company that is financing its expenditures with cash from operations than one that does it by selling its assets. Information about cash flows helps users decide whether a company has enough cash to pay its existing debts as they mature. It is also relied upon to evaluate a company's ability to meet unexpected obligations and pursue unexpected opportunities. External information users especially want to assess a company's ability to take advantage of new business opportunities. Internal users such as managers use cash flow information to plan day-to-day operating activities and make long-term investment decisions.

Macy's striking turnaround is an example of how analysis and management of cash flows can lead to improved financial stability. Several years ago Macy's obtained temporary protection from bankruptcy, at which time it desperately needed to improve its cash flows. It did so by engaging in aggressive cost-cutting measures. As a result, Macy's annual cash flow rose to $210 million, up from a negative cash flow of $38.9 million in the prior year. Macy's eventually met its financial obligations and then successfully merged with **Federated Department Stores**.

The case of **W. T. Grant Co.** is a classic example of the importance of cash flow information in predicting a company's future performance and financial strength. Grant reported net income of more than $40 million per year for three consecutive years. At that same time, it was experiencing an alarming decrease in cash provided by operations. For instance, net cash outflow was more than $90 million by the end of that three-year period. Grant soon went bankrupt. Users who relied solely on Grant's income numbers were unpleasantly surprised. This reminds us that cash flows as well as income statement and balance sheet information are crucial in making business decisions.

> **Decision Insight**
>
> **Cash Multiple**   Some experts who value private companies do so on the basis of a multiple of operating cash flow. Medium-sized private companies usually sell for five to seven times their operating cash flows. Larger companies often command higher multiples.

Measurement of Cash Flows

Cash flows are defined to include both *cash* and *cash equivalents*. The statement of cash flows explains the difference between the beginning and ending balances of cash and cash equivalents. We continue to use the phrases *cash flows* and the *statement of cash flows,* but we must remember that both phrases refer to cash and cash equivalents. Recall that a cash equivalent must satisfy two criteria: (1) be readily convertible to a known amount of cash and (2) be sufficiently close to its maturity so its market value is unaffected by interest rate changes. In most cases, a debt security must be within three months of its maturity to satisfy these criteria. Companies must disclose and follow a clear policy for determining cash and cash equivalents and apply it consistently from period to period. **American Express**, for example, defines its cash equivalents as "time deposits and other highly liquid investments with original maturities of 90 days or less."

> **Decision Insight**
>
> **Cash Flow**   "A lender must have a complete understanding of a borrower's cash flows to assess both the borrowing needs and repayment sources. This requires information about the major types of cash inflows and outflows. I have seen many companies, whose financial statements indicate good profitability, experience severe financial problems because the owners or managers lacked a good understanding of cash flows."—Mary E. Garza, **Bank of America**.

Classification of Cash Flows

Since cash and cash equivalents are combined, the statement of cash flows does not report transactions between cash and cash equivalents such as cash paid to purchase cash equivalents and cash received from selling cash equivalents. However, all other cash receipts and cash payments are classified and reported on the statement as operating, investing, or financing activities. Individual cash receipts and payments for each of these three categories are labeled to identify their originating transactions or events. A net cash inflow (source) occurs when the receipts in a category exceed the payments. A net cash outflow (use) occurs when the payments in a category exceed the receipts.

C2 Distinguish between operating, investing, and financing activities.

Operating Activities   **Operating activities** include those transactions and events that determine net income. Examples are the production and purchase of merchandise, the sale of goods and services to customers, and the expenditures to administer the business. Not all items in income, such as unusual gains and losses, are operating activities (we discuss these exceptions later in the chapter). Exhibit 16.1 lists the more common cash inflows and outflows from operating activities. (Although cash receipts and cash payments from buying and selling trading securities are often reported under operating activities, new standards require that these receipts and payments be classified based on the nature and purpose of those securities.)

Exhibit 16.1

Cash Flows from Operating Activities

Cash Inflows

From customers for cash sales
From borrowers for interest
From collections on credit sales
From cash dividends received
From lawsuit settlements

Operating Activities

Cash Outflows

Operating Activities

To salaries and wages
To suppliers for goods and services
To lenders for interest
To governments for taxes and fines
To charities

Point: Investing activities exclude transactions in trading securities.

Point: Common errors include misclassification of *cash dividends received* and *cash interest received* as investing activities and *cash interest paid* as financing. The FASB requires these cash flows be reported as operating activities.

Investing Activities   **Investing activities** generally include those transactions and events that affect long-term assets, namely, the purchase and sale of long-term assets. They also include the (1) purchase and sale of short-term investments other than cash equivalents and trading securities and (2) lending and collecting money for notes receivable. Exhibit 16.2 lists examples of cash flows from investing activities. Proceeds from collecting the principal amounts of notes deserve special mention. If the note results from sales to customers, its cash receipts are classed as operating activities whether short term or long term. If the note results from a loan to another party apart from sales, however, the cash receipts from collecting the note principal are classed as an investing activity. The FASB requires the collection of interest on loans be reported as an operating activity.

Exhibit 16.2

Cash Flows from Investing Activities

Cash Inflows

From selling available-for-sale securities
From collecting principal on loans
From selling (discounting) of notes
From selling long-term productive assets
From selling held-to-maturity securities

Investing Activities

Cash Outflows

Investing Activities

To make loans to others
To purchase long-term productive assets
To purchase held-to-maturity securities
To purchase available-for-sale securities

Point: Interest payments on a loan are classified as operating activities, but payments of loan principal are financing activities.

Financing Activities   **Financing activities** include those transactions and events that affect long-term liabilities and equity. Examples are (1) obtaining cash from issuing debt and repaying the amounts borrowed and (2) receiving cash from or distributing cash to owners. These activities involve transactions with a company's owners and creditors. They also often involve borrowing and repaying principal amounts relating to both short- and long-term debt. Notice that payments of interest expense are classified as operating activities. Also, cash payments to settle credit purchases of merchandise, whether on account or by note, are operating activities. Exhibit 16.3 lists examples of cash flows from financing activities.

Exhibit 16.3

Cash Flows from
Financing Activities

Noncash Investing and Financing

When important investing and financing activities do not affect cash receipts or payments, they are still disclosed at the bottom of the statement of cash flows or in a note to the statement because of their importance and the *full-disclosure principle*. One example of such a transaction is the purchase of long-term assets using a long-term note payable. This transaction involves both investing and financing activities but does not affect any cash inflow or outflow and is not reported in any of the three sections of the statement of cash flows. This disclosure rule also extends to transactions with partial cash receipts or payments.

To illustrate, assume that Goorin purchases land for $12,000 by paying $5,000 cash and trading in used equipment with a $7,000 market value. The investing section of the statement of cash flows reports only the $5,000 cash outflow for the land purchase. The $12,000 investing transaction is only partially described in the body of the statement of cash flows, yet this information is potentially important to users because it changes the makeup of assets. Goorin could either describe the transaction in a note or include a small schedule at the bottom of its statement that lists the $12,000 land purchase along with the cash financing of $5,000 and a $7,000 trade-in of used equipment. As another example, Borg Co. acquired $900,000 of assets in exchange for $200,000 cash and a $700,000 long-term note, which is reported as follows:

C3 Identify and disclose noncash investing and financing activities.

Point: A stock dividend transaction involving a transfer from retained earnings to common stock or a credit to contributed capital is *not* considered a noncash investing and financing activity because the company receives no consideration for shares issued.

Decision Maker	Answer—p. 652

Entrepreneur   You are considering purchasing a start-up business that recently reported a $110,000 annual net loss and a $225,000 annual net cash inflow. How are these results possible?

Fair value of assets acquired	$900,000
Less cash paid	200,000
Liabilities incurred or assumed	$700,000

Exhibit 16.4 lists transactions commonly disclosed as noncash investing and financing activities.

- Retirement of debt by issuing equity stock.
- Conversion of preferred stock to common stock.
- Lease of assets in a capital lease transaction.
- Purchase of long-term assets by issuing a note or bond.
- Exchange of noncash assets for other noncash assets.
- Purchase of noncash assets by issuing equity or debt.

Exhibit 16.4

Examples of Noncash Investing and Financing Activities

Format of the Statement of Cash Flows

Accounting standards require companies to include a statement of cash flows in a complete set of financial statements. This statement must report information about a company's cash receipts and cash payments during the period. Exhibit 16.5 shows the usual format. A company must report cash flows from three activities: operating, investing, and financing. The statement explains how transactions and events impact the prior period-end cash (and cash equivalents) balance to produce its current period-end balance.

C4 Describe the format of the statement of cash flows.

Exhibit 16.5

Format of the Statement of Cash Flows

COMPANY NAME
Statement of Cash Flows
For *period* Ended *date*

Cash flows from operating activities
  [List of individual inflows and outflows]
  Net cash provided (used) by operating activities . . . . $ #
Cash flows from investing activities
  [List of individual inflows and outflows]
  Net cash provided (used) by investing activities . . . .   #
Cash flows from financing activities
  [List of individual inflows and outflows]
  Net cash provided (used) by financing activities . . . .   #
Net increase (decrease) in cash . . . . $ #
Cash (and equivalents) balance at prior period-end . . . .   #
Cash (and equivalents) balance at current period-end . . . . $ #

Separate schedule or note disclosure of any "noncash investing and financing transactions" is required.

Global: International standards also require a statement of cash flows separated into operating, investing, and financing activities.

Quick Check
Answers—p. 652

1. Does a statement of cash flows report the cash payments to purchase cash equivalents? Does it report the cash receipts from selling cash equivalents?
2. Identify the categories of cash flows reported separately on the statement of cash flows.
3. Identify the cash activity category for each transaction: (*a*) purchase equipment for cash, (*b*) cash payment of wages, (*c*) sale of common stock for cash, (*d*) receipt of cash dividends from stock investment, (*e*) cash collection from customers, (*f*) bonds issuance for cash.

Preparing the Statement of Cash Flows

P1   **Prepare a statement of cash flows.**

Step 1: Compute net increase or decrease in cash

Step 2: Compute net cash from operating activities

Step 3: Compute net cash from investing activities

Step 4: Compute net cash from financing activities

Step 5: Prove and report beginning and ending cash balances

Preparing a statement of cash flows involves five steps: (1) compute the net increase or decrease in cash; (2) compute and report net cash provided (used) by operating activities (using either the direct or indirect method; both are explained); (3) compute and report net cash provided (used) by investing activities; (4) compute and report net cash provided (used) by financing activities; and (5) compute net cash flow by combining net cash provided (used) by operating, investing, and financing activities and then *prove it* by adding it to the beginning cash balance to show that it equals the ending cash balance. Important noncash investing and financing activities are disclosed in either a note or a separate schedule to the statement.

Computing the net increase or net decrease in cash is a simple but crucial computation. It equals the current period's cash balance minus the prior period's cash balance. This is the *bottom-line* figure for the statement of cash flows and is a check on the accuracy of one's work. The information we need to prepare a statement of cash flows comes from various sources including comparative balance sheets at the beginning and end of the period, and an income statement for the period. There are two alternative approaches to preparing the statement: (1) analyzing the Cash account and (2) analyzing noncash accounts.

Analyzing the Cash Account   A company's cash receipts and cash payments are recorded in the Cash account in its general ledger. The Cash account is therefore a natural place to look for information about cash flows from operating, investing, and financing activities. To illustrate, review the summarized Cash T-account of Genesis, Inc., in Exhibit 16.6. Individual cash transactions are summarized in this Cash account according to the major types of cash receipts and cash payments. For instance, only the total of cash receipts from all customers is listed. Individual cash transactions underlying these totals can number in the thousands. Accounting software programs are available to provide summarized cash accounts.

Preparing a statement of cash flows from Exhibit 16.6 requires determining whether an individual cash inflow or outflow is an operating, investing, or financing activity, and then listing each by activity. This yields the statement shown in Exhibit 16.7. However, preparing

Exhibit 16.6
Summarized Cash Account

the statement of cash flows from an analysis of the summarized Cash account has two limitations. First, most companies have many individual cash receipts and payments, making it difficult to review them all. Accounting software minimizes this burden, but it is still a task requiring professional judgment for many transactions. Second, the Cash account does not usually carry an adequate description of each cash transaction, making assignment of all cash transactions according to activity difficult.

Point: View the change in cash as a *target* number that you will fully explain and prove in the statement of cash flows.

Exhibit 16.7
Statement of Cash Flows—Direct Method

GENESIS
Statement of Cash Flows
For Year Ended December 31, 2008

Cash flows from operating activities		
Cash received from customers	$570,000	
Cash paid for merchandise	(319,000)	
Cash paid for wages and other operating expenses	(218,000)	
Cash paid for interest	(8,000)	
Cash paid for taxes	(5,000)	
Net cash provided by operating activities		$20,000
Cash flows from investing activities		
Cash received from sale of plant assets	12,000	
Cash paid for purchase of plant assets	(10,000)	
Net cash provided by investing activities		2,000
Cash flows from financing activities		
Cash received from issuing stock	15,000	
Cash paid to retire bonds	(18,000)	
Cash paid for dividends	(14,000)	
Net cash used in financing activities		(17,000)
Net increase in cash		$ 5,000
Cash balance at prior year-end		12,000
Cash balance at current year-end		$17,000

Analyzing Noncash Accounts A second approach to preparing the statement of cash flows is analyzing noncash accounts. This approach uses the fact that when a company records cash inflows and outflows with debits and credits to the Cash account (see Exhibit 16.6), it also records credits and debits in noncash accounts (reflecting double-entry accounting). Many of these noncash accounts are balance sheet accounts, for instance, from the sale of land for cash. Others are revenue and expense accounts that are closed to equity. For instance, the sale of services for cash yields a credit to Services Revenue that is closed to Retained Earnings for a corporation. In sum, *all cash transactions eventually affect noncash balance sheet accounts*. Thus, we can determine cash inflows and outflows by analyzing changes in noncash balance sheet accounts.

Exhibit 16.8 uses the accounting equation to show the relation between the Cash account and the noncash balance sheet accounts. This exhibit starts with the accounting equation at the top. It is then expanded in line (2) to separate cash from noncash asset accounts. Line (3) moves noncash asset accounts to the right-hand side of the equality where they are subtracted. This

Global: Some countries require a statement of funds flow instead of a statement of cash flows; *funds* are often defined as *working capital* (current assets minus current liabilities).

Exhibit 16.8

Relation between Cash and
Noncash Accounts

shows that cash equals the sum of the liability and equity accounts *minus* the noncash asset accounts. Line (4) points out that *changes* on one side of the accounting equation equal *changes* on the other side. It shows that we can explain changes in cash by analyzing changes in the noncash accounts consisting of liability accounts, equity accounts, and noncash assets accounts. By analyzing noncash balance sheet accounts and any related income statement accounts, we can prepare a statement of cash flows.

Information to Prepare the Statement   Information to prepare the statement of cash flows usually comes from three sources: (1) comparative balance sheets, (2) current income statement, and (3) additional information. Comparative balance sheets are used to compute changes in noncash accounts from the beginning to the end of the period. The current income statement is used to help compute cash flows from operating activities. Additional information often includes details on transactions and events that help explain both the cash flows and noncash investing and financing activities.

Decision Insight

e-Cash Every credit transaction on the Net leaves a trail that a hacker or a marketer can pick up. Enter e-cash—or digital money. The encryption of e-cash protects your money from snoops and thieves and cannot be traced, even by the issuing bank.

Cash Flows from Operating

Indirect and Direct Methods of Reporting

Cash flows provided (used) by operating activities are reported in one of two ways: the *direct method* or the *indirect method*. **These two different methods apply only to the operating activities section.**

The **direct method** separately lists each major item of operating cash receipts (such as cash received from customers) and each major item of operating cash payments (such as cash paid for merchandise). The cash payments are subtracted from cash receipts to determine the net cash provided (used) by operating activities. The operating activities section of Exhibit 16.7 reflects the direct method of reporting operating cash flows.

The **indirect method** reports net income and then adjusts it for items necessary to obtain net cash provided (used) by operating activities. It does *not* report individual items of cash inflows and cash outflows from operating activities. Instead, the indirect method reports the necessary adjustments to reconcile net income to net cash provided (used) by operating activities. The operating activities section for Genesis prepared under the indirect method is shown in Exhibit 16.9.

Cash flows from operating activities		
Net income	$ 38,000	
Adjustments to reconcile net income to net cash provided by operating activities		
Increase in accounts receivable	(20,000)	
Increase in merchandise inventory	(14,000)	
Increase in prepaid expenses	(2,000)	
Decrease in accounts payable	(5,000)	
Decrease in interest payable	(1,000)	
Increase in income taxes payable	10,000	
Depreciation expense	24,000	
Loss on sale of plant assets	6,000	
Gain on retirement of bonds	(16,000)	
Net cash provided by operating activities		**$20,000**

Exhibit 16.9

Operating Activities Section—Indirect Method

The net cash amount provided by operating activities is *identical* under both the direct and indirect methods. This equality always exists. The difference in these methods is with the computation and presentation of this amount. The FASB recommends the direct method, but because it is not required and the indirect method is arguably easier to compute, nearly all companies report operating cash flows using the indirect method.

To illustrate, we prepare the operating activities section of the statement of cash flows for Genesis. Exhibit 16.10 shows the December 31, 2007 and 2008, balance sheets of Genesis along with its 2008 income statement. We use this information to prepare a statement of cash flows that explains the $5,000 increase in cash for 2008 as reflected in its balance sheets. This $5,000 is computed as Cash of $17,000 at the end of 2008 minus Cash of $12,000 at the end of 2007. Genesis discloses additional information about 2008 transactions:

a. The accounts payable balances result from merchandise inventory purchases.

b. Purchased plant assets costing $70,000 by paying $10,000 cash and issuing $60,000 of bonds payable.

c. Sold plant assets with an original cost of $30,000 and accumulated depreciation of $12,000 for $12,000 cash, yielding a $6,000 loss.

d. Received cash of $15,000 from issuing 3,000 shares of common stock.

e. Paid $18,000 cash to retire bonds with a $34,000 book value, yielding a $16,000 gain.

f. Declared and paid cash dividends of $14,000.

> *The next section describes the indirect method. Appendix 16B describes the direct method. An instructor can choose to cover either one or both methods. Neither section depends on the other.*

Application of the Indirect Method of Reporting

Net income is computed using accrual accounting, which recognizes revenues when earned and expenses when incurred. Revenues and expenses do not necessarily reflect the receipt and payment of cash. The indirect method of computing and reporting net cash flows from operating activities involves adjusting the net income figure to obtain the net cash provided (used) by operating activities. This includes subtracting noncash increases (credits) from net income and adding noncash charges (debits) back to net income.

To illustrate, the indirect method begins with Genesis's net income of $38,000 and adjusts it to obtain net cash provided (used) by operating activities of $20,000. Exhibit 16.11 shows the results of the indirect method of reporting operating cash flows, which adjusts net income for three types of adjustments. There are adjustments ① to reflect changes in noncash current assets and current liabilities related to operating activities, ② to income statement items involving operating activities that do not affect cash inflows or outflows, and ③ to eliminate gains and losses resulting from investing and financing activities (not part of operating activities). This section describes each of these adjustments.

Point: To better understand the direct and indirect methods of reporting operating cash flows, identify similarities and differences between Exhibits 16.7 and 16.11.

Topic Tackler

PLUS

16-2

P2 Compute cash flows from operating activities using the indirect method.

Point: *Noncash credits* refer to *revenue amounts* reported on the income statement that are *not collected in cash* this period. *Noncash charges* refer to *expense amounts* reported on the income statement that are *not paid* this period.

Exhibit 16.10

Financial Statements

GENESIS Income Statement For Year Ended December 31, 2008		
Sales		$590,000
Cost of goods sold	$300,000	
Wages and other operating expenses	216,000	
Interest expense	7,000	
Depreciation expense	24,000	(547,000)
		43,000
Other gains (losses)		
Gain on retirement of bonds	16,000	
Loss on sale of plant assets	(6,000)	10,000
Income before taxes		53,000
Income taxes expense		(15,000)
Net income		$ 38,000

GENESIS Balance Sheets December 31, 2008 and 2007		
	2008	2007
Assets		
Current assets		
Cash	$ 17,000	$ 12,000
Accounts receivable	60,000	40,000
Merchandise inventory	84,000	70,000
Prepaid expenses	6,000	4,000
Total current assets	167,000	126,000
Long-term assets		
Plant assets	250,000	210,000
Accumulated depreciation	(60,000)	(48,000)
Total assets	$357,000	$288,000
Liabilities		
Current liabilities		
Accounts payable	$ 35,000	$ 40,000
Interest payable	3,000	4,000
Income taxes payable	22,000	12,000
Total current liabilities	60,000	56,000
Long-term bonds payable	90,000	64,000
Total liabilities	150,000	120,000
Equity		
Common stock, $5 par	95,000	80,000
Retained earnings	112,000	88,000
Total equity	207,000	168,000
Total liabilities and equity	$357,000	$288,000

① **Adjustments for Changes in Current Assets and Current Liabilities** This section describes adjustments for changes in noncash current assets and current liabilities.

Adjustments for changes in noncash current assets. Changes in noncash current assets are normally the result of operating activities. Examples are sales affecting accounts receivable and asset usage affecting prepaid rent. Decreases in noncash current assets yield the following adjustment:

Decreases in noncash current assets are added to net income.

To see the logic for this adjustment, consider that a decrease in a noncash current asset such as accounts receivable suggests more available cash at the end of the period compared to the beginning. This is so because a decrease in accounts receivable implies higher cash receipts than reflected in sales. We add these higher cash receipts (from decreases in noncash current assets) to net income when computing cash flow from operations.

In contrast, an increase in noncash current assets such as accounts receivable implies less cash receipts than reflected in sales. As another example, an increase in prepaid rent indicates that more cash is paid for rent than is deducted as rent expense. Increases in noncash current assets yield the following adjustment:

Increases in noncash current assets are subtracted from net income.

To illustrate, these adjustments are applied to the noncash current assets in Exhibit 16.10.

Accounts receivable. Accounts Receivable *increase* $20,000, from a beginning balance of $40,000 to an ending balance of $60,000. This increase implies that Genesis collects less cash

Point: Operating activities are typically those that determine income, which are often reflected in changes in current assets and current liabilities.

than is reported in sales. That is, some of these sales were in the form of accounts receivable and that amount increased during the period. To see this it is helpful to use *account analysis*. This usually involves setting up a T-account and reconstructing its major entries to compute cash receipts or payments. The following reconstructed Accounts Receivable T-account reveals the lower amount of cash receipts compared to sales:

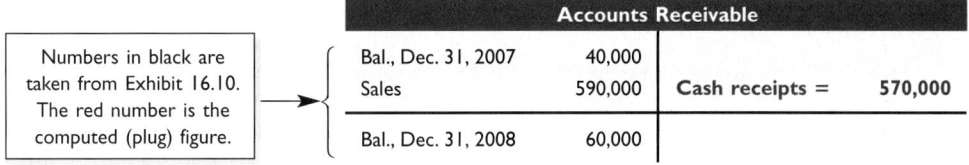

Accounts Receivable			
Bal., Dec. 31, 2007	40,000		
Sales	590,000	Cash receipts =	570,000
Bal., Dec. 31, 2008	60,000		

Numbers in black are taken from Exhibit 16.10. The red number is the computed (plug) figure.

Notice that sales are $20,000 greater than the cash receipts. This $20,000—as reflected in the $20,000 increase in Accounts Receivable—is subtracted from net income when computing cash provided by operating activities (see Exhibit 16.11).

Merchandise inventory. Merchandise inventory *increases* by $14,000, from a $70,000 beginning balance to an $84,000 ending balance. This increase implies that Genesis had a larger amount of cash purchases than cost of goods sold. This larger amount of cash purchases is in the form of inventory, as reflected in the following account analysis:

Merchandise Inventory			
Bal., Dec. 31, 2007	70,000		
Purchases =	314,000	Cost of goods sold	300,000
Bal., Dec. 31, 2008	84,000		

GENESIS Statement of Cash Flows For Year Ended December 31, 2008		
Cash flows from operating activities		
Net income	$ 38,000	
Adjustments to reconcile net income to net cash provided by operating activities		
① Increase in accounts receivable	(20,000)	
Increase in merchandise inventory	(14,000)	
Increase in prepaid expenses	(2,000)	
Decrease in accounts payable	(5,000)	
Decrease in interest payable	(1,000)	
Increase in income taxes payable	10,000	
② Depreciation expense	24,000	
③ Loss on sale of plant assets	6,000	
Gain on retirement of bonds	(16,000)	
Net cash provided by operating activities		$20,000
Cash flows from investing activities		
Cash received from sale of plant assets	12,000	
Cash paid for purchase of plant assets	(10,000)	
Net cash provided by investing activities		2,000
Cash flows from financing activities		
Cash received from issuing stock	15,000	
Cash paid to retire bonds	(18,000)	
Cash paid for dividends	(14,000)	
Net cash used in financing activities		(17,000)
Net increase in cash		$ 5,000
Cash balance at prior year-end		12,000
Cash balance at current year-end		$17,000

Exhibit 16.11

Statement of Cash Flows— Indirect Method

Point: Refer to Exhibit 16.10 and identify the $5,000 change in cash. This change is what the statement of cash flows explains; it serves as a check figure.

The amount by which purchases exceed cost of goods sold—as reflected in the $14,000 increase in inventory—is subtracted from net income when computing cash provided by operating activities (see Exhibit 16.11).

Prepaid expenses. Prepaid expenses *increase* $2,000, from a $4,000 beginning balance to a $6,000 ending balance, implying that Genesis's cash payments exceed its recorded prepaid expenses. These higher cash payments increase the amount of Prepaid Expenses, as reflected in its reconstructed T-account:

Prepaid Expenses			
Bal., Dec. 31, 2007	4,000		
Cash payments =	**218,000**	Wages and other operating exp.	216,000
Bal., Dec. 31, 2008	6,000		

The amount by which cash payments exceed the recorded operating expenses—as reflected in the $2,000 increase in Prepaid Expenses—is subtracted from net income when computing cash provided by operating activities (see Exhibit 16.11).

Adjustments for changes in current liabilities.   Changes in current liabilities are normally the result of operating activities. An example is a purchase that affects accounts payable. Increases in current liabilities yield the following adjustment to net income when computing operating cash flows:

Increases in current liabilities are added to net income.

To see the logic for this adjustment, consider that an increase in the Accounts Payable account suggests that cash payments are less than the related (cost of goods sold) expense. As another example, an increase in wages payable implies that cash paid for wages is less than the recorded wages expense. Since the recorded expense is greater than the cash paid, we add the increase in wages payable to net income to compute net cash flow from operations.

Conversely, when current liabilities decrease, the following adjustment is required:

Decreases in current liabilities are subtracted from net income.

To illustrate, this adjustment is applied to the current liabilities in Exhibit 16.10.

Accounts payable. Accounts Payable *decrease* $5,000, from a beginning balance of $40,000 to an ending balance of $35,000. This decrease implies that cash payments to suppliers exceed purchases by $5,000 for the period, which is reflected in the reconstructed Accounts Payable T-account:

Accounts Payable			
		Bal., Dec. 31, 2007	40,000
Cash payments =	**319,000**	Purchases	314,000
		Bal., Dec. 31, 2008	35,000

The amount by which cash payments exceed purchases—as reflected in the $5,000 decrease in Accounts Payable—is subtracted from net income when computing cash provided by operating activities (see Exhibit 16.11).

Interest payable. Interest Payable *decreases* $1,000, from a $4,000 beginning balance to a $3,000 ending balance. This decrease indicates that cash paid for interest exceeds interest expense by $1,000, which is reflected in the Interest Payable T-account:

Interest Payable			
		Bal., Dec. 31, 2007	4,000
Cash paid for interest =	**8,000**	Interest expense	7,000
		Bal., Dec. 31, 2008	3,000

The amount by which cash paid exceeds recorded expense—as reflected in the $1,000 decrease in Interest Payable—is subtracted from net income (see Exhibit 16.11).

Income taxes payable. Income Taxes Payable *increase* $10,000, from a $12,000 beginning balance to a $22,000 ending balance. This increase implies that reported income taxes exceed the cash paid for taxes, which is reflected in the Income Taxes Payable T-account:

Income Taxes Payable			
		Bal., Dec. 31, 2007	12,000
Cash paid for taxes =	5,000	Income taxes expense	15,000
		Bal., Dec. 31, 2008	22,000

The amount by which cash paid falls short of the reported taxes expense—as reflected in the $10,000 increase in Income Taxes Payable—is added to net income when computing cash provided by operating activities (see Exhibit 16.11).

Adjustments for Changes in Current Assets and Current Liabilities		
Account	Increases	Decreases
Noncash current assets	Deduct from NI	Add to NI
Current liabilities	Add to NI	Deduct from NI

② **Adjustments for Operating Items Not Providing or Using Cash**   The income statement usually includes some expenses that do not reflect cash outflows in the period. Examples are depreciation, amortization, depletion, and bad debts expense. The indirect method for reporting operating cash flows requires that

Expenses with no cash outflows are added back to net income.

To see the logic of this adjustment, recall that items such as depreciation, amortization, depletion, and bad debts originate from debits to expense accounts and credits to noncash accounts. These entries have *no* cash effect, and we add them back to net income when computing net cash flows from operations. Adding them back cancels their deductions.

Similarly, when net income includes revenues that do not reflect cash inflows in the period, the indirect method for reporting operating cash flows requires that

Revenues with no cash inflows are subtracted from net income.

We apply these adjustments to the Genesis operating items that do not provide or use cash.

Depreciation.   Depreciation expense is the only Genesis operating item that has no effect on cash flows in the period. We must add back the $24,000 depreciation expense to net income when computing cash provided by operating activities. (We later explain that the cash outflow to acquire a plant asset is reported as an investing activity.)

③ **Adjustments for Nonoperating Items**   Net income often includes losses that are not part of operating activities but are part of either investing or financing activities. Examples are a loss from the sale of a plant asset and a loss from retirement of a bond payable. The indirect method for reporting operating cash flows requires that

Nonoperating losses are added back to net income.

To see the logic, consider that items such as a plant asset sale and a bond retirement are normally recorded by recognizing the cash, removing all plant asset or bond accounts, and recognizing any loss or gain. The cash received or paid is not part of operating activities but is part of either investing or financing activities. *No* operating cash flow effect occurs. However, because the nonoperating loss is a deduction in computing net income, we need to add it back to net income when computing cash flow from operations. Adding it back cancels the deduction.

Similarly, when net income includes gains not part of operating activities, the indirect method for reporting operating cash flows requires that

Point: An income statement reports revenues, gains, expenses, and losses on an accrual basis. The statement of cash flows reports cash received and cash paid for operating, financing, and investing activities.

Nonoperating gains are subtracted from net income.

To illustrate these adjustments, we consider the nonoperating items of Genesis.

Loss on sale of plant assets.   Genesis reports a $6,000 loss on sale of plant assets as part of net income. This loss is a proper deduction in computing income, but it is *not part of operating activities*. Instead, a sale of plant assets is part of investing activities. Thus, the $6,000 nonoperating loss is added back to net income (see Exhibit 16.11). Adding it back cancels the loss. We later explain how to report the cash inflow from the asset sale in investing activities.

Gain on retirement of debt.   A $16,000 gain on retirement of debt is properly included in net income, but it is *not part of operating activities*. This means the $16,000 nonoperating gain must be subtracted from net income to obtain net cash provided by operating activities (see Exhibit 16.11). Subtracting it cancels the recorded gain. We later describe how to report the cash outflow to retire debt.

Summary of Adjustments for Indirect Method

Exhibit 16.12 summarizes the most common adjustments to net income when computing net cash provided (used) by operating activities under the indirect method.

Decision Insight

Cash or Income   The difference between net income and operating cash flows can be large and reflect on the quality of earnings. This bar chart shows net income and operating cash flows of four companies. Operating cash flows can be either higher or lower than net income.

Exhibit 16.12

Summary of Selected Adjustments for Indirect Method

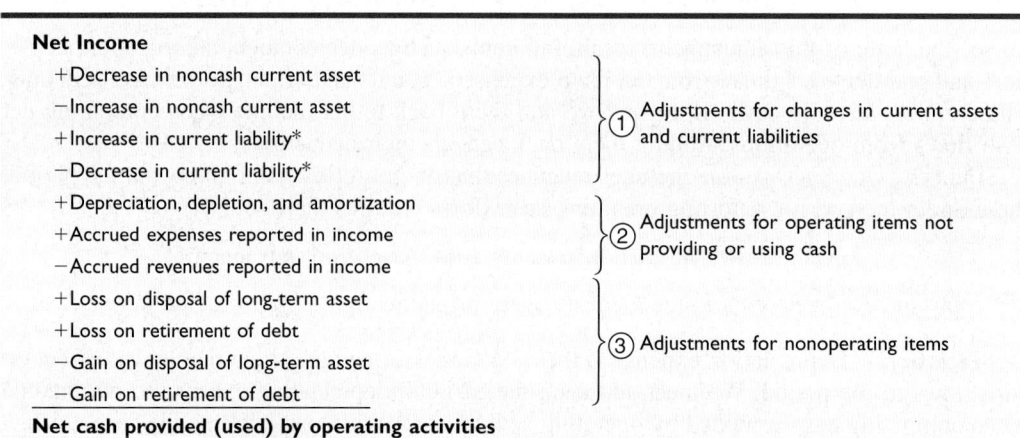

Net Income
 +Decrease in noncash current asset
 −Increase in noncash current asset
 +Increase in current liability*
 −Decrease in current liability*
 +Depreciation, depletion, and amortization
 +Accrued expenses reported in income
 −Accrued revenues reported in income
 +Loss on disposal of long-term asset
 +Loss on retirement of debt
 −Gain on disposal of long-term asset
 −Gain on retirement of debt
 Net cash provided (used) by operating activities

① Adjustments for changes in current assets and current liabilities
② Adjustments for operating items not providing or using cash
③ Adjustments for nonoperating items

* Excludes current portion of long-term debt and any (nonsales-related) short-term notes payable—both are financing activities.

The computations in determining cash provided (used) by operating activities are different for the indirect and direct methods, but the result is identical. Both methods yield the same $20,000 figure for cash from operating activities for Genesis; see Exhibits 16.7 and 16.11.

Quick Check

Answers—p. 652

4. Determine net cash provided (used) by operating activities using the following data: net income, $74,900; decrease in accounts receivable, $4,600; increase in inventory, $11,700; decrease in accounts payable, $1,000; loss on sale of equipment, $3,400; payment of cash dividends, $21,500.

5. Why are expenses such as depreciation and amortization added to net income when cash flow from operating activities is computed by the indirect method?

6. A company reports net income of $15,000 that includes a $3,000 gain on the sale of plant assets. Why is this gain subtracted from net income in computing cash flow from operating activities using the indirect method?

Cash Flows from Investing

The third major step in preparing the statement of cash flows is to compute and report cash flows from investing activities. We normally do this by identifying changes in (1) all noncurrent asset accounts and (2) the current accounts for both notes receivable and investments in securities (excluding trading securities). We then analyze changes in these accounts to determine their effect, if any, on cash and report the cash flow effects in the investing activities section of the statement of cash flows. **Reporting of investing activities is identical under the direct method and indirect method.**

Three-Stage Process of Analysis

Information to compute cash flows from investing activities is usually taken from beginning and ending balance sheets and the income statement. We use a three-stage process to determine cash provided (used) by investing activities: (1) identify changes in investing-related accounts, (2) explain these changes using reconstruction analysis, and (3) report their cash flow effects.

Analysis of Noncurrent Assets

Information about the Genesis transactions provided earlier reveals that the company both purchased and sold plant assets during the period. Both transactions are investing activities and are analyzed for their cash flow effects in this section.

P3 Determine cash flows from both investing and financing activities.

Plant Asset Transactions   The first stage in analyzing the Plant Assets account and its related Accumulated Depreciation is to identify any changes in these accounts from comparative balance sheets in Exhibit 16.10. This analysis reveals a $40,000 increase in plant assets from $210,000 to $250,000 and a $12,000 increase in accumulated depreciation from $48,000 to $60,000.

The second stage is to explain these changes. Items *b* and *c* of the additional information for Genesis (page 629) are relevant in this case. Recall that the Plant Assets account is affected by both asset purchases and sales, while its Accumulated Depreciation account is normally increased from depreciation and decreased from the removal of accumulated depreciation in asset sales. To explain changes in these accounts and to identify their cash flow effects, we prepare *reconstructed entries* from prior transactions; *they are not the actual entries by the preparer.*

To illustrate, item *b* reports that Genesis purchased plant assets of $70,000 by issuing $60,000 in bonds payable to the seller and paying $10,000 in cash. The reconstructed entry for analysis of item *b* follows:

Point: Investing activities include (1) purchasing and selling long-term assets, (2) lending and collecting on notes receivable, and (3) purchasing and selling short-term investments other than cash equivalents and trading securities.

Point: Financing and investing info is available in ledger accounts to help explain changes in comparative balance sheets. Post references lead to relevant entries and explanations.

Reconstruction	Plant Assets..............................	70,000	
	Bonds Payable		60,000
	Cash..............................		**10,000**

Assets = Liabilities + Equity
+70,000   +60,000
−10,000

This entry reveals a $10,000 cash outflow for plant assets and a $60,000 noncash investing and financing transaction involving bonds exchanged for plant assets.

Next, item *c* reports that Genesis sold plant assets costing $30,000 (with $12,000 of accumulated depreciation) for $12,000 cash, resulting in a $6,000 loss. The reconstructed entry for analysis of item *c* follows:

Reconstruction	**Cash**	**12,000**	
	Accumulated Depreciation	12,000	
	Loss on Sale of Plant Assets	6,000	
	Plant Assets		30,000

Assets = Liabilities + Equity
+12,000   −6,000
−30,000
+12,000

This entry reveals a $12,000 cash inflow from assets sold. The $6,000 loss is computed by comparing the asset book value to the cash received and does not reflect any cash inflow or outflow. We also reconstruct the entry for Depreciation Expense using information from the income statement:

Assets = Liabilities + Equity
−24,000   −24,000

Reconstruction	Depreciation Expense	24,000	
	Accumulated Depreciation		24,000

This entry shows that Depreciation Expense results in no cash flow effect. These three reconstructed entries are reflected in the following plant asset and related T-accounts.

Plant Assets			
Bal., Dec. 31, 2007	210,000		
Purchase	70,000	Sale	30,000
Bal., Dec. 31, 2008	250,000		

Accumulated Depreciation—Plant Assets			
		Bal., Dec. 31, 2007	48,000
Sale	12,000	Depr. expense	24,000
		Bal., Dec. 31, 2008	60,000

Example: If a plant asset costing $40,000 with $37,000 of accumulated depreciation is sold at a $1,000 loss, what is the cash flow? What is the cash flow if this asset is sold at a gain of $3,000? *Answers:* +$2,000; +$6,000.

This reconstruction analysis is complete in that the change in plant assets from $210,000 to $250,000 is fully explained by the $70,000 purchase and the $30,000 sale. Also, the change in accumulated depreciation from $48,000 to $60,000 is fully explained by depreciation expense of $24,000 and the removal of $12,000 in accumulated depreciation from an asset sale. (*Note:* Preparers of the statement of cash flows have the entire ledger and additional information at their disposal, but for brevity reasons only the information needed for reconstructing accounts is given.)

The third stage looks at the reconstructed entries for identification of cash flows. The two identified cash flow effects are reported in the investing section of the statement as follows (also see Exhibit 16.7 or 16.11):

Cash flows from investing activities	
Cash received from sale of plant assets	$12,000
Cash paid for purchase of plant assets	(10,000)

Also, the $60,000 portion of the purchase described in item *b* and financed by issuing bonds is a noncash investing and financing activity. It is reported in a note or in a separate schedule to the statement as follows:

Noncash investing and financing activity	
Purchased plant assets with issuance of bonds	$60,000

Analysis of Other Assets

Many other asset transactions (including those involving current notes receivable and investments in certain securities) are considered investing activities and can affect a company's cash flows. Since Genesis did not enter into other investing activities impacting assets, we do not need to extend our analysis to these other assets. If such transactions did exist, we would analyze them using the same three-stage process illustrated for plant assets.

Quick Check	Answer—p. 652

7. Equipment costing $80,000 with accumulated depreciation of $30,000 is sold at a loss of $10,000. What is the cash receipt from this sale? In what section of the statement of cash flows is this transaction reported?

Cash Flows from Financing

The fourth major step in preparing the statement of cash flows is to compute and report cash flows from financing activities. We normally do this by identifying changes in all noncurrent liability accounts (including the current portion of any notes and bonds) and the equity accounts. These accounts include long-term debt, notes payable, bonds payable, common stock, and retained earnings. Changes in these accounts are then analyzed using available information to determine their effect, if any, on cash. Results are reported in the financing activities section of the statement. **Reporting of financing activities is identical under the direct method and indirect method.**

Three-Stage Process of Analysis

We again use a three-stage process to determine cash provided (used) by financing activities: (1) identify changes in financing-related accounts, (2) explain these changes using reconstruction analysis, and (3) report their cash flow effects.

Analysis of Noncurrent Liabilities

Information about Genesis provided earlier reveals two transactions involving noncurrent liabilities. We analyzed one of those, the $60,000 issuance of bonds payable to purchase plant assets. This transaction is reported as a significant noncash investing and financing activity in a note or a separate schedule to the statement of cash flows. The other remaining transaction involving noncurrent liabilities is the cash retirement of bonds payable.

Point: Financing activities generally refer to changes in the noncurrent liability and the equity accounts. Examples are (1) receiving cash from issuing debt or repaying amounts borrowed and (2) receiving cash from or distributing cash to owners.

Bonds Payable Transactions The first stage in analysis of bonds is to review the comparative balance sheets from Exhibit 16.10. This analysis reveals an increase in bonds payable from $64,000 to $90,000.

The second stage explains this change. Item *e* of the additional information for Genesis (page 629) reports that bonds with a carrying value of $34,000 are retired for $18,000 cash, resulting in a $16,000 gain. The reconstructed entry for analysis of item *e* follows:

Reconstruction	Bonds Payable	34,000	
	Gain on retirement of debt		16,000
	Cash		**18,000**

Assets	= Liabilities +	Equity
−18,000	−34,000	+16,000

This entry reveals an $18,000 cash outflow for retirement of bonds and a $16,000 gain from comparing the bonds payable carrying value to the cash received. This gain does not reflect any cash inflow or outflow. Also, item *b* of the additional information reports that Genesis purchased plant assets costing $70,000 by issuing $60,000 in bonds payable to the seller and paying $10,000 in cash. We reconstructed this entry when analyzing investing activities: It showed a $60,000 increase to bonds payable that is reported as a noncash investing and financing transaction. The Bonds Payable account reflects (and is fully explained by) these reconstructed entries as follows:

Bonds Payable			
		Bal., Dec. 31, 2007	64,000
Retired bonds	34,000	**Issued bonds**	**60,000**
		Bal., Dec. 31, 2008	90,000

The third stage is to report the cash flow effect of the bond retirement in the financing section of the statement as follows (also see Exhibit 16.7 or 16.11):

Cash flows from financing activities
Cash paid to retire bonds . . . . $(18,000)

Analysis of Equity

The Genesis information reveals two transactions involving equity accounts. The first is the issuance of common stock for cash. The second is the declaration and payment of cash dividends. We analyze both.

Common Stock Transactions   The first stage in analyzing common stock is to review the comparative balance sheets from Exhibit 16.10, which reveals an increase in common stock from $80,000 to $95,000.

The second stage explains this change. Item *d* of the additional information (page 629) reports that 3,000 shares of common stock are issued at par for $5 per share. The reconstructed entry for analysis of item *d* follows:

Assets = Liabilities + Equity
+15,000   +15,000

| Reconstruction | Cash .... | 15,000 | |
| | Common Stock .... | | 15,000 |

This entry reveals a $15,000 cash inflow from stock issuance and is reflected in (and explains) the Common Stock account as follows:

Common Stock		
	Bal., Dec. 31, 2007	80,000
	Issued stock	**15,000**
	Bal., Dec. 31, 2008	95,000

The third stage discloses the cash flow effect from stock issuance in the financing section of the statement as follows (also see Exhibit 16.7 or 16.11):

Cash flows from financing activities
Cash received from issuing stock $15,000

Retained Earnings Transactions   The first stage in analyzing the Retained Earnings account is to review the comparative balance sheets from Exhibit 16.10. This reveals an increase in retained earnings from $88,000 to $112,000.

The second stage explains this change. Item *f* of the additional information (page 629) reports that cash dividends of $14,000 are paid. The reconstructed entry follows:

Assets = Liabilities + Equity
−14,000   −14,000

| Reconstruction | Retained Earnings......................... | 14,000 | |
| | Cash.................................. | | 14,000 |

This entry reveals a $14,000 cash outflow for cash dividends. Also note that the Retained Earnings account is impacted by net income of $38,000. (Net income was analyzed under the operating section of the statement of cash flows.) The reconstructed Retained Earnings account follows:

Retained Earnings			
		Bal., Dec. 31, 2007	88,000
Cash dividend	**14,000**	**Net income**	**38,000**
		Bal., Dec. 31, 2008	112,000

The third stage reports the cash flow effect from the cash dividend in the financing section of the statement as follows (also see Exhibit 16.7 or 16.11):

Cash flows from financing activities
Cash paid for dividends . . . . $(14,000)

We now have identified and explained all of the Genesis cash inflows and cash outflows and one noncash investing and financing transaction. Specifically, our analysis has reconciled changes in all noncash balance sheet accounts.

Proving Cash Balances

The fifth and final step in preparing the statement is to report the beginning and ending cash balances and prove that the *net change in cash* is explained by operating, investing, and financing cash flows. This step is shown here for Genesis.

Net cash provided by operating activities	$ 20,000
Net cash provided by investing activities	2,000
Net cash used in financing activities	(17,000)
Net increase in cash	**$ 5,000**
Cash balance at 2007 year-end	12,000
Cash balance at 2008 year-end	$ 17,000

The preceding table shows that the $5,000 net increase in cash, from $12,000 at the beginning of the period to $17,000 at the end, is reconciled by net cash flows from operating ($20,000 inflow), investing ($2,000 inflow), and financing ($17,000 outflow) activities. This is formally reported at the bottom of the statement of cash flows as shown in both Exhibits 16.7 and 16.11.

Decision Maker   Answer—p. 652

Reporter Management is in labor contract negotiations and grants you an interview. It highlights a recent $600,000 net loss that involves a $930,000 extraordinary loss and a total net cash outflow of $550,000 (which includes net cash outflows of $850,000 for investing activities and $350,000 for financing activities). What is your assessment of this company?

Cash Flow Analysis   **Decision Analysis**

Analyzing Cash Sources and Uses

Most managers stress the importance of understanding and predicting cash flows for business decisions. Creditors evaluate a company's ability to generate cash before deciding whether to lend money. Investors also assess cash inflows and outflows before buying and selling stock. Information in the statement of cash flows helps address these and other questions such as (1) How much cash is generated from or used in operations? (2) What expenditures are made with cash from operations? (3) What is the source of cash for debt payments? (4) What is the source of cash for distributions to owners? (5) How is the increase in investing activities financed? (6) What is the source of cash for new plant assets? (7) Why is cash flow from operations different from income? (8) How is cash from financing used?

A1 Analyze the statement of cash flows.

To effectively answer these questions, it is important to separately analyze investing, financing, and operating activities. To illustrate, consider data from three different companies in Exhibit 16.13. These companies operate in the same industry and have been in business for several years.

Decision Insight

Free Cash Flows Cash-based valuation of a company is theoretically equal to earnings-based valuation, but it usually yields a different value due to practical limitations. One limitation is the measurement of cash flows that are "free" for distribution to shareholders. These *free cash flows* are defined as cash flows available to shareholders after operating asset reinvestments and debt payments. Growth and financial flexibility depend on adequate free cash flow.

Exhibit 16.13

Cash Flows of Competing
Companies

($ thousands)	BMX	ATV	Trex
Cash provided (used) by operating activities	$90,000	$40,000	$(24,000)
Cash provided (used) by investing activities			
Proceeds from sale of plant assets			26,000
Purchase of plant assets	(48,000)	(25,000)	
Cash provided (used) by financing activities			
Proceeds from issuance of debt			13,000
Repayment of debt	(27,000)		
Net increase (decrease) in cash	$15,000	$15,000	$ 15,000

Each company generates an identical $15,000 net increase in cash, but its sources and uses of cash flows
are very different. BMX's operating activities provide net cash flows of $90,000, allowing it to purchase
plant assets of $48,000 and repay $27,000 of its debt. ATV's operating activities provide $40,000 of cash
flows, limiting its purchase of plant assets to $25,000. Trex's $15,000 net cash increase is due to selling
plant assets and incurring additional debt. Its operating activities yield a net cash outflow of $24,000.
Overall, analysis of these cash flows reveals that BMX is more capable of generating future cash flows
than is ATV or Trex.

Cash Flow on Total Assets

A2 Compute and apply the
cash flow on total
assets ratio.

Cash flow information has limitations, but it can help measure a company's ability to meet its obligations, pay dividends, expand operations, and obtain financing. Users often compute and analyze a cash-
based ratio similar to return on total assets except that its numerator is net cash flows from operating
activities. The **cash flow on total assets** ratio is in Exhibit 16.14.

Exhibit 16.14

Cash Flow on Total Assets

$$\text{Cash flow on total assets} = \frac{\text{Cash flow from operations}}{\text{Average total assets}}$$

Exhibit 16.15

Nike's Cash Flow on Total Assets

Year	Cash Flow on Total Assets	Return on Total Assets
2005	18.8%	14.5%
2004	20.6	12.8
2003	13.9	7.1
2002	17.6	10.8
2001	11.2	10.1

This ratio reflects actual cash flows and is not
affected by accounting income recognition and
measurement. It can help business decision makers estimate the amount and timing of cash flows
when planning and analyzing operating activities.

To illustrate, the 2005 cash flow on total assets
ratio for **Nike** is 18.8%—see Exhibit 16.15. Is an
18.8% ratio good or bad? To answer this question,
we compare this ratio with the ratios of prior years
(we could also compare its ratio with those of its
competitors and the market). Nike's cash flow on
total assets ratio for several prior years is in the second column of Exhibit 16.15. Results show that its
18.8% return is higher than each of the prior years'
returns except 2004.

As an indicator of *earnings quality,* some analysts
compare the cash flow on total assets ratio to the return on total assets ratio. Nike's return on total assets
is provided in the third column of Exhibit 16.15. Nike's
cash flow on total assets ratio exceeds its return on total assets in each of the five years, leading some analysts to infer that Nike's earnings quality is high for
that period because more earnings are realized in the
form of cash.

Decision Insight

Cash Flow Ratios Analysts use various other cash-based ratios:

(1) $\text{Cash coverage of growth} = \dfrac{\text{Operating cash flow}}{\text{Cash outflow for plant assets}}$

where a low ratio (less than 1) implies cash inadequacy to meet asset growth,
whereas a high ratio implies cash adequacy for asset growth.

(2) $\text{Operating cash flow to sales} = \dfrac{\text{Operating cash flow}}{\text{Net sales}}$

when this ratio substantially and consistently differs from the operating
income to net sales ratio, the risk of accounting improprieties increases.

Demonstration Problem

Umlauf's comparative balance sheets, income statement, and additional information follow.

UMLAUF COMPANY
Balance Sheets
December 31, 2008 and 2007

	2008	2007
Assets		
Cash	$ 43,050	$ 23,925
Accounts receivable	34,125	39,825
Merchandise inventory	156,000	146,475
Prepaid expenses	3,600	1,650
Equipment	135,825	146,700
Accum. depreciation—Equipment	(61,950)	(47,550)
Total assets	$310,650	$311,025
Liabilities and Equity		
Accounts payable	$ 28,800	$ 33,750
Income taxes payable	5,100	4,425
Dividends payable	0	4,500
Bonds payable	0	37,500
Common stock, $10 par	168,750	168,750
Retained earnings	108,000	62,100
Total liabilities and equity	$310,650	$311,025

UMLAUF COMPANY
Income Statement
For Year Ended December 31, 2008

Sales		$446,100
Cost of goods sold	$222,300	
Other operating expenses	120,300	
Depreciation expense	25,500	(368,100)
		78,000
Other gains (losses)		
Loss on sale of equipment	3,300	
Loss on retirement of bonds	825	(4,125)
Income before taxes		73,875
Income taxes expense		(13,725)
Net income		$ 60,150

Additional Information

a. Equipment costing $21,375 with accumulated depreciation of $11,100 is sold for cash.

b. Equipment purchases are for cash.

c. Accumulated Depreciation is affected by depreciation expense and the sale of equipment.

d. The balance of Retained Earnings is affected by dividend declarations and net income.

e. All sales are made on credit.

f. All merchandise inventory purchases are on credit.

g. Accounts Payable balances result from merchandise inventory purchases.

h. Prepaid expenses relate to "other operating expenses."

Required

1. Prepare a statement of cash flows using the indirect method for year 2008.

2.ᴮ Prepare a statement of cash flows using the direct method for year 2008.

Planning the Solution

- Prepare two blank statements of cash flows with sections for operating, investing, and financing activities using the (1) indirect method format and (2) direct method format.

- Compute the cash paid for equipment and the cash received from the sale of equipment using the additional information provided along with the amount for depreciation expense and the change in the balances of equipment and accumulated depreciation. Use T-accounts to help chart the effects of the sale and purchase of equipment on the balances of the Equipment account and the Accumulated Depreciation account.

- Compute the effect of net income on the change in the Retained Earnings account balance. Assign the difference between the change in retained earnings and the amount of net income to dividends declared. Adjust the dividends declared amount for the change in the Dividends Payable balance.

- Compute cash received from customers, cash paid for merchandise, cash paid for other operating expenses, and cash paid for taxes as illustrated in the chapter.

- Enter the cash effects of reconstruction entries to the appropriate section(s) of the statement.

- Total each section of the statement, determine the total net change in cash, and add it to the beginning balance to get the ending balance of cash.

Solution to Demonstration Problem

Supporting computations for cash receipts and cash payments.

(1)	*Cost of equipment sold	$ 21,375
	Accumulated depreciation of equipment sold	(11,100)
	Book value of equipment sold	10,275
	Loss on sale of equipment	(3,300)
	Cash received from sale of equipment	$ 6,975
	Cost of equipment sold	$ 21,375
	Less decrease in the equipment account balance	(10,875)
	Cash paid for new equipment	$ 10,500
(2)	Loss on retirement of bonds	$ 825
	Carrying value of bonds retired	37,500
	Cash paid to retire bonds	$ 38,325
(3)	Net income	$ 60,150
	Less increase in retained earnings	45,900
	Dividends declared	14,250
	Plus decrease in dividends payable	4,500
	Cash paid for dividends	$ 18,750
(4)B	Sales	$ 446,100
	Add decrease in accounts receivable	5,700
	Cash received from customers	$451,800
(5)B	Cost of goods sold	$ 222,300
	Plus increase in merchandise inventory	9,525
	Purchases	231,825
	Plus decrease in accounts payable	4,950
	Cash paid for merchandise	$236,775
(6)B	Other operating expenses	$ 120,300
	Plus increase in prepaid expenses	1,950
	Cash paid for other operating expenses	$122,250
(7)B	Income taxes expense	$ 13,725
	Less increase in income taxes payable	(675)
	Cash paid for income taxes	$ 13,050

* Supporting T-account analysis for part 1 follows:

Equipment			
Bal., Dec. 31, 2007	146,700		
Cash purchase	10,500	Sale	21,375
Bal., Dec. 31, 2008	135,825		

Accumulated Depreciation—Equipment			
		Bal., Dec. 31, 2007	47,550
Sale	11,100	Depr. expense	25,500
		Bal., Dec. 31, 2008	61,950

UMLAUF COMPANY
Statement of Cash Flows (Indirect Method)
For Year Ended December 31, 2008

Cash flows from operating activities		
Net income	$60,150	
Adjustments to reconcile net income to net cash provided by operating activities		
Decrease in accounts receivable	5,700	
Increase in merchandise inventory	(9,525)	
Increase in prepaid expenses	(1,950)	
Decrease in accounts payable	(4,950)	
Increase in income taxes payable	675	
Depreciation expense	25,500	

[continued on next page]

[continued from previous page]

Loss on sale of plant assets	3,300	
Loss on retirement of bonds	825	
Net cash provided by operating activities		$79,725
Cash flows from investing activities		
Cash received from sale of equipment	6,975	
Cash paid for equipment	(10,500)	
Net cash used in investing activities		(3,525)
Cash flows from financing activities		
Cash paid to retire bonds payable	(38,325)	
Cash paid for dividends	(18,750)	
Net cash used in financing activities		(57,075)
Net increase in cash		$19,125
Cash balance at prior year-end		23,925
Cash balance at current year-end		$43,050

UMLAUF COMPANY
Statement of Cash Flows (Direct Method)
For Year Ended December 31, 2008

Cash flows from operating activities		
Cash received from customers	$451,800	
Cash paid for merchandise	(236,775)	
Cash paid for other operating expenses	(122,250)	
Cash paid for income taxes	(13,050)	
Net cash provided by operating activities		$79,725
Cash flows from investing activities		
Cash received from sale of equipment	6,975	
Cash paid for equipment	(10,500)	
Net cash used in investing activities		(3,525)
Cash flows from financing activities		
Cash paid to retire bonds payable	(38,325)	
Cash paid for dividends	(18,750)	
Net cash used in financing activities		(57,075)
Net increase in cash		$19,125
Cash balance at prior year-end		23,925
Cash balance at current year-end		$43,050

APPENDIX

Spreadsheet Preparation of the Statement of Cash Flows

16A

This appendix explains how to use a spreadsheet to prepare the statement of cash flows under the indirect method.

Preparing the Indirect Method Spreadsheet

Analyzing noncash accounts can be challenging when a company has a large number of accounts and many operating, investing, and financing transactions. A *spreadsheet,* also called *work sheet* or *working paper,* can help us organize the information needed to prepare a statement of cash flows. A spreadsheet also makes it easier to check the accuracy of our work. To illustrate, we return to the comparative balance sheets and

P4   Illustrate use of a spreadsheet to prepare a statement of cash flows.

income statement shown in Exhibit 16.10. Information needed for the spreadsheet in preparing the statement of cash flows along with identifying letters *a* through *m* follow:

  a. Net income is $38,000.

  b. Accounts receivable increase by $20,000.

  c. Merchandise inventory increases by $14,000.

  d. Prepaid expenses increase by $2,000.

  e. Accounts payable decrease by $5,000.

  f. Interest payable decreases by $1,000.

  g. Income taxes payable increase by $10,000.

  h. Depreciation expense is $24,000.

  i. Plant assets costing $30,000 with accumulated depreciation of $12,000 are sold for $12,000 cash. This yields a loss on sale of assets of $6,000.

  j. Bonds with a book value of $34,000 are retired with a cash payment of $18,000, yielding a $16,000 gain on retirement.

  k. Plant assets costing $70,000 are purchased with a cash payment of $10,000 and an issuance of bonds payable for $60,000.

  l. Issued 3,000 shares of common stock for $15,000 cash.

  m. Paid cash dividends of $14,000.

    Exhibit 16A.1 shows the indirect method spreadsheet for Genesis. We enter both beginning and ending balance sheet amounts on the spreadsheet. We also enter information in the Analysis of Changes columns (keyed to the additional information items *a* through *m*) to explain changes in the accounts and determine the cash flows for operating, investing, and financing activities. Information about noncash investing and financing activities is reported near the bottom.

Entering the Analysis of Changes on the Spreadsheet

The following sequence of procedures is used to complete the spreadsheet after the beginning and ending balances of the balance sheet accounts are entered:

① Enter net income as the first item in the Statement of Cash Flows section for computing operating cash inflow (debit) and as a credit to Retained Earnings.

② In the Statement of Cash Flows section, adjustments to net income are entered as debits if they increase cash flows and as credits if they decrease cash flows. Applying this same rule, adjust net income for the change in each noncash current asset and current liability account related to operating activities. For each adjustment to net income, the offsetting debit or credit must help reconcile the beginning and ending balances of a current asset or current liability account.

③ Enter adjustments to net income for income statement items not providing or using cash in the period. For each adjustment, the offsetting debit or credit must help reconcile a noncash balance sheet account.

④ Adjust net income to eliminate any gains or losses from investing and financing activities. Because the cash from a gain must be excluded from operating activities, the gain is entered as a credit in the operating activities section. Losses are entered as debits. For each adjustment, the related debit and/or credit must help reconcile balance sheet accounts and involve reconstructed entries to show the cash flow from investing or financing activities.

⑤ After reviewing any unreconciled balance sheet accounts and related information, enter the remaining reconciling entries for investing and financing activities. Examples are purchases of plant assets, issuances of long-term debt, stock issuances, and dividend payments. Some of these may require entries in the noncash investing and financing section of the spreadsheet (reconciled).

⑥ Check accuracy by totaling the Analysis of Changes columns and by determining that the change in each balance sheet account has been explained (reconciled).

We illustrate these steps in Exhibit 16A.1 for Genesis:

Point: Analysis of the changes on the spreadsheet are summarized as:

1. Cash flows from operating activities generally affect net income, current assets, and current liabilities.

2. Cash flows from investing activities generally affect noncurrent asset accounts.

3. Cash flows from financing activities generally affect noncurrent liability and equity accounts.

Step	Entries
①	(*a*)
②	(*b*) through (*g*)
③	(*h*)
④	(*i*) through (*j*)
⑤	(*k*) through (*m*)

Exhibit 16A.1

Spreadsheet for Preparing Statement of Cash Flows—Indirect Method

					File Edit View Insert Format Tools Data Accounting Window Help

GENESIS
Spreadsheet for Statement of Cash Flows–Indirect Method
For Year Ended December 31, 2008

		Dec. 31, 2007		Analysis of Changes — Debit		Credit	Dec. 31, 2008
8	**Balance Sheet—Debits**						
9	Cash	$ 12,000					$ 17,000
10	Accounts receivable	40,000	(b)	$ 20,000			60,000
11	Merchandise inventory	70,000	(c)	14,000			84,000
12	Prepaid expenses	4,000	(d)	2,000			6,000
13	Plant assets	210,000	(k1)	70,000	(i)	$ 30,000	250,000
14		$336,000					$417,000
16	**Balance Sheet—Credits**						
17	Accumulated depreciation	$ 48,000	(i)	12,000	(h)	24,000	$ 60,000
18	Accounts payable	40,000	(e)	5,000			35,000
19	Interest payable	4,000	(f)	1,000			3,000
20	Income taxes payable	12,000			(g)	10,000	22,000
21	Bonds payable	64,000	(j)	34,000	(k2)	60,000	90,000
22	Common stock, $5 par value	80,000			(l)	15,000	95,000
23	Retained earnings	88,000	(m)	14,000	(a)	38,000	112,000
24		$336,000					$417,000
26	**Statement of Cash Flows**						
27	Operating activities						
28	Net income		(a)	38,000			
29	Increase in accounts receivable				(b)	20,000	
30	Increase in merchandise inventory				(c)	14,000	
31	Increase in prepaid expenses				(d)	2,000	
32	Decrease in accounts payable				(e)	5,000	
33	Decrease in interest payable				(f)	1,000	
34	Increase in income taxes payable		(g)	10,000			
35	Depreciation expense		(h)	24,000			
36	Loss on sale of plant assets		(i)	6,000			
37	Gain on retirement of bonds				(j)	16,000	
38	Investing activities						
39	Receipts from sale of plant assets		(i)	12,000			
40	Payment for purchase of plant assets				(k1)	10,000	
41	Financing activities						
42	Payment to retire bonds				(j)	18,000	
43	Receipts from issuing stock		(l)	15,000			
44	Payment of cash dividends				(m)	14,000	
46	**Noncash Investing and Financing Activities**						
47	Purchase of plant assets with bonds		(k2)	60,000	(k1)	60,000	
48				$337,000		$337,000	

Sheet1 / Sheet2 / Sheet3 /

Since adjustments *i, j,* and *k* are more challenging, we show them in the following debit and credit format. These entries are for purposes of our understanding; they are *not* the entries actually made in the journals. Changes in the Cash account are identified as sources or uses of cash.

i.	Loss from sale of plant assets	6,000	
	Accumulated depreciation	12,000	
	Receipt from sale of plant assets **(source of cash)**	12,000	
	Plant assets		30,000
	To describe sale of plant assets.		

[continued on next page]

[continued from previous page]

j.	Bonds payable...................................	34,000	
	Payments to retire bonds **(use of cash)**................		18,000
	Gain on retirement of bonds		16,000
	To describe retirement of bonds.		
k1.	Plant assets.....................................	70,000	
	Payment to purchase plant assets **(use of cash)**		10,000
	Purchase of plant assets financed by bonds		60,000
	To describe purchase of plant assets.		
k2.	Purchase of plant assets financed by bonds.................	60,000	
	Bonds payable		60,000
	To issue bonds for purchase of assets.		

APPENDIX

16B Direct Method of Reporting Operating Cash Flows

P5   Compute cash flows from operating activities using the direct method.

We compute cash flows from operating activities under the direct method by adjusting accrual-based income statement items to the cash basis. The usual approach is to adjust income statement accounts related to operating activities for changes in their related balance sheet accounts as follows:

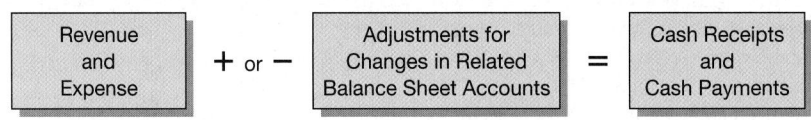

The framework for reporting cash receipts and cash payments for the operating section of the cash flow statement under the direct method is as in Exhibit 16B.1. We consider cash receipts first and then cash payments.

Exhibit 16B.1

Major Classes of Operating Cash Flows

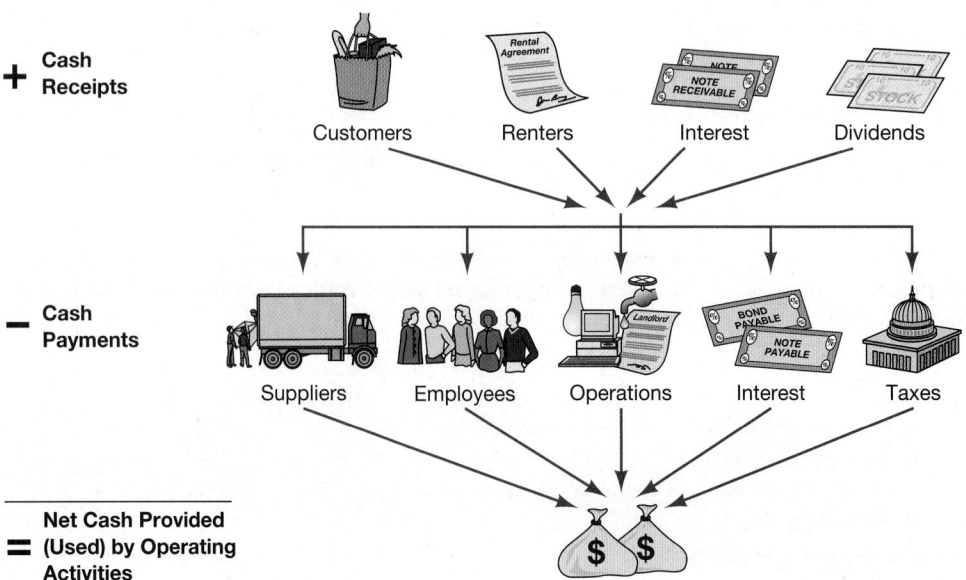

Operating Cash Receipts

A review of Exhibit 16.10 and the additional information reported by Genesis suggests only one potential cash receipt: sales to customers. This section, therefore, starts with sales to customers as reported on the income statement and then adjusts it as necessary to obtain cash received from customers to report on the statement of cash flows.

Cash Received from Customers   If all sales are for cash, the amount received from customers equals the sales reported on the income statement. When some or all sales are on account, however, we must adjust the amount of sales for the change in Accounts Receivable. It is often helpful to use *account analysis* to do this. This usually involves setting up a T-account and reconstructing its major entries, with emphasis on cash receipts and payments. To illustrate, we use a T-account that includes accounts receivable balances for Genesis on December 31, 2007 and 2008. The beginning balance is $40,000 and the ending balance is $60,000. Next, the income statement shows sales of $590,000, which we enter on the debit side of this account. We now can reconstruct the Accounts Receivable account to determine the amount of cash received from customers as follows:

Point: An accounts receivable increase implies cash received from customers is less than sales (the converse is also true).

Accounts Receivable			
Bal., Dec. 31, 2007	40,000		
Sales	590,000	Cash receipts =	570,000
Bal., Dec. 31, 2008	60,000		

This T-account shows that the Accounts Receivable balance begins at $40,000 and increases to $630,000 from sales of $590,000, yet its ending balance is only $60,000. This implies that cash receipts from customers are $570,000, computed as $40,000 + $590,000 − [?] = $60,000. This computation can be rearranged to express cash received as equal to sales of $590,000 minus a $20,000 increase in accounts receivable. This computation is summarized as a general rule in Exhibit 16B.2. The statement of cash flows in Exhibit 16.7 reports the $570,000 cash received from customers as a cash inflow from operating activities.

Example: If the ending balance of accounts receivable is $20,000 (instead of $60,000), what is cash received from customers? *Answer:* $610,000

$$\text{Cash received from customers} = \text{Sales} - \begin{cases} + \text{ Decrease in accounts receivable} \\ \quad\quad\quad\quad\text{or} \\ - \text{ Increase in accounts receivable} \end{cases}$$

Exhibit 16B.2

Formula to Compute Cash Received from Customers—Direct Method

Other Cash Receipts   While Genesis's cash receipts are limited to collections from customers, we often see other types of cash receipts, most commonly cash receipts involving rent, interest, and dividends. We compute cash received from these items by subtracting an increase in their respective receivable or adding a decrease. For instance, if rent receivable increases in the period, cash received from renters is less than rent revenue reported on the income statement. If rent receivable decreases, cash received is more than reported rent revenue. The same logic applies to interest and dividends. The formulas for these computations are summarized later in this appendix.

Point: Net income and cash flows from operations are different. Net income is measured using accrual accounting. Cash flows from operations are measured using cash basis accounting.

Operating Cash Payments

A review of Exhibit 16.10 and the additional Genesis information shows four operating expenses: cost of goods sold; wages and other operating expenses; interest expense; and taxes expense. We analyze each expense to compute its cash amounts for the statement of cash flows. (We then examine depreciation and the other losses and gains.)

Cash Paid for Merchandise   We compute cash paid for merchandise by analyzing both cost of goods sold and merchandise inventory. If all merchandise purchases are for cash and the ending balance of Merchandise Inventory is unchanged from the beginning balance, the amount of cash paid for merchandise equals cost of goods sold—an uncommon situation. Instead, there normally is some change in the Merchandise Inventory balance. Also, some or all merchandise purchases are often made on credit, and this yields changes in the Accounts Payable balance. When the balances of both Merchandise Inventory and Accounts Payable change, we must adjust the cost of goods sold for changes in both accounts to compute cash paid for merchandise. This is a two-step adjustment.

First, we use the change in the account balance of Merchandise Inventory, along with the cost of goods sold amount, to compute cost of purchases for the period. An increase in merchandise inventory implies that we bought more than we sold, and we add this inventory increase to cost of goods sold to compute cost of purchases. A decrease in merchandise inventory implies that we bought less than we sold, and we subtract the inventory decrease from cost of goods sold to compute purchases. We illustrate the *first step* by reconstructing the Merchandise Inventory account of Genesis:

Merchandise Inventory			
Bal., Dec. 31, 2007	70,000		
Purchases =	314,000	Cost of goods sold	300,000
Bal., Dec. 31, 2008	84,000		

The beginning balance is $70,000, and the ending balance is $84,000. The income statement shows that cost of goods sold is $300,000, which we enter on the credit side of this account. With this information, we determine the amount for cost of purchases to be $314,000. This computation can be rearranged to express cost of purchases as equal to cost of goods sold of $300,000 plus the $14,000 increase in inventory.

The second step uses the change in the balance of Accounts Payable, and the amount of cost of purchases, to compute cash paid for merchandise. A decrease in accounts payable implies that we paid for more goods than we acquired this period, and we would then add the accounts payable decrease to cost of purchases to compute cash paid for merchandise. An increase in accounts payable implies that we paid for less than the amount of goods acquired, and we would subtract the accounts payable increase from purchases to compute cash paid for merchandise. The *second step* is applied to Genesis by reconstructing its Accounts Payable account:

Accounts Payable			
		Bal., Dec. 31, 2007	40,000
Cash payments =	319,000	Purchases	314,000
		Bal., Dec. 31, 2008	35,000

Example: If the ending balances of Inventory and Accounts Payable are $60,000 and $50,000, respectively (instead of $84,000 and $35,000), what is cash paid for merchandise? *Answer:* $280,000

Its beginning balance of $40,000 plus purchases of $314,000 minus an ending balance of $35,000 yields cash paid of $319,000 (or $40,000 + $314,000 − [?] = $35,000). Alternatively, we can express cash paid for merchandise as equal to purchases of $314,000 plus the $5,000 decrease in accounts payable. The $319,000 cash paid for merchandise is reported on the statement of cash flows in Exhibit 16.7 as a cash outflow under operating activities.

We summarize this two-step adjustment to cost of goods sold to compute cash paid for merchandise inventory in Exhibit 16B.3.

Exhibit 16B.3

Two Steps to Compute Cash Paid for Merchandise—Direct Method

Cash Paid for Wages and Operating Expenses (excluding depreciation)

The income statement of Genesis shows wages and other operating expenses of $216,000 (see Exhibit 16.10). To compute cash paid for wages and other operating expenses, we adjust this amount for any changes in their related balance sheet accounts. We begin by looking for any prepaid expenses and accrued liabilities related to wages and other operating expenses in the balance sheets of Genesis in

Exhibit 16.10. The balance sheets show prepaid expenses but no accrued liabilities. Thus, the adjustment is limited to the change in prepaid expenses. The amount of adjustment is computed by assuming that all cash paid for wages and other operating expenses is initially debited to Prepaid Expenses. This assumption allows us to reconstruct the Prepaid Expenses account:

Prepaid Expenses			
Bal., Dec. 31, 2007	4,000		
Cash payments =	**218,000**	Wages and other operating exp.	216,000
Bal., Dec. 31, 2008	6,000		

Prepaid Expenses increase by $2,000 in the period, meaning that cash paid for wages and other operating expenses exceeds the reported expense by $2,000. Alternatively, we can express cash paid for wages and other operating expenses as equal to its reported expenses of $216,000 plus the $2,000 increase in prepaid expenses.[1]

Point: A decrease in prepaid expenses implies that reported expenses include an amount(s) that did not require a cash outflow in the period.

Exhibit 16B.4 summarizes the adjustments to wages (including salaries) and other operating expenses. The Genesis balance sheet did not report accrued liabilities, but we include them in the formula to explain the adjustment to cash when they do exist. A decrease in accrued liabilities implies that we paid cash for more goods or services than received this period, so we add the decrease in accrued liabilities to the expense amount to obtain cash paid for these goods or services. An increase in accrued liabilities implies that we paid cash for less than what was acquired, so we subtract this increase in accrued liabilities from the expense amount to get cash paid.

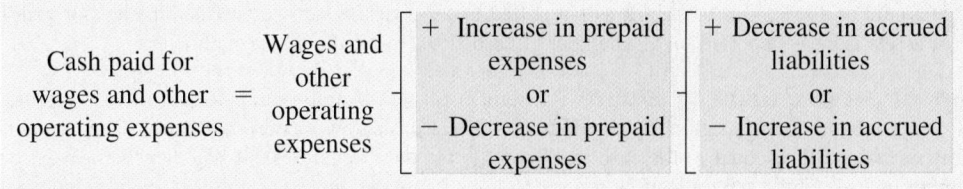

Exhibit 16B.4

Formula to Compute Cash Paid for Wages and Operating Expenses—Direct Method

Cash Paid for Interest and Income Taxes   Computing operating cash flows for interest and taxes is similar to that for operating expenses. Both require adjustments to their amounts reported on the income statement for changes in their related balance sheet accounts. We begin with the Genesis income statement showing interest expense of $7,000 and income taxes expense of $15,000. To compute the cash paid, we adjust interest expense for the change in interest payable and then the income taxes expense for the change in income taxes payable. These computations involve reconstructing both liability accounts:

Interest Payable			
		Bal., Dec. 31, 2007	4,000
Cash paid for interest =	**8,000**	Interest expense	7,000
		Bal., Dec. 31, 2008	3,000

Income Taxes Payable			
		Bal., Dec. 31, 2007	12,000
Cash paid for taxes =	**5,000**	Income taxes expense	15,000
		Bal., Dec. 31, 2008	22,000

These accounts reveal cash paid for interest of $8,000 and cash paid for income taxes of $5,000. The formulas to compute these amounts are in Exhibit 16B.5. Both of these cash payments are reported as operating cash outflows on the statement of cash flows in Exhibit 16.7.

---

[1] The assumption that all cash payments for wages and operating expenses are initially debited to Prepaid Expenses is not necessary for our analysis to hold. If cash payments are debited directly to the expense account, the total amount of cash paid for wages and other operating expenses still equals the $216,000 expense plus the $2,000 increase in Prepaid Expenses (which arise from end-of-period adjusting entries).

Exhibit 16B.5

Formulas to Compute Cash Paid for Both Interest and Taxes—Direct Method

Analysis of Additional Expenses, Gains, and Losses   Genesis has three additional items reported on its income statement: depreciation, loss on sale of assets, and gain on retirement of debt. We must consider each for its potential cash effects.

Depreciation Expense   Depreciation expense is $24,000. It is often called a *noncash expense* because depreciation has no cash flows. Depreciation expense is an allocation of an asset's depreciable cost. The cash outflow with a plant asset is reported as part of investing activities when it is paid for. Thus, depreciation expense is *never* reported on a statement of cash flows using the direct method, nor is depletion or amortization expense.

Loss on Sale of Assets   Sales of assets frequently result in gains and losses reported as part of net income, but the amount of recorded gain or loss does *not* reflect any cash flows in these transactions. Asset sales result in cash inflow equal to the cash amount received, regardless of whether the asset was sold at a gain or a loss. This cash inflow is reported under investing activities. Thus, the loss or gain on a sale of assets is *never* reported on a statement of cash flows using the direct method.

Gain on Retirement of Debt   Retirement of debt usually yields a gain or loss reported as part of net income, but that gain or loss does *not* reflect cash flow in this transaction. Debt retirement results in cash outflow equal to the cash paid to settle the debt, regardless of whether the debt is retired at a gain or loss. This cash outflow is reported under financing activities; the loss or gain from retirement of debt is *never* reported on a statement of cash flows using the direct method.

Point: The direct method is usually viewed as *user friendly* because less accounting knowledge is required to understand and use it.

Summary of Adjustments for Direct Method

Exhibit 16B.6 summarizes common adjustments for net income to yield net cash provided (used) by operating activities under the direct method.

Exhibit 16B.6

Summary of Selected Adjustments for Direct Method

Item	From Income Statement	Adjustments to Obtain Cash Flow Numbers	
Receipts			
From sales	Sales Revenue	+Decrease in Accounts Receivable −Increase in Accounts Receivable	
From rent	Rent Revenue	+Decrease in Rent Receivable −Increase in Rent Receivable	
From interest	Interest Revenue	+Decrease in Interest Receivable −Increase in Interest Receivable	
From dividends	Dividend Revenue	+Decrease in Dividends Receivable −Increase in Dividends Receivable	
Payments			
To suppliers	Cost of Goods Sold	+Increase in Inventory −Decrease in Inventory	+Decrease in Accounts Payable −Increase in Accounts Payable
For operations	Operating Expense	+Increase in Prepaids −Decrease in Prepaids	+Decrease in Accrued Liabilities −Increase in Accrued Liabilities
To employees	Wages (Salaries) Expense	+Decrease in Wages (Salaries) Payable −Increase in Wages (Salaries) Payable	
For interest	Interest Expense	+Decrease in Interest Payable −Increase in Interest Payable	
For taxes	Income Tax Expense	+Decrease in Income Tax Payable −Increase in Income Tax Payable	

Direct Method Format of Operating Activities Section

Exhibit 16.7 shows the Genesis statement of cash flows using the direct method. Major items of cash inflows and cash outflows are listed separately in the operating activities section. The format requires that operating cash outflows be subtracted from operating cash inflows to get net cash provided (used) by operating activities. The FASB recommends that the operating activities section of the statement of cash flows be reported using the direct method, which is considered more useful to financial statement users. *However, the FASB requires a reconciliation of net income to net cash provided (used) by operating activities when the direct method is used* (which can be reported in the notes). This reconciliation is similar to preparation of the operating activities section of the statement of cash flows using the indirect method.

Point: Some preparers argue that it is easier to prepare a statement of cash flows using the indirect method. This likely explains its greater frequency in financial statements.

Quick Check
Answers—p. 652

8. Net sales in a period are $590,000, beginning accounts receivable are $120,000, and ending accounts receivable are $90,000. What cash amount is collected from customers in the period?

9. The Merchandise Inventory account balance decreases in the period from a beginning balance of $32,000 to an ending balance of $28,000. Cost of goods sold for the period is $168,000. If the Accounts Payable balance increases $2,400 in the period, what is the cash amount paid for merchandise inventory?

10. Wages and other operating expenses total $112,000. Beginning-of-period prepaid expenses totaled $1,200, and its ending balance is $4,200. The end-of-period wages payable equal $5,600, whereas there were no accrued liabilities at period-end. How much cash is paid for wages and other operating expenses?

Summary

C1 Explain the purpose and importance of cash flow information. The main purpose of the statement of cash flows is to report the major cash receipts and cash payments for a period. This includes identifying cash flows as relating to either operating, investing, or financing activities. Most business decisions involve evaluating activities that provide or use cash.

C2 Distinguish between operating, investing, and financing activities. Operating activities include transactions and events that determine net income. Investing activities include transactions and events that mainly affect long-term assets. Financing activities include transactions and events that mainly affect long-term liabilities and equity.

C3 Identify and disclose noncash investing and financing activities. Noncash investing and financing activities must be disclosed either in a note or a separate schedule to the statement of cash flows. Examples are the retirement of debt by issuing equity and the exchange of a note payable for plant assets.

C4 Describe the format of the statement of cash flows. The statement of cash flows separates cash receipts and payments into operating, investing, or financing activities.

A1 Analyze the statement of cash flows. To understand and predict cash flows, users stress identification of the sources and uses of cash flows by operating, investing, and financing activities. Emphasis is on operating cash flows since they derive from continuing operations.

A2 Compute and apply the cash flow on total assets ratio. The cash flow on total assets ratio is defined as operating cash flows divided by average total assets. Analysis of current and past values for this ratio can reflect a company's ability to yield regular and positive cash flows. It is also viewed as a measure of earnings quality.

P1 Prepare a statement of cash flows. Preparation of a statement of cash flows involves five steps: (1) Compute the net increase or decrease in cash; (2) compute net cash provided (used) by operating activities (*using either the direct or indirect method*); (3) compute net cash provided (used) by investing activities; (4) compute net cash provided (used) by financing activities; and (5) report the beginning and ending cash balance and prove that it is explained by net cash flows. Noncash investing and financing activities are also disclosed.

P2 Compute cash flows from operating activities using the indirect method. The indirect method for reporting net cash provided (used) by operating activities starts with net income and then adjusts it for three items: (1) changes in noncash current assets and current liabilities related to operating activities, (2) revenues and expenses not providing (using) cash, and (3) gains and losses from investing and financing activities.

P3 Determine cash flows from both investing and financing activities. Cash flows from both investing and financing activities are determined by identifying the cash flow effects of transactions and events affecting each balance sheet account related to these activities. All cash flows from these activities are identified when we can explain changes in these accounts from the beginning to the end of the period.

P4^A Illustrate use of a spreadsheet to prepare a statement of cash flows. A spreadsheet is a useful tool in preparing a statement of cash flows. Six key steps (see appendix) are applied when using the spreadsheet to prepare the statement.

P5^B Compute cash flows from operating activities using the direct method. The direct method for reporting net cash provided (used) by operating activities lists major operating cash inflows less cash outflows to yield net cash inflow or outflow from operations.

Entrepreneur Several factors might explain an increase in net cash flows when a net loss is reported, including (1) early recognition of expenses relative to revenues generated (such as research and development), (2) cash advances on long-term sales contracts not yet recognized in income, (3) issuances of debt or equity for cash to finance expansion, (4) cash sale of assets, (5) delay of cash payments, and (6) cash prepayment on sales. Analysis needs to focus on the components of both the net loss and the net cash flows and their implications for future performance.

Reporter Your initial reaction based on the company's $600,000 loss with a $550,000 decrease in net cash flows is not positive. However, closer scrutiny reveals a more positive picture of this company's performance. Cash flow from operating activities is $650,000, computed as [?] − $850,000 − $350,000 = $(550,000). You also note that net income *before* the extraordinary loss is $330,000, computed as [?] − $930,000 = $(600,000).

Guidance Answers to **Quick Checks**

1. No to both. The statement of cash flows reports changes in the sum of cash plus cash equivalents. It does not report transfers between cash and cash equivalents.

2. The three categories of cash inflows and outflows are operating activities, investing activities, and financing activities.

3. **a.** Investing   **c.** Financing   **e.** Operating
   b. Operating   **d.** Operating   **f.** Financing

4. $74,900 + $4,600 − $11,700 − $1,000 + $3,400 = $70,200

5. Expenses such as depreciation and amortization do not require current cash outflows. Therefore, adding these expenses back to

net income eliminates these noncash items from the net income number, converting it to a cash basis.

6. A gain on the sale of plant assets is subtracted from net income because a sale of plant assets is not an operating activity; it is an investing activity for the amount of cash received from its sale. Also, such a gain yields no cash effects.

7. $80,000 − $30,000 − $10,000 = $40,000 cash receipt. The $40,000 cash receipt is reported as an investing activity.

8. $590,000 + ($120,000 − $90,000) = $620,000

9. $168,000 − ($32,000 − $28,000) − $2,400 = $161,600

10. $112,000 + ($4,200 − $1,200) − $5,600 = $109,400

Multiple Choice Quiz   Answers on p. 671   mhhe.com/wildFAP18e

Multiple Choice Quizzes A and B are available at the book's Website.

1. A company uses the indirect method to determine its cash flows from operating activities. Use the following information to determine its net cash provided or used by operating activities.

Net income	$15,200
Depreciation expense	10,000
Cash payment on note payable	8,000
Gain on sale of land	3,000
Increase in inventory	1,500
Increase in accounts payable	2,850

   a. $23,550 used by operating activities
   b. $23,550 provided by operating activities

   c. $15,550 provided by operating activities
   d. $42,400 provided by operating activities
   e. $20,850 provided by operating activities

2. A machine with a cost of $175,000 and accumulated depreciation of $94,000 is sold for $87,000 cash. The amount reported as a source of cash under cash flows from investing activities is:
   a. $81,000.
   b. $6,000.
   c. $87,000.
   d. Zero; this is a financing activity.
   e. Zero; this is an operating activity.

3. A company settles a long-term note payable plus interest by paying $68,000 cash toward the principal amount and $5,440

cash for interest. The amount reported as a use of cash under cash flows from financing activities is:
a. Zero; this is an investing activity.
b. Zero; this is an operating activity.
c. $73,440.
d. $68,000.
e. $5,440.

4. The following information is available regarding a company's annual salaries and wages. What amount of cash is paid for salaries and wages?

Salaries and wages expense	$255,000
Salaries and wages payable, prior year-end	8,200
Salaries and wages payable, current year-end	10,900

a. $252,300
b. $257,700

c. $255,000
d. $274,100
e. $235,900

5. The following information is available for a company. What amount of cash is paid for merchandise for the current year?

Cost of goods sold	$545,000
Merchandise inventory, prior year-end	105,000
Merchandise inventory, current year-end	112,000
Accounts payable, prior year-end	98,500
Accounts payable, current year-end	101,300

a. $545,000
b. $554,800
c. $540,800
d. $535,200
e. $549,200

Superscript letter A(B) denotes assignments based on Appendix 16A (16B).

Discussion Questions

1. What is the reporting purpose of the statement of cash flows? Identify at least two questions that this statement can answer.

2. Describe the direct method of reporting cash flows from operating activities.

3. When a statement of cash flows is prepared using the direct method, what are some of the operating cash flows?

4. Describe the indirect method of reporting cash flows from operating activities.

5. What are some investing activities reported on the statement of cash flows?

6. What are some financing activities reported on the statement of cash flows?

7. Where on the statement of cash flows is the payment of cash dividends reported?

8. Assume that a company purchases land for $100,000, paying $20,000 cash and borrowing the remainder with a long-term note payable. How should this transaction be reported on a statement of cash flows?

9. On June 3, a company borrows $50,000 cash by giving its bank a 160-day, interest-bearing note. On the statement of cash flows, where should this be reported?

10. If a company reports positive net income for the year, can it also show a net cash outflow from operating activities? Explain.

11. Is depreciation a source of cash flow?

12. Refer to **Best Buy**'s statement of cash flows in Appendix A. (*a*) Which method is used to compute its net cash provided by operating activities? (*b*) While its balance sheet shows an increase in receivables from fiscal years 2004 to 2005, why is this increase in receivables subtracted when computing net cash provided by operating activities for the year ended February 26, 2005?

13. Refer to **Circuit City**'s statement of cash flows in Appendix A. What are its cash flows from financing activities for the year ended February 28, 2005? List items and amounts.

14. Refer to **Apple**'s statement of cash flows in Appendix A. What investing activities result in cash outflows for the year ended September 25, 2004? List items and amounts.

 Red numbers denote Discussion Questions that involve decision-making.

The statement of cash flows is one of the four primary financial statements.
1. Describe the content and layout of a statement of cash flows, including its three sections.
2. List at least three transactions classified as investing activities in a statement of cash flows.
3. List at least three transactions classified as financing activities in a statement of cash flows.
4. List at least three transactions classified as significant noncash financing and investing activities in the statement of cash flows.

QUICK STUDY

QS 16-1
Statement of cash flows
C1 C2 C3

QS 16-2

Transaction classification by activity

C2

Classify the following cash flows as operating, investing, or financing activities.

1. Sold long-term investments for cash.
2. Received cash payments from customers.
3. Paid cash for wages and salaries.
4. Purchased inventories for cash.
5. Paid cash dividends.

6. Issued common stock for cash.
7. Received cash interest on a note.
8. Paid cash interest on outstanding bonds.
9. Received cash from sale of land at a loss.
10. Paid cash for property taxes on building.

QS 16-3

Computing cash from operations (indirect)

P2

Use the following information to determine this company's cash flows from operating activities using the indirect method.

KATAHN COMPANY Selected Balance Sheet Information December 31, 2008 and 2007		
	2008	**2007**
Current assets		
Cash	$84,650	$26,800
Accounts receivable	25,000	32,000
Inventory	60,000	54,100
Current liabilities		
Accounts payable	30,400	25,700
Income taxes payable	2,050	2,200

KATAHN COMPANY Income Statement For Year Ended December 31, 2008		
Sales		$515,000
Cost of goods sold		331,600
Gross profit		183,400
Operating expenses		
Depreciation expense	$ 36,000	
Other expenses	121,500	157,500
Income before taxes		25,900
Income taxes expense		7,700
Net income		$ 18,200

QS 16-4

Computing cash from asset sales

P3

The following selected information is from Ellerby Company's comparative balance sheets.

At December 31	2008	2007
Furniture	$132,000	$ 184,500
Accumulated depreciation—Furniture	(88,700)	(110,700)

The income statement reports depreciation expense for the year of $18,000. Also, furniture costing $52,500 was sold for its book value. Compute the cash received from the sale of the furniture.

QS 16-5

Computing financing cash flows

P3

The following selected information is from the Princeton Company's comparative balance sheets.

At December 31	2008	2007
Common stock, $10 par value	$105,000	$100,000
Paid-in capital in excess of par	567,000	342,000
Retained earnings	313,500	287,500

Princeton's net income for the year ended December 31, 2008, was $48,000.

1. Compute the cash received from the sale of its common stock during 2008.
2. Compute the cash paid for dividends during 2008.

QS 16-6

Computing cash from operations (indirect)   P2

Use the following balance sheets and income statement to answer QS 16-6 through QS 16-11.

Use the indirect method to prepare the cash provided (used) from operating activities section only of the statement of cash flows.

CRUZ, INC.
Comparative Balance Sheets
December 31, 2008

	2008	2007
Assets		
Cash	$ 94,800	$ 24,000
Accounts receivable, net	41,000	51,000
Inventory	85,800	95,800
Prepaid expenses	5,400	4,200
Furniture	109,000	119,000
Accum. depreciation—Furniture	(17,000)	(9,000)
Total assets	$319,000	$285,000
Liabilities and Equity		
Accounts payable	$ 15,000	$ 21,000
Wages payable	9,000	5,000
Income taxes payable	1,400	2,600
Notes payable (long-term)	29,000	69,000
Common stock, $5 par value	229,000	179,000
Retained earnings	35,600	8,400
Total liabilities and equity	$319,000	$285,000

CRUZ, INC.
Income Statement
For Year Ended December 31, 2008

Sales		$488,000
Cost of goods sold		314,000
Gross profit		174,000
Operating expenses		
Depreciation expense	$37,600	
Other expenses	89,100	126,700
Income before taxes		47,300
Income taxes expense		17,300
Net income		$ 30,000

Refer to the data in QS 16-6.
Furniture costing $55,000 is sold at its book value in 2008. Acquisitions of furniture total $45,000 cash, on which no depreciation is necessary because it is acquired at year-end. What is the cash inflow related to the sale of furniture?

QS 16-7
Computing cash from asset sales P3

Refer to the data in QS 16-6.
1. Assume that all common stock is issued for cash. What amount of cash dividends is paid during 2008?
2. Assume that no additional notes payable are issued in 2008. What cash amount is paid to reduce the notes payable balance in 2008?

QS 16-8
Computing financing cash outflows P3

Refer to the data in QS 16-6.
1. How much cash is received from sales to customers for year 2008?
2. What is the net increase or decrease in cash for year 2008?

QS 16-9[B]
Computing cash received from customers P5

Refer to the data in QS 16-6.
1. How much cash is paid to acquire merchandise inventory during year 2008?
2. How much cash is paid for operating expenses during year 2008?

QS 16-10[B]
Computing operating cash outflows P5

Refer to the data in QS 16-6.
Use the direct method to prepare the cash provided (used) from operating activities section only of the statement of cash flows.

QS 16-11[B]
Computing cash from operations (direct) P5

Financial data from three competitors in the same industry follow.
1. Which of the three competitors is in the strongest position as shown by its statement of cash flows?
2. Analyze and discuss the strength of Peña's cash flow on total assets ratio to that of Garcia.

QS 16-12
Analyses of sources and uses of cash A1 A2

($ thousands)	Peña	Garcia	Piniella
Cash provided (used) by operating activities	$ 70,000	$ 60,000	$ (24,000)
Cash provided (used) by investing activities			
Proceeds from sale of operating assets			26,000
Purchase of operating assets	(28,000)	(34,000)	
Cash provided (used) by financing activities			
Proceeds from issuance of debt			23,000
Repayment of debt	(6,000)		
Net increase (decrease) in cash	$ 36,000	$ 26,000	$ 25,000
Average total assets	$ 790,000	$ 625,000	$ 300,000

QS 16-13^A

Noncash accounts
on a spreadsheet   P4

When a spreadsheet for a statement of cash flows is prepared, all changes in noncash balance sheet accounts are fully explained on the spreadsheet. Explain how these noncash balance sheet accounts are used to fully account for cash flows on a spreadsheet.

QS 16-14

Computing cash flows from
operations (indirect)

P2

For each of the following separate cases, compute cash flows from operations. The list includes all balance sheet accounts related to operating activities.

	Case A	Case B	Case C
Net income	$ 4,000	$100,000	$72,000
Depreciation expense	30,000	8,000	24,000
Accounts receivable increase (decrease)	40,000	20,000	(4,000)
Inventory increase (decrease)	(20,000)	(10,000)	10,000
Accounts payable increase (decrease)	24,000	(22,000)	14,000
Accrued liabilities increase (decrease)	(44,000)	12,000	(8,000)

QS 16-15

Computing cash flows from
investing

P3

Compute cash flows from investing activities using the following information.

Sale of short-term investments	$ 6,000
Cash collections from customers	16,000
Purchase of used equipment	5,000
Depreciation expense	2,000

QS 16-16

Computing cash flows from
financing

P3

Compute cash flows from financing activities using the following information.

Additional short-term borrowings	$20,000
Purchase of short-term investments	5,000
Cash dividends paid	16,000
Interest paid	8,000

EXERCISES

Exercise 16-1

Cash flow from
operations (indirect)

P2

Salud Company reports net income of $400,000 for the year ended December 31, 2008. It also reports $80,000 depreciation expense and a $20,000 gain on the sale of machinery. Its comparative balance sheets reveal a $40,000 increase in accounts receivable, $6,000 increase in accounts payable, $12,000 decrease in prepaid expenses, and $2,000 decrease in wages payable.

Required

Prepare only the operating activities section of the statement of cash flows for 2008 using the *indirect method*.

The following transactions and events occurred during the year. Assuming that this company uses the *indirect method* to report cash provided by operating activities, indicate where each item would appear on its statement of cash flows by placing an *x* in the appropriate column.

Exercise 16-2
Cash flow classification
(indirect)   C2   C3   P2

	Statement of Cash Flows			Noncash Investing and Financing Activities	Not Reported on Statement or in Notes
	Operating Activities	Investing Activities	Financing Activities		
a. Paid cash to purchase inventory.	____	____	____	____	____
b. Purchased land by issuing common stock.	____	____	____	____	____
c. Accounts receivable decreased in the year.	____	____	____	____	____
d. Sold equipment for cash, yielding a loss.	____	____	____	____	____
e. Recorded depreciation expense.	____	____	____	____	____
f. Income taxes payable increased in the year.	____	____	____	____	____
g. Declared and paid a cash dividend.	____	____	____	____	____
h. Accounts payable decreased in the year	____	____	____	____	____
i. Paid cash to settle bond payable	____	____	____	____	____
j. Prepaid expenses increased in the year	____	____	____	____	____

The following transactions and events occurred during the year. Assuming that this company uses the *direct method* to report cash provided by operating activities, indicate where each item would appear on the statement of cash flows by placing an *x* in the appropriate column.

Exercise 16-3[B]
Cash flow classification
(direct)   C2   C3   P5

	Statement of Cash Flows			Noncash Investing and Financing Activities	Not Reported on Statement or in Notes
	Operating Activities	Investing Activities	Financing Activities		
a. Retired long-term bonds payable by issuing common stock	____	____	____	____	____
b. Recorded depreciation expense.	____	____	____	____	____
c. Paid cash dividend that was declared in a prior period.	____	____	____	____	____
d. Sold inventory for cash.	____	____	____	____	____
e. Borrowed cash from bank by signing a 9-month note payable.	____	____	____	____	____
f. Paid cash to purchase a patent.	____	____	____	____	____
g. Accepted six-month note receivable in exchange for plant assets.	____	____	____	____	____
h. Paid cash toward accounts payable.	____	____	____	____	____
i. Collected cash from sales.	____	____	____	____	____
j. Paid cash to acquire treasury stock.	____	____	____	____	____

Olhstead Company's calendar-year 2008 income statement shows the following: Net Income, $374,000; Depreciation Expense, $44,000; Amortization Expense, $7,200; Gain on Sale of Plant Assets, $6,000. An examination of the company's current assets and current liabilities reveals the following changes (all from operating activities): Accounts Receivable decrease, $17,100; Merchandise Inventory decrease, $42,000; Prepaid Expenses increase, $4,700; Accounts Payable decrease, $8,200; Other Payables increase, $1,200. Use the *indirect method* to compute cash flow from operating activities.

Exercise 16-4
Cash flows from operating
activities (indirect)

P2

Exercise 16-5[B]
Computation of cash
flows (direct)

P5

For each of the following three separate cases, use the information provided about the calendar-year 2008 operations of Alberto Company to compute the required cash flow information.

Case A: Compute cash received from customers:

Sales	$515,000
Accounts receivable, December 31, 2007	27,200
Accounts receivable, December 31, 2008	33,600

Case B: Compute cash paid for rent:

Rent expense	$139,800
Rent payable, December 31, 2007	7,800
Rent payable, December 31, 2008	6,200

Case C: Compute cash paid for merchandise:

Cost of goods sold	$525,000
Merchandise inventory, December 31, 2007	158,600
Accounts payable, December 31, 2007	66,700
Merchandise inventory, December 31, 2008	130,400
Accounts payable, December 31, 2008	82,000

Exercise 16-6
Cash flows from operating
activities (indirect)

P2

Use the following income statement and information about changes in noncash current assets and current liabilities to prepare only the cash flows from operating activities section of the statement of cash flows using the *indirect* method.

ABBECK COMPANY
Income Statement
For Year Ended December 31, 2008

Sales		$1,828,000
Cost of goods sold		991,000
Gross profit		837,000
Operating expenses		
Salaries expense	$245,535	
Depreciation expense	44,200	
Rent expense	49,600	
Amortization expenses—Patents	4,200	
Utilities expense	18,125	361,660
		475,340
Gain on sale of equipment		6,200
Net income		$ 481,540

Changes in current asset and current liability accounts for the year that relate to operations follow.

Accounts receivable	$30,500 increase		Accounts payable	$12,500 decrease
Merchandise inventory	25,000 increase		Salaries payable	3,500 decrease

Exercise 16-7[B]
Cash flows from operating
activities (direct)   P5

Refer to the information about Abbeck Company in Exercise 16-6.
Use the *direct method* to prepare only the cash provided (used) by operating activities section of the statement of cash flows.

Exercise 16-8
Cash flows from investing
activities

P3

Use the following information to determine a company's cash flows from investing activities.
 a. Equipment with a book value of $65,300 and an original cost of $133,000 was sold at a loss of $14,000.
 b. Paid $89,000 cash for a new truck.
 c. Sold land costing $154,000 for $198,000 cash, yielding a gain of $44,000.
 d. Long-term investments in stock were sold for $60,800 cash, yielding a gain of $4,150.

Use the following information to determine a company's cash flows from financing activities.

a. Net income was $35,000.

b. Issued common stock for $64,000 cash.

c. Paid cash dividend of $14,600.

d. Paid $50,000 cash to settle a bond payable at its $50,000 maturity value.

e. Paid $12,000 cash to acquire its treasury stock.

f. Purchased equipment for $39,000 cash.

Exercise 16-9
Cash flows from financing activities

P3

Use the following financial statements and additional information to (1) prepare a statement of cash flows for the year ended June 30, 2008, using the *indirect method,* and (2) compute the cash flow on total assets ratio for Ikiban for its fiscal year 2008.

Exercise 16-10
Preparation of statement of cash flows (indirect)

C2 A2 P1 P2 P3

IKIBAN INC.
Comparative Balance Sheets
June 30, 2008 and 2007

	2008	2007
Assets		
Cash	$ 87,500	$ 44,000
Accounts receivable, net	65,000	51,000
Inventory	63,800	86,500
Prepaid expenses	4,400	5,400
Equipment	124,000	115,000
Accum. depreciation—Equipment	(27,000)	(9,000)
Total assets	$317,700	$292,900
Liabilities and Equity		
Accounts payable	$ 25,000	$ 30,000
Wages payable	6,000	15,000
Income taxes payable	3,400	3,800
Notes payable (long term)	30,000	60,000
Common stock, $5 par value	220,000	160,000
Retained earnings	33,300	24,100
Total liabilities and equity	$317,700	$292,900

IKIBAN INC.
Income Statement
For Year Ended June 30, 2008

Sales		$678,000
Cost of goods sold		411,000
Gross profit		267,000
Operating expenses		
Depreciation expense	$58,600	
Other expenses	67,000	
Total operating expenses		125,600
		141,400
Other gains (losses)		
Gain on sale of equipment		2,000
Income before taxes		143,400
Income taxes expense		43,890
Net income		$ 99,510

Additional Information

a. A $30,000 note payable is retired at its carrying (book) value in exchange for cash.

b. The only changes affecting retained earnings are net income and cash dividends paid.

c. New equipment is acquired for $57,600 cash.

d. Received cash for the sale of equipment that had cost $48,600, yielding a $2,000 gain.

e. Prepaid Expenses and Wages Payable relate to Other Expenses on the income statement.

f. All purchases and sales of merchandise inventory are on credit.

Refer to the data in Exercise 16-10.
Using the *direct method,* prepare the statement of cash flows for the year ended June 30, 2008.

Exercise 16-11[B]
Preparation of statement of cash flows (direct) C2 P1 P3 P5

Exercise 16-12ᴮ

Preparation of statement of
cash flows (direct) and
supporting note

C2 C3 C4 P1

Use the following information about the cash flows of Ferron Company to prepare a complete statement
of cash flows (*direct method*) for the year ended December 31, 2008. Use a note disclosure for any noncash investing and financing activities.

Cash and cash equivalents balance, December 31, 2007	$ 40,000
Cash and cash equivalents balance, December 31, 2008	148,000
Cash received as interest	3,500
Cash paid for salaries	76,500
Bonds payable retired by issuing common stock (no gain or loss on retirement)	185,500
Cash paid to retire long-term notes payable	100,000
Cash received from sale of equipment	60,250
Cash received in exchange for six-month note payable	35,000
Land purchased by issuing long-term note payable	105,250
Cash paid for store equipment	24,750
Cash dividends paid	10,000
Cash paid for other expenses	20,000
Cash received from customers	495,000
Cash paid for merchandise	254,500

Exercise 16-13ᴮ

Preparation of statement of
cash flows (direct) from
Cash T-account

C2 A1 P1 P3 P5

The following summarized Cash T-account reflects the total debits and total credits to the Cash account
of Thomas Corporation for calendar year 2008.

(1) Use this information to prepare a complete statement of cash flows for year 2008. The cash provided
(used) by operating activities should be reported using the *direct method.*

(2) Refer to the statement of cash flows prepared for part 1 to answer the following questions *a* through
d: (*a*) Which section—operating, investing, or financing—shows the largest cash (i) inflow and (ii) outflow? (*b*) What is the largest individual item among the investing cash outflows? (*c*) Are the cash proceeds larger from issuing notes or issuing stock? (*d*) Does the company have a net cash inflow or outflow from borrowing activities?

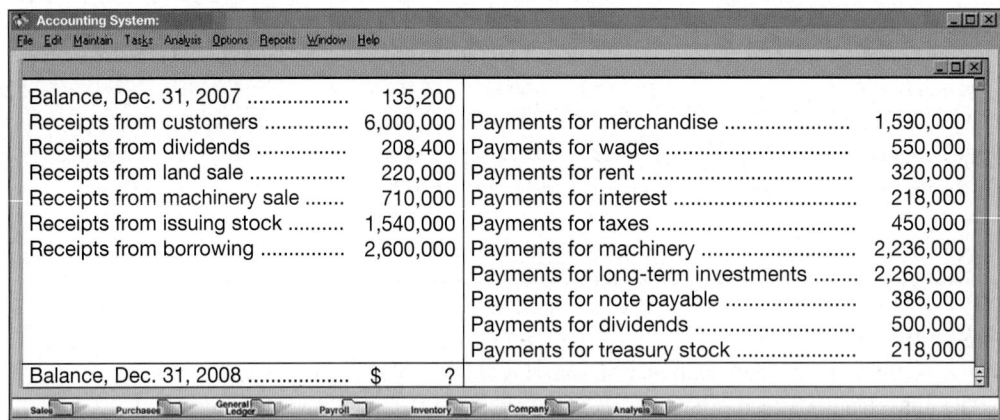

Accounting System:			
File Edit Maintain Tasks Analysis Options Reports Window Help			
Balance, Dec. 31, 2007	135,200		
Receipts from customers	6,000,000	Payments for merchandise	1,590,000
Receipts from dividends	208,400	Payments for wages	550,000
Receipts from land sale	220,000	Payments for rent	320,000
Receipts from machinery sale	710,000	Payments for interest	218,000
Receipts from issuing stock	1,540,000	Payments for taxes	450,000
Receipts from borrowing	2,600,000	Payments for machinery	2,236,000
		Payments for long-term investments	2,260,000
		Payments for note payable	386,000
		Payments for dividends	500,000
		Payments for treasury stock	218,000
Balance, Dec. 31, 2008	$?		

Sales   Purchases   General Ledger   Payroll   Inventory   Company   Analysis

---

Exercise 16-14

Reporting cash flows from
operations (indirect)

C4 P2

Hampton Company reports the following information.

Sales		$160,000
Expenses		
Cost of goods sold	100,000	
Salaries expense	24,000	
Depreciation expense	12,000	
Net income		$ 24,000
Accounts receivable increase		$ 10,000
Inventory decrease		16,000
Salaries payable increase		1,000

Required

Prepare the operating activities section of the statement of cash flows for Hampton Company using the indirect method.

Arundel Company disclosed the following income statement and balance sheet information.

Exercise 16-15
Reporting and interpreting cash flows from operations (indirect)

C4   P2

Revenues	$100,000
Expenses	
Salaries expense	84,000
Utilities expense	14,000
Depreciation expense	14,600
Other expenses	3,400
Net loss	$(16,000)
Accounts receivable decrease	$ 24,000
Purchased a machine	10,000
Salaries payable increase	18,000
Other accrued liabilities decrease	8,000

Required

1. Prepare the operating activities section of the statement of cash flows for Arundel Company using the indirect method.

2. What were the major reasons that Arundel Company was able to report a net loss but positive cash flow from operations?

3. Of the potential causes of differences between cash flow from operations and net income, which are the most important to investors?

Forten Company, a merchandiser, recently completed its calendar-year 2008 operations. For the year, (1) all sales are credit sales, (2) all credits to Accounts Receivable reflect cash receipts from customers, (3) all purchases of inventory are on credit, (4) all debits to Accounts Payable reflect cash payments for inventory, and (5) Other Expenses are paid in advance and are initially debited to Prepaid Expenses. Forten's balance sheets and income statement follow:

PROBLEM SET A

Problem 16-1A
Statement of cash flows
(indirect method)

C2   C3   A1   P1   P2   P3

FORTEN COMPANY
Comparative Balance Sheets
December 31, 2008 and 2007

	2008	2007
Assets		
Cash	$ 49,800	$ 73,500
Accounts receivable	65,810	50,625
Merchandise inventory	275,656	251,800
Prepaid expenses	1,250	1,875
Equipment	157,500	108,000
Accum. depreciation—Equipment	(36,625)	(46,000)
Total assets	$513,391	$439,800
Liabilities and Equity		
Accounts payable	$ 53,141	$114,675
Short-term notes payable	10,000	6,000
Long-term notes payable	65,000	48,750
Common stock, $5 par value	162,750	150,250
Paid-in capital in excess		
of par, common stock	37,500	0
Retained earnings	185,000	120,125
Total liabilities and equity	$513,391	$439,800

FORTEN COMPANY
Income Statement
For Year Ended December 31, 2008

Sales		$582,500
Cost of goods sold		285,000
Gross profit		297,500
Operating expenses		
Depreciation expense	$ 20,750	
Other expenses	132,400	153,150
Other gains (losses)		
Loss on sale of equipment		5,125
Income before taxes		139,225
Income taxes expense		24,250
Net income		$114,975

Additional Information on Year 2008 Transactions

a. The loss on the cash sale of equipment was $5,125 (details in *b*).

b. Sold equipment costing $46,875, with accumulated depreciation of $30,125, for $11,625 cash.

c. Purchased equipment costing $96,375 by paying $30,000 cash and signing a long-term note payable for the balance.

d. Borrowed $4,000 cash by signing a short-term note payable.

e. Paid $50,125 cash to reduce the long-term notes payable.

f. Issued 2,500 shares of common stock for $20 cash per share.

g. Declared and paid cash dividends of $50,100.

Required

Check Cash from operating
activities, $40,900

1. Prepare a complete statement of cash flows; report its operating activities using the *indirect method*. Disclose any noncash investing and financing activities in a note.

Analysis Component

2. Analyze and discuss the statement of cash flows prepared in part 1, giving special attention to the wisdom of the cash dividend payment.

Problem 16-2A[A]
Cash flows spreadsheet
(indirect method)

P1 P2 P3 P4

Refer to the information reported about Forten Company in Problem 16-1A.

Required

Prepare a complete statement of cash flows using a spreadsheet as in Exhibit 16A.1; report its operating activities using the indirect method. Identify the debits and credits in the Analysis of Changes columns with letters that correspond to the following list of transactions and events.

a. Net income was $114,975.

b. Accounts receivable increased.

c. Merchandise inventory increased.

d. Prepaid expenses decreased.

e. Accounts payable decreased.

f. Depreciation expense was $20,750.

g. Sold equipment costing $46,875, with accumulated depreciation of $30,125, for $11,625 cash. This yielded a loss of $5,125.

h. Purchased equipment costing $96,375 by paying $30,000 cash and **(i.)** by signing a long-term note payable for the balance.

j. Borrowed $4,000 cash by signing a short-term note payable.

k. Paid $50,125 cash to reduce the long-term notes payable.

l. Issued 2,500 shares of common stock for $20 cash per share.

Check Analysis of Changes column
totals, $600,775

m. Declared and paid cash dividends of $50,100.

Problem 16-3A[B]
Statement of cash flows (direct
method) C3 P1 P3 P5

Check Cash used in financing
activities, $(46,225)

Refer to Forten Company's financial statements and related information in Problem 16-1A.

Required

Prepare a complete statement of cash flows; report its operating activities according to the *direct method*. Disclose any noncash investing and financing activities in a note.

Problem 16-4A
Statement of cash flows (indirect
method) C3 P1 P2 P3

mhhe.com/wildFAP18e

Golden Corp., a merchandiser, recently completed its 2008 operations. For the year, (1) all sales are credit sales, (2) all credits to Accounts Receivable reflect cash receipts from customers, (3) all purchases of inventory are on credit, (4) all debits to Accounts Payable reflect cash payments for inventory, (5) Other Expenses are all cash expenses, and (6) any change in Income Taxes Payable reflects the accrual and cash payment of taxes. Golden's balance sheets and income statement follow.

GOLDEN CORPORATION
Comparative Balance Sheets
December 31, 2008 and 2007

	2008	2007
Assets		
Cash	$ 164,000	$107,000
Accounts receivable	83,000	71,000
Merchandise inventory	601,000	526,000
Equipment	335,000	299,000
Accum. depreciation—Equipment	(158,000)	(104,000)
Total assets	$1,025,000	$899,000
Liabilities and Equity		
Accounts payable	$ 87,000	$ 71,000
Income taxes payable	28,000	25,000
Common stock, $2 par value	592,000	568,000
Paid-in capital in excess		
of par value, common stock	196,000	160,000
Retained earnings	122,000	75,000
Total liabilities and equity	$1,025,000	$899,000

GOLDEN CORPORATION
Income Statement
For Year Ended December 31, 2008

Sales		$1,792,000
Cost of goods sold		1,086,000
Gross profit		706,000
Operating expenses		
Depreciation expense	$ 54,000	
Other expenses	494,000	548,000
Income before taxes		158,000
Income taxes expense		22,000
Net income		$ 136,000

Additional Information on Year 2008 Transactions

a. Purchased equipment for $36,000 cash.

b. Issued 12,000 shares of common stock for $5 cash per share.

c. Declared and paid $89,000 in cash dividends.

Required

Prepare a complete statement of cash flows; report its cash inflows and cash outflows from operating activities according to the *indirect method*.

Check Cash from operating activities, $122,000

Refer to the information reported about Golden Corporation in Problem 16-4A.

Required

Prepare a complete statement of cash flows using a spreadsheet as in Exhibit 16A.1; report operating activities under the indirect method. Identify the debits and credits in the Analysis of Changes columns with letters that correspond to the following list of transactions and events.

a. Net income was $136,000.

b. Accounts receivable increased.

c. Merchandise inventory increased.

d. Accounts payable increased.

e. Income taxes payable increased.

f. Depreciation expense was $54,000.

g. Purchased equipment for $36,000 cash.

h. Issued 12,000 shares at $5 cash per share.

i. Declared and paid $89,000 of cash dividends.

Problem 16-5A[A]

Cash flows spreadsheet (indirect method)

P1 P2 P3 P4

mhhe.com/wildFAP18e

Check Analysis of Changes column totals, $481,000

Refer to Golden Corporation's financial statements and related information in Problem 16-4A.

Required

Prepare a complete statement of cash flows; report its cash flows from operating activities according to the *direct method*.

Problem 16-6A[B]

Statement of cash flows (direct method)   P1 P3 P5

mhhe.com/wildFAP18e

Check Cash used in financing activities, $(29,000)

Problem 16-7A
Computing cash flows from operations (indirect)

C4 P2

Lansing Company's 2008 income statement and selected balance sheet data at December 31, 2007 and 2008, follow ($ thousands).

LANSING COMPANY
Selected Balance Sheet Accounts

At Decmber 31	2008	2007
Accounts receivable	$560	$580
Inventory	198	154
Accounts payable	440	460
Salaries payable	88	70
Utilities payable	22	16
Prepaid insurance	26	28
Prepaid rent	22	18

LANSING COMPANY
Income Statement

Sales revenue	$97,200
Expenses	
Cost of goods sold	42,000
Depreciation expense	12,000
Salaries expense	18,000
Rent expense	9,000
Insurance expense	3,800
Interest expense	3,600
Utilities expense	2,800
Net income	$ 6,000

Required

Check Cash from operating activities, $17,978

Prepare the cash flows from operating activities section of the company's 2008 statement of cash flows using the indirect method.

Problem 16-8A[B]
Computing cash flows from operations (direct)

C4 P5

Refer to the information in Problem 16-7A.

Required

Prepare the cash flows from operating activities section of the company's 2008 statement of cash flows using the direct method.

PROBLEM SET B

Problem 16-1B
Statement of cash flows (indirect method)

C2 C3 A1 P1 P2 P3

Gazelle Corporation, a merchandiser, recently completed its calendar-year 2008 operations. For the year, (1) all sales are credit sales, (2) all credits to Accounts Receivable reflect cash receipts from customers, (3) all purchases of inventory are on credit, (4) all debits to Accounts Payable reflect cash payments for inventory, and (5) Other Expenses are paid in advance and are initially debited to Prepaid Expenses. Gazelle's balance sheets and income statement follow.

GAZELLE CORPORATION
Income Statement
For Year Ended December 31, 2008

Sales		$1,185,000
Cost of goods sold		595,000
Gross profit		590,000
Operating expenses		
Depreciation expense	$ 38,600	
Other expenses	362,850	
Total operating expenses		401,450
		188,550
Other gains (losses)		
Loss on sale of equipment		2,100
Income before taxes		186,450
Income taxes expense		28,350
Net income		$ 158,100

GAZELLE CORPORATION
Comparative Balance Sheets
December 31, 2008 and 2007

	2008	2007
Assets		
Cash	$123,450	$ 61,550
Accounts receivable	77,100	80,750
Merchandise inventory	240,600	250,700
Prepaid expenses	15,100	17,000
Equipment	262,250	200,000
Accum. depreciation—Equipment	(110,750)	(95,000)
Total assets	$607,750	$515,000
Liabilities and Equity		
Accounts payable	$17,750	$102,000
Short-term notes payable	15,000	10,000
Long-term notes payable	100,000	77,500
Common stock, $5 par	215,000	200,000
Paid-in capital in excess of par, common stock	30,000	0
Retained earnings	230,000	125,500
Total liabilities and equity	$607,750	$515,000

Additional Information on Year 2008 Transactions

a. The loss on the cash sale of equipment was $2,100 (details in *b*).

b. Sold equipment costing $51,000, with accumulated depreciation of $22,850, for $26,050 cash.

c. Purchased equipment costing $113,250 by paying $43,250 cash and signing a long-term note payable for the balance.

d. Borrowed $5,000 cash by signing a short-term note payable.

e. Paid $47,500 cash to reduce the long-term notes payable.

f. Issued 3,000 shares of common stock for $15 cash per share.

g. Declared and paid cash dividends of $53,600.

Required

1. Prepare a complete statement of cash flows; report its operating activities using the *indirect method*. Disclose any noncash investing and financing activities in a note.

Check Cash from operating activities, $130,200

Analysis Component

2. Analyze and discuss the statement of cash flows prepared in part 1, giving special attention to the wisdom of the cash dividend payment.

Refer to the information reported about Gazelle Corporation in Problem 16-1B.

Problem 16-2B[A]
Cash flows spreadsheet
(indirect method)

P1 P2 P3 P4

Required

Prepare a complete statement of cash flows using a spreadsheet as in Exhibit 16A.1; report its operating activities using the *indirect method*. Identify the debits and credits in the Analysis of Changes columns with letters that correspond to the following list of transactions and events.

a. Net income was $158,100.

b. Accounts receivable decreased.

c. Merchandise inventory decreased.

d. Prepaid expenses decreased.

e. Accounts payable decreased.

f. Depreciation expense was $38,600.

g. Sold equipment costing $51,000, with accumulated depreciation of $22,850, for $26,050 cash. This yielded a loss of $2,100.

h. Purchased equipment costing $113,250 by paying $43,250 cash and **(i.)** by signing a long-term note payable for the balance.

j. Borrowed $5,000 cash by signing a short-term note payable.

k. Paid $47,500 cash to reduce the long-term notes payable.

l. Issued 3,000 shares of common stock for $15 cash per share.

m. Declared and paid cash dividends of $53,600.

Check Analysis of Changes column totals, $681,950

Refer to Gazelle Corporation's financial statements and related information in Problem 16-1B.

Problem 16-3B[B]
Statement of cash flows (direct method) C3 P1 P3 P5

Required

Prepare a complete statement of cash flows; report its operating activities according to the *direct method*. Disclose any noncash investing and financing activities in a note.

Check Cash used in financing activities, $51,100

Problem 16-4B
Statement of cash flows
(indirect method)

C3   P1   P2   P3

Satu Co., a merchandiser, recently completed its 2008 operations. For the year, (1) all sales are credit sales, (2) all credits to Accounts Receivable reflect cash receipts from customers, (3) all purchases of inventory are on credit, (4) all debits to Accounts Payable reflect cash payments for inventory, (5) Other Expenses are cash expenses, and (6) any change in Income Taxes Payable reflects the accrual and cash payment of taxes. Satu's balance sheets and income statement follow.

SATU COMPANY
Comparative Balance Sheets
December 31, 2008 and 2007

	2008	2007
Assets		
Cash	$ 58,750	$ 28,400
Accounts receivable	20,222	25,860
Merchandise inventory	165,667	140,320
Equipment	107,750	77,500
Accum. depreciation—Equipment	(46,700)	(31,000)
Total assets	$305,689	$241,080
Liabilities and Equity		
Accounts payable	$ 20,372	$157,530
Income taxes payable	2,100	6,100
Common stock, $5 par value	40,000	25,000
Paid-in capital in excess of par, common stock	68,000	20,000
Retained earnings	175,217	32,450
Total liabilities and equity	$305,689	$241,080

SATU COMPANY
Income Statement
For Year Ended December 31, 2008

Sales		$750,800
Cost of goods sold		269,200
Gross profit		481,600
Operating expenses		
Depreciation expense	$ 15,700	
Other expenses	173,933	189,633
Income before taxes		291,967
Income taxes expense		89,200
Net income		$202,767

Additional Information on Year 2008 Transactions

a. Purchased equipment for $30,250 cash.

b. Issued 3,000 shares of common stock for $21 cash per share.

c. Declared and paid $60,000 of cash dividends.

Required

Check Cash from operating activities, $57,600

Prepare a complete statement of cash flows; report its cash inflows and cash outflows from operating activities according to the *indirect method*.

Problem 16-5B[A]
Cash flows spreadsheet
(indirect method)

P1   P2   P3   P4

Refer to the information reported about Satu Company in Problem 16-4B.

Required

Prepare a complete statement of cash flows using a spreadsheet as in Exhibit 16A.1; report operating activities under the *indirect method*. Identify the debits and credits in the Analysis of Changes columns with letters that correspond to the following list of transactions and events.

a. Net income was $202,767.

b. Accounts receivable decreased.

c. Merchandise inventory increased.

d. Accounts payable decreased.

e. Income taxes payable decreased.

f. Depreciation expense was $15,700.

g. Purchased equipment for $30,250 cash.

h. Issued 3,000 shares at $21 cash per share.

i. Declared and paid $60,000 of cash dividends.

Check Analysis of Changes column totals, $543,860

Refer to Satu Company's financial statements and related information in Problem 16-4B.

Required

Prepare a complete statement of cash flows; report its cash flows from operating activities according to the *direct method.*

Problem 16-6B^B
Statement of cash flows
(direct method)   P1   P3   P5

Check   Cash provided by financing activities, $3,000

Salt Lake Company's 2008 income statement and selected balance sheet data at December 31, 2007 and 2008, follow ($ thousands).

Problem 16-7B
Computing cash flows from operations (indirect)

C4   P2

SALT LAKE COMPANY
Income Statement

Sales revenue	$156,000
Expenses	
Cost of goods sold	72,000
Depreciation expense	32,000
Salaries expense	20,000
Rent expense	5,000
Insurance expense	2,600
Interest expense	2,400
Utilities expense	2,000
Net income	$ 20,000

SALT LAKE COMPANY
Selected Balance Sheet Accounts

At December 31	2008	2007
Accounts receivable	$360	$300
Inventory	86	98
Accounts payable	240	260
Salaries payable	90	60
Utilities payable	20	0
Prepaid insurance	14	18
Prepaid rent	10	20

Required

Prepare the cash flows from operating activities section of the company's 2008 statement of cash flows using the indirect method.

Check   Cash from operating activities, $51,996

Refer to the information in Problem 16-7B.

Required

Prepare the cash flows from operating activities section of the company's 2008 statement of cash flows using the direct method.

Problem 16-8B^B
Computing cash flows from operations (direct)

C4   P5

 Problem Set C is available at the book's Website to further reinforce and assess your learning.

PROBLEM SET C

(This serial problem began in Chapter 1 and continues through most of the book. If previous chapter segments were not completed, the serial problem can begin at this point. It is helpful, but not necessary, for you to use the Working Papers that accompany the book.)

SERIAL PROBLEM

Success Systems

SP 16   Adriana Lopez, owner of Success Systems, decides to prepare a statement of cash flows for her business. (Although the serial problem allowed for various ownership changes in earlier chapters, we will prepare the statement of cash flows using the following financial data.)

SUCCESS SYSTEMS
Income Statement
For Three Months Ended March 31, 2008

Computer services revenue		$31,850
Net sales		20,345
Total revenue		52,195
Cost of goods sold	$14,272	
Depreciation expense—Office equipment	625	
Depreciation expense—Computer equipment	1,250	
Wages expense	3,900	
Insurance expense	600	
Rent expense	2,625	
Computer supplies expense	2,075	
Advertising expense	800	
Mileage expense	512	
Repairs expense—Computer	1,200	
Total expenses		27,859
Net income		$24,336

SUCCESS SYSTEMS
Comparative Balance Sheets
December 31, 2007, and March 31, 2008

	2008	2007
Assets		
Cash	$ 87,266	$ 80,260
Accounts receivable	24,400	5,800
Merchandise Inventory	680	0
Computer supplies	1,950	775
Prepaid insurance	1,200	1,800
Prepaid rent	875	875
Office equipment	10,000	10,000
Accumulated depreciation—Office equipment	(1,250)	(625)
Computer equipment	25,000	25,000
Accumulated depreciation—Computer equipment	(2,500)	(1,250)
Total assets	$147,621	$122,635
Liabilities and Equity		
Accounts payable	$ 0	$ 2,100
Wages payable	1,050	600
Unearned computer service revenue	0	2,500
Common stock	120,000	110,000
Retained earnings	26,571	7,435
Total liabilities and equity	$147,621	$122,635

Required

Prepare a statement of cash flows for Success Systems using the *indirect method* for the three months ended March 31, 2008. Recall that the owner Adriana Lopez contributed $10,000 to the business in exchange for additional stock in the first quarter of 2008 and has received $5,200 in cash dividends.

BEYOND THE NUMBERS

REPORTING IN ACTION

C4 A1

BTN 16-1   Refer to **Best Buy**'s financial statements in Appendix A to answer the following.

1. Is Best Buy's statement of cash flows prepared under the direct method or the indirect method? How do you know?
2. For each fiscal year 2005, 2004, and 2003, is the amount of cash provided by operating activities more or less than the cash paid for dividends?
3. What is the largest amount in reconciling the difference between net income and cash flow from operating activities in 2005? In 2004? In 2003?
4. Identify the largest cash flows for investing and for financing activities in 2005 and in 2004.

Fast Forward

5. Obtain Best Buy's financial statements for a fiscal year ending after February 26, 2005, from either its Website (BestBuy.com) or the SEC's EDGAR database (www.sec.gov). Since February 26, 2005, what are Best Buy's largest cash outflows and cash inflows in the investing and in the financing sections of its statement of cash flow?

BTN 16-2 Key comparative figures ($ millions) for **Best Buy** and **Circuit City** follow.

	Best Buy			Circuit City		
Key Figures	Current Year	I Year Prior	2 Years Prior	Current Year	I Year Prior	2 Years Prior
Operating cash flows	$ 1,841	$1,369	$ 778	$ 456	$(126)	$(163)
Total assets	10,294	8,652	7,694	3,789	3,731	3,841

Required

1. Compute the recent two years' cash flow on total assets ratios for both Best Buy and Circuit City.
2. What does the cash flow on total assets ratio measure?
3. Which company has the higher cash flow on total assets ratio for the periods shown?
4. Does the cash flow on total assets ratio reflect on the quality of earnings? Explain.

BTN 16-3 Lisa Gish is preparing for a meeting with her banker. Her business is finishing its fourth year of operations. In the first year, it had negative cash flows from operations. In the second and third years, cash flows from operations were positive. However, inventory costs rose significantly in year 4, and cash flows from operations will probably be down 25%. Gish wants to secure a line of credit from her banker as a financing buffer. From experience, she knows the banker will scrutinize operating cash flows for years 1 through 4 and will want a projected number for year 5. Gish knows that a steady progression upward in operating cash flows for years 1 through 4 will help her case. She decides to use her discretion as owner and considers several business actions that will turn her operating cash flow in year 4 from a decrease to an increase over year 3.

Required

1. Identify two business actions Gish might take to improve cash flows from operations.
2. Comment on the ethics and possible consequences of Gish's decision to pursue these actions.

BTN 16-4 Your friend, Jessica Willard, recently completed the second year of her business and just received annual financial statements from her accountant. Willard finds the income statement and balance sheet informative but does not understand the statement of cash flows. She says the first section is especially confusing because it contains a lot of additions and subtractions that do not make sense to her. Willard adds, "The income statement tells me the business is more profitable than last year and that's most important. If I want to know how cash changes, I can look at comparative balance sheets."

Required

Write a half-page memorandum to your friend explaining the purpose of the statement of cash flows. Speculate as to why the first section is so confusing and how it might be rectified.

BTN 16-5 Access the April 29, 2005, filing of the 10-K report (for fiscal year ending January 29, 2005) of **J. Crew Group, Inc.**, at www.sec.gov.

Required

1. Does J. Crew use the direct or indirect method to construct its consolidated statement of cash flows?
2. For the fiscal year ended January 29, 2005, what is the largest item in reconciling the net loss to cash flow provided by operations?
3. In recent years J. Crew has recorded several net losses. Has the company been more successful in generating operating cash flows over this time period than in generating net income?
4. In the year ended January 29, 2005, what was the largest cash outflow for investing activities and for financing activities?
5. What items does J. Crew report as supplementary cash flow information?
6. Does J. Crew report any noncash financing activities?

TEAMWORK IN ACTION

C1 C4 A1 P2 P5

BTN 16-6   Team members are to coordinate and independently answer one question within each of the following three sections. Team members should then report to the team and confirm or correct team-mates' answers.

1. Answer *one* of the following questions about the statement of cash flows.

   a. What are this statement's reporting objectives?

   b. What two methods are used to prepare it? Identify similarities and differences between them.

   c. What steps are followed to prepare the statement?

   d. What types of analyses are often made from this statement's information?

2. Identify and explain the adjustment from net income to obtain cash flows from operating activities using the indirect method for *one* of the following items.

   a. Noncash operating revenues and expenses.

   b. Nonoperating gains and losses.

   c. Increases and decreases in noncash current assets.

   d. Increases and decreases in current liabilities.

3.[B]Identify and explain the formula for computing cash flows from operating activities using the direct method for *one* of the following items.

   a. Cash receipts from sales to customers.

   b. Cash paid for merchandise inventory.

   c. Cash paid for wages and operating expenses.

   d. Cash paid for interest and taxes.

Note: For teams of more than four, some pairing within teams is necessary. Use as an in-class activity or as an assignment. If used in class, specify a time limit on each part. Conclude with reports to the entire class, using team rotation. Each team can prepare responses on a transparency.

BusinessWeek ACTIVITY

A1

BTN 16-7   Read the article "Amazon.com's Split Personality" by Nicholas G. Carr in the June 9, 2005, issue of *BusinessWeek*. (The book's Website provides a free link.) Also, access **Amazon.com**'s most recent financial statements from **www.sec.gov**.

Required

1. In what order does Amazon.com present its financial statements? How does this ordering compare to other companies' financial statements that you have seen?

2. Why do you believe Amazon.com presents its financial statements in the order it does?

3. What is Jeff Bezo's perception of the relative importance of the cash flow statement and the income statement? Explain.

ENTREPRENEURIAL DECISION

C1 A1

BTN 16-8   Review the chapter's opener involving **Ashtae Products, Inc**.

Required

1. In a business such as Ashtae Products, monitoring cash flow is always a priority. Even though Ashtae has about $5 million in annual sales and earns a positive net income, explain how cash flow can lag behind earnings?

2. Ashtae is a closely held corporation. What are potential sources of financing for its future expansion?

C2 A1

BTN 16-9   Jenna and Matt Wilder are completing their second year operating Mountain High, a downhill ski area and resort. Mountain High reports a net loss of $(10,000) for its second year, which includes an $85,000 extraordinary loss from fire. This past year also involved major purchases of plant assets for renovation and expansion, yielding a year-end total asset amount of $800,000. Mountain High's net cash outflow for its second year is $(5,000); a summarized version of its statement of cash flows follows:

Net cash flow provided by operating activities	$295,000
Net cash flow used by investing activities	(310,000)
Net cash flow provided by financing activities	10,000

Required

Write a one-page memorandum to the Wilders evaluating Mountain High's current performance and assessing its future. Give special emphasis to cash flow data and their interpretation.

BTN 16-10 Visit **The Motley Fool**'s Website (**Fool.com**). Click on the sidebar link titled *Fool's School*. Identify and select the link *How to Value Stocks*.

HITTING THE ROAD

C1

Required

1. How does the Fool's school define cash flow?
2. Per the school's instruction, why do analysts focus on earnings before interest and taxes (EBIT)?
3. Visit other links at this Website that interest you such as "A Journey through the Balance Sheet," or find out what the "Fool's Ratio" is. Write a half-page report on what you find.

BTN 16-11 Key comparative information for **Dixons** (**Dixons-Group.com**) follows.

GLOBAL DECISION

C1 C2 C4

Dixons

(£ millions)	Current Year	I Year Prior	2 Years Prior
Operating cash flows	£ 328	£ 340	£ 340
Total assets	3,874	4,158	4,081

Required

1. Compute the recent two years' cash flow on total assets ratio for Dixons.
2. How does Dixons' ratio compare to Best Buy and Circuit City's ratios from BTN 16-2?

ANSWERS TO MULTIPLE CHOICE QUIZ

1. b;

Net income	$15,200
Depreciation expense	10,000
Gain on sale of land	(3,000)
Increase in inventory	(1,500)
Increase in accounts payable	2,850
Net cash provided by operations	$23,550

2. c; cash received from sale of machine is reported as an investing activity.

3. d; FASB requires cash interest paid to be reported under operating.

4. a; Cash paid for salaries and wages = $255,000 + $8,200 − $10,900 = $252,300

5. e; Increase in inventory = $112,000 − $105,000 = $7,000
Increase in accounts payable = $101,300 − $98,500 = $2,800
Cash paid for merchandise = $545,000 + $7,000 − $2,800 = $549,200

17

Analysis of Financial Statements

A Look Back

Chapter 16 focused on reporting and analyzing cash inflows and cash outflows. We explained how to prepare, analyze, and interpret the statement of cash flows.

A Look at This Chapter

This chapter emphasizes the analysis and interpretation of financial statement information. We learn to apply horizontal, vertical, and ratio analyses to better understand company performance and financial condition.

A Look Ahead

Chapter 18 introduces us to managerial accounting. We discuss its purposes, concepts, and roles in helping managers gather and organize information for decisions. We also explain basic management principles.

Learning Objectives

CAP

Conceptual

C1 Explain the purpose of analysis. *(p. 674)*

C2 Identify the building blocks of analysis. *(p. 675)*

C3 Describe standards for comparisons in analysis. *(p. 676)*

C4 Identify the tools of analysis. *(p. 676)*

Analytical

A1 Summarize and report results of analysis. *(p. 694)*

A2 *Appendix 17A*—Explain the form and assess the content of a complete income statement. *(p. 697)*

Procedural

P1 Explain and apply methods of horizontal analysis. *(p. 676)*

P2 Describe and apply methods of vertical analysis. *(p. 681)*

P3 Define and apply ratio analysis. *(p. 685)*

"What goes on at The Motley Fool every day is similar to what goes on in a library"
—Tom Gardner (David Gardner on left)

Fools and Their Money

ALEXANDRIA, VA—In Shakespeare's Elizabethan comedy *As You Like It*, only the fool could speak truthfully to the King without getting his head lopped off. Inspired by Shakespeare's stage character, Tom and David Gardner vowed to become modern-day fools who tell it like it is. With under $10,000 in startup money, the brothers launched **The Motley Fool (Fool.com).** And befitting of a Shakespearean play, the two say they are "dedicated to educating, amusing, and enriching individuals in search of the truth."

The Gardners do not fear the wrath of any King, real or fictional. They are intent on exposing the truth, as they see it, "that the financial world preys on ignorance and fear." As Tom explains, "There is such a great need in the general populace for financial information." Who can argue, given their brilliant success through practically every medium; including their Website, radio shows, newspaper columns, online store, investment newsletters, and global expansion.

Despite the brothers' best efforts, however, ordinary people still do not fully use information contained in financial statements. For instance, discussions keep appearing on The Motley Fool's online bulletin board that can be easily resolved using reliable and available accounting data. So, it would seem that the Fools must continue their work of "educating and enriching" individuals.

Resembling The Motley Fools' objectives, this chapter introduces horizontal and vertical analyses—tools used to reveal crucial trends and insights from financial information. It also expands on ratio analysis, which gives insight into a company's financial condition and performance. By arming ourselves with the information contained in this chapter and the investment advice of The Motley Fool, *we* can be sure to not play the fool in today's financial world.

[Sources: *Motley Fool Website,* May 2006; *Entrepreneur,* July 1997; *What to do with Your Money Now,* June 2002; *USA Weekend,* July 2004]

Chapter Preview

This chapter shows how to use information in financial statements to evaluate a company's financial performance and condition. We describe the purpose of financial statement analysis, its basic building blocks, the information available, standards for comparisons, and tools of analysis. The chapter emphasizes three major analysis tools: horizontal analysis, vertical analysis, and ratio analysis. We illustrate the application of each of these tools using **Best Buy**'s financial statements. We also introduce comparative analysis using **Circuit City**'s financial statements. This chapter expands and organizes the ratio analyses introduced at the end of each chapter.

Analysis of Financial Statements

Basics of Analysis	Horizontal Analysis	Vertical Analysis	Ratio Analysis
• Purpose • Building blocks • Information • Standards for comparisons • Tools	• Comparative balance sheets • Comparative income statements • Trend analysis	• Common-size balance sheet • Common-size income statement • Common-size graphics	• Liquidity and efficiency • Solvency • Profitability • Market prospects • Ratio summary

Basics of Analysis

Financial statement analysis applies analytical tools to general-purpose financial statements and related data for making business decisions. It involves transforming accounting data into more useful information. Financial statement analysis reduces our reliance on hunches, guesses, and intuition as well as our uncertainty in decision making. It does not lessen the need for expert judgment; instead, it provides us an effective and systematic basis for making business decisions. This section describes the purpose of financial statement analysis, its information sources, the use of comparisons, and some issues in computations.

Purpose of Analysis

C1 Explain the purpose of analysis.

Internal users of accounting information are those involved in strategically managing and operating the company. They include managers, officers, internal auditors, consultants, budget directors, and market researchers. The purpose of financial statement analysis for these users is to provide strategic information to improve company efficiency and effectiveness in providing products and services.

External users of accounting information are *not* directly involved in running the company. They include shareholders, lenders, directors, customers, suppliers, regulators, lawyers, brokers, and the press. External users rely on financial statement analysis to make better and more informed decisions in pursuing their own goals.

We can identify other uses of financial statement analysis. Shareholders and creditors assess company prospects to make investing and lending decisions. A board of directors analyzes financial statements in monitoring management's decisions. Employees and unions use financial statements in labor negotiations. Suppliers use financial statement information in establishing credit terms. Customers analyze financial statements in deciding whether to establish supply relationships. Public utilities set customer rates by analyzing financial statements. Auditors use financial statements in assessing the "fair presentation" of their clients' financial

Point: Financial statement analysis tools are also used for personal financial investment decisions.

Point: Financial statement analysis is a topic on the CPA, CMA, CIA, and CFA exams.

reports. Analyst services such as **Dun & Bradstreet**, **Moody's**, and **Standard & Poor's** use financial statements in making buy-sell recommendations and in setting credit ratings. The common goal of these users is to evaluate company performance and financial condition. This includes evaluating (1) past and current performance, (2) current financial position, and (3) future performance and risk.

Building Blocks of Analysis

Financial statement analysis focuses on one or more elements of a company's financial condition or performance. Our analysis emphasizes four areas of inquiry—with varying degrees of importance. These four areas are described and illustrated in this chapter and are considered the *building blocks* of financial statement analysis:

C2 Identify the building blocks of analysis.

- **Liquidity** and **efficiency**—ability to meet short-term obligations and to efficiently generate revenues.
- **Solvency**—ability to generate future revenues and meet long-term obligations.
- **Profitability**—ability to provide financial rewards sufficient to attract and retain financing.
- **Market prospects**—ability to generate positive market expectations.

Applying the building blocks of financial statement analysis involves determining (1) the objectives of analysis and (2) the relative emphasis among the building blocks. We distinguish among these four building blocks to emphasize the different aspects of a company's financial condition or performance, yet we must remember that these areas of analysis are interrelated. For instance, a company's operating performance is affected by the availability of financing and short-term liquidity conditions. Similarly, a company's credit standing is not limited to satisfactory short-term liquidity but depends also on its profitability and efficiency in using assets. Early in our analysis, we need to determine the relative emphasis of each building block. Emphasis and analysis can later change as a result of evidence collected.

Decision Insight

Chips and Brokers The phrase *blue chips* refers to stock of big, profitable companies. The phrase comes from poker; where the most valuable chips are blue. The term *brokers* refers to those who execute orders to buy or sell stock. The term comes from wine retailers—individuals who broach (break) wine casks.

Information for Analysis

Some users, such as managers and regulatory authorities, are able to receive special financial reports prepared to meet their analysis needs. However, most users must rely on **general-purpose financial statements** that include the (1) income statement, (2) balance sheet, (3) statement of stockholders' equity (or statement of retained earnings), (4) statement of cash flows, and (5) notes to these statements.

Financial reporting refers to the communication of financial information useful for making investment, credit, and other business decisions. Financial reporting includes not only general-purpose financial statements but also information from SEC 10-K or other filings, press releases, shareholders' meetings, forecasts, management letters, auditors' reports, and Webcasts.

Management's Discussion and Analysis (MD&A) is one example of useful information outside traditional financial statements. **Best Buy**'s MD&A (available at <u>BestBuy.com</u>), for example, begins with an overview and strategic initiatives. It then discusses operating results followed by liquidity and capital resources—roughly equivalent to investing and financing. The final few parts discuss special financing arrangements, key accounting policies, interim results, and the next year's outlook. The MD&A is an excellent starting point in understanding a company's business activities.

Decision Insight

Analysis Online Many Websites offer free access and screening of companies by key numbers such as earnings, sales, and book value. For instance, **Standard & Poor's** has information for more than 10,000 stocks (<u>StandardPoor.com</u>) that is accessible by its programs.

Standards for Comparisons

C3   Describe standards for comparisons in analysis.

When interpreting measures from financial statement analysis, we need to decide whether the measures indicate good, bad, or average performance. To make such judgments, we need standards (benchmarks) for comparisons that include the following:

■ *Intracompany*—The company under analysis can provide standards for comparisons based on its own prior performance and relations between its financial items. **Best Buy**'s current net income, for instance, can be compared with its prior years' net income and in relation to its revenues or total assets.

■ *Competitor*—One or more direct competitors of the company being analyzed can provide standards for comparisons. **Coca-Cola**'s profit margin, for instance, can be compared with **PepsiCo**'s profit margin.

■ *Industry*—Industry statistics can provide standards of comparisons. Such statistics are available from services such as **Dun & Bradstreet**, **Standard & Poor's**, and **Moody's**.

■ *Guidelines (rules of thumb)*—General standards of comparisons can develop from experience. Examples are the 2:1 level for the current ratio or 1:1 level for the acid-test ratio. Guidelines, or rules of thumb, must be carefully applied because context is crucial.

Point: Each chapter's *Reporting in Action* problems engage students in *intracompany* analysis, whereas *Comparative Analysis* problems require competitor analysis (Best Buy vs. Circuit City).

All of these comparison standards are useful when properly applied, yet measures taken from a selected competitor or group of competitors are often best. Intracompany and industry measures are also important. Guidelines or rules of thumb should be applied with care, and then only if they seem reasonable given past experience and industry norms.

Quick Check
Answers—p. 700

1. Who are the intended users of general-purpose financial statements?
2. General-purpose financial statements consist of what information?
3. Which of the following is *least* useful as a basis for comparison when analyzing ratios? (*a*) Company results from a different economic setting. (*b*) Standards from past experience. (*c*) Rule-of-thumb standards. (*d*) Industry averages.
4. What is the preferred basis of comparison for ratio analysis?

Tools of Analysis

C4   Identify the tools of analysis.

Three of the most common tools of financial statement analysis are

1. **Horizontal analysis**—Comparison of a company's financial condition and performance across time.
2. **Vertical analysis**—Comparison of a company's financial condition and performance to a base amount.
3. **Ratio analysis**—Measurement of key relations between financial statement items.

The remainder of this chapter describes these analysis tools and how to apply them.

Horizontal Analysis

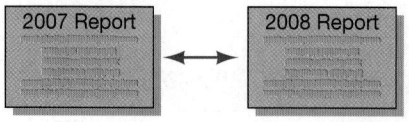

Analysis of any single financial number is of limited value. Instead, much of financial statement analysis involves identifying and describing relations between numbers, groups of numbers, and changes in those numbers. Horizontal analysis refers to examination of financial statement data *across time*. [The term *horizontal analysis* arises from the left-to-right (or right-to-left) movement of our eyes as we review comparative financial statements across time.]

Comparative Statements

P1   Explain and apply methods of horizontal analysis.

Comparing amounts for two or more successive periods often helps in analyzing financial statements. **Comparative financial statements** facilitate this comparison by showing financial amounts in side-by-side columns on a single statement, called a *comparative format*. Using figures from **Best Buy**'s financial statements, this section explains how to compute dollar changes and percent changes for comparative statements.

Topic Tackler

PLUS

17-1

Computation of Dollar Changes and Percent Changes   Comparing financial statements over relatively short time periods—two to three years—is often done by analyzing changes in line items. A change analysis usually includes analyzing absolute dollar amount changes and percent changes. Both analyses are relevant because dollar changes can yield large percent changes inconsistent with their importance. For instance, a 50% change from a base figure of $100 is less important than the same percent change from a base amount of $100,000 in the same statement. Reference to dollar amounts is necessary to retain a proper perspective and to assess the importance of changes. We compute the *dollar change* for a financial statement item as follows:

Example: What is a more significant change, a 70% increase on a $1,000 expense or a 30% increase on a $400,000 expense? *Answer:* The 30% increase.

$$\text{Dollar change} = \text{Analysis period amount} - \text{Base period amount}$$

Analysis period is the point or period of time for the financial statements under analysis, and *base period* is the point or period of time for the financial statements used for comparison purposes. The prior year is commonly used as a base period. We compute the *percent change* by dividing the dollar change by the base period amount and then multiplying this quantity by 100 as follows:

$$\text{Percent change } (\%) = \frac{\text{Analysis period amount} - \text{Base period amount}}{\text{Base period amount}} \times 100$$

We can always compute a dollar change, but we must be aware of a few rules in working with percent changes. To illustrate, look at four separate cases in this chart:

Case	Analysis Period	Base Period	Change Analysis Dollar	Change Analysis Percent
A	$ 1,500	$(4,500)	$ 6,000	—
B	(1,000)	2,000	(3,000)	—
C	8,000	—	8,000	—
D	0	10,000	(10,000)	(100%)

When a negative amount appears in the base period and a positive amount in the analysis period (or vice versa), we cannot compute a meaningful percent change; see cases A and B. Also, when no value is in the base period, no percent change is computable; see case C. Finally, when an item has a value in the base period and zero in the analysis period, the decrease is 100 percent; see case D.

Example: When there is a value in the base period and zero in the analysis period, the decrease is 100%. Why isn't the reverse situation an increase of 100%? *Answer:* A 100% increase of zero is still zero.

It is common when using horizontal analysis to compare amounts to either average or median values from prior periods (average and median values smooth out erratic or unusual fluctuations).[1] We also commonly round percents and ratios to one or two decimal places, but practice on this matter is not uniform. Computations are as

Decision Insight

Ticker Prices   *Ticker prices* refer to a band of moving data on a monitor carrying up-to-the-minute stock prices. The phrase comes from *ticker tape*, a 1-inch-wide strip of paper spewing stock prices from a printer that ticked as it ran. Most of today's investors have never seen actual ticker tape, but the phrase survives.

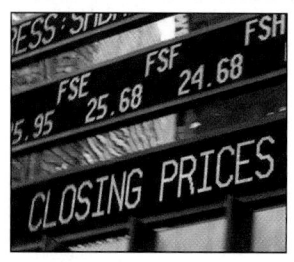

---

[1] *Median* is the middle value in a group of numbers. For instance, if five prior years' incomes are (in 000s) $15, $19, $18, $20, and $22, the median value is $19. When there are two middle numbers, we can take their average. For instance, if four prior years' sales are (in 000s) $84, $91, $96, and $93, the median is $92 (computed as the average of $91 and $93).

detailed as necessary, which is judged by whether rounding potentially affects users' decisions. Computations should not be excessively detailed so that important relations are lost among a mountain of decimal points and digits.

Comparative Balance Sheets   Comparative balance sheets consist of balance sheet amounts from two or more balance sheet dates arranged side by side. Its usefulness is often improved by showing each item's dollar change and percent change to highlight large changes.

Analysis of comparative financial statements begins by focusing on items that show large dollar or percent changes. We then try to identify the reasons for these changes and, if possible, determine whether they are favorable or unfavorable. We also follow up on items with small changes when we expected the changes to be large.

Exhibit 17.1 shows comparative balance sheets for **Best Buy**. A few items stand out. All asset categories substantially increase, which is probably not surprising because Best Buy is a growth company. At least part of the increase in liquid assets is from the 10.2% increase in current liabilities and the cash inflows from employee stock options; see the financing activities

Point: Spreadsheet programs can help with horizontal, vertical, and ratio analyses, including graphical depictions of financial relations. The key is using this information effectively for business decisions.

Point: Business consultants use comparative statement analysis to provide management advice.

Exhibit 17.1

Comparative Balance Sheets

BEST BUY Comparative Balance Sheets February 26, 2005, and February 28, 2004				
(in millions)	2005	2004	Dollar Change	Percent Change
Assets				
Cash and cash equivalents	$ 470	$ 245	$ 225	91.8%
Short-term investments	2,878	2,355	523	22.2
Receivables, net	375	343	32	9.3
Merchandise inventories	2,851	2,607	244	9.4
Other current assets	329	174	155	89.1
Total current assets	6,903	5,724	1,179	20.6
Property and equipment	4,192	3,574	618	17.3
Less accumulated depreciation	1,728	1,330	398	29.9
Net property and equipment	2,464	2,244	220	9.8
Goodwill	513	477	36	7.5
Tradename	40	37	3	8.1
Long-term investments	148	—	148	—
Other long-term assets	226	170	56	32.9
Total assets	$10,294	$8,652	$1,642	19.0
Liabilities				
Accounts payable	$ 2,824	$2,460	364	14.8
Unredeemed gift card liabilities	410	300	110	36.7
Accrued compensation and related expenses	234	269	(35)	(13.0)
Accrued liabilities	844	724	120	16.6
Accrued income taxes	575	380	195	51.3
Current portion of long-term debt	72	368	(296)	(80.4)
Total current liabilities	4,959	4,501	458	10.2
Long-term liabilities	358	247	111	44.9
Long-term debt	528	482	46	9.5
Shareholders' equity				
Common stock	33	32	1	3.1
Additional paid-in capital	952	836	116	13.9
Retained earnings	3,315	2,468	847	34.3
Accumulated other comprehensive income	149	86	63	73.3
Total shareholders' equity	4,449	3,422	1,027	30.0
Total liabilities and shareholders' equity	$10,294	$8,652	$1,642	19.0

section of the statement of cash flows. Of course, substantial asset growth (19.0%) must be accompanied by future income to validate Best Buy's growth strategy.

We likewise see substantial increases on the financing side, the most notable ones being current and long-term liabilities totaling about $569 million. Much of this is reflected in the increase in current assets and property and equipment. Best Buy also reinvested much of its income as reflected in the $847 million increase in retained earnings. Again, we must monitor the increases in investing and financing activities to be sure they are reflected in increased operating performance.

Comparative Income Statements   Comparative income statements are prepared similarly to comparative balance sheets. Amounts for two or more periods are placed side by side, with additional columns for dollar and percent changes. Exhibit 17.2 shows Best Buy's comparative income statements.

Exhibit 17.2

Comparative Income Statements

BEST BUY Comparative Income Statements For Years Ended February 26, 2005, and February 28, 2004				
(in millions, except per share data)	2005	2004	Dollar Change	Percent Change
Revenues	$27,433	$24,548	$2,885	11.8%
Cost of goods sold	20,938	18,677	2,261	12.1
Gross profit	6,495	5,871	624	10.6
Selling, general & administrative expenses	5,053	4,567	486	10.6
Operating income	1,442	1,304	138	10.6
Net interest income (expense)	1	(8)	9	—
Earnings from continuing operations before income taxes	1,443	1,296	147	11.3
Income tax expense	509	496	13	2.6
Earnings from continuing operations	934	800	134	16.8
Loss from discontinued operations, net of tax	—	(29)	29	(100.0)
Gain (loss) on disposal of discontinued operations	50	(66)	116	—
Net earnings	$ 984	$ 705	$ 279	39.6
Basic earnings per share	$ 3.02	$ 2.18	0.84	38.5
Diluted earnings per share	$ 2.94	$ 2.13	0.81	38.0

Best Buy has substantial revenue growth of 11.8% in 2005. This finding helps support management's growth strategy as reflected in the comparative balance sheets. Equally impressive is its ability to control cost of sales and general and administrative expenses, which increased 12.1% and 10.6%, respectively. Best Buy's net income growth of 39.6% on revenue growth of 11.8% is impressive.

Point: Percent change can also be computed by dividing the current period by the prior period and subtracting 1.0. For example, the 11.8% revenue increase of Exhibit 17.2 is computed as: ($27,433/$24,548) − 1.

Trend Analysis

Trend analysis, also called *trend percent analysis* or *index number trend analysis,* is a form of horizontal analysis that can reveal patterns in data across successive periods. It involves computing trend percents for a series of financial numbers and is a variation on the use of percent changes. The difference is that trend analysis does not subtract the base period amount in the numerator. To compute trend percents, we do the following:

1. Select a *base period* and assign each item in the base period a weight of 100%.
2. Express financial numbers as a percent of their base period number.

Specifically, a *trend percent,* also called an *index number,* is computed as follows:

Point: *Index* refers to the comparison of the analysis period to the base period. Percents determined for each period are called *index numbers.*

$$\text{Trend percent (\%)} = \frac{\text{Analysis period amount}}{\text{Base period amount}} \times 100$$

To illustrate trend analysis, we use the **Best Buy** data in Exhibit 17.3.

Exhibit 17.3
Revenues and Expenses

(in millions)	2005	2004	2003	2002	2001
Revenues	$27,433	$24,548	$20,943	$17,711	$15,189
Cost of goods sold	20,938	18,677	15,998	13,941	12,177
Selling, general & administrative expenses	5,053	4,567	3,935	2,862	2,401

These data are from Best Buy's *Selected Financial Data* section. The base period is 2001 and the trend percent is computed in each subsequent year by dividing that year's amount by its 2001 amount. For instance, the revenue trend percent for 2005 is 180.6%, computed as $27,433/$15,189. The trend percents—using the data from Exhibit 17.3—are shown in Exhibit 17.4.

Exhibit 17.4
Trend Percents for Revenues and Expenses

	2005	2004	2003	2002	2001
Revenues	180.6%	161.6%	137.9%	116.6%	100%
Cost of goods sold	171.9	153.4	131.4	114.5	100%
Selling, general & administrative expenses	210.5	190.2	163.9	119.2	100%

Point: Trend analysis expresses a percent of base, not a percent of change.

Exhibit 17.5
Trend Percent Lines for Revenues and Expenses of Best Buy

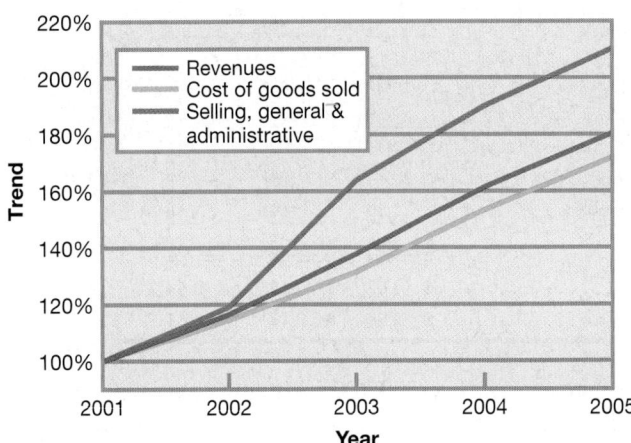

Graphical depictions often aid analysis of trend percents. Exhibit 17.5 shows the trend percents from Exhibit 17.4 in a *line graph*, which can help us identify trends and detect changes in direction or magnitude. It reveals that the trend line for revenues consistently exceeds that for cost of goods sold. Moreover, the magnitude of that difference has consistently grown. This result bodes well for Best Buy because its cost of goods sold are by far its largest cost, and the company shows an ability to control these expenses as it expands. The line graph also reveals a consistent increase in each of these accounts, which is typical of growth companies. The trend line for selling, general and administrative expenses is troubling because it exceeds the revenue trend line in all years. The good news is that nearly all of that upward shift in costs occured in one year (2003). In other years, management appears to have limited those costs to not exceed revenue growth.

Exhibit 17.6 compares **Best Buy**'s revenue trend line to that of **Circuit City** for this same period. Best Buy's revenues sharply increased over this time period while those of Circuit City were flat. These data indicate that Best Buy's products and services have met with considerable consumer acceptance.

Exhibit 17.6
Trend Percent Lines—Best Buy vs. Circuit City

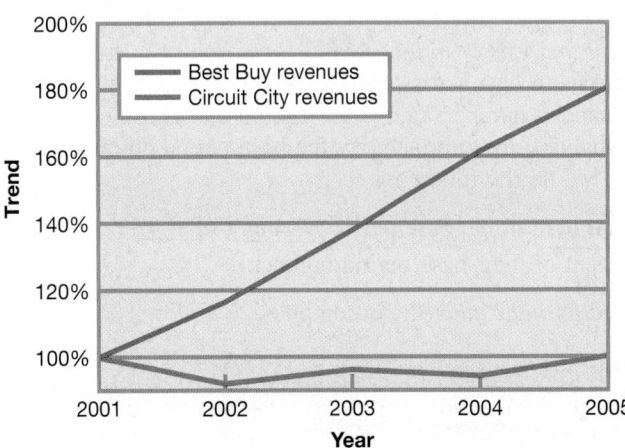

Trend analysis of financial statement items can include comparisons of relations between items on different financial statements. For instance, Exhibit 17.7 compares Best Buy's revenues and total assets. The rate of increase in total assets (212.7%) is greater than the increase in revenues (180.6%) since 2001. Is this result favorable or not? It suggests that Best Buy was less efficient in using its assets in 2005. Management apparently is expecting future years' revenues to compensate for this asset growth.

($ millions)	2005	2001	Trend Percent (2005 vs. 2001)
Revenues	$27,433	$15,189	180.6%
Total assets	10,294	4,840	212.7

Exhibit 17.7

Revenue and Asset Data for Best Buy

Overall we must remember that an important role of financial statement analysis is identifying questions and areas of interest, which often direct us to important factors bearing on a company's future. Accordingly, financial statement analysis should be seen as a continuous process of refining our understanding and expectations of company performance and financial condition.

Decision Maker   Answer—p. 700

Auditor   Your tests reveal a 3% increase in sales from $200,000 to $206,000 and a 4% decrease in expenses from $190,000 to $182,400. Both changes are within your "reasonableness" criterion of ±5%, and thus you don't pursue additional tests. The audit partner in charge questions your lack of follow-up and mentions the *joint relation* between sales and expenses. To what is the partner referring?

Vertical Analysis

Vertical analysis is a tool to evaluate individual financial statement items or a group of items in terms of a specific base amount. We usually define a key aggregate figure as the base, which for an income statement is usually revenue and for a balance sheet is usually total assets. This section explains vertical analysis and applies it to Best Buy. [The term *vertical analysis* arises from the up-down (or down-up) movement of our eyes as we review common-size financial statements. Vertical analysis is also called *common-size analysis*.]

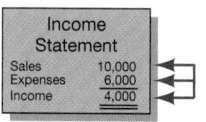

Income Statement
Sales   10,000
Expenses   6,000
Income   4,000

Common-Size Statements

The comparative statements in Exhibits 17.1 and 17.2 show the change in each item over time, but they do not emphasize the relative importance of each item. We use **common-size financial statements** to reveal changes in the relative importance of each financial statement item. All individual amounts in common-size statements are redefined in terms of common-size percents. A *common-size percent* is measured by dividing each individual financial statement amount under analysis by its base amount:

P2   Describe and apply methods of vertical analysis.

$$\text{Common-size percent (\%)} = \frac{\text{Analysis amount}}{\text{Base amount}} \times 100$$

Common-Size Balance Sheets   Common-size statements express each item as a percent of a *base amount,* which for a common-size balance sheet is usually total assets. The base amount is assigned a value of 100%. (This implies that the total amount of liabilities plus equity equals 100% since this amount equals total assets.) We then compute a common-size percent for each asset, liability, and equity item using total assets as the base amount. When we present a company's successive balance sheets in this way, changes in the mixture of assets, liabilities, and equity are apparent.

Exhibit 17.8 shows common-size comparative balance sheets for Best Buy. Some relations that stand out on both a magnitude and percentage basis include (1) a nearly twofold increase in cash and equivalents, (2) a 2.4% decline in inventories as a percentage of assets, (3) a 2%

Point: The *base* amount in common-size analysis is an *aggregate* amount from the same period's financial statement.

Point: Common-size statements often are used to compare two or more companies in the same industry.

Exhibit 17.8

Common-Size Comparative
Balance Sheets

BEST BUY
Common-Size Comparative Balance Sheets
February 26, 2005, and February 28, 2004

($ millions)	2005	2004	Common-Size Percents* 2005	2004
Assets				
Cash and cash equivalents	$ 470	$ 245	4.6%	2.8%
Short-term investments	2,878	2,355	28.0	27.2
Receivables, net	375	343	3.6	4.0
Merchandise inventories	2,851	2,607	27.7	30.1
Other current assets	329	174	3.2	2.0
Total current assets	6,903	5,724	67.1	66.2
Property and equipment	4,192	3,574	40.7	41.3
Less accumulated depreciation	1,728	1,330	16.8	15.4
Net property and equipment	2,464	2,244	23.9	25.9
Goodwill	513	477	5.0	5.5
Tradename	40	37	0.4	0.4
Long-term investments	148	—	1.4	0.0
Other long-term assets	226	170	2.2	2.0
Total assets	$10,294	$8,652	100.0%	100.0%
Liabilities				
Accounts payable	$ 2,824	$2,460	27.4%	28.4%
Unredeemed gift card liabilities	410	300	4.0	3.5
Accrued compensation and related expenses	234	269	2.3	3.1
Accrued liabilities	844	724	8.2	8.4
Accrued income taxes	575	380	5.6	4.4
Current portion of long-term debt	72	368	0.7	4.3
Total current liabilities	4,959	4,501	48.2	52.0
Long-term liabilities	358	247	3.5	2.9
Long-term debt	528	482	5.1	5.6
Shareholders' equity				
Common stock	33	32	0.3	0.4
Additional paid-in capital	952	836	9.2	9.7
Retained earnings	3,315	2,468	32.2	28.5
Accumulated other comprehensive income	149	86	1.4	1.0
Total shareholders' equity	4,449	3,422	43.2	39.6
Total liabilities and shareholders' equity	$10,294	$8,652	100.0%	100.0%

* Percents are rounded to tenths and thus may not exactly sum to totals and subtotals.

decrease in net property and equipment as a percentage of assets, (4) a decline in the current portion of long-term debt, and (5) a marked increase in retained earnings. Most of these changes are characteristic of a successful growth/stable company. The concern, if any, is whether Best Buy can continue to generate sufficient revenues and income to support its asset buildup within a very competitive industry.

Common-Size Income Statements   Analysis also benefits from use of a common-size income statement. Revenues is usually the base amount, which is assigned a value of 100%. Each common-size income statement item appears as a percent of revenues. If we think of the 100% revenues amount as representing one sales dollar, the remaining items show how each revenue dollar is distributed among costs, expenses, and income.

Exhibit 17.9 shows common-size comparative income statements for each dollar of Best Buy's revenues. The past two years' common-size numbers are similar. The good news is that Best Buy

Point: Common-size statements are also useful in comparing firms that report in different currencies.

Global: International companies sometimes disclose "convenience" financial statements, which are statements translated in other languages and currencies. However, these statements rarely adjust for differences in accounting principles across countries.

BEST BUY Common-Size Comparative Income Statements For Years Ended February 26, 2005, and February 28, 2004			Common-Size Percents*	
($ millions)	2005	2004	2005	2004
Revenues	$27,433	$24,548	100.0%	100.0%
Cost of goods sold	20,938	18,677	76.3	76.1
Gross profit	6,495	5,871	23.7	23.9
Selling, general & administrative expenses	5,053	4,567	18.4	18.6
Operating income	1,442	1,304	5.3	5.3
Net interest income (expense)	1	(8)	0.0	(0.0)
Earnings from continuing operations before income taxes	1,443	1,296	5.3	5.3
Income tax expense	509	496	1.9	2.0
Earnings from continuing operations	934	800	3.4	3.3
Loss from discontinued operations, net of tax	—	(29)	—	(0.1)
Gain (loss) on disposal of discontinued operations	50	(66)	0.2	(0.3)
Net earnings	$ 984	$ 705	3.6%	2.9%

Exhibit 17.9

Common-Size Comparative
Income Statements

* Percents are rounded to tenths and thus may not exactly sum to totals and subtotals.

has been able to squeeze an extra 0.7 cent in earnings per revenue dollar—evidenced by the 2.9% to 3.6% rise in earnings as a percentage of revenues. This implies that management is effectively controlling costs and/or the company is reaping growth benefits, so-called *economies of scale*. The bad news is that gross profit lost 0.2 cent per revenue dollar—evidenced by the 23.9% to 23.7% decline in gross profit as a percentage of revenues. This is a concern given the price-competitive electronics market. Analysis here shows that common-size percents for successive income statements can uncover potentially important changes in a company's expenses. Evidence of no changes, especially when changes are expected, is also informative.

Common-Size Graphics

Two of the most common tools of common-size analysis are trend analysis of common-size statements and graphical analysis. The trend analysis of common-size statements is similar to that of comparative statements discussed under vertical analysis. It is not illustrated here because the only difference is the substitution of common-size percents for trend percents. Instead, this section discusses graphical analysis of common-size statements.

An income statement readily lends itself to common-size graphical analysis. This is so because revenues affect nearly every item in an income statement. Exhibit 17.10 shows **Best Buy**'s 2005 common-size income statement in graphical form. This pie chart highlights the contribution of each component of revenues for *earnings from continuing operations.*

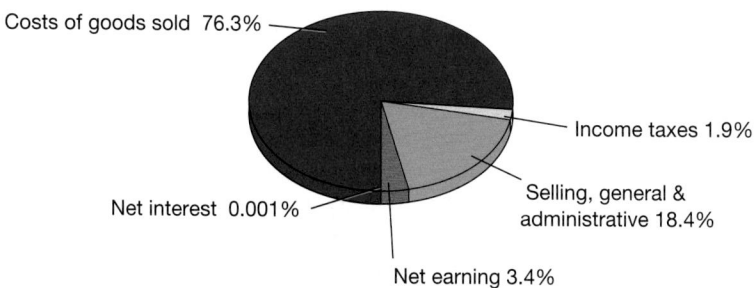

Exhibit 17.10

Common-Size Graphic of
Income Statement

Exhibit 17.11 previews more complex graphical analyses available and the insights they provide. The data for this exhibit are taken from **Best Buy**'s *Segments* footnote. Best Buy has two reportable segments: domestic and international.

Exhibit 17.11

Revenue and Operating Income Breakdown by Segment

The upper bar in Exhibit 17.11 shows the percent of revenues from each segment. The major revenue source is Domestic (89.7%). The lower bar shows the percent of operating income from each segment. Although International provides 10.3% of revenues, it provides only 3.4% of operating income. This type of information can help users in determining strategic analyses and actions.

Exhibit 17.12

Common-Size Graphic of Asset Components

Graphical analysis is also useful in identifying (1) sources of financing including the distribution among current liabilities, noncurrent liabilities, and equity capital and (2) focuses of investing activities, including the distribution among current and noncurrent assets. As illustrative, Exhibit 17.12 shows a common-size graphical display of Best Buy's assets. Common-size balance sheet analysis can be extended to examine the composition of these subgroups. For instance, in assessing liquidity of current assets, knowing what proportion of current assets consists of inventories is usually important, and not simply what proportion inventories are of total assets.

Common-size financial statements are also useful in comparing different companies. Exhibit 17.13 shows common-size graphics of both Best Buy and Circuit City on financing sources. This graphic highlights the much larger percent of equity financing (and less current liability financing) for Circuit City than for Best Buy. Comparison of a company's common-size statements with competitors' or industry common-size statistics alerts us to differences in the structure or distribution of its financial statements but not to their dollar magnitude.

Exhibit 17.13

Common-Size Graphic of Financing Sources— Competitor Analysis

Ratio Analysis

Ratios are among the more widely used tools of financial analysis because they provide clues to and symptoms of underlying conditions. A ratio can help us uncover conditions and trends difficult to detect by inspecting individual components making up the ratio. Ratios, like other analysis tools, are usually future oriented; that is, they are often adjusted for their probable future trend and magnitude, and their usefulness depends on skillful interpretation.

A ratio expresses a mathematical relation between two quantities. It can be expressed as a percent, rate, or proportion. For instance, a change in an account balance from $100 to $250 can be expressed as (1) 150%, (2) 2.5 times, or (3) 2.5 to 1 (or 2.5:1). Computation of a ratio is a simple arithmetic operation, but its interpretation is not. To be meaningful, a ratio must refer to an economically important relation. For example, a direct and crucial relation exists between an item's sales price and its cost. Accordingly, the ratio of cost of goods sold to sales is meaningful. In contrast, no obvious relation exists between freight costs and the balance of long-term investments.

This section describes an important set of financial ratios and its application. The selected ratios are organized into the four building blocks of financial statement analysis: (1) liquidity and efficiency, (2) solvency, (3) profitability, and (4) market prospects. All of these ratios were explained at relevant points in prior chapters. The purpose here is to organize and apply them under a summary framework. We use four common standards, in varying degrees, for comparisons: intracompany, competitor, industry, and guidelines.

Liquidity and Efficiency

Liquidity refers to the availability of resources to meet short-term cash requirements. It is affected by the timing of cash inflows and outflows along with prospects for future performance. Analysis of liquidity is aimed at a company's funding requirements. *Efficiency* refers to how productive a company is in using its assets. Efficiency is usually measured relative to how much revenue is generated from a certain level of assets.

Both liquidity and efficiency are important and complementary. If a company fails to meet its current obligations, its continued existence is doubtful. Viewed in this light, all other measures of analysis are of secondary importance. Although accounting measurements assume the company's continued existence, our analysis must always assess the validity of this assumption using liquidity measures. Moreover, inefficient use of assets can cause liquidity problems. A lack of liquidity often precedes lower profitability and fewer opportunities. It can foretell a loss of owner control or of investment. To a company's creditors, lack of liquidity can yield delays in collecting interest and principal payments or the loss of amounts due them. A company's customers and suppliers of goods and services also are affected by short-term liquidity problems. Implications include a company's inability to execute contracts and potential damage to important customer and supplier relationships. This section describes and illustrates key ratios relevant to assessing liquidity and efficiency.

Working Capital and Current Ratio   The amount of current assets less current liabilities is called **working capital,** or *net working capital.* A company needs adequate working capital to meet current debts, to carry sufficient inventories, and to take advantage of cash discounts. A company that runs low on working capital is less likely to meet current obligations or to continue operating. When evaluating a company's working capital, we must not only look at the dollar amount of current assets less current liabilities, but also at their ratio. Chapter 3 defined the *current ratio* as follows:

$$\text{Current ratio} = \frac{\text{Current assets}}{\text{Current liabilities}}$$

Drawing on information in Exhibit 17.1, **Best Buy**'s working capital and current ratio for both 2005 and 2004 are shown in Exhibit 17.14. **Circuit City**'s (and the Industry) current ratio of 2.13 (1.8) is shown in the margin. Best Buy's ratio (1.39) is lower than either of the comparison

P3   Define and apply ratio analysis.

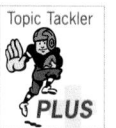

17-2

Point: Some sources for industry norms are *Annual Statement Studies* by Robert Morris Associates, *Industry Norms & Key Business Ratios* by Dun & Bradstreet, *Standard & Poor's Industry Surveys,* and MarketGuide.com.

Exhibit 17.14

Best Buy's Working Capital and
Current Ratio

Circuit City (Industry)
Current ratio = 2.13 (1.8)

($ millions)	2005	2004
Current assets	$ 6,903	$ 5,724
Current liabilities	4,959	4,501
Working capital	$1,944	$1,223
Current ratio		
$6,903/$4,959	1.39 to 1	
$5,724/$4,501		1.27 to 1

ratios, but it does not appear in danger of defaulting on loan payments. A high current ratio suggests a strong liquidity position and an ability to meet current obligations. A company can, however, have a current ratio that is too high. An excessively high current ratio means that the company has invested too much in current assets compared to its current obligations. An excessive investment in current assets is not an efficient use of funds because current assets normally generate a low return on investment (compared with long-term assets).

Many users apply a guideline of 2:1 (or 1.5:1) for the current ratio in helping evaluate a company's debt-paying ability. A company with a 2:1 or higher current ratio is generally thought to be a good credit risk in the short run. Such a guideline or any analysis of the current ratio must recognize at least three additional factors: (1) type of business, (2) composition of current assets, and (3) turnover rate of current asset components.

Type of business. A service company that grants little or no credit and carries few inventories can probably operate on a current ratio of less than 1:1 if its revenues generate enough cash to pay its current liabilities. On the other hand, a company selling high-priced clothing or furniture requires a higher ratio because of difficulties in judging customer demand and cash receipts. For instance, if demand falls, inventory may not generate as much cash as expected. Accordingly, analysis of the current ratio should include a comparison with ratios from successful companies in the same industry and from prior periods. We must also recognize that a company's accounting methods, especially choice of inventory method, affect the current ratio. For instance, when costs are rising, a company using LIFO tends to report a smaller amount of current assets than when using FIFO.

Composition of current assets. The composition of a company's current assets is important to an evaluation of short-term liquidity. For instance, cash, cash equivalents, and short-term investments are more liquid than accounts and notes receivable. Also, short-term receivables normally are more liquid than inventory. Cash, of course, can be used to immediately pay current debts. Items such as accounts receivable and inventory, however, normally must be converted into cash before payment is made. An excessive amount of receivables and inventory weakens a company's ability to pay current liabilities. The acid-test ratio (see below) can help with this assessment.

Point: When a firm uses LIFO in a period of rising costs, the standard for an adequate current ratio usually is lower than if it used FIFO.

Decision Maker

Answer—p. 700

Banker A company requests a one-year, $200,000 loan for expansion. This company's current ratio is 4:1, with current assets of $160,000. Key competitors carry a current ratio of about 1.9:1. Using this information, do you approve the loan application? Does your decision change if the application is for a 10-year loan?

Turnover rate of assets. Asset turnover measures a company's efficiency in using its assets. One relevant measure of asset efficiency is the revenue generated. A measure of total asset turnover is revenues divided by total assets, but evaluation of turnover for individual assets is also useful. We discuss both receivables turnover and inventory turnover on the next page.

Acid-Test Ratio   Quick assets are cash, short-term investments, and current receivables. These are the most liquid types of current assets. The *acid-test ratio,* also called *quick ratio,* was introduced in Chapter 5 and it reflects on short-term liquidity.

$$\text{Acid-test ratio} = \frac{\text{Cash} + \text{Short-term investments} + \text{Current receivables}}{\text{Current liabilities}}$$

Global: Ratio analysis helps overcome most currency translation problems, but it does *not* overcome differences in accounting principles.

Best Buy's acid-test ratio is computed in Exhibit 17.15. Best Buy's 2005 acid-test ratio (0.75) is slightly less than that for both Circuit City (0.93) and the 1:1 common guideline for an acceptable acid-test ratio, but it is greater than the industry 0.7. Similar to analysis of the current ratio, we need to consider other factors. For instance, the frequency with which a company converts its current assets into cash affects its working capital requirements. This implies that analysis of short-term liquidity should also include an analysis of receivables and inventories, which we consider next.

($ millions)	2005	2004
Cash and equivalents	$ 470	$ 245
Short-term investments	2,878	2,355
Current receivables	375	343
Total quick assets	$3,723	$2,943
Current liabilities	$4,959	$4,501
Acid-test ratio		
$3,723/$4,959	0.75 to 1	
$2,943/$4,501		0.65 to 1

Exhibit 17.15

Acid-Test Ratio

Circuit City (Industry)
Acid-test ratio = 0.93 (0.7)

Accounts Receivable Turnover We can measure how frequently a company converts its receivables into cash by computing the *accounts receivable turnover*. As explained in Chapter 9, it is computed as follows.

$$\text{Accounts receivable turnover} = \frac{\text{Net sales}}{\text{Average accounts receivable}}$$

Short-term receivables from customers are often included in the denominator along with accounts receivable. Also, accounts receivable turnover is more precise if credit sales are used for the numerator, but external users generally use net sales (or net revenues) because information about credit sales is typically not reported. Best Buy's 2005 accounts receivable turnover is computed as follows ($ millions).

Point: Some users prefer using gross accounts receivable (before subtracting the allowance for doubtful accounts) to avoid the influence of a manager's bad debts estimates.

$$\frac{\$27,433}{(\$375 + \$343)/2} = 76.4 \text{ times}$$

Circuit City
Accounts receivable turnover = 61.0

Best Buy's value of 76.4 is larger than Circuit City's 61.0. Accounts receivable turnover is high when accounts receivable are quickly collected. A high turnover is favorable because it means the company need not commit large amounts of funds to accounts receivable. However, an accounts receivable turnover can be too high; this can occur when credit terms are so restrictive that they negatively affect sales volume.

Point: Ending accounts receivable can be substituted for the average balance in computing accounts receivable turnover if the difference between ending and average receivables is small.

Inventory Turnover How long a company holds inventory before selling it affects working capital requirements. One measure of this effect is *inventory turnover*, also called *merchandise turnover* or *merchandise inventory turnover*, which is defined in Chapter 6 as:

$$\text{Inventory turnover} = \frac{\text{Cost of goods sold}}{\text{Average inventory}}$$

Using Best Buy's cost of goods sold and inventories information, we compute its inventory turnover for 2005 as follows (if the beginning and ending inventories for the year do not represent the usual inventory amount, an average of quarterly or monthly inventories can be used).

$$\frac{\$20,938}{(\$2,851 + \$2,607)/2} = 7.67 \text{ times}$$

Circuit City (Industry)
Inventory turnover = 5.31 (5.0)

Best Buy's inventory turnover of 7.67 is higher than Circuit City's 5.31. A company with a high turnover requires a smaller investment in inventory than one producing the same sales with a lower turnover. Inventory turnover can be too high, however, if the inventory a company keeps is so small that it restricts sales volume.

Days' Sales Uncollected   Accounts receivable turnover provides insight into how frequently a company collects its accounts. Days' sales uncollected is one measure of this activity, which is defined in Chapter 8 as:

$$\text{Days' sales uncollected} = \frac{\text{Accounts receivable}}{\text{Net sales}} \times 365$$

Any short-term notes receivable from customers are normally included in the numerator. Best Buy's 2005 days' sales uncollected follows.

$$\frac{\$375}{\$27,433} \times 365 = 4.99 \text{ days}$$

Circuit City
Day's sales uncollected = 6.03

Circuit City's days' sales uncollected of 6.03 days is longer than the 4.99 days for Best Buy. Days' sales uncollected is more meaningful if we know company credit terms. A rough guideline states that days' sales uncollected should not exceed $1\frac{1}{3}$ times the days in its (1) credit period, *if* discounts are not offered or (2) discount period, *if* favorable discounts are offered.

Days' Sales in Inventory   Chapter 6 explained how *days' sales in inventory* is a useful measure in evaluating inventory liquidity. Days' sales in inventory is linked to inventory in a way that days' sales uncollected is linked to receivables. We compute days' sales in inventory as follows.

$$\text{Days' sales in inventory} = \frac{\text{Ending inventory}}{\text{Cost of goods sold}} \times 365$$

Best Buy's days' sales in inventory for 2005 follows.

$$\frac{\$2,851}{\$20,938} \times 365 = 49.7 \text{ days}$$

Circuit City
Days' sales in inventory = 67.4

Point: *Average collection period* is estimated by dividing 365 by the accounts receivable turnover ratio. For example, 365 divided by an accounts receivable turnover of 6.1 indicates a 60-day average collection period.

If the products in Best Buy's inventory are in demand by customers, this formula estimates that its inventory will be converted into receivables (or cash) in 49.7 days. If all of Best Buy's sales were credit sales, the conversion of inventory to receivables in 49.7 days *plus* the conversion of receivables to cash in 4.99 days implies that inventory will be converted to cash in about 54.69 days (49.7 + 4.99).

Total Asset Turnover   *Total asset turnover* reflects a company's ability to use its assets to generate sales and is an important indication of operating efficiency. We explained in Chapter 10 the computation of this ratio as follows.

$$\text{Total asset turnover} = \frac{\text{Net sales}}{\text{Average total assets}}$$

Best Buy's total asset turnover for 2005 follows and is better than Circuit City's.

$$\frac{\$27,433}{(\$10,294 + \$8,652)/2} = 2.90 \text{ times}$$

Circuit City
Total asset turnover = 2.79

Solvency

Solvency refers to a company's long-run financial viability and its ability to cover long-term obligations. All of a company's business activities—financing, investing, and operating—affect its solvency. Analysis of solvency is long term and uses less precise but more encompassing measures than liquidity. One of the most important components of solvency analysis is the composition of a company's capital structure. *Capital structure* refers to a company's financing sources. It ranges from relatively permanent equity financing to riskier or more temporary short-term financing. Assets represent security for financiers, ranging from loans secured by specific assets to the assets available as general security to unsecured creditors. This section describes the tools of solvency analysis. Our analysis focuses on a company's ability to both meet its obligations and provide security to its creditors *over the long run*. Indicators of this ability include *debt* and *equity* ratios, the relation between *pledged assets and secured liabilities,* and the company's capacity to earn sufficient income to *pay fixed interest charges.*

Debt and Equity Ratios   One element of solvency analysis is to assess the portion of a company's assets contributed by its owners and the portion contributed by creditors. This relation is reflected in the debt ratio described in Chapter 2. The *debt ratio* expresses total liabilities as a percent of total assets. The **equity ratio** provides complementary information by expressing total equity as a percent of total assets. **Best Buy**'s debt and equity ratios follow.

Point: For analysis purposes, Minority Interest is usually added to equity.

($ millions)	2005	Ratios	
Total liabilities	$ 5,845	56.8%	[Debt ratio]
Total equity	4,449	43.2	[Equity ratio]
Total liabilities and equity	$10,294	100.0%	

Circuit City
Debt ratio = 44.9%
Equity ratio = 55.1%

Best Buy's financial statements reveal more debt than equity. A company is considered less risky if its capital structure (equity and long-term debt) contains more equity. One risk factor is the required payment for interest and principal when debt is outstanding. Another factor is the greater the stockholder financing, the more losses a company can absorb through equity before the assets become inadequate to satisfy creditors' claims. From the stockholders' point of view, if a company earns a return on borrowed capital that is higher than the cost of borrowing, the difference represents increased income to stockholders. The inclusion of debt is described as *financial leverage* because debt can have the effect of increasing the return to stockholders. Companies are said to be highly leveraged if a large portion of their assets is financed by debt.

Point: Bank examiners from the FDIC and other regulatory agencies use debt and equity ratios to monitor compliance with regulatory capital requirements imposed on banks and S&Ls.

Debt-to-Equity Ratio   We explained in Chapter 14 how to use the ratio of total liabilities to equity as another measure of solvency. We compute the ratio as follows.

$$\text{Debt-to-equity ratio} = \frac{\text{Total liabilities}}{\text{Total equity}}$$

Best Buy's debt-to-equity ratio for 2005 is

$$\$5,845/\$4,449 = 1.31$$

Best Buy's 1.31 debt-to-equity ratio is larger than the 0.82 ratio for Circuit City and the industry ratio of 0.99. Consistent with our inferences from the debt ratio, Best Buy's capital structure has more debt than equity, which increases risk. Recall that debt must be repaid with interest, while equity does not. These debt requirements can be burdensome when the industry and/or the economy experience a downturn. The larger debt-to-equity ratio also implies less opportunity to expand through use of debt financing.

Decision Insight

Bears and Bulls   A *bear market* is a declining market. The phrase comes from bear-skin jobbers who often sold the skins before the bears were caught. The term *bear* was then used to describe investors who sold shares they did not own in anticipation of a price decline. A *bull market* is a rising market. This phrase comes from the once popular sport of bear and bull baiting. The term *bull* came to mean the opposite of *bear*.

Times Interest Earned   The amount of income before deductions for interest expense and income taxes is the amount available to pay interest expense. Chapter 11 explained that the following *times interest earned* ratio reflects the creditors' risk of loan repayments with interest.

Point: The times interest earned ratio and the debt and equity ratios are of special interest to bank lending officers.

$$\text{Times interest earned} = \frac{\text{Income before interest expense and income taxes}}{\text{Interest expense}}$$

The larger this ratio, the less risky is the company for creditors. One guideline says that creditors are reasonably safe if the company earns its fixed interest expense two or more times each year. Best Buy's times interest earned ratio follows; its value suggests that its creditors have little risk of nonrepayment.

Circuit City
Times interest earned = 47.4

$$\frac{\$934 + \$44 \text{ (see Best Buy note \#6)} + \$509}{\$44} = 33.8$$

Profitability

We are especially interested in a company's ability to use its assets efficiently to produce profits (and positive cash flows). *Profitability* refers to a company's ability to generate an adequate return on invested capital. Return is judged by assessing earnings relative to the level and sources of financing. Profitability is also relevant to solvency. This section describes key profitability measures and their importance to financial statement analysis.

Profit Margin   A company's operating efficiency and profitability can be expressed by two components. The first is *profit margin,* which Chapter 3 explained reflects a company's ability to earn net income from sales. It is measured by expressing net income as a percent of sales (*sales* and *revenues* are similar terms). **Best Buy**'s profit margin follows.

Circuit City
Profit margin = 0.6%

$$\text{Profit margin} = \frac{\text{Net income}}{\text{Net sales}} = \frac{\$984}{\$27,433} = 3.6\%$$

To evaluate profit margin, we must consider the industry. For instance, an appliance company might require a profit margin between 10% and 15%; whereas a retail supermarket might require a profit margin of 1% or 2%. Both profit margin and *total asset turnover* make up the two basic components of operating efficiency. These ratios reflect on management because managers are ultimately responsible for operating efficiency. The next section explains how we use both measures to analyze return on total assets.

Return on Total Assets   *Return on total assets* is defined as follows.

$$\text{Return on total assets} = \frac{\text{Net income}}{\text{Average total assets}}$$

Best Buy's 2005 return on total assets is

$$\frac{\$984}{(\$10,294 + \$8,652)/2} = 10.4\%$$

Circuit City (Industry)
Return on total assets = 1.6% (3.1)

Best Buy's 10.4% return on total assets is lower than that for many businesses but is higher than Circuit City's return of 1.6% and the industry's 3.1% return. We also should evaluate any trend in the rate of return.

Point: Many analysts add back *Interest expense* $\times$ *(1 − Tax rate)* to net income in computing return on total assets.

The following equation shows the important relation between profit margin, total asset turnover, and return on total assets.

$$\text{Profit margin} \times \text{Total asset turnover} = \text{Return on total assets}$$

or

$$\frac{\text{Net income}}{\text{Net sales}} \times \frac{\text{Net sales}}{\text{Average total assets}} = \frac{\text{Net income}}{\text{Average total assets}}$$

Both profit margin and total asset turnover contribute to overall operating efficiency, as measured by return on total assets. If we apply this formula to Best Buy, we get

$$3.6\% \times 2.90 = 10.4\%$$

Circuit City: 0.6% × 2.79 = 1.6%
(with rounding)

This analysis shows that Best Buy's superior return on assets to that of Circuit City is driven by its higher profit margin.

Return on Common Stockholders' Equity   Perhaps the most important goal in operating a company is to earn net income for its owner(s). *Return on common stockholders' equity* measures a company's success in reaching this goal and is defined as follows.

$$\text{Return on common stockholders' equity} = \frac{\text{Net income} - \text{Preferred dividends}}{\text{Average common stockholders' equity}}$$

Best Buy's 2005 return on common stockholders' equity is computed as follows:

$$\frac{\$984 - \$0}{(\$4,449 + \$3,422)/2} = 25.0\%$$

Circuit City
Return on common stockholders'
equity = 2.9%

The denominator in this computation is the book value of common equity (including any minority interest). In the numerator, the dividends on cumulative preferred stock are subtracted whether they are declared or are in arrears. If preferred stock is noncumulative, its dividends are subtracted only if declared.

Decision Insight

Wall Street   *Wall Street* is synonymous with financial markets, but its name comes from the street location of the original New York Stock Exchange. The street's name derives from stockades built by early settlers to protect New York from pirate attacks.

Market Prospects

Market measures are useful for analyzing corporations with publicly traded stock. These market measures use stock price, which reflects the market's (public's) expectations for the company. This includes expectations of both company return and risk—as the market perceives it.

Price-Earnings Ratio   Computation of the *price-earnings ratio* was explained in Chapter 13 as follows.

$$\text{Price-earnings ratio} = \frac{\text{Market price per common share}}{\text{Earnings per share}}$$

Point: PE ratio can be viewed as an indicator of the market's expected growth and risk for a stock. High expected risk suggests a low PE ratio. High expected growth suggests a high PE ratio.

Predicted earnings per share for the next period is often used in the denominator of this computation. Reported earnings per share for the most recent period is also commonly used. In both cases, the ratio is used as an indicator of the future growth and risk of a company's earnings as perceived by the stock's buyers and sellers.

The market price of Best Buy's common stock at the start of fiscal year 2006 was $51.69. Using Best Buy's $3.02 basic earnings per share, we compute its price-earnings ratio as follows (some analysts compute this ratio using the median of the low and high stock price).

Circuit City
PE (year-end) = 48.8

$$\frac{\$51.69}{\$3.02} = 17.1$$

Point: Some investors avoid stocks with high PE ratios under the belief they are "overpriced." Alternatively, some investors *sell these stocks short*—hoping for price declines.

Best Buy's price-earnings ratio is slightly higher than the norm. (Circuit City's ratio is high due to its abnormally low earnings.) Best Buy's middle-of-the-pack ratio likely reflects investors' expectations of continued growth but normal earnings.

Dividend Yield   *Dividend yield* is used to compare the dividend-paying performance of different investment alternatives. We compute dividend yield as explained in Chapter 13 as follows.

$$\text{Dividend yield} = \frac{\text{Annual cash dividends per share}}{\text{Market price per share}}$$

Best Buy's dividend yield, based on its fiscal year-end market price per share of $51.69 and its policy of $0.42 cash dividends per share, is computed as follows.

Circuit City
Dividend yield = 0.4%

$$\frac{\$0.42}{\$51.69} = 0.8\%$$

Some companies do not declare and pay dividends because they wish to reinvest the cash.

Summary of Ratios

Point: Corporate PE ratios and dividend yields are found in daily stock market quotations listed in *The Wall Street Journal, Investor's Business Daily,* or other publications and Web services.

Exhibit 17.16 summarizes the major financial statement analysis ratios illustrated in this chapter and throughout the book. This summary includes each ratio's title, its formula, and the purpose for which it is commonly used.

Quick Check
Answers—p. 700

10. Which ratio best reflects a company's ability to meet immediate interest payments? (*a*) Debt ratio. (*b*) Equity ratio. (*c*) Times interest earned.

11. Which ratio best measures a company's success in earning net income for its owner(s)? (*a*) Profit margin. (*b*) Return on common stockholders' equity. (*c*) Price-earnings ratio. (*d*) Dividend yield.

12. If a company has net sales of $8,500,000, net income of $945,000, and total asset turnover of 1.8 times, what is its return on total assets?

Exhibit 17.16

Financial Statement Analysis Ratios*

Ratio	Formula	Measure of
Liquidity and Efficiency		
Current ratio	$= \dfrac{\text{Current assets}}{\text{Current liabilities}}$	Short-term debt-paying ability
Acid-test ratio	$= \dfrac{\text{Cash + Short-term investments + Current receivables}}{\text{Current liabilities}}$	Immediate short-term debt-paying ability
Accounts receivable turnover	$= \dfrac{\text{Net sales}}{\text{Average accounts receivable}}$	Efficiency of collection
Inventory turnover	$= \dfrac{\text{Cost of goods sold}}{\text{Average inventory}}$	Efficiency of inventory management
Days' sales uncollected	$= \dfrac{\text{Accounts receivable}}{\text{Net sales}} \times 365$	Liquidity of receivables
Days' sales in inventory	$= \dfrac{\text{Ending inventory}}{\text{Cost of goods sold}} \times 365$	Liquidity of inventory
Total asset turnover	$= \dfrac{\text{Net sales}}{\text{Average total assets}}$	Efficiency of assets in producing sales
Solvency		
Debt ratio	$= \dfrac{\text{Total liabilities}}{\text{Total assets}}$	Creditor financing and leverage
Equity ratio	$= \dfrac{\text{Total equity}}{\text{Total assets}}$	Owner financing
Debt-to-equity ratio	$= \dfrac{\text{Total liabilities}}{\text{Total equity}}$	Debt versus equity financing
Times interest earned	$= \dfrac{\text{Income before interest expense and income taxes}}{\text{Interest expense}}$	Protection in meeting interest payments
Profitability		
Profit margin ratio	$= \dfrac{\text{Net income}}{\text{Net sales}}$	Net income in each sales dollar
Gross margin ratio	$= \dfrac{\text{Net sales} - \text{Cost of goods sold}}{\text{Net sales}}$	Gross margin in each sales dollar
Return on total assets	$= \dfrac{\text{Net income}}{\text{Average total assets}}$	Overall profitability of assets
Return on common stockholders' equity	$= \dfrac{\text{Net income} - \text{Preferred dividends}}{\text{Average common stockholders' equity}}$	Profitability of owner investment
Book value per common share	$= \dfrac{\text{Shareholders' equity applicable to common shares}}{\text{Number of common shares outstanding}}$	Liquidation at reported amounts
Basic earnings per share	$= \dfrac{\text{Net income} - \text{Preferred dividends}}{\text{Weighted-average common shares outstanding}}$	Net income per common share
Market Prospects		
Price-earnings ratio	$= \dfrac{\text{Market price per common share}}{\text{Earnings per share}}$	Market value relative to earnings
Dividend yield	$= \dfrac{\text{Annual cash dividends per share}}{\text{Market price per share}}$	Cash return per common share

* Additional ratios also examined in previous chapters included credit risk ratio; plant asset useful life; plant asset age; days' cash expense coverage; cash coverage of growth; cash coverage of debt; free cash flow; cash flow on total assets; and payout ratio. Many of these are defined on the back inside cover of the book.

Decision Analysis   **Analysis Reporting**

A1   Summarize and report
     results of analysis.

Understanding the purpose of financial statement analysis is crucial to the usefulness of any analysis. This understanding leads to efficiency of effort, effectiveness in application, and relevance in focus. The purpose of most financial statement analyses is to reduce uncertainty in business decisions through a rigorous and sound evaluation. A *financial statement analysis report* helps by directly addressing the building blocks of analysis and by identifying weaknesses in inference by requiring explanation: It forces us to organize our reasoning and to verify its flow and logic. A report also serves as a communication link with readers, and the writing process reinforces our judgments and vice versa. Finally, the report helps us (re)evaluate evidence and refine conclusions on key building blocks. A good analysis report usually consists of six sections:

1. **Executive summary**—brief focus on important analysis results and conclusions.
2. **Analysis overview**—background on the company, its industry, and its economic setting.
3. **Evidential matter**—financial statements and information used in the analysis, including ratios, trends, comparisons, statistics, and all analytical measures assembled; often organized under the building blocks of analysis.
4. **Assumptions**—identification of important assumptions regarding a company's industry and economic environment, and other important assumptions for estimates.
5. **Key factors**—list of important favorable and unfavorable factors, both quantitative and qualitative, for company performance; usually organized by areas of analysis.
6. **Inferences**—forecasts, estimates, interpretations, and conclusions drawing on all sections of the report.

Decision Insight

Short Selling   *Short selling* refers to selling stock before you buy it. Here's an example: You borrow 100 shares of Nike stock, sell them in the market at $40 each, and receive money from their sale. You then wait. You hope that Nike's stock price falls to, say, $35 each and you can replace the borrowed stock for less money than you sold it for, reaping a profit of $5 each less any transaction costs.

We must remember that the user dictates relevance, meaning that the analysis report should include a brief table of contents to help readers focus on those areas most relevant to their decisions. All irrelevant matter must be eliminated. For example, decades-old details of obscure transactions and detailed miscues of the analysis are irrelevant. Ambiguities and qualifications to avoid responsibility or hedging inferences must be eliminated. Finally, writing is important. Mistakes in grammar and errors of fact compromise the report's credibility.

Demonstration Problem

Use the following financial statements of Precision Co. to complete these requirements.

1. Prepare comparative income statements showing the percent increase or decrease for year 2009 in comparison to year 2008.
2. Prepare common-size comparative balance sheets for years 2009 and 2008.
3. Compute the following ratios as of December 31, 2009, or for the year ended December 31, 2009, and identify its building block category for financial statement analysis.

   a. Current ratio   **g.** Debt-to-equity ratio
   b. Acid-test ratio   **h.** Times interest earned
   c. Accounts receivable turnover   **i.** Profit margin ratio
   d. Days' sales uncollected   **j.** Total asset turnover
   e. Inventory turnover   **k.** Return on total assets
   f. Debt ratio   **l.** Return on common stockholders' equity

PRECISION COMPANY Comparative Balance Sheets December 31, 2009 and 2008		
	2009	2008
Assets		
Current assets		
Cash	$ 79,000	$ 42,000
Short-term investments	65,000	96,000
Accounts receivable, net	120,000	100,000
Merchandise inventory	250,000	265,000
Total current assets	514,000	503,000
Plant assets		
Store equipment, net	400,000	350,000
Office equipment, net	45,000	50,000
Buildings, net	625,000	675,000
Land	100,000	100,000
Total plant assets	1,170,000	1,175,000
Total assets	$1,684,000	$1,678,000
Liabilities		
Current liabilities		
Accounts payable	$ 164,000	$ 190,000
Short-term notes payable	75,000	90,000
Taxes payable	26,000	12,000
Total current liabilities	265,000	292,000
Long-term liabilities		
Notes payable (secured by mortgage on buildings)	400,000	420,000
Total liabilities	665,000	712,000
Stockholders' Equity		
Common stock, $5 par value	475,000	475,000
Retained earnings	544,000	491,000
Total stockholders' equity	1,019,000	966,000
Total liabilities and equity	$1,684,000	$1,678,000

PRECISION COMPANY Comparative Income Statements For Years Ended December 31, 2009 and 2008		
	2009	2008
Sales	$2,486,000	$2,075,000
Cost of goods sold	1,523,000	1,222,000
Gross profit	963,000	853,000
Operating expenses		
Advertising expense	145,000	100,000
Sales salaries expense	240,000	280,000
Office salaries expense	165,000	200,000
Insurance expense	100,000	45,000
Supplies expense	26,000	35,000
Depreciation expense	85,000	75,000
Miscellaneous expenses	17,000	15,000
Total operating expenses	778,000	750,000
Operating income	185,000	103,000
Interest expense	44,000	46,000
Income before taxes	141,000	57,000
Income taxes	47,000	19,000
Net income	$ 94,000	$ 38,000
Earnings per share	$ 0.99	$ 0.40

Planning the Solution

- Set up a four-column income statement; enter the 2009 and 2008 amounts in the first two columns and then enter the dollar change in the third column and the percent change from 2008 in the fourth column.
- Set up a four-column balance sheet; enter the 2009 and 2008 year-end amounts in the first two columns and then compute and enter the amount of each item as a percent of total assets.
- Compute the required ratios using the data provided. Use the average of beginning and ending amounts when appropriate (see Exhibit 17.16 for definitions).

Solution to Demonstration Problem

1.

PRECISION COMPANY Comparative Income Statements For Years Ended December 31, 2009 and 2008				
			Increase (Decrease) in 2009	
	2009	2008	Amount	Percent
Sales	$2,486,000	$2,075,000	$411,000	19.8%
Cost of goods sold	1,523,000	1,222,000	301,000	24.6
Gross profit	963,000	853,000	110,000	12.9
Operating expenses				
Advertising expense	145,000	100,000	45,000	45.0
Sales salaries expense	240,000	280,000	(40,000)	(14.3)
Office salaries expense	165,000	200,000	(35,000)	(17.5)

[continued on next page]

[continued from previous page]

Insurance expense	100,000	45,000	55,000	122.2
Supplies expense	26,000	35,000	(9,000)	(25.7)
Depreciation expense	85,000	75,000	10,000	13.3
Miscellaneous expenses	17,000	15,000	2,000	13.3
Total operating expenses	778,000	750,000	28,000	3.7
Operating income	185,000	103,000	82,000	79.6
Interest expense	44,000	46,000	(2,000)	(4.3)
Income before taxes	141,000	57,000	84,000	147.4
Income taxes	47,000	19,000	28,000	147.4
Net income	$ 94,000	$ 38,000	$ 56,000	147.4
Earnings per share	$ 0.99	$ 0.40	$ 0.59	147.5

2.

PRECISION COMPANY
Common-Size Comparative Balance Sheets
December 31, 2009 and 2008

	December 31 2009	December 31 2008	Common-Size Percents 2009*	Common-Size Percents 2008*
Assets				
Current assets				
Cash	$ 79,000	$ 42,000	4.7%	2.5%
Short-term investments	65,000	96,000	3.9	5.7
Accounts receivable, net	120,000	100,000	7.1	6.0
Merchandise inventory	250,000	265,000	14.8	15.8
Total current assets	514,000	503,000	30.5	30.0
Plant Assets				
Store equipment, net	400,000	350,000	23.8	20.9
Office equipment, net	45,000	50,000	2.7	3.0
Buildings, net	625,000	675,000	37.1	40.2
Land	100,000	100,000	5.9	6.0
Total plant assets	1,170,000	1,175,000	69.5	70.0
Total assets	$1,684,000	$1,678,000	100.0	100.0
Liabilities				
Current liabilities				
Accounts payable	$ 164,000	$ 190,000	9.7%	11.3%
Short-term notes payable	75,000	90,000	4.5	5.4
Taxes payable	26,000	12,000	1.5	0.7
Total current liabilities	265,000	292,000	15.7	17.4
Long-term liabilities				
Notes payable (secured by mortgage on buildings)	400,000	420,000	23.8	25.0
Total liabilities	665,000	712,000	39.5	42.4
Stockholders' Equity				
Common stock, $5 par value	475,000	475,000	28.2	28.3
Retained earnings	544,000	491,000	32.3	29.3
Total stockholders' equity	1,019,000	966,000	60.5	57.6
Total liabilities and equity	$1,684,000	$1,678,000	100.0	100.0

* Columns do not always exactly add to 100 due to rounding.

3. **Ratios for 2009:**
   a. Current ratio: $514,000/$265,000 = 1.9:1 (liquidity and efficiency)
   b. Acid-test ratio: ($79,000 + $65,000 + $120,000)/$265,000 = 1.0:1 (liquidity and efficiency)
   c. Average receivables: ($120,000 + $100,000)/2 = $110,000
      Accounts receivable turnover: $2,486,000/$110,000 = 22.6 times (liquidity and efficiency)
   d. Days' sales uncollected: ($120,000/$2,486,000) × 365 = 17.6 days (liquidity and efficiency)
   e. Average inventory: ($250,000 + $265,000)/2 = $257,500
      Inventory turnover: $1,523,000/$257,500 = 5.9 times (liquidity and efficiency)

f. Debt ratio: $665,000/$1,684,000 = 39.5% (solvency)

g. Debt-to-equity ratio: $665,000/$1,019,000 = 0.65 (solvency)

h. Times interest earned: $185,000/$44,000 = 4.2 times (solvency)

i. Profit margin ratio: $94,000/$2,486,000 = 3.8% (profitability)

j. Average total assets: ($1,684,000 + $1,678,000)/2 = $1,681,000
Total asset turnover: $2,486,000/$1,681,000 = 1.48 times (liquidity and efficiency)

k. Return on total assets: $94,000/$1,681,000 = 5.6% or 3.8% × 1.48 = 5.6% (profitability)

l. Average total common equity: ($1,019,000 + $966,000)/2 = $992,500
Return on common stockholders' equity: $94,000/$992,500 = 9.5% (profitability)

APPENDIX

Sustainable Income

17A

When a company's revenue and expense transactions are from normal, continuing operations, a simple income statement is usually adequate. When a company's activities include income-related events not part of its normal, continuing operations, it must disclose information to help users understand these events and predict future performance. To meet these objectives, companies separate the income statement into continuing operations, discontinued segments, extraordinary items, comprehensive income, and earnings per share. For illustration, Exhibit 17A.1 shows such an income statement for ComUS. These separate distinctions help us measure *sustainable income,* which is the income level most likely to continue into the future. Sustainable income is commonly used in PE ratios and other market-based measures of performance.

Continuing Operations

The first major section (①) shows the revenues, expenses, and income from continuing operations. Users especially rely on this information to predict future operations. Many users view this section as the most important. Earlier chapters explained the items comprising income from continuing operations.

A2 Explain the form and assess the content of a complete income statement.

Discontinued Segments

A **business segment** is a part of a company's operations that serves a particular line of business or class of customers. A segment has assets, liabilities, and financial results of operations that can be distinguished from those of other parts of the company. A company's gain or loss from selling or closing down a segment is separately reported. Section ② of Exhibit 17A.1 reports both (1) income from operating the discontinued segment for the current period prior to its disposal and (2) the loss from disposing of the segment's net assets. The income tax effects of each are reported separately from the income taxes expense in section ①.

Extraordinary Items

Section ③ reports **extraordinary gains and losses,** which are those that are *both unusual* and *infrequent.* An **unusual gain or loss** is abnormal or otherwise unrelated to the company's regular activities and environment. An **infrequent gain or loss** is not expected to recur given the company's operating environment. Reporting extraordinary items in a separate category helps users predict future performance, absent the effects of extraordinary items. Items usually considered extraordinary include (1) expropriation (taking away) of property by a foreign government, (2) condemning of property by a domestic government body, (3) prohibition against using an asset by a newly enacted law, and (4) losses and gains from an unusual and infrequent calamity ("act of God"). Items *not* considered extraordinary include (1) write-downs

Exhibit 17A.1

Income Statement (all-inclusive) for a Corporation

ComUS Income Statement For Year Ended December 31, 2008		
Net sales		$8,478,000
Operating expenses		
Cost of goods sold	$5,950,000	
Depreciation expense	35,000	
Other selling, general, and administrative expenses	515,000	
Interest expense	20,000	
① Total operating expenses		(6,520,000)
Other gains (losses)		
Loss on plant relocation		(45,000)
Gain on sale of surplus land		72,000
Income from continuing operations before taxes		1,985,000
Income taxes expense		(595,500)
Income from continuing operations		1,389,500
Discontinued segment		
② Income from operating Division A (net of $180,000 taxes)	420,000	
Loss on disposal of Division A (net of $66,000 tax benefit)	(154,000)	266,000
Income before extraordinary items		1,655,500
Extraordinary items		
③ Gain on land expropriated by state (net of $61,200 taxes)	198,800	
Loss from earthquake damage (net of $270,000 tax benefit)	(630,000)	(431,200)
Net income		$1,224,300
Earnings per common share (200,000 outstanding shares)		
Income from continuing operations		$ 6.95
Discontinued operations		1.33
④ Income before extraordinary items		8.28
Extraordinary items		(2.16)
Net income (basic earnings per share)		$ 6.12

of inventories and write-offs of receivables, (2) gains and losses from disposing of segments, and (3) financial effects of labor strikes.

  Gains and losses that are neither unusual nor infrequent are reported as part of continuing operations. Gains and losses that are *either* unusual *or* infrequent, but *not* both, are reported as part of continuing operations *but* after the normal revenues and expenses.

Earnings per Share

The final section ④ of the income statement in Exhibit 17A.1 reports earnings per share for each of the three subcategories of income (continuing operations, discontinued segments, and extraordinary items) when they exist. Earnings per share is discussed in Chapter 13.

Changes in Accounting Principles

Point: Changes in principles are sometimes required when new accounting standards are issued.

The *consistency principle* directs a company to apply the same accounting principles across periods. Yet a company can change from one acceptable accounting principle (such as FIFO, LIFO, or weighted-average) to another as long as the change improves the usefulness of information in its financial statements. A footnote would describe the accounting change and why it is an improvement.

Decision Maker

Answer—p. 700

Small Business Owner You own an orange grove near Jacksonville, Florida. A bad frost destroys about one-half of your oranges. You are currently preparing an income statement for a bank loan. Can you claim the loss of oranges as extraordinary?

  Changes in accounting principles require retrospective application to prior periods' financial statements. *Retrospective application* involves applying a different accounting principle to prior periods as if that principle had always been used. Retrospective application enhances the consistency of financial information between periods, which improves the usefulness of information, especially with comparative analyses. (Prior to 2005, the cumulative effect of changes in accounting principles was recognized in net income in the period of the change.) Accounting standards also require that *a change in depreciation, amortization, or depletion method for long-term operating assets is accounted for as a change in accounting estimate*—that is, prospectively over current and future periods. This reflects the notion that an entity should change its depreciation, amortization, or depletion method only with changes in estimated asset benefits, the pattern of benefit usage, or information about those benefits.

Comprehensive Income

Comprehensive income is net income plus certain gains and losses that bypass the income statement. These items are recorded directly to equity. Specifically, comprehensive income equals the change in equity for the period, excluding investments from and distributions (dividends) to its stockholders. For **Best Buy**, it is computed as follows:

Net income	$ 984
Accumulated other comprehensive income	63
Comprehensive income	$1,047

The most common items included in *accumulated other comprehensive income, or AOCI*, are unrealized gains and losses on available-for-sale securities, foreign currency translation adjustments, and minimum pension liability adjustments. (Detailed computations for these items are in advanced courses.) Analysts disagree on how to treat these items. Some analysts believe that AOCI items should not be considered when predicting future performance, and some others believe AOCI items should be considered as they reflect on company and managerial performance. Whatever our position, we must be familiar with what AOCI items are as they are commonly reported in financial statements. Best Buy reports its comprehensive income in its statement of shareholders' equity (see Appendix A).

Quick Check
Answers—p. 700

13. Which of the following is an extraordinary item? (*a*) a settlement paid to a customer injured while using the company's product, (*b*) a loss to a plant from damages caused by a meteorite, or (*c*) a loss from selling old equipment.
14. Identify the four major sections of an income statement that are potentially reportable.
15. A company using FIFO for the past 15 years decides to switch to LIFO. The effect of this event on prior years' net income is (*a*) reported as if the new method had always been used; (*b*) ignored because it is a change in an accounting estimate; or (*c*) reported on the current year income statement.

Summary

C1 Explain the purpose of analysis. The purpose of financial statement analysis is to help users make better business decisions. Internal users want information to improve company efficiency and effectiveness in providing products and services. External users want information to make better and more informed decisions in pursuing their goals. The common goals of all users are to evaluate a company's (1) past and current performance, (2) current financial position, and (3) future performance and risk.

C2 Identify the building blocks of analysis. Financial statement analysis focuses on four "building blocks" of analysis: (1) liquidity and efficiency—ability to meet short-term obligations and efficiently generate revenues; (2) solvency—ability to generate future revenues and meet long-term obligations; (3) profitability—ability to provide financial rewards sufficient to attract and retain

financing; and (4) market prospects—ability to generate positive market expectations.

C3 Describe standards for comparisons in analysis. Standards for comparisons include (1) intracompany—prior performance and relations between financial items for the company under analysis; (2) competitor—one or more direct competitors of the company; (3) industry—industry statistics; and (4) guidelines (rules of thumb)—general standards developed from past experiences and personal judgments.

C4 Identify the tools of analysis. The three most common tools of financial statement analysis are (1) horizontal analysis—comparing a company's financial condition and performance across time; (2) vertical analysis—comparing a company's financial condition and performance to a base amount such as revenues or total assets; and (3) ratio analysis—using and quantifying key relations among financial statement items.

A1 **Summarize and report results of analysis.** A financial statement analysis report is often organized around the building blocks of analysis. A good report separates interpretations and conclusions of analysis from the information underlying them. An analysis report often consists of six sections: (1) executive summary, (2) analysis overview, (3) evidential matter, (4) assumptions, (5) key factors, and (6) inferences.

A2[A] **Explain the form and assess the content of a complete income statement.** An income statement has four *potential* sections: (1) continuing operations, (2) discontinued segments, (3) extraordinary items, and (4) earnings per share.

P1 **Explain and apply methods of horizontal analysis.** Horizontal analysis is a tool to evaluate changes in data across time. Two important tools of horizontal analysis are comparative statements and trend analysis. Comparative statements show amounts for two or more successive periods, often with changes disclosed in both absolute and percent terms. Trend analysis is used to reveal important changes occurring from one period to the next.

P2 **Describe and apply methods of vertical analysis.** Vertical analysis is a tool to evaluate each financial statement item or group of items in terms of a base amount. Two tools of vertical analysis are common-size statements and graphical analyses. Each item in common-size statements is expressed as a percent of a base amount. For the balance sheet, the base amount is usually total assets, and for the income statement, it is usually sales.

P3 **Define and apply ratio analysis.** Ratio analysis provides clues to and symptoms of underlying conditions. Ratios, properly interpreted, identify areas requiring further investigation. A ratio expresses a mathematical relation between two quantities such as a percent, rate, or proportion. Ratios can be organized into the building blocks of analysis: (1) liquidity and efficiency, (2) solvency, (3) profitability, and (4) market prospects.

Guidance Answers to **Decision Maker**

Auditor   The *joint relation* referred to is the combined increase in sales and the decrease in expenses yielding more than a 5% increase in income. Both *individual* accounts (sales and expenses) yield percent changes within the ±5% acceptable range. However, a joint analysis suggests a different picture. For example, consider a joint analysis using the profit margin ratio. The client's profit margin is 11.46% ($206,000 − $182,400/$206,000) for the current year compared with 5.0% ($200,000 − $190,000/$200,000) for the prior year—yielding a 129% increase in profit margin! This is what concerns the partner, and it suggests expanding audit tests to verify or refute the client's figures.

Banker   Your decision on the loan application is positive for at least two reasons. First, the current ratio suggests a strong ability to meet short-term obligations. Second, current assets of $160,000 and a current ratio of 4:1 imply current liabilities of $40,000 (one-fourth of current assets) and a working capital excess of $120,000. This working capital excess is 60% of the loan amount. However, if the application is for a 10-year loan, our decision is less optimistic. The current ratio and working capital suggest a good safety margin, but indications of inefficiency in operations exist. In particular, a 4:1 current ratio is more than double its key competitors' ratio. This is characteristic of inefficient asset use.

Small Business Owner   The frost loss is probably not extraordinary. Jacksonville experiences enough recurring frost damage to make it difficult to argue this event is both unusual and infrequent. Still, you want to highlight the frost loss and hope the bank views this uncommon event separately from continuing operations.

Guidance Answers to **Quick Checks**

1. General-purpose financial statements are intended for a variety of users interested in a company's financial condition and performance—users without the power to require specialized financial reports to meet their specific needs.

2. General-purpose financial statements include the income statement, balance sheet, statement of stockholders' (owner's) equity, and statement of cash flows plus the notes related to these statements.

3. *a*

4. Data from one or more direct competitors are usually preferred for comparative purposes.

5. *d*

6. Percents on comparative income statements show the increase or decrease in each item from one period to the next. On common-size comparative income statements, each item is shown as a percent of net sales for that period.

7. *c*

8. (*a*) ($820,000 + $240,000 + $470,000)/
       ($350,000 + $180,000) = 2.9 to 1.

(*b*) ($820,000 + $240,000)/($350,000 + $180,000) = 2:1.

9. (*a*) $2,500,000/[($290,000 + $240,000)/2] = 9.43 times.

(*b*) ($290,000/$2,500,000) × 365 = 42 days.

(*c*) $750,000/[($530,000 + $470,000)/2] = 1.5 times.

(*d*) ($530,000/$750,000) × 365 = 258 days.

10. *c*

11. *b*

12. Profit margin $\times$ $\dfrac{\text{Total asset}}{\text{turnover}}$ = $\dfrac{\text{Return on}}{\text{total assets}}$

$$\frac{\$945,000}{\$8,500,000} \times 1.8 = 20\%$$

13. (*b*)

14. The four (potentially reportable) major sections are income from continuing operations, discontinued segments, extraordinary items, and earnings per share.

15. (*a*); known as retrospective application.

Key Terms

Key Terms are available at the book's Website for learning and testing in an online Flashcard Format.

Business segment (p. 697)
Common-size financial statement (p. 681)
Comparative financial statements (p. 676)
Efficiency (p. 675)
Equity ratio (p. 689)
Extraordinary gains and losses (p. 697)
Financial reporting (p. 675)

Financial statement analysis (p. 674)
General-purpose financial statements (p. 675)
Horizontal analysis (p. 676)
Infrequent gain or loss (p. 697)
Liquidity (p. 675)
Market prospects (p. 675)

Profitability (p. 675)
Ratio analysis (p. 676)
Solvency (p. 675)
Unusual gain or loss (p. 697)
Vertical analysis (p. 676)
Working capital (p. 685)

Multiple Choice Quiz   Answers on p. 717   mhhe.com/wildFAP18e

Multiple Choice Quizzes A and B are available at the book's Website.

1. A company's sales in 2007 were $300,000 and in 2008 were $351,000. Using 2007 as the base year, the sales trend percent for 2008 is:
 a. 17%
 b. 85%
 c. 100%
 d. 117%
 e. 48%

Use the following information for questions 2 through 5.

GALLOWAY COMPANY
Balance Sheet
December 31, 2008

Assets

Cash	$ 86,000
Accounts receivable	76,000
Merchandise inventory	122,000
Prepaid insurance	12,000
Long-term investments	98,000
Plant assets, net	436,000
Total assets	$830,000

Liabilities and Equity

Current liabilities	$124,000
Long-term liabilities	90,000
Common stock	300,000
Retained earnings	316,000
Total liabilities and equity	$830,000

2. What is Galloway Company's current ratio?
 a. 0.69
 b. 1.31
 c. 3.88
 d. 6.69
 e. 2.39

3. What is Galloway Company's acid-test ratio?
 a. 2.39
 b. 0.69
 c. 1.31
 d. 6.69
 e. 3.88

4. What is Galloway Company's debt ratio?
 a. 25.78%
 b. 100.00%
 c. 74.22%
 d. 137.78%
 e. 34.74%

5. What is Galloway Company's equity ratio?
 a. 25.78%
 b. 100.00%
 c. 34.74%
 d. 74.22%
 e. 137.78%

Superscript letter ᴬ denotes assignments based on Appendix 17A.

Discussion Questions

1. What is the difference between comparative financial statements and common-size comparative statements?

2. Which items are usually assigned a 100% value on (a) a common-size balance sheet and (b) a common-size income statement?

3. Explain the difference between financial reporting and financial statements.

4. What three factors would influence your evaluation as to whether a company's current ratio is good or bad?

5. Suggest several reasons why a 2:1 current ratio may not be adequate for a particular company.

6. Why is working capital given special attention in the process of analyzing balance sheets?

7. What does the number of days' sales uncollected indicate?

8. What does a relatively high accounts receivable turnover indicate about a company's short-term liquidity?

9. Why is a company's capital structure, as measured by debt and equity ratios, important to financial statement analysts?

10. How does inventory turnover provide information about a company's short-term liquidity?

11. What ratios would you compute to evaluate management performance?

12. Why must the ratio of pledged assets to secured liabilities be interpreted with caution?

13. Why would a company's return on total assets be different from its return on common stockholders' equity?

14. Where on the income statement does a company report an unusual gain not expected to occur more often than once every two years or so?

15. Use **Best Buy**'s financial statements in Appendix A to compute its return on total assets for the years ended February 26, 2005, and February 28, 2004. Total assets at March, 2003, were $7,694 (in millions).

16. Refer to **Circuit City**'s financial statements in Appendix A to compute its equity ratio as of February 28, 2005 and February 29, 2004.

17. Refer to **Apple**'s financial statements in Appendix A. Compute its profit margin for the fiscal year ended September 25, 2004.

 Red numbers denote Discussion Questions that involve decision-making.

QUICK STUDY

QS 17-1
Financial reporting   C1

Which of the following items (1) through (9) are part of financial reporting but are *not* included as part of general-purpose financial statements? (1) stock price information and analysis, (2) statement of cash flows, (3) management discussion and analysis of financial performance, (4) income statement, (5) company news releases, (6) balance sheet, (7) financial statement notes, (8) statement of shareholders' equity, (9) prospectus.

QS 17-2
Standard of comparison   C3

What are four possible standards of comparison used to analyze financial statement ratios? Which of these is generally considered to be the most useful? Which one is least likely to provide a good basis for comparison?

QS 17-3
Common-size and trend percents

P1   P2

Use the following information for Ciolino Corporation to determine (1) the 2007 and 2008 common-size percents for cost of goods sold using net sales as the base and (2) the 2007 and 2008 trend percents for net sales using 2007 as the base year.

($ thousands)	2008	2007
Net sales	$202,800	$116,200
Cost of goods sold	110,600	61,400

QS 17-4
Horizontal analysis

P1

Compute the annual dollar changes and percent changes for each of the following accounts.

	2008	2007
Short-term investments	$220,000	$160,000
Accounts receivable	38,000	44,000
Notes payable	60,000	0

QS 17-5
Building blocks of analysis

C2   C4   P3

Match the ratio to the building block of financial statement analysis to which it best relates.

A. Liquidity and efficiency   **C.** Profitability
B. Solvency   **D.** Market prospects

1. _____ Book value per common share   **6.** _____ Gross margin ratio
2. _____ Days' sales in inventory   **7.** _____ Acid-test ratio
3. _____ Accounts receivable turnover   **8.** _____ Equity ratio
4. _____ Debt-to-equity   **9.** _____ Return on total assets
5. _____ Times interest earned   **10.** _____ Dividend yield

1. Which two short-term liquidity ratios measure how frequently a company collects its accounts?

2. What measure reflects the difference between current assets and current liabilities?

3. Which two ratios are key components in measuring a company's operating efficiency? Which ratio summarizes these two components?

QS 17-6
Identifying financial ratios

C4   P3

For each ratio listed, identify whether the change in ratio value from 2007 to 2008 is usually regarded as favorable or unfavorable.

QS 17-7
Ratio interpretation

P3

Ratio	2008	2007	Ratio	2008	2007
1. Profit margin	9%	8%	5. Accounts receivable turnover	5.5	6.7
2. Debt ratio	47%	42%	6. Basic earnings per share	$1.25	$1.10
3. Gross margin	34%	46%	7. Inventory turnover	3.6	3.4
4. Acid-test ratio	1.00	1.15	8. Dividend yield	2%	1.2%

A review of the notes payable files discovers that three years ago the company reported the entire amount of a payment (principal and interest) on an installment note payable as interest expense. This mistake had a material effect on the amount of income in that year. How should the correction be reported in the current year financial statements?

QS 17-8^A
Error adjustments

A2

Compute trend percents for the following financial items, using 2006 as the base year. State whether the situation as revealed by the trends appears to be favorable or unfavorable for each item.

EXERCISES

Exercise 17-1
Computation and analysis of trend percents

P1

	2010	2009	2008	2007	2006
Sales	$282,880	$270,800	$252,600	$234,560	$150,000
Cost of goods sold	128,200	122,080	115,280	106,440	67,000
Accounts receivable	18,100	17,300	16,400	15,200	9,000

Common-size and trend percents for Skelton Company's sales, cost of goods sold, and expenses follow. Determine whether net income increased, decreased, or remained unchanged in this three-year period.

Exercise 17-2
Determination of income effects from common-size and trend percents

P1 P2

	Common-Size Percents			Trend Percents		
	2009	2008	2007	2009	2008	2007
Sales	100.0%	100.0%	100.0%	105.4%	104.2%	100.0%
Cost of goods sold	63.4	61.9	59.1	103.0	101.1	100.0
Total expenses	15.3	14.8	15.1	95.0	91.0	100.0

Express the following comparative income statements in common-size percents and assess whether or not this company's situation has improved in the most recent year.

Exercise 17-3
Common-size percent computation and interpretation

P2

MACHIKO CORPORATION Comparative Income Statements For Years Ended December 31, 2008 and 2007		
	2008	2007
Sales	$740,000	$625,000
Cost of goods sold	560,300	290,800
Gross profit	179,700	334,200
Operating expenses	128,200	218,500
Net income	$ 51,500	$115,700

Exercise 17-4

Analysis of short-term
financial condition

A1   P3

The following information is available for Morgan Company and Parker Company, similar firms operating
in the same industry. Write a half-page report comparing Morgan and Parker using the available information. Your discussion should include their ability to meet current obligations and to use current assets
efficiently.

Team Project: Assume
that the two companies apply
for a one-year loan from the
team. Identify additional
information the companies
must provide before the
team can make a loan
decision.

	Morgan			Parker		
	2009	2008	2007	2009	2008	2007
Current ratio	1.7	1.6	2.1	3.2	2.7	1.9
Acid-test ratio	1.0	1.1	1.2	2.8	2.5	1.6
Accounts receivable turnover	30.5	25.2	29.2	16.4	15.2	16.0
Merchandise inventory turnover	24.2	21.9	17.1	14.5	13.0	12.6
Working capital	$70,000	$58,000	$52,000	$131,000	$103,000	$78,000

Exercise 17-5

Analysis of efficiency and
financial leverage

A1   P3

Roak Company and Clay Company are similar firms that operate in the same industry. Clay began operations in 2008 and Roak in 2005. In 2010, both companies pay 7% interest on their debt to creditors.
The following additional information is available.

	Roak Company			Clay Company		
	2010	2009	2008	2010	2009	2008
Total asset turnover	3.1	2.8	3.0	1.7	1.5	1.2
Return on total assets	9.0%	9.6%	8.8%	5.9%	5.6%	5.3%
Profit margin ratio	2.4%	2.5%	2.3%	2.8%	3.0%	2.9%
Sales	$410,000	$380,000	$396,000	$210,000	$170,000	$110,000

Write a half-page report comparing Roak and Clay using the available information. Your analysis should
include their ability to use assets efficiently to produce profits. Also comment on their success in
employing financial leverage in 2010.

Exercise 17-6

Common-size percents

P2

Simeon Company's year-end balance sheets follow. Express the balance sheets in common-size percents.
Round amounts to the nearest one-tenth of a percent. Analyze and comment on the results.

At December 31	2009	2008	2007
Assets			
Cash	$ 31,800	$ 35,625	$ 37,800
Accounts receivable, net	89,500	62,500	50,200
Merchandise inventory	112,500	82,500	54,000
Prepaid expenses	10,700	9,375	5,000
Plant assets, net	278,500	255,000	230,500
Total assets	$523,000	$445,000	$377,500
Liabilities and Equity			
Accounts payable	$129,900	$ 75,250	$ 51,250
Long-term notes payable secured by			
mortgages on plant assets	98,500	101,500	83,500
Common stock, $10 par value	163,500	163,500	163,500
Retained earnings	131,100	104,750	79,250
Total liabilities and equity	$523,000	$445,000	$377,500

Refer to Simeon Company's balance sheets in Exercise 17-6. Analyze its year-end short-term liquidity position at the end of 2009, 2008, and 2007 by computing (1) the current ratio and (2) the acid-test ratio. Comment on the ratio results.

Exercise 17-7
Liquidity analysis

P3

Refer to the Simeon Company information in Exercise 17-6. The company's income statements for the years ended December 31, 2009 and 2008, follow. Assume that all sales are on credit and then compute: (1) days' sales uncollected, (2) accounts receivable turnover, (3) inventory turnover, and (4) days' sales in inventory. Comment on the changes in the ratios from 2008 to 2009.

Exercise 17-8
Liquidity analysis and interpretation

P3

For Year Ended December 31		2009		2008
Sales		$673,500		$532,000
Cost of goods sold	$411,225		$345,500	
Other operating expenses	209,550		134,980	
Interest expense	12,100		13,300	
Income taxes	9,525		8,845	
Total costs and expenses		642,400		502,625
Net income		$ 31,100		$ 29,375
Earnings per share		$ 1.90		$ 1.80

Refer to the Simeon Company information in Exercises 17-6 and 17-8. Compare the company's long-term risk and capital structure positions at the end of 2009 and 2008 by computing these ratios: (1) debt and equity ratios, (2) debt-to-equity ratio, and (3) times interest earned. Comment on these ratio results.

Exercise 17-9
Risk and capital structure analysis

P3

Refer to Simeon Company's financial information in Exercises 17-6 and 17-8. Evaluate the company's efficiency and profitability by computing the following for 2009 and 2008: (1) profit margin ratio, (2) total asset turnover, and (3) return on total assets. Comment on these ratio results.

Exercise 17-10
Efficiency and profitability analysis P3

Refer to Simeon Company's financial information in Exercises 17-6 and 17-8. Additional information about the company follows. To help evaluate the company's profitability, compute and interpret the following ratios for 2009 and 2008: (1) return on common stockholders' equity, (2) price-earnings ratio on December 31, and (3) dividend yield.

Exercise 17-11
Profitability analysis

P3

Common stock market price, December 31, 2009	$30.00
Common stock market price, December 31, 2008	28.00
Annual cash dividends per share in 2009	0.29
Annual cash dividends per share in 2008	0.24

In 2008, Randa Merchandising, Inc., sold its interest in a chain of wholesale outlets, taking the company completely out of the wholesaling business. The company still operates its retail outlets. A listing of the major sections of an income statement follows:

A. Income (loss) from continuing operations
B. Income (loss) from operating, or gain (loss) from disposing, a discontinued segment
C. Extraordinary gain (loss)

Indicate where each of the following income-related items for this company appears on its 2008 income statement by writing the letter of the appropriate section in the blank beside each item.

Exercise 17-12^A
Income statement categories

A2

Section	Item	Debit	Credit
_____	1. Net sales		$2,900,000
_____	2. Gain on state's condemnation of company property (net of tax)		230,000
_____	3. Cost of goods sold	$1,480,000	
_____	4. Income taxes expense	217,000	
_____	5. Depreciation expense	232,500	
_____	6. Gain on sale of wholesale business segment (net of tax)		775,000
_____	7. Loss from operating wholesale business segment (net of tax)	444,000	
_____	8. Salaries expense	640,000	

Exercise 17-13[A]

Income statement presentation

A2

Use the financial data for Randa Merchandising, Inc., in Exercise 17-12 to prepare its income statement for calendar year 2008. (Ignore the earnings per share section.)

PROBLEM SET A

Problem 17-1A

Ratios, common-size statements, and trend percents

P1 P2 P3

mhhe.com/wildFAP18e

Selected comparative financial statements of Korbin Company follow.

KORBIN COMPANY Comparative Income Statements For Years Ended December 31, 2009, 2008, and 2007			
	2009	**2008**	**2007**
Sales	$555,000	$340,000	$278,000
Cost of goods sold	283,500	212,500	153,900
Gross profit	271,500	127,500	124,100
Selling expenses	102,900	46,920	50,800
Administrative expenses	50,668	29,920	22,800
Total expenses	153,568	76,840	73,600
Income before taxes	117,932	50,660	50,500
Income taxes	40,800	10,370	15,670
Net income	$ 77,132	$ 40,290	$ 34,830

KORBIN COMPANY Comparative Balance Sheets December 31, 2009, 2008, and 2007			
	2009	**2008**	**2007**
Assets			
Current assets	$ 52,390	$ 37,924	$ 51,748
Long-term investments	0	500	3,950
Plant assets, net	100,000	96,000	60,000
Total assets	$152,390	$134,424	$115,698
Liabilities and Equity			
Current liabilities	$ 22,800	$ 19,960	$ 20,300
Common stock	72,000	72,000	60,000
Other paid-in capital	9,000	9,000	6,000
Retained earnings	48,590	33,464	29,398
Total liabilities and equity	$152,390	$134,424	$115,698

Required

1. Compute each year's current ratio.

2. Express the income statement data in common-size percents.

3. Express the balance sheet data in trend percents with 2007 as the base year.

Check   (3) 2009, Total assets trend, 131.71%

Analysis Component

4. Comment on any significant relations revealed by the ratios and percents computed.

Selected comparative financial statements of Haroun Company follow.

Problem 17-2A

Calculation and analysis of trend percents

A1   P1

HAROUN COMPANY Comparative Income Statements ($000) For Years Ended December 31, 2009–2003							
	2009	2008	2007	2006	2005	2004	2003
Sales	$1,694	$1,496	$1,370	$1,264	$1,186	$1,110	$928
Cost of goods sold	1,246	1,032	902	802	752	710	586
Gross profit	448	464	468	462	434	400	342
Operating expenses	330	256	234	170	146	144	118
Net income	$ 118	$ 208	$ 234	$ 292	$ 288	$ 256	$224

HAROUN COMPANY Comparative Balance Sheets ($000) December 31, 2009–2003							
	2009	2008	2007	2006	2005	2004	2003
Assets							
Cash	$ 58	$ 78	$ 82	$ 84	$ 88	$ 86	$ 89
Accounts receivable, net	490	514	466	360	318	302	216
Merchandise inventory	1,838	1,364	1,204	1,032	936	810	615
Other current assets	36	32	14	34	28	28	9
Long-term investments	0	0	0	146	146	146	146
Plant assets, net	2,020	2,014	1,752	944	978	860	725
Total assets	$4,442	$4,002	$3,518	$2,600	$2,494	$2,232	$1,800
Liabilities and Equity							
Current liabilities	$1,220	$1,042	$ 718	$ 614	$ 546	$ 522	$ 282
Long-term liabilities	1,294	1,140	1,112	570	580	620	400
Common stock	1,000	1,000	1,000	850	850	650	650
Other paid-in capital	250	250	250	170	170	150	150
Retained earnings	678	570	438	396	348	290	318
Total liabilities and equity	$4,442	$4,002	$3,518	$2,600	$2,494	$2,232	$1,800

Required

1. Compute trend percents for all components of both statements using 2003 as the base year.

Check   (1) 2009, Total assets trend, 246.8%

Analysis Component

2. Analyze and comment on the financial statements and trend percents from part 1.

Plum Corporation began the month of May with $700,000 of current assets, a current ratio of 2.50:1, and an acid-test ratio of 1.10:1. During the month, it completed the following transactions (the company uses a perpetual inventory system).

May   2   Purchased $50,000 of merchandise inventory on credit.
     8   Sold merchandise inventory that cost $55,000 for $110,000 cash.
   10   Collected $20,000 cash on an account receivable.
   15   Paid $22,000 cash to settle an account payable.

Problem 17-3A

Transactions, working capital, and liquidity ratios

P3

mhhe.com/wildFAP18e

17   Wrote off a $5,000 bad debt against the Allowance for Doubtful Accounts account.
22   Declared a $1 per share cash dividend on the 50,000 shares of outstanding common stock.
26   Paid the dividend declared on May 22.
27   Borrowed $100,000 cash by giving the bank a 30-day, 10% note.
28   Borrowed $80,000 cash by signing a long-term secured note.
29   Used the $180,000 cash proceeds from the notes to buy new machinery.

Required

Prepare a table showing Plum's (1) current ratio, (2) acid-test ratio, and (3) working capital, after each transaction. Round ratios to hundredths.

Problem 17-4A
Calculation of financial
statement ratios

P3

mhhe.com/wildFAP18e

Selected year-end financial statements of Cabot Corporation follow. (All sales were on credit; selected balance sheet amounts at December 31, 2007, were inventory, $48,900; total assets, $189,400; common stock, $90,000; and retained earnings, $22,748.)

CABOT CORPORATION
Income Statement
For Year Ended December 31, 2008

Sales	$448,600
Cost of goods sold	297,250
Gross profit	151,350
Operating expenses	98,600
Interest expense	4,100
Income before taxes	48,650
Income taxes	19,598
Net income	$ 29,052

CABOT CORPORATION
Balance Sheet
December 31, 2008

Assets		Liabilities and Equity	
Cash	$ 10,000	Accounts payable	$ 17,500
Short-term investments	8,400	Accrued wages payable	3,200
Accounts receivable, net	29,200	Income taxes payable	3,300
Notes receivable (trade)*	4,500	Long-term note payable, secured	
Merchandise inventory	32,150	by mortgage on plant assets	63,400
Prepaid expenses	2,650	Common stock	90,000
Plant assets, net	153,300	Retained earnings	62,800
Total assets	$240,200	Total liabilities and equity	$240,200

* These are short-term notes receivable arising from customer (trade) sales.

Required

Compute the following: (1) current ratio, (2) acid-test ratio, (3) days' sales uncollected, (4) inventory turnover, (5) days' sales in inventory, (6) debt-to-equity ratio, (7) times interest earned, (8) profit margin ratio, (9) total asset turnover, (10) return on total assets, and (11) return on common stockholders' equity.

Problem 17-5A
Comparative ratio
analysis   A1   P3

Summary information from the financial statements of two companies competing in the same industry follows.

	Barco Company	Kyan Company			Barco Company	Kyan Company
Data from the current year-end balance sheets				**Data from the current year's income statement**		
Assets				Sales	$770,000	$880,200
Cash	$ 19,500	$ 34,000		Cost of goods sold	585,100	632,500
Accounts receivable, net	37,400	57,400		Interest expense	7,900	13,000
Current notes receivable (trade)	9,100	7,200		Income tax expense	14,800	24,300
Merchandise inventory	84,440	132,500		Net income	$162,200	$210,400
Prepaid expenses	5,000	6,950		Basic earnings per share	$ 4.51	$ 5.11
Plant assets, net	290,000	304,400				
Total assets	$445,440	$542,450				
				Beginning-of-year balance sheet data		
Liabilities and Equity				Accounts receivable, net	$ 29,800	$ 54,200
Current liabilities	$ 61,340	$ 93,300		Current notes receivable (trade)	0	0
Long-term notes payable	80,800	101,000		Merchandise inventory	55,600	107,400
Common stock, $5 par value	180,000	206,000		Total assets	398,000	382,500
Retained earnings	123,300	142,150		Common stock, $5 par value	180,000	206,000
Total liabilities and equity	$445,440	$542,450		Retained earnings	98,300	93,600

Required

1. For both companies compute the (*a*) current ratio, (*b*) acid-test ratio, (*c*) accounts (including notes) receivable turnover, (*d*) inventory turnover, (*e*) days' sales in inventory, and (*f*) days' sales uncollected. Identify the company you consider to be the better short-term credit risk and explain why.

2. For both companies compute the (*a*) profit margin ratio, (*b*) total asset turnover, (*c*) return on total assets, and (*d*) return on common stockholders' equity. Assuming that each company paid cash dividends of $3.80 per share and each company's stock can be purchased at $75 per share, compute their (*e*) price-earnings ratios and (*f*) dividend yields. Identify which company's stock you would recommend as the better investment and explain why.

Check (1) Kyan: Accounts receivable turnover, 14.8; Inventory turnover, 5.3

(2) Barco: Profit margin, 21.1%; PE, 16.6

Selected account balances from the adjusted trial balance for Olinda Corporation as of its calendar year-end December 31, 2005, follow.

Problem 17-6A[A]

Income statement computations and format

A2

	Debit	Credit
a. Interest revenue		$ 14,000
b. Depreciation expense—Equipment	$ 34,000	
c. Loss on sale of equipment	25,850	
d. Accounts payable		44,000
e. Other operating expenses	106,400	
f. Accumulated depreciation—Equipment		71,600
g. Gain from settlement of lawsuit		44,000
h. Accumulated depreciation—Buildings		174,500
i. Loss from operating a discontinued segment (pretax)	18,250	
j. Gain on insurance recovery of tornado damage (pretax and extraordinary)		29,120
k. Net sales		998,500
l. Depreciation expense—Buildings	52,000	
m. Correction of overstatement of prior year's sales (pretax)	16,000	
n. Gain on sale of discontinued segment's assets (pretax)		34,000
o. Loss from settlement of lawsuit	23,750	
p. Income taxes expense		
q. Cost of goods sold	482,500	

Required

Answer each of the following questions by providing supporting computations.

1. Assume that the company's income tax rate is 30% for all items. Identify the tax effects and after-tax amounts of the four items labeled pretax.

2. What is the amount of income from continuing operations before income taxes? What is the amount of the income taxes expense? What is the amount of income from continuing operations?

3. What is the total amount of after-tax income (loss) associated with the discontinued segment?

4. What is the amount of income (loss) before the extraordinary items?

5. What is the amount of net income for the year?

PROBLEM SET B

Problem 17-1B

Ratios, common-size statements, and trend percents

P1   P2   P3

Selected comparative financial statement information of Bluegrass Corporation follows.

BLUEGRASS CORPORATION Comparative Income Statements For Years Ended December 31, 2009, 2008, and 2007			
	2009	**2008**	**2007**
Sales	$198,800	$166,000	$143,800
Cost of goods sold	108,890	86,175	66,200
Gross profit	89,910	79,825	77,600
Selling expenses	22,680	19,790	18,000
Administrative expenses	16,760	14,610	15,700
Total expenses	39,440	34,400	33,700
Income before taxes	50,470	45,425	43,900
Income taxes	6,050	5,910	5,300
Net income	$ 44,420	$ 39,515	$ 38,600

BLUEGRASS CORPORATION Comparative Balance Sheets December 31, 2009, 2008, and 2007			
	2009	**2008**	**2007**
Assets			
Current assets	$ 54,860	$ 32,660	$ 36,300
Long-term investments	0	1,700	10,600
Plant assets, net	112,810	113,660	79,000
Total assets	$167,670	$148,020	$125,900
Liabilities and Equity			
Current liabilities	$ 22,370	$ 19,180	$ 16,500
Common stock	46,500	46,500	37,000
Other paid-in capital	13,850	13,850	11,300
Retained earnings	84,950	68,490	61,100
Total liabilities and equity	$167,670	$148,020	$125,900

Required

1. Compute each year's current ratio.

2. Express the income statement data in common-size percents.

3. Express the balance sheet data in trend percents with 2007 as the base year.

Analysis Component

4. Comment on any significant relations revealed by the ratios and percents computed.

Selected comparative financial statements of Tripoly Company follow.

TRIPOLY COMPANY Comparative Income Statements ($000) For Years Ended December 31, 2009–2003							
	2009	2008	2007	2006	2005	2004	2003
Sales	$560	$610	$630	$680	$740	$770	$860
Cost of goods sold	276	290	294	314	340	350	380
Gross profit	284	320	336	366	400	420	480
Operating expenses	84	104	112	126	140	144	150
Net income	$200	$216	$224	$240	$260	$276	$330

TRIPOLY COMPANY Comparative Balance Sheets ($000) December 31, 2009–2003							
	2009	2008	2007	2006	2005	2004	2003
Assets							
Cash	$ 44	$ 46	$ 52	$ 54	$ 60	$ 62	$ 68
Accounts receivable, net	130	136	140	144	150	154	160
Merchandise inventory	166	172	178	180	186	190	208
Other current assets	34	34	36	38	38	40	40
Long-term investments	36	30	26	110	110	110	110
Plant assets, net	510	514	520	412	420	428	454
Total assets	$920	$932	$952	$938	$964	$984	$1,040
Liabilities and Equity							
Current liabilities	$148	$156	$186	$190	$210	$260	$ 280
Long-term liabilities	92	120	142	148	194	214	260
Common stock	160	160	160	160	160	160	160
Other paid-in capital	70	70	70	70	70	70	70
Retained earnings	450	426	394	370	330	280	270
Total liabilities and equity	$920	$932	$952	$938	$964	$984	$1,040

Problem 17-2B
Calculation and analysis of
trend percents

A1 P1

Required

1. Compute trend percents for all components of both statements using 2003 as the base year.

Check (1) 2009, Total assets trend, 88.5%

Analysis Component

2. Analyze and comment on the financial statements and trend percents from part 1.

Koto Corporation began the month of June with $300,000 of current assets, a current ratio of 2.5:1, and an acid-test ratio of 1.4:1. During the month, it completed the following transactions (the company uses a perpetual inventory system).

Problem 17-3B
Transactions, working capital, and
liquidity ratios

P3

June 1 Sold merchandise inventory that cost $75,000 for $120,000 cash.
    3 Collected $88,000 cash on an account receivable.
    5 Purchased $150,000 of merchandise inventory on credit.
    7 Borrowed $100,000 cash by giving the bank a 60-day, 10% note.
   10 Borrowed $120,000 cash by signing a long-term secured note.
   12 Purchased machinery for $275,000 cash.
   15 Declared a $1 per share cash dividend on the 80,000 shares of outstanding common stock.
   19 Wrote off a $5,000 bad debt against the Allowance for Doubtful Accounts account.
   22 Paid $12,000 cash to settle an account payable.
   30 Paid the dividend declared on June 15.

Check June 1: Current ratio, 2.88;
Acid-test, 2.40

June 30: Working capital,
$(10,000); Current ratio, 0.97

Required

Prepare a table showing the company's (1) current ratio, (2) acid-test ratio, and (3) working capital after each transaction. Round ratios to hundredths.

Problem 17-4B
Calculation of financial
statement ratios

P3

Selected year-end financial statements of Overton Corporation follow. (All sales were on credit; selected balance sheet amounts at December 31, 2007, were inventory, $17,400; total assets, $94,900; common stock, $35,500; and retained earnings, $18,800.)

OVERTON CORPORATION
Income Statement
For Year Ended December 31, 2008

Sales	$315,500
Cost of goods sold	236,100
Gross profit	79,400
Operating expenses	49,200
Interest expense	2,200
Income before taxes	28,000
Income taxes	4,200
Net income	$ 23,800

OVERTON CORPORATION
Balance Sheet
December 31, 2008

Assets		Liabilities and Equity	
Cash	$ 6,100	Accounts payable	$ 11,500
Short-term investments	6,900	Accrued wages payable	3,300
Accounts receivable, net	12,100	Income taxes payable	2,600
Notes receivable (trade)*	3,000	Long-term note payable, secured	
Merchandise inventory	13,500	by mortgage on plant assets	30,000
Prepaid expenses	2,000	Common stock, $5 par value	35,000
Plant assets, net	73,900	Retained earnings	35,100
Total assets	$117,500	Total liabilities and equity	$117,500

* These are short-term notes receivable arising from customer (trade) sales.

Required

Check Acid-test ratio, 1.6 to 1;
Inventory turnover, 15.3

Compute the following: (1) current ratio, (2) acid-test ratio, (3) days' sales uncollected, (4) inventory turnover, (5) days' sales in inventory, (6) debt-to-equity ratio, (7) times interest earned, (8) profit margin ratio, (9) total asset turnover, (10) return on total assets, and (11) return on common stockholders' equity.

Problem 17-5B
Comparative
ratio analysis   A1   P3

Summary information from the financial statements of two companies competing in the same industry follows.

	Fargo Company	Ball Company		Fargo Company	Ball Company
Data from the current year-end balance sheets			**Data from the current year's income statement**		
Assets			Sales	$393,600	$667,500
Cash	$ 20,000	$ 36,500	Cost of goods sold	290,600	480,000
Accounts receivable, net	77,100	70,500	Interest expense	5,900	12,300
Current notes receivable (trade)	11,600	9,000	Income tax expense	5,700	12,300
Merchandise inventory	86,800	82,000	Net income	33,850	61,700
Prepaid expenses	9,700	10,100	Basic earnings per share	1.27	2.19
Plant assets, net	176,900	252,300			
Total assets	$382,100	$460,400			
			Beginning-of-year balance sheet data		
Liabilities and Equity			Accounts receivable, net	$ 72,200	$ 73,300
Current liabilities	$ 90,500	$ 97,000	Current notes receivable (trade)	0	0
Long-term notes payable	93,000	93,300	Merchandise inventory	105,100	80,500
Common stock, $5 par value	133,000	141,000	Total assets	383,400	443,000
Retained earnings	65,600	129,100	Common stock, $5 par value	133,000	141,000
Total liabilities and equity	$382,100	$460,400	Retained earnings	49,100	109,700

Required

1. For both companies compute the (*a*) current ratio, (*b*) acid-test ratio, (*c*) accounts (including notes) receivable turnover, (*d*) inventory turnover, (*e*) days' sales in inventory, and (*f*) days' sales uncollected. Identify the company you consider to be the better short-term credit risk and explain why.

2. For both companies compute the (*a*) profit margin ratio, (*b*) total asset turnover, (*c*) return on total assets, and (*d*) return on common stockholders' equity. Assuming that each company paid cash dividends of $1.50 per share and each company's stock can be purchased at $25 per share, compute their (*e*) price-earnings ratios and (*f*) dividend yields. Identify which company's stock you would recommend as the better investment and explain why.

Check (1) Fargo: Accounts receivable turnover, 4.9; Inventory turnover, 3.0

(2) Ball: Profit margin, 9.2%; PE, 11.4

Selected account balances from the adjusted trial balance for Harbor Corp. as of its calendar year-end December 31, 2008, follow.

Problem 17-6B[A]

Income statement computations and format

A2

	Debit	Credit
a. Accumulated depreciation—Buildings		$ 400,000
b. Interest revenue		20,000
c. Net sales		2,640,000
d. Income taxes expense	$?	
e. Loss on hurricane damage (pretax and extraordinary)	64,000	
f. Accumulated depreciation—Equipment		220,000
g. Other operating expenses	328,000	
h. Depreciation expense—Equipment	100,000	
i. Loss from settlement of lawsuit	36,000	
j. Gain from settlement of lawsuit		68,000
k. Loss on sale of equipment	24,000	
l. Loss from operating a discontinued segment (pretax)	120,000	
m. Depreciation expense—Buildings	156,000	
n. Correction of overstatement of prior year's expense (pretax)		48,000
o. Cost of goods sold	1,040,000	
p. Loss on sale of discontinued segment's assets (pretax)	180,000	
q. Accounts payable		132,000

Required

Answer each of the following questions by providing supporting computations.

1. Assume that the company's income tax rate is 25% for all items. Identify the tax effects and after-tax amounts of the four items labeled pretax.

2. What is the amount of income from continuing operations before income taxes? What is the amount of income taxes expense? What is the amount of income from continuing operations?

3. What is the total amount of after-tax income (loss) associated with the discontinued segment?

4. What is the amount of income (loss) before the extraordinary items?

5. What is the amount of net income for the year?

Check (3) $(225,000)

(4) $558,000

(5) $510,000

 Problem Set C is available at the book's Website to reinforce and assess your learning.

PROBLEM SET C

(This serial problem began in Chapter 1 and continues through most of the book. If previous chapter segments were not completed, the serial problem can begin at this point. It is helpful, but not necessary, for you to use the Working Papers that accompany the book.)

SERIAL PROBLEM

Success Systems

SP 17 Use the following selected data from Success Systems' income statement for the three months ended March 31, 2008, and from its March 31, 2008, balance sheet to complete the requirements below: computer services revenue, $31,850; net (goods) sales, $20,345; total sales and revenue, $52,195; cost of goods sold, $14,272; net income, $24,336; quick assets, $111,666; current assets, $116,371; total assets, $147,621; current liabilities, $1,050; total liabilities, $1,050; and total equity, $146,571.

Required

1. Compute the gross margin ratio (both with and without services revenue) and net profit margin ratio.
2. Compute the current ratio and acid-test ratio.
3. Compute the debt ratio and equity ratio.
4. What percent of its assets are current? What percent are long term?

BEYOND THE NUMBERS

REPORTING IN ACTION

A1 P1 P2

BTN 17-1   Refer to **Best Buy**'s financial statements in Appendix A to answer the following.

1. Using 2003 as the base year, compute trend percents for fiscal years 2003, 2004, and 2005 for revenues, cost of sales, selling general and administrative expenses, income taxes, and net income. (Round to the nearest whole percent.)
2. Compute common-size percents for fiscal years 2005 and 2004 for the following categories of assets: (*a*) total current assets, (*b*) property and equipment, net, and (*c*) intangible assets. (Round to the nearest tenth of a percent.)
3. Comment on any significant changes across the years for the income statement trends computed in part 1 and the balance sheet percents computed in part 2.

Fast Forward

4. Access Best Buy's financial statements for fiscal years ending after February 26, 2005, from Best Buy's Website (**BestBuy.com**) or the SEC database (**www.SEC.gov**). Update your work for parts 1, 2, and 3 using the new information accessed.

COMPARATIVE ANALYSIS

C3 P2

BTN 17-2   Key comparative figures ($ millions) for both **Best Buy** and **Circuit City** follow.

Key Figures	Best Buy	Circuit City
Cash and equivalents	$ 470	$ 880
Accounts receivable, net	375	173
Inventories	2,851	1,460
Retained earnings	3,315	1,247
Costs of sales	20,938	7,904
Revenues	27,433	10,472
Total assets	10,294	3,789

Required

1. Compute common-size percents for both companies using the data provided.
2. Which company retains a higher portion of cumulative net income in the company?
3. Which company has a higher gross margin ratio on sales?
4. Which company holds a higher percent of its total assets as inventory?

ETHICS CHALLENGE

A1

BTN 17-3   As Beacon Company controller, you are responsible for informing the board of directors about its financial activities. At the board meeting, you present the following information.

	2009	2008	2007
Sales trend percent	147.0%	135.0%	100.0%
Selling expenses to sales	10.1%	14.0%	15.6%
Sales to plant assets ratio	3.8 to 1	3.6 to 1	3.3 to 1
Current ratio	2.9 to 1	2.7 to 1	2.4 to 1
Acid-test ratio	1.1 to 1	1.4 to 1	1.5 to 1
Inventory turnover	7.8 times	9.0 times	10.2 times
Accounts receivable turnover	7.0 times	7.7 times	8.5 times
Total asset turnover	2.9 times	2.9 times	3.3 times
Return on total assets	10.4%	11.0%	13.2%
Return on stockholders' equity	10.7%	11.5%	14.1%
Profit margin ratio	3.6%	3.8%	4.0%

After the meeting, the company's CEO holds a press conference with analysts in which she mentions the following ratios.

	2009	2008	2007
Sales trend percent	147.0%	135.0%	100.0%
Selling expenses to sales	10.1%	14.0%	15.6%
Sales to plant assets ratio	3.8 to 1	3.6 to 1	3.3 to 1
Current ratio	2.9 to 1	2.7 to 1	2.4 to 1

Required

1. Why do you think the CEO decided to report 4 ratios instead of the 11 prepared?

2. Comment on the possible consequences of the CEO's reporting of the ratios selected.

BTN 17-4 Each team is to select a different industry, and each team member is to select a different company in that industry and acquire its financial statements. Use those statements to analyze the company, including at least one ratio from each of the four building blocks of analysis. When necessary, use the financial press to determine the market price of its stock. Communicate with teammates via a meeting, e-mail, or telephone to discuss how different companies compare to each other and to industry norms. The team is to prepare a single one-page memorandum reporting on its analysis and the conclusions reached.

COMMUNICATING IN PRACTICE

C2 A1 P3

BTN 17-5 Access the March 7, 2005, filing of the 2004 10-K report of the **Hershey Foods Corporation** (ticker HSY) at www.sec.gov and complete the following requirements.

TAKING IT TO THE NET

C4 P3

Required

Compute or identify the following profitability ratios of Hershey for its years ending December 31, 2004, *and* December 31, 2003. Interpret its profitability using the following ratio results.

1. Profit margin ratio

2. Gross profit ratio

3. Return on total assets (*Note:* Total assets in 2002 were $3,480,551,000.)

4. Return on common stockholders' equity (*Note:* Total shareholders' equity in 2002 was $1,371,703,000.)

5. Basic earnings per share

BTN 17-6 A team approach to learning financial statement analysis is often useful.

TEAMWORK IN ACTION

C2 P1 P2 P3

Required

1. Each team should write a description of horizontal and vertical analysis that all team members agree with and understand. Illustrate each description with an example.

2. *Each* member of the team is to select *one* of the following categories of ratio analysis. Explain what the ratios in that category measure. Choose one ratio from the category selected, present its formula, and explain what it measures.

   a. Liquidity and efficiency   **c.** Profitability

   b. Solvency   **d.** Market prospects

3. Each team member is to present his or her notes from part 2 to teammates. Team members are to confirm or correct other teammates' presentation.

Hint: Pairing within teams may be necessary for part 2. Use as an in-class activity or as an assignment. Consider presentations to the entire class using team rotation with transparencies.

BTN 17-7 Read the article "Hollinger's Troubles, in Black and White," by Louis Lavelle in the September 2, 2004, issue of *BusinessWeek*. (The book's Website provides a free link.)

***BusinessWeek* ACTIVITY**

C1 C4

Required

What are the suggestions that Lavelle has for stockholders to identify a potentially troubled company?

ENTREPRENEURIAL DECISION

A1 P1 P2 P3

BTN 17-8   Assume that David and Tom Gardner of **The Motley Fool** (**Fool.com**) have impressed you since you first heard of their rather improbable rise to prominence in financial circles. You learn of a staff opening at The Motley Fool and decide to apply for it. Your resume is successfully screened from the thousands received and you advance to the interview process. You learn that the interview consists of analyzing the following financial facts and answering analysis questions. (*Note:* The data are taken from a small merchandiser in outdoor recreational equipment.)

	2008	2007	2006
Sales trend percents	137.0%	125.0%	100.0%
Selling expenses to sales	9.8%	13.7%	15.3%
Sales to plant assets ratio	3.5 to 1	3.3 to 1	3.0 to 1
Current ratio	2.6 to 1	2.4 to 1	2.1 to 1
Acid-test ratio	0.8 to 1	1.1 to 1	1.2 to 1
Merchandise inventory turnover	7.5 times	8.7 times	9.9 times
Accounts receivable turnover	6.7 times	7.4 times	8.2 times
Total asset turnover	2.6 times	2.6 times	3.0 times
Return on total assets	8.8%	9.4%	11.1%
Return on equity	9.75%	11.50%	12.25%
Profit margin ratio	3.3%	3.5%	3.7%

Required

Use these data to answer each of the following questions with explanations.

1. Is it becoming easier for the company to meet its current liabilities on time and to take advantage of any available cash discounts? Explain.
2. Is the company collecting its accounts receivable more rapidly? Explain.
3. Is the company's investment in accounts receivable decreasing? Explain.
4. Is the company's investment in plant assets increasing? Explain.
5. Is the owner's investment becoming more profitable? Explain.
6. Did the dollar amount of selling expenses decrease during the three-year period? Explain.

HITTING THE ROAD

C1 P3

BTN 17-9   You are to devise an investment strategy to enable you to accumulate $1,000,000 by age 65. Start by making some assumptions about your salary. Next compute the percent of your salary that you will be able to save each year. If you will receive any lump-sum monies, include those amounts in your calculations. Historically, stocks have delivered average annual returns of 10–11%. Given this history, you should probably not assume that you will earn above 10% on the money you invest. It is not necessary to specify exactly what types of assets you will buy for your investments; just assume a rate you expect to earn. Use the future value tables in Appendix B to calculate how your savings will grow. Experiment a bit with your figures to see how much less you have to save if you start at, for example, age 25 versus age 35 or 40. (For this assignment, do not include inflation in your calculations.)

GLOBAL DECISION

A1

Dixons

BTN 17-10   **Dixons**, **Best Buy**, and **Circuit City** are competitors in the global marketplace. Visit the Dixons' Website (**Dixons-Group.com**) and access its most recent annual report.

Required

Review Dixons' Website and skim through its annual report. Compare its annual report to one of its U.S. competitor's reports (Best Buy or Circuit City) presented in Appendix A. Identify five ways that the U.K. company's report or its Website differs from that of its U.S. competitors.

ANSWERS TO MULTIPLE CHOICE QUIZ

1. d; ($351,000/$300,000) × 100 = 117%

2. e; ($86,000 + $76,000 + $122,000 + $12,000)/$124,000 = 2.39

3. c; ($86,000 + $76,000)/$124,000 = 1.31

4. a; ($124,000 + $90,000)/$830,000 = 25.78%

5. d; ($300,000 + $316,000)/$830,000 = 74.22%

18

Managerial Accounting Concepts and Principles

A Look Back

Chapter 17 described the analysis and interpretation of financial statement information. We applied horizontal, vertical, and ratio analyses to better understand company performance and financial condition.

A Look at This Chapter

We begin our study of managerial accounting by explaining its purpose and describing its major characteristics. We also discuss cost concepts and describe how they help managers gather and organize information for making decisions. The reporting of manufacturing activities is also discussed.

A Look Ahead

The remaining chapters discuss the types of decisions managers must make and how managerial accounting helps with those decisions. The first of these chapters, Chapter 19, considers how we measure costs assigned to certain types of projects.

Learning Objectives

CAP

Conceptual

C1 Explain the purpose and nature of managerial accounting. (p. 720)

C2 Describe the lean business model. (p. 723)

C3 Describe accounting concepts useful in classifying costs. (p. 725)

C4 Define product and period costs and explain how they impact financial statements. (p. 726)

C5 Explain how balance sheets and income statements for manufacturing and merchandising companies differ. (p. 728)

C6 Explain manufacturing activities and the flow of manufacturing costs. (p. 732)

Analytical

A1 Compute cycle time and cycle efficiency, and explain their importance to production management (p. 735)

Procedural

P1 Compute cost of goods sold for a manufacturer. (p. 730)

P2 Prepare a manufacturing statement and explain its purpose and links to financial statements. (p. 733)

> "I've transitioned from being a fan of the guitar, to a guitar builder, to being a guitar CEO"
> —Chris Griffiths

Good Vibrations

ST. JOHN'S, NEWFOUNDLAND—"I've always had a mechanical curiosity," admits Chris Griffiths. "I was always one of those kids who took apart the alarm clock and spread out all the pieces. I was always really curious as to what made things work." In his curiosity Chris found his passion: guitars and what makes them tick. "If I was home and unemployed, I'd just be playing guitar anyway!"

Says Chris of his early start building guitars, "I've got my little chisel, and I've got my little stack of sandpaper, and I'm going to do it. I thought, well, that's great, man." But Chris had bigger dreams. "I wanted to do something really, really different, and really innovative. I was looking for a competitive advantage." Chris' innovation was a one-piece injection-molded structure he called *Griffiths Active Bracing System*™ that would be encased in the guitar body. "I didn't know what I was doing," admits Chris. "I was making it up as I was going along."

What Chris did was revolutionize the way to make guitars, and make them better. "Because all the braces are made out of one piece they vibrate as a single unit," explains Chris. "All of a sudden, it comes alive acoustically." His startup, **Garrison Guitars (GarrisonGuitars.com),** manufactures guitars using Chris's bracing system. "Whether you bake pies or you build guitars or you cut hair," explains Chris, "[you build] a business infrastructure around that. It

was the best thing that ever happened to me." It is also the best thing for Chris' customers. "It's all about adding value for the consumer. We offer exceptional value by building quality instruments and by providing outstanding service and support," says Chris.

Chris believes basic managerial principles, product and period costs, and manufacturing statements are like another language to most people. But he also realizes entrepreneurial success often depends on embracing, understanding, and applying these concepts. Knowing your manufacturing activities and cost flows is not easy, notes Chris, but the cost of not understanding those concepts is far greater. "In a typical guitar factory it would take you about two and a half hours to make [the bracing] components," says Chris. "We make this component in 45 seconds. I'm no accountant, but apparently that's pretty good!"

Chris believes entrepreneurs fill a void by creating a niche, and then monitoring and controlling production while meeting customer needs. But Chris strikes a cautionary note for any would-be entrepreneur in his line of work. Without applying managerial accounting principles and lean manufacturing, says Chris, "It's just a building, a bunch of machines, and a pile of wood." Now there's advice that sounds really great, man.

[Sources: *Garrison Guitars Website*, May 2006; *Entrepreneur*, December 2005; *Innovation Strategy Website*, March 2003; *Association for Manufacturing Excellence Website*, March 2006; *Composites News Supersite*, January 2005]

Managerial accounting, like financial accounting, provides information to help users make better decisions. However, managerial accounting and financial accounting differ in important ways, which this chapter explains. This chapter also compares the accounting and reporting practices used by manufacturing and merchandising companies. A merchandising company sells products without changing their condition. A manufacturing

company buys raw materials and turns them into finished products for sale to customers. A third type of company earns revenues by providing services rather than products. The skills, tools, and techniques developed for measuring a manufacturing company's activities apply to service companies as well. The chapter concludes by explaining the flow of manufacturing activities and preparing the manufacturing statement.

Managerial Accounting Concepts and Principles

Managerial Accounting Basics
- Purpose of managerial accounting
- Nature of managerial accounting
- Managerial decisions
- Managerial accounting in business

Managerial Cost Concepts
- Types of cost classifications
- Identification of cost classifications
- Cost concepts for service companies

Reporting Manufacturing Activities
- Balance sheet
- Income statement
- Flow of activities
- Manufacturing statement

Managerial Accounting Basics

Managerial accounting is an activity that provides financial and nonfinancial information to an organization's managers and other internal decision makers. This section explains the purpose of managerial accounting (also called *management accounting*) and compares it with financial accounting. The main purpose of the financial accounting system is to prepare general-purpose financial statements. That information is incomplete for internal decision makers who manage organizations.

Purpose of Managerial Accounting

C1 Explain the purpose and nature of managerial accounting.

The purpose of both managerial accounting and financial accounting is providing useful information to decision makers. They do this by collecting, managing, and reporting information in demand by their users. Both areas of accounting also share the common practice of reporting monetary information, although managerial accounting includes the reporting of nonmonetary information. They even report some of the same information. For instance, a company's financial statements contain information useful for both its managers (insiders) and other persons interested in the company (outsiders).

The remainder of this book looks carefully at managerial accounting information, how to gather it, and how managers use it. We consider the concepts and procedures used to determine the costs of products and services as well as topics such as budgeting, break-even analysis, product costing, profit planning, and cost analysis. Information about the costs of products and services is important for many decisions that managers make. These decisions include predicting the future costs of a product or service. Predicted costs are used in product pricing, profitability analysis, and in deciding whether to make or buy a product or component. More generally, much of managerial accounting involves gathering information about costs for planning and control decisions.

Planning is the process of setting goals and making plans to achieve them. Companies formulate long-term strategic plans that usually span a 5- to 10-year horizon and then refine them with medium-term and short-term plans. Strategic plans usually set a firm's long-term direction by developing a road map based on opportunities such as new products, new markets, and capital investments. A strategic plan's goals and objectives are broadly defined given its long-term orientation. Medium- and short-term plans are more operational in nature. They translate the strategic plan into actions. These plans are more concrete and consist of better defined objectives and goals. A short-term plan often covers a one-year period that, when translated in monetary terms, is known as a budget.

Control is the process of monitoring planning decisions and evaluating an organization's activities and employees. It includes the measurement and evaluation of actions, processes, and outcomes. Feedback provided by the control function allows managers to revise their plans. Measurement of actions and processes also allows managers to take corrective actions to avoid undesirable outcomes. For example, managers periodically compare actual results with planned results. Exhibit 18.1 portrays the important management functions of planning and control.

Point: Costs are important to managers because they impact both the financial position and profitability of a business. Managerial accounting assists in analysis, planning, and control of costs.

Exhibit 18.1
Planning and Control

Monitoring

Feedback

Planning
- Strategic aims
- Long- & short-term
- Annual budgets

Control
- Measurement
- Evaluation
- Oversight

Managers use information to plan and control business activities. In later chapters, we explain how managers also use this information to direct and improve business operations.

Nature of Managerial Accounting

Managerial accounting has its own special characteristics. To understand these characteristics, we compare managerial accounting to financial accounting; they differ in at least seven important ways. These differences are summarized in Exhibit 18.2. This section discusses each of these characteristics.

Exhibit 18.2
Key Differences between Managerial Accounting and Financial Accounting

"This company's outlook is good. I'll buy its shares."

"This department is doing well. We'll expand its product line."

	Financial Accounting	Managerial Accounting
1. Users and decision makers	Investors, creditors, and other users external to the organization	Managers, employees, and decision makers internal to the organization
2. Purpose of information	Assist external users in making investment, credit, and other decisions	Assist managers in making planning and control decisions
3. Flexibility of practice	Structured and often controlled by GAAP	Relatively flexible (no GAAP constraints)
4. Timeliness of information	Often available only after an audit is complete	Available quickly without the need to wait for an audit
5. Time dimension	Focus on historical information with some predictions	Many projections and estimates; historical information also presented
6. Focus of information	Emphasis on whole organization	Emphasis on an organization's projects, processes, and subdivisions
7. Nature of information	Monetary information	Mostly monetary; but also nonmonetary information

Point: It is desirable to accumulate information for management reports in a database separate from financial accounting records.

Users and Decision Makers Companies accumulate, process, and report financial accounting and managerial accounting information for different groups of decision makers. Financial accounting information is primarily provided to external users including investors, creditors, analysts, and regulators. External users rarely have a major role in managing a company's daily activities. Managerial accounting information is primarily provided to internal users who are responsible for making and implementing decisions about a company's business activities.

Purpose of Information Investors, creditors, and other external users of financial accounting information must often decide whether to invest in or lend to a company. If they have already done so, they must decide whether to continue owning the company or carrying the loan. Internal decision makers must plan a company's future. They seek to take advantage of opportunities or to overcome obstacles. They also try to control activities and ensure their effective and efficient implementation. Managerial accounting information helps these internal users make both planning and control decisions.

Point: The *Institute of Management Accountants* issues statements that govern the practice of managerial accounting. Accountants who pass a qualifying exam are awarded the CMA.

Flexibility of Practice External users compare companies by using financial reports and need protection against false or misleading information. Accordingly, financial accounting relies on accepted principles that are enforced through an extensive set of rules and guidelines, or GAAP. Internal users need managerial accounting information for planning and controlling their company's activities rather than for external comparisons. They require different types of information depending on the activity. This makes standardizing managerial accounting systems across companies difficult. Instead, managerial accounting systems are flexible. The design of a company's managerial accounting system largely depends on the nature of the business and the arrangement of its internal operations. Managers can decide for themselves what information they want and how they want it reported. Even within a single company, different managers often design their own systems to meet their special needs. The important question a manager must ask is whether the information being collected and reported is useful for planning, decision making, and control purposes.

Point: Financial statements are usually issued several weeks after the period-end. GAAP requires the reporting of important events that occur while the statements are being prepared. These events are called *subsequent events*.

Point: Independent auditors test the integrity of managerial accounting records when they are used in preparing financial statements.

Timeliness of Information Formal financial statements reporting past transactions and events are not immediately available to outside parties. Independent certified public accountants often must *audit* a company's financial statements before it provides them to external users. Thus, because audits often take several weeks to complete, financial reports to outsiders usually are not available until well after the period-end. However, managers can quickly obtain managerial accounting information. External auditors need not review it. Estimates and projections are acceptable. To get information quickly, managers often accept less precision in reports. As an example, an early internal report to management prepared right after the year-end could report net income for the year between $4.2 and $4.8 million. An audited income statement could later show net income for the year at $4.6 million. The internal report is not precise, but its information can be more useful because it is available earlier.

Internal auditing plays an important role in managerial accounting. Internal auditors evaluate the flow of information not only inside but also outside the company. Managers are responsible for preventing and detecting fraudulent activities in their companies.

Time Dimension To protect external users from false expectations, financial reports deal primarily with results of both past activities and current conditions. While some predictions such as service lives and salvage values of plant assets are necessary, financial accounting avoids predictions whenever possible. Managerial accounting regularly includes predictions of conditions and events. As an example, one important managerial

---

Decision Ethics   Answer—p. 741

Production Manager You invite three friends to a restaurant. When the dinner check arrives, David, a self-employed entrepreneur, picks it up saying, "Here, let me pay. I'll deduct it as a business expense on my tax return." Denise, a salesperson, takes the check from David's hand and says, "I'll put this on my company's credit card. It won't cost us anything." Derek, a factory manager for a company, laughs and says, "Neither of you understands. I'll put this on my company's credit card and call it overhead on a cost-plus contract my company has with a client." (*A cost-plus contract means the company receives its costs plus a percent of those costs.*) Adds Derek, "That way, my company pays for dinner *and* makes a profit." Who should pay the bill? Why?

accounting report is a budget, which predicts revenues, expenses, and other items. If managerial accounting reports were restricted to the past and present, managers would be less able to plan activities and less effective in managing and evaluating current activities.

Focus of Information   Companies often organize into divisions and departments, but investors rarely can buy shares in one division or department. Nor do creditors lend money to a company's single division or department. Instead, they own shares in or make loans to the entire company. Financial accounting focuses primarily on a company as a whole as depicted in Exhibit 18.3. The focus of managerial accounting is different. While top-level managers are responsible for managing the whole company, most other managers are responsible for much smaller sets of activities. These middle-level and lower-level managers need managerial accounting reports dealing with specific activities, projects, and subdivisions for which they are responsible. For instance, division sales managers are directly responsible only for the results achieved in their divisions. Accordingly, division sales managers need information about results achieved in their own divisions to improve their performance. This information includes the level of success achieved by each individual or department in each division as depicted in Exhibit 18.4.

Exhibit 18.3
Focus of External Reports

Exhibit 18.4
Focus of Internal Reports

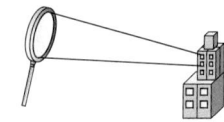

Nature of Information   Both financial and managerial accounting systems report monetary information. Managerial accounting systems also report considerable nonmonetary information. Monetary information is an important part of managerial decisions, and nonmonetary information plays a crucial role, especially when monetary effects are difficult to measure. Common examples of nonmonetary information are the quality and delivery criteria of purchasing decisions.

Managerial Decision Making

The previous section emphasized differences between financial and managerial accounting, but they are not entirely separate. Similar information is useful to both external and internal users. For instance, information about costs of manufacturing products is useful to all users in making decisions. Also, both financial and managerial accounting affect peoples' actions. For example, **Trek**'s design of a sales compensation plan affects the behavior of its salesforce. It also must estimate the dual effects of promotion and sales compensation plans on buying patterns of customers. These estimates impact the equipment purchase decisions for manufacturing and can affect the supplier selection criteria established by purchasing. Thus, financial and managerial accounting systems do more than measure; they also affect people's decisions and actions.

Managerial Accounting in Business

We have explained the importance of managerial accounting for internal decision making. Although the analytical tools and techniques of managerial accounting have always been useful, their relevance and importance continue to increase. This is so because of changes in the business environment. This section describes some of these changes and their impact on managerial accounting.

C2   Describe the lean business model.

Lean Business Model   Two important factors have encouraged companies to be more effective and efficient in running their operations. First, there is an increased emphasis on *customers* as the most important constituent of a business. Customers expect to derive a certain value for the money they spend to buy products and services. Specifically, they expect that their suppliers will offer them the right service (or product) at the right time and the right price. This implies that companies accept the notion of **customer orientation,** which means that employees understand the changing needs and wants of their customers and align their management and operating practices accordingly.

Second, our *global economy* expands competitive boundaries, thereby providing customers more choices. The global economy also produces changes in business activities. One notable case that reflects these changes in customer demand and global competition is auto manufacturing. The top three Japanese auto manufacturers (**Honda**, **Nissan**, and **Toyota**) once controlled more than 40% of the U.S. auto market. Customers perceived that Japanese auto manufacturers provided value not available from other manufacturers. Many European and North American auto manufacturers responded to this challenge and regained much of the lost market share.

Companies must be alert to these and other factors. Many companies have responded by adopting the **lean business model,** whose goal is to *eliminate waste* while "satisfying the customer" and "providing a positive return" to the company.

Lean Practices   **Continuous improvement** rejects the notions of "good enough" or "acceptable" and challenges employees and managers to continuously experiment with new and improved business practices. This has led companies to adopt practices such as total quality management (TQM) and just-in-time (JIT) manufacturing. The philosophy underlying both practices is continuous improvement; the difference is in the focus.

Point: Goals of a TQM process include reduced waste, better inventory control, fewer defects, and continuous improvement. Just-in-time concepts have similar goals.

Total quality management focuses on quality improvement and applies this standard to all aspects of business activities. In doing so, managers and employees seek to uncover waste in business activities including accounting activities such as payroll and disbursements. To encourage an emphasis on quality, the U.S. Congress established the Malcolm Baldrige National Quality Award (MBQNA). Entrants must conduct a thorough analysis and evaluation of their business using guidelines from the Baldrige committee. **Ritz Carlton Hotel** is a recipient of the Baldrige award in the service category. The company applies a core set of values, collectively called *The Gold Standards,* to improve customer service.

Point: The time between buying raw materials and selling finished goods is called *throughput time.*

Just-in-time manufacturing is a system that acquires inventory and produces only when needed. An important aspect of JIT is that companies manufacture products only after they receive an order (a *demand-pull* system) and then deliver the customer's requirements on time. This means that processes must be aligned to eliminate any delays and inefficiencies including inferior inputs and outputs. Companies must also establish good relations and communications with their suppliers. On the downside, JIT is more susceptible to disruption than traditional systems. As one example, several **General Motors** plants were temporarily shut down due to a strike at an assembly division; the plants supplied components *just in time* to the assembly division.

Point: Many industries can benefit from a JIT system.

Implications for Managerial Accounting   Adopting the lean business model can be challenging because to foster its implementation, all systems and procedures that a company follows must be realigned. Managerial accounting has an important role to play by providing accurate cost and performance information. Companies must understand the nature and sources of cost and must develop systems that capture costs accurately. Developing such a system is important to measuring the "value" provided to customers. The price that customers pay for acquiring goods and services is an important determinant of value. In turn, the costs a company incurs are key determinants of price. All else being equal, the better a company is at controlling its costs, the better its performance.

Managerial Cost Concepts

An organization incurs many different types of costs that are classified differently, depending on management needs (different costs for different purposes). We can classify costs on the basis of their (1) behavior, (2) traceability, (3) controllability, (4) relevance, and (5) function. This section explains each concept for assigning costs to products and services.

C3 Describe accounting concepts useful in classifying costs.

Types of Cost Classifications

Classification by Behavior At a basic level, a cost can be classified as fixed or variable. A **fixed cost** does not change with changes in the volume of activity (within a range of activity known as an activity's *relevant range*). For example, straight-line depreciation on equipment is a fixed cost. A **variable cost** changes in proportion to changes in the volume of activity. Sales commissions computed as a percent of sales revenue are variable costs. Additional examples of fixed and variable costs for a bike manufacturer are provided in Exhibit 18.5. When cost items are combined, total cost can be fixed, variable, or mixed. *Mixed* refers to a combination of fixed and variable costs. Equipment rental often includes a fixed cost for some minimum amount and a variable cost based on amount of usage. Classification of costs by behavior is helpful in cost-volume-profit analyses and short-term decision making. We discuss these in Chapters 22 and 25.

Topic Tackler PLUS
18-1

Exhibit 18.5

Fixed and Variable Costs

Fixed Cost: Rent for Rocky Mountain Bikes' building is $22,000, and doesn't change with the number of bikes produced.

Variable Cost: Cost of bicycle tires is variable with the number of bikes produced—this cost is $15 per pair.

Classification by Traceability A cost is often traced to a **cost object,** which is a product, process, department, or customer to which costs are assigned. **Direct costs** are those traceable to a single cost object. For example, if a product is a cost object, its material and labor costs are usually directly traceable. **Indirect costs** are those that cannot be traced to a single cost object. An example of an indirect cost is a maintenance plan that benefits two or more departments. Exhibit 18.6 identifies examples of both direct and indirect costs for the maintenance department in a manufacturing plant. Classification of costs by traceability is useful for cost allocation. This is discussed in Chapter 21.

Exhibit 18.6

Direct and Indirect Costs of a Maintenance Department

Direct Costs
- Salaries of maintenance department employees
- Equipment purchased by maintenance department
- Materials purchased by maintenance department
- Maintenance department equipment depreciation

Indirect Costs
- Factory accounting
- Factory administration
- Factory rent
- Factory managers' salary
- Factory light and heat
- Factory internal audit
- Factory intranet

Decision Maker   Answer—p. 741

Entrepreneur   You wish to trace as many of your assembly department's direct costs as possible. You can trace 90% of them in an economical manner. To trace the other 10%, you need sophisticated and costly accounting software. Do you purchase this software?

Exhibit 18.7

Controllability of Costs

Senior Manager
Controls costs of investment in land, buildings, and equipment.

Supervisor
Controls daily expenses such as supplies, maintenance, and overtime.

Point: Opportunity costs are not recorded by the accounting system.

Decision Maker   Answer—p. 741

Purchase Manager   You are evaluating two potential suppliers of seats for the manufacturing of motorcycles. One supplier (A) quotes a $145 price per seat and ensures 100% quality standards and on-time delivery. The second supplier (B) quotes a $115 price per seat but does not give any written assurances on quality or delivery. You decide to contract with the second supplier (B), saving $30 per seat. Does this decision have opportunity costs?

C4   Define product and period costs and explain how they impact financial statements.

Point: Only costs of production and purchases are classed as product costs.

Point: Product costs are either in the income statement as part of cost of goods sold or in the balance sheet as inventory. Period costs appear only on the income statement under operating expenses. See Exhibit 18.8.

Classification by Controllability   A cost can be defined as **controllable** or **not controllable.** Whether a cost is controllable or not depends on the employee's responsibilities, as shown in Exhibit 18.7. This is referred to as *hierarchical levels* in management, or *pecking order.* For example, investments in machinery are controllable by upper-level managers but not lower-level managers. Many daily operating expenses such as overtime often are controllable by lower-level managers. Classification of costs by controllability is especially useful for assigning responsibility to and evaluating managers.

Classification by Relevance   A cost can be classified by relevance by identifying it as either a sunk cost or an out-of-pocket cost. A **sunk cost** has already been incurred and cannot be avoided or changed. It is irrelevant to future decisions. One example is the cost of a company's office equipment previously purchased. An **out-of-pocket cost** requires a future outlay of cash and is relevant for decision making. Future purchases of equipment involve out-of-pocket costs. A discussion of relevant costs must also consider opportunity costs. An **opportunity cost** is the potential benefit lost by choosing a specific action from two or more alternatives. One example is a student giving up wages from a job to attend evening classes. Consideration of opportunity cost is important when, for example, an insurance company must decide whether to outsource its payroll function or maintain it internally. This is discussed in Chapter 25.

Classification by Function   Another cost classification (for manufacturers) is capitalization as inventory or to expense as incurred. Costs capitalized as inventory are called **product costs,** which refer to expenditures necessary and integral to finished products. They include direct materials, direct labor, and indirect manufacturing costs called *overhead costs*. Product costs pertain to activities carried out to manufacture the product. Costs expensed are called **period costs,** which refer to expenditures identified more with a time period than with finished products. They include selling and general administrative expenses. Period costs pertain to activities that are not part of the manufacturing process. A distinction between product and period costs is important because period costs are expensed in the income statement and product costs are assigned to inventory on the balance sheet until that inventory is sold. An ability to understand and identify product costs and period costs is crucial to using and interpreting a *manufacturing statement* described later in this chapter.

Exhibit 18.8 shows the different effects of product and period costs. Period costs flow directly to the current income statement as expenses. They are not reported as assets. Product costs are first assigned to inventory. Their final treatment depends on when inventory is sold or disposed of. Product costs assigned to finished goods that are sold in year 2007 are reported on the 2007 income statement as part of cost of goods sold. Product costs assigned to unsold inventory are carried forward on the balance sheet at the end of year 2007. If this inventory is sold in year 2008, product costs assigned to it are reported as part of cost of goods sold in that year's income statement.

The difference between period and product costs explains why the year 2007 income statement does not report operating expenses related to either factory workers' wages or depreciation on factory buildings and equipment. Instead, both costs are combined with the cost of raw materials to compute the product cost of finished goods. A portion of these manufacturing costs

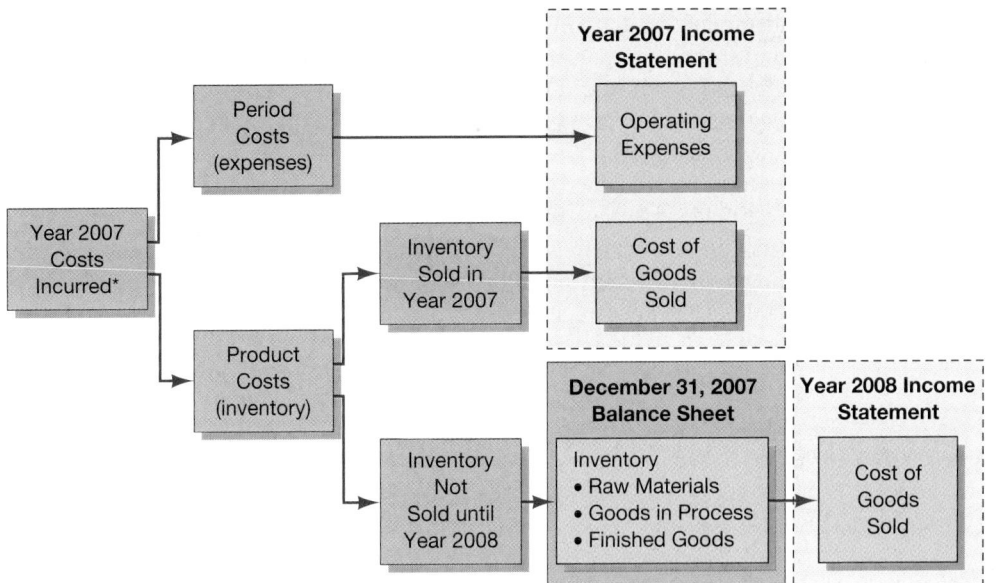

Exhibit 18.8

Period and Product Costs in Financial Statements

* This diagram excludes costs to acquire assets other than inventory.

(related to the goods sold) is reported in the year 2007 income statement as part of Cost of Goods Sold. The other portion is reported on the balance sheet at the end of that year as part of Inventory. The portion assigned to inventory could be included in any or all of raw materials, goods in process, or finished goods inventories.

Point: For a team approach to identifying period and product costs, see *Teamwork in Action* in the *Beyond the Numbers* section.

Identification of Cost Classification

It is important to understand that a cost can be classified using any one (or combination) of the five different means described here. To do this we must understand costs and operations. Specifically, for the five classifications, we must be able to identify the *activity* for behavior, *cost object* for traceability, *management hierarchical level* for controllability, *opportunity cost* for relevance, and *benefit period* for function. Factory rent, for instance, can be classified as a product cost; it is fixed with respect to number of units produced, it is indirect with respect to the product, and it is not controllable by a production supervisor. Potential multiple classifications are shown in Exhibit 18.9 using different cost items incurred in manufacturing mountain bikes. The finished bike is the cost object. Proper allocation of these costs and the managerial decisions based on cost data depend on a correct cost classification.

Point: All expenses of service companies are period costs because these companies do not have inventory.

Cost Item	By Behavior	By Traceability	By Function
Bicycle tires	Variable	Direct	Product
Wages of assembly worker*	Variable	Direct	Product
Advertising	Fixed	Indirect	Period
Production manager's salary	Fixed	Indirect	Product
Office depreciation	Fixed	Indirect	Period

Exhibit 18.9

Examples of Multiple Cost Classifications

* Although an assembly worker's wages are classified as variable costs, their actual behavior depends on how workers are paid and whether their wages are based on a union contract (such as piece rate or monthly wages).

Cost Concepts for Service Companies

The cost concepts described are generally applicable to service organizations. For example, consider **Southwest Airlines.** Its cost of beverages for passengers is a variable cost based on number of passengers. The cost of leasing an aircraft is fixed with respect to number of

Service Costs

- Beverages and snacks
- Cleaning fees
- Pilot and co-pilot salaries
- Attendant salaries
- Fuel and oil costs
- Travel agent fees
- Ground crew salaries

passengers. We can also trace a flight crew's salary to a specific flight whereas we likely cannot trace wages for the ground crew to a specific flight. Classification by function (such as product versus period costs) is not relevant to service companies because services are not inventoried. Instead, costs incurred by a service firm are expensed in the reporting period when incurred.

Managers in service companies must understand and apply cost concepts. They seek and rely on accurate cost estimates for many decisions. For example, an airline manager must often decide between canceling or rerouting flights. The manager must also be able to estimate costs saved by canceling a flight versus rerouting. Knowledge of fixed costs is equally important. We explain more about the cost requirements for these and other managerial decisions in Chapter 25.

Quick Check
Answers—p. 741

5. Which type of cost behavior increases total costs when volume of activity increases?

6. How could traceability of costs improve managerial decisions?

Reporting Manufacturing Activities

Companies with manufacturing activities differ from both merchandising and service companies. The main difference between merchandising and manufacturing companies is that merchandisers buy goods ready for sale while manufacturers produce goods from materials and labor. **Payless** is an example of a merchandising company. It buys and sells shoes without physically changing them. **Adidas** is primarily a manufacturer of shoes, apparel, and accessories. It purchases materials such as leather, cloth, dye, plastic, rubber, glue, and laces and then uses employees' labor to convert these materials to products. **Southwest Airlines** is a service company that transports people and items.

Manufacturing activities differ from both selling merchandise and providing services. Also, the financial statements for manufacturing companies differ slightly. This section considers some of these differences and compares them to accounting for a merchandising company.

Manufacturer's Balance Sheet

C5 Explain how balance sheets and income statements for manufacturing and merchandising companies differ.

Manufacturers carry several unique assets and usually have three inventories instead of the single inventory that merchandisers carry. Exhibit 18.10 shows three different inventories in the current asset section of the balance sheet for Rocky Mountain Bikes, a manufacturer. The three inventories are raw materials, goods in process, and finished goods.

Raw Materials Inventory   **Raw materials inventory** refers to the goods a company acquires to use in making products. It uses raw materials in two ways: directly and indirectly. Most raw materials physically become part of a product and are identified with specific units or batches of a product. Raw materials used directly in a product are called *direct materials*. Other materials used to support production processes are sometimes not as clearly identified with specific units or batches of product. These materials are called **indirect materials** be-

Point: Reducing the size of inventories saves storage costs and frees money for other uses.

cause they are not clearly identified with specific product units or batches. Items used as indirect materials often appear on a balance sheet as factory supplies or are included in raw materials. Some direct materials are classified as indirect materials when their costs are low (insignificant). Examples include screws and nuts used in assembling mountain bikes and staples and glue used in manufacturing shoes. Using the *materiality principle,* individually tracing the costs of each of these materials and classifying them separately as direct materials does not make much economic sense. For

Inventories of Rocky Mountain Bikes

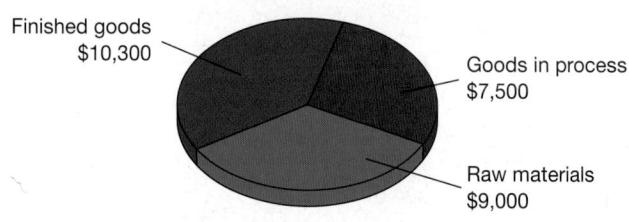

Finished goods
$10,300

Goods in process
$7,500

Raw materials
$9,000

Exhibit 18.10

Balance Sheet for a Manufacturer

ROCKY MOUNTAIN BIKES			
Balance Sheet			
December 31, 2008			
Assets		**Liabilities and Equity**	
Current assets		Current liabilities	
Cash	$ 11,000	Accounts payable	$ 14,000
Accounts receivable, net	30,150	Wages payable	540
Raw materials inventory	**9,000**	Interest payable	2,000
Goods in process inventory	**7,500**	Income taxes payable	32,600
Finished goods inventory	**10,300**	Total current liabilities	49,140
Factory supplies	350	Long-term liabilities	
Prepaid insurance	300	Long-term notes payable	50,000
Total current assets	68,600	Total liabilities	99,140
Plant assets			
Small tools	1,100	Stockholders' equity	
Delivery equipment, net	5,000	Common stock, $1.2 par	24,000
Office equipment, net	1,300	Paid-in capital	76,000
Factory machinery, net	65,500	Retained earnings	49,760
Factory building, net	86,700	Total stockholders' equity	149,760
Land	9,500	Total liabilities and equity	$248,900
Total plant assets, net	169,100		
Intangible assets (patents), net	11,200		
Total assets	$248,900		

instance, keeping detailed records of the amount of glue used to manufacture one shoe is not cost beneficial.

Goods in Process Inventory   Another inventory held by manufacturers is **goods in process inventory,** also called *work in process inventory.* It consists of products in the process of being manufactured but not yet complete. The amount of goods in process inventory depends on the type of production process. If the time required to produce a unit of product is short, the goods in process inventory is likely small, but if weeks or months are needed to produce a unit, the goods in process inventory is usually larger.

Finished Goods Inventory   A third inventory owned by a manufacturer is **finished goods inventory,** which consists of completed products ready for sale. This inventory is similar to merchandise inventory owned by a merchandising company. Manufacturers also often own unique plant assets such as small tools, factory buildings, factory equipment, and patents to manufacture products. The balance sheet in Exhibit 18.10 shows that Rocky Mountain Bikes owns all of these assets. Some manufacturers invest millions or even billions of dollars in production facilities and patents. **Briggs & Stratton's** recent balance sheet shows about $500 million net investment in land, buildings, machinery and equipment, much of which involves production facilities. It manufactures more racing engines than any other company in the world.

Manufacturer's Income Statement

The main difference between the income statement of a manufacturer and that of a merchandiser involves the items making up cost of goods sold. Exhibit 18.11 compares the components of cost of goods sold for a manufacturer and a merchandiser. A merchandiser adds cost of

Exhibit 18.11

Cost of Goods Sold
Computation

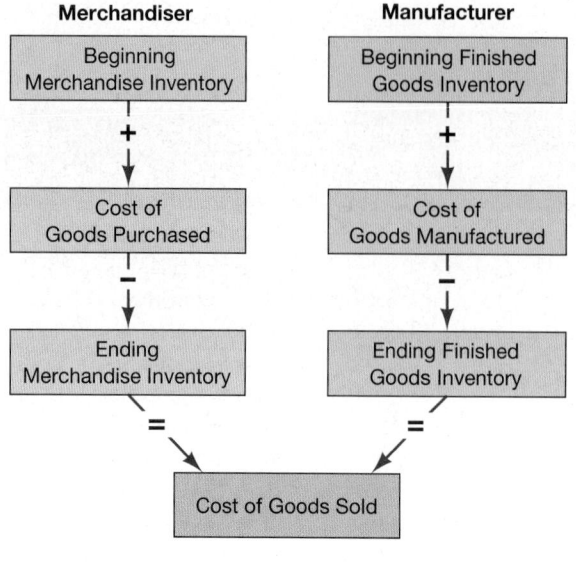

goods purchased to beginning merchandise inventory and then subtracts ending merchandise inventory to get cost of goods sold. A manufacturer adds cost of goods manufactured to beginning finished goods inventory and then subtracts ending finished goods inventory to get cost of goods sold.

A merchandiser often uses the term *merchandise* inventory; a manufacturer often uses the term *finished goods* inventory. A manufacturer's inventories of raw materials and goods in process are not included in finished goods because they are not available for sale. A manufacturer also shows cost of goods *manufactured* instead of cost of goods *purchased.* This difference occurs because a manufacturer produces its goods instead of purchasing them ready for sale. We show later in this chapter how to derive cost of goods manufactured from the manufacturing statement.

P1   Compute cost of goods sold for a manufacturer.

The Cost of Goods Sold section for both a merchandiser (Tele-Mart) and a manufacturer (Rocky Mountain Bikes) is shown in Exhibit 18.12 to highlight these differences. The remaining income statement sections are similar.

Exhibit 18.12

Cost of Goods Sold for a
Merchandiser and Manufacturer

Merchandising Company		Manufacturing Company	
Cost of goods sold		Cost of goods sold	
Beginning *merchandise* inventory	$ 14,200	**Beginning *finished goods* inventory**	$ 11,200
Cost of merchandise *purchased*	234,150	**Cost of goods *manufactured***	170,500
Goods available for sale	248,350	Goods available for sale	181,700
Less ending *merchandise* inventory	12,100	**Less ending *finished goods* inventory**	10,300
Cost of goods sold	$236,250	Cost of goods sold	$171,400

* Cost of goods manufactured is reported in the income statement of Exhibit 18.14.

18-2

Although the cost of goods sold computations are similar, the numbers in these computations reflect different activities. A merchandiser's cost of goods purchased is the cost of buying products to be sold. A manufacturer's cost of goods manufactured is the sum of direct materials, direct labor, and factory overhead costs incurred in producing products. The remainder of this section further explains these three manufacturing costs and describes prime and conversion costs.

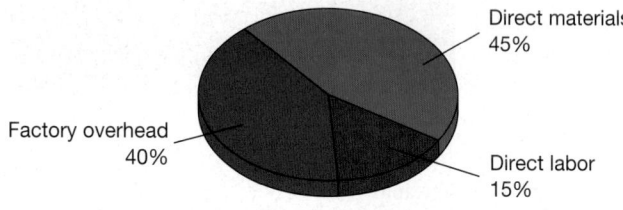

Direct Materials   **Direct materials** are tangible components of a finished product. **Direct material costs** are the expenditures for direct materials that are separately and readily traced through the manufacturing process to finished goods. Examples of direct materials in manufacturing a mountain bike include its tires, seat, frame, pedals, brakes, cables, gears, and handlebars. The chart in the margin shows that direct materials generally make up about 45% of manufacturing costs in today's products, but this amount varies across industries and companies.

Direct Labor **Direct labor** refers to the efforts of employees who physically convert materials to finished product. **Direct labor costs** are the wages and salaries for direct labor that are separately and readily traced through the manufacturing process to finished goods. Examples of direct labor in manufacturing a mountain bike include operators directly involved in converting raw materials into finished products (welding, painting, forming) and assembly workers who attach materials such as tires, seats, pedals, and brakes to the bike frames. Costs of other workers on the assembly line who assist direct laborers are classified as **indirect labor costs**. **Indirect labor** refers to manufacturing workers' efforts not linked to specific units or batches of the product.

Point: Indirect labor costs are part of factory overhead.

Factory Overhead **Factory overhead** consists of all manufacturing costs that are not direct materials or direct labor. **Factory overhead costs** cannot be separately or readily traced to finished goods. These costs include indirect materials and indirect labor, costs not directly traceable to the product. Overtime paid to direct laborers is also included in overhead because overtime is due to delays, interruptions, or constraints not necessarily identifiable to a specific product or batches of product. Factory overhead costs also include maintenance of the mountain bike factory, supervision of its employees, repairing manufacturing equipment, factory utilities (water, gas, electricity), production manager's salary, factory rent, depreciation on factory buildings and equipment, factory insurance, property taxes on factory buildings and equipment, and factory accounting and legal services. Factory overhead does *not* include selling and administrative expenses because they are not incurred in manufacturing products. These expenses are called *period costs* and are recorded as expenses on the income statement when incurred.

Point: Factory overhead is also called *manufacturing overhead.*

Prime and Conversion Costs Direct material costs and direct labor costs are also called **prime costs**—expenditures directly associated with the manufacture of finished goods. Direct labor costs and overhead costs are called **conversion costs**—expenditures incurred in the process of converting raw materials to finished goods. Direct labor costs are considered both prime costs and conversion costs. Exhibit 18.13 conveys the relation between prime and conversion costs and their components of direct material, direct labor, and factory overhead.

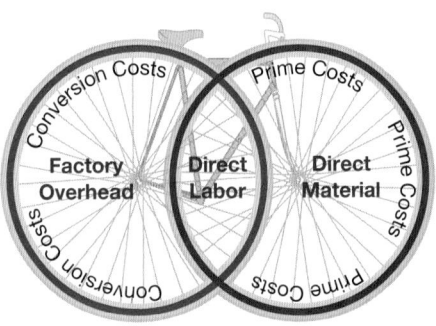

Exhibit 18.13

Prime and Conversion Costs and Their Makeup

Point: Prime costs = Direct materials + Direct labor. Conversion costs = Direct labor + Factory overhead.

Reporting Performance Exhibit 18.14 shows the income statement for Rocky Mountain Bikes. Its operating expenses include sales salaries, office salaries, and depreciation of delivery and office equipment. Operating expenses do not include manufacturing costs such as factory workers' wages and depreciation of production equipment and the factory buildings. These manufacturing costs are reported as part of cost of goods manufactured and included in cost of goods sold. We explained why and how this is done in the section Classification by Function.

Point: Manufacturers treat costs such as depreciation and rent as product costs if they are related to manufacturing.

Quick Check	Answers—p. 741

7. What are the three types of inventory on a manufacturing company's balance sheet?

8. How does cost of goods sold differ for merchandising versus manufacturing companies?

Exhibit 18.14

Income Statement for a
Manufacturer

ROCKY MOUNTAIN BIKES		
Income Statement		
For Year Ended December 31, 2008		
Sales		$310,000
Cost of goods sold		
Finished goods inventory, Dec. 31, 2007	$ 11,200	
Cost of goods manufactured	**170,500**	
Goods available for sale	181,700	
Less finished goods inventory, Dec. 31, 2008	10,300	
Cost of goods sold		171,400
Gross profit		138,600
Operating expenses		
Selling expenses		
Sales salaries expense	18,000	
Advertising expense	5,500	
Delivery wages expense	12,000	
Shipping supplies expense	250	
Insurance expense—Delivery equipment	300	
Depreciation expense—Delivery equipment	2,100	
Total selling expenses		38,150
General and administrative expenses		
Office salaries expense	15,700	
Miscellaneous expense	200	
Bad debts expense	1,550	
Office supplies expense	100	
Depreciation expense—Office equipment	200	
Interest expense	4,000	
Total general and administrative expenses		21,750
Total operating expenses		59,900
Income before income taxes		78,700
Income taxes expense		32,600
Net income		$ 46,100
Net income per common share (20,000 shares)		$ 2.31

Flow of Manufacturing Activities

C6 Explain manufacturing
activities and the flow of
manufacturing costs.

To understand manufacturing and its reports, we must first understand the flow of manufacturing activities and costs. Exhibit 18.15 shows the flow of manufacturing activities for a manufacturer. This exhibit has three important sections: *materials activity, production activity,* and *sales activity.* We explain each activity in this section.

Materials Activity The far left side of Exhibit 18.15 shows the flow of raw materials. Manufacturers usually start a period with some beginning raw materials inventory carried over from the previous period. The company then acquires additional raw materials in the current period. Adding these purchases to beginning inventory gives total raw materials available for use in production. These raw materials are then either used in production in the current period or remain in inventory at the end of the period for use in future periods.

Production Activity The middle section of Exhibit 18.15 describes production activity. Four factors come together in production: beginning goods in process inventory, direct materials, direct labor, and overhead. Beginning goods in process inventory consists of partly assembled products from the previous period. Production activity results in products that are either finished or remain unfinished. The cost of finished products makes up the cost of goods manufactured for the current period. Unfinished products are identified as ending goods in

Point: Knowledge of managerial accounting provides us a means of measuring manufacturing costs and is a sound foundation for studying advanced business topics.

Point: The series of activities that add value to a company's products or services is called a **value chain.**

Exhibit 18.15

Activities and Cost Flows in Manufacturing

process inventory. The cost of unfinished products consists of direct materials, direct labor, and factory overhead, and is reported on the current period's balance sheet. The costs of both finished goods manufactured and goods in process are *product costs.*

Sales Activity The company's sales activity is portrayed in the far right side of Exhibit 18.15. Newly completed units are combined with beginning finished goods inventory to make up total finished goods available for sale in the current period. The cost of finished products sold is reported on the income statement as cost of goods sold. The cost of products not sold is reported on the current period's balance sheet as ending finished goods inventory.

Manufacturing Statement

A company's manufacturing activities are described in a **manufacturing statement,** also called the *schedule of manufacturing activities* or the *schedule of cost of goods manufactured.* The manufacturing statement summarizes the types and amounts of costs incurred in a company's manufacturing process. Exhibit 18.16 shows the manufacturing statement for Rocky Mountain Bikes. The statement is divided into four parts: *direct materials, direct labor, overhead,* and *computation of cost of goods manufactured.* We describe each of these parts in this section.

P2 Prepare a manufacturing statement and explain its purpose and links to financial statements.

① The manufacturing statement begins by computing direct materials used. We start by adding beginning raw materials inventory of $8,000 to the current period's purchases of $86,500. This yields $94,500 of total raw materials available for use. A physical count of inventory shows $9,000 of ending raw materials inventory. This implies a total cost of raw materials used during the period of $85,500 ($94,500 total raw materials available for use − $9,000 ending inventory). (*Note:* All raw materials are direct materials for Rocky Mountain Bikes.)

② The second part of the manufacturing statement reports direct labor costs. Rocky Mountain Bikes had total direct labor costs of $60,000 for the period. This amount includes payroll taxes and fringe benefits.

"My boss wants us to appeal to a younger and hipper crowd. So, I'd like to get a tattoo that says-- 'Accounting rules!'"

Exhibit 18.16

Manufacturing Statement

ROCKY MOUNTAIN BIKES
Manufacturing Statement
For Year Ended December 31, 2008

Direct materials			
①	Raw materials inventory, Dec. 31, 2007	$ 8,000	
	Raw materials purchases	86,500	
	Raw materials available for use	94,500	
	Less raw materials inventory, Dec. 31, 2008	9,000	
	Direct materials used		$ 85,500
② {	**Direct labor**		60,000
	Factory overhead		
③	Indirect labor	9,000	
	Factory supervision	6,000	
	Factory utilities	2,600	
	Repairs—Factory equipment	2,500	
	Property taxes—Factory building	1,900	
	Factory supplies used	600	
	Factory insurance expired	1,100	
	Small tools written off	200	
	Depreciation expense—Factory equipment	3,500	
	Depreciation expense—Factory building	1,800	
	Amortization expense—Patents	800	
	Total factory overhead		30,000
④	Total manufacturing costs		175,500
	Add goods in process inventory, Dec. 31, 2007		2,500
	Total cost of goods in process		178,000
	Less goods in process inventory, Dec. 31, 2008		7,500
	Cost of goods manufactured		$170,500

Point: Direct material and direct labor costs increase with increases in production volume and are called *variable costs*. Overhead can be both variable and fixed. When overhead costs vary with production, they are called *variable overhead*. When overhead costs don't vary with production, they are called *fixed overhead*.

Point: Manufacturers sometimes report variable and fixed overhead separately in the manufacturing statement to provide more information to managers about cost behavior.

③ The third part of the manufacturing statement reports overhead costs. The statement lists each important factory overhead item and its cost. Total factory overhead cost for the period is $30,000. Some companies report only *total* factory overhead on the manufacturing statement and attach a separate schedule listing individual overhead costs.

④ The final section of the manufacturing statement computes and reports the *cost of goods manufactured*. (Total manufacturing costs for the period are $175,500 [$85,500 + $60,000 + $30,000], the sum of direct materials used and direct labor and overhead costs incurred.) This amount is first added to beginning goods in process inventory. This gives the total goods in process inventory of $178,000 ($175,500 + $2,500). We then compute the current period's cost of goods manufactured of $170,500 by taking the $178,000 total goods in process and subtracting the $7,500 cost of ending goods in process inventory that consists of direct materials, direct labor, and factory overhead. The cost of goods manufactured amount is also called *net cost of goods manufactured* or *cost of goods completed*. Exhibit 18.14 shows that this item and amount are listed in the Cost of Goods Sold section of Rocky Mountain Bikes' income statement.

A managerial accounting system records costs and reports them in various reports that eventually determine financial statements. Exhibit 18.17 shows how overhead costs flow through the system: from an initial listing of specific costs, to a section of the manufacturing statement, to the reporting on the income statement.

Management uses information in the manufacturing statement to plan and control the company's manufacturing activities. To provide timely information for decision making, the statement is often prepared monthly, weekly, or even daily. In anticipation of its Xbox 360 release, **Microsoft** grew its finished goods inventories from $271 million in 2004 to $422 million in

Exhibit 18.17

Overhead Cost Flows across Accounting Reports

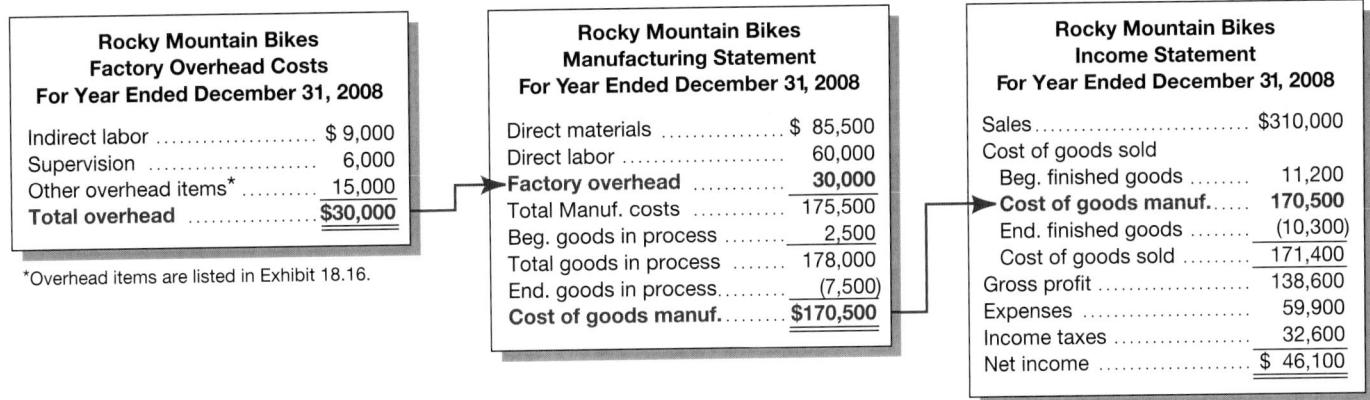

Rocky Mountain Bikes Factory Overhead Costs For Year Ended December 31, 2008	
Indirect labor	$ 9,000
Supervision	6,000
Other overhead items*	15,000
Total overhead	**$30,000**

*Overhead items are listed in Exhibit 18.16.

Rocky Mountain Bikes Manufacturing Statement For Year Ended December 31, 2008	
Direct materials	$ 85,500
Direct labor	60,000
Factory overhead	30,000
Total Manuf. costs	175,500
Beg. goods in process	2,500
Total goods in process	178,000
End. goods in process	(7,500)
Cost of goods manuf.	**$170,500**

Rocky Mountain Bikes Income Statement For Year Ended December 31, 2008	
Sales	$310,000
Cost of goods sold	
Beg. finished goods	11,200
Cost of goods manuf.	170,500
End. finished goods	(10,300)
Cost of goods sold	171,400
Gross profit	138,600
Expenses	59,900
Income taxes	32,600
Net income	$ 46,100

2005. The manufacturing statement contains information useful to external users but is not a general-purpose financial statement. Companies rarely publish the manufacturing statement because managers view this information as proprietary and potentially harmful to them if released to competitors.

Cycle Time and Cycle Efficiency   Decision Analysis

As lean manufacturing practices help companies move toward just-in-time manufacturing, it is important for these companies to reduce the time to manufacture their products and to improve manufacturing efficiency. One metric that measures that time element is **cycle time (CT)**. A definition of cycle time is in Exhibit 18.18.

A1 Compute cycle time and cycle efficiency, and explain their importance to production management.

Cycle time = Process time + Inspection time + Move time + Wait time

Exhibit 18.18
Cycle Time

Process time is the time spent producing the product. *Inspection time* is the time spent inspecting (1) raw materials when received, (2) goods in process while in production, and (3) finished goods prior to shipment. *Move time* is the time spent moving (1) raw materials from storage to production and (2) goods in process from factory location to another factory location. *Wait time* is the time that an order or job sits with no production applied to it; this can be due to order delays, bottlenecks in production, and poor scheduling.

Process time is considered **value-added time** because it is the only activity in cycle time that adds value to the product from the customer's perspective. The other three time activities are considered **non-value-added time** because they add no value to the customer.

Companies strive to reduce non-value-added time to improve **cycle efficiency (CE)**. Cycle efficiency is the ratio of value-added time to total cycle time—see Exhibit 18.19.

Exhibit 18.19

Cycle Efficiency

$$\text{Cycle efficiency} = \frac{\text{Value-added time}}{\text{Cycle time}}$$

To illustrate, assume that Rocky Mountain Bikes receives and produces an order for 500 Tracker® mountain bikes. Assume that the following times were measured during production of this order.

Process time	1.8 days
Inspection time	0.5 days
Move time	0.7 days
Wait time	3.0 days

In this case, cycle time is 6.0 days, computed as 1.8 days + 0.5 days + 0.7 days + 3.0 days. Also, cycle efficiency is 0.3, or 30%, computed as 1.8 days divided by 6.0 days. This means that Rocky Mountain Bikes spends 30% of its time working on the product (value-added time). The other 70% is spent on non-value-added activities.

If a company has a CE of 1, it means that its time is spent entirely on value-added activities. If the CE is low, the company should evaluate its production process to see if it can identify ways to reduce non-value-added activities. The 30% CE for Rocky Mountain Bikes is low and its management should look for ways to reduce non-value-added activities.

Demonstration Problem 1: Cost Behavior and Classification

Understanding the classification and assignment of costs is important. Consider a company that manufactures computer chips. It incurs the following costs in manufacturing chips and in operating the company.

1. Plastic board used to mount the chip, $3.50 each.
2. Assembly worker pay of $15 per hour to attach chips to plastic board.
3. Salary for factory maintenance workers who maintain factory equipment.
4. Factory supervisor pay of $55,000 per year to supervise employees.
5. Real estate taxes paid on the factory, $14,500.
6. Real estate taxes paid on the company office, $6,000.
7. Depreciation costs on machinery used by workers, $30,000.
8. Salary paid to the chief financial officer, $95,000.
9. Advertising costs of $7,800 paid to promote products.
10. Salespersons' commissions of $0.50 for each assembled chip sold.
11. Management has the option to rent the manufacturing plant to six local hospitals to store medical records instead of producing and assembling chips.

Classify each cost in the following table according to the categories listed in the table header. A cost can be classified under more than one category. For example, the plastic board used to mount chips is classified as a direct material product cost and as a direct unit cost.

	Period Costs	Product Costs			Unit Cost Classification		Sunk Cost	Opportunity Cost
Cost	Selling and Administrative	Direct Material (prime cost)	Direct Labor (prime and conversion)	Factory Overhead (conversion cost)	Direct	Indirect		
1. Plastic board used to mount the chip, $3.50 each		✔			✔			

Solution to Demonstration Problem 1

Cost*	Period Costs Selling and Administrative	Product Costs			Unit Cost Classification		Sunk Cost	Opportunity Cost
		Direct Material (prime cost)	Direct Labor (prime and conversion)	Factory Overhead (conversion cost)	Direct	Indirect		
1.		✔			✔			
2.			✔		✔			
3.				✔		✔		
4.				✔		✔		
5.				✔		✔		
6.	✔							
7.				✔		✔	✔	
8.	✔							
9.	✔							
10.	✔							
11.								✔

* Costs 1 through 11 refer to the 11 cost items described at the beginning of the problem.

Demonstration Problem 2: Reporting for Manufacturers

A manufacturing company's balance sheet and income statement differ from those for a merchandising or service company.

Required

1. Fill in the [BLANK] descriptors on the partial balance sheets for both the manufacturing company and the merchandising company. Explain why a different presentation is required.

Manufacturing Company

ADIDAS GROUP
Partial Balance Sheet
December 31, 2008

Current assets
Cash $10,000
[BLANK] 8,000
[BLANK] 5,000
[BLANK] 7,000
Supplies 500
Prepaid insurance 500
Total current assets $31,000

Merchandising Company

PAYLESS SHOE OUTLET
Partial Balance Sheet
December 31, 2008

Current assets
Cash .... $ 5,000
[BLANK] 12,000
Supplies 500
Prepaid insurance 500
Total current assets $18,000

2. Fill in the [BLANK] descriptors on the income statements for the manufacturing company and the merchandising company. Explain why a different presentation is required.

Manufacturing Company

ADIDAS GROUP
Partial Income Statement
For Year Ended December 31, 2008

Sales	$200,000
Cost of goods sold	
Finished goods inventory, Dec. 31, 2007	10,000
[BLANK]	120,000
Goods available for sale	130,000
Finished goods inventory, Dec. 31, 2008	(7,000)
Cost of goods sold	123,000
Gross profit	$ 77,000

Merchandising Company

PAYLESS SHOE OUTLET
Partial Income Statement
For Year Ended December 31, 2008

Sales	$190,000
Cost of goods sold	
Merchandise inventory, Dec. 31, 2007	8,000
[BLANK]	108,000
Goods available for sale	116,000
Merchandise inventory, Dec. 31, 2008	(12,000)
Cost of goods sold	104,000
Gross profit	$ 86,000

3. The manufacturer's cost of goods manufactured is the sum of (a) _____, (b) _____, and (c) _____ costs incurred in producing the product.

Solution to Demonstration Problem 2

1. Inventories for a manufacturer and for a merchandiser.

Manufacturing Company

ADIDAS GROUP
Partial Balance Sheet
December 31, 2008

Current assets	
Cash	$10,000
Raw materials inventory	8,000
Goods in process inventory	5,000
Finished goods inventory	7,000
Supplies	500
Prepaid insurance	500
Total current assets	$31,000

Merchandising Company

PAYLESS SHOE OUTLET
Partial Balance Sheet
December 31, 2008

Current assets	
Cash	$ 5,000
Merchandise inventory	12,000
Supplies	500
Prepaid insurance	500
Total current assets	$18,000

Explanation: A manufacturing company must control and measure three types of inventories: raw materials, goods in process, and finished goods. In the sequence of making a product, the raw materials move into production—called *goods in process inventory*—and then to finished goods. All raw materials and goods in process inventory at the end of each accounting period are considered current assets. All unsold finished inventory is considered a current asset at the end of each accounting period. The merchandising company must control and measure only one type of inventory, purchased goods.

2. Cost of goods sold for a manufacturer and for a merchandiser.

Manufacturing Company

ADIDAS GROUP
Partial Income Statement
For Year Ended December 31, 2008

Sales	$200,000
Cost of goods sold	
Finished goods inventory, Dec. 31, 2007	10,000
Cost of goods manufactured	120,000
Goods available for sale	130,000
Finished goods inventory, Dec. 31, 2008	(7,000)
Cost of goods sold	123,000
Gross profit	$ 77,000

Merchandising Company

PAYLESS SHOE OUTLET
Partial Income Statement
For Year Ended December 31, 2008

Sales	$190,000
Cost of goods sold	
Merchandise inventory, Dec. 31, 2007	8,000
Cost of purchases	108,000
Goods available for sale	116,000
Merchandise inventory, Dec. 31, 2008	(12,000)
Cost of goods sold	104,000
Gross profit	$ 86,000

Explanation: Manufacturing and merchandising companies use different reporting terms. In particular, the terms *finished goods* and *cost of goods manufactured* are used to reflect the production of goods, yet the concepts and techniques of reporting cost of goods sold for a manufacturing company and merchandising company are similar.

3. A manufacturer's cost of goods manufactured is the sum of (a) *direct material,* (b) *direct labor,* and (c) *factory overhead* costs incurred in producing the product.

Demonstration Problem 3: Manufacturing Statement

The following account balances and other information are from SUNN Corporation's accounting records for year-end December 31, 2008. Use this information to prepare (1) a table listing factory overhead costs, (2) a manufacturing statement (show only the total factory overhead cost), and (3) an income statement.

Advertising expense	$ 85,000	Goods in process inventory, Dec. 31, 2007	$ 8,000
Amortization expense—Patents	16,000	Goods in process inventory, Dec. 31, 2008	9,000
Bad debts expense	28,000	Income taxes	53,400
Depreciation expense—Office equipment	37,000	Indirect labor	26,000
Depreciation expense—Factory building	133,000	Interest expense	25,000
Depreciation expense—Factory equipment	78,000	Miscellaneous expense	55,000
Direct labor	250,000	Property taxes on factory equipment	14,000
Factory insurance expired	62,000	Raw materials inventory, Dec. 31, 2007	60,000
Factory supervision	74,000	Raw materials inventory, Dec. 31, 2008	78,000
Factory supplies used	21,000	Raw materials purchases	313,000
Factory utilities	115,000	Repairs expense—Factory equipment	31,000
Finished goods inventory, Dec. 31, 2007	15,000	Salaries expense	150,000
Finished goods inventory, Dec. 31, 2008	12,500	Sales	1,630,000

Planning the Solution

- Analyze the account balances and select those that are part of factory overhead costs.
- Arrange these costs in a table that lists factory overhead costs for the year.
- Analyze the remaining costs and select those related to production activity for the year; selected costs should include the materials and goods in process inventories and direct labor.
- Prepare a manufacturing statement for the year showing the calculation of the cost of materials used in production, the cost of direct labor, and the total factory overhead cost. When presenting overhead cost on this statement, report only total overhead cost from the table of overhead costs for the year. Show the costs of beginning and ending goods in process inventory to determine cost of goods manufactured.
- Organize the remaining revenue and expense items into the income statement for the year. Combine cost of goods manufactured from the manufacturing statement with the finished goods inventory amounts to compute cost of goods sold for the year.

Solution to Demonstration Problem 3

SUNN CORPORATION Factory Overhead Costs For Year Ended December 31, 2008	
Amortization expense—Patents	$ 16,000
Depreciation expense—Factory building	133,000
Depreciation expense—Factory equipment	78,000
Factory insurance expired	62,000
Factory supervision	74,000
Factory supplies used	21,000

SUNN CORPORATION Manufacturing Statement For Year Ended December 31, 2008		
Direct materials		
Raw materials inventory, Dec. 31, 2007		$ 60,000
Raw materials purchase		313,000
Raw materials available for use		373,000
Less raw materials inventory, Dec. 31, 2008		78,000
Direct materials used		295,000

[continued on next page]

[continued from previous page]

Factory utilities	115,000
Indirect labor	26,000
Property taxes on factory equipment	14,000
Repairs expense—Factory equipment	31,000
Total factory overhead	$570,000

Direct labor	250,000
Factory overhead	570,000
Total manufacturing costs	1,115,000
Goods in process inventory, Dec. 31, 2007	8,000
Total cost of goods in process	1,123,000
Less goods in process inventory, Dec. 31, 2008	9,000
Cost of goods manufactured	$1,114,000

SUNN CORPORATION
Income Statement
For Year Ended December 31, 2008

Sales		$1,630,000
Cost of goods sold		
Finished goods inventory, Dec. 31, 2007	$ 15,000	
Cost of goods manufactured	1,114,000	
Goods available for sale	1,129,000	
Less finished goods inventory, Dec. 31, 2008	12,500	
Cost of goods sold		1,116,500
Gross profit		513,500
Operating expenses		
Advertising expense	85,000	
Bad debts expense	28,000	
Depreciation expense—Office equipment	37,000	
Interest expense	25,000	
Miscellaneous expense	55,000	
Salaries expense	150,000	
Total operating expenses		380,000
Income before income taxes		133,500
Income taxes		53,400
Net income		$ 80,100

Summary

C1 Explain the purpose and nature of managerial accounting. The purpose of managerial accounting is to provide useful information to management and other internal decision makers. It does this by collecting, managing, and reporting both monetary and nonmonetary information in a manner useful to internal users. Major characteristics of managerial accounting include (1) focus on internal decision makers, (2) emphasis on planning and control, (3) flexibility, (4) timeliness, (5) reliance on forecasts and estimates, (6) focus on segments and projects, and (7) reporting both monetary and nonmonetary information.

C2 Describe the lean business model. The main purpose of the lean business model is the elimination of waste. Concepts such as total quality management and just-in-time production often aid in effective application of the model.

C3 Describe accounting concepts useful in classifying costs. We can classify costs on the basis of their (1) behavior—fixed vs. variable, (2) traceability—direct vs. indirect, (3) controllability—controllable vs. uncontrollable, (4) relevance—sunk vs. out of pocket, and (5) function—product vs. period. A cost can be classified in more than one way, depending on the purpose for which the cost is being determined. These classifications help to understand cost patterns, analyze performance, and plan operations.

C4 Define product and period costs and explain how they impact financial statements. Costs that are capitalized because they are expected to have future value are called *product costs;* costs that are expensed are called *period costs.* This classification is important because it affects the amount of costs expensed in the income statement and the amount of costs assigned to inventory on the balance sheet. Product costs are commonly made up of direct materials, direct labor, and overhead. Period costs include selling and administrative expenses.

C5 Explain how balance sheets and income statements for manufacturing and merchandising companies differ. The main difference is that manufacturers usually carry three inventories on their balance sheets—raw materials, goods in process, and finished goods—instead of one inventory that merchandisers carry. The main difference between income statements of manufacturers and merchandisers is the items making up cost of goods sold. A merchandiser adds beginning merchandise inventory to cost of goods purchased and then subtracts ending merchandise inventory to get cost of goods sold. A manufacturer adds beginning finished goods inventory to cost of goods manufactured and then subtracts ending finished goods inventory to get cost of goods sold.

C6 Explain manufacturing activities and the flow of manufacturing costs. Manufacturing activities consist of materials, production, and sales activities. The materials activity consists of the purchase and issuance of materials to production. The production activity consists of converting materials into finished goods. At this stage in the process, the materials, labor, and overhead costs have been incurred and the manufacturing statement is prepared. The sales activity consists of selling some or all of finished goods available for sale. At this stage, the cost of goods sold is determined.

A1 Compute cycle time and cycle efficiency, and explain their importance to production management. It is important for companies to reduce the time to produce their products and to

improve manufacturing efficiency. One measure of that time is cycle time (CT), defined as Process time + Inspection time + Move time + Wait time. Process time is value-added time, the others are non-value-added time. Cycle efficiency (CE) is the ratio of value-added time to total cycle time. If CE is low, management should evaluate its production process to see if it can reduce non-value-added activities.

P1 Compute cost of goods sold for a manufacturer. A manufacturer adds beginning finished goods inventory to cost of goods manufactured and then subtracts ending finished goods inventory to get cost of goods sold.

P2 Prepare a manufacturing statement and explain its purpose and links to financial statements. The manufacturing statement reports computation of cost of goods manufactured for the period. It begins by showing the period's costs for direct materials, direct labor, and overhead and then adjusts these numbers for the beginning and ending inventories of the goods in process to yield cost of goods manufactured.

Guidance Answers to **Decision Maker** and **Decision Ethics**

Production Manager   It appears that all three friends want to pay the bill with someone else's money. David is using money belonging to the tax authorities, Denise is taking money from her company, and Derek is defrauding the client. To prevent such practices, companies have internal audit mechanisms. Many companies also adopt ethical codes of conduct to help guide employees. We must recognize that some entertainment expenses are justifiable and even encouraged. For example, the tax law allows certain deductions for entertainment that have a business purpose. Corporate policies also sometimes allow and encourage reimbursable spending for social activities, and contracts can include entertainment as allowable costs. Nevertheless, without further details, payment for this bill should be made from personal accounts.

Entrepreneur   Tracing all costs directly to cost objects is always desirable, but you need to be able to do so in an economically feasible

manner. In this case, you are able to trace 90% of the assembly department's direct costs. It may not be economical to spend more money on a new software to trace the final 10% of costs. You need to make a cost-benefit trade-off. If the software offers benefits beyond tracing the remaining 10% of the assembly department's costs, your decision should consider this.

Purchase Manager   Opportunity costs relate to the potential quality and delivery benefits given up by not choosing supplier (A). Selecting supplier (B) might involve future costs of poor-quality seats (inspection, repairs, and returns). Also, potential delivery delays could interrupt work and increase manufacturing costs. Your company could also incur sales losses if the product quality of supplier (B) is low. As purchase manager, you are responsible for these costs and must consider them in making your decision.

Guidance Answers to **Quick Checks**

1. *d*

2. Financial accounting information is intended for users external to an organization such as investors, creditors, and government authorities. Managerial accounting focuses on providing information to managers, officers, and other decision makers within the organization.

3. No, GAAP do not control the practice of managerial accounting. Unlike external users, the internal users need managerial accounting information for planning and controlling business activities rather than for external comparison. Different types of information are required, depending on the activity. Therefore it is difficult to standardize managerial accounting.

4. Under TQM, all managers and employees should strive toward higher standards in their work and in the products and services they offer to customers.

5. Variable costs increase when volume of activity increases.

6. By being able to trace costs to cost objects (say, to products and departments), managers better understand the total costs

associated with a cost object. This is useful when managers consider making changes to the cost object (such as when dropping the product or expanding the department).

7. Raw materials inventory, goods in process inventory, and finished goods inventory.

8. The cost of goods sold for merchandising companies includes all costs of acquiring the merchandise; the cost of goods sold for manufacturing companies includes the three costs of manufacturing: direct materials, direct labor, and overhead.

9. *a*

10. No; companies rarely report a manufacturing statement.

11. Beginning goods in process inventory is added to total manufacturing costs to yield total goods in process. Ending goods in process inventory is subtracted from total goods in process to yield cost of goods manufactured for the period.

Key Terms   mhhe.com/wildFAP18e

Key Terms are available at the book's Website for learning and testing in an online Flashcard Format.

Continuous improvement (p. 724)
Control (p. 721)
Controllable or not controllable cost (p. 726)
Conversion costs (p. 731)
Cost object (p. 725)
Customer orientation (p. 723)
Cycle efficiency (CE) (p. 735)
Cycle time (CT) (p. 735)
Direct costs (p. 725)
Direct labor (p. 731)
Direct labor costs (p. 731)
Direct material (p. 730)
Direct material costs (p. 730)

Factory overhead (p. 731)
Factory overhead costs (p. 731)
Finished goods inventory (p. 729)
Fixed cost (p. 725)
Goods in process inventory (p. 729)
Indirect costs (p. 725)
Indirect labor (p. 731)
Indirect labor costs (p. 731)
Indirect material (p. 728)
Just-in-time (JIT) manufacturing (p. 724)
Lean business model (p. 724)
Managerial accounting (p. 720)
Manufacturing statement (p. 733)
Non-value-added time (p. 735)

Opportunity cost (p. 726)
Out-of-pocket cost (p. 726)
Period costs (p. 726)
Planning (p. 721)
Prime costs (p. 731)
Product costs (p. 726)
Raw materials inventory (p. 728)
Sunk cost (p. 726)
Total quality management (TQM) (p. 724)
Value-added time (p. 735)
Value chain (p. 732)
Variable cost (p.725)

Multiple Choice Quiz   Answers on p. 759   mhhe.com/wildFAP18e

Personal Interactive Quizzes A and B are available at the book's Website.

1. Continuous improvement
   a. Is used to reduce inventory levels.
   b. Is applicable only in service businesses.
   c. Rejects the notion of "good enough."
   d. Is used to reduce ordering costs.
   e. Is applicable only in manufacturing businesses.

2. A direct cost is one that is
   a. Variable with respect to the cost object.
   b. Traceable to the cost object.
   c. Fixed with respect to the cost object.
   d. Allocated to the cost object.
   e. A period cost.

3. Costs that are incurred as part of the manufacturing process, but are not clearly traceable to the specific unit of product or batches of product are called
   a. Period costs.
   b. Factory overhead.
   c. Sunk costs.
   d. Opportunity costs.
   e. Fixed costs.

4. The three major cost components of manufacturing a product are
   a. Direct materials, direct labor, and factory overhead.
   b. Period costs, product costs, and sunk costs.
   c. Indirect labor, indirect materials, and fixed expenses.
   d. Variable costs, fixed costs, and period costs.
   e. Opportunity costs, sunk costs, and direct costs.

5. A company reports the following for the current year.

Finished goods inventory, beginning year	$6,000
Finished goods inventory, ending year	3,200
Cost of goods sold	7,500

Its cost of goods manufactured for the current year is
   a. $1,500.
   b. $1,700.
   c. $7,500.
   d. $2,800.
   e. $4,700.

Discussion Questions

1. Describe the managerial accountant's role in business planning, control, and decision making.

2. Distinguish between managerial and financial accounting on
   a. Users and decision makers   **b.** Purpose of information

   c. Flexibility of practice   **e.** Focus of information
   d. Time dimension   **f.** Nature of information

3. Identify the usual changes that a company must make when it adopts a customer orientation.

4. Distinguish between direct material and indirect material.

5. Distinguish between direct labor and indirect labor.

6. Distinguish between (a) factory overhead and (b) selling and administrative overhead.

7. What product cost is listed as both a prime cost and a conversion cost?

8. Assume that you tour **Apple**'s factory where it makes its products. List three direct costs and three indirect costs that you are likely to see.

9. Should we evaluate a manager's performance on the basis of controllable or noncontrollable costs? Why?

10. Explain why knowledge of cost behavior is useful in product performance evaluation.

11. Explain why product costs are capitalized but period costs are expensed in the current accounting period.

12. Explain how business activities and inventories for a manufacturing company, a merchandising company, and a service company differ.

13. Why does managerial accounting often involve working with numerous predictions and estimates?

14. How do an income statement and a balance sheet for a manufacturing company and a merchandising company differ?

15. Besides inventories, what other assets often appear on manufacturers' balance sheets but not on merchandisers' balance sheets?

16. Why does a manufacturing company require three different inventory categories?

17. Manufacturing activities of a company are described in the _____. This statement summarizes the types and amounts of costs incurred in its manufacturing _____.

18. What are the three categories of manufacturing costs?

19. List several examples of factory overhead.

20. List the four components of a manufacturing statement and provide specific examples of each for **Apple**.

21. Prepare a proper title for the annual "manufacturing statement" of **Apple**. Does the date match the balance sheet or income statement? Why?

22. Describe the relations among the income statement, the manufacturing statement, and a detailed listing of factory overhead costs.

23. Define and describe *cycle time* and identify the components of cycle time.

24. Explain the difference between value-added time and non-value-added time.

25. Define and describe *cycle efficiency*.

26. Can management of a company such as **Best Buy** use cycle time and cycle efficiency as useful measures of performance? Explain.

27. Access **Anheuser-Busch**'s 2004 annual report (10-K) for fiscal year ended December 31, 2004, at the SEC's EDGAR database (**SEC.gov**) or its Website (**Anheuser-Busch.com**). From its balance sheet, identify the titles and amounts of its inventory components.

Red numbers denote Discussion Questions that involve decision-making.

Managerial accounting (choose one):

1. Provides information to aid management in planning and controlling business activities.

2. Provides information that is widely available to all interested parties.

3. Is directed at reporting aggregate data on the company as a whole.

4. Must follow generally accepted accounting principles.

QUICK STUDY

QS 18-1
Managerial accounting defined
C1

Identify whether each description most likely applies to managerial or financial accounting.

1. _____ It is directed at external users in making investment, credit, and other decisions.

2. _____ Its information is often available only after an audit is complete.

3. _____ Its primary focus is on the organization as a whole.

4. _____ Its principles and practices are very flexible.

5. _____ Its primary users are company managers.

QS 18-2
Managerial accounting versus financial accounting
C1

Match each lean business concept with its best description by entering its letter in the blank.

1. _____ Just-in-time manufacturing

2. _____ Continuous improvements

3. _____ Customer orientation

4. _____ Total quality management

A. Inventory is acquired or produced only as needed.

B. Flexible product designs can be modified to accommodate customer choices.

C. Every manager and employee constantly looks for ways to improve company operations.

D. Focuses on quality throughout the production process.

QS 18-3
Lean business concepts
C2

QS 18-4

Fixed and variable costs

C3

Which of these statements is true regarding fixed and variable costs?

1. Fixed costs stay the same and variable costs increase in total as activity volume increases.

2. Fixed costs increase and variable costs decrease in total as activity volume decreases.

3. Both fixed and variable costs stay the same in total as activity volume increases.

4. Both fixed and variable costs increase as activity volume increases.

QS 18-5

Direct and indirect costs

C3

Verdi Company produces sporting equipment, including leather footballs. Identify each of the following costs as direct or indirect if the cost object is a football produced by Verdi.

1. Electricity used in the production plant.

2. Labor used on the football production line.

3. Salary of manager who supervises the entire plant.

4. Depreciation on equipment used to produce footballs.

5. Leather used to produce footballs.

QS 18-6

Product and period costs

C4

Which of these statements is true regarding product and period costs?

1. Sales commission is a product cost and depreciation on factory equipment is a product cost.

2. Factory maintenance is a product cost and sales commission is a period cost.

3. Sales commission is a product cost and factory rent is a period cost.

4. Factory wages is a product cost and direct material is a period cost.

QS 18-7

Inventory reporting for manufacturers

C5

Three inventory categories are reported on a manufacturing company's balance sheet: (*a*) raw materials, (*b*) goods in process, and (*c*) finished goods. Identify the usual order in which these inventory items are reported on the balance sheet.

1. (*b*)(*c*)(*a*)   **2.** (*c*)(*b*)(*a*)   **3.** (*a*)(*b*)(*c*)   **4.** (*b*)(*a*)(*c*)

QS 18-8

Cost of goods sold   P1

A company has year-end cost of goods manufactured of $4,000, beginning finished goods inventory of $500, and ending finished goods inventory of $750. Its cost of goods sold is

1. $4,250   **2.** $4,000   **3.** $3,750   **4.** $3,900

QS 18-9

Manufacturing flows identified

C6

Identify the usual sequence of manufacturing activities by filling in the blank (1, 2, or 3) corresponding to its order: _____ Production activities; _____ Sales activities; _____ Materials activities.

QS 18-10

Cost of goods manufactured

P2

Prepare the manufacturing statement for Briton Company using the following information.

Direct materials	$190,500
Direct labor	63,150
Factory overhead costs	24,000
Goods in process, Dec. 31, 2007	157,600
Goods in process, Dec. 31, 2008	142,750

QS 18-11

Manufacturing cycle time and efficiency

A1

Compute and interpret (*a*) manufacturing cycle time and (*b*) manufacturing cycle efficiency using the following information.

Process time	15.0 hours
Inspection time	2.0 hours
Move time	6.5 hours
Wait time	36.5 hours

Compute cost of goods sold for year 2008 using the following information.

Finished goods inventory, Dec. 31, 2007	$345,000
Goods in process inventory, Dec. 31, 2007	83,500
Goods in process inventory, Dec. 31, 2008	72,300
Cost of goods manufactured, year 2008	918,700
Finished goods inventory, Dec. 31, 2008	283,600

QS 18-12
Cost of goods sold

P1

EXERCISES

Both managerial accounting and financial accounting provide useful information to decision makers. Indicate in the following chart the most likely source of information for each business decision (a decision can require major input from both sources).

Exercise 18-1
Sources of accounting information

C1

	Primary Information Source	
Business Decision	**Managerial**	**Financial**
Report financial performance to board of directors	_____	_____
Estimate product cost for a new line of shoes	_____	_____
Plan the budget for next quarter	_____	_____
Measure profitability of all individual stores	_____	_____
Prepare financial reports according to GAAP	_____	_____
Determine amount of dividends to pay stockholders	_____	_____
Determine location and size for a new plant	_____	_____
Evaluate a purchasing department's performance	_____	_____

Complete the following statements by filling in the blanks.

1. _____ is the process of setting goals and making plans to achieve them.

2. _____ is the process of monitoring planning decisions and evaluating an organization's activities and employees.

3. _____ _____ usually covers a period of 5 to 10 years.

4. _____ _____ usually covers a period of one year.

Exercise 18-2
Planning and control descriptions

C1

In the following chart, compare financial accounting and managerial accounting by describing how each differs for the items listed. Be specific in your responses.

Exercise 18-3
Characteristics of financial accounting and managerial accounting

C1

	Financial Accounting	**Managerial Accounting**
1. Users and decision makers	_____	_____
2. Purpose of information	_____	_____
3. Flexibility of practice	_____	_____
4. Timeliness of information	_____	_____
5. Time dimension	_____	_____
6. Focus of information	_____	_____
7. Nature of information	_____	_____

Customer orientation means that a company's managers and employees respond to customers' changing wants and needs. A manufacturer of plastic fasteners has created a customer satisfaction survey that it asks each of its customers to complete. The survey asks about the following factors: (A) lead time; (B) delivery; (C) price; (D) product performance. Each factor is to be rated as unsatisfactory, marginal, average, satisfactory, very satisfied.

Exercise 18-4
Customer orientation in practice

C2

a. Match the competitive forces 1 through 4 to the factors on the survey. A factor can be matched to more than one competitive force.

Survey Factor	Competitive Force
A. Lead time	_____ **1.** Time
B. Delivery	_____ **2.** Quality
C. Price	_____ **3.** Cost
D. Product performance	_____ **4.** Flexibility of service

b. How can managers of this company use the information from this customer satisfaction survey to better meet competitive forces and satisfy their customers?

Exercise 18-5
Management concepts

C2

Following are three separate events affecting the managerial accounting systems for different companies. Match the management concept(s) that the company is likely to adopt for the event identified. There is some overlap in the meaning of customer orientation and total quality management and, therefore, some responses can include more than one concept.

Event	Management Concept
_____ 1. The company starts reporting measures on customer complaints and product returns from customers.	a. Total quality management (TQM)
_____ 2. The company starts reporting measures such as the percent of defective products and the number of units scrapped.	b. Just-in-time (JIT) system
_____ 3. The company starts measuring inventory turnover and discontinues elaborate inventory records. Its new focus is to pull inventory through the system.	c. Continuous improvement (CI)
	d. Customer orientation (CO)

Exercise 18-6
Cost analysis and identification

C3   C4

Georgia Pacific, a manufacturer, incurs the following costs. (1) Classify each cost as either a product or a period cost. If a product cost, identify it as a prime and/or conversion cost. (2) Classify each product cost as either a direct cost or an indirect cost using the product as the cost object.

Cost	Product Cost		Period Cost	Direct Cost	Indirect Cost
	Prime	Conversion			
Direct materials used	_____	_____	_____	_____	_____
State and federal income taxes	_____	_____	_____	_____	_____
Payroll taxes for production supervisor	_____	_____	_____	_____	_____
Amortization of patents on factory machine	_____	_____	_____	_____	_____
Accident insurance on factory workers	_____	_____	_____	_____	_____
Wages to assembly workers	_____	_____	_____	_____	_____
Factory utilities	_____	_____	_____	_____	_____
Small tools used	_____	_____	_____	_____	_____
Bad debts expense	_____	_____	_____	_____	_____
Depreciation—Factory building	_____	_____	_____	_____	_____
Advertising	_____	_____	_____	_____	_____
Office supplies used	_____	_____	_____	_____	_____

Exercise 18-7
Cost classifications   C3

(1) Identify each of the five cost classifications discussed in the chapter. (2) List two purposes of identifying these separate cost classifications.

Exercise 18-8
Cost analysis and classification

C3

Listed here are product costs for the production of soccer balls. (1) Classify each cost (a) as either fixed or variable and (b) as either direct or indirect. (2) What pattern do you see regarding the relation between costs classified by behavior and costs classified by traceability?

Product Cost	Cost by Behavior		Cost by Traceability	
	Variable	Fixed	Direct	Indirect
Annual flat fee paid for office security	___	___		
Leather cover for soccer balls	___	___	___	___
Lace to hold leather together	___	___	___	___
Wages of assembly workers	___	___	___	___
Taxes on factory	___	___	___	___
Coolants for machinery	___	___	___	___
Machinery depreciation	___	___	___	___

Current assets for two different companies at calendar year-end 2008 are listed here. One is a manufacturer, Salomon Skis Mfg., and the other, Sun Fresh Foods, is a grocery distribution company. (1) Identify which set of numbers relates to the manufacturer and which to the merchandiser. (2) Prepare the current asset section for each company from this information. Discuss why the current asset section for these two companies is different.

Exercise 18-9
Balance sheet identification and preparation
C5

Account	Company 1	Company 2
Cash	$ 7,000	$ 5,000
Raw materials inventory	—	42,000
Merchandise inventory	45,000	—
Goods in process inventory	—	30,000
Finished goods inventory	—	50,000
Accounts receivable, net	62,000	75,000
Prepaid expenses	1,500	900

Compute cost of goods sold for each of these two companies for the year ended December 31, 2008.

Exercise 18-10
Cost of goods sold computation
C5   P1

	Viking Retail	Log Homes Manufacturing
1		
2		
3 Beginning inventory		
4 Merchandise	$275,000	
5 Finished goods		$450,000
6 Cost of purchases	500,000	
7 Cost of goods manufactured		900,000
8 Ending inventory		
9 Merchandise	115,000	
10 Finished goods		375,000
11		

Check   Viking COGS, $660,000

Using the following data, compute (1) the cost of goods manufactured and (2) the cost of goods sold for both Garcia Company and Culpepper Company.

Exercise 18-11
Cost of goods manufactured and cost of goods sold computation

P1   P2

	Garcia Company	Culpepper Company
Beginning finished goods inventory	$12,000	$16,450
Beginning goods in process inventory	14,500	19,950
Beginning raw materials inventory	7,250	9,000
Rental cost on factory equipment	27,000	22,750
Direct labor	19,000	35,000
Ending finished goods inventory	17,650	13,300
Ending goods in process inventory	22,000	16,000

[continued on next page]

[continued from previous page]

Ending raw materials inventory	5,300	7,200
Factory utilities	9,000	12,000
Factory supplies used	8,200	3,200
General and administrative expenses	21,000	43,000
Indirect labor	1,250	7,660
Repairs—Factory equipment	4,780	1,500
Raw materials purchases	33,000	52,000
Sales salaries	50,000	46,000

Check Garcia COGS, $91,030

Exercise 18-12
Components of accounting reports

C6 P2

For each of the following account balances for a manufacturing company, place a ✔ in the appropriate column indicating that it appears on the balance sheet, the income statement, the manufacturing statement, and/or a detailed listing of factory overhead costs. Assume that the income statement shows the calculation of cost of goods sold and the manufacturing statement shows only the total amount of factory overhead. (An account balance can appear on more than one report.)

	Account	Balance Sheet	Income Statement	Manufacturing Statement	Overhead Report
3	Accounts receivable				
4	Computer supplies used in office				
5	Beginning finished goods inventory				
6	Beginning goods in process inventory				
7	Beginning raw materials inventory				
8	Cash				
9	Depreciation expense—Factory building				
10	Depreciation expense—Factory equipment				
11	Depreciation expense—Office building				
12	Depreciation expense—Office equipment				
13	Direct labor				
14	Ending finished goods inventory				
15	Ending goods in process inventory				
16	Ending raw materials inventory				
17	Factory maintenance wages				
18	Computer supplies used in factory				
19	Income taxes				
20	Insurance on factory building				
21	Rent cost on office building				
22	Office supplies used				
23	Property taxes on factory building				
24	Raw materials purchases				
25	Sales				

Exercise 18-13
Manufacturing statement preparation P2

Given the following selected account balances of Shanta Company, prepare its manufacturing statement for the year ended on December 31, 2008. Include a listing of the individual overhead account balances in this statement.

Sales	$1,250,000
Raw materials inventory, Dec. 31, 2007	37,000
Goods in process inventory, Dec. 31, 2007	53,900
Finished goods inventory, Dec. 31, 2007	62,750
Raw materials purchases	175,600
Direct labor	225,000
Factory computer supplies used	17,840
Indirect labor	47,000
Repairs—Factory equipment	5,250
Rent cost of factory building	57,000
Advertising expense	94,000
General and administrative expenses	129,300
Raw materials inventory, Dec. 31, 2008	42,700
Goods in process inventory, Dec. 31, 2008	41,500
Finished goods inventory, Dec. 31, 2008	67,300

Check Cost of goods manufactured, $534,390

Use the information in Exercise 18-13 to prepare an income statement for Shanta Company (a manufacturer). Assume that its cost of goods manufactured is $534,390.

Exercise 18-14
Income statement
preparation   P2

The following chart shows how costs flow through a business as a product is manufactured. Some boxes in the flowchart show cost amounts. Compute the cost amounts for boxes that contain question marks.

Exercise 18-15
Cost flows in manufacturing

C6   P2

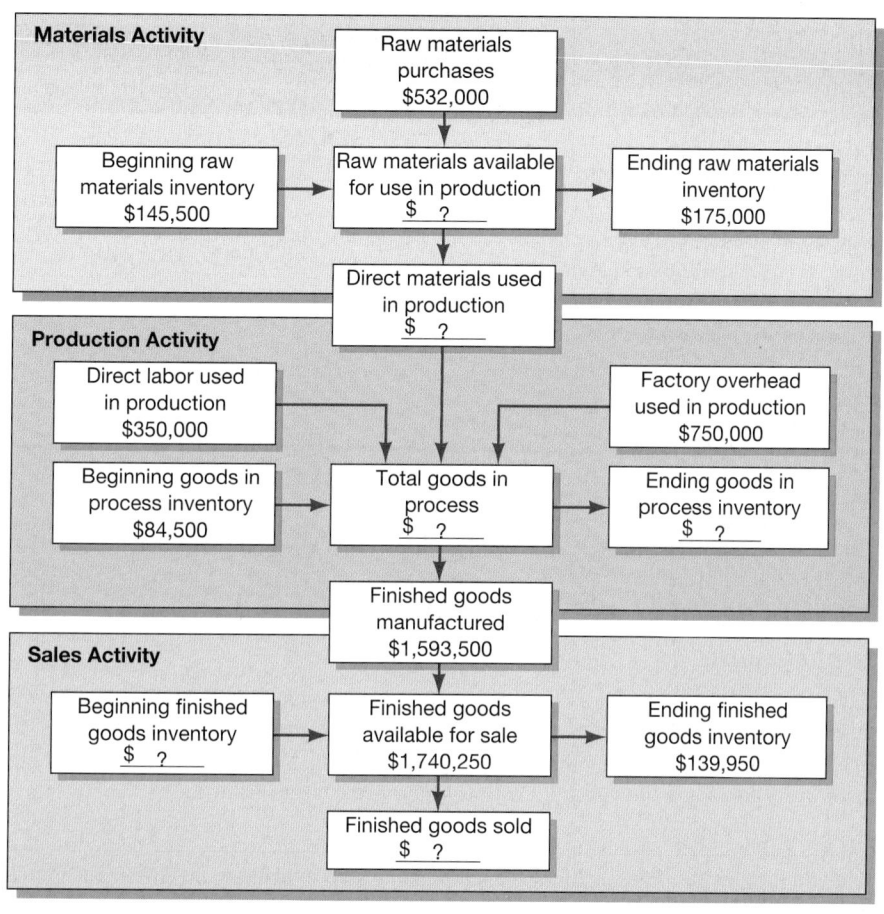

This chapter explained the purpose of managerial accounting in the context of the current business environment. Review the *automobile* section of your local newspaper; the Sunday paper is often best. Review advertisements of sport utility vehicles and identify the manufacturers that offer these products and the factors on which they compete.

PROBLEM SET A

Problem 18-1A
Managerial accounting role

C1   C2

Required

Discuss the potential contributions and responsibilities of the managerial accounting professional in helping an automobile manufacturer succeed. (*Hint:* Think about information and estimates that a managerial accountant might provide new entrants into the sports utility market.)

Many fast food restaurants compete on lean business concepts. Match each of the following activities at a fast food restaurant with the lean business concept it strives to achieve.

Problem 18-2A
Lean business concepts

C2

_____ **1.** Courteous employees

_____ **2.** Food produced to order

_____ **3.** New product development

_____ **4.** Clean tables and floors

_____ **5.** Orders filled within 3 minutes

_____ **6.** Standardized food making processes

_____ **7.** Customer satisfaction surveys

a. Total quality management (TQM)

b. Just-in-time (JIT)

c. Continuous improvement (CI)

[continued on next page]

_____ **8.** Continually changing menus

_____ **9.** Drive-through windows

_____ **10.** Standardized menus from location to location

Problem 18-3A

Cost computation, classification, and analysis

C3

Listed here are the total costs associated with the production of 1,000 drum sets manufactured by DrumBeat. The drum sets sell for $500 each.

Costs	Cost by Behavior		Cost by Function	
	Variable	**Fixed**	**Product**	**Period**
Plastic for casing—$17,000	$17,000		$17,000	
Wages of assembly workers—$82,000				
Property taxes on factory—$5,000				
Accounting staff salaries—$35,000				
Drum stands (1,000 stands outsourced)—$26,000				
Rent cost of equipment for sales staff—$10,000				
Upper management salaries—$125,000				
Annual flat fee for maintenance service—$10,000				
Sales commissions—$15 per unit				
Machinery depreciation—$40,000				

Required

Check   (1) Total variable cost, $125,000

1. Classify each cost and its amount as (*a*) either fixed or variable and (*b*) either product or period (the first cost is completed as an example).

2. Compute the manufacturing cost per drum set.

Analysis Component

3. Assume that 1,200 drum sets are produced in the next month. What do you predict will be the total cost of plastic for the casings and the per-unit cost of the plastic for the casings? Explain.

4. Assume that 1,200 drum sets are produced in the next month. What do you predict will be the total cost of property taxes and the per-unit cost of the property taxes? Explain.

Problem 18-4A

Cost classification and explanation

C3 C4

Assume that you must make a presentation to the marketing staff explaining the difference between product and period costs. Your supervisor tells you the marketing staff would also like clarification regarding prime and conversion costs and an explanation of how these terms fit with product and period cost. You are told that many on the staff are unable to classify costs in their merchandising activities.

Required

Prepare a one-page memorandum to your supervisor outlining your presentation to the marketing staff.

Problem 18-5A

Opportunity cost estimation and application

C1 C3

Refer to *Decision Maker,* **Purchase Manager,** in this chapter. Assume that you are the motorcycle manufacturer's managerial accountant. The purchasing manager asks you about preparing an estimate of the related costs for buying motorcycle seats from supplier (B). She tells you this estimate is needed because unless dollar estimates are attached to nonfinancial factors, such as lost production time, her supervisor will not give it full attention. The manager also shows you the following information.

- Production output is 1,000 motorcycles per year based on 250 production days a year.
- Production time per day is 8 hours at a cost of $2,000 per hour to run the production line.
- Lost production time due to poor quality is 1%.
- Satisfied customers purchase, on average, three motorcycles during a lifetime.
- Satisfied customers recommend the product, on average, to 5 other people.
- Marketing predicts that using seat (B) will result in 5 lost customers per year from repeat business and referrals.
- Average contribution margin per motorcycle is $3,000.

Required

Estimate the costs (including opportunity costs) of buying motorcycle seats from supplier (B). This problem requires that you think creatively and make reasonable estimates and, therefore, there could be more than one correct answer. (*Hint:* Reread the answer to *Decision Maker* and compare the cost savings for buying from supplier [B] to the sum of lost customer revenue from repeat business and referrals and the cost of lost production time.)

Check Estimated cost of lost production time, $40,000

Notaro's Boot Company makes specialty boots for the rodeo circuit. On December 31, 2007, the company had (*a*) 300 pairs of boots in finished goods inventory and (*b*) 1,200 heels at a cost of $8 each in raw materials inventory. During 2008, the company purchased 35,000 additional heels at $8 each and manufactured 16,600 pairs of boots.

Problem 18-6A
Ending inventory computation and evaluation

C2 C5

Required

1. Determine the unit and dollar amounts of raw materials inventory in heels at December 31, 2008.

Check (1) Ending (heel) inventory, $24,000 (3,000 units)

Analysis Component

2. Write a one-half page memorandum to the production manager explaining why a just-in-time inventory system for heels should be considered. Include the amount of working capital that can be reduced at December 31, 2008, if the ending heel raw material inventory is cut in half.

Shown here are annual financial data at December 31, 2008, taken from two different companies.

	Sports World Retail	Sno-Board Manufacturing
Beginning inventory		
Merchandise	$200,000	
Finished goods		$500,000
Cost of purchases	300,000	
Cost of goods manufactured		875,000
Ending inventory		
Merchandise	175,000	
Finished goods		225,000

Problem 18-7A
Inventory computation and reporting

C3 C5 P1

mhhe.com/wildFAP18e

Required

1. Compute the cost of goods sold section of the income statement at December 31, 2008, for each company. Include proper title and format in the solution.

2. Write a half-page memorandum to your instructor (*a*) identifying the inventory accounts and (*b*) describing where each is reported on the income statement and balance sheet for both companies.

Check (1) Sno-Board's cost of goods sold, $1,150,000

The following calendar year-end information is taken from the December 31, 2008, adjusted trial balance and other records of DeLeon Company.

Problem 18-8A
Manufacturing and income statements; inventory analysis P2

Advertising expense	$ 28,750	Direct labor	675,480
Depreciation expense—Office equipment	7,250	Income taxes expense	233,725
Depreciation expense—Selling equipment	8,600	Indirect labor	56,875
Depreciation expense—Factory equipment	33,550	Miscellaneous production costs	8,425
Factory supervision	102,600	Office salaries expense	63,000
Factory supplies used	7,350	Raw materials purchases	925,000
Factory utilities	33,000	Rent expense—Office space	22,000
Inventories		Rent expense—Selling space	26,100
Raw materials, December 31, 2007	166,850	Rent expense—Factory building	76,800
Raw materials, December 31, 2008	182,000	Maintenance expense—Factory equipment	35,400
Goods in process, December 31, 2007	15,700	Sales	4,525,000
Goods in process, December 31, 2008	19,380	Sales discounts	62,500
Finished goods, December 31, 2007	167,350	Sales salaries expense	392,560
Finished goods, December 31, 2008	136,490		

Required

1. Prepare the company's 2008 manufacturing statement.

2. Prepare the company's 2008 income statement that reports separate categories for (*a*) selling expenses and (*b*) general and administrative expenses.

Analysis Component

3. Compute the (*a*) inventory turnover and (*b*) days' sales in inventory for both its raw materials inventory and its finished goods inventory (see Chapter 6). Discuss some possible reasons for differences between these ratios for the two types of inventories.

Problem 18-9A
Manufacturing cycle time and efficiency

A1

Oakwood Company produces oak bookcases to customer order. Oakwood received an order from a customer to produce 5,000 bookcases. The following information is available for the production of the bookcases.

Process time	6.0 days
Inspection time	0.8 days
Move time	3.2 days
Wait time	5.0 days

Required

1. Compute the company's manufacturing cycle time.

2. Compute the company's manufacturing cycle efficiency. Interpret your answer.

Analysis Component

3. Assume that Oakwood wishes to increase its manufacturing cycle efficiency to 0.75. What are some ways that Oakwood can accomplish this?

PROBLEM SET B

Problem 18-1B
Managerial accounting role

C1 C2

This chapter described the purpose of managerial accounting in the context of the current business environment. Review the *home electronics* section of your local newspaper; the Sunday paper is often best. Review advertisements of home electronics and identify the manufacturers that offer these products and the factors on which they compete.

Required

Discuss the potential contributions and responsibilities of the managerial accounting professional in helping a home electronics manufacturer succeed. (*Hint:* Think about information and estimates that a managerial accountant might provide new entrants into the home electronics market.)

Problem 18-2B
Lean business concepts

C2

Eastman-Kodak manufactures digital cameras and must compete on lean manufacturing concepts. Match each of the following activities that it engages in with the lean manufacturing concept it strives to achieve.

_____ **1.** Lenses are received daily based on customer orders.

_____ **2.** Customers receive a satisfaction survey with each camera purchased.

_____ **3.** The manufacturing process is standardized and documented.

_____ **4.** Cameras are produced in small lots, and only to customer order.

_____ **5.** Manufacturing facilities are arranged to reduce move time and wait time.

_____ **6.** Kodak conducts focus groups to determine new features that customers want in digital cameras.

a. Total quality management (TQM)

b. Just-in-time (JIT)

c. Continuous improvement (CI)

[continued on next page]

_____ **7.** Orders received are filled within two business days.

_____ **8.** Kodak works with suppliers to reduce inspection time of incoming materials.

_____ **9.** Kodak monitors the market to determine what features its competitors are offering on digital cameras.

_____ **10.** Kodak asks production workers for ideas to improve production.

Listed here are the total costs associated with the production of 15,000 CDs manufactured by Hip-Hop. The CDs sell for $18 each.

Problem 18-3B

Cost computation, classification, and analysis

C3

Costs	Cost by Behavior		Cost by Function	
	Variable	Fixed	Product	Period
Plastic for CDs—$1,500	$1,500		$1,500	
Wages of assembly workers—$30,000				
Cost of factory rent—$6,750				
Systems staff salaries—$15,000				
Labeling (12,000 outsourced)—$3,750				
Cost of office equipment rent—$1,050				
Upper management salaries—$120,000				
Annual fixed fee for cleaning service—$4,520				
Sales commissions—$0.50 per CD				
Machinery depreciation—$18,000				

Required

1. Classify each cost and its amount as (_a_) either fixed or variable and (_b_) either product or period.

2. Compute the manufacturing cost per CD.

Check (2) Total variable manufacturing cost, $35,250

Analysis Component

3. Assume that 10,000 CDs are produced in the next month. What do you predict will be the total cost of plastic for the CDs and the per-unit cost of the plastic for the CDs? Explain.

4. Assume that 10,000 CDs are produced in the next month. What do you predict will be the total cost of factory rent and the per-unit cost of the factory rent? Explain.

Assume that you must make a presentation to a client explaining the difference between prime and conversion costs. The client makes and sells 200,000 cookies per week. The client tells you that her sales staff also would like a clarification regarding product and period costs. She tells you that most of the staff lack training in managerial accounting.

Problem 18-4B

Cost classification and explanation

C3   C4

Required

Prepare a one-page memorandum to your client outlining your planned presentation to her sales staff.

Refer to _Decision Maker,_ **Purchase Manager,** in this chapter. Assume that you are the motorcycle manufacturer's managerial accountant. The purchasing manager asks you about preparing an estimate of the related costs for buying motorcycle seats from supplier (B). She tells you this estimate is needed because unless dollar estimates are attached to nonfinancial factors such as lost production time, her supervisor will not give it full attention. The manager also shows you the following information.

Problem 18-5B

Opportunity cost estimation and application

C1   C3

- Production output is 1,000 motorcycles per year based on 250 production days a year.
- Production time per day is 8 hours at a cost of $500 per hour to run the production line.
- Lost production time due to poor quality is 1%.
- Satisfied customers purchase, on average, three motorcycles during a lifetime.
- Satisfied customers recommend the product, on average, to four other people.
- Marketing predicts that using seat (B) will result in four lost customers per year from repeat business and referrals.
- Average contribution margin per motorcycle is $4,000.

Required

Check Cost of lost customer revenue, $16,000

Estimate the costs (including opportunity costs) of buying motorcycle seats from supplier (B). This problem requires that you think creatively and make reasonable estimates and, therefore, there could be more than one correct answer. (*Hint:* Reread the answer to *Decision Maker,* and compare the cost savings for buying from supplier [B] to the sum of lost customer revenue from repeat business and referrals and the cost of lost production time.)

Problem 18-6B
Ending inventory computation and evaluation

C2 C5

Check (1) Ending (blade) inventory, $120,000 (6,000 units)

Sharp Edges makes specialty skates for the ice skating circuit. On December 31, 2007, the company had (*a*) 1,500 skates in finished goods inventory and (*b*) 2,500 blades at a cost of $20 each in raw materials inventory. During 2008, Sharp Edges purchased 45,000 additional blades at $20 each and manufactured 20,750 pairs of skates.

Required

1. Determine the unit and dollar amounts of raw materials inventory in blades at December 31, 2008.

Analysis Component

2. Write a one-half page memorandum to the production manager explaining why a just-in-time inventory system for blades should be considered. Include the amount of working capital that can be reduced at December 31, 2008, if the ending blade raw material inventory is cut in half.

Problem 18-7B
Inventory computation and reporting

C3 C5 P1

Shown here are annual financial data at December 31, 2008, taken from two different companies.

	Badger Retail	Naima Manufacturing
Beginning inventory		
Merchandise	$100,000	
Finished goods		$300,000
Cost of purchases	250,000	
Cost of goods manufactured		586,000
Ending inventory		
Merchandise	150,000	
Finished goods		200,000

Required

Check (1) Badger cost of goods sold, $200,000

1. Compute the cost of goods sold section of the income statement at December 31, 2008, for each company. Include proper title and format in the solution.

2. Write a half-page memorandum to your instructor (*a*) identifying the inventory accounts and (*b*) identifying where each is reported on the income statement and balance sheet for both companies.

Problem 18-8B
Manufacturing and income statements; analysis of inventories

P2

The following calendar year-end information is taken from the December 31, 2008, adjusted trial balance and other records of Elegant Furniture.

Advertising expense	$ 20,250		Direct labor	562,500
Depreciation expense—Office equipment	8,440		Income taxes expense	136,700
Depreciation expense—Selling equipment	10,125		Indirect labor	59,000
Depreciation expense—Factory equipment	35,400		Miscellaneous production costs	8,440
Factory supervision	121,500		Office salaries expense	70,875
Factory supplies used	6,060		Raw materials purchases	894,375
Factory utilities	37,500		Rent expense—Office space	23,625
Inventories			Rent expense—Selling space	27,000
Raw materials, December 31, 2007	40,375		Rent expense—Factory building	93,500
Raw materials, December 31, 2008	70,430		Maintenance expense—Factory equipment	30,375
Goods in process, December 31, 2007	12,500		Sales	5,000,000
Goods in process, December 31, 2008	14,100		Sales discounts	57,375
Finished goods, December 31, 2007	177,200		Sales salaries expense	295,300
Finished goods, December 31, 2008	141,750			

Required

1. Prepare the company's 2008 manufacturing statement.

2. Prepare the company's 2008 income statement that reports separate categories for (*a*) selling expenses and (*b*) general and administrative expenses.

Check (1) Cost of goods manufactured, $1,816,995

Analysis Component

3. Compute the (*a*) inventory turnover and (*b*) days' sales in inventory for both its raw materials inventory and its finished goods inventory (see Chapter 6). Discuss some possible reasons for differences between these ratios for the two types of inventories.

Best Ink produces ink-jet printers for personal computers. Best Ink received an order for 500 printers from a customer. The following information is available for this order.

Problem 18-9B
Manufacturing cycle time and efficiency

A1

Process time	16.0 hours
Inspection time	3.5 hours
Move time	9.0 hours
Wait time	21.5 hours

Required

1. Compute the company's manufacturing cycle time.

2. Compute the company's manufacturing cycle efficiency. Interpret your answer.

Analysis Component

3. Assume that Best Ink wishes to increase its manufacturing cycle efficiency to 0.80. What are some ways that Best Ink can accomplish this?

 Problem Set C is available at the book's Website to reinforce and assess your learning. **PROBLEM SET C**

(This serial problem began in Chapter 1 and continues through most of the book. If previous chapter segments were not completed, the serial problem can begin at this point. It is helpful, but not necessary, for you to use the Working Papers that accompany the book.)

SERIAL PROBLEM

Success Systems

SP 18 Adriana Lopez, owner of Success Systems, decides to diversify her business by also manufacturing computer workstation furniture.

Required

1. Classify the following manufacturing costs of Success Systems by behavior and traceability.

Product Costs	Cost by Behavior		Cost by Traceability	
	Variable	Fixed	Direct	Indirect
Glue to assemble workstation component parts	___	___	___	___
Laminate coverings for desktops	___	___	___	___
Wages of desk assembler	___	___	___	___
Taxes on assembly workshop	___	___	___	___
Depreciation on tools	___	___	___	___
Electricity for workshop	___	___	___	___
Monthly flat fee to clean workshop	___	___	___	___

2. Prepare a manufacturing statement for Success Systems for the month ended January 31, 2009. Assume the following manufacturing costs:

Direct materials: $2,125

Factory overhead: $460

Direct labor: $852

Beginning goods in process: none (December 31, 2008)

Ending goods in process: $1,796 (January 31, 2009)

Beginning finished goods inventory: none (December 31, 2008)

Ending finished goods inventory: $344 (January 31, 2009)

Check   (3) COGS, $1,297

3. Prepare the cost of goods sold section of a partial income statement for Success Systems for the month ended January 31, 2009.

BEYOND THE NUMBERS

REPORTING IN ACTION

C1 C2

BTN 18-1   Managerial accounting is more than recording, maintaining, and reporting financial results. Managerial accountants must provide managers with both financial and nonfinancial information including estimates, projections, and forecasts. There are many accounting estimates that management accountants must make, and **Best Buy** must notify shareholders of these estimates.

Required

1. Access and read Best Buy's "Critical Accounting Estimates" section (5 pages), which is part of its *Management's Discussion and Analysis of Financial Condition and Results of Operations* section, from either its annual report or its 10-K for the year ended February 26, 2005 [BestBuy.com]. What are some of the accounting estimates that Best Buy made in preparing its financial statements? What are some of the effects if the actual results of Best Buy differ from its assumptions?

2. What is the management accountant's role in determining those estimates?

Fast Forward

3. Access **Best Buy**'s annual report for a fiscal year ending after February 26, 2005, from either its Website [BestBuy.com] or the SEC's EDGAR database [www.sec.gov]. Answer the questions in parts (1) and (2) after reading the current MD&A section. Identify any major changes.

COMPARATIVE ANALYSIS

C1 C2

BTN 18-2   **Best Buy** and **Circuit City** are both merchandisers that rely on customer satisfaction. Access and read (1) Best Buy's "Strategic Initiatives" section [1 page] and (2) Circuit City's "Fiscal 2006 Outlook" section [2 pages]. Both sections are located in the respective company's *Management Discussion and Analysis of Financial Condition and Results of Operations* section from the annual report or 10-K. The Best Buy report is for the year ended February 26, 2005, and the Circuit City report is for the year ended February 28, 2005.

Required

1. Identify the strategic initiatives that each company put forward in its desire to better compete and succeed in the marketplace.

2. For each of these strategic initiatives for both companies, explain how it reflects (or does not reflect) a customer satisfaction focus.

BTN 18-3   Assume that you are the managerial accountant at Infostore, a manufacturer of hard drives, CDs, and diskettes. Its reporting year-end is December 31. The chief financial officer is concerned about having enough cash to pay the expected income tax bill because of poor cash flow management. On November 15, the purchasing department purchased excess inventory of CD raw materials in anticipation of rapid growth of this product beginning in January. To decrease the company's tax liability, the chief financial officer tells you to record the purchase of this inventory as part of supplies and expense it in the current year; this would decrease the company's tax liability by increasing expenses.

ETHICS CHALLENGE

C1 C3 C4

Required

1. In which account should the purchase of CD raw materials be recorded?

2. How should you respond to this request by the chief financial officer?

BTN 18-4   Write a one-page memorandum to a prospective college student about salary expectations for graduates in business. Compare and contrast the expected salaries for accounting (including different subfields such as public, corporate, tax, audit, and so forth), marketing, management, and finance majors. Prepare a graph showing average starting salaries (and those for experienced professionals in those fields if available). To get this information, stop by your school's career services office; libraries also have this information. The Website **JobStar.org** (click on *Salary Info*) also can get you started.

COMMUNICATING IN PRACTICE

BTN 18-5   Managerial accounting professionals follow a code of ethics. As a member of the Institute of Management Accountants, the managerial accountant must comply with Standards of Ethical Conduct.

TAKING IT TO THE NET

C1 C2

Required

Identify, print, and read the *Ethical Standards* posted at **www.IMAnet.org**. (Search using "ethical standards.")

BTN 18-6   The following calendar-year information is taken from the December 31, 2008, adjusted trial balance and other records of Dahlia Company.

TEAMWORK IN ACTION

C6 P2

Advertising expense	$ 19,125	Direct labor	650,750
Depreciation expense—Office equipment	8,750	Indirect labor	60,000
Depreciation expense—Selling equipment	10,000	Miscellaneous production costs	8,500
Depreciation expense—Factory equipment	32,500	Office salaries expense	100,875
Factory supervision	122,500	Raw materials purchases	872,500
Factory supplies used	15,750	Rent expense—Office space	21,125
Factory utilities	36,250	Rent expense—Selling space	25,750
Inventories		Rent expense—Factory building	79,750
Raw materials, December 31, 2007	177,500	Maintenance expense—Factory equipment	27,875
Raw materials, December 31, 2008	168,125	Sales	3,275,000
Goods in process, December 31, 2007	15,875	Sales discounts	57,500
Goods in process, December 31, 2008	14,000	Sales salaries expense	286,250
Finished goods, December 31, 2007	164,375		
Finished goods, December 31, 2008	129,000		

Required

1. *Each* team member is to be responsible for computing **one** of the following amounts. You are not to duplicate your teammates' work. Get any necessary amounts from teammates. Each member is to explain the computation to the team in preparation for reporting to class.

   a. Materials used.   **d.** Total cost of goods in process.

   b. Factory overhead.   **e.** Cost of goods manufactured.

   c. Total manufacturing costs.

2. Check your cost of goods manufactured with the instructor. If it is correct, proceed to part (3).

3. *Each* team member is to be responsible for computing **one** of the following amounts. You are not to duplicate your teammates' work. Get any necessary amounts from teammates. Each member is to explain the computation to the team in preparation for reporting to class.

   a. Net sales.   **d.** Total operating expenses.

   b. Cost of goods sold.   **e.** Net income or loss before taxes.

   c. Gross profit.

Point: Provide teams with transparencies and markers for presentation purposes.

BusinessWeek
ACTIVITY

C1 C2

BTN 18-7   Read the article "A CEO Explains 'the Concept of Lean'" in the July 19, 2005, issue of *BusinessWeek*. (The book's Website provides a free link.)

Required

1. What advantages does Donald E. Washkewicz see in **Parker Hannifin**'s change to a lean manufacturing environment? Explain.

2. Explain why the lean manufacturing environment does not reduce operating efficiencies.

ENTREPRENEURIAL DECISION

C1 C3

BTN 18-8   Chris Griffiths of **Garrison Guitars** must understand his manufacturing costs to effectively operate and succeed as a profitable and efficient company.

Required

1. What are the three main categories of manufacturing costs that Chris must monitor and control? Provide examples of each.

2. How can Chris make the Garrison Guitars' manufacturing process more cost effective? Provide examples of two useful managerial measures of time and efficiency.

HITTING THE ROAD

C1 C4

BTN 18-9   Visit your favorite fast-food restaurant. Observe its business operations.

Required

1. Describe all business activities from the time a customer arrives to the time that customer departs.

2. List all costs you can identify with the separate activities described in part 1.

3. Classify each cost from part 2 as fixed or variable, and explain your classification.

GLOBAL DECISION

Dixons

BTN 18-10   Access **Dixons'** annual report for the year ended May 1, 2004 (**Dixons-Group.com**). Read the section "Corporate Governance" dealing with the responsibilities of the board of directors.

Required

1. Identify the responsibilities of Dixons' board of directors.

2. How would management accountants be involved in assisting the board of directors in carrying out their responsibilities? Explain.

ANSWERS TO MULTIPLE CHOICE QUIZ

1. c
2. b
3. b
4. a
5. Beginning finished goods + Cost of goods manufactured (COGM) −
Ending finished goods = Cost of goods sold
$6,000 + COGM − $3,200 = $7,500
COGM = <u>$4,700</u>

19

Job Order Cost Accounting

A Look Back

Chapter 18 introduced managerial accounting and explained basic cost concepts. We also described the lean business model and the reporting of manufacturing activities, including the manufacturing statement.

A Look at This Chapter

We begin this chapter by describing a cost accounting system. We then explain the procedures used to determine costs using a job order costing system. We conclude with a discussion of over- and underapplied overhead.

A Look Ahead

Chapter 20 focuses on measuring costs in process production companies. We explain process production, describe how to assign costs to processes, and compute and analyze cost per equivalent unit.

Learning Objectives

CAP

Conceptual

C1 Explain the cost accounting system. (p. 762)

C2 Describe important features of job order production. (p. 762)

C3 Explain job cost sheets and how they are used in job order cost accounting. (p. 764)

Analytical

A1 Apply job order costing in pricing services. (p. 774)

Procedural

P1 Describe and record the flow of materials costs in job order cost accounting. (p. 765)

P2 Describe and record the flow of labor costs in job order cost accounting. (p. 767)

P3 Describe and record the flow of overhead costs in job order cost accounting. (p. 769)

P4 Determine adjustments for overapplied and underapplied factory overhead. (p. 773)

"We're saving lives . . . it's awesome"
—Sandra Johnson
(Marco Johnson on left)

Business of Saving Lives

LANCASTER, CA—Witnessing needless injury and death, firefighter Marco Johnson began teaching first aid and CPR courses. Although he was performing a valuable community service, Marco wanted to do more. "I wish someone would start CPR or first aid before we get on the scene," says Marco of the anguish he sometimes feels at the site of an accident. "I think maybe a few more lives could be saved," he says. "Knowing the basics of CPR and first aid saves lives."

So Marco and his wife, Sandra, started **Antelope Valley Medical College (AVMedicalCollege.com),** a company devoted to training people in life-saving procedures. Sandra's tasks were to find clients and set times and places for instruction. "We made simple fliers and went right to daycare providers," says Marco. "[Then] we went to large corporations because we knew there were OSHA laws that had to be met."

But the early days brought several challenges. Marco and Sandra needed to monitor and control job costs for their training programs. Success depended not only on securing clients, but also on maintaining cost controls and emphasizing quality instruction. "There were times," says Marco, "when we looked at each other and said, 'What did we get ourselves into?' My wife would schedule appointments and

I would teach classes between shifts and on my days off," recalls Marco. Yet the couple carefully handled labor and overhead costs and soon grew profitable.

Today, the company uses state-of-the-art job order cost accounting to track program costs. This includes tracking the costs of labor and overhead, and managing those expenses. Cost accounting procedures help Marco and Sandra avoid the mistakes made by startups that fail to use costing techniques and then experience run-away costs. Recruiting top-notch personnel also controls labor costs. "[We] make sure they have a passion for what they're doing," insists Marco. "We want people at our institutions and our schools to care."

"We're saving lives," says Sandra. "It's awesome to know I was part of that with my husband." The public clearly agrees with their cause. After just eight years in business, annual revenues of Antelope Valley Medical College is projected to be over $7 million. Yet Marco and Sandra have never lost sight of their core mission. "Do whatever it takes," say Marco and Sandra. "It can mean the difference between life and death."

[Sources: *Antelope Valley Medical College Website,* May 2006; *Entrepreneur,* November and October 2004; *Black Enterprise,* 2003; *Kiplinger,* February 2005; *Making It!,* April 2005]

This chapter introduces a cost accounting system for assigning costs to the flow of goods through a production process. We then describe the details of a *job order cost accounting system*. Job order costing is frequently used by manufacturers of custom products or providers of custom services.

Manufacturers that use job order costing typically base it on a perpetual inventory system, which provides a continuous record of materials, goods in process, and finished goods inventories.

Job Order Cost Accounting

This section describes a cost accounting system and job order production and costing.

Cost Accounting System

C1   Explain the cost accounting system.

An ever-increasing number of companies use a cost accounting system to generate timely and accurate inventory information. A **cost accounting system** records manufacturing activities using a *perpetual* inventory system, which continuously updates records for costs of materials, goods in process, and finished goods inventories. A cost accounting system also provides timely information about inventories and manufacturing costs per unit of product. This is especially helpful for managers' efforts to control costs and determine selling prices. (A **general accounting system** records manufacturing activities using a *periodic* inventory system. Some companies still use a general accounting system, but its use is declining as competitive forces and customer demands have increased pressures on companies to better manage inventories.)

Point: Cost accounting systems accumulate costs and then assign them to products and services.

The two basic types of cost accounting systems are *job order cost accounting* and *process cost accounting.* We describe job order cost accounting in this chapter. Process cost accounting is explained in Chapter 20.

Job Order Production

C2   Describe important features of job order production.

Many companies produce products individually designed to meet the needs of a specific customer. Each customized product is manufactured separately and its production is called **job order production,** or *job order manufacturing* (also called *customized production,* which is the production of products in response to special orders). Examples of such products include special-order machines, a factory building, custom jewelry, wedding invitations, and artwork.

The production activities for a customized product represent a **job.** The principle of customization is equally applicable to both manufacturing *and* service companies. Most service companies meet customers' needs by performing a custom service for a specific customer. Examples of such services include an accountant auditing a client's financial statements, an

Topic Tackler

PLUS

interior designer remodeling an office, a wedding consultant planning and supervising a reception, and a lawyer defending a client. Whether the setting is manufacturing or services, job order operations involve meeting the needs of customers by producing or performing custom jobs.

Boeing's aerospace division is one example of a job order production system. Its primary business is twofold: (1) design, develop, and integrate space carriers and (2) provide systems engineering and integration of Department of Defense (DoD) systems. Many of its orders are customized and produced through job order operations.

When a job involves producing more than one unit of a custom product, it is often called a **job lot.** Products produced as job lots could include benches for a church, imprinted T-shirts for a 10K race or company picnic, or advertising signs for a chain of stores. Although these orders involve more than one unit, the volume of production is typically low, such as 50 benches, 200 T-shirts, or 100 signs. Another feature of job order production is the diversity, often called *heterogeneity,* of the products produced. Namely, each customer order is likely to differ from another in some important respect. These variations can be minor or major.

Point: Many professional examinations including the CPA and CMA exams require knowledge of job order and process cost accounting.

Events in Job Order Costing

The initial event in a normal job order operation is the receipt of a customer order for a custom product. This causes the company to begin work on a job. A less common case occurs when management decides to begin work on a job before it has a signed contract. This is referred to as *jobs produced on speculation.*

The first step in both cases is to predict the cost to complete the job. This cost depends on the product design prepared by either the customer or the producer. The second step is to negotiate a sales price and decide whether to pursue the job. Other than for government or other cost-plus contracts, the selling price is determined by market factors. Producers evaluate the market price, compare it to cost, and determine whether the profit on the job is reasonable. If the profit is not reasonable, the producer would determine a desired **target cost.** The third step is for the producer to schedule production of the job to meet the customer's needs and to fit within its own production constraints. Preparation of this work schedule should consider workplace facilities including equipment, personnel, and supplies. Once this schedule is complete, the producer can place orders for raw materials. Production occurs as materials and labor are applied to the job.

> **Decision Insight**
>
> **Custom Design**   Managers once saw companies as the center of a solar system orbited by suppliers and customers. Now the customer has become the center of the business universe. Companies such as **Dell** encourage consumers to customize products. Soon consumers may be able to personalize almost any product, from cellular phones to appliances to furniture.

Point: Some jobs are priced on a *cost-plus basis:* The customer pays the manufacturer for costs incurred on the job plus a negotiated amount or rate of profit.

An overview of job order production activity is shown in Exhibit 19.1. This exhibit shows the March production activity of Road Warriors, which manufactures security-equipped cars and trucks. The company converts any vehicle by giving it a diversity of security items such as alarms, reinforced exterior, bulletproof glass, and bomb detectors. The company began by catering to high-profile celebrities, but it now caters to anyone who desires added security in a vehicle.

Job order production for Road Warriors requires materials, labor, and overhead costs. Recall that direct materials are goods used in manufacturing that are clearly identified with a particular job. Similarly, direct labor is effort devoted to a particular job. Overhead costs support production of more than one job. Common overhead items are depreciation on factory buildings and equipment, factory supplies, supervision, maintenance, cleaning, and utilities.

Exhibit 19.1 shows that materials, labor, and overhead are added to Jobs B15, B16, B17, B18, and B19 during March. Road Warriors completed Jobs B15, B16, and B17 in March and delivered Jobs B15 and B16 to customers. At the end of March, Jobs B18 and B19 remain in goods in process inventory and Job B17 is in finished goods

> **Decision Insight**
>
> **Target Costing**   Many producers determine a target cost for their jobs. Target cost is determined as follows: Expected selling price − Desired profit = Target cost. If the projected target cost of the job as determined by job costing is too high, the producer can apply *value engineering,* which is a method of determining ways to reduce job cost until the target cost is met.

Exhibit 19.1

Job Order Production Activities

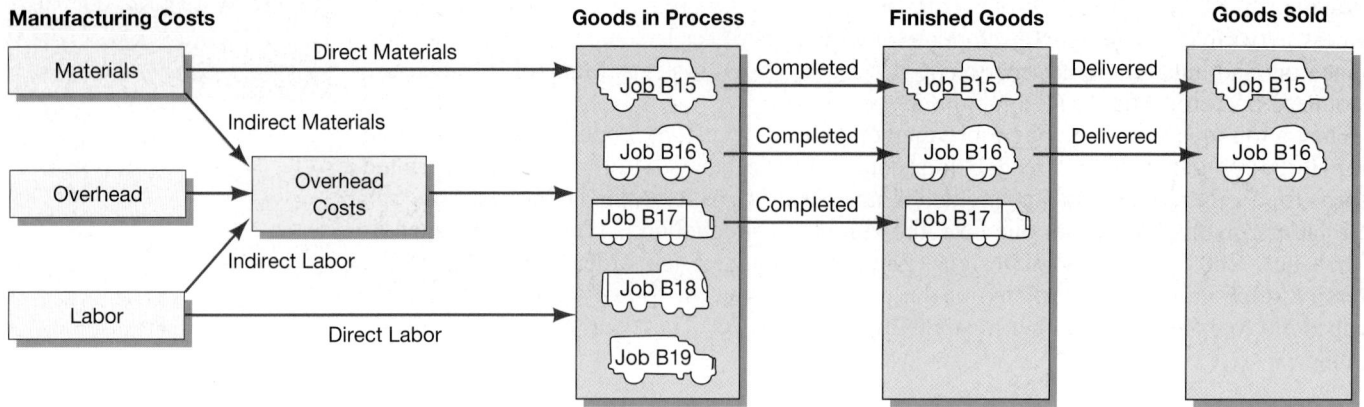

C3   Explain job cost sheets
and how they are used
in job order cost accounting.

Point: Factory overhead consists of costs (other than direct materials and direct labor) that ensure the production activities are carried out.

inventory. Both labor and materials costs are also separated into their direct and indirect components. Their indirect amounts are added to overhead. Total overhead cost is then allocated to the various jobs.

Job Cost Sheet

General ledger accounts usually do not provide the accounting information that managers of job order cost operations need to plan and control production activities. This is so because the needed information often requires more detailed data. Such detailed data are usually stored in subsidiary records controlled by general ledger accounts. Subsidiary records store information about raw materials, overhead costs, jobs in process, finished goods, and other items. This section describes the use of these records.

A major aim of a **job order cost accounting system** is to determine the cost of producing each job or job lot. In the case of a job lot, the system also aims to compute the cost per unit. The accounting system must include separate records for each job to accomplish this, and it must capture information about costs incurred and charge these costs to each job.

A **job cost sheet** is a separate record maintained for each job. Exhibit 19.2 shows a job cost sheet for an alarm system that Road Warriors produced for a customer. This job cost sheet identifies the customer, the job number assigned, the product, and key dates. Costs incurred on the job are immediately recorded on this sheet. When each job is complete, the supervisor enters the date of completion, records any remarks, and signs the sheet. The job cost sheet in Exhibit 19.2 classifies costs as direct materials, direct labor, or overhead. It shows that a total of $600 in direct materials is added to Job B15 on four different dates. It also shows seven entries for direct labor costs that total $1,000. Road Warriors *allocates* (also termed *applies, assigns,* or *charges*) factory overhead costs of $1,600 to this job using an allocation rate of 160% of direct labor cost (160% × $1,000)—we discuss overhead allocation later in this chapter.

While a job is being produced, its accumulated costs are kept in **Goods in Process Inventory.** The collection of job cost sheets for all jobs in process makes up a subsidiary ledger controlled by the Goods in Process Inventory account in the general ledger. Managers use job cost sheets to monitor costs incurred to date and to predict and control costs for each job.

When a job is finished, its job cost sheet is completed and moved from the jobs in process file to the finished jobs file. This latter file acts as a subsidiary ledger controlled by the **Finished**

Exhibit 19.2

Job Cost Sheet

```
Accounting System: Exhibit 19-2                                    _ □ x
File  Edit  Maintain  Tasks  Analysis  Options  Reports  Window  Help
Road Warriors                              Los Angeles, California  _ □ x
```

•Job Cost Sheet•

Customer's Name _Carroll Connor_   Job No. _B15_

Address _1542 High Point Dr._   City & State _Portland, Oregon_

Job Description _Level I Alarm System on Ford Expedition_

Date promised _March 15_   Date started _March 3_   Date completed _March 11_

Direct Materials			Direct Labor			Overhead		
Date	Requisition	Cost	Date	Time Ticket	Cost	Date	Rate	Cost
3/3/2008	R-4698	100.00	3/3/2008	L-3393	120.00	3/11/2008	160% of	1,600.00
3/7/2008	R-4705	225.00	3/4/2008	L-3422	150.00		Direct	
3/9/2008	R-4725	180.00	3/5/2008	L-3456	180.00		Labor	
3/10/2008	R-4777	95.00	3/8/2008	L-3479	60.00		Cost	
			3/9/2008	L-3501	90.00			
			3/10/2008	L-3535	240.00			
			3/11/2008	L-3559	160.00			
Total		600.00	Total		1,000.00	Total		1,600.00

REMARKS: _Completed job on March 11, and shipped to customer_
on March 15. Met all specifications and requirements.

SUMMARY:

Materials	600.00
Labor	1,000.00
Overhead	1,600.00
Total cost	3,200.00

Signed: _C. Luther, Supervisor_

```
Sales   Purchases   General   Payroll   Inventory   Company   Analysis
                    Ledger
```

Goods Inventory account. When a finished job is delivered to a customer, the job cost sheet is moved to a permanent file supporting the total cost of goods sold. This permanent file contains records from both current and prior periods.

Point: Documents (electronic and paper) are crucial in a job order system, and the job cost sheet is a cornerstone. Understanding it aids in grasping concepts of capitalizing product costs and product cost flow.

Quick Check

Answers—p. 779

1. Which of these products is likely to involve job order production? (a) inexpensive watches, (b) racing bikes, (c) bottled soft drinks, or (d) athletic socks.

2. What is the difference between a job and a job lot?

3. Which of these statements is correct? (a) The collection of job cost sheets for unfinished jobs makes up a subsidiary ledger controlled by the Goods in Process Inventory account, (b) Job cost sheets are financial statements provided to investors, or (c) A separate job cost sheet is maintained in the general ledger for each job in process.

4. What three costs are normally accumulated on job cost sheets?

Job Order Cost Flows and Reports

Materials Cost Flows and Documents

This section focuses on the flow of materials costs and the related documents in a job order cost accounting system. We begin analysis of the flow of materials costs by examining Exhibit 19.3. When materials are first received from suppliers, the employees count and inspect them and record the items' quantity and cost on a receiving report. The receiving report serves as the *source document* for recording materials received in both a materials ledger card and in the general ledger. In nearly all job order cost systems, **materials ledger cards** (or files) are perpetual records that are updated each time units are purchased and each time units are issued for use in production.

Materials

P1 Describe and record the flow of materials costs in job order cost accounting.

Point: Some companies certify certain suppliers based on the quality of their materials. Goods received from these suppliers are not always inspected by the purchaser to save costs.

Exhibit 19.3

Materials Cost Flows through
Subsidiary Records

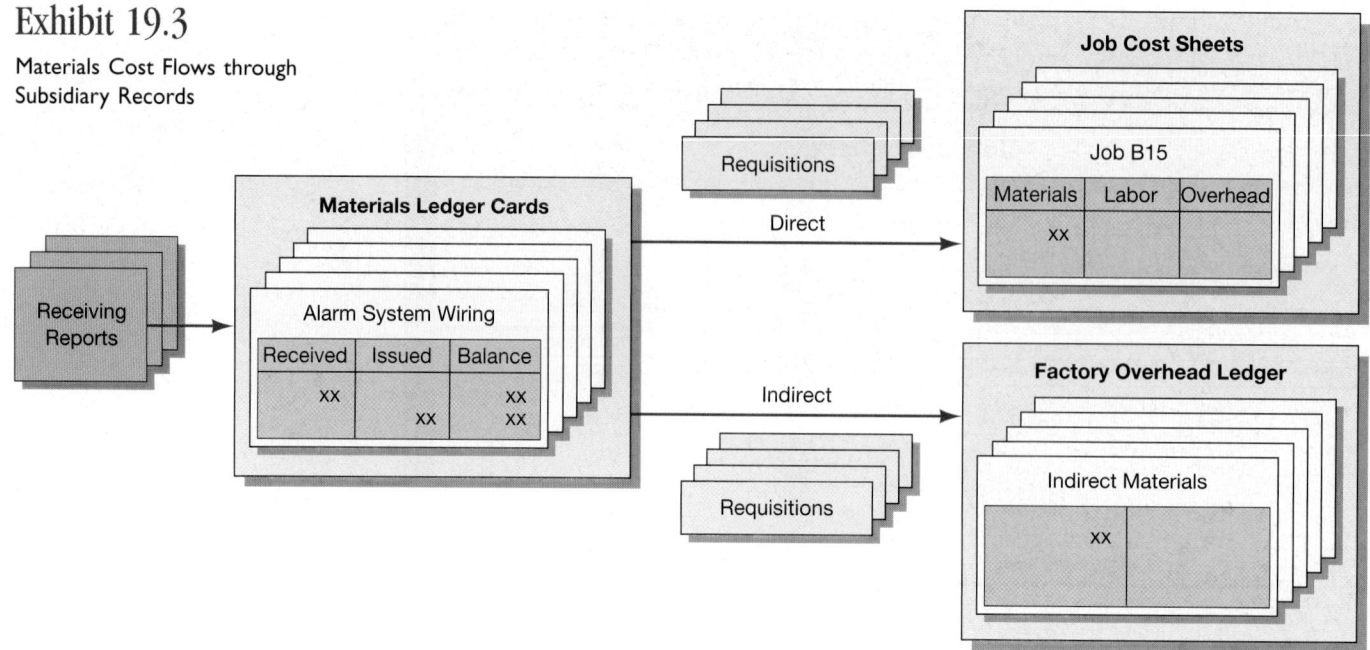

To illustrate the purchase of materials, Road Warriors acquired $450 of wiring and related materials on March 7, 2008. This purchase is recorded as follows.

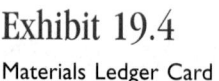

Assets = Liabilities + Equity
+450   +450

Mar. 4	Raw Materials Inventory—M-347.	450	
	Accounts Payable		450
	To record purchase of materials for production.		

Exhibit 19.3 shows that materials can be requisitioned for use either on a specific job (direct materials) or as overhead (indirect materials). Cost of direct materials flows from the materials ledger card to the job cost sheet. The cost of indirect materials flows from the materials ledger card to the Indirect Materials account in the factory overhead ledger, which is a subsidiary ledger controlled by the Factory Overhead account in the general ledger.

Exhibit 19.4 shows a materials ledger card for material received and issued by Road Warriors. The card identifies the item as alarm system wiring and shows the item's stock number, its location in the storeroom, information about the maximum and minimum quantities that should be available, and the reorder quantity. For example, alarm system wiring is issued and recorded on March 7, 2008. The job cost sheet in Exhibit 19.2 showed that Job B15 used this wiring.

Exhibit 19.4

Materials Ledger Card

Road Warriors

Item ___Alarm system wiring___   Stock No. ___M–347___   Location in Storeroom ___Bin 137___

Maximum quantity ___5 units___   Minimum quantity ___1 unit___   Quantity to reorder ___2 units___

	Received				Issued				Balance		
Date	Receiving Report Number	Units	Unit Price	Total Price	Requi- sition Number	Units	Unit Price	Total Price	Units	Unit Price	Total Price
									1	225.00	225.00
3/ 4/2008	C-7117	2	225.00	450.00					3	225.00	675.00
3/ 7/2008					R-4705	1	225.00	225.00	2	225.00	450.00

When materials are needed in production, a production manager prepares a **materials requisition** and sends it to the materials manager. The requisition shows the job number, the type of material, the quantity needed, and the signature of the manager authorized to make the requisition. Exhibit 19.5 shows the materials requisition for alarm system wiring for Job B15. To see how this requisition ties to the flow of costs, compare the information on the requisition with the March 7, 2008, data in Exhibits 19.2 and 19.4.

Road Warriors

MATERIALS REQUISITION NUMBER R–4705

Job No. **B15**	Date **3/7/2008**
Material Stock No. **M–347**	Material Description **Alarm system wiring**
Quantity Requested **1**	Requested By **C. Luther**

===

Quantity Provided **1**	Date Provided **3/7/2008**
Filled By **M. Bateman**	Material Received By **C. Luther**
Remarks	

Exhibit 19.5

Materials Requisition

The use of alarm system wiring on Job B15 yields the following entry (locate this cost item in the job cost sheet shown in Exhibit 19.2).

Mar. 7	Goods in Process Inventory—Job B15.	225	
	Raw Materials Inventory—M-347		225
	To record use of material on Job B15.		

Assets = Liabilities + Equity
+225
−225

This entry is posted both to its general ledger accounts and to subsidiary records. Posting to subsidiary records includes a debit to a job cost sheet and a credit to a materials ledger card. (*Note:* An entry to record use of indirect materials is the same as that for direct materials *except* the debit is to Factory Overhead. In the subsidiary factory overhead ledger, this entry is posted to Indirect Materials.)

Point: Requisitions are often accumulated and recorded in one entry. The frequency of entries depends on the job, the industry, and management procedures.

Labor Cost Flows and Documents

Exhibit 19.6 shows the flow of labor costs from clock cards and the Factory Payroll account to subsidiary records of the job order cost accounting system. Recall that costs in subsidiary records give detailed information needed to manage and control operations.

Labor

P2 Describe and record the flow of labor costs in job order cost accounting.

The flow of costs in Exhibit 19.6 begins with **clock cards.** Employees commonly use these cards to record the number of hours worked, and they serve as source documents for entries to record labor costs. Clock card data on the number of hours worked is used at the end of each pay period to determine total labor cost. This amount is then debited to the Factory Payroll account, a temporary account containing the total payroll cost (both direct and indirect). Payroll cost is later allocated to both specific jobs and overhead.

Point: Indirect materials are included in overhead on the job cost sheet. Assigning overhead costs to products is described in the next section.

According to clock card data, workers earned $1,500 for the week ended March 5. Illustrating the flow of labor costs, the accrual and payment of these wages are recorded as follows.

Mar. 6	Factory payroll.	1,500	
	Cash		1,500
	To record the weekly payroll.		

Assets = Liabilities + Equity
−1,500   −1,500

Exhibit 19.6

Labor Cost Flows through
Subsidiary Records

*"It's on Corporate Standard Time...
It loses an hour of your pay every day."*

To assign labor costs to specific jobs and to overhead, we must know how each employee's time is used and its costs. Source documents called **time tickets** usually capture these data. Employees regularly fill out time tickets to report how much time they spent on each job. An employee who works on several jobs during a day completes a separate time ticket for each job. Tickets are also prepared for time charged to overhead as indirect labor. A supervisor signs an employee's time ticket to confirm its accuracy.

Exhibit 19.7 shows a time ticket reporting the time a Road Warrior employee spent working on Job B15. The employee's supervisor signed the ticket to confirm its accuracy. The hourly rate and total labor cost are computed after the time ticket is turned in. To see the effect of this time ticket on the job cost sheet, look at the entry dated March 8, 2008, in Exhibit 19.2.

Exhibit 19.7

Time Ticket

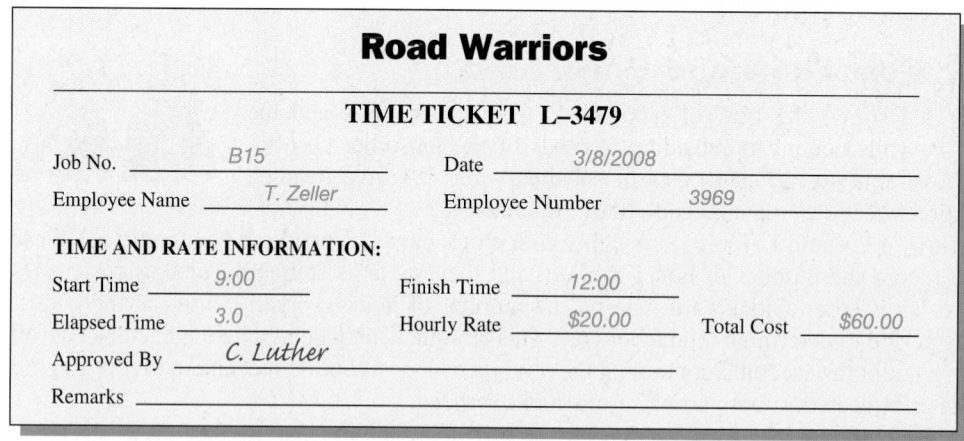

When time tickets report labor used on a specific job, this cost is recorded as direct labor. The following entry records the data from the time ticket in Exhibit 19.7.

Assets = Liabilities + Equity
+60   +60

	Mar. 8	Goods in Process Inventory—Job B15	60	
		Factory Payroll		60
		To record direct labor used on Job B15.		

The debit in this entry is posted both to the general ledger account and to the appropriate job cost sheet. (*Note:* An entry to record indirect labor is the same as for direct labor *except* that it debits Factory Overhead and credits Factory Payroll. In the subsidiary factory overhead ledger, the debit in this entry is posted to the Indirect Labor account.)

Point: In the accounting equation, we treat accounts such as Factory Overhead and Factory Payroll as temporary accounts, which hold various expenses until they are allocated to balance sheet or income statement accounts.

Overhead Cost Flows and Documents

Factory overhead (or simply overhead) cost flows are shown in Exhibit 19.8. Factory overhead includes all production costs other than direct materials and direct labor. Two sources of overhead costs are indirect materials and indirect labor. These costs are recorded from requisitions for indirect materials and time tickets for indirect labor. Two other sources of overhead are (1) vouchers authorizing payments for items such as supplies or utilities and (2) adjusting entries for costs such as depreciation.

Overhead

P3 Describe and record the flow of overhead costs in job order cost accounting.

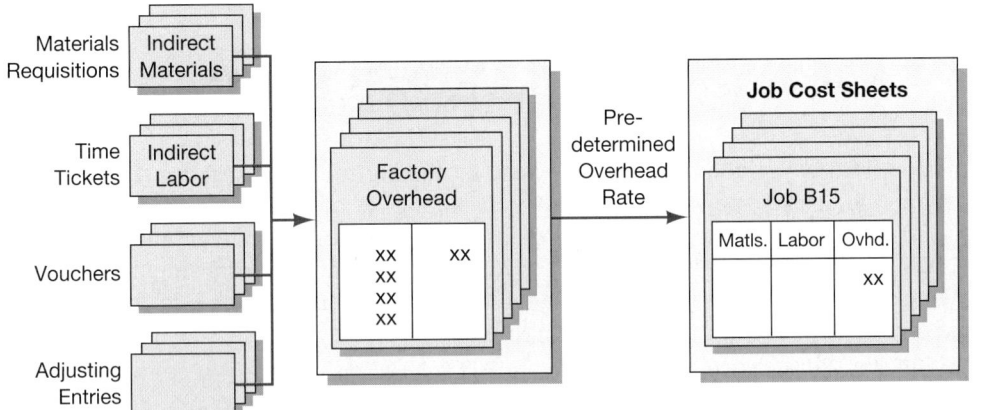

Exhibit 19.8

Overhead Cost Flows through Subsidiary Records

Factory overhead usually includes many different costs and, thus, a separate account for each is often maintained in a subsidiary factory overhead ledger. This ledger is controlled by the Factory Overhead account in the general ledger. Factory Overhead is a temporary account that accumulates costs until they are allocated to jobs.

Recall that overhead costs are recorded with debits to the Factory Overhead account and with credits to other accounts such as Cash, Accounts Payable, and Accumulated Depreciation—Equipment. In the subsidiary factory overhead ledger, the debits are posted to their respective accounts such as Depreciation Expense—Equipment, Insurance Expense—Warehouse, or Amortization Expense—Patents.

To illustrate the recording of overhead, the following two entries reflect the depreciation of factory equipment and the accrual of utilities, respectively, for the week ended March 6.

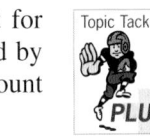
Topic Tackler
PLUS
19-2

Mar. 6	Factory Overhead	600	
	Accumulated Depreciation—Equipment		600
	To record depreciation on factory equipment.		
Mar. 6	Factory Overhead	250	
	Utilities Payable.		250
	To record the accrual of factory utilities.		

Assets = Liabilities + Equity
−600   −600

Assets = Liabilities + Equity
                +250   −250

Exhibit 19.8 shows that overhead costs flow from the Factory Overhead account to job cost sheets. Because overhead is made up of costs not directly associated with specific jobs or job lots, we cannot determine the dollar amount incurred on a specific job. We know, however, that overhead costs represent a necessary part of business activities. If a job cost is to include all costs needed to complete the job, some amount of overhead must be included. Given the difficulty in determining the overhead amount for a specific job, however, we allocate overhead to individual jobs in some reasonable manner.

We generally allocate overhead by linking it to another factor used in production, such as direct labor or machine hours. The factor to which overhead costs are linked is known as the

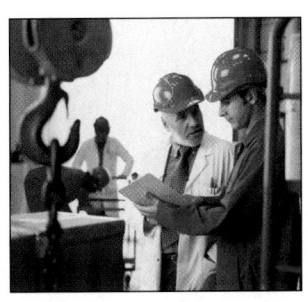

allocation base. A manager must think carefully about how many and which allocation bases to use. This managerial decision influences the accuracy with which overhead costs are allocated to individual jobs. In Exhibit 19.2, overhead is expressed as 160% of direct labor. We then allocate overhead by multiplying 160% by the estimated amount of direct labor on the jobs.

We cannot wait until the end of a period to allocate overhead to jobs because perpetual inventory records are part of the job order costing system (demanding up-to-date costs). Instead, we must predict overhead in advance and assign it to jobs so that a job's total costs can be estimated prior to its completion. This estimated cost is useful for managers in many decisions including setting prices. Being able to estimate overhead in advance requires a **predetermined overhead rate,** also called *predetermined overhead allocation* (or *application*) *rate.* This rate requires an estimate of total overhead cost and an allocation factor such as total direct labor cost before the start of the period. Exhibit 19.9 shows the usual formula for computing a predetermined overhead rate (estimates are commonly based on annual amounts). This rate is used during the period to allocate overhead to jobs. It is common for companies to use multiple activity (allocation) bases and multiple predetermined overhead rates for different types of products and services.

Exhibit 19.9

Predetermined Overhead Allocation Rate Formula

$$\text{Predetermined overhead rate} = \frac{\text{Estimated overhead costs}}{\text{Estimated activity base}}$$

Example: If management predicts total direct labor costs of $100,000 and total overhead costs of $200,000, what is its predetermined overhead rate? *Answer:* 200% of direct labor cost.

To illustrate, Road Warriors allocates overhead by linking it to direct labor. At the start of the current period, management predicts total direct labor costs of $125,000 and total overhead costs of $200,000. Using these estimates, management computes its predetermined overhead rate as 160% of direct labor cost ($200,000 ÷ $125,000). Specifically, reviewing the job order cost sheet in Exhibit 19.2, we see that $1,000 of direct labor went into Job B15. We then use the predetermined overhead rate of 160% to allocate $1,600 of overhead to this job. The entry to record this allocation is

Assets = Liabilities + Equity
+1,600   +1,600

Mar. 11	Goods in Process Inventory—Job B15............	1,600	
	Factory Overhead.......................		1,600
	To assign overhead to Job B15.		

Decision Ethics

Answer—p. 778

Web Consultant You are working on seven client engagements. Two clients reimburse your firm for actual costs plus a 10% markup. The other five pay a fixed fee for services. Your firm's costs include overhead allocated at $47 per labor hour. The managing partner of your firm instructs you to record as many labor hours as possible to the two markup engagements by transferring labor hours from the other five. What do you do?

Since the allocation rate for overhead is estimated at the start of a period, the total amount assigned to jobs during a period rarely equals the amount actually incurred. We explain how this difference is treated later in this chapter.

Summary of Cost Flows

We showed journal entries for charging Goods in Process Inventory (Job B15) with the cost of (1) direct materials requisitions, (2) direct labor time tickets, and (3) factory overhead. We made separate entries for each of these costs, but they are usually recorded in one entry. Specifically, materials requisitions are often collected for a day or a week and recorded with a single entry summarizing them. The same is done with labor time tickets. When summary entries are made, supporting schedules of the jobs charged and the types of materials used provide the basis for postings to subsidiary records.

To show all production cost flows for a period and their related entries, we again look at Road Warriors' activities. Exhibit 19.10 shows costs linked to all of Road Warriors' production activities for March. Road Warriors did not have any jobs in process at the beginning of March, but it did apply materials, labor, and overhead costs to five new jobs in March. Jobs B15 and B16 are completed and delivered to customers in March, Job B17 is completed but not delivered, and Jobs B18 and B19 are still in process. Exhibit 19.10 also shows purchases of raw materials for $2,750, labor costs incurred for $5,300, and overhead costs of $6,720.

The upper part of Exhibit 19.11 shows the flow of these costs through general ledger accounts and the end-of-month balances in key subsidiary records. Arrow lines are numbered

Exhibit 19.10

Job Order Costs of All Production Activities

ROAD WARRIORS **Job Order Manufacturing Costs** **For Month Ended March 31, 2008**							
			Overhead		**Goods in**	**Finished**	**Cost of Goods**
Explanation	**Materials**	**Labor**	**Incurred**	**Allocated**	**Process**	**Goods**	**Sold**
Job B15	$ 600	$1,000		$1,600			$3,200
Job B16	300	800		1,280			2,380
Job B17	500	1,100		1,760		$3,360	
Job B18	150	700		1,120	$1,970		
Job B19	250	600		960	1,810		
Total job costs	1,800	4,200		$6,720	$3,780	$3,360	$5,580
Indirect materials	550		$ 550				
Indirect labor		1,100	1,100				
Other overhead			5,070				
Total costs used in production	2,350	$5,300	$6,720				
Ending materials inventory	1,400						
Materials available	3,750						
Less beginning materials inventory	(1,000)						
Materials purchased	$2,750						

Exhibit 19.11

Job Order Cost Flows and Ending Job Cost Sheets

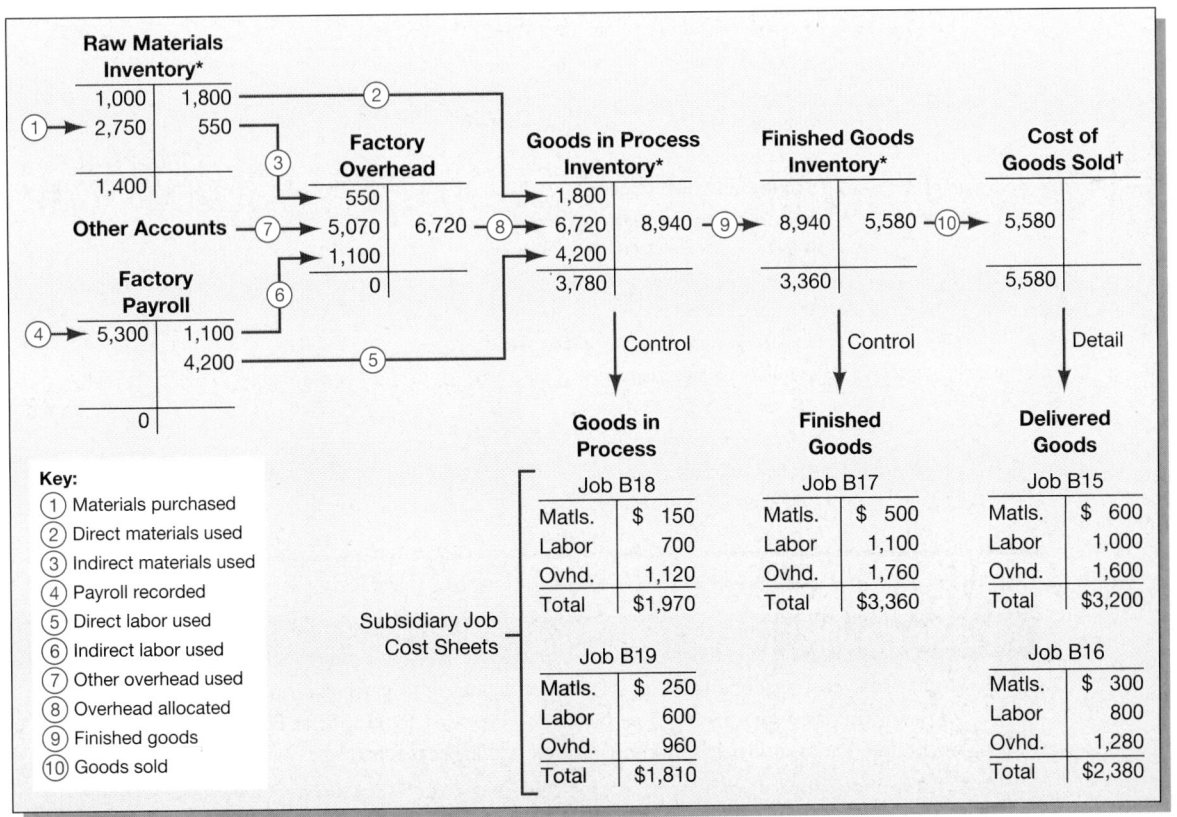

* The ending balances in the inventory accounts are carried to the balance sheet.

† The Cost of Goods Sold balance is carried to the income statement.

Answer—p. 779

Decision Maker

Entrepreneur   Competitors' prices on one of your product segments are lower than yours. Of the total product cost used in setting your prices, 53% is overhead allocated using direct labor hours. You believe that product costs are distorted and wonder whether there is a better way to allocate overhead and to set product price. What do you suggest?

to show the flows of costs for March. Each numbered cost flow reflects several entries made in March. The lower part of Exhibit 19.11 shows summarized job cost sheets and their status at the end of March. The sum of costs assigned to the jobs in process ($1,970 + $1,810) equals the $3,780 balance in Goods in Process Inventory shown in Exhibit 19.10. Also, costs assigned to Job B17 equal the $3,360 balance in Finished Goods Inventory. The sum of costs assigned to Jobs B15 and B16 ($3,200 + $2,380) equals the $5,580 balance in Cost of Goods Sold.

Exhibit 19.12 shows each cost flow with a single entry summarizing the actual individual entries made in March. Each entry is numbered to link with the arrow lines in Exhibit 19.11.

Exhibit 19.12

Entries for Job Order Production Costs*

①	Raw Materials Inventory..........................	2,750	
	Accounts Payable		2,750
	Acquired materials on credit for factory use.		
②	Goods in Process Inventory	1,800	
	Raw Materials Inventory		1,800
	To assign costs of direct materials used.		
③	Factory Overhead	550	
	Raw Materials Inventory		550
	To record use of indirect materials.		
④	Factory Payroll	5,300	
	Cash (and other accounts)		5,300
	To record salaries and wages of factory workers (including various payroll liabilities).		
⑤	Goods in Process Inventory	4,200	
	Factory Payroll		4,200
	To assign costs of direct labor used.		
⑥	Factory Overhead	1,100	
	Factory Payroll		1,100
	To record indirect labor costs as overhead.		
⑦	Factory Overhead	5,070	
	Cash (and other accounts)		5,070
	To record factory overhead costs such as insurance, utilities, rent, and depreciation.		
⑧	Goods in Process Inventory	6,720	
	Factory Overhead...........................		6,720
	To apply overhead at 160% of direct labor.		
⑨	Finished Goods Inventory.........................	8,940	
	Goods in Process Inventory....................		8,940
	To record completion of Jobs B15, B16, and B17.		
⑩	Cost of Goods Sold..............................	5,580	
	Finished Goods Inventory		5,580
	To record sale of Jobs B15 and B16.		

Point: *Actual* overhead is debited to Factory Overhead. *Allocated* overhead is credited to Factory Overhead.

* Transactions are numbered to be consistent with arrow lines in Exhibit 19.11.

Quick Check   Answers—p. 779

5. In job order cost accounting, which account is debited in recording a raw materials requisition? (*a*) Raw Materials Inventory, (*b*) Raw Materials Purchases, (*c*) Goods in Process Inventory if for a job, or (*d*) Goods in Process Inventory if they are indirect materials.

6. What are four sources of information for recording costs in the Factory Overhead account?

7. Why does job order cost accounting require a predetermined overhead rate?

8. What events result in a debit to Factory Payroll? What events result in a credit?

Adjustment of Overapplied or Underapplied Overhead

Refer to the debits in the Factory Overhead account in Exhibit 19.11 (or Exhibit 19.12). The total cost of factory overhead incurred during March is $6,720 ($550 + $5,070 + $1,100). The $6,720 exactly equals the amount assigned to goods in process inventory (see arrow line ⑧). Therefore, the overhead incurred equals the overhead applied in March. The amount of overhead incurred rarely equals the amount of overhead applied, however, because a job order cost accounting system uses a predetermined overhead rate in applying factory overhead costs to jobs. This rate is determined using estimated amounts before the period begins, and estimates rarely equal the exact amounts actually incurred. This section explains what we do when too much or too little overhead is applied to jobs.

Underapplied Overhead

When less overhead is applied than is actually incurred, the remaining debit balance in the Factory Overhead account at the end of the period is called **underapplied overhead.** To illustrate, assume that Road Warriors actually incurred *other overhead costs* of $5,550 instead of the $5,070 shown in Exhibit 19.11. This yields an actual total overhead cost of $7,200 in March. Since the amount of overhead applied was only $6,720, the Factory Overhead account is left with a $480 debit balance as shown in the ledger account in Exhibit 19.13.

P4   Determine adjustments for overapplied and underapplied factory overhead.

Factory Overhead				Acct. No. 540	
Date	Explanation	Debit	Credit	Balance	
Mar. 31	Indirect materials cost	550		550 Dr.	
31	Indirect labor cost	1,100		1,650 Dr.	
31	Other overhead cost	5,550		7,200 Dr.	
31	Overhead costs applied to jobs		6,720	480 Dr.	

Exhibit 19.13

Underapplied Overhead in the Factory Overhead Ledger Account

The $480 debit balance reflects manufacturing costs not assigned to jobs. This means that the balances in Goods in Process Inventory, Finished Goods Inventory, and Cost of Goods Sold do not include all production costs incurred. When the underapplied overhead amount is immaterial, it is allocated (closed) to the Cost of Goods Sold account with the following adjusting entry.[1]

Example: If we do not adjust for underapplied overhead, will net income be overstated or understated? *Answer:* Overstated.

Mar. 31	Cost of Goods Sold.........................	480	
	Factory Overhead......................		480
	To adjust for underapplied overhead costs.		

Assets = Liabilities + Equity
−480
+480

The $480 debit (increase) to Cost of Goods Sold reduces income by $480.

---

[1] When the underapplied (or overapplied) overhead is significant, the amount is normally allocated to the Cost of Goods Sold, Finished Goods Inventory, and Goods in Process Inventory accounts. The preferred method of allocating underapplied (or overapplied) overhead in this case is one consistent with the allocation method used in the period. For Road Warriors, underapplied overhead is allocated to jobs based on direct labor. Jobs B15 and B16, which are sold, account for 42.8% of the total direct labor cost in March. Also, 26.2% of direct labor was consumed by B17, which is in Finished Goods inventory, and the remaining 31% was consumed by Jobs B18 and B19, which are in Goods in Process inventory. These percents are multiplied by $480 to compute the amount of underapplied overhead allocated to each account (for example, 42.8% of $480, or $205, is allocated to the Cost of Goods Sold account). The following adjusting entry records this allocation.

Mar. 31	Goods in Process Inventory......................	149	
	Finished Goods Inventory	126	
	Cost of Goods Sold...........................	205	
	Factory Overhead........................		480
	To adjust for underapplied overhead costs.		

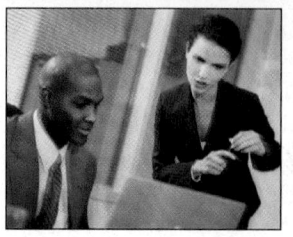
Overapplied Overhead

When the overhead applied in a period exceeds the overhead incurred, the resulting credit balance in the Factory Overhead account is called **overapplied overhead.** We treat overapplied overhead at the end of the period in the same way we treat underapplied overhead, except that we debit Factory Overhead and credit Cost of Good Sold for the amount.

Quick Check   Answers—p. 779

9. In a job order cost accounting system, why does the Factory Overhead account usually have an overapplied or underapplied balance at period-end?

10. When the Factory Overhead account has a debit balance at period-end, does this reflect overapplied or underapplied overhead?

Decision Analysis   Pricing for Services

A1 Apply job order costing in pricing services.

The chapter described job order costing mainly using a manufacturing setting. However, these concepts and procedures are applicable to a service setting. Consider AdWorld, an advertising agency that develops Web-based ads for small firms. Each of its customers has unique requirements, so costs for each individual job must be tracked separately.

AdWorld uses two types of labor: Web designers ($65 per hour) and computer staff ($50 per hour). It also incurs overhead costs that it assigns using two different predetermined overhead allocation rates: $125 per designer hour and $96 per staff hour. For each job, AdWorld must estimate the number of designer and staff hours needed. Then total costs pertaining to each job are determined using the procedures in the chapter. (*Note:* Most service firms have neither the category of materials cost nor inventory.)

To illustrate, a manufacturer of golf balls requested a quote from AdWorld for an advertising engagement. AdWorld estimates that the job will require 43 designer hours and 61 staff hours, with the following total estimated cost for this job.

Direct Labor		
Designers (43 hours × $65)	$ 2,795	
Staff (61 hours × $50)	3,050	
Total direct labor		$ 5,845
Overhead		
Designer related (43 hours × $125)	5,375	
Staff related (61 hours × $96)	5,856	
Total overhead		11,231
Total estimated job cost		$17,076

Decision Maker   Answer—p. 779

Sales Manager As AdWorld's sales manager, assume that you estimate costs pertaining to a proposed job as $17,076. Your normal pricing policy is to apply a markup of 18% from total costs. However, you learn that three other agencies are likely to bid for the same job, and that their quotes will range from $16,500 to $22,000. What price should you quote? What factors other than cost must you consider?

AdWorld can use this cost information to help determine the price quote for the job (see *Decision Maker, Sales Manager,* scenario in the margin).

Another source of information that AdWorld must consider is the market, that is, how much competitors will quote for this job. Competitor information is often unavailable; therefore, AdWorld's managers must use estimates based on their assessment of the competitive environment.

Demonstration Problem—Job Order Costing

The following information reflects Walczak Company's job order production activities for May.

Raw materials purchases	$16,000
Factory payroll cost	15,400
Overhead costs incurred	
Indirect materials	5,000
Indirect labor	3,500
Other factory overhead	9,500

Walczak's predetermined overhead rate is 150% of direct labor cost. Costs are allocated to the three jobs worked on during May as follows.

	Job 401	Job 402	Job 403
In-process balances on April 30			
Direct materials	$3,600		
Direct labor	1,700		
Applied overhead	2,550		
Costs during May			
Direct materials	3,550	$3,500	$1,400
Direct labor	5,100	6,000	800
Applied overhead	?	?	?
Status on May 31	Finished (sold)	Finished (unsold)	In process

Required

1. Determine the total cost of:
   a. The April 30 inventory of jobs in process.
   b. Materials used during May.
   c. Labor used during May.
   d. Factory overhead incurred and applied during May and the amount of any over- or underapplied overhead on May 31.
   e. Each job as of May 31, the May 31 inventories of both goods in process and finished goods, and the goods sold during May.
2. Prepare summarized journal entries for the month to record:
   a. Materials purchases (on credit), the factory payroll (paid with cash), indirect materials, indirect labor, and the other factory overhead (paid with cash).
   b. Assignment of direct materials, direct labor, and overhead costs to the Goods in Process Inventory account. (Use separate debit entries for each job.)
   c. Transfer of each completed job to the Finished Goods Inventory account.
   d. Cost of goods sold.
   e. Removal of any underapplied or overapplied overhead from the Factory Overhead account. (Assume the amount is not material.)
3. Prepare a manufacturing statement for May.

Planning the Solution

- Determine the cost of the April 30 goods in process inventory by totaling the materials, labor, and applied overhead costs for Job 401.
- Compute the cost of materials used and labor by totaling the amounts assigned to jobs and to overhead.

- Compute the total overhead incurred by summing the amounts for the three components. Compute the amount of applied overhead by multiplying the total direct labor cost by the predetermined overhead rate. Compute the underapplied or overapplied amount as the difference between the actual cost and the applied cost.
- Determine the total cost charged to each job by adding the costs incurred in April (if any) to the cost of materials, labor, and overhead applied during May.
- Group the costs of the jobs according to their completion status.
- Record the direct materials costs assigned to the three jobs, using a separate Goods in Process Inventory account for each job; do the same for the direct labor and the applied overhead.
- Transfer costs of Jobs 401 and 402 from Goods in Process Inventory to Finished Goods.
- Record the costs of Job 401 as cost of goods sold.
- Record the transfer of underapplied overhead from the Factory Overhead account to the Cost of Goods Sold account.
- On the manufacturing statement, remember to include the beginning and ending goods in process inventories and to deduct the underapplied overhead.

Solution to Demonstration Problem

1. Total cost of

a. April 30 inventory of jobs in process (Job 401).

Direct materials	$3,600
Direct labor	1,700
Applied overhead	2,550
Total cost	$7,850

b. Materials used during May.

Direct materials	
Job 401	$ 3,550
Job 402	3,500
Job 403	1,400
Total direct materials	8,450
Indirect materials	5,000
Total materials used	$13,450

c. Labor used during May.

Direct labor	
Job 401	$ 5,100
Job 402	6,000
Job 403	800
Total direct labor	11,900
Indirect labor	3,500
Total labor used	$15,400

d. Factory overhead incurred in May.

Actual overhead	
Indirect materials	$ 5,000
Indirect labor	3,500
Other factory overhead	9,500
Total actual overhead	18,000
Overhead applied (150% × $11,900)	17,850
Underapplied overhead	$ 150

e. Total cost of each job.

	401	402	403
In-process costs from April			
Direct materials	$ 3,600		
Direct labor	1,700		
Applied overhead*	2,550		
Cost incurred in May			
Direct materials	3,550	$ 3,500	$1,400
Direct labor	5,100	6,000	800
Applied overhead*	7,650	9,000	1,200
Total costs	$24,150	$18,500	$3,400

* Equals 150% of the direct labor cost.

Total cost of the May 31 inventory of goods in process (Job 403) = $3,400

Total cost of the May 31 inventory of finished goods (Job 402) = $18,500

Total cost of goods sold during May (Job 401) = $24,150

2. Journal entries.

a.

Raw Materials Inventory	16,000	
Accounts Payable		16,000
To record materials purchases.		
Factory Payroll	15,400	
Cash		15,400
To record factory payroll.		
Factory Overhead	5,000	
Raw Materials Inventory		5,000
To record indirect materials.		
Factory Overhead	3,500	
Factory Payroll		3,500
To record indirect labor.		
Factory Overhead	9,500	
Cash		9,500
To record other factory overhead.		

b. Assignment of costs to Goods in Process Inventory.

Goods in Process Inventory (Job 401)	3,550	
Goods in Process Inventory (Job 402)	3,500	
Goods in Process Inventory (Job 403)	1,400	
Raw Materials Inventory		8,450
To assign direct materials to jobs.		
Goods in Process Inventory (Job 401)	5,100	
Goods in Process Inventory (Job 402)	6,000	
Goods in Process Inventory (Job 403)	800	
Factory Payroll		11,900
To assign direct labor to jobs.		
Goods in Process Inventory (Job 401)	7,650	
Goods in Process Inventory (Job 402)	9,000	
Goods in Process Inventory (Job 403)	1,200	
Factory Overhead		17,850
To apply overhead to jobs.		

c. Transfer of completed jobs to Finished Goods Inventory.

Finished Goods Inventory	42,650	
Goods in Process Inventory (Job 401)		24,150
Goods in Process Inventory (Job 402)		18,500
To record completion of jobs.		

d.

Cost of Goods Sold	24,150	
Finished Goods Inventory		24,150
To record sale of Job 401.		

e.

Cost of Goods Sold	150	
Factory Overhead		150
To assign underapplied overhead.		

3.

WALCZAK COMPANY Manufacturing Statement For Month Ended May 31		
Direct materials		$ 8,450
Direct labor		11,900
Factory overhead		
Indirect materials	$5,000	
Indirect labor	3,500	
Other factory overhead	9,500	18,000
Total production costs		38,350
Add goods in process, April 30		7,850
Total cost of goods in process		46,200
Less goods in process, May 31		3,400
Less underapplied overhead		150
Cost of goods manufactured		$42,650

> Note how underapplied overhead is reported. Overapplied overhead is similarly reported, but is added.

Summary

C1 Explain the cost accounting system. A cost accounting system records production activities using a perpetual inventory system, which continuously updates records for transactions and events that affect inventory costs.

C2 Describe important features of job order production.
Certain companies called *job order manufacturers* produce custom-made products for customers. These customized products are produced in response to a customer's orders. A job order manufacturer produces products that usually are different and, typically, produced in low volumes. The production systems of job order companies are flexible and are not highly standardized.

C3 Explain job cost sheets and how they are used in job order cost accounting. In a job order cost accounting system, the costs of producing each job are accumulated on a separate job cost sheet. Costs of direct materials, direct labor, and overhead are accumulated separately on the job cost sheet and then added to determine the total cost of a job. Job cost sheets for jobs in process, finished jobs, and jobs sold make up subsidiary records controlled by general ledger accounts.

A1 Apply job order costing in pricing services. Job order costing can usefully be applied to a service setting. The resulting job cost estimate can then be used to help determine a price for services.

P1 Describe and record the flow of materials costs in job order cost accounting. Costs of materials flow from receiving reports to materials ledger cards and then to either job cost sheets or the Indirect Materials account in the factory overhead ledger.

P2 Describe and record the flow of labor costs in job order cost accounting. Costs of labor flow from clock cards to the Factory Payroll account and then to either job cost sheets or the Indirect Labor account in the factory overhead ledger.

P3 Describe and record the flow of overhead costs in job order cost accounting. Overhead costs are accumulated in the Factory Overhead account that controls the subsidiary factory overhead ledger. Then, using a predetermined overhead rate, overhead costs are charged to jobs.

P4 Determine adjustments for overapplied and underapplied factory overhead. At the end of each period, the Factory Overhead account usually has a residual debit (underapplied overhead) or credit (overapplied overhead) balance. If the balance is not material, it is transferred to Cost of Goods Sold, but if it is material, it is allocated to Goods in Process Inventory, Finished Goods Inventory, and Cost of Goods Sold.

Guidance Answers to **Decision Maker** and **Decision Ethics**

Management Consultant Service companies (such as this consulting firm) do not recognize goods in process inventory or finished goods inventory—an important difference between service and manufacturing companies. For the two jobs that are 60% complete, you could recognize revenues and costs at 60% of the total expected amounts. This means you could recognize revenue of $7,200 (0.60 × $12,000) and costs of $6,000 (0.60 × $10,000), yielding net income of $1,200 from each job.

Web Consultant The partner has a monetary incentive to *manage* the numbers and assign more costs to the two cost-plus engagements. This also would reduce costs on the fixed-price engagements. To act in such a manner is unethical. As a professional and an honest person, it is your responsibility to engage in ethical behavior. You must not comply with the partner's instructions. If the partner insists you act in an unethical manner, you should report the matter to a higher authority in the organization.

Entrepreneur An inadequate cost system can distort product costs. You should review overhead costs in detail. Once you know the different cost elements in overhead, you can classify them into groups such as material related, labor related, or machine related. Other groups can also be formed (we discuss this in Chapter 21). Once you have classified overhead items into groups, you can better establish overhead allocation bases and use them to compute predetermined overhead rates. These multiple rates and bases can then be used to assign overhead costs to products. This will likely improve product pricing.

Sales Manager The price based on AdWorld's normal pricing policy is $20,150 ($17,076 × 1.18), which is within the price range offered by competitors. One option is to apply normal pricing policy and quote a price of $20,150. On the other hand, assessing the competition, particularly in terms of their service quality and other benefits they might offer, would be useful. Although price is an input customers use to select suppliers, factors such as quality and timeliness (responsiveness) of suppliers are important. Accordingly, your price can reflect such factors.

Guidance Answers to **Quick Checks**

1. *b*

2. A job is a special order for a custom product. A job lot consists of a quantity of identical, special-order items.

3. *a*

4. Three costs normally accumulated on a job cost sheet are direct materials, direct labor, and factory overhead.

5. *c*

6. Four sources of factory overhead are materials requisitions, time tickets, vouchers, and adjusting entries.

7. Since a job order cost accounting system uses perpetual inventory records, overhead costs must be assigned to jobs before the

end of a period. This requires the use of a predetermined overhead rate.

8. Debits are recorded when wages and salaries of factory employees are paid or accrued. Credits are recorded when direct labor costs are assigned to jobs and when indirect labor costs are transferred to the Factory Overhead account.

9. Overapplied or underapplied overhead usually exists at the end of a period because application of overhead is based on estimates of overhead and another variable such as direct labor. Estimates rarely equal actual amounts incurred.

10. A debit balance reflects underapplied factory overhead.

Key Terms   mhhe.com/wildFAP18e

Key Terms are available at the book's Website for learning and testing in an online Flashcard Format.

Clock card (p. 767)
Cost accounting system (p. 762)
Finished Goods Inventory (p. 764)
General accounting system (p. 762)
Goods in Process Inventory (p. 764)
Job (p. 762)

Job cost sheet (p. 764)
Job lot (p. 763)
Job order cost accounting system (p. 764)
Job order production (p. 762)
Materials ledger card (p. 765)

Materials requisition (p. 767)
Overapplied overhead (p. 774)
Predetermined overhead rate (p. 770)
Target cost (p. 763)
Time ticket (p. 768)
Underapplied overhead (p. 773)

Multiple Choice Quiz   Answers on p. 795   mhhe.com/wildFAP18e

Multiple Choice Quizzes A and B are available at the book's Website.

1. A company's predetermined overhead allocation rate is 150% of its direct labor costs. How much overhead is applied to a job that requires total labor costs of $30,000?
  a. $15,000
  b. $30,000
  c. $45,000
  d. $60,000
  e. $75,000

2. A company's cost accounting system uses direct labor costs to apply overhead to goods in process and finished goods inventories. Its production costs for the period are: direct

materials, $45,000; direct labor, $35,000; and overhead applied, $38,500. What is its predetermined overhead allocation rate?
  a. 10%
  b. 110%
  c. 86%
  d. 91%
  e. 117%

3. A company's ending inventory of finished goods has a total cost of $10,000 and consists of 500 units. If the overhead applied to these goods is $4,000, and the predetermined overhead rate is 80% of direct labor costs, how much direct materials cost was incurred in producing these 500 units?

a. $10,000
b. $ 6,000
c. $ 4,000
d. $ 5,000
e. $ 1,000

4. A company's Goods in Process Inventory T-account follows.

Goods in Process Inventory			
Beginning balance	9,000		
Direct materials	94,200		
Direct labor	59,200	?	Finished goods
Overhead applied	31,600		
Ending balance	17,800		

The cost of units transferred to Finished Goods inventory is

a. $193,000
b. $211,800
c. $185,000
d. $144,600
e. $176,200

5. At the end of its current year, a company learned that its overhead was underapplied by $1,500 and that this amount is not considered material. Based on this information, the company should

a. Close the $1,500 to Finished Goods Inventory.
b. Close the $1,500 to Cost of Goods Sold.
c. Carry the $1,500 to the next period.
d. Do nothing about the $1,500 because it is not material and it is likely that overhead will be overapplied by the same amount next year.
e. Carry the $1,500 to the Income Statement as "Other Expense."

Discussion Questions

1. Why must a company estimate the amount of factory overhead assigned to individual jobs or job lots?

2. The chapter used a percent of labor cost to assign factory overhead to jobs. Identify another factor (or base) a company might reasonably use to assign overhead costs.

3. What information is recorded on a job cost sheet? How do management and employees use job cost sheets?

4. In a job order cost accounting system, what records serve as a subsidiary ledger for Goods in Process Inventory? For Finished Goods Inventory?

5. What journal entry is recorded when a materials manager receives a materials requisition and then issues materials (both direct and indirect) for use in the factory?

6. How does the materials requisition help safeguard a company's assets?

7. What is the difference between a clock card and a time ticket?

8. What events cause debits to be recorded in the Factory Overhead account? What events cause credits to be recorded in the Factory Overhead account?

9. What account(s) is(are) used to eliminate overapplied or underapplied overhead from the Factory Overhead account, assuming the amount is not material?

10. Assume that **Apple** produces a batch of 1,000 iPods. Does it account for this as 1,000 individual jobs or as a job lot? Explain (consider costs and benefits).

11. Why must a company prepare a predetermined overhead rate when using job order cost accounting?

12. How would a hospital apply job order costing? Explain.

13. **Harley-Davidson** manufactures 30 luxury-model motorcycles. Does it account for these motorcycles as 30 individual jobs or as a job lot? Explain.   **Harley-Davidson**

 Red numbers denote Discussion Questions that involve decision-making.

QUICK STUDY

QS 19-1
Factory overhead rates   P3

A company incurred the following manufacturing costs this period: direct labor, $468,000; direct materials, $354,500; and factory overhead, $117,000. Compute overhead cost as a percent of (1) direct labor and (2) direct materials. Round percents to the nearest whole number.

QS 19-2
Jobs and job lots

C2

Determine which products are most likely to be manufactured as a job and which as a job lot.

1. A hand-crafted table.
2. A 90-foot motor yacht.
3. Wedding dresses for a chain of stores.
4. A custom-designed home.
5. Hats imprinted with company logo.
6. Little League trophies.

QS 19-3
Job cost computation

C3

The following information is from the materials requisitions and time tickets for Job 9-1005 completed by Great Bay Boats. The requisitions are identified by code numbers starting with the letter Q and the time tickets start with W. At the start of the year, management estimated that overhead cost would equal 110% of direct labor cost for each job. Determine the total cost on the job cost sheet for Job 9-1005.

Date	Document	Amount
7/1/2008	Q-4698	$1,250
7/1/2008	W-3393	600
7/5/2008	Q-4725	1,000
7/5/2008	W-3479	450
7/10/2008	W-3559	300

During the current month, a company that uses a job order cost accounting system purchases $50,000 in raw materials for cash. It then uses $12,000 of raw materials indirectly as factory supplies and uses $32,000 of raw materials as direct materials. Prepare entries to record these three transactions.

QS 19-4
Direct materials journal entries
P1

During the current month, a company that uses a job order cost accounting system incurred a monthly factory payroll of $80,000, paid in cash. Of this amount, $40,000 is classified as indirect labor and the remainder as direct. Prepare entries to record these transactions.

QS 19-5
Direct labor journal entries   P2

During the current month, a company that uses a job order cost accounting system incurred a monthly factory payroll of $175,000, paid in cash. Of this amount, $44,000 is classified as indirect labor and the remainder as direct for the production of a job lot. Factory overhead is applied at 90% of direct labor. Prepare the entry to apply factory overhead to this job lot.

QS 19-6
Factory overhead journal entries
P3

A company allocates overhead at a rate of 150% of direct labor cost. Actual overhead cost for the current period is $950,000, and direct labor cost is $600,000. Prepare the entry to close over- or underapplied overhead to cost of goods sold.

QS 19-7
Entry for over- or underapplied overhead   P4

The left column lists the titles of documents and accounts used in job order cost accounting. The right column presents short descriptions of the purposes of the documents. Match each document in the left column to its numbered description in the right column.

EXERCISES

Exercise 19-1
Documents in job order cost accounting
C2 C3 P1 P2 P3

A. Factory Payroll account
B. Materials ledger card
C. Time ticket
D. Voucher
E. Materials requisition
F. Factory Overhead account
G. Clock card

_____ **1.** Shows amount of time an employee works on a job.
_____ **2.** Temporarily accumulates incurred labor costs until they are assigned to specific jobs or to overhead.
_____ **3.** Shows only total time an employee works each day.
_____ **4.** Perpetual inventory record of raw materials received, used, and available for use.
_____ **5.** Shows amount approved for payment of an overhead or other cost.
_____ **6.** Temporarily accumulates the cost of incurred overhead until the cost is assigned to specific jobs.
_____ **7.** Communicates the need for materials to complete a job.

As of the end of June, the job cost sheets at Racing Wheels, Inc., show the following total costs accumulated on three custom jobs.

Exercise 19-2
Analysis of cost flows
C2 P1 P2 P3

	Job 102	Job 103	Job 104
Direct materials	$15,000	$33,000	$27,000
Direct labor	8,000	14,200	21,000
Overhead	4,000	7,100	10,500

Job 102 was started in production in May and the following costs were assigned to it in May: direct materials, $6,000; direct labor, $1,800; and overhead, $900. Jobs 103 and 104 are started in June. Overhead cost is applied with a predetermined rate based on direct labor cost. Jobs 102 and 103 are finished in June, and Job 104 is expected to be finished in July. No raw materials are used indirectly in June. Using this information, answer the following questions.

1. What is the cost of the raw materials requisitioned in June for each of the three jobs?
2. How much direct labor cost is incurred during June for each of the three jobs?
3. What predetermined overhead rate is used during June?
4. How much total cost is transferred to finished goods during June?

Check (4) $81,300

Exercise 19-3

Overhead rate; costs assigned to jobs

P3

Check   (2) $22,710

In December 2007, Shire Computer's management establishes the year 2008 predetermined overhead rate based on direct labor cost. The information used in setting this rate includes estimates that the company will incur $747,500 of overhead costs and $575,000 of direct labor cost in year 2008. During March 2008, Shire began and completed Job No. 13-56.

1. What is the predetermined overhead rate for year 2008?

2. Use the information on the following job cost sheet to determine the total cost of the job.

JOB COST SHEET

| Customer's Name | Keiser Co. | | | | Job No. | 13-56 |

Job Description   5 plasma monitors—61 inch

	Direct Materials			Direct Labor		Overhead Costs Applied	
Date	Requisition No.	Amount	Time-Ticket No.	Amount	Rate	Amount
Mar. 8	4-129	$5,000	T-306	$ 700		
Mar. 11	4-142	7,020	T-432	1,250		
Mar. 18	4-167	3,330	T-456	1,250		
Totals						

Exercise 19-4

Analysis of costs assigned to goods in process

P3

Lorenzo Company uses a job order cost accounting system that charges overhead to jobs on the basis of direct material cost. At year-end, the Goods in Process Inventory account shows the following.

Accounting System

File Edit Maintain Tasks Analysis Options Reports Window Help

Goods in Process Inventory   Acct. No. 121

Date	Explanation	Debit	Credit	Balance
2008				
Dec. 31	Direct materials cost	1,500,000		1,500,000
31	Direct labor cost	300,000		1,800,000
31	Overhead costs	600,000		2,400,000
31	To finished goods		2,350,000	50,000

Sales   Purchases   General Ledger   Payroll   Inventory   Company   Analysis

Check   (2) Direct labor cost, $8,000

1. Determine the overhead rate used (based on direct material cost).

2. Only one job remained in the goods in process inventory at December 31, 2008. Its direct materials cost is $30,000. How much direct labor cost and overhead cost are assigned to it?

Exercise 19-5

Cost flows in a job order cost system

C3   P3

The following information is available for Lock-Safe Company, which produces special-order security products and uses a job order cost accounting system.

	April 30	May 31
Inventories		
Raw materials	$43,000	$ 52,000
Goods in process	10,200	21,300
Finished goods	63,000	35,600
Activities and information for May		
Raw materials purchases (paid with cash)		210,000
Factory payroll (paid with cash)		345,000
Factory overhead		
Indirect materials		15,000
Indirect labor		80,000
Other overhead costs		120,000
Sales (received in cash)		1,400,000
Predetermined overhead rate based on direct labor cost		70%

Compute the following amounts for the month of May.

1. Cost of direct materials used.   **4.** Cost of goods sold.*

2. Cost of direct labor used.   **5.** Gross profit.

3. Cost of goods manufactured.   **6.** Overapplied or underapplied overhead.

*Do not consider any underapplied or overapplied overhead.

Check   (3) $625,400

Use information in Exercise 19-5 to prepare journal entries for the following events in May.

1. Raw materials purchases for cash.

2. Direct materials usage.

3. Indirect materials usage.

4. Factory payroll costs in cash.

5. Direct labor usage.

6. Indirect labor usage.

7. Factory overhead excluding indirect materials and indirect labor (record credit to Other Accounts).

8. Application of overhead to goods in process.

9. Transfer of finished jobs to the finished goods inventory.

10. Sale and delivery of finished goods to customers for cash (record unadjusted cost of sales).

11. Allocation (closing) of overapplied or underapplied overhead to Cost of Goods Sold.

Exercise 19-6
Journal entries for a job order cost accounting system

P1   P2   P3   P4

In December 2007, Infovision established its predetermined overhead rate for movies produced during year 2008 by using the following cost predictions: overhead costs, $1,680,000, and direct labor costs, $480,000. At year end 2008, the company's records show that actual overhead costs for the year are $1,652,000. Actual direct labor cost had been assigned to jobs as follows.

Exercise 19-7
Factory overhead computed, applied, and adjusted

P3   P4

Movies completed and released	$425,000
Movies still in production	50,000
Total actual direct labor cost	$475,000

1. Determine the predetermined overhead rate for year 2008.

2. Set up a T-account for overhead and enter the overhead costs incurred and the amounts applied to movies during the year using the predetermined overhead rate.

3. Determine whether overhead is overapplied or underapplied (and the amount) during the year.

4. Prepare the adjusting entry to allocate any over- or underapplied overhead to Cost of Goods Sold.

Check   (3) $10,500 overapplied

In December 2007, Cardozo Company established its predetermined overhead rate for jobs produced during year 2008 by using the following cost predictions: overhead costs, $750,000, and direct labor costs, $625,000. At year end 2008, the company's records show that actual overhead costs for the year are $830,000. Actual direct labor cost had been assigned to jobs as follows.

Exercise 19-8
Factory overhead computed, applied, and adjusted

P3   P4

Jobs completed and sold	$513,750
Jobs in finished goods inventory	102,750
Jobs in goods in process inventory	68,500
Total actual direct labor cost	$685,000

1. Determine the predetermined overhead rate for year 2008.

2. Set up a T-account for Factory Overhead and enter the overhead costs incurred and the amounts applied to jobs during the year using the predetermined overhead rate.

3. Determine whether overhead is overapplied or underapplied (and the amount) during the year.

4. Prepare the adjusting entry to allocate any over- or underapplied overhead to Cost of Goods Sold.

5. Prepare the adjusting entry to allocate any over- or underapplied overhead to Cost of Goods Sold, Finished Goods Inventory, and Goods in Process Inventory.

Check   (3) $8,000 underapplied

Sunrise Company applies factory overhead based on direct labor costs. The company incurred the following costs during 2008: direct materials costs, $650,000; direct labor costs, $3,000,000; and factory overhead costs applied, $1,800,000.

Exercise 19-9
Overhead rate calculation, allocation, and analysis   P3

1. Determine the company's predetermined overhead rate for year 2008.

2. Assuming that the company's $71,000 ending Goods in Process Inventory account for year 2008 had $20,000 of direct labor costs, determine the inventory's direct materials costs.

3. Assuming that the company's $490,000 ending Finished Goods Inventory account for year 2008 had $250,000 of direct materials costs, determine the inventory's direct labor costs and its overhead costs.

Exercise 19-10
Costs allocated to ending inventories

P3

Deschamps Company's ending Goods in Process Inventory account consists of 5,000 units of partially completed product, and its Finished Goods Inventory account consists of 12,000 units of product. The factory manager determines that Goods in Process Inventory includes direct materials cost of $10 per unit and direct labor cost of $7 per unit. Finished goods are estimated to have $12 of direct materials cost per unit and $9 of direct labor cost per unit. The company established the predetermined overhead rate using the following predictions: estimated direct labor cost, $300,000, and estimated factory overhead, $375,000. The company allocates factory overhead to its goods in process and finished goods inventories based on direct labor cost. During the period, the company incurred these costs: direct materials, $535,000; direct labor, $290,000; and factory overhead applied, $362,500.

1. Determine the predetermined overhead rate.

2. Compute the total cost of the two ending inventories.

3. Compute cost of goods sold for the year (assume no beginning inventories and no underapplied or overapplied overhead).

Exercise 19-11
Cost-based pricing

A1

Hansel Corporation has requested bids from several architects to design its new corporate headquarters. Frey Architects is one of the firms bidding on the job. Frey estimates that the job will require the following direct labor.

	Labor	Estimated Hours	Hourly Rate
1			
2	Architects	150	$300
3	Staff	300	75
4	Clerical	500	20
5			

Frey applies overhead to jobs at 175% of direct labor cost. Frey would like to earn at least $80,000 profit on the architectural job. Based on past experience and market research, it estimates that the competition will bid between $285,000 and $350,000 for the job.

1. What is Frey's estimated cost of the architectural job?

2. What bid would you suggest that Frey submit?

PROBLEM SET A

Problem 19-1A
Production costs computed and recorded; reports prepared

C3 P1 P2 P3 P4

Ciolino Co.'s March 31 inventory of raw materials is $80,000. Raw materials purchases in April are $500,000, and factory payroll cost in April is $363,000. Overhead costs incurred in April are: indirect materials, $50,000; indirect labor, $23,000; factory rent, $32,000; factory utilities, $19,000; and factory equipment depreciation, $51,000. The predetermined overhead rate is 50% of direct labor cost. Job 306 is sold for $635,000 cash in April. Costs of the three jobs worked on in April follow.

	Job 306	Job 307	Job 308
Balances on March 31			
Direct materials	$ 29,000	$ 35,000	
Direct labor	20,000	18,000	
Applied overhead	10,000	9,000	
Costs during April			
Direct materials	135,000	220,000	$100,000
Direct labor	85,000	150,000	105,000
Applied overhead	?	?	?
Status on April 30	Finished (sold)	Finished (unsold)	In process

Required

1. Determine the total of each production cost incurred for April (direct labor, direct materials, and applied overhead), and the total cost assigned to each job (including the balances from March 31).

2. Prepare journal entries for the month of April to record the following.

    a. Materials purchases (on credit), factory payroll (paid in cash), and actual overhead costs including indirect materials and indirect labor. (Factory rent and utilities are paid in cash.)

    b. Assignment of direct materials, direct labor, and applied overhead costs to the Goods in Process Inventory.

    c. Transfer of Jobs 306 and 307 to the Finished Goods Inventory.

    d. Cost of goods sold for Job 306.

    e. Revenue from the sale of Job 306.

    f. Assignment of any underapplied or overapplied overhead to the Cost of Goods Sold account. (The amount is not material.)

                   Check   (2f) $5,000 underapplied

3. Prepare a manufacturing statement for April (use a single line presentation for direct materials and show the details of overhead cost).

                   (3) Cost of goods manufactured, $828,500

4. Compute gross profit for April. Show how to present the inventories on the April 30 balance sheet.

Analysis Component

5. The over- or underapplied overhead is closed to Cost of Goods Sold. Discuss how this adjustment impacts business decision-making regarding individual jobs or batches of jobs.

Farina Bay's computer system generated the following trial balance on December 31, 2008. The company's manager knows something is wrong with the trial balance because it does not show any balance for Goods in Process Inventory but does show balances for the Factory Payroll and Factory Overhead accounts.

Problem 19-2A

Source documents, journal entries, overhead, and financial reports

P1   P2   P3   P4

	Debit	Credit
Cash	$102,000	
Accounts receivable	75,000	
Raw materials inventory	80,000	
Goods in process inventory	0	
Finished goods inventory	15,000	
Prepaid rent	3,000	
Accounts payable		$ 17,000
Notes payable		25,000
Common stock		50,000
Retained earnings		271,000
Sales		373,000
Cost of goods sold	218,000	
Factory payroll	68,000	
Factory overhead	115,000	
Operating expenses	60,000	
Totals	$736,000	$736,000

After examining various files, the manager identifies the following six source documents that need to be processed to bring the accounting records up to date.

Materials requisition 21-3010:	$10,200 direct materials to Job 402
Materials requisition 21-3011:	$18,600 direct materials to Job 404
Materials requisition 21-3012:	$5,600 indirect materials
Labor time ticket 6052:	$36,000 direct labor to Job 402
Labor time ticket 6053:	$23,800 direct labor to Job 404
Labor time ticket 6054:	$8,200 indirect labor

Jobs 402 and 404 are the only units in process at year-end. The predetermined overhead rate is 200% of direct labor cost.

Required

1. Use information on the six source documents to prepare journal entries to assign the following costs.

    a. Direct materials costs to Goods in Process Inventory.

    b. Direct labor costs to Goods in Process Inventory.

    c. Overhead costs to Goods in Process Inventory.

   d. Indirect materials costs to the Factory Overhead account.

   e. Indirect labor costs to the Factory Overhead account.

2. Determine the revised balance of the Factory Overhead account after making the entries in part 1. Determine whether there is any under- or overapplied overhead for the year. Prepare the adjusting entry to allocate any over- or underapplied overhead to Cost of Goods Sold, assuming the amount is not material.

3. Prepare a revised trial balance.

4. Prepare an income statement for year 2008 and a balance sheet as of December 31, 2008.

Analysis Component

5. Assume that the $5,600 on materials requisition 21-3012 should have been direct materials charged to Job 404. Without providing specific calculations, describe the impact of this error on the income statement for 2008 and the balance sheet at December 31, 2008.

Problem 19-3A

Source documents, journal entries, and accounts in job order cost accounting

P1 P2 P3

Widmer Watercraft's predetermined overhead rate for year 2008 is 200% of direct labor. Information on the company's production activities during May 2008 follows.

a. Purchased raw materials on credit, $200,000.

b. Paid $126,000 cash for factory wages.

c. Paid $15,000 cash to a computer consultant to reprogram factory equipment.

d. Materials requisitions record use of the following materials for the month.

Job 136	$ 48,000
Job 137	32,000
Job 138	19,200
Job 139	22,400
Job 140	6,400
Total direct materials	128,000
Indirect materials	19,500
Total materials used	$147,500

e. Time tickets record use of the following labor for the month.

Job 136	$ 12,000
Job 137	10,500
Job 138	37,500
Job 139	39,000
Job 140	3,000
Total direct labor	102,000
Indirect labor	24,000
Total	$126,000

f. Applied overhead to Jobs 136, 138, and 139.

g. Transferred Jobs 136, 138, and 139 to Finished Goods.

h. Sold Jobs 136 and 138 on credit at a total price of $525,000.

i. The company incurred the following overhead costs during the month (credit Prepaid Insurance for expired factory insurance).

Depreciation of factory building	$68,000
Depreciation of factory equipment	36,500
Expired factory insurance	10,000
Accrued property taxes payable	35,000

j. Applied overhead at month-end to the Goods in Process (Jobs 137 and 140) using the predetermined overhead rate of 200% of direct labor cost.

Required

1. Prepare a job cost sheet for each job worked on during the month. Use the following simplified form.

```
┌─────────────────────────────────┐
│  Job No. _____              │
│                                 │
│  Materials . . . . . . . .  $_____ │
│                                 │
│  Labor . . . . . . . . . .   _____ │
│                                 │
│  Overhead . . . . . . .      _____ │
│                                 │
│  Total cost . . . . . . .  $_____ │
└─────────────────────────────────┘
```

2. Prepare journal entries to record the events and transactions *a* through *j*.

3. Set up T-accounts for each of the following general ledger accounts, each of which started the month with a zero balance: Raw Materials Inventory; Goods in Process Inventory; Finished Goods Inventory; Factory Payroll; Factory Overhead; Cost of Goods Sold. Then post the journal entries to these T-accounts and determine the balance of each account.

4. Prepare a report showing the total cost of each job in process and prove that the sum of their costs equals the Goods in Process Inventory account balance. Prepare similar reports for Finished Goods Inventory and Cost of Goods Sold.

Check (2f) Cr. Factory Overhead, $177,000

Check (4) Finished Goods Inventory, $139,400

In December 2007, Yerbury Company's manager estimated next year's total direct labor cost assuming 50 persons working an average of 2,000 hours each at an average wage rate of $25 per hour. The manager also estimated the following manufacturing overhead costs for year 2008.

Indirect labor	$ 319,200
Factory supervision	240,000
Rent on factory building	140,000
Factory utilities	88,000
Factory insurance expired	68,000
Depreciation—Factory equipment	480,000
Repairs expense—Factory equipment	60,000
Factory supplies used	68,800
Miscellaneous production costs	36,000
Total estimated overhead costs	$1,500,000

Problem 19-4A
Overhead allocation and adjustment using a predetermined overhead rate

C3 P3 P4

mhhe.com/wildFAP18e

At the end of 2008, records show the company incurred $1,520,000 of actual overhead costs. It completed and sold five jobs with the following direct labor costs: Job 201, $604,000; Job 202, $563,000; Job 203, $298,000; Job 204, $716,000; and Job 205, $314,000. In addition, Job 206 is in process at the end of 2008 and had been charged $17,000 for direct labor. No jobs were in process at the end of 2007. The company's predetermined overhead rate is based on direct labor cost.

Required

1. Determine the following.
  a. Predetermined overhead rate for year 2008.
  b. Total overhead cost applied to each of the six jobs during year 2008.
  c. Over- or underapplied overhead at year-end 2008.

2. Assuming that any over- or underapplied overhead is not material, prepare the adjusting entry to allocate any over- or underapplied overhead to Cost of Goods Sold at the end of year 2008.

Check (1c) $12,800 underapplied
(2) Cr. Factory Overhead $12,800

If the working papers that accompany this book are unavailable, do not attempt to solve this problem.
Sager Company manufactures variations of its product, a technopress, in response to custom orders from its customers. On May 1, the company had no inventories of goods in process or finished goods but held the following raw materials.

Problem 19-5A
Production transactions; subsidiary records; and source documents

P1 P2 P3 P4

Material M	200 units @ $250 =	$50,000
Material R	95 units @ 180 =	17,100
Paint	55 units @ 75 =	4,125
Total cost		$71,225

On May 4, the company began working on two technopresses: Job 102 for Worldwide Company and Job 103 for Reuben Company.

Required

Follow the instructions in this list of activities and complete the sheets provided in the working papers.

a. Purchased raw materials on credit and recorded the following information from receiving reports and invoices.

> Receiving Report No. 426, Material M, 250 units at $250 each.
> Receiving Report No. 427, Material R, 90 units at $180 each.

Instructions: Record these purchases with a single journal entry and post it to general ledger T-accounts, using the transaction letter *a* to identify the entry. Enter the receiving report information on the materials ledger cards.

b. Requisitioned the following raw materials for production.

> Requisition No. 35, for Job 102, 135 units of Material M.
> Requisition No. 36, for Job 102, 72 units of Material R.
> Requisition No. 37, for Job 103, 70 units of Material M.
> Requisition No. 38, for Job 103, 38 units of Material R.
> Requisition No. 39, for 15 units of paint.

Instructions: Enter amounts for direct materials requisitions on the materials ledger cards and the job cost sheets. Enter the indirect material amount on the materials ledger card and record a debit to the Indirect Materials account in the subsidiary factory overhead ledger. Do not record a journal entry at this time.

c. Received the following employee time tickets for work in May.

> Time tickets Nos. 1 to 10 for direct labor on Job 102, $90,000.
> Time tickets Nos. 11 to 30 for direct labor on Job 103, $65,000.
> Time tickets Nos. 31 to 36 for equipment repairs, $19,250.

Instructions: Record direct labor from the time tickets on the job cost sheets and then debit indirect labor to the Indirect Labor account in the subsidiary factory overhead ledger. Do not record a journal entry at this time.

d. Paid cash for the following items during the month: factory payroll, $174,250, and miscellaneous overhead items, $102,000.

Instructions: Record these payments with journal entries and then post them to the general ledger accounts. Also record a debit in the Miscellaneous Overhead account in the subsidiary factory overhead ledger.

e. Finished Job 102 and transferred it to the warehouse. The company assigns overhead to each job with a predetermined overhead rate equal to 80% of direct labor cost.

Instructions: Enter the allocated overhead on the cost sheet for Job 102, fill in the cost summary section of the cost sheet, and then mark the cost sheet "Finished." Prepare a journal entry to record the job's completion and its transfer to Finished Goods and then post it to the general ledger accounts.

f. Delivered Job 102 and accepted the customer's promise to pay $400,000 within 30 days.

Instructions: Prepare journal entries to record the sale of Job 102 and the cost of goods sold. Post them to the general ledger accounts.

g. Applied overhead to Job 103 based on the job's direct labor to date.

Instructions: Enter overhead on the job cost sheet but do not make a journal entry at this time.

Check (h) Dr. Goods in Process Inventory, $71,050

h. Recorded the total direct and indirect materials costs as reported on all the requisitions for the month.

Instructions: Prepare a journal entry to record these costs and post it to general ledger accounts.

i. Recorded the total direct and indirect labor costs as reported on all time tickets for the month.

Instructions: Prepare a journal entry to record these costs and post it to general ledger accounts.

j. Recorded the total overhead costs applied to jobs.

Check Balance in Factory Overhead, $1,625 Cr., overapplied

Instructions: Prepare a journal entry to record the allocation of these overhead costs and post it to general ledger accounts.

Tavella Co.'s August 31 inventory of raw materials is $150,000. Raw materials purchases in September are $400,000, and factory payroll cost in September is $220,000. Overhead costs incurred in September are: indirect materials, $30,000; indirect labor, $14,000; factory rent, $20,000; factory utilities, $12,000; and factory equipment depreciation, $30,000. The predetermined overhead rate is 50% of direct labor cost. Job 114 is sold for $380,000 cash in September. Costs for the three jobs worked on in September follow.

PROBLEM SET B

Problem 19-1B
Production costs computed and recorded; reports prepared

C3   P1   P2   P3   P4

	Job 114	Job 115	Job 116
Balances on August 31			
Direct materials	$ 14,000	$ 18,000	
Direct labor	18,000	16,000	
Applied overhead	9,000	8,000	
Costs during September			
Direct materials	100,000	170,000	$ 80,000
Direct labor	30,000	68,000	120,000
Applied overhead	?	?	?
Status on September 30	Finished (sold)	Finished (unsold)	In process

Required

1. Determine the total of each production cost incurred for September (direct labor, direct materials, and applied overhead), and the total cost assigned to each job (including the balances from August 31).

2. Prepare journal entries for the month of September to record the following.

   a. Materials purchases (on credit), factory payroll (paid in cash), and actual overhead costs including indirect materials and indirect labor. (Factory rent and utilities are paid in cash.)

   b. Assignment of direct materials, direct labor, and applied overhead costs to Goods in Process Inventory.

   c. Transfer of Jobs 114 and 115 to the Finished Goods Inventory.

   d. Cost of Job 114 in the Cost of Goods Sold account.

   e. Revenue from the sale of Job 114.

   f. Assignment of any underapplied or overapplied overhead to the Cost of Goods Sold account. (The amount is not material.)

3. Prepare a manufacturing statement for September (use a single line presentation for direct materials and show the details of overhead cost).

4. Compute gross profit for September. Show how to present the inventories on the September 30 balance sheet.

Check (2f) $3,000 overapplied

(3) Cost of goods manufactured, $500,000

Analysis Component

5. The over- or underapplied overhead adjustment is closed to Cost of Goods Sold. Discuss how this adjustment impacts business decision making regarding individual jobs or batches of jobs.

Swisher Company's computer system generated the following trial balance on December 31, 2008. The company's manager knows that the trial balance is wrong because it does not show any balance for Goods in Process Inventory but does show balances for the Factory Payroll and Factory Overhead accounts.

Problem 19-2B
Source documents, journal entries, overhead, and financial reports

P1   P2   P3   P4

	Debit	Credit
Cash	$ 48,000	
Accounts receivable	42,000	
Raw materials inventory	26,000	
Goods in process inventory	0	
Finished goods inventory	9,000	
Prepaid rent	3,000	
Accounts payable		$ 10,500
Notes payable		13,500
Common stock		30,000
Retained earnings		87,000
Sales		180,000
Cost of goods sold	105,000	

[continued on next page]

[continued from previous page]

Factory payroll	16,000	
Factory overhead	27,000	
Operating expenses	45,000	
Totals	$321,000	$321,000

After examining various files, the manager identifies the following six source documents that need to be processed to bring the accounting records up to date.

Materials requisition 94-231:	$4,600 direct materials to Job 603
Materials requisition 94-232:	$7,600 direct materials to Job 604
Materials requisition 94-233:	$2,100 indirect materials
Labor time ticket 765:	$5,000 direct labor to Job 603
Labor time ticket 766:	$8,000 direct labor to Job 604
Labor time ticket 777:	$3,000 indirect labor

Jobs 603 and 604 are the only units in process at year-end. The predetermined overhead rate is 200% of direct labor cost.

Required

1. Use information on the six source documents to prepare journal entries to assign the following costs.
   a. Direct materials costs to Goods in Process Inventory.
   b. Direct labor costs to Goods in Process Inventory.
   c. Overhead costs to Goods in Process Inventory.
   d. Indirect materials costs to the Factory Overhead account.
   e. Indirect labor costs to the Factory Overhead account.

Check (2) $6,100 underapplied overhead

2. Determine the revised balance of the Factory Overhead account after making the entries in part 1. Determine whether there is under- or overapplied overhead for the year. Prepare the adjusting entry to allocate any over- or underapplied overhead to Cost of Goods Sold, assuming the amount is not material.

(3) T. B. totals, $321,000

3. Prepare a revised trial balance.

(4) Net income, $23,900

4. Prepare an income statement for year 2008 and a balance sheet as of December 31, 2008.

Analysis Component

5. Assume that the $2,100 indirect materials on materials requisition 94-233 should have been direct materials charged to Job 604. Without providing specific calculations, describe the impact of this error on the income statement for 2008 and the balance sheet at December 31, 2008.

Problem 19-3B
Source documents, journal entries, and accounts in job order cost accounting

P1 P2 P3

Prescott Company's predetermined overhead rate is 200% of direct labor. Information on the company's production activities during September 2008 follows.
a. Purchased raw materials on credit, $125,000.
b. Paid $84,000 cash for factory wages.
c. Paid $11,000 cash for miscellaneous factory overhead costs.
d. Materials requisitions record use of the following materials for the month.

Job 487	$30,000
Job 488	20,000
Job 489	12,000
Job 490	14,000
Job 491	4,000
Total direct materials	80,000
Indirect materials	12,000
Total materials used	$92,000

e. Time tickets record use of the following labor for the month.

Job 487	$ 8,000
Job 488	7,000
Job 489	25,000
Job 490	26,000
Job 491	2,000
Total direct labor	68,000
Indirect labor	16,000
Total	$84,000

f. Allocated overhead to Jobs 487, 489, and 490.

g. Transferred Jobs 487, 489, and 490 to Finished Goods.

h. Sold Jobs 487 and 489 on credit for a total price of $340,000.

i. The company incurred the following overhead costs during the month (credit Prepaid Insurance for expired factory insurance).

Depreciation of factory building	$37,000
Depreciation of factory equipment	21,000
Expired factory insurance	7,000
Accrued property taxes payable	31,000

j. Applied overhead at month-end to the Goods in Process (Jobs 488 and 491) using the predetermined overhead rate of 200% of direct labor cost.

Required

1. Prepare a job cost sheet for each job worked on in the month. Use the following simplified form.

Job No. _____	
Materials	$ _____
Labor	_____
Overhead	_____
Total cost	$ _____

2. Prepare journal entries to record the events and transactions *a* through *j*.

3. Set up T-accounts for each of the following general ledger accounts, each of which started the month with a zero balance: Raw Materials Inventory, Goods in Process Inventory, Finished Goods Inventory, Factory Payroll, Factory Overhead, Cost of Goods Sold. Then post the journal entries to these T-accounts and determine the balance of each account.

4. Prepare a report showing the total cost of each job in process and prove that the sum of their costs equals the Goods in Process Inventory account balance. Prepare similar reports for Finished Goods Inventory and Cost of Goods Sold.

Check (2f) Cr. Factory Overhead, $118,000

(4) Finished Goods Inventory, $92,000

In December 2007, Pavelka Company's manager estimated next year's total direct labor cost assuming 50 persons working an average of 2,000 hours each at an average wage rate of $15 per hour. The manager also estimated the following manufacturing overhead costs for year 2008.

Problem 19-4B
Overhead allocation and adjustment using a predetermined overhead rate

C3 P3 P4

Indirect labor	$159,600
Factory supervision	120,000
Rent on factory building	70,000
Factory utilities	44,000
Factory insurance expired	34,000
Depreciation—Factory equipment	240,000
Repairs expense—Factory equipment	30,000
Factory supplies used	34,400
Miscellaneous production costs	18,000
Total estimated overhead costs	$750,000

At the end of 2008, records show the company incurred $725,000 of actual overhead costs. It completed and sold five jobs with the following direct labor costs: Job 625, $354,000; Job 626, $330,000; Job 627, $175,000; Job 628, $420,000; and Job 629, $184,000. In addition, Job 630 is in process at the end of 2008 and had been charged $10,000 for direct labor. No jobs were in process at the end of 2007. The company's predetermined overhead rate is based on direct labor cost.

Required

1. Determine the following.
   a. Predetermined overhead rate for year 2008.
   b. Total overhead cost applied to each of the six jobs during year 2008.
   c. Over- or underapplied overhead at year-end 2008.

Check (1c) $11,500 overapplied

(2) Dr. Factory Overhead, $11,500

2. Assuming that any over- or underapplied overhead is not material, prepare the adjusting entry to allocate any over- or underapplied overhead to Cost of Goods Sold at the end of year 2008.

Problem 19-5B
Production transactions; subsidiary records; and source documents

P1 P2 P3 P4

If the working papers that accompany this book are unavailable, do not attempt to solve this problem. King Company produces variations of its product, a megatron, in response to custom orders from its customers. On June 1, the company had no inventories of goods in process or finished goods but held the following raw materials.

Material M	120 units @ $200 =	$24,000
Material R	80 units @ 160 =	12,800
Paint	44 units @ 72 =	3,168
Total cost		$39,968

On June 3, the company began working on two megatrons: Job 450 for Encinita Company and Job 451 for Fargo, Inc.

Required

Follow instructions in this list of activities and complete the sheets provided in the working papers.

a. Purchased raw materials on credit and recorded the following information from receiving reports and invoices.

> Receiving Report No. 20, Material M, 150 units at $200 each.
> Receiving Report No. 21, Material R, 70 units at $160 each.

Instructions: Record these purchases with a single journal entry and post it to general ledger T-accounts, using the transaction letter *a* to identify the entry. Enter the receiving report information on the materials ledger cards.

b. Requisitioned the following raw materials for production.

> Requisition No. 223, for Job 450, 80 units of Material M.
> Requisition No. 224, for Job 450, 60 units of Material R.
> Requisition No. 225, for Job 451, 40 units of Material M.
> Requisition No. 226, for Job 451, 30 units of Material R.
> Requisition No. 227, for 12 units of paint.

Instructions: Enter amounts for direct materials requisitions on the materials ledger cards and the job cost sheets. Enter the indirect material amount on the materials ledger card and record a debit to the Indirect Materials account in the subsidiary factory overhead ledger. Do not record a journal entry at this time.

c. Received the following employee time tickets for work in June.

> Time tickets Nos. 1 to 10 for direct labor on Job 450, $40,000.
> Time tickets Nos. 11 to 20 for direct labor on Job 451, $32,000.
> Time tickets Nos. 21 to 24 for equipment repairs, $12,000.

Instructions: Record direct labor from the time tickets on the job cost sheets and then debit indirect labor to the Indirect Labor account in the subsidiary factory overhead ledger. Do not record a journal entry at this time.

d. Paid cash for the following items during the month: factory payroll, $84,000, and miscellaneous overhead items, $36,800.

Instructions: Record these payments with journal entries and post them to the general ledger accounts. Also record a debit in the Miscellaneous Overhead account in the subsidiary factory overhead ledger.

e. Finished Job 450 and transferred it to the warehouse. The company assigns overhead to each job with a predetermined overhead rate equal to 70% of direct labor cost.

Instructions: Enter the allocated overhead on the cost sheet for Job 450, fill in the cost summary section of the cost sheet, and then mark the cost sheet "Finished." Prepare a journal entry to record the job's completion and its transfer to Finished Goods and then post it to the general ledger accounts.

f. Delivered Job 450 and accepted the customer's promise to pay $290,000 within 30 days.

Instructions: Prepare journal entries to record the sale of Job 450 and the cost of goods sold. Post them to the general ledger accounts.

g. Applied overhead cost to Job 451 based on the job's direct labor used to date.

Instructions: Enter overhead on the job cost sheet but do not make a journal entry at this time.

h. Recorded the total direct and indirect materials costs as reported on all the requisitions for the month.

Instructions: Prepare a journal entry to record these costs and post it to general ledger accounts.

Check (h) Dr. Goods in Process Inventory, $38,400

i. Recorded the total direct and indirect labor costs as reported on all time tickets for the month.

Instructions: Prepare a journal entry to record these costs and post it to general ledger accounts.

j. Recorded the total overhead costs applied to jobs.

Instructions: Prepare a journal entry to record the allocation of these overhead costs and post it to general ledger accounts.

Check Balance in Factory Overhead, $736 Cr., overapplied

 Problem Set C is available at the book's Website to reinforce and assess your learning.   **PROBLEM SET C**

(This serial problem began in Chapter 1 and continues through most of the book. If previous chapter segments were not completed, the serial problem can begin at this point. It is helpful, but not necessary, for you to use the Working Papers that accompany the book.)

SERIAL PROBLEM

Success Systems

SP 19   The computer workstation furniture manufacturing that Adriana Lopez started in January 2009, is progressing well. As of the end of June, Success Systems' job cost sheets show these total costs accumulated on three furniture jobs.

	Job 6.02	Job 6.03	Job 6.04
Direct materials	$3,000	$6,600	$5,400
Direct labor	1,600	2,840	4,200
Overhead	800	1,420	2,100

Job 6.02 was started in production in May, and these costs were assigned to it in May: direct materials, $1,200; direct labor, $360; and overhead, $180. Jobs 6.03 and 6.04 were started in June. Overhead cost is applied with a predetermined rate based on direct labor costs. Jobs 6.02 and 6.03 are finished in June, and Job 6.04 is expected to be finished in July. No raw materials are used indirectly in June.

Required

1. What is the cost of the raw materials used in June for each of the three jobs and in total?

2. How much total direct labor cost is incurred in June?

3. What predetermined overhead rate is used in June?

4. How much cost is transferred to finished goods inventory in June?

Check (1) Total materials, $13,800

(3) 50%

BEYOND THE NUMBERS

BTN 19-1   Best Buy's financial statements and notes in Appendix A provide evidence of growth potential in its domestic sales.

REPORTING IN ACTION

C2

Required

1. Identify at least two types of costs that will predictably increase as a percent of sales with growth in domestic sales.

2. Explain why you believe the types of costs identified for part 1 will increase, and describe how you might assess Best Buy's success with these costs. (*Hint:* You might consider the gross margin ratio.)

Fast Forward

3. Access Best Buy's annual report for a fiscal year ending after February 26, 2005, from its Website [**BestBuy.com**] or the SEC's EDGAR database [**www.sec.gov**]. Review and report its growth in sales along with its cost and income levels (including its gross margin ratio).

COMPARATIVE ANALYSIS

C1

BTN 19-2   Retailers as well as manufacturers can apply just-in-time (JIT) to their inventory management. Both **Best Buy** and **Circuit City** want to know the impact of a JIT inventory system for their operating cash flows. Review each company's statement of cash flows in Appendix A to answer the following.

Required

1. Identify the impact on operating cash flows (increase or decrease) for changes in inventory levels (increase or decrease) for both companies for each of the three most recent years.

2. What impact would a JIT inventory system have on both Best Buy's and Circuit City's operating income? Link the answer to your response for part 1.

3. Would the move to a JIT system have a one-time or recurring impact on operating cash flow?

ETHICS CHALLENGE

P3

Point: Students could compare responses and discuss differences in concerns with allocating overhead.

BTN 19-3   An accounting professional requires at least two skill sets. The first is to be technically competent. Knowing how to capture, manage, and report information is a necessary skill. Second, the ability to assess manager and employee actions and biases for accounting analysis is another skill. For instance, knowing how a person is compensated helps anticipate information biases. Draw on these skills and write a one-half page memo to the financial officer on the following practice of allocating overhead.

Background: Assume that your company sells portable housing to both general contractors and the government. It sells jobs to contractors on a bid basis. A contractor asks for three bids from different manufacturers. The combination of low bid and high quality wins the job. However, jobs sold to the government are bid on a cost-plus basis. This means price is determined by adding all costs plus a profit based on cost at a specified percent, such as 10%. You observe that the amount of overhead allocated to government jobs is higher than that allocated to contract jobs. These allocations concern you and motivate your memo.

COMMUNICATING IN PRACTICE

C2   C3

Point: Have students present a mock interview, one assuming the role of the president of the company and the other the applicant.

BTN 19-4   Assume that you are preparing for a second interview with a manufacturing company. The company is impressed with your credentials but has indicated that it has several qualified applicants. You anticipate that in this second interview, you must show what you offer over other candidates. You learn the company currently uses a periodic inventory system and is not satisfied with the timeliness of its information and its inventory management. The company manufactures custom-order holiday decorations and display items. To show your abilities, you plan to recommend that it use a cost accounting system.

Required

In preparation for the interview, prepare notes outlining the following:

1. Your cost accounting system recommendation and why it is suitable for this company.

2. A general description of the documents that the proposed cost accounting system requires.

3. How the documents in part 2 facilitate the operation of the cost accounting system.

TAKING IT TO THE NET

C2

BTN 19-5   Many contractors work on custom jobs that require a job order costing system.

Required

Access the Website **AEC.Geac.com** and under *Job Cost Accounting* click on *The Construction Manager*. Prepare a one-page memorandum for the CEO of a construction company providing information about the job order costing software this company offers. Would you recommend that the company purchase this software?

TEAMWORK IN ACTION

C2

BTN 19-6   Consider the activities undertaken by a medical clinic in your area.

Required

1. Do you consider a job order cost accounting system appropriate for the clinic?

2. Identify as many factors as possible to lead you to conclude that it uses a job order system.

BTN 19-7 Read the article "Ikea—How the Swedish Retailer Became a Global Cult Brand" in the November 14, 2005, issue of *BusinessWeek*.

Required

Identify the reasons why **Ikea** can offer low-cost products to its customers.

BusinessWeek
ACTIVITY

C1   C2

BTN 19-8 Refer to the chapter opener regarding Marco and Sandra Johnson and their company, **Antelope Valley Medical College**. All successful businesses track their costs. It is especially important for a startup business to monitor and control its costs. Marco and Sandra hope to track all costs associated with each training course taught at their college.

Required

1. How can Marco and Sandra apply a job order costing system for Antelope Valley Medical College to monitor the costs of each course? Can they apply the same system to monitor the profitability of each course taught? Explain.

2. Assume that Marco and Sandra use a job order costing system at Antelope Valley Medical College. Identify the three basic cost categories. List at least two typical costs that will fall into each cost category.

ENTREPRENEURIAL DECISION

C2

BTN 19-9 Job order cost accounting is frequently used by home builders.

Required

1. You (or your team) are to prepare a job cost sheet for a single-family home under construction. List four items of both direct materials and direct labor. Explain how you think overhead should be applied.

2. Contact a builder and compare your job cost sheet to this builder's job cost sheet. If possible, speak to that company's accountant. Write your findings in a short report.

HITTING THE ROAD

C3   P2   P3   P4

BTN 19-10 **Dixons**, **Circuit City**, and **Best Buy** are competitors in the global marketplace. Access Dixons' annual report (**Dixons-Group.com**) for the year ended May 1, 2004. The following information is available for Dixons.

(£ millions)	Current Year	One Year Prior	Two Years Prior
Inventories	£777.7	£699.9	£615.7

Required

1. Determine the change in Dixons' inventories for the last two years. Then identify the impact on net resources generated by operating activities (increase or decrease) for changes in inventory levels (increase or decrease) for Dixons for the last two years.

2. Would a move to a JIT system likely impact Dixons more than it would Best Buy or Circuit City? Explain.

GLOBAL DECISION

C1

ANSWERS TO MULTIPLE CHOICE QUIZ

1. c; $30,000 \times 150\% = \underline{\$45,000}$

2. b; $38,500/\$35,000 = \underline{110\%}$

3. e; Direct materials + Direct labor + Overhead = Total cost;
   Direct materials + ($4,000/.80) + $4,000 = $10,000
   Direct materials = $\underline{\$1,000}$

4. e; $9,000 + $94,200 + $59,200 + $31,600 − Finished goods = $17,800
   Thus, finished goods = $\underline{\$176,200}$

5. b

20

Process Cost Accounting

A Look Back

Chapter 18 introduced managerial accounting and described cost concepts and the reporting of manufacturing activities. Chapter 19 explained job order costing—an important cost accounting system for customized products and services.

A Look at This Chapter

This chapter focuses on how to measure and account for costs in process operations. We explain process production, describe how to assign costs to processes, and compute cost per equivalent unit for a process.

A Look Ahead

Chapter 21 explains how to allocate factory overhead costs to different products and introduces the activity-based costing method of overhead allocation. It also explains responsibility accounting and measures of departmental performance.

Learning Objectives

CAP

Conceptual

C1 Explain process operations and the way they differ from job order operations. (p. 798)

C2 Define equivalent units and explain their use in process cost accounting. (p. 805)

C3 Explain the four steps in accounting for production activity in a period. (p. 806)

C4 Define a process cost summary and describe its purposes. (p. 809)

C5 *Appendix 20A*—Explain and illustrate the four steps in accounting for production activity using FIFO. (p. 816)

Analytical

A1 Compare process cost accounting and job order cost accounting. (p. 799)

A2 Explain and illustrate a hybrid costing system. (p. 813)

Procedural

P1 Record the flow of direct materials costs in process cost accounting. (p. 802)

P2 Record the flow of direct labor costs in process cost accounting. (p. 802)

P3 Record the flow of factory overhead costs in process cost accounting. (p. 803)

P4 Compute equivalent units produced in a period. (p. 805)

P5 Prepare a process cost summary. (p. 809)

P6 Record the transfer of completed goods to Finished Goods Inventory and Cost of Goods Sold. (p. 811)

"Once you make a mistake that costs you a lot of money . . . you never forget it"
—Cristina Bartolucci (on left is Laura DeLuisa)

Decision Feature

Styling to the DuWop Tune

GLENDALE, CA—A few years ago, Cristina Bartolucci and Laura DeLuisa were making their livings as hair and makeup artists on Hollywood movie sets. They had no idea they would soon become makeup moguls. "We had this problem," explains Cristina. "Stars would go out late, eat too much . . . drink too much . . . and arrive on the set at 5 AM with tired, puffy eyes, and then expect us to make them look flawless and wide awake." So the pair headed into Laura's kitchen and developed *I Gels*—naturally cool gel discs filled with botanicals that, when placed on the eyes, are soothing and help with dark circles and puffiness. Cristina and Laura promptly started their makeup company called **DuWop (DuWop.com),** meaning "two Italian girls."

"If it weren't for *I Gels,* I don't know if we'd be here," says Laura. Although *I Gels* were an instant hit, it took a lot of hard work. Cristina and Laura had to learn about production operations and suppliers. A big part of their success, they say, was learning the skills needed to monitor and control the costs of materials, labor, and overhead applied to production processes. Cristina and Laura also adopted a hands-on managerial style. "The UPS truck would arrive and we'd start flinging parcels," jokes Laura. But they feel their highly involved approach to production management is necessary. "[If] you make a

mistake that costs you a lot of money, you risk losing your company," says Cristina.

Cristina and Laura also developed their abilities to prepare and interpret process cost summaries on their production activities. Sales are important, they admit, but without cost controls, income is quickly eaten away. "[We] fix problems right away," says Cristina. Suppliers of materials presented special challenges, explains Laura. "I'd actually gotten bullied by a few suppliers. [And] they'd talk us into things that we really didn't need," she says. Yet the pair's focus on cost management helped curtail the risks of making bad decisions, and they stayed committed to improving process operations and tracking all costs.

DuWop began with the advantage of having a natural research lab. "On the packaging it says, 'Not tested on animals, only on actors,' and that's the truth," says Laura. They also focused on satisfying customers. "Some of our most devoted customers are people who have had suggestions about how to make a product better," says Cristina. The DuWop duo listens intently to its actor-customers to grow their beloved business. "I don't believe in giving up," says Laura. Adds Cristina, "I love what I'm doing."

[Sources: *DuWop Website,* May 2006; *Entrepreneur,* November and October 2004; *CPC Packaging,* February 2005; *Health and Beauty,* November 2001; *Factio,* July 2005; *Oprah Winfrey Show,* 2003]

The type of product or service a company offers determines its cost accounting system. Job order costing is used to account for custom products and services that meet the demands of a particular customer. Not all products are manufactured in this way; many carry standard designs so that one unit is no different than any other unit. Such a system often produces large numbers of units on a continuous basis, all of which pass through similar processes. This chapter describes how to use a process cost accounting system to account for these types of products. It also explains how costs are accumulated for each process and then assigned to units passing through those processes. This information helps to understand and estimate the cost of each process as well as find ways to reduce costs and improve processes.

Process Cost Accounting

Process Operations	Process Cost Accounting	Equivalent Units of Production (EUP)	Process Costing Illustration
• Comparison of job order and process operations • Organization of process operations • GenX Company—An Illustration	• Direct and indirect costs • Accounting for materials costs • Accounting for labor costs • Accounting for factory overhead	• Accounting for goods in process • Differences between EUP for materials and that for labor and overhead	• Physical flow of units • EUP • Cost per EUP • Cost reconciliation • Process cost summary • Transfers to finished goods and to cost of goods sold

Process Operations

C1 Explain process operations and the way they differ from job order operations.

Process operations, also called *process manufacturing* or *process production,* is the mass production of products in a continuous flow of steps. This means that products pass through a series of sequential processes. Petroleum refining is a common example of process operations. Crude oil passes through a series of steps before it is processed into different grades of petroleum. **Exxon Mobil**'s oil activities reflect a process operation. An important characteristic of process operations is the high level of standardization necessary if the system is to produce large volumes of products. Process operations also extend to services. Examples include mail sorting in large post offices and order processing in large mail-order firms such as **L.L. Bean**. The common feature in these service organizations is that operations are performed in a sequential manner using a series of standardized processes. Other companies using process operations include **Kellogg** (cereals), **Pfizer** (drugs), **Procter & Gamble** (household products), **Xerox** (copiers), **Coca-Cola** (softdrinks), **Heinz** (ketchup), and **Hershey** (chocolate).

Each of these examples of products and services involves operations having a series of *processes,* or steps. Each process involves a different set of activities. A production operation that processes chemicals, for instance, might include the four steps shown in Exhibit 20.1. Understanding such processes for companies with process operations is crucial for measuring their costs.

Exhibit 20.1

Process Operations: Chemicals

Comparing Job Order and Process Operations

Job order and process operations can be considered as two ends of a continuum. Important features of both systems are shown in Exhibit 20.2. We often describe job order and process operations with manufacturing examples, but they both apply to service companies. In a job order costing system, the measurement focus is on the individual job or batch. In a process costing system, the measurement focus is on the process itself and the standardized units produced.

A1 Compare process cost accounting and job order cost accounting.

Exhibit 20.2

Comparing Job Order and Process Operations

Job Order Systems	Process Systems
• Custom orders	• Repetitive operations
• Heterogeneous products and services	• Homogeneous products and services
• Low production volume	• High production volume
• High product flexibility	• Low product flexibility
• Low to medium standardization	• High standardization

Organization of Process Operations

In a process operation, each process is identified as a separate *production department, workstation,* or *work center.* With the exception of the first process or department, each receives the output from the prior department as a partially processed product. Depending on the nature of the process, a company applies direct labor, overhead, and, perhaps, additional direct materials to move the product toward completion. Only the final process or department in the series produces finished goods ready for sale to customers.

Tracking costs for several related departments can seem complex. Yet because process costing procedures are applied to the activity of each department or process separately, we need only consider one process at a time. This simplifies the procedures.

When the output of one department becomes an input to another department, as is the case in sequential processing, we simply transfer the costs associated with those units from the first department into the next. We repeat these steps from department to department until the final process is complete. At that point the accumulated costs are transferred with the product from Goods in Process Inventory to Finished Goods Inventory. The next section illustrates a company with a single process, but the methods illustrated apply to a multiprocess scenario as each department's costs are handled separately for each department.

GenX Company— An Illustration

The GenX Company illustrates process operations. It produces Profen®, an over-the-counter pain reliever for athletes. GenX sells Profen to wholesale distributors who in turn sell it to retailers. Profen is produced by mixing its active

Decision Insight

Accounting for Health   Many service companies use process departments to perform specific tasks for consumers. Hospitals, for instance, have radiology and physical therapy facilities with special equipment and trained employees. When patients need services, they are processed through departments to receive prescribed care. Service companies need process cost accounting information as much as manufacturers to estimate costs of services, to plan future operations, to control costs, and to determine customer charges.

ingredient, Profelene, with flavorings and preservatives, molding it into Profen tablets, and packaging the tablets. Exhibit 20.3 shows a summary floor plan of the GenX factory, which has five areas.

☐1 *Storeroom*—materials are received and then distributed when requisitioned.

☐2 *Production support offices*—used by administrative and maintenance employees who support manufacturing operations.

☐3 *Locker rooms*—workers change from street clothes into sanitized uniforms before working in the factory.

☐4 *Production floor*—area where the powder is processed into tablets.

☐5 *Warehouse*—finished products are stored before being shipped to wholesalers.

Point: Robots, computers, and online information are common in today's factory.

Exhibit 20.3

Floor Plan of GenX's Factory

The first step in process manufacturing is to decide when to produce a product. Management determines the types and quantities of materials and labor needed and then schedules the work. Based on these plans, production begins. The flowchart in Exhibit 20.4 shows the production steps for GenX. The following sections explain how GenX uses a process cost accounting system to compute these costs. Many of the explanations refer to this exhibit and its numbered cost flows ① through ⑩. (*Hint:* The amounts for the numbered cost flows in Exhibit 20.4 are summarized in Exhibit 20.21. Those amounts are explained in the following pages, but it can help to refer to Exhibit 20.21 as we proceed through the explanations.)

Exhibit 20.4

Process Operations and Costs: GenX

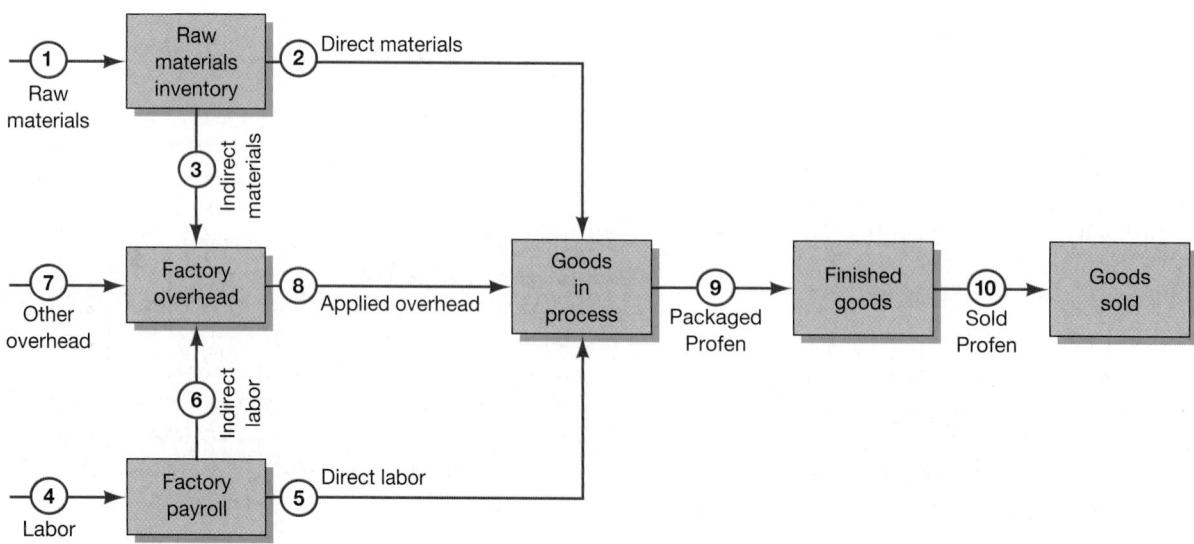

Process Cost Accounting

Process and job order operations are similar in that both combine materials, labor, and overhead in the process of producing products. They differ in how they are organized and managed. The measurement focus in a job order costing system is on the individual job or batch, whereas in a process costing system, it is on the individual process. Regardless of the measurement focus, we are ultimately interested in determining the cost per unit of product (or service) resulting from either system.

Specifically, the **job order cost accounting system** assigns direct materials, direct labor, and overhead to jobs. The total job cost is then divided by the number of units to compute a cost per unit for that job. The **process cost accounting system** assigns direct materials, direct labor, and overhead to specific processes (or departments). The total costs associated with each process are then divided by the number of units passing through that process to determine the cost per equivalent unit (defined later in the chapter) for that process. Differences in the way these two systems apply materials, labor, and overhead costs are highlighted in Exhibit 20.5.

Point: The cost object in a job order system is the specific job; the cost object in a process costing system is the process.

Job order operations

Process operations

Exhibit 20.5

Comparing Job Order and Process Cost Accounting Systems

Direct and Indirect Costs

Like job order operations, process cost accounting systems use the concepts of direct and indirect costs. Materials and labor that can be traced to specific processes are assigned to those processes as direct costs. Materials and labor that cannot be traced to a specific process are indirect costs and are assigned to overhead. Some costs classified as overhead in a job order system may be classified as direct costs in process cost accounting. For example, depreciation of a machine used entirely by one process is a direct cost of that process.

Point: If a cost can be traced to the cost object, it is direct; if it cannot, it is indirect.

Decision Insight

JIT Boon to Process Operations   Companies that adopt JIT manufacturing often organize their production system as a series of sequential processes. One survey found 60% of companies that converted to JIT used process operations; this compares to only 20% before converting to JIT.

Accounting for Materials Costs

P1   Record the flow of direct
     materials costs in process
cost accounting.

In Exhibit 20.4, arrow line ① reflects the arrival of materials at GenX's factory. These materials include Profelene, flavorings, preservatives, and packaging. They also include supplies for the production support office. GenX uses a perpetual inventory system and makes all purchases on credit. The summary entry for receipts of raw materials in April follows (dates in journal entries numbered ① through ⑩ are omitted because they are summary entries, often reflecting two or more transactions or events).

Assets = Liabilities + Equity
+11,095   +11,095

①	Raw Materials Inventory	11,095
	Accounts Payable	11,095
	Acquired materials on credit for factory use.	

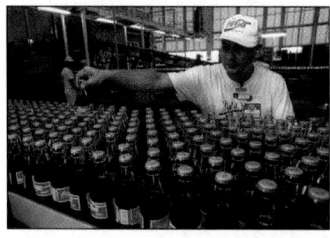

Arrow line ② in Exhibit 20.4 reflects the flow of direct materials to production, where they are used to produce Profen. Most direct materials are physically combined into the finished product; the remaining direct materials include those used and clearly linked with a specific process. The manager of a process usually obtains materials by submitting a *materials requisition* to the materials storeroom manager. In some situations, materials move continuously from raw materials inventory through the manufacturing process. **Pepsi Bottling**, for instance, uses a process in which inventory moves continuously through the system. In these cases, a **materials consumption report** summarizes the materials used by a department during a reporting period and replaces materials requisitions. The entry to record the use of direct materials by GenX's production department in April follows.

Assets = Liabilities + Equity
+9,900
−9,900

②	Goods in Process Inventory	9,900
	Raw Materials Inventory	9,900
	To assign costs of direct materials used in production.	

This entry transfers costs from one asset account to another asset account. (When two or more production departments exist, a company uses two or more Goods in Process Inventory accounts to separately accumulate costs incurred by each.)

In Exhibit 20.4, the arrow line ③ reflects the flow of indirect materials from the storeroom to factory overhead. These materials are not clearly linked with any specific production process or department but are used to support overall production activity. The following entry records the cost of indirect materials used by GenX in April.

Example: What types of materials might the flow of arrow line ③ in Exhibit 20.4 reflect? *Answer:* Goggles, gloves, protective clothing, recordkeeping supplies, and cleaning supplies.

Assets = Liabilities + Equity
−1,195   −1,195

③	Factory Overhead	1,195
	Raw Materials Inventory	1,195
	To record indirect materials used in April.	

After the entries for both direct and indirect materials are posted, the Raw Materials Inventory account appears as shown in Exhibit 20.6. The April 30 balance sheet reports the $4,000 Raw Materials Inventory account as a current asset.

Exhibit 20.6

Raw Materials Inventory

Raw Materials Inventory				Acct. No. 132		
Date		Explanation		Debit	Credit	Balance
Mar.	31	Balance			·	4,000
Apr.	30	Materials purchases		11,095		15,095
	30	Direct materials usage			9,900	5,195
	30	Indirect materials usage			1,195	4,000

Accounting for Labor Costs

P2   Record the flow of direct
     labor costs in process
cost accounting.

Exhibit 20.4 shows GenX factory payroll costs as reflected in arrow line ④. Total labor costs of $8,920 are paid in cash and are recorded in the Factory Payroll account.

④	Factory Payroll.............................	8,920		Assets = Liabilities + Equity
	Cash		8,920	−8,920 −8,920
	To record factory wages for April.			

Time reports from the production department and the production support office triggered this entry. (For simplicity, we do not separately identify withholdings and additional payroll taxes for employees.) In a process operation, the direct labor of a production department includes all labor used exclusively by that department. This is the case even if the labor is not applied to the product itself. If a production department in a process operation, for instance, has a full-time manager and a full-time maintenance worker, their salaries are direct labor costs of that process and are not factory overhead.

Arrow line ⑤ in Exhibit 20.4 shows GenX's use of direct labor in the production department. The following entry transfers April's direct labor costs from the Factory Payroll account to the Goods in Process Inventory account.

⑤	Goods in Process Inventory	5,700		Assets = Liabilities + Equity
	Factory Payroll		5,700	+5,700 +5,700
	To assign costs of direct labor used in production.			

Arrow line ⑥ in Exhibit 20.4 reflects GenX's indirect labor costs. These employees provide clerical, maintenance, and other services that help produce Profen efficiently. For example, they order materials, deliver them to the factory floor, repair equipment, operate and program computers used in production, keep payroll and other production records, clean up, and move the finished goods to the warehouse. The following entry charges these indirect labor costs to factory overhead.

Point: A department's indirect labor cost might include an allocated portion of the salary of a manager who supervises two or more departments. Allocation of costs between departments is discussed in Chapter 21.

⑥	Factory Overhead	3,220		Assets = Liabilities + Equity
	Factory Payroll		3,220	−3,220
	To record indirect labor as overhead.			+3,220

After these entries for both direct and indirect labor are posted, the Factory Payroll account appears as shown in Exhibit 20.7. The Factory Payroll account is now closed and ready to receive entries for May.

Factory Payroll			Acct. No. 530		
Date	**Explanation**	**Debit**	**Credit**	**Balance**	
Mar.	31	Balance			0
Apr.	30	Total payroll for April	8,920		8,920
	30	Direct labor costs		5,700	3,220
	30	Indirect labor costs		3,220	0

Exhibit 20.7

Factory Payroll

Accounting for Factory Overhead

Overhead costs other than indirect materials and indirect labor are reflected by arrow line ⑦ in Exhibit 20.4. These overhead items include the costs of insuring production assets, renting the factory building, using factory utilities, and depreciating equipment not directly related to a specific process. The following entry records overhead costs for April.

P3 Record the flow of factory overhead costs in process cost accounting.

⑦	Factory Overhead	2,425		Assets = Liabilities + Equity
	Prepaid Insurance		180	−180 +645 −2,425
	Utilities Payable		645	−750
	Cash		750	−850
	Accumulated Depreciation—Factory Equipment ..		850	
	To record overhead items incurred in April.			

After this entry is posted, the Factory Overhead account balance is $6,840, comprising indirect materials of $1,195, indirect labor of $3,220, and $2,425 of other overhead.

Arrow line ⑧ in Exhibit 20.4 reflects the application of factory overhead to production. Factory overhead is applied to processes by relating overhead cost to another variable such as direct labor hours or machine hours used. In some situations, a single allocation basis such as direct labor hours (or a single rate for the entire plant) fails to provide useful allocations. As a result, management can use different rates for different production departments. Based on an analysis of its operations, GenX applies its April overhead at a rate of 120% of direct labor cost, as shown in Exhibit 20.8.

Exhibit 20.8

Applying Factory Overhead

	Direct Labor Cost	Predetermined Rate	Overhead Applied
Production Department	$5,700	120%	$6,840

GenX records its applied overhead with the following entry.

⑧	Goods in Process Inventory	6,840	
	Factory Overhead.		6,840
	Allocated overhead costs to production at 120% of direct labor cost.		

Decision Ethics

Answer—p. 821

Budget Officer   You are working to identify the direct and indirect costs of a new processing department that has several machines. This department's manager instructs you to classify a majority of the costs as indirect to take advantage of the direct labor-based overhead allocation method so it will be charged a lower amount of overhead (because of its small direct labor cost). This would penalize other departments with higher allocations. It also will cause the performance ratings of managers in these other departments to suffer. What action do you take?

After posting this entry, the Factory Overhead account appears as shown in Exhibit 20.9. For GenX, the amount of overhead applied equals the actual overhead incurred during April. In most cases, using a predetermined overhead rate leaves an overapplied or underapplied balance in the Factory Overhead account. At the end of the period, this overapplied or underapplied balance should be either closed to the Cost of Goods Sold account or allocated among the Cost of Goods Sold, the Goods in Process Inventory, and the Finished Goods Inventory. Procedures for this allocation are the same as that described in Chapter 19 for job order cost accounting systems.

Exhibit 20.9

Factory Overhead

Factory Overhead						Acct. No. 540
Date		Explanation		Debit	Credit	Balance
Mar.	31	Balance				0
Apr.	30	Indirect materials usage		1,195		1,195
	30	Indirect labor costs		3,220		4,415
	30	Other overhead costs		2,425		6,840
	30	Applied to production departments			6,840	0

Quick Check

Answers—p. 822

1. A process operation (*a*) is another name for a job order operation, (*b*) does not use the concepts of direct materials or direct labor, or (*c*) typically produces large quantities of homogenous products or services.

2. Under what conditions is a process cost accounting system more suitable for measuring production costs than a job order cost accounting system?

3. When direct materials are assigned and used in production, the entry to record their use includes (*a*) a credit to Goods in Process Inventory, (*b*) a debit to Goods in Process Inventory, or (*c*) a debit to Raw Materials Inventory.

4. What are the three cost categories incurred by both job order and process operations?

5. How many Goods in Process Inventory accounts are needed in a process cost system?

Equivalent Units of Production

We explained how materials, labor, and overhead costs for a period are accumulated in the Goods in Process Inventory account, but we have not explained the arrow lines labeled ⑨ and ⑩ in Exhibit 20.4. These lines reflect the transfer of products from the production department to finished goods inventory, and from finished goods inventory to cost of goods sold. To determine the costs recorded for these flows, we must first determine the cost per unit of product and then apply this result to the number of units transferred.

C2 Define equivalent units and explain their use in process cost accounting.

Topic Tackler
PLUS
20-1

Accounting for Goods in Process

If a process has *no beginning and no ending goods in process inventory,* the unit cost of goods transferred out of a process is computed as follows.

> **Total cost assigned to the process (direct materials, direct labor, and overhead)**
> **Total number of units started and finished in the period**

If a process has a beginning or ending inventory of partially processed units (or both), then the total cost assigned to the process must be allocated to all completed and incomplete units worked on during the period. Therefore, the denominator must measure the entire production activity of the process for the period, called **equivalent units of production** (or **EUP**), a phrase that refers to the number of units that could have been started *and* completed given the cost incurred during a period. This measure is then used to compute the cost per equivalent unit and to assign costs to finished goods and goods in process inventory.

To illustrate, assume that GenX adds (or introduces) 100 units into its process during a period. Suppose at the end of that period, the production supervisor determines that those 100 units are 60% of the way through the process. Therefore, equivalent units of production for that period total 60 EUP (100 units × 60%). This means that with the resources used to put 100 units 60% of the way through the process we could have started and completed 60 whole units.

Differences in Equivalent Units for Materials, Labor, and Overhead

In many processes, the equivalent units of production for direct materials are not the same with respect to direct labor and overhead. To illustrate, consider a 5-step process operation shown in Exhibit 20.10.

P4 Compute equivalent units produced in a period.

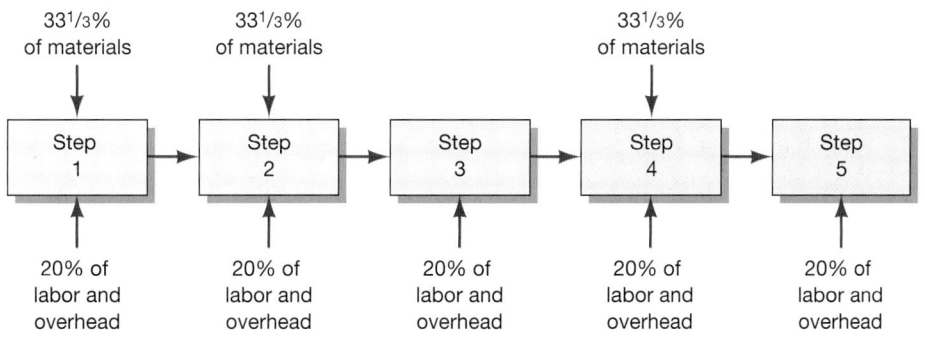

Exhibit 20.10

An Illustrative 5-Step Process Operation

This exhibit shows that one-third of the direct material cost is added at each of three steps: 1, 2, and 4. One-fifth of the direct labor cost is added at each of the five steps. One-fifth of the overhead also is added at each step because overhead is applied as a percent of direct labor for this company.

When units finish step 1, they are one-third complete with respect to direct materials but only one-fifth complete with respect to direct labor and overhead. When they finish step 2,

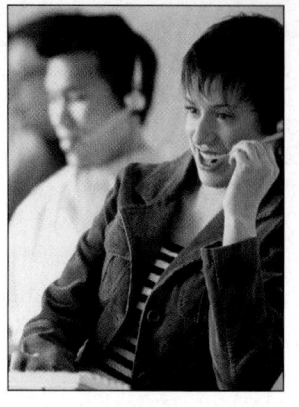

they are two-thirds complete with respect to direct materials but only two-fifths complete with respect to direct labor and overhead. When they finish step 3, they remain two-thirds complete with respect to materials but are now three-fifths complete with respect to labor and overhead. When they finish step 4, they are 100% complete with respect to materials (all direct materials have been added) but only four-fifths complete with respect to labor and overhead.

For example, if 300 units of product are started and processed through step 1 of Exhibit 20.10, they are said to be one-third complete *with respect to materials*. Expressed in terms of equivalent finished units, the processing of these 300 units is equal to finishing 100 EUP with respect to materials (300 units × 33⅓%). However, only one-fifth of direct labor and overhead has been applied to the 300 units at the end of step 1. This means that the equivalent units of production *with respect to labor and overhead* total 60 EUP (300 units × 20%).

Process Costing Illustration

This section applies process costing concepts and procedures to GenX. **This illustration uses the weighted average method for inventory costs. The FIFO method is illustrated in Appendix 20A.** (Assume a weighted average cost flow for all computations and assignments in this chapter unless explicitly stated differently. When using a just-in-time inventory system, different inventory methods yield similar results because inventories are immaterial.)

C3 Explain the four steps in accounting for production activity in a period.

Exhibit 20.11 shows selected information from the production department for the month of April. Accounting for a department's activity for a period includes four steps involving analysis of (1) physical flow, (2) equivalent units, (3) cost per equivalent unit, and (4) cost assignment and reconciliation. The next sections describe each step.

Exhibit 20.11

Production Data

Beginning goods in process inventory (March 31)	
Units of product	30,000
Percentage of completion—Direct materials	100%
Percentage of completion—Direct labor	40%
Direct materials costs	$ 3,300
Direct labor costs	$ 600
Factory overhead costs applied (120% of direct labor)	$ 720
Activities during the current period (April)	
Units started this period	90,000
Units transferred out (completed)	100,000
Direct materials costs	$ 9,900
Direct labor costs	$ 5,700
Factory overhead costs applied (120% of direct labor)	$ 6,840
Ending goods in process inventory (April 30)	
Units of product	20,000
Percentage of completion—Direct materials	100%
Percentage of completion—Direct labor	25%

Step 1: Determine Physical Flow of Units

A *physical flow reconciliation* is a report that reconciles (1) the physical units started in a period with (2) the physical units completed in that period. A physical flow reconciliation for GenX is shown in Exhibit 20.12 for April.

Units to Account For		Units Accounted For	
Beginning goods in process inventory	30,000 units	Units completed and transferred out	100,000 units
Units started this period	90,000 units	Ending goods in process inventory . . .	20,000 units
Total units to account for . . .	**120,000 units**	Total units accounted for	**120,000 units**

reconciled

Exhibit 20.12

Physical Flow Reconciliation

The weighted average method does not require us to separately track the units in beginning work in process from those units started this period. Instead, the units are treated as part of a large pool with an average cost per unit.

Step 2: Compute Equivalent Units of Production

The second step is to compute *equivalent units of production* for direct materials, direct labor, and factory overhead for April. Overhead is applied using direct labor as the allocation base for GenX. This also implies that equivalent units are the same for both labor and overhead.

GenX used its direct materials, direct labor, and overhead to make finished units of Profen and to begin processing some units that are not yet complete. We must convert the physical units measure to equivalent units based on how each input has been used. Equivalent units are computed by multiplying the number of physical units by the percentage of completion for each input—see Exhibit 20.13.

Equivalent Units of Production	Direct Materials	Direct Labor	Factory Overhead
Equivalent units completed and transferred out (100,000 × 100%)	100,000 EUP	100,000 EUP	100,000 EUP
Equivalent units for ending goods in process			
Direct materials (20,000 × 100%)	20,000		
Direct labor (20,000 × 25%)		5,000	
Factory overhead (20,000 × 25%)			5,000
Equivalent units of production	120,000 EUP	105,000 EUP	105,000 EUP

Exhibit 20.13

Equivalent Units of Production— Weighted Average

The first row of Exhibit 20.13 reflects units transferred out in April. The production department entirely completed its work on the 100,000 units transferred out. These units have 100% of the materials, labor, and overhead required, or 100,000 equivalent units of each input (100,000 × 100%).

The second row references the ending goods in process, and rows three, four, and five break it down by materials, labor, and overhead. For direct materials, the units in ending goods in process inventory (20,000 physical units) include all materials required, so there are 20,000 equivalent units (20,000 × 100%) of materials in the unfinished physical units. Regarding labor, the units in ending goods in process inventory include 25% of the labor required, which implies 5,000 equivalent units of labor (20,000 × 25%). These units are only 25% complete and labor is used uniformly through the process. Overhead is applied on the basis of direct labor for GenX, so equivalent units for overhead is computed identically to labor (20,000 × 25%).

The final row reflects the whole units of product that could have been manufactured with the amount of inputs used to create some complete and some incomplete units. For GenX, the amount of inputs used to produce 100,000 complete units and to start 20,000 additional units is equivalent to the amount of direct materials in 120,000 whole units, the amount of direct labor in 105,000 whole units, the amount of overhead in 105,000 whole units.

Step 3: Compute Cost per Equivalent Unit

Equivalent units of production for each product (from step 2) is used to compute the average cost per equivalent unit. Under the **weighted average method,** the computation of EUP does not separate the units in beginning inventory from those started this period; similarly, this method combines the costs of beginning goods in process inventory with the costs incurred in the current period. This process is illustrated in Exhibit 20.14.

Exhibit 20.14

Cost per Equivalent Unit of Production—Weighted Average

Cost per Equivalent Unit of Production	Direct Materials	Direct Labor	Factory Overhead
Costs of beginning goods in process inventory	$ 3,300	$ 600	$ 720
Costs incurred this period	9,900	5,700	6,840
Total costs	$13,200	$6,300	$7,560
÷ Equivalent units of production (from Step 2)	120,000 EUP	105,000 EUP	105,000 EUP
= Cost per equivalent unit of production	$0.11 per EUP*	$0.06 per EUP†	$0.072 per EUP‡

*$13,200 ÷ 120,000 EUP   †$6,300 ÷ 105,000 EUP   ‡$7,560 ÷ 105,000 EUP

For direct materials, the cost averages $0.11 per EUP, computed as the sum of direct materials cost from beginning goods in process inventory ($3,300) and the direct materials cost incurred in April ($9,900), and this sum ($13,200) is then divided by the 120,000 EUP for materials (from step 2). The costs per equivalent unit for labor and overhead are similarly computed. Specifically, direct labor cost averages $0.06 per EUP, computed as the sum of labor cost in beginning goods in process inventory ($600) and the labor costs incurred in April ($5,700), and this sum ($6,300) divided by 105,000 EUP for labor. Overhead costs averages $0.072 per EUP, computed as the sum of overhead cost in the beginning goods in process inventory ($720) and the overhead costs applied in April ($6,840), and this sum ($7,560) divided by 105,000 EUP for overhead.

Step 4: Assign and Reconcile Costs

Topic Tackler
PLUS

20-2

The EUP from Step 2 and the cost per EUP from Step 3 are used in Step 4 to assign costs to (a) units that production completed and transferred to finished goods and (b) units that remain in process. This is illustrated in Exhibit 20.15.

Exhibit 20.15

Report of Costs Accounted For—Weighted Average

Cost of units completed and transferred out		
Direct materials (100,000 EUP × $0.11 per EUP)	$11,000	
Direct labor (100,000 EUP × $0.06 per EUP)	6,000	
Factory overhead (100,000 EUP × $0.072 per EUP)	7,200	
Cost of units completed this period		$ 24,200
Cost of ending goods in process inventory		
Direct materials (20,000 EUP × $0.11 per EUP)	2,200	
Direct labor (5,000 EUP × $0.06 per EUP)	300	
Factory overhead (5,000 EUP × $0.072 per EUP)	360	
Cost of ending goods in process inventory		2,860
Total costs accounted for		**$27,060**

Cost of Units Completed and Transferred   The 100,000 units completed and transferred to finished goods inventory required 100,000 EUP of direct materials. Thus, we assign $11,000 (100,000 EUP × $0.11 per EUP) of direct materials cost to those units. Similarly, those units had received 100,000 EUP of direct labor and 100,000 EUP of factory overhead (recall Exhibit 20.13). Thus, we assign $6,000 (100,000 EUP × $0.06 per EUP) of direct labor and $7,200 (100,000 EUP × $0.072 per EUP) of overhead to those units. The total cost of the 100,000 completed and transferred units is $24,200 ($11,000 + $6,000 + $7,200) and their average cost per unit is $0.242 ($24,200 ÷ 100,000 units).

Cost of Units for Ending Goods in Process   There are 20,000 incomplete units in goods in process inventory at period-end. For direct materials, those units have 20,000 EUP of material (from step 2) at a cost of $0.11 per EUP (from step 3), which yields the materials cost of goods in process inventory of $2,200 (20,000 EUP × $0.11 per EUP). For direct labor, the in-process units have 25% of the required labor, or 5,000 EUP (from step 2). Using the $0.06 labor cost per EUP (from step 3) we obtain the labor cost of goods in process inventory of $300 (5,000 EUP × $0.06 per EUP). For overhead, the in-process units reflect 5,000 EUP (from step 2). Using the $0.072 overhead cost per EUP (from step 3) we obtain overhead costs with in-process inventory of $360 (5,000 EUP × $0.072 per EUP). Total cost of goods in process inventory at period-end is $2,860 ($2,200 + $300 + $360).

As a check, management verifies that total costs assigned to those units completed and transferred plus the costs of those in process (from Exhibit 20.15) equal the costs incurred by production. Exhibit 20.16 shows the costs incurred by production this period. We then reconcile the *costs accounted for* in Exhibit 20.15 with the *costs to account for* in Exhibit 20.16.

Exhibit 20.16

Report of Costs to Account For—Weighted Average

Cost of beginning goods in process inventory		
Direct materials	$3,300	
Direct labor	600	
Factory overhead	720	$ 4,620
Cost incurred this period		
Direct materials	9,900	
Direct labor	5,700	
Factory overhead	6,840	22,440
Total costs to account for		**$27,060**

At GenX, the production department manager is responsible for $27,060 in costs: $4,620 that is assigned to the goods in process at the start of the period plus $22,440 of materials, labor, and overhead incurred in the period. At period-end, that manager must show where these costs are assigned. The manager for GenX reports that $2,860 are assigned to units in process and $24,200 are assigned to units completed (per Exhibit 20.15). The sum of these amounts equals $27,060. Thus, the total *costs to account for* equals the total *costs accounted for* (minor differences can sometimes occur from rounding).

Process Cost Summary   An important managerial accounting report for a process cost accounting system is the **process cost summary** (also called *production report*), which is prepared separately for each process or production department. Three reasons for the summary are to (1) help department managers control and monitor their departments, (2) help factory managers evaluate department managers' performances, and (3) provide cost information for financial statements. A process cost summary achieves these purposes by describing the costs charged to each department, reporting the equivalent units of production achieved by each department, and determining the costs assigned to each department's output. For our purposes, it is prepared using a combination of Exhibits 20.13, 20.14, 20.15, and 20.16.

C4 Define a process cost summary and describe its purposes.

The process cost summary for GenX is shown in Exhibit 20.17. The report is divided into three sections. Section ① lists the total costs charged to the department, including direct materials, direct labor, and overhead costs incurred, as well as the cost of the beginning goods in process inventory. Section ② describes the equivalent units of production for the department. Equivalent units for materials, labor, and overhead are in separate columns. It also reports direct materials, direct labor, and overhead costs per equivalent unit. Section ③ allocates total costs among units worked on in the period. The $24,200 is the total cost of goods transferred out of the department, and the $2,860 is the cost of partially processed ending inventory units. The assigned costs are then added to show that the total $27,060 cost charged to the department in section ① is now assigned to the units in section ③.

P5 Prepare a process cost summary.

Exhibit 20.17

Process Cost Summary

GenX COMPANY
Process Cost Summary
For Month Ended April 30, 2008

Costs Charged to Production

① Costs of beginning goods in process

Direct materials	$3,300	
Direct labor	600	
Factory overhead	720	$ 4,620

Costs incurred this period

Direct materials	9,900	
Direct labor	5,700	
Factory overhead	6,840	22,440
Total costs to account for		$27,060

Unit Cost Information

Units to account for:		Units accounted for:	
Beginning goods in process	30,000	Completed and transferred out	100,000
Units started this period	90,000	Ending goods in process	20,000
Total units to account for	120,000	Total units accounted for	120,000

Equivalent Units of Production (EUP)	Direct Materials	Direct Labor	Factory Overhead
Units completed and transferred out	100,000 EUP	100,000 EUP	100,000 EUP
Units of ending goods in process			
② Direct materials (20,000 × 100%)	20,000		
Direct labor (20,000 × 25%)		5,000	
Factory overhead (20,000 × 25%)			5,000
Equivalent units of production	120,000 EUP	105,000 EUP	105,000 EUP

Cost per EUP	Direct Materials	Direct Labor	Factory Overhead
Costs of beginning goods in process	$ 3,300	$ 600	$ 720
Costs incurred this period	9,900	5,700	6,840
Total costs	$13,200	$6,300	$7,560
÷ EUP	120,000 EUP	105,000 EUP	105,000 EUP
Cost per EUP	$0.11 per EUP	$0.06 per EUP	$0.072 per EUP

Cost Assignment and Reconciliation

Costs transferred out (cost of goods manufactured)

Direct materials (100,000 EUP × $0.11 per EUP)	$11,000	
Direct labor (100,000 EUP × $0.06 per EUP)	6,000	
Factory overhead (100,000 EUP × $0.072 per EUP)	7,200	$ 24,200

③ Costs of ending goods in process

Direct materials (20,000 EUP × $0.11 per EUP)	2,200	
Direct labor (5,000 EUP × $0.06 per EUP)	300	
Factory overhead (5,000 EUP × $0.072 per EUP)	360	2,860
Total costs accounted for		$27,060

reconciled

Quick Check

Answers—p. 822

6. Equivalent units are (*a*) a measure of a production department's productivity in using direct materials, direct labor, or overhead; (*b*) units of a product produced by a foreign competitor that are similar to units produced by a domestic company; or (*c*) generic units of a product similar to brand name units of a product.

7. Interpret the meaning of a department's equivalent units with respect to direct labor.

8. A department began the period with 8,000 units that were one-fourth complete with respect to direct labor. It completed 58,000 units, and ended with 6,000 units that were one-third complete with respect to direct labor. What were its direct labor equivalent units for the period using the weighted average method?

9. A process cost summary for a department has three sections. What information is presented in each of them?

Transfers to Finished Goods Inventory and Cost of Goods Sold

Arrow line ⑨ in Exhibit 20.4 reflects the transfer of completed products from production to finished goods inventory. The process cost summary shows that the 100,000 units of finished Profen are assigned a cost of $24,200. The entry to record this transfer is:

P6 Record the transfer of completed goods to Finished Goods Inventory and Cost of Goods Sold.

⑨	Finished Goods Inventory....................	24,200	
	Goods in Process Inventory................		24,200
	To record transfer of completed units.		

Assets = Liabilities + Equity
+24,200
−24,200

The credit to Goods in Process Inventory reduces that asset balance to reflect that 100,000 units are no longer in production. The cost of these units has been transferred to Finished Goods Inventory, which is recognized as a $24,200 increase in this asset. After this entry is posted, there remains a balance of $2,860 in the Goods in Process Inventory account, which is the amount computed in Step 4 previously. The cost of units transferred from Goods in Process Inventory to Finished Goods Inventory is called the **cost of goods manufactured.** Exhibit 20.18 reveals the activities in the Goods in Process Inventory account for this period. The ending balance of this account equals the cost assigned to the partially completed units in section ③ of Exhibit 20.17.

Goods in Process Inventory			Acct. No. 134		
Date		Explanation	Debit	Credit	Balance
Mar.	31	Balance			4,620
Apr.	30	Direct materials usage	9,900		14,520
	30	Direct labor costs incurred	5,700		20,220
	30	Factory overhead applied	6,840		27,060
	30	Transfer completed product to warehouse		24,200	2,860

Exhibit 20.18

Goods in Process Inventory

Arrow line ⑩ in Exhibit 20.4 reflects the sale of finished goods. Assume that GenX sold 106,000 units of Profen this period, and that its beginning inventory of finished goods consisted of 26,000 units with a cost of $6,292. Also assume that its ending finished goods inventory consists of 20,000 units at a cost of $4,840. Using this information, we can compute its cost of goods sold for April as shown in Exhibit 20.19.

Beginning finished goods inventory	$ 6,292
+ Cost of goods manufactured this period	24,200
= Cost of goods available for sale	$30,492
− Ending finished goods inventory	4,840
= Cost of goods sold	$25,652

Exhibit 20.19

Cost of Goods Sold

The summary entry to record cost of goods sold for this period follows.

⑩	Cost of Goods Sold........................	25,652	
	Finished Goods Inventory		25,652
	To record cost of goods sold for April.		

Assets = Liabilities + Equity
−25,652   −25,652

The Finished Goods Inventory account now appears as shown in Exhibit 20.20.

Finished Goods Inventory			Acct. No. 135		
Date		Explanation	Debit	Credit	Balance
Mar.	31	Balance			6,292
Apr.	30	Transfer in cost of goods manufactured	24,200		30,492
	30	Cost of goods sold		25,652	4,840

Exhibit 20.20

Finished Goods Inventory

Summary of Cost Flows   Exhibit 20.21 shows GenX's manufacturing cost flows for April. Each of these cost flows and the entries to record them have been explained. The flow of costs through the accounts reflects the flow of production activities and products.

Exhibit 20.21*

Cost Flows through GenX

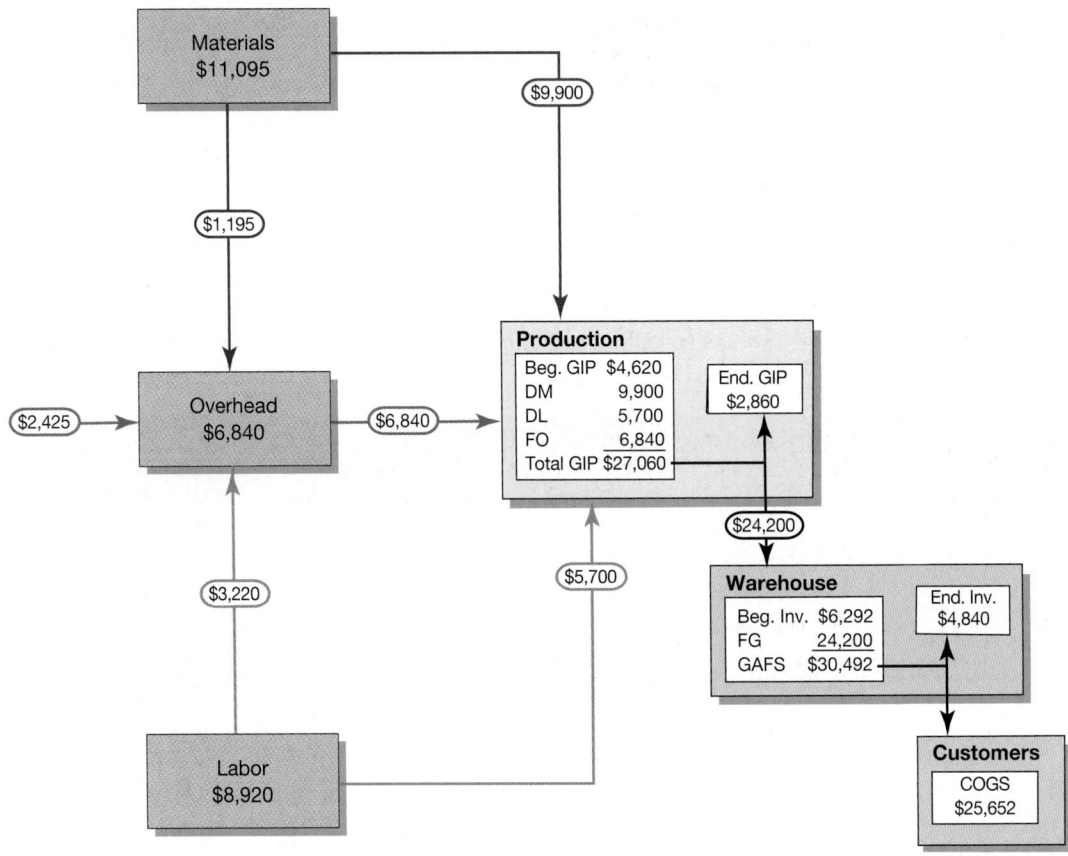

*Abbreviations: GIP (goods in process); DM (direct materials); DL (direct labor); FO (factory overhead); FG (finished goods); GAFS (goods available for sale); COGS (cost of goods sold).

Effect of Lean Business Model on Process Operations

Adopting lean business practices often yields changes in process operations. Management concerns with throughput and just-in-time manufacturing, for instance, cause boundary lines between departments to blur. In some cases, higher quality and better efficiency are obtained by entirely reorganizing production processes. For example, instead of producing different types of computers in a series of departments, a separate work center for each computer can be established in one department. When such a re-arrangement occurs, the process cost accounting system is changed to account for each work center's costs.

To illustrate, when a company adopts a just-in-time inventory system, its inventories can be minimal. If raw materials are not ordered or received until needed, a Raw Materials Inventory

Decision Insight

Lean Machine   Attention to customer orientation has led to improved processes for companies. A manufacturer of control devices improved quality and reduced production time by forming teams to study processes and suggest improvements. Another company set up project groups to evaluate its production processes.

account may be unnecessary. Instead, materials cost is immediately debited to the Goods in Process Inventory account. Similarly, a Finished Goods Inventory account may not be needed. Instead, cost of finished goods may be immediately debited to the Cost of Goods Sold account.

Decision Insight

Best of Both   Customer orientation demands both flexibility and standardization. Flexibility allows companies to supply products or services to a customer's specifications as in a job order setting, and standardization helps achieve efficiencies and lower costs as in a process operation.

Hybrid Costing System   Decision Analysis

This chapter explained the process costing system and contrasted it with the job order costing system. Many organizations use a *hybrid system* that contains features of both process and job order operations. A recent survey of manufacturers revealed that a majority use hybrid systems.

A2   Explain and illustrate a hybrid costing system.

To illustrate, consider a car manufacturer's assembly line. On one hand, the line resembles a process operation in that the assembly steps for each car are nearly identical. On the other hand, the specifications of most cars have several important differences. At the **Ford** Mustang plant, each car assembled on a given day can be different from the previous car and the next car. This means that the costs of materials (subassemblies or components) for each car can differ. Accordingly, while the conversion costs (direct labor and overhead) can be accounted for using a process costing system, the component costs (direct materials) are accounted for using a job order system (separately for each car or type of car).

A hybrid system of processes requires a *hybrid costing system* to properly cost products or services. In the Ford plant, the assembly costs per car are readily determined using process costing. The costs of additional components can then be added to the assembly costs to determine each car's total cost (as in job order costing). To illustrate, consider the following information for a daily assembly process at Ford.

Assembly process costs	
Direct materials	$10,600,000
Direct labor	$5,800,000
Factory overhead	$6,200,000
Number of cars assembled	1,000
Costs of three different types of steering wheels	$240, $330, $480
Costs of three different types of seats	$620, $840, $1,360

The assembly process costs $22,600 per car. Depending on the type of steering wheel and seats the customer requests, the cost of a car can range from $23,460 to $24,440 (a $980 difference).

Today companies are increasingly trying to standardize processes while attempting to meet individual customer needs. To the extent that differences among individual customers' requests are large, understanding the costs to satisfy those requests is important. Thus, monitoring and controlling both process and job order costs are important.

Decision Ethics   Answer—p. 821

Entrepreneur   You operate a process production company making similar products for three different customers. One customer demands 100% quality inspection of products at your location before shipping. The added costs of that inspection are spread across all customers, not just the one demanding it. If you charge the added costs to that customer, you could lose that customer and experience a loss. Moreover, your other two customers have agreed to pay 110% of full costs. What actions (if any) do you take?

Demonstration Problem

Pennsylvania Company produces a product that passes through a single production process. Then, completed products are transferred to finished goods in its warehouse. Information related to its manufacturing activities for July follows.

Raw Materials

Beginning inventory	$100,000
Raw materials purchased on credit	211,400
Direct materials used	(190,000)
Indirect materials used	(51,400)
Ending inventory	$ 70,000

Factory Payroll

Direct labor incurred	$ 55,500
Indirect labor incurred	50,625
Total payroll (paid in cash)	$106,125

Factory Overhead

Indirect materials used	$ 51,400
Indirect labor used	50,625
Other overhead costs	71,725
Total factory overhead incurred	$173,750

Factory Overhead Applied

Overhead applied (200% of direct labor)	$111,000

Production Department

Beginning goods in process inventory (units)	5,000
Percentage completed—Materials	100%
Percentage completed—Labor and overhead	60%
Beginning goods in process inventory (costs)	
Direct materials used	$ 20,000
Direct labor incurred	9,600
Overhead applied (200% of direct labor)	19,200
Total costs of beginning goods in process	$ 48,800
Units started this period	20,000
Units completed this period	17,000
Ending goods in process inventory (units)	8,000
Percentage completed—Materials	100%
Percentage completed—Labor and overhead	20%

Finished Goods Inventory

Beginning finished goods inventory	$ 96,400
Cost transferred in from production	321,300
Cost of goods sold	(345,050)
Ending finished goods inventory	$ 72,650

Required

1. Prepare a physical flow reconciliation for July as illustrated in Exhibit 20.12.
2. Compute the equivalent units of production in July for direct materials, direct labor, and factory overhead.
3. Compute the costs per equivalent units of production in July for direct materials, direct labor, and factory overhead.
4. Prepare a report of costs accounted for and a report of costs to account for.
5. Prepare summary journal entries to record the transactions and events of July for (a) raw materials purchases, (b) direct materials usage, (c) indirect materials usage, (d) factory payroll costs, (e) direct labor usage, (f) indirect labor usage, (g) other overhead costs (credit Other Accounts), (h) application of overhead to production, (i) transfer of finished goods from production, and (j) the cost of goods sold.

Planning the Solution

- Track the physical flow to determine the number of units completed in July.
- Compute the equivalent unit of production for direct materials, direct labor, and factory overhead.
- Compute the costs per equivalent unit of production with respect to direct materials, direct labor, and overhead; and determine the cost per unit for each.
- Compute the total cost of the goods transferred to production by using the equivalent units and unit costs. Determine (a) the cost of the beginning in-process inventory, (b) the materials, labor, and overhead costs added to the beginning in-process inventory, and (c) the materials, labor, and overhead costs added to the units started and completed in the month.
- Determine cost of goods sold using balances in finished goods and cost of units completed this period.
- Use the information to record the summary journal entries for July.

Solution to Demonstration Problem

1. Physical Flow Reconciliation

Units to Account For		Units Accounted For	
Beginning goods in process inventory	5,000 units	Units completed and transferred out	17,000 units
Units started this period	20,000 units	Ending goods in process inventory	8,000 units
Total units to account for	**25,000 units**	Total units accounted for	**25,000 units**

reconciled

2. Equivalent Units of Production

Equivalent Units of Production	Direct Materials	Direct Labor	Factory Overhead
Equivalent units completed and transferred out	17,000 EUP	17,000 EUP	17,000 EUP
Equivalent units in ending goods in process			
Direct materials (8,000 × 100%)	8,000		
Direct labor (8,000 × 20%)		1,600	
Factory overhead (8,000 × 20%)			1,600
Equivalent units of production	25,000 EUP	18,600 EUP	18,600 EUP

3. Costs per Equivalent Unit of Production

Costs per Equivalent Unit of Production	Direct Materials	Direct Labor	Factory Overhead
Costs of beginning goods in process	$ 20,000	$ 9,600	$ 19,200
Costs incurred this period	190,000	55,500	111,000**
Total costs	$210,000	$65,100	$130,200
÷ Equivalent units of production (from part 2) .	25,000 EUP	18,600 EUP	18,600 EUP
= Costs per equivalent unit of production	$8.40 per EUP	$3.50 per EUP	$7.00 per EUP

**Factory overhead applied

4. Reports of *Costs Accounted For* and of *Costs to Account For*

Report of Costs Accounted For		
Cost of units transferred out (cost of goods manufactured)		
Direct materials ($8.40 per EUP × 17,000 EUP)	$142,800	
Direct labor ($3.50 per EUP × 17,000 EUP)	59,500	
Factory overhead ($7.00 per EUP × 17,000 EUP)	119,000	
Cost of units completed this period		$ 321,300
Cost of ending goods in process inventory		
Direct materials ($8.40 per EUP × 8,000 EUP)	67,200	
Direct labor ($3.50 per EUP × 1,600 EUP)	5,600	
Factory overhead ($7.00 per EUP × 1,600 EUP)	11,200	
Cost of ending goods in process inventory		84,000
Total costs accounted for		**$405,300**

Report of Costs to Account For		
Cost of beginning goods in process inventory		
Direct materials	$ 20,000	
Direct labor	9,600	
Factory overhead	19,200	$ 48,800
Cost incurred this period		
Direct materials	190,000	
Direct labor	55,500	
Factory overhead	111,000	356,500
Total costs to account for		**$405,300**

reconciled

5. Summary journal entries for the transactions and events in July.

a.	Raw Materials Inventory	211,400	
	Accounts Payable		211,400
	To record raw materials purchases.		
b.	Goods in Process Inventory	190,000	
	Raw Materials Inventory		190,000
	To record direct materials usage.		
c.	Factory Overhead	51,400	
	Raw Materials Inventory		51,400
	To record indirect materials usage.		

[continued on next page]

[continued from previous page]

d.	Factory Payroll...............................	106,125	
	Cash		106,125
	To record factory payroll costs.		
e.	Goods in Process Inventory	55,500	
	Factory Payroll		55,500
	To record direct labor usage.		
f.	Factory Overhead	50,625	
	Factory Payroll		50,625
	To record indirect labor usage.		
g.	Factory Overhead	71,725	
	Other Accounts		71,725
	To record other overhead costs.		
h.	Goods in Process Inventory	111,000	
	Factory Overhead.......................		111,000
	To record application of overhead.		
i.	Finished Goods Inventory.....................	321,300	
	Goods in Process Inventory................		321,300
	To record transfer of finished goods from production.		
j.	Cost of Goods Sold..........................	345,050	
	Finished Goods Inventory		345,050
	To record cost of goods sold.		

APPENDIX

20A FIFO Method of Process Costing

C5 Explain and illustrate the four steps in accounting for production activity using FIFO

The **FIFO method** of process costing assigns costs to units assuming a first-in, first-out flow of product. The objectives, concepts, and journal entries (not amounts) are the same as for the weighted average method, but computation of equivalent units of production and cost assignment are slightly different.

Exhibit 20A.1 shows selected information from GenX's production department for the month of April. Accounting for a department's activity for a period includes four steps: (1) determine physical flow, (2) compute equivalent units, (3) compute cost per equivalent unit, and (4) determine cost assignment and reconciliation. This appendix describes each of these steps using the FIFO method for process costing.

Exhibit 20A.1

Production Data

Beginning goods in process inventory (March 31)	
Units of product	30,000
Percentage of completion—Direct materials	100%
Percentage of completion—Direct labor	65%
Direct materials costs	$ 3,300
Direct labor costs	$ 600
Factory overhead costs applied (120% of direct labor)	$ 720
Activities during the current period (April)	
Units started this period	90,000
Units transferred out (completed)	100,000
Direct materials costs	$ 9,900
Direct labor costs	$ 5,700
Factory overhead costs applied (120% of direct labor)	$ 6,840
Ending goods in process inventory (April 30)	
Units of product	20,000
Percentage of completion—Direct materials	100%
Percentage of completion—Direct labor	25%

Step 1: Determine Physical Flow of Units

A *physical flow reconciliation* is a report that reconciles (1) the physical units started in a period with (2) the physical units completed in that period. The physical flow reconciliation for GenX is shown in Exhibit 20A.2 for April.

Units to Account For		Units Accounted For	
Beginning goods in process inventory	30,000 units	Units completed and transferred out	100,000 units
Units started this period	90,000 units	Ending goods in process inventory . . .	20,000 units
Total units to account for . . .	**120,000 units**	Total units accounted for	**120,000 units**

reconciled

Exhibit 20A.2

Physical Flow Reconciliation

FIFO assumes that the 100,000 units transferred to finished goods during April include the 30,000 units from the beginning goods in process inventory. The remaining 70,000 units transferred out are from units started in April. Of the total 90,000 units started in April, 70,000 were completed, leaving 20,000 units unfinished at period-end.

Step 2: Compute Equivalent Units of Production—FIFO

GenX used its direct materials, direct labor, and overhead both to make complete units of Profen and to start some units that are not yet complete. We need to convert the physical measure of units to equivalent units based on how much of each input has been used. We do this by multiplying the number of physical units by the percentage of processing applied to those units in the current period; this is done for each input (materials, labor, and overhead). The FIFO method accounts for cost flow in a sequential manner—earliest costs are the first to flow out. (This is different from the weighted average method, which combines prior period costs—those in beginning Goods in Process Inventory—with costs incurred in the current period.)

Three distinct groups of units must be considered in determining the equivalent units of production under the FIFO method: (a) units in beginning Goods in Process Inventory that were completed this period, (b) units started *and* completed this period, and (c) units in ending Goods in Process Inventory. We must determine how much material, labor, and overhead are used for each of these unit groups. These computations are shown in Exhibit 20A.3. The remainder of this section explains these computations.

Equivalent Units of Production	Direct Materials	Direct Labor	Factory Overhead
(a) Equivalent units to complete beginning goods in process			
Direct materials (30,000 × 0%)	0 EUP		
Direct labor (30,000 × 35%)		10,500 EUP	
Factory overhead (30,000 × 35%)			10,500 EUP
(b) Equivalent units started and completed*	70,000	70,000	70,000
(c) Equivalent units in ending goods in process			
Direct materials (20,000 × 100%)	20,000		
Direct labor (20,000 × 25%)		5,000	
Factory overhead (20,000 × 25%)			5,000
Equivalent units of production	90,000 EUP	85,500 EUP	85,500 EUP

Exhibit 20A.3

Equivalent Units of Production—FIFO

*Units completed this period	100,000 units
Less units in beginning goods in process	30,000
Units started and completed this period	70,000 units

(a) Beginning Goods in Process Under FIFO, we assume that production first completes any units started in the prior period. There were 30,000 physical units in beginning goods in process inventory. Those units were 100% complete with respect to direct materials as of the end of the prior period. This means that no materials (0%) are needed in April to complete those 30,000 units. So, the equivalent units of *materials* to complete beginning goods in process are zero (30,000 × 0%)—see first row under row "(a)" in Exhibit 20A.3. The units in process as of April 1 had already been through

65% of production prior to this period and need only go through the remaining 35% of production. The equivalent units of *labor* to complete the beginning goods in process are 10,500 (30,000 × 35%)—see second row under row "(a)." This implies that the amount of labor required this period to complete the 30,000 units started in the prior period is the amount of labor needed to make 10,500 units, start-to-finish. Finally, overhead is applied based on direct labor costs, so GenX computes equivalent units for overhead as it would for direct labor.

(b) Units Started and Completed This Period   After completing any beginning goods in process, FIFO assumes that production begins on newly started units. GenX began work on 90,000 new units this period. Of those units, 20,000 remain incomplete at period-end. This means that 70,000 of the units started in April were completed in April. These complete units have received 100% of materials, labor, and overhead. Exhibit 20A.3 reflects this by including 70,000 equivalent units (70,000 × 100%) of materials, labor, and overhead in its equivalent units of production—see row "(b)."

(c) Ending Goods in Process   The 20,000 units started in April that GenX was not able to complete by period-end consumed materials, labor, and overhead. Specifically, those 20,000 units received 100% of materials and, therefore, the equivalent units of materials in ending goods in process inventory are 20,000 (20,000 × 100%)—see first row under row "(c)." For labor and overhead, the units in ending goods in process were 25% complete in production. This means the equivalent units of labor and overhead for those units is 5,000 (20,000 × 25%) as GenX incurs labor and overhead costs uniformly throughout its production process. Finally, for each input (direct materials, direct labor, and factory overhead), the equivalent units for each of the unit groups (a), (b), and (c) are added to determine the total equivalent units of production with respect to each—see final row in Exhibit 20A.3.

Step 3: Compute Cost per Equivalent Unit—FIFO

To compute cost per equivalent unit, we take the product costs (for each of direct materials, direct labor, and factory overhead from Exhibit 20A.1) added in April and divide by the equivalent units of production from Step 2. Exhibit 20A.4 illustrates these computations.

Exhibit 20A.4

Cost per Equivalent Unit of Production—FIFO

Cost per Equivalent Unit of Production	Direct Materials	Direct Labor	Factory Overhead
Costs incurred this period	$9,900	$5,700	$6,840
÷ Equivalent units of production (from Step 2)	90,000 EUP	85,500 EUP	85,500 EUP
Cost per equivalent unit of production	$0.11 per EUP	$0.067 per EUP	$0.08 per EUP

It is essential to compute costs per equivalent unit for *each* input because production inputs are added at different times in the process. The FIFO method computes the cost per equivalent unit based solely on this period's EUP and costs (unlike the weighted average method which adds in the costs of the beginning goods in process inventory).

Step 4: Assign and Reconcile Costs

The equivalent units determined in Step 2 and the cost per equivalent unit computed in Step 3 are both used to assign costs (1) to units that the production department completed and transferred to finished goods and (2) to units that remain in process at period-end.

In Exhibit 20A.5, under the section for cost of units transferred out, we see that the cost of units completed in April includes the $4,620 cost carried over from March for work already applied to the 30,000 units that make up beginning Goods in Process Inventory, plus the $2,430 incurred in April to complete those units. This section also includes the $17,990 of cost assigned to the 70,000 units started and completed this period. Thus, the total cost of goods manufactured in April is $24,154 ($4,620 + $1,544 + $17,990). The average cost per unit for goods completed in April is $0.242 ($24,154 ÷ 100,000 completed units).

The computation for cost of ending goods in process inventory is in the lower part of Exhibit 20A.5. The cost of units in process includes materials, labor, and overhead costs corresponding to the percentage of these resources applied to those incomplete units in April. That cost of $2,935 ($2,200 + $335 + $400) also is the ending balance for the Goods in Process Inventory account.

Exhibit 20A.5

Report of Costs Accounted
For—FIFO

Cost of units transferred out (cost of goods manufactured)		
Cost of beginning goods in process inventory		$ 4,620
Cost to complete beginning goods in process		
Direct materials ($0.11 per EUP × 0 EUP)	$ 0	
Direct labor ($0.067 per EUP × 10,500 EUP)	704	
Factory overhead ($0.08 per EUP × 10,500 EUP)	840	1,544
Cost of units started and completed this period		
Direct materials ($0.11 per EUP × 70,000 EUP)	7,700	
Direct labor ($0.067 per EUP × 70,000 EUP)	4,690	
Factory overhead ($0.08 per EUP × 70,000 EUP)	5,600	17,990
Total cost of units finished this period		24,154
Cost of ending goods in process inventory		
Direct materials ($0.11 per EUP × 20,000 EUP)	2,200	
Direct labor ($0.067 per EUP × 5,000 EUP)	335	
Factory overhead ($0.08 per EUP × 5,000 EUP)	400	
Total cost of ending goods in process inventory		2,935
Total costs accounted for		**$27,089**

Management verifies that the total costs assigned to units transferred out and units still in process equal the total costs incurred by production. We reconcile the costs accounted for (in Exhibit 20A.5) to the costs that production was charged for as shown in Exhibit 20A.6.

Exhibit 20A.6

Report of Costs to
Account—FIFO

Cost of beginning goods in process inventory		
Direct materials	$3,300	
Direct labor	600	
Factory overhead	720	$ 4,620
Costs incurred this period		
Direct materials	9,900	
Direct labor	5,700	
Factory overhead	6,840	22,440
Total costs to account for		**$27,060**

The production manager is responsible for $27,060 in costs: $4,620 that had been assigned to the department's Goods in Process Inventory as of April 1 plus $22,440 of materials, labor, and overhead costs the department incurred in April. At period-end, the manager must identify where those costs were assigned. The production manager can report that there was $24,154 of cost assigned to units completed in April and $2,935 assigned to units still in process at period-end. The sum of these amounts is $29 different from the $27,060 total costs incurred by production due to rounding in Step 3—rounding errors are common and not a concern.

The final report is the process cost summary, which summarizes key information from Exhibits 20A.3, 20A.4, 20A.5, and 20A.6. Reasons for the summary are to (1) help managers control and monitor costs, (2) help upper management assess department manager performance, and (3) provide cost information for financial reporting. The process cost summary, using FIFO, for GenX is in Exhibit 20A.7. Section ① lists the total costs charged to the department, including direct materials, direct labor, and overhead costs incurred, as well as the cost of the beginning goods in process inventory. Section ② describes the equivalent units of production for the department. Equivalent units for materials, labor, and overhead are in separate columns. It also reports direct materials, direct labor, and overhead costs per equivalent unit. Section ③ allocates total costs among units worked on in the period.

Decision Maker   Answer—p. 822

Cost Manager As cost manager for an electronics manufacturer, you apply a process costing system using FIFO. Your company plans to adopt a just-in-time system and eliminate inventories. What is the impact of the use of FIFO (versus the weighted-average method) given these plans?

Exhibit 20A.7
Process Cost Summary

GenX COMPANY
Process Cost Summary
For Month Ended April 30, 2008

Costs charged to production

Costs of beginning goods in process inventory

Direct materials	$3,300	
Direct labor	600	
Factory overhead	720	$ 4,620

Costs incurred this period

Direct materials	9,900	
Direct labor	5,700	
Factory overhead	6,840	22,440
Total costs to account for		$27,060

Unit cost information

Units to account for		Units accounted for	
Beginning goods in process	30,000	Transferred out	100,000
Units started this period	90,000	Ending goods in process	20,000
Total units to account for	120,000	Total units accounted for	120,000

Equivalent units of production	Direct Materials	Direct Labor	Factory Overhead
Equivalent units to complete beginning goods in process			
Direct materials (30,000 × 0%)	0 EUP		
Direct labor (30,000 × 35%)		10,500 EUP	
Factory overhead (30,000 × 35%)			10,500 EUP
Equivalent units started and completed	70,000	70,000	70,000
Equivalent units in ending goods in process			
Direct materials (20,000 × 100%)	20,000		
Direct labor (20,000 × 25%)		5,000	
Factory overhead (20,000 × 25%)			5000
Equivalent units of production	90,000 EUP	85,500 EUP	85,500 EUP

Cost per equivalent unit of production	Direct Materials	Direct Labor	Factory Overhead
Costs incurred this period	$9,900	$5,700	$6,840
÷ Equivalent units of production	90,000 EUP	85,500 EUP	85,500 EUP
Cost per equivalent unit of production	$0.11 per EUP	$0.067 per EUP	$0.08 per EUP

Cost assignment and reconciliation

(cost of units completed and transferred out)

Cost of beginning goods in process		$ 4,620
Cost to complete beginning goods in process		
Direct materials ($0.11 per EUP × 0 EUP)	$ 0	
Direct labor ($0.067 per EUP × 10,500 EUP)	704	
Factory overhead ($0.08 per EUP × 10,500 EUP)	840	1,544
Cost of units started and completed this period		
Direct Materials ($0.11 per EUP × 70,000 EUP)	7,700	
Direct Labor ($0.067 per EUP × 70,000 EUP)	4,690	
Factory overhead ($0.08 per EUP × 70,000 EUP)	5,600	17,990
Total cost of units finished this period		24,154

Cost of ending goods in process

Direct materials ($0.11 per EUP × 20,000 EUP)	2,200	
Direct labor ($0.067 per EUP × 5,000 EUP)	335	
Factory overhead ($0.08 per EUP × 5,000 EUP)	400	
Total cost of ending goods in process		2,935
Total costs accounted for		$27,089*

reconciled

* $29 difference due to rounding

Summary

C1 **Explain process operations and the way they differ from job order operations.** Process operations produce large quantities of similar products or services by passing them through a series of processes, or steps, in production. Like job order operations, they combine direct materials, direct labor, and overhead in the operations. Unlike job order operations that assign the responsibility for each job to a manager, process operations assign the responsibility for each *process* to a manager.

C2 **Define equivalent units and explain their use in process cost accounting.** Equivalent units of production measure the activity of a process as the number of units that would be completed in a period if all effort had been applied to units that were started and finished. This measure of production activity is used to compute the cost per equivalent unit and to assign costs to finished goods and goods in process inventory.

C3 **Explain the four steps in accounting for production activity in a period.** The four steps involved in accounting for production activity in a period are (1) recording the physical flow of units, (2) computing the equivalent units of production, (3) computing the cost per equivalent unit of production, and (4) reconciling costs. The last step involves assigning costs to finished goods and goods in process inventory for the period.

C4 **Define a process cost summary and describe its purposes.** A process cost summary reports on the activities of a production process or department for a period. It describes the costs charged to the department, the equivalent units of production for the department, and the costs assigned to the output. The report aims to (1) help managers control their departments, (2) help factory managers evaluate department managers' performances, and (3) provide cost information for financial statements.

C5 **Explain and illustrate the four steps in accounting for production activity using FIFO.** The FIFO method for process costing is applied and illustrated to (1) report the physical flow of units, (2) compute the equivalent units of production, (3) compute the cost per equivalent unit of production, and (4) assign and reconcile costs.

A1 **Compare process cost accounting and job order cost accounting.** Process and job order manufacturing operations are similar in that both combine materials, labor, and factory overhead to produce products or services. They differ in the way they are organized and managed. In job order operations, the job order cost accounting system assigns materials, labor, and overhead to specific jobs. In process operations, the process cost accounting system assigns materials, labor, and overhead to specific processes. The total costs associated with each process are then divided by the number of units passing through that process to get cost per

equivalent unit. The costs per equivalent unit for all processes are added to determine the total cost per unit of a product or service.

A2 **Explain and illustrate a hybrid costing system.** A hybrid costing system contains features of both job order and process costing systems. Generally, certain direct materials are accounted for by individual products as in job order costing, but direct labor and overhead costs are accounted for similar to process costing.

P1 **Record the flow of direct materials costs in process cost accounting.** Materials purchased are debited to a Raw Materials Inventory account. As direct materials are issued to processes, they are separately accumulated in a Goods in Process Inventory account for that process.

P2 **Record the flow of direct labor costs in process cost accounting.** Direct labor costs are initially debited to the Factory Payroll account. The total amount in it is then assigned to the goods in process inventory account pertaining to each process.

P3 **Record the flow of factory overhead costs in process cost accounting.** The different factory overhead items are first accumulated in the Factory Overhead account and are then allocated, using a predetermined overhead rate, to the different processes. The allocated amount is debited to the goods in process inventory account pertaining to each process.

P4 **Compute equivalent units produced in a period.** To compute equivalent units, determine the number of units that would have been finished if all materials (or labor or overhead) had been used to produce units that were started and completed during the period. The costs incurred by a process are divided by its equivalent units to yield cost per unit.

P5 **Prepare a process cost summary.** A process cost summary includes the physical flow of units, equivalent units of production, costs per equivalent unit, and a cost reconciliation. It reports the units and costs to account for during the period and how they were accounted for during the period. In terms of units, the summary includes the beginning goods in process inventory and the units started during the month. These units are accounted for in terms of the goods completed and transferred out, and the ending goods in process inventory. With respect to costs, the summary includes materials, labor, and overhead costs assigned to the process during the period. It shows how these costs are assigned to goods completed and transferred out, and to ending goods in process inventory.

P6 **Record the transfer of completed goods to Finished Goods Inventory and Cost of Goods Sold.** As units complete the final process and are eventually sold, their accumulated cost is transferred to Finished Goods Inventory and finally to Cost of Goods Sold.

Budget Officer By instructing you to classify a majority of costs as indirect, the manager is passing some of his department's costs to a common overhead pool that other departments will partially absorb. Since overhead costs are allocated on the basis of direct labor for this company and the new department has a relatively low direct labor cost, the new department will be assigned less overhead. Such action

suggests unethical behavior by this manager. You must object to such reclassification. If this manager refuses to comply, you must inform someone in a more senior position.

Entrepreneur By spreading the added quality-related costs across three customers, the entrepreneur is probably trying to remain competitive with respect to the customer that demands the 100% quality inspection. Moreover, the entrepreneur is partly covering the added costs by recovering 2/3 of them from the other two customers who are paying 110% of total costs. This act likely breaches the trust placed by the two customers in this entrepreneur's application of its costing system. The costing system should be changed, and the entrepreneur should consider renegotiating the pricing and/or quality-

test agreement with this one customer (at the risk of losing this currently loss-producing customer).

Cost Manager Differences between the FIFO and weighted-average methods are greatest when large work in process inventories exist and when costs fluctuate. The method used if inventories are eliminated does not matter; both produce identical costs.

Guidance Answers to **Quick Checks**

1. *c*

2. When a company produces large quantities of similar products/services, a process cost system is often more suitable.

3. *b*

4. The costs are direct materials, direct labor, and overhead.

5. A goods in process inventory account is needed for *each* production department.

6. *a*

7. Equivalent units with respect to direct labor are the number of units that would have been produced if all labor had been used on units that were started and finished during the period.

8.

Units completed and transferred out	58,000 EUP
Units of ending goods in process	
Direct labor (6,000 × 1/3)	2,000 EUP
Units of production	60,000 EUP

9. The first section shows the costs charged to the department. The second section describes the equivalent units produced by the department. The third section shows the assignment of total costs to units worked on during the period.

Key Terms   mhhe.com/wildFAP18e

Key Terms are available at the book's Website for learning and testing in an online Flashcard Format.

Cost of goods manufactured (p. 811)
Equivalent units of production (EUP) (p. 805)
FIFO method (p. 816)

Job order cost accounting system (p. 801)
Materials consumption report (p. 802)
Process cost accounting system (p. 801)

Process cost summary (p. 809)
Process operations (p. 798)
Weighted average method (p. 808)

Multiple Choice Quiz   Answers on p. 839   mhhe.com/wildFAP18e

Multiple Choice Quizzes A and B are available at the book's Website.

1. Equivalent units of production are equal to
  a. Physical units that were completed this period from all effort being applied to them.
  b. The number of units introduced into the process this period.
  c. The number of finished units actually completed this period.
  d. The number of units that could have been started and completed given the cost incurred.
  e. The number of units in the process at the end of the period.

2. Recording the cost of raw materials purchased for use in a process costing system includes a
  a. Credit to Raw Materials Inventory.
  b. Debit to Goods in Process Inventory.
  c. Debit to Factory Overhead.
  d. Credit to Factory Overhead.
  e. Debit to Raw Materials Inventory.

3. The production department started the month with a beginning goods in process inventory of $20,000. During the month, it was assigned the following costs: direct materials, $152,000; direct labor, $45,000; overhead applied at the rate of 40% of direct labor cost. Inventory with a cost of $218,000 was transferred to finished goods. The ending balance of goods in process inventory is
  a. $330,000
  b. $ 17,000
  c. $220,000
  d. $112,000
  e. $118,000

4. A company's beginning work in process inventory consists of 10,000 units that are 20% complete with respect to direct labor costs. A total of 40,000 units are completed this period.

There are 15,000 units in goods in process, one-third complete for direct labor, at period-end. The equivalent units of production (EUP) with respect to direct labor at period-end, assuming the weighted average method, are

a. 45,000 EUP
b. 40,000 EUP
c. 5,000 EUP
d. 37,000 EUP
e. 43,000 EUP

5. Assume the same information as in question 4. Also assume that beginning work in process had $6,000 in direct labor cost; and that $84,000 in direct labor is added during this period. What is the cost per EUP for labor?

a. $0.50 per EUP
b. $1.87 per EUP
c. $2.00 per EUP
d. $2.10 per EUP
e. $2.25 per EUP

Assume weighted-average inventory method is used for all assignments unless stated differently.
Superscript letter [A] denotes assignments based on Appendix 20A.

Discussion Questions

1. Can services be delivered by means of process operations? Support your answer with an example.

2. What is the main factor for a company in choosing between the job order costing and process costing accounting systems? Give two likely applications of each system.

3. Identify the control document for materials flow when a materials requisition slip is not used.

4. The focus in a job order costing system is the job or batch. Identify the main focus in process costing.

5. Are the journal entries that match cost flows to product flows in process costing primarily the same or much different than those in job order costing? Explain.

6. Explain in simple terms the notion of equivalent units of production (EUP). Why is it necessary to use EUP in process costing?

7. What are the two main inventory methods used in process costing? What are the differences between these methods?

8. Why is it possible for direct labor in process operations to include the labor of employees who do not work directly on products or services?

9. Assume that a company produces a single product by processing it first through a single production department. Direct labor costs flow through what accounts in this company's process cost system?

10. After all labor costs for a period are allocated, what balance should remain in the Factory Payroll account?

11. Is it possible to have under- or overapplied overhead costs in a process cost accounting system? Explain.

12. Explain why equivalent units of production for both direct labor and overhead can be the same as, and why they can be different from, equivalent units for direct materials.

13. List the four steps in accounting for production activity in a reporting period (for process operations).

14. What purposes does a process cost summary serve?

15. Are there situations where **Best Buy** can use process costing? Identify at least one and explain it.

16. **Apple** produces iMacs with a multiple production line. Identify and list some of its production processing steps and departments.

 Red numbers denote Discussion Questions that involve decision-making.

For each of the following products and services, indicate whether it is most likely produced in a process operation or in a job order operation.

1. Door hinges
2. Cut flower arrangements
3. House paints
4. Concrete swimming pools
5. Custom tailored suits
6. Grand pianos
7. Wall clocks
8. Sport shirts
9. Bolts and nuts
10. Folding chairs

QUICK STUDY

QS 20-1
Matching of product to cost accounting system
C1

Blanche's Boxes makes cardboard shipping cartons in a single operation. This period, Blanche purchased $62,000 in raw materials. Its production department requisitioned $50,000 of those materials for use in producing cartons. Prepare journal entries to record its (1) purchase of raw materials and (2) requisition of direct materials.

QS 20-2
Recording costs of direct materials
P1

Refer to information in QS 20-2. Blanche's Boxes incurred $135,000 in factory payroll costs, of which $125,000 was direct labor. Prepare journal entries to record its (1) total factory payroll incurred and (2) direct labor used in production.

QS 20-3
Recording costs of direct labor
P2

QS 20-4
Recording costs of factory overhead

P3

Refer to information in QS 20-2 and QS 20-3. Blanche's Boxes requisitions $9,000 of indirect materials from its raw materials and used $10,000 of indirect labor in its production of boxes. Also, it incurred $156,000 of other factory overhead costs. It applies factory overhead at the rate of 140% of direct labor costs. Prepare journal entries to record its (1) indirect materials requisitioned, (2) indirect labor used in production, (3) other factory overhead costs incurred, and (4) application of overhead to production.

QS 20-5
Recording transfer of costs to finished goods   P5

Refer to information in QS 20-2, QS 20-3, and QS 20-4. Blanche's Boxes completed 20,000 boxes costing $275,000 and transferred them to finished goods. Prepare its journal entry to record the transfer of the boxes from production to finished goods inventory.

QS 20-6
Computing equivalent units of production

P4

The following refers to units processed in Sunflower Printing's binding department in March. Compute the total equivalent units of production with respect to labor for March using the weighted average inventory method.

	Units of Product	Percent of Labor Added
Beginning goods in process	150,000	80%
Goods started	310,000	100
Goods completed	340,000	100
Ending goods in process	120,000	25

QS 20-7
Computing EUP cost C4 P5

The cost of beginning inventory plus the costs added during the period should equal the cost of units _____ plus the cost of _____.

QS 20-8
Hybrid costing system A2

Explain a hybrid costing system. Identify a product or service operation that might well fit a hybrid costing system.

QS 20-9[A]
Computing equivalent units—FIFO C2 P4

Refer to QS 20-6 and compute the total equivalent units of production with respect to labor for March using the FIFO inventory method.

EXERCISES

Exercise 20-1
Terminology in process cost accounting

C1 A1 P1 P2 P3

Match each of the following items A through G with the best numbered description of its purpose.

A. Factory Overhead account
B. Process cost summary
C. Equivalent units of production
D. Goods in Process Inventory
E. Raw Materials Inventory account
F. Materials requisition
G. Finished Goods Inventory account

_____ **1.** Notifies the materials manager to send materials to a production department.

_____ **2.** Holds costs of indirect materials, indirect labor, and similar costs until assigned to production.

_____ **3.** Holds costs of direct materials, direct labor, and applied overhead until products are transferred from production to finished goods (or another department).

_____ **4.** Standardizes partially completed units into equivalent completed units.

_____ **5.** Holds costs of finished products until sold to customers.

_____ **6.** Describes the activity and output of a production department for a period.

_____ **7.** Holds costs of materials until they are used in production or as factory overhead.

Exercise 20-2
Journal entries in process cost accounting

P1 P2 P3

Wooden Toy Company manufactures toy trucks. Prepare journal entries to record its following production activities for January.

1. Purchased $80,000 of raw materials on credit.
2. Used $42,000 of direct materials in production.
3. Used $22,500 of indirect materials.

4. Incurred total labor cost of $95,000, which is paid in cash.

5. Used $75,000 of direct labor in production.

6. Used $20,000 of indirect labor.

7. Incurred overhead costs of $38,750 (paid in cash).

8. Applied overhead at 110% of direct labor costs.

9. Transferred completed products with a cost of $135,600 to finished goods inventory.

10. Sold $315,000 of products on credit. Their cost is $175,000.

Check (8) Cr. Factory Overhead, $82,500

The following journal entries are recorded in Kiesha Co.'s process cost accounting system. Kiesha produces apparel and accessories. Overhead is applied to production based on direct labor cost for the period. Prepare a brief explanation (including any overhead rates applied) for each journal entry *a* through *j*.

Exercise 20-3
Interpretation of journal entries in process cost accounting

P1   P2   P3   P6

a.	Raw Materials Inventory	52,000	
	Accounts Payable		52,000
b.	Goods in Process Inventory	42,000	
	Raw Materials Inventory		42,000
c.	Goods in Process Inventory	26,000	
	Factory Payroll		26,000
d.	Factory Payroll	32,000	
	Cash		32,000
e.	Factory Overhead	10,000	
	Cash		10,000
f.	Factory Overhead	10,000	
	Raw Materials Inventory		10,000
g.	Factory Overhead	6,000	
	Factory Payroll		6,000
h.	Goods in Process Inventory	32,500	
	Factory Overhead		32,500
i.	Finished Goods Inventory	88,000	
	Goods in Process Inventory		88,000
j.	Accounts Receivable	250,000	
	Sales		250,000
	Cost of Goods Sold	100,000	
	Finished Goods Inventory		100,000

Laffer Lumber produces bagged bark for use in landscaping. Production involves packaging bark chips in plastic bags in a bagging department. The following information describes production operations for October.

Exercise 20-4
Recording cost flows in a process cost system

P1   P2   P3   P6

	Bagging Department
Direct materials used	$ 522,000
Direct labor used	$ 130,000
Predetermined overhead rate (based on direct labor)	175%
Goods transferred from bagging to finished goods	$(595,000)

The company's revenue for the month totaled $950,000 from credit sales, and its cost of goods sold for the month is $540,000. Prepare summary journal entries dated October 31 to record its October production activities for (1) direct material usage, (2) direct labor usage, (3) overhead allocation, (4) goods transfer from production to finished goods, and (5) sales.

Check (3) Cr. Factory Overhead, $227,500

Exercise 20-5

Computing equivalent units of production—weighted average

C2   P4

Check   (2) EUP for materials, 365,600

During April, the production department of a process manufacturing system completed a number of units of a product and transferred them to finished goods. Of these transferred units, 60,000 were in process in the production department at the beginning of April and 240,000 were started and completed in April. April's beginning inventory units were 60% complete with respect to materials and 40% complete with respect to labor. At the end of April, 82,000 additional units were in process in the production department and were 80% complete with respect to materials and 30% complete with respect to labor.

1. Compute the number of units transferred to finished goods.

2. Compute the number of equivalent units with respect to both materials used and labor used in the production department for April using the weighted-average method.

Exercise 20-6

Costs assigned to output and inventories—weighted average

C3   P4   P5

Check   (2) Costs accounted for, $1,666,730

The production department described in Exercise 20-5 had $850,000 of direct materials and $650,000 of direct labor cost charged to it during April. Also, its beginning inventory included $118,840 of direct materials cost and $47,890 of direct labor.

1. Compute the direct materials cost and the direct labor cost per equivalent unit for the department.

2. Using the weighted average method, assign April's costs to the department's output; specifically, its units transferred to finished goods and its ending goods in process inventory.

Exercise 20-7ᴬ

Computing equivalent units of production—FIFO

C5   P4

Refer to the information in Exercise 20-5 to compute the number of equivalent units with respect to both materials used and labor used in the production department for April using the FIFO method.

Exercise 20-8ᴬ

Costs assigned to output—FIFO

C5   P4   P5

Refer to the information in Exercise 20-6 and complete its parts (1) and (2) using the FIFO method.

Exercise 20-9

Equivalent units computed—weighted average

C2   P4   P5

Check   (3) EUP for materials, 88,000

The production department in a process manufacturing system completed 80,000 units of product and transferred them to finished goods during a recent period. Of these units, 24,000 were in process at the beginning of the period. The other 56,000 units were started and completed during the period. At period-end, 16,000 units were in process. Compute the department's equivalent units of production with respect to direct materials under each of three separate assumptions:

1. All direct materials are added to products when processing begins.

2. Direct materials are added to products evenly throughout the process. Beginning goods in process inventory was 50% complete, and ending goods in process inventory was 75% complete.

3. One-half of direct materials is added to products when the process begins and the other half is added when the process is 75% complete as to direct labor. Beginning goods in process inventory is 40% complete as to direct labor and ending goods in process inventory is 60% complete as to direct labor.

Exercise 20-10ᴬ

Equivalent units computed—FIFO

C5

Check   (3) EUP for materials, 76,000

Refer to the information in Exercise 20-9 and complete it for each of the 3 separate assumptions using the FIFO method for process costing.

Exercise 20-11

Flowchart of costs for a process operation   P1   P2   P3   P6

The following flowchart shows the August production activity of the Spalding Company. Use the amounts shown on the flowchart to compute the missing four numbers identified by blanks.

Production

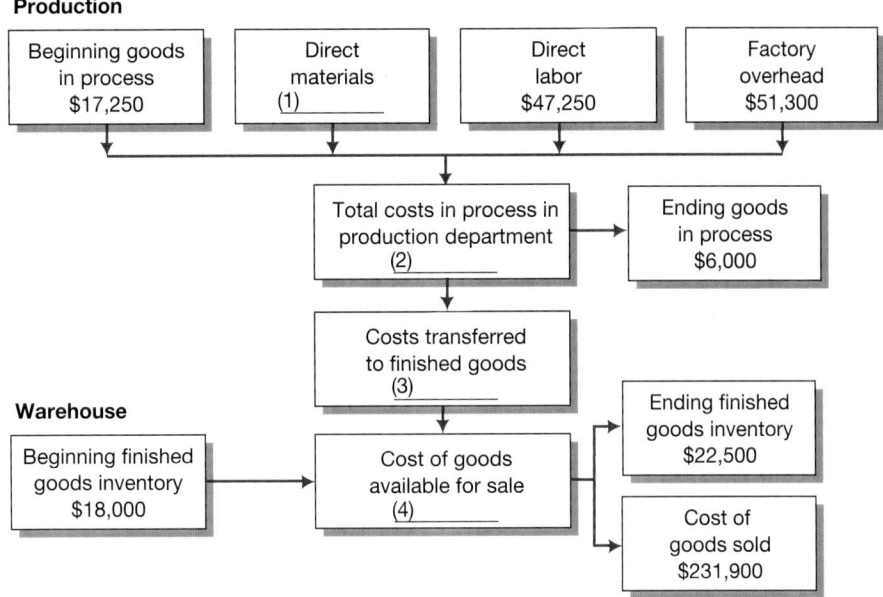

Warehouse

The following partially completed process cost summary describes the July production activities of Ashad Company. Its production output is sent to its warehouse for shipping. Prepare its process cost summary using the weighted average method.

Exercise 20-12
Completing a process cost summary

P5

Equivalent Units of Production	Direct Materials	Direct Labor	Factory Overhead
Units transferred out	32,000	32,000	32,000
Units of ending goods in process	2,500	1,500	1,500
Equivalent units of production	34,500	33,500	33,500

Costs per EUP	Direct Materials	Direct Labor	Factory Overhead
Costs of beginning goods in process	$ 18,550	$ 760	$ 1,520
Costs incurred this period	357,500	62,890	125,780
Total costs	$376,050	$63,650	$127,300

Units in beginning goods in process	2,000
Units started this period	32,500
Units completed and transferred out	32,000
Units in ending goods in process	2,500

Hi-Test Company uses the weighted average method of process costing to assign production costs to its products. Information for September follows. Assume that all materials are added at the beginning of its production process, and that direct labor and factory overhead are added uniformly throughout the process.

Exercise 20-13
Process costing—weighted average

P1 P2 P6

Goods in process inventory, September 1 (2,000 units, 100% complete with respect to direct materials, 80% complete with respect to direct labor and overhead; includes $45,000 of direct material cost, $25,600 in direct labor cost, $30,720 overhead cost)	$101,320
Units started in September	28,000
Units completed and transferred to finished goods inventory	23,000
Goods in process inventory, September 30 (? units, 100% complete with respect to direct materials, 40% complete with respect to direct labor and overhead)	?

[continued on next page]

828 Chapter 20 Process Cost Accounting

[continued from previous page]

Costs incurred in September	
Direct materials	$375,000
Direct labor	$155,000
Overhead applied at 120% of direct labor cost	?

Required

Fill in the blanks labeled *a* through *uu* in the following process cost summary.

Check (c) $817,320

HI-TEST COMPANY
Process Cost Summary
For Month Ended September 30

Costs Charged to Production

Costs of beginning goods in process

Direct materials	$ 45,000	
Direct labor	25,600	
Factory overhead	30,720	$101,320

Costs incurred this period

Direct materials	$375,000	
Direct labor	155,000	
Factory overhead	(a)_____	(b)_____
Total costs to account for		(c)_____

Unit Cost Information

Units to account for		Units accounted for	
Beginning goods in process	2,000	Completed and transferred out	23,000
Units started this period	28,000	Ending goods in process	(d)_____
Total units to account for	(e)_____	Total units accounted for	(f)_____

Equivalent Units of Production (EUP)				Direct Materials	Direct Labor	Factory Overhead
Units completed and transferred out				(g)_____ EUP	(h)_____ EUP	(i)_____ EUP
Units of ending goods in process						
Materials	(j)_____	×	100%	(k)_____ EUP		
Direct labor	(l)_____	×	40%		(m)_____ EUP	
Factory overhead	(n)_____	×	40%			(o)_____ EUP
Equivalent units of production (EUP)				(p)_____ EUP	(q)_____ EUP	(r)_____ EUP

Cost per EUP	Direct Materials	Direct Labor	Factory Overhead
Costs of beginning goods in process	$ 45,000	$ 25,600	$30,720
Costs incurred this period	375,000	155,000	(s)_____
Total costs	$420,000	$180,600	(t)_____
÷ EUP	(u)_____	(v)_____	(w)_____
Cost per EUP	(x)_____	(y)_____	(z)_____

(z) $8.40 per EUP

Cost Assignment and Reconciliation

Costs transferred out	Cost/EUP	×	EUP		
Direct materials	(aa)_____	×	(bb)_____	(cc)_____	
Direct labor	(dd)_____	×	(ee)_____	(ff)_____	
Factory overhead	(gg)_____	×	(hh)_____	(ii)_____	
Costs of goods completed and transferred out					(jj)_____
Costs of ending goods in process					
Direct materials	(kk)_____	×	(ll)_____	(mm)_____	
Direct labor	(nn)_____	×	(oo)_____	(pp)_____	
Factory overhead	(qq)_____	×	(rr)_____	(ss)_____	
Costs of ending goods in process					(tt)_____
Total costs accounted for					(uu)_____

Sierra Company manufactures woven blankets and accounts for product costs using process costing. The following information is available regarding its May inventories.

PROBLEM SET A

Problem 20-1A
Production cost flow and
measurement; journal entries

P1   P2   P3   P6

	Beginning Inventory	Ending Inventory
Raw materials inventory	$ 60,000	$ 92,500
Goods in process inventory	435,000	515,000
Finished goods inventory	633,000	605,000

The following additional information describes the company's production activities for May.

Raw materials purchases (on credit)	$ 250,000
Factory payroll cost (paid in cash)	1,530,000
Other overhead cost (Other Accounts credited)	87,000
Materials used	
Direct	$ 157,500
Indirect	60,000
Labor used	
Direct	$ 780,000
Indirect	750,000
Overhead rate as a percent of direct labor	115%
Sales (on credit)	$2,500,000

Required

1. Compute the cost of (a) products transferred from production to finished goods, and (b) goods sold.

2. Prepare summary journal entries dated May 31 to record the following production activities during May: (a) raw materials purchases, (b) direct materials usage, (c) indirect materials usage, (d) payroll costs, (e) direct labor costs, (f) indirect labor costs, (g) other overhead costs, (h) overhead applied, (i) goods transferred from production to finished goods, and (j) sale of finished goods.

Check   (1b) Cost of goods sold
$1,782,500

Victory Company uses weighted-average process costing to account for its production costs. Direct labor is added evenly throughout the process. Direct materials are added at the beginning of the process. During November, Victory transferred 700,000 units of product to finished goods. At the end of November, the goods in process inventory consists of 180,000 units that are 30% complete with respect to labor. Beginning inventory had $420,000 of direct materials and $139,000 of direct labor cost. The direct labor cost added in November is $2,220,000, and the direct materials cost added is $3,254,000.

Problem 20-2A
Cost per equivalent unit; costs
assigned to products

P4   P5

mhhe.com/wildFAP18e

Required

1. Determine the equivalent units of production with respect to (a) direct labor and (b) direct materials.

2. Compute both the direct labor cost and the direct materials cost per equivalent unit.

3. Compute both direct labor cost and direct materials cost assigned to (a) units completed and transferred out, and (b) ending goods in process inventory.

Check   (2) Direct labor cost per
equivalent unit, $4.50

(3b) $783,000

Analysis Component

4. Victory sells and ships all units to customers as soon as they are completed. Assume that an error is made in determining the percentage of completion for units in ending inventory. Instead of being 30% complete with respect to labor, they are actually 60% complete. Write a one-page memo to the plant manager describing how this error affects its November financial statements.

Problem 20-3A
Journalizing in process costing;
equivalent units and costs

P1 P2 P3 P4 P6

Elliott Company produces large quantities of a standardized product. The following information is available for its production activities for March.

Raw materials		Factory overhead incurred	
Beginning inventory	$ 16,000	Indirect materials used	$ 70,000
Raw materials purchased (on credit)	250,000	Indirect labor used	45,000
Direct materials used	(168,000)	Other overhead costs	164,790
Indirect materials used	(70,000)	Total factory overhead incurred	$279,790
Ending inventory	$ 28,000		
		Factory overhead applied	
Factory payroll		**(140% of direct labor cost)**	
Direct labor used	$199,850	Total factory overhead applied	$279,790
Indirect labor used	45,000		
Total payroll cost (paid in cash)	$244,850		

Additional information about units and costs of production activities follows.

Units		Costs		
Beginning goods in process inventory	2,000	Beginning goods in process inventory		
Started	20,000	Direct materials	$2,500	
Ending goods in process inventory	5,000	Direct labor	2,650	
		Factory overhead	3,710	$ 8,860
Status of ending goods in process inventory		Direct materials added		168,000
Materials—Percent complete	100%	Direct labor added		199,850
Labor and overhead—Percent complete	35%	Overhead applied (140% of direct labor)		279,790
		Total costs		$656,500
		Ending goods in process inventory		$ 84,110

During March, 10,000 units of finished goods are sold for $120 cash each. Cost information regarding finished goods follows.

Beginning finished goods inventory	$150,000
Cost transferred in	572,390
Cost of goods sold	(592,390)
Ending finished goods inventory	$130,000

Required

1. Prepare journal entries dated March 31 to record the following March activities: (a) purchase of raw materials, (b) direct materials usage, (c) indirect materials usage, (d) factory payroll costs, (e) direct labor costs used in production, (f) indirect labor costs, (g) other overhead costs—credit Other Accounts, (h) overhead applied, (i) goods transferred to finished goods, and (j) sale of finished goods.

Check (2) Cost per equivalent unit: materials, $7.75; labor, $10.80; overhead, $15.12

2. Prepare a process cost summary report for this company, showing costs charged to production, units cost information, equivalent units of production, cost per EUP, and its cost assignment and reconciliation.

Analysis Component

3. Elliott provides incentives to its department managers by paying monthly bonuses based on their success in controlling costs per equivalent unit of production. Assume that the production department underestimates the percentage of completion for units in ending inventory with the result that its equivalent units of production in ending inventory for March are understated. What impact does this error have on the March bonuses paid to the production managers? What impact, if any, does this error have on April bonuses?

Fast Co. produces its product through a single processing department. Direct materials are added at the
of production, and direct labor and overhead are added evenly throughout the process. The company
monthly reporting periods for its weighted-average process cost accounting system. Its Goods in Pr
Inventory account follows after entries for direct materials, direct labor, and overhead costs for Oc

Goods in Process Inventory				Acct. No. 133
Date	Explanation	Debit	Credit	Balance
Oct. 1	Balance			335,930
31	Direct materials	102,050		437,980
31	Direct labor	408,200		846,180
31	Applied overhead	244,920		1,091,100

Its beginning goods in process consisted of $59,450 of direct materials, $172,800 of direct labor, and
$103,680 of factory overhead. During October, the company started 140,000 units and transferred 150,000
units to finished goods. At the end of the month, the goods in process inventory consisted of 20,000 units
that were 80% complete.

Required

1. Prepare the company's process cost summary for October using the weighted average method.

2. Prepare the journal entry dated October 31 to transfer the cost of the completed units to finished
goods inventory.

Check (1) Costs transferred to finished goods, $982,500

Tamar Co. manufactures a single product in one department. All direct materials are added at the beginning of the manufacturing process. Direct labor and overhead are added evenly throughout the process.
Tamar uses monthly reporting periods for its weighted average process cost accounting. During May, the
company completed and transferred 22,200 units of product to finished goods inventory. Its 3,000 units of
beginning goods in process consisted of $19,800 of direct materials, $123,300 of direct labor, and $98,640
of factory overhead. It has 2,400 units (100% complete with respect to direct materials and 80% complete
with respect to direct labor and overhead) in process at month-end. After entries to record direct materials,
direct labor, and overhead for May, the company's Goods in Process Inventory account follows.

Problem 20-5A
Process cost summary;
equivalent units; cost estimates

P4 P5

Goods in Process Inventory				Acct. No. 133
Date	Explanation	Debit	Credit	Balance
May 1	Balance			241,740
31	Direct materials	496,800		738,540
31	Direct labor	1,203,300		1,941,840
31	Applied overhead	962,640		2,904,480

Required

1. Prepare the company's process cost summary for May.

2. Prepare the journal entry dated May 31 to transfer the cost of completed units to finished goods inventory.

Analysis Components

3. The cost accounting process depends on numerous estimates.

  a. Identify two major estimates that determine the cost per equivalent unit.

  b. In what direction might you anticipate a bias from management for each estimate in part 3a (assume that management compensation is based on maintaining low inventory amounts)? Explain
your answer.

Check (1) EUP for labor and overhead, 24,120 EUP

(2) Cost transferred to finished goods, $2,664,000

Refer to the data in Problem 20-5A. Assume that Tamar uses the FIFO method to account for its process
costing system. The following additional information is available:

• Beginning goods in process consisted of 3,000 units that were 100% complete with respect to direct
materials and 40% complete with respect to direct labor and overhead.

• Of the 22,200 units completed, 3,000 were from beginning goods in process. The remaining 19,200
were units started and completed during May.

Problem 20-6A[A]
Process cost summary; equivalent
units; and cost estimates

C5 P5 P6

Required

1. Prepare the company's process cost summary for May using FIFO.

2. Prepare the journal entry dated May 31 to transfer the cost of completed units to finished goods inventory.

and
0 EUP

ansferred to
goods, $2,667,840

PROBLEM SET B

Problem 20-1B

Production cost flow and measurement; journal entries

P1 P2 P3 P6

Dream Toys Company manufactures dolls and accounts for product costs using process costing. The following information is available regarding its June inventories.

	Beginning Inventory	Ending Inventory
Raw materials inventory	$ 72,000	$110,000
Goods in process inventory	156,000	250,000
Finished goods inventory	160,000	198,000

The following additional information describes the company's production activities for June.

Raw materials purchases (on credit)	$ 200,000
Factory payroll cost (paid in cash)	400,000
Other overhead cost (Other Accounts credited)	170,500
Materials used	
Direct	$ 120,000
Indirect	42,000
Labor used	
Direct	$ 350,000
Indirect	50,000
Overhead rate as a percent of direct labor	75%
Sales (on credit)	$1,000,000

Required

Check (1b) Cost of goods sold, $600,500

1. Compute the cost of (a) products transferred from production to finished goods, and (b) goods sold.

2. Prepare journal entries dated June 30 to record the following production activities during June: (a) raw materials purchases, (b) direct materials usage, (c) indirect materials usage, (d) payroll costs, (e) direct labor costs, (f) indirect labor costs, (g) other overhead costs, (h) overhead applied, (i) goods transferred from production to finished goods, and (j) sale of finished goods.

Problem 20-2B

Cost per equivalent unit; costs assigned to products

P4 P5

Abraham Company uses process costing to account for its production costs. Direct labor is added evenly throughout the process. Direct materials are added at the beginning of the process. During September, the production department transferred 80,000 units of product to finished goods. Beginning goods in process had $58,000 of direct materials and $86,400 of direct labor cost. At the end of September, the goods in process inventory consists of 8,000 units that are 25% complete with respect to labor. The direct materials cost added in September is $712,000, and direct labor cost added is $1,980,000.

Required

Check (2) Direct labor cost per equivalent unit, $25.20

(3b) $120,400

1. Determine the equivalent units of production with respect to (a) direct labor and (b) direct materials.

2. Compute both the direct labor cost and the direct materials cost per equivalent unit.

3. Compute both direct labor cost and direct materials cost assigned to (a) units completed and transferred out, and (b) ending goods in process inventory.

Analysis Component

4. Abraham sells and ships all units to customers as soon as they are completed. Assume that an error is made in determining the percentage of completion for units in ending inventory. Instead of being 25% complete with respect to labor, they are actually 75% complete. Write a one-page memo to the plant manager describing how this error affects its September financial statements.

Oslo Company produces large quantities of a standardized product. The following information is available for its production activities for May.

Problem 20-3B
Journalizing in process costing; equivalent units and costs

P1 P2 P3 P4 P6

Raw materials

Beginning inventory	$ 32,000
Raw materials purchased (on credit)	221,120
Direct materials used	(197,120)
Indirect materials used	(40,560)
Ending inventory	$ 15,440

Factory payroll

Direct labor used	$123,680
Indirect labor used	36,320
Total payroll cost (paid in cash)	$160,000

Factory overhead incurred

Indirect materials used	$ 40,560
Indirect labor used	36,320
Other overhead costs	34,432
Total factory overhead incurred	$111,312

Factory overhead applied
(90% of direct labor cost)

Total factory overhead applied	$111,312

Additional information about units and costs of production activities follows.

Units

Beginning goods in process inventory	4,000
Started	12,000
Ending goods in process inventory	3,000

Status of ending goods in process inventory

Materials—Percent complete	100%
Labor and overhead—Percent complete	100%

Costs

Beginning goods in process inventory

Direct materials	$2,880	
Direct labor	2,820	
Factory overhead	2,538	$ 8,238
Direct materials added		197,120
Direct labor added		123,680
Overhead applied (90% of direct labor)		111,312
Total costs		$440,350
Ending goods in process inventory		$ 50,610

During May, 10,000 units of finished goods are sold for $120 cash each. Cost information regarding finished goods follows.

Beginning finished goods inventory	$ 148,400
Cost transferred in from production	389,740
Cost of goods sold	(474,540)
Ending finished goods inventory	$ 63,600

Required

1. Prepare journal entries dated May 31 to record the following May activities: (a) purchase of raw materials, (b) direct materials usage, (c) indirect materials usage, (d) factory payroll costs, (e) direct labor costs used in production, (f) indirect labor costs, (g) other overhead costs—credit Other Accounts, (h) overhead applied, (i) goods transferred to finished goods, and (j) sale of finished goods.

2. Prepare a process cost summary report for this company, showing costs charged to production, units cost information, equivalent units of production, cost per EUP, and its cost assignment and reconciliation.

Check (2) Cost per equivalent unit: materials, $12.50; labor, $9.20; overhead, $8.28

Analysis Component

3. Oslo provides incentives to its department managers by paying monthly bonuses based on their success in controlling costs per equivalent unit of production. Assume that production overestimates the percentage of completion for units in ending inventory with the result that its equivalent units of production in ending inventory for May are overstated. What impact does this error have on bonuses paid to the managers of the production department? What impact, if any, does this error have on these managers' June bonuses?

Problem 20-4B
Process cost summary; equivalent units

P4 P5 P6

Braun Company produces its product through a single processing department. Direct materials are added at the beginning of the process. Direct labor and overhead are added to the product evenly throughout the process. The company uses monthly reporting periods for its weighted-average process cost accounting. Its Goods in Process Inventory account follows after entries for direct materials, direct labor, and overhead costs for November.

Goods in Process Inventory					Acct. No. 133
Date		Explanation	Debit	Credit	Balance
Nov.	1	Balance			21,300
	30	Direct materials	116,400		137,700
	30	Direct labor	426,800		564,500
	30	Applied overhead	640,200		1,204,700

The 7,500 units of beginning goods in process consisted of $6,800 of direct materials, $5,800 of direct labor, and $8,700 of factory overhead. During November, the company finished and transferred 100,000 units of its product to finished goods. At the end of the month, the goods in process inventory consisted of 12,000 units that were 25% complete with respect to direct labor and factory overhead and 100% complete with respect to direct materials.

Required

Check (1) Cost transferred to finished goods, $1,160,000

1. Prepare the company's process cost summary for November using the weighted average method.
2. Prepare the journal entry dated November 30 to transfer the cost of the completed units to finished goods inventory.

Problem 20-5B
Process cost summary; equivalent units; cost estimates

P4 P5

Switch Co. manufactures a single product in one department. Direct labor and overhead are added evenly throughout the process. Direct materials are added as needed. The company uses monthly reporting periods for its weighted average process cost accounting. During January, Switch completed and transferred 220,000 units of product to finished goods inventory. Its 10,000 units of beginning goods in process consisted of $7,500 of direct materials, $14,240 of direct labor, and $35,600 of factory overhead. 40,000 units (50% complete with respect to direct materials and 30% complete with respect to direct labor and overhead) are in process at month-end. After entries for direct materials, direct labor, and overhead for January, the company's Goods in Process Inventory account follows.

Goods in Process Inventory					Acct. No. 133
Date		Explanation	Debit	Credit	Balance
Jan.	1	Balance			57,340
	31	Direct materials	112,500		169,840
	31	Direct labor	176,000		345,840
	31	Applied overhead	440,000		785,840

Required

Check (1) EUP for labor and overhead, 232,000
(2) Cost transferred to finished goods, $741,400

1. Prepare the company's process cost summary for January.
2. Prepare the journal entry dated January 31 to transfer the cost of completed units to finished goods inventory.

Analysis Components

3. The cost accounting process depends on several estimates.
   a. Identify two major estimates that affect the cost per equivalent unit.
   b. In what direction might you anticipate a bias from management for each estimate in part 3a (assume that management compensation is based on maintaining low inventory amounts)? Explain your answer.

Refer to information in Problem 20-5B. Assume that Switch uses the FIFO method to account for its process costing system. The following additional information is available.

- Beginning goods in process consists of 10,000 units that were 75% complete with respect to direct materials and 60% complete with respect to direct labor and overhead.
- Of the 220,000 units completed, 10,000 were from beginning goods in process; the remaining 210,000 were units started and completed during January.

Required

1. Prepare the company's process cost summary for January using FIFO. Round cost per EUP to one-tenth of a cent.

2. Prepare the journal entry dated January 31 to transfer the cost of completed units to finished goods inventory.

Problem Set C is available at the book's Website to further reinforce and assess your learning.

(This serial problem began in Chapter 1 and continues through most of the book. If previous chapter segments were not completed, the serial problem can begin at this point.)

SP 20 The computer workstation furniture manufacturing that Adriana Lopez started is progressing well. At this point, Adriana is using a job order costing system to account for the production costs of this product line. Adriana has heard about process costing and is wondering whether process costing might be a better method for her to keep track of and monitor her production costs.

Required

1. What are the features that distinguish job order costing from process costing?

2. Do you believe that Adriana should continue to use job order costing or switch to process costing for her workstation furniture manufacturing? Explain.

CP 20 Corked Bat Company manufactures baseball bats. In addition to its goods in process inventories, Corked Bat maintains inventories of raw materials and finished goods. It uses raw materials as direct materials in production and as indirect materials. Its factory payroll costs include direct labor for production and indirect labor. All materials are added at the beginning of the process, and direct labor and factory overhead are applied uniformly throughout the production process.

Required

You are to maintain records and produce measures of inventories to reflect the July events of this company. All computations of unit costs are rounded to the nearest penny and all other dollar amounts to the nearest whole dollar. Set up the following general ledger accounts and enter the June 30 balances: Raw Materials Inventory, $50,000; Goods in Process Inventory, $16,270 ($5,320 of direct materials, $7,300 of direct labor, and $3,650 of overhead); Finished Goods Inventory, $220,000; Sales, $0; Cost of Goods Sold, $0; Factory Payroll, $0; and Factory Overhead, $0.

1. Prepare journal entries to record the following July transactions and events.

   a. Purchased raw materials for $250,000 cash (the company uses a perpetual inventory system).

   b. Used raw materials as follows: direct materials, $104,880; and indirect materials, $20,000.

   c. Incurred factory payroll cost of $454,500 paid in cash (ignore taxes).

   d. Assigned factory payroll costs as follows: direct labor, $404,500; and indirect labor, $50,000.

   e. Incurred additional factory overhead costs of $160,000 paid in cash.

   f. Allocated factory overhead to production at 50% of direct labor costs.

Check (2) EUP for overhead, 28,400

2. Information about the July inventories follows. Use this information with that from part 1 to prepare a process cost summary, assuming the weighted average method is used.

Units	
Beginning inventory	10,000 units
Started	28,000 units
Ending inventory	16,000 units
Beginning inventory	
Materials—Percent complete	100%
Labor and overhead—Percent complete	75%
Ending inventory	
Materials—Percent complete	100%
Labor and overhead—Percent complete	40%

3. Using results from part 2 and the available information, make computations and prepare journal entries to record the following:

(3a) $542,300

    a. Total costs transferred to finished goods for July (label entry g).

    b. Sale of finished goods costing $531,400 for $1,250,000 in cash (label entry h).

4. Post entries from parts 1 and 3 to the ledger accounts set up at the beginning of the problem.

5. Compute the amount of gross profit from the sales in July. (*Note:* Add any underapplied overhead to, or deduct any overapplied overhead from, cost of goods sold. Ignore the corresponding journal entry.)

BEYOND THE NUMBERS

REPORTING IN ACTION

C2

BTN 20-1 **Best Buy** reports in notes to its financial statements that, in addition to its merchandise sold, it includes the following costs (among others) in cost of goods sold: freight expenses associated with moving inventories from vendors to distribution centers, costs of services provided, customer shipping and handling expenses, costs associated with operating their distribution network, and freight expenses associated with moving merchandise from distribution centers to retail stores.

Required

1. Why do you believe Best Buy includes these costs in its cost of goods sold?

2. What effect does this cost accounting policy for its cost of goods sold have on Best Buy's financial statements and any analysis of these statements? Explain.

Fast Forward

3. Access Best Buy's financial statements for fiscal years after February 26, 2005, from its Website (**BestBuy.com**) or the SEC's EDGAR Website (**sec.gov**). Review its footnote relating to Cost of Goods Sold and Selling, General, and Administrative Expense. Has Best Buy changed its policy with respect to what costs are included in cost of goods sold? Explain.

COMPARATIVE ANALYSIS

C1

BTN 20-2 Retailers such as **Best Buy** and **Circuit City** usually work to maintain a high-quality and low-cost operation. One ratio routinely computed for this assessment is the cost of goods sold divided by total expenses. A decline in this ratio can mean that the company is spending too much on selling and administrative activities. An increase in this ratio beyond a reasonable level can mean that the company is not spending enough on selling activities. (Assume for this analysis that total expenses equal cost of goods sold plus selling, general, and administrative expenses.)

Required

1. For both Best Buy and Circuit City, refer to Appendix A and compute the ratio of cost of goods sold to total expenses for their two most recent fiscal years.

2. Comment on the similarities or differences in the ratio results across both years and companies.

BTN 20-3   Many accounting and accounting-related professionals are skilled in financial analysis, but most are not skilled in manufacturing. This is especially the case for process manufacturing environments (for example, a bottling plant or chemical factory). To provide professional accounting and financial services, one must understand the industry, product, and processes. We have an ethical responsibility to develop this understanding before offering services to clients in these areas.

ETHICS CHALLENGE

C1   C3

Required

Write a one-page action plan, in memorandum format, on how you would obtain an understanding of key business processes of a company that hires you to provide financial services. The memorandum should specify an industry, a product, and one selected process and should draw on at least one reference, such as a professional journal or industry magazine.

BTN 20-4   You hire a new assistant production manager whose prior experience is with a company that produced goods to order. Your company engages in continuous production of homogeneous products that go through various production processes. Your new assistant e-mails you questioning some cost classifications on an internal report, specifically why the costs of some materials that do not actually become part of the finished product, including some labor costs not directly associated with producing the product, are classified as direct costs. Respond to this concern via memorandum.

COMMUNICATING IN PRACTICE

A1   C1   P1   P2

BTN 20-5   Many companies acquire software to help them monitor and control their costs and as an aid to their accounting systems. One company that supplies such software is **proDacapo** (**prodacapo.com**). There are many other such vendors. Access proDacapo's Website, click on "Process Management" and review the information displayed.

TAKING IT TO THE NET

C1   C3

Required

How is process management software helpful to businesses? Explain with reference to costs, efficiency, and examples, if possible.

BTN 20-6   The purpose of this team activity is to ensure that each team member understands process operations and the related accounting entries. Find the activities and flows identified in Exhibit 20.4 with numbers ①–⑩. Pick a member of the team to start by describing activity number ① in this exhibit, then verbalizing the related journal entry, and describing how the amounts in the entry are computed. The other members of the team are to agree or disagree; discussion is to continue until all members express understanding. Rotate to the next numbered activity and next team member until all activities and entries have been discussed. If at any point a team member is uncertain about an answer, the team member may pass and get back in the rotation when he or she can contribute to the team's discussion.

TEAMWORK IN ACTION

C1   P1   P2   P3   P6

BTN 20-7   Read the article "Global or Local? Make it Both," from the August 22, 2005, issue of *BusinessWeek*. (The book's Website provides a free link to the article.)

BusinessWeek **ACTIVITY**

C1   C3

Required

1. How does Gianfranco Zaccai define *global* products? Does he imply that the products must be the same the world over? Explain.
2. How do global product choices depend on flexibility of mass production?
3. What are some examples of companies who found that their assumptions about international customers were incorrect? Identify and briefly discuss them.

**ENTREPRENEURIAL
DECISION**

C4

BTN 20-8   Read the chapter opener regarding **DuWop**. Cristina Bartolucci commented that some suppliers tried to bully them and talk them into buying items that they did not really need.

Required

How do unnecessary raw materials inventories affect profitability? If the items are not used in production, how can they affect profits? Explain.

**HITTING THE
ROAD**

C3

Point: The class can compare and discuss the different processes studied and the answers provided.

BTN 20-9   In process costing, the process is analyzed first and then a unit measure is computed in the form of equivalent units for direct materials, direct labor, overhead, and all three combined. The same analysis applies to both manufacturing and service processes.

Required

Visit your local **U.S. Mail** center. Look into the backroom and you will see several ongoing processes. Select one process, such as sorting, and list the costs associated with this process. Your list should include materials, labor, and overhead; be specific. Classify each cost as fixed or variable. At the bottom of your list, outline how overhead should be assigned to your identified process. The following format (with an example) is suggested.

Cost Description	Direct Material	Direct Labor	Overhead	Variable Cost	Fixed Cost
Manual sorting		X		X	
⋮					
Overhead allocation suggestions:					

GLOBAL DECISION

C1

BTN 20-10   **Dixons**, **Best Buy**, and **Circuit City** are competitors in the global marketplace. Selected data for each of these companies follow.

	Dixons*		Best Buy[†]		Circuit City[†]	
	Current Year	Prior Year	Current Year	Prior Year	Current Year	Prior Year
Cost of goods sold	£5,806	£5,127	$20,938	$18,677	$ 7,904	$7,573
General, selling, and administrative expenses	378	365	5,053	4,567	2,457	2,277
Total expenses	£6,184	£5,492	$25,991	$23,244	$10,361	$9,850

* millions of pounds
[†] millions of dollars

Required

1. Review the discussion of the importance of the cost of goods sold divided by total expenses ratio in BTN 20-2. Compute the cost of goods sold to total expenses ratio for all three companies for the two years of data provided.
2. Comment on the similarities or differences in the ratio results across years and companies.

ANSWERS TO MULTIPLE CHOICE QUIZ

1. d

2. e

3. b; $20,000 + $152,000 + $45,000 + $18,000 − $218,000 = $17,000

4. a; 40,000 + (15,000 × 1/3) = 45,000 EUP

5. c; ($6,000 + $84,000) ÷ 45,000 EUP = $2 per EUP

21

Cost Allocation and Performance Measurement

A Look Back

Chapter 20 focused on how to measure and account for costs in process operations. It explained process production, described how to assign costs to processes, and computed cost per equivalent unit.

A Look at This Chapter

This chapter describes cost allocation and activity-based costing. It identifies managerial reports useful in directing a company's activities. It also describes responsibility accounting, measuring departmental performance, and allocating common costs across departments.

A Look Ahead

Chapter 22 looks at cost behavior and explains how its identification is useful to managers in performing cost-volume-profit analyses. It also shows how to apply cost-volume-profit analysis for managerial decisions.

Learning Objectives

CAP

Conceptual

C1 Explain departmentalization and the role of departmental accounting. (p. 848)

C2 Distinguish between direct and indirect expenses. (p. 849)

C3 Identify bases for allocating indirect expenses to departments. (p. 850)

C4 Explain controllable costs and responsibility accounting. (p. 855)

C5 *Appendix 21A—*Describe allocation of joint costs across products. (p. 861)

Analytical

A1 Analyze investment centers using return on total assets. (p. 858)

Procedural

P1 Assign overhead costs using two-stage cost allocation. (p. 842)

P2 Assign overhead costs using activity-based costing. (p. 844)

P3 Prepare departmental income statements. (p. 851)

P4 Prepare departmental contribution reports. (p. 854)

> "If you put enough energy into your dream, you can make anything happen"
> —Jim Bonaminio

The Wizard of Odd

FAIRFIELD, OH—Jim Bonaminio built his roadside produce stand while living in an abandoned gas station. "I would get up and leave at 4 in the morning to buy everything fresh [and] my wife opened the market at 8 a.m.," recalls Jim. "By 10 o'clock at night, we'd be sitting on the bed balancing the register receipts . . . we worked seven days a week." The fruit of those early efforts is **Jungle Jim's International Market (JungleJim.com).** Jim and his wife now serve more than 50,000 customers (Jim calls them "Foodies" and his store "Foodieland") each week, and annual sales are near $100 million.

Jungle Jim's is no Wal-Mart wannabe, but it is arguably America's wackiest supermarket. Yet there is a plan to Jim's madness. Instead of trying to beat the big chains at the price-squeezing game, Jim's is a funhouse maze of a store. A seven-foot Elvis lion sings "Jailhouse Rock," an antique fire engine rests atop cases of hot sauce, port-a-potties lead to fancy restrooms, and Robin Hood greets customers with English food set within a 30-foot-tall Sherwood Forest. This is just a sampling. Jim is already working on a plan to install the old monorail acquired from Paramount's Kings Island.

"If you don't go out on a limb, then you're just like everybody else," insists Jim. "The stuff I've collected—all sorts of weird stuff—gets reused. We make it fit into the craziness." Despite the wackiness, his store's defining trait is specialty food departments reflecting nearly 100 countries. Jungle Jim's stocks more than 140,000 items, including 1,600 cheeses, 8,500 wines, 800 beers, 1,000 hot sauces, and an entire acre of produce! More than several dozen ethnic departments make up his 300,000 square foot Foodieland.

This diversity of departments requires cost management. Jim is first and foremost a businessman. "I hire professional people to run the departments," says Jim. "I offer suggestions. They run with the ball. I block and add my creative craziness." Jim has successfully merged cost controls and departmental and individual responsibility into his store. He closely monitors direct, indirect, and controllable costs and allocates them to departments and products. Jim knows how departments and products are performing and their contribution margins. Says Jim about his employees, "[they're] always looking for ways to make money . . . [I want them] to be the best in each food department."

Yet cost management has not curtailed Jim's fun-loving approach to business. "I'm trying to create something that has never been done," says Jim. "I just want to see if I can do it and have fun."

[Sources: *Jungle Jim's Website*, May 2006; *BusinessWeek*, April 2005; *Country Living*, November 2004; *Miamian*, Summer 2004; *Design*, May 2004; *Smithsonian*, October 2000; *Plain Dealer*, November 2004]

This chapter describes how to allocate costs shared by more than one product across those different products and how to allocate indirect costs of shared items such as utilities, advertising, and rent. The chapter also describes activity-based costing and how it traces the costs of individual activities. This knowledge helps managers better understand how to assign costs and assess company performance. The chapter also introduces additional managerial accounting reports useful in managing a company's activities and explains how and why management divides companies into departments.

Cost Allocation and Performance Measurement

Overhead Cost Allocation Methods

- Two-stage cost allocation
- Activity-based cost allocation
- Comparison of allocation methods

Departmental Accounting

- Motivation for departmentalization
- Departmental evaluation
- Departmental reporting and analysis

Departmental Expense Allocation

- Direct and indirect expenses
- Allocation of indirect expenses
- Departmental income statements
- Departmental contribution to overhead

Responsibility Accounting

- Controllable versus direct costs
- Responsibility accounting system

Section 1—Allocating Costs for Product Costing

This first of two sections in this chapter focuses on alternatives for allocation of costs to products and services. We explain and illustrate two basic methods: (1) traditional two-state cost allocation and (2) activity-based cost allocation. The second section describes and illustrates the allocation of costs for performance evaluation.

Overhead Cost Allocation Methods

P1 Assign overhead costs using two-stage cost allocation.

Point: Use of a single overhead allocation rate is known as using a *plantwide rate.*

We previously explained how to assign overhead costs to jobs (and processes) by using a predetermined overhead rate per unit of an allocation base such as direct labor cost. When a single overhead rate is used on a companywide basis, all overhead is lumped together, and a predetermined overhead rate per unit of an allocation base is computed and used to assign overhead to jobs (and processes). The use of a single predetermined overhead rate suggests that this allocation process is simple. In reality, it can be complicated. This chapter explains the traditional two-stage cost allocation procedure and then introduces the activity-based cost allocation procedure.

Two-Stage Cost Allocation

An organization incurs overhead costs in many activities. These activities can be identified with various departments, which can be broadly classified as either operating or service departments.

Operating departments perform an organization's main functions. For example, an accounting firm's main functions usually include auditing, tax, and advisory services. Similarly, the production and selling departments of a manufacturing firm perform its main functions and serve as operating departments. *Service departments* provide support to an organization's operating departments. Examples of service departments are payroll, human resource management, accounting, and executive management. Service departments do not engage in activities that generate revenues, yet their support is crucial for the operating departments' success. In this section, we apply a two-stage cost allocation procedure to assign (1) service department costs to operating departments and (2) operating department costs, including those assigned from service departments, to the organization's output.

Illustration of Two-Stage Cost Allocation   Exhibit 21.1 shows the two-stage cost allocation procedure. This exhibit uses data from **AutoGrand**, a custom automobile manufacturer. AutoGrand has five manufacturing-related departments: janitorial, maintenance, factory accounting, machining, and assembly. Expenses incurred by each of these departments are considered product costs. There are three service departments—janitorial, maintenance, and factory accounting; each incurs expenses of $10,000, $15,000 and $8,000, respectively. As shown in Exhibit 21.1, the first stage of the two-stage procedure involves allocating the costs of the three service departments to the two operating departments (machining and assembly). The two operating departments use the resources of these service departments.

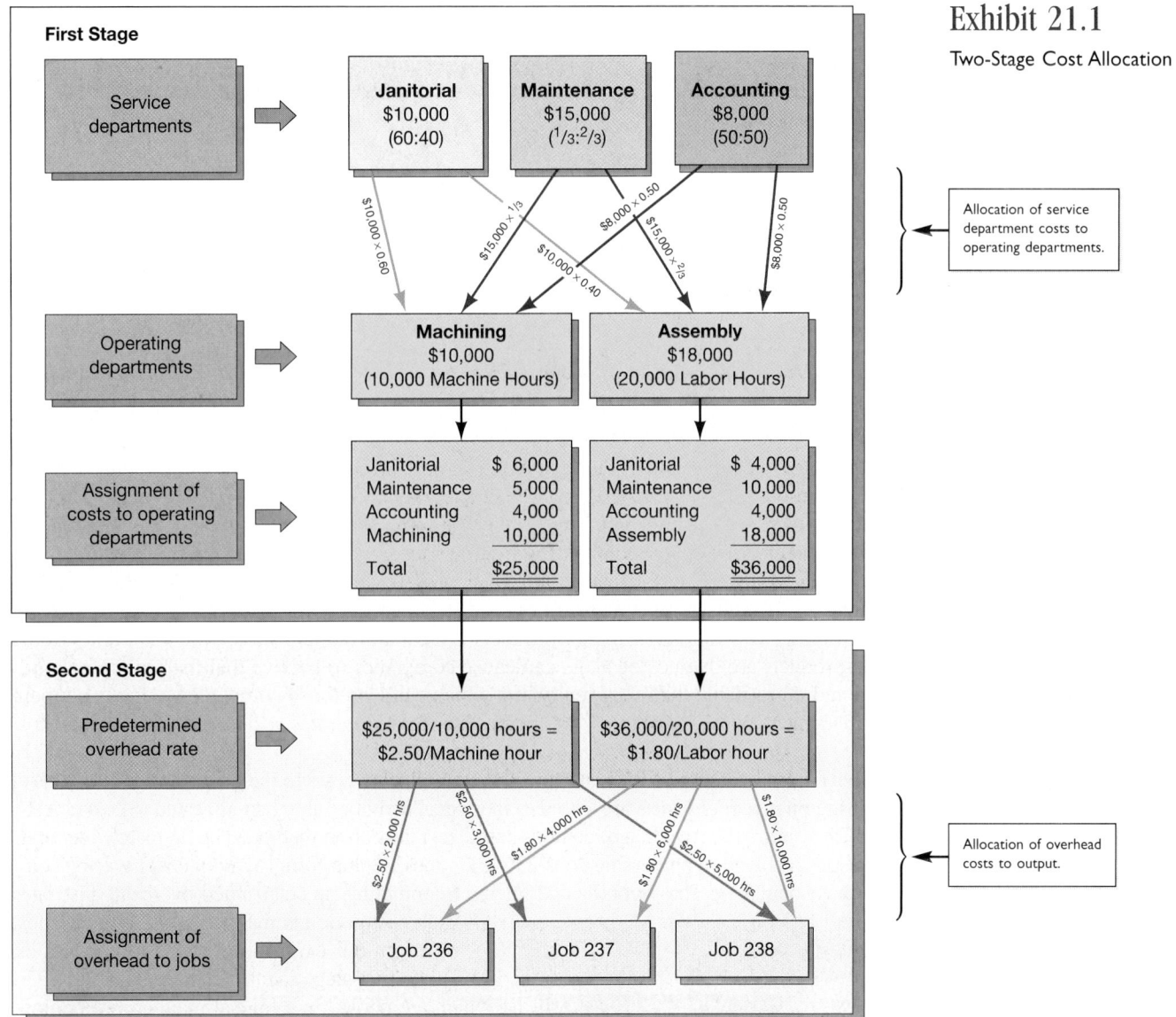

Exhibit 21.1
Two-Stage Cost Allocation

To illustrate the first stage of cost allocation, we use the janitorial department. Its costs are allocated to machining and assembly in the ratio 60:40. This means that 60%, or $6,000, of janitorial costs are assigned to the machining department and 40%, or $4,000, to the assembly department. The expenses incurred by the maintenance and factory accounting departments are similarly assigned to machining and assembly. We then add the expenses directly incurred by each operating department to these assigned costs to determine the total expenses for each operating department. This yields total costs of $25,000 for machining and $36,000 for assembly.

In the second stage, predetermined overhead rates are computed for each operating department. The allocation base is machine hours for machining and labor hours for assembly. The

Point: Use of a separate overhead allocation rate for each department is known as using *departmental rates.*

predetermined overhead rate is $2.50 per machine hour for the machining department and $1.80 per labor hour for the assembly department. These predetermined overhead rates are then used to assign overhead to output.

To illustrate this second stage, assume that three jobs were started and finished in a recent month. These jobs consumed resources as follows: Job 236—2,000 machine hours in machining and 4,000 labor hours in assembly; Job 237—3,000 machine hours and 6,000 labor hours; Job 238—5,000 machine hours and 10,000 labor hours. The overhead assigned to these three jobs is shown with the arrow lines in the bottom row of Exhibit 21.1.

Exhibit 21.2 summarizes these allocations. Total overhead allocated to Jobs 236, 237, and 238, is $12,200, $18,300, and $30,500, respectively. These allocated costs sum to $61,000, which is the total amount of overhead started with.

Exhibit 21.2

Assignment of Overhead Costs to Output

	Job 236	Job 237	Job 238	Department Totals
Machining				
$2.50 × 2,000 hours	$ 5,000			
$2.50 × 3,000 hours		$ 7,500		
$2.50 × 5,000 hours			$12,500	$25,000
Assembly				
$1.80 × 4,000 hours	7,200			
$1.80 × 6,000 hours		10,800		
$1.80 × 10,000 hours			18,000	36,000
Total overhead assigned	$12,200	$18,300	$30,500	$61,000

Activity-Based Cost Allocation

P2 Assign overhead costs using activity-based costing.

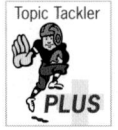

Topic Tackler

PLUS

21-1

Point: A survey found that most respondents believe that activity-based costing is worth the investment because of improved management decisions.

For companies with only one product, or with multiple products that use about the same amount of indirect resources, using a single overhead cost rate based on volume is adequate. Multiple overhead rates can further improve on cost allocations. Yet, when a company has many products that consume different amounts of indirect resources, even the multiple overhead rate system based on volume is often inadequate. Such a system usually fails to reflect the products' different uses of indirect resources and often distorts products costs.

Specifically, low-volume complex products are usually undercosted, whereas high-volume simpler products are overcosted. This can cause companies to believe that their complex products are more profitable than they really are, which can lead those companies to focus on them to the detriment of high-volume simpler products. This creates a demand for a better cost allocation system for these indirect (overhead) costs.

Activity-based costing (ABC) attempts to better allocate costs to the proper users of overhead by focusing on *activities*. Costs are traced to individual activities and then allocated to cost objects. Exhibit 21.3 shows the (two-stage) activity-based cost allocation method. The first stage identifies the activities involved in processing Jobs 236, 237, and 238 and forms activity cost *pools* by combining those activities. The second stage involves computing predetermined overhead cost rates for each cost pool and then assigning costs to jobs.

We begin our explanation at the top of Exhibit 21.3. The first stage identifies individual activities, which are pooled in a logical manner into homogenous groups, or *cost pools*. A homogenous cost pool consists of activities that belong to the same process and/or are caused by the same cost driver. An **activity cost driver,** or simply *cost driver,* is a factor that causes the cost of an activity to go up or down. For example, preparing an invoice, checking it, and dispatching it are activities of the "invoicing" process and can therefore be grouped in a single cost pool. Moreover, the number of invoices processed likely drives the costs of these activities.

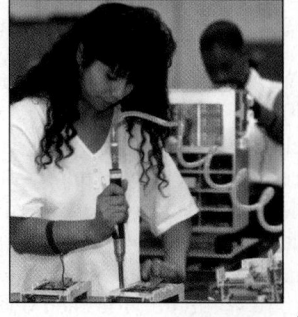

Exhibit 21.3

Activity-Based Cost Allocation

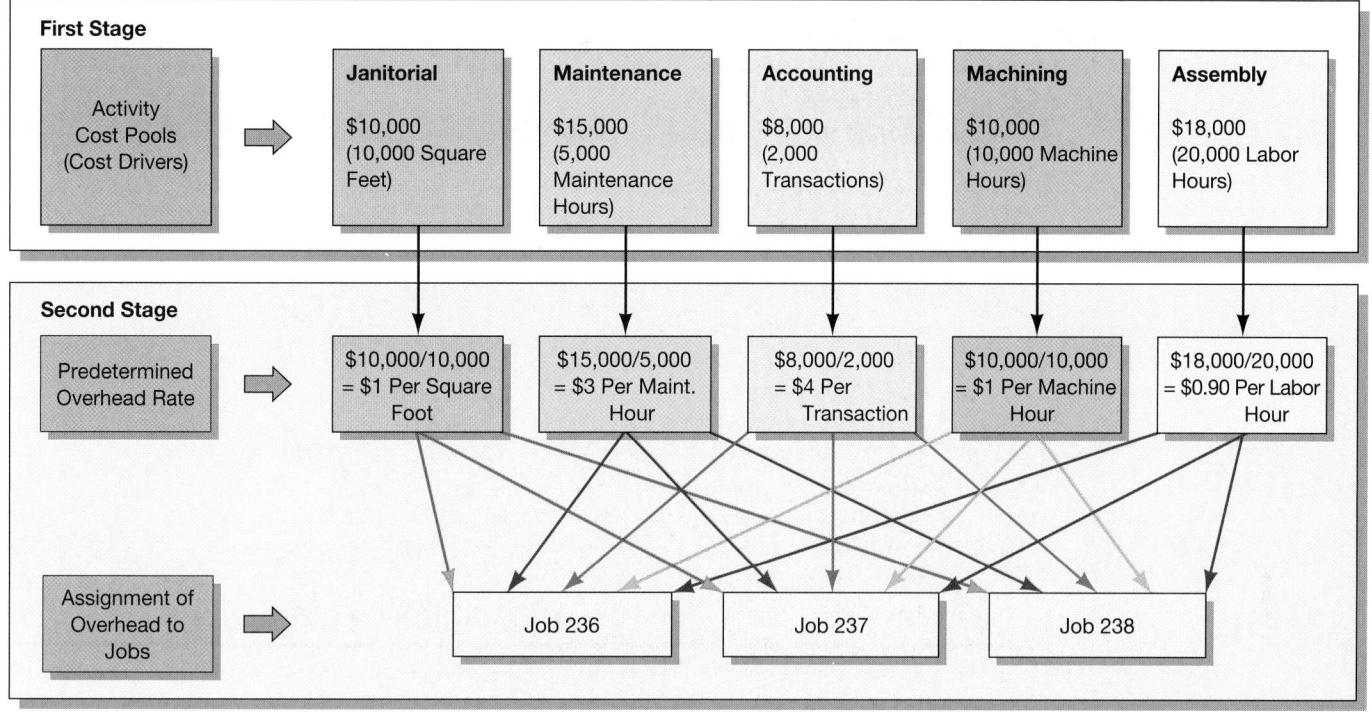

An **activity cost pool** is a temporary account accumulating the costs a company incurs to support an identified set of activities. Costs accumulated in an activity cost pool include the variable and fixed costs of the activities in the pool. Variable costs pertain to resources acquired as needed (such as materials); fixed costs pertain to resources acquired in advance (such as equipment). An activity cost pool account is handled like a factory overhead account.

In the second stage, after all activity costs are accumulated in an activity cost pool account, overhead rates are computed. Then, costs are allocated to cost objects (users) based on cost drivers (allocation bases).

Point: A cost driver is different from an allocation base. An allocation base is used as a basis for assigning overhead but need not have a cause-effect relation with the costs assigned. However, a cost driver has a cause-effect relation with the cost assigned.

Illustration of Activity-Based Costing   To illustrate, let's return to AutoGrand's three jobs. Assume that resources used to complete Jobs 236, 237, and 238 are shown in Exhibit 21.4.

Resources Used	Job 236	Job 237	Job 238
Square feet of space	5,000	3,000	2,000
Maintenance hours	2,500	1,500	1,000
Number of transactions	500	700	800
Machine hours	2,000	3,000	5,000
Direct labor hours	4,000	6,000	10,000

Exhibit 21.4

Activity Resource Use

The $61,000 of total costs are assigned to these three jobs using activity-based costing as shown in Exhibit 21.5 (rates are taken from the second stage of Exhibit 21.3). Comparing Exhibits 21.2 and 21.5, we see that the costs assigned to the three jobs vary markedly depending on whether two-stage (departmental) cost allocation or activity-based costing is used. Costs assigned to Job 236 go from $12,200 using two-stage cost allocation to $20,100 under activity-based costing. Costs assigned to Job 238 decline from $30,500 to $22,200. These differences in assigned amounts result from more accurately tracing costs to each job using activity-based costing where the allocation bases reflect actual cost drivers.

Exhibit 21.5

Activity-Based Assignment of Overhead to Output

	Job 236	Job 237	Job 238	Activity Totals
Janitorial				
$1.00 × 5,000 sq. ft.	$ 5,000			
$1.00 × 3,000 sq. ft.		$ 3,000		
$1.00 × 2,000 sq. ft.			$ 2,000	$10,000
Maintenance				
$3.00 × 2,500 maint. hrs.	7,500			
$3.00 × 1,500 maint. hrs.		4,500		
$3.00 × 1,000 maint. hrs.			3,000	15,000
Factory Accounting				
$4.00 × 500 transactions	2,000			
$4.00 × 700 transactions		2,800		
$4.00 × 800 transactions			3,200	8,000
Machining				
$1.00 × 2,000 machine hrs.	2,000			
$1.00 × 3,000 machine hrs.		3,000		
$1.00 × 5,000 machine hrs.			5,000	10,000
Assembly				
$0.90 × 4,000 labor hrs.	3,600			
$0.90 × 6,000 labor hrs.		5,400		
$0.90 × 10,000 labor hrs.			9,000	18,000
Total overhead assigned	$20,100	$18,700	$22,200	$61,000

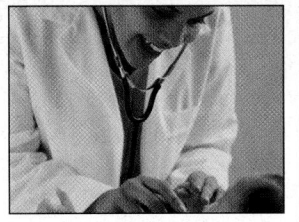

Comparison of Two-Stage and Activity-Based Cost Allocation

Traditional cost systems capture overhead costs by individual department (or function) and accumulate these costs in one or more overhead accounts. Companies then assign these overhead costs using a single allocation base such as direct labor or multiple volume-based allocation bases. Unfortunately, traditional cost systems have tended to use allocation bases that are often not closely related to the way these costs are actually incurred.

In contrast, activity-based cost systems capture costs by individual activity. These activities and their costs are then accumulated into activity cost pools. A company selects a cost driver (allocation base) for each activity pool. It uses this cost driver to assign the accumulated activity costs to cost objects (such as jobs or products) benefiting from the activity.

An activity-based costing system commonly consists of more allocation bases as compared to a traditional cost system. For example, a Chicago-based manufacturer currently uses nearly 20 different activity cost drivers to assign overhead costs to its products. Exhibit 21.6 lists common examples of overhead cost pools and their usual cost drivers.

Activity-based costing is especially effective when the same department or departments produce many different types of products. For instance, more complex products often require more help from service departments such as engineering, maintenance, and materials handling. If the same amount of direct labor is applied to the complex and simple products, a traditional overhead allocation system assigns the same overhead cost to both. With activity-based costing, however, the complex products are assigned a larger portion of overhead. The difference in overhead assigned can affect product pricing, make-or-buy, and other managerial decisions.

Activity-based costing encourages managers to focus on *activities* as well as the use of those

Activity Cost Pool	Cost Driver
Materials purchasing	Number of purchase orders
Materials handling	Number of materials requisitions
Personnel processing	Number of employees hired or laid off
Equipment depreciation	Number of products produced or hours of use
Quality inspection	Number of units inspected
Indirect labor in setting up equipment	Number of setups required
Engineering costs for product modifications	Number of modifications (engineering change orders)

Exhibit 21.6

Cost Pools and Cost Drivers in Activity-Based Costing

activities. For instance, assume AutoGrand can reduce the number of transactions processed in Factory Accounting to 1,500 (375 transactions for Job 236, 525 transactions for Job 237, and 600 transactions for Job 238) and that through continuous improvement it can reduce costs of processing those transactions to $4,500. The resulting rate to process a transaction is $3 per transaction ($4,500/1,500 transactions—down from $4 per Exhibit 21.3). The cost of transaction processing is reduced for all jobs (Job 236, $1,125; Job 237, $1,575; Job 238, $1,800). However, if those accounting costs were grouped in a single overhead cost pool, it is more difficult to identify cost savings and understand their effects on product costs.

Activity-based costing requires managers to look at each item and encourages them to manage each cost to increase the benefit from each dollar spent. It also encourages managers to cooperate because it shows how their efforts are interrelated. This results in *activity-based management.*

Decision Ethics   Answer—p. 863

Accounting Officer   Your company produces expensive garments, whose production involves many complex and specialized activities. Your general manager recently learned about activity-based costing (ABC) and asks your advice. However, your supervisor does not want to disturb the existing cost system and instructs you to prepare a report stating that "implementation of ABC is a complicated process involving too many steps and not worth the effort." You believe ABC will actually help the company identify sources of costs and control them. What action do you take?

Quick Check   Answers—p. 863

1. What is a cost driver?
2. When activity-based costing is used rather than traditional allocation methods, (a) managers must identify cost drivers for various items of overhead cost, (b) individual cost items in service departments are allocated directly to products or services, (c) managers can direct their attention to the activities that drive overhead cost, or (d) all of the above.

Section 2—Allocating Costs for Performance Evaluation

This second section of the chapter describes and illustrates allocation of costs for performance evaluation. We begin with departmental accounting and expense allocations and conclude with responsibility accounting.

Departmental Accounting

Companies are divided into *departments,* also called *subunits,* when they are too large to be managed effectively as a single unit. Managerial accounting for departments has two main goals. The first is to set up a **departmental accounting system** to provide information for managers to evaluate the profitability or cost effectiveness of each department's activities. The second goal is to set up a **responsibility accounting system** to control costs and expenses and evaluate managers' performances by assigning costs and expenses to the managers responsible for controlling them. Departmental and responsibility accounting systems are related and share much information.

Motivation for Departmentalization

C1 Explain departmentalization and the role of departmental accounting.

Many companies are so large and complex that they are broken into separate divisions for efficiency and/or effectiveness purposes. Divisions then are usually organized into separate departments. When a company is departmentalized, each department is often placed under the direction of a manager. As a company grows, management often divides departments into new departments so that responsibilities for a department's activities do not overwhelm the manager's ability to oversee and control them. A company also creates departments to take advantage of the skills of individual managers. Departments are broadly classified as either operating or service departments.

Departmental Evaluation

Point: To improve profitability, **Sears, Roebuck & Co.** eliminated several departments, including its catalog division.

Topic Tackler

PLUS

21-2

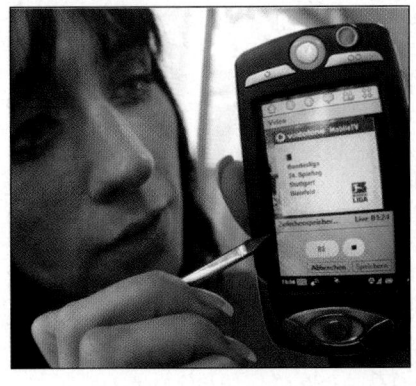

Point: Selling departments are often treated as *revenue centers;* their managers are responsible for maximizing sales revenues.

When a company is divided into departments, managers need to know how each department is performing. The accounting system must supply information about resources used and outputs achieved by each department. This requires a system to measure and accumulate revenue and expense information for each department whenever possible.

Departmental information is rarely distributed publicly because of its potential usefulness to competitors. Information about departments is prepared for internal managers to help control operations, appraise performance, allocate resources, and plan strategy. If a department is highly profitable, management may decide to expand its operations, or if a department is performing poorly, information about revenues or expenses can suggest useful changes.

More companies are emphasizing customer satisfaction as a main responsibility of many departments. This has led to changes in the measures reported. Increasingly, financial measurements are being supplemented with quality and customer satisfaction indexes. **Motorola**, for instance, uses two key measures: the number of defective parts per million parts produced and the percent of orders delivered on time to customers. (Note that some departments have only "internal customers.")

Financial information used to evaluate a department depends on whether it is evaluated as a profit center or a cost center. A **profit center** incurs costs and generates revenues; selling departments are often evaluated as profit centers. A **cost center** incurs costs without directly generating revenues. The manufacturing departments of a manufacturer and its service departments such as accounting, advertising, and purchasing, are all cost centers.

Evaluating managers' performance depends on whether they are responsible for profit centers or cost centers. Profit center managers are judged on their abilities to generate revenues in excess of the department's costs. They are assumed to influence both revenue generation and cost incurrence. Cost center managers are judged on their abilities to control costs by keeping them within a satisfactory range under an assumption that only they influence costs.

Decision Insight

Nonfinancial Measures A majority of companies now report nonfinancial performance measures to management. Common measures are cycle time, defect rate, on-time deliveries, inventory turnover, customer satisfaction, and safety. When nonfinancial measures are used with financial measures, the performance measurement system resembles a *balanced scorecard.* Many of these companies also use activity-based management as part of their performance measurement system.

Departmental Reporting and Analysis

Companies use various measures (financial and nonfinancial) and reporting formats to evaluate their departments. The type and form of information depend on management's focus and philosophy. **Hewlett-Packard**'s statement of corporate objectives, for instance, indicates that its goal is to satisfy customer needs. Its challenge is to set up managerial accounting systems to provide relevant feedback for evaluating performance in terms of its stated objectives. Also, the means used to obtain information about departments depend on how extensively a company uses computer and information technology.

When accounts are not maintained separately in the general ledger by department, a company can create departmental information by using a *departmental spreadsheet analysis*. For example, after recording sales in its usual manner, a company can compute daily total sales by department and enter these totals on a sales spreadsheet. At period-end, column totals of the spreadsheet show sales by department. The combined total of all columns equals the balance of the Sales account. A merchandiser that uses a spreadsheet analysis of department sales often uses separate spreadsheets to accumulate sales, sales returns, purchases, and purchases returns by department. If each department keeps a count of its inventory, it can also compute its gross profit (assuming it's a profit center).

Point: Many retailers use a point-of-sales system capturing sales data and creating requests to release inventory from the warehouse and order more merchandise. **Wal-Mart**'s sales system not only collects data for internal use but also is used by **Procter & Gamble** to plan its production and product deliveries to **Wal-Mart**.

Point: **Link Wood Products**, a manufacturer of lawn and garden products, records each sale by department on a spreadsheet. Daily totals are accumulated in another spreadsheet to obtain monthly totals by department.

Quick Check

Answers—p. 863

3. What is the difference between a departmental accounting system and a responsibility accounting system?
4. Service departments (a) manufacture products, (b) make sales directly to customers, (c) produce revenues, (d) assist operating departments.
5. Explain the difference between a cost center and a profit center. Cite an example of each.

Departmental Expense Allocation

When a company computes departmental profits, it confronts some accounting challenges that involve allocating its expenses across its operating departments.

Direct and Indirect Expenses

Direct expenses are costs readily traced to a department because they are incurred for that department's sole benefit. They require no allocation across departments. For example, the salary of an employee who works in only one department is a direct expense of that one department.

Indirect expenses are costs that are incurred for the joint benefit of more than one department and cannot be readily traced to only one department. For example, if two or more departments share a single building, all enjoy the benefits of the expenses for rent, heat, and light. Indirect expenses are allocated across departments benefiting from them when we need information about departmental profits. Ideally, we allocate indirect expenses by using a cause-effect relation. When we cannot identify cause-effect relations, we allocate each indirect expense on a basis approximating the relative benefit each department receives. Measuring the benefit for each department from an indirect expense can be difficult.

C2 Distinguish between direct and indirect expenses.

Point: Utility expense has elements of both direct and indirect expenses.

Illustration of Indirect Expense Allocation To illustrate how to allocate an indirect expense, we consider a retail store that purchases janitorial services from an outside company. Management allocates this cost across the store's three departments according to the floor space each occupies. Costs of janitorial services for a recent month are $300. Exhibit 21.7 shows the square feet of floor space each department occupies. The store computes the percent of total square feet allotted to each department and uses it to allocate the $300 cost.

Department	Square Feet	Percent of Total	Allocated Cost
Jewelry	2,400	60%	$180
Watch repair	600	15	45
China and silver	1,000	25	75
Totals	4,000	100%	$300

Exhibit 21.7

Indirect Expense Allocation

Specifically, because the jewelry department occupies 60% of the floor space, 60% of the total $300 cost is assigned to it. The same procedure is applied to the other departments. When the allocation process is complete, these and other allocated costs are deducted from the gross profit for each department to determine net income for each. One consideration in allocating costs is to motivate managers and employees to behave as desired. As a result, a cost incurred in one department might be best allocated to other departments when one of the other departments caused the cost.

Allocation of Indirect Expenses

This section describes how to identify the bases used to allocate indirect expenses across departments. No standard rule identifies the best basis because expense allocation involves several factors, and the relative importance of these factors varies across departments and organizations. Judgment is required, and people do not always agree. In our discussion, note the parallels between activity-based costing and the departmental expense allocation procedures described here.

Wages and Salaries Employee wages and salaries can be either direct or indirect expenses. If their time is spent entirely in one department, their wages are direct expenses of that department. However, if employees work for the benefit of more than one department, their wages are indirect expenses and must be allocated across the departments benefited. An employee's contribution to a department usually depends on the number of hours worked in contributing to that department. Thus, a reasonable basis for allocating employee wages and salaries is the *relative amount of time spent in each department*. In the case of a supervisor who manages more than one department, recording the time spent in each department may not always be practical. Instead, a company can allocate the supervisor's salary to departments on the basis of the number of employees in each department—a reasonable basis if a supervisor's main task is managing people. Another basis of allocation is on sales across departments, also a reasonable basis if a supervisor's job reflects on departmental sales.

Rent and Related Expenses Rent expense for a building is reasonably allocated to a department on the basis of floor space it occupies. Location can often make some floor space more valuable than other space. Thus, the allocation method can charge departments that occupy more valuable space a higher expense per square foot. Ground floor retail space, for instance, is often more valuable than basement or upper-floor space because all customers pass departments near the entrance but fewer go beyond the first floor. When no precise measures of floor space values exist, basing allocations on data such as customer traffic and real estate assessments is helpful. When a company owns its building, its expenses for depreciation, taxes, insurance, and other related building expenses are allocated like rent expense.

Advertising Expenses Effective advertising of a department's products increases its sales and customer traffic. Moreover, advertising products for some departments usually helps other departments' sales because customers also often buy unadvertised products. Thus, many stores treat advertising as an indirect expense allocated on the basis of each department's proportion of total sales. For example, a department with 10% of a store's total sales is assigned 10% of advertising expense. Another method is to analyze each advertisement to compute the Web/newspaper space or TV/radio time devoted to the products of a department and charge that department for the proportional costs of advertisements. Management must consider whether this more detailed and costly method is justified.

Equipment and Machinery Depreciation Depreciation on equipment and machinery used only in one department is a direct expense of that department. Depreciation on equipment and machinery used by more than one department is an indirect expense to be allocated across departments. Accounting for each department's depreciation expense requires a company to keep records showing which departments use specific assets. The number of hours that a department uses equipment and machinery is a reasonable basis for allocating depreciation.

Utilities Expenses   Utilities expenses such as heating and lighting are usually allocated on the basis of floor space occupied by departments. This practice assumes their use is uniform across departments. When this is not so, a more involved allocation can be necessary, although there is often a trade-off between the usefulness of more precise allocations and the effort to compute them.

Service Department Expenses   To generate revenues, operating departments require support services provided by departments such as personnel, payroll, advertising, and purchasing. Such service departments are typically evaluated as cost centers because they do not produce revenues. (Evaluating them as profit centers requires the use of a system that "charges" user departments a price that then serves as the "revenue" generated by service departments.) A departmental accounting system can accumulate and report costs incurred directly by each service department for this purpose. The system then allocates a service department's expenses to operating departments benefiting from them. This is often done, for example, using traditional two-stage cost allocation (see Exhibit 21.1). Exhibit 21.8 shows some commonly used bases for allocating service department expenses to operating departments.

Service Department	Common Allocation Bases
Office expenses	Number of employees or sales in each department
Personnel expenses	Number of employees in each department
Payroll expenses	Number of employees in each department
Advertising expenses	Sales or amount of advertising charged directly to each department
Purchasing costs	Dollar amounts of purchases or number of purchase orders processed
Cleaning expenses	Square feet of floor space occupied
Maintenance expenses	Square feet of floor space occupied

Exhibit 21.8

Bases for Allocating Service Department Expenses

Departmental Income Statements

An income statement can be prepared for each operating department once expenses have been assigned to it. Its expenses include both direct expenses and its share of indirect expenses. For this purpose, compiling all expenses incurred in service departments before assigning them to operating departments is useful. We illustrate the steps to prepare departmental income statements using **A-1 Hardware** and its five departments. Two of them (office and purchasing) are service departments and the other three (hardware, housewares, and appliances) are operating (selling) departments. Allocating costs to operating departments and preparing departmental income statements involves four steps.

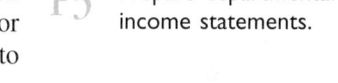

P3   Prepare departmental income statements.

Step 1   Step 1 accumulates direct expenses for each service and operating department as shown in Exhibit 21.9. Direct expenses include salaries, wages, and other expenses that each department incurs but does not share with any other department. This information is accumulated in departmental expense accounts.

Direct Expenses	Direct Expenses	Direct Expenses	Direct Expenses	Direct Expenses
General office	Purchasing	Hardware	Housewares	Appliances

Exhibit 21.9

Step 1: Direct Expense Accumulation

Step 2   Step 2 allocates indirect expenses across all departments using the allocation base identified for each expense as shown in Exhibit 21.10. Indirect expenses can include items such as depreciation, rent, advertising, and any other expenses that cannot be directly assigned to a department. Indirect expenses are recorded in expense accounts, and costs are allocated using a *departmental expense allocation spreadsheet* described in step 3.

Exhibit 21.10

Step 2: Indirect Expense
Allocation

Step 3   Step 3 allocates expenses of the service departments (office and purchasing) to the operating departments. Exhibit 21.11 reflects the allocation of service department expenses using the allocation base(s).

Exhibit 21.11

Step 3: Service Department
Expense Allocation to Operating
Departments

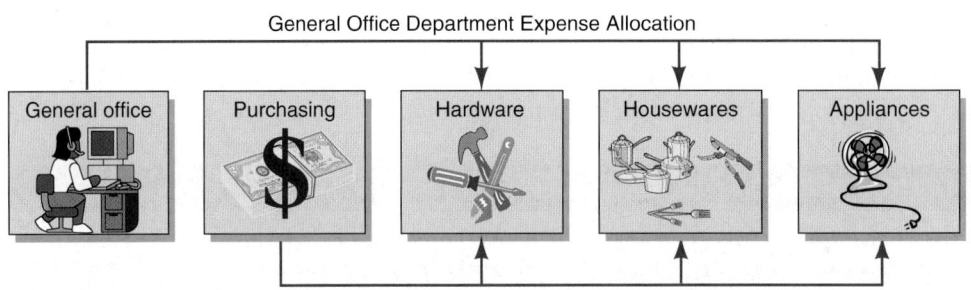

Exhibit 21.12

Departmental Expense
Allocation Spreadsheet

Computations for both steps 2 and 3 are commonly made using a departmental expense allocation spreadsheet as shown in Exhibit 21.12.[1] The first two sections of this spreadsheet list direct expenses and indirect expenses by department. The third section lists the service

File Edit View Insert Format Tools Data Window Help							

A-1 HARDWARE
Departmental Expense Allocations
For Year Ended December 31, 2008

	Allocation Base	Expense Account Balance	General Office Dept.	Purchasing Dept.	Hardware Dept.	House- wares Dept.	Appliances Dept.
Direct expenses							
Salaries expense..................	Payroll records	$51,900	$13,300	$8,200	$15,600	$ 7,000	$ 7,800
Depreciation—Equipment......	Depreciation records	1,500	500	300	400	100	200
Supplies expense..................	Requisitions...........................	900	200	100	300	200	100
Indirect expenses							
Rent expense	Amount and value of space..	12,000	600	600	4,860	3,240	2,700
Utilities expense.....................	Floor space............................	2,400	300	300	810	540	450
Advertising expense...............	Sales......................................	1,000			500	300	200
Insurance expense.................	Value of insured assets	2,500	400	200	900	600	400
Total department expenses		72,200	15,300	9,700	23,370	11,980	11,850
Service department expenses							
General office department.....	Sales......................................		(15,300)		↳7,650	↳4,590	↳3,060
Purchasing department	Purchase orders....................			(9,700)	↗3,880	↗2,630	↗3,190
Total expenses allocated to operating departments.......................................		$72,200	$ 0	$ 0	$34,900	$19,200	$18,100

Sheet1 / Sheet2 / Sheet3

---

[1] In some cases we allocate a service department's expenses to other service departments when they use its services. For example, expenses of a payroll office benefit all service and operating departments and can be assigned to all departments. Nearly all examples and assignment materials in this book allocate service expenses only to operating departments for simplicity.

department expenses and their allocations to operating departments. The allocation bases are identified in the second column, and total expense amounts are reported in the third column.

The departmental expense allocation spreadsheet is useful in implementing the first three steps. To illustrate, first (step 1) the three direct expenses of salaries, depreciation, and supplies are accumulated in each of the five departments.

Second (step 2), the four indirect expenses of rent, utilities, advertising, and insurance are allocated to all departments using the allocation bases identified. For example, consider rent allocation. Exhibit 21.13 lists the five departments' square footage of space occupied. The two service departments (office and purchasing) occupy 25% of the total space (3,000 sq. feet/12,000 sq. feet). However, they are located near the back of the building, which is of lower value than space near the front that is occupied by operating departments. Management estimates that space near the back accounts for $1,200 of the total rent expense of $12,000. Exhibit 21.14 shows how we allocate the $1,200 rent expense between these two service departments in proportion to their

Exhibit 21.13
Departments' Square Footages

General office	1,500 sq. ft.
Purchasing	1,500 sq. ft.
Hardware	4,050 sq. ft.
Housewares	2,700 sq. ft.
Appliances	2,250 sq. ft.
Total	12,000 sq. ft.

Exhibit 21.14
Allocating Indirect (Rent) Expense to Service Departments

Department	Square Feet	Percent of Total	Allocated Cost
General office	1,500	50.0%	$ 600
Purchasing	1,500	50.0	600
Totals	3,000	100.0%	$1,200

square footage. We then allocate the remaining $10,800 of rent expense to the three operating departments as shown in Exhibit 21.15. We continue step 2 by allocating the $2,400 of utilities expense to all departments based on the square footage occupied as shown in

Exhibit 21.15
Allocating Indirect (Rent) Expense to Operating Departments

Department	Square Feet	Percent of Total	Allocated Cost
Hardware	4,050	45.0%	$ 4,860
Housewares	2,700	30.0	3,240
Appliances	2,250	25.0	2,700
Totals	9,000	100.0%	$10,800

Exhibit 21.16. The rows in Exhibit 21.12 for rent and utilities expenses show the amounts from Exhibits 21.14, 21.15, and 21.16. The allocations of the two other indirect expenses of advertising and insurance are similarly computed. Note that because advertising expense is allocated on the basis of sales and because service departments do not have sales, it is allocated only to the three operating departments.

Exhibit 21.16
Allocating Indirect (Utilities) Expense to All Departments

Department	Square Feet	Percent of Total	Allocated Cost
General office	1,500	12.50%	$ 300
Purchasing	1,500	12.50	300
Hardware	4,050	33.75	810
Housewares	2,700	22.50	540
Appliances	2,250	18.75	450
Totals	12,000	100.00%	$2,400

Third (step 3), total expenses of the two service departments are allocated to the three operating departments using the allocation bases shown in the final three rows of Exhibit 21.12.

Step 4   When the departmental expense spreadsheet is complete, the amounts in the operating department columns are used to prepare departmental income statements as shown in Exhibit 21.17. This exhibit uses the spreadsheet for its operating expenses; information on sales and cost of goods sold comes from departmental records.

Exhibit 21.17

Departmental Income Statements

A-1 HARDWARE Departmental Income Statements For Year Ended December 31, 2008				
	Hardware Department	Housewares Department	Appliances Department	Combined
Sales	$119,500	$71,700	$47,800	$239,000
Cost of goods sold	73,800	43,800	30,200	147,800
Gross profit	45,700	27,900	17,600	91,200
Operating expenses				
Salaries expense	15,600	7,000	7,800	30,400
Depreciation expense—Equipment	400	100	200	700
Supplies expense	300	200	100	600
Rent expense	4,860	3,240	2,700	10,800
Utilities expense	810	540	450	1,800
Advertising expense	500	300	200	1,000
Insurance expense	900	600	400	1,900
Share of general office expenses	7,650	4,590	3,060	15,300
Share of purchasing expenses	3,880	2,630	3,190	9,700
Total operating expenses	34,900	19,200	18,100	72,200
Net income (loss)	**$10,800**	**$8,700**	**$ (500)**	**$19,000**

Departmental Contribution to Overhead

Data from departmental income statements are not always best for evaluating each department's performance, especially when indirect expenses are a large portion of total expenses and when weaknesses in assumptions and decisions in allocating indirect expenses can markedly affect net income. In these and other cases, we might better evaluate department performance using the **departmental contribution to overhead,** which is a report of the amount of sales less *direct* expenses.[2]

The upper half of Exhibit 21.18 shows a departmental contribution to overhead as part of an expanded income statement. This format is common when reporting departmental contributions

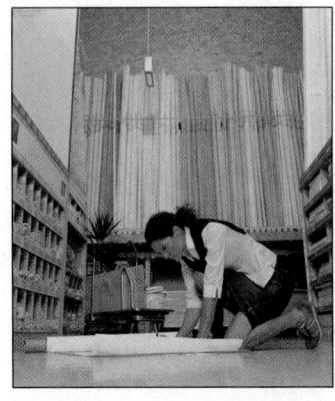

to overhead. Using the information in Exhibits 21.17 and 21.18, we can evaluate the profitability of the three operating departments. For instance, let's compare the performance of the appliances department as described in these two exhibits. Exhibit 21.17 shows a $500 net loss resulting from this department's operations, but Exhibit 21.18 shows a $9,500 positive contribution to overhead, which is 19.9% of sales. The contribution of the appliances department is not as large as that of the other selling departments, but a $9,500 contribution to overhead is better than a $500 loss. This tells us that the appliances department is not a money loser. On the contrary, it is contributing $9,500 toward defraying total indirect expenses of $40,500.

---

[2] A department's contribution is said to be "to overhead" because of the practice of considering all indirect expenses as overhead. Thus, the excess of a department's sales over direct expenses is a contribution toward at least a portion of its total overhead.

Exhibit 21.18

Departmental Contribution to Overhead

A-1 HARDWARE Income Statement Showing Departmental Contribution to Overhead For Year Ended December 31, 2008				
	Hardware Department	Housewares Department	Appliances Department	Combined
Sales	$119,500	$ 71,700	$47,800	$239,000
Cost of goods sold	73,800	43,800	30,200	147,800
Gross profit	45,700	27,900	17,600	91,200
Direct expenses				
Salaries expense	15,600	7,000	7,800	30,400
Depreciation expense—Equipment	400	100	200	700
Supplies expense	300	200	100	600
Total direct expenses	16,300	7,300	8,100	31,700
Departmental contributions to overhead	**$ 29,400**	**$20,600**	**$ 9,500**	**$ 59,500**
Indirect expenses				
Rent expense				10,800
Utilities expense				1,800
Advertising expense				1,000
Insurance expense				1,900
General office department expense				15,300
Purchasing department expense				9,700
Total indirect expenses				40,500
Net income				$ 19,000
Contribution as percent of sales	24.6%	28.7%	19.9%	24.9%

Quick Check

Answers—p. 863

6. If a company has two operating (selling) departments (shoes and hats) and two service departments (payroll and advertising), which of the following statements is correct? (a) Wages incurred in the payroll department are direct expenses of the shoe department, (b) Wages incurred in the payroll department are indirect expenses of the operating departments, or (c) Advertising department expenses are allocated to the other three departments.

7. Which of the following bases can be used to allocate supervisors' salaries across operating departments? (a) Hours spent in each department, (b) number of employees in each department, (c) sales achieved in each department, or (d) any of the above, depending on which information is most relevant and accessible.

8. What three steps are used to allocate expenses to operating departments?

9. An income statement showing departmental contribution to overhead, (a) subtracts indirect expenses from each department's revenues, (b) subtracts only direct expenses from each department's revenues, or (c) shows net income for each department.

Responsibility Accounting

Departmental accounting reports often provide data used to evaluate a department's performance, but are they useful in assessing how well a department *manager* performs? Neither departmental income nor its contribution to overhead may be useful because many expenses can be outside a manager's control. Instead, we often evaluate a manager's performance using responsibility accounting reports that describe a department's activities in terms of **controllable costs.**[3] A cost is controllable if a manager has the power to determine or at least significantly

C4 Explain controllable costs and responsibility accounting.

---

[3] The terms *cost* and *expense* are often used interchangeably in managerial accounting, but they are not necessarily the same. *Cost* often refers to the monetary outlay to acquire some resource that can have present and future benefit. *Expense* usually refers to an expired cost. That is, as the benefit of a resource expires, a portion of its cost is written off as an expense.

affect the amount incurred. **Uncontrollable costs** are not within the manager's control or influence.

Controllable versus Direct Costs

Controllable costs are not always the same as direct costs. Direct costs are readily traced to a department, but the department manager might or might not control their amounts. For example, department managers often have little or no control over depreciation expense because they cannot affect the amount of equipment assigned to their departments. Also, department managers rarely control their own salaries. However, they can control or influence items such as the cost of supplies used in their department. When evaluating managers' performances, we should use data reflecting their departments' outputs along with their controllable costs and expenses.

Distinguishing between controllable and uncontrollable costs depends on the particular manager and time period under analysis. For example, the cost of property insurance is usually not controllable at the department manager's level but by the executive responsible for obtaining the company's insurance coverage. Likewise, this executive might not control costs resulting from insurance policies already in force. However, when a policy expires, this executive can renegotiate a replacement policy and then controls these costs. Therefore, all costs are controllable at some management level if the time period is sufficiently long. We must use good judgment in identifying controllable costs.

Responsibility Accounting System

A *responsibility accounting system* uses the concept of controllable costs to assign managers the responsibility for costs and expenses under their control. Prior to each reporting period, a company prepares plans that identify costs and expenses under each manager's control. These plans are called **responsibility accounting budgets.** To ensure the cooperation of managers and the reasonableness of budgets, managers should be involved in preparing their budgets.

A responsibility accounting system also involves performance reports. A **responsibility accounting performance report** accumulates and reports costs and expenses that a manager is responsible for and their budgeted amounts. Management's analysis of differences between budgeted amounts and actual costs and expenses often results in corrective or strategic managerial actions. Upper-level management uses performance reports to evaluate the effectiveness of lower-level managers in controlling costs and expenses and keeping them within budgeted amounts.

A responsibility accounting system recognizes that control over costs and expenses belongs to several levels of management. We illustrate this by considering the organization chart in Exhibit 21.19. The lines in this chart connecting the managerial positions reflect channels of authority. For example, the four department managers of this consulting firm (benchmarking, cost management, outsourcing, and service) are responsible for controllable costs and expenses incurred in their departments, but these same costs are subject to the overall control of the vice president (VP) for operational consulting. Similarly, this VP's costs are subject to the control of the executive vice president (EVP) for operations, the president, and, ultimately, the board of directors.

Exhibit 21.19

Organizational Responsibility Chart

At lower levels, managers have limited responsibility and relatively little control over costs and expenses. Performance reports for low-level management typically cover few controllable costs. Responsibility and control broaden for higher-level managers; therefore, their reports span a wider range of costs. However, reports to higher-level managers seldom contain the details reported to their subordinates but are summarized for two reasons: (1) lower-level managers are often responsible for these detailed costs and (2) detailed reports can obscure broader, more important issues facing a company.

Exhibit 21.20 shows summarized performance reports for the three management levels identified in Exhibit 21.19. Exhibit 21.20 shows that costs under the control of the benchmarking department manager are totaled and included among controllable costs of the VP for operational consulting. Also, costs under the control of the VP are totaled and included among controllable costs of the EVP for operations. In this way, a responsibility accounting system provides relevant information for each management level.

Executive Vice President, Operations

Exhibit 21.20

Responsibility Accounting Performance Reports

For July

Controllable Costs	Budgeted Amount	Actual Amount	Over (Under) Budget
Salaries, VPs	$ 80,000	$ 80,000	$ 0
Quality control costs	21,000	22,400	1,400
Office costs	29,500	28,800	(700)
Operational consulting	276,700	279,500	2,800 ◄
Strategic consulting	390,000	380,600	(9,400)
Totals	$ 797,200	$ 791,300	$(5,900)

Vice President, Operational Consulting

For July

Controllable Costs	Budgeted Amount	Actual Amount	Over (Under) Budget
Salaries, department managers	$ 75,000	$ 78,000	$ 3,000
Depreciation	10,600	10,600	0
Insurance	6,800	6,300	(500)
► Benchmarking department	79,600	79,900	300
Cost management department	61,500	60,200	(1,300)
Outsourcing department	24,300	24,700	400
Service department	18,900	19,800	900
Totals	$276,700	$279,500	$2,800

Manager, Benchmarking Department

For July

Controllable Costs	Budgeted Amount	Actual Amount	Over (Under) Budget
Salaries	$ 51,600	$ 52,500	$ 900
Supplies	8,000	7,800	(200)
Other controllable costs	20,000	19,600	(400)
Totals	$ 79,600	$ 79,900	$ 300

Technological advances increase our ability to produce vast amounts of information that often exceeds our ability to use it. Good managers select relevant data for planning and controlling the areas under their responsibility. A good responsibility accounting system makes every effort to provide relevant information to the right person (the one who controls the cost) at the right time (before a cost is out of control).

Decision Analysis | Investment Center Return on Total Assets

A1 Analyze investment centers using return on total assets.

Topic Tackler

PLUS

21-3

We discussed the classification of departments and divisions as profit centers or cost centers. Another way is to classify (and evaluate) a department as an **investment center.** An investment center manager is responsible for effectively using the center's assets to generate income for the center.

A measure often used to evaluate the performance of an investment center manager is the **investment center return on total assets,** also called *return on investment*. This measure is computed as a **center's net income divided by the center's average total assets.** To illustrate, if a center with an average investment of $1 million yields a net income of $210,000, its return on total assets is 21%.

Decision Maker

Answer—p. 863

Center Manager Your center's usual return on total assets is 19%. You are considering two new investments for your center. The first requires a $250,000 average investment and is expected to yield annual net income of $50,000. The second requires a $1 million average investment with an expected annual net income of $175,000. Do you pursue either?

Top management can use a center's return on total assets to assess how well its manager has utilized the center's assets to generate returns for the company. Top management can also compare performance across departments and/or divisions using this measure. Many companies establish a center's target return on total assets and reward managers based on whether they meet targets. In addition, center managers often use the center's return on total assets to decide whether to invest additional resources in the center.

Demonstration Problem

Management requests departmental income statements for Hacker's Haven, a computer store that has five departments. Three are operating departments (hardware, software, and repairs) and two are service departments (general office and purchasing).

	General Office	Purchasing	Hardware	Software	Repairs
Sales	—	—	$960,000	$600,000	$840,000
Cost of goods sold	—	—	500,000	300,000	200,000
Direct expenses					
Payroll	$60,000	$45,000	80,000	25,000	325,000
Depreciation	6,000	7,200	33,000	4,200	9,600
Supplies	15,000	10,000	10,000	2,000	25,000

The departments incur several indirect expenses. To prepare departmental income statements, the indirect expenses must be allocated across the five departments. Then the expenses of the two service departments must be allocated to the three operating departments. Total cost amounts and the allocation bases for each indirect expense follow.

Indirect Expense	Total Cost	Allocation Basis
Rent	$150,000	Square footage occupied
Utilities	50,000	Square footage occupied
Advertising	125,000	Dollars of sales
Insurance	30,000	Value of assets insured
Service departments		
General office	?	Number of employees
Purchasing	?	Dollars of cost of goods sold

The following additional information is needed for indirect expense allocations.

Department	Square Feet	Sales	Insured Assets	Employees	Cost of Goods Sold
General office	500		$ 60,000		
Purchasing	500		72,000		
Hardware	4,000	$ 960,000	330,000	5	$ 500,000
Software	3,000	600,000	42,000	5	300,000
Repairs	2,000	840,000	96,000	10	200,000
Totals	10,000	$2,400,000	$600,000	20	$1,000,000

Required

1. Prepare a departmental expense allocation spreadsheet for Hacker's Haven.
2. Prepare a departmental income statement reporting net income for each operating department and for all operating departments combined.

Planning the Solution

- Set up and complete four tables to allocate the indirect expenses—one each for rent, utilities, advertising, and insurance.
- Allocate the departments' indirect expenses using a spreadsheet like the one in Exhibit 21.12. Enter the given amounts of the direct expenses for each department. Then enter the allocated amounts of the indirect expenses that you computed.
- Complete two tables for allocating the general office and purchasing department costs to the three operating departments. Enter these amounts on the spreadsheet and determine the total expenses allocated to the three operating departments.
- Prepare departmental income statements like the one in Exhibit 21.17. Show sales, cost of goods sold, gross profit, individual expenses, and net income for each of the three operating departments and for the combined company.

Solution to Demonstration Problem

Allocations of the four indirect expenses across the five departments.

Rent	Square Feet	Percent of Total	Allocated Cost
General office	500	5.0%	$ 7,500
Purchasing	500	5.0	7,500
Hardware	4,000	40.0	60,000
Software	3,000	30.0	45,000
Repairs	2,000	20.0	30,000
Totals	10,000	100.0%	$150,000

Utilities	Square Feet	Percent of Total	Allocated Cost
General office	500	5.0%	$ 2,500
Purchasing	500	5.0	2,500
Hardware	4,000	40.0	20,000
Software	3,000	30.0	15,000
Repairs	2,000	20.0	10,000
Totals	10,000	100.0%	$50,000

Advertising	Sales Dollars	Percent of Total	Allocated Cost
Hardware	$ 960,000	40.0%	$ 50,000
Software	600,000	25.0	31,250
Repairs	840,000	35.0	43,750
Totals	$2,400,000	100.0%	$125,000

Insurance	Assets Insured	Percent of Total	Allocated Cost
General office	$ 60,000	10.0%	$ 3,000
Purchasing	72,000	12.0	3,600
Hardware	330,000	55.0	16,500
Software	42,000	7.0	2,100
Repairs	96,000	16.0	4,800
Totals	$600,000	100.0%	$30,000

1. Allocations of service department expenses to the three operating departments.

General Office Allocations to	Employees	Percent of Total	Allocated Cost
Hardware	5	25.0%	$23,500
Software	5	25.0	23,500
Repairs	10	50.0	47,000
Totals	20	100.0%	$94,000

Purchasing Allocations to	Cost of Goods Sold	Percent of Total	Allocated Cost
Hardware	$ 500,000	50.0%	$37,900
Software	300,000	30.0	22,740
Repairs	200,000	20.0	15,160
Totals	$1,000,000	100.0%	$75,800

HACKER'S HAVEN
Departmental Expense Allocations
For Year Ended December 31, 2008

	Allocation Base	Expense Account Balance	General Office Dept.	Purchasing Dept.	Hardware Dept.	Software Dept.	Repairs Dept.
Direct Expenses							
Payroll		$ 535,000	$ 60,000	$ 45,000	$ 80,000	$ 25,000	$ 325,000
Depreciation		60,000	6,000	7,200	33,000	4,200	9,600
Supplies		62,000	15,000	10,000	10,000	2,000	25,000
Indirect Expenses							
Rent	Square ft.	150,000	7,500	7,500	60,000	45,000	30,000
Utilities	Square ft.	50,000	2,500	2,500	20,000	15,000	10,000
Advertising	Sales	125,000	—	—	50,000	31,250	43,750
Insurance	Assets	30,000	3,000	3,600	16,500	2,100	4,800
Total expenses		1,012,000	94,000	75,800	269,500	124,550	448,150
Service Department Expenses							
General office	Employees		(94,000)		23,500	23,500	47,000
Purchasing	Goods sold			(75,800)	37,900	22,740	15,160
Total expenses allocated to operating departments		$1,012,000	$ 0	$ 0	$330,900	$170,790	$510,310

2. Departmental income statements for Hacker's Haven.

HACKER'S HAVEN
Departmental Income Statements
For Year Ended December 31, 2008

	Hardware	Software	Repairs	Combined
Sales	$ 960,000	$ 600,000	$ 840,000	$2,400,000
Cost of goods sold	500,000	300,000	200,000	1,000,000
Gross profit	460,000	300,000	640,000	1,400,000
Expenses				
Payroll	80,000	25,000	325,000	430,000
Depreciation	33,000	4,200	9,600	46,800
Supplies	10,000	2,000	25,000	37,000
Rent	60,000	45,000	30,000	135,000
Utilities	20,000	15,000	10,000	45,000
Advertising	50,000	31,250	43,750	125,000
Insurance	16,500	2,100	4,800	23,400
Share of general office	23,500	23,500	47,000	94,000
Share of purchasing	37,900	22,740	15,160	75,800
Total expenses	330,900	170,790	510,310	1,012,000
Net income	$129,100	$129,210	$129,690	$ 388,000

Joint Costs and Their Allocation

21A

Most manufacturing processes involve **joint costs,** which refer to costs incurred to produce or purchase two or more products at the same time. A joint cost is like an indirect expense in the sense that more than one cost object share it. For example, a sawmill company incurs a joint cost when it buys logs that it cuts into lumber as shown in Exhibit 21A.1. The joint cost includes the logs (raw material) and its cutting (conversion) into boards classified as Clear, Select, No. 1 Common, No. 2 Common, No. 3 Common, and other types of lumber and by-products.

C5 Describe allocation of joint costs across products.

When a joint cost is incurred, a question arises as to whether to allocate it to different products resulting from it. The answer is that when management wishes to estimate the costs of individual products, joint costs are included and must be allocated to these joint products. However, when management needs information to help decide whether to sell a product at a certain point in the production process or to process it further, the joint costs are ignored.

Exhibit 21A.1

Joint Products from Logs

Financial statements prepared according to GAAP must assign joint costs to products. To do this, management must decide how to allocate joint costs across products benefiting from these costs. If some products are sold and others remain in inventory, allocating joint costs involves assigning costs to both cost of goods sold and ending inventory.

The two usual methods to allocate joint costs are the (1) *physical basis* and (2) the *value basis.* The physical basis typically involves allocating joint cost using physical characteristics such as the ratio of pounds, cubic feet, or gallons of each joint product to the total pounds, cubic feet, or gallons of all joint products flowing from the cost. This method is not preferred because the resulting cost allocations do not reflect the relative market values the joint cost generates. The preferred approach is the value basis, which allocates joint cost in proportion to the sales value of the output produced by the process at the "split-off point"; see Exhibit 21A.1.

Physical Basis Allocation of Joint Cost   To illustrate the physical basis of allocating a joint cost, we consider a sawmill that bought logs for $30,000. When cut, these logs produce 100,000 board feet of lumber in the grades and amounts shown in Exhibit 21A.2. The logs produce 20,000 board feet of No. 3 Common lumber, which is 20% of the total. With physical allocation, the No. 3 Common lumber is assigned 20% of the $30,000 cost of the logs, or $6,000 ($30,000 × 20%). Because this low-grade lumber sells for $4,000, this allocation gives a $2,000 loss from its production and sale. The physical basis for allocating joint costs does not reflect the extra value flowing into some products or the inferior value flowing into others. That is, the portion of a log that produces Clear and Select grade lumber is worth more than the portion used to produce the three grades of common lumber, but the physical basis fails to reflect this.

Exhibit 21A.2

Allocating Joint Costs on a Physical Basis

Grade of Lumber	Board Feet Produced	Percent of Total	Allocated Cost	Sales Value	Gross Profit
Clear and Select	10,000	10.0%	$ 3,000	$12,000	$ 9,000
No. 1 Common	30,000	30.0	9,000	18,000	9,000
No. 2 Common	40,000	40.0	12,000	16,000	4,000
No. 3 Common	20,000	20.0	6,000	4,000	(2,000)
Totals	100,000	100.0%	$30,000	$50,000	$20,000

Value Basis Allocation of Joint Cost Exhibit 21A.3 illustrates the value basis method of allocation. It determines the percents of the total costs allocated to each grade by the ratio of each grade's sales value to the total sales value of $50,000 (sales value is the unit selling price multiplied by the number of units produced). The Clear and Select lumber grades receive 24% of the total cost ($12,000/$50,000) instead of the 10% portion using a physical basis. The No. 3 Common lumber receives only 8% of the total cost, or $2,400, which is much less than the $6,000 assigned to it using the physical basis.

Exhibit 21A.3

Allocating Joint Costs on a Value Basis

Grade of Lumber	Sales Value	Percent of Total	Allocated Cost	Gross Profit
Clear and Select	$12,000	24.0%	$ 7,200	$ 4,800
No. 1 Common	18,000	36.0	10,800	7,200
No. 2 Common	16,000	32.0	9,600	6,400
No. 3 Common	4,000	8.0	2,400	1,600
Totals	$50,000	100.0%	$30,000	$20,000

Example: Refer to Exhibit 21A.3. If the sales value of Clear and Select lumber is changed to $10,000, what is the revised ratio of the market value of No. 1 Common to the total? *Answer:* $18,000/$48,000 = 37.5%

An outcome of value basis allocation is that *each* grade produces exactly the same 40% gross profit at the split-off point. This 40% rate equals the gross profit rate from selling all the lumber made from the $30,000 logs for a combined price of $50,000.

Quick Check

Answer—p. 863

12. A company produces three products, B1, B2, and B3. The joint cost incurred for the current month for these products is $180,000. The following data relate to this month's production:

Product	Units Produced	Unit Sales Value
B1	96,000	$3.00
B2	64,000	6.00
B3	32,000	9.00

The amount of joint cost allocated to product B3 using the value basis allocation is (*a*) $30,000, (*b*) $54,000, or (*c*) $90,000.

Summary

C1 Explain departmentalization and the role of departmental accounting. Companies are divided into departments when they are too large to be effectively managed as a single unit. Operating departments carry out an organization's main functions. Service departments support the activities of operating departments. Departmental accounting systems provide information for evaluating departmental performance.

C2 Distinguish between direct and indirect expenses.
Direct expenses are traced to a specific department and are incurred for the sole benefit of that department. Indirect expenses benefit more than one department. Indirect expenses are allocated to departments when computing departmental net income.

C3 Identify bases for allocating indirect expenses to departments. Ideally, we allocate indirect expenses by using a cause-effect relation for the allocation base. When a cause-effect relation is not identifiable, each indirect expense is allocated on a basis reflecting the relative benefit received by each department.

C4 Explain controllable costs and responsibility accounting. A controllable cost is one that is influenced by a specific management level. The total expenses of operating a department often include some items a department manager does not control.

Responsibility accounting systems provide information for evaluating the performance of department managers. A responsibility accounting system's performance reports for evaluating department managers should include only the expenses (and revenues) that each manager controls.

C5 Describe allocation of joint costs across products. A joint cost refers to costs incurred to produce or purchase two or more products at the same time. When income statements are prepared, joint costs are usually allocated to the resulting joint products using either a physical or value basis.

A1 Analyze investment centers using return on total assets. A measure often used to evaluate an investment center manager is the *investment center return on total assets,* also called *return on investment.* This measure is computed as the center's net income divided by the center's average total assets.

P1 Assign overhead costs using two-stage cost allocation. In the traditional two-stage cost allocation procedure, service department costs are first assigned to operating departments. Then, in the second stage, a predetermined overhead allocation rate is computed for each operating department and is used to assign overhead to output.

P2 **Assign overhead costs using activity-based costing.** In activity-based costing, the costs of related activities are collected and then pooled in some logical manner into activity cost pools. After all activity costs have been accumulated in an activity cost pool account, users of the activity, termed *cost objects,* are assigned a portion of the total activity cost using a cost driver (allocation base).

P3 **Prepare departmental income statements.** Each profit center (department) is assigned its expenses to yield its own income statement. These costs include its direct expenses and its share of indirect expenses. The departmental income statement lists its revenues and costs of goods sold to determine gross profit. Its operating expenses (direct expenses and its indirect expenses allocated to the department) are deducted from gross profit to yield departmental net income.

P4 **Prepare departmental contribution reports.** The departmental contribution report is similar to the departmental income statement in terms of computing the gross profit for each department. Then the direct operating expenses for each department are deducted from gross profit to determine the contribution generated by each department. Indirect operating expenses are deducted *in total* from the company's combined contribution.

Guidance Answers to **Decision Maker** and **Decision Ethics**

Director of Operations You should collect details on overhead items and review them to see whether direct labor drives these costs. If it does not, overhead might be improperly assigned to departments. The situation also provides an opportunity to consider other overhead allocation bases, including use of activity-based costing.

Accounting Officer You should not author a report that you disagree with. You are responsible for ascertaining all the facts of ABC (implementation procedures, advantages and disadvantages, and costs). You should then approach your supervisor with these facts and suggest that you would like to modify the report to request, for example, a pilot test. The pilot test will allow you to further assess the suitability of ABC. Your suggestion might be rejected, at which time you may wish to speak with a more senior-level manager.

Center Manager We must first realize that the two investment opportunities are not comparable on the basis of absolute dollars of income or on assets. For instance, the second investment provides a higher income in absolute dollars but requires a higher investment. Accordingly, we need to compute return on total assets for each alternative: (1) $50,000 ÷ $250,000 = 20%, and (2) $175,000 ÷ $1 million = 17.5%. Alternative 1 has the higher return and is preferred over alternative 2. Do you pursue one, both, or neither? Because alternative 1's return is higher than the center's usual return of 19%, it should be pursued, assuming its risks are acceptable. Also, since alternative 1 requires a small investment, top management is likely to be more agreeable to pursuing it. Alternative 2's return is lower than the usual 19% and is not likely to be acceptable.

Guidance Answers to **Quick Checks**

1. Cost drivers are the factors that have a cause-effect relation with costs (or activities that pertain to costs).
2. *d*
3. A departmental accounting system provides information used to evaluate the performance of *departments*. A responsibility accounting system provides information used to evaluate the performance of *department managers.*
4. *d*
5. A cost center, such as a service department, incurs costs without directly generating revenues. A profit center, such as a product division, incurs costs but also generates revenues.
6. *b*

7. *d*
8. (1) Assign the direct expenses to each department. (2) Allocate indirect expenses to all departments. (3) Allocate the service department expenses to the operating departments.
9. *b*
10. No, because many expenses that enter into these calculations are beyond the manager's control, and managers should not be evaluated using costs they do not control.
11. *c*
12. *b*; $180,000 × ([32,000 × $9]/[96,000 × $3 + 64,000 × $6 + 32,000 × $9]) = $54,000.

Key Terms

mhhe.com/wildFAP18e

Key Terms are available at the book's Website for learning and testing in an online Flashcard Format.

Multiple Choice Quizzes A and B are available at the book's Website.

I. A retailer has three departments—housewares, appliances, and clothing—and buys advertising that benefits all departments. Advertising expense is $150,000 for the year, and departmental sales for the year follow: housewares, $356,250; appliances, $641,250; clothing, $427,500. How much advertising expense is allocated to appliances if allocation is based on departmental sales?
  a. $37,500
  b. $67,500
  c. $45,000
  d. $150,000
  e. $641,250

2. An activity-based costing system
  a. Does not require the level of detail that a traditional costing system requires.
  b. Does not enable the calculation of unit cost data.
  c. Allocates costs to products on the basis of activities performed on them.
  d. Cannot be used by a service company.
  e. Allocates costs to products based on the number of direct labor hours used.

3. A company produces two products, Grey and Red. The following information is available relating to those two products. Assume that the company's total setup cost is $162,000. Using activity-based costing, how much setup cost is allocated to each unit of Grey?

	Grey	Red
Units produced	500	40,000
Number of setups	50	100
Direct labor hours per unit	15	15

  a. $1,080
  b. $ 72
  c. $ 162
  d. $2,000
  e. $ 108

4. A company operates three retail departments as profit centers, and the following information is available for each. Which department has the largest dollar amount of departmental contribution to overhead and what is the dollar amount contributed?

Department	Sales	Cost of Goods Sold	Direct Expenses	Allocated Indirect Expenses
X	$500,000	$350,000	$50,000	$40,000
Y	200,000	75,000	20,000	50,000
Z	350,000	150,000	75,000	10,000

  a. Department Y, $ 55,000
  b. Department Z, $125,000
  c. Department X, $500,000
  d. Department Z, $200,000
  e. Department X, $ 60,000

5. Using the data in question 4, Department X's contribution to overhead as a percentage of sales is
  a. 20%
  b. 30%
  c. 12%
  d. 48%
  e. 32%

Superscript letter ^A denotes assignments based on Appendix 21A.

Discussion Questions

I. Why are many companies divided into departments?

2. Complete the following for a traditional two-stage allocation system: In the first stage, service department costs are assigned to _____ departments. In the second stage, a predetermined overhead rate is computed for each operating department and used to assign overhead to _____.

3. What is the difference between operating departments and service departments?

4. What is activity-based costing? What is its goal?

5. Identify at least four typical cost pools for activity-based costing in most organizations.

6. In activity-based costing, costs in a cost pool are allocated to _____ using predetermined overhead rates.

7. What company circumstances especially encourage use of activity-based costing?

8. What are two main goals in managerial accounting for reporting on and analyzing departments?

9. Is it possible to evaluate a cost center's profitability? Explain.

10. What is the difference between direct and indirect expenses?

11. Suggest a reasonable basis for allocating each of the following indirect expenses to departments: (a) salary of a supervisor who manages several departments, (b) rent, (c) heat, (d) electricity for lighting, (e) janitorial services, (f) advertising, (g) expired insurance on equipment, and (h) property taxes on equipment.

12. How is a department's contribution to overhead measured?

13. What are controllable costs?

14. Controllable and uncontrollable costs must be identified with a particular _____ and a definite _____ period.

15. Why should managers be closely involved in preparing their responsibility accounting budgets?

16. In responsibility accounting, who receives timely cost reports and specific cost information? Explain.

17.ᴬWhat is a joint cost? How are joint costs usually allocated among the products produced from them?

18.ᴬGive two examples of products with joint costs.

19. Each retail store of **Best Buy** has several departments. Why is it useful for its management to (a) collect accounting information about each department and (b) treat each department as a profit center?

20. **Apple** delivers its products to locations around the world. List three controllable and three uncontrollable costs for its delivery department.

 Red numbers denote Discussion Questions that involve decision-making.

In each blank next to the following terms, place the identifying letter of its best description.

1. _____ Cost center

2. _____ Investment center

3. _____ Departmental accounting system

4. _____ Operating department

5. _____ Profit center

6. _____ Responsibility accounting system

7. _____ Service department

A. Incurs costs without directly yielding revenues.

B. Provides information used to evaluate the performance of a department manager.

C. Holds manager responsible for revenues, costs, and investments.

D. Engages directly in manufacturing or in making sales directly to customers.

E. Does not directly manufacture products but contributes to profitability of the entire company.

F. Incurs costs and also generates revenues.

G. Provides information used to evaluate the performance of a department.

QUICK STUDY

QS 21-1
Allocation and measurement terms

C1 C2 C3 C4 A1

For each of the following types of indirect expenses and service department expenses, identify one allocation basis that could be used to distribute it to the departments indicated.

1. Computer service expenses of production scheduling for operating departments.

2. General office department expenses of the operating departments.

3. Maintenance department expenses of the operating departments.

4. Electric utility expenses of all departments.

QS 21-2
Basis for cost allocation

C3

The following is taken from Antuan Co.'s internal records of its factory with two operating departments. The cost driver for indirect labor and supplies is direct labor costs, and the cost driver for the remaining overhead items is number of hours of machine use. Compute the total amount of overhead cost allocated to Operating Department 1 using activity-based costing.

QS 21-3
Activity-based costing and overhead cost allocation

P2

	Direct Labor	Machine Use Hours
Operating department 1	$ 9,400	1,200
Operating department 2	6,600	2,000
Totals	$16,000	3,200

Factory overhead costs	
Rent and utilities	$ 6,100
Indirect labor	2,700
General office expense	2,000
Depreciation—Equipment	1,500
Supplies	1,300
Total factory overhead	$13,600

Check   Dept. 1 allocation, $5,950

QS 21-4
Departmental contribution to overhead
P4

Use the information in the following table to compute each department's contribution to overhead (both in dollars and as a percent). Which department contributes the largest dollar amount to total overhead? Which contributes the highest percent (as a percent of sales)?

	Dept. A	Dept. B	Dept. C
Sales	$53,000	$180,000	$84,000
Cost of goods sold	34,185	103,700	49,560
Gross profit	18,815	76,300	34,440
Total direct expenses	3,660	37,060	7,386
Contribution to overhead	$	$	$
Contribution percent	%	%	%

QS 21-5
Investment center analysis
A1

Compute return on assets for each of these **Best Buy** divisions (each is an investment center). Comment on the relative performance of each investment center.

Investment Center	Net Income	Average Assets	Return on Assets
Cameras and camcorders	$4,500,000	$20,000,000	_____
Phones and communications	1,500,000	12,500,000	_____
Computers and accessories	800,000	10,000,000	_____

QS 21-6ᴬ
Joint cost allocation
C5

A company purchases a 10,020 square foot commercial building for $325,000 and spends an additional $50,000 to divide the space into two separate rental units and prepare it for rent. Unit A, which has the desirable location on the corner and contains 3,340 square feet, will be rented for $1.00 per square foot. Unit B contains 6,680 square feet and will be rented for $0.75 per square foot. How much of the joint cost should be assigned to Unit B using the value basis of allocation?

EXERCISES

Exercise 21-1
Departmental expense allocations
P1   C3

Woh Che Co. has four departments: materials, personnel, manufacturing, and packaging. In a recent month, the four departments incurred three shared indirect expenses. The amounts of these indirect expenses and the bases used to allocate them follow.

Indirect Expense	Cost	Allocation Base
Supervision	$ 82,500	Number of employees
Utilities	50,000	Square feet occupied
Insurance	22,500	Value of assets in use
Total	$155,000	

Departmental data for the company's recent reporting period follow.

Department	Employees	Square Feet	Asset Values
Materials	27	25,000	$ 6,000
Personnel	9	5,000	1,200
Manufacturing	63	55,000	37,800
Packaging	51	15,000	15,000
Total	150	100,000	$60,000

(1) Use this information to allocate each of the three indirect expenses across the four departments. (2) Prepare a summary table that reports the indirect expenses assigned to each of the four departments.

Provo Company produces two types of glass shelving, rounded edge and squared edge, on the same production line. For the current period, the company reports the following data.

	Rounded Edge	Squared Edge	Total
Direct materials	$ 9,500	$21,600	$ 31,100
Direct labor	6,100	11,900	18,000
Overhead (300% of direct labor cost)	18,300	35,700	54,000
Total cost	$33,900	$69,200	$103,100
Quantity produced	10,500 ft.	14,100 ft.	
Average cost per ft.	$ 3.23	$ 4.91	

Exercise 21-2
Activity-based costing
of overhead

P2

Provo's controller wishes to apply activity-based costing (ABC) to allocate the $54,000 of overhead costs incurred by the two product lines to see whether cost per foot would change markedly from that reported above. She has collected the following information.

Overhead Cost Category (Activity Cost Pool)	Cost
Supervision	$ 2,700
Depreciation of machinery	28,300
Assembly line preparation	23,000
Total overhead	$54,000

She has also collected the following information about the cost drivers for each category (cost pool) and the amount of each driver used by the two product lines.

Overhead Cost Category (Activity Cost Pool)	Driver	Usage		
		Rounded Edge	Squared Edge	Total
Supervision	Direct labor cost($)	$6,100	$11,900	$18,000
Depreciation of machinery	Machine hours	250 hours	750 hours	1,000 hours
Assembly line preparation	Setups (number)	20 times	105 times	125 times

Use this information to (1) assign these three overhead cost pools to each of the two products using ABC, (2) determine average cost per foot for each of the two products using ABC, and (3) compare the average cost per foot under ABC with the average cost per foot under the current method for each product. For part 3, explain why a difference between the two cost allocation methods exists.

Check   (2) Rounded edge, $2.60; Squared edge, $5.38

Truck Market pays $130,000 rent each year for its two-story building. The space in this building is occupied by five departments as specified here.

Exercise 21-3
Rent expense allocated
to departments

P1   C3

Paint department	1,440 square feet of first-floor space
Engine department	3,360 square feet of first-floor space
Window department	2,016 square feet of second-floor space
Electrical department	960 square feet of second-floor space
Accessory department	1,824 square feet of second-floor space

The company allocates 65% of total rent expense to the first floor and 35% to the second floor, and then allocates rent expense for each floor to the departments occupying that floor on the basis of space occupied. Determine the rent expense to be allocated to each department. (Round percents to the nearest one-tenth and dollar amounts to the nearest whole dollar.)

Check   Allocated to Paint Dept., $25,350

Exercise 21-4

Departmental expense
allocation spreadsheet

C3　P1

Overland Cycle Shop has two service departments (advertising and administration) and two operating departments (cycles and clothing). During 2008, the departments had the following direct expenses and occupied the following amount of floor space.

Department	Direct Expenses	Square Feet
Advertising	$ 18,000	1,120
Administrative	25,000	1,400
Cycles	103,000	7,140
Clothing	15,000	4,340

The advertising department developed and distributed 120 advertisements during the year. Of these, 90 promoted cycles and 30 promoted clothing. The store sold $350,000 of merchandise during the year. Of this amount, $273,000 is from the cycles department, and $77,000 is from the clothing department. The utilities expense of $64,000 is an indirect expense to all departments. Prepare a departmental expense allocation spreadsheet for Overland Cycle Shop. The spreadsheet should assign (1) direct expenses to each of the four departments, (2) the $64,000 of utilities expense to the four departments on the basis of floor space occupied, (3) the advertising department's expenses to the two operating departments on the basis of the number of ads placed that promoted a department's products, and (4) the administrative department's expenses to the two operating departments based on the amount of sales. Provide supporting computations for the expense allocations.

Check　Total expenses allocated to
Cycles Dept., $177,472

Exercise 21-5

Service department
expenses allocated to
operating departments　P3

The following is a partially completed lower section of a departmental expense allocation spreadsheet for Cozy Bookstore. It reports the total amounts of direct and indirect expenses allocated to its five departments. Complete the spreadsheet by allocating the expenses of the two service departments (advertising and purchasing) to the three operating departments.

File Edit View Insert Format Tools Data Window Help

	Allocation Base	Expense Account Balance	Advertising Dept.	Purchasing Dept.	Books Dept.	Magazines Dept.	Newspapers Dept.
1			Allocation of Expenses to Departments				
5 Total department expenses..........		$698,000	$24,000	$34,000	$425,000	$90,000	$125,000
6 **Service department expenses**							
7 　Advertising department.............Sales			?		?	?	?
8 　Purchasing department............Purch. orders				?	?	?	?
9 Total expenses allocated to							
10 　operating departments..............		?	$ 0	$ 0	?	?	?

Advertising and purchasing department expenses are allocated to operating departments on the basis of dollar sales and purchase orders, respectively. Information about the allocation bases for the three operating departments follows.

Department	Sales	Purchase Orders
Books	$495,000	516
Magazines	198,000	360
Newspapers	207,000	324
Total	$900,000	1,200

Check　Total expenses allocated to
Books Dept., $452,820

Exercise 21-6

Indirect payroll expense allocated
to departments

C3

Jessica Porter works in both the jewelry department and the hosiery department of a retail store. Porter assists customers in both departments and arranges and stocks merchandise in both departments. The store allocates Porter's $30,000 annual wages between the two departments based on a sample of the time worked in the two departments. The sample is obtained from a diary of hours worked that Porter kept in a randomly chosen two-week period. The diary showed the following hours and activities spent in the two departments. Allocate Porter's annual wages between the two departments.

Selling in jewelry department		51 hours
Arranging and stocking merchandise in jewelry department		6 hours
Selling in hosiery department		12 hours
Arranging and stocking merchandise in hosiery department		7 hours
Idle time spent waiting for a customer to enter one of the selling departments		4 hours

Check   Assign $7,500 to Hosiery

Maryanne Dinardo manages an auto dealership's service department. The recent month's income statement for her department follows. (1) Analyze the items on the income statement and identify those that definitely should be included on a performance report used to evaluate Dinardo's performance. List them and explain why you chose them. (2) List and explain the items that should definitely be excluded. (3) List the items that are not definitely included or excluded and explain why they fall into that category.

Exercise 21-7
Managerial performance evaluation
C4

Revenues		
Sales of parts	$ 72,000	
Sales of services	105,000	$177,000
Costs and expenses		
Cost of parts sold	30,000	
Building depreciation	9,300	
Income taxes allocated to department	8,700	
Interest on long-term debt	7,500	
Manager's salary	12,000	
Payroll taxes	8,100	
Supplies	15,900	
Utilities	4,400	
Wages (hourly)	16,000	
Total costs and expenses		111,900
Departmental net income		$ 65,100

You must prepare a return on investment analysis for the regional manager of Fast & Great Burgers. This growing chain is trying to decide which outlet of two alternatives to open. The first location (A) requires a $1,000,000 investment and is expected to yield annual net income of $160,000. The second location (B) requires a $600,000 investment and is expected to yield annual net income of $108,000. Compute the return on investment for each Fast & Great Burgers alternative and then make your recommendation in a one-half page memorandum to the regional manager. (The chain currently generates an 18% return on total assets.)

Exercise 21-8
Investment center analysis
A1

Heart & Home Properties is developing a subdivision that includes 600 home lots. The 450 lots in the Canyon section are below a ridge and do not have views of the neighboring canyons and hills; the 150 lots in the Hilltop section offer unobstructed views. The expected selling price for each Canyon lot is $55,000 and for each Hilltop lot is $110,000. The developer acquired the land for $4,000,000 and spent another $3,500,000 on street and utilities improvements. Assign the joint land and improvement costs to the lots using the value basis of allocation and determine the average cost per lot.

Exercise 21-9^A
Joint real estate costs assigned
C5

Check   Total Hilltop cost, $3,000,000

Pirate Seafood Company purchases lobsters and processes them into tails and flakes. It sells the lobster tails for $21 per pound and the flakes for $14 per pound. On average, 100 pounds of lobster are processed into 52 pounds of tails and 22 pounds of flakes, with 26 pounds of waste. Assume that Pirate purchased 2,400 pounds of lobster for $4.50 per pound and processed the lobsters with an additional labor cost of $1,800. No materials or labor costs are assigned to the waste. If 1,096 pounds of tails and 324 pounds of flakes are sold, what is (1) the allocated cost of the sold items and (2) the allocated cost of the ending inventory? Pirate allocates joint costs on a value basis. (Round the dollar cost per pound to the nearest thousandth.)

Exercise 21-10^A
Joint product costs assigned
C5

Check   (2) Inventory cost, $2,268

PROBLEM SET A

Problem 21-1A
Allocation of building occupancy costs to departments

C3   P1

mhhe.com/wildFAP18e

National Bank has several departments that occupy both floors of a two-story building. The departmental accounting system has a single account, Building Occupancy Cost, in its ledger. The types and amounts of occupancy costs recorded in this account for the current period follow.

Depreciation—Building	$18,000
Interest—Building mortgage	27,000
Taxes—Building and land	9,000
Gas (heating) expense	3,000
Lighting expense	3,000
Maintenance expense	6,000
Total occupancy cost	$66,000

The building has 4,000 square feet on each floor. In prior periods, the accounting manager merely divided the $66,000 occupancy cost by 8,000 square feet to find an average cost of $8.25 per square foot and then charged each department a building occupancy cost equal to this rate times the number of square feet that it occupied.

Diane Linder manages a first-floor department that occupies 1,000 square feet, and Juan Chiro manages a second-floor department that occupies 1,800 square feet of floor space. In discussing the departmental reports, the second-floor manager questions whether using the same rate per square foot for all departments makes sense because the first-floor space is more valuable. This manager also references a recent real estate study of average local rental costs for similar space that shows first-floor space worth $30 per square foot and second-floor space worth $20 per square foot (excluding costs for heating, lighting, and maintenance).

Required

1. Allocate all occupancy costs to the Linder and Chiro departments using the current allocation method.

Check (2) Total occupancy cost to Linder, $9,600

2. Allocate the depreciation, interest, and taxes occupancy costs to the Linder and Chiro departments in proportion to the relative market values of the floor space. Allocate the heating, lighting, and maintenance costs to the Linder and Chiro departments in proportion to the square feet occupied (ignoring floor space market values).

Analysis Component

3. Which allocation method would you prefer if you were a manager of a second-floor department? Explain.

Problem 21-2A
Activity-based costing

P2

Patient Health is an outpatient surgical clinic that was profitable for many years, but Medicare has cut its reimbursements by as much as 50%. As a result, the clinic wants to better understand its costs. It decides to prepare an activity-based cost analysis, including an estimate of the average cost of both general surgery and orthopedic surgery. The clinic's three cost centers and their cost drivers follow.

Cost Center	Cost	Cost Driver	Driver Quantity
Professional salaries	$2,000,000	Professional hours	10,000
Patient services and supplies	37,500	Number of patients	500
Building cost	300,000	Square feet	2,000

The two main surgical units and their related data follow.

Service	Hours	Square Feet*	Patients
General surgery	2,500	720	400
Orthopedic surgery	7,500	1,280	100

* Orthopedic surgery requires more space for patients, supplies, and equipment.

Required

1. Compute the cost per cost driver for each of the three cost centers.

Check (2) Average cost of general (orthopedic) surgery, $1,595 ($16,995) per patient

2. Use the results from part 1 to allocate costs from each of the three cost centers to both the general surgery and the orthopedic surgery units. Compute total cost and average cost per patient for both the general surgery and the orthopedic surgery units.

Analysis Component

3. Without providing computations, would the average cost of general surgery be higher or lower if all center costs were allocated based on the number of patients? Explain.

Williams Co. began operations in January 2008 with two operating (selling) departments and one service (office) department. Its departmental income statements follow.

Problem 21-3A

Departmental income statements; forecasts

P3

mhhe.com/wildFAP18e

WILLIAMS COMPANY Departmental Income Statements For Year Ended December 31, 2008			
	Clock	**Mirror**	**Combined**
Sales	$130,000	$55,000	$185,000
Cost of goods sold	63,700	34,100	97,800
Gross profit	66,300	20,900	87,200
Direct expenses			
Sales salaries	20,000	7,000	27,000
Advertising	1,200	500	1,700
Store supplies used	900	400	1,300
Depreciation—Equipment	1,500	300	1,800
Total direct expenses	23,600	8,200	31,800
Allocated expenses			
Rent expense	7,020	3,780	10,800
Utilities expense	2,600	1,400	4,000
Share of office department expenses	10,500	4,500	15,000
Total allocated expenses	20,120	9,680	29,800
Total expenses	43,720	17,880	61,600
Net income	$ 22,580	$ 3,020	$ 25,600

Williams plans to open a third department in January 2009 that will sell paintings. Management predicts that the new department will generate $50,000 in sales with a 55% gross profit margin and will require the following direct expenses: sales salaries, $8,000; advertising, $800; store supplies, $500; and equipment depreciation, $200. It will fit the new department into the current rented space by taking some square footage from the other two departments. When opened the new painting department will fill one-fifth of the space presently used by the clock department and one-fourth used by the mirror department. Management does not predict any increase in utilities costs, which are allocated to the departments in proportion to occupied space (or rent expense). The company allocates office department expenses to the operating departments in proportion to their sales. It expects the painting department to increase total office department expenses by $7,000. Since the painting department will bring new customers into the store, management expects sales in both the clock and mirror departments to increase by 8%. No changes for those departments' gross profit percents or their direct expenses are expected except for store supplies used, which will increase in proportion to sales.

Required

Prepare departmental income statements that show the company's predicted results of operations for calendar year 2009 for the three operating (selling) departments and their combined totals. (Round percents to the nearest one-tenth and dollar amounts to the nearest whole dollar.)

Check 2009 forecasted combined net income (sales), $43,472 ($249,800)

Billie Whitehorse, the plant manager of Travel Free's Indiana plant, is responsible for all of that plant's costs other than her own salary. The plant has two operating departments and one service department. The camper and trailer operating departments manufacture different products and have their own managers. The office department, which Whitehorse also manages, provides services equally to the two operating departments. A budget is prepared for each operating department and the office department. The company's responsibility accounting system must assemble information to present budgeted and actual costs in performance reports for each operating department manager and the plant manager. Each performance report includes only those costs that a particular operating department manager can control: raw materials, wages, supplies used, and equipment depreciation. The plant manager is responsible for the department managers' salaries, utilities, building rent, office salaries other than her own, and other

Problem 21-4A

Responsibility accounting performance reports; controllable and budgeted costs

C4 P4

office costs plus all costs controlled by the two operating department managers. The annual departmental budgets and actual costs for the two operating departments follow.

	Budget			Actual		
	Campers	Trailers	Combined	Campers	Trailers	Combined
Raw materials	$195,000	$275,000	$ 470,000	$194,200	$273,200	$ 467,400
Employee wages	104,000	205,000	309,000	106,600	206,400	313,000
Dept. manager salary	43,000	52,000	95,000	44,000	53,500	97,500
Supplies used	33,000	90,000	123,000	31,700	91,600	123,300
Depreciation—Equip.	60,000	125,000	185,000	60,000	125,000	185,000
Utilities	3,600	5,400	9,000	3,300	5,000	8,300
Building rent	5,700	9,300	15,000	5,300	8,700	14,000
Office department costs	68,750	68,750	137,500	67,550	67,550	135,100
Totals	$513,050	$830,450	$1,343,500	$512,650	$830,950	$1,343,600

The office department's annual budget and its actual costs follow.

	Budget	Actual
Plant manager salary	$ 80,000	$ 82,000
Other office salaries	32,500	30,100
Other office costs	25,000	23,000
Totals	$137,500	$135,100

Required

1. Prepare responsibility accounting performance reports like those in Exhibit 21.20 that list costs controlled by the following:

Check   (1a) $500 total over budget

   a. Manager of the camper department.

   b. Manager of the trailer department.

(1c) Indiana plant controllable costs, $1,900 total under budget

   c. Manager of the Indiana plant.

In each report, include the budgeted and actual costs and show the amount that each actual cost is over or under the budgeted amount.

Analysis Component

2. Did the plant manager or the operating department managers better manage costs? Explain.

Problem 21-5Aᴬ
Allocation of joint costs

C5

Georgia Orchards produced a good crop of peaches this year. After preparing the following income statement, Georgia believes it should have given its No. 3 peaches to charity and saved its efforts.

GEORGIA ORCHARDS Income Statement For Year Ended December 31, 2008				
	No. 1	No. 2	No. 3	Combined
Sales (by grade)				
No. 1: 300,000 lbs. @ $1.50/lb	$450,000			
No. 2: 300,000 lbs. @ $1.00/lb		$300,000		
No. 3: 750,000 lbs. @ $0.25/lb			$ 187,500	
Total sales				$937,500
Costs				
Tree pruning and care @ $0.30/lb	90,000	90,000	225,000	405,000
Picking, sorting, and grading @ $0.15/lb	45,000	45,000	112,500	202,500
Delivery costs @ $0.05/lb	15,000	15,000	37,500	67,500
Total costs	150,000	150,000	375,000	675,000
Net income (loss)	$300,000	$150,000	$(187,500)	$262,500

In preparing this statement, Georgia allocated joint costs among the grades on a physical basis as an equal amount per pound. Georgia's delivery cost records show that $30,000 of the $67,500 relates to crating the No. 1 and No. 2 peaches and hauling them to the buyer. The remaining $37,500 of delivery costs is for crating the No. 3 peaches and hauling them to the cannery.

Required

1. Prepare reports showing cost allocations on a sales value basis to the three grades of peaches. Separate the delivery costs into the amounts directly identifiable with each grade. Then allocate any shared delivery costs on the basis of the relative sales value of each grade.

2. Using your answers to part 1, prepare an income statement using the joint costs allocated on a sales value basis.

Check (1) $129,600 tree pruning and care costs allocated to No. 2

(2) Net income from No. 1 & No. 2 peaches, $140,400 & $93,600

Analysis Component

3. Do you think delivery costs fit the definition of a joint cost? Explain.

Harmon's has several departments that occupy all floors of a two-story building that includes a basement floor. Harmon rented this building under a long-term lease negotiated when rental rates were low. The departmental accounting system has a single account, Building Occupancy Cost, in its ledger. The types and amounts of occupancy costs recorded in this account for the current period follow.

PROBLEM SET B

Problem 21-1B
Allocation of building occupancy costs to departments

C3   P1

Building rent	$400,000
Lighting expense	25,000
Cleaning expense	40,000
Total occupancy cost	$465,000

The building has 7,500 square feet on each of the upper two floors but only 5,000 square feet in the basement. In prior periods, the accounting manager merely divided the $465,000 occupancy cost by 20,000 square feet to find an average cost of $23.25 per square foot and then charged each department a building occupancy cost equal to this rate times the number of square feet that it occupies.

Jordan Style manages a department that occupies 2,000 square feet of basement floor space. In discussing the departmental reports with other managers, she questions whether using the same rate per square foot for all departments makes sense because different floor space has different values. Style checked a recent real estate report of average local rental costs for similar space that shows first-floor space worth $40 per square foot, second-floor space worth $20 per square foot, and basement space worth $10 per square foot (excluding costs for lighting and cleaning).

Required

1. Allocate all occupancy costs to Style's department using the current allocation method.

2. Allocate the building rent cost to Style's department in proportion to the relative market value of the floor space. Allocate to Style's department the lighting and heating costs in proportion to the square feet occupied (ignoring floor space market values).

Check (2) Total costs allocated to Style's Dept., $22,500

Analysis Component

3. Which allocation method would you prefer if you were a manager of a basement department?

Wooddale Landscaping has enjoyed profits for many years, but new competition has cut service revenue by as much as 30%. As a result, the company wants to better understand its costs. It decides to prepare an activity-based cost analysis, including an estimate of the average cost of both general landscaping services and custom design landscaping services. The company's three cost centers and their cost drivers follow.

Problem 21-2B
Activity-based costing

P2

Cost Center	Cost	Cost Driver	Driver Quantity
Professional salaries	$600,000	Professional hours	10,000
Customer supplies	150,000	Number of customers	800
Building cost	240,000	Square feet	2,500

The two main landscaping units and their related data follow.

Service	Hours	Square Feet*	Customers
General landscaping	2,500	1,000	600
Custom design landscaping	7,500	1,500	200

* Custom design landscaping requires more space for equipment, supplies, and planning.

Required

1. Compute the cost per cost driver for each of the three cost centers.

Check (2) Average cost of general (custom) landscaping, $597.50 ($3,157.50) per customer

2. Use the results from part 1 to allocate costs from each of the three cost centers to both the general landscaping and the custom design landscaping units. Compute total cost and average cost per customer for both the general landscaping and the custom design landscaping units.

Analysis Component

3. Without providing computations, would the average cost of general landscaping be higher or lower if all center costs were allocated based on the number of customers? Explain.

Problem 21-3B
Departmental income statements; forecasts

P3

Bonanza Entertainment began operations in January 2008 with two operating (selling) departments and one service (office) department. Its departmental income statements follow.

BONANZA ENTERTAINMENT Departmental Income Statements For Year Ended December 31, 2008			
	Movies	**Video Games**	**Combined**
Sales	$600,000	$200,000	$800,000
Cost of goods sold	420,000	154,000	574,000
Gross profit	180,000	46,000	226,000
Direct expenses			
Sales salaries	37,000	15,000	52,000
Advertising	12,500	6,000	18,500
Store supplies used	4,000	1,000	5,000
Depreciation—Equipment	4,500	3,000	7,500
Total direct expenses	58,000	25,000	83,000
Allocated expenses			
Rent expense	41,000	9,000	50,000
Utilities expense	7,380	1,620	9,000
Share of office department expenses	56,250	18,750	75,000
Total allocated expenses	104,630	29,370	134,000
Total expenses	162,630	54,370	217,000
Net income (loss)	$ 17,370	$ (8,370)	$ 9,000

Bonanza plans to open a third department in January 2009 that will sell compact discs. Management predicts that the new department will generate $300,000 in sales with a 35% gross profit margin and will require the following direct expenses: sales salaries, $18,000; advertising, $10,000; store supplies, $2,000; and equipment depreciation, $1,200. The company will fit the new department into the current rented space by taking some square footage from the other two departments. When opened, the new compact disc department will fill one-fourth of the space presently used by the movie department and one-third of the space used by the video game department. Management does not predict any increase in utilities costs, which are allocated to the departments in proportion to occupied space (or rent expense). The company allocates office department expenses to the operating departments in proportion to their sales. It expects the compact disc department to increase total office department expenses by $10,000. Since the compact disc department will bring new customers into the store, management expects sales in both the movie and video game departments to increase by 8%. No changes for those departments' gross profit percents or for their direct expenses are expected, except for store supplies used, which will increase in proportion to sales.

Required

Prepare departmental income statements that show the company's predicted results of operations for calendar year 2009 for the three operating (selling) departments and their combined totals. (Round percents to the nearest one-tenth and dollar amounts to the nearest whole dollar.)

Check 2009 forecasted movies net income (sales), $52,450 ($648,000)

Britney Brown, the plant manager of LMN Co.'s Chicago plant, is responsible for all of that plant's costs other than her own salary. The plant has two operating departments and one service department. The refrigerator and dishwasher operating departments manufacture different products and have their own managers. The office department, which Brown also manages, provides services equally to the two operating departments. A monthly budget is prepared for each operating department and the office department. The company's responsibility accounting system must assemble information to present budgeted and actual costs in performance reports for each operating department manager and the plant manager. Each performance report includes only those costs that a particular operating department manager can control: raw materials, wages, supplies used, and equipment depreciation. The plant manager is responsible for the department managers' salaries, utilities, building rent, office salaries other than her own, and other office costs plus all costs controlled by the two operating department managers. The April departmental budgets and actual costs for the two operating departments follow.

Problem 21-4B
Responsibility accounting performance reports; controllable and budgeted costs

C4   P4

	Budget			Actual		
	Refrigerators	Dishwashers	Combined	Refrigerators	Dishwashers	Combined
Raw materials	$400,000	$200,000	$ 600,000	$385,000	$202,000	$ 587,000
Employee wages	170,000	80,000	250,000	174,700	81,500	256,200
Dept. manager salary	55,000	49,000	104,000	55,000	46,500	101,500
Supplies used	15,000	9,000	24,000	14,000	9,700	23,700
Depreciation—Equip.	53,000	37,000	90,000	53,000	37,000	90,000
Utilities	30,000	18,000	48,000	34,500	20,700	55,200
Building rent	63,000	17,000	80,000	65,800	16,500	82,300
Office department costs	70,500	70,500	141,000	75,000	75,000	150,000
Totals	$856,500	$480,500	$1,337,000	$857,000	$488,900	$1,345,900

The office department's budget and its actual costs for April follow.

	Budget	Actual
Plant manager salary	$ 80,000	$ 85,000
Other office salaries	40,000	35,200
Other office costs	21,000	29,800
Totals	$141,000	$150,000

Required

1. Prepare responsibility accounting performance reports like those in Exhibit 21.20 that list costs controlled by the following:

   a. Manager of the refrigerator department.

   b. Manager of the dishwasher department.

   c. Manager of the Chicago plant.

In each report, include the budgeted and actual costs for the month and show the amount by which each actual cost is over or under the budgeted amount.

Check (1a) $11,300 total under budget

(1c) Chicago plant controllable costs, $3,900 total over budget

Analysis Component

2. Did the plant manager or the operating department managers better manage costs? Explain.

Problem 21-5B[A]
Allocation of joint costs

C5

Rita and Rick Redding own and operate a tomato grove. After preparing the following income statement, Rita believes they should have offered the No. 3 tomatoes to the public for free and saved themselves time and money.

RITA AND RICK REDDING Income Statement For Year Ended December 31, 2008				
	No. 1	No. 2	No. 3	Combined
Sales (by grade)				
No. 1: 500,000 lbs. @ $1.80/lb	$900,000			
No. 2: 400,000 lbs. @ $1.25/lb		$500,000		
No. 3: 100,000 lbs. @ $0.40/lb			$ 40,000	
Total sales				$1,440,000
Costs				
Land preparation, seeding, and cultivating @ $0.70/lb	350,000	280,000	70,000	700,000
Harvesting, sorting, and grading @ $0.04/lb	20,000	16,000	4,000	40,000
Delivery costs @ $0.02/lb	10,000	7,000	3,000	20,000
Total costs	380,000	303,000	77,000	760,000
Net income (loss)	$520,000	$197,000	$(37,000)	$680,000

In preparing this statement, Rita and Rick allocated joint costs among the grades on a physical basis as an equal amount per pound. Also, their delivery cost records show that $17,000 of the $20,000 relates to crating the No. 1 and No. 2 tomatoes and hauling them to the buyer. The remaining $3,000 of delivery costs is for crating the No. 3 tomatoes and hauling them to the cannery.

Required

Check (1) $1,120 harvesting, sorting and grading costs allocated to No. 3

1. Prepare reports showing cost allocations on a sales value basis to the three grades of tomatoes. Separate the delivery costs into the amounts directly identifiable with each grade. Then allocate any shared delivery costs on the basis of the relative sales value of each grade. (Round percents to the nearest one-tenth and dollar amounts to the nearest whole dollar.)

(2) Net income from No. 1 & No. 2 tomatoes, $426,569 & $237,151

2. Using your answers to part 1, prepare an income statement using the joint costs allocated on a sales value basis.

Analysis Component

3. Do you think delivery costs fit the definition of a joint cost? Explain.

PROBLEM SET C

Problem Set C is available at the book's Website to further reinforce and assess your learning.

BEYOND THE NUMBERS

REPORTING IN ACTION

C4

BTN 21-1 Review **Best Buy**'s income statement in Appendix A and identify its revenues for the years ended February 26, 2005, February 28, 2004, and March 1, 2003. For the year ended February 26, 2005, Best Buy reports the following product revenue mix. (Assume that its product revenue mix is the same for each of the three years reported when answering the requirements.)

Home Office	Entertainment Software	Consumer Electronics	Appliances
34%	21%	39%	6%

Required

1. Compute the amount of revenue from each of its product lines for the years ended February 26, 2005, February 28, 2004, and March 1, 2003.

2. If Best Buy wishes to evaluate each of its product lines, how can it allocate its operating expenses to each of them to determine each product line's profitability?

Fast Forward

3. Access Best Buy's annual report for a fiscal year ending after February 26, 2005, from its Website (**BestBuy.com**) or the SEC's EDGAR database (**sec.gov**). Compute its revenues for its product lines for the most recent year(s). Compare those results to those from part 1. How has its product mix changed?

BTN 21-2   **Best Buy** and **Circuit City** compete across the country in several markets. The most common competitive markets for these two companies are by location.

**COMPARATIVE
ANALYSIS**

P3

Required

1. Design a three-tier responsibility accounting organizational chart assuming that you have available internal information for both companies. Use Exhibit 21.19 as an example. The goal of this assignment is to design a reporting framework for the companies; numbers are not required. Limit your reporting framework to sales activity only.
2. Explain why it is important to have similar performance reports when comparing performance within a company (and across different companies). Be specific in your response.

BTN 21-3   Senior Security Co. offers a range of security services for senior citizens. Each type of service is considered within a separate department. Mary Pincus, the overall manager, is compensated partly on the basis of departmental performance by staying within the quarterly cost budget. She often revises operations to make sure departments stay within budget. Says Pincus, "I will not go over budget even if it means slightly compromising the level and quality of service. These are minor compromises that don't significantly affect my clients, at least in the short term."

**ETHICS
CHALLENGE**

P3

Required

1. Is there an ethical concern in this situation? If so, which parties are affected? Explain.
2. Can Mary Pincus take action to eliminate or reduce any ethical concerns? Explain.
3. What is Senior Security's ethical responsibility in offering professional services?

BTN 21-4   Improvement Station is a national home improvement chain with more than 100 stores throughout the country. The manager of each store receives a salary plus a bonus equal to a percent of the store's net income for the reporting period. The following net income calculation is on the Denver store manager's performance report for the recent monthly period.

**COMMUNICATING
IN PRACTICE**

C4 C5 P3

Sales	$2,500,000
Cost of goods sold	800,000
Wages expense	500,000
Utilities expense	200,000
Home office expense	75,000
Net income	$925,000
Manager's bonus (0.5%)	$ 4,625

In previous periods, the bonus had also been 0.5%, but the performance report had not included any charges for the home office expense, which is now assigned to each store as a percent of its sales.

Required

Assume that you are the national office manager. Write a one-half page memorandum to your store managers explaining why home office expense is in the new performance report.

TAKING IT TO THE NET
A1

BTN 21-5 This chapter described and used spreadsheets to prepare various managerial reports (see Exhibit 21-12). You can download from Websites various tutorials showing how spreadsheets are used in managerial accounting and other business applications.

Required

1. Check out the Website <u>Lacher.com</u>. Scroll down and open its table of contents. Select "Business Solutions Tutorials" and identify and list three tutorials for review.
2. Describe in a one-half page memorandum to your instructor how the applications described in each tutorial are helpful in business and managerial decision making.

TEAMWORK IN ACTION
C1 C2

BTN 21-6 Activity-based costing (ABC) is increasingly popular as a useful managerial tool to (1) measure the cost of resources consumed and (2) assign cost to products and services. This managerial tool has been available to accounting and business decision makers for more than 25 years.

Required

Break into teams and identify at least three likely reasons that activity-based costing has gained popularity in recent years. Be prepared to present your answers in a class discussion. (*Hint:* What changes have occurred in products and services over the past 25 years?)

BusinessWeek ACTIVITY
C4

BTN 21-7 Read the article "The Easiest Commute of All" from the December 12, 2005, issue of *BusinessWeek*. (The book's Website provides free access to the article.)

Required

1. Why are many workers becoming remote workers?
2. Are there advantages for a company to have these remote workers?
3. How can a manager assess a worker's productivity if the worker is not on site?

ENTREPRENEURIAL DECISION
P3

BTN 21-8 **Jungle Jim's International Market** has grown considerably since Jim Bonaminio began with his roadside produce stand. Jim now operates a gigantic supermarket with many departments and activities.

Required

1. How can Jim Bonaminio use departmental income statements to assist him in understanding and controlling his supermarket operations?
2. Are departmental income statements always the best measure of a department's performance? Explain.

HITTING THE ROAD
P3

BTN 21-9 Visit a local movie theater and check out both its concession area and its showing areas. The manager of a theater must confront questions such as:
- How much return do we earn on concessions?
- What types of movies generate the greatest sales?
- What types of movies generate the greatest net income?

Required

Assume that you are the new accounting manager for a 16-screen movie theater. You are to set up a responsibility accounting reporting framework for the theater.

1. Recommend how to segment the different departments of a movie theater for responsibility reporting.
2. Propose an expense allocation system for heat, rent, insurance, and maintenance costs of the theater.

BTN 21-10   Key segment data from **Dixons** (<u>Dixons-Group.com</u>) follow.

GLOBAL DECISION

Segment, for Year Ended (£ millions)	Net Sales May 1, 2004	Net Sales May 3, 2003	Operating Income May 1, 2004	Operating Income May 3, 2003
United Kingdom retail	£4,697.9	£4,524.5	£254.2	£238.0
International retail	1,760.1	1,195.3	63.6	40.1
Totals	£6,458.0	£5,719.8	£317.8	£278.1

Required

1. Compute the growth (in percent) for Dixons' total net sales from fiscal year 2003 to 2004.
2. Compute the growth (in percent) for each segment's net sales from fiscal year 2003 to 2004.
3. Which segment's net sales grew the fastest?
4. Which segment was most profitable?
5. How can Dixons' managers use this information?

Dixons

ANSWERS TO MULTIPLE CHOICE QUIZ

1. b; [$641,250/($356,250 + $641,250 + $427,500)] × $150,000 = $67,500
2. c;
3. e; $162,000 × 50/150 setups = $54,000; $54,000/500 units = $108 per Grey unit. (Red is $2.70 per unit.)
4. b;

	Department X	Department Y	Department Z
Sales	$500,000	$200,000	$350,000
Cost of goods sold	350,000	75,000	150,000
Gross profit	150,000	125,000	200,000
Direct expenses ..	50,000	20,000	75,000
Departmental contribution ...	$100,000	$105,000	$125,000

5. a; $100,000/$500,000 = 20%

22

Cost-Volume-Profit Analysis

A Look Back

Chapter 21 focused on cost allocation, activity-based costing, and performance measurement. We identified ways to measure and analyze company activities, its departments, and its managers.

A Look at This Chapter

This chapter shows how information on both costs and sales behavior is useful to managers in performing cost-volume-profit analysis. This analysis is an important part of successful management and sound business decisions.

A Look Ahead

Chapter 23 introduces and describes the budgeting process and its importance to management. It also explains the master budget and its usefulness to the planning of future company activities.

Learning Objectives

CAP

Conceptual

C1 Describe different types of cost behavior in relation to production and sales volume. (p. 882)

C2 Identify assumptions in cost-volume-profit analysis and explain their impact. (p. 890)

C3 Describe several applications of cost-volume-profit analysis. (p. 892)

Analytical

A1 Compare the scatter diagram, high-low, and regression methods of estimating costs. (p. 887)

A2 Compute contribution margin and describe what it reveals about a company's cost structure. (p. 888)

A3 Analyze changes in sales using the degree of operating leverage. (p. 896)

Procedural

P1 Determine cost estimates using three different methods. (p. 885)

P2 Compute break-even point for a single product company. (p. 888)

P3 Graph costs and sales for a single product company. (p. 890)

P4 Compute break-even point for a multiproduct company. (p. 895)

"There is no store in any of the Chinatowns across the U.S. that carries our products"
—Xiaoning Wang

Sprouting Fruits of China

NEW YORK, NY—Xiaoning Wang launched Brooklyn-based **ChinaSprout (ChinaSprout.com)** to provide the best educational and cultural products and community services to people interested in Chinese culture. It all began when Wang and her husband wanted to educate their own son, Simon, about the culture of Chinese people. The couple soon grew frustrated, however, by a lack of quality educational products and services. They also discovered many friends and neighbors who were similarly dismayed.

With $6,000 and a dream, Wang and her husband started their merchandising business of buying and distributing products from China. They promoted their Website by printing flyers and passing them out at cultural events. Word quickly spread and business soared.

"When I started ChinaSprout," says Wang, "I never dreamed that it would grow as fast as it did and develop such an enormous following." The business quickly required cost controls to maintain the quality and service that loyal customers expected. Wang focused on cost behavior and on identifying variable and fixed costs. She says this type of analysis is crucial to understanding break-even points and maintaining the right product mix. "This wonderful mix allows us to expand our categories of products offered," says Wang. "That selection has grown to over 3,000 products in more than 150 different shopping categories."

Wang's keen sense for business and Chinese culture gives her unique insight into how product costs relate to sales volume and profits. As a result, ChinaSprout does not only achieve its break-even point, it markedly exceeds it. Wang also tracks individual products in her multiproduct offerings. With a focus on cost-volume-profit analysis, Wang says she is able to expand and continually look for "culturally relevant products and services to an increasing number of Chinese American families, schools, museums, and stores."

"ChinaSprout has become the most popular destination for Chinese cultural and educational products," says Wang. Each product must pass a cost-volume-profit and break-even analysis. This yields a unique product offering. "There is no store in any of the Chinatowns across the U.S. that carries our products," says Wang proudly. Moreover, "most of our products are sourced directly from China."

Customer satisfaction is equally important. Wang explains how ChinaSprout constantly draws on feedback collected from its customers. "A key success factor ... is to keep in contact with your customers," says Wang. It has been a "great pleasure and joy to serve such an open-hearted and multicultural community. *Xiexie and Xin Nian Kuai Le!*" she exclaims.

[Sources: *ChinaSprout Website,* May 2006; *Earnshaw's Magazine,* August 2003; *National Association of Women Business Owners,* March 2003; *Multichannel Merchant,* June 2002; *ShopSite Website,* 2006]

This chapter describes different types of costs and shows how changes in a company's operating volume affect these costs. The chapter also analyzes a company's costs and sales to understand how different operating strategies affect profit or loss. Managers use this type of analysis to forecast what will happen if changes are made to costs, sales volume, selling prices, or product mix. They then use these forecasts to select the best business strategy for the company.

Cost-Volume-Profit Analysis

Identifying Cost Behavior
- Fixed costs
- Variable costs
- Mixed costs
- Step-wise costs
- Curvilinear costs

Measuring Cost Behavior
- Scatter diagrams
- High-low method
- Least-squares regression
- Comparison of cost estimation methods

Using Break-Even Analysis
- Computing break-even
- Preparing a cost-volume-profit chart
- Making assumptions in cost-volume-profit analysis

Applying Cost-Volume-Profit Analysis
- Computing income from sales and costs
- Computing sales for target income
- Computing margin of safety
- Using sensitivity analysis
- Computing multiproduct break-even

Identifying Cost Behavior

Planning a company's future activities and events is a crucial phase in successful management. One of the first steps in planning is to predict the volume of activity, the costs to be incurred, sales to be made, and profit to be received. An important tool to help managers carry out this step is **cost-volume-profit (CVP) analysis,** which helps them predict how changes in costs and sales levels affect income. In its basic form, CVP analysis involves computing the sales level at which a company neither earns an income nor incurs a loss, called the *break-even point.* For this reason, this basic form of cost-volume-profit analysis is often called *break-even analysis.* Managers use variations of CVP analysis to answer questions such as these:

Point: *Profit* is another term for *income.*

- What sales volume is needed to earn a target income?
- What is the change in income if selling prices decline and sales volume increases?
- How much does income increase if we install a new machine to reduce labor costs?
- What is the income effect if we change the sales mix of our products or services?

Consequently, cost-volume-profit analysis is useful in a wide range of business decisions.
    Conventional cost-volume-profit analysis requires management to classify all costs as either *fixed* or *variable* with respect to production or sales volume. The remainder of this section discusses the concepts of fixed and variable cost behavior as they relate to CVP analysis.

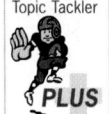

Topic Tackler

PLUS

22-1

C1 Describe different types of cost behavior in relation to production and sales volume.

Fixed Costs

A *fixed cost* remains unchanged in amount when the volume of activity varies from period to period within a relevant range. For example, $5,000 in monthly rent paid for a factory building remains the same whether the factory operates with a single eight-hour shift or around the clock with three shifts. This means that rent cost is the same each month at any level of output from zero to the plant's full productive capacity. Notice that while *total* fixed cost does not change as the level of production changes the fixed cost *per unit* of output decreases as volume increases. For instance, if 20 units are produced when monthly rent is $5,000, the average rent cost per unit is $250 (computed as $5,000/20 units). When production increases to 100 units per month, the average cost per unit decreases to $50 (computed as $5,000/100 units). The average cost decreases to $10 per unit if production increases to 500 units per month. Common examples of fixed costs include depreciation, property taxes, office salaries, and many service department costs.

Decision Insight

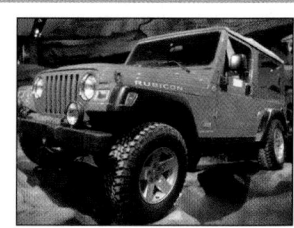

Cost Driven Fixed costs were a driving force behind the **Daimler-Benz** and **Chrysler** merger. The auto business has huge fixed costs, mainly in plant and equipment. This means that with higher sales volume, fixed costs can be spread over more units. This yields lower fixed costs (and price) per auto.

When production volume and costs are graphed, units of product are usually plotted on the *horizontal axis* and dollars of cost are plotted on the *vertical axis*. Fixed costs then are represented as a horizontal line because they remain constant at all levels of production. To illustrate, the graph in Exhibit 22.1 shows that fixed costs remain at $32,000 at all production levels up to the company's monthly capacity of 2,000 units of output. The *relevant range* for fixed costs in Exhibit 22.1 is 0 to 2,000 units. If the relevant range changes (that is, production capacity extends beyond this range), the amount of fixed costs will likely change.

Example: If the fixed cost line in Exhibit 22.1 is shifted upward, does the total cost line shift up, down, or remain in the same place? *Answer:* It shifts up by the same amount.

Exhibit 22.1

Relations of Fixed and Variable Costs to Volume

Example: If the level of fixed costs in Exhibit 22.1 changes, does the slope of the total cost line change? *Answer:* No, the slope doesn't change. The total cost line is simply shifted upward or downward.

Variable Costs

A *variable cost* changes in proportion to changes in volume of activity. The direct materials cost of a product is one example of a variable cost. If one unit of product requires materials costing $20, total materials costs are $200 when 10 units of product are manufactured, $400 for 20 units, $600 for 30 units, and so on. Notice that variable cost *per unit* remains constant but the *total* amount of variable cost changes with the level of production. In addition to direct materials, common variable costs include direct labor (if employees are paid per unit), sales commissions, shipping costs, and some overhead costs.

When variable costs are plotted on a graph of cost and volume, they appear as a straight line starting at the zero cost level. This straight line is upward (positive) sloping. The line rises as volume of activity increases. A variable cost line using a $20 per unit cost is graphed in Exhibit 22.1.

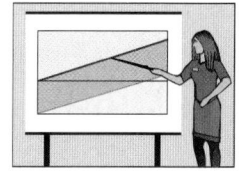

Point: Fixed costs are constant in total but vary (decline) per unit as more units are produced. Variable costs vary in total but are fixed per unit.

Mixed Costs

A **mixed cost** includes both fixed and variable cost components. For example, compensation for sales representatives often includes a fixed monthly salary and a variable commission based on sales. The total cost line in Exhibit 22.1 is a mixed cost. Like a fixed cost, it is greater than zero when volume is zero, but unlike a fixed cost, it increases steadily in proportion to increases in volume. The mixed cost line in Exhibit 22.1 starts on the vertical axis at the $32,000 fixed cost point. Thus, at the zero volume level, total cost equals the fixed costs. As the activity level increases, the mixed cost line increases at an amount equal to the variable cost per unit. This line is highest when volume of activity is at 2,000 units (the end point of the relevant range). In CVP analysis, mixed costs are often separated into fixed and variable components. The fixed component is added to other fixed costs, and the variable component is added to other variable costs.

Step-Wise Costs

A **step-wise cost** reflects a step pattern in costs. Salaries of production supervisors often behave in a step-wise manner in that their salaries are fixed within a *relevant range* of the current production volume. However, if production volume expands significantly (for example, with the addition of another shift), additional supervisors must be hired. This means that the total cost for supervisory salaries goes up by a lump-sum amount. Similarly, if volume takes another significant step up, supervisory salaries will increase by another lump sum. This behavior reflects a step-wise cost, also known as *stair-step costs,* which is graphed in Exhibit 22.2. See how it is flat within ranges (steps). Then, when volume significantly changes, it shifts to another level for that range (step).

Exhibit 22.2

Step-Wise and
Curvilinear Costs

In a conventional CVP analysis, a step-wise cost is usually treated as either a fixed cost or a variable cost. This treatment involves manager judgment and depends on the width of the range and the expected volume. To illustrate, suppose after the production of every 25 snowboards, an operator lubricates the finishing machine. The cost of this lubricant reflects a step-wise pattern. Also, suppose that after the production of every 1,000 units, the snowboard cutting tool is replaced. Again, this is a step-wise cost. Note that the range of 25 snowboards is much narrower than the range of 1,000 snowboards. Some managers might treat the lubricant cost as a variable cost and the cutting tool cost as a fixed cost.

Point: Computer spreadsheets are important and effective tools for CVP analysis and for analyzing alternative "what-if" strategies.

Curvilinear Costs

A variable cost, as explained, is a *linear* cost; that is, it increases at a constant rate as volume of activity increases. A **curvilinear cost,** also called *nonlinear cost,* increases at a nonconstant rate as volume increases. When graphed, curvilinear costs appear as a curved line. Exhibit 22.2 shows a curvilinear cost beginning at zero when production is zero and then increasing at different rates.

An example of a curvilinear cost is total direct labor cost when workers are paid by the hour. At low to medium levels of production, adding more employees allows each of them to specialize by doing certain tasks repeatedly instead of doing several different tasks. This often yields additional units of output at lower costs. A point is eventually reached at which adding more employees creates inefficiencies. For instance, a large crew demands more time and effort in communicating and coordinating their efforts. While adding employees in this case increases

Point: Cost-volume-profit analysis helped Rod Canion, Jim Harris, and Bill Murto raise start-up capital of $20 million to launch **Compaq Computer.** They showed that break-even volumes were attainable within the first year.

output, the labor cost per unit increases, and the total labor cost goes up at a steeper slope. This pattern is seen in Exhibit 22.2 where the curvilinear cost curve starts at zero, rises, flattens out, and then increases at a faster rate as output nears the maximum.

Quick Check
Answers—p. 899

1. Which of the following statements is typically true? (*a*) Variable cost per unit increases as volume increases, (*b*) fixed cost per unit decreases as volume increases, or (*c*) a curvilinear cost includes both fixed and variable elements.

2. Describe the behavior of a fixed cost.

3. If cost per unit of activity remains constant (fixed), why is it called a variable cost?

Measuring Cost Behavior

Identifying and measuring cost behavior requires careful analysis and judgment. An important part of this process is to identify costs that can be classified as either fixed or variable, which often requires analysis of past cost behavior. Three methods are commonly used to analyze past costs: scatter diagrams, high-low method, and least-squares regression. Each method is discussed in this section using the unit and cost data shown in Exhibit 22.3, which is taken from a start-up company that uses units produced as the activity base in estimating cost behavior.

P1   Determine cost estimates using three different methods.

Scatter Diagrams

Scatter diagrams display past cost and unit data in graphical form. In preparing a scatter diagram, units are plotted on the horizontal axis and cost is plotted on the vertical axis. Each individual point on a scatter diagram reflects the cost and number of units for a prior period. In Exhibit 22.4, the prior 12 months' cost and number of units are graphed. Each point reflects total costs incurred and units produced for one of those months. For instance, the point labeled March had units produced of 25,000 and costs of $25,000.

Month	Units Produced	Total Cost
January	17,500	$20,500
February	27,500	21,500
March	25,000	25,000
April	35,000	21,500
May	47,500	25,500
June	22,500	18,500
July	30,000	23,500
August	52,500	28,500
September	37,500	26,000
October	57,500	26,000
November	62,500	31,000
December	67,500	29,000

Exhibit 22.3

Data for Estimating Cost Behavior

Exhibit 22.4

Scatter Diagram

The **estimated line of cost behavior** is drawn on a scatter diagram to reflect the relation between cost and unit volume. This line best visually "fits" the points in a scatter diagram. Fitting this line demands judgment. The line drawn in Exhibit 22.4 intersects the vertical axis at approximately $16,000, which reflects fixed cost. To compute variable cost per unit, or the slope, we perform three steps. First, we select any two points on the horizontal axis (units), say 0 and 40,000. Second, we draw a vertical line from each of these points to intersect the estimated line of cost behavior. The point on the vertical axis (cost) corresponding to the 40,000 units point that intersects the estimated line is roughly $24,000. Similarly, the cost corresponding to zero units is $16,000 (the fixed cost point). Third, we compute the slope of the line, or variable cost, as the change in cost divided by the change in units. Exhibit 22.5 shows this computation.

Exhibit 22.5

Variable Cost per Unit
(Scatter Diagram)

Example: In Exhibits 22.4 and 22.5, if units are projected at 30,000, what is predicted cost? *Answer:* Approximately $22,000.

$$\frac{\textbf{Change in cost}}{\textbf{Change in units}} = \frac{\$24,000 - \$16,000}{40,000 - 0} = \frac{\$8,000}{40,000} = \$0.20 \text{ per unit}$$

Variable cost is $0.20 per unit. Thus, the cost equation that management will use to estimate costs for different unit levels is **$16,000 plus $0.20 per unit**.

High-Low Method

The **high-low method** is a way to estimate the cost equation by graphically connecting the two cost amounts at the highest and lowest unit volumes. In our case, the lowest number of units is 17,500, and the highest is 67,500. The costs corresponding to these unit volumes are $20,500 and $29,000, respectively (see data in Exhibit 22.3). The estimated line of cost behavior for the high-low method is then drawn by connecting these two points on the scatter diagram corresponding to the lowest and highest unit volumes as follows.

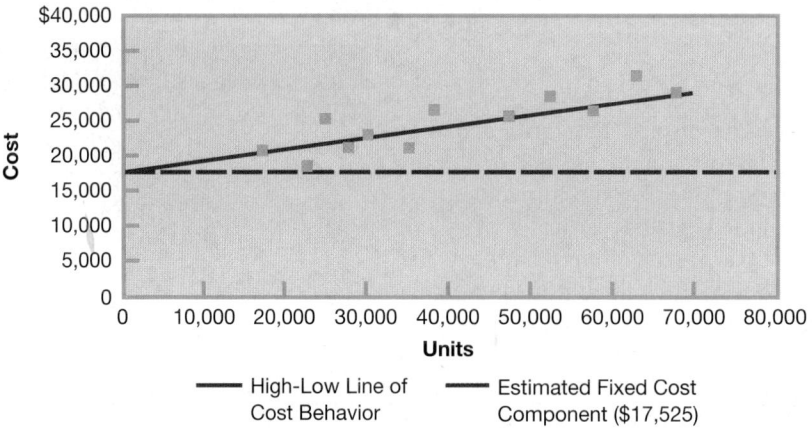

Point: Note that the high-low method identifies the high and low points of the volume (activity) base, and the costs linked with those extremes—which may not be the highest and lowest costs.

The variable cost per unit is determined as the change in cost divided by the change in units and uses the data from the high and low unit volumes. This results in a slope, or variable cost per unit, of $0.17 as computed in Exhibit 22.6.

Exhibit 22.6

Variable Cost per Unit
(High-Low Method)

$$\frac{\textbf{Change in cost}}{\textbf{Change in units}} = \frac{\$29,000 - \$20,500}{67,500 - 17,500} = \frac{\$8,500}{50,000} = \$0.17 \text{ per unit}$$

To estimate fixed cost for the high-low method, we use the knowledge that total cost equals fixed cost plus variable cost per unit times the number of units. Then, we pick either the high or low point to determine fixed cost. This computation is shown in Exhibit 22.7—where we use the high point (67,500 units) in determining fixed cost of $17,525. By coincidence, use of the low point (17,500 units) yields the same fixed cost estimate: $20,500 = Fixed cost + ($0.17 per unit × 17,500), or Fixed cost = $17,525.

Exhibit 22.7

Fixed Cost (High-Low Method)

Total cost = Fixed cost + (Variable cost × Units)

$29,000 = Fixed cost + ($0.17 per unit × 67,500 units)

Then,

Fixed cost = $17,525

Thus, the cost equation used to estimate costs at different units is **$17,525 plus $0.17 per unit**. This cost equation differs slightly from that determined from the scatter diagram method. A deficiency of the high-low method is that it ignores all cost points except the highest and lowest. The result is less precision because the high-low method uses the most extreme points rather than the more usual conditions likely to recur.

Least-Squares Regression

Least-squares regression is a statistical method for identifying cost behavior. For our purposes, we use the cost equation estimated from this method but leave the computational details for more advanced courses. Such computations for least-squares regression are readily done using most spreadsheet programs or calculators.

The regression cost equation for the data presented in Exhibit 22.3 is **$16,947 plus $0.19 per unit**; that is, fixed cost is estimated as $16,947 and variable cost at $0.19 per unit. Both costs are reflected in the following graph.

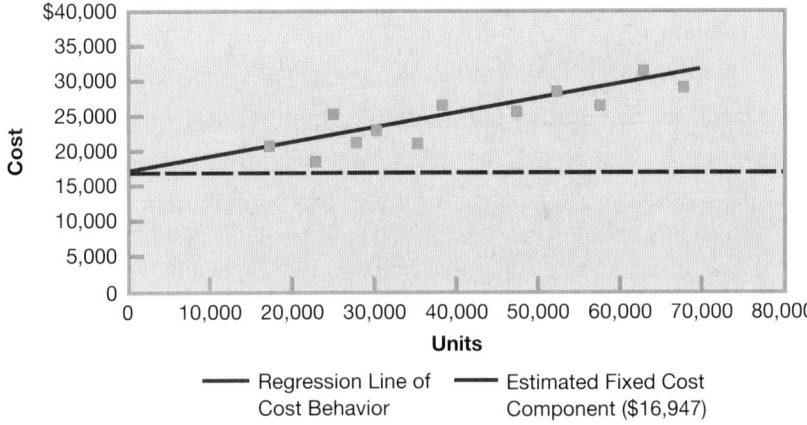

— Regression Line of   — Estimated Fixed Cost
    Cost Behavior   Component ($16,947)

Comparison of Cost Estimation Methods

The three cost estimation methods result in slightly different estimates of fixed and variable costs as summarized in Exhibit 22.8. Estimates from the scatter diagram are based on a visual fit of the cost line and are subject to interpretation. Estimates from the high-low method use only two sets of values corresponding to the lowest and highest unit volumes. Estimates from least-squares regression use a statistical technique and all available data points.

A1   Compare the scatter diagram, high-low, and regression methods of estimating costs.

Exhibit 22.8

Comparison of Cost Estimation Methods

Estimation Method	Fixed Cost	Variable Cost
Scatter diagram	$16,000	$0.20 per unit
High-low method	17,525	0.17 per unit
Least-squares regression	16,947	0.19 per unit

We must remember that all three methods use *past data.* Thus, cost estimates resulting from these methods are only as good as the data used for estimation. Managers must establish that the data are reliable in deriving cost estimates for the future.

Quick Check   Answers—p. 899

4. Which of the following methods is likely to yield the most precise estimated line of cost behavior? (*a*) high-low, (*b*) least-squares regression, or (*c*) scatter diagram.

5. What is the primary weakness of the high-low method?

6. Using conventional CVP analysis, a mixed cost should be (*a*) disregarded, (*b*) treated as a fixed cost, or (*c*) separated into fixed and variable components.

Using Break-Even Analysis

Break-even analysis is a special case of cost-volume-profit analysis. This section describes break-even analysis by computing the break-even point and preparing a CVP (or break-even) chart.

Contribution Margin and Its Measures

A2 Compute contribution margin and describe what it reveals about a company's cost structure.

We explained how managers classify costs by behavior. This often refers to classifying costs as being fixed or variable with respect to volume of activity. In manufacturing companies, volume of activity usually refers to the number of units produced. We then classify a cost as either fixed or variable, depending on whether total cost changes as the number of units produced changes. Once we separate costs by behavior, we can then compute a product's contribution margin. **Contribution margin per unit,** or *unit contribution margin,* is the amount a product's unit selling price exceeds its total unit variable cost. This excess amount contributes to covering fixed costs and generating profits on a per unit basis. Exhibit 22.9 shows the contribution margin per unit formula.

Exhibit 22.9

Contribution Margin per Unit

Contribution margin per unit = Sales price per unit − Total variable cost per unit

Users often use contribution margin in the form of a **contribution margin ratio,** which is the percent of a unit's selling price that exceeds total unit variable cost. It can be interpreted as the percent of each sales dollar that remains after deducting total unit variable cost. Exhibit 22.10 shows the formula for the contribution margin ratio.

Exhibit 22.10

Contribution Margin Ratio

$$\text{Contribution margin ratio} = \frac{\text{Contribution margin per unit}}{\text{Sales price per unit}}$$

To illustrate the use of contribution margin, let's consider **Rydell,** which sells footballs for $100 per unit and incurs variable costs of $70 per unit sold. Its fixed costs are $24,000 per month with monthly capacity of 1,800 units (footballs). Rydell's contribution margin per unit is $30, which is computed as follows.

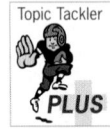

Topic Tackler

PLUS

22-2

Selling price per unit	$100
Variable cost per unit	70
Contribution margin per unit	$ 30

Decision Maker   Answer—p. 899

Sales Manager   You are evaluating orders from two customers but can accept only one of the orders because of your company's limited capacity. The first order is for 100 units of a product with a contribution margin ratio of 60% and a selling price of $1,000. The second order is for 500 units of a product with a contribution margin ratio of 20% and a selling price of $800. The incremental fixed costs are the same for both orders. Which order do you accept?

Its contribution margin ratio is 30%, computed as $30/$100. This reveals that for each unit sold, Rydell has $30 that contribute to covering fixed cost and profit. If we consider sales in dollars, a contribution margin of 30% implies that for each $1 in sales, Rydell has $0.30 that contributes to fixed cost and profit.

Computing Break-Even Point

The **break-even point** is the sales level at which a company neither earns a profit nor incurs a loss. The concept of break-even is applicable to nearly all organizations, activities, and events. One of the most important items of information when launching a project is whether it will break even, that is, whether sales will at least cover total costs. The break-even point can be expressed in either units or dollars of sales.

P2 Compute break-even point for a single product company.

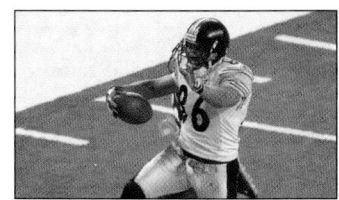

To illustrate the computation of break-even analysis, let's again look at Rydell, which sells footballs for $100 per unit and incurs $70 of variable costs per unit sold. Its fixed costs are $24,000 per month. Rydell breaks even for the month when it sells 800 footballs (sales volume of $80,000). We compute this break-even point using the formula in Exhibit 22.11. This formula uses the contribution margin per unit, which for Rydell is $30 ($100 − $70). From this we can compute break-even sales volume as $24,000/$30, or 800 units per month.

$$\text{Break-even point in units} = \frac{\text{Fixed costs}}{\text{Contribution margin per unit}}$$

Exhibit 22.11

Formula for Computing Break-Even Sales (in units)[1]

At a price of $100 per unit, monthly sales of 800 units yields sales dollars of $80,000 (called *break-even sales dollars*). This $80,000 break-even sales can be computed directly using the formula in Exhibit 22.12.

$$\text{Break-even point in dollars} = \frac{\text{Fixed costs}}{\text{Contribution margin ratio}}$$

Exhibit 22.12

Formula for Computing Break-Even Sales (in dollars)[2]

Rydell's break-even point in dollars is computed as $24,000/0.30, or $80,000 of monthly sales. To verify that Rydell's break-even point equals $80,000 (or 800 units), we prepare a simplified income statement in Exhibit 22.13. It shows that the $80,000 revenue from sales of 800 units exactly equals the sum of variable and fixed costs.

Exhibit 22.13

Contribution Margin Income Statement for Break-Even Sales

RYDELL COMPANY	
Contribution Margin Income Statement (at Break-even)	
For Month Ended January 31, 2008	
Sales (800 units at $100 each)	$80,000
Variable costs (800 units at $70 each)	56,000
Contribution margin	24,000
Fixed costs	24,000
Net income	$ 0

The statement in Exhibit 22.13 is called a *contribution margin income statement.* It differs in format from a conventional income statement in two ways. First, it separately classifies costs and expenses as variable or fixed. Second, it reports contribution margin (Sales − Variable costs). The contribution margin income statement format is used in this chapter's assignment materials because of its usefulness in CVP analysis.

---

[1] To obtain this formula, we define S = Sales in units; R = Revenue per unit; F = Fixed costs per period; V = Variable cost per unit; $S \times R$ = Dollar sales; $S \times V$ = Total variable cost; and contribution margin per unit = $R - V$. At break-even, net income is zero, so therefore,

$$\text{Sales} = \text{Fixed costs} + \text{Variable costs}$$
$$(S \times R) = F + (S \times V)$$
$$(S \times R) - (S \times V) = F$$
$$S \times (R - V) = F$$
$$S = F/(R - V)$$
$$S = F/\text{Contribution margin per unit}$$

[2] To obtain this formula, recall that: Contribution margin ratio = $(R - V)/R$. Then, at break-even,

$$S = F/(R - V) \text{ [from footnote 1]}$$
$$S \times R = (F \times R)/(R - V)$$
$$S \times R = F \times [R/(R - V)]$$
$$S \times R = F/[(R - V)/R]$$
$$S \times R = F/\text{Contribution margin ratio}$$

Preparing a Cost-Volume-Profit Chart

P3 Graph costs and sales for a single product company.

Exhibit 22.14 is a graph of Rydell's cost-volume-profit relations. This graph is called a **cost-volume-profit (CVP) chart,** or a *break-even chart* or *break-even graph.* The horizontal axis is the number of units produced and sold and the vertical axis is dollars of sales and costs. The lines in the chart depict both sales and costs at different output levels.

Exhibit 22.14

Cost-Volume-Profit Chart

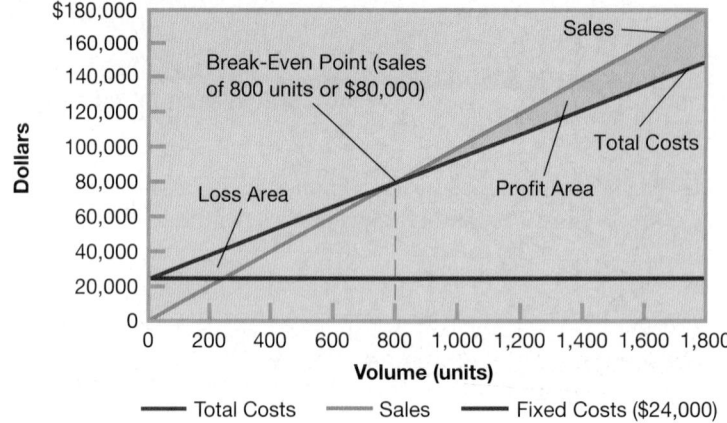

We follow three steps to prepare a CVP chart, which can also be drawn with computer programs that convert numeric data to graphs:

1. Plot fixed costs on the vertical axis ($24,000 for Rydell). Draw a horizontal line at this level to show that fixed costs remain unchanged regardless of output volume (drawing this fixed cost line is not essential to the chart).

2. Draw the total (variable plus fixed) costs line for a relevant range of volume levels. This line starts at the fixed costs level on the vertical axis because total costs equal fixed costs at zero volume. The slope of the total cost line equals the variable cost per unit ($70). To draw the line, compute the total costs for any volume level, and connect this point with the vertical axis intercept ($24,000). Do not draw this line beyond the productive capacity for the planning period (1,800 units for Rydell).

3. Draw the sales line. Start at the origin (zero units and zero dollars of sales) and make the slope of this line equal to the selling price per unit ($100). To sketch the line, compute dollar sales for any volume level and connect this point with the origin. Do not extend this line beyond the productive capacity. Total sales will be at the highest level at maximum capacity.

Example: In Exhibit 22.14, the sales line intersects the total cost line at 800 units. At what point would the two lines intersect if selling price is increased by 20% to $120 per unit? *Answer:* $24,000/ ($120 − $70) = 480 units

The total costs line and the sales line intersect at 800 units in Exhibit 22.14, which is the break-even point, the point where total dollar sales of $80,000 equals the sum of both fixed and variable costs ($80,000).

On either side of the break-even point, the vertical distance between the sales line and the total costs line at any specific volume reflects the profit or loss expected at that point. At volume levels to the left of the break-even point, this vertical distance is the amount of the expected loss because the total costs line is above the total sales line. At volume levels to the right of the break-even point, the vertical distance represents the expected profit because the total sales line is above the total costs line.

Making Assumptions in Cost-Volume-Profit Analysis

C2 Identify assumptions in cost-volume-profit analysis and explain their impact.

Cost-volume-profit analysis assumes that relations can normally be expressed as simple lines similar to those in Exhibits 22.4 and 22.14. Such assumptions allow users to answer several important questions, but the usefulness of the answers depends on the validity of three assumptions: (1) constant selling price per unit, (2) constant variable costs per unit, and (3) constant total fixed costs. These assumptions are not always realistic, but they do not necessarily limit the usefulness of CVP analysis as a way to better understand costs and sales. This section discusses these assumptions and other issues for CVP analysis.

Working with Assumptions   The behavior of individual costs and sales often is not perfectly consistent with CVP assumptions. If the expected costs and sales behavior differ from the assumptions, the results of CVP analysis can be limited. Still, we can perform useful analyses in spite of limitations with these assumptions for several reasons.

Summing costs can offset individual deviations.   Deviations from assumptions with individual costs are often minor when these costs are summed. That is, individual variable cost items may not be perfectly variable, but when we sum these variable costs, their individual deviations can offset each other. This means the assumption of variable cost behavior can be proper for total variable costs. Similarly, an assumption that total fixed costs are constant can be proper even when individual fixed cost items are not exactly constant.

> **Point:** CVP analysis can be very useful for business decision making even when its assumptions are not strictly met.

CVP is applied to a relevant range of operations.   Sales, variable costs, and fixed costs often are reasonably reflected in straight lines on a graph when the assumptions are applied over a relevant range. The **relevant range of operations** is the normal operating range for a business. Except for unusually difficult or prosperous times, management typically plans for operations within a range of volume neither close to zero nor at maximum capacity. The relevant range excludes extremely high and low operating levels that are unlikely to occur. The validity of assuming that a specific cost is fixed or variable is more acceptable when operations are within the relevant range. As shown in Exhibit 22.2, a curvilinear cost can be treated as variable and linear if the relevant range covers volumes where it has a nearly constant slope. If the normal range of activity changes, some costs might need reclassification.

CVP analysis yields estimates.   CVP analysis yields approximate answers to questions about costs, volumes, and profits. These answers do not have to be precise because the analysis makes rough estimates about the future. As long as managers understand that CVP analysis gives estimates, it can be a useful tool for starting the planning process. Other qualitative factors also must be considered.

Working with Output Measures   CVP analysis usually describes the level of activity in terms of *sales volume,* which can be expressed in terms of either units sold or dollar sales. However, other measures of output exist. For instance, a manufacturer can use the number of units produced as a measure of output. Also, to simplify analysis, we sometimes assume that production level is the same as the sales level. That is, inventory levels do not change. This often is justified by arguing that CVP analysis provides only approximations.

> **Example:** If selling price declines, what happens to the break-even point? *Answer:* It increases.

Quick Check
Answers—p. 899

7. Fixed cost divided by the contribution margin ratio yields the (*a*) break-even point in dollars, (*b*) contribution margin per unit, or (*c*) break-even point in units.

8. A company sells a product for $90 per unit with variable costs of $54 per unit. What is the contribution margin ratio?

9. Refer to Quick Check (8). If fixed costs for the period are $90,000, what is the break-even point in dollars?

10. What three basic assumptions are used in CVP analysis?

Applying Cost-Volume-Profit Analysis

Managers consider a variety of strategies in planning business operations. Cost-volume-profit analysis is useful in helping managers evaluate the likely effects of these strategies, which is the focus of this section.

Computing Income from Sales and Costs

C3   Describe several applications of cost-volume-profit analysis.

An important question managers often need an answer to is "What is the predicted income from a predicted level of sales?" To answer this, we look at four variables in CVP analysis. These variables and their relations to income (pretax) are shown in Exhibit 22.15. We use these relations to compute expected income from predicted sales and cost levels.

Exhibit 22.15

Income Relations in CVP Analysis

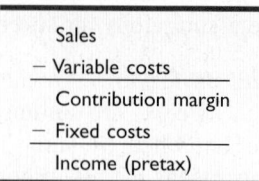

Sales
— Variable costs
    Contribution margin
— Fixed costs
    Income (pretax)

To illustrate, let's assume that Rydell's management expects to sell 1,500 units in January 2008. What is the amount of income if this sales level is achieved? Following Exhibit 22.15, we compute Rydell's expected income in Exhibit 22.16.

Exhibit 22.16

Computing Expected Pretax Income from Expected Sales

RYDELL COMPANY
Contribution Margin Income Statement
For Month Ended January 31, 2008

Sales (1,500 units at $100 each)	$150,000
Variable costs (1,500 units at $70 each)	105,000
Contribution margin	45,000
Fixed costs	24,000
Income (pretax)	$ 21,000

The $21,000 income is pretax. To find the amount of *after-tax* income from selling 1,500 units, management must apply the proper tax rate. Assume that the tax rate is 25%. Then, we can prepare the after-tax income statement shown in Exhibit 22.17. We can also compute pretax income as after-tax income divided by (1 − tax rate); for Rydell, this is $15,750/(1 − 0.25), or $21,000.

Exhibit 22.17

Computing Expected After-Tax Income from Expected Sales

RYDELL COMPANY
Contribution Margin Income Statement
For Month Ended January 31, 2008

Sales (1,500 units at $100 each)	$150,000
Variable costs (1,500 units at $70 each)	105,000
Contribution margin	45,000
Fixed costs	24,000
Pretax income	21,000
Income taxes (25%)	5,250
Net income (after tax)	$ 15,750

Management then assesses whether this income is an adequate return on assets invested. Management should also consider whether sales and income can be increased by raising or lowering prices. CVP analysis is a good tool for addressing these kinds of "what-if" questions.

Computing Sales for a Target Income

"How many units must I sell to earn $50,000?"

Many companies' annual plans are based on certain income targets (sometimes called *budgets*). Rydell's income target for this year is to increase income by 10% over the prior year. When prior year income is known, Rydell easily computes its target income. CVP analysis helps to determine the sales level needed to achieve the target income. Computing this sales level is important because planning for the year is then based on this level. We use the formula shown in Exhibit 22.18 to compute sales for a target *after-tax* income.

$$\text{Dollar sales at target after-tax income} = \frac{\text{Fixed costs} + \text{Target pretax income}}{\text{Contribution margin ratio}}$$

Exhibit 22.18

Computing Sales (dollars) for a Target After-Tax Income[3]

To illustrate, Rydell has monthly fixed costs of $24,000 and a 30% contribution margin ratio. Assume that it sets a target monthly after-tax income of $9,000 when the tax rate is 25%. This means the pretax income is targeted at $12,000 [$9,000/(1 − 0.25)] with a tax expense of $3,000. Using the formula in Exhibit 22.18, we find that $120,000 of sales is needed to produce a $9,000 after-tax income as shown in Exhibit 22.19.

Example: If variable costs decline, what happens to the break-even point? *Answer:* It decreases.

$$\text{Dollar sales at target after-tax income} = \frac{\$24,000 + \$12,000}{30\%} = \$120,000$$

Exhibit 22.19

Rydell's Dollar Sales for a Target Income

We can alternatively compute *unit sales* instead of dollar sales. To do this, we substitute *contribution margin per unit* for the contribution margin ratio in the denominator. This gives the number of units to sell to reach the target after-tax income. Exhibit 22.20 illustrates this for Rydell. The two computations in Exhibits 22.19 and 22.20 are equivalent because sales of 1,200 units at $100 per unit equals $120,000 of sales.

Point: Break-even is a special case of the formulas in Exhibits 22.18 and 22.20; simply set target pretax income to $0 and the formulas reduce to those in Exhibits 22.11 and 22.12.

$$\text{Unit sales at target aftertax income} = \frac{\text{Fixed costs} + \text{Target pretax income}}{\text{Contribution margin per unit}}$$
$$= \frac{\$24,000 + \$12,000}{\$30} = 1,200 \text{ units}$$

Exhibit 22.20

Computing Sales (units) for a Target After-Tax Income

Computing the Margin of Safety

All companies wish to sell more than the break-even number of units. The excess of expected sales over the break-even sales level is called a company's **margin of safety,** the amount that sales can drop before the company incurs a loss. It can be expressed in units, dollars, or even as a percent of the predicted level of sales. To illustrate, if Rydell's expected sales are $100,000, the margin of safety is $20,000 above break-even sales of $80,000. As a percent, the margin of safety is 20% of expected sales as shown in Exhibit 22.21.

> **Decision Ethics**   Answer—p. 899
>
> **Supervisor** Your team is conducting a cost-volume-profit analysis for a new product. Different sales projections have different incomes. One member suggests picking numbers yielding favorable income because any estimate is "as good as any other." Another member points to a scatter diagram of 20 months' production on a comparable product and suggests dropping unfavorable data points for cost estimation. What do you do?

---

[3] To obtain this formula, we define S = Sales in units; R = Revenue per unit; F = Fixed costs per period; V = Variable cost per unit; N = Target net income; T = Income taxes; $S \times R$ = Dollar sales; $S \times V$ = Total variable cost; and the Contribution margin ratio = $(R - V)/R$. The after-tax target net income is then defined as:

$$(S \times R) - F - (S \times V) - T = N$$
$$(S \times R) - (S \times V) = F + N + T$$
$$S \times (R - V) = F + N + T$$
$$S = (F + N + T)/(R - V)$$
$$S \times R = [(F + N + T) \times R]/(R - V)$$
$$S \times R = (F + N + T) \times [R/(R - V)]$$
$$S \times R = (F + N + T)/[(R - V)/R]$$
$$S \times R = (F + N + T)/\text{Contribution margin ratio}$$

Exhibit 22.21

Computing Margin of Safety (in percent)

$$\text{Margin of safety (in percent)} = \frac{\text{Expected sales} - \text{Break-even sales}}{\text{Expected sales}}$$

$$= \frac{\$100,000 - \$80,000}{\$100,000} = 20\%$$

Management must assess whether the margin of safety is adequate in light of factors such as sales variability, competition, consumer tastes, and economic conditions.

Using Sensitivity Analysis

Knowing the effects of changing some estimates used in CVP analysis is often useful because they are *estimates,* not actual values. For instance, we might want to know what happens if we reduce a product's selling price to increase sales. Or we might want to know what happens to income if we automate a currently manual process. We can use CVP analysis to predict income if we can describe how these changes affect a company's fixed costs, variable costs, selling price, and volume.

To illustrate, assume that Rydell Company is looking into buying a new machine that would increase monthly fixed costs from $24,000 to $30,000 but decrease variable costs from $70 per unit to $60 per unit. The machine is used to produce output whose selling price will remain unchanged at $100. This results in increases in both the unit contribution margin and the contribution margin ratio. The revised contribution margin per unit is $40 ($100 − $60), and the revised contribution margin ratio is 40% of selling price ($40/$100). Using CVP analysis, Rydell's revised break-even point in dollars would be $75,000 as computed in Exhibit 22.22.

Decision Insight

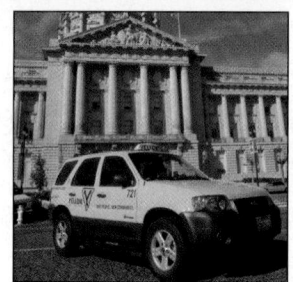

Eco-CVP Ford Escape, Toyota Prius, and Honda Insight are hybrids. Many promise to save owners $1,000 or more a year in fuel costs relative to comparables and they generate less greenhouse gases. Are these models economically feasible? Analysts estimate that **Ford** can break even with its Escape when a $3,000 premium is paid over comparable gas-based models.

Example: If fixed costs decline, what happens to the break-even point? *Answer:* It decreases.

Exhibit 22.22

Revising Breakeven When Changes Occur

$$\text{Revised break-even point in dollars} = \frac{\text{Revised fixed costs}}{\text{Revised contribution margin ratio}} = \frac{\$30,000}{40\%} = \$75,000$$

Point: Price competition led paging companies to give business to resellers—companies that lease services at a discount and then resell to subscribers. **Paging Network** charged some resellers under $1 per month, less than a third of what is needed to break even. Its CEO now admits the low-price strategy was flawed.

The revised fixed costs and the revised contribution margin ratio can be used to address other issues including computation of (1) expected income for a given sales level and (2) the sales level needed to earn a target income. Another use of sensitivity analysis is to generate different sets of revenue and cost estimates that are *optimistic, pessimistic,* and *most likely*. Different CVP analyses based on these estimates provide different scenarios that management can analyze and use in planning business strategy.

Quick Check

Answers—pp. 899–900

11. A company has fixed costs of $50,000 and a 25% contribution margin ratio. What dollar sales are necessary to achieve an after-tax net income of $120,000 if the tax rate is 20%? (*a*) $800,000, (*b*) $680,000, or (*c*) $600,000.

12. If a company's contribution margin ratio decreases from 50% to 25%, what can be said about unit sales needed to achieve the same target income level?

13. What is a company's margin of safety?

Computing Multiproduct Break-Even Point

To this point, we have looked only at cases where the company sells a single product or service. This was to keep the basic CVP analysis simple. However, many companies sell multiple products or services, and we can modify the CVP analysis for use in these cases. An important assumption in a multiproduct setting is that the sales mix of different products is known and remains constant during the planning period. **Sales mix** is the ratio (proportion) of the sales volumes for the various products. For instance, if a company normally sells 10,000 footballs, 5,000 softballs, and 4,000 basketballs per month, its sales mix can be expressed as 10:5:4 for footballs, softballs, and basketballs.

P4 Compute break-even point for a multiproduct company.

To apply multiproduct CVP analysis, we need to estimate the break-even point by using a **composite unit,** which consists of a specific number of units of each product in proportion to their expected sales mix. Multiproduct CVP analysis treats this composite unit as a single product. To illustrate, let's look at **Hair-Today,** a styling salon that offers three cuts: basic, ultra, and budget in the ratio of 4 basic units to 2 ultra units to 1 budget unit (expressed as 4:2:1). Management wants to estimate its break-even point for next year. Unit selling prices for these three cuts are basic, $10; ultra, $16; and budget, $8. Using the 4:2:1 sales mix, the selling price of a composite unit of the three products is computed as follows.

4 units of basic @ $10 per unit	$ 40
2 units of ultra @ $16 per unit	32
1 unit of budget @ $8 per unit	8
Selling price of a composite unit	**$80**

Hair-Today's fixed costs are $96,000 per year, and its variable costs of the three products are basic, $6.50; ultra, $9.00; and budget, $4.00. Variable costs for a composite unit of these products follow.

Point: Selling prices and variable costs are usually expressed in per unit amounts. Fixed costs are usually expressed in total amounts.

4 units of basic @ $6.50 per unit	$ 26
2 units of ultra @ $9.00 per unit	18
1 unit of budget @ $4.00 per unit	4
Variable costs of a composite unit	**$48**

Hair-Today's $32 contribution margin for a composite unit is computed by subtracting the variable costs of a composite unit ($48) from its selling price ($80). We then use the contribution margin to determine Hair-Today's break-even point in composite units in Exhibit 22.23.

$$\text{Break-even point in composite units} = \frac{\text{Fixed costs}}{\text{Contribution margin per composite unit}}$$

$$= \frac{\$96,000}{\$32} = 3,000 \text{ composite units}$$

Exhibit 22.23

Break-Even Point in Composite Units

This computation implies that Hair-Today breaks even when it sells 3,000 composite units. To determine how many units of each product it must sell to break even, we multiply the number of units of each product in the composite by 3,000 as follows.

Point: The break-even point in dollars for Exhibit 22.23 is: $96,000/($32/$80) = $240,000.

Basic:	4 × 3,000	. . . .	12,000 units
Ultra:	2 × 3,000	. . . .	6,000 units
Budget:	1 × 3,000	. . . .	3,000 units

Exhibit 22.24 verifies these results by showing Hair-Today's sales and costs at this break-even point using a contribution margin income statement.

Exhibit 22.24

Multiproduct Break-Even Income Statement

HAIR-TODAY Forecasted Contribution Margin Income Statement (at Breakeven)				
	Basic	Ultra	Budget	Totals
Sales				
Basic (12,000 @ $10)	$120,000			
Ultra (6,000 @ $16)		$96,000		
Budget (3,000 @ $8)			$24,000	
Total sales				$240,000
Variable costs				
Basic (12,000 @ $6.50)	78,000			
Ultra (6,000 @ $9)		54,000		
Budget (3,000 @ $4)			12,000	
Total variable costs				144,000
Contribution margin	$ 42,000	$42,000	$12,000	96,000
Fixed costs				96,000
Net income				$ 0

Decision Maker

Answer—p. 899

Entrepreneur   A CVP analysis indicates that your start-up, which markets electronic products, will break even with the current sales mix and price levels. You have a target income in mind. What analysis might you perform to assess likelihood for achieving this income?

A CVP analysis using composite units can be used to answer a variety of planning questions. Once a product mix is set, all answers are based on the assumption that the mix remains constant at all relevant sales levels as other factors in the analysis do. We also can vary the sales mix to see what happens under alternative strategies.

Quick Check

Answers—p. 900

14. The sales mix of a company's two products, X and Y, is 2:1. Unit variable costs for both products are $2, and unit sales price is $5 for X and $4 for Y. What is the contribution margin per composite unit? (a) $5, (b) $10, or (c) $8.

15. What additional assumption about sales mix must be made in doing a conventional CVP analysis for a company that produces and sells more than one product?

Decision Analysis   **Degree of Operating Leverage**

A3   Analyze changes in sales using the degree of operating leverage.

CVP analysis is especially useful when management begins the planning process and wishes to predict outcomes of alternative strategies. These strategies can involve changes in selling prices, fixed costs, variable costs, sales volume, and product mix. Managers are interested in seeing the effects of changes in some or all of these factors.

One goal of all managers is to get maximum benefits from their fixed costs. Managers would like to use 100% of their output capacity so that fixed costs are spread over the largest number of units. This would decrease fixed cost per unit and increase income. The extent, or relative size, of fixed costs in the total cost structure is known as **operating leverage.** Companies having a higher proportion of fixed costs in their total cost structure are said to have higher operating leverage. An example of this is a company that chooses to automate its processes instead of using direct labor, increasing its fixed costs and lowering its variable costs. A useful managerial measure to help assess the effect of changes in the level of sales on income is the **degree of operating leverage (DOL)** defined as:

DOL = Total contribution margin (in dollars)/Pretax income

To illustrate, let's return to Rydell Company. At a sales level of 1,200 units, Rydell's total contribution margin is $36,000 (1,200 units × $30 contribution margin per unit). Its pretax income, after subtracting fixed costs of $24,000, is $12,000 ($36,000 − $24,000). Rydell's degree of operating leverage at this sales level is 3.0, computed as contribution margin divided by pretax income ($36,000/$12,000). We then use DOL to measure the effect of changes in the level of sales on pretax income. For instance, suppose Rydell expects sales to increase by 10%. If this increase is within the relevant range of operations, we can expect this 10% increase in sales to result in a 30% increase in pretax income computed as DOL multiplied by the increase in sales (3.0 × 10%). Similar analyses can be done for expected decreases in sales.

Demonstration Problem

Sport Caps Co. manufactures and sells caps for different sporting events. The fixed costs of operating the company are $150,000 per month, and the variable costs for caps are $5 per unit. The caps are sold for $8 per unit. The fixed costs provide a production capacity of up to 100,000 caps per month.

Required

1. Use the formulas in the chapter to compute the following:
   a. Contribution margin per cap.
   b. Break-even point in terms of the number of caps produced and sold.
   c. Amount of net income at 30,000 caps sold per month (ignore taxes).
   d. Amount of net income at 85,000 caps sold per month (ignore taxes).
   e. Number of caps to be produced and sold to provide $45,000 of after-tax income, assuming an income tax rate of 25%.
2. Draw a CVP chart for the company, showing cap output on the horizontal axis. Identify (a) the break-even point and (b) the amount of pretax income when the level of cap production is 70,000. (Omit the fixed cost line.)
3. Use the formulas in the chapter to compute the
   a. Contribution margin ratio.
   b. Break-even point in terms of sales dollars.
   c. Amount of net income at $250,000 of sales per month (ignore taxes).
   d. Amount of net income at $600,000 of sales per month (ignore taxes).
   e. Dollars of sales needed to provide $45,000 of after-tax income, assuming an income tax rate of 25%.

Planning the Solution

- Identify the formulas in the chapter for the required items expressed in units and solve them using the data given in the problem.
- Draw a CVP chart that reflects the facts in the problem. The horizontal axis should plot the volume in units up to 100,000, and the vertical axis should plot the total dollars up to $800,000. Plot the total cost line as upward sloping, starting at the fixed cost level ($150,000) on the vertical axis and increasing until it reaches $650,000 at the maximum volume of 100,000 units. Verify that the break-even point (where the two lines cross) equals the amount you computed in part 1.
- Identify the formulas in the chapter for the required items expressed in dollars and solve them using the data given in the problem.

Solution to Demonstration Problem

1. a. Contribution margin per cap   = Selling price per unit − Variable cost per unit
      = $8 − $5 = $\underline{\underline{\$3}}$

   b. Break-even point in caps $= \dfrac{\text{Fixed costs}}{\text{Contribution margin per cap}} = \dfrac{\$150,000}{\$3} = \underline{\underline{50,000 \text{ caps}}}$

   c. Net income at 30,000 caps sold   = (Units × Contribution margin per unit) − Fixed costs
      = (30,000 × $3) − $150,000 = $\underline{\underline{\$(60,000) \text{ loss}}}$

   d. Net income at 85,000 caps sold   = (Units × Contribution margin per unit) − Fixed costs
      = (85,000 × $3) − $150,000 = $\underline{\underline{\$105,000 \text{ profit}}}$

e. Pretax income $= \$45,000/(1 - 0.25) = \$60,000$
Income taxes $= \$60,000 \times 25\% = \$15,000$

$$\text{Units needed for } \$45,000 \text{ income} = \frac{\text{Fixed costs} + \text{Target pretax income}}{\text{Contribution margin per cap}}$$
$$= \frac{\$150,000 + \$60,000}{\$3} = \underline{\underline{70,000 \text{ caps}}}$$

2. CVP chart.

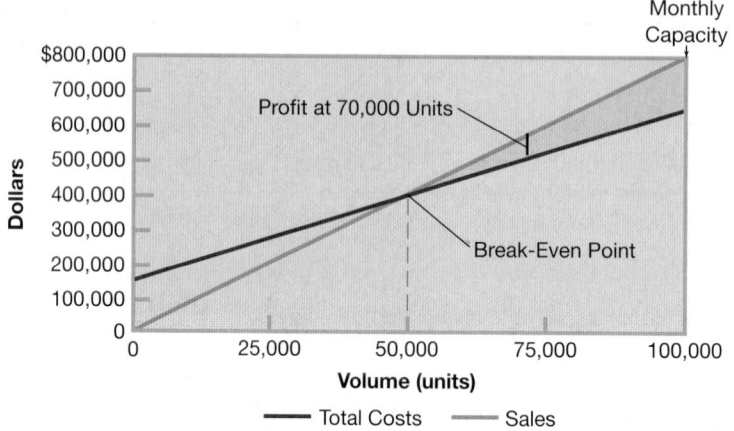

3. a. Contribution margin ratio $= \dfrac{\text{Contribution margin per unit}}{\text{Selling price per unit}} = \dfrac{\$3}{\$8} = \underline{\underline{0.375, \text{ or } 37.5\%}}$

b. Break-even point in dollars $= \dfrac{\text{Fixed costs}}{\text{Contribution margin ratio}} = \dfrac{\$150,000}{37.5\%} = \underline{\underline{\$400,000}}$

c. Net income at sales of \$250,000 $= (\text{Sales} \times \text{Contribution margin ratio}) - \text{Fixed costs}$
$= (\$250,000 \times 37.5\%) - \$150,000 = \underline{\underline{\$(56,250) \text{ loss}}}$

d. Net income at sales of \$600,000 $= (\text{Sales} \times \text{Contribution margin ratio}) - \text{Fixed costs}$
$= (\$600,000 \times 37.5\%) - \$150,000 = \underline{\underline{\$75,000 \text{ income}}}$

e. Dollars of sales to yield \$45,000 after-tax income $= \dfrac{\text{Fixed costs} + \text{Target pretax income}}{\text{Contribution margin ratio}}$
$= \dfrac{\$150,000 + \$60,000}{37.5\%} = \underline{\underline{\$560,000}}$

Summary

C1 Describe different types of cost behavior in relation to production and sales volume. Cost behavior is described in terms of how its amount changes in relation to changes in volume of activity within a relevant range. Fixed costs remain constant to changes in volume. Total variable costs change in direct proportion to volume changes. Mixed costs display the effects of both fixed and variable components. Step-wise costs remain constant over a small volume range, then change by a lump sum and remain constant over another volume range, and so on. Curvilinear costs change in a nonlinear relation to volume changes.

C2 Identify assumptions in cost-volume-profit analysis and explain their impact. Conventional cost-volume-profit analysis is based on assumptions that the product's selling price remains constant and that variable and fixed costs behave in a manner consistent with their variable and fixed classifications.

C3 Describe several applications of cost-volume-profit analysis. Cost-volume-profit analysis can be used to predict what can happen under alternative strategies concerning sales volume, selling prices, variable costs, or fixed costs. Applications include "what-if" analysis, computing sales for a target income, and break-even analysis.

A1 Compare the scatter diagram, high-low, and regression methods of estimating costs. Cost estimates from a scatter diagram are based on a visual fit of the cost line. Estimates from the high-low method are based only on costs corresponding to the lowest and highest sales. The least-squares regression method is a statistical technique and uses all data points.

A2 Compute contribution margin and describe what it reveals about a company's cost structure. Contribution margin per unit is a product's sales price less its total variable costs. Contribution margin ratio is a product's contribution margin per unit divided by its sales price. Unit contribution margin is the amount received from each sale that contributes to fixed costs and income. The contribution margin ratio reveals what portion of each sales dollar is available as contribution to fixed costs and income.

A3 **Analyze changes in sales using the degree of operating leverage.** The extent, or relative size, of fixed costs in a company's total cost structure is known as *operating leverage*. One tool useful in assessing the effect of changes in sales on income is the degree of operating leverage, or DOL. DOL is the ratio of the contribution margin divided by pretax income. This ratio can be used to determine the expected percent change in income given a percent change in sales.

P1 **Determine cost estimates using three different methods.** Three different methods used to estimate costs are the scatter diagram, the high-low method, and least-squares regression. All three methods use past data to estimate costs.

P2 **Compute break-even point for a single product company.** A company's break-even point for a period is the sales volume at

which total revenues equal total costs. To compute a break-even point in terms of sales units, we divide total fixed costs by the contribution margin per unit. To compute a break-even point in terms of sales dollars, divide total fixed costs by the contribution margin ratio.

P3 **Graph costs and sales for a single product company.** The costs and sales for a company can be graphically illustrated using a CVP chart. In this chart, the horizontal axis represents the number of units sold and the vertical axis represents dollars of sales or costs. Straight lines are used to depict both costs and sales on the CVP chart.

P4 **Compute break-even point for a multiproduct company.** CVP analysis can be applied to a multiproduct company by expressing sales volume in terms of composite units. A composite unit consists of a specific number of units of each product in proportion to their expected sales mix. Multiproduct CVP analysis treats this composite unit as a single product.

Guidance Answers to **Decision Maker** and **Decision Ethics**

Sales Manager The contribution margin per unit for the first order is $600 (60% of $1,000); the contribution margin per unit for the second order is $160 (20% of $800). You are likely tempted to accept the first order based on its high contribution margin per unit, but you must compute total contribution margin based on the number of units sold for each order. Total contribution margin is $60,000 ($600 per unit × 100 units) and $80,000 ($160 per unit × 500 units) for the two orders, respectively. The second order provides the largest return in absolute dollars and is the order you would accept. Another factor to consider in your selection is the potential for a long-term relationship with these customers including repeat sales and growth.

Operations Manager Without the availability of past data, none of the three methods described in the chapter can be used to measure cost behavior. Instead, the manager must investigate whether data from similar manufacturers can be accessed. This is likely difficult due to the sensitive nature of such data. In the absence of data, the manager should develop a list of the different production inputs and identify input-output relations. This provides guidance to the manager in measuring cost behavior. After several months, actual cost data will be available for analysis.

Supervisor Your dilemma is whether to go along with the suggestions to "manage" the numbers to make the project look like it will achieve sufficient profits. You should not succumb to these suggestions. Many people will likely be affected negatively if you manage the predicted numbers and the project eventually is unprofitable. Moreover, if it does fail, an investigation would likely reveal that data in the proposal were "fixed" to make it look good. Probably the only benefit from managing the numbers is the short-term payoff of pleasing those who proposed the product. One way to deal with this dilemma is to prepare several analyses showing results under different assumptions and then let senior management make the decision.

Entrepreneur You must first compute the level of sales required to achieve the desired net income. Then you must conduct sensitivity analysis by varying the price, sales mix, and cost estimates. Results from the sensitivity analysis provide information you can use to assess the possibility of reaching the target sales level. For instance, you might have to pursue aggressive marketing strategies to push the high-margin products, or you might have to cut prices to increase sales and profits, or another strategy might emerge.

Guidance Answers to **Quick Checks**

1. *b*

2. A fixed cost remains unchanged in total amount regardless of output levels. However, fixed *cost per unit* declines with increased output.

3. Such a cost is considered variable because the *total* cost changes in proportion to volume changes.

4. *b*

5. The high-low method ignores all costs and sales (activity-base) volume data points except the costs corresponding to the highest and lowest (most extreme) sales (activity-base) volume.

6. *c*

7. *a*

8. ($90 − $54)/$90 = 40%

9. $90,000/40% = $225,000

10. Three basic CVP assumptions are that (1) selling price per unit is constant, (2) variable costs per unit are constant, and (3) total fixed costs are constant.

11. a; Two steps are required for explanation:

(1) Pretax income = $120,000/(1 − 0.20) = $150,000

(2) $\dfrac{\$50,000 + \$150,000}{25\%} = \$800,000$

12. If the contribution margin ratio decreases from 50% to 25%, unit sales would have to double.

13. A company's margin of safety is the excess of the predicted sales level over its break-even sales level.

14. *c*; Selling price of a composite unit:

2 units of X @ $5 per unit $10
1 unit of Y @ $4 per unit   4
Selling price of a composite unit $14

Variable costs of a composite unit:

2 units of X @ $2 per unit $4
1 unit of Y @ $2 per unit   2
Variable costs of a composite unit $6

Therefore, contribution margin per composite unit is $8.

15. It must be assumed that the sales mix remains unchanged at all sales levels in the relevant range.

Key Terms   mhhe.com/wildFAP18e

Key Terms are available at the book's Website for learning and testing in an online Flashcard Format.

Break-even point (p. 888)
Composite unit (p. 895)
Contribution margin per unit (p. 888)
Contribution margin ratio (p. 888)
Cost-volume-profit (CVP) analysis (p. 882)
Cost-volume-profit (CVP) chart (p. 890)

Curvilinear cost (p. 884)
Degree of operating leverage (DOL) (p. 896)
Estimated line of cost behavior (p. 885)
High-low method (p. 886)
Least-squares regression (p. 887)
Margin of safety (p. 893)

Mixed cost (p. 883)
Operating leverage (p. 896)
Relevant range of operations (p. 891)
Sales mix (p. 895)
Scatter diagram (p. 885)
Step-wise cost (p. 884)

Multiple Choice Quiz   Answers on p. 913   mhhe.com/wildFAP18e

Multiple Choice Quizzes A and B are available at the book's Website.

1. A company's only product sells for $150 per unit. Its variable costs per unit are $100, and its fixed costs total $75,000. What is its contribution margin per unit?
   a. $50
   b. $250
   c. $100
   d. $150
   e. $25

2. Using information from question 1, what is the company's contribution margin ratio?
   a. 66⅔%
   b. 100%
   c. 50%
   d. 0%
   e. 33⅓%

3. Using information from question 1, what is the company's break-even point in units?
   a. 500 units
   b. 750 units

   c. 1,500 units
   d. 3,000 units
   e. 1,000 units

4. A company's forecasted sales are $300,000 and its sales at break-even are $180,000. Its margin of safety in dollars is:
   a. $180,000
   b. $120,000
   c. $480,000
   d. $60,000
   e. $300,000

5. A product sells for $400 per unit and its variable costs per unit are $260. The company's fixed costs are $840,000. If the company desires $70,000 pretax income, what is the required dollar sales?
   a. $2,400,000
   b. $200,000
   c. $2,600,000
   d. $2,275,000
   e. $1,400,000

Discussion Questions

1. How is cost-volume-profit analysis useful?

2. What is a variable cost? Identify two variable costs.

3. When output volume increases, do variable costs per unit increase, decrease, or stay the same within the relevant range of activity? Explain.

4. When output volume increases, do fixed costs per unit increase, decrease, or stay the same within the relevant range of activity? Explain.

5. How do step-wise costs and curvilinear costs differ?

6. Define and describe *contribution margin* per unit.

7. Define and explain the *contribution margin ratio*.

8. Describe the contribution margin ratio in layperson's terms.

9. In performing CVP analysis for a manufacturing company, what simplifying assumption is usually made about the volume of production and the volume of sales?

10. What two arguments tend to justify classifying all costs as either fixed or variable even though individual costs might not behave exactly as classified?

11. How does assuming that operating activity occurs within a relevant range affect cost-volume-profit analysis?

12. List three methods to measure cost behavior.

13. How is a scatter diagram used to identify and measure the behavior of a company's costs?

14. In cost-volume-profit analysis, what is the estimated profit at the break-even point?

15. Assume that a straight line on a CVP chart intersects the vertical axis at the level of fixed costs and has a positive slope that rises with each additional unit of volume by the amount of the variable costs per unit. What does this line represent?

16. Why are fixed costs depicted as a horizontal line on a CVP chart?

17. Each of two similar companies has sales of $20,000 and total costs of $15,000 for a month. Company A's total costs include $10,000 of variable costs and $5,000 of fixed costs. If Company B's total costs include $4,000 of variable costs and $11,000 of fixed costs, which company will enjoy more profit if sales double?

18. _____ of _____ reflects expected sales in excess of the level of break-even sales.

19. **Apple** produces iPods for sale. Identify some of the variable and fixed product costs associated with that production. [*Hint:* Limit costs to product costs.]

20. Should **Best Buy** use single product or multiproduct break-even analysis? Explain.

21. **Apple** is thinking of expanding sales of its most popular MacIntosh model by 65%. Do you expect its variable and fixed costs for this model to stay within the relevant range? Explain.

 Red numbers denote Discussion Questions that involve decision-making.

Determine whether each of the following is best described as a fixed, variable, or mixed cost with respect to product units.

1. Rubber used to manufacture athletic shoes.

2. Maintenance of factory machinery.

3. Packaging expense.

4. Wages of an assembly-line worker paid on the basis of acceptable units produced.

5. Factory supervisor's salary.

6. Taxes on factory building.

7. Depreciation expense of warehouse.

QUICK STUDY

QS 22-1
Cost behavior identification
C1

Listed here are four series of separate costs measured at various volume levels. Examine each series and identify whether it is best described as a fixed, variable, step-wise, or curvilinear cost. (It can help to graph the cost series.)

QS 22-2
Cost behavior identification
C1

Volume (Units)	Series 1	Series 2	Series 3	Series 4
0	$ 0	$450	$ 800	$100
100	800	450	800	105
200	1,600	450	800	120
300	2,400	450	1,600	145
400	3,200	450	1,600	190
500	4,000	450	2,400	250
600	4,800	450	2,400	320

This scatter diagram reflects past maintenance hours and their corresponding maintenance costs.

QS 22-3
Cost behavior estimation
C1 P1

[Scatter diagram: Maintenance Costs (y-axis, $0 to $12,000 in $2,000 increments) versus Maintenance Hours (x-axis, 0 to 5,000 in 1,000 increments)]

1. Draw an estimated line of cost behavior.

2. Estimate the fixed and variable components of maintenance costs.

QS 22-4
Cost behavior estimation—
high-low method

C1 P1

The following information is available for a company's maintenance cost over the last seven months. Using the high-low method, estimate both the fixed and variable components of its maintenance cost.

Month	Maintenance Hours	Maintenance Cost
June	9	$5,450
July	18	6,900
August	12	5,100
September	15	6,000
October	21	6,900
November	24	8,100
December	6	3,600

QS 22-5
Contribution margin ratio

A2

Compute and interpret the contribution margin ratio using the following data: sales, $5,000; total variable cost, $3,000.

QS 22-6
Contribution margin per unit
and break-even units   A2   P2

SBD Phone Company sells its cordless phone for $90 per unit. Fixed costs total $162,000, and variable costs are $36 per unit. Determine (1) contribution margin per unit and (2) break-even point in units.

QS 22-7
Contribution margin ratio
and break-even dollars   P2

Refer to QS 22-6. Determine (1) contribution margin ratio and (2) break-even point in dollars.

QS 22-8
CVP analysis and target income

C3 P2

Refer to QS 22-6. Assume that SBD Phone Co. is subject to a 30% income tax rate. Compute the units of product that must be sold to earn after-tax income of $140,000.

QS 22-9
CVP assumptions

C2

Which one of the following is an assumption that underlies cost-volume-profit analysis?
1. Selling price per unit must change in proportion to the number of units sold.
2. All costs have approximately the same relevant range.
3. For costs classified as variable, the costs per unit of output must change constantly.
4. For costs classified as fixed, the costs per unit of output must remain constant.

QS 22-10
Operating leverage analysis   A3

A high proportion of Company A's total costs are variable with respect to units sold; a high proportion of Company B's total costs are fixed with respect to units sold. Which company is likely to have a higher degree of operating leverage (DOL)? Explain.

QS 22-11
Multiproduct break-even   P4

Page-Me-Now Company manufactures and sells two products, green beepers and gold beepers, in the ratio of 5:3. Fixed costs are $85,000, and the contribution margin per composite unit is $125. What number of both green and gold beepers is sold at the break-even point?

EXERCISES

Exercise 22-1
Measurement of cost behavior
using a scatter diagram

P1

A company reports the following information about its sales and its cost of sales. Each unit of its product sells for $500. Use these data to prepare a scatter diagram. Draw an estimated line of cost behavior and determine whether the cost appears to be variable, fixed, or mixed.

Period	Sales	Cost of Sales
1	$22,500	$15,150
2	17,250	11,250
3	15,750	10,500
4	11,250	8,250
5	13,500	9,000
6	18,750	14,250

Following are five graphs representing various cost behaviors. (1) Identify whether the cost behavior in each graph is mixed, step-wise, fixed, variable, or curvilinear. (2) Identify the graph (by number) that best illustrates each cost behavior: (a) Factory policy requires one supervisor for every 30 factory workers; (b) real estate taxes on factory; (c) electricity charge that includes the standard monthly charge plus a charge for each kilowatt hour; (d) commissions to salespersons; and (e) costs of hourly paid workers that provide substantial gains in efficiency when a few workers are added but gradually smaller gains in efficiency when more workers are added.

Exercise 22-2
Cost behavior in graphs

C1

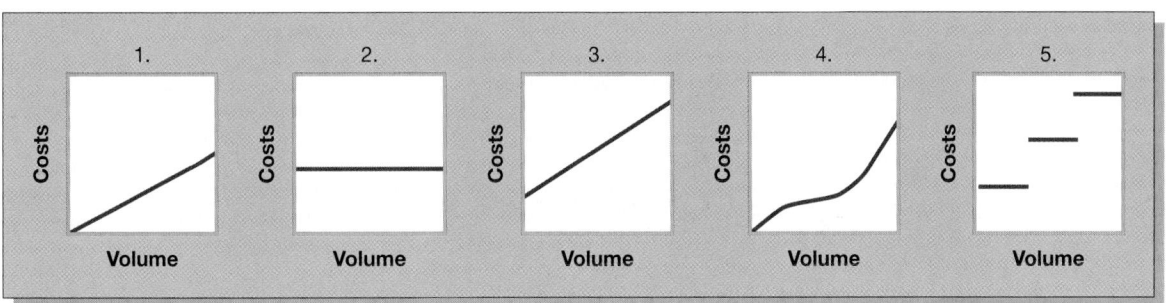

The left column lists several cost classifications. The right column presents short definitions of those costs. In the blank space beside each of the numbers in the right column, write the letter of the cost best described by the definition.

Exercise 22-3
Cost behavior defined

C1

A. Total cost

B. Mixed cost

C. Variable cost

D. Curvilinear cost

E. Step-wise cost

F. Fixed cost

_____ **1.** This cost is the combined amount of all the other costs.

_____ **2.** This cost remains constant over a limited range of volume; when it reaches the end of its limited range, it changes by a lump sum and remains at that level until it exceeds another limited range.

_____ **3.** This cost has a component that remains the same over all volume levels and another component that increases in direct proportion to increases in volume.

_____ **4.** This cost increases when volume increases, but the increase is not constant for each unit produced.

_____ **5.** This cost remains constant over all volume levels within the productive capacity for the planning period.

_____ **6.** This cost increases in direct proportion to increases in volume; its amount is constant for each unit produced.

Following are five series of costs A through E measured at various volume levels. Examine each series and identify which is fixed, variable, mixed, step-wise, or curvilinear.

Exercise 22-4
Cost behavior identification

C1

Volume (Units)	Series A	Series B	Series C	Series D	Series E
0	$ 0	$2,500	$ 0	$1,000	$5,000
400	3,600	3,100	6,000	1,000	5,000
800	7,200	3,700	6,600	2,000	5,000
1,200	10,800	4,300	7,200	2,000	5,000
1,600	14,400	4,900	8,200	3,000	5,000
2,000	18,000	5,500	9,600	3,000	5,000
2,400	21,600	6,100	13,500	4,000	5,000

Bloom Company management predicts that it will incur fixed costs of $160,000 and earn pretax income of $164,000 in the next period. Its expected contribution margin ratio is 25%. Use this information to compute the amounts of (1) total dollar sales and (2) total variable costs.

Exercise 22-5
Predicting sales and variable costs using contribution margin   C3

Exercise 22-6

Scatter diagram and measurement of cost behavior

P1

Use the following information about sales and costs to prepare a scatter diagram. Draw a cost line that reflects the behavior displayed by this cost. Determine whether the cost is variable, step-wise, fixed, mixed, or curvilinear.

Period	Sales	Costs	Period	Sales	Costs
1	$760	$590	9	$580	$390
2	800	560	10	320	240
3	200	230	11	240	230
4	400	400	12	720	550
5	480	390	13	280	260
6	620	550	14	440	410
7	680	590	15	380	260
8	540	430			

Exercise 22-7

Contribution margin, break-even, and CVP chart

P2 P3 A2

Bloom Company manufactures a single product that sells for $180 per unit and whose total variable costs are $135 per unit. The company's annual fixed costs are $562,500. (1) Use this information to compute the company's (a) contribution margin, (b) contribution margin ratio, (c) break-even point in units, and (d) break-even point in dollars of sales. (2) Draw a CVP chart for the company.

Exercise 22-8

Income reporting and break-even analysis   C3

Refer to Exercise 22-7. (1) Prepare a contribution margin income statement for Bloom Company showing sales, variable costs, and fixed costs at the break-even point. (2) If Bloom's fixed costs increase by $135,000, what amount of sales (in dollars) is needed to break even? Explain.

Exercise 22-9

Computing sales to achieve target income   C3

Bloom Company management (in Exercise 22-7) targets an annual after-tax income of $810,000. The company is subject to a 20% income tax rate. Assume that fixed costs remain at $562,500. Compute the (1) unit sales to earn the target after-tax net income and (2) dollar sales to earn the target after-tax net income.

Exercise 22-10

Forecasted income statement

C3

Check   Forecast income, $1,470,000

Bloom Company sales manager (in Exercise 22-7) predicts that annual sales of the company's product will soon reach 40,000 units and its price will increase to $200 per unit. According to the production manager, the variable costs are expected to increase to $140 per unit but fixed costs will remain at $562,500. The income tax rate is 20%. What amounts of pretax and after-tax income can the company expect to earn from these predicted changes? (*Hint:* Prepare a forecasted contribution margin income statement as in Exhibit 22.17.)

Exercise 22-11

Predicting unit and dollar sales

C3

Nombre Company management predicts $390,000 of variable costs, $430,000 of fixed costs, and a pretax income of $155,000 in the next period. Management also predicts that the contribution margin per unit will be $9. Use this information to compute the (1) total expected dollar sales for next period and (2) number of units expected to be sold next period.

Exercise 22-12

Computation of variable and fixed costs; CVP chart   P3

Cooper Company expects to sell 200,000 units of its product next year, which would generate total sales of $17 million. Management predicts that pretax net income for next year will be $1,250,000 and that the contribution margin per unit will be $25. (1) Use this information to compute next year's total expected (a) variable costs and (b) fixed costs. (2) Prepare a CVP chart from this information.

Exercise 22-13

Operating leverage computed and applied

A3

Company A is a manufacturer with current sales of $3,000,000 and a 60% contribution margin. Its fixed costs equal $1,300,000. Company B is a consulting firm with current service revenues of $3,000,000 and a 25% contribution margin. Its fixed costs equal $250,000. Compute the degree of operating leverage (DOL) for each company. Identify which company benefits more from a 20% increase in sales and explain why.

Exercise 22-14

CVP analysis using composite units   P4

Check   (3) 1,000 units

Handy Home sells windows and doors in the ratio of 8:2 (windows:doors). The selling price of each window is $200 and of each door is $500. The variable cost of a window is $125 and of a door is $350. Fixed costs are $900,000. Use this information to determine the (1) selling price per composite unit, (2) variable costs per composite unit, (3) break-even point in composite units, and (4) number of units of each product that will be sold at the break-even point.

The following costs result from the production and sale of 1,000 drum sets manufactured by Tom Thompson Company for the year ended December 31, 2008. The drum sets sell for $500 each. The company has a 25% income tax rate.

Problem 22-1A
Contribution margin income statement and contribution margin ratio

A2

Variable production costs	
Plastic for casing	$ 17,000
Wages of assembly workers	82,000
Drum stands	26,000
Variable selling costs	
Sales commissions	15,000
Fixed manufacturing costs	
Taxes on factory	5,000
Factory maintenance	10,000
Factory machinery depreciation	40,000
Fixed selling and administrative costs	
Lease of equipment for sales staff	10,000
Accounting staff salaries	35,000
Administrative management salaries	125,000

Check   (1) Net income, $101,250

Required

1. Prepare a contribution margin income statement for the company.

2. Compute its contribution margin per unit and its contribution margin ratio.

Analysis Component

3. Interpret the contribution margin and contribution margin ratio from part 2.

Xcite Equipment Co. manufactures and markets a number of rope products. Management is considering the future of Product XT, a special rope for hang gliding, that has not been as profitable as planned. Since Product XT is manufactured and marketed independently of the other products, its total costs can be precisely measured. Next year's plans call for a $200 selling price per 100 yards of XT rope. Its fixed costs for the year are expected to be $270,000, up to a maximum capacity of 700,000 yards. Forecasted variable costs are $140 per 100 yards of XT rope.

Problem 22-2A
CVP analysis and charting

P2   P3

mhhe.com/wildFAP18e

Required

1. Estimate Product XT's break-even point in terms of (a) sales units and (b) sales dollars.

Check   (1) Break-even sales, 4,500 units or $900,000

2. Prepare a CVP chart for Product XT like that in Exhibit 22.14. Use 700,000 yards as the maximum number of sales units on the horizontal axis of the graph, and $1,400,000 as the maximum dollar amount on the vertical axis.

3. Prepare a contribution margin income statement showing sales, variable costs, and fixed costs for Product XT at the break-even point.

Alden Co.'s monthly sales and cost data for its operating activities of the past year follow. Management wants to use these data to predict future fixed and variable costs.

Problem 22-3A
Scatter diagram and cost behavior estimation

P1

Period	Sales	Total Cost	Period	Sales	Total Cost
1	$320,000	$160,000	7	$340,000	$220,000
2	160,000	100,000	8	280,000	160,000
3	280,000	220,000	9	80,000	64,000
4	200,000	100,000	10	160,000	140,000
5	300,000	230,000	11	100,000	100,000
6	200,000	120,000	12	110,000	80,000

Required

1. Prepare a scatter diagram for these data with sales volume (in $) plotted on the horizontal axis and total cost plotted on the vertical axis.

2. Estimate both the variable costs per sales dollar and the total monthly fixed costs using the high-low method. Draw the total costs line on the scatter diagram in part 1.

Check (3) Variable costs, $0.60 per sales dollar; Fixed costs, $16,000

3. Use the estimated line of cost behavior and results from part 2 to predict future total costs when sales volume is (a) $200,000 and (b) $300,000.

Problem 22-4A

Break-even analysis; income targeting and forecasting

C3　P2

Astro Co. sold 20,000 units of its only product and incurred a $50,000 loss (ignoring taxes) for the current year as shown below. During a planning session for year 2009's activities, the production manager notes that variable costs can be reduced 50% by installing a machine that automates several operations. To obtain these savings, the company must increase its annual fixed costs by $200,000. The maximum output capacity of the company is 40,000 units per year.

ASTRO COMPANY	
Contribution Margin Income Statement	
For Year Ended December 31, 2008	
Sales	$1,000,000
Variable costs	800,000
Contribution margin	200,000
Fixed costs	250,000
Net loss	$ (50,000)

Required

1. Compute the break-even point in dollar sales for year 2008.

2. Compute the predicted break-even point in dollar sales for year 2009 assuming the machine is installed and there is no change in unit sales price.

Check (3) Net income, $150,000

3. Prepare a forecasted contribution margin income statement for 2009 that shows the expected results with the machine installed. Assume that the unit sales price and the number of units sold will not change and no income taxes.

(4) Required sales, $1,083,333 or 21,667 units

4. Compute the sales level required in both dollars and units to earn $140,000 of after-tax income in 2009 with the machine installed and no change in unit sales price. Assume that the income tax rate is 30%. (*Hint:* Use procedures in Exhibits 22.18 and 22.20.)

(5) Net income, $140,000 (rounded)

5. Prepare a forecasted contribution margin income statement that shows the results at the sales level computed in part 4. Assume an income tax rate of 30%.

Problem 22-5A

Break-even analysis, different cost structures, and income calculations

C3

Vanna Co. produces and sells two products, T and O. It manufactures these products in separate factories and markets them through different channels. They have no shared costs. This year, Vanna sold 50,000 units of each product. Sales and costs for each product follow.

	Product T	Product O
Sales	$2,000,000	$2,000,000
Variable costs	1,600,000	250,000
Contribution margin	400,000	1,750,000
Fixed costs	125,000	1,475,000
Income before taxes	275,000	275,000
Income taxes (32% rate)	88,000	88,000
Net income	$ 187,000	$ 187,000

Required

1. Compute the break-even point in dollar sales for each product.

2. Assume that the company expects sales of each product to decline to 30,000 units next year with no change in unit sales price. Prepare forecasted financial results for next year following the format of the contribution margin income statement as shown above with columns for each of the two products (assume a 32% tax rate). Also, assume that any loss before taxes yields a 32% tax savings.

3. Assume that the company expects sales of each product to increase to 60,000 units next year with no change in unit sales price. Prepare forecasted financial results for next year following the format of the contribution margin income statement as shown above with columns for each of the two products (assume a 32% tax rate).

Check (2) After-tax income: T, $78,200; O, $(289,000)

(3) After-tax income: T, $241,400; O, $425,000

Analysis Component

4. If sales greatly decrease, which product would experience a greater loss? Explain.

5. Describe some factors that might have created the different cost structures for these two products.

This year Bertrand Company sold 40,000 units of its only product for $25 per unit. Manufacturing and selling the product required $200,000 of fixed manufacturing costs and $325,000 of fixed selling and administrative costs. Its per unit variable costs follow.

Problem 22-6A
Analysis of price, cost, and volume changes for contribution margin and net income

C3 P2

mhhe.com/wildFAP18e

Material	$8.00
Direct labor (paid on the basis of completed units)	5.00
Variable overhead costs	1.00
Variable selling and administrative costs	0.50

Next year the company will use new material, which will reduce material costs by 50% and direct labor costs by 60% and will not affect product quality or marketability. Management is considering an increase in the unit sales price to reduce the number of units sold because the factory's output is nearing its annual output capacity of 45,000 units. Two plans are being considered. Under plan 1, the company will keep the price at the current level and sell the same volume as last year. This plan will increase income because of the reduced costs from using the new material. Under plan 2, the company will increase price by 20%. This plan will decrease unit sales volume by 10%. Under both plans 1 and 2, the total fixed costs and the variable costs per unit for overhead and for selling and administrative costs will remain the same.

Required

1. Compute the break-even point in dollar sales for both (a) plan 1 and (b) plan 2.

2. Prepare a forecasted contribution margin income statement with two columns showing the expected results of plan 1 and plan 2. The statements should report sales, total variable costs, contribution margin, total fixed costs, income before taxes, income taxes (30% rate), and net income.

Check (1) Break-even: Plan 1, $750,000; Plan 2, $700,000

(2) Net income: Plan 1, $122,500; Plan 2, $199,500

Patriot Co. manufactures and sells three products: red, white, and blue. Their unit sales prices are red, $20; white, $35; and blue, $65. The per unit variable costs to manufacture and sell these products are red, $12; white, $22; and blue, $50. Their sales mix is reflected in a ratio of 5:4:2 (red:white:blue). Annual fixed costs shared by all three products are $250,000. One type of raw material has been used to manufacture all three products. The company has developed a new material of equal quality for less cost. The new material would reduce variable costs per unit as follows: red, by $6; white, by $12; and blue, by $10. However, the new material requires new equipment, which will increase annual fixed costs by $50,000. (Round answers to whole composite unit.)

Problem 22-7A
Break-even analysis with composite units

P4 C3

Required

1. If the company continues to use the old material, determine its break-even point in both sales units and sales dollars of each individual product.

2. If the company uses the new material, determine its new break-even point in both sales units and sales dollars of each individual product.

Check (1) Old plan break-even, 2,050 composite units

(2) New plan break-even, 1,364 composite units

Analysis Component

3. What insight does this analysis offer management for long-term planning?

PROBLEM SET B

Problem 22-1B

Contribution margin income statement and contribution margin ratio

A2

The following costs result from the production and sale of 12,000 CD sets manufactured by Gilmore Company for the year ended December 31, 2008. The CD sets sell for $18 each. The company has a 25% income tax rate.

Variable manufacturing costs	
Plastic for CD sets	$ 1,500
Wages of assembly workers	30,000
Labeling	3,000
Variable selling costs	
Sales commissions	6,000
Fixed manufacturing costs	
Rent on factory	6,750
Factory cleaning service	4,520
Factory machinery depreciation	20,000
Fixed selling and administrative costs	
Lease of office equipment	1,050
Systems staff salaries	15,000
Administrative management salaries	120,000

Required

Check (1) Net income, $6,135

1. Prepare a contribution margin income statement for the company.

2. Compute its contribution margin per unit and its contribution margin ratio.

Analysis Component

3. Interpret the contribution margin and contribution margin ratio from part 2.

Problem 22-2B

CVP analysis and charting

P2 P3

Hip-Hop Co. manufactures and markets several products. Management is considering the future of one product, electronic keyboards, that has not been as profitable as planned. Since this product is manufactured and marketed independently of the other products, its total costs can be precisely measured. Next year's plans call for a $350 selling price per unit. The fixed costs for the year are expected to be $42,000, up to a maximum capacity of 700 units. Forecasted variable costs are $210 per unit.

Required

Check (1) Break-even sales, 300 units or $105,000

1. Estimate the keyboards' break-even point in terms of (a) sales units and (b) sales dollars.

2. Prepare a CVP chart for keyboards like that in Exhibit 22.14. Use 700 keyboards as the maximum number of sales units on the horizontal axis of the graph, and $250,000 as the maximum dollar amount on the vertical axis.

3. Prepare a contribution margin income statement showing sales, variable costs, and fixed costs for keyboards at the break-even point.

Problem 22-3B

Scatter diagram and cost behavior estimation

P1

Kyo Co.'s monthly sales and costs data for its operating activities of the past year follow. Management wants to use these data to predict future fixed and variable costs.

Period	Sales	Total Cost	Period	Sales	Total Cost
1	$195	$ 97	7	$145	$ 93
2	125	87	8	185	105
3	105	73	9	135	85
4	155	89	10	85	58
5	95	81	11	175	95
6	215	110	12	115	79

Required

1. Prepare a scatter diagram for these data with sales volume (in $) plotted on the horizontal axis and total costs plotted on the vertical axis.

2. Estimate both the variable costs per sales dollar and the total monthly fixed costs using the high-low method. Draw the total costs line on the scatter diagram in part 1.

3. Use the estimated line of cost behavior and results from part 2 to predict future total costs when sales volume is (a) $100 and (b) $170.

Check   (3) Variable costs, $0.40 per sales dollar; Fixed costs, $24

Rivera Co. sold 20,000 units of its only product and incurred a $50,000 loss (ignoring taxes) for the current year as shown below. During a planning session for year 2009's activities, the production manager notes that variable costs can be reduced 50% by installing a machine that automates several operations. To obtain these savings, the company must increase its annual fixed costs by $150,000. The maximum output capacity of the company is 40,000 units per year.

Problem 22-4B
Break-even analysis; income targeting and forecasting

C3   P2

RIVERA COMPANY	
Contribution Margin Income Statement	
For Year Ended December 31, 2008	
Sales	$750,000
Variable costs	600,000
Contribution margin	150,000
Fixed costs	200,000
Net loss	$ (50,000)

Required

1. Compute the break-even point in dollar sales for year 2008.

2. Compute the predicted break-even point in dollar sales for year 2009 assuming the machine is installed and no change in unit sales price. (Round the change in variable costs to a whole number.)

3. Prepare a forecasted contribution margin income statement for 2009 that shows the expected results with the machine installed. Assume that the unit sales price and the number of units sold will not change and no income taxes.

4. Compute the sales level required in both dollars and units to earn $140,000 of after-tax income in 2009 with the machine installed and no change in unit sales price. Assume that the income tax rate is 30%. (*Hint:* Use procedures in Exhibits 22.18 and 22.20.)

5. Prepare a forecasted contribution margin income statement that shows the results at the sales level computed in part 4. Assume an income tax rate of 30%.

Check   (3) Net income, $100,000

(4) Required sales, $916,667 or 24,445 units

(5) Net income, $140,000 (rounded)

Mingei Co. produces and sells two products, BB and TT. It manufactures these products in separate factories and markets them through different channels. They have no shared costs. This year, Mingei Co. sold 50,000 units of each product. Sales and costs for each product follow.

Problem 22-5B
Break-even analysis, different cost structures, and income calculations

C3

	Product BB	Product TT
Sales	$800,000	$800,000
Variable costs	560,000	100,000
Contribution margin	240,000	700,000
Fixed costs	100,000	560,000
Income before taxes	140,000	140,000
Income taxes (32% rate)	44,800	44,800
Net income	$ 95,200	$ 95,200

Required

1. Compute the break-even point in dollar sales for each product.

2. Assume that the company expects sales of each product to decline to 33,000 units next year with no change in unit sales price. Prepare forecasted financial results for next year following the format of the contribution margin income statement as shown above with columns for each of the two products (assume a 32% tax rate, and that any loss before taxes yields a 32% tax savings).

3. Assume that the company expects sales of each product to increase to 64,000 units next year with no change in unit sales price. Prepare forecasted financial results for next year following the format of the contribution margin income statement as shown above with columns for each of the two products (assume a 32% tax rate).

Check   (2) After-tax income: BB, $39,712; TT, $(66,640)

(3) After-tax income: BB, $140,896; TT, $228,480

Analysis Component

4. If sales greatly increase, which product would experience a greater increase in profit? Explain.

5. Describe some factors that might have created the different cost structures for these two products.

Problem 22-6B
Analysis of price, cost, and volume changes for contribution margin and net income

C3   P2

This year Best Company earned a disappointing 5.6% after-tax return on sales from marketing 100,000 units of its only product. The company buys its product in bulk and repackages it for resale at the price of $20 per unit. Best incurred the following costs this year.

Total variable unit costs	$800,000
Total variable packaging costs	$100,000
Fixed costs	$950,000
Income tax rate	25%

The marketing manager claims that next year's results will be the same as this year's unless some changes are made. The manager predicts the company can increase the number of units sold by 80% if it reduces the selling price by 20% and upgrades the packaging. This change would increase variable packaging costs by 20%. Increased sales would allow the company to take advantage of a 25% quantity purchase discount on the cost of the bulk product. Neither the packaging change nor the volume discount would affect fixed costs, which provide an annual output capacity of 200,000 units.

Required

Check (1) Break-even for new strategy, $1,727,273

         (2) Net income: Existing strategy, $112,500; New strategy, $475,500

1. Compute the break-even point in dollar sales under the (a) existing business strategy and (b) new strategy that alters both unit sales price and variable costs.

2. Prepare a forecasted contribution margin income statement with two columns showing the expected results of (a) the existing strategy and (b) changing to the new strategy. The statements should report sales, total variable costs (unit and packaging), contribution margin, fixed costs, income before taxes, income taxes, and net income. Also determine the after-tax return on sales for these two strategies.

Problem 22-7B
Break-even analysis with composite units

P4   C3

Milano Co. manufactures and sells three products: product 1, product 2, and product 3. Their unit sales prices are product 1, $40; product 2, $30; and product 3, $20. The per unit variable costs to manufacture and sell these products are product 1, $30; product 2, $15; and product 3, $8. Their sales mix is reflected in a ratio of 6:4:2. Annual fixed costs shared by all three products are $270,000. One type of raw material has been used to manufacture products 1 and 2. The company has developed a new material of equal quality for less cost. The new material would reduce variable costs per unit as follows: product 1 by $10, and product 2, by $5. However, the new material requires new equipment, which will increase annual fixed costs by $50,000.

Required

Check (1) Old plan break-even, 1,875 composite units

         (2) New plan break-even, 1,429 composite units

1. If the company continues to use the old material, determine its break-even point in both sales units and sales dollars of each individual product.

2. If the company uses the new material, determine its new break-even point in both sales units and sales dollars of each individual product.

Analysis Component

3. What insight does this analysis offer management for long-term planning?

PROBLEM SET C

 Problem Set C is available at the book's Website to further reinforce and assess your learning.

SERIAL PROBLEM

Success Systems

(This serial problem began in Chapter 1 and continues through most of the book. If previous chapter segments were not completed, the serial problem can begin at this point. It is helpful, but not necessary, for you to use the Working Papers that accompany the book.)

SP 22   Success Systems sells upscale modular desk units and office chairs in the ratio of 2:1 (desk unit: chair). The selling price is $1,250 per desk unit and $500 per chair. The variable cost is $750 per desk unit and $250 per chair. Fixed costs are $60,000.

Required

1. Compute the selling price per composite unit.

2. Compute the variable costs per composite unit.

3. Compute the break-even point in composite units.

Check   (3) 48 composite units

4. Compute the number of units of each product that would be sold at the break-even point.

BEYOND THE NUMBERS

BTN 22-1   **Best Buy** offers services to customers that help them use products they purchase from Best Buy. One of these services is its Geek Squad, which is Best Buy's 24-Hour Computer Support Task Force. As you complete the following requirements, assume that the Geek Squad uses many of Best Buy's existing resources such as its purchasing department and its buildings and equipment.

REPORTING IN ACTION

C1

Required

1. Identify several of the variable, mixed, and fixed costs that the Geek Squad is likely to incur in carrying out its services.

2. Assume that Geek Squad revenues are expected to grow by 25% in the next year. How do you expect the costs identified in part 1 to change, if at all?

3. How is your answer to part 2 different from many of the examples discussed in the chapter? (*Hint:* Consider how the contribution margin ratio changes as volume—sales or customers served—increases.)

BTN 22-2   Both **Best Buy** and **Circuit City** sell numerous consumer products, and each of these companies has a different product mix.

COMPARATIVE ANALYSIS

P2   C3   A2

Required

1. Assume the following data are available for both companies. Compute each company's break-even point in unit sales. (Each company sells many products at many different selling prices, and each has its own variable costs. This assignment assumes an *average* selling price per unit and an *average* cost per item.)

	Best Buy	Circuit City
Average selling price per item sold	$45	$20
Average variable cost per item sold	$34	$15
Total fixed costs	$5,053 million	$2,457 million

2. If unit sales were to decline, which company would experience the larger decline in operating profit? Explain.

BTN 22-3   Labor costs of an auto repair mechanic are seldom based on actual hours worked. Instead, the amount paid a mechanic is based on an industry average of time estimated to complete a repair job. The repair shop bills the customer for the industry average amount of time at the repair center's billable cost per hour. This means a customer can pay, for example, $120 for two hours of work on a car when the actual time worked was only one hour. Many experienced mechanics can complete repair jobs well under the industry average. The average data are compiled by engineering studies and surveys conducted in the auto repair business. Assume that you are asked to complete such a survey for a repair center. The survey calls for objective input, and many questions require detailed cost data and analysis. The mechanics and owners know you have the survey and encourage you to complete it in a way that increases the average billable hours for repair work.

ETHICS CHALLENGE

C1

Required

Write a one-page memorandum to the mechanics and owners that describes the direct labor analysis you will undertake in completing this survey.

**COMMUNICATING
IN PRACTICE**

C2

BTN 22-4　Several important assumptions underlie CVP analysis. Assumptions often help simplify and focus our analysis of sales and costs. A common application of CVP analysis is as a tool to forecast sales, costs, and income.

Required

Assume that you are actively searching for a job. Prepare a one-half page report identifying (1) three assumptions relating to your expected revenue (salary) and (2) three assumptions relating to your expected costs for the first year of your new job. Be prepared to discuss your assumptions in class.

**TAKING IT TO
THE NET**

C1　C3

BTN 22-5　Access and review the entrepreneurial information at **Business Owner's Toolkit** [Toolkit.cch.com]. Access and review its *New Business Cash Needs Estimate* under the **Business Tools** menu bar or similar worksheets related to controls of cash and costs.

Required

Write a one-half page report that describes the information and resources available at the Business Owner's Toolkit to help the owner of a start-up business to control and monitor its costs.

**TEAMWORK IN
ACTION**

C2

BTN 22-6　A local movie theater owner explains to you that ticket sales on weekends and evenings are strong, but attendance during the weekdays, Monday through Thursday, is poor. The owner proposes to offer a contract to the local grade school to show educational materials at the theater for a set charge per student during school hours. The owner asks your help to prepare a CVP analysis listing the cost and sales projections for the proposal. The owner must propose to the school's administration a charge per child. At a minimum, the charge per child needs to be sufficient for the theater to break even.

Required

Your team is to prepare two separate lists of questions that enable you to complete a reliable CVP analysis of this situation. One list is to be answered by the school's administration, the other by the owner of the movie theater.

***BusinessWeek*
ACTIVITY**

C3

BTN 22-7　Read the article, "McNealy: Why Sun Is Back," in the December 2, 2005, issue of *BusinessWeek*. (The book's Website provides free access to the article.)

Required

1. What has been **Sun Microsystems**' business model over the past years?

2. How has their business model changed recently?

3. How can a company profit by giving its product away?

**ENTREPRENEURIAL
DECISION**

C1

BTN 22-8　Xiaoning Wang is a diligent businesswoman. She continually searches for new product additions to further increase the profitability of **ChinaSprout**. She discusses broadly a method she applies for deciding what products to add and not add to her product lines.

Required

1. What information should Wang search for to help her decide whether to add or not add new products to her existing product lines?

2. What managerial tools are available to her to help make the decisions in part 1?

**HITTING THE
ROAD**

P4

BTN 22-9　Multiproduct break-even analysis is often viewed differently when actually applied in practice. You are to visit a local fast-food restaurant and count the number of items on the menu. To apply multiproduct break-even analysis to the restaurant, similar menu items must often be fit into groups. A reasonable approach is to classify menu items into approximately five groups, for example, drink group. We then estimate average selling price and average variable cost to compute average contribution margin. (*Hint:* The contribution margin ratio on drinks is about 90%.)

Required

1. Prepare a one-year multiproduct break-even analysis for the restaurant you visit. Begin by establishing groups. Next, estimate each group's volume and contribution margin. These estimates are necessary to compute each group's contribution margin. Assume that annual fixed costs in total are $500,000 per year. (*Hint:* You must develop your own estimates on volume and contribution margin for each group to obtain the break-even point and sales.)

2. Prepare a one-page report on the results of your analysis. Comment on the volume of sales necessary to break even at a fast-food restaurant.

BTN 22-10 Access and review **Dixons'** Website (**Dixons-Group.com**) to answer the following questions.

GLOBAL DECISION

C3

Dixons

1. Do you believe that Dixons' managers use single product CVP analysis or multiproduct break-even point analysis? Explain.

2. How does the addition of a new product line affect Dixons' CVP analysis?

3. How does the addition of a new store affect Dixons' CVP analysis?

ANSWERS TO MULTIPLE CHOICE QUIZ

1. a; $150 − $100 = $50

2. e; ($150 − $100)/$150 = 33⅓%

3. c; $75,000/$50 CM per unit = 1,500 units

4. b; $300,000 − $180,000 = $120,000

5. c; Contribution margin ratio = ($400 − $260)/$400 = 0.35
   Targeted sales = ($840,000 + $70,000)/0.35 = $2,600,000

23

Master Budgets and Planning

A Look Back

Chapter 22 looked at cost behavior and its use by managers in performing cost-volume-profit analysis. It also illustrated the application of cost-volume-profit analysis.

A Look at This Chapter

This chapter explains the importance of budgeting and describes the master budget and its preparation. It also discusses the value of the master budget to the planning of future business activities.

A Look Ahead

Chapter 24 focuses on flexible budgets, standard costs, and variance reporting. It explains the usefulness of these procedures and reports for business decisions.

Learning Objectives

CAP

Conceptual

C1 Describe the importance and benefits of budgeting. (p. 916)

C2 Explain the process of budget administration. (p. 918)

C3 Describe a master budget and the process of preparing it. (p. 920)

Analytical

A1 Analyze expense planning using activity-based budgeting. (p. 929)

Procedural

P1 Prepare each component of a master budget and link each to the budgeting process. (p. 922)

P2 Link both operating and capital expenditures budgets to budgeted financial statements. (p. 926)

P3 Appendix 23A—Prepare production and manufacturing budgets. (p. 935)

"We were making a unique new product . . . into a category that had a lot of potential for growth"
—Stephen Sullivan (on right; on left is Brian Cousins)

Reaching for the Clouds

JACKSON, WY—It all started when Stephen Sullivan got a pair of pants as a gift. The pants were made of Schoeller® fabric, which is durable, lightweight, and comfortable. "I wore those pants for three years," Stephen recalls. "They reminded me of my Mom's old stretch ski pants and how much she wore them and loved them." Stephen and his friend, Brian Cousins, were working for an outdoor retailer when they devised a plan to develop and market high-performance, multisport mountain apparel called **Cloudveil** (**Cloudveil.com**)—Cloudveil Dome is a peak in the Tetons.

Stephen quit his day job to research outdoor apparel and learn everything about marketing and operating their new business. While Stephen bartended during evenings to make ends meet, Brian went to work for an apparel manufacturer to learn the production and financial side of the business. "One of the smartest things we did early on was realize we didn't know everything," explains Stephen. "Then we set out to find others who did."

With their plans and dreams came budgets. In the early stages, however, the pair admits their budgeting process and planning were not ideal. "The thinking was, 'Let's be a clothing company and go buy some sewing machines.' [We now know] that style of thinking is archaic," says Stephen. "I can't even sew!" confesses Brian.

The friends now attend more seriously to master budgets and the budgeting process. They say budgets help formalize business expectations and objectives. They also help direct employees and put everyone on the same page. "We did not want the investment in labor or overhead," explains Stephen. Consequently, the pair budgeted for that type of operation and planned accordingly. They also communicated their expectations and plans to employees. To make such a system successful requires trust, an understanding of the process, and knowledge of how decisions impact the budgeted financial statements, says Stephen.

As Cloudveil continues to expand, master budgets and planning remain integral to decisions. Stephen explains that the company must "continue to innovate through design that benefits the discerning outdoor consumer . . . while nurturing and servicing the growing demand." Cloudveil's budgeting and planning process led them to obtain additional funds to expand. "That is so huge for our business," says Stephen. "Bringing this money into the business has really freed up our minds to do what we do best." These friends believe in their tag line: *Live Close to Your Dreams!*

[Sources: *Cloudveil Website*, May 2006; *Entrepreneur*, November 2002; *Outdoor Retailer Magazine*, 2001; *Denver Post*, 2005; *Northwestern Magazine*, Fall 2004]

Management seeks to turn its strategies into action plans. These action plans include financial details that are compiled in a master budget. The budgeting process serves several purposes, including motivating employees and communicating with them. The budget process also helps coordinate a company's activities toward common goals and is useful in evaluating results and management performance. This chapter explains how to prepare a master budget and use it as a formal plan of a company's future activities. The ability to prepare this type of plan is of enormous help in starting and operating a company. Such planning gives managers a glimpse into the future, and it can help translate ideas into actions.

Master Budgets and Planning

Budget Process
- Strategic budgeting
- Benchmarking budgets
- Budgeting and human behavior
- Budgeting as a management tool
- Budgeting communication

Budget Administration
- Budget committee
- Budget reporting
- Budget timing

Master Budget
- Master budget components
- Operating budgets
- Capital expenditures budget
- Financial budgets

Budget Process

Strategic Budgeting

Most companies prepare long-term strategic plans spanning 5 to 10 years. They then fine-tune them in preparing medium-term and short-term plans. Strategic plans usually set a company's long-term direction. They provide a road map for the future about potential opportunities such as new products, markets, and investments. The strategic plan can be inexact, given its long-term focus. Medium- and short-term plans are more operational and translate strategic plans into actions. These action plans are fairly concrete and consist of defined objectives and goals.

C1 Describe the importance and benefits of budgeting.

Short-term financial plans are called *budgets* and typically cover a one-year period. A **budget** is a formal statement of a company's future plans. It is usually expressed in monetary terms because the economic or financial aspects of the business are the primary factors driving management's decisions. All managers should be involved in **budgeting,** the process of planning future business actions and expressing them as formal plans. Managers who plan carefully and formalize plans in a budgeting process increase the likelihood of both personal and company success. (Although most firms prepare annual budgets, it is not unusual for organizations to prepare three-year and five-year budgets that are revised at least annually.)

The relevant focus of a budgetary analysis is the future. Management must focus on future transactions and events and the opportunities available. A focus on the future is important because the pressures of daily operating problems often divert management's attention and take precedence over planning. A good budgeting system counteracts this tendency by formalizing the planning process and demanding relevant input. Budgeting makes planning an explicit management responsibility.

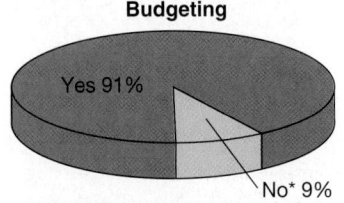

Companies Performing Annual Budgeting

Yes 91%

No* 9%

*Most of the 9% have eliminated annual budgeting in favor of rolling or continual budgeting.

Benchmarking Budgets

The control function requires management to evaluate (benchmark) business operations against some norm. Evaluation involves comparing actual results against one of two usual alternatives: (1) past performance or (2) expected performance.

An evaluation assists management in identifying problems and taking corrective actions if necessary. Evaluation using expected, or budgeted, performance is potentially superior to using past performance to decide whether actual results trigger a need for corrective actions. This is so because past performance fails to consider several changes that can affect current and future activities. Changes in economic conditions, shifts in competitive advantages within the industry, new product developments, increased or decreased advertising, and other factors reduce the usefulness of comparisons with past results. In hi-tech industries, for instance, increasing competition, technological advances, and other innovations often reduce the usefulness of performance comparisons across years.

Budgeted performance is computed after careful analysis and research that attempts to anticipate and adjust for changes in important company, industry, and economic factors. Therefore, budgets usually provide management an effective control and monitoring system.

Point: Managers can evaluate performance by preparing reports that compare actual results to budgeted plans.

Budgeting and Human Behavior

Budgeting provides standards for evaluating performance and can affect the attitudes of employees evaluated by them. It can be used to create a positive effect on employees' attitudes, but it can also create negative effects if not properly applied. Budgeted levels of performance, for instance, must be realistic to avoid discouraging employees. Personnel who will be evaluated should be consulted and involved in preparing the budget to increase their commitment to meeting it. Performance evaluations must allow the affected employees to explain the reasons for apparent performance deficiencies.

The budgeting process has three important guidelines: (1) Employees affected by a budget should be consulted when it is prepared (*participatory budgeting*), (2) goals reflected in a budget should be attainable, and (3) evaluations should be made carefully with opportunities to explain any failures. Budgeting can be a positive motivating force when these guidelines are followed. Budgeted performance levels can provide goals for employees to attain or even exceed as they carry out their responsibilities. This is especially important in organizations that consider the annual budget a "sacred" document.

Point: The practice of involving employees in the budgeting process is known as *participatory budgeting*.

Decision Insight

Budgets Exposed When companies go public and trade their securities on an organized exchange, management usually develops specific future plans and budgets. For this purpose, companies often develop detailed six- to twelve-month budgets and less-detailed budgets spanning 2 to 5 years.

Budgeting as a Management Tool

An important management objective in large companies is to ensure that activities of all departments contribute to meeting the company's overall goals. This requires coordination. Budgeting provides a way to achieve this coordination.

We describe later in this chapter that a company's budget, or operating plan, is based on its objectives. This operating plan starts with the sales budget, which drives all other budgets including production, materials, labor, and overhead. The budgeting process coordinates the activities of these various departments to meet the company's overall goals.

Budgeting Communication

Managers of small companies can adequately explain business plans directly to employees through conversations and other informal communications. However, conversations can create uncertainty and confusion if not supported by clear documentation of the plans. A written budget is preferred and can inform employees in all types of organizations about management's plans. The budget can also communicate management's specific action plans for the employees in the budget period.

Decision Ethics   Answer—p. 937

Budget Staffer Your company's earnings for the current period will be far below the budgeted amount reported in the press. One of your superiors, who is aware of the upcoming earnings shortfall, has accepted a management position with a competitor. This superior is selling her shares of the company. What are your ethical concerns, if any?

Budget Administration

Budget Committee

C2 Explain the process of budget administration.

The task of preparing a budget should not be the sole responsibility of any one department. Similarly, the budget should not be simply handed down as top management's final word. Instead, budget figures and budget estimates developed through a *bottom-up* process usually are more useful. This includes, for instance, involving the sales department in preparing sales estimates. Likewise, the production department should have initial responsibility for preparing its own expense budget. Without active employee involvement in preparing budget figures, there is a risk these employees will feel that the numbers fail to reflect their special problems and needs.

Most budgets should be developed by a bottom-up process, but the budgeting system requires central guidance. This guidance is supplied by a budget committee of department heads and other executives responsible for seeing that budgeted amounts are realistic and coordinated. If a department submits initial budget figures not reflecting efficient performance, the budget committee should return them with explanatory comments on how to improve them. Then the originating department must either adjust its proposals or explain why they are acceptable. Communication between the originating department and the budget committee should continue as needed to ensure that both parties accept the budget as reasonable, attainable, and desirable.

Point: In a large company, developing a budget through a bottom-up process can involve hundreds of employees and take several weeks to finalize.

The concept of continuous improvement applies to budgeting as well as production. **BP**, one of the world's largest energy companies, streamlined its monthly budget report from a one-inch-thick stack of monthly control reports to a tidy, two-page flash report on monthly earnings and key production statistics. The key to this efficiency gain was the integration of new budgeting and cost allocation processes with its strategic planning process. BP's controller explained the new role of the finance department with respect to the budgetary control process as follows: "there's less of an attitude that finance's job is to control. People really have come to see that our job is to help attain business objectives."

Budget Reporting

The budget period usually coincides with the accounting period. Most companies prepare at least an annual budget, which reflects the objectives for the next year. To provide specific guidance, the annual budget usually is separated into quarterly or monthly budgets. These short-term budgets allow management to periodically evaluate performance and take needed corrective action.

Managers can compare actual results to budgeted amounts in a report such as that shown in Exhibit 23.1. This report shows actual amounts, budgeted amounts, and their differences. A difference is called a *variance*. Management examines variances to identify areas for improvement and corrective action.

Budget Timing

The time period required for the annual budgeting process can vary considerably. For example, budgeting for 2009 can begin as early as January 2008 or as late as December 2008. Large, complex organizations usually require a longer time to prepare their budgets than do smaller organizations. This is so because considerable effort is required to coordinate the different units (departments) within large organizations.

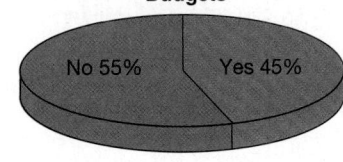

Companies Using Rolling Budgets

No 55%   Yes 45%

Many companies apply **continuous budgeting** by preparing **rolling budgets.** As each monthly or quarterly budget period goes by, these companies revise their entire set of budgets for the months or quarters remaining and add new monthly or quarterly budgets to replace the ones that have lapsed. At any point in time, monthly or quarterly budgets are available for the

ECCENTRIC MUSIC Income Statement with Variations from Budget For Month Ended April 30, 2008			
	Actual	**Budget**	**Variance**
Net sales	$60,500	$57,150	$+3,350
Cost of goods sold	41,350	39,100	+2,250
Gross profit	19,150	18,050	+1,100
Operating expenses			
Selling expenses			
Sales salaries	6,250	6,000	+250
Advertising	900	800	+100
Store supplies	550	500	+50
Depreciation—Store equipment	1,600	1,600	
Total selling expenses	9,300	8,900	+400
General and administrative expenses			
Office salaries	2,000	2,000	
Office supplies used	165	150	+15
Rent	1,100	1,100	
Insurance	200	200	
Depreciation—Office equipment	100	100	
Total general and administrative expenses	3,565	3,550	+15
Total operating expenses	12,865	12,450	+415
Net income	$ 6,285	$ 5,600	$ +685

Exhibit 23.1

Comparing Actual Performance with Budgeted Performance

Example: Assume that you must explain variances to top management. Which variances in Exhibit 23.1 would you research and why? *Answer:* Sales and cost of goods sold—due to their large variances.

next 12 months or four quarters. Exhibit 23.2 shows rolling budgets prepared at the end of five consecutive periods. The first set (at top) is prepared in December 2007 and covers the four calendar quarters of 2008. In March 2008, the company prepares another rolling budget for the next four quarters through March 2009. This same process is repeated every three months. As a result, management is continuously planning ahead.

Exhibit 23.2

Rolling Budgets

Exhibit 23.2 reflects an annual budget composed of four quarters prepared four times per year using the most recent information available. For example, the budget for the fourth quarter of 2008 is prepared in December 2007 and revised in March, June, and September of 2008. When continuous budgeting is not used, the fourth-quarter budget is nine months old and perhaps out of date when applied.

Decision Insight

Budget Calendar   Many companies use long-range operating budgets. For large companies, three groups usually determine or influence the budgets: creditors, directors, and management. All three are interested in the companies' future cash flows and earnings. The annual budget process often begins six months or more before the budget is due to the board of directors. A typical budget calendar, shown here, provides insight into the budget process during a typical calendar year.

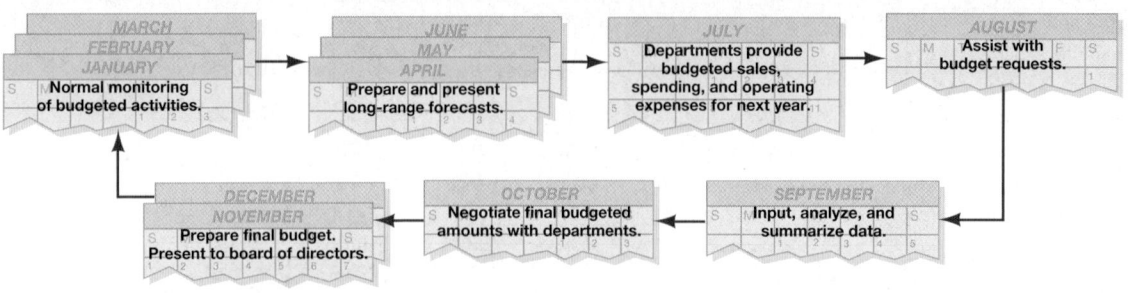

Quick Check

Answers—p. 937

1. What are the major benefits of budgeting?
2. What is the main responsibility of the budget committee?
3. What is the usual time period covered by a budget?
4. What are rolling budgets?

Master Budget

C3   Describe a master budget and the process of preparing it.

A **master budget** is a formal, comprehensive plan for a company's future. It contains several individual budgets that are linked with each other to form a coordinated plan.

Master Budget Components

The master budget typically includes individual budgets for sales, purchases, production, various expenses, capital expenditures, and cash. Managers often express the expected financial results of these planned activities with both a budgeted income statement for the budget period and a budgeted balance sheet for the end of the budget period. The usual number and types of budgets included in a master budget depend on the company's size and complexity. A master budget should include, at a minimum, the budgets listed in Exhibit 23.3. In addition to these individual budgets, managers often include supporting calculations and additional tables with the master budget.

Decision Insight

Budgeting Targets   Budgeting is a crucial part of any acquisition. Analysis begins by projecting annual sales volume and prices. It then estimates cost of sales, expenses, and income for the next several years. Using the present value of this projected income stream, buyers determine an offer price.

Exhibit 23.3

Basic Components of a Master Budget

- **Operating budgets**
  - *Sales budget*
  - For merchandisers add: *Merchandise purchases budget* (units to be purchased)
  - For manufacturers add: *Production budget* (units to be produced)
    - *Manufacturing budget* (manufacturing costs)
  - *Selling expense budget*
  - *General and administrative expense budget*
- **Capital expenditures budget** (expenditures for plant assets)
- **Financial budgets**
  - *Cash budget* (cash receipts and disbursements)
  - *Budgeted income statement*
  - *Budgeted balance sheet*

Some budgets require the input of other budgets. For example, the merchandise purchases budget cannot be prepared until the sales budget has been prepared because the number of units to be purchased depends on how many units are expected to be sold. As a result, we often must sequentially prepare budgets within the master budget.

A typical sequence for a quarterly budget consists of the five steps in Exhibit 23.4. Any stage in this budgeting process might reveal undesirable outcomes, so changes often must be made to prior budgets by repeating the previous steps. For instance, an early version of the cash budget could show an insufficient amount of cash unless cash outlays are reduced. This could yield a reduction in planned equipment purchases. A preliminary budgeted balance sheet could also reveal too much debt from an ambitious capital expenditures budget. Findings such as these often result in revised plans and budgets.

Topic Tackler

PLUS

23-1

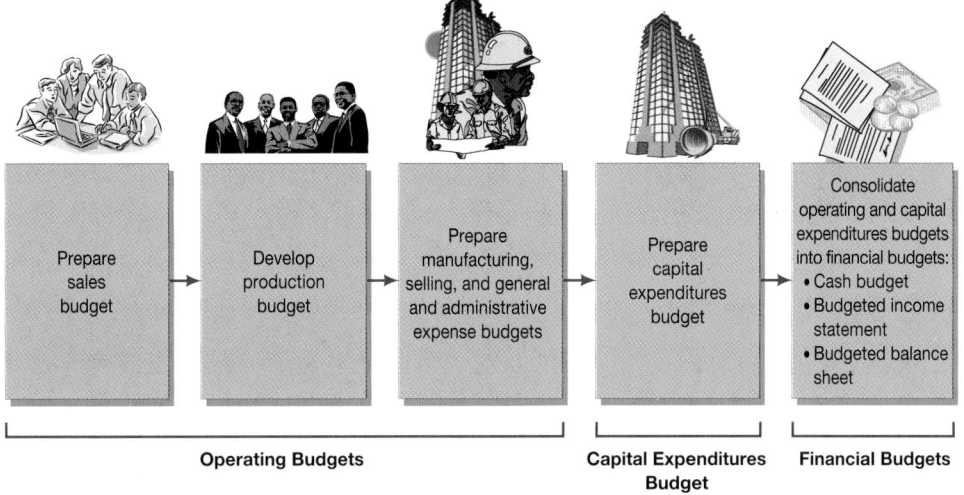

Operating Budgets   **Capital Expenditures**   **Financial Budgets**
                                        Budget

Exhibit 23.4

Master Budget Sequence

The remainder of this section explains how Hockey Den (HD), a retailer of youth hockey sticks, prepares its master budget. Its master budget includes operating, capital expenditures, and cash budgets for each month in each quarter. It also includes a budgeted income statement for each quarter and a budgeted balance sheet as of the last day of each quarter. We show how HD prepares budgets for October, November, and December 2008. Exhibit 23.5 presents HD's balance sheet at the start of this budgeting period, which we often refer to as we prepare the component budgets.

Exhibit 23.5

Balance Sheet Prior to the Budgeting Periods

HOCKEY DEN
Balance Sheet
September 30, 2008

Assets

Cash		$ 20,000
Accounts receivable		42,000
Inventory (900 units @ $60)		54,000
Equipment*	$200,000	
Less accumulated depreciation	36,000	164,000
Total assets		$280,000

Liabilities and Equity

Liabilities		
Accounts payable	$ 58,200	
Income taxes payable (due 10/31/2008)	20,000	
Note payable to bank	10,000	$ 88,200
Stockholders' equity		
Common stock	150,000	
Retained earnings	41,800	191,800
Total liabilities and equity		$280,000

* Equipment is depreciated on a straight-line basis over 10 years (salvage value is $20,000).

Operating Budgets

P1   Prepare each component of a master budget and link each to the budgeting process.

This section explains HD's preparation of operating budgets. Its operating budgets consist of the sales budget, merchandise purchases budget, selling expense budget, and general and administrative expense budget. HD does not prepare production and manufacturing budgets because it is a merchandiser. (The preparation of production budgets and manufacturing budgets is described in Appendix 23A.)

Sales Budget   The first step in preparing the master budget is planning the **sales budget,** which shows the planned sales units and the expected dollars from these sales. The sales budget is the starting point in the budgeting process because plans for most departments are linked to sales.

The sales budget should emerge from a careful analysis of forecasted economic and market conditions, business capacity, proposed selling expenses (such as advertising), and predictions of unit sales. A company's sales personnel are usually asked to develop predictions of sales for each territory and department because people normally feel a greater commitment to goals they help set. Another advantage to this participatory budgeting approach is that it draws on knowledge and experience of people involved in the activity.

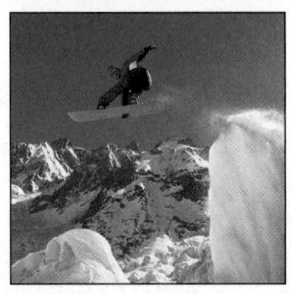

To illustrate, in September 2008, HD sold 700 hockey sticks at $100 per unit. After considering sales predictions and market conditions, HD prepares its sales budget for the next quarter (three months) plus one extra month (see Exhibit 23.6). The sales budget includes January 2009 because the purchasing department relies on estimated January sales to decide on December 2008 inventory purchases. The sales budget in Exhibit 23.6 includes forecasts of both unit sales and unit prices. Some sales budgets are expressed only in total sales dollars, but most are more detailed. Management finds it useful to know budgeted units and unit prices for many different products, regions, departments, and sales representatives.

Exhibit 23.6

Sales Budget for Planned Unit and Dollar Sales

HOCKEY DEN Monthly Sales Budget October 2008–January 2009			
	Budgeted Unit Sales	Budgeted Unit Price	Budgeted Total Sales
September 2008 (actual)	700	$100	$ 70,000
October 2008	1,000	$100	$100,000
November 2008	800	100	80,000
December 2008	1,400	100	140,000
Totals for the quarter	3,200	100	$320,000
January 2009	900	100	$ 90,000

Merchandise Purchases Budget   Companies use various methods to help managers make inventory purchasing decisions. These methods recognize that the number of units added to inventory depends on budgeted sales volume. Whether a company manufactures or purchases the product it sells, budgeted future sales volume is the primary factor in most inventory management decisions. A company must also consider its inventory system and other factors that we discuss next.

Just-in-time inventory systems.   Managers of *just-in-time* (JIT) inventory systems use sales budgets for short periods (often as few as one or two days) to order just enough merchandise or materials to satisfy the immediate sales demand. This keeps the amount of inventory to a minimum (or zero in an ideal situation). A JIT system minimizes the costs of maintaining inventory, but it is practical only if customers are content to order in advance or if managers can accurately determine short-term sales demand. Suppliers also must be able and willing to ship small quantities regularly and promptly.

Point: Accurate estimates of future sales are crucial in a JIT system.

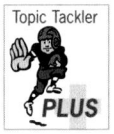
Topic Tackler

PLUS

23-2

Safety stock inventory systems.   Market conditions and manufacturing processes for some products do not allow use of a just-in-time system. Companies in these cases maintain sufficient inventory to reduce the risk and cost of running short. This practice requires enough purchases to satisfy the budgeted sales amounts and to maintain a **safety stock,** a quantity of inventory that provides protection against lost sales caused by unfulfilled demands from customers or delays in shipments from suppliers.

Merchandise purchases budget preparation.   A merchandiser usually expresses a **merchandise purchases budget** in both units and dollars. Exhibit 23.7 shows the general layout for this budget in equation form. If this formula is expressed in units and only one product is involved, we can compute the number of dollars of inventory to be purchased for the budget by multiplying the units to be purchased by the cost per unit.

| Inventory to be purchased | **=** | Budgeted ending inventory | **+** | Budgeted cost of sales for the period | **—** | Budgeted beginning inventory |

Exhibit 23.7

General Formula for a Merchandise Purchases Budget

To illustrate, after assessing the cost of keeping inventory along with the risk and cost of inventory shortages, HD decided that the number of units in its inventory at each month-end should equal 90% of next month's predicted sales. For example, inventory at the end of October should equal 90% of budgeted November sales, and the November ending inventory should equal 90% of budgeted December sales, and so on. Also, HD's suppliers expect the September 2008 per unit cost of $60 to remain unchanged through January 2009. This information along with knowledge of 900 units in inventory at September 30 (see Exhibit 23.5) allows the company to prepare the merchandise purchases budget shown in Exhibit 23.8.

Example: Assume Hockey Den adopts a JIT system in purchasing merchandise. How will its sales budget differ from its merchandise purchases budget? *Answer:* The two budgets will be similar because future inventory should be near zero.

Exhibit 23.8

Merchandise Purchases Budget

HOCKEY DEN Merchandise Purchases Budget October 2008–December 2008			
	October	November	December
Next month's budgeted sales (units)	800	1,400	900
Ratio of inventory to future sales	× 90%	× 90%	× 90%
Budgeted ending inventory (units)	720	1,260	810
Add budgeted sales (units)	1,000	800	1,400
Required units of available merchandise	1,720	2,060	2,210
Deduct beginning inventory (units)	900	720	1,260
Units to be purchased	820	1,340	950
Budgeted cost per unit	$ 60	$ 60	$ 60
Budgeted cost of merchandise purchases	$49,200	$80,400	$57,000

The first three lines of HD's merchandise purchases budget determine the required ending inventories (in units). Budgeted unit sales are then added to the desired ending inventory to give the required units of available merchandise. We then subtract beginning inventory to determine the budgeted number of units to be purchased. The last line is the budgeted cost of the purchases, computed by multiplying the number of units to be purchased by the predicted cost per unit.

Example: If ending inventory in Exhibit 23.8 is required to equal 80% of next month's predicted sales, how many units must be purchased each month? *Answer:* Budgeted ending inventory: Oct. = 640 units; Nov. = 1,120 units; Dec. = 720 units. Required purchases: Oct. = 740 units; Nov. = 1,280 units; Dec. = 1,000 units.

We already indicated that some budgeting systems describe only the total dollars of budgeted sales. Likewise, a system can express a merchandise purchases budget only in terms of the total cost of merchandise to be purchased, omitting the number of units to be purchased. This method assumes a constant relation between sales and cost of goods sold. HD, for instance, might assume the expected cost of goods sold to be 60% of sales, computed from the budgeted unit cost of $60 and the budgeted sales price of $100. However, it still must consider the effects of changes in beginning and ending inventories in determining the amounts to be purchased.

Selling Expense Budget   The **selling expense budget** is a plan listing the types and amounts of selling expenses expected during the budget period. Its initial responsibility usually rests with the vice president of marketing or an equivalent sales manager. The selling expense budget is normally created to provide sufficient selling expenses to meet sales goals reflected in the sales budget. Predicted selling expenses are based on both the sales budget and the experience of previous periods. After some or all of the master budget is prepared, management might decide that projected sales volume is inadequate. If so, subsequent adjustments in the sales budget can require corresponding adjustments in the selling expense budget.

To illustrate, HD's selling expense budget is in Exhibit 23.9. The firm's selling expenses consist of commissions paid to sales personnel and a $2,000 monthly salary paid to the sales manager. Sales commissions equal 10% of total sales and are paid in the month sales occur. Sales commissions are variable with respect to sales volume, but the sales manager's salary is fixed. No advertising expenses are budgeted for this particular quarter.

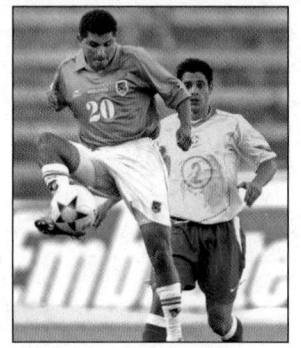

Decision Insight

Goals and Budgets   France Telecom failed to properly budget and coordinate its efforts for World Cup ticket sales. It assigned 60 of its operators to take orders for the few thousand tickets available to U.K. citizens. In the first 60 minutes after the phone lines opened, **British Telecom** logged an amazing four million call attempts. The odds of a U.K. soccer fan getting through to the ticket hotline were around one in two million.

Exhibit 23.9

Selling Expense Budget

HOCKEY DEN				
Selling Expense Budget				
October 2008–December 2008				
	October	**November**	**December**	**Totals**
Budgeted sales	$100,000	$80,000	$140,000	$320,000
Sales commission percent	× 10%	× 10%	× 10%	× 10%
Sales commissions	10,000	8,000	14,000	32,000
Salary for sales manager	2,000	2,000	2,000	6,000
Total selling expenses	$ 12,000	$10,000	$ 16,000	$ 38,000

Example: If sales commissions in Exhibit 23.9 are increased, which budgets are affected? *Answer:* Selling expenses budget, cash budget, and budgeted income statement.

General and Administrative Expense Budget   The **general and administrative expense budget** plans the predicted operating expenses not included in the selling expenses budget. General and administrative expenses can be either variable or fixed with respect to sales volume. The office manager responsible for general administration often is responsible for preparing the initial general and administrative expense budget.

Interest expense and income tax expense are often classified as general and administrative expenses in published income statements, but normally cannot be planned at this stage of the budgeting process. The prediction of interest expense follows the preparation of the cash budget and the decisions regarding debt. The predicted income tax expense depends on the budgeted amount of pretax income. Both interest and income taxes are usually beyond the control of the office manager. As a result, they are not used in comparison to the budget to evaluate that person's performance.

Exhibit 23.10 shows HD's general and administrative expense budget. It includes salaries of $54,000 per year, or $4,500 per month (paid each month when they are earned). Using information in Exhibit 23.5, the depreciation on equipment is computed as $18,000 per year [($200,000 − $20,000)/10 years], or $1,500 per month ($18,000/12 months).

HOCKEY DEN General and Administrative Expense Budget October 2008–December 2008				
	October	November	December	Totals
Administrative salaries	$4,500	$4,500	$4,500	$13,500
Depreciation of equipment	1,500	1,500	1,500	4,500
Total general and administrative expenses	$6,000	$6,000	$6,000	$18,000

Exhibit 23.10

General and Administrative Expense Budget

Example: In Exhibit 23.10, how would a rental agreement of $5,000 per month plus 1% of sales affect the general and administrative expense budget? (Budgeted sales are in Exhibit 23.6.) *Answer: Rent expense:* Oct. = $6,000; Nov. = $5,800; Dec. = $6,400; Total = $18,200; *Revised total general and administrative expenses:* Oct. = $12,000; Nov. = $11,800; Dec. = $12,400; Total = $36,200.

Quick Check

Answers—p. 937

5. What is a master budget?

6. A master budget (a) always includes a manufacturing budget specifying the units to be produced; (b) is prepared with a process starting with the operating budgets and continues with the capital expenditures budget and then financial budgets; or (c) is prepared with a process ending with the sales budget.

7. What are the three primary categories of budgets in the master budget?

8. In preparing monthly budgets for the third quarter, a company budgeted sales of 120 units for July and 140 units for August. Management wants each month's ending inventory to be 60% of next month's sales. The June 30 inventory consists of 50 units. How many units of product for July acquisition should the merchandise purchases budget specify for the third quarter? (a) 84, (b) 120, (c) 154, or (d) 204.

9. How do the operating budgets for merchandisers and manufacturers differ?

10. How does a just-in-time inventory system differ from a safety stock system?

Capital Expenditures Budget

The **capital expenditures budget** lists dollar amounts to be both received from plant asset disposals and spent to purchase additional plant assets to carry out the budgeted business activities. It is usually prepared after the operating budgets. Since a company's plant assets determine its productive capacity, this budget is usually affected by long-range plans for the business. Yet the process of preparing a sales or purchases budget can reveal that the company requires more (or less) capacity, which implies more (or less) plant assets.

Capital budgeting is the process of evaluating and planning for capital (plant asset) expenditures. This is an important management task because these expenditures often involve long-run commitments of large amounts, affect predicted cash flows, and impact future debt and equity financing. This means that the capital expenditures budget is often linked with management's evaluation of the company's ability to take on more debt. We describe capital budgeting in Chapter 25.

Hockey Den does not anticipate disposal of any plant assets through December 2008, but it does plan to acquire additional equipment for $25,000 cash near the end of December 2008. This is the only budgeted capital expenditure from October 2008 through January 2009. Thus, no separate budget is shown. The cash budget in Exhibit 23.11 reflects this $25,000 planned expenditure.

Exhibit 23.11
Cash Budget

HOCKEY DEN Cash Budget October 2008–December 2008	October	November	December
Beginning cash balance	$ 20,000	$ 20,000	$ 22,272
Cash receipts from customers (Exhibit 23.12)	82,000	92,000	104,000
Total cash available	102,000	112,000	126,272
Cash disbursements			
Payments for merchandise (Exhibit 23.13)	58,200	49,200	80,400
Sales commissions (Exhibit 23.9)	10,000	8,000	14,000
Salaries			
Sales (Exhibit 23.9)	2,000	2,000	2,000
Administrative (Exhibit 23.10)	4,500	4,500	4,500
Income taxes payable (Exhibit 23.5)	20,000		
Dividends ($150,000 × 2%)		3,000	
Interest on bank loan			
October ($10,000 × 1%)	100		
November ($22,800 × 1%)		228	
Purchase of equipment			25,000
Total cash disbursements	94,800	66,928	125,900
Preliminary cash balance	$ 7,200	$ 45,072	$ 372
Additional loan from bank	12,800		19,628
Repayment of loan to bank		22,800	
Ending cash balance	$ 20,000	$ 22,272	$ 20,000
Loan balance, end of month	$ 22,800	$ 0	$ 19,628

Example: If the minimum ending cash balance in Exhibit 23.11 is changed to $25,000 for each month, what is the projected loan balance at Dec. 31, 2008?
Answer:

Loan balance, Oct. 31	$27,800
November interest	278
November payment	25,022
Loan balance, Nov. 30	2,778
December interest	28
Additional loan in Dec.	21,928
Loan balance, Dec. 31	24,706

P2 Link both operating and capital expenditures budgets to budgeted financial statements.

Financial Budgets

After preparing its operating and capital expenditures budgets, a company uses information from these budgets to prepare at least three financial budgets: the cash budget, budgeted income statement, and budgeted balance sheet.

Cash Budget   After developing budgets for sales, merchandise purchases, expenses, and capital expenditures, the next step is to prepare the **cash budget,** which shows expected cash inflows and outflows during the budget period. It is especially important to maintain a cash balance necessary to meet ongoing obligations. By preparing a cash budget, management can prearrange loans to cover anticipated cash shortages before they are needed. A cash budget also helps management avoid a cash balance that is too large. Too much cash is undesirable because it earns a relatively low (if any) return.

When preparing a cash budget, we add expected cash receipts to the beginning cash balance and deduct expected cash disbursements. If the expected ending cash balance is inadequate, additional cash requirements appear in the budget as planned increases from short-term loans. If the expected ending cash balance exceeds the desired balance, the excess is used to repay loans or to acquire short-term investments. Information for preparing the cash budget is mainly taken from the operating and capital expenditures budgets.

To illustrate, Exhibit 23.11 presents HD's cash budget. The beginning cash balance for October is taken from the September 30, 2008, balance sheet in Exhibit 23.5. The remainder of this section describes the computations in the cash budget.

We begin with reference to HD's budgeted sales (Exhibit 23.6). Analysis of past sales indicates that 40% of the firm's sales are for cash. The remaining 60% are credit sales; these customers are expected to pay in full in the month following the sales. We now can compute the budgeted cash receipts from customers as shown in Exhibit 23.12. October's budgeted cash receipts consist of $40,000 from expected cash sales ($100,000 × 40%) plus the anticipated

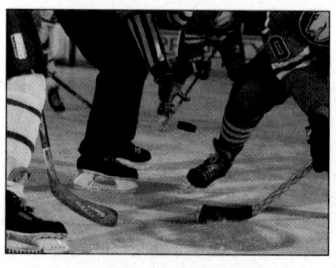

	September	October	November	December
Sales	$70,000	$100,000	$80,000	$140,000
Less ending accounts receivable (60%)	42,000	60,000	48,000	84,000
Cash receipts from				
Cash sales (40% of sales)		40,000	32,000	56,000
Collections of prior month's receivables		42,000	60,000	48,000
Total cash receipts		$ 82,000	$92,000	$104,000

Exhibit 23.12

Computing Budgeted Cash Receipts

collection of $42,000 of accounts receivable from the end of September. Each month's cash receipts from customers are transferred to the second line of Exhibit 23.11.

Next, we see that HD's merchandise purchases are entirely on account. It makes full payment during the month following its purchases. Therefore, cash disbursements for purchases can be computed from the September 30, 2008, balance sheet (Exhibit 23.5) and the merchandise purchases budget (Exhibit 23.8). This computation is shown in Exhibit 23.13.

October payments (September 30 balance)	$58,200
November payments (October purchases)	49,200
December payments (November purchases)	80,400

Exhibit 23.13

Computing Cash Disbursements for Purchases

The monthly budgeted cash disbursements for sales commissions and salaries are taken from the selling expense budget (Exhibit 23.9) and the general and administrative expense budget (Exhibit 23.10). The cash budget is unaffected by depreciation as reported in the general and administrative expenses budget.

Income taxes are due and payable in October as shown in the September 30, 2008, balance sheet (Exhibit 23.5). The cash budget in Exhibit 23.11 shows this $20,000 expected payment in October. Predicted income tax expense for the quarter ending December 31 is 40% of net income and is due in January 2009. It is therefore not reported in the October–December 2008 cash budget but in the budgeted income statement as income tax expense and on the budgeted balance sheet as income tax liability.

Hockey Den also pays a cash dividend equal to 2% of the par value of common stock in the second month of each quarter. The cash budget in Exhibit 23.11 shows a November payment of $3,000 for this purpose (2% of $150,000; see Exhibit 23.5).

Hockey Den has an agreement with its bank that promises additional loans at each month-end, if necessary, to keep a minimum cash balance of $20,000. If the cash balance exceeds $20,000 at a month-end, HD uses the excess to repay loans. Interest is paid at each month-end at the rate of 1% of the beginning balance of these loans. For October, this payment is 1% of the $10,000 amount reported in the balance sheet of Exhibit 23.5. For November, HD expects to pay interest of $228, computed as 1% of the $22,800 expected loan balance at October 31. No interest is budgeted for December because the company expects to repay the loans in full at the end of November. Exhibit 23.11 shows that the October 31 cash balance declines to $7,200 (before any loan-related activity). This amount is less than the $20,000 minimum. Hockey Den will bring this balance up to the minimum by borrowing $12,800 with a short-term note. At the end of November, the budget shows an expected cash balance of $45,072 before any loan activity. This means that HD expects to repay $22,800 of debt. The equipment purchase budgeted for December reduces the expected

Decision Insight

Netting Cash   The Hockey Company—whose brands include CCM, JOFA, and KOHO—reported net cash outflows for investing activities of $32 million. Much of this amount was a prepayment to the **NHL** for a 10-year license agreement.

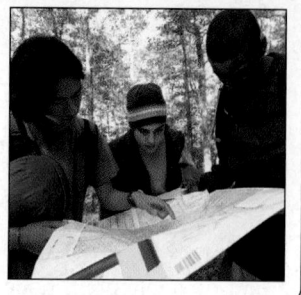

cash balance to $372, far below the $20,000 minimum. The company expects to borrow $19,628 in that month to reach the minimum desired ending balance.

Budgeted Income Statement   One of the final steps in preparing the master budget is to summarize the income effects. The **budgeted income statement** is a managerial accounting report showing predicted amounts of sales and expenses for the budget period. Information needed for preparing a budgeted income statement is primarily taken from already prepared budgets. The volume of information summarized in the budgeted income statement is so large for some companies that they often use spreadsheets to accumulate the budgeted transactions and classify them by their effects on income. We condense HD's budgeted income statement and show it in Exhibit 23.14. All information in this exhibit is taken from earlier budgets. Also, we now can predict the amount of income tax expense for the quarter, computed as 40% of the budgeted pretax income. This amount is included in the cash budget and/or the budgeted balance sheet as necessary.

Exhibit 23.14

Budgeted Income Statement

HOCKEY DEN		
Budgeted Income Statement		
For Three Months Ended December 31, 2008		
Sales (Exhibit 23.6, 3,200 units @ $100)		$320,000
Cost of goods sold (3,200 units @ $60)		192,000
Gross profit		128,000
Operating expenses		
Sales commissions (Exhibit 23.9)	$32,000	
Sales salaries (Exhibit 23.9)	6,000	
Administrative salaries (Exhibit 23.10)	13,500	
Depreciation on equipment (Exhibit 23.10)	4,500	
Interest expense (Exhibit 23.11)	328	56,328
Income before income taxes		71,672
Income tax expense ($71,672 × 40%)		28,669
Net income		$ 43,003

Budgeted Balance Sheet   The final step in preparing the master budget is summarizing the company's financial position. The **budgeted balance sheet** shows predicted amounts for the company's assets, liabilities, and equity as of the end of the budget period. HD's budgeted balance sheet in Exhibit 23.15 is prepared using information from the other budgets. The sources of amounts are reported in the notes to the budgeted balance sheet.[1]

---

[1] An eight-column spreadsheet, or work sheet, can be used to prepare a budgeted balance sheet (and income statement). The first two columns show the ending balance sheet amounts from the period prior to the budget period. The budgeted transactions and adjustments are entered in the third and fourth columns in the same manner as adjustments are entered on an ordinary work sheet. After all budgeted transactions and adjustments have been entered, the amounts in the first two columns are combined with the budget amounts in the third and fourth columns and sorted to the proper Income Statement (fifth and sixth columns) and Balance Sheet columns (seventh and eighth columns). Amounts in these columns are used to prepare the budgeted income statement and balance sheet.

Exhibit 23.15

Budgeted Balance Sheet

HOCKEY DEN
Budgeted Balance Sheet
December 31, 2008

Assets

Cash[a]		$ 20,000
Accounts receivable[b]		84,000
Inventory[c]		48,600
Equipment[d]	$225,000	
Less accumulated depreciation[e]	40,500	184,500
Total assets		$337,100

Liabilities and Equity

Liabilities		
Accounts payable[f]	$ 57,000	
Income taxes payable[g]	28,669	
Bank loan payable[h]	19,628	$105,297
Stockholders' equity		
Common stock[i]	150,000	
Retained earnings[j]	81,803	231,803
Total liabilities and equity		$337,100

[a] Ending balance for December from the cash budget in Exhibit 23.11.

[b] 60% of $140,000 sales budgeted for December from the sales budget in Exhibit 23.6.

[c] 810 units in budgeted December ending inventory at the budgeted cost of $60 per unit (from the purchases budget in Exhibit 23.8).

[d] September 30 balance of $200,000 from the beginning balance sheet in Exhibit 23.5 plus $25,000 cost of new equipment from the cash budget in Exhibit 23.11.

[e] September 30 balance of $36,000 from the beginning balance sheet in Exhibit 23.5 plus $4,500 expense from the general and administrative expense budget in Exhibit 23.10.

[f] Budgeted cost of purchases for December from the purchases budget in Exhibit 23.8.

[g] Income tax expense from the budgeted income statement for the fourth quarter in Exhibit 23.14.

[h] Budgeted December 31 balance from the cash budget in Exhibit 23.11.

[i] Unchanged from the beginning balance sheet in Exhibit 23.5.

[j] September 30 balance of $41,800 from the beginning balance sheet in Exhibit 23.5 plus budgeted net income of $43,003 from the budgeted income statement in Exhibit 23.14 minus budgeted cash dividends of $3,000 from the cash budget in Exhibit 23.11.

Quick Check

Answers—p. 937

11. In preparing a budgeted balance sheet, (*a*) plant assets are determined by analyzing the capital expenditures budget and the balance sheet from the beginning of the budget period, (*b*) liabilities are determined by analyzing the general and administrative expense budget, or (*c*) retained earnings are determined from information contained in the cash budget and the balance sheet from the beginning of the budget period.

12. What sequence is followed in preparing the budgets that constitute the master budget?

Activity-Based Budgeting

Decision Analysis

Activity-based budgeting (ABB) is a budget system based on expected activities. Knowledge of expected activities and their levels for the budget period enables management to plan for resources required to perform the activities. To illustrate, we consider the budget of a company's accounting department. Traditional budgeting systems list items such as salaries, supplies, equipment, and utilities. Such an itemized budget informs management of the use of the funds budgeted (for example, salaries), but management cannot assess the basis for increases or decreases in budgeted amounts as compared to prior periods. Accordingly, management often makes across-the-board cuts or increases. In contrast, ABB requires management to list activities performed by, say, the accounting department such as auditing, tax reporting, financial reporting, and cost accounting. Exhibit 23.16 contrasts a

A1 Analyze expense planning using activity-based budgeting.

Exhibit 23.16

Activity-Based Budgeting versus
Traditional Budgeting (for an
accounting department)

Activity-Based Budget		Traditional Budget	
Auditing	$ 58,000	Salaries	$152,000
Tax reporting	71,000	Supplies	22,000
Financial reporting	63,000	Depreciation	36,000
Cost accounting	32,000	Utilities	14,000
Total	$224,000	Total	$224,000

traditional budget with an activity-based budget for a company's accounting department. An understanding of the resources required to perform the activities, the costs associated with these resources, and the way resource use changes with changes in activity levels allows management to better assess how expenses will change to accommodate changes in activity levels. Moreover, by knowing the relation between activities and costs, management can attempt to reduce costs by eliminating nonvalue-added activities.

Decision Maker

Answer—p. 937

Environmental Manager You hold the new position of environmental control manager for a chemical company. You are asked to develop a budget for your job and identify job responsibilities. How do you proceed?

Demonstration Problem

Wild Wood Company's management asks you to prepare its master budget using the following information. The budget is to cover the months of April, May, and June of 2008.

WILD WOOD COMPANY
Balance Sheet
March 31, 2008

Assets		Liabilities and Equity	
Cash	$ 50,000	Accounts payable	$156,000
Accounts receivable	175,000	Short-term notes payable	12,000
Inventory	126,000	Total current liabilities	168,000
Total current assets	351,000	Long-term note payable	200,000
Equipment, gross	480,000	Total liabilities	368,000
Accumulated depreciation	(90,000)	Common stock	235,000
Equipment, net	390,000	Retained earnings	138,000
		Total stockholders' equity	373,000
Total assets	$741,000	Total liabilities and equity	$741,000

Additional Information

a. Sales for March total 10,000 units. Each month's sales are expected to exceed the prior month's results by 5%. The product's selling price is $25 per unit.

b. Company policy calls for a given month's ending inventory to equal 80% of the next month's expected unit sales. The March 31 inventory is 8,400 units, which complies with the policy. The purchase price is $15 per unit.

c. Sales representatives' commissions are 12.5% of sales and are paid in the month of the sales. The sales manager's monthly salary will be $3,500 in April and $4,000 per month thereafter.

d. Monthly general and administrative expenses include $8,000 administrative salaries, $5,000 depreciation, and 0.9% monthly interest on the long-term note payable.

e. The company expects 30% of sales to be for cash and the remaining 70% on credit. Receivables are collected in full in the month following the sale (none is collected in the month of the sale).

f. All merchandise purchases are on credit, and no payables arise from any other transactions. One month's purchases are fully paid in the next month.

g. The minimum ending cash balance for all months is $50,000. If necessary, the company borrows enough cash using a short-term note to reach the minimum. Short-term notes require an interest payment of 1% at each month-end (before any repayment). If the ending cash balance exceeds the minimum, the excess will be applied to repaying the short-term notes payable balance.

h. Dividends of $100,000 are to be declared and paid in May.

i. No cash payments for income taxes are to be made during the second calendar quarter. Income taxes will be assessed at 35% in the quarter.

j. Equipment purchases of $55,000 are scheduled for June.

Required

Prepare the following budgets and other financial information as required:

  1. Sales budget, including budgeted sales for July.

  2. Purchases budget, the budgeted cost of goods sold for each month and quarter, and the cost of the June 30 budgeted inventory.

  3. Selling expense budget.

  4. General and administrative expense budget.

  5. Expected cash receipts from customers and the expected June 30 balance of accounts receivable.

  6. Expected cash payments for purchases and the expected June 30 balance of accounts payable.

  7. Cash budget.

  8. Budgeted income statement.

  9. Budgeted statement of retained earnings.

10. Budgeted balance sheet.

Planning the Solution

- The sales budget shows expected sales for each month in the quarter. Start by multiplying March sales by 105% and then do the same for the remaining months. July's sales are needed for the purchases budget. To complete the budget, multiply the expected unit sales by the selling price of $25 per unit.

- Use these results and the 80% inventory policy to budget the size of ending inventory for April, May, and June. Add the budgeted sales to these numbers and subtract the actual or expected beginning inventory for each month. The result is the number of units to be purchased each month. Multiply these numbers by the per unit cost of $15. Find the budgeted cost of goods sold by multiplying the unit sales in each month by the $15 cost per unit. Compute the cost of the June 30 ending inventory by multiplying the expected units available at that date by the $15 cost per unit.

- The selling expense budget has only two items. Find the amount of the sales representatives' commissions by multiplying the expected dollar sales in each month by the 12.5% commission rate. Then include the sales manager's salary of $3,500 in April and $4,000 in May and June.

- The general and administrative expense budget should show three items. Administrative salaries are fixed at $8,000 per month, and depreciation is $5,000 per month. Budget the monthly interest expense on the long-term note by multiplying its $200,000 balance by the 0.9% monthly interest rate.

- Determine the amounts of cash sales in each month by multiplying the budgeted sales by 30%. Add to this amount the credit sales of the prior month (computed as 70% of prior month's sales). April's cash receipts from collecting receivables equals the March 31 balance of $175,000. The expected June 30 accounts receivable balance equals 70% of June's total budgeted sales.

- Determine expected cash payments on accounts payable for each month by making them equal to the merchandise purchases in the prior month. The payments for April equal the March 31 balance of accounts payable shown on the beginning balance sheet. The June 30 balance of accounts payable equals merchandise purchases for June.

- Prepare the cash budget by combining the given information and the amounts of cash receipts and cash payments on account that you computed. Complete the cash budget for each month by either borrowing enough to raise the preliminary balance to the minimum or paying off short-term debt as much as the balance allows without falling below the minimum. Show the ending balance of the short-term note in the budget.

- Prepare the budgeted income statement by combining the budgeted items for all three months. Determine the income before income taxes and multiply it by the 35% rate to find the quarter's income tax expense.

- The budgeted statement of retained earnings should show the March 31 balance plus the quarter's net income minus the quarter's dividends.

- The budgeted balance sheet includes updated balances for all items that appear in the beginning balance sheet and an additional liability for unpaid income taxes. Amounts for all asset, liability, and equity accounts can be found either in the budgets, other calculations, or by adding amounts found there to the beginning balances.

Solution to Demonstration Problem

1. Sales budget

	April	May	June	July
Prior period's unit sales	10,000	10,500	11,025	11,576
Plus 5% growth	500	525	551	579
Projected unit sales	10,500	11,025	11,576	12,155

	April	May	June	Quarter
Projected unit sales	10,500	11,025	11,576	
Selling price per unit	× $25	× $25	× $25	
Projected sales	$262,500	$275,625	$289,400	$827,525

2. Purchases budget

	April	May	June	Quarter
Next period's unit sales (part 1)	11,025	11,576	12,155	
Ending inventory percent	× 80%	× 80%	× 80%	
Desired ending inventory	8,820	9,261	9,724	
Current period's unit sales (part 1)	10,500	11,025	11,576	
Units to be available	19,320	20,286	21,300	
Less beginning inventory	8,400	8,820	9,261	
Units to be purchased	10,920	11,466	12,039	
Budgeted cost per unit	× $15	× $15	× $15	
Projected purchases	$163,800	$171,990	$180,585	$516,375

Budgeted cost of goods sold

	April	May	June	Quarter
This period's unit sales (part 1)	10,500	11,025	11,576	
Budgeted cost per unit	× $15	× $15	× $15	
Projected cost of goods sold	$157,500	$165,375	$173,640	$496,515

Budgeted inventory for June 30

Units (part 2)	9,724
Cost per unit	× $15
Total	$145,860

3. Selling expense budget

	April	May	June	Quarter
Budgeted sales (part 1)	$262,500	$275,625	$289,400	$827,525
Commission percent	× 12.5%	× 12.5%	× 12.5%	× 12.5%
Sales commissions	32,813	34,453	36,175	103,441
Manager's salary	3,500	4,000	4,000	11,500
Projected selling expenses	$ 36,313	$ 38,453	$ 40,175	$114,941

4. General and administrative expense budget

	April	May	June	Quarter
Administrative salaries	$ 8,000	$ 8,000	$ 8,000	$24,000
Depreciation	5,000	5,000	5,000	15,000
Interest on long-term note payable (0.9% × $200,000)	1,800	1,800	1,800	5,400
Projected expenses	$14,800	$14,800	$14,800	$44,400

5. Expected cash receipts from customers

	April	May	June	Quarter
Budgeted sales (part 1)	$262,500	$275,625	$289,400	
Ending accounts receivable (70%)	$183,750	$192,938	$202,580	
Cash receipts				
Cash sales (30%)	$ 78,750	$ 82,687	$ 86,820	$248,257
Collections of prior period's receivables	175,000	183,750	192,938	551,688
Total cash to be collected	$253,750	$266,437	$279,758	$799,945

6. Expected cash payments to suppliers

	April	May	June	Quarter
Cash payments (equal to prior period's purchases)	$156,000	$163,800	$171,990	$491,790
Expected June 30 balance of accounts payable (June purchases)			$180,585	

7. Cash budget

	April	May	June
Beginning cash balance	$ 50,000	$ 89,517	$ 50,000
Cash receipts (part 5)	253,750	266,437	279,758
Total cash available	303,750	355,954	329,758
Cash payments			
Payments for merchandise (part 6)	156,000	163,800	171,990
Sales commissions (part 3)	32,813	34,453	36,175
Salaries			
Sales (part 3)	3,500	4,000	4,000
Administrative (part 4)	8,000	8,000	8,000
Interest on long-term note (part 4)	1,800	1,800	1,800
Dividends		100,000	
Equipment purchase			55,000
Interest on short-term notes			
April ($12,000 × 1.0%)	120		
June ($6,099 × 1.0%)			61
Total cash payments	202,233	312,053	277,026
Preliminary balance	101,517	43,901	52,732
Additional loan		6,099	
Loan repayment	(12,000)		(2,732)
Ending cash balance	$ 89,517	$ 50,000	$ 50,000
Ending short-term notes	$ 0	$ 6,099	$ 3,367

8.

WILD WOOD COMPANY		
Budgeted Income Statement		
For Quarter Ended June 30, 2008		
Sales (part 1)		$ 827,525
Cost of goods sold (part 2)		496,515
Gross profit		331,010
Operating expenses		
Sales commissions (part 3)	$103,441	
Sales salaries (part 3)	11,500	
Administrative salaries (part 4)	24,000	
Depreciation (part 4)	15,000	
Interest on long-term note (part 4)	5,400	
Interest on short-term notes (part 7)	181	
Total operating expenses		159,522
Income before income taxes		171,488
Income taxes (35%)		60,021
Net income		$ 111,467

9.

WILD WOOD COMPANY	
Budgeted Statement of Retained Earnings	
For Quarter Ended June 30, 2008	
Beginning retained earnings (given)	$138,000
Net income (part 8)	111,467
	249,467
Less cash dividends (given)	100,000
Ending retained earnings	$149,467

10.

WILD WOOD COMPANY		
Budgeted Balance Sheet		
June 30, 2008		
Assets		
Cash (part 7)		$ 50,000
Accounts receivable (part 5)		202,580
Inventory (part 2)		145,860
Total current assets		398,440
Equipment (given plus purchase)	$535,000	
Less accumulated depreciation (given plus expense)	105,000	430,000
Total assets		$828,440
Liabilities and Equity		
Accounts payable (part 6)		$180,585
Short-term notes payable (part 7)		3,367
Income taxes payable (part 8)		60,021
Total current liabilities		243,973
Long-term note payable (given)		200,000
Total liabilities		443,973
Common stock (given)		235,000
Retained earnings (part 9)		149,467
Total stockholders' equity		384,467
Total liabilities and equity		$828,440

Production and Manufacturing Budgets

23A

Unlike a merchandising company, a manufacturer must prepare a **production budget** instead of a merchandise purchases budget. A production budget, which shows the number of units to be produced each month, is similar to merchandise purchases budgets except that the number of units to be purchased each month (as shown in Exhibit 23.8) is replaced by the number of units to be manufactured each month. A production budget does not show costs; it is *always expressed in units of product*. Exhibit 23A.1 shows the production budget for **Toronto Sticks Company** (**TSC**), a manufacturer of hockey sticks. TSC is an exclusive supplier of hockey sticks to Hockey Den, meaning that TSC uses HD's budgeted sales figures (Exhibit 23.6) to determine its production and manufacturing budgets.

P3   Prepare production and manufacturing budgets.

Exhibit 23A.1

Production Budget

TSC Production Budget October 2008–December 2008	October	November	December
Next period's budgeted sales (units)	800	1,400	900
Ratio of inventory to future sales	× 90%	× 90%	× 90%
Budgeted ending inventory (units)	720	1,260	810
Add budgeted sales for the period (units)	1,000	800	1,400
Required units of available production	1,720	2,060	2,210
Deduct beginning inventory (units)	(900)	(720)	(1,260)
Units to be produced	820	1,340	950

A **manufacturing budget** shows the budgeted costs for direct materials, direct labor, and overhead. It is based on the budgeted production volume from the production budget. The manufacturing budget for most companies consists of three individual budgets: direct materials budget, direct labor budget, and overhead budget. Exhibits 23A.2–23A.4 show these three manufacturing budgets for TSC. These budgets yield the total expected cost of goods to be manufactured in the budget period.

The *direct materials budget* is driven by the budgeted materials needed to satisfy each month's production requirement. To this we must add the desired ending inventory requirements. The desired ending inventory of direct materials as shown in Exhibit 23A.2 is 50% of next month's budgeted materials requirements of wood. For instance, in October 2008, an ending inventory of 335 units of material is desired (50% of November's 670 units). The desired ending inventory for December 2008 is 225 units,

Exhibit 23A.2

Direct Materials Budget

TSC Direct Materials Budget October 2008–December 2008	October	November	December
Budget production (units)	820	1,340	950
Materials requirements per unit	× 0.5	× 0.5	× 0.5
Materials needed for production (units)	410	670	475
Add budgeted ending inventory (units)	335	237.5	225
Total materials requirements (units)	745	907.5	700
Deduct beginning inventory (units)	(205)	(335)	(237.5)
Materials to be purchased (units)	540	572.5	462.5
Material price per unit	$ 20	$ 20	$ 20
Total cost of direct materials purchases	$10,800	$11,450	$9,250

computed from the direct material requirement of 450 units for a production level of 900 units in January 2009. The total materials requirements are computed by adding the desired ending inventory figures to that month's budgeted production material requirements. For October 2008, the total materials requirement is 745 units (335 + 410). From the total materials requirement, we then subtract the units of materials available in beginning inventory. For October 2008, the materials available from September 2008 are computed as 50% of October's materials requirements to satisfy production, or 205 units (50% of 410). Therefore, direct materials purchases in October 2008 are budgeted at 540 units (745 − 205). See Exhibit 23A.2.

TSC's *direct labor budget* is shown in Exhibit 23A.3. About 15 minutes of labor time is required to produce one unit. Labor is paid at the rate of $12 per hour. Budgeted labor hours are computed by multiplying the budgeted production level for each month by one-quarter (0.25) of an hour. Direct labor cost is then computed by multiplying budgeted labor hours by the labor rate of $12 per hour.

Exhibit 23A.3

Direct Labor Budget

TSC Direct Labor Budget October 2008–December 2008	October	November	December
Budgeted production (units)	820	1,340	950
Labor requirements per unit (hours)	× 0.25	× 0.25	× 0.25
Total labor hours needed	205	335	237.5
Labor rate (per hour)	$ 12	$ 12	$ 12
Labor dollars	$2,460	$4,020	$2,850

TSC's *factory overhead budget* is shown in Exhibit 23A.4. The variable portion of overhead is assigned at the rate of $2.50 per unit of production. The fixed portion stays constant at $1,500 per month. The budget in Exhibit 23A.4 is in condensed form; most overhead budgets are more detailed, listing each overhead cost item.

Exhibit 23A.4

Factory Overhead Budget

TSC Factory Overhead Budget October 2008–December 2008	October	November	December
Budgeted production (units)	820	1,340	950
Variable factory overhead rate	× $2.50	× $2.50	× $2.50
Budgeted variable overhead	2,050	3,350	2,375
Budgeted fixed overhead	1,500	1,500	1,500
Budgeted total overhead	$3,550	$4,850	$3,875

Summary

C1 Describe the importance and benefits of budgeting. Planning is a management responsibility of critical importance to business success. Budgeting is the process management uses to formalize its plans. Budgeting promotes management analysis and focuses its attention on the future. Budgeting also provides a basis for evaluating performance, serves as a source of motivation, is a means of coordinating activities, and communicates management's plans and instructions to employees.

C2 Explain the process of budget administration. Budgeting is a detailed activity that requires administration. At least three aspects are important: budget committee, budget reporting, and budget timing. A budget committee oversees the budget preparation. The budget period pertains to the time period for which the budget is prepared such as a year or month.

C3 Describe a master budget and the process of preparing it. A master budget is a formal overall plan for a company. It consists of plans for business operations and capital expenditures, plus the financial results of those activities. The budgeting process begins with a sales budget. Based on expected sales volume, companies can budget purchases, selling expenses, and administrative expenses. Next, the capital expenditures budget is prepared, followed by the cash budget and budgeted financial statements. Manufacturers also must budget production quantities, materials purchases, labor costs, and overhead.

A1 Analyze expense planning using activity-based budgeting. Activity-based budgeting requires management to identify activities performed by departments, plan necessary activity levels, identify resources required to perform these activities, and budget the resources.

P1   **Prepare each component of a master budget and link each to the budgeting process.** The term *master budget* refers to a collection of individual component budgets. Each component budget is designed to guide persons responsible for activities covered by that component. A master budget must reflect the components of a company and their interaction in pursuit of company goals.

P2   **Link both operating and capital expenditures budgets to budgeted financial statements.** The operating budgets, capital expenditures budget, and cash budget contain much of the infor-

mation to prepare a budgeted income statement for the budget period and a budgeted balance sheet at the end of the budget period. Budgeted financial statements show the expected financial consequences of the planned activities described in the budgets.

P3^A   **Prepare production and manufacturing budgets.** A manufacturer must prepare a *production budget* instead of a purchases budget. A *manufacturing budget* shows the budgeted production costs for direct materials, direct labor, and overhead.

Guidance Answers to **Decision Maker** and **Decision Ethics**

Budget Staffer   Your superior's actions appear unethical because she is using private information for personal gain. As a budget staffer, you are low in the company's hierarchical structure and probably unable to confront this superior directly. You should inform an individual with a position of authority within the organization about your concerns.

Entrepreneur   You must deal with two issues. First, because fashions and designs frequently change, you cannot heavily rely on previous budgets. As a result, you must carefully analyze the market to understand what designs are in vogue. This will help you plan the product mix and estimate demand. The second issue is the

budgeting period. An annual sales budget may be unreliable because tastes can quickly change. Your best bet might be to prepare monthly and quarterly sales budgets that you continuously monitor and revise.

Environmental Manager   You are unlikely to have data on this new position to use in preparing your budget. In this situation, you can use activity-based budgeting. This requires developing a list of activities to conduct, the resources required to perform these activities, and the expenses associated with these resources. You should challenge yourself to be absolutely certain that the listed activities are necessary and that the listed resources are required.

Guidance Answers to **Quick Checks**

1. Major benefits include promoting a focus on the future; providing a basis for evaluating performance; providing a source of motivation; coordinating the departments of a business; and communicating plans and instructions.

2. The budget committee's responsibility is to provide guidance to ensure that budget figures are realistic and coordinated.

3. Budget periods usually coincide with accounting periods and therefore cover a month, quarter, or a year. Budgets can also be prepared for longer time periods, such as five years.

4. Rolling budgets are budgets that are periodically revised in the ongoing process of continuous budgeting.

5. A master budget is a comprehensive or overall plan for the company that is generally expressed in monetary terms.

6. *b*

7. The master budget includes operating budgets, the capital expenditures budget, and financial budgets.

8. *c*; Computed as $(60\% \times 140) + 120 - 50 = 154$.

9. Merchandisers prepare merchandise purchases budgets; manufacturers prepare production and manufacturing budgets.

10. A just-in-time system keeps the level of inventory to a minimum and orders merchandise or materials to meet immediate sales demand. A safety stock system maintains an inventory that is large enough to meet sales demands plus an amount to satisfy unexpected sales demands and an amount to cover delayed shipments from suppliers.

11. *a*

12. (a) Operating budgets (such as sales, selling expense, and administrative budgets), (b) capital expenditures budget, (c) financial budgets: cash budget, budgeted income statement, and budgeted balance sheet.

Key Terms   mhhe.com/wildFAP18e

Key Terms are available at the book's Website for learning and testing in an online Flashcard Format.

Activity-based budgeting (ABB) (p. 929)
Budget (p. 916)
Budgeted balance sheet (p. 928)
Budgeted income statement (p. 928)
Budgeting (p. 916)
Capital expenditures budget (p. 925)

Cash budget (p. 926)
Continuous budgeting (p. 918)
General and administrative expense budget (p. 924)
Manufacturing budget (p. 935)
Master budget (p. 920)

Merchandise purchases budget (p. 923)
Production budget (p. 935)
Rolling budgets (p. 918)
Safety stock (p. 923)
Sales budget (p. 922)
Selling expense budget (p. 924)

Multiple Choice Quiz   Answers on p. 951   mhhe.com/wildFAP18e

Multiple Choice Quizzes A and B are available at the book's Website.

1. A plan that reports the units or costs of merchandise to be purchased by a merchandising company during the budget period is called a
   a. Capital expenditures budget.
   b. Cash budget.
   c. Merchandise purchases budget.
   d. Selling expenses budget.
   e. Sales budget.

2. A hardware store has budgeted sales of $36,000 for its power tool department in July. Management wants to have $7,000 in power tool inventory at the end of July. Its beginning inventory of power tools is expected to be $6,000. What is the budgeted dollar amount of merchandise purchases?
   a. $36,000
   b. $43,000
   c. $42,000
   d. $35,000
   e. $37,000

3. A store has the following budgeted sales for the next five months.

May	$210,000
June	186,000
July	180,000
August	220,000
September	240,000

   Cash sales are 25% of total sales and all credit sales are expected to be collected in the month following the sale. The total amount of cash expected to be received from customers in September is

   a. $240,000
   b. $225,000
   c. $ 60,000
   d. $165,000
   e. $220,000

4. A plan that shows the expected cash inflows and cash outflows during the budget period, including receipts from loans needed to maintain a minimum cash balance and repayments of such loans, is called
   a. A rolling budget.
   b. An income statement.
   c. A balance sheet.
   d. A cash budget.
   e. An operating budget.

5.[A] The following sales are predicted for a company's next four months.

	September	October	November	December
Unit sales ..	480	560	600	480

   Each month's ending inventory of finished goods should be 30% of the next month's sales. At September 1, the finished goods inventory is 140 units. The budgeted production of units for October is

   a. 572 units.
   b. 560 units.
   c. 548 units.
   d. 600 units.
   e. 180 units.

Superscript letter [A] denotes assignments based on Appendix 23A.

Discussion Questions

1. Identify at least three roles that budgeting plays in helping managers control and monitor a business.
2. What two common benchmarks can be used to evaluate actual performance? Which of the two is generally more useful?
3. What is the benefit of continuous budgeting?
4. Identify three usual time horizons for short-term planning and budgets.
5. Why should each department participate in preparing its own budget?
6. How does budgeting help management coordinate and plan business activities?
7. Why is the sales budget so important to the budgeting process?
8. What is a selling expense budget? What is a capital expenditures budget?
9. Budgeting promotes good decision making by requiring managers to conduct _____ and by focusing their attention on the _____.

10. What is a cash budget? Why must operating budgets and the capital expenditures budget be prepared before the cash budget?
11.[A] What is the difference between a production budget and a manufacturing budget?
12. Would a manager of a **Best Buy** retail store participate more in budgeting than a manager at the corporate offices? Explain.
13. Does the manager of a local **Circuit City** retail store participate in long-term budgeting? Explain.
14. Assume that **Apple**'s iMac division is charged with preparing a master budget. Identify the participants—for example, the sales manager for the sales budget—and describe the information each person provides in preparing the master budget.

Red numbers denote Discussion Questions that involve decision-making.

Which one of the following sets of items are all necessary components of the master budget?

1. Operating budgets, historical income statement, and budgeted balance sheet.

2. Prior sales reports, capital expenditures budget, and financial budgets.

3. Sales budget, operating budgets, and historical financial budgets.

4. Operating budgets, financial budgets, and capital expenditures budget.

QS 23-1
Components of a master budget
C3

The motivation of employees is one goal of budgeting. Identify three guidelines that organizations should follow if budgeting is to serve effectively as a source of motivation for employees.

QS 23-2
Budget motivation   C1

Montel Company's July sales budget calls for sales of $600,000. The store expects to begin July with $50,000 of inventory and to end the month with $40,000 of inventory. Gross margin is typically 40% of sales. Determine the budgeted cost of merchandise purchases for July.

QS 23-3
Purchases budget   P1

Good management includes good budgeting. (1) Explain why the bottom-up approach to budgeting is considered a more successful management technique than a top-down approach. (2) Provide an example of implementation of the bottom-up approach to budgeting.

QS 23-4
Budgeting process   C2

Lighthouse Company anticipates total sales for June and July of $420,000 and $398,000, respectively. Cash sales are normally 60% of total sales. Of the credit sales, 20% are collected in the same month as the sale, 70% are collected during the first month after the sale, and the remaining 10% are collected in the second month. Determine the amount of accounts receivable reported on Lighthouse's budgeted balance sheet as of July 31.

QS 23-5
Computing budgeted accounts receivable
P2

Use the following information to prepare a cash budget for the month ended on March 31 for Gado Company. The budget should show expected cash receipts and cash disbursements for the month of March and the balance expected on March 31.

a. Beginning cash balance on March 1, $72,000.

b. Cash receipts from sales, $300,000.

c. Budgeted cash disbursements for purchases, $140,000.

d. Budgeted cash disbursements for salaries, $80,000.

e. Other budgeted cash expenses, $45,000.

f. Cash repayment of bank loan, $20,000.

QS 23-6
Cash budget
P1   P2

Activity-based budgeting is a budget system based on *expected activities*. (1) Describe activity-based budgeting, and explain its preparation of budgets. (2) How does activity-based budgeting differ from traditional budgeting?

QS 23-7
Activity-based budgeting
A1

Forrest Company manufactures watches and has a JIT policy that ending inventory must equal 10% of the next month's sales. It estimates that October's actual ending inventory will consist of 40,000 watches. November and December sales are estimated to be 400,000 and 350,000 watches, respectively. Compute the number of watches to be produced that would appear on Forrest's production budget for the month of November.

QS 23-8[A]
Production budget
P3

Walker Company prepares monthly budgets. The current budget plans for a September ending inventory of 30,000 units. Company policy is to end each month with merchandise inventory equal to a specified percent of budgeted sales for the following month. Budgeted sales and merchandise purchases for the three most recent months follow. (1) Prepare the merchandise purchases budget for the months of July, August, and September. (2) Compute the ratio of ending inventory to the next month's sales for each budget prepared in part 1. (3) How many units are budgeted for sale in October?

Exercise 23-1
Preparation of merchandise purchases budgets (for three periods)

C3   P1

	Sales (Units)	Purchases (Units)
July	180,000	200,250
August	315,000	308,250
September	270,000	259,500

Check   July budgeted ending inventory, $47,250

Exercise 23-2
Preparation of cash budgets
(for three periods)

C3 P2

Kayak Co. budgeted the following cash receipts and cash disbursements for the first three months of next year.

	Cash Receipts	Cash Disbursements
January	$525,000	$475,000
February	400,000	350,000
March	450,000	525,000

Check January ending cash balance, $30,000

According to a credit agreement with the company's bank, Kayak promises to have a minimum cash balance of $30,000 at each month-end. In return, the bank has agreed that the company can borrow up to $150,000 at an annual interest rate of 12%, paid on the last day of each month. The interest is computed based on the beginning balance of the loan for the month. The company has a cash balance of $30,000 and a loan balance of $60,000 at January 1. Prepare monthly cash budgets for each of the first three months of next year.

Exercise 23-3
Preparation of a cash budget

C3 P2

Use the following information to prepare the July cash budget for Acco Co. It should show expected cash receipts and cash disbursements for the month and the cash balance expected on July 31.

a. Beginning cash balance on July 1: $50,000.

b. Cash receipts from sales: 30% is collected in the month of sale, 50% in the next month, and 20% in the second month after sale (uncollectible accounts are negligible and can be ignored). Sales amounts are: May (actual), $1,720,000; June (actual), $1,200,000; and July (budgeted), $1,400,000.

c. Payments on merchandise purchases: 60% in the month of purchase and 40% in the month following purchase. Purchases amounts are: June (actual), $700,000; and July (budgeted), $750,000.

d. Budgeted cash disbursements for salaries in July: $275,000.

e. Budgeted depreciation expense for July: $36,000.

f. Other cash expenses budgeted for July: $200,000.

g. Accrued income taxes due in July: $80,000.

Check Ending cash balance, $122,400

h. Bank loan interest due in July: $6,600.

Exercise 23-4
Preparing a budgeted income
statement and balance sheet

C3 P2

Use the information in Exercise 23-3 and the following additional information to prepare a budgeted income statement for the month of July and a budgeted balance sheet for July 31.

a. Cost of goods sold is 55% of sales.

b. Inventory at the end of June is $80,000 and at the end of July is $60,000.

c. Salaries payable on June 30 are $50,000 and are expected to be $60,000 on July 31.

d. The equipment account balance is $1,600,000 on July 31. On June 30, the accumulated depreciation on equipment is $280,000.

e. The $6,600 cash payment of interest represents the 1% monthly expense on a bank loan of $660,000.

f. Income taxes payable on July 31 are $30,720, and the income tax rate applicable to the company is 30%.

Check Net income, $71,680; Total assets, $2,686,400

g. The only other balance sheet accounts are: Common Stock, with a balance of $600,000 on June 30; and Retained Earnings, with a balance of $964,000 on June 30.

Exercise 23-5
Computing budgeted cash
payments for purchases

C3 P2

Hardy Company's cost of goods sold is consistently 60% of sales. The company plans to carry ending merchandise inventory for each month equal to 20% of the next month's budgeted cost of goods sold. All merchandise is purchased on credit, and 50% of the purchases made during a month is paid for in that month. Another 35% is paid for during the first month after purchase, and the remaining 15% is paid for during the second month after purchase. Expected sales are: August (actual), $325,000; September (actual), $320,000; October (estimated), $250,000; November (estimated), $310,000. Use this information to determine October's expected cash payments for purchases. (*Hint:* Use the layout of Exhibit 23.8, but revised for the facts given here.)

Check Budgeted purchases: August, $194,400; October, $157,200

Exercise 23-6
Computing budgeted purchases
and costs of goods sold

C3 P1 P2

Quick Dollar Company purchases all merchandise on credit. It recently budgeted the following month-end accounts payable balances and merchandise inventory balances. Cash payments on accounts payable during each month are expected to be: May, $1,600,000; June, $1,490,000; July, $1,425,000; and August, $1,495,000. Use the available information to compute the budgeted amounts of (1) merchandise purchases for June, July, and August, and (2) cost of goods sold for June, July, and August.

	Accounts Payable	Merchandise Inventory
May 31	$150,000	$250,000
June 30	200,000	400,000
July 31	235,000	300,000
August 31	195,000	330,000

Check June purchases, $1,540,000; June cost of goods sold, $1,390,000

Big Sound, a merchandising company specializing in home computer speakers, budgets its monthly cost of goods sold to equal 70% of sales. Its inventory policy calls for ending inventory in each month to equal 20% of the next month's budgeted cost of goods sold. All purchases are on credit, and 25% of the purchases in a month is paid for in the same month. Another 60% is paid for during the first month after purchase, and the remaining 15% is paid for in the second month after purchase. The following sales budgets are set: July, $350,000; August, $290,000; September, $320,000; October, $275,000; and November, $265,000. Compute the following: (1) budgeted merchandise purchases for July, August, September, and October; (2) budgeted payments on accounts payable for September and October; and (3) budgeted ending balances of accounts payable for September and October.

Exercise 23-7
Computing budgeted accounts payable and purchases P1 P2

Check July purchases, $236,600; Sept. payments on accts. pay., $214,235

Electro Company manufactures an innovative automobile transmission for electric cars. Management predicts that ending inventory for the first quarter will be 75,000 units. The following unit sales of the transmissions are expected during the rest of the year: second quarter, 450,000 units; third quarter, 525,000 units; and fourth quarter, 475,000 units. Company policy calls for the ending inventory of a quarter to equal 20% of the next quarter's budgeted sales. Prepare a production budget for both the second and third quarters that shows the number of transmissions to manufacture.

Exercise 23-8[A]
Preparing production budgets (for two periods) P3

Check Second quarter production, 480,000

Kegler's Supply is a merchandiser of three different products. The company's February 28 inventories are footwear, 20,000 units; sports equipment, 80,000 units; and apparel, 50,000 units. Management believes that excessive inventories have accumulated for all three products. As a result, a new policy dictates that ending inventory in any month should equal 30% of the expected unit sales for the following month. Expected sales in units for March, April, May, and June follow.

PROBLEM SET A

Problem 23-1A
Preparation and analysis of merchandise purchases budgets

C3 P1

mhhe.com/wildFAP18e

	Budgeted Sales in Units			
	March	April	May	June
Footwear	15,000	25,000	32,000	35,000
Sports equipment	70,000	90,000	95,000	90,000
Apparel	40,000	38,000	37,000	25,000

Required

1. Prepare a merchandise purchases budget (in units) for each product for each of the months of March, April, and May.

Check (1) March budgeted purchases Footwear, 2,500; Sports equip., 17,000; Apparel, 1,400

Analysis Component

2. The purchases budgets in part 1 should reflect fewer purchases of all three products in March compared to those in April and May. What factor caused fewer purchases to be planned? Suggest business conditions that would cause this factor to both occur and impact the company in this way.

During the last week of August, Oneida Company's owner approaches the bank for a $100,000 loan to be made on September 2 and repaid on November 30 with annual interest of 12%, for an interest cost of $3,000. The owner plans to increase the store's inventory by $80,000 during September and needs the loan to pay for inventory acquisitions. The bank's loan officer needs more information about Oneida's ability to repay the loan and asks the owner to forecast the store's November 30 cash position. On September 1, Oneida is expected to have a $5,000 cash balance, $148,000 of accounts receivable, and $125,000 of accounts payable. Its budgeted sales, merchandise purchases, and various cash disbursements for the next three months follow.

Problem 23-2A
Preparation of cash budgets (for three periods)

C3 P2

mhhe.com/wildFAP18e

File Edit View Insert Format Tools Data Window Help			
Budgeted Figures*	**September**	**October**	**November**
Sales	$250,000	$375,000	$400,000
Merchandise purchases	240,000	225,000	200,000
Cash disbursements			
Payroll	20,000	22,000	24,000
Rent	10,000	10,000	10,000
Other cash expenses	35,000	30,000	20,000
Repayment of bank loan			100,000
Interest on the bank loan			3,000

* Operations began in August; August sales were $215,000 and purchases were $125,000.

The budgeted September merchandise purchases include the inventory increase. All sales are on account. The company predicts that 25% of credit sales is collected in the month of the sale, 45% in the month following the sale, 20% in the second month, 9% in the third, and the remainder is uncollectible. Applying these percents to the August credit sales, for example, shows that $96,750 of the $215,000 will be collected in September, $43,000 in October, and $19,350 in November. All merchandise is purchased on credit; 80% of the balance is paid in the month following a purchase, and the remaining 20% is paid in the second month. For example, of the $125,000 August purchases, $100,000 will be paid in September and $25,000 in October.

Check Budgeted cash balance: September, $99,250; October, $69,500; November, $22,600

Required

Prepare a cash budget for September, October, and November for Oneidia Company. Show supporting calculations as needed.

Problem 23-3A
Preparation and analysis of cash budgets with supporting inventory and purchases budgets

C3   P2

Aztec Company sells its product for $180 per unit. Its actual and projected sales follow.

	Units	Dollars
April (actual)	4,000	$ 720,000
May (actual)	2,000	360,000
June (budgeted)	6,000	1,080,000
July (budgeted)	5,000	900,000
August (budgeted)	3,800	684,000

All sales are on credit. Recent experience shows that 20% of credit sales is collected in the month of the sale, 50% in the month after the sale, 28% in the second month after the sale, and 2% proves to be uncollectible. The product's purchase price is $110 per unit. All purchases are payable within 12 days. Thus, 60% of purchases made in a month is paid in that month and the other 40% is paid in the next month. Aztec has a policy to maintain an ending monthly inventory of 20% of the next month's unit sales plus a safety stock of 100 units. The April 30 and May 31 actual inventory levels are consistent with this policy. Selling and administrative expenses for the year are $1,320,000 and are paid evenly throughout the year in cash. The company's minimum cash balance at month-end is $100,000. This minimum is maintained, if necessary, by borrowing cash from the bank. If the balance exceeds $100,000, the company repays as much of the loan as it can without going below the minimum. This type of loan carries an annual 12% interest rate. On May 31, the loan balance is $25,000, and the company's cash balance is $100,000.

Required

Check (1) Cash collections: June, $597,600; July, $820,800

1. Prepare a table that shows the computation of cash collections of its credit sales (accounts receivable) in each of the months of June and July.

2. Prepare a table that shows the computation of budgeted ending inventories (in units) for April, May, June, and July.

(3) Budgeted purchases: May, $308,000; June, $638,000

3. Prepare the merchandise purchases budget for May, June, and July. Report calculations in units and then show the dollar amount of purchases for each month.

4. Prepare a table showing the computation of cash payments on product purchases for June and July.

(5) Budgeted ending loan balance: June, $43,650; July, $0

5. Prepare a cash budget for June and July, including any loan activity and interest expense. Compute the loan balance at the end of each month.

Analysis Component

6. Refer to your answer to part 5. Aztec's cash budget indicates the company will need to borrow more than $18,000 in June and will be able to pay it back in July. Suggest some reasons that knowing this information in May would be helpful to management.

Merline, a one-product mail-order firm, buys its product for $75 per unit and sells it for $150 per unit. The sales staff receives a 10% commission on the sale of each unit. Its December income statement follows.

Problem 23-4A

Preparation and analysis of budgeted income statements

C3 P2

MERLINE COMPANY Income Statement For Month Ended December 31, 2008	
Sales	$2,250,000
Cost of goods sold	1,125,000
Gross profit	1,125,000
Expenses	
Sales commissions (10%)	225,000
Advertising	250,000
Store rent	30,000
Administrative salaries	45,000
Depreciation	50,000
Other expenses	10,000
Total expenses	610,000
Net income	$ 515,000

Management expects December's results to be repeated in January, February, and March of 2009 without any changes in strategy. Management, however, has an alternative plan. It believes that unit sales will increase at a rate of 10% *each* month for the next three months (beginning with January) if the item's selling price is reduced to $125 per unit and advertising expenses are increased by 15% and remain at that level for all three months. The cost of its product will remain at $75 per unit, the sales staff will continue to earn a 10% commission, and the remaining expenses will stay the same.

Required

1. Prepare budgeted income statements for each of the months of January, February, and March that show the expected results from implementing the proposed changes. Use a three-column format, with one column for each month.

Check (1) Budgeted net income:
January, $196,250; February, $258,125;
March, $326,187

Analysis Component

2. Use the budgeted income statements from part 1 to recommend whether management should implement the proposed changes. Explain.

Near the end of 2008, the management of Dimsdale Sports Co., a merchandising company, prepared the following estimated balance sheet for December 31, 2008.

Problem 23-5A

Preparation of a complete master budget

C2 C3 P1 P2

DIMSDALE SPORTS COMPANY Estimated Balance Sheet December 31, 2008		
Assets		
Cash		$ 36,000
Accounts receivable		525,000
Inventory		150,000
Total current assets		711,000
Equipment	$540,000	
Less accumulated depreciation	67,500	472,500
Total assets		$1,183,500

[continued on next page]

[continued from previous page]

Liabilities and Equity		
Accounts payable	$360,000	
Bank loan payable	15,000	
Taxes payable (due 3/15/2009)	90,000	
Total liabilities		$ 465,000
Common stock	472,500	
Retained earnings	246,000	
Total stockholders' equity		718,500
Total liabilities and equity		$1,183,500

To prepare a master budget for January, February, and March of 2009, management gathers the following information.

a. Dimsdale Sports' single product is purchased for $30 per unit and resold for $55 per unit. The expected inventory level of 5,000 units on December 31, 2008, is more than management's desired level for 2009, which is 20% of the next month's expected sales (in units). Expected sales are: January, 7,000 units; February, 9,000 units; March, 11,000 units; and April, 10,000 units.

b. Cash sales and credit sales represent 25% and 75%, respectively, of total sales. Of the credit sales, 60% is collected in the first month after the month of sale and 40% in the second month after the month of sale. For the December 31, 2008, accounts receivable balance, $125,000 is collected in January and the remaining $400,000 is collected in February.

c. Merchandise purchases are paid for as follows: 20% in the first month after the month of purchase and 80% in the second month after the month of purchase. For the December 31, 2008, accounts payable balance, $80,000 is paid in January and the remaining $280,000 is paid in February.

d. Sales commissions equal to 20% of sales are paid each month. Sales salaries (excluding commissions) are $60,000 per year.

e. General and administrative salaries are $144,000 per year. Maintenance expense equals $2,000 per month and is paid in cash.

f. Equipment reported in the December 31, 2008, balance sheet was purchased in January 2008. It is being depreciated over eight years under the straight-line method with no salvage value. The following amounts for new equipment purchases are planned in the coming quarter: January, $36,000; February, $96,000; and March, $28,800. This equipment will be depreciated under the straight-line method over eight years with no salvage value. A full month's depreciation is taken for the month in which equipment is purchased.

g. The company plans to acquire land at the end of March at a cost of $150,000, which will be paid with cash on the last day of the month.

h. Dimsdale Sports has a working arrangement with its bank to obtain additional loans as needed. The interest rate is 12% per year, and interest is paid at each month-end based on the beginning balance. Partial or full payments on these loans can be made on the last day of the month. The company has agreed to maintain a minimum ending cash balance of $25,000 in each month.

i. The income tax rate for the company is 40%. Income taxes on the first quarter's income will not be paid until April 15.

Required

Prepare a master budget for each of the first three months of 2009; include the following component budgets (show supporting calculations as needed, and round amounts to the nearest dollar):

1. Monthly sales budgets (showing both budgeted unit sales and dollar sales).

2. Monthly merchandise purchases budgets.

3. Monthly selling expense budgets.

4. Monthly general and administrative expense budgets.

5. Monthly capital expenditures budgets.

6. Monthly cash budgets.

7. Budgeted income statement for the entire first quarter (not for each month).

8. Budgeted balance sheet as of March 31, 2009.

Check (2) Budgeted purchases: January, $114,000; February, $282,000

(3) Budgeted selling expenses: January, $82,000; February, $104,000

(6) Ending cash bal.: January, $30,100; February, $210,300

(8) Budgeted total assets at March 31, $1,568,650

Black Diamond Company produces snow skis. Each ski requires 2 pounds of carbon fiber. The company's management predicts that 5,000 skis and 6,000 pounds of carbon fiber will be in inventory on June 30 of the current year and that 150,000 skis will be sold during the next (third) quarter. Management wants to end the third quarter with 3,500 skis and 4,000 pounds of carbon fiber in inventory. Carbon fiber can be purchased for $15 per pound.

Problem 23-6A[A]
Preparing production and direct materials budgets
C3   P3

Required

1. Prepare the third-quarter production budget for skis.
2. Prepare the third-quarter direct materials (carbon fiber) budget; include the dollar cost of purchases.

Check   (1) Units manuf., 148,500;
(2) Cost of carbon fiber purchases, $4,425,000

H2O Sports Corp. is a merchandiser of three different products. The company's March 31 inventories are water skis, 40,000 units; tow ropes, 90,000 units; and life jackets, 150,000 units. Management believes that excessive inventories have accumulated for all three products. As a result, a new policy dictates that ending inventory in any month should equal 10% of the expected unit sales for the following month. Expected sales in units for April, May, June, and July follow.

PROBLEM SET B

Problem 23-1B
Preparation and analysis of merchandise purchases budgets

C3   P1

	Budgeted Sales in Units			
	April	May	June	July
Water skis	70,000	90,000	130,000	100,000
Tow ropes	100,000	90,000	110,000	100,000
Life jackets	160,000	190,000	200,000	120,000

Required

1. Prepare a merchandise purchases budget (in units) for each product for each of the months of April, May, and June.

Analysis Component

2. The purchases budgets in part 1 should reflect fewer purchases of all three products in April compared to those in May and June. What factor caused fewer purchases to be planned? Suggest business conditions that would cause this factor to both occur and affect the company as it has.

Check   (1) April budgeted purchases:
Water skis, 39,000; Tow ropes, 19,000;
Life jackets, 29,000

During the last week of March, Sony Stereo's owner approaches the bank for an $80,000 loan to be made on April 1 and repaid on June 30 with annual interest of 12%, for an interest cost of $2,400. The owner plans to increase the store's inventory by $60,000 in April and needs the loan to pay for inventory acquisitions. The bank's loan officer needs more information about Sony Stereo's ability to repay the loan and asks the owner to forecast the store's June 30 cash position. On April 1, Sony Stereo is expected to have a $3,000 cash balance, $135,000 of accounts receivable, and $100,000 of accounts payable. Its budgeted sales, merchandise purchases, and various cash disbursements for the next three months follow.

Problem 23-2B
Preparation of cash budgets (for three periods)

C3   P2

File   Edit   View   Insert   Format   Tools   Data   Window   Help

	Budgeted Figures*	April	May	June
1	**Budgeted Figures***	**April**	**May**	**June**
2	Sales	$220,000	$300,000	$380,000
3	Merchandise purchases	210,000	180,000	220,000
4	Cash disbursements			
5	Payroll	16,000	17,000	18,000
6	Rent	6,000	8,000	6,000
7	Other cash expenses	64,000	8,000	7,000
8	Repayment of bank loan			80,000
9	Interest on the bank loan.........			2,400
10				

* Operations began in March; March sales were $180,000 and purchases were $100,000.

The budgeted April merchandise purchases include the inventory increase. All sales are on account. The company predicts that 25% of credit sales is collected in the month of the sale, 45% in the month following the sale, 20% in the second month, 9% in the third, and the remainder is uncollectible. Applying these percents to the March credit sales, for example, shows that $81,000 of the $180,000 will be collected in April, $36,000 in May, and $16,200 in June. All merchandise is purchased on credit; 80% of the balance is paid in the month following a purchase and the remaining 20% is paid in the second month. For example, of the $100,000 March purchases, $80,000 will be paid in April and $20,000 in May.

Check Budgeted cash balance: April, $53,000; May, $44,000; June, $34,800

Required

Prepare a cash budget for April, May, and June for Sony Stereo. Show supporting calculations as needed.

Problem 23-3B

Preparation and analysis of cash budgets with supporting inventory and purchases budgets

C3   P2

Connick Company sells its product for $22 per unit. Its actual and projected sales follow.

	Units	Dollars
January (actual)	18,000	$396,000
February (actual)	22,500	495,000
March (budgeted)	19,000	418,000
April (budgeted)	18,750	412,500
May (budgeted)	21,000	462,000

All sales are on credit. Recent experience shows that 40% of credit sales is collected in the month of the sale, 35% in the month after the sale, 23% in the second month after the sale, and 2% proves to be uncollectible. The product's purchase price is $12 per unit. All purchases are payable within 21 days. Thus, 30% of purchases made in a month is paid in that month and the other 70% is paid in the next month. Connick has a policy to maintain an ending monthly inventory of 20% of the next month's unit sales plus a safety stock of 100 units. The January 31 and February 28 actual inventory levels are consistent with this policy. Selling and administrative expenses for the year are $1,920,000 and are paid evenly throughout the year in cash. The company's minimum cash balance for month-end is $50,000. This minimum is maintained, if necessary, by borrowing cash from the bank. If the balance exceeds $50,000, the company repays as much of the loan as it can without going below the minimum. This type of loan carries an annual 12% interest rate. At February 28, the loan balance is $12,000, and the company's cash balance is $50,000.

Required

Check (1) Cash collections: March, $431,530; April, $425,150

1. Prepare a table that shows the computation of cash collections of its credit sales (accounts receivable) in each of the months of March and April.
2. Prepare a table showing the computations of budgeted ending inventories (units) for January, February, March, and April.

(3) Budgeted purchases: February, $261,600; March, $227,400

3. Prepare the merchandise purchases budget for February, March, and April. Report calculations in units and then show the dollar amount of purchases for each month.
4. Prepare a table showing the computation of cash payments on product purchases for March and April.

(5) Ending cash balance: March, $58,070, April, $94,920

5. Prepare a cash budget for March and April, including any loan activity and interest expense. Compute the loan balance at the end of each month.

Analysis Component

6. Refer to your answer to part 5. Connick's cash budget indicates whether the company must borrow additional funds at the end of March. Suggest some reasons that knowing this information in February would be helpful to management.

Problem 23-4B

Preparation and analysis of budgeted income statements

C3   P2

Comp-Media buys its product for $60 and sells it for $130 per unit. The sales staff receives a 10% commission on the sale of each unit. Its June income statement follows.

COMP-MEDIA COMPANY Income Statement For Month Ended June 30, 2008	
Sales	$1,300,000
Cost of goods sold	600,000
Gross profit	700,000
Expenses	
Sales commissions (10%)	130,000
Advertising	200,000

[continued on next page]

[continued from previous page]

Store rent	24,000
Administrative salaries	40,000
Depreciation	50,000
Other expenses	12,000
Total expenses	456,000
Net income	$ 244,000

Management expects June's results to be repeated in July, August, and September without any changes in strategy. Management, however, has another plan. It believes that unit sales will increase at a rate of 10% *each* month for the next three months (beginning with July) if the item's selling price is reduced to $115 per unit and advertising expenses are increased by 25% and remain at that level for all three months. The cost of its product will remain at $60 per unit, the sales staff will continue to earn a 10% commission, and the remaining expenses will stay the same.

Required

1. Prepare budgeted income statements for each of the months of July, August, and September that show the expected results from implementing the proposed changes. Use a three-column format, with one column for each month.

Check Budgeted net income: July, $102,500; August, $150,350; September, $202,985

Analysis Component

2. Use the budgeted income statements from part 1 to recommend whether management should implement the proposed plan. Explain.

Near the end of 2008, the management of Isle Corp., a merchandising company, prepared the following estimated balance sheet for December 31, 2008.

Problem 23-5B
Preparation of a complete master budget

C2 C3 P1 P2

ISLE CORPORATION
Estimated Balance Sheet
December 31, 2008

Assets

Cash		$ 36,000
Accounts receivable		525,000
Inventory		150,000
Total current assets		711,000
Equipment	$540,000	
Less accumulated depreciation	67,500	472,500
Total assets		$1,183,500

Liabilities and Equity

Accounts payable	$360,000	
Bank loan payable	15,000	
Taxes payable (due 3/15/2009)	90,000	
Total liabilities		$ 465,000
Common stock	472,500	
Retained earnings	246,000	
Total stockholders' equity		718,500
Total liabilities and equity		$1,183,500

To prepare a master budget for January, February, and March of 2009, management gathers the following information.

a. Isle Corp.'s single product is purchased for $30 per unit and resold for $45 per unit. The expected inventory level of 5,000 units on December 31, 2008, is more than management's desired level for 2009, which is 25% of the next month's expected sales (in units). Expected sales are: January, 6,000 units; February, 8,000 units; March, 10,000 units; and April, 9,000 units.

b. Cash sales and credit sales represent 25% and 75%, respectively, of total sales. Of the credit sales, 60% is collected in the first month after the month of sale and 40% in the second month after the month of sale. For the $525,000 accounts receivable balance at December 31, 2008, $315,000 is collected in January 2009 and the remaining $210,000 is collected in February 2009.

c. Merchandise purchases are paid for as follows: 20% in the first month after the month of purchase and 80% in the second month after the month of purchase. For the $360,000 accounts payable balance at December 31, 2008, $72,000 is paid in January 2009 and the remaining $288,000 is paid in February 2009.

d. Sales commissions equal to 20% of sales are paid each month. Sales salaries (excluding commissions) are $90,000 per year.

e. General and administrative salaries are $144,000 per year. Maintenance expense equals $3,000 per month and is paid in cash.

f. Equipment reported in the December 31, 2008, balance sheet was purchased in January 2008. It is being depreciated over 8 years under the straight-line method with no salvage value. The following amounts for new equipment purchases are planned in the coming quarter: January, $72,000; February, $96,000; and March, $28,800. This equipment will be depreciated using the straight-line method over 8 years with no salvage value. A full month's depreciation is taken for the month in which equipment is purchased.

g. The company plans to acquire land at the end of March at a cost of $150,000, which will be paid with cash on the last day of the month.

h. Isle Corp. has a working arrangement with its bank to obtain additional loans as needed. The interest rate is 12% per year, and interest is paid at each month-end based on the beginning balance. Partial or full payments on these loans can be made on the last day of the month. Isle has agreed to maintain a minimum ending cash balance of $36,000 in each month.

i. The income tax rate for the company is 40%. Income taxes on the first quarter's income will not be paid until April 15.

Required

Prepare a master budget for each of the first three months of 2009; include the following component budgets (show supporting calculations as needed, and round amounts to the nearest dollar):

1. Monthly sales budgets (showing both budgeted unit sales and dollar sales).

Check (2) Budgeted purchases: January, $90,000; February, $255,000;
(3) Budgeted selling expenses: January, $61,500; February, $79,500

2. Monthly merchandise purchases budgets.

3. Monthly selling expense budgets.

4. Monthly general and administrative expense budgets.

5. Monthly capital expenditures budgets.

(6) Ending cash bal.: January, $182,850; February, $107,850
(8) Budgeted total assets at March 31, $1,346,875

6. Monthly cash budgets.

7. Budgeted income statement for the entire first quarter (not for each month).

8. Budgeted balance sheet as of March 31, 2009.

Problem 23-6B[A]
Preparing production and direct materials budgets

C3 P3

NSA Company produces baseball bats. Each bat requires 3 pounds of aluminum alloy. Management predicts that 8,000 bats and 15,000 pounds of aluminum alloy will be in inventory on March 31 of the current year and that 250,000 bats will be sold during this year's second quarter. Management wants to end the second quarter with 6,000 finished bats and 12,000 pounds of aluminum alloy in inventory. Aluminum alloy can be purchased for $4 per pound.

Required

Check (1) Units manuf., 248,000;
(2) Cost of aluminum purchases, $2,964,000

1. Prepare the second-quarter production budget for bats.

2. Prepare the second-quarter direct materials (aluminum alloy) budget; include the dollar cost of purchases.

PROBLEM SET C

 Problem Set C is available at the book's Website to further reinforce and assess your learning.

SERIAL PROBLEM

Success Systems

(This serial problem began in Chapter 1 and continues through most of the book. If previous chapter segments were not completed, the serial problem can begin at this point. It is helpful, but not necessary, for you to use the Working Papers that accompany the book.)

SP 23 Adriana Lopez expects second quarter 2009 sales of her new line of computer furniture to be the same as the first quarter's sales (reported below) without any changes in strategy. Monthly sales averaged 40 desk units (sales price of $1,250) and 20 chairs (sales price of $500).

```
╔══════════════════════════════════════╗
║           SUCCESS SYSTEMS            ║
║       Segment Income Statement*      ║
║     For Quarter Ended March 31, 2009 ║
╚══════════════════════════════════════╝
```

Sales†	$180,000
Cost of goods sold‡	105,000
Gross profit	75,000
Expenses	
Sales commissions (10%)	18,000
Advertising expenses	9,000
Other fixed expenses	18,000
Total expenses	45,000
Net income	$ 30,000

* Reflects revenue and expense activity only related to the computer furniture segment.

† Revenue: (120 desks × $1,250) + (60 chairs × $500) = $150,000 + $30,000 = $180,000

‡ Cost of goods sold: (120 desks × $750) + (60 chairs × $250) = $90,000 + $15,000 = $105,000

Lopez believes that sales will increase each month for the next three months (April, 44 desks, 22 chairs; May, 48 desks, 24 chairs; June, 52 desks, 26 chairs) *if* selling prices are reduced to $1,125 for desks and $375 for chairs, and advertising expenses are increased by 25% and remain at that level for all three months. The products' cost will remain at $750 for desks and $250 for chairs. The sales staff will continue to earn a 10% commission, and the fixed costs per month will remain at $5,000.

Required

1. Prepare budgeted income statements for each of the months of April, May, and June that show the expected results from implementing the proposed changes. Use a three-column format, with one column for each month.

   Check   (1) Budgeted income: April, $3,725; May, $4,950

2. Use the budgeted income statements from part 1 to recommend whether Lopez should implement the proposed changes. Explain.

BEYOND THE NUMBERS

BTN 23-1   Financial statements often serve as a starting point in formulating budgets. You are assigned to review **Best Buy**'s financial statements to determine its cash paid for dividends in the current year and the budgeted cash needed to pay its next year's dividend.

Required

1. Which financial statement(s) reports the amount of (a) cash dividends paid and (b) annual cash dividends declared? Explain where on the statement(s) this information is reported.
2. Indicate the amount of cash dividends (a) paid in the year ended February 26, 2005, and (b) to be paid (budgeted for) next year under the assumption that annual cash dividends equal 20% of the prior year's net income.

REPORTING IN ACTION

P2   C2   C3

Fast Forward

3. Access Best Buy's financial statements for a fiscal year ending after February 26, 2005, from either its Website [BestBuy.com] or the SEC's EDGAR database [www.SEC.gov]. Compare your answer for part 2 with actual cash dividends paid for its fiscal year ended 2006. Compute the error, if any, in your estimate. Speculate as to why dividends were higher or lower than budgeted.

**COMPARATIVE
ANALYSIS**

P2

BTN 23-2 One source of cash savings for a company is improved management of inventory. To illustrate, assume that **Best Buy** and **Circuit City** both have $250,000 per month in sales in the Virginia area, and both forecast this level of sales per month for the next 24 months. Also assume that both Best Buy and Circuit City have a 20% contribution margin and equal fixed costs, and that cost of goods sold is the only variable cost. Assume that the main difference between Best Buy and Circuit City is the distribution system. Best Buy uses a just-in-time system and requires ending inventory of only 10% of next month's sales in inventory at each month-end. However, Circuit City is building an improved distribution system and currently requires 40% of next month's sales in inventory at each month-end.

Required

1. Compute the amount by which Circuit City can reduce its inventory level if it can match Best Buy's system of maintaining an inventory equal to 10% of next month's sales. (*Hint:* Focus on the facts given and only on the Virginia area.)
2. Explain how the analysis in part 1 that shows ending inventory levels for both the 40% and 10% required inventory policies can help justify a just-in-time inventory system. You can assume a 15% interest cost for resources that are tied up in ending inventory.

**ETHICS
CHALLENGE**

C1 C2

BTN 23-3 Both the budget process and budgets themselves can impact management actions, both positively and negatively. For instance, a common practice among not-for-profit organizations and government agencies is for management to spend any amounts remaining in a budget at the end of the budget period, a practice often called "use it or lose it." The view is that if a department manager does not spend the budgeted amount, top management will reduce next year's budget by the amount not spent. To avoid losing budget dollars, department managers often spend all budgeted amounts regardless of the value added to products or services. All of us pay for the costs associated with this budget system.

Required

Write a one-half page report to a local not-for-profit organization or government agency offering a solution to the "use it or lose it" budgeting problem.

**COMMUNICATING
IN PRACTICE**

P1

BTN 23-4 The sales budget is usually the first and most crucial of the component budgets in a master budget because all other budgets usually rely on it for planning purposes.

Required

Assume that your company's sales staff provides information on expected sales and selling prices for items making up the sales budget. Prepare a one-page memorandum to your supervisor outlining concerns with the sales staff's input in the sales budget when its compensation is at least partly tied to these budgets. More generally, explain the importance of assessing any potential bias in information provided to the budget process.

**TAKING IT TO
THE NET**

C2 P1 P2

BTN 23-5 Access an e-budgets Website at **HelmsmanGroup.com** (by **FRx Corporation**). Review the information at this site; click on the link *CFO Tour* and examine the information provided.

Required

1. Assume the role of a senior manager in a large, multidivision company. What are the benefits of using e-budgets?
2. As a senior manager, what concerns do you have with the concept and application of e-budgets?

**TEAMWORK IN
ACTION**

A1

BTN 23-6 Your team is to prepare a budget report outlining the costs of attending college (full-time) for the next two semesters (30 hours) or three quarters (45 hours). This budget's focus is solely on attending college; do not include personal items in the team's budget. Your budget must include tuition, books, supplies, club fees, food, housing, and all costs associated with travel to and from college. This budgeting exercise is similar to the initial phase in activity-based budgeting. Include a list of any assumptions you use in completing the budget. Be prepared to present your budget in class.

BTN 23-7 Read the article "Get Thee to a Budget" from the March 14, 2005, issue of *Business Week*. (This book's Website provides free access to this article.)

BusinessWeek
ACTIVITY

C2 A1

Required

What advantages do new business owners who prepare budgets have over those who do not?

BTN 23-8 **Cloudveil** currently produces high-performance, multisport mountain apparel. Assume that Stephen Sullivan and Brian Cousins are considering producing a new line of apparel for high-altitude camping. They plan on meeting with a financial institution for potential funding and have been asked by its loan officers for their business plan.

ENTREPRENEURIAL DECISION

C1

Required

1. What should Cloudveil's business plan include?

2. How can budgeting help the owners efficiently develop and operate their business?

BTN 23-9 To help understand the factors impacting a sales budget, you are to visit three businesses with the same ownership or franchise membership. Record the selling prices of two identical products at each location, such as regular and premium gas sold at **Chevron** stations. You are likely to find a difference in prices for at least one of the three locations you visit.

HITTING THE ROAD

C3 P1

Required

1. Identify at least three external factors that must be considered when setting the sales budget. (*Note:* There is a difference between internal and external factors that impact the sales budget.)

2. What factors might explain any differences identified in the prices of the businesses you visited?

BTN 23-10 Access **Dixons'** income statement (**Dixons-Group.com**) for the year ended May 1, 2004.

GLOBAL DECISION

Dixons

Required

1. Is Dixons' administrative expense budget likely to be an important budget in its master budgeting process? Explain.

2. Identify three types of expenses that would be reported as administrative expenses on Dixons' income statement.

3. Who likely has the initial responsibility for Dixons' administrative expense budget? Explain.

ANSWERS TO MULTIPLE CHOICE QUIZ

1. c

2. e; Budgeted purchases = $36,000 + $7,000 − $6,000 = $37,000

3. b; Cash collected = 25% of September sales + 75% of August sales = (0.25 × $240,000) + (0.75 × $220,000) = $225,000

4. d

5. a; 560 units + (0.30 × 600 units) − (0.30 × 560 units) = 572 units

24

Flexible Budgets and Standard Costs

Learning Objectives

CAP

Standards for Performance Apparel

BALTIMORE, MD—Kevin Plank's company, **Under Armour (UnderArmour.com)**, manufactures a polyester blend fabric that whisks perspiration away from the skin. "There was a void in apparel and I decided to fill it," says Kevin. He invested his life savings of $20,000 and began working out of his grandma's basement. In the process, Kevin launched an entirely new sportswear category from sweaty undergarments.

As sales grew, Kevin partnered with a factory in Ohio that had excess capacity and hit it off with the factory manager, Sal Fasciana. Sal spent many evenings and weekends teaching Kevin about manufacturing, cost management, and accounting. It was Sal who introduced Kevin to budgets and variances. "I said, 'OK, kid. This is the way it's going to be done,'" recalls Sal. To save money for investing in his new company, Kevin even moved into a spare room in Sal and his wife's home, living on Sal's lasagna and Froot Loops.

Kevin applied what Sal taught him. He ensured the budgeted numbers were sensible and focused on meeting quality standards regarding materials, labor, and overhead. "We can only be concerned about ourselves and the job [that] we do," insists Kevin. The company adheres to tight standards variances. For instance, when a new product failed to meet standards, Kevin quickly pulled it and Under Armour took a $600,000 hit

in inventory. Says Kevin, "It's hard to take a $600,000 hit [but] money can be replaced." Kevin adheres to strict budgets and standards because, as he puts it, "The best product we manufacture is our story." Lose the story, and a company's edge is next.

A commitment to performance reporting and quality standards is propelling Under Armour's sales toward $300 million and shattering Kevin's most optimistic budget goals. "It's about educating consumers ... investing in the product." Kevin also applies cost analysis and variances, flexible and fixed budgets, and performance reports. Sales variances are especially crucial to production pricing because the polyester-blend fabric that Kevin uses costs two to three times as much as cotton.

"When I first started... I was a young punk who thought he knew everything," explains Kevin. Although Kevin admits that insight and ingenuity are vital, he knows accounting reports must show profits for long-term success. "Most people out there are saying we're going to trip up at some point," says Kevin. "Our job is to prove them wrong." He might also prove Thomas Edison right: genius is 99 percent perspiration and 1 percent inspiration.

[Sources: *Under Armour Website,* May 2006; *Entrepreneur,* November 2003; *FastCompany,* 2005 and 2002; *USA Today,* December 2004; *Inc.com,* 2003 and 2004; *All Headline News,* August 2005; *Baltimore Business Journal,* February 2006]

Budgeting helps organize and formalize management's planning activities. This chapter extends the study of budgeting to look more closely at the use of budgets to evaluate performance. Evaluations are important for controlling and monitoring business activities. This chapter also describes and illustrates the use of standard costs and variance analyses. These managerial tools are useful for both evaluating and controlling organizations and for the planning of future activities.

Flexible Budgets

Budgetary Process	**Flexible Budget Reports**
• Control and reporting	• Purpose
• Fixed budget performance report	• Preparation
• Evaluation	• Flexible budget performance report

Standard Costs

Materials and Labor Standards	**Cost Variances**	**Overhead Standards and Variances**
• Identifying materials and labor standards	• Analysis process	• Setting overhead standards
• Setting standard costs	• Computation	• Using variance analysis
	• Materials and labor variances	• Computing variances

Section 1—Flexible Budgets

This section introduces fixed budgets and fixed budget performance reports. It then introduces flexible budgets and flexible budget performance reports and illustrates their advantages.

Budgetary Process

A master budget reflects management's planned objectives for a future period. The preparation of a master budget is based on a predicted level of activity such as sales volume for the budget period. This section discusses the effects on the usefulness of budget reports when the actual level of activity differs from the predicted level.

Budgetary Control and Reporting

Budgetary control refers to management's use of budgets to monitor and control a company's operations. This includes using budgets to see that planned objectives are met. **Budget reports** contain relevant information that compares actual results to planned activities. This comparison is motivated by a need to both monitor performance and control activities. Budget reports are sometimes viewed as progress reports, or *report cards,* on management's performance in achieving planned objectives. These reports can be prepared at any time and for any period. Three common periods for a budget report are a month, quarter, and year.

Point: Budget reports are often used as a base to determine bonuses of managers.

The budgetary control process involves at least four steps: (1) develop the budget from planned objectives, (2) compare actual results to budgeted amounts and analyze any differences, (3) take corrective and strategic actions, and (4) establish new planned objectives and prepare a new budget. Exhibit 24.1 shows this continual process of budgetary control. Budget

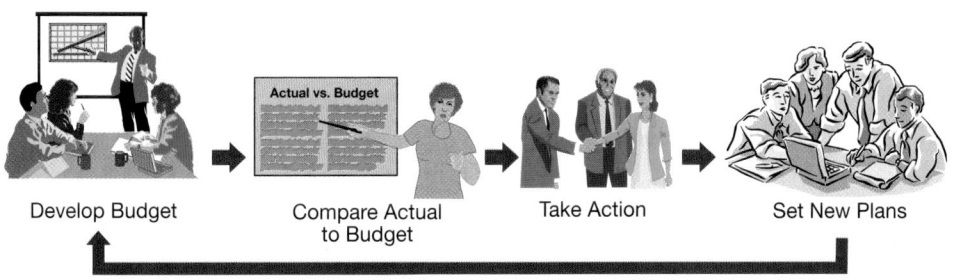

| Develop Budget | Compare Actual to Budget | Take Action | Set New Plans |

Exhibit 24.1

Process of Budgetary Control

reports and related documents are effective tools for managers to obtain the greatest benefits from this budgetary process.

Fixed Budget Performance Report

In a fixed budgetary control system, the master budget is based on a single prediction for sales volume or other activity level. The budgeted amount for each cost essentially assumes that a specific (or *fixed*) amount of sales will occur. A **fixed budget,** also called *static budget,* is based on a single predicted amount of sales or other measure of activity.

One benefit of a budget is its usefulness in comparing actual results with planned activities. Information useful for analysis is often presented for comparison in a performance report. As shown in Exhibit 24.2, a **fixed budget performance report** for Optel compares actual results for January 2008 with the results expected under its fixed budget that predicted 10,000 (composite) units of sales. Optel manufactures inexpensive eyeglasses, frames, contact lens, and related supplies. For this report, its production volume equals sales volume (its inventory level did not change).

Exhibit 24.2

Fixed Budget
Performance Report

OPTEL Fixed Budget Performance Report For Month Ended January 31, 2008	Fixed Budget	Actual Results	Variances*
Sales (in units)	10,000	12,000	
Sales (in dollars)	$100,000	$125,000	$25,000 F
Cost of goods sold			
Direct materials	10,000	13,000	3,000 U
Direct labor	15,000	20,000	5,000 U
Overhead			
Factory supplies	2,000	2,100	100 U
Utilities	3,000	4,000	1,000 U
Depreciation—Machinery	8,000	8,000	0
Supervisory salaries	11,000	11,000	0
Selling expenses			
Sales commissions	9,000	10,800	1,800 U
Shipping expenses	4,000	4,300	300 U
General and administrative expenses			
Office supplies	5,000	5,200	200 U
Insurance expenses	1,000	1,200	200 U
Depreciation—Office equipment	7,000	7,000	0
Administrative salaries	13,000	13,000	0
Total expenses	88,000	99,600	11,600 U
Income from operations	$ 12,000	$ 25,400	$13,400 F

* F = Favorable variance; and U = Unfavorable variance.

This type of performance report designates differences between budgeted and actual results as variances. We see the letters *F* and *U* located beside the numbers in the third number column of this report. Their meanings are as follows:

F = **Favorable variance**   When compared to budget, the actual cost or revenue contributes to a *higher* income. That is, actual revenue is higher than budgeted revenue, or actual cost is lower than budgeted cost.

U = **Unfavorable variance**   When compared to budget, the actual cost or revenue contributes to a *lower* income; actual revenue is lower than budgeted revenue, or actual cost is higher than budgeted cost.

This convention is common in practice and is used throughout this chapter.

Example: How is it that the favorable sales variance in Exhibit 24.2 is linked with so many unfavorable cost and expense variances? *Answer:* Costs have increased with the increase in sales.

Budget Reports for Evaluation

A primary use of budget reports is as a tool for management to monitor and control operations. Evaluation by Optel management is likely to focus on a variety of questions that might include these:

■ Why is actual income from operations $13,400 higher than budgeted?
■ Are amounts paid for each expense item too high?
■ Is manufacturing using too much direct material?
■ Is manufacturing using too much direct labor?

The performance report in Exhibit 24.2 provides little help in answering these questions because actual sales volume is 2,000 units higher than budgeted. A manager does not know if this higher level of sales activity is the cause of variations in total dollar sales and expenses or if other factors have influenced these amounts. This inability of fixed budget reports to adjust for changes in activity levels is a major limitation of a fixed budget performance report. That is, it fails to show whether actual costs are out of line due to a change in actual sales volume or some other factor.

Flexible Budget Reports

Purpose of Flexible Budgets

A1   Compare fixed and flexible budgets.

To help address limitations with the fixed budget performance report, particularly from the effects of changes in sales volume, management can use a flexible budget. A **flexible budget,** also called a *variable budget,* is a report based on predicted amounts of revenues and expenses corresponding to the actual level of output. Flexible budgets are useful both before and after the period's activities are complete.

A flexible budget prepared before the period is often based on several levels of activity. Budgets for those different levels can provide a "what if" look at operations. The different levels often include both a best case and worst case scenario. This allows management to make adjustments to avoid or lessen the effects of the worst case scenario.

A flexible budget prepared after the period helps management evaluate past performance. It is especially useful for such an evaluation because it reflects budgeted revenues and costs based on the actual level of activity. Thus, comparisons of actual results with budgeted performance are more likely to identify the causes of any differences. This can help managers focus attention on real problem areas and implement corrective actions. This is in contrast to a fixed budget, whose primary purpose is to assist managers in planning future activities and whose numbers are based on a single predicted amount of budgeted sales or production.

Topic Tackler

PLUS

24-1

Preparation of Flexible Budgets

A flexible budget is designed to reveal the effects of volume of activity on revenues and costs. To prepare a flexible budget, management relies on the distinctions between fixed and variable costs. Recall that the cost per unit of activity remains constant for variable costs so that the total amount of a variable cost changes in direct proportion to a change in activity level. The total amount of fixed cost remains unchanged regardless of changes in the level of activity within a relevant (normal) operating range. (Assume that costs can be reasonably classified as variable or fixed within a relevant range.)

When we create the numbers constituting a flexible budget, we express each variable cost as either a constant amount per unit of sales or as a percent of a sales dollar. In the case of a fixed cost, we express its budgeted amount as the total amount expected to occur at any sales volume within the relevant range.

Exhibit 24.3 shows a set of flexible budgets for Optel in January 2008. Seven of its expenses are classified as variable costs. Its remaining five expenses are fixed costs. These classifications result from management's investigation of each expense. Variable and fixed expense categories are *not* the same for every company, and we must avoid drawing conclusions from specific cases. For example, depending on the nature of a company's operations, office supplies expense can be either fixed or variable with respect to sales.

P1 Prepare a flexible budget and interpret a flexible budget performance report.

Point: Usefulness of a flexible budget depends on valid classification of variable and fixed costs. Some costs are mixed and must be analyzed to determine their variable and fixed portions.

Exhibit 24.3

Flexible Budgets

	Flexible Budget Variable Amount per Unit	Flexible Budget Total Fixed Cost	Flexible Budget for Unit Sales of 10,000	Flexible Budget for Unit Sales of 12,000	Flexible Budget for Unit Sales of 14,000
OPTEL Flexible Budgets For Month Ended January 31, 2008					
Sales	$10.00		$100,000	$120,000	$140,000
Variable costs					
Direct materials	1.00		10,000	12,000	14,000
Direct labor	1.50		15,000	18,000	21,000
Factory supplies	0.20		2,000	2,400	2,800
Utilities	0.30		3,000	3,600	4,200
Sales commissions	0.90		9,000	10,800	12,600
Shipping expenses	0.40		4,000	4,800	5,600
Office supplies	0.50		5,000	6,000	7,000
Total variable costs	4.80		48,000	57,600	67,200
Contribution margin	$ 5.20		$ 52,000	$ 62,400	$ 72,800
Fixed costs					
Depreciation—Machinery		$ 8,000	8,000	8,000	8,000
Supervisory salaries		11,000	11,000	11,000	11,000
Insurance expense		1,000	1,000	1,000	1,000
Depreciation—Office equipment		7,000	7,000	7,000	7,000
Administrative salaries		13,000	13,000	13,000	13,000
Total fixed costs		$40,000	40,000	40,000	40,000
Income from operations			$ 12,000	$ 22,400	$ 32,800

The layout for the flexible budgets in Exhibit 24.3 follows a *contribution margin format*— beginning with sales followed by variable costs and then fixed costs. Both the expected individual and total variable costs are reported and then subtracted from sales. The difference between sales and variable costs equals contribution margin. The expected amounts of fixed costs are listed next, followed by the expected income from operations before taxes.

Example: Using Exhibit 24.3, what is the budgeted income from operations for unit sales of (a) 11,000 and (b) 13,000? *Answers:* $17,200 for unit sales of 11,000. $27,600 for unit sales of 13,000.

The first and second number columns of Exhibit 24.3 show the flexible budget amounts for variable costs per unit and each fixed cost for any volume of sales in the relevant range. The third, fourth, and fifth columns show the flexible budget amounts computed for three different sales volumes. For instance, the third column's flexible budget is based on 10,000 units. These numbers are the same as those in the fixed budget of Exhibit 24.2 because the expected volumes are the same for these two budgets.

Recall that Optel's actual sales volume for January is 12,000 units. This sales volume is 2,000 units more than the 10,000 units originally predicted in the master budget. When differences between actual and predicted volume arise, the usefulness of a flexible budget is apparent. For instance, compare the flexible budget for 10,000 units in the third column (which is the same as the fixed budget in Exhibit 24.2) with the flexible budget for 12,000 units in the fourth column. The higher levels for both sales and variable costs reflect nothing more than the increase in sales activity. Any budget analysis comparing actual with planned results that ignores this information is less useful to management.

To illustrate, when we evaluate Optel's performance, we need to prepare a flexible budget showing actual and budgeted values at 12,000 units. As part of a complete profitability analysis, managers could compare the actual income of $25,400 (from Exhibit 24.2) with the $22,400 income expected at the actual sales volume of 12,000 units (from Exhibit 24.3). This results in a total income variance of $3,000 to be explained and interpreted. This variance is markedly different from the $13,400 variance identified in Exhibit 24.2 using a fixed budget. After receiving the flexible budget based on January's actual volume, management must determine what caused this $3,000 difference. The next section describes a flexible budget performance report that provides guidance in this analysis.

Point: Flexible budgeting allows a budget to be prepared at the *actual* output level. Performance reports are then prepared comparing the flexible budget to actual revenues and costs.

Point: A flexible budget yields an "apples to apples" comparison because budgeted activity levels are the same as the actual.

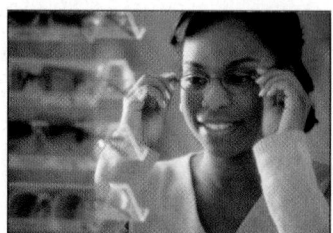

Flexible Budget Performance Report

A **flexible budget performance report** lists differences between actual performance and budgeted performance based on actual sales volume or other activity level. This report helps direct management's attention to those costs or revenues that differ substantially from budgeted amounts. Exhibit 24.4 shows Optel's flexible budget performance report for January. We prepare this report after the actual volume is known to be 12,000 units. This report shows a $5,000 favorable variance in total dollar sales. Because actual and budgeted volumes are both 12,000 units, the $5,000 sales variance must have resulted from a higher than expected selling price. Further analysis of the facts surrounding this $5,000 sales variance reveals a favorable sales variance per unit of nearly $0.42 as shown here:

Actual average price per unit (rounded to cents)	$125,000/12,000 = $10.42
Budgeted price per unit	$120,000/12,000 = 10.00
Favorable sales variance per unit	$5,000/12,000 = $ 0.42

The other variances in Exhibit 24.4 also direct management's attention to areas where corrective actions can help control Optel's operations. Each expense variance is analyzed as the sales variance was. We can think of each expense as the joint result of using a given number of units of input and paying a specific price per unit of input.

Each variance in Exhibit 24.4 is due in part to a difference between *actual price* per unit of input and *budgeted price* per unit of input. This is a **price variance.** Each variance also can be due in part to a difference between *actual quantity* of input used and *budgeted quantity* of input. This is a **quantity variance.** We explain more about this breakdown, known as **variance analysis,** later in the standard costs section.

Decision Maker   Answer—p. 978

Entrepreneur   The heads of both strategic consulting and tax consulting divisions of your financial services firm complain to you about the unfavorable variances on their performance reports. "We worked on more consulting assignments than planned. It's not surprising our costs are higher than expected. To top it off, this report characterizes our work as *poor!*" How do you respond?

Exhibit 24.4

Flexible Budget
Performance Report

OPTEL Flexible Budget Performance Report For Month Ended January 31, 2008	Flexible Budget	Actual Results	Variances*
Sales (12,000 units)	$120,000	$125,000	$5,000 F
Variable costs			
Direct materials	12,000	13,000	1,000 U
Direct labor	18,000	20,000	2,000 U
Factory supplies	2,400	2,100	300 F
Utilities	3,600	4,000	400 U
Sales commissions	10,800	10,800	0
Shipping expenses	4,800	4,300	500 F
Office supplies	6,000	5,200	800 F
Total variable costs	57,600	59,400	1,800 U
Contribution margin	62,400	65,600	3,200 F
Fixed costs			
Depreciation—Machinery	8,000	8,000	0
Supervisory salaries	11,000	11,000	0
Insurance expense	1,000	1,200	200 U
Depreciation—Office equipment	7,000	7,000	0
Administrative salaries	13,000	13,000	0
Total fixed costs	40,000	40,200	200 U
Income from operations	$ 22,400	$ 25,400	$3,000 F

* F = Favorable variance; and U = Unfavorable variance.

Quick Check

Answers—p. 978

1. A flexible budget (a) shows fixed costs as constant amounts of cost per unit of activity, (b) shows variable costs as constant amounts of cost per unit of activity, or (c) is prepared based on one expected amount of budgeted sales or production.
2. What is the initial step in preparing a flexible budget?
3. What is the main difference between a fixed and a flexible budget?
4. What is contribution margin?

Section 2—Standard Costs

Standard costs are preset costs for delivering a product or service under normal conditions. These costs are established by personnel, engineering, and accounting studies using past experiences and data. Management uses these costs to assess the reasonableness of actual costs incurred for producing the product or service. When actual costs vary from standard costs, management follows up to identify potential problems and take corrective actions.

Standard costs are often used in preparing budgets because they are the anticipated costs incurred under normal conditions. Terms such as *standard materials cost, standard labor cost,* and *standard overhead cost* are often used to refer to amounts budgeted for direct materials, direct labor, and overhead.

C1 Define *standard costs* and explain their computation and uses.

Point: Since standard costs are often budgeted costs, they can be used to prepare both fixed budgets and flexible budgets.

Materials and Labor Standards

This section explains how to set materials and labor standards and how to prepare a standard cost card.

Identifying Standard Costs

Point: Business practice often uses the word *budget* when speaking of total amounts and *standard* when discussing per unit amounts.

Managerial accountants, engineers, personnel administrators, and other managers combine their efforts to set standard costs. To identify standards for direct labor costs, we can conduct time and motion studies for each labor operation in the process of providing a product or service. From these studies, management can learn the best way to perform the operation and then set the standard labor time required for the operation under normal conditions. Similarly, standards for materials are set by studying the quantity, grade, and cost of each material used. Standards for overhead costs are explained later in the chapter.

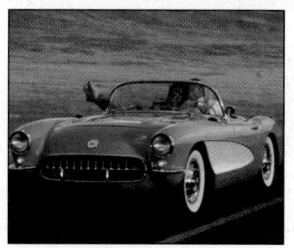

Decision Insight

Cruis'n Standards The **Corvette** consists of hundreds of parts for which engineers set standards. Various types of labor are also involved in its production, including machining, assembly, painting, and welding, and standards are set for each. Actual results are periodically compared with standards to assess performance.

Regardless of the care used in setting standard costs and in revising them as conditions change, actual costs frequently differ from standard costs, often as a result of one or more factors. For instance, the actual quantity of material used can differ from the standard, or the price paid per unit of material can differ from the standard. Quantity and price differences from standard amounts can also occur for labor. That is, the actual labor time and actual labor rate can vary from what was expected. The same analysis applies to overhead costs.

Setting Standard Costs

Example: What factors might be considered when deciding whether to revise standard costs? *Answer:* Changes in the processes and/or resources needed to carry out the processes.

Point: Companies promoting continuous improvement strive to achieve ideal standards by eliminating inefficiencies and waste.

To illustrate the setting of a standard cost, we consider a professional league baseball bat manufactured by ProBat. Its engineers have determined that manufacturing one bat requires 0.90 kgs. of high-grade wood. They also expect some loss of material as part of the process because of inefficiencies and waste. This results in adding an *allowance* of 0.10 kgs., making the standard requirement 1.0 kg. of wood for each bat.

The 0.90 kgs. portion is called an *ideal standard;* it is the quantity of material required if the process is 100% efficient without any loss or waste. Reality suggests that some loss of material usually occurs with any process. The standard of 1.0 kg. is known as the *practical standard,* the quantity of material required under normal application of the process.

High-grade wood can be purchased at a standard price of $25 per kg. The purchasing department sets this price as the expected price for the budget period. To determine this price, the purchasing department considers factors such as the quality of materials, future economic conditions, supply factors (shortages and excesses), and any available discounts. The engineers also decide that two hours of labor time (after including allowances) are required to manufacture a bat. The wage rate is $20 per hour (better than average skilled labor is required). ProBat assigns all overhead at the rate of $10 per labor hour. The standard costs of direct materials, direct labor, and overhead for one bat are as shown in Exhibit 24.5 in what is called a *standard cost card.* These cost amounts are then used to prepare manufacturing budgets for a budgeted level of production.

Exhibit 24.5

Standard Cost Card

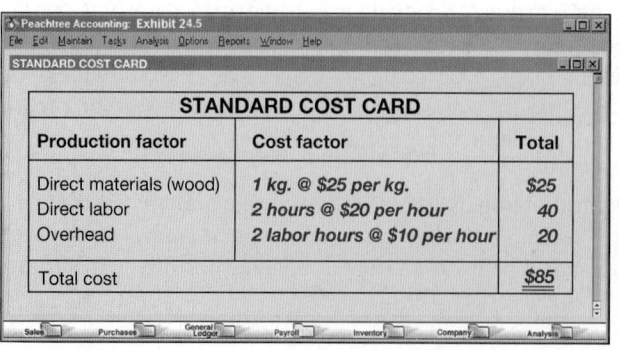

STANDARD COST CARD

Production factor	Cost factor	Total
Direct materials (wood)	1 kg. @ $25 per kg.	$25
Direct labor	2 hours @ $20 per hour	40
Overhead	2 labor hours @ $10 per hour	20
Total cost		$85

Cost Variances

A **cost variance,** also simply called a *variance,* is the difference between actual and standard costs. A cost variance can be favorable or unfavorable. A variance from standard cost is considered favorable if actual cost is less than standard cost. It is considered unfavorable if actual cost is more than standard cost.[1] This section discusses variance analysis.

C2 Describe variances and what they reveal about performance.

Cost Variance Analysis

Variances are usually identified in performance reports. When a variance occurs, management wants to determine the factors causing it. This often involves analysis, evaluation, and explanation. The results of these efforts should enable management to assign responsibility for the variance and then to take actions to correct the situation.

To illustrate, Optel's standard materials cost for producing 12,000 units of its product is $12,000. Its actual materials cost for January proved to be $13,000. The $1,000 unfavorable variance raises questions that call for answers that, in turn, can lead to changes to correct the situation and eliminate this variance in the next period. A performance report often identifies the existence of a problem, but we must follow up with further investigation to see what can be done to improve future performance.

Exhibit 24.6 shows the flow of events in the effective management of variance analysis. It shows four steps: (1) preparing a standard cost performance report, (2) computing and analyzing variances, (3) identifying questions and their explanations, and (4) taking corrective and strategic actions. These variance analysis steps are interrelated and are frequently applied in good organizations.

Prepare Reports   Analyze Variances   Questions and Answers   Take Action

Exhibit 24.6

Variance Analysis

Cost Variance Computation

Management needs information about the factors causing a cost variance, but first it must properly compute the variance. In its most simple form, a cost variance (CV) is computed as the difference between actual cost (AC) and standard cost (SC) as shown in Exhibit 24.7.

Cost Variance (CV) = **Actual Cost** (AC) − **Standard Cost** (SC)

where:

Actual Cost (AC) = **Actual Quantity** (AQ) × **Actual Price** (AP)

Standard Cost (SC) = **Standard Quantity** (SQ) × **Standard Price** (SP)

Exhibit 24.7

Cost Variance Formulas

A cost variance is further defined by its components. Actual quantity (AQ) is the input (material or labor) used to manufacture the quantity of output. Standard quantity (SQ) is the expected input for the quantity of output. Actual price (AP) is the amount paid to acquire the input (material or labor), and standard price (SP) is the expected price.

---

[1] Short-term favorable variances can sometimes lead to long-term unfavorable variances. For instance, if management spends less than the budgeted amount on maintenance or insurance, the performance report would show a favorable variance. Cutting these expenses can lead to major losses in the long run if machinery wears out prematurely or insurance coverage proves inadequate.

Point: Price and quantity variances for direct labor are nearly always referred to as *rate* and *efficiency variances,* respectively.

Two main factors cause a cost variance: (1) the difference between actual price and standard price results in a *price* (or rate) *variance* and (2) the difference between actual quantity and standard quantity results in a *quantity* (or usage or efficiency) *variance.* To assess the impacts of these two factors on a cost variance, we use the formula in Exhibit 24.8.

Exhibit 24.8

Price Variance and Quantity Variance Formulas

These formulas identify the sources of the cost variance. Managers sometimes find it useful to apply an alternative (but equivalent) computation for the price and quantity variances as shown in Exhibit 24.9.

Exhibit 24.9

Alternative Price Variance and Quantity Variance Formulas

Price Variance (PV) = [Actual Price (AP) − Standard Price (SP)] × Actual Quantity (AQ)

Quantity Variance (QV) = [Actual Quantity (AQ) − Standard Quantity (SQ)] × Standard Price (SP)

The results from applying the formulas in Exhibits 24.8 and 24.9 are identical.

Materials and Labor Variances

P2 Compute materials and labor variances.

We illustrate the computation of the materials and labor cost variances using data from **G-Max,** a company that makes specialty golf equipment and accessories for individual customers. This company has set the following standard quantities and prices for materials and labor per unit for one of its hand-crafted golf clubheads:

Direct materials (1 lb. per unit at $1 per lb.)	$1.00
Direct labor (1 hr. per unit at $8 per hr.)	8.00
Total standard direct cost per unit	$9.00

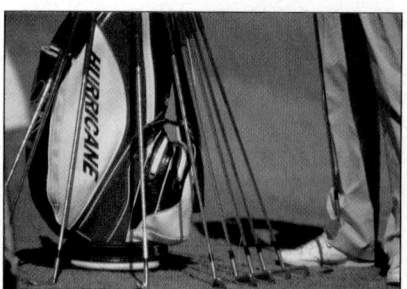

Materials Cost Variances   During May 2008, G-Max budgeted to produce 4,000 clubheads (units). It actually produced only 3,500 units. It used 3,600 pounds of direct materials (titanium) costing $1.05 per pound, meaning its total materials cost was $3,780. This information allows us to compute both actual and standard direct materials costs for G-Max's 3,500 units and its direct materials cost variance as follows:

Topic Tackler

PLUS

24-2

Actual cost	3,600 lbs. @ $1.05 per lb.	= $3,780
Standard cost	3,500 lbs. @ $1.00 per lb.	= 3,500
Direct materials cost variance (unfavorable)		= $ 280

The materials price and quantity variances for these G-Max clubheads are computed and shown in Exhibit 24.10.

Actual Cost AQ × AP 3,600 lbs. × $1.05 $3,780	AQ × SP 3,600 lbs. × $1.00 $3,600	Standard Cost SQ × SP 3,500 lbs. × $1.00 $3,500

$180 U
Price Variance

$100 U
Quantity Variance

$280 U
Total Direct Materials Variance

Exhibit 24.10

Materials Price and Quantity Variances

The $180 unfavorable price variance results from paying 5 cents more than the standard price, computed as 3,600 lbs. × $0.05. The $100 unfavorable quantity variance is due to using 100 lbs. more materials than the standard quantity, computed as 100 lbs. × $1. The total direct materials variance is $280 and is unfavorable. This information allows management to ask the responsible individuals for explanations and corrective actions.

The purchasing department is usually responsible for the price paid for materials. Responsibility for explaining the price variance in this case rests with the purchasing manager if a price higher than standard caused the variance. The production department is usually responsible for the amount of material used and in this case is responsible for explaining why the process used more than the standard amount of materials.

Variance analysis presents challenges. For instance, the production department could have used more than the standard amount of material because its quality did not meet specifications and led to excessive waste. In this case, the purchasing manager is responsible for explaining why inferior materials were acquired. However, the production manager is responsible for explaining what happened if analysis shows that waste was due to inefficiencies, not poor quality material.

In evaluating price variances, managers must recognize that a favorable price variance can indicate a problem with poor product quality. **Redhook Ale**, a micro brewery in the Pacific Northwest, can probably save 10% to 15% in material prices by buying six-row barley malt instead of the better two-row from Washington's Yakima valley. Attention to quality, however, has helped Redhook Ale become the only craft brewer to be "kosher" certified. Redhook's purchasing activities are judged on both the quality of the materials and the purchase price variance. This stand on quality has helped Redhook report increases in both sales and gross margin.

Labor Cost Variances   Labor cost for a specific product or service depends on the number of hours worked (quantity) and the wage rate paid to employees (price). When actual amounts for a task differ from standard, the labor cost variance can be divided into a rate (price) variance and an efficiency (quantity) variance.

To illustrate, G-Max's direct labor standard for 3,500 units of its hand-crafted clubheads is one hour per unit, or 3,500 hours at $8 per hour. Since only 3,400 hours at $8.30 per hour were actually used to complete the units, the actual and standard labor costs are

Actual cost	3,400 hrs. @ $8.30 per hr.	= $28,220
Standard cost	3,500 hrs. @ $8.00 per hr.	= 28,000
Direct labor cost variance (unfavorable)		= $ 220

This analysis shows that actual cost is merely $220 over the standard and suggests no immediate concern. Computing both the labor rate and efficiency variances reveals a different picture, however, as shown in Exhibit 24.11.

Exhibit 24.11

Labor Rate and
Efficiency Variances*

* AH is actual direct labor hours: AR is actual wage rate; SH is standard direct labor hours allowed for actual output; SR is standard wage rate.

Example: Compute the rate variance and the efficiency variance for Exhibit 24.11 if 3,700 actual hours are used at an actual price of $7.50 per hour. *Answer:* $1,850 favorable labor rate variance and $1,600 unfavorable labor efficiency variance.

The analysis in Exhibit 24.11 shows that an $800 favorable efficiency variance results from using 100 fewer direct labor hours than standard for the units produced, but this favorable variance is more than offset by a wage rate that is $0.30 higher than standard. The personnel administrator or possibly the production manager needs to explain why the wage rate is higher than expected. The production manager should also explain how the labor hours were reduced. If this experience can be repeated and transferred to other departments, more savings are possible.

One possible explanation of these labor rate and efficiency variances is the use of workers with different skill levels. If this is the reason, senior management must discuss the implications with the production manager who has the responsibility to assign workers to tasks with the appropriate skill level. In this case, an investigation might show that higher skilled workers were used to produce 3,500 units of handcrafted clubheads. As a result, fewer labor hours might be required for the work, but the wage rate paid these workers is higher than standard because of their greater skills. The effect of this strategy is a higher than standard total cost, which would require actions to remedy the situation or adjust the standard.

Decision Maker

Answer—p. 978

Human Resource Manager   You receive the manufacturing variance report for June and discover a large unfavorable labor efficiency (quantity) variance. What factors do you investigate to identify its possible causes?

Quick Check

Answers—p. 978

5. A standard cost (a) changes in direct proportion to changes in the level of activity, (b) is an amount incurred at the actual level of production for the period, or (c) is an amount incurred under normal conditions to provide a product or service.

6. What is a cost variance?

7. The following information is available for York Company.

Actual direct labor hours per unit	2.5 hours
Standard direct labor hours per unit	2.0 hours
Actual production (units)	2,500 units
Budgeted production (units)	3,000 units
Actual rate per hour	$3.10
Standard rate per hour	$3.00

The labor efficiency variance is (a) $3,750 U, (b) $3,750 F, or (c) $3,875 U.

8. Refer to Quick Check 7; the labor rate variance is (a) $625 F or (b) $625 U.

9. If a materials quantity variance is favorable and a materials price variance is unfavorable, can the total materials cost variance be favorable?

Overhead Standards and Variances

When standard costs are used, a predetermined overhead rate is used to assign standard overhead costs to products or services produced. This predetermined rate is often based on some overhead allocation base (such as standard labor cost, standard labor hours, or standard machine hours).

Setting Overhead Standards

Standard overhead costs are the amounts expected to occur at a certain activity level. Unlike direct materials and direct labor, overhead includes fixed costs and variable costs. This results in the average overhead cost per unit changing as the predicted volume changes. Since standard costs are also budgeted costs, they must be established before the reporting period begins. Standard overhead costs are therefore average per unit costs based on the predicted activity level.

To establish the standard overhead cost rate, management uses the same cost structure it used to construct a flexible budget at the end of a period. This cost structure identifies the different overhead cost components and classifies them as variable or fixed. To get the standard overhead rate, management selects a level of activity (volume) and predicts total overhead cost. It then divides this total by the allocation base to get the standard rate. Standard direct labor hours expected to be used to produce the predicted volume is a common allocation base and is used in this section.

Point: Managers consider the types of overhead costs when choosing the basis for assigning overhead costs to products.

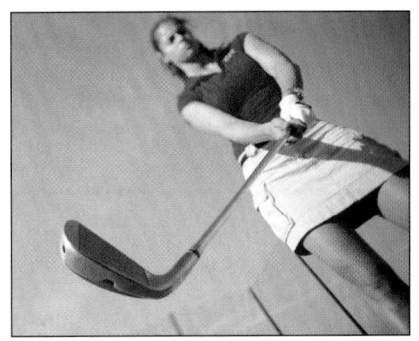

To illustrate, Exhibit 24.12 shows the overhead cost structure used to develop G-Max's flexible overhead budgets for May 2008. The predetermined standard overhead rate for May is set before the month begins. The first two number columns list the per unit amounts of variable costs and the monthly amounts of fixed costs. The four right-most columns show the costs expected to occur at four different levels of activity. The predetermined overhead rate per labor hour is smaller as volume of activity increases because fixed costs remain constant.

G-Max managers predicted an 80% activity level for May, or a production volume of 4,000 clubheads. At this volume, they budget $8,000 as the May total overhead. This choice implies a $2 per unit (labor hour) average overhead cost ($8,000/4,000 units). Since G-Max has a standard of one direct labor hour per unit, the predetermined standard overhead rate for May is $2 per standard direct labor hour. The variable overhead rate remains constant at $1 per direct labor hour regardless of the budgeted production level. The fixed overhead rate changes according to the budgeted production volume. For instance, for the predicted level of 4,000 units of production, the fixed rate is $1 per hour ($4,000 fixed costs/4,000 units). For a production level of 5,000 units, however, the fixed rate is $0.80 per hour.

Point: Variable costs per unit remain constant, but fixed costs per unit decline with increases in volume. This means the average total overhead cost per unit declines with increases in volume.

When choosing the predicted activity level, management considers many factors. The level can be set as high as 100% of capacity, but this is rare. Factors causing the activity level to be less than full capacity include difficulties in scheduling work, equipment under repair or maintenance, and insufficient product demand. Good long-run management practices often call for some plant capacity in excess of current operating needs to allow for special opportunities and demand changes.

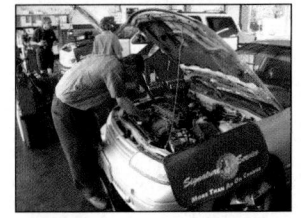

Exhibit 24.12

Flexible Overhead Budgets

	G-MAX Flexible Overhead Budgets For Month Ended May 31, 2008					
	Flexible Budget		Flexible Budget at 70% Capacity	Flexible Budget at 80% Capacity	Flexible Budget at 90% Capacity	Flexible Budget at 100% Capacity
	Variable Amount per Unit	Total Fixed Cost				
Production (in units)	I unit		3,500	4,000	4,500	5,000
Factory overhead						
Variable costs						
Indirect labor	$0.40/unit		$1,400	$1,600	$1,800	$2,000
Indirect materials	0.30/unit		1,050	1,200	1,350	1,500
Power and lights	0.20/unit		700	800	900	1,000
Maintenance	0.10/unit		350	400	450	500
Total variable overhead costs	$1.00/unit		3,500	4,000	4,500	5,000
Fixed costs (per month)						
Building rent		$1,000	1,000	1,000	1,000	1,000
Depreciation—Machinery		1,200	1,200	1,200	1,200	1,200
Supervisory salaries		1,800	1,800	1,800	1,800	1,800
Total fixed overhead costs		$4,000	4,000	4,000	4,000	4,000
Total factory overhead			$7,500	$8,000	$8,500	$9,000
Standard direct labor hours	I hr./unit		3,500 hrs.	4,000 hrs.	4,500 hrs.	5,000 hrs.
Predetermined overhead rate per standard direct labor hour			$ 2.14	$ 2.00	$ 1.89	$ 1.80

P3   Compute overhead variances.

Using Overhead Cost Variance Analysis

When standard costs are used, the cost accounting system applies overhead to the good units produced using the predetermined standard overhead rate. At period-end, the difference between the total overhead cost applied to products and the total overhead cost actually incurred is called an **overhead cost variance,** which is defined in Exhibit 24.13.

Exhibit 24.13

Overhead Cost Variance

> **Overhead cost variance (OCV) = Actual overhead incurred (AOI) − Standard overhead applied (SOA)**

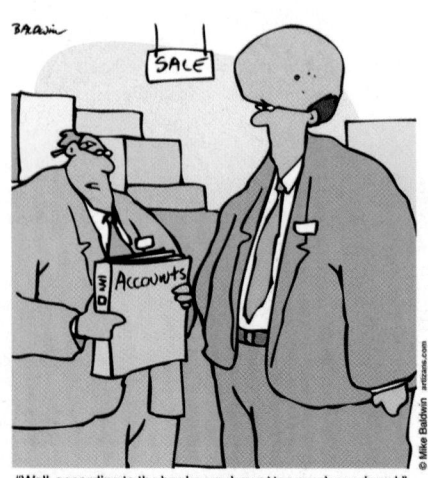

"Well, according to the books, you've got too much overhead."

To help identify factors causing the overhead cost variance, managers analyze this variance separately for variable and fixed overhead. The results provide information useful for taking strategic actions to improve company performance. Similar to analysis of direct materials and direct labor variances, both the variable and fixed overhead variances can be separated into useful components as shown in Exhibit 24.14.

A **spending variance** occurs when management pays an amount different than the standard price to acquire an item. For instance, the actual wage rate paid to indirect labor might be higher than the standard rate. Similarly, actual supervisory salaries might be different than expected. Spending variances such as these cause management to investigate the reasons that the amount paid differs from the standard. Both variable and fixed overhead costs can yield their own spending variances. Analyzing variable overhead includes computing an **efficiency variance,** which occurs when standard direct labor hours (the allocation base) expected for actual production differ from the actual direct labor hours used. This efficiency

Variable Overhead Variance*

Actual Overhead		Applied Overhead
AH × AVR	AH × SVR	SH × SVR

Spending Variance

Efficiency Variance

Variable Overhead Variance

* AH = actual direct labor hours; AVR = actual variable overhead rate; SH = standard direct labor hours; SVR = standard variable overhead rate.

Fixed Overhead Variance

Actual Overhead	Budgeted Overhead	Applied Overhead

Spending Variance

Volume Variance

Fixed Overhead Variance

Exhibit 24.14

Variable and Fixed
Overhead Variances

variance reflects on the cost-effectiveness in using the overhead allocation base (such as direct labor).

A **volume variance** occurs when a difference occurs between the actual volume of production and the standard volume of production. The budgeted fixed overhead amount is the same regardless of the volume of production (within the relevant range). This budgeted amount is computed based on standard direct labor hours that the budgeted production volume allows. The applied overhead is based, however, on the standard direct labor hours allowed for the actual volume of production. A difference between budgeted and actual production volumes results in a difference in the standard direct labor hours allowed for these two production levels. This situation yields a volume variance different from zero.

We can combine the variable overhead spending variance, the fixed overhead spending variance, and the variable overhead efficiency variance to get **controllable variance;** see Exhibit 24.15. The controllable variance is so named because it refers to activities usually under management control.

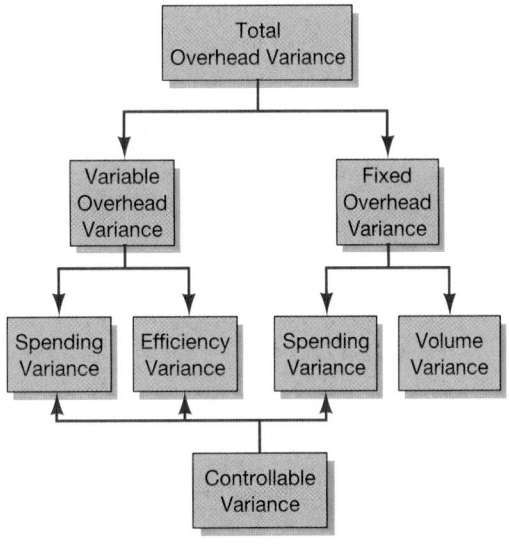

Exhibit 24.15

Framework for Understanding
Total Overhead Variance

Computing Overhead Cost Variances

To illustrate how to compute overhead cost variances, return to the G-Max data. We know that it actually produced 3,500 units when 4,000 units were budgeted. Additional G-Max data show that actual overhead cost incurred is $7,650 (variable portion of $3,650; fixed portion of $4,000). Using this information, we can compute overhead variances for both variable and fixed overhead.

Variable Overhead Cost Variances Recall that G-Max applies overhead based on direct labor hours as the allocation base. We know that it used 3,400 direct labor hours to produce 3,500 units. This compares favorably to the standard requirement of 3,500 direct labor hours at one labor hour per unit. We compute and separate G-Max's variable overhead cost variances as shown in Exhibit 24.16.

Exhibit 24.16

Computing Variable Overhead Cost Variances

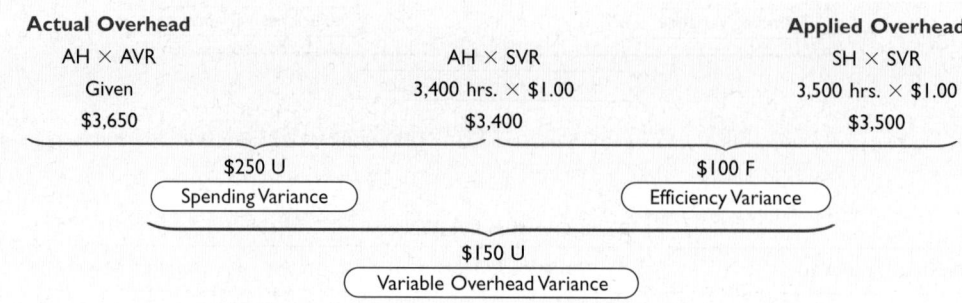

The $3,650 actual variable overhead from G-Max's cost records is used to compute the actual variable overhead rate of $1.07 per direct labor hour ($3,650/3,400 direct labor hours). This reveals that, on average, G-Max incurred $0.07 more per direct labor hour in variable overhead than the standard rate. The middle column of Exhibit 24.16 is computed by multiplying the 3,400 actual direct labor hours by the $1 standard rate per direct labor hour. The applied overhead is computed by multiplying the 3,500 standard hours allowed for actual production by the $1 standard rate per direct labor hour.

Fixed Overhead Cost Variances   G-Max reports that it incurred $4,000 in actual fixed overhead; this amount equals the budgeted fixed overhead for May (see Exhibit 24.12). G-Max's budgeted fixed overhead application rate is $1 per hour ($4,000/4,000 direct labor hours), but the actual production level is only 3,500 units. Using this information, we can compute the fixed overhead cost variances shown in Exhibit 24.17. The applied fixed overhead is computed by multiplying 3,500 standard hours allowed for the actual production by the $1 fixed overhead allocation rate. Exhibit 24.17 reveals that the fixed overhead spending variance is zero and the volume variance is $500. The volume variance occurs because 500 fewer units are produced than budgeted; namely, 80% of the manufacturing capacity is budgeted but only 70% is used.

Exhibit 24.17

Computing Fixed Overhead Cost Variances

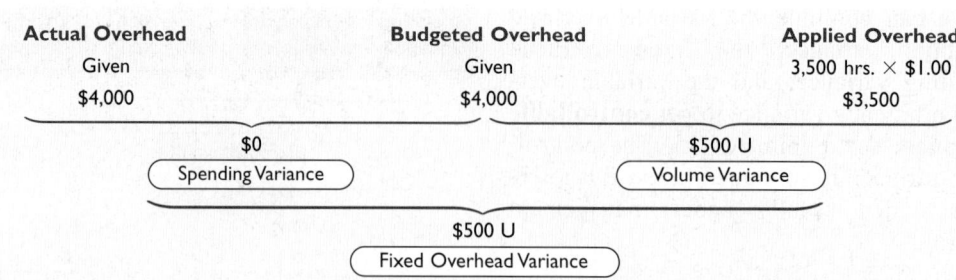

We show this volume variance graphically in Exhibit 24.18. The upward-sloping line reflects the amount of fixed overhead costs applied to the units produced in May using the predetermined fixed overhead rate. The uppermost horizontal line reflects the $4,000 of total fixed costs budgeted for May. These two lines cross at the planned operating volume of 4,000 units. When unit volume is 3,500 units, the overhead-costs-applied line falls $500 below the budgeted fixed overhead line. This shortfall is the volume variance.

An unfavorable volume variance implies that the company did not reach its predicted operating level. Management needs to know why the actual level of performance differs from the

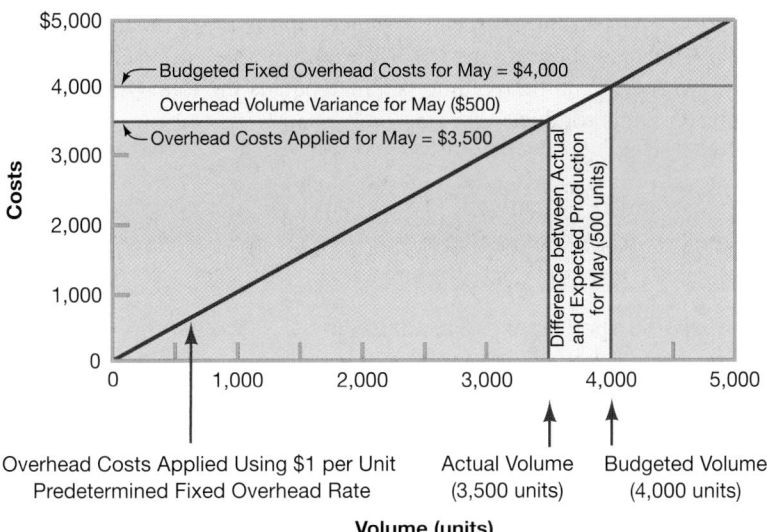

Exhibit 24.18

Fixed Overhead Volume Variance

expected level. The main purpose of the volume variance is to identify what portion of the total variance is caused by failing to meet the expected volume level. This information permits management to focus on the controllable variance.

A complete overhead variance report provides managers information about specific overhead costs and how they differ from budgeted amounts. Exhibit 24.19 shows G-Max's overhead variance report for May. It reveals that (1) fixed costs and maintenance cost were incurred as expected, (2) costs for indirect labor and power and lights were higher than expected, and (3) indirect materials cost was less than expected.

Using information from Exhibits 24.16 and 24.17, we can compute the total controllable overhead variance as $150 unfavorable ($250 U + $100 F + $0). This amount is also readily

Exhibit 24.19

Overhead Variance Report

G-MAX
Overhead Variance Report
For Month Ended May 31, 2008

Volume Variance

Expected production level	80% of capacity
Production level achieved	70% of capacity
Volume variance	$500 (unfavorable)

Controllable Variance	Flexible Budget	Actual Results	Variances*
Variable overhead costs			
Indirect labor	$1,400	$1,525	$125 U
Indirect materials	1,050	1,025	25 F
Power and lights	700	750	50 U
Maintenance	350	350	0
Total variable overhead costs	3,500	3,650	150 U†
Fixed overhead costs			
Building rent	1,000	1,000	0
Depreciation—Machinery	1,200	1,200	0
Supervisory salaries	1,800	1,800	0
Total fixed overhead costs	4,000	4,000	0‡
Total overhead costs	$7,500	$7,650	$150 U

* F = Favorable variance; and U = Unfavorable variance.

† Total variable overhead (spending and efficiency) variance.

‡ Fixed overhead spending variance.

available from Exhibit 24.19. The overhead variance report shows the total volume variance as $500 unfavorable (shown at the top) and the $150 unfavorable controllable variance. The sum of the controllable variance and the volume variance equals the total (fixed and variable) overhead variance of $650 unfavorable.

Extensions of Standard Costs

This section extends the application of standard costs for control purposes, for service companies, and for accounting systems.

Standard Costs for Control

C3 Explain how standard cost information is useful for management by exception.

To control business activities, top management must be able to affect the actions of lower-level managers responsible for the company's revenues and costs. After preparing a budget and establishing standard costs, management should take actions to gain control when actual costs differ from standard or budgeted amounts.

Reports such as the ones illustrated in this chapter call management's attention to variances from business plans and other standards. When managers use these reports to focus on problem areas, the budgeting process contributes to the control function. In using budgeted performance reports, practice of management by exception is often useful. **Management by exception** means that managers focus attention on the most significant variances and give less attention to areas where performance is reasonably close to the standard. This practice leads management to concentrate on the exceptional or irregular situations. Management by exception is especially useful when directed at controllable items.

Standard Costs for Services

Many managers use standard costs and variance analysis to investigate manufacturing costs. Many managers also recognize that standard costs and variances can help them control *non manufacturing* costs. Companies providing services instead of products can benefit from the use of standard costs. Application of standard costs and variances can be readily adapted to nonmanufacturing situations. To illustrate, many service providers use standard costs to help control expenses. First, they use standard costs as a basis for budgeting all services. Second, they use periodic performance reports to compare actual results to standards. Third, they use these reports to identify significant variances within specific areas of responsibility. Fourth, they implement the appropriate control procedures.

Standard Cost Accounting System

We have shown how companies use standard costs in management reports. Most standard cost systems also record these costs and variances in accounts. This practice simplifies recordkeeping and helps in preparing reports. Although we do not need knowledge of standard cost accounting practices to understand standard costs and their use, we must know how to interpret the accounts in which standard costs and variances are recorded. The entries in this section briefly illustrate the important aspects of this process for G-Max's standard costs and variances for May.

P4 Prepare journal entries for standard costs and account for price and quantity variances.

The first of these entries records standard materials cost incurred in May in the Goods in Process Inventory account. This part of the entry is similar to the usual accounting entry, but the amount of the debit equals the standard cost ($3,500) instead of the actual cost ($3,780). This entry credits Raw Materials Inventory for actual cost. The difference between standard and actual costs is recorded with debits to two separate materials variance accounts (recall Exhibit 24.10). Both the materials price and quantity variances are recorded as debits because they reflect additional costs higher than the standard cost (if actual costs were less than the standard, they are recorded as credits). This treatment (debit) reflects their unfavorable effect because they represent higher costs and lower income.

May 31	Goods in Process Inventory	3,500	
	Direct Materials Price Variance*	**180**	
	Direct Materials Quantity Variance	**100**	
	Raw Materials Inventory		3,780
	To charge production for standard quantity of materials used (3,500 lbs.) at the standard price ($1 per lb.), and to record material price and material quantity variances.		

Assets = Liabilities + Equity
+3,500   −100
−3,780   −180

* Many companies record the materials price variance when materials are purchased. For simplicity, we record both the materials price and quantity variances when materials are issued to production.

The second entry debits Goods in Process Inventory for the standard labor cost of the goods manufactured during May ($28,000). Actual labor cost ($28,220) is recorded with a credit to the Factory Payroll account. The difference between standard and actual labor costs is explained by two variances (see Exhibit 24.11). The direct labor rate variance is unfavorable and is debited to that account. The direct labor efficiency variance is favorable and is credited. The direct labor efficiency variance is favorable because it represents a lower cost and a higher net income.

May 31	Goods in Process Inventory	28,000	
	Direct Labor Rate Variance	**1,020**	
	Direct Labor Efficiency Variance		**800**
	Factory Payroll		28,220
	To charge production with 3,500 standard hours of direct labor at the standard $8 per hour rate, and to record the labor rate and efficiency variances.		

Assets = Liabilities + Equity
+28,000   +28,220
                          − 1,020
                          +   800

The entry to assign standard predetermined overhead to the cost of goods manufactured must debit the $7,000 predetermined amount to the Goods in Process Inventory account. The $7,650 actual overhead costs are debited to the Factory Overhead account. Thus, when Factory Overhead is applied to Goods in Process Inventory, the amount applied is debited to the Goods in Process Inventory account and credited to the Factory Overhead account. To account for the difference between actual and standard costs, the entry includes a $250 debit to the Variable Overhead Spending Variance, a $100 credit to the Variable Overhead Efficiency Variance, and a $500 debit to the Volume Variance (recall Exhibits 24.16 and 24.17). An alternative (simpler) approach, shown here, is to record the difference with a $150 debit to the Controllable Variance account and a $500 debit to the Volume Variance account (recall from Exhibit 24.15 that controllable variance is the sum of both variable overhead variances and the fixed overhead spending variance).

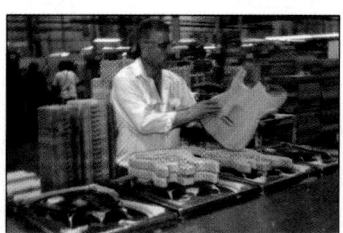

Assets = Liabilities + Equity
+7,000   +7,650
                   − 150
                   − 500

May 31	Goods in Process Inventory	7,000	
	Controllable Variance	150	
	Volume Variance	500	
	Factory Overhead		7,650

*To apply overhead at the standard rate of
$2 per standard direct labor hour (3,500 hours),
and to record overhead variances.*

The balances of these six different variance accounts accumulate until the end of the accounting period. As a result, the unfavorable variances of some months offset the favorable variances of others.

These variance account balances, which reflect results of the period's various transactions and events, are closed at period-end. If the variances are *material,* they are added to or subtracted from the balances of the Goods in Process Inventory, the Finished Goods Inventory, and the Cost of Goods Sold accounts. If the amounts are *immaterial,* they are added to or subtracted from the balance of the Cost of Goods Sold account. This process is similar to that shown in Chapter 19 for eliminating an underapplied or overapplied balance in the Factory Overhead account. (*Note:* These variance balances, which represent differences between actual and standard costs, must be added to or subtracted from the materials, labor, and overhead costs recorded. In this way, the recorded costs equal the actual costs incurred in the period; a company must use actual costs in external financial statements prepared in accordance with generally accepted accounting principles.)

Quick Check
Answers—p. 978

10. Under what conditions is an overhead volume variance considered favorable?

11. To use management by exception with standard costs, a company (a) must record standard costs in its accounting, (b) should compute variances from flexible budget amounts to allow management to focus its attention on significant differences between actual and budgeted results, or (c) should analyze only variances for direct materials and direct labor.

12. A company uses a standard cost accounting system. Prepare the journal entry to record these direct materials variances:

Direct materials cost actually incurred	$73,200
Direct materials quantity variance (favorable)	3,800
Direct materials price variance (unfavorable)	1,300

13. If standard costs are recorded in the manufacturing accounts, how are recorded variances treated at the end of an accounting period?

Decision Analysis   **Sales Variances**

A2   Analyze changes in sales from expected amounts.

This chapter explained the computation and analysis of cost variances. A similar variance analysis can be applied to sales. To illustrate, consider the following sales data from G-Max for two of its golf products, Excel golf balls and Big Bert® drivers.

	Budgeted	Actual
Sales of Excel golf balls (units)	1,000 units	1,100 units
Sales price per Excel golf ball	$ 10	$ 10.50
Sales of Big Bert® drivers (units)	150 units	140 units
Sales price per Big Bert® driver	$ 200	$ 190

Using this information, we compute both the *sales price variance* and the *sales volume variance* as shown in Exhibit 24.20. The total sales price variance is $850 unfavorable, and the total sales volume variance is $1,000 unfavorable. Neither variance implies anything positive about these two products. Further analysis of these total sales variances reveals that both the sales price and sales volume variances for Excel golf balls are favorable, meaning that both the unfavorable total sales price variance and the unfavorable total sales volume variance are due to the Big Bert driver.

Excel Golf Balls	Actual Results	Flexible Budget	Fixed Budget
Sales units (balls)	1,100	1,100	1,000
Sales dollars (balls)	$11,550	$11,000	$10,000
	$550 F		$1,000 F
	Sales Price Variance		Sales Volume Variance
Big Bert® Drivers			
Sales units (drivers)	140	140	150
Sales dollars (drivers)	$26,600	$28,000	$30,000
	$1,400 U		$2,000 U
	Sales Price Variance		Sales Volume Variance
Total	$850 U		$1,000 U

Exhibit 24.20

Computing Sales Variances

Managers use sales variances for planning and control purposes. The sales variance information is used to plan future actions to avoid unfavorable variances. G-Max sold 90 total combined units (both balls and drivers) more than planned, but these 90 units were not sold in the proportion budgeted. G-Max sold fewer than the budgeted quantity of the higher priced driver, which contributed to the unfavorable total sales variances. Managers use such detail to question what caused the company to sell more golf balls and fewer drivers. Managers also use this information to evaluate and even reward their salespeople. Extra compensation is paid to salespeople who contribute to a higher profit margin. Finally, with multiple products, the sales volume variance can be separated into a *sales mix variance* and a *sales quantity variance*. The sales mix variance is the difference between the actual and budgeted sales mix of the products. The sales quantity variance is the difference between the total actual and total budgeted quantity of units sold.

Decision Maker

Answer—p. 978

Sales Manager   The current performance report reveals a large favorable sales volume variance but an unfavorable sales price variance. You did not expect to see a large increase in sales volume. What steps do you take to analyze this situation?

Demonstration Problem

Pacific Company provides the following information about its budgeted and actual results for June 2008. Although the expected June volume was 25,000 units produced and sold, the company actually produced and sold 27,000 units as detailed here:

	Budget (25,000 units)	Actual (27,000 units)
Selling price	$5.00 per unit	$5.23 per unit
Variable costs (per unit)		
Direct materials	1.24 per unit	1.12 per unit
Direct labor	1.50 per unit	1.40 per unit
Factory supplies*	0.25 per unit	0.37 per unit
Utilities*	0.50 per unit	0.60 per unit
Selling costs	0.40 per unit	0.34 per unit

[continued on next page]

[continued from previous page]

Fixed costs (per month)		
Depreciation—Machinery*	$3,750	$3,710
Depreciation—Building*	2,500	2,500
General liability insurance	1,200	1,250
Property taxes on office equipment	500	485
Other administrative expense	750	900

* Indicates factory overhead item; $0.75 per unit or $3 per direct labor hour for variable overhead, and $0.25 per unit or $1 per direct labor hour for fixed overhead.

Standard costs based on expected output of 25,000 units

	Per Unit of Output	Quantity to Be Used	Total Cost
Direct materials, 4 oz. @ $0.31/oz.	$1.24/unit	100,000 oz.	$31,000
Direct labor, 0.25 hrs. @ $6.00/hr.	1.50/unit	6,250 hrs.	37,500
Overhead	1.00/unit		25,000

Actual costs incurred to produce 27,000 units

	Per Unit of Output	Quantity Used	Total Cost
Direct materials, 4 oz. @ $0.28/oz.	$1.12/unit	108,000 oz.	$30,240
Direct labor, 0.20 hrs. @ $7.00/hr.	1.40/unit	5,400 hrs.	37,800
Overhead	1.20/unit		32,400

Standard costs based on expected output of 27,000 units

	Per Unit of Output	Quantity to Be Used	Total Cost
Direct materials, 4 oz. @ $0.31/oz.	$1.24/unit	108,000 oz.	$33,480
Direct labor, 0.25 hrs. @ $6.00/hr.	1.50/unit	6,750 hrs.	40,500
Overhead			26,500

Required

1. Prepare June flexible budgets showing expected sales, costs, and net income assuming 20,000, 25,000, and 30,000 units of output produced and sold.

2. Prepare a flexible budget performance report that compares actual results with the amounts budgeted if the actual volume had been expected.

3. Apply variance analysis for direct materials, for direct labor, and for overhead.

Planning the Solution

- Prepare a table showing the expected results at the three specified levels of output. Compute the variable costs by multiplying the per unit variable costs by the expected volumes. Include fixed costs at the given amounts. Combine the amounts in the table to show total variable costs, contribution margin, total fixed costs, and income from operations.

- Prepare a table showing the actual results and the amounts that should be incurred at 27,000 units. Show any differences in the third column and label them with an *F* for favorable if they increase income or a *U* for unfavorable if they decrease income.

- Using the chapter's format, compute these total variances and the individual variances requested:
  - Total materials variance (including the direct materials quantity variance and the direct materials price variance).

- Total direct labor variance (including the direct labor efficiency variance and rate variance).
- Total overhead variance (including both variable and fixed overhead variances and their component variances).

Solution to Demonstration Problem

1.

PACIFIC COMPANY
Flexible Budgets
For Month Ended June 30, 2008

	Flexible Budget		Flexible Budget for Unit Sales of 20,000	Flexible Budget for Unit Sales of 25,000	Flexible Budget for Unit Sales of 30,000
	Variable Amount per Unit	Total Fixed Cost			
Sales	$5.00		$100,000	$125,000	$150,000
Variable costs					
Direct materials	1.24		24,800	31,000	37,200
Direct labor	1.50		30,000	37,500	45,000
Factory supplies	0.25		5,000	6,250	7,500
Utilities	0.50		10,000	12,500	15,000
Selling costs	0.40		8,000	10,000	12,000
Total variable costs	3.89		77,800	97,250	116,700
Contribution margin	$1.11		22,200	27,750	33,300
Fixed costs					
Depreciation—Machinery		$3,750	3,750	3,750	3,750
Depreciation—Building		2,500	2,500	2,500	2,500
General liability insurance		1,200	1,200	1,200	1,200
Property taxes on office equipment		500	500	500	500
Other administrative expense		750	750	750	750
Total fixed costs		$8,700	8,700	8,700	8,700
Income from operations			$ 13,500	$ 19,050	$ 24,600

2.

PACIFIC COMPANY
Flexible Budget Performance Report
For Month Ended June 30, 2008

	Flexible Budget	Actual Results	Variance*
Sales (27,000 units)	$135,000	$141,210	$6,210 F
Variable costs			
Direct materials	33,480	30,240	3,240 F
Direct labor	40,500	37,800	2,700 F
Factory supplies	6,750	9,990	3,240 U
Utilities	13,500	16,200	2,700 U
Selling costs	10,800	9,180	1,620 F
Total variable costs	105,030	103,410	1,620 F
Contribution margin	29,970	37,800	7,830 F
Fixed costs			
Depreciation—Machinery	3,750	3,710	40 F
Depreciation—Building	2,500	2,500	0
General liability insurance	1,200	1,250	50 U
Property taxes on office equipment	500	485	15 F
Other administrative expense	750	900	150 U
Total fixed costs	8,700	8,845	145 U
Income from operations	$ 21,270	$ 28,955	$7,685 F

* F = Favorable variance; and U = Unfavorable variance.

3. Variance analysis of materials, labor, and overhead costs.

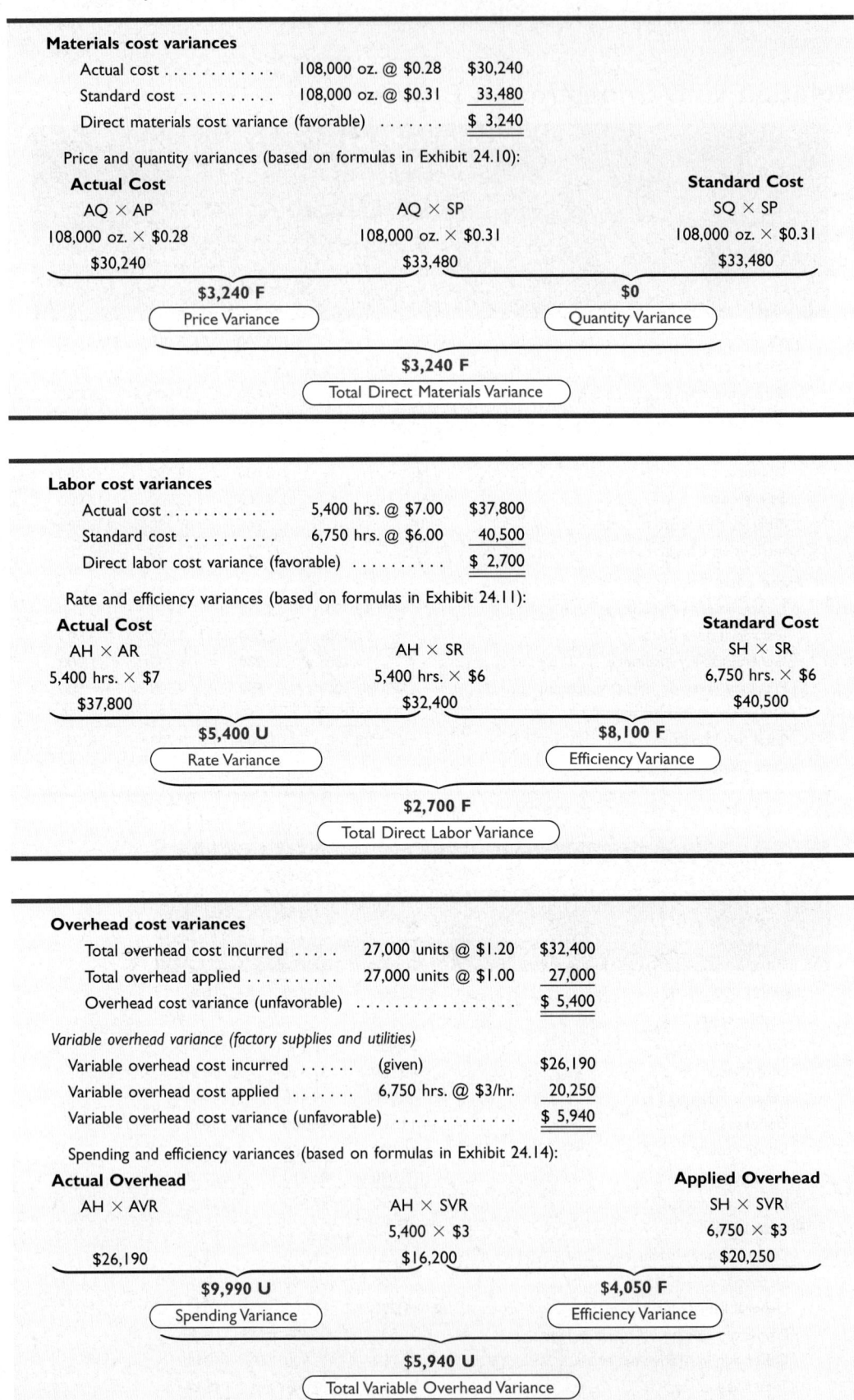

Materials cost variances

Actual cost	108,000 oz. @ $0.28	$30,240
Standard cost	108,000 oz. @ $0.31	33,480
Direct materials cost variance (favorable)		$ 3,240

Price and quantity variances (based on formulas in Exhibit 24.10):

Actual Cost		**Standard Cost**
AQ × AP	AQ × SP	SQ × SP
108,000 oz. × $0.28	108,000 oz. × $0.31	108,000 oz. × $0.31
$30,240	$33,480	$33,480

$3,240 F
(Price Variance)

$0
(Quantity Variance)

$3,240 F
(Total Direct Materials Variance)

Labor cost variances

Actual cost	5,400 hrs. @ $7.00	$37,800
Standard cost	6,750 hrs. @ $6.00	40,500
Direct labor cost variance (favorable)		$ 2,700

Rate and efficiency variances (based on formulas in Exhibit 24.11):

Actual Cost		**Standard Cost**
AH × AR	AH × SR	SH × SR
5,400 hrs. × $7	5,400 hrs. × $6	6,750 hrs. × $6
$37,800	$32,400	$40,500

$5,400 U
(Rate Variance)

$8,100 F
(Efficiency Variance)

$2,700 F
(Total Direct Labor Variance)

Overhead cost variances

Total overhead cost incurred	27,000 units @ $1.20	$32,400
Total overhead applied	27,000 units @ $1.00	27,000
Overhead cost variance (unfavorable)		$ 5,400

Variable overhead variance (factory supplies and utilities)

Variable overhead cost incurred	(given)	$26,190
Variable overhead cost applied	6,750 hrs. @ $3/hr.	20,250
Variable overhead cost variance (unfavorable)		$ 5,940

Spending and efficiency variances (based on formulas in Exhibit 24.14):

Actual Overhead		**Applied Overhead**
AH × AVR	AH × SVR	SH × SVR
	5,400 × $3	6,750 × $3
$26,190	$16,200	$20,250

$9,990 U
(Spending Variance)

$4,050 F
(Efficiency Variance)

$5,940 U
(Total Variable Overhead Variance)

[continued on next page]

[continued from previous page]

Fixed overhead (depreciation on machinery and building)

Fixed overhead cost incurred	(given)	$ 6,210
Fixed overhead cost applied	6,750 hrs. @ $1/hr.	6,750
Fixed overhead cost variance (favorable)		$ 540

Spending and volume variances (based on formulas in Exhibit 24.14):

We can also compute

Controllable variance: $5,900 U (both spending variances plus efficiency variance)

Volume variance: 500 F (identified as above)

Summary

C1 **Define *standard costs* and explain their computation and uses.** Standard costs are the normal costs that should be incurred to produce a product or perform a service. They should be based on a careful examination of the processes used to produce a product or perform a service as well as the quantities and prices that should be incurred in carrying out those processes. On a performance report, standard costs (which are flexible budget amounts) are compared to actual costs, and the differences are presented as variances.

C2 **Describe variances and what they reveal about performance.** Management can use variances to monitor and control activities. Total cost variances can be broken into price and quantity variances to direct management's attention to those responsible for quantities used and prices paid.

C3 **Explain how standard cost information is useful for management by exception.** Standard cost accounting provides management information about costs that differ from budgeted (expected) amounts. Performance reports disclose the costs or areas of operations that have significant variances from budgeted amounts. This allows managers to focus attention on the exceptions and less attention on areas proceeding normally.

A1 **Compare fixed and flexible budgets.** A fixed budget shows the revenues and costs expected to occur at a specified volume level. If actual volume is at some other level, the amounts in the fixed budget do not provide a reasonable basis for evaluating actual performance. A flexible budget expresses variable costs in per unit terms so that it can be used to develop budgeted amounts for any volume level within the relevant range. Thus, managers compute budgeted amounts for evaluation after a period for the volume that actually occurred.

A2 **Analyze changes in sales from expected amounts.** Actual sales can differ from budgeted sales, and managers can inves-

tigate this difference by computing both the sales price and sales volume variances. The *sales price variance* refers to that portion of total variance resulting from a difference between actual and budgeted selling prices. The *sales volume variance* refers to that portion of total variance resulting from a difference between actual and budgeted sales quantities.

P1 **Prepare a flexible budget and interpret a flexible budget performance report.** To prepare a flexible budget, we express each variable cost as a constant amount per unit of sales (or as a percent of sales dollar). In contrast, the budgeted amount of each fixed cost is expressed as a total amount expected to occur at any sales volume within the relevant range. The flexible budget is then determined using these computations and amounts for fixed and variable costs at the expected sales volume.

P2 **Compute materials and labor variances.** Materials and labor variances are due to differences between the actual costs incurred and the budgeted costs. The price (or rate) variance is computed by comparing the actual cost with the flexible budget amount that should have been incurred to acquire the actual quantity of resources. The quantity (or efficiency) variance is computed by comparing the flexible budget amount that should have been incurred to acquire the actual quantity of resources with the flexible budget amount that should have been incurred to acquire the standard quantity of resources.

P3 **Compute overhead variances.** Overhead variances are due to differences between the actual overhead costs incurred and the overhead applied to production. An overhead spending variance arises when the actual amount incurred differs from the budgeted amount of overhead. An overhead efficiency (or volume) variance arises when the flexible overhead budget amount differs from the overhead applied to production. It is important to realize that overhead is assigned using an overhead allocation base, meaning that an efficiency variance (in the case of variable overhead) is a result of the overhead application base being used more or less efficiently than planned.

P4   **Prepare journal entries for standard costs and account for price and quantity variances.** When a company records standard costs in its accounts, the standard costs of materials, labor, and overhead are debited to the Goods in Process Inventory account. Based on an analysis of the material, labor, and overhead costs, each quantity variance, price variance, volume variance, and controllable variance is recorded in a separate account. At period-end, if the variances are material, they are allocated among the balances of the Goods in Process Inventory, Finished Goods Inventory, and Cost of Goods Sold accounts. If they are not material, they are simply debited or credited to the Cost of Goods Sold account.

Guidance Answers to **Decision Maker** and **Decision Ethics**

Entrepreneur   From the complaints, this performance report appears to compare actual results with a fixed budget. This comparison is useful in determining whether the amount of work actually performed was more or less than planned, but it is not useful in determining whether the divisions were more or less efficient than planned. If the two consulting divisions worked on more assignments than expected, some costs will certainly increase. Therefore, you should prepare a flexible budget using the actual number of consulting assignments and then compare actual performance to the flexible budget.

Human Resource Manager   As HR manager, you should investigate the causes for any labor-related variances although you may not be responsible for them. An unfavorable labor efficiency variance occurs because more labor hours than standard were used during the period. There are at least three possible reasons for this: (1) materials quality could be poor, resulting in more labor consumption due to rework, (2) unplanned interruptions (strike, breakdowns, accidents) could have occurred during the period, and (3) the production manager could have used a different labor mix to expedite orders. This new labor mix could have consisted of a larger proportion of untrained labor, which resulted in more labor hours.

Internal Auditor   Although the manager's actions might not be unethical, this action is undesirable. The internal auditor should report this behavior, possibly recommending that for the purchase of such discretionary items, the manager must provide budgetary requests using an activity-based budgeting process. The internal auditor would then be given full authority to verify this budget request.

Sales Manager   The unfavorable sales price variance suggests that actual prices were lower than budgeted prices. As the sales manager, you want to know the reasons for a lower than expected price. Perhaps your salespeople lowered the price of certain products by offering quantity discounts. You then might want to know what prompted them to offer the quantity discounts (perhaps competitors were offering discounts). You want to break the sales volume variance into both the sales mix and sales quantity variances. You could find that although the sales quantity variance is favorable, the sales mix variance is not. Then you need to investigate why actual sales mix differs from budgeted sales mix.

Guidance Answers to **Quick Checks**

1. *b*

2. The first step is classifying each cost as variable or fixed.

3. A fixed budget is prepared using an expected volume of sales or production. A flexible budget is prepared using the actual volume of activity.

4. Contribution margin equals sales less variable costs.

5. *c*

6. It is the difference between actual cost and standard cost.

7. *a*; Total actual hours: $2,500 \times 2.5 = 6,250$
    Total standard hours: $2,500 \times 2.0 = 5,000$
    Efficiency variance = $(6,250 - 5,000) \times \$3.00$
                  $= \$3,750$ U

8. *b*; Rate variance = $(\$3.10 - \$3.00) \times 6,250 = \$625$ U

9. Yes, this will occur when the materials quantity variance is more than the materials price variance.

10. The overhead volume variance is favorable when the actual operating level is higher than the expected level.

11. *b*

12.

Goods in Process Inventory	75,700	
Direct Materials Price Variance	1,300	
Direct Materials Quantity Variance		3,800
Raw Materials Inventory		73,200

13. If the variances are material, they should be prorated among the Goods in Process Inventory, Finished Goods Inventory, and Cost of Goods Sold accounts. If they are not material, they can be closed to Cost of Goods Sold.

Key Terms   mhhe.com/wildFAP18e

Key Terms are available at the book's Website for learning and testing in an online Flashcard Format.

Budgetary control (p. 954)
Budget report (p. 954)
Controllable variance (p. 967)
Cost variance (p. 961)
Efficiency variance (p. 966)
Favorable variance (p. 956)
Fixed budget (p. 955)

Fixed budget performance report (p. 955)
Flexible budget (p. 956)
Flexible budget performance report (p. 958)
Management by exception (p. 970)
Overhead cost variance (p. 966)
Price variance (p. 958)

Quantity variance (p. 958)
Spending variance (p. 966)
Standard costs (p. 959)
Unfavorable variance (p. 956)
Variance analysis (p. 958)
Volume variance (p. 967)

Multiple Choice Quiz   Answers on p. 995   mhhe.com/wildFAP18e

Multiple Choice Quizzes A and B are available at the book's Website.

1. A company predicts its production and sales will be 24,000 units. At that level of activity, its fixed costs are budgeted at $300,000, and its variable costs are budgeted at $246,000. If its activity level declines to 20,000 units, what will be its fixed costs and its variable costs?
 a. Fixed, $300,000; Variable, $246,000
 b. Fixed, $250,000; Variable, $205,000
 c. Fixed, $300,000; Variable, $205,000
 d. Fixed, $250,000; Variable, $246,000
 e. Fixed, $300,000; Variable, $300,000

2. Using the following information about a single-product company, compute its total actual cost of direct materials used.
 • Direct materials standard cost: 5 lbs. × $2 per lb. = $10.
 • Total direct materials cost variance: $15,000 unfavorable.
 • Actual direct materials used: 300,000 lbs.
 • Actual units produced: 60,000 units.
 a. $585,000
 b. $600,000
 c. $300,000
 d. $315,000
 e. $615,000

3. A company uses four hours of direct labor to produce a product unit. The standard direct labor cost is $20 per hour. This period the company produced 20,000 units and used 84,160 hours of direct labor at a total cost of $1,599,040. What is its labor rate variance for the period?
 a. $83,200 F
 b. $84,160 U

 c. $84,160 F
 d. $83,200 U
 e. $ 960 F

4. A company's standard for a unit of its single product is $6 per unit in variable overhead (4 hours × $1.50 per hour). Actual data for the period shows variable overhead costs of $150,000 and production of 24,000 units. Its total variable overhead cost variance is
 a. $ 6,000 F
 b. $ 6,000 U
 c. $114,000 U
 d. $114,000 F
 e. $ 0

5. A company's standard for a unit of its single product is $4 per unit in fixed overhead ($24,000 total/6,000 units budgeted). Actual data for the period shows total actual fixed overhead of $24,100 and production of 4,800 units. Its volume variance is
 a. $4,800 U
 b. $4,800 F
 c. $ 100 U
 d. $ 100 F
 e. $4,900 U

Discussion Questions

1. What limits the usefulness to managers of fixed budget performance reports?

2. Identify the main purpose of a flexible budget for managers.

3. Prepare a flexible budget performance report title (in proper form) for Spalding Company for the calendar year 2008. Why is a proper title important for this or any report?

4. What type of analysis does a flexible budget performance report help management perform?

5. In what sense can a variable cost be considered constant?

6. What department is usually responsible for a direct labor rate variance? What department is usually responsible for a direct labor efficiency variance? Explain.

7. What is a price variance? What is a quantity variance?

8. What is the purpose of using standard costs?

9. In an analysis of fixed overhead cost variances, what is the volume variance?

10. What is the predetermined standard overhead rate? How is it computed?

11. In general, variance analysis is said to provide information about _____ and _____ variances.

12. In an analysis of overhead cost variances, what is the controllable variance and what causes it?

13. What is the relation among standard costs, flexible budgets, variance analysis, and management by exception?

14. How can the manager of a music department of a Best Buy retail store use flexible budgets to enhance performance?

15. Is it possible for a retail store such as Circuit City to use variances in analyzing its operating performance? Explain.

16. Assume that Apple is budgeted to operate at 80% of capacity but actually operates at 75% of capacity. What effect will the 5% deviation have on its controllable variance? Its volume variance?

 Red numbers denote Discussion Questions that involve decision-making.

QUICK STUDY

QS 24-1

Flexible budget performance report

P1

Beech Company reports the following selected financial results for May. For the level of production achieved in May, the budgeted amounts would be: sales, $1,300,000; variable costs, $750,000; and fixed costs, $300,000. Prepare a flexible budget performance report for May.

Sales (150,000 units)	$1,275,000
Variable costs	712,500
Fixed costs	300,000

QS 24-2

Labor cost variances

C2 P2

Frontera Company's output for the current period results in a $20,000 unfavorable direct labor rate variance and a $10,000 unfavorable direct labor efficiency variance. Production for the current period was assigned a $400,000 standard direct labor cost. What is the actual total direct labor cost for the current period?

QS 24-3

Materials cost variances

C2 P2

Juan Company's output for the current period was assigned a $150,000 standard direct materials cost. The direct materials variances included a $12,000 favorable price variance and a $2,000 favorable quantity variance. What is the actual total direct materials cost for the current period?

QS 24-4

Materials cost variances

C2 P2

For the current period, Kayenta Company's manufacturing operations yield a $4,000 unfavorable price variance on its direct materials usage. The actual price per pound of material is $78; the standard price is $77.50. How many pounds of material are used in the current period?

QS 24-5

Management by exception

C3

Managers use *management by exception* for control purposes. (1) Describe the concept of management by exception. (2) Explain how standard costs help managers apply this concept to monitor and control costs.

QS 24-6

Overhead cost variances   P3

Alvarez Company's output for the current period yields a $20,000 favorable overhead volume variance and a $60,400 unfavorable overhead controllable variance. Standard overhead charged to production for the period is $225,000. What is the actual total overhead cost incurred for the period?

Refer to the information in QS 24-6. Alvarez records standard costs in its accounts. Prepare the journal entry to charge overhead costs to the Goods in Process Inventory account and to record any variances.

QS 24-7
Preparing overhead entries P4

Farad Company specializes in selling used SUVs. During the first six months of 2008, the dealership sold 50 SUVs at an average price of $9,000 each. The budget for the first six months of 2008 was to sell 45 SUVs at an average price of $9,500 each. Compute the dealership's sales price variance and sales volume variance for the first six months of 2008.

QS 24-8
Computing sales price and volume variances
A2

Tempo Company's fixed budget for the first quarter of calendar year 2008 reveals the following. Prepare flexible budgets following the format of Exhibit 24.3 that show variable costs per unit, fixed costs, and three different flexible budgets for sales volumes of 6,000, 7,000, and 8,000 units.

EXERCISES

Exercise 24-1
Preparation of flexible budgets
P1

Sales (7,000 units)		$2,800,000
Cost of goods sold		
Direct materials	$280,000	
Direct labor	490,000	
Production supplies	175,000	
Plant manager salary	65,000	1,010,000
Gross profit		1,790,000
Selling expenses		
Sales commissions	140,000	
Packaging	154,000	
Advertising	125,000	419,000
Administrative expenses		
Administrative salaries	85,000	
Depreciation—Office equip.	35,000	
Insurance	20,000	
Office rent	36,000	176,000
Income from operations		$1,195,000

Check Income (at 6,000 units), $972,000

JPAK Company manufactures and sells mountain bikes. It normally operates eight hours a day, five days a week. Using this information, classify each of the following costs as fixed or variable. If additional information would affect your decision, describe the information.

Exercise 24-2
Classification of costs as fixed or variable
P1

a. Depreciation on tools
b. Pension cost
c. Bike frames
d. Screws for assembly

e. Management salaries
f. Incoming shipping expenses
g. Office supplies
h. Taxes on property

i. Gas used for heating
j. Direct labor
k. Repair expense for tools

Solitaire Company's fixed budget performance report for June follows. The $315,000 budgeted expenses include $294,000 variable expenses and $21,000 fixed expenses. Actual expenses include $27,000 fixed expenses. Prepare a flexible budget performance report that shows any variances between budgeted results and actual results. List fixed and variable expenses separately.

Exercise 24-3
Preparation of a flexible budget performance report
A1

	Fixed Budget	Actual Results	Variances
Sales (in units)	8,400	10,800	
Sales (in dollars)	$420,000	$540,000	$120,000 F
Total expenses	315,000	378,000	63,000 U
Income from operations	$105,000	$162,000	$ 57,000 F

Check Income variance, $21,000 F

Exercise 24-4

Preparation of a flexible budget performance report

A1

Bay City Company's fixed budget performance report for July follows. The $647,500 budgeted expenses include $487,500 variable expenses and $160,000 fixed expenses. Actual expenses include $158,000 fixed expenses. Prepare a flexible budget performance report showing any variances between budgeted and actual results. List fixed and variable expenses separately.

	Fixed Budget	Actual Results	Variances
Sales (in units)	7,500	7,200	
Sales (in dollars)	$750,000	$737,000	$13,000 U
Total expenses	647,500	641,000	6,500 F
Income from operations	$102,500	$ 96,000	$ 6,500 U

Check Income variance, $4,000 F

Exercise 24-5

Computation and interpretation of labor variances

C2　P2　

Check October rate variance, $3,250 U

After evaluating Null Company's manufacturing process, management decides to establish standards of 3 hours of direct labor per unit of product and $15 per hour for the labor rate. During October, the company uses 16,250 hours of direct labor at a $247,000 total cost to produce 5,600 units of product. In November, the company uses 22,000 hours of direct labor at a $335,500 total cost to produce 6,000 units of product. (1) Compute the rate variance, the efficiency variance, and the total direct labor cost variance for each of these two months. (2) Interpret the October direct labor variances.

Exercise 24-6

Computation and interpretation of overhead variances

C2　P3　

Sedona Company set the following standard costs for one unit of its product for 2008.

Direct material (20 lbs. @ $2.50 per lb.)	$ 50.00
Direct labor (10 hrs. @ $8.00 per hr.)	80.00
Factory variable overhead (10 hrs. @ $4.00 per hr.)	40.00
Factory fixed overhead (10 hrs. @ $1.60 per hr.)	16.00
Standard cost	$186.00

The $5.60 ($4.00 + $1.60) total overhead rate per direct labor hour is based on an expected operating level equal to 75% of the factory's capacity of 50,000 units per month. The following monthly flexible budget information is also available.

	Operating Levels		
	70%	75%	80%
Budgeted output (units)	35,000	37,500	40,000
Budgeted labor (standard hours)	350,000	375,000	400,000
Budgeted overhead (dollars)			
Variable overhead	$1,400,000	$1,500,000	$1,600,000
Fixed overhead	600,000	600,000	600,000
Total overhead	$2,000,000	$2,100,000	$2,200,000

During the current month, the company operated at 70% of capacity, employees worked 340,000 hours, and the following actual overhead costs are incurred.

Variable overhead costs	$1,375,000
Fixed overhead costs	628,600
Total overhead costs	$2,003,600

(1) Show how the company computed its predetermined overhead application rate per hour for total overhead, variable overhead, and fixed overhead. (2) Compute and interpret the variable overhead spending and efficiency variances. (3) Compute and interpret the fixed overhead spending and volume variances.

Hart Company made 3,000 bookshelves using 22,000 board feet of wood costing $266,200. The company's direct materials standards for one bookshelf are 8 board feet of wood at $12 per board foot. (1) Compute the direct materials variances incurred in manufacturing these bookshelves. (2) Interpret the direct materials variances.

Exercise 24-7
Computation and interpretation of materials variances

C2   P2

Check   Price variance, $2,200 U

Refer to Exercise 24-7. Hart Company records standard costs in its accounts and its material variances in separate accounts when it assigns materials costs to the Goods in Process Inventory account. (1) Show the journal entry that both charges the direct materials costs to the Goods in Process Inventory account and records the materials variances in their proper accounts. (2) Assume that Hart's material variances are the only variances accumulated in the accounting period and that they are immaterial. Prepare the adjusting journal entry to close the variance accounts at period-end. (3) Identify the variance that should be investigated according to the management by exception concept. Explain.

Exercise 24-8
Materials variances recorded and closed

C3   P4

Check   (2) Cr. to cost of goods sold, $21,800

World Company expects to operate at 80% of its productive capacity of 50,000 units per month. At this planned level, the company expects to use 25,000 standard hours of direct labor. Overhead is allocated to products using a predetermined standard rate based on direct labor hours. At the 80% capacity level, the total budgeted cost includes $50,000 fixed overhead cost and $275,000 variable overhead cost. In the current month, the company incurred $305,000 actual overhead and 22,000 actual labor hours while producing 35,000 units. Compute the (1) total overhead variance, (2) overhead volume variance, and (3) overhead controllable variance.

Exercise 24-9
Computation of volume and controllable overhead variances

P3

Check   (3) $14,375 U

Comp Wiz sells computers. During May 2008, it sold 350 computers at a $1,200 average price each. The May 2008 budget included sales of 365 computers at an average price of $1,100 each. (1) Compute the sales price variance and the sales volume variance for May 2008. (2) Interpret the findings.

Exercise 24-10
Computing and interpreting sales variances A2

Trico Company set the following standard unit costs for its single product.

PROBLEM SET A

Problem 24-1A
Computation of materials, labor, and overhead variances

C2   P2   P3

mhhe.com/wildFAP18e

Direct materials (30 lbs. @ $4 per lb.)	$120.00
Direct labor (5 hrs. @ $14 per hr.)	70.00
Factory overhead—Variable (5 hrs. @ $8 per hr.)	40.00
Factory overhead—Fixed (5 hrs. @ $10 per hr.)	50.00
Total standard cost	$280.00

The predetermined overhead rate is based on a planned operating volume of 80% of the productive capacity of 60,000 units per quarter. The following flexible budget information is available.

	Operating Levels		
	70%	**80%**	**90%**
Production in units	42,000	48,000	54,000
Standard direct labor hours	210,000	240,000	270,000
Budgeted overhead			
Fixed factory overhead	$2,400,000	$2,400,000	$2,400,000
Variable factory overhead	$1,680,000	$1,920,000	$2,160,000

During the current quarter, the company operated at 90% of capacity and produced 54,000 units of product; actual direct labor totaled 265,000 hours. Units produced are assigned the following standard costs:

Direct materials (1,620,000 lbs. @ $4 per lb.)	$ 6,480,000
Direct labor (270,000 hrs. @ $14 per hr.)	3,780,000
Factory overhead (270,000 hrs. @ $18 per hr.)	4,860,000
Total standard cost	$15,120,000

Actual costs incurred during the current quarter follow:

Direct materials (1,615,000 lbs. @ $4.10)	$ 6,621,500
Direct labor (265,000 hrs. @ $13.75)	3,643,750
Fixed factory overhead costs	2,350,000
Variable factory overhead costs	2,200,000
Total actual costs	$14,815,250

Required

Check (1) Materials variances:
Price, $161,500 U; Quantity, $20,000 F.
(2) Labor variances: Rate,
$66,250 F; Efficiency, $70,000 F

1. Compute the direct materials cost variance, including its price and quantity variances.
2. Compute the direct labor variance including its rate and efficiency variances.
3. Compute these variances: (a) variable overhead spending and efficiency, (b) fixed overhead spending and volume, and (c) total overhead controllable.

Problem 24-2A
Preparation and analysis
of a flexible budget

P1   A1

Phoenix Company's 2008 master budget included the following fixed budget report. It is based on an expected production and sales volume of 15,000 units.

PHOENIX COMPANY Fixed Budget Report For Year Ended December 31, 2008		
Sales		$3,000,000
Cost of goods sold		
Direct materials	$975,000	
Direct labor	225,000	
Machinery repairs (variable cost)	60,000	
Depreciation—Plant equipment	300,000	
Utilities ($45,000 is variable)	195,000	
Plant management salaries	200,000	1,955,000
Gross profit		1,045,000
Selling expenses		
Packaging	75,000	
Shipping	105,000	
Sales salary (fixed annual amount)	250,000	430,000
General and administrative expenses		
Advertising expense	125,000	
Salaries	241,000	
Entertainment expense	90,000	456,000
Income from operations		$ 159,000

Required

Check (2) Budgeted income at
16,000 units, $260,000

1. Classify all items listed in the fixed budget as variable or fixed. Also determine their amounts per unit or their amounts for the year, as appropriate.
2. Prepare flexible budgets (see Exhibit 24.3) for the company at sales volumes of 14,000 and 16,000 units.
3. The company's business conditions are improving. One possible result is a sales volume of approximately 18,000 units. The company president is confident that this volume is within the relevant range of existing capacity. How much would operating income increase over the 2008 budgeted amount of $159,000 if this level is reached without increasing capacity?

(4) Potential operating loss,
$(144,000)

4. An unfavorable change in business is remotely possible; in this case, production and sales volume for 2008 could fall to 12,000 units. How much income (or loss) from operations would occur if sales volume falls to this level?

Refer to information in Problem 24-2A. Phoenix Company's actual income statement for 2008 follows.

PHOENIX COMPANY Statement of Income from Operations For Year Ended December 31, 2008		
Sales (18,000 units)		$3,648,000
Cost of goods sold		
Direct materials	$1,185,000	
Direct labor	278,000	
Machinery repairs (variable cost)	63,000	
Depreciation—Plant equipment	300,000	
Utilities (fixed cost is $147,500)	200,500	
Plant management salaries	210,000	2,236,500
Gross profit		1,411,500
Selling expenses		
Packaging	87,500	
Shipping	118,500	
Sales salary (annual)	268,000	474,000
General and administrative expenses		
Advertising expense	132,000	
Salaries	241,000	
Entertainment expense	93,500	466,500
Income from operations		$ 471,000

Problem 24-3A
Preparation and analysis of a flexible budget performance report

P1 A2

mhhe.com/wildFAP18e

Required

1. Prepare a flexible budget performance report for 2008.

Analysis Component

2. Analyze and interpret both the (a) sales variance and (b) direct materials variance.

Check (1) Variances: Fixed costs, $36,000 U; Income, $9,000 F

Antuan Company set the following standard costs for one unit of its product.

Direct materials (6 lbs. @ $5 per lb.)	$ 30
Direct labor (2 hrs. @ $17 per hr.)	34
Overhead (2 hrs. @ $18.50 per hr.)	37
Total standard cost	$101

Problem 24-4A
Flexible budget preparation; computation of materials, labor, and overhead variances; and overhead variance report

P1 P2 P3 C2

The predetermined overhead rate ($18.50 per direct labor hour) is based on expected volume of 75% of the factory's capacity of 20,000 units per month. Following are the company's budgeted overhead costs per month at the 75% level.

Overhead Budget (75% capacity)		
Variable overhead costs		
Indirect materials	$ 45,000	
Indirect labor	180,000	
Power	45,000	
Repairs and maintenance	90,000	
Total variable overhead costs		$360,000
Fixed overhead costs		
Depreciation—Building	24,000	
Depreciation—Machinery	80,000	
Taxes and insurance	12,000	
Supervision	79,000	
Total fixed overhead costs		195,000
Total overhead costs		$555,000

The company incurred the following actual costs when it operated at 75% of capacity in October.

Direct materials (91,000 lbs. @ $5.10 per lb.)		$ 464,100
Direct labor (30,500 hrs. @ $17.25 per hr.)		526,125
Overhead costs		
Indirect materials	$ 44,250	
Indirect labor	177,750	
Power	43,000	
Repairs and maintenance	96,000	
Depreciation—Building	24,000	
Depreciation—Machinery	75,000	
Taxes and insurance	11,500	
Supervision	89,000	560,500
Total costs		$1,550,725

Required

1. Examine the monthly overhead budget to (a) determine the costs per unit for each variable overhead item and its total per unit costs, and (b) identify the total fixed costs per month.

2. Prepare flexible overhead budgets (as in Exhibit 24.12) for October showing the amounts of each variable and fixed cost at the 65%, 75%, and 85% capacity levels.

3. Compute the direct materials cost variance, including its price and quantity variances.

4. Compute the direct labor cost variance, including its rate and efficiency variances.

5. Compute the (a) variable overhead spending and efficiency variances, (b) fixed overhead spending and volume variances, and (c) total overhead controllable variance.

6. Prepare a detailed overhead variance report (as in Exhibit 24.19) that shows the variances for individual items of overhead.

Check   (2) Budgeted total overhead at 13,000 units, $507,000.

     (3) Materials variances: Price, $9,100 U; Quantity, $5,000 U.

     (4) Labor variances: Rate, $7,625 U; Efficiency, $8,500 U

Problem 24-5A
Materials, labor, and overhead variances; and overhead variance report

C2   P2   P3

Kegler Company has set the following standard costs per unit for the product it manufactures.

Direct materials (15 lbs. @ $4 per lb.)	$ 60.00
Direct labor (3 hrs. @ $15 per hr.)	45.00
Overhead (3 hrs. @ $3.85 per hr.)	11.55
Total standard cost	$116.55

The predetermined overhead rate is based on a planned operating volume of 80% of the productive capacity of 10,000 units per month. The following flexible budget information is available.

	Operating Levels		
	70%	**80%**	**90%**
Production in units	7,000	8,000	9,000
Standard direct labor hours	21,000	24,000	27,000
Budgeted overhead			
Variable overhead costs			
Indirect materials	$13,125	$ 15,000	$16,875
Indirect labor	21,000	24,000	27,000
Power	5,250	6,000	6,750
Maintenance	2,625	3,000	3,375
Total variable costs	42,000	48,000	54,000
Fixed overhead costs			
Rent of factory building	15,000	15,000	15,000
Depreciation—Machinery	10,000	10,000	10,000
Supervisory salaries	19,400	19,400	19,400
Total fixed costs	44,400	44,400	44,400
Total overhead costs	$86,400	$ 92,400	$98,400

During May, the company operated at 90% of capacity and produced 9,000 units, incurring the following actual costs.

Direct materials (138,000 lbs. @ $3.75 per lb.)		$ 517,500
Direct labor (31,000 hrs. @ $15.10 per hr.)		468,100
Overhead costs		
Indirect materials	$15,000	
Indirect labor	26,500	
Power	6,750	
Maintenance	4,000	
Rent of factory building	15,000	
Depreciation—Machinery	10,000	
Supervisory salaries	22,000	99,250
Total costs		$1,084,850

Required

1. Compute the direct materials variance, including its price and quantity variances.
2. Compute the direct labor variance, including its rate and efficiency variances.
3. Compute these variances: (a) variable overhead spending and efficiency, (b) fixed overhead spending and volume, and (c) total overhead controllable.
4. Prepare a detailed overhead variance report (as in Exhibit 24.19) that shows the variances for individual items of overhead.

Check (1) Materials variances: Price, $34,500 F; Quantity, $12,000 U.
(2) Labor variances: Rate, $3,100 U; Efficiency, $60,000 U.

Boss Company's standard cost accounting system recorded this information from its December operations.

Problem 24-6A
Materials, labor, and overhead variances recorded and analyzed

C3 P4

Standard direct materials cost	$100,000
Direct materials quantity variance (unfavorable)	3,000
Direct materials price variance (favorable)	500
Actual direct labor cost	90,000
Direct labor efficiency variance (favorable)	7,000
Direct labor rate variance (unfavorable)	1,200
Actual overhead cost	375,000
Volume variance (unfavorable)	12,000
Controllable variance (unfavorable)	9,000

Required

1. Prepare December 30 journal entries to record the company's costs and variances for the month.

Check (1) Dr. Goods in Process Inventory (for overhead), $354,000

Analysis Component

2. Identify the areas that would attract the attention of a manager who uses management by exception. Explain what action(s) the manager should consider.

Kryll Company set the following standard unit costs for its single product.

PROBLEM SET B

Problem 24-1B
Computation of materials, labor, and overhead variances

C2 P2 P3

Direct materials (25 lbs. @ $4 per lb.)	$100.00
Direct labor (6 hrs. @ $8 per hr.)	48.00
Factory overhead—Variable (6 hrs. @ $5 per hr.)	30.00
Factory overhead—Fixed (6 hrs. @ $7 per hr.)	42.00
Total standard cost	$220.00

The predetermined overhead rate is based on a planned operating volume of 80% of the productive capacity of 60,000 units per quarter. The following flexible budget information is available.

	Operating Levels		
	70%	**80%**	**90%**
Production in units	42,000	48,000	54,000
Standard direct labor hours	252,000	288,000	324,000
Budgeted overhead			
Fixed factory overhead	$2,016,000	$2,016,000	$2,016,000
Variable factory overhead	1,260,000	1,440,000	1,620,000

During the current quarter, the company operated at 70% of capacity and produced 42,000 units of product; direct labor hours worked were 250,000. Units produced are assigned the following standard costs:

Direct materials (1,050,000 lbs. @ $4 per lb.)	$4,200,000
Direct labor (252,000 hrs. @ $8 per hr.)	2,016,000
Factory overhead (252,000 hrs. @ $12 per hr.)	3,024,000
Total standard cost	$9,240,000

Actual costs incurred during the current quarter follow:

Direct materials (1,000,000 lbs. @ $4.25)	$4,250,000
Direct labor (250,000 hrs. @ $7.75)	1,937,500
Fixed factory overhead costs	1,960,000
Variable factory overhead costs	1,200,000
Total actual costs	$9,347,500

Required

Check (1) Materials variances:
Price, $250,000 U; Quantity, $200,000 F.
(2) Labor variances: Rate, $62,500 F;
Efficiency, $16,000 F

1. Compute the direct materials cost variance, including its price and quantity variances.
2. Compute the direct labor variance, including its rate and efficiency variances.
3. Compute these variances: (a) variable overhead spending and efficiency, (b) fixed overhead spending and volume, and (c) total overhead controllable.

Problem 24-2B
Preparation and analysis of a flexible budget

P1 A1

Tohono Company's 2008 master budget included the following fixed budget report. It is based on an expected production and sales volume of 20,000 units.

TOHONO COMPANY
Fixed Budget Report
For Year Ended December 31, 2008

Sales		$3,000,000
Cost of goods sold		
Direct materials	$1,200,000	
Direct labor	260,000	
Machinery repairs (variable cost)	57,000	
Depreciation—Machinery	250,000	
Utilities (25% is variable cost)	200,000	
Plant manager salaries	140,000	2,107,000
Gross profit		893,000
Selling expenses		
Packaging	80,000	
Shipping	116,000	
Sales salary (fixed annual amount)	160,000	356,000
General and administrative expenses		
Advertising	81,000	
Salaries	241,000	
Entertainment expense	90,000	412,000
Income from operations		$ 125,000

Required

1. Classify all items listed in the fixed budget as variable or fixed. Also determine their amounts per unit or their amounts for the year, as appropriate.

2. Prepare flexible budgets (see Exhibit 24.3) for the company at sales volumes of 18,000 and 24,000 units.

Check (2) Budgeted income at 24,000 units, $372,400

3. The company's business conditions are improving. One possible result is a sales volume of approximately 28,000 units. The company president is confident that this volume is within the relevant range of existing capacity. How much would operating income increase over the 2008 budgeted amount of $125,000 if this level is reached without increasing capacity?

4. An unfavorable change in business is remotely possible; in this case, production and sales volume for 2008 could fall to 14,000 units. How much income (or loss) from operations would occur if sales volume falls to this level?

(4) Potential operating loss, $(246,100)

Refer to information in Problem 24-2B. Tohono Company's actual income statement for 2008 follows.

Problem 24-3B
Preparation and analysis of a flexible budget performance report

P1 A2

TOHONO COMPANY
Statement of Income from Operations
For Year Ended December 31, 2008

Sales (24,000 units)		$3,648,000
Cost of goods sold		
Direct materials	$1,400,000	
Direct labor	360,000	
Machinery repairs (variable cost)	60,000	
Depreciation—Machinery	250,000	
Utilities (variable cost, $64,000)	218,000	
Plant manager salaries	155,000	2,443,000
Gross profit		1,205,000
Selling expenses		
Packaging	90,000	
Shipping	124,000	
Sales salary (annual)	162,000	376,000
General and administrative expenses		
Advertising expense	104,000	
Salaries	232,000	
Entertainment expense	100,000	436,000
Income from operations		$ 393,000

Required

1. Prepare a flexible budget performance report for 2008.

Check (1) Variances: Fixed costs, $45,000 U; Income, $20,600 F

Analysis Component

2. Analyze and interpret both the (a) sales variance and (b) direct materials variance.

SunCoast Company set the following standard costs for one unit of its product.

Problem 24-4B
Flexible budget preparation; computation of materials, labor, and overhead variances; and overhead variance report

P1 P2 P3 C2

Direct materials (4.5 lb. @ $6 per lb.)	$27
Direct labor (1.5 hrs. @ $12 per hr.)	18
Overhead (1.5 hrs. @ $16 per hr.)	24
Total standard cost	$69

The predetermined overhead rate ($16.00 per direct labor hour) is based on an expected volume of 75% of the factory's capacity of 20,000 units per month. Following are the company's budgeted overhead costs per month at the 75% level.

Overhead Budget (75% capacity)		
Variable overhead costs		
Indirect materials	$22,500	
Indirect labor	90,000	
Power	22,500	
Repairs and maintenance	45,000	
Total variable overhead costs		$180,000
Fixed overhead costs		
Depreciation—Building	24,000	
Depreciation—Machinery	72,000	
Taxes and insurance	18,000	
Supervision	66,000	
Total fixed overhead costs		180,000
Total overhead costs		$360,000

The company incurred the following actual costs when it operated at 75% of capacity in December.

Direct materials (69,000 lbs. @ $6.10)		$ 420,900
Direct labor (22,800 hrs. @ $12.30)		280,440
Overhead costs		
Indirect materials	$21,600	
Indirect labor	82,260	
Power	23,100	
Repairs and maintenance	46,800	
Depreciation—Building	24,000	
Depreciation—Machinery	75,000	
Taxes and insurance	16,500	
Supervision	66,000	355,260
Total costs		$1,056,600

Required

Check (2) Budgeted total overhead at 17,000 units, $384,000

(3) Materials variances: Price, $6,900 U; Quantity, $9,000 U

(4) Labor variances: Rate, $6,840 U; Efficiency, $3,600 U

1. Examine the monthly overhead budget to (a) determine the costs per unit for each variable overhead item and its total per unit costs, and (b) identify the total fixed costs per month.
2. Prepare flexible overhead budgets (as in Exhibit 24.12) for December showing the amounts of each variable and fixed cost at the 65%, 75%, and 85% capacity levels.
3. Compute the direct materials cost variance, including its price and quantity variances.
4. Compute the direct labor cost variance, including its rate and efficiency variances.
5. Compute the (a) variable overhead spending and efficiency variances, (b) fixed overhead spending and volume variances, and (c) total overhead controllable variance.
6. Prepare a detailed overhead variance report (as in Exhibit 24.19) that shows the variances for individual items of overhead.

Problem 24-5B
Materials, labor, and overhead variances; and overhead variance report

C2 P2 P3

Guadelupe Company has set the following standard costs per unit for the product it manufactures.

Direct materials (10 lbs. @ $3.00 per lb.)	$30.00
Direct labor (4 hr. @ $6 per hr.)	24.00
Overhead (4 hr. @ $2.50 per hr.)	10.00
Total standard cost	$64.00

The predetermined overhead rate is based on a planned operating volume of 80% of the productive capacity of 10,000 units per month. The following flexible budget information is available.

	Operating Levels		
	70%	80%	90%
Production in units	7,000	8,000	9,000
Standard direct labor hours	28,000	32,000	36,000
Budgeted overhead			
Variable overhead costs			
Indirect materials	$ 8,750	$10,000	$11,250
Indirect labor	14,000	16,000	18,000
Power	3,500	4,000	4,500
Maintenance	1,750	2,000	2,250
Total variable costs	28,000	32,000	36,000
Fixed overhead costs			
Rent of factory building	12,000	12,000	12,000
Depreciation—Machinery	20,000	20,000	20,000
Taxes and insurance	2,400	2,400	2,400
Supervisory salaries	13,600	13,600	13,600
Total fixed costs	48,000	48,000	48,000
Total overhead costs	$76,000	$80,000	$84,000

During March, the company operated at 90% of capacity and produced 9,000 units, incurring the following actual costs.

Direct materials (92,000 lbs. @ $2.95 per lb.)		$ 271,400
Direct labor (37,600 hrs. @ $6.05 per hr.)		227,480
Overhead costs		
Indirect materials	$10,000	
Indirect labor	16,000	
Power	4,500	
Maintenance	3,000	
Rent of factory building	12,000	
Depreciation—Machinery	19,200	
Taxes and insurance	3,000	
Supervisory salaries	14,000	81,700
Total costs		$580,580

Required

1. Compute the direct materials cost variance, including its price and quantity variances.
2. Compute the direct labor variance, including its rate and efficiency variances.
3. Compute these variances: (a) variable overhead spending and efficiency, (b) fixed overhead spending and volume, and (c) total overhead controllable.
4. Prepare a detailed overhead variance report (as in Exhibit 24.19) that shows the variances for individual items of overhead.

Check (1) Materials variances: Price, $4,600 F; Quantity, $6,000 U.
(2) Labor variances: Rate, $1,880 U; Efficiency, $9,600 U

Kenya Company's standard cost accounting system recorded this information from its June operations.

Problem 24-6B
Materials, labor, and overhead variances recorded and analyzed

C3   P4

Standard direct materials cost	$130,000
Direct materials quantity variance (favorable)	5,000
Direct materials price variance (favorable)	1,500
Actual direct labor cost	65,000
Direct labor efficiency variance (favorable)	3,000
Direct labor rate variance (unfavorable)	500
Actual overhead cost	250,000
Volume variance (unfavorable)	12,000
Controllable variance (unfavorable)	8,000

Required

1. Prepare journal entries dated June 30 to record the company's costs and variances for the month.

Analysis Component

2. Identify the areas that would attract the attention of a manager who uses management by exception. Describe what action(s) the manager should consider.

PROBLEM SET C

Problem Set C is available at the book's Website to further reinforce and assess your learning.

SERIAL PROBLEM

Success Systems

(This serial problem began in Chapter 1 and continues through most of the book. If previous chapter segments were not completed, the serial problem can begin at this point. It is helpful, but not necessary, for you to use the Working Papers that accompany the book.)

SP 24 Success Systems' second quarter 2009 fixed budget performance report for its computer furniture operations follows. The $174,150 budgeted expenses include $144,900 variable expenses and $29,250 fixed expenses. The actual expenses include $30,000 fixed expenses. Prepare a flexible budget performance report that shows any variances between budgeted results and actual results. List fixed and variable expenses separately.

	Fixed Budget	Actual Results	Variances
Desk sales (in units)	144	150	
Chair sales (in units)	72	80	
Desk sales (in dollars)	$162,000	$169,500	$7,500 F
Chair sales (in dollars)	$ 27,000	$ 30,000	$3,000 F
Total expenses	$174,150	$182,450	$8,300 U
Income from operations	$ 14,850	$ 17,050	$2,200 F

BEYOND THE NUMBERS

**REPORTING IN
ACTION**

C1

BTN 24-1 Analysis of flexible budgets and standard costs emphasizes the importance of a similar unit of measure for meaningful comparisons and evaluations. When **Best Buy** compiles its financial reports in compliance with GAAP, it applies the same unit of measurement, U.S. dollars, for most measures of business operations. One issue for Best Buy is how best to adjust account values for its subsidiaries that compile financial reports in currencies other than the U.S. dollar.

Required

1. Read Best Buy's Note 1 in Appendix A and identify the financial statement where it reports foreign currency translation.

2. Record the annual amount of its foreign currency translation adjustment and its ending balance for the three fiscal years 2002 through 2005.

Fast Forward

3. Access Best Buy's financial statements for a fiscal year ending after February 26, 2005, from either its Website [**BestBuy.com**] or the SEC's EDGAR database [**www.sec.gov**]. (a) Identify its foreign currency translation adjustment. (b) Does this adjustment increase or decrease net income? Explain.

BTN 24-2   The usefulness of budgets, variances, and related analyses often depends on the accuracy of management's estimates of future sales activity.

COMPARATIVE ANALYSIS

A2

Required

1. Identify and record the prior three years' sales (in dollars) for both **Best Buy** and **Circuit City** using their financial statements in Appendix A.

2. Using the data in part 1, predict both companies' sales activity for the next two to three years. (If possible, compare your predictions to actual sales figures for these years.)

BTN 24-3   Setting materials, labor, and overhead standards is challenging. If standards are set too low, companies might purchase inferior products and employees might not work to their full potential. If standards are set too high, companies could be unable to offer a quality product at a profitable rate and employees could be overworked. The ethical challenge is to set a high but reasonable standard. Assume that as a manager, you are asked to set the standard materials price and quantity for the new 1,000 CKB Mega-Max chip, a technically advanced product. To properly set the price and quantity standards, you assemble a team of specialists to provide input.

ETHICS CHALLENGE

C1

Required

Identify four types of specialists that you would assemble to provide information to help set the materials price and quantity standards. Briefly explain why you chose each individual.

BTN 24-4   The reason we use the words *favorable* and *unfavorable* when evaluating variances is made clear when we look at the closing of accounts. To see this, consider that (1) all variance accounts are closed at the end of each period (temporary accounts), (2) a favorable variance is always a credit balance, and (3) an unfavorable variance is always a debit balance. Write a one-half page memorandum to your instructor with three parts that answer the three following requirements. (Assume that variance accounts are closed to Cost of Goods Sold.)

COMMUNICATING IN PRACTICE

P4   C2

Required

1. Does Cost of Goods Sold increase or decrease when closing a favorable variance? Does gross margin increase or decrease when a favorable variance is closed to Cost of Goods Sold? Explain.

2. Does Cost of Goods Sold increase or decrease when closing an unfavorable variance? Does gross margin increase or decrease when an unfavorable variance is closed to Cost of Goods Sold? Explain.

3. Explain the meaning of a favorable variance and an unfavorable variance.

BTN 24-5   Access iSixSigma's Website (iSixSigma.com) to search for and read information about *benchmarking* to complete the following requirements.

TAKING IT TO THE NET

C1

Required

1. Write a one-paragraph explanation (in layperson's terms) of benchmarking.

2. How does standard costing relate to benchmarking?

TEAMWORK IN ACTION

C2

BTN 24-6   Many service industries link labor rate and time (quantity) standards with their processes. One example is the standard time to board an aircraft. The reason time plays such an important role in the service industry is that it is viewed as a competitive advantage: best service in the shortest amount of time. Although the labor rate component is difficult to observe, the time component of a service delivery standard is often readily apparent, for example, "Lunch will be served in less than five minutes, or it is free."

Required

Break into teams and select two service industries for your analysis. Identify and describe all the time elements each industry uses to create a competitive advantage.

***BusinessWeek* ACTIVITY**

C2

BTN 24-7   Read the article "The Shrinking Productivity Factor" from the December 28, 2005, issue of *BusinessWeek*. (The book's Website provides free access to the article.)

Required

1. The article predicts that worker productivity will increase in 2006. Which labor variance—the rate or efficiency variance—would this affect? How would it be affected?
2. The article predicts that labor costs will increase in 2006. Which labor variance—the rate or efficiency variance—would this affect? How would it be affected?
3. If productivity increases and labor costs increase, what is your prediction for a company's total labor costs? Explain.

ENTREPRENEURIAL DECISION

C1 C2

BTN 24-8   Entrepreneur Kevin Plank of **Under Armour** has implemented a costing system with standard costs for direct materials, direct labor, and overhead costs. Two comments frequently are mentioned in relation to standard costing and variance analysis: "Variances are not explanations" and "Management's goal is not to minimize variances."

Required

Write Kevin Plank a short memo interpreting these two comments.

HITTING THE ROAD

C1

BTN 24-9   Training employees to use standard amounts of materials in production is common. Typically, large companies invest in this training but small organizations do not. One can observe these different practices in a trip to two different pizza businesses. Visit both a local pizza business and a national pizza chain business and then complete the following.

Required

1. Observe and record the number of raw material items used to make a typical cheese pizza. Also observe how the person making the pizza applies each item when preparing the pizza.
2. Record any differences in how items are applied between the two businesses.
3. Estimate which business is more profitable from your observations. Explain.

GLOBAL DECISION

Dixons

BTN 24-10   Access the annual report of **Dixons** (at **Dixons-Group.com**) for the year ended May 1, 2004. The usefulness of its budgets, variances, and related analyses depends on the accuracy of management's estimates of future sales activity.

Required

1. Identify and record the prior two years' sales (in pounds) for Dixons from its income statement.
2. Using the data in part 1, predict sales activity for Dixons for the next two years. Explain your prediction process.

ANSWERS TO MULTIPLE CHOICE QUIZ

1. c; Fixed costs remain at $300,000; Variable costs = ($246,000/24,000 units) × 20,000 units = $205,000.

2. e; Budgeted direct materials + Unfavorable variance = Actual cost of direct materials used; or, 60,000 units × $10 per unit = $600,000 + $15,000 U = $615,000.

3. c; (AH × AR) − (AH × SR) = $1,599,040 – (84,160 hours × $20 per hour) = $84,160 F.

4. b; Actual variable overhead − Variable overhead applied to production = Variable overhead cost variance; or, $150,000 − (96,000 hours × $1.50 per hour) = $6,000 U.

5. a; Budgeted fixed overhead − Fixed overhead applied to production = Volume variance; or, $24,000 − (4,800 units × $4 per unit) = $4,800 U.

25

Capital Budgeting and Managerial Decisions

A Look Back

Chapter 24 discussed flexible budgets, variance analysis, and standard costs. It explained how management uses each to control and monitor business activities.

A Look at This Chapter

This chapter focuses on evaluating capital budgeting decisions. It also explains several tools and procedures used in making and evaluating short-term managerial decisions.

> "If you're good at what you do and you are focused ... it will happen to you"
> —Art Alaniz

Reaching for the Sky

EDINBURG, TX—Art Alaniz credits his Mexican-immigrant parents and their work ethic for much of his success. "I failed at my first two entrepreneurial attempts," explains Art. With his parents' help, says Art, "I picked myself up, dusted myself off, and went back in there." Art launched his current company, **Progressive Telecom (ProgressiveTelecom.com),** from a spare room in his mother's house. His mother, says Art, "always supported us and our dreams, [although she] speaks little English and has little formal education."

"I've always wanted to own my own business," recalls Art. "I started by advertising in the newspaper that I buy used Cell phones. Then I would refurbish them and sell them." Sales skyrocketed along with the proliferation of cell phones. The business quickly outgrew his mother's house. "We were doing good numbers," says Art. "Our company [went] from selling 20 to 50 phones to selling 20,000."

Soon, capital budgeting decisions became important for the financial health of his business as it built warehouses, juggled a large inventory, and determined the product mix it would carry. Art also implemented payback periods and return rates as a way to narrow business opportunities and to improve decision making.

Many new business questions also emerged, explains Art. Do we take this one-time deal? Do we scrap or rework certain inventory? Do we sell or further process particular items? What is the best product mix? These questions needed answers. Art learned to focus on relevant costs and incremental revenue concepts to arrive at a solution for these cases. "It was tough and is still," admits Art. "I know what I want to accomplish and I keep moving forward."

With an attention to managerial decisions and budgeting, this 34-year-old entrepreneur has guided the rapid growth of his company. In less than 10 years, Progressive Telecom's sales are nearing a remarkable $40 million.

Art still faces key business decisions every day, such as financing requirements, hurdle rates, payback periods, rates of return, net present values, and break-even time. But none of these faze him anymore. "What's the worst that could happen?" asks Art. "I have to start over again. That's not too difficult." We know he'll just pick himself up, dust himself off, and get right back in there.

[Sources: *Progressive Telecom Website,* May 2006; *The Monitor,* November 2004; *Entrepreneur,* November and October 2004; *PRNewswire,* October 2003; *TradeRoots.org Website,* March 2006; *Small Business Administration,* March 2006]

Making business decisions involves choosing between alternative courses of action. Many factors affect business decisions, yet analysis typically focuses on finding the alternative that offers the highest return on investment or the greatest reduction in costs. Some decisions are based on little more than an intuitive understanding of the situation because available information is too limited to allow a more systematic analysis. In other cases, intangible factors such as convenience, prestige, and environmental considerations are more important than strictly quantitative factors. In all situations, managers can reach a sounder decision if they identify the consequences of alternative choices in financial terms. This chapter explains several methods of analysis that can help managers make those business decisions.

Section 1—Capital Budgeting

C1 Explain the importance of capital budgeting.

The capital expenditures budget is management's plan for acquiring and selling plant assets. **Capital budgeting** is the process of analyzing alternative long-term investments and deciding which assets to acquire or sell. These decisions can involve developing a new product or process, buying a new machine or a new building, or acquiring an entire company. An objective for these decisions is to earn a satisfactory return on investment.

Capital budgeting decisions require careful analysis because they are usually the most difficult and risky decisions that managers make. These decisions are difficult because they require predicting events that will not occur until well into the future. Many of these predictions are tentative and potentially unreliable. Specifically, a capital budgeting decision is risky because (1) the outcome is uncertain, (2) large amounts of money are usually involved, (3) the investment involves a long-term commitment, and (4) the decision could be difficult or impossible to reverse, no matter how poor it turns out to be. Risk is especially high for investments in technology due to innovations and uncertainty.

Managers use several methods to evaluate capital budgeting decisions. Nearly all of these methods involve predicting cash inflows and cash outflows of proposed investments, assessing the risk of and returns on those flows, and then choosing the investments to make. Management often restates future cash flows in terms of their present value. This approach applies the time value of money: A dollar today is worth more than a dollar tomorrow. Similarly, a dollar tomorrow is worth less than a dollar today. The process of restating future cash flows in terms of their present value is called *discounting*. The time value of money is important when evaluating capital investments, but managers sometimes apply evaluation methods that ignore present value. This section describes four methods for comparing alternative investments.

Point: The nature of capital spending has changed with the business environment. Budgets for information technology have increased from about 25% of corporate capital spending 20 years ago to an estimated 35% today.

Methods Not Using Time Value of Money

All investments, whether they involve the purchase of a machine or another long-term asset, are expected to produce net cash flows. *Net cash flow* is cash inflows minus cash outflows. Sometimes managers perform simple analyses of the financial feasibility of an investment's net cash flow without using the time value of money. This section explains two of the most common methods in this category: (1) payback period and (2) accounting rate of return.

Payback Period

An investment's **payback period (PBP)** is the expected time period to recover the initial investment amount. Managers prefer investing in assets with shorter payback periods to reduce the risk of an unprofitable investment over the long run. Acquiring assets with short payback periods reduces a company's risk from potentially inaccurate long-term predictions of future cash flows.

P1   Compute payback period and describe its use.

Computing Payback Period with Even Cash Flows   To illustrate use of the payback period for an investment with even cash flows, we look at data from FasTrac, a manufacturer of exercise equipment and supplies. (*Even cash flows* are cash flows that are the same each and every year; *uneven cash flows* are cash flows that are not all equal in amount.) FasTrac is considering several different capital investments, one of which is to purchase a machine to use in manufacturing a new product. This machine costs $16,000 and is expected to have an eight-year life with no salvage value. Management predicts this machine will produce 1,000 units of product each year and that the new product will be sold for $30 per unit. Exhibit 25.1 shows the expected annual net cash flows for this asset over its life as well as the expected annual revenues and expenses (including depreciation and income taxes) from investing in the machine.

Decision Insight	
Payback Phones Profits of telecoms declined as too much capital investment chased too little revenue. Telecom success depends on new technology, and communications gear is evolving at a dizzying rate. Consequently, managers of telecoms often demand short payback periods and large expected net cash flows to compensate for the investment risk.	

Exhibit 25.1

Cash Flow Analysis

FASTRAC Cash Flow Analysis—Machinery Investment January 15, 2008	Expected Accrual Figures	Expected Net Cash Flows
Annual sales of new product	$30,000	$30,000
Deduct annual expenses		
Cost of materials, labor, and overhead (except depreciation)	15,500	15,500
Depreciation—Machinery	2,000	
Additional selling and administrative expenses	9,500	9,500
Annual pretax accrual income	3,000	
Income taxes (30%)	900	900
Annual net income	$ 2,100	
Annual net cash flow		**$ 4,100**

The amount of net cash flow from the machinery is computed by subtracting expected cash outflows from expected cash inflows. The cash flows column of Exhibit 25.1 excludes all noncash revenues and expenses. Depreciation is FasTrac's, only noncash item. Alternatively, managers can adjust the projected net income for revenue and expense items that do not affect

Point: Annual net cash flow in Exhibit 25.1 equals net income plus depreciation (a noncash expense).

cash flows. For FasTrac, this means taking the $2,100 net income and adding back the $2,000 depreciation.

The formula for computing the payback period of an investment that yields even net cash flows is in Exhibit 25.2.

Exhibit 25.2

Payback Period Formula with Even Cash Flows

$$\text{Payback period} = \frac{\text{Cost of investment}}{\text{Annual net cash flow}}$$

The payback period reflects the amount of time for the investment to generate enough net cash flow to return (or pay back) the cash initially invested to purchase it. FasTrac's payback period for this machine is just under four years:

$$\text{Payback period} = \frac{\$16,000}{\$4,100} = 3.9 \text{ years}$$

Example: If an alternative machine (with different technology) yields a payback period of 3.5 years, which one does a manager choose? Answer: The alternative (3.5 is less than 3.9).

The initial investment is fully recovered in 3.9 years, or just before reaching the halfway point of this machine's useful life of eight years.

Computing Payback Period with Uneven Cash Flows   Computing the payback period in the prior section assumed even net cash flows. What happens if the net cash flows are uneven? In this case, the payback period is computed using the *cumulative total of net cash flows*. The word *cumulative* refers to the addition of each period's net cash flows as we progress through time. To illustrate, consider data for another investment that FasTrac is considering. This machine is predicted to generate uneven net cash flows over the next eight years. The relevant data and payback period computation are shown in Exhibit 25.3.

Exhibit 25.3

Payback Period Calculation with Uneven Cash Flows

Period*	Expected Net Cash Flows	Cumulative Net Cash Flows
Year 0	$(16,000)	$(16,000)
Year 1	3,000	(13,000)
Year 2	4,000	(9,000)
Year 3	4,000	(5,000)
Year 4	4,000	(1,000)
Year 5	5,000	4,000
Year 6	3,000	7,000
Year 7	2,000	9,000
Year 8	2,000	11,000
		Payback period = 4.2 years

* All cash inflows and outflows occur uniformly during the year.

Example: Find the payback period in Exhibit 25.3 if net cash flows for the first 4 years are:
Year 1 = $6,000; Year 2 = $5,000;
Year 3 = $4,000; Year 4 = $3,000.
Answer: 3.33 years

Year 0 refers to the period of initial investment in which the $16,000 cash outflow occurs at the end of year 0 to acquire the machinery. By the end of year 1, the cumulative net cash flow is reduced to $(13,000), computed as the $(16,000) initial cash outflow plus year 1's $3,000 cash inflow. This process continues throughout the asset's life. The cumulative net cash flow amount changes from negative to positive in year 5. Specifically, at the end of year 4, the cumulative net cash flow is $(1,000). As soon as FasTrac receives net cash inflow of $1,000 during the fifth year, it has fully recovered the investment. If we assume that cash flows are received uniformly *within* each year, receipt of the $1,000 occurs about one-fifth of the way through the year. This is computed as $1,000 divided by year 5's total net cash flow of $5,000, or 0.20. This yields a payback period of 4.2 years, computed as 4 years plus 0.20 of year 5.

Using the Payback Period   Companies desire a short payback period to increase return and reduce risk. The more quickly a company receives cash, the sooner it is available for other uses and the less time it is at risk of loss. A shorter payback period also improves the company's ability to respond to unanticipated changes and lowers its risk of having to keep an unprofitable investment.

Payback period should never be the only consideration in evaluating investments. This is so because it ignores at least two important factors. First, it fails to reflect differences in the timing of net cash flows within the payback period. In Exhibit 25.3, FasTrac's net cash flows in the first five years were $3,000, $4,000, $4,000, $4,000, and $5,000. If another investment had predicted cash flows of $9,000, $3,000, $2,000, $1,800, and $1,000 in these five years, its payback period would also be 4.2 years, but this second alternative could be more desirable because it provides cash more quickly. The second important factor is that the payback period ignores *all* cash flows after the point where its costs are fully recovered. For example, one investment might pay back its cost in 3 years but stop producing cash after 4 years. A second investment might require 5 years to pay back its cost yet continue to produce net cash flows for another 15 years. A focus on only the payback period would mistakenly lead management to choose the first investment over the second.

"So what if I underestimated costs and overestimated revenues? It all averages out in the end."

Quick Check

Answers—p. 1020

1. Capital budgeting is (*a*) concerned with analyzing alternative sources of capital, including debt and equity, (*b*) an important activity for companies when considering what assets to acquire or sell, or (*c*) best done by intuitive assessments of the value of assets and their usefulness.

2. Why are capital budgeting decisions often difficult?

3. A company is considering purchasing equipment costing $75,000. Future annual net cash flows from this equipment are $30,000, $25,000, $15,000, $10,000, and $5,000. The payback period is (*a*) 4 years, (*b*) 3.5 years, or (*c*) 3 years.

4. If depreciation is an expense, why is it added back to an investment's net income to compute the net cash flow from that investment?

5. If two investments have the same payback period, are they equally desirable? Explain.

Accounting Rate of Return

The **accounting rate of return,** also called *return on average investment,* is computed by dividing a project's after-tax net income by the average amount invested in it. To illustrate, we return to FasTrac's $16,000 machinery investment described in Exhibit 25.1. We first compute (1) the after-tax net income and (2) the average amount invested. The $2,100 after-tax net income is already available from Exhibit 25.1. To compute the average amount invested, we assume that net cash flows are received evenly throughout each year. Thus, the average investment for each year is computed as the average of its beginning and ending book values. If FasTrac's $16,000 machine is depreciated $2,000 each year, the average amount invested in the machine for each year is computed as shown in Exhibit 25.4. The average for any year is the average of the beginning and ending book values.

P2 Compute accounting rate of return and explain its use.

	Beginning Book Value	Annual Depreciation	Ending Book Value	Average Book Value
Year 1	$16,000	$2,000	$14,000	$15,000
Year 2	14,000	2,000	12,000	13,000
Year 3	12,000	2,000	10,000	11,000
Year 4	10,000	2,000	8,000	9,000
Year 5	8,000	2,000	6,000	7,000
Year 6	6,000	2,000	4,000	5,000
Year 7	4,000	2,000	2,000	3,000
Year 8	2,000	2,000	0	1,000
All years				$ 8,000

Exhibit 25.4

Computing Average Amount Invested

Next we need the average book value for the asset's entire life. This amount is computed by taking the average of the individual yearly averages. This average equals $8,000, computed as $64,000 (the sum of the individual years' averages) divided by eight years (see last column of Exhibit 25.4).

Point: General formula for *annual average investment* is the sum of individual years' average book values divided by the number of years of the planned investment.

If a company uses straight-line depreciation, we can find the average amount invested by using the formula in Exhibit 25.5. Because FasTrac uses straight-line depreciation, its average amount invested for the eight years equals the sum of the book value at the beginning of the asset's investment period and the book value at the end of its investment period, divided by 2, as shown in Exhibit 25.5.

Exhibit 25.5

Computing Average Amount Invested under Straight-Line Depreciation

$$\text{Annual average investment} = \frac{\text{Beginning book value} + \text{Ending book value}}{2}$$
(straight-line case only)
$$= \frac{\$16,000 + \$0}{2} = \$8,000$$

If an investment has a salvage value, the average amount invested when using straight-line depreciation is computed as (Beginning book value + Salvage value)/2.

Once we determine the after-tax net income and the average amount invested, the accounting rate of return on the investment can be computed from the annual after-tax net income divided by the average amount invested, as shown in Exhibit 25.6.

Exhibit 25.6

Accounting Rate of Return Formula

$$\text{Accounting rate of return} = \frac{\text{Annual after-tax net income}}{\text{Annual average investment}}$$

This yields an accounting rate of return of 26.25% ($2,100/$8,000). FasTrac management must decide whether a 26.25% accounting rate of return is satisfactory. To make this decision, we must factor in the investment's risk. For instance, we cannot say an investment with a 26.25% return is preferred over one with a lower return unless we recognize any differences in risk. Thus, an investment's return is satisfactory or unsatisfactory only when it is related to returns from other investments with similar lives and risk.

When accounting rate of return is used to choose among capital investments, the one with the least risk, the shortest payback period, and the highest return for the longest time period is often identified as the best. However, use of accounting rate of return to evaluate investment opportunities is limited because it bases the amount invested on book values (not predicted market values) in future periods. Accounting rate of return is also limited when an asset's net incomes are expected to vary from year to year. This requires computing the rate using *average* annual net incomes, yet this accounting rate of return fails to distinguish between two investments with the same average annual net income but different amounts of income in early years versus later years or different levels of income variability.

Quick Check

Answers—p. 1020

6. The following data relate to a company's decision on whether to purchase a machine:

Cost	$180,000
Salvage value	15,000
Annual after-tax net income	40,000

The machine's accounting rate of return, assuming the even receipt of its net cash flows during the year and use of straight-line depreciation, is (a) 22%, (b) 41%, or (c) 21%.

7. Is a 15% accounting rate of return for a machine a good rate?

Methods Using Time Value of Money

This section describes two methods that help managers with capital budgeting decisions and that use the time value of money: (1) net present value and (2) internal rate of return. *(To apply these methods, you need a basic understanding of the concept of present value. An expanded*

explanation of present value concepts is in Appendix B near the end of the book. You can use the present value tables at the end of Appendix B to solve many of this chapter's assignments that use the time value of money.)

Net Present Value

Net present value analysis applies the time value of money to future cash inflows and cash out-flows so management can evaluate a project's benefits and costs at one point in time. Specifically, **net present value (NPV)** is computed by discounting the future net cash flows from the investment at the project's required rate of return and then subtracting the initial amount invested.

To illustrate, let's return to FasTrac's proposed machinery purchase described in Exhibit 25.1. Does this machine provide a satisfactory return while recovering the amount invested? Recall that the machine requires a $16,000 investment and is expected to provide $4,100 annual net cash inflows for the next eight years. If we assume that net cash flows from this machine are received at each year-end and that FasTrac requires a 12% annual return, net present value can be computed as in Exhibit 25.7.

P3   Compute net present value and describe its use.

Point: The assumption of end-of-year cash flows simplifies computations and is common in practice.

	Net Cash Flows*	Present Value of 1 at 12%†	Present Value of Net Cash Flows
Year 1	$ 4,100	0.8929	$ 3,661
Year 2	4,100	0.7972	3,269
Year 3	4,100	0.7118	2,918
Year 4	4,100	0.6355	2,606
Year 5	4,100	0.5674	2,326
Year 6	4,100	0.5066	2,077
Year 7	4,100	0.4523	1,854
Year 8	4,100	0.4039	1,656
Totals	$32,800		$20,367
Amount invested			**(16,000)**
Net present value			**$ 4,367**

Exhibit 25.7

Net Present Value Calculation with Equal Cash Flows

* Cash flows occur at the end of each year.

† Present value of 1 factors are taken from Table B.1 in Appendix B.

The first number column of Exhibit 25.7 shows the annual net cash flows. Present value of 1 factors, also called *discount factors,* are shown in the second column. Taken from Table B.1 in Appendix B, they assume that net cash flows are received at each year-end. *(To simplify present value computations and for assignment material at the end of this chapter, we assume that net cash flows are received at each year-end.)* Annual net cash flows from the first column of Exhibit 25.7 are multiplied by the discount factors in the second column to give present values shown in the third column. The last three lines of this exhibit show the final NPV computations. The asset's $16,000 initial cost is deducted from the $20,367 total present value of all future net cash flows to give this asset's NPV of $4,367. The machine is thus expected to (1) recover its cost, (2) provide a 12% compounded return, and (3) generate $4,367 above cost. We summarize this analysis by saying the present value of this machine's future net cash flows to FasTrac exceeds the $16,000 investment by $4,367.

Point: The amount invested includes all costs that must be incurred to get the asset in its proper location and ready for use.

Example: What is the net present value in Exhibit 25.7 if a 10% return is applied? *Answer:* $5,873

Net Present Value Decision Rule   The decision rule in applying NPV is as follows: When an asset's expected cash flows are discounted at the required rate and yield a *positive* net present value, the asset should be acquired. This decision rule is reflected in the graphic at the right. When comparing several investment opportunities of about the same cost and same risk, we prefer the one with the highest positive net present value.

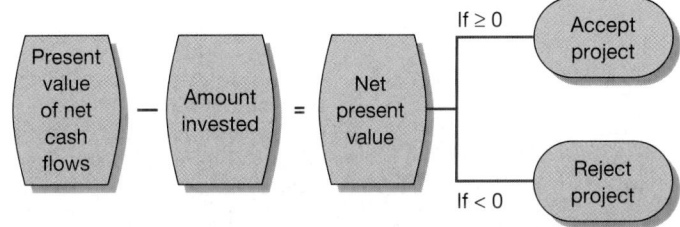

> ### Decision Ethics
>
> Answer—p. 1020
>
> **Systems Manager** Top management adopts a policy requiring purchases in excess of $5,000 to be submitted with cash flow projections to the cost analyst for capital budget approval. As systems manager, you want to upgrade your computers at a $25,000 cost. You consider submitting several orders all under $5,000 to avoid the approval process. You believe the computers will increase profits and wish to avoid a delay. What do you do?

Simplifying Computations The computations in Exhibit 25.7 use separate present value of 1 factors for each of the eight years. Each year's net cash flow is multiplied by its present value of 1 factor to determine its present value. The individual present values for each of the eight net cash flows are added to give the asset's total present value. This computation can be simplified in two ways if annual net cash flows are equal in amount. One way is to add the eight annual present value of 1 factors for a total of 4.9676 and multiply this amount by the annual $4,100 net cash flow to get the $20,367 total present value of net cash flows.[1] A second simplification is to use a calculator with compound interest functions or a spreadsheet program. Whatever procedure you use, it is important to understand the concepts behind these computations.

Uneven Cash Flows Net present value analysis can also be applied when net cash flows are uneven (unequal). To illustrate, assume that FasTrac can choose only one capital investment from among projects A, B, and C. Each project requires the same $12,000 initial investment. Future net cash flows for each project are shown in the first three number columns of Exhibit 25.8.

Exhibit 25.8

Net Present Value Calculation with Uneven Cash Flows

	Net Cash Flows			Present Value of 1 at 10%	Present Value of Net Cash Flows		
	A	B	C		A	B	C
Year 1	$ 5,000	$ 8,000	$ 1,000	0.9091	$ 4,546	$ 7,273	$ 909
Year 2	5,000	5,000	5,000	0.8264	4,132	4,132	4,132
Year 3	5,000	2,000	9,000	0.7513	3,757	1,503	6,762
Totals	$15,000	$15,000	$15,000		12,435	12,908	11,803
Amount invested					(12,000)	(12,000)	(12,000)
Net present value ...					$ 435	$ 908	$ (197)

The three projects in Exhibit 25.8 have the same expected total net cash flows of $15,000. Project A is expected to produce equal amounts of $5,000 each year. Project B is expected to produce a larger amount in the first year. Project C is expected to produce a larger amount in the third year. The fourth column of Exhibit 25.8 shows the present value of 1 factors from Table B.1 assuming 10% required return.

Computations in the right-most columns show that Project A has a $435 positive NPV. Project B has the largest NPV of $908 because it brings in cash more quickly. Project C has a $(197) *negative* NPV because its larger cash inflows are delayed. If FasTrac requires a 10% return, it should reject Project C because its NPV implies a return *under* 10%. If only one project can be accepted, project B appears best because it yields the highest NPV.

Salvage Value and Accelerated Depreciation FasTrac predicted the $16,000 machine to have zero salvage value at the end of its useful life (recall Exhibit 25.1). In many

---

[1] We can simplify this computation using Table B.3, which gives the present value of 1 to be received periodically for a number of periods. To determine the present value of these eight annual receipts discounted at 12%, go down the 12% column of Table B.3 to the factor on the eighth line. This cumulative discount factor, also known as an *annuity* factor, is 4.9676. We then compute the $20,367 present value for these eight annual $4,100 receipts, computed as 4.9676 × $4,100.

cases, assets are expected to have salvage values. If so, this amount is an additional net cash inflow received at the end of the final year of the asset's life. All other computations remain the same.

Depreciation computations also affect net present value analysis. FasTrac computes depreciation using the straight-line method. Accelerated depreciation is also commonly used, especially for income tax reports. Accelerated depreciation produces larger depreciation deductions in the early years of an asset's life and smaller deductions in later years. This pattern results in smaller income tax payments in early years and larger payments in later years. Accelerated depreciation does not change the basics of a present value analysis, but it can change the result. Using accelerated depreciation for tax reporting affects the NPV of an asset's cash flows because it produces larger net cash inflows in the early years of the asset's life and smaller ones in later years. Being able to use accelerated depreciation for tax reporting always makes an investment more desirable because early cash flows are more valuable than later ones.

Example: When is it appropriate to use different discount rates for different projects? *Answer:* When risk levels are different.

Use of Net Present Value   In deciding whether to proceed with a capital investment project, we approve the proposal if the NPV is positive but reject it if the NPV is negative. When considering several projects of similar investment amounts and risk levels, we can compare the different projects' NPVs and rank them on the basis of their NPVs. However, if the amount invested differs substantially across projects, the NPV is of limited value for comparison purposes. To illustrate, suppose that Project X requires a $1 million investment and provides a $100,000 NPV. Project Y requires an investment of only $100,000 and returns a $75,000 NPV. Ranking on the basis of NPV puts Project X ahead of Y, yet X's NPV is only 10% of the initial investment whereas Y's NPV is 75% of its investment. We must also remember that when reviewing projects with different risks, we computed the NPV of individual projects using different discount rates. The higher the risk, the higher the discount rate.

Internal Rate of Return

Another means to evaluate capital investments is to use the **internal rate of return,** which equals the rate that yields an NPV of zero for an investment. This means that if we compute the total present value of a project's net cash flows using the IRR as the discount rate and then subtract the initial investment from this total present value, we get a zero NPV.

To illustrate, we use the data for FasTrac's Project A from Exhibit 25.8 to compute its IRR. Exhibit 25.9 shows the two-step process in computing IRR.

P4   Compute internal rate of return and explain its use.

Step 1: Compute the present value factor for the investment project.

$$\textbf{Present value factor} = \frac{\textbf{Amount invested}}{\textbf{Net cash flows}} = \frac{\$12,000}{\$5,000} = 2.4000$$

Step 2: Identify the discount rate (IRR) yielding the present value factor

Search Table B.3 for a present value factor of 2.4000 in the three-year row (equaling the 3-year project duration). The 12% discount rate yields a present value factor of 2.4018. This implies that the IRR is approximately 12%.*

Exhibit 25.9

Computing Internal Rate of Return (with even cash flows)

* Since the present value factor of 2.4000 is not exactly equal to the 12% factor of 2.4018, we can more precisely
   estimate the IRR as follows:

Discount rate	Present Value Factor from Table B.3
12%	2.4018
15%	2.2832
	0.1186 = difference

$$\text{Then, IRR} = 12\% + \left[(15\% - 12\%) \times \frac{2.4018 - 2.4000}{0.1186} \right] = \underline{\underline{12.05\%}}$$

When cash flows are equal, as with Project A, we compute the present value factor (as shown in Exhibit 25.9) by dividing the initial investment by its annual net cash flows. We then use an annuity table to determine the discount rate equal to this present value factor. For FasTrac's Project A, we look across the three-period row of Table B.3 and find that the discount rate corresponding to the present value factor of 2.4000 roughly equals the 2.4018 value for the 12% rate. This row is reproduced here:

Present Value of an Annuity of 1 for Three Periods

		Rate			
Periods	1%	5%	10%	12%	15%
3	2.9410	2.7232	2.4869	2.4018	2.2832

The 12% rate is the Project's IRR. A more precise IRR estimate can be computed following the procedure shown in the note to Exhibit 25.9. Spreadsheet software and calculators can also compute this IRR.

Uneven Cash Flows   If net cash flows are uneven, we must use trial and error to compute the IRR. We do this by selecting any reasonable discount rate and computing the NPV. If the amount is positive (negative), we recompute the NPV using a higher (lower) discount rate. We continue these steps until we reach a point where two consecutive computations result in NPVs having different signs (positive and negative). Because the NPV is zero using IRR, we know that the IRR lies between these two discount rates. We can then estimate its value. Spreadsheet programs and calculators can do these computations for us.

Decision Insight

Fun-IRR   Many theme parks use both financial and nonfinancial criteria to evaluate their investments in new rides and activities. The use of IRR is a major part of this evaluation. This requires good estimates of future cash inflows and outflows. It also requires risk assessments of the uncertainty of the future cash flows.

C2   Describe the selection of a hurdle rate for an investment.

Use of Internal Rate of Return   When we use the IRR to evaluate a project, we compare it to a predetermined **hurdle rate,** which is a minimum acceptable rate of return and is applied as follows.

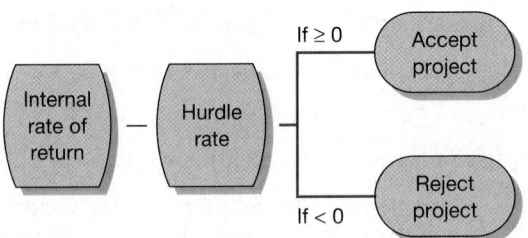

Example: How can management evaluate the risk of an investment? *Answer:* It must assess the uncertainty of future cash flows.

Top management selects the hurdle rate to use in evaluating capital investments. Financial formulas aid in this selection, but the choice of a minimum rate is subjective and left to management. For projects financed from borrowed funds, the hurdle rate must exceed the interest rate paid on these funds. The return on an investment must cover its interest and provide an additional profit to reward the company for its risk. For instance, if money is borrowed at 10%, an average risk investment often requires an after-tax return of 15% (or 5% above the borrowing rate). Remember that lower-risk investments require a lower rate of return compared with higher-risk investments.

If the project is internally financed, the hurdle rate is often based on actual returns from comparable projects. If the IRR is higher than the hurdle rate, the project is accepted. Multiple projects are often ranked by the extent to which their IRR exceeds the hurdle rate. The hurdle rate for individual projects is often different, depending on the risk involved. IRR is not subject to the limitations of NPV when comparing projects with different amounts invested because the IRR is expressed as a percent rather than as an absolute dollar value in NPV.

Decision Maker   Answer—p. 1020

Entrepreneur You are developing a new product and you use a 12% discount rate to compute its NPV. Your banker, from whom you hope to obtain a loan, expresses concern that your discount rate is too low. How do you respond?

Comparison of Capital Budgeting Methods

We explained four methods that managers use to evaluate capital investment projects. How do these methods compare with each other? Exhibit 25.10 addresses that question. Neither the payback period nor the accounting rate of return considers the time value of money. On the other hand, both the net present value and the internal rate of return do.

Exhibit 25.10

Comparing Capital Budgeting Methods

	Payback Period	Accounting Rate of Return	Net Present Value	Internal Rate of Return
Measurement basis	■ Cash flows	■ Accrual income	■ Cash flows ■ Profitability	■ Cash flows ■ Profitability
Measurement unit	■ Years	■ Percent	■ Dollars	■ Percent
Strengths	■ Easy to understand	■ Easy to understand	■ Reflects time value of money	■ Reflects time value of money
	■ Allows comparison of projects	■ Allows comparison of projects	■ Reflects varying risks over project's life	■ Allows comparisons of dissimilar projects
Limitations	■ Ignores time value of money	■ Ignores time value of money	■ Difficult to compare dissimilar projects	■ Ignores varying risks over life of project
	■ Ignores cash flows after payback period	■ Ignores annual rates over life of project		

The payback period is probably the simplest method. It gives managers an estimate of how soon they will recover their initial investment. Managers sometimes use this method when they have limited cash to invest and a number of projects to choose from. The accounting rate of return yields a percent measure computed using accrual income instead of cash flows. The accounting rate of return is an average rate for the entire investment period. Net present value considers all estimated net cash flows for the project's expected life. It can be applied to even and uneven cash flows and can reflect changes in the level of risk over a project's life. Since it yields a dollar measure, comparing projects of unequal sizes is more difficult. The internal rate of return considers all cash flows from a project. It is readily computed when the cash flows are even but requires some trial and error estimation when cash flows are uneven. Because the IRR is a percent measure, it is readily used to compare projects with different investment amounts. However, IRR does not reflect changes in risk over a project's life.

Decision Insight

And the Winner Is . . .
How do we choose among the methods for evaluating capital investments? Management surveys consistently show the internal rate of return (IRR) as the most popular method followed by the payback period and net present value (NPV). Few companies use the accounting rate of return (ARR), but nearly all use more than one method.

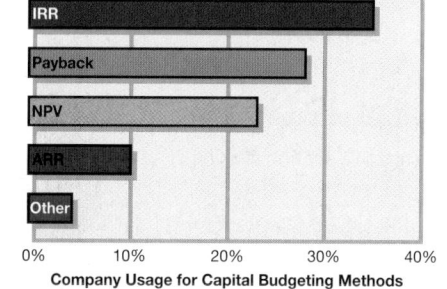

Company Usage for Capital Budgeting Methods

Quick Check   Answers—p. 1020

8. A company can invest in only one of two projects, A or B. Each project requires a $20,000
investment and is expected to generate end-of-period, annual cash flows as follows:

	Year 1	Year 2	Year 3	Total
Project A	$12,000	$8,500	$4,000	$24,500
Project B	4,500	8,500	13,000	26,000

Assuming a discount rate of 10%, which project has the higher net present value?

9. Two investment alternatives are expected to generate annual cash flows with the same net
present value (assuming the same discount rate applied to each). Using this information, can you
conclude that the two alternatives are equally desirable?

10. When two investment alternatives have the same total expected cash flows but differ
in the timing of those flows, which method of evaluating those investments is superior,
(a) accounting rate of return or (b) net present value?

Section 2—Managerial Decisions

This section focuses on methods that use accounting information to make several important
managerial decisions. Most of these involve short-term decisions. This differs from methods
used for longer-term managerial decisions that are described in the first section of this chapter
and in several other chapters of this book.

Decisions and Information

This section explains how managers make decisions and the information relevant to those
decisions.

Decision Making

Managerial decision making involves five steps: (1) define the decision task, (2) identify
alternative courses of action, (3) collect relevant information and evaluate each alternative,
(4) select the preferred course of action, and (5) analyze and assess decisions made. These five
steps are illustrated in Exhibit 25.11.

Exhibit 25.11

Managerial Decision Making

| Define Task and Goal | Identify Alternative Actions | Collect Relevant Information | Select Course of Action | Analyze and Assess Decision |

Both managerial and financial accounting information play an important role in most management decisions. The accounting system is expected to provide primarily *financial* information such as performance reports and budget analyses for decision making. *Nonfinancial* information is also relevant, however; it includes information on environmental effects, political
sensitivities, and social responsibility.

Relevant Costs

Most financial measures of revenues and costs from accounting systems are based on historical costs. Although historical costs are important and useful for many tasks such as product pricing and the control and monitoring of business activities, we sometimes find that an analysis of *relevant costs,* or *avoidable costs,* is especially useful. Three types of costs are pertinent to our discussion of relevant costs: sunk costs, out-of-pocket costs, and opportunity costs.

A *sunk cost* arises from a past decision and cannot be avoided or changed; it is irrelevant to future decisions. An example is the cost of computer equipment previously purchased by a company. Most of a company's allocated costs, including fixed overhead items such as depreciation and administrative expenses, are sunk costs.

An *out-of-pocket cost* requires a future outlay of cash and is relevant for current and future decision making. These costs are usually the direct result of management's decisions. For instance, future purchases of computer equipment involve out-of-pocket costs.

An *opportunity cost* is the potential benefit lost by taking a specific action when two or more alternative choices are available. An example is a student giving up wages from a job to attend summer school. Companies continually must choose from alternative courses of action. For instance, a company making standardized products might be approached by a customer to supply a special (nonstandard) product. A decision to accept or reject the special order must consider not only the profit to be made from the special order but also the profit given up by devoting time and resources to this order instead of pursuing an alternative project. The profit given up is an opportunity cost. Consideration of opportunity costs is important. The implications extend to internal resource allocation decisions. For instance, a computer manufacturer must decide between internally manufacturing a chip versus buying it externally. In another case, management of a multidivisional company must decide whether to continue operating or close a particular division.

Besides relevant costs, management must also consider the relevant benefits associated with a decision. **Relevant benefits** refer to the additional or *incremental* revenue generated by selecting a particular course of action over another. For instance, a student must decide the relevant benefits of taking one course over another. In sum, both relevant costs and relevant benefits are crucial to managerial decision making.

C3 Describe the importance of relevant costs for short-term decisions.

Example: Depreciation and amortization are allocations of the original cost of plant and intangible assets. Are they out-of-pocket costs? *Answer:* No; they are sunk costs.

Point: Opportunity costs are not entered in accounting records. This does not reduce their relevance for managerial decisions.

Managerial Decision Scenarios

Managers experience many different scenarios that require analyzing alternative actions and making a decision. We describe several different types of decision scenarios in this section. We set these tasks in the context of FasTrac, the exercise supplies and equipment manufacturer introduced earlier. *We treat each of these decision tasks as separate from each other.*

A1 Evaluate short-term managerial decisions using relevant costs.

Additional Business

FasTrac is operating at its normal level of 80% of full capacity. At this level, it produces and sells approximately 100,000 units of product annually. Its per unit and annual total costs are shown in Exhibit 25.12.

	Per Unit	Annual Total
Sales (100,000 units)	$10.00	$1,000,000
Direct materials	(3.50)	(350,000)
Direct labor	(2.20)	(220,000)
Overhead	(1.10)	(110,000)
Selling expenses	(1.40)	(140,000)
Administrative expenses	(0.80)	(80,000)
Total costs and expenses	(9.00)	(900,000)
Operating income	$ 1.00	$ 100,000

Exhibit 25.12

Selected Operating Income Data

A current buyer of FasTrac's products wants to purchase additional units of its product and export them to another country. This buyer offers to buy 10,000 units of the product at $8.50 per unit, or $1.50 less than the current price. The offer price is low, but FasTrac is considering the proposal because this sale would be several times larger than any single previous sale and it would use idle capacity. Also, the units will be exported, so this new business will not affect current sales.

To determine whether to accept or reject this order, management needs to know whether accepting the offer will increase net income. The analysis in Exhibit 25.13 shows that if management relies on per unit historical costs, it would reject the sale because it yields a loss. However, historical costs are *not* relevant to this decision. Instead, the relevant costs are the additional costs called **incremental costs.** These costs, also called *differential costs,* are the additional costs incurred if a company pursues a certain course of action. FasTrac's incremental costs are those related to the added volume that this new order would bring.

Exhibit 25.13

Analysis of Additional Business Using Historical Costs

	Per Unit	Total
Sales (10,000 additional units)	$ 8.50	$ 85,000
Direct materials	(3.50)	(35,000)
Direct labor	(2.20)	(22,000)
Overhead	(1.10)	(11,000)
Selling expenses	(1.40)	(14,000)
Administrative expenses	(0.80)	(8,000)
Total costs and expenses	(9.00)	(90,000)
Operating loss	$(0.50)	$ (5,000)

To make its decision, FasTrac must analyze the costs of this new business in a different manner. The following information regarding the order is available:

■ Manufacturing 10,000 additional units requires direct materials of $3.50 per unit and direct labor of $2.20 per unit (same as for all other units).

■ Manufacturing 10,000 additional units adds $5,000 of incremental overhead costs for power, packaging, and indirect labor (all variable costs).

■ Incremental commissions and selling expenses from this sale of 10,000 additional units would be $2,000 (all variable costs).

■ Incremental administrative expenses of $1,000 for clerical efforts are needed (all fixed costs) with the sale of 10,000 additional units.

We use this information, as shown in Exhibit 25.14, to assess how accepting this new business will affect FasTrac's income.

Exhibit 25.14

Analysis of Additional Business Using Relevant Costs

	Current Business	Additional Business	Combined
Sales	$1,000,000	$ 85,000	$1,085,000
Direct materials	(350,000)	(35,000)	(385,000)
Direct labor	(220,000)	(22,000)	(242,000)
Overhead	(110,000)	(5,000)	(115,000)
Selling expenses	(140,000)	(2,000)	(142,000)
Administrative expense	(80,000)	(1,000)	(81,000)
Total costs and expenses	(900,000)	(65,000)	(965,000)
Operating income	$ 100,000	$ 20,000	$ 120,000

Example: Exhibit 25.14 uses quantitative information. Suggest some qualitative factors to be considered when deciding whether to accept this project. *Answer:* (1) Impact on relationships with other customers and (2) Improved relationship with customer buying additional units.

The analysis of relevant costs in Exhibit 25.14 suggests that the additional business be accepted. It would provide $85,000 of added revenue while incurring only $65,000 of added costs. This would yield $20,000 of additional pretax income, or a pretax profit margin of 23.5%. More generally, FasTrac would increase its income with any price that exceeded $6.50 per unit ($65,000 incremental cost/10,000 additional units).

An analysis of the incremental costs pertaining to the additional volume is always relevant for this type of decision. We must proceed cautiously, however, when the additional volume approaches or exceeds the factory's existing available capacity. If the additional volume requires the company to expand its capacity by obtaining more equipment, more space, or more personnel, the incremental costs could quickly exceed the incremental revenue. Another cautionary note is the effect on existing sales. All new units of the extra business will be sold outside FasTrac's normal domestic sales channels. If accepting additional business would cause existing sales to decline, this information must be included in our analysis. The contribution margin lost from a decline in sales is an opportunity cost. If future cash flows over several time periods are affected, their net present value also must be computed and used in this analysis.

The key point is that management must not blindly use historical costs, especially allocated overhead costs. Instead, the accounting system needs to provide information about the incremental costs to be incurred if the additional business is accepted.

Decision Maker   Answer—p. 1020

Partner You are a partner in a small accounting firm that specializes in keeping the books and preparing taxes for clients. A local restaurant is interested in obtaining these services from your firm. Identify factors that are relevant in deciding whether to accept the engagement.

Make or Buy

The managerial decision to make or buy a component for one of its current products is commonplace and depends on incremental costs. To illustrate, FasTrac has excess productive capacity it can use to manufacture Part 417, a component of the main product it sells. The part is currently purchased and delivered to the plant at a cost of $1.20 per unit. FasTrac estimates that making Part 417 would cost $0.45 for direct materials, $0.50 for direct labor, and an undetermined amount for overhead. The task is to determine how much overhead to add to these costs so we can decide whether to make or buy Part 417. If FasTrac's normal predetermined overhead application rate is 100% of direct labor cost, we might be tempted to conclude that overhead cost is $0.50 per unit, computed as 100% of the $0.50 direct labor cost. We would then mistakenly conclude that total cost is $1.45 ($0.45 of materials + $0.50 of labor + $0.50 of overhead). A wrong decision in this case would be to conclude that the company is better off buying the part at $1.20 each than making it for $1.45 each.

Topic Tackler

PLUS

25-2

Instead, as we explained earlier, only incremental overhead costs are relevant in this situation. Thus, we must compute an *incremental overhead rate.* Incremental overhead costs might include, for example, additional power for operating machines, extra supplies, added cleanup costs, materials handling, and quality control. We can prepare a per unit analysis in this case as shown in Exhibit 25.15.

We can see that if incremental overhead costs are less than $0.25 per unit, the total cost of making the component is less than the purchase price of $1.20 and FasTrac should make the part. FasTrac's decision rule in this case is that any amount of overhead less than $0.25 per unit yields a total cost for Part 417 that is less than the $1.20 purchase price. FasTrac must consider several nonfinancial

	Make	Buy
Direct materials	$0.45	—
Direct labor	0.50	—
Overhead costs	[?]	—
Purchase price	—	$1.20
Total incremental costs . .	**$0.95 + [?]**	**$1.20**

Exhibit 25.15

Make or Buy Analysis

factors in the make or buy decision, including product quality, timeliness of delivery (especially in a just-in-time setting), reactions of customers and suppliers, and other intangibles such as employee morale and workload. It must also consider whether making the part requires incremental fixed costs to expand plant capacity. When these added factors are considered, small cost differences may not matter.

Scrap or Rework

Managers often must make a decision on whether to scrap or rework products in process. Remember that costs already incurred in manufacturing the units of a product that do not meet quality standards are sunk costs that have been incurred and cannot be changed. Sunk costs are irrelevant in any decision on whether to sell the substandard units as scrap or to rework them to meet quality standards.

To illustrate, assume that FasTrac has 10,000 defective units of a product that have already cost $1 per unit to manufacture. These units can be sold as is (as scrap) for $0.40 each, or they can be reworked for $0.80 per unit and then sold for their full price of $1.50 each. Should FasTrac sell the units as scrap or rework them?

To make this decision, management must recognize that the already incurred manufacturing costs of $1 per unit are sunk (unavoidable). These costs are *entirely irrelevant* to the decision. In addition, we must be certain that all costs of reworking defects, including interfering with normal operations, are accounted for in our analysis. For instance, reworking the defects means that FasTrac is unable to manufacture 10,000 *new* units with an incremental cost of $1 per unit and a selling price of $1.50 per unit, meaning it incurs an opportunity cost equal to the lost $5,000 net return from making and selling 10,000 new units. This opportunity cost is the difference between the $15,000 revenue (10,000 units × $1.50) from selling these new units and their $10,000 manufacturing costs (10,000 units × $1). Our analysis is reflected in Exhibit 25.16.

Exhibit 25.16

Scrap or Rework Analysis

	Scrap	Rework
Sale of scrapped/reworked units	$ 4,000	$ 15,000
Less costs to rework defects		(8,000)
Less opportunity cost of not making new units		**(5,000)**
Incremental net income	$4,000	$ 2,000

The analysis yields a $2,000 difference in favor of scrapping the defects, yielding a total incremental net income of $4,000. If we had failed to include the opportunity costs of $5,000, the rework option would have shown an income of $7,000 instead of $2,000, mistakenly making the reworking appear more favorable than scrapping.

11. A company receives a special order for 200 units that requires stamping the buyer's name on each unit, yielding an additional fixed cost of $400 to its normal costs. Without the order, the company is operating at 75% of capacity and produces 7,500 units of product at the following costs:

Direct materials	$37,500
Direct labor	60,000
Overhead (30% variable)	20,000
Selling expenses (60% variable)	25,000

The special order will not affect normal unit sales and will not increase fixed overhead and selling expenses. Variable selling expenses on the special order are reduced to one-half the normal amount. The price per unit necessary to earn $1,000 on this order is (*a*) $14.80, (*b*) $15.80, (*c*) $19.80, (*d*) $20.80, or (*e*) $21.80.

12. What are the incremental costs of accepting additional business?

Sell or Process

The managerial decision to sell partially completed products as is or to process them further for sale depends significantly on relevant costs. To illustrate, suppose that FasTrac has 40,000 units of partially finished Product Q. It has already spent $0.75 per unit to manufacture these 40,000 units at a $30,000 total cost. FasTrac can sell the 40,000 units to another manufacturer as raw material for $50,000. Alternatively, it can process them further and produce finished products X, Y, and Z at an incremental cost of $2 per unit. The added processing yields the products and revenues shown in Exhibit 25.17. FasTrac must decide whether the added revenues from selling finished products X, Y, and Z exceed the costs of finishing them.

Exhibit 25.18 shows the two-step analysis for this decision. First, FasTrac computes its incremental revenue from further processing Q into products X, Y, and Z. This amount is the difference between the $220,000 revenue from the further processed products and the $50,000 FasTrac will give up by not selling Q as is (a $50,000 opportunity cost). Second, FasTrac computes its incremental costs from further processing Q into X, Y, and Z. This amount is $80,000 (40,000 units × $2 incremental cost). The analysis shows that FasTrac can earn incremental net income of $90,000 from a decision to further process Q. (Notice that the earlier incurred $30,000 manufacturing cost for the 40,000 units of Product Q does not appear in Exhibit 25.18 because it is a sunk cost and as such is irrelevant to the decision.)

Product	Price	Units	Revenues
Product X	$4.00	10,000	$ 40,000
Product Y	6.00	22,000	132,000
Product Z	8.00	6,000	48,000
Spoilage	—	2,000	0
Totals		40,000	$220,000

Exhibit 25.17

Revenues from Processing Further

Revenue if processed	$220,000
Revenue if sold as is	(50,000)
Incremental revenue	170,000
Cost to process	(80,000)
Incremental net income	**$ 90,000**

Exhibit 25.18

Sell or Process Analysis

Example: Does the decision change if incremental costs in Exhibit 25.18 increase to $4 per unit and the opportunity cost increases to $95,000? *Answer:* Yes. There is now an incremental net loss of $35,000.

Sales Mix Selection

When a company sells a mix of products, some are likely to be more profitable than others. Management is often wise to concentrate sales efforts on more profitable products. If production facilities or other factors are limited, an increase in the production and sale of one product usually requires reducing the production and sale of others. In this case, management must identify the most profitable combination, or *sales mix* of products. To identify the best sales mix, management must know the contribution margin of each product, the facilities required to produce each product, any constraints on these facilities, and its markets.

To illustrate, assume that FasTrac makes and sells two products, A and B. The same machines are used to produce both products. A and B have the following selling prices and variable costs per unit:

	Product A	Product B
Selling price per unit	$5.00	$7.50
Variable costs per unit	3.50	5.50
Contribution margin per unit	$1.50	$2.00

The variable costs are included in the analysis because they are the incremental costs of producing these products within the existing capacity of 100,000 machine hours per month. We consider three separate cases.

Case 1: Assume that (1) each product requires 1 machine hour per unit for production and (2) the markets for these products are unlimited. Under these conditions, FasTrac should produce as much of Product B as it can because of its larger contribution margin of $2 per unit. At full capacity, FasTrac would produce $200,000 of total contribution margin per month, computed as $2 per unit times 100,000 machine hours.

Case 2: Assume that (1) Product A requires 1 machine hour per unit, (2) Product B requires 2 machine hours per unit, and (3) the markets for these products are unlimited. Under these conditions, FasTrac should produce as much of Product A as it can because it has a contribution margin of $1.50 per machine hour compared with only $1 per machine hour for Product B. Exhibit 25.19 shows the relevant analysis.

Exhibit 25.19

Sales Mix Analysis

	Product A	Product B
Selling price per unit	$ 5.00	$ 7.50
Variable costs per unit	3.50	5.50
Contribution margin per unit	$ 1.50	$ 2.00
Machine hours per unit	1.0	2.0
Contribution margin per machine hour	**$1.50**	**$1.00**

Example: For Case 2, if Product B's variable costs per unit increase to $6, Product A's variable costs per unit decrease to $3, and the same machine hours per unit are used, which product should FasTrac produce? *Answer:* Product A. Its contribution margin of $2 per machine hour is higher than B's $.75 per machine hour.

Point: A method called *linear programming* is useful for finding the optimal sales mix for several products subject to many market and production constraints. This method is described in advanced courses.

At its full capacity of 100,000 machine hours, FasTrac would produce 100,000 units of Product A, yielding $150,000 of total contribution margin per month. In contrast, if it uses all 100,000 hours to produce Product B, only 50,000 units would be produced yielding a contribution margin of $100,000. These results suggest that when a company faces excess demand and limited capacity, only the most profitable product per input should be manufactured.

Case 3: The need for a mix of different products arises when market demand is not sufficient to allow a company to sell all that it produces. For instance, assume that (1) Product A requires 1 machine hour per unit, (2) Product B requires 2 machine hours per unit, and (3) the market for Product A is limited to 80,000 units. Under these conditions, FasTrac should produce no more than 80,000 units of Product A. This would leave another 20,000 machine hours of capacity for making Product B. FasTrac should use this spare capacity to produce 10,000 units of Product B. This sales mix would maximize FasTrac's total contribution margin per month at an amount of $140,000.

Segment Elimination

When a segment such as a department or division is performing poorly, management must consider eliminating it. Segment information on either net income (loss) or its contribution to overhead is not sufficient for this decision. Instead, we must look at the segment's avoidable expenses and unavoidable expenses. **Avoidable expenses,** also called *escapable expenses,* are amounts the company would not incur if it eliminated the segment. **Unavoidable**

expenses, also called *inescapable expenses,* are amounts that would continue even if the segment is eliminated.

To illustrate, FasTrac considers eliminating its treadmill division because its $48,300 total expenses are higher than its $47,800 sales. Classification of this division's operating expenses into avoidable or unavoidable expenses is shown in Exhibit 25.20.

	Total	Avoidable Expenses	Unavoidable Expenses
Cost of goods sold	$ 30,000	$ 30,000	—
Direct expenses			
Salaries expense	7,900	7,900	—
Depreciation expense—Equipment	200	—	$ 200
Indirect expenses			
Rent and utilities expense	3,150	—	3,150
Advertising expense	400	400	—
Insurance expense	400	300	100
Service department costs			
Share of office department expenses	3,060	2,200	860
Share of purchasing expenses	3,190	1,000	2,190
Total	**$48,300**	**$41,800**	**$6,500**

Exhibit 25.20

Classification of Segment Operating Expenses for Analysis

FasTrac's analysis shows that it can avoid $41,800 expenses if it eliminates the treadmill division. Because this division's sales are $47,800, eliminating it will cause FasTrac to lose $6,000 of income. *Our decision rule is that a segment is a candidate for elimination if its revenues are less than its avoidable expenses.* Avoidable expenses can be viewed as the costs to generate this segment's revenues.

When considering elimination of a segment, we must assess its impact on other segments. A segment could be unprofitable on its own, but it might still contribute to other segments' revenues and profits. It is possible then to continue a segment even when its revenues are less than its avoidable expenses. Similarly, a profitable segment might be discontinued if its space, assets, or staff can be more profitably used by expanding existing segments or by creating new ones. Our decision to keep or eliminate a segment requires a more complex analysis than simply looking at a segment's performance report. Such reports provide useful information, but they do not provide all the information necessary for this decision.

Example: How can insurance be classified as either avoidable or unavoidable? *Answer:* Depends on whether the assets insured can be removed and the premiums canceled.

Example: Give an example of a segment that a company might profitably use to attract customers even though it might incur a loss. *Answer:* Warranty and post-sales services.

Qualitative Decision Factors

Managers must consider qualitative factors in making managerial decisions. Consider a decision on whether to buy a component from an outside supplier or continue to make it. Several qualitative decision factors must be considered. For example, the quality, delivery, and reputation of the proposed supplier are important. The effects from deciding not to make the component can include potential layoffs and impaired worker morale. Consider another situation in which a company is considering a one-time sale to a new customer at a special low price. Qualitative factors to consider in this situation include the effects of a low price on the company's image and the threat that regular customers might demand a similar price. The company must also consider whether this customer is really a one-time customer. If not, can it continue to offer this low price in the long run? Clearly, management cannot rely solely on financial data to make such decisions.

Quick Check   Answers—p. 1020

15. What is the difference between avoidable and unavoidable expenses?

16. A segment is a candidate for elimination if (*a*) its revenues are less than its avoidable expenses, (*b*) it has a net loss, (*c*) its unavoidable expenses are higher than its revenues.

Decision Analysis   **Break-Even Time**

A2 Analyze a capital investment project using break-even time.

The first section of this chapter explained several methods to evaluate capital investments. Break-even time of an investment project is a variation of the payback period method that overcomes the limitation of not using the time value of money. **Break-even time (BET)** is a time-based measure used to evaluate a capital investment's acceptability. Its computation yields a measure of expected time, reflecting the time period until the *present value* of the net cash flows from an investment equals the initial cost of the investment. In basic terms, break-even time is computed by restating future cash flows in terms of present values and then determining the payback period using these present values.

To illustrate, we return to the FasTrac case described in Exhibit 25.1 involving a $16,000 investment in machinery. The annual net cash flows from this investment are projected at $4,100 for eight years. Exhibit 25.21 shows the computation of break-even time for this investment decision.

Exhibit 25.21

Break-Even Time Analysis*

Year	Cash Flows	Present Value of 1 at 10%	Present Value of Cash Flows	Cumulative Present Value of Cash Flows
0	$(16,000)	1.0000	$(16,000)	$(16,000)
1	4,100	0.9091	3,727	(12,273)
2	4,100	0.8264	3,388	(8,885)
3	4,100	0.7513	3,080	(5,805)
4	4,100	0.6830	2,800	(3,005)
5	4,100	0.6209	2,546	**(459)**
6	4,100	0.5645	2,314	**1,855**
7	4,100	0.5132	2,104	3,959
8	4,100	0.4665	1,913	5,872

* The time of analysis is the start of year 1 (same as end of year 0). All cash flows occur at the end of each year.

The right-most column of this exhibit shows that break-even time is between 5 and 6 years, or about 5.2 years. This is the time the project takes to break even after considering the time value of money (recall that the payback period computed without considering the time value of money was 3.9 years). We interpret this as cash flows earned after 5.2 years contribute to a positive net present value that, in this case, eventually amounts to $5,872.

Decision Maker   Answer—p. 1020

Investment Manager Management asks you, the investment manager, to evaluate three alternative investments. Investment recovery time is crucial because cash is scarce. The time value of money is also important. Which capital budgeting method(s) do you use to assess the investments?

Break-even time is a useful measure for managers because it identifies the point in time when they can expect the cash flows to begin to yield net positive returns. Managers expect a positive net present value from an investment if break-even time is less than the investment's estimated life. The method allows managers to compare and rank alternative investments, giving the project with the shortest break-even time the highest rank.

Demonstration Problem

Determine the appropriate action in each of the following managerial decision situations.

1. Packer Company is operating at 80% of its manufacturing capacity of 100,000 product units per year. A chain store has offered to buy an additional 10,000 units at $22 each and sell them to customers so as not to compete with Packer Company. The following data are available.

Costs at 80% Capacity	Per Unit	Total
Direct materials	$ 8.00	$ 640,000
Direct labor	7.00	560,000
Overhead (fixed and variable)	12.50	1,000,000
Totals	$27.50	$2,200,000

In producing 10,000 additional units, fixed overhead costs would remain at their current level but incremental variable overhead costs of $3 per unit would be incurred. Should the company accept or reject this order?

2. Green Company uses Part JR3 in manufacturing its products. It has always purchased this part from a supplier for $40 each. It recently upgraded its own manufacturing capabilities and has enough excess capacity (including trained workers) to begin manufacturing Part JR3 instead of buying it. The company prepares the following cost projections of making the part, assuming that overhead is allocated to the part at the normal predetermined rate of 200% of direct labor cost.

Direct materials	$11
Direct labor	15
Overhead (fixed and variable) (200% of direct labor)	30
Total	$56

The required volume of output to produce the part will not require any incremental fixed overhead. Incremental variable overhead cost will be $17 per unit. Should the company make or buy this part?

3. Gold Company's manufacturing process causes a relatively large number of defective parts to be produced. The defective parts can be (a) sold for scrap, (b) melted to recover the recycled metal for reuse, or (c) reworked to be good units. Reworking defective parts reduces the output of other good units because no excess capacity exists. Each unit reworked means that one new unit cannot be produced. The following information reflects 500 defective parts currently available.

Proceeds of selling as scrap	$2,500
Additional cost of melting down defective parts	400
Cost of purchases avoided by using recycled metal from defects	4,800
Cost to rework 500 defective parts	
Direct materials	0
Direct labor	1,500
Incremental overhead	1,750
Cost to produce 500 new parts	
Direct materials	6,000
Direct labor	5,000
Incremental overhead	3,200
Selling price per good unit	40

Should the company melt the parts, sell them as scrap, or rework them?

4. White Company can invest in one of two projects, TD1 or TD2. Each project requires an initial investment of $100,000 and produces the year-end cash inflows shown in the following table. Use net present values to determine which project, if any, should be chosen. Assume that the company requires a 10% return from its investments.

	Net Cash Flows	
	TD1	TD2
Year 1	$ 20,000	$ 40,000
Year 2	30,000	40,000
Year 3	70,000	40,000
Totals	$120,000	$120,000

Planning the Solution

- Determine whether Packer Company should accept the additional business by finding the incremental costs of materials, labor, and overhead that will be incurred if the order is accepted. Omit fixed costs that the order will not increase. If the incremental revenue exceeds the incremental cost, accept the order.

- Determine whether Green Company should make or buy the component by finding the incremental cost of making each unit. If the incremental cost exceeds the purchase price, the component should be purchased. If the incremental cost is less than the purchase price, make the component.

- Determine whether Gold Company should sell the defective parts, melt them down and recycle the metal, or rework them. To compare the three choices, examine all costs incurred and benefits received from the alternatives in working with the 500 defective units versus the production of 500 new units. For the scrapping alternative, include the costs of producing 500 new units and subtract the $2,500 proceeds from selling the old ones. For the melting alternative, include the costs of melting the defective units, add the net cost of new materials in excess over those obtained from recycling, and add the direct labor and overhead costs. For the reworking alternative, add the costs of direct labor and incremental overhead. Select the alternative that has the lowest cost. The cost assigned to the 500 defective units is sunk and not relevant in choosing among the three alternatives.

- Compute White Company's net present value of each investment using a 10% discount rate.

Solution to Demonstration Problem

1. This decision involves accepting additional business. Since current unit costs are $27.50, it appears initially as if the offer to sell for $22 should be rejected, but the $27.50 cost includes fixed costs. When the analysis includes only *incremental* costs, the per unit cost is as shown in the following table. The offer should be accepted because it will produce $4 of additional profit per unit (computed as $22 price less $18 incremental cost), which yields a total profit of $40,000 for the 10,000 additional units.

Direct materials	$ 8.00
Direct labor	7.00
Variable overhead (given)	3.00
Total incremental cost	$18.00

2. For this make or buy decision, the analysis must not include the $13 nonincremental overhead per unit ($30 − $17). When only the $17 incremental overhead is included, the relevant unit cost of manufacturing the part is shown in the following table. It would be better to continue buying the part for $40 instead of making it for $43.

Direct materials	$11.00
Direct labor	15.00
Variable overhead	17.00
Total incremental cost	$43.00

3. The goal of this scrap or rework decision is to identify the alternative that produces the greatest net benefit to the company. To compare the alternatives, we determine the net cost of obtaining 500 marketable units as follows:

Incremental Cost to Produce 500 Marketable Units	Sell as Is	Melt and Recycle	Rework Units
Direct materials			
New materials	$ 6,000	$6,000	
Recycled metal materials		(4,800)	
Net materials cost		1,200	
Melting costs		400	
Total direct materials cost	6,000	1,600	
Direct labor	5,000	5,000	$1,500
Incremental overhead	3,200	3,200	1,750
Cost to produce 500 marketable units	14,200	9,800	3,250
Less proceeds of selling defects as scrap	(2,500)		
Opportunity costs*			5,800
Net cost	$11,700	$9,800	$9,050

* The $5,800 opportunity cost is the lost contribution margin from not being able to produce and sell 500 units because of reworking, computed as ($40 − $28.40) × 500 units.

The incremental cost of 500 marketable parts is smallest if the defects are reworked.

4. TD1:

	Net Cash Flows	Present Value of 1 at 10%	Present Value of Net Cash Flows
Year 1	$ 20,000	0.9091	$ 18,182
Year 2	30,000	0.8264	24,792
Year 3	70,000	0.7513	52,591
Totals	$120,000		95,565
Amount invested			(100,000)
Net present value			**$ (4,435)**

TD2:

	Net Cash Flows	Present Value of 1 at 10%	Present Value of Net Cash Flows
Year 1	$ 40,000	0.9091	$ 36,364
Year 2	40,000	0.8264	33,056
Year 3	40,000	0.7513	30,052
Totals	$120,000		99,472
Amount invested			(100,000)
Net present value			**$ (528)**

White Company should not invest in either project. Both are expected to yield a negative net present value, and it should invest only in positive net present value projects.

Summary

C1 Explain the importance of capital budgeting. Capital budgeting is the process of analyzing alternative investments and deciding which assets to acquire or sell. It involves predicting the cash flows to be received from the alternatives, evaluating their merits, and then choosing which ones to pursue.

C2 Describe the selection of a hurdle rate for an investment. Top management should select the hurdle (discount) rate to use in evaluating capital investments. The required hurdle rate should be at least higher than the interest rate on money borrowed because the return on an investment must cover the interest and provide an additional profit to reward the company for risk.

C3 Describe the importance of relevant costs for short-term decisions. A company must rely on relevant costs pertaining to alternative courses of action rather than historical costs. Out-of-pocket expenses and opportunity costs are relevant because these are avoidable; sunk costs are irrelevant because they result from past decisions and are therefore unavoidable. Managers must also consider the relevant benefits associated with alternative decisions.

A1 Evaluate short-term managerial decisions using relevant costs. Relevant costs are useful in making decisions such as to accept additional business, make or buy, and sell as is or process further. For example, the relevant factors in deciding whether to produce and sell additional units of product are incremental costs and incremental revenues from the additional volume.

A2 Analyze a capital investment project using break-even time. Break-even time (BET) is a method for evaluating capital investments by restating future cash flows in terms of their present values (discounting the cash flows) and then calculating the payback period using these present values of cash flows.

P1 Compute payback period and describe its use. One way to compare potential investments is to compute and compare their payback periods. The payback period is an estimate of the expected time before the cumulative net cash inflow from the investment equals its initial cost. A payback period analysis fails to reflect risk of the cash flows, differences in the timing of cash flows within the payback period, and cash flows that occur after the payback period.

P2 Compute accounting rate of return and explain its use. A project's accounting rate of return is computed by dividing the expected annual after-tax net income by the average amount of investment in the project. When the net cash flows are received evenly throughout each period and straight-line depreciation is used, the average investment is computed as the average of the investment's initial book value and its salvage value.

P3 Compute net present value and describe its use. An investment's net present value is determined by predicting the future cash flows it is expected to generate, discounting them at a rate that represents an acceptable return, and then by subtracting the investment's initial cost from the sum of the present values. This technique can deal with any pattern of expected cash flows and applies a superior concept of return on investment.

P4 Compute internal rate of return and explain its use. The internal rate of return (IRR) is the discount rate that results in a zero net present value. When the cash flows are equal, we can compute the present value factor corresponding to the IRR by dividing the initial investment by the annual cash flows. We then use the annuity tables to determine the discount rate corresponding to this present value factor.

Guidance Answers to **Decision Maker** and **Decision Ethics**

Systems Manager   Your dilemma is whether to abide by rules designed to prevent abuse or to bend them to acquire an investment that you believe will benefit the firm. You should not pursue the latter action because breaking up the order into small components is dishonest and there are consequences of being caught at a later stage. Develop a proposal for the entire package and then do all you can to expedite its processing, particularly by pointing out its benefits. When faced with controls that are not working, there is rarely a reason to overcome its shortcomings by dishonesty. A direct assault on those limitations is more sensible and ethical.

Entrepreneur   The banker is probably concerned because new products are risky and should therefore be evaluated using a higher rate of return. You should conduct a thorough technical analysis and obtain detailed market data and information about any similar products available in the market. These factors might provide sufficient information to support the use of a lower return. You must convince yourself that the risk level is consistent with the discount rate used.

You should also be confident that your company has the capacity and the resources to handle the new product.

Partner   You should identify the differences between existing clients and this potential client. A key difference is that the restaurant business has additional inventory components (groceries, vegetables, meats, etc.) and is likely to have a higher proportion of depreciable assets. These differences imply that the partner must spend more hours auditing the records and understanding the business, regulations, and standards that pertain to the restaurant business. Such differences suggest that the partner must use a different "formula" for quoting a price to this potential client vis-à-vis current clients.

Investment Manager   You should probably focus on either the payback period or break-even time because both the time value of money and recovery time are important. Break-even time method is superior because it accounts for the time value of money, which is an important consideration in this decision.

Guidance Answers to **Quick Checks**

1. *b*

2. A capital budgeting decision is difficult because (1) the outcome is uncertain, (2) large amounts of money are usually involved, (3) a long-term commitment is required, and (4) the decision could be difficult or impossible to reverse.

3. *b*

4. Depreciation expense is subtracted from revenues in computing net income but does not use cash and should be added back to net income to compute net cash flows.

5. Not necessarily. One investment can continue to generate cash flows beyond the payback period for a longer time period than the other. The timing of their cash flows within the payback period also can differ.

6. *b*; Annual average investment = ($180,000 + $15,000)/2
= $97,500
Accounting rate of return = $40,000/$97,500 = 41%

7. For this determination, we need to compare it to the returns expected from alternative investments with similar risk.

8. Project A has the higher net present value as follows:

Year	Present Value of 1 at 10%	Project A Net Cash Flows	Project A Present Value of Net Cash Flows	Project B Net Cash Flows	Project B Present Value of Net Cash Flows
1	0.9091	$12,000	$10,909	$ 4,500	$ 4,091
2	0.8264	8,500	7,024	8,500	7,024
3	0.7513	4,000	3,005	13,000	9,767
Totals		$24,500	$20,938	$26,000	$20,882
Amount invested			(20,000)		(20,000)
Net present value			**$ 938**		**$ 882**

9. No, the information is too limited to draw that conclusion. For example, one investment could be riskier than the other, or one could require a substantially larger initial investment.

10. *b*

11. *e*; Variable costs per unit for this order of 200 units follow:

Direct materials ($37,500/7,500)	$ 5.00
Direct labor ($60,000/7,500)	8.00
Variable overhead [(0.30 × $20,000)/7,500]	0.80
Variable selling expenses [(0.60 × $25,000 × 0.5)/7,500]	1.00
Total variable costs per unit	$14.80

Cost to produce special order: (200 × $14.80) + $400
= $3,360.
Price per unit to earn $1,000: ($3,360 + $1,000)/200 = 21.80.

12. They are the additional (new) costs of accepting new business.

13. *d*;

	Incremental benefits		Incremental costs
Alpha	$300 ($600 − $300)	>	$150 (given)
Beta	$450 ($900 − $450)	>	$300 (given)
Gamma	$150 ($425 − $275)	>	$125 (given)
Delta	$ 60 ($210 − $150)	<	$ 75 (given)

14. A sunk cost is *never* relevant because it results from a past decision and is already incurred.

15. Avoidable expenses are ones a company will not incur by eliminating a segment; unavoidable expenses will continue even after a segment is eliminated.

16. *a*

Key Terms

mhhe.com/wildFAP18e

Key Terms are available at the book's Website for learning and testing in an online Flashcard Format.

Accounting rate of return (p. 1001)
Avoidable expense (p. 1014)
Break-even time (BET) (p. 1016)
Capital budgeting (p. 998)

Hurdle rate (p. 1006)
Incremental cost (p. 1010)
Internal rate of return (IRR) (p. 1005)
Net present value (NPV) (p. 1003)

Payback period (PBP) (p. 999)
Relevant benefits (p. 1009)
Unavoidable expense (p. 1014)

Multiple Choice Quiz

Answers on p. 1036   mhhe.com/wildFAP18e

Multiple Choice Quizzes A and B are available at the book's Website.

1. A company inadvertently produced 3,000 defective MP3 players. The players cost $12 each to produce. A recycler offers to purchase the defective players as they are for $8 each. The production manager reports that the defects can be corrected for $10 each, enabling them to be sold at their regular market price of $19 each. The company should:
  a. Correct the defect and sell them at the regular price.
  b. Sell the players to the recycler for $8 each.
  c. Sell 2,000 to the recycler and repair the rest.
  d. Sell 1,000 to the recycler and repair the rest.
  e. Throw the players away.

2. A company's productive capacity is limited to 480,000 machine hours. Product X requires 10 machine hours to produce; and Product Y requires 2 machine hours to produce. Product X sells for $32 per unit and has variable costs of $12 per unit; Product Y sells for $24 per unit and has variable costs of $10 per unit. Assuming that the company can sell as many of either product as it produces, it should:
  a. Produce X and Y in the ratio of 57% and 43%.
  b. Produce X and Y in the ratio of 83% X and 17% Y.
  c. Produce equal amounts of Product X and Product Y.
  d. Produce only Product X.
  e. Produce only Product Y.

3. A company receives a special one-time order for 3,000 units of its product at $15 per unit. The company has excess capacity and it currently produces and sells the units at $20 each to its regular customers. Production costs are $13.50 per unit, which

includes $9 of variable costs. To produce the special order, the company must incur additional fixed costs of $5,000. Should the company accept the special order?
  a. Yes, because incremental revenue exceeds incremental costs.
  b. No, because incremental costs exceed incremental revenue.
  c. No, because the units are being sold for $5 less than the regular price.
  d. Yes, because incremental costs exceed incremental revenue.
  e. No, because incremental cost exceeds $15 per unit when total costs are considered.

4. A company is considering the purchase of equipment for $270,000. Projected annual cash inflow from this equipment is $61,200 per year. The payback period is:
  a. 0.2 years
  b. 5.0 years
  c. 4.4 years
  d. 2.3 years
  e. 3.9 years

5. A company buys a machine for $180,000 that has an expected life of nine years and no salvage value. The company expects an annual net income (after taxes of 30%) of $8,550. What is the accounting rate of return?
  a. 4.75%
  b. 42.75%
  c. 2.85%
  d. 9.50%
  e. 6.65%

Discussion Questions

1. What is capital budgeting?
2. Identify four reasons that capital budgeting decisions by managers are risky.
3. Capital budgeting decisions require careful analysis because they are generally the _____ _____ and _____ decisions that management faces.
4. Identify two disadvantages of using the payback period for comparing investments.
5. Why is an investment more attractive to management if it has a shorter payback period?

6. What is the average amount invested in a machine during its predicted five-year life if it costs $200,000 and has a $20,000 salvage value? Assume that net income is received evenly throughout each year and straight-line depreciation is used.
7. If the present value of the expected net cash flows from a machine, discounted at 10%, exceeds the amount to be invested, what can you say about the investment's expected rate of return? What can you say about the expected rate of return if the present value of the net cash flows, discounted at 10%, is less than the investment amount?

8. Why is the present value of $100 that you expect to receive one year from today worth less than $100 received today? What is the present value of $100 that you expect to receive one year from today, discounted at 12%?

9. Why should managers set the required rate of return higher than the rate at which money can be borrowed when making a typical capital budgeting decision?

10. Why does the use of the accelerated depreciation method (instead of straight line) for income tax reporting increase an investment's value?

11. What is an out-of-pocket cost? What is an opportunity cost? Are opportunity costs recorded in the accounting records?

12. Why are sunk costs irrelevant in deciding whether to sell a product in its present condition or to make it into a new product through additional processing?

13. Identify the incremental costs incurred by **Best Buy** for shipping one additional iPod from a warehouse to a retail store along with the store's normal order of 75 iPods.

14. Circuit City is considering expanding a store. Identify three methods management can use to evaluate whether to expand.

15. Assume that **Apple** manufactures and sells 500,000 units of a product at $30 per unit in domestic markets. It costs $20 per unit to manufacture ($13 variable cost per unit, $7 fixed cost per unit). Can you describe a situation under which the company is willing to sell an additional 25,000 units of the product in an international market at $15 per unit?

 Red numbers denote Discussion Questions that involve decision-making.

QUICK STUDY

QS 25-1
Analyzing payback periods   P1

Park Company is considering two alternative investments. The payback period is 3.5 years for Investment A and 4 years for Investment B. (1) If management relies on the payback period, which investment is preferred? (2) Why might Park's analysis of these two alternatives lead to the selection of B over A?

QS 25-2
Payback period   P1

Freeman Company is considering an investment that requires immediate payment of $27,000 and provides expected cash inflows of $9,000 annually for four years. What is the investment's payback period?

QS 25-3
Computation of
net present value   P3

If Quail Company invests $50,000 today, it can expect to receive $10,000 at the end of each year for the next seven years plus an extra $6,000 at the end of the seventh year. What is the net present value of this investment assuming a required 10% return on investments?

QS 25-4
Computation of
accounting rate of return   P2

Peng Company is considering an investment expected to generate an average net income after taxes of $1,950 for three years. The investment costs $45,000 and has an estimated $6,000 salvage value. Compute the accounting rate of return for this investment.

QS 25-5
Selection of sales mix

C3   A1

Excel Memory Company can sell all units of computer memory X and Y that it can produce, but it has limited production capacity. It can produce two units of X per hour or three units of Y per hour, and it has 4,000 production hours available. Contribution margin is $5 for Product X and $4 for Product Y. What is the most profitable sales mix for this company?

QS 25-6
Analysis of incremental costs

C3   A1

Kando Company incurs a $9 per unit cost for Product A, which it currently manufactures and sells for $13.50 per unit. Instead of manufacturing and selling this product, Kando can purchase Product B for $5 per unit and sell it for $12 per unit. If it does so, unit sales would remain unchanged and $5 of the $9 per unit costs assigned to Product A would be eliminated. Should the company continue to manufacture Product A or purchase Product B for resale?

QS 25-7
Computation of break-even time

A2

Quick Feet, a shoe manufacturer, is evaluating the costs and benefits of new equipment that would custom fit each pair of athletic shoes. The customer would have his or her foot scanned by digital computer equipment; this information would be used to cut the raw materials to provide the customer a perfect fit. The new equipment costs $150,000 and is expected to generate an additional $52,500 in cash flows for five years. A bank will make a $150,000 loan to the company at a 10% interest rate for this equipment's purchase. Use the following table to determine the break-even time for this equipment.

Year	Cash Flows*	Present Value of 1 at 10%	Present Value of Cash Flows	Cumulative Present Value of Cash Flows
0	$(150,000)	1.0000		
1	52,500	0.9091		
2	52,500	0.8264		
3	52,500	0.7513		
4	52,500	0.6830		
5	52,500	0.6209		

* All cash flows occur at year-end.

EXERCISES

Compute the payback period for each of these two separate investments:

a. A new operating system for an existing machine is expected to cost $520,000 and have a useful life of six years. The system yields an incremental after-tax income of $150,000 each year after deducting its straight-line depreciation. The predicted salvage value of the system is $10,000.

b. A machine costs $380,000, has a $20,000 salvage value, is expected to last eight years, and will generate an after-tax income of $60,000 per year after straight-line depreciation.

Exercise 25-1
Payback period computation; even cash flows
P1

Beyer Company is considering the purchase of an asset for $180,000. It is expected to produce the following net cash flows. The cash flows occur evenly throughout each year. Compute the payback period for this investment.

	Year 1	Year 2	Year 3	Year 4	Year 5	Total
Net cash flows	$60,000	$40,000	$70,000	$120,000	$38,000	$328,000

Exercise 25-2
Payback period computation; uneven cash flows
P1

Check 3.083 years

A machine can be purchased for $150,000 and used for 5 years, yielding the following net incomes. In projecting net incomes, double-declining balance depreciation is applied, using a 5-year life and a zero salvage value. Compute the machine's payback period. Ignore taxes.

	Year 1	Year 2	Year 3	Year 4	Year 5
Net incomes	$10,000	$25,000	$50,000	$37,500	$100,000

Exercise 25-3
Payback period computation; declining-balance depreciation
P1

Check 2.265 years

A machine costs $700,000 and is expected to yield an after-tax net income of $52,000 each year. Management predicts this machine has a 10-year service life and a $100,000 salvage value, and it uses straight-line depreciation. Compute this machine's accounting rate of return.

Exercise 25-4
Accounting rate of return   P2

B2B Co. is considering the purchase of equipment that would allow the company to add a new product to its line. The equipment is expected to cost $360,000 with a 6-year life and no salvage value. It will be depreciated on a straight-line basis. The company expects to sell 144,000 units of the equipment's product each year. The expected annual income related to this equipment follows. Compute the (1) payback period and (2) accounting rate of return for this equipment.

Exercise 25-5
Payback period and accounting rate of return on investment
P1   P2

Sales	$225,000
Costs	
Materials, labor, and overhead (except depreciation)	120,000
Depreciation on new equipment	30,000
Selling and administrative expenses	22,500
Total costs and expenses	172,500
Pretax income	52,500
Income taxes (30%)	15,750
Net income	$ 36,750

Check   (1) 5.39 years (2) 20.42%

Exercise 25-6

Computing net present value   P3

After evaluating the risk of the investment described in Exercise 25-5, B2B Co. concludes that it must earn at least an 8% return on this investment. Compute the net present value of this investment.

Exercise 25-7

Computation and interpretation of net present value and internal rate of return

P3   P4

Phoenix Company can invest in each of three cheese-making projects: C1, C2, and C3. Each project requires an initial investment of $228,000 and would yield the following annual cash flows.

	C1	C2	C3
Year 1	$ 12,000	$ 96,000	$180,000
Year 2	108,000	96,000	60,000
Year 3	168,000	96,000	48,000
Totals	$288,000	$288,000	$288,000

(1) Assuming that the company requires a 12% return from its investments, use net present value to determine which projects, if any, should be acquired. (2) Using the answer from part 1, explain whether the internal rate of return is higher or lower than 12% for project C2. (3) Compute the internal rate of return for project C2.

Check   (3) IRR = 13%

Exercise 25-8

Decision to accept additional business or not

C3   A1

Farrow Co. expects to sell 150,000 units of its product in the next period with the following results.

Sales (150,000 units)	$2,250,000
Costs and expenses	
Direct materials	300,000
Direct labor	600,000
Overhead	150,000
Selling expenses	225,000
Administrative expenses	385,500
Total costs and expenses	1,660,500
Net income	$ 589,500

The company has an opportunity to sell 15,000 additional units at $12 per unit. The additional sales would not affect its current expected sales. Direct materials and labor costs would be the same for the additional units as they are for the regular units. However, the additional volume would create the following incremental costs: (1) total overhead would increase by 15% and (2) administrative expenses would increase by $64,500. Prepare an analysis to determine whether the company should accept or reject the offer to sell additional units at the reduced price of $12 per unit.

Check   Income increase, $3,000

Gilberto Company currently manufactures one of its crucial parts at a cost of $4.45 per unit. This cost is based on a normal production rate of 65,000 units per year. Variable costs are $1.95 per unit, fixed costs related to making this part are $65,000 per year, and allocated fixed costs are $58,500 per year. Allocated fixed costs are unavoidable whether the company makes or buys the part. Gilberto is considering buying the part from a supplier for a quoted price of $3.50 per unit guaranteed for a three-year period. Should the company continue to manufacture the part, or should it buy the part from the outside supplier? Support your answer with analyses.

Exercise 25-9
Make or buy decision

C3 A1

Check $35,750 increased costs to buy

Cobe Company has already manufactured 28,000 units of Product A at a cost of $28 per unit. The 28,000 units can be sold at this stage for $700,000. Alternatively, it can be further processed at a $420,000 total additional cost and be converted into 5,600 units of Product B and 11,200 units of Product C. Per unit selling price for Product B is $105 and for Product C is $70. Prepare an analysis that shows whether the 28,000 units of Product A should be processed further or not.

Exercise 25-10
Sell or process decision

C3 A1

Suresh Co. expects its five departments to yield the following income for next year.

Exercise 25-11
Analysis of income effects from eliminating departments

C3 A1

	Dept. M	Dept. N	Dept. O	Dept. P	Dept. T
Sales	$63,000	$ 35,000	$56,000	$42,000	$ 28,000
Expenses					
Avoidable	9,800	36,400	22,400	14,000	37,800
Unavoidable	51,800	12,600	4,200	29,400	9,800
Total expenses	61,600	49,000	26,600	43,400	47,600
Net income (loss)	$ 1,400	$(14,000)	$29,400	$ (1,400)	$(19,600)

Recompute and prepare the departmental income statements (including a combined total column) for the company under each of the following separate scenarios: Management (1) does not eliminate any department, (2) eliminates departments with expected net losses, and (3) eliminates departments with sales dollars that are less than avoidable expenses. Explain your answers to parts 2 and 3.

Check Total income (loss):
(2) $(21,000), (3) $7,000

Colt Company owns a machine that can produce two specialized products. Production time for Product TLX is two units per hour and for Product MTV is five units per hour. The machine's capacity is 2,750 hours per year. Both products are sold to a single customer who has agreed to buy all of the company's output up to a maximum of 4,700 units of Product TLX and 2,500 units of Product MTV. Selling prices and variable costs per unit to produce the products follow. Determine (1) the company's most profitable sales mix and (2) the contribution margin that results from that sales mix.

Exercise 25-12
Sales mix determination and analysis

C3 A1

	Product TLX	Product MTV
Selling price per unit	$15.00	$9.50
Variable costs per unit	4.80	5.50

Check (2) $56,450

This chapter explained two methods to evaluate investments using recovery time, the payback period and break-even time (BET). Refer to QS 25-7 and (1) compute the recovery time for both the payback period and break-even time, (2) discuss the advantage(s) of break-even time over the payback period, and (3) list two conditions under which payback period and break-even time are similar.

Exercise 25-13
Comparison of payback and BET

P1 A2

PROBLEM SET A

Problem 25-1A
Computation of payback period, accounting rate of return, and net present value

P1 P2 P3

mhhe.com/wildFAP18e

Factor Company is planning to add a new product to its line. To manufacture this product, the company needs to buy a new machine at a $480,000 cost with an expected four-year life and a $20,000 salvage value. All sales are for cash, and all costs are out of pocket except for depreciation on the new machine. Additional information includes the following.

Expected annual sales of new product	$1,840,000
Expected annual costs of new product	
Direct materials	480,000
Direct labor	672,000
Overhead excluding straight-line depreciation on new machine	336,000
Selling and administrative expenses	160,000
Income taxes	30%

Required

Check (4) 21.56%

(5) $107,356

1. Compute straight-line depreciation for each year of this new machine's life.
2. Determine expected net income and net cash flow for each year of this machine's life.
3. Compute this machine's payback period, assuming that cash flows occur evenly throughout each year.
4. Compute this machine's accounting rate of return, assuming that income is earned evenly throughout each year.
5. Compute the net present value for this machine using a discount rate of 7% and assuming that cash flows occur at each year-end. (*Hint:* Salvage value is a cash inflow at the end of the asset's life.)

Problem 25-2A
Analysis and computation of payback period, accounting rate of return, and net present value

P1 P2 P3

Most Company has an opportunity to invest in one of two new projects. Project Y requires a $350,000 investment for new machinery with a four-year life and no salvage value. Project Z requires a $350,000 investment for new machinery with a three-year life and no salvage value. The two projects yield the following predicted annual results. The company uses straight-line depreciation, and cash flows occur evenly throughout each year.

	Project Y	Project Z
Sales	$350,000	$280,000
Expenses		
Direct materials	49,000	35,000
Direct labor	70,000	42,000
Overhead including depreciation	126,000	126,000
Selling and administrative expenses	25,000	25,000
Total expenses	270,000	228,000
Pretax income	80,000	52,000
Income taxes (30%)	24,000	15,600
Net income	$ 56,000	$ 36,400

Required

Check For Project Y: (2) 2.44 years,
(3) 32%, (4) $125,286

1. Compute each project's annual expected net cash flows.
2. Determine each project's payback period.
3. Compute each project's accounting rate of return.
4. Determine each project's net present value using 8% as the discount rate. For part 4 only, assume that cash flows occur at each year-end.

Analysis Component

5. Identify the project you would recommend to management and explain your choice.

Manning Corporation is considering a new project requiring a $90,000 investment in test equipment with no salvage value. The project would produce $66,000 of pretax income before depreciation at the end of each of the next six years. The company's income tax rate is 40%. In compiling its tax return and computing its income tax payments, the company can choose between the two alternative depreciation schedules shown in the table.

Problem 25-3A
Computation of cash flows and net present values with alternative depreciation methods

P3

	Straight-Line Depreciation	MACRS Depreciation*
Year 1	$ 9,000	$18,000
Year 2	18,000	28,800
Year 3	18,000	17,280
Year 4	18,000	10,368
Year 5	18,000	10,368
Year 6	9,000	5,184
Totals	$90,000	$90,000

* The modified accelerated cost recovery system (MACRS) for depreciation is discussed in Chapter 10.

Required

1. Prepare a five-column table that reports amounts (assuming use of straight-line depreciation) for each of the following for each of the six years: (a) pretax income before depreciation, (b) straight-line depreciation expense, (c) taxable income, (d) income taxes, and (e) net cash flow. Net cash flow equals the amount of income before depreciation minus the income taxes.

2. Prepare a five-column table that reports amounts (assuming use of MACRS depreciation) for each of the following for each of the six years: (a) pretax income before depreciation, (b) MACRS depreciation expense, (c) taxable income, (d) income taxes, and (e) net cash flow. Net cash flow equals the income amount before depreciation minus the income taxes.

3. Compute the net present value of the investment if straight-line depreciation is used. Use 10% as the discount rate.

4. Compute the net present value of the investment if MACRS depreciation is used. Use 10% as the discount rate.

Check Net present value:
(3) $108,518, (4) $110,303

Analysis Component

5. Explain why the MACRS depreciation method increases this project's net present value.

Jones Products manufactures and sells to wholesalers approximately 400,000 packages per year of underwater markers at $6 per package. Annual costs for the production and sale of this quantity are shown in the table.

Problem 25-4A
Analysis of income effects of additional business

C3 A1

mhhe.com/wildFAP18e

Direct materials	$ 576,000
Direct labor	144,000
Overhead	320,000
Selling expenses	150,000
Administrative expenses	100,000
Total costs and expenses	$1,290,000

A new wholesaler has offered to buy 50,000 packages for $5.20 each. These markers would be marketed under the wholesaler's name and would not affect Jones Products' sales through its normal channels. A study of the costs of this additional business reveals the following:

- Direct materials costs are 100% variable.
- Per unit direct labor costs for the additional units would be 50% higher than normal because their production would require overtime pay at one-and-one-half times the usual labor rate.
- 25% of the normal annual overhead costs are fixed at any production level from 350,000 to 500,000 units. The remaining 75% of the annual overhead cost is variable with volume.

- Accepting the new business would involve no additional selling expenses.
- Accepting the new business would increase administrative expenses by a $5,000 fixed amount.

Required

Prepare a three-column comparative income statement that shows the following:

1. Annual operating income without the special order (column 1).

2. Annual operating income received from the new business only (column 2).

3. Combined annual operating income from normal business and the new business (column 3).

Check Operating income:
(1) $1,110,000, (2) $126,000

Problem 25-5A

Analysis of sales mix strategies

C3 A1

Edgerron Company is able to produce two products, G and B, with the same machine in its factory. The following information is available.

	Product G	Product B
Selling price per unit	$120	$160
Variable costs per unit	40	90
Contribution margin per unit	$ 80	$ 70
Machine hours to produce 1 unit	0.4 hours	1.0 hours
Maximum unit sales per month	600 units	200 units

The company presently operates the machine for a single eight-hour shift for 22 working days each month. Management is thinking about operating the machine for two shifts, which will increase its productivity by another eight hours per day for 22 days per month. This change would require $15,000 additional fixed costs per month.

Required

1. Determine the contribution margin per machine hour that each product generates.

2. How many units of Product G and Product B should the company produce if it continues to operate with only one shift? How much total contribution margin does this mix produce each month?

3. If the company adds another shift, how many units of Product G and Product B should it produce? How much total contribution margin would this mix produce each month? Should the company add the new shift? Explain.

Check Units of Product G: (2) 440,
(3) 600, (4) 700

4. Suppose that the company determines that it can increase Product G's maximum sales to 700 units per month by spending $12,000 per month in marketing efforts. Should the company pursue this strategy and the double shift? Explain.

Problem 25-6A

Analysis of possible elimination of a department

C3 A1

Elegant Decor Company's management is trying to decide whether to eliminate Department 200, which has produced losses or low profits for several years. The company's 2008 departmental income statement shows the following.

ELEGANT DECOR COMPANY
Departmental Income Statements
For Year Ended December 31, 2008

	Dept. 100	Dept. 200	Combined
Sales	$436,000	$290,000	$726,000
Cost of goods sold	262,000	207,000	469,000
Gross profit	174,000	83,000	257,000
Operating expenses			
Direct expenses			
Advertising	17,000	12,000	29,000
Store supplies used	4,000	3,800	7,800
Depreciation—Store equipment	5,000	3,300	8,300
Total direct expenses	26,000	19,100	45,100

[continued on next page]

[continued from previous page]

Allocated expenses			
Sales salaries	65,000	39,000	104,000
Rent expense	9,440	4,720	14,160
Bad debts expense	9,900	8,100	18,000
Office salary	18,720	12,480	31,200
Insurance expense	2,000	1,100	3,100
Miscellaneous office expenses	2,400	1,600	4,000
Total allocated expenses	107,460	67,000	174,460
Total expenses	133,460	86,100	219,560
Net income (loss)	$ 40,540	$ (3,100)	$ 37,440

In analyzing whether to eliminate Department 200, management considers the following:

a. The company has one office worker who earns $600 per week, or $31,200 per year, and four sales-clerks who each earn $500 per week, or $26,000 per year.

b. The full salaries of two salesclerks are charged to Department 100. The full salary of one sales clerk is charged to Department 200. The salary of the fourth clerk, who works half-time in both departments, is divided evenly between the two departments.

c. Eliminating Department 200 would avoid the sales salaries and the office salary currently allocated to it. However, management prefers another plan. Two salesclerks have indicated that they will be quitting soon. Management believes that their work can be done by the other two clerks if the one office worker works in sales half-time. Eliminating Department 200 will allow this shift of duties. If this change is implemented, half the office worker's salary would be reported as sales salaries and half would be reported as office salary.

d. The store building is rented under a long-term lease that cannot be changed. Therefore, Department 100 will use the space and equipment currently used by Department 200.

e. Closing Department 200 will eliminate its expenses for advertising, bad debts, and store supplies; 70% of the insurance expense allocated to it to cover its merchandise inventory; and 25% of the miscellaneous office expenses presently allocated to it.

Required

1. Prepare a three-column report that lists items and amounts for (a) the company's total expenses (including cost of goods sold)—in column 1, (b) the expenses that would be eliminated by closing Department 200—in column 2, and (c) the expenses that will continue—in column 3.

2. Prepare a forecasted annual income statement for the company reflecting the elimination of Department 200 assuming that it will not affect Department 100's sales and gross profit. The statement should reflect the reassignment of the office worker to one-half time as a salesclerk.

Analysis Component

3. Reconcile the company's combined net income with the forecasted net income assuming that Department 200 is eliminated (list both items and amounts). Analyze the reconciliation and explain why you think the department should or should not be eliminated.

Cortino Company is planning to add a new product to its line. To manufacture this product, the company needs to buy a new machine at a $300,000 cost with an expected four-year life and a $20,000 salvage value. All sales are for cash and all costs are out of pocket, except for depreciation on the new machine. Additional information includes the following.

Expected annual sales of new product	$1,150,000
Expected annual costs of new product	
Direct materials	300,000
Direct labor	420,000
Overhead excluding straight-line depreciation on new machine	210,000
Selling and administrative expenses	100,000
Income taxes	30%

Check (1) Total expenses:
(a) $688,560, (b) $284,070

(2) Forecasted net income without Department 200, $31,510

PROBLEM SET B

Problem 25-1B
Computation of payback period, accounting rate of return, and net present value

P1   P2   P3

Required

1. Compute straight-line depreciation for each year of this new machine's life.

2. Determine expected net income and net cash flow for each year of this machine's life.

3. Compute this machine's payback period, assuming that cash flows occur evenly throughout each year.

4. Compute this machine's accounting rate of return, assuming that income is earned evenly throughout each year.

5. Compute the net present value for this machine using a discount rate of 7% and assuming that cash flows occur at each year-end. (*Hint:* Salvage value is a cash inflow at the end of the asset's life.)

Check   (4) 21.88%

(5) $70,915

Problem 25-2B

Analysis and computation of payback period, accounting rate of return, and net present value

P1   P2   P3

Aikman Company has an opportunity to invest in one of two projects. Project A requires a $240,000 investment for new machinery with a four-year life and no salvage value. Project B also requires a $240,000 investment for new machinery with a three-year life and no salvage value. The two projects yield the following predicted annual results. The company uses straight-line depreciation, and cash flows occur evenly throughout each year.

	Project A	Project B
Sales	$250,000	$200,000
Expenses		
Direct materials	35,000	25,000
Direct labor	50,000	30,000
Overhead including depreciation	90,000	90,000
Selling and administrative expenses	18,000	18,000
Total expenses	193,000	163,000
Pretax income	57,000	37,000
Income taxes (30%)	17,100	11,100
Net income	$ 39,900	$ 25,900

Required

1. Compute each project's annual expected net cash flows.

2. Determine each project's payback period.

3. Compute each project's accounting rate of return.

4. Determine each project's net present value using 8% as the discount rate. For part 4 only, assume that cash flows occur at each year-end.

Check   For Project A: (2) 2.4 years, (3) 33.3%, (4) $90,879

Analysis Component

5. Identify the project you would recommend to management and explain your choice.

Problem 25-3B

Computation of cash flows and net present values with alternative depreciation methods

P3

Grossman Corporation is considering a new project requiring a $30,000 investment in an asset having no salvage value. The project would produce $12,000 of pretax income before depreciation at the end of each of the next six years. The company's income tax rate is 40%. In compiling its tax return and computing its income tax payments, the company can choose between two alternative depreciation schedules as shown in the table.

	Straight-Line Depreciation	MACRS Depreciation*
Year 1	$ 3,000	$ 6,000
Year 2	6,000	9,600
Year 3	6,000	5,760
Year 4	6,000	3,456
Year 5	6,000	3,456
Year 6	3,000	1,728
Totals	$30,000	$30,000

* The modified accelerated cost recovery system (MACRS) for depreciation is discussed in Chapter 10.

Required

1. Prepare a five-column table that reports amounts (assuming use of straight-line depreciation) for each of the following items for each of the six years: (a) pretax income before depreciation, (b) straight-line depreciation expense, (c) taxable income, (d) income taxes, and (e) net cash flow. Net cash flow equals the amount of income before depreciation minus the income taxes.

2. Prepare a five-column table that reports amounts (assuming use of MACRS depreciation) for each of the following items for each of the six years: (a) income before depreciation, (b) MACRS depreciation expense, (c) taxable income, (d) income taxes, and (e) net cash flow. Net cash flow equals the amount of income before depreciation minus the income taxes.

3. Compute the net present value of the investment if straight-line depreciation is used. Use 10% as the discount rate.

Check Net present value:
(3) $10,041, (4) $10,635

4. Compute the net present value of the investment if MACRS depreciation is used. Use 10% as the discount rate.

Analysis Component

5. Explain why the MACRS depreciation method increases the net present value of this project.

Windmire Company manufactures and sells to local wholesalers approximately 300,000 units per month at a sales price of $4 per unit. Monthly costs for the production and sale of this quantity follow.

Problem 25-4B
Analysis of income effects of additional business

C3 A1

Direct materials	$ 384,000
Direct labor	96,000
Overhead	288,000
Selling expenses	120,000
Administrative expenses	80,000
Total costs and expenses	$ 968,000

A new out-of-state distributor has offered to buy 50,000 units next month for $3.44 each. These units would be marketed in other states and would not affect Windmire's sales through its normal channels. A study of the costs of this new business reveals the following:

- Direct materials costs are 100% variable.

- Per unit direct labor costs for the additional units would be 50% higher than normal because their production would require time-and-a-half overtime pay to meet the distributor's deadline.

- Twenty-five percent of the normal annual overhead costs are fixed at any production level from 250,000 to 400,000 units. The remaining 75% is variable with volume.

- Accepting the new business would involve no additional selling expenses.

- Accepting the new business would increase administrative expenses by a $4,000 fixed amount.

Required

Prepare a three-column comparative income statement that shows the following:

1. Monthly operating income without the special order (column 1).

2. Monthly operating income received from the new business only (column 2).

3. Combined monthly operating income from normal business and the new business (column 3).

Check Operating income:
(1) $232,000, (2) $44,000

Sung Company is able to produce two products, R and T, with the same machine in its factory. The following information is available.

Problem 25-5B
Analysis of sales mix strategies

C3 A1

	Product R	Product T
Selling price per unit	$ 60	$ 80
Variable costs per unit	20	45
Contribution margin per unit	$ 40	$ 35
Machine hours to produce 1 unit	0.4 hours	1.0 hours
Maximum unit sales per month	550 units	175 units

The company presently operates the machine for a single eight-hour shift for 22 working days each month. Management is thinking about operating the machine for two shifts, which will increase its productivity by another eight hours per day for 22 days per month. This change would require $3,250 additional fixed costs per month.

Required

1. Determine the contribution margin per machine hour that each product generates.

2. How many units of Product R and Product T should the company produce if it continues to operate with only one shift? How much total contribution margin does this mix produce each month?

Check Units of Product R: (2) 440, (3) 550, (4) 675

3. If the company adds another shift, how many units of Product R and Product T should it produce? How much total contribution margin would this mix produce each month? Should the company add the new shift? Explain.

4. Suppose that the company determines that it can increase Product R's maximum sales to 675 units per month by spending $4,500 per month in marketing efforts. Should the company pursue this strategy and the double shift? Explain.

Problem 25-6B

Analysis of possible elimination of a department

C3   A1

Esme Company's management is trying to decide whether to eliminate Department Z, which has produced low profits or losses for several years. The company's 2008 departmental income statement shows the following.

	Dept. A	Dept. Z	Combined
ESME COMPANY			
Departmental Income Statements			
For Year Ended December 31, 2008			
Sales	$700,000	$175,000	$875,000
Cost of goods sold	461,300	125,100	586,400
Gross profit	238,700	49,900	288,600
Operating expenses			
Direct expenses			
Advertising	27,000	3,000	30,000
Store supplies used	5,600	1,400	7,000
Depreciation—Store equipment	14,000	7,000	21,000
Total direct expenses	46,600	11,400	58,000
Allocated expenses			
Sales salaries	70,200	23,400	93,600
Rent expense	22,080	5,520	27,600
Bad debts expense	21,000	4,000	25,000
Office salary	20,800	5,200	26,000
Insurance expense	4,200	1,400	5,600
Miscellaneous office expenses	1,700	2,500	4,200
Total allocated expenses	139,980	42,020	182,000
Total expenses	186,580	53,420	240,000
Net income (loss)	$ 52,120	$ (3,520)	$ 48,600

In analyzing whether to eliminate Department Z, management considers the following items:

a. The company has one office worker who earns $500 per week or $26,000 per year and four salesclerks who each earn $450 per week or $23,400 per year.

b. The full salaries of three salesclerks are charged to Department A. The full salary of one salesclerk is charged to Department Z.

c. Eliminating Department Z would avoid the sales salaries and the office salary currently allocated to it. However, management prefers another plan. Two salesclerks have indicated that they will be quitting soon. Management believes that their work can be done by the two remaining clerks if the one office worker works in sales half time. Eliminating Department Z will allow this shift of duties. If this change is implemented, half the office worker's salary would be reported as sales salaries and half would be reported as office salary.

d. The store building is rented under a long-term lease that cannot be changed. Therefore, Department A will use the space and equipment currently used by Department Z.

e. Closing Department Z will eliminate its expenses for advertising, bad debts, and store supplies; 65% of the insurance expense allocated to it to cover its merchandise inventory; and 30% of the miscellaneous office expenses presently allocated to it.

Required

1. Prepare a three-column report that lists items and amounts for (a) the company's total expenses (including cost of goods sold)—in column 1, (b) the expenses that would be eliminated by closing Department Z—in column 2, and (c) the expenses that will continue—in column 3.

2. Prepare a forecasted annual income statement for the company reflecting the elimination of Department Z assuming that it will not affect Department A's sales and gross profit. The statement should reflect the reassignment of the office worker to one-half time as a salesclerk.

Analysis Component

3. Reconcile the company's combined net income with the forecasted net income assuming that Department Z is eliminated (list both items and amounts). Analyze the reconciliation and explain why you think the department should or should not be eliminated.

Check (1) Total expenses: (a) $826,400, (b) $181,960

(2) Forecasted net income without Department Z, $55,560

 Problem Set C is available at the book's Website to further reinforce and assess your learning.

PROBLEM SET C

(This serial problem began in Chapter 1 and continues through most of the book. If previous chapter segments were not completed, the serial problem can begin at this point. It is helpful, but not necessary, that you use the Working Papers that accompany the book.)

SERIAL PROBLEM

Success Systems

SP 25 Adriana Lopez is considering the purchase of equipment for Success Systems that would allow the company to add a new product to its computer furniture line. The equipment is expected to cost $240,000 and to have a six-year life and no salvage value. It will be depreciated on a straight-line basis. Success Systems expects to sell 100 units of the equipment's product each year. The expected annual income related to this equipment follows.

Sales	$300,000
Costs	
Materials, labor, and overhead (except depreciation)	160,000
Depreciation on new equipment	40,000
Selling and administrative expenses	30,000
Total costs and expenses	230,000
Pretax income	70,000
Income taxes (30%)	21,000
Net income	$ 49,000

Required

Compute the (1) payback period and (2) accounting rate of return for this equipment.

BEYOND THE NUMBERS

BTN 25-1 In fiscal 2005, **Best Buy** invested $145 million in store-related projects that included store remodels, relocations, expansions, and various merchandising projects. Assume that these projects have a seven-year life, and that Best Buy requires a 15% internal rate of return on these projects.

REPORTING IN ACTION

C1 A1 P3

Required

1. What is the amount of annual cash flows that Best Buy must earn from these projects to have a 15% internal rate of return? (*Hint:* Identify the seven-period, 15% factor from the present value of an annuity table, and then divide $145 million by this factor to get the annual cash flows necessary.)

Fast Forward

2. Access Best Buy's financial statements for fiscal years ended after February 26, 2005, from its Website (**BestBuy.com**) or the SEC's Website (**SEC.gov**).

   a. Determine the amount that Best Buy invested in similar store-related projects for the most recent year.

   b. Assume a seven-year life and a 15% internal rate of return. What is the amount of cash flows that Best Buy must earn on these new projects?

COMPARATIVE ANALYSIS

C3

BTN 25-2   **Best Buy** and **Circuit City** sell several different products; most are profitable but some are not. Teams of employees in each company make advertising, investment, and product mix decisions. A certain portion of advertising for both companies is on a local basis to a target audience.

Required

1. Find one major advertisement of a product or group of products for each company in your local newspaper. Contact the newspaper and ask the approximate cost of this ad space (for example, cost of one page or one-half page of advertising).

2. Estimate how many products this advertisement must sell to justify its cost. Begin by taking the product's sales price advertised for each company and assume a 20% contribution margin.

3. Prepare a one-half page memorandum explaining the importance of effective advertising when making a product mix decision. Be prepared to present your ideas in class.

ETHICS CHALLENGE

P3

BTN 25-3   A consultant commented that "too often the numbers look good but feel bad." This comment often stems from estimation error common to capital budgeting proposals that relate to future cash flows. Three reasons for this error often exist. First, reliably predicting cash flows several years into the future is very difficult. Second, the present value of cash flows many years into the future (say, beyond 10 years) is often very small. Third, it is difficult for personal biases and expectations not to unduly influence present value computations.

Required

1. Compute the present value of $100 to be received in 10 years assuming a 12% discount rate.

2. Why is understanding the three reasons mentioned for estimation errors important when evaluating investment projects? Link this response to your answer for part 1.

COMMUNICATING IN PRACTICE

P1 P2 P3 P4

BTN 25-4   Payback period, accounting rate of return, net present value, and internal rate of return are common methods to evaluate capital investment opportunities. Assume that your manager asks you to identify the type of measurement basis and unit that each method offers and to list the advantages and disadvantages of each. Present your response in memorandum format of less than one page.

TAKING IT TO THE NET

BTN 25-5   Many companies must determine whether to internally produce their component parts or to outsource them. Further, some companies now outsource key components to international providers. Access the Website **BizBrim.com** and review the available information on outsourcing—especially as it relates to both the advantages and the negative effects of outsourcing.

Required

1. What does Bizbrim identify as the major advantages and the major disadvantages of outsourcing?

2. Does it seem that Bizbrim is generally in favor of or opposed to outsourcing? Explain.

TEAMWORK IN ACTION

P1 P3

BTN 25-6   Break into teams and identify four reasons that an international airline such as **Southwest**, **Northwest**, or **American** would invest in a project when its direct analysis using both payback period and net present value indicate it to be a poor investment. (*Hint:* Think about qualitative factors.) Provide an example of an investment project supporting your answer.

BTN 25-7 Read the article "Don't Be Afraid to Ask" by Liz Ryan in the December 27, 2005, issue of *BusinessWeek*. (The book's Website provides free access to the article.) This article deals with various business decision-making activities.

BusinessWeek
ACTIVITY
C1

Required

1. What role does asking the right question have in the management decision-making process?
2. How do the methods described in this chapter fit into the "don't be afraid to ask" framework?

BTN 25-8 Art Alaniz of **Progressive Telecom** buys used cell phones, refurbishes them, and resells them. He often must decide whether to scrap or rework his inventory. Assume that he purchases 1,000 cell phones from a recycler at a cost of $3,000. Art says the phones include 400 units of Model XR and 600 units of Model CT. Each of the Models can either be (1) refurbished and sold or (2) disassembled and the components sold to wholesalers. Details of each model's estimated refurbishing costs, value after refurbishing, cost to disassemble, and value if disassembled follow.

**ENTREPRENEURIAL
DECISION**
A1

	Model XR	Model CT
Cost to refurbish phones for resale	$18,500	$20,000
Resale value of phones after refurbishing	20,000	27,000
Cost to disassemble for component resale	1,500	1,800
Resale value of disassembled components	4,000	6,000

Required

1. Compute the incremental revenue from each model if Alaniz decides to refurbush the cell phones for resale.
2. Compute the incremental revenue from each model if Alaniz disassembles the cell phones for component resale.
3. What business decision should Alaniz implement for each model? Explain.

BTN 25-9 Visit or call a local auto dealership and inquire about leasing a car. Ask about the down payment and the required monthly payments. You will likely find the salesperson does not discuss the cost to purchase this car but focuses on the affordability of the monthly payments. This chapter gives you the tools to compute the cost of this car using the lease payment schedule in present dollars and to estimate the profit from leasing for an auto dealership.

**HITTING THE
ROAD**
C1 P3

Required

1. Compare the cost of leasing the car to buying it in present dollars using the information from the dealership you contact. (Assume you will make a final payment at the end of the lease and then own the car.)
2. Is it more costly to lease or buy the car? Support your answer with computations.

BTN 25-10 Access **Dixons'** 2004 annual report dated May 1, 2004, from its Website **DixonsGroup.com**. Identify its report on social responsibility.

GLOBAL DECISION
C1

Dixons

Required

1. Dixons reports that it recycled 2,611 tons of cardboard, paper, and plastic. Further, it reports a reduced amount of average emissions from its company cars. Efforts such as these can be costly to a company. Why would a company like Dixons pursue these costly efforts?
2. Dixons reports that it is working to recycle old appliances from its customers. This activity would be a costly undertaking for the company. Why would Dixons initiate such a program?

ANSWERS TO MULTIPLE CHOICE QUIZ

1. a; Reworking provides incremental revenue of $11 per unit ($19 − $8); and, it costs $10 to rework them. The company is better off by $1 per unit when it reworks these products and sells them at the regular price.

2. e; Product X has a $2 contribution margin per machine hour [($32 − $12)/ 10 MH]; Product Y has a $7 contribution margin per machine hour [($24 − $10)/2 MH]. It should produce as much of Product Y as possible.

3. a; Total revenue from the special order = 3,000 units × $15 per unit = $45,000; and, Total costs for the special order = (3,000 units × $9 per unit) + $5,000 = $32,000. Net income from the special order = $45,000 − $32,000 = $13,000. Thus, yes, it should accept the order.

4. c; Payback = $270,000/$61,200 per year = 4.4 years.

5. d; Accounting rate of return = $8,550/[($180,000 + $0)/2] = 9.5%.

A Financial Statement Information

This appendix includes financial information for (1) **Best Buy**, (2) **Circuit City**, and (3) **Apple Computer**. This information is taken from their annual 10-K reports filed with the SEC. An **annual report** is a summary of a company's financial results for the year along with its current financial condition and future plans. This report is directed to external users of financial information, but it also affects the actions and decisions of internal users.

A company uses an annual report to showcase itself and its products. Many annual reports include attractive photos, diagrams, and illustrations related to the company. The primary objective of annual reports, however, is the *financial section,* which communicates much information about a company, with most data drawn from the accounting information system. The layout of an annual report's financial section is fairly established and typically includes the following:

- Letter to Shareholders
- Financial History and Highlights
- Management Discussion and Analysis
- Management's Report on Financial Statements and on Internal Controls
- Report of Independent Accountants (Auditor's Report) and on Internal Controls
- Financial Statements
- Notes to Financial Statements
- List of Directors and Officers

This appendix provides the financial statements for Best Buy (plus selected notes), Circuit City, and Apple Computer. The appendix is organized as follows:

- **Best Buy A-2** through **A-18**
- **Circuit City A-19** through **A-23**
- **Apple Computer A-24** through **A-28**

Many assignments at the end of each chapter refer to information in this appendix. We encourage readers to spend time with these assignments; they are especially useful in showing the relevance and diversity of financial accounting and reporting.

Special note: The SEC maintains the EDGAR (**E**lectronic **D**ata **G**athering, **A**nalysis, and **R**etrieval) database at www.sec.gov. The **Form 10-K** is the annual report form for most companies. It provides electronically accessible information. The **Form 10-KSB** is the annual report form filed by "small businesses." It requires slightly less information than the Form 10-K. One of these forms must be filed within 90 days after the company's fiscal year-end. (Forms 10-K405, 10-KT, 10-KT405, and 10-KSB405 are slight variations of the usual form due to certain regulations or rules.)

Financial Report

Selected Financial Data

The following table presents our selected financial data. Certain prior-year amounts have been reclassified to conform to the current-year presentation. All fiscal years presented reflect the classification of Musicland's financial results as discontinued operations.

Five-Year Financial Highlights

$ in millions, except per share amounts

Fiscal Year	2005	2004	2003	2002	2001
Consolidated Statements of Earnings Data					
Revenue	$27,433	$24,548	$20,943	$17,711	$15,189
Operating income	1,442	1,304	1,010	908	611
Earnings from continuing operations	934	800	622	570	401
Loss from discontinued operations, net of tax	—	(29)	(441)	—	(5)
Gain (loss) on disposal of discontinued operations, net of tax	50	(66)	—	—	—
Cumulative effect of change in accounting principles, net of tax	—	—	(82)	—	—
Net earnings	984	705	99	570	396
Per Share Data					
Continuing operations	$2.79	$2.41	$1.90	$1.77	$1.26
Discontinued operations	—	(0.09)	(1.34)	—	(0.02)
Gain (loss) on disposal of discontinued operations	0.15	(0.20)	—	—	—
Cumulative effect of accounting changes	—	—	(0.25)	—	—
Net earnings	2.94	2.13	0.31	1.77	1.24
Cash dividends declared and paid	0.42	0.40	—	—	—
Common stock price:					
High	62.20	62.70	53.75	51.47	59.25
Low	43.87	25.55	16.99	22.42	14.00
Operating Statistics					
Comparable store sales change	4.3%	7.1%	2.4%	1.9%	4.9%
Gross profit rate	23.7%	23.9%	23.6%	20.0%	18.5%
Selling, general and administrative expense rate	18.4%	18.6%	18.8%	14.9%	14.5%
Operating income rate	5.3%	5.3%	4.8%	5.1%	4.0%
Year-End Data					
Current ratio	1.4	1.3	1.3	1.2	1.1
Total assets	$10,294	$8,652	$7,694	$7,367	$4,840
Long-term debt, including current portion	600	850	834	820	296
Total shareholders' equity	4,449	3,422	2,730	2,521	1,822
Number of stores					
U.S. Best Buy stores	668	608	548	481	419
Magnolia Audio Video stores	20	22	19	13	13
International stores	144	127	112	95	—
Total retail square footage (000s)					
U.S. Best Buy stores	28,260	26,421	24,243	21,599	19,010
Magnolia Audio Video stores	194	218	189	133	133
International stores	3,139	2,800	2,375	1,923	—

Fiscal 2001 included 53 weeks. All other periods presented included 52 weeks.

Consolidated Balance Sheets

$ in millions, except per share amounts

Assets	February 26, 2005	February 28, 2004
Current Assets		
Cash and cash equivalents	$ 470	$ 245
Short-term investments	2,878	2,355
Receivables	375	343
Merchandise inventories	2,851	2,607
Other current assets	329	174
Total current assets	6,903	5,724
Property and Equipment		
Land and buildings	506	484
Leasehold improvements	1,139	861
Fixtures and equipment	2,458	2,151
Property under master and capital lease	89	78
	4,192	3,574
Less accumulated depreciation	1,728	1,330
Net property and equipment	2,464	2,244
Goodwill	513	477
Tradename	40	37
Long-Term Investments	148	—
Other Assets	226	170
Total Assets	$10,294	$8,652
Liabilities and Shareholders' Equity		
Current Liabilities		
Accounts payable	$ 2,824	$2,460
Unredeemed gift card liabilities	410	300
Accrued compensation and related expenses	234	269
Accrued liabilities	844	724
Accrued income taxes	575	380
Current portion of long-term debt	72	368
Total current liabilities	4,959	4,501
Long-Term Liabilities	358	247
Long-Term Debt	528	482
Shareholders' Equity		
Preferred stock, $1.00 par value: Authorized — 400,000 shares; Issued and outstanding — none	—	—
Common stock, $.10 par value: Authorized — 1 billion shares; Issued and outstanding — 328,342,000 and 324,648,000 shares, respectively	33	32
Additional paid-in capital	952	836
Retained earnings	3,315	2,468
Accumulated other comprehensive income	149	86
Total shareholders' equity	4,449	3,422
Total Liabilities and Shareholders' Equity	$10,294	$8,652

See Notes to Consolidated Financial Statements.

Consolidated Statements of Earnings
$ in millions, except per share amounts

For the Fiscal Years Ended	February 26, 2005	February 28, 2004	March 1, 2003
Revenue	$27,433	$24,548	$20,943
Cost of goods sold	20,938	18,677	15,998
Gross profit	6,495	5,871	4,945
Selling, general and administrative expenses	5,053	4,567	3,935
Operating income	1,442	1,304	1,010
Net interest income (expense)	1	(8)	4
Earnings from continuing operations before income tax expense	1,443	1,296	1,014
Income tax expense	509	496	392
Earnings from continuing operations	934	800	622
Loss from discontinued operations (Note 2), net of $17 and $119 tax	—	(29)	(441)
Gain (loss) on disposal of discontinued operations (Note 2)	50	(66)	—
Cumulative effect of change in accounting principle for goodwill (Note 1), net of $24 tax	—	—	(40)
Cumulative effect of change in accounting principle for vendor allowances (Note 1), net of $26 tax	—	—	(42)
Net earnings	$ 984	$ 705	$ 99
Basic earnings (loss) per share:			
Continuing operations	$ 2.87	$ 2.47	$ 1.93
Discontinued operations	—	(0.09)	(1.37)
Gain (loss) on disposal of discontinued operations	0.15	(0.20)	—
Cumulative effect of accounting changes	—	—	(0.25)
Basic earnings per share	$ 3.02	$ 2.18	$ 0.31
Diluted earnings (loss) per share:[1]			
Continuing operations	$ 2.79	$ 2.41	$ 1.90
Discontinued operations	—	(0.09)	(1.34)
Gain (loss) on disposal of discontinued operations	0.15	(0.20)	—
Cumulative effect of accounting changes	—	—	(0.25)
Diluted earnings per share	$ 2.94	$ 2.13	$ 0.31
Basic weighted average common shares outstanding (in millions)	325.9	323.3	321.1
Diluted weighted average common shares outstanding (in millions)[1]	336.6	333.9	330.7

[1] The calculation of diluted earnings per share assumes the conversion of our convertible debentures due in 2022 into 5.8 million shares of common stock and adds back related after-tax interest expense of $6.5 for all periods presented.

See Notes to Consolidated Financial Statements.

Consolidated Statements of Changes in Shareholders' Equity

$ and shares in millions

	Common Shares	Common Stock	Additional Paid-In Capital	Retained Earnings	Accumulated Other Comprehensive Income (Loss)	Total
Balances at March 2, 2002	319	$31	$ 702	$1,794	$ (6)	$2,521
Net earnings	—	—	—	99	—	99
Other comprehensive income (loss), net of tax:						
Foreign currency translation adjustments	—	—	—	—	34	34
Other	—	—	—	—	(1)	(1)
Total comprehensive income						132
Stock options exercised	3	1	43	—	—	44
Tax benefit from stock options exercised	—	—	33	—	—	33
Balances at March 1, 2003	322	32	778	1,893	27	2,730
Net earnings	—	—	—	705	—	705
Foreign currency translation adjustments	—	—	—	—	59	59
Total comprehensive income						764
Stock options exercised	5	—	114	—	—	114
Tax benefit from stock options exercised	—	—	41	—	—	41
Vesting of restricted stock awards	—	—	3	—	—	3
Common stock dividends, $0.40 per share	—	—	—	(130)	—	(130)
Repurchase of common stock	(2)	—	(100)	—	—	(100)
Balances at February 28, 2004	325	32	836	2,468	86	3,422
Net earnings	—	—	—	984	—	984
Other comprehensive income, net of tax:						
Foreign currency translation adjustments	—	—	—	—	59	59
Other	—	—	—	—	4	4
Total comprehensive income						1,047
Stock options exercised	6	1	219	—	—	220
Tax benefit from stock options exercised and employee stock purchase plan	—	—	60	—	—	60
Issuance of common stock under employee stock purchase plan	1	—	36	—	—	36
Vesting of restricted stock awards	—	—	1	—	—	1
Common stock dividends, $0.42 per share	—	—	—	(137)	—	(137)
Repurchase of common stock	(4)	—	(200)	—	—	(200)
Balances at February 26, 2005	328	$33	$ 952	$3,315	$149	$4,449

See Notes to Consolidated Financial Statements.

Consolidated Statements of Cash Flows
$ in millions

For the Fiscal Years Ended	February 26, 2005	February 28, 2004	March 1, 2003
Operating Activities			
Net earnings	$ 984	$ 705	$ 99
(Gain) loss from and disposal of discontinued operations, net of tax	(50)	95	441
Cumulative effect of change in accounting principles, net of tax	—	—	82
Earnings from continuing operations	934	800	622
Adjustments to reconcile earnings from continuing operations to total cash provided by operating activities from continuing operations:			
Depreciation	459	385	310
Asset impairment charges	22	22	11
Deferred income taxes	(28)	(14)	(37)
Other	23	16	15
Changes in operating assets and liabilities, net of acquired assets and liabilities:			
Receivables	(30)	(27)	(89)
Merchandise inventories	(240)	(507)	(256)
Other assets	(190)	(25)	(21)
Accounts payable	347	272	(5)
Other liabilities	243	250	117
Accrued income taxes	301	197	111
Total cash provided by operating activities from continuing operations	1,841	1,369	778
Investing Activities			
Additions to property and equipment	(502)	(545)	(725)
Purchases of available-for-sale securities	(7,789)	(2,989)	(1,844)
Sales of available-for-sale securities	7,118	2,175	1,610
Other, net	7	1	49
Total cash used in investing activities from continuing operations	(1,166)	(1,358)	(910)
Financing Activities			
Long-term debt payments	(371)	(17)	(13)
Issuance of common stock under employee stock purchase plan and for the exercise of stock options	256	114	40
Repurchase of common stock	(200)	(100)	—
Dividends paid	(137)	(130)	—
Net proceeds from issuance of long-term debt	—	—	18
Other, net	(7)	46	(15)
Total cash (used in) provided by financing activities from continuing operations	(459)	(87)	30
Effect of Exchange Rate Changes on Cash	9	1	—
Net Cash Used in Discontinued Operations	—	(53)	(79)
Increase (Decrease) in Cash and Cash Equivalents	225	(128)	(181)
Cash and Cash Equivalents at Beginning of Year	245	373	554
Cash and Cash Equivalents at End of Year	$ 470	$ 245	$ 373
Supplemental Disclosure of Cash Flow Information			
Income tax paid	$ 241	$ 306	$ 283
Interest paid	35	22	24
Capital and financing lease obligations incurred	117	26	—

See Notes to Consolidated Financial Statements.

Best Buy

SELECTED Notes to Consolidated Financial Statements

$ in millions, except per share amounts

1.   Summary of Significant Accounting Policies

Description of Business

Best Buy Co., Inc. is a specialty retailer of consumer electronics, home-office products, entertainment software, appliances and related services.

We operate two reportable segments: Domestic and International. The Domestic segment is comprised of U.S. Best Buy and Magnolia Audio Video operations. At February 26, 2005, we operated 668 U.S. Best Buy stores in 48 states and the District of Columbia. At February 26, 2005, we operated 20 Magnolia Audio Video stores in California, Washington and Oregon. The International segment is comprised of Future Shop and Best Buy operations in Canada. At February 26, 2005, we operated 114 Future Shop stores throughout all Canadian provinces and 30 Canadian Best Buy stores in Ontario, Alberta, British Columbia, Manitoba and Saskatchewan. Future Shop and Canadian Best Buy stores offer products and services similar to those offered by U.S. Best Buy stores except that Canadian Best Buy stores do not sell appliances.

In support of our retail store operations, we also operate Geek Squad, a computer repair and service provider, and Web sites for each of our brands (BestBuy.com, BestBuyCanada.ca, FutureShop.ca, MagnoliaAV.com and GeekSquad.com).

Fiscal Year

Our fiscal year ends on the Saturday nearest the end of February. Fiscal 2005, 2004 and 2003 each included 52 weeks.

Cash and Cash Equivalents

Cash primarily consists of cash on hand and bank deposits. Cash equivalents primarily consist of money market accounts and other highly liquid investments with an original maturity of three months or less when purchased. We carry these investments at cost, which approximates market value. The amount of cash equivalents at February 26, 2005, and February 28, 2004, was $156 and $73, respectively, and the weighted average interest rates were 2.9% and 0.9%, respectively.

Outstanding checks in excess of funds on deposit totaled $393 and $351 at February 26, 2005, and February 28, 2004, respectively, and are reflected as current liabilities.

Merchandise Inventories

Merchandise inventories are recorded at the lower of average cost or market. In-bound freight-related costs from our vendors are included as part of the net cost of merchandise inventories. Also included in the cost of inventory are certain vendor allowances that are not a reimbursement of specific, incremental and identifiable costs to promote a vendor's products. Other costs associated with acquiring, storing and transporting merchandise inventories to our retail stores are expensed as incurred and included in cost of goods sold.

Our inventory loss reserve represents anticipated physical inventory losses (e.g., theft) that have occurred since the last physical inventory date. Independent physical inventory counts are taken on a regular basis to ensure that the inventory reported in our consolidated financial statements is accurately stated. During the interim period between physical inventory counts, we reserve for anticipated physical inventory losses on a location-by-location basis.

Property and Equipment

Property and equipment are recorded at cost. We compute depreciation using the straight-line method over the estimated useful lives of the assets. Leasehold improvements are depreciated over the shorter of their estimated useful lives or the period from the date the assets are placed in service to the end of the initial lease

$ in millions, except per share amounts

term. Accelerated depreciation methods are generally used for income tax purposes.

Repairs and maintenance costs are charged directly to expense as incurred. Major renewals or replacements that substantially extend the useful life of an asset are capitalized and depreciated.

Estimated useful lives by major asset category are as follows:

Asset	Life (in years)
Buildings	30-40
Leasehold improvements	10-25
Fixtures and equipment	3-15
Property under master and capital lease	3-35

Goodwill and Intangible Assets

Goodwill

Goodwill is the excess of the purchase price over the fair value of identifiable net assets acquired in business combinations accounted for under the purchase method. Effective March 3, 2002, we adopted SFAS No. 142, *Goodwill and Other Intangible Assets,* which eliminated the systematic amortization of goodwill. This Statement also requires that we review goodwill for impairment at adoption and at least annually thereafter.

During the fourth quarter of fiscal 2005, we completed our annual impairment testing of our goodwill and tradename, using the same valuation techniques as described above, and determined there was no impairment.

Tradename

We have an indefinite-lived intangible asset related to our Future Shop tradename that totaled $40 and $37 at February 26, 2005, and February 28, 2004, respectively, which is included in the International segment. The change in the indefinite-lived intangible asset balance from February 28, 2004, was the result of fluctuations in foreign currency exchange rates.

Lease Rights

Lease rights, representing costs incurred to acquire the lease of a specific commercial property, are recorded at cost and are amortized to rent expense over the remaining lease term, which ranges up to 16 years, beginning with the date we take possession of the property.

The gross cost and accumulated amortization of lease rights were $27 and $29; and $9 and $6, respectively, at February 26, 2005, and February 28, 2004, respectively. Lease rights amortization was $4, $4 and $2 for fiscal 2005, 2004 and 2003, respectively. Current lease rights amortization is expected to be approximately $3 for each of the next five fiscal years.

Income Taxes

We account for income taxes under the liability method. Under this method, deferred tax assets and liabilities are recognized for the estimated future tax consequences attributable to differences between the financial statement carrying amounts of existing assets and liabilities and their respective tax bases, and operating loss and tax credit carryforwards. Deferred tax assets and liabilities are measured using enacted income tax rates in effect for the year in which those temporary differences are expected to be recovered or settled. The effect on deferred tax assets and liabilities of a change in income tax rates is recognized in our statement of earnings in the period that includes the enactment date. A valuation allowance is recorded to reduce the carrying amounts of deferred tax assets if it is more likely than not that such assets will not be realized.

Long-Term Liabilities

The major components of long-term liabilities at February 26, 2005, and February 28, 2004, included deferred compensation plan liabilities, long-term rent-related liabilities, deferred income taxes and advances received under vendor alliance programs.

Foreign Currency

Foreign currency denominated assets and liabilities are translated into U.S. dollars using the exchange rates in effect at the balance sheet date. Results of operations and cash flows are translated using the average exchange rates throughout the period. The effect of exchange rate

$ in millions, except per share amounts

fluctuations on translation of assets and liabilities is included as a component of shareholders' equity in accumulated other comprehensive income. Gains and losses from foreign currency transactions, which are included in SG&A, have not been significant.

Revenue Recognition

We recognize revenue from the sale of merchandise at the time the customer takes possession of the merchandise. We recognize service revenue at the time the service is provided, the sales price is fixed or determinable, and collectibility is reasonably assured. Proceeds from the sale of gift cards are deferred until the customer uses the gift card to acquire merchandise or services. Amounts billed to customers for shipping and handling are included in revenue. An allowance has been established for estimated sales returns.

We sell extended service contracts on behalf of an unrelated third party. In jurisdictions where we are not deemed to be the obligor on the contract, commissions are recognized in revenue at the time of sale. In jurisdictions where we are deemed to be the obligor on the contract, commissions are recognized in revenue ratably over the term of the service contract.

Sales Incentives

We frequently offer sales incentives that entitle our customers to receive a reduction in the price of a product or service. Sales incentives include discounts, coupons and other offers that entitle a customer to receive a reduction in the price of a product or service by submitting a claim for a refund or rebate. For sales incentives in which we are the obligor, the reduction in revenue is recognized at the time the product is sold.

We have a customer loyalty program which allows members to earn points for each purchase completed at U.S. Best Buy stores. Points earned enable members to receive a certificate that may be redeemed on future purchases at U.S. Best Buy stores. The value of points earned by our loyalty program members is included in accrued liabilities and recorded as a reduction of revenue at the time the points are earned, based on the percentage of points that are projected to be redeemed.

Costs of Goods Sold and Selling, General and Administrative Expenses

The following table illustrates the primary costs classified in each major expense category.

Cost of Goods Sold	SG&A
<ul><li>Total cost of products sold including:<ul><li>— Freight expenses associated with moving merchandise inventories from our vendors to our distribution centers;</li><li>— Vendor allowances that are not a reimbursement of specific, incremental and identifiable costs to promote a vendor's products;</li></ul></li><li>Costs of services provided;</li><li>Physical inventory losses;</li><li>Markdowns;</li><li>Customer shipping and handling expenses;</li><li>Costs associated with operating our distribution network, including payroll and benefit costs, occupancy costs, and depreciation; and</li><li>Freight expenses associated with moving merchandise inventories from our distribution centers to our retail stores.</li></ul>	<ul><li>Payroll and benefit costs for retail and corporate employees;</li><li>Occupancy costs of retail, services and corporate facilities;</li><li>Depreciation related to retail, services and corporate assets;</li><li>Advertising;</li><li>Vendor allowances that are a reimbursement of specific, incremental and identifiable costs to promote a vendor's products;</li><li>Outside service fees;</li><li>Long-lived asset impairment charges; and</li><li>Other administrative costs, such as credit card service fees, supplies, and travel and lodging.</li></ul>

$ in millions, except per share amounts

Advertising Costs

Advertising costs, which are included in SG&A, are expensed the first time the advertisement runs. Advertising costs consist primarily of print and television advertisements as well as promotional events. Gross advertising expenses, before expense reimbursement from vendor allowances, for fiscal 2005, 2004 and 2003 were $712, $675 and $567, respectively.

Stock-Based Compensation

We have a stock-based compensation plan that includes stock options and restricted stock. We also have an employee stock purchase plan. The table below illustrates the effect on net earnings and earnings per share as if we had applied the fair value recognition provisions of SFAS No. 123 to stock-based compensation for each of the last three fiscal years.

	2005	2004	2003
Net earnings, as reported	$ 984	$ 705	$ 99
Add: Stock-based compensation expense included in reported net earnings, net of tax[1]	(1)	5	1
Deduct: Stock-based compensation expense determined under fair value method for all awards, net of tax[2]	(60)	(101)	(85)
Net earnings, pro forma	$ 923	$ 609	$ 15
Earnings per share:			
Basic — as reported	$3.02	$2.18	$0.31
Basic — pro forma	$2.83	$1.88	$0.05
Diluted — as reported	$2.94	$2.13	$0.31
Diluted — pro forma	$2.80	$1.88	$0.05

[1]   Amounts represent the after-tax compensation costs for restricted stock awards.

[2]   In the fourth quarter of fiscal 2005, we increased our expected participant stock option forfeiture rate as a result of transferring to a third-party provider certain corporate employees, and the departure of certain senior executives. This higher level of expected stock option forfeitures reduced our fiscal 2005 pro forma stock-based compensation expense. Fiscal 2005 pro forma stock-based compensation expense may not be indicative of future stock-based compensation expense.

2.   Discontinued Operations

In fiscal 2004, we sold our interest in Musicland. The buyer assumed all of Musicland's liabilities, including approximately $500 in lease obligations, in exchange for all of the capital stock of Musicland and paid no cash consideration. The transaction also resulted in the transfer of all of Musicland's assets, other than a distribution center in Franklin, Indiana, and selected nonoperating assets. The loss from discontinued operations for fiscal 2004 included a loss on the disposal of discontinued operations (which was primarily noncash) of $66, net of tax, related to the sale of Musicland. In connection with the sale, Musicland purchased transition support services from us for approximately one year from the date of the sale.

In accordance with SFAS No. 144, Musicland's financial results are reported separately as discontinued operations for all periods presented.

During fiscal 2003, we recorded an after-tax, noncash impairment charge of $308 for the full write-off of goodwill related to our acquisition of Musicland. In addition, we recorded an after-tax, noncash charge of $8 for the change in our method of accounting for Musicland vendor allowances. The charges are classified as cumulative effects of changes in accounting principles in discontinued operations (see Note 1, *Summary of Significant Accounting Policies*).

Also during fiscal 2003, in accordance with SFAS No. 144, we recorded a pre-tax impairment charge of $166 related to a reassessment of the carrying value of

$ in millions, except per share amounts

Musicland's long-lived assets. The $166 charge was recorded in loss before income taxes, in the table below. We determined fair values utilizing widely accepted valuation techniques, including discounted cash flows. We based fair values on the then-current expectations for the business in light of the then-existing retail environment and the uncertainty associated with future trends in prerecorded music products.

The financial results of Musicland, included in discontinued operations, were as follows:

For the Fiscal Years Ended	Feb. 26, 2005	Feb. 28, 2004[1]	March 1, 2003
Revenue	$—	$354	$1,727
Loss before income taxes	—	(46)	(244)
Loss before the disposal and the cumulative effect of accounting changes, net of $17 and $119 tax, respectively	—	(29)	(125)
Gain (loss) on disposal of discontinued operations[2]	50	(66)	—
Cumulative effect of change in accounting principles, net of $5 tax	—	—	(316)
Gain (loss) from discontinued operations, net of tax	$50	$ (95)	$ (441)

[1] Fiscal 2004 includes operating results from March 2, 2003, through June 16, 2003, the date we sold our interest in Musicland.

[2] Fiscal 2005 gain on disposal of discontinued operations represents the reversal of valuation allowances on deferred tax assets as described below. Fiscal 2004 loss on disposal of discontinued operations is net of $25 tax benefit offset by a $25 valuation allowance.

3. Investments in Debt Securities

Our short-term and long-term investments are comprised of municipal and United States government debt securities. In accordance with SFAS No. 115, *Accounting for Certain Investments in Debt and Equity Securities,* and based on our ability to market and sell these instruments, we classify auction-rate debt securities and other investments in debt securities as available-for-sale and carry them at amortized cost. Auction-rate debt securities are long-term bonds that are similar to short-term instruments because their interest rates are reset periodically and investments in these securities can be sold for cash on the auction date. We classify auction-rate debt securities as short-term or long-term investments based on the reset dates.

In accordance with our investment policy, we place our investments in debt securities with issuers who have high-quality credit and limit the amount of investment exposure to any one issuer. We seek to preserve principal and minimize exposure to interest-rate fluctuations by limiting default risk, market risk and reinvestment risk.

On an annual basis, we review the key characteristics of our debt securities portfolio and their classification in accordance with GAAP. If a decline in the fair value of a security is deemed by management to be other than temporary, the cost basis of the investment is written down to fair value, and the amount of the write-down is included in the determination of income.

During our annual review in the fourth quarter of fiscal 2005, we reclassified our auction-rate debt securities from cash and cash equivalents to short-term investments or long-term investments, as appropriate, for all periods presented. The amortized cost of the securities reclassified for fiscal 2004 was $2,355. The unrealized gain on the securities in conjunction with this reclassification was not significant.

We also revised the presentation in the consolidated statements of cash flows for the years ended February 28, 2004, and March 1, 2003, to reflect the gross purchases and sales of these securities as investing activities rather than as a component of cash and cash equivalents, which is consistent with the presentation for the fiscal year ended February 26, 2005.

$ in millions, except per share amounts

The carrying amount of our investments in debt securities approximated fair value of February 26, 2005, and February 28, 2004, respectively, due to the rapid turnover of our portfolio and the highly liquid nature of these investments. Therefore, there were no significant unrealized holding gains or losses.

The following table presents the amortized principal amounts, related weighted average interest rates, maturities and major security types for our investments in debt securities:

	February 26, 2005		February 28, 2004	
	Amortized Principal Amount	Weighted Average Interest Rate	Amortized Principal Amount	Weighted Average Interest Rate
Short-term investments (less than one year)	$2,878	3.22%	$2,355	1.59%
Long-term investments (one to three years)	148	3.73%	—	—
Total	$3,026		$2,355	
Municipal debt securities	$3,019		$2,355	
Debt securities issued by U.S. Treasury and other U.S. government entities	7		—	
Total	$3,026		$2,355	

4. Debt

	Feb. 26, 2005	Feb. 28, 2004
Convertible subordinated debentures, unsecured, due 2022, initial interest rate 2.25%	$402	$ 402
Convertible debentures, unsecured, due 2021, interest rate 2.75%[1]	—	353
Master lease obligations, due 2006, interest rate 5.9%	55	58
Capital lease obligations, due 2005, interest rates ranging from 5.5% to 8.0%	13	16
Financing lease obligations, due 2008 to 2022, interest rates ranging from 5.6% to 6.0%[2]	107	—
Mortgage and other debt, interest rates ranging from 1.8% to 8.9%	23	21
Total debt	600	850
Less: current portion	(72)	(368)
Total long-term debt	$528	$ 482

[1] In June 2004, we redeemed our convertible debentures due in 2021, for $355. No gain or loss was incurred.

[2] In fiscal 2005, we recorded $107 of financing leases as a result of our review of our lease accounting practices. See Note 7, *Leases*, for further information.

The mortgage and other debt are secured by certain property and equipment with a net book value of $98 and $97 at February 26, 2005, and February 28, 2004, respectively.

Convertible Debentures

In January 2002, we sold convertible subordinated debentures having an aggregate principal amount of $402. The proceeds from the offering, net of $6 in offering expenses, were $396. The debentures mature in 2022 and are callable at par, at our option, for cash on or after January 15, 2007.

Holders may require us to purchase all or a portion of their debentures on January 15, 2007; January 15, 2012; and January 15, 2017, at a purchase price equal

$ in millions, except per share amounts

to 100% of the principal amount of the debentures plus accrued and unpaid interest up to but not including the date of purchase. We have the option to settle the purchase price in cash, stock, or a combination of cash and stock.

The debentures will be convertible into shares of our common stock at a conversion rate of 14.4927 shares per $0.001 principal amount of debentures, equivalent to an initial conversion price of $69.00 per share, if the closing price of our common stock exceeds a specified price for a specified period of time, if our credit rating falls below specified levels, if the debentures are called for redemption or if certain specified corporate transactions occur. At February 26, 2005, none of the criteria for conversion had been met. The debentures have an initial interest rate of 2.25% per annum. The interest rate may be reset, but not below 2.25% or above 3.25%, on July 15, 2006; July 15, 2011; and July 15, 2016. One of our subsidiaries has guaranteed the convertible debentures.

Credit Facilities

We have a $200 bank revolving credit facility which is guaranteed by certain of our subsidiaries. The facility expires on December 22, 2009. Borrowings under this facility are unsecured and bear interest at rates specified in the credit agreement. We also pay certain facility and agent fees. The agreement contains convenants that require us to maintain certain financial ratios.

Other

The fair value of long-term debt approximated $603 and $902 as of February 26, 2005, and February 28, 2004, respectively, based on the ask prices quoted from external sources, compared with carrying values of $600 and $850, respectively.

The future maturities of long-term debt, including master and capitalized leases, consist of the following:

Fiscal Year	
2006	$ 72
2007[1]	415
2008	14
2009	14
2010	20
Thereafter	65
	$600

[1] Holders of our debentures due in 2022 may require us to purchase all or a portion of their debentures on January 15, 2007. The table above assumes that all holders of our debentures exercise their redemption options.

5. Shareholders Equity Stock Compensation Plans

Outstanding options were granted at exercise prices equal to the fair market value of our common stock on the date of grant and have a 10-year term. Options issued to employees generally vest over a four-year period. Options issued to our directors vest immediately upon grant.

Earnings per Share

Basic earnings per share is computed based on the weighted average number of common shares outstanding. Diluted earnings per share is computed based on the weighted average number of common shares outstanding adjusted by the number of additional shares that would have been outstanding had the potentially dilutive common shares been issued. Potentially dilutive shares of common stock include stock options, unvested restricted stock awards, shares issuable under our ESPP as well as common shares that would have resulted from the assumed conversion of our convertible debentures (see Note 4, *Debt*). Since the potentially dilutive shares related to the convertible debentures are included in the calculation, the related interest, net of tax, is added back to income from continuing operations, as the interest would not have been paid if the convertible debentures were converted to common stock.

$ in millions, except per share amounts

The following table presents a reconciliation of the numerators and denominators of basic and diluted earnings per share from continuing operations for fiscal 2005, 2004 and 2003:

	2005	2004	2003
Numerator:			
Earnings from continuing operations, basic	$ 934	$ 800	$ 622
Adjustment for assumed dilution:			
Interest on convertible debentures due in 2022, net of tax	7	6	6
Earnings from continuing operations, diluted	$ 941	$ 806	$ 628
Denominator (in millions):			
Weighted average common shares outstanding	325.9	323.3	321.1
Effect of dilutive securities:			
Shares from assumed conversion of convertible debentures	5.8	5.8	5.8
Stock options and other	4.9	4.8	3.8
Weighted average common shares outstanding, assuming dilution	336.6	333.9	330.7
Basic earnings per share — continuing operations	$ 2.87	$ 2.47	$ 1.93
Diltuted earnings per share — continuing operations	$ 2.79	$ 2.41	$ 1.90

Repurchase of Common Stock

In June 2004, our Board authorized the purchase of up to $500 of our common stock from time to time through open market purchases. The $500 share repurchase program, which became effective on June 24, 2004, terminated and replaced the $400 share repurchase program authorized by our Board in fiscal 2000.

In April 2005, our Board authorized the purchase of up to $1.5 billion of our common stock from time to time through open market purchases. This share repurchase program has no stated expiration date. The $1.5 billion share repurchase program terminated and replaced the $500 share repurchase program authorized by our Board in June 2004.

During fiscal 2005, we purchased and retired 2.3 million shares at a cost of $118 under the $500 share repurchase program, and 1.6 million shares at a cost of $82 under the $400 share repurchase program.

Comprehensive Income

Comprehensive income is computed as net earnings plus certain other items that are recorded directly to shareholders' equity. The only significant other item included in comprehensive income is foreign currency translation adjustments. Foreign currency translation adjustments do not include a provision for income tax because earnings from foreign operations are considered to be indefinitely reinvested outside the U.S. Investment gains/losses were not significant.

$ in millions, except per share amounts

6. Net Interest Income (Expense)

Net interest income (expense) for fiscal 2005, 2004 and 2003 was comprised of the following

	2005	2004	2003
Interest expense[1]	$(44)	$(32)	$(30)
Capitalized interest	—	1	5
Interest income	45	23	23
Net interest income (expense)	1	(8)	(2)
Interest expense allocated to discontinued operations[2]	—	—	(6)
Net interest income (expense) from continuing operations	$ 1	$ (8)	$ 4

[1]   Fiscal 2005 interest expense includes $21 of expense related to our lease accounting corrections.

[2]   We allocated interest expense to discontinued operations based upon debt that was attributable to Musicland's operation.

7. Leases

We lease portions of our corporate facilities and conduct the majority of our retail and distribution operations from leased locations. The leases require payment of real estate taxes, insurance and common area maintenance, in addition to rent. The terms of our lease agreements generally range up to 20 years. Most of the leases contain renewal options and escalation clauses, and certain store leases require contingent rents based on specified percentages of revenue. Other leases contain covenants related to the maintenance of financial ratios.

For leases that contain predetermined fixed escalations of the minimum rent, we recognize the related rent expense on a straight-line basis from the date we take possession of the property to the end of the initial lease term. We record any difference between the straight-line rent amounts and amounts payable under the leases as part of deferred rent, in accrued liabilities or long-term liabilities, as appropriate.

Cash or lease incentives (tenant allowances) received upon entering into certain store leases are recognized on a straight-line basis as a reduction to rent from the date we take possession of the property though the end of the initial lease term. We record the unamortized portion of tenant allowances as a part of deferred rent, in accrued liabilities or long-term liabilities, as appropriate.

At February 26, 2005, and February 28, 2004, deferred rent included in accrued liabilities was approximately $11 and $3, respectively, and deferred rent included in long-term liabilities was approximately $171 and $73, respectively.

We also lease certain equipment under noncancelable operating and capital leases. Assets acquired under capital leases are depreciated over the shorter of the useful life of the asset or the initial lease term.

Rental expense for all operating leases, during the past three fiscal years, including leases of property and equipment, was as follows:

	2005	2004	2003
Net rent expense for continuing operations	$501	$468	$440

$ in millions, except per share amounts

The future minimum lease payments under our capital, financing and operating leases by fiscal year (not including contingent rentals) as of February 26, 2005, are as follows:

Fiscal Year	Capital Leases	Financing Leases	Operating Leases
2006	$ 6	$ 16	$ 541
2007	2	15	541
2008	2	15	524
2009	2	14	511
2010	2	14	486
Thereafter	1	79	3,247
Subtotal	15	153	$5,850
Less: imputed interest	(2)	(46)	
Present value of lease obligations	$13	$107	

8. Benefit Plans

We sponsor retirement savings plans for employees meeting certain age and service requirements. The plans provide for company-matching contributions, which are subject to annual approval by our Board. The total matching contributions were $14, $13 and $13 in fiscal 2005, 2004 and 2003, respectively.

9. Income Taxes

Income tax expense was comprised of the following for the past three fiscal years:

	2005	2004	2003
Current:			
Federal	$502	$456	$375
State	36	49	51
Foreign	(1)	5	3
	537	510	429
Deferred:			
Federal	(4)	(9)	(22)
State	(20)	(1)	(3)
Foreign	(4)	(4)	(12)
	(28)	(14)	(37)
Income tax expense	$509	$496	$392

Deferred taxes are the result of differences between the bases of assets and liabilities for financial reporting and income tax purposes.

10. Segments

We operate two reportable segments: Domestic and International. The Domestic segment is comprised of U.S. Best Buy and Magnolia Audio Video operations. The International segment is comprised of Future Shop and Best Buy operations in Canada. Our segments are evaluated on an operating income basis, and a stand-alone tax provision is not calculated for each segment.

The following table presents our business segment information for continuing operations.

	2005
Revenue	
Domestic	$24,616
International	2,817
Total revenue	$27,433
Operating Income	
Domestic	$ 1,393
International	49
Total operating income	1,442
Net interest income (expense)	1
Earnings from continuing operations before income tax expense	$ 1,443
Assets	
Domestic	$ 8,372
International	1,922
Total assets	$10,294

$ in millions, except per share amounts

11. Contingencies and Commitments

Contingencies

We are involved in various other legal proceedings arising in the normal course of conducting business. We believe the amounts provided in our consolidated financial statements, as prescribed by GAAP, are adequate in light of the probable and estimable liabilities. The resolution of those proceedings is not expected to have a material impact on our results of operation or financial condition.

Commitments

In 2004, we engaged Accenture LLP to assist us with improving our operational capabilities and reducing our costs in the Human Resources and Information Systems areas. Our future contractual obligations to Accenture are expected to range from $124 to $235 per year through 2011, the end of the contract period. Prior to our engagement of Accenture, a significant portion of these costs were incurred as part of normal operations.

We had outstanding letters of credit for purchase obligations with a fair value of $92 as of February 26, 2005.

As of February 26, 2005, we had commitments for the purchase and construction of facilities valued at approximately $83. Also, as of February 26, 2005, we had entered into lease commitments for land and buildings for 73 future locations. These lease commitments with real estate developers provide for minimum rentals ranging from 10 to 20 years, which if consummated based on current cost estimates, will approximate $53 annually over the lease terms.

We assumed a liability for certain extended service contracts when we acquired Future Shop in fiscal 2002. We established an accrued liability for the acquired extended service contracts based on historical trends in product failure rates and the expected material and labor costs necessary to provide the services. The remaining terms of these acquired extended service contracts vary by product and extend through fiscal 2007. The estimated remaining liability for acquired extended service contracts at February 26, 2005, was $9. Subsequent to the acquisition, all new extended service contracts were sold on behalf of an unrelated third party, without recourse.

Financial Report

CONSOLIDATED BALANCE SHEETS

(Amounts in thousands except share data)	At February 28 or 29 2005	2004
ASSETS		
CURRENT ASSETS:		
Cash and cash equivalents	$ 879,660	$ 783,471
Short-term investments	125,325	–
Accounts receivable, net of allowance for doubtful accounts of $120 and $547	172,995	170,568
Retained interests in securitized receivables	–	425,678
Merchandise inventory	1,459,520	1,517,256
Deferred income taxes	29,518	–
Prepaid expenses and other current assets	18,697	22,088
TOTAL CURRENT ASSETS	2,685,715	2,919,061
Property and equipment, net	738,802	677,107
Deferred income taxes	73,558	88,146
Goodwill	215,884	–
Other intangible assets	31,331	–
Other assets	44,092	46,212
TOTAL ASSETS	$3,789,382	$3,730,526
LIABILITIES AND STOCKHOLDERS' EQUITY		
CURRENT LIABILITIES:		
Accounts payable	$ 961,718	$ 833,825
Accrued expenses and other current liabilities	228,966	149,605
Accrued income taxes	72,274	71,163
Deferred income taxes	–	79,422
Current installments of long-term debt	888	1,115
Liabilities of discontinued operations	–	3,068
TOTAL CURRENT LIABILITIES	1,263,846	1,138,198
Long-term debt, excluding current installments	11,522	22,691
Accrued straight-line rent and deferred rent credits	230,426	206,784
Accrued lease termination costs	104,234	75,722
Other liabilities	91,920	63,170
TOTAL LIABILITIES	1,701,948	1,506,565
STOCKHOLDERS' EQUITY:		
Common stock, $0.50 par value; 525,000,000 shares authorized; 188,150,383 shares issued and outstanding (203,899,395 in 2004)	94,075	101,950
Capital in excess of par value	721,038	922,600
Retained earnings	1,247,221	1,199,411
Accumulated other comprehensive income	25,100	–
TOTAL STOCKHOLDERS' EQUITY	2,087,434	2,223,961
Commitments and contingent liabilities [NOTES 12, 13 AND 16]		
TOTAL LIABILITIES AND STOCKHOLDERS' EQUITY	$3,789,382	$3,730,526

See accompanying notes to consolidated financial statements.

CIRCUIT CITY

CONSOLIDATED STATEMENTS OF OPERATIONS

(Amounts in thousands except per share data)	2005	%	2004	%	2003	%
NET SALES AND OPERATING REVENUES	$10,472,364	100.0	$9,857,057	100.0	$10,054,864	100.0
Cost of sales, buying and warehousing	7,903,641	75.5	7,573,049	76.8	7,647,992	76.1
GROSS PROFIT	2,568,723	24.5	2,284,008	23.2	2,406,872	23.9
Finance income	5,564	0.1	32,693	0.3	27,292	0.3
Selling, general and administrative expenses	2,457,032	23.5	2,277,479	23.1	2,385,310	23.7
Stock-based compensation expense	19,400	0.2	38,658	0.4	53,251	0.5
Interest expense	2,066	–	1,804	–	1,093	–
Earnings (loss) from continuing operations before income taxes	95,789	0.9	(1,240)	–	(5,490)	(0.1)
Income tax provision (benefit)	35,878	0.3	(453)	–	(181)	–
NET EARNINGS (LOSS) FROM CONTINUING OPERATIONS	59,911	0.6	(787)	–	(5,309)	(0.1)
NET EARNINGS (LOSS) FROM DISCONTINUED OPERATIONS	1,747	–	(88,482)	(0.9)	87,572	0.9
NET EARNINGS (LOSS)	$ 61,658	0.6	$ (89,269)	(0.9)	$ 82,263	0.8
Net earnings (loss) from discontinued operations attributed to:						
Circuit City common stock	$ 1,747		$ (88,482)		$ 65,264	
CarMax Group common stock	$ –		$ –		$ 22,308	
Weighted average common shares:						
Circuit City:						
Basic	193,466		205,865		207,217	
Diluted	196,227		205,865		207,217	
CarMax Group:						
Basic	–		–		37,023	
Diluted	–		–		38,646	
NET EARNINGS (LOSS) PER SHARE:						
Basic:						
Continuing operations	$ 0.31		$ –		$ (0.03)	
Discontinued operations attributed to Circuit City common stock	0.01		(0.43)		0.31	
	$ 0.32		$ (0.43)		$ 0.29	
Discontinued operations attributed to CarMax Group common stock	$ –		$ –		$ 0.60	
Diluted:						
Continuing operations	$ 0.31		$ –		$ (0.03)	
Discontinued operations attributed to Circuit City common stock	0.01		(0.43)		0.31	
	$ 0.31		$ (0.43)		$ 0.29	
Discontinued operations attributed to CarMax Group common stock	$ –		$ –		$ 0.58	

Years Ended February 28 or 29

See accompanying notes to consolidated financial statements.

CIRCUIT CITY

CONSOLIDATED STATEMENTS OF STOCKHOLDERS' EQUITY AND COMPREHENSIVE INCOME

(Amounts in thousands except per share data)	Shares Outstanding Circuit City	CarMax Group	Common Stock Circuit City	CarMax Group	Capital In Excess of Par Value	Retained Earnings	Accumulated Other Comprehensive Income	Total
BALANCE AT FEBRUARY 28, 2002	208,823	36,851	$104,411	$ 18,426	$893,537	$1,744,129	$ —	$2,760,503
Net earnings and comprehensive income	—	—	—	—	—	82,263	—	82,263
Compensation for stock options	—	—	—	—	34,637	—	—	34,637
Exercise of common stock options	311	246	156	123	5,035	—	—	5,314
Shares issued under employee stock purchase plans	457	—	229	—	7,400	—	—	7,629
Shares issued under stock incentive plans	843	—	421	—	17,207	—	—	17,628
Tax effect from stock issued	—	—	—	—	5,986	—	—	5,986
Cancellation of restricted stock	(479)	(8)	(240)	(4)	(8,081)	—	—	(8,325)
Unearned compensation restricted stock	—	—	—	—	9,830	—	—	9,830
Cash dividends — common stock ($0.07 per share)	—	—	—	—	—	(14,687)	—	(14,687)
Distribution of CarMax, Inc. common stock to stockholders	—	(37,089)	—	(18,545)	—	(536,765)	—	(555,310)
Special dividend from CarMax	—	—	—	—	—	28,400	—	28,400
BALANCE AT FEBRUARY 28, 2003	209,955	—	104,977	—	965,551	1,303,340	—	2,373,868
Net loss and comprehensive loss	—	—	—	—	—	(89,269)	—	(89,269)
Repurchases of common stock	(9,266)	—	(4,633)	—	(79,720)	—	—	(84,353)
Compensation for stock options	—	—	—	—	24,184	—	—	24,184
Exercise of common stock options	1,369	—	685	—	11,843	—	—	12,528
Shares issued under stock incentive plans	2,546	—	1,273	—	19,312	—	—	20,585
Tax effect from stock issued	—	—	—	—	(10,595)	—	—	(10,595)
Cancellation of restricted stock	(705)	—	(352)	—	(10,074)	—	—	(10,426)
Unearned compensation restricted stock	—	—	—	—	2,099	—	—	2,099
Cash dividends — common stock ($0.07 per share)	—	—	—	—	—	(14,660)	—	(14,660)
BALANCE AT FEBRUARY 29, 2004	203,899	—	101,950	—	922,600	1,199,411	—	2,223,961
Comprehensive income:								
Net earnings	—	—	—	—	—	61,658	—	61,658
Other comprehensive income, net of taxes:								
Foreign currency translation adjustment (net of deferred taxes of $13,707)	—	—	—	—	—	—	25,100	25,100
Comprehensive income								86,758
Repurchases of common stock	(19,163)	—	(9,582)	—	(250,250)	—	—	(259,832)
Compensation for stock options	—	—	—	—	18,739	—	—	18,739
Exercise of common stock options	3,489	—	1,745	—	26,761	—	—	28,506
Shares issued under stock incentive plans	723	—	361	—	7,393	—	—	7,754
Tax effect from stock issued	—	—	—	—	(1,564)	—	—	(1,564)
Cancellation of restricted stock	(798)	—	(399)	—	(6,378)	—	—	(6,777)
Shares issued in acquisition of InterTAN, Inc.	—	—	—	—	6,498	—	—	6,498
Unearned compensation restricted stock	—	—	—	—	(2,761)	—	—	(2,761)
Cash dividends — common stock ($0.07 per share)	—	—	—	—	—	(13,848)	—	(13,848)
BALANCE AT FEBRUARY 28, 2005	188,150	—	$ 94,075	$ —	$721,038	$1,247,221	$25,100	$2,087,434

See accompanying notes to consolidated financial statements.

CONSOLIDATED STATEMENTS OF CASH FLOWS

(Amounts in thousands)	2005	2004	2003
		Years Ended February 28 or 29	
OPERATING ACTIVITIES:			
Net earnings (loss)	$ **61,658**	$ (89,269)	$ 82,263
Adjustments to reconcile net earnings (loss) to net cash provided by (used in) operating activities of continuing operations:			
Net (earnings) loss from discontinued operations	**(1,747)**	88,482	(87,572)
Depreciation and amortization	**154,788**	197,607	159,800
Stock option expense	**18,739**	24,184	30,823
Amortization of restricted stock awards	**(434)**	13,395	20,828
(Gain) loss on dispositions of property and equipment	**(206)**	7,500	15,659
Provision for deferred income taxes	**(116,455)**	(35,618)	(18,664)
Changes in operating assets and liabilities:			
(Increase) decrease in accounts receivable, net	**(65,112)**	(30,183)	6,229
Decrease (increase) in retained interests in securitized receivables	**32,867**	(186,537)	(92,888)
Decrease (increase) in merchandise inventory	**159,278**	(107,520)	(175,493)
Decrease (increase) in prepaid expenses and other current assets	**7,148**	(3,923)	21,081
Decrease (increase) in other assets	**3,925**	12,553	(26,181)
Increase (decrease) in accounts payable	**101,991**	(85,727)	(58,041)
Increase (decrease) in accrued expenses and other current liabilities, and accrued income taxes	**36,008**	50,577	(48,069)
Increase in other long-term liabilities	**63,549**	18,966	7,116
NET CASH PROVIDED BY (USED IN) OPERATING ACTIVITIES OF CONTINUING OPERATIONS	**455,879**	(125,513)	(163,109)
INVESTING ACTIVITIES:			
Proceeds from the sale of the private-label operation	**475,857**	–	–
Acquisitions, net of cash acquired of $30,615	**(268,774)**	–	–
Purchases of property and equipment	**(269,166)**	(175,769)	(150,757)
Proceeds from sales of property and equipment	**106,369**	40,427	59,888
Purchases of investment securities	**(125,325)**	–	–
NET CASH USED IN INVESTING ACTIVITIES OF CONTINUING OPERATIONS	**(81,039)**	(135,342)	(90,869)
FINANCING ACTIVITIES:			
Payments on short-term debt	**(1,853)**	–	(397)
Principal payments on long-term debt	**(28,008)**	(1,458)	(24,865)
Repurchases of common stock	**(259,832)**	(84,353)	–
Issuances of Circuit City common stock, net	**27,156**	11,391	8,901
Issuances of CarMax Group common stock, net	–	–	298
Dividends paid	**(13,848)**	(14,660)	(14,687)
NET CASH USED IN FINANCING ACTIVITIES OF CONTINUING OPERATIONS	**(276,385)**	(89,080)	(30,750)
CASH (USED IN) PROVIDED BY DISCONTINUED OPERATIONS:			
BANKCARD OPERATION	**(4,282)**	248,736	(94,533)
CARMAX OPERATION	–	–	26,185
DIVX OPERATION	–	–	(10,500)
EFFECT OF EXCHANGE RATE CHANGES ON CASH	**2,016**	–	–
Increase (decrease) in cash and cash equivalents	**96,189**	(101,199)	(363,576)
Cash and cash equivalents at beginning of year	**783,471**	884,670	1,248,246
CASH AND CASH EQUIVALENTS AT END OF YEAR	$ **879,660**	$ 783,471	$ 884,670

See accompanying notes to consolidated financial statements.

CIRCUIT CITY

CONSOLIDATED BALANCE SHEETS

(In millions, except share amounts)

	September 25, 2004	September 27, 2003
ASSETS:		
Current assets:		
Cash and cash equivalents	$2,969	$3,396
Short-term investments	2,495	1,170
Accounts receivable, less allowances of $47 and $49, respectively	774	766
Inventories	101	56
Deferred tax assets	231	190
Other current assets	485	309
Total current assets	7,055	5,887
Property, plant, and equipment, net	707	669
Goodwill	80	85
Acquired intangible assets	17	24
Other assets	191	150
Total assets	$8,050	$6,815
LIABILITIES AND SHAREHOLDERS' EQUITY:		
Current liabilities:		
Accounts payable	$1,451	$1,154
Accrued expenses	1,229	899
Current debt	—	304
Total current liabilities	2,680	2,357
Deferred tax liabilities and other non-current liabilities	294	235
Total liabilities	2,974	2,592
Shareholders' equity:		
Common stock, no par value; 900,000,000 shares authorized; 391,443,617 and 366,726,584 shares issued and outstanding, respectively	2,514	1,926
Deferred stock compensation	(93)	(62)
Retained earnings	2,670	2,394
Accumulated other comprehensive income (loss)	(15)	(35)
Total shareholders' equity	5,076	4,223
Total liabilities and shareholders' equity	$8,050	$6,815

See accompanying notes to consolidated financial statements.

CONSOLIDATED STATEMENTS OF OPERATIONS
(In millions, except share and per share amounts)

Three fiscal years ended September 25, 2004	2004	2003	2002
Net sales	$ 8,279	$ 6,207	$ 5,742
Cost of sales	6,020	4,499	4,139
Gross margin	2,259	1,708	1,603
Operating expenses:			
Rescarch and development	489	471	446
Selling, general, and administrative	1,421	1,212	1,109
Restructuring costs	23	26	30
Purchased in-process research and development	—	—	1
Total operating expenses	1,933	1,709	1,586
Operating income (loss)	326	(1)	17
Other income and expense:			
Gains (losses) on non-current investments, net	4	10	(42)
Interest and other income, net	53	83	112
Total other income and expense	57	93	70
Income before provision for income taxes	383	92	87
Provision for income taxes	107	24	22
Income before accounting changes	276	68	65
Cumulative effects of accounting changes, net of income taxes	—	1	—
Net income	$ 276	$ 69	$ 65
Earnings per common share before accounting changes:			
Basic	$ 0.74	$ 0.19	$ 0.18
Diluted	$ 0.71	$ 0.19	$ 0.18
Earnings per common share:			
Basic	$ 0.74	$ 0.19	$ 0.18
Diluted	$ 0.71	$ 0.19	$ 0.18
Shares used in computing earnings per share (in thousands):			
Basic	371,590	360,631	355,022
Diluted	387,311	363,466	361,785

See accompanying notes to consolidated financial statements.

CONSOLIDATED STATEMENTS OF SHAREHOLDERS' EQUITY

(In millions, except share amounts which are in thousands)

	Common Stock		Deferred Stock Compensation	Retained Earnings	Accumulated Other Comprehensive Income (Loss)	Total Shareholders' Equity
	Shares	Amount				
Balances as of September 29, 2001	350,922	$1,693	$(11)	$2,260	$(22)	$3,920
Components of comprehensive income:						
Net income	—	—	—	65	—	65
Change in foreign currency translation . .	—	—	—	—	5	5
Change in unrealized gain on available-for-sale securities, net of tax	—	—	—	—	(17)	(17)
Change in unrealized gain on derivative investments, net of tax	—	—	—	—	(15)	(15)
Total comprehensive income						38
Amortization of deferred stock compensation	—	—	4	—	—	4
Common stock issued under stock plans . .	8,037	105	—	—	—	105
Tax benefit related to stock options	—	28	—	—	—	28
Balances as of September 28, 2002	358,959	$1,826	$ (7)	$2,325	$(49)	$4,095
Components of comprehensive income:						
Net income	—	—	—	69	—	69
Change in foreign currency translation . .	—	—	—	—	31	31
Change in unrealized gain on available-for-sale securities, net of tax	—	—	—	—	(12)	(12)
Change in unrealized gain on derivative investments, net of tax	—	—	—	—	(5)	(5)
Total comprehensive income						83
Amortization of deferred stock compensation	—	—	15	—	—	15
Write-off of deferred stock compensation .	—	—	5	—	—	5
Common stock issued under stock plans . .	9,299	128	(75)	—	—	53
Settlement of forward purchase agreement .	(1,531)	(35)	—	—	—	(35)
Tax benefit related to stock options	—	7	—	—	—	7
Balances as of September 27, 2003	366,727	$1,926	$(62)	$2,394	$(35)	$4,223
Components of comprehensive income:						
Net income	—	—	—	276	—	276
Change in foreign currency translation . .	—	—	—	—	13	13
Change in unrealized gain on available-for-sale securities, net of tax	—	—	—	—	(5)	(5)
Change in unrealized loss on derivative investments, net of tax	—	—	—	—	12	12
Total comprehensive income						296
Issuance of restricted stock units	—	64	(64)	—	—	—
Adjustment to common stock related to a prior year acquisition	(79)	(2)	—	—	—	(2)
Amortization of deferred stock compensation	—	—	33	—	—	33
Common stock issued under stock plans . .	24,796	427	—	—	—	427
Tax benefit related to stock options	—	99	—	—	—	99
Balances as of September 25, 2004	391,444	$2,514	$(93)	$2,670	$(15)	$5,076

See accompanying notes to consolidated financial statements.

CONSOLIDATED STATEMENTS OF CASH FLOWS

(In millions)

Three fiscal years ended September 25, 2004	2004	2003	2002
Cash and cash equivalents, beginning of the year............	$ 3,396	$ 2,252	$ 2,310
Operating Activities:			
Net income.......................................	276	69	65
Cumulative effects of accounting changes, net of taxes...........	—	(1)	—
Adjustments to reconcile net income to cash generated by operating activities:			
Depreciation, amortization and accretion..................	150	113	114
Stock-based compensation expense	33	16	5
Non-cash restructuring	5	12	8
Provision for (benefit from) deferred income taxes............	20	(11)	(34)
Loss on disposition of property, plant, and equipment	7	2	7
Gains on sales of short-term investments, net	(1)	(21)	(7)
(Gains) losses on non-current investments, net..............	(4)	(10)	42
Gain on forward purchase agreement	—	(6)	—
Purchased in-process research and development..............	—	—	1
Changes in operating assets and liabilities:			
Accounts receivable	(8)	(201)	(99)
Inventories	(45)	(11)	(34)
Other current assets.............................	(176)	(34)	(114)
Other assets..................................	(39)	(30)	(11)
Accounts payable	297	243	110
Other liabilities	419	159	36
Cash generated by operating activities	934	289	89
Investing Activities:			
Purchases of short-term investments	(3,270)	(2,648)	(4,144)
Proceeds from maturities of short-term investments............	1,141	2,446	2,846
Proceeds from sales of short-term investments..............	801	1,116	1,254
Proceeds from sales of non-current investments.............	5	45	25
Purchases of property, plant, and equipment	(176)	(164)	(174)
Cash used for business acquisitions....................	—	—	(52)
Other.......................................	11	33	(7)
Cash generated by (used for) investing activities	(1,488)	828	(252)
Financing Activities:			
Payment of long-term debt..........................	(300)	—	—
Proceeds from issuance of common stock	427	53	105
Cash used for repurchase of common stock................	—	(26)	—
Cash generated by financing activities	127	27	105
Increase (decrease) in cash and cash equivalents	(427)	1,144	(58)
Cash and cash equivalents, end of the year	$ 2,969	$ 3,396	$ 2,252
Supplemental cash flow disclosures:			
Cash paid during the year for interest	$ 10	$ 20	$ 20
Cash paid (received) for income taxes, net................	$ (7)	$ 45	$ 11

See accompanying notes to consolidated financial statements.

B

Time Value of Money

CAP

Conceptual

C1 Describe the earning of interest and the concepts of present and future values. *(p. B-2)*

Procedural

P1 Apply present value concepts to a single amount by using interest tables. *(p. B-3)*

P2 Apply future value concepts to a single amount by using interest tables. *(p. B-5)*

P3 Apply present value concepts to an annuity by using interest tables. *(p. B-6)*

P4 Apply future value concepts to an annuity by using interest tables. *(p. B-7)*

Appendix Preview

The concepts of present and future values are important to modern business activity. The purpose of this appendix is to explain, illustrate, and compute present and future values. This appendix applies these concepts with reference to both business and everyday activities.

Present and Future Value Concepts

C1 Describe the earning of interest and the concepts of present and future values.

The old saying "Time is money" reflects the notion that as time passes, the values of our assets and liabilities change. This change is due to *interest,* which is a borrower's payment to the owner of an asset for its use. The most common example of interest is a savings account asset. As we keep a balance of cash in the account, it earns interest that the financial institution pays us. An example of a liability is a car loan. As we carry the balance of the loan, we accumulate interest costs on it. We must ultimately repay this loan with interest.

Present and future value computations enable us to measure or estimate the interest component of holding assets or liabilities over time. The present value computation is important when we want to know the value of future-day assets *today.* The future value computation is important when we want to know the value of present-day assets *at a future date.* The first section focuses on the present value of a single amount. The second section focuses on the future value of a single amount. Then both the present and future values of a series of amounts (called an *annuity*) are defined and explained.

Present Value of a Single Amount

We graphically express the present value, called p, of a single future amount, called f, that is received or paid at a future date in Exhibit B.1.

Exhibit B.1

Present Value of a Single Amount Diagram

The formula to compute the present value of a single amount is shown in Exhibit B.2, where p = present value; f = future value; i = rate of interest per period; and n = number of periods. (Interest is also called the *discount,* and an interest rate is also called the *discount rate.*)

Exhibit B.2

Present Value of a Single Amount Formula

$$p = \frac{f}{(1 + i)^n}$$

To illustrate present value concepts, assume that we need $220 one period from today. We want to know how much we must invest now, for one period, at an interest rate of 10% to provide for this $220. For this illustration, the p, or present value, is the unknown amount—the specifics are shown graphically as follows:

Conceptually, we know p must be less than $220. This is obvious from the answer to this question: Would we rather have $220 today or $220 at some future date? If we had $220 today, we could invest it and see it grow to something more than $220 in the future. Therefore, we would prefer the $220 today. This means that if we were promised $220 in the future, we would take less than $220 today. But how much less? To answer that question, we compute an estimate of the present value of the $220 to be received one period from now using the formula in Exhibit B.2 as follows:

$$p = \frac{f}{(1 + i)^n} = \frac{\$220}{(1 + 0.10)^1} = \$200$$

We interpret this result to say that given an interest rate of 10%, we are indifferent between $200 today or $220 at the end of one period.

We can also use this formula to compute the present value for *any number of periods*. To illustrate, consider a payment of $242 at the end of two periods at 10% interest. The present value of this $242 to be received two periods from now is computed as follows:

$$p = \frac{f}{(1 + i)^n} = \frac{\$242}{(1 + 0.10)^2} = \$200$$

Together, these results tell us we are indifferent between $200 today, or $220 one period from today, or $242 two periods from today given a 10% interest rate per period.

The number of periods (n) in the present value formula does not have to be expressed in years. Any period of time such as a day, a month, a quarter, or a year can be used. Whatever period is used, the interest rate (i) must be compounded for the same period. This means that if a situation expresses n in months and i equals 12% per year, then i is transformed into interest earned per month (or 1%). In this case, interest is said to be *compounded monthly.*

A present value table helps us with present value computations. It gives us present values (factors) for a variety of both interest rates (i) and periods (n). Each present value in a present value table assumes that the future value (f) equals 1. When the future value (f) is different from 1, we simply multiply the present value (p) from the table by that future value to give us the estimate. The formula used to construct a table of present values for a single future amount of 1 is shown in Exhibit B.3.

$$p = \frac{1}{(1 + i)^n}$$

Exhibit B.3

Present Value of 1 Formula

This formula is identical to that in Exhibit B.2 except that f equals 1. Table B.1 at the end of this appendix is such a present value table. It is often called a **present value of 1 table**. A present value table involves three factors: p, i, and n. Knowing two of these three factors allows us to compute the third. (A fourth is f, but as already explained, we need only multiply the 1 used in the formula by f.) To illustrate the use of a present value table, consider three cases.

P1   Apply present value concepts to a single amount by using interest tables.

Case 1 (solve for p when knowing i and n). To show how we use a present value table, let's look again at how we estimate the present value of $220 (the f value) at the end of one period ($n = 1$) where the interest rate (i) is 10%. To solve this case, we go to the present value table (Table B.1) and look in the row for 1 period and in the column for 10% interest. Here we find a present value (p) of 0.9091 based on a future value of 1. This means, for instance, that $1 to be received one period from today at 10% interest is worth $0.9091 today. Since the future value in this case is not $1 but $220, we multiply the 0.9091 by $220 to get an answer of $200.

Case 2 (solve for n when knowing p and i). To illustrate, assume a $100,000 future value ($f$) that is worth $13,000 today ($p$) using an interest rate of 12% (i) but where n is unknown. In particular, we want to know how many periods (n) there are between the present value and the future value. To put this in context, it would fit a situation in which we want to retire with $100,000 but currently have only $13,000 that is earning a 12% return. How long will it be before we can retire? To answer this, we go to Table B.1 and look in the 12% interest column. Here we find a column of present values (p) based on a future value of 1. To use the present value table for this solution, we must divide $13,000 ($p$) by $100,000 ($f$), which equals 0.1300. This is necessary because *a present value table defines* f *equal to 1, and* p *as a fraction of 1.* We look for a value nearest to 0.1300 (p), which we find in the row for 18 periods (n). This means that the present value of $100,000 at the end of 18 periods at 12% interest is $13,000 or, alternatively stated, we must work 18 more years.

Case 3 (solve for i when knowing p and n). In this case, we have, say, a $120,000 future value ($f$) worth $60,000 today ($p$) when there are nine periods (n) between the present and future values, but the interest rate is unknown. As an example, suppose we want to retire with $120,000, but we have only $60,000 and hope to retire in nine years. What interest rate must we earn to retire with $120,000 in nine years? To answer this, we go to the present value table (Table B.1) and look in the row for nine periods. To use the present value table, we must divide $60,000 ($p$) by $120,000 ($f$), which equals 0.5000. Recall that this step is necessary because a present value table defines f equal to 1 and p as a fraction of 1. We look for a value in the row for nine periods that is nearest to 0.5000 (p), which we find in the column for 8% interest (i). This means that the present value of $120,000 at the end of nine periods at 8% interest is $60,000 or, in our example, we must earn 8% annual interest to retire in nine years.

Decision Insight

Keep That Job   Lottery winners often never work again. Kenny Dukes, a recent Georgia lottery winner, doesn't have that option. He is serving parole for burglary charges, and Georgia requires its parolees to be employed (or in school). Dukes had to choose between $31 million in 30 annual payments or $16 million in one lump sum ($10.6 million after-tax); he chose the latter.

Quick Check   Answer—p. B-8

1. A company is considering an investment expected to yield $70,000 after six years. If this company demands an 8% return, how much is it willing to pay for this investment?

Future Value of a Single Amount

We must modify the formula for the present value of a single amount to obtain the formula for the future value of a single amount. In particular, we multiply both sides of the equation in Exhibit B.2 by $(1 + i)^n$ to get the result shown in Exhibit B.4.

Exhibit B.4

Future Value of a Single
Amount Formula

$$f = p \times (1 + i)^n$$

The future value (f) is defined in terms of p, i, and n. We can use this formula to determine that $200 ($p$) invested for 1 ($n$) period at an interest rate of 10% (i) yields a future value of

$220 as follows:

$$f = p \times (1 + i)^n$$
$$= \$200 \times (1 + 0.10)^1$$
$$= \$220$$

This formula can also be used to compute the future value of an amount for *any number of periods* into the future. To illustrate, assume that $200 is invested for three periods at 10%. The future value of this $200 is $266.20, computed as follows:

$$f = p \times (1 + i)^n$$
$$= \$200 \times (1 + 0.10)^3$$
$$= \$266.20$$

A future value table makes it easier for us to compute future values (f) for many different combinations of interest rates (i) and time periods (n). Each future value in a future value table assumes the present value (p) is 1. As with a present value table, if the future amount is something other than 1, we simply multiply our answer by that amount. The formula used to construct a table of future values (factors) for a single amount of 1 is in Exhibit B.5.

P2 **Apply future value concepts to a single amount by using interest tables.**

$$f = (1 + i)^n$$

Exhibit B.5

Future Value of 1 Formula

Table B.2 at the end of this appendix shows a table of future values for a current amount of 1. This type of table is called a **future value of 1 table**.

There are some important relations between Tables B.1 and B.2. In Table B.2, for the row where $n = 0$, the future value is 1 for each interest rate. This is so because no interest is earned when time does not pass. Also notice that Tables B.1 and B.2 report the same information but in a different manner. In particular, one table is simply the *inverse* of the other. To illustrate this inverse relation, let's say we invest $100 annually for a period of five years at 12% per year. How much do we expect to have after five years? We can answer this question using Table B.2 by finding the future value (f) of 1, for five periods from now, compounded at 12%. From that table we find $f = 1.7623$. If we start with $100, the amount it accumulates to after five years is $176.23 ($100 \times 1.7623$). We can alternatively use Table B.1. Here we find that the present value (p) of 1, discounted five periods at 12%, is 0.5674. Recall the inverse relation between present value and future value. This means that $p = 1/f$ (or equivalently, $f = 1/p$). We can compute the future value of $100 invested for five periods at 12% as follows: $f = \$100 \times (1/0.5674) = \$176.24$.

A future value table involves three factors: f, i, and n. Knowing two of these three factors allows us to compute the third. To illustrate, consider these three possible cases.

Case 1 (solve for f when knowing i and n). Our preceding example fits this case. We found that $100 invested for five periods at 12% interest accumulates to $176.24.

Case 2 (solve for n when knowing f and i). In this case, we have, say, $2,000 ($p$) and we want to know how many periods (n) it will take to accumulate to $3,000 ($f$) at 7% ($i$) interest. To answer this, we go to the future value table (Table B.2) and look in the 7% interest column. Here we find a column of future values (f) based on a present value of 1. To use a future value table, we must divide $3,000 ($f$) by $2,000 ($p$), which equals 1.500. This is necessary because *a future value table defines* p *equal to 1, and* f *as a multiple of 1*. We look for a value nearest to 1.50 (f), which we find in the row for six periods (n). This means that $2,000 invested for six periods at 7% interest accumulates to $3,000.

Case 3 (solve for i when knowing f and n). In this case, we have, say, $2,001 ($p$) and in nine years ($n$), we want to have $4,000 ($f$). What rate of interest must we earn to accomplish this? To answer that, we go to Table B.2 and search in the row for nine periods. To use a future value table, we must divide $4,000 ($f$) by $2,001 ($p$), which equals 1.9990. Recall that this is necessary because a future value table defines p equal to 1 and f as a multiple of 1. We look for a value nearest to 1.9990 (f), which we find in the column for 8% interest (i). This means that $2,001 invested for nine periods at 8% interest accumulates to $4,000.

| **Quick Check** | Answer—p. B-8 |

2. Assume that you win a $150,000 cash sweepstakes. You decide to deposit this cash in an account earning 8% annual interest, and you plan to quit your job when the account equals $555,000. How many years will it be before you can quit working?

Present Value of an Annuity

An *annuity* is a series of equal payments occurring at equal intervals. One example is a series of three annual payments of $100 each. An *ordinary annuity* is defined as equal end-of-period payments at equal intervals. An ordinary annuity of $100 for 3 periods and its present value (p) are illustrated in Exhibit B.6.

Exhibit B.6

Present Value of an Ordinary Annuity Diagram

P3 Apply present value concepts to an annuity by using interest tables.

One way to compute the present value of an ordinary annuity is to find the present value of each payment using our present value formula from Exhibit B.3. We then add each of the three present values. To illustrate, let's look at three $100 payments at the end of each of the next three periods with an interest rate of 15%. Our present value computations are

$$p = \frac{\$100}{(1 + 0.15)^1} + \frac{\$100}{(1 + 0.15)^2} + \frac{\$100}{(1 + 0.15)^3} = \$228.32$$

This computation is identical to computing the present value of each payment (from Table B.1) and taking their sum or, alternatively, adding the values from Table B.1 for each of the three payments and multiplying their sum by the $100 annuity payment.

A more direct way is to use a present value of annuity table. Table B.3 at the end of this appendix is one such table. This table is called a **present value of an annuity of 1 table**. If we look at Table B.3 where $n = 3$ and $i = 15\%$, we see the present value is 2.2832. This means that the present value of an annuity of 1 for three periods, with a 15% interest rate, equals 2.2832.

A present value of an annuity formula is used to construct Table B.3. It can also be constructed by adding the amounts in a present value of 1 table. To illustrate, we use Tables B.1 and B.3 to confirm this relation for the prior example:

From Table B.1		From Table B.3	
$i = 15\%, n = 1$	0.8696		
$i = 15\%, n = 2$	0.7561		
$i = 15\%, n = 3$	0.6575		
Total	2.2832	$i = 15\%, n = 3$	2.2832

We can also use business calculators or spreadsheet programs to find the present value of an annuity.

Quick Check   Answer—p. B-8

3. A company is considering an investment paying $10,000 every six months for three years. The first payment would be received in six months. If this company requires an 8% annual return, what is the maximum amount it is willing to pay for this investment?

Future Value of an Annuity

The future value of an *ordinary annuity* is the accumulated value of each annuity payment with interest as of the date of the final payment. To illustrate, let's consider the earlier annuity of three annual payments of $100. Exhibit B.7 shows the point in time for the future value (f). The first payment is made two periods prior to the point when future value is determined, and the final payment occurs on the future value date.

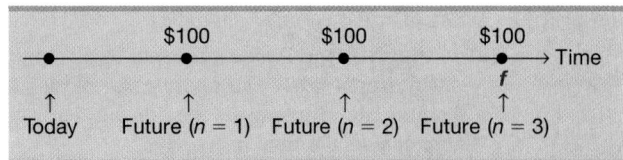

Exhibit B.7

Future Value of an Ordinary Annuity Diagram

One way to compute the future value of an annuity is to use the formula to find the future value of *each* payment and add them. If we assume an interest rate of 15%, our calculation is

$$f = \$100 \times (1 + 0.15)^2 + \$100 \times (1 + 0.15)^1 + \$100 \times (1 + 0.15)^0 = \$347.25$$

This is identical to using Table B.2 and summing the future values of each payment, or by adding the future values of the three payments of 1 and multiplying the sum by $100.

A more direct way is to use a table showing future values of annuities. Such a table is called a **future value of an annuity of 1 table**. Table B.4 at the end of this appendix is one such table. Note that in Table B.4 when $n = 1$, the future values equal 1 ($f = 1$) for all rates of interest. This is so because such an annuity consists of only one payment and the future value is determined on the date of that payment—no time passes between the payment and its future value. The future value of an annuity formula is used to construct Table B.4. We can also construct it by adding the amounts from a future value of 1 table. To illustrate, we use Tables B.2 and B.4 to confirm this relation for the prior example:

P4   Apply future value concepts to an annuity by using interest tables.

From Table B.2		From Table B.4	
$i = 15\%, n = 0$	1.0000		
$i = 15\%, n = 1$	1.1500		
$i = 15\%, n = 2$	1.3225		
Total	3.4725	$i = 15\%, n = 3$	3.4725

Note that the future value in Table B.2 is 1.0000 when $n = 0$, but the future value in Table B.4 is 1.0000 when $n = 1$. Is this a contradiction? No. When $n = 0$ in Table B.2, the future value is determined on the date when a single payment occurs. This means that no interest is earned because no time has passed, and the future value equals the payment. Table B.4 describes annuities with equal payments occurring at the end of each period. When $n = 1$, the annuity has one payment, and its future value equals 1 on the date of its final and only payment. Again, no time passes between the payment and its future value date.

Quick Check

Answer—p. B-8

4. A company invests $45,000 per year for five years at 12% annual interest. Compute the value of this annuity investment at the end of five years.

Summary

C1 Describe the earning of interest and the concepts of present and future values. Interest is payment by a borrower to the owner of an asset for its use. Present and future value computations are a way for us to estimate the interest component of holding assets or liabilities over a period of time.

P1 Apply present value concepts to a single amount by using interest tables. The present value of a single amount received at a future date is the amount that can be invested now at the specified interest rate to yield that future value.

P2 Apply future value concepts to a single amount by using interest tables. The future value of a single amount invested at a specified rate of interest is the amount that would accumulate by the future date.

P3 Apply present value concepts to an annuity by using interest tables. The present value of an annuity is the amount that can be invested now at the specified interest rate to yield that series of equal periodic payments.

P4 Apply future value concepts to an annuity by using interest tables. The future value of an annuity invested at a specific rate of interest is the amount that would accumulate by the date of the final payment.

Guidance Answers to **Quick Checks**

1. $70,000 × 0.6302 = $44,114 (use Table B.1, $i = 8\%$, $n = 6$).

2. $555,000/$150,000 = 3.7000; Table B.2 shows this value is not achieved until after 17 years at 8% interest.

3. $10,000 × 5.2421 = $52,421 (use Table B.3, $i = 4\%$, $n = 6$).

4. $45,000 × 6.3528 = $285,876 (use Table B.4, $i = 12\%$, $n = 5$).

QUICK STUDY

QS B-1

Identifying interest rates in tables

C1

Assume that you must make future value estimates using the *future value of 1 table* (Table B.2). Which interest rate column do you use when working with the following rates?

1. 8% compounded quarterly

2. 12% compounded annually

3. 6% compounded semiannually

4. 12% compounded monthly

QS B-2

Interest rate on an investment   P1

Ken Francis is offered the possibility of investing $2,745 today and in return to receive $10,000 after 15 years. What is the annual rate of interest for this investment? (Use Table B.1.)

QS B-3

Number of periods of an investment   P1

Megan Brink is offered the possibility of investing $6,651 today at 6% interest per year in a desire to accumulate $10,000. How many years must Brink wait to accumulate $10,000? (Use Table B.1.)

QS B-4

Present value of an amount   P1

Flaherty is considering an investment that, if paid for immediately, is expected to return $140,000 five years from now. If Flaherty demands a 9% return, how much is she willing to pay for this investment?

CII, Inc., invests $630,000 in a project expected to earn a 12% annual rate of return. The earnings will be reinvested in the project each year until the entire investment is liquidated 10 years later. What will the cash proceeds be when the project is liquidated?

QS B-5
Future value
of an amount P2

Beene Distributing is considering a project that will return $150,000 annually at the end of each year for six years. If Beene demands an annual return of 7% and pays for the project immediately, how much is it willing to pay for the project?

QS B-6
Present value
of an annuity P3

Claire Fitch is planning to begin an individual retirement program in which she will invest $1,500 at the end of each year. Fitch plans to retire after making 30 annual investments in the program earning a return of 10%. What is the value of the program on the date of the last payment?

QS B-7
Future value
of an annuity P4

Bill Thompson expects to invest $10,000 at 12% and, at the end of a certain period, receive $96,463. How many years will it be before Thompson receives the payment? (Use Table B.2.)

EXERCISES

Exercise B-1
Number of periods
of an investment P2

Ed Summers expects to invest $10,000 for 25 years, after which he wants to receive $108,347. What rate of interest must Summers earn? (Use Table B.2.)

Exercise B-2
Interest rate on
an investment P2

Jones expects an immediate investment of $57,466 to return $10,000 annually for eight years, with the first payment to be received one year from now. What rate of interest must Jones earn? (Use Table B.3.)

Exercise B-3
Interest rate on
an investment P3

Keith Riggins expects an investment of $82,014 to return $10,000 annually for several years. If Riggins earns a return of 10%, how many annual payments will he receive? (Use Table B.3.)

Exercise B-4
Number of periods
of an investment P3

Algoe expects to invest $1,000 annually for 40 years to yield an accumulated value of $154,762 on the date of the last investment. For this to occur, what rate of interest must Algoe earn? (Use Table B.4.)

Exercise B-5
Interest rate on
an investment P4

Kate Beckwith expects to invest $10,000 annually that will earn 8%. How many annual investments must Beckwith make to accumulate $303,243 on the date of the last investment? (Use Table B.4.)

Exercise B-6
Number of periods
of an investment P4

Sam Weber finances a new automobile by paying $6,500 cash and agreeing to make 40 monthly payments of $500 each, the first payment to be made one month after the purchase. The loan bears interest at an annual rate of 12%. What is the cost of the automobile?

Exercise B-7
Present value
of an annuity P3

Spiller Corp. plans to issue 10%, 15-year, $500,000 par value bonds payable that pay interest semiannually on June 30 and December 31. The bonds are dated December 31, 2008, and are issued on that date. If the market rate of interest for the bonds is 8% on the date of issue, what will be the total cash proceeds from the bond issue?

Exercise B-8
Present value of bonds

P1 P3

McAdams Company expects to earn 10% per year on an investment that will pay $606,773 six years from now. Use Table B.1 to compute the present value of this investment.

Exercise B-9
Present value
of an amount P1

Exercise B-10
Present value of
an amount and
of an annuity   P1 P3

Compute the amount that can be borrowed under each of the following circumstances:

1. A promise to repay $90,000 seven years from now at an interest rate of 6%.

2. An agreement made on February 1, 2008, to make three separate payments of $20,000 on February 1 of 2009, 2010, and 2011. The annual interest rate is 10%.

Exercise B-11
Present value
of an amount   P1

On January 1, 2008, a company agrees to pay $20,000 in three years. If the annual interest rate is 10%, determine how much cash the company can borrow with this agreement.

Exercise B-12
Present value
of an amount   P1

Find the amount of money that can be borrowed today with each of the following separate debt agreements *a* through *f*:

Case	Single Future Payment	Number of Periods	Interest Rate
a.	$40,000	3	4%
b.	75,000	7	8
c.	52,000	9	10
d.	18,000	2	4
e.	63,000	8	6
f.	89,000	5	2

Exercise B-13
Present values of annuities

P3

C&H Ski Club recently borrowed money and agrees to pay it back with a series of six annual payments of $5,000 each. C&H subsequently borrows more money and agrees to pay it back with a series of four annual payments of $7,500 each. The annual interest rate for both loans is 6%.

1. Use Table B.1 to find the present value of these two separate annuities. (Round amounts to the nearest dollar.)

2. Use Table B.3 to find the present value of these two separate annuities.

Exercise B-14
Present value with semiannual
compounding

C1 P3

Otto Co. borrows money on April 30, 2008, by promising to make four payments of $13,000 each on November 1, 2008; May 1, 2009; November 1, 2009; and May 1, 2010.

1. How much money is Otto able to borrow if the interest rate is 8%, compounded semiannually?

2. How much money is Otto able to borrow if the interest rate is 12%, compounded semiannually?

3. How much money is Otto able to borrow if the interest rate is 16%, compounded semiannually?

Exercise B-15
Future value
of an amount   P2

Mark Welsch deposits $7,200 in an account that earns interest at an annual rate of 8%, compounded quarterly. The $7,200 plus earned interest must remain in the account 10 years before it can be withdrawn. How much money will be in the account at the end of 10 years?

Exercise B-16
Future value
of an annuity   P4

Kelly Malone plans to have $50 withheld from her monthly paycheck and deposited in a savings account that earns 12% annually, compounded monthly. If Malone continues with her plan for two and one-half years, how much will be accumulated in the account on the date of the last deposit?

Exercise B-17
Future value of
an amount plus
an annuity   P2 P4

Starr Company decides to establish a fund that it will use 10 years from now to replace an aging production facility. The company will make a $100,000 initial contribution to the fund and plans to make quarterly contributions of $50,000 beginning in three months. The fund earns 12%, compounded quarterly. What will be the value of the fund 10 years from now?

Exercise B-18
Future value of
an amount   P2

Catten, Inc., invests $163,170 today earning 7% per year for nine years. Use Table B.2 to compute the future value of the investment nine years from now.

For each of the following situations, identify (1) the case as either (*a*) a present or a future value and (*b*) a single amount or an annuity, (2) the table you would use in your computations (but do not solve the problem), and (3) the interest rate and time periods you would use.

a. You need to accumulate $10,000 for a trip you wish to take in four years. You are able to earn 8% compounded semiannually on your savings. You plan to make only one deposit and let the money accumulate for four years. How would you determine the amount of the one-time deposit?

b. Assume the same facts as in part (*a*) except that you will make semiannual deposits to your savings account.

c. You want to retire after working 40 years with savings in excess of $1,000,000. You expect to save $4,000 a year for 40 years and earn an annual rate of interest of 8%. Will you be able to retire with more than $1,000,000 in 40 years? Explain.

d. A sweepstakes agency names you a grand prize winner. You can take $225,000 immediately or elect to receive annual installments of $30,000 for 20 years. You can earn 10% annually on any investments you make. Which prize do you choose to receive?

Exercise B-19
Using present and future value tables

C1   P1   P2   P3   P4

Table B.1

Present Value of 1

$$p = 1/(1 + i)^n$$

Periods	1%	2%	3%	4%	5%	6%	7%	8%	9%	10%	12%	15%
1	0.9901	0.9804	0.9709	0.9615	0.9524	0.9434	0.9346	0.9259	0.9174	0.9091	0.8929	0.8696
2	0.9803	0.9612	0.9426	0.9246	0.9070	0.8900	0.8734	0.8573	0.8417	0.8264	0.7972	0.7561
3	0.9706	0.9423	0.9151	0.8890	0.8638	0.8396	0.8163	0.7938	0.7722	0.7513	0.7118	0.6575
4	0.9610	0.9238	0.8885	0.8548	0.8227	0.7921	0.7629	0.7350	0.7084	0.6830	0.6355	0.5718
5	0.9515	0.9057	0.8626	0.8219	0.7835	0.7473	0.7130	0.6806	0.6499	0.6209	0.5674	0.4972
6	0.9420	0.8880	0.8375	0.7903	0.7462	0.7050	0.6663	0.6302	0.5963	0.5645	0.5066	0.4323
7	0.9327	0.8706	0.8131	0.7599	0.7107	0.6651	0.6227	0.5835	0.5470	0.5132	0.4523	0.3759
8	0.9235	0.8535	0.7894	0.7307	0.6768	0.6274	0.5820	0.5403	0.5019	0.4665	0.4039	0.3269
9	0.9143	0.8368	0.7664	0.7026	0.6446	0.5919	0.5439	0.5002	0.4604	0.4241	0.3606	0.2843
10	0.9053	0.8203	0.7441	0.6756	0.6139	0.5584	0.5083	0.4632	0.4224	0.3855	0.3220	0.2472
11	0.8963	0.8043	0.7224	0.6496	0.5847	0.5268	0.4751	0.4289	0.3875	0.3505	0.2875	0.2149
12	0.8874	0.7885	0.7014	0.6246	0.5568	0.4970	0.4440	0.3971	0.3555	0.3186	0.2567	0.1869
13	0.8787	0.7730	0.6810	0.6006	0.5303	0.4688	0.4150	0.3677	0.3262	0.2897	0.2292	0.1625
14	0.8700	0.7579	0.6611	0.5775	0.5051	0.4423	0.3878	0.3405	0.2992	0.2633	0.2046	0.1413
15	0.8613	0.7430	0.6419	0.5553	0.4810	0.4173	0.3624	0.3152	0.2745	0.2394	0.1827	0.1229
16	0.8528	0.7284	0.6232	0.5339	0.4581	0.3936	0.3387	0.2919	0.2519	0.2176	0.1631	0.1069
17	0.8444	0.7142	0.6050	0.5134	0.4363	0.3714	0.3166	0.2703	0.2311	0.1978	0.1456	0.0929
18	0.8360	0.7002	0.5874	0.4936	0.4155	0.3503	0.2959	0.2502	0.2120	0.1799	0.1300	0.0808
19	0.8277	0.6864	0.5703	0.4746	0.3957	0.3305	0.2765	0.2317	0.1945	0.1635	0.1161	0.0703
20	0.8195	0.6730	0.5537	0.4564	0.3769	0.3118	0.2584	0.2145	0.1784	0.1486	0.1037	0.0611
25	0.7798	0.6095	0.4776	0.3751	0.2953	0.2330	0.1842	0.1460	0.1160	0.0923	0.0588	0.0304
30	0.7419	0.5521	0.4120	0.3083	0.2314	0.1741	0.1314	0.0994	0.0754	0.0573	0.0334	0.0151
35	0.7059	0.5000	0.3554	0.2534	0.1813	0.1301	0.0937	0.0676	0.0490	0.0356	0.0189	0.0075
40	0.6717	0.4529	0.3066	0.2083	0.1420	0.0972	0.0668	0.0460	0.0318	0.0221	0.0107	0.0037

Table B.2

Future Value of 1

$$f = (1 + i)^n$$

Periods	1%	2%	3%	4%	5%	6%	7%	8%	9%	10%	12%	15%
0	1.0000	1.0000	1.0000	1.0000	1.0000	1.0000	1.0000	1.0000	1.0000	1.0000	1.0000	1.0000
1	1.0100	1.0200	1.0300	1.0400	1.0500	1.0600	1.0700	1.0800	1.0900	1.1000	1.1200	1.1500
2	1.0201	1.0404	1.0609	1.0816	1.1025	1.1236	1.1449	1.1664	1.1881	1.2100	1.2544	1.3225
3	1.0303	1.0612	1.0927	1.1249	1.1576	1.1910	1.2250	1.2597	1.2950	1.3310	1.4049	1.5209
4	1.0406	1.0824	1.1255	1.1699	1.2155	1.2625	1.3108	1.3605	1.4116	1.4641	1.5735	1.7490
5	1.0510	1.1041	1.1593	1.2167	1.2763	1.3382	1.4026	1.4693	1.5386	1.6105	1.7623	2.0114
6	1.0615	1.1262	1.1941	1.2653	1.3401	1.4185	1.5007	1.5869	1.6771	1.7716	1.9738	2.3131
7	1.0721	1.1487	1.2299	1.3159	1.4071	1.5036	1.6058	1.7138	1.8280	1.9487	2.2107	2.6600
8	1.0829	1.1717	1.2668	1.3686	1.4775	1.5938	1.7182	1.8509	1.9926	2.1436	2.4760	3.0590
9	1.0937	1.1951	1.3048	1.4233	1.5513	1.6895	1.8385	1.9990	2.1719	2.3579	2.7731	3.5179
10	1.1046	1.2190	1.3439	1.4802	1.6289	1.7908	1.9672	2.1589	2.3674	2.5937	3.1058	4.0456
11	1.1157	1.2434	1.3842	1.5395	1.7103	1.8983	2.1049	2.3316	2.5804	2.8531	3.4785	4.6524
12	1.1268	1.2682	1.4258	1.6010	1.7959	2.0122	2.2522	2.5182	2.8127	3.1384	3.8960	5.3503
13	1.1381	1.2936	1.4685	1.6651	1.8856	2.1329	2.4098	2.7196	3.0658	3.4523	4.3635	6.1528
14	1.1495	1.3195	1.5126	1.7317	1.9799	2.2609	2.5785	2.9372	3.3417	3.7975	4.8871	7.0757
15	1.1610	1.3459	1.5580	1.8009	2.0789	2.3966	2.7590	3.1722	3.6425	4.1772	5.4736	8.1371
16	1.1726	1.3728	1.6047	1.8730	2.1829	2.5404	2.9522	3.4259	3.9703	4.5950	6.1304	9.3576
17	1.1843	1.4002	1.6528	1.9479	2.2920	2.6928	3.1588	3.7000	4.3276	5.0545	6.8660	10.7613
18	1.1961	1.4282	1.7024	2.0258	2.4066	2.8543	3.3799	3.9960	4.7171	5.5599	7.6900	12.3755
19	1.2081	1.4568	1.7535	2.1068	2.5270	3.0256	3.6165	4.3157	5.1417	6.1159	8.6128	14.2318
20	1.2202	1.4859	1.8061	2.1911	2.6533	3.2071	3.8697	4.6610	5.6044	6.7275	9.6463	16.3665
25	1.2824	1.6406	2.0938	2.6658	3.3864	4.2919	5.4274	6.8485	8.6231	10.8347	17.0001	32.9190
30	1.3478	1.8114	2.4273	3.2434	4.3219	5.7435	7.6123	10.0627	13.2677	17.4494	29.9599	66.2118
35	1.4166	1.9999	2.8139	3.9461	5.5160	7.6861	10.6766	14.7853	20.4140	28.1024	52.7996	133.1755
40	1.4889	2.2080	3.2620	4.8010	7.0400	10.2857	14.9745	21.7245	31.4094	45.2593	93.0510	267.8635

$$p = \left[1 - \frac{1}{(1 + i)^n}\right]/i$$

Table B.3

Present Value of an Annuity of 1

Periods	1%	2%	3%	4%	5%	6%	7%	8%	9%	10%	12%	15%
1	0.9901	0.9804	0.9709	0.9615	0.9524	0.9434	0.9346	0.9259	0.9174	0.9091	0.8929	0.8696
2	1.9704	1.9416	1.9135	1.8861	1.8594	1.8334	1.8080	1.7833	1.7591	1.7355	1.6901	1.6257
3	2.9410	2.8839	2.8286	2.7751	2.7232	2.6730	2.6243	2.5771	2.5313	2.4869	2.4018	2.2832
4	3.9020	3.8077	3.7171	3.6299	3.5460	3.4651	3.3872	3.3121	3.2397	3.1699	3.0373	2.8550
5	4.8534	4.7135	4.5797	4.4518	4.3295	4.2124	4.1002	3.9927	3.8897	3.7908	3.6048	3.3522
6	5.7955	5.6014	5.4172	5.2421	5.0757	4.9173	4.7665	4.6229	4.4859	4.3553	4.1114	3.7845
7	6.7282	6.4720	6.2303	6.0021	5.7864	5.5824	5.3893	5.2064	5.0330	4.8684	4.5638	4.1604
8	7.6517	7.3255	7.0197	6.7327	6.4632	6.2098	5.9713	5.7466	5.5348	5.3349	4.9676	4.4873
9	8.5660	8.1622	7.7861	7.4353	7.1078	6.8017	6.5152	6.2469	5.9952	5.7590	5.3282	4.7716
10	9.4713	8.9826	8.5302	8.1109	7.7217	7.3601	7.0236	6.7101	6.4177	6.1446	5.6502	5.0188
11	10.3676	9.7868	9.2526	8.7605	8.3064	7.8869	7.4987	7.1390	6.8052	6.4951	5.9377	5.2337
12	11.2551	10.5753	9.9540	9.3851	8.8633	8.3838	7.9427	7.5361	7.1607	6.8137	6.1944	5.4206
13	12.1337	11.3484	10.6350	9.9856	9.3936	8.8527	8.3577	7.9038	7.4869	7.1034	6.4235	5.5831
14	13.0037	12.1062	11.2961	10.5631	9.8986	9.2950	8.7455	8.2442	7.7862	7.3667	6.6282	5.7245
15	13.8651	12.8493	11.9379	11.1184	10.3797	9.7122	9.1079	8.5595	8.0607	7.6061	6.8109	5.8474
16	14.7179	13.5777	12.5611	11.6523	10.8378	10.1059	9.4466	8.8514	8.3126	7.8237	6.9740	5.9542
17	15.5623	14.2919	13.1661	12.1657	11.2741	10.4773	9.7632	9.1216	8.5436	8.0216	7.1196	6.0472
18	16.3983	14.9920	13.7535	12.6593	11.6896	10.8276	10.0591	9.3719	8.7556	8.2014	7.2497	6.1280
19	17.2260	15.6785	14.3238	13.1339	12.0853	11.1581	10.3356	9.6036	8.9501	8.3649	7.3658	6.1982
20	18.0456	16.3514	14.8775	13.5903	12.4622	11.4699	10.5940	9.8181	9.1285	8.5136	7.4694	6.2593
25	22.0232	19.5235	17.4131	15.6221	14.0939	12.7834	11.6536	10.6748	9.8226	9.0770	7.8431	6.4641
30	25.8077	22.3965	19.6004	17.2920	15.3725	13.7648	12.4090	11.2578	10.2737	9.4269	8.0552	6.5660
35	29.4086	24.9986	21.4872	18.6646	16.3742	14.4982	12.9477	11.6546	10.5668	9.6442	8.1755	6.6166
40	32.8347	27.3555	23.1148	19.7928	17.1591	15.0463	13.3317	11.9246	10.7574	9.7791	8.2438	6.6418

$$f = [(1 + i)^n - 1]/i$$

Table B.4

Future Value of an Annuity of 1

Periods	1%	2%	3%	4%	5%	6%	7%	8%	9%	10%	12%	15%
1	1.0000	1.0000	1.0000	1.0000	1.0000	1.0000	1.0000	1.0000	1.0000	1.0000	1.0000	1.0000
2	2.0100	2.0200	2.0300	2.0400	2.0500	2.0600	2.0700	2.0800	2.0900	2.1000	2.1200	2.1500
3	3.0301	3.0604	3.0909	3.1216	3.1525	3.1836	3.2149	3.2464	3.2781	3.3100	3.3744	3.4725
4	4.0604	4.1216	4.1836	4.2465	4.3101	4.3746	4.4399	4.5061	4.5731	4.6410	4.7793	4.9934
5	5.1010	5.2040	5.3091	5.4163	5.5256	5.6371	5.7507	5.8666	5.9847	6.1051	6.3528	6.7424
6	6.1520	6.3081	6.4684	6.6330	6.8019	6.9753	7.1533	7.3359	7.5233	7.7156	8.1152	8.7537
7	7.2135	7.4343	7.6625	7.8983	8.1420	8.3938	8.6540	8.9228	9.2004	9.4872	10.0890	11.0668
8	8.2857	8.5830	8.8923	9.2142	9.5491	9.8975	10.2598	10.6366	11.0285	11.4359	12.2997	13.7268
9	9.3685	9.7546	10.1591	10.5828	11.0266	11.4913	11.9780	12.4876	13.0210	13.5795	14.7757	16.7858
10	10.4622	10.9497	11.4639	12.0061	12.5779	13.1808	13.8164	14.4866	15.1929	15.9374	17.5487	20.3037
11	11.5668	12.1687	12.8078	13.4864	14.2068	14.9716	15.7836	16.6455	17.5603	18.5312	20.6546	24.3493
12	12.6825	13.4121	14.1920	15.0258	15.9171	16.8699	17.8885	18.9771	20.1407	21.3843	24.1331	29.0017
13	13.8093	14.6803	15.6178	16.6268	17.7130	18.8821	20.1406	21.4953	22.9534	24.5227	28.0291	34.3519
14	14.9474	15.9739	17.0863	18.2919	19.5986	21.0151	22.5505	24.2149	26.0192	27.9750	32.3926	40.5047
15	16.0969	17.2934	18.5989	20.0236	21.5786	23.2760	25.1290	27.1521	29.3609	31.7725	37.2797	47.5804
16	17.2579	18.6393	20.1569	21.8245	23.6575	25.6725	27.8881	30.3243	33.0034	35.9497	42.7533	55.7175
17	18.4304	20.0121	21.7616	23.6975	25.8404	28.2129	30.8402	33.7502	36.9737	40.5447	48.8837	65.0751
18	19.6147	21.4123	23.4144	25.6454	28.1324	30.9057	33.9990	37.4502	41.3013	45.5992	55.7497	75.8364
19	20.8109	22.8406	25.1169	27.6712	30.5390	33.7600	37.3790	41.4463	46.0185	51.1591	63.4397	88.2118
20	22.0190	24.2974	26.8704	29.7781	33.0660	36.7856	40.9955	45.7620	51.1601	57.2750	72.0524	102.4436
25	28.2432	32.0303	36.4593	41.6459	47.7271	54.8645	63.2490	73.1059	84.7009	98.3471	133.3339	212.7930
30	34.7849	40.5681	47.5754	56.0849	66.4388	79.0582	94.4608	113.2832	136.3075	164.4940	241.3327	434.7451
35	41.6603	49.9945	60.4621	73.6522	90.3203	111.4348	138.2369	172.3168	215.7108	271.0244	431.6635	881.1702
40	48.8864	60.4020	75.4013	95.0255	120.7998	154.7620	199.6351	259.0565	337.8824	442.5926	767.0914	1,779.0903

Glossary

Absorption costing Costing method that assigns both variable and fixed costs to products.

Accelerated depreciation method Method that produces larger depreciation charges in the early years of an asset's life and smaller charges in its later years. *(p. 392)*

Account Record within an accounting system in which increases and decreases are entered and stored in a specific asset, liability, equity, revenue, or expense. *(p. 49)*

Account balance Difference between total debits and total credits (including the beginning balance) for an account. *(p. 53)*

Account form balance sheet Balance sheet that lists assets on the left side and liabilities and equity on the right. *(p. 18)*

Account payable Liability created by buying goods or services on credit; backed by the buyer's general credit standing. *(p. 50)*

Accounting Information and measurement system that identifies, records, and communicates relevant information about a company's business activities. *(p. 4)*

Accounting cycle Recurring steps performed each accounting period, starting with analyzing transactions and continuing through the post-closing trial balance (or reversing entries). *(p. 144)*

Accounting equation Equality involving a company's assets, liabilities, and equity; Assets = Liabilities + Equity; also called *balance sheet equation*. *(p. 12)*

Accounting information system People, records, and methods that collect and process data from transactions and events, organize them in useful forms, and communicate results to decision makers. *(p. 266)*

Accounting period Length of time covered by financial statements; also called *reporting period*. *(p. 92)*

Accounting rate of return Rate used to evaluate the acceptability of an investment; equals the after-tax periodic income from a project divided by the average investment in the asset; also called *rate of return on average investment*. *(p. 1001)*

Accounts payable ledger Subsidiary ledger listing individual creditor (supplier) accounts. *(p. 271)*

Accounts receivable Amounts due from customers for credit sales; backed by the customer's general credit standing. *(p. 354)*

Accounts receivable ledger Subsidiary ledger listing individual customer accounts. *(p. 271)*

Accounts receivable turnover Measure of both the quality and liquidity of accounts receivable; indicates how often receivables are received and collected during the period; computed by dividing net sales by average accounts receivable. *(p. 368)*

Accrual basis accounting Accounting system that recognizes revenues when earned and expenses when incurred; the basis for GAAP. *(p. 93)*

Accrued expenses Costs incurred in a period that are both unpaid and unrecorded; adjusting entries for recording accrued expenses involve increasing expenses and increasing liabilities. *(p. 99)*

Accrued revenues Revenues earned in a period that are both unrecorded and not yet received in cash (or other assets); adjusting entries for recording accrued revenues involve increasing assets and increasing revenues. *(p. 100)*

Accumulated depreciation Cumulative sum of all depreciation expense recorded for an asset. *(p. 97)*

Acid-test ratio Ratio used to assess a company's ability to settle its current debts with its most liquid assets; defined as quick assets (cash, short-term investments, and current receivables) divided by current liabilities. *(p. 193)*

Activity-based budgeting (ABB) Budget system based on expected activities. *(p. 929)*

Activity-based costing (ABC) Cost allocation method that focuses on activities performed; traces costs to activities and then assigns them to cost objects. *(p. 844)*

Activity cost driver Variable that causes an activity's cost to go up or down; a causal factor. *(p. 844)*

Activity cost pool Temporary account that accumulates costs a company incurs to support an activity. *(p. 845)*

Adjusted trial balance List of accounts and balances prepared after period-end adjustments are recorded and posted. *(p. 103)*

Adjusting entry Journal entry at the end of an accounting period to bring an asset or liability account to its proper amount and update the related expense or revenue account. *(p. 94)*

Aging of accounts receivable Process of classifying accounts receivable by how long they are past due for purposes of estimating uncollectible accounts. *(p. 362)*

Allowance for Doubtful Accounts Contra asset account with a balance approximating uncollectible accounts receivable; also called *Allowance for Uncollectible Accounts*. *(p. 359)*

Allowance method Procedure that (a) estimates and matches bad debts expense with its sales for the period and/or (b) reports accounts receivable at estimated realizable value. *(p. 359)*

Amortization Process of allocating the cost of an intangible asset to expense over its estimated useful life. *(p. 401)*

Annual financial statements Financial statements covering a one-year period; often based on a calendar year, but any consecutive 12-month (or 52-week) period is acceptable. *(p. 93)*

Annual report Summary of a company's financial results for the year with its current financial condition and future plans; directed to external users of financial information. *(p. A-1)*

Annuity Series of equal payments at equal intervals. *(p. 562)*

Appropriated retained earnings Retained earnings separately reported to inform stockholders of funding needs. *(p. 517)*

Assets Resources a business owns or controls that are expected to provide current and future benefits to the business. *(p. 12)*

Audit Analysis and report of an organization's accounting system, its records, and its reports using various tests. *(p. 11)*

Authorized stock Total amount of stock that a corporation's charter authorizes it to issue. *(p. 503)*

Available-for-sale (AFS) securities Investments in debt and equity securities that are not classified as trading securities or held-to-maturity securities. *(p. 590)*

Average cost See *weighted average.* *(p. 230)*

Avoidable expense Expense (or cost) that is relevant for decision making; expense that is not incurred if a department, product, or service is eliminated. *(p. 1014)*

Bad debts Accounts of customers who do not pay what they have promised to pay; an expense of selling on credit; also called *uncollectible accounts. (p. 358)*

Balance column account Account with debit and credit columns for recording entries and another column for showing the balance of the account after each entry. *(p. 56)*

Balance sheet Financial statement that lists types and dollar amounts of assets, liabilities, and equity at a specific date. *(p. 17)*

Balance sheet equation (See *accounting equation.*) *(p. 12)*

Bank reconciliation Report that explains the difference between the book (company) balance of cash and the cash balance reported on the bank statement. *(p. 326)*

Bank statement Bank report on the depositor's beginning and ending cash balances, and a listing of its changes, for a period. *(p. 325)*

Basic earnings per share Net income less any preferred dividends and then divided by weighted-average common shares outstanding. *(p. 518)*

Batch processing Accumulating source documents for a period of time and then processing them all at once such as once a day, week, or month. *(p. 281)*

Bearer bonds Bonds made payable to whoever holds them (the *bearer*); also called *unregistered bonds. (p. 557)*

Benchmarking Practice of comparing and analyzing company financial performance or position with other companies or standards.

Betterments Expenditures to make a plant asset more efficient or productive; also called *improvements. (p. 397)*

Bond Written promise to pay the bond's par (or face) value and interest at a stated contract rate; often issued in denominations of $1,000. *(p. 544)*

Bond certificate Document containing bond specifics such as issuer's name, bond par value, contract interest rate, and maturity date. *(p. 546)*

Bond indenture Contract between the bond issuer and the bondholders; identifies the parties' rights and obligations. *(p. 546)*

Book value Asset's acquisition costs less its accumulated depreciation (or depletion, or amortization); also sometimes used synonymously as the *carrying value* of an account. *(pp. 97 & 391)*

Book value per common share Recorded amount of equity applicable to common shares divided by the number of common shares outstanding. *(p. 520)*

Book value per preferred share Equity applicable to preferred shares (equals its call price [or par value if it is not callable] plus any cumulative dividends in arrears) divided by the number of preferred shares outstanding. *(p. 520)*

Bookkeeping (See *recordkeeping.*) *(p. 5)*

Break-even point Output level at which sales equals fixed plus variable costs; where income equals zero. *(p. 888)*

Break-even time (BET) Time-based measurement used to evaluate the acceptability of an investment; equals the time expected to pass before the present value of the net cash flows from an investment equals its initial cost. *(p. 1016)*

Budget Formal statement of future plans, usually expressed in monetary terms. *(p. 916)*

Budget report Report comparing actual results to planned objectives; sometimes used as a progress report. *(p. 954)*

Budgetary control Management use of budgets to monitor and control company operations. *(p. 954)*

Budgeted balance sheet Accounting report that presents predicted amounts of the company's assets, liabilities, and equity balances as of the end of the budget period. *(p. 928)*

Budgeted income statement Accounting report that presents predicted amounts of the company's revenues and expenses for the budget period. *(p. 928)*

Budgeting Process of planning future business actions and expressing them as formal plans. *(p. 916)*

Business An organization of one or more individuals selling products and/or services for profit. *(p. 10)*

Business entity principle Principle that requires a business to be accounted for separately from its owner(s) and from any other entity. *(p. 10)*

Business segment Part of a company that can be separately identified by the products or services that it provides or by the geographic markets that it serves; also called *segment. (p. 697)*

C corporation Corporation that does not qualify for nor elect to be treated as a proprietorship or partnership for income tax purposes and therefore is subject to income taxes; also called *C corp. (p. 474)*

Call price Amount that must be paid to call and retire a callable preferred stock or a callable bond. *(p. 513)*

Callable bonds Bonds that give the issuer the option to retire them at a stated amount prior to maturity. *(p. 557)*

Callable preferred stock Preferred stock that the issuing corporation, at its option, may retire by paying the call price plus any dividends in arrears. *(p. 513)*

Canceled checks Checks that the bank has paid and deducted from the depositor's account. *(p. 326)*

Capital budgeting Process of analyzing alternative investments and deciding which assets to acquire or sell. *(p. 998)*

Capital expenditures Additional costs of plant assets that provide material benefits extending beyond the current period; also called *balance sheet expenditures. (p. 396)*

Capital expenditures budget Plan that lists dollar amounts to be both received from disposal of plant assets and spent to purchase plant assets. *(p. 925)*

Capital leases Long-term leases in which the lessor transfers substantially all risk and rewards of ownership to the lessee. *(p. 568)*

Capital stock General term referring to a corporation's stock used in obtaining capital (owner financing). *(p. 503)*

Capitalize Record the cost as part of a permanent account and allocate it over later periods. *(p. 396)*

Carrying value of bonds Net amount at which bonds are reported on the balance sheet; equals the par value of the bonds less any unamortized discount or plus any unamortized premium; also called *carrying amount* or *book value. (p. 548)*

Cash Includes currency, coins, and amounts on deposit in bank checking or savings accounts. *(p. 317)*

Cash basis accounting Accounting system that recognizes revenues when cash is received and records expenses when cash is paid. *(p. 93)*

Cash budget Plan that shows expected cash inflows and outflows during the budget period, including receipts from loans needed to maintain a minimum cash balance and repayments of such loans. *(p. 926)*

Cash disbursements journal Special journal normally used to record all payments of cash; also called *cash payments journal. (p. 278)*

Cash discount Reduction in the price of merchandise granted by a seller to a buyer when payment is made within the discount period. *(p. 181)*

Cash equivalents Short-term, investment assets that are readily convertible to a known cash amount or sufficiently close to their maturity date (usually within 90 days) so that market value is not sensitive to interest rate changes. *(p. 317)*

Cash flow on total assets Ratio of operating cash flows to average total assets; not sensitive to income recognition and measurement; partly reflects earnings quality. *(p. 640)*

Cash Over and Short Income statement account used to record cash overages and cash shortages arising from errors in cash receipts or payments. *(p. 318)*

Cash receipts journal Special journal normally used to record all receipts of cash. *(p. 275)*

Change in an accounting estimate Change in an accounting estimate that results from new information, subsequent developments, or improved judgment that impacts current and future periods. *(pp. 395 & 517)*

Chart of accounts List of accounts used by a company; includes an identification number for each account. *(p. 52)*

Check Document signed by a depositor instructing the bank to pay a specified amount to a designated recipient. *(p. 323)*

Check register Another name for a cash disbursements journal when the journal has a column for check numbers. *(pp. 279 & 334)*

Classified balance sheet Balance sheet that presents assets and liabilities in relevant subgroups, including current and noncurrent classifications. *(p. 145)*

Clock card Source document used to record the number of hours an employee works and to determine the total labor cost for each pay period. *(p. 767)*

Closing entries Entries recorded at the end of each accounting period to transfer end-of-period balances in revenue, gain, expense, loss, and withdrawal (dividend for a corporation) accounts to the capital account (to retained earnings for a corporation). *(p. 141)*

Closing process Necessary end-of-period steps to prepare the accounts for recording the transactions of the next period. *(p. 140)*

Columnar journal Journal with more than one column. *(p. 272)*

Common stock Corporation's basic ownership share; also generically called *capital stock. (pp. 11 & 502)*

Common-size financial statement Statement that expresses each amount as a percent of a base amount. In the balance sheet, total assets is usually the base and is expressed as 100%. In the income statement, net sales is usually the base. *(p. 681)*

Comparative financial statement Statement with data for two or more successive periods placed in side-by-side columns, often with changes shown in dollar amounts and percents. *(p. 676)*

Compatibility principle Information system principle that prescribes an accounting system to conform with a company's activities, personnel, and structure. *(p. 267)*

Complex capital structure Capital structure that includes outstanding rights or options to purchase common stock, or securities that are convertible into common stock. *(p. 519)*

Components of accounting systems Five basic components of accounting systems are source documents, input devices, information processors, information storage, and output devices. *(p. 267)*

Composite unit Generic unit consisting of a specific number of units of each product; unit comprised in proportion to the expected sales mix of its products. *(p. 895)*

Compound journal entry Journal entry that affects at least three accounts. *(p. 59)*

Comprehensive income Net change in equity for a period, excluding owner investments and distributions. *(p. 593)*

Computer hardware Physical equipment in a computerized accounting information system. *(p. 268)*

Computer network Linkage giving different users and different computers access to common databases and programs. *(p. 281)*

Computer software Programs that direct operations of computer hardware. *(p. 268)*

Conservatism principle Principle that prescribes the less optimistic estimate when two estimates are about equally likely. *(p. 234)*

Consignee Receiver of goods owned by another who holds them for purposes of selling them for the owner. *(p. 224)*

Consignor Owner of goods who ships them to another party who will sell them for the owner. *(p. 224)*

Consistency principle Principle that prescribes use of the same accounting method(s) over time so that financial statements are comparable across periods. *(p. 232)*

Consolidated financial statements Financial statements that show all (combined) activities under the parent's control, including those of any subsidiaries. *(p. 593)*

Contingent liability Obligation to make a future payment if, and only if, an uncertain future event occurs. *(p. 439)*

Continuous budgeting Practice of preparing budgets for a selected number of future periods and revising those budgets as each period is completed. *(p. 918)*

Continuous improvement Concept requiring every manager and employee continually to look to improve operations. *(p. 724)*

Contra account Account linked with another account and having an opposite normal balance; reported as a subtraction from the other account's balance. *(p. 97)*

Contract rate Interest rate specified in a bond indenture (or note); multiplied by the par value to determine the interest paid each period; also called *coupon rate, stated rate,* or *nominal rate. (p. 547)*

Contributed capital Total amount of cash and other assets received from stockholders in exchange for stock; also called *paid-in capital.*

Contributed capital in excess of par value Difference between the par value of stock and its issue price when issued at a price above par.

Contribution margin Sales revenue less total variable costs.

Contribution margin income statement Income statement that separates variable and fixed costs; highlights the contribution margin, which is sales less variable expenses.

Contribution margin per unit Amount that the sale of one unit contributes toward recovering fixed costs and earning profit; defined as sales price per unit minus variable expense per unit. *(p. 888)*

Contribution margin ratio Product's contribution margin divided by its sale price. *(p. 888)*

Control Process of monitoring planning decisions and evaluating the organization's activities and employees. *(p. 721)*

Control principle Information system principle that prescribes an accounting system to aid managers in controlling and monitoring business activities. *(p. 266)*

Controllable costs Costs that a manager has the power to control or at least strongly influence. *(pp. 726 & 855)*

Controllable variance Combination of both overhead spending variances (variable and fixed) and the variable overhead efficiency variance. *(p. 967)*

Controlling account General ledger account, the balance of which (after posting) equals the sum of the balances in its related subsidiary ledger. *(p. 271)*

Conversion costs Expenditures incurred in converting raw materials to finished goods; includes direct labor costs and overhead costs. *(p. 731)*

Convertible bonds Bonds that bondholders can exchange for a set number of the issuer's shares. *(p. 557)*

Convertible preferred stock Preferred stock with an option to exchange it for common stock at a specified rate. *(p. 513)*

Copyright Right giving the owner the exclusive privilege to publish and sell musical, literary, or artistic work during the creator's life plus 70 years. *(p. 402)*

Corporation Business that is a separate legal entity under state or federal laws with owners called *shareholders* or *stockholders. (pp. 11 & 500)*

Cost All normal and reasonable expenditures necessary to get an asset in place and ready for its intended use. *(p. 387)*

Cost accounting system Accounting system for manufacturing activities based on the perpetual inventory system. *(p. 762)*

Cost-benefit principle Information system principle that prescribes the benefits from an activity in an accounting system to outweigh the costs of that activity. *(p. 267)*

Cost center Department that incurs costs but generates no revenues; common example is the accounting or legal department. *(p. 848)*

Cost object Product, process, department, or customer to which costs are assigned. *(p. 725)*

Cost of goods available for sale Consists of beginning inventory plus net purchases of a period. *(p. 200)*

Cost of goods manufactured Total manufacturing costs (direct materials, direct labor, and factory overhead) for the period plus beginning goods in process less ending goods in process; also called *net cost of goods manufactured* and *cost of goods completed. (p. 811)*

Cost of goods sold Cost of inventory sold to customers during a period; also called *cost of sales. (p. 179)*

Cost principle Accounting principle that prescribes financial statement information to be based on actual costs incurred in business transactions. *(p. 9)*

Cost variance Difference between the actual incurred cost and the standard cost. *(p. 961)*

Cost-volume-profit (CVP) analysis Planning method that includes predicting the volume of activity, the costs incurred, sales earned, and profits received. *(p. 882)*

Coupon bonds Bonds with interest coupons attached to their certificates; bondholders detach coupons when they mature and present them to a bank or broker for collection. *(p. 557)*

Credit Recorded on the right side; an entry that decreases asset and expense accounts, and increases liability, revenue, and most equity accounts; abbreviated Cr. *(p. 53)*

Credit memorandum Notification that the sender has credited the recipient's account in the sender's records. *(p. 187)*

Credit period Time period that can pass before a customer's payment is due. *(p. 181)*

Credit terms Description of the amounts and timing of payments that a buyer (debtor) agrees to make in the future. *(p. 181)*

Creditors Individuals or organizations entitled to receive payments. *(p. 50)*

Cumulative preferred stock Preferred stock on which undeclared dividends accumulate until paid; common stockholders cannot receive dividends until cumulative dividends are paid. *(p. 511)*

Current assets Cash and other assets expected to be sold, collected, or used within one year or the company's operating cycle, whichever is longer. *(p. 146)*

Current liabilities Obligations due to be paid or settled within one year or the company's operating cycle, whichever is longer. *(pp. 147 & 429)*

Current portion of long-term debt Portion of long-term debt due within one year or the operating cycle, whichever is longer; reported under current liabilities. *(p. 437)*

Current ratio Ratio used to evaluate a company's ability to pay its short-term obligations, calculated by dividing current assets by current liabilities. *(p. 148)*

Curvilinear cost Cost that changes with volume but not at a constant rate. *(p. 884)*

Customer orientation Company position that its managers and employees be in tune with the changing wants and needs of consumers. *(p. 723)*

CVP chart Graphic representation of cost-volume-profit relations. *(p. 890)*

Cycle efficiency (CE) A measure of production efficiency, which is defined as value-added (process) time divided by total cycle time. *(p. 735)*

Cycle time (CT) A measure of the time to produce a product or service, which is the sum of process time, inspection time, move time, and wait time; also called *throughput time.* *(p. 735)*

Date of declaration Date the directors vote to pay a dividend. *(p. 507)*

Date of payment Date the corporation makes the dividend payment. *(p. 507)*

Date of record Date directors specify for identifying stockholders to receive dividends. *(p. 507)*

Days' sales in inventory Estimate of number of days needed to convert inventory into receivables or cash; equals ending inventory divided by cost of goods sold and then multiplied by 365; also called *days' stock on hand.* *(p. 236)*

Days' sales uncollected Measure of the liquidity of receivables computed by dividing the current balance of receivables by the annual credit (or net) sales and then multiplying by 365; also called *days' sales in receivables.* *(p. 329)*

Debit Recorded on the left side; an entry that increases asset and expense accounts, and decreases liability, revenue, and most equity accounts; abbreviated Dr. *(p. 53)*

Debit memorandum Notification that the sender has debited the recipient's account in the sender's records. *(p. 182)*

Debt ratio Ratio of total liabilities to total assets; used to reflect risk associated with a company's debts. *(p. 67)*

Debt-to-equity ratio Defined as total liabilities divided by total equity; shows the proportion of a company financed by non-owners (creditors) in comparison with that financed by owners. *(p. 558)*

Debtors Individuals or organizations that owe money. *(p. 49)*

Declining-balance method Method that determines depreciation charge for the period by multiplying a depreciation rate (often twice the straight-line rate) by the asset's beginning-period book value. *(p. 392)*

Deferred income tax liability Corporation income taxes that are deferred until future years because of temporary differences between GAAP and tax rules. *(p. 451)*

Degree of operating leverage (DOL) Ratio of contribution margin divided by pretax income; used to assess the effect on income of changes in sales. *(p. 896)*

Departmental accounting system Accounting system that provides information useful in evaluating the profitability or cost effectiveness of a department. *(p. 847)*

Departmental contribution to overhead Amount by which a department's revenues exceed its direct expenses. *(p. 854)*

Depletion Process of allocating the cost of natural resources to periods when they are consumed and sold. *(p. 400)*

Deposit ticket Lists items such as currency, coins, and checks deposited and their corresponding dollar amounts. *(p. 323)*

Deposits in transit Deposits recorded by the company but not yet recorded by its bank. *(p. 326)*

Depreciable cost Cost of a plant asset less its salvage value. *(p. 390)*

Depreciation Expense created by allocating the cost of plant and equipment to periods in which they are used; represents the expense of using the asset. *(pp. 97 & 389)*

Diluted earnings per share Earnings per share calculation that requires dilutive securities be added to the denominator of the basic EPS calculation. *(p. 519)*

Dilutive securities Securities having the potential to increase common shares outstanding; examples are options, rights, convertible bonds, and convertible preferred stock. *(p. 519)*

Direct costs Costs incurred for the benefit of one specific cost object. *(p. 725)*

Direct expenses Expenses traced to a specific department (object) that are incurred for the sole benefit of that department. *(p. 849)*

Direct labor Efforts of employees who physically convert materials to finished product. *(p. 731)*

Direct labor costs Wages and salaries for direct labor that are separately and readily traced through the production process to finished goods. *(p. 731)*

Direct material Raw material that physically becomes part of the product and is clearly identified with specific products or batches of product. *(p. 730)*

Direct material costs Expenditures for direct material that are separately and readily traced through the production process to finished goods. *(p. 730)*

Direct method Presentation of net cash from operating activities for the statement of cash flows that lists major operating cash receipts less major operating cash payments. *(p. 628)*

Direct write-off method Method that records the loss from an uncollectible account receivable at the time it is determined to be uncollectible; no attempt is made to estimate bad debts. *(p. 358)*

Discount on bonds payable Difference between a bond's par value and its lower issue price or carrying value; occurs when the contract rate is less than the market rate. *(p. 547)*

Discount on note payable Difference between the face value of a note payable and the (lesser) amount borrowed; reflects the added interest to be paid on the note over its life.

Discount on stock Difference between the par value of stock and its issue price when issued at a price below par value. *(p. 505)*

Discount period Time period in which a cash discount is available and the buyer can make a reduced payment. *(p. 181)*

Discount rate Expected rate of return on investments; also called *cost of capital, hurdle rate,* or *required rate of return.* *(p. B-2)*

Discounts lost Expenses resulting from not taking advantage of cash discounts on purchases. *(p. 335)*

Dividend in arrears Unpaid dividend on cumulative preferred stock; must be paid before any regular dividends on preferred stock and before any dividends on common stock. *(p. 511)*

Dividend yield Ratio of the annual amount of cash dividends distributed to common shareholders relative to the common stock's market value (price). *(p. 519)*

Dividends Corporation's distributions of assets to its owners.

Double-declining-balance (DDB) depreciation Depreciation equals beginning book value multiplied by 2 times the straight-line rate. *(p. 392)*

Double-entry accounting Accounting system in which each transaction affects at least two accounts and has at least one debit and one credit. *(p. 53)*

Double taxation Corporate income is taxed and then its later distribution through dividends is normally taxed again for shareholders. *(p. 11)*

Earnings (See *net income.*) *(p. 13)*

Earnings per share (EPS) Amount of income earned by each share of a company's outstanding common stock; also called *net income per share.* *(p. 518)*

Effective interest method Allocates interest expense over the bond life to yield a constant rate of interest; interest expense for a period is found by multiplying the balance of the liability at the beginning of the period by the bond market rate at issuance; also called *interest method.* *(p. 563)*

Efficiency Company's productivity in using its assets; usually measured relative to how much revenue a certain level of assets generates. *(p. 675)*

Efficiency variance Difference between the actual quantity of an input and the standard quantity of that input. *(p. 966)*

Electronic funds transfer (EFT) Use of electronic communication to transfer cash from one party to another. *(p. 324)*

Employee benefits Additional compensation paid to or on behalf of employees, such as premiums for medical, dental, life, and disability insurance, and contributions to pension plans. *(p. 437)*

Employee earnings report Record of an employee's net pay, gross pay, deductions, and year-to-date payroll information. *(p. 448)*

Enterprise resource planning (ERP) software Programs that manage a company's vital operations, which range from order taking to production to accounting. *(p. 281)*

Entity Organization that, for accounting purposes, is separate from other organizations and individuals. *(p. 10)*

EOM Abbreviation for *end of month;* used to describe credit terms for credit transactions. *(p. 181)*

Equity Owner's claim on the assets of a business; equals the residual interest in an entity's assets after deducting liabilities; also called *net assets.* *(p. 12)*

Equity method Accounting method used for long-term investments when the investor has "significant influence" over the investee. *(p. 592)*

Equity ratio Portion of total assets provided by equity, computed as total equity divided by total assets. *(p. 689)*

Equity securities with controlling influence Long-term investment when the investor is able to exert controlling influence over the investee; investors owning 50% or more of voting stock are presumed to exert controlling influence. *(p. 593)*

Equity securities with significant influence Long-term investment when the investor is able to exert significant influence over the investee; investors owning 20 percent or more (but less than 50 percent) of voting stock are presumed to exert significant influence. *(p. 591)*

Equivalent units of production (EUP) Number of units that would be completed if all effort during a period had been applied to units that were started and finished. *(p. 805)*

Estimated liability Obligation of an uncertain amount that can be reasonably estimated. *(p. 437)*

Estimated line of cost behavior Line drawn on a graph to visually fit the relation between cost and sales. *(p. 885)*

Ethics Codes of conduct by which actions are judged as right or wrong, fair or unfair, honest or dishonest. *(p. 8)*

Events Happenings that both affect an organization's financial position and can be reliably measured. *(p. 13)*

Expanded accounting equation Assets = Liabilities + Equity; Equity equals [Owner capital − Owner withdrawals + Revenues − Expenses] for a non-corporation; Equity equals [Contributed capital + Retained earnings + Revenues − Expenses] for a corporation where dividends are subtracted from retained earnings. *(p. 13)*

Expenses Outflows or using up of assets as part of operations of a business to generate sales. *(p. 13)*

External transactions Exchanges of economic value between one entity and another entity. *(p. 13)*

External users Persons using accounting information who are not directly involved in running the organization. *(p. 5)*

Extraordinary gains or losses Gains or losses reported separately from continuing operations because they are both unusual and infrequent. *(p. 697)*

Extraordinary repairs Major repairs that extend the useful life of a plant asset beyond prior expectations; treated as a capital expenditure. *(p. 397)*

Factory overhead Factory activities supporting the production process that are not direct material or direct labor; also called *overhead* and *manufacturing overhead.* *(p. 731)*

Factory overhead costs Expenditures for factory overhead that cannot be separately or readily traced to finished goods; also called *overhead costs*. *(p. 73)*

Favorable variance Difference in actual revenues or expenses from the budgeted amount that contributes to a higher income. *(p. 956)*

Federal depository bank Bank authorized to accept deposits of amounts payable to the federal government. *(p. 446)*

Federal Insurance Contributions Act (FICA) Taxes Taxes assessed on both employers and employees; for Social Security and Medicare programs. *(p. 434)*

Federal Unemployment Taxes (FUTA) Payroll taxes on employers assessed by the federal government to support its unemployment insurance program. *(p. 436)*

FIFO method (See *first-in, first-out.*) *(p. 816)*

Financial accounting Area of accounting mainly aimed at serving external users. *(p. 5)*

Financial Accounting Standards Board (FASB) Independent group of full-time members responsible for setting accounting rules. *(p. 9)*

Financial leverage Earning a higher return on equity by paying dividends on preferred stock or interest on debt at a rate lower than the return earned with the assets from issuing preferred stock or debt; also called *trading on the equity.* *(p. 513)*

Financial reporting Process of communicating information relevant to investors, creditors, and others in making investment, credit, and business decisions. *(p. 675)*

Financial statement analysis Application of analytical tools to general-purpose financial statements and related data for making business decisions. *(p. 674)*

Financial statements Includes the balance sheet, income statement, statement of owner's (or stockholders') equity, and statement of cash flows. *(p. 17)*

Financing activities Transactions with owners and creditors that include obtaining cash from issuing debt, repaying amounts borrowed, and obtaining cash from or distributing cash to owners. *(p. 624)*

Finished goods inventory Account that controls the finished goods files, which acts as a subsidiary ledger (of the Inventory account) in which the costs of finished goods that are ready for sale are recorded. *(pp. 729 & 764)*

First-in, first-out (FIFO) Method to assign cost to inventory that assumes items are sold in the order acquired; earliest items purchased are the first sold. *(p. 229)*

Fiscal year Consecutive 12-month (or 52-week) period chosen as the organization's annual accounting period. *(p. 93)*

Fixed budget Planning budget based on a single predicted amount of volume; unsuitable for evaluations if the actual volume differs from predicted volume. *(p. 955)*

Fixed budget performance report Report that compares actual revenues and costs with fixed budgeted amounts and identifies the differences as favorable or unfavorable variances. *(p. 955)*

Fixed cost Cost that does not change with changes in the volume of activity. *(p. 725)*

Flexibility principle Information system principle that prescribes an accounting system be able to adapt to changes in the company, its operations, and needs of decision makers. *(p. 267)*

Flexible budget Budget prepared (using actual volume) once a period is complete that helps managers evaluate past performance; uses fixed and variable costs in determining total costs. *(p. 956)*

Flexible budget performance report Report that compares actual revenues and costs with their variable budgeted amounts based on actual sales volume (or other level of activity) and identifies the differences as variances. *(p. 958)*

FOB Abbreviation for *free on board;* the point when ownership of goods passes to the buyer; *FOB shipping point* (or *factory*) means the buyer pays shipping costs and accepts ownership of goods when the seller transfers goods to carrier; *FOB destination* means the seller pays shipping costs and buyer accepts ownership of goods at the buyer's place of business. *(p. 183)*

Foreign exchange rate Price of one currency stated in terms of another currency. *(p. 599)*

Form 940 IRS form used to report an employer's federal unemployment taxes (FUTA) on an annual filing basis. *(p. 446)*

Form 941 IRS form filed to report FICA taxes owed and remitted. *(p. 444)*

Form 10-K (or 10-KSB) Annual report form filed with SEC by businesses (small businesses) with publicly-traded securities. *(p. A-1)*

Form W-2 Annual report by an employer to each employee showing the employee's wages subject to FICA and federal income taxes along with amounts withheld. *(p. 446)*

Form W-4 Withholding allowance certificate, filed with the employer, identifying the number of withholding allowances claimed. *(p. 448)*

Franchises Privileges granted by a company or government to sell a product or service under specified conditions. *(p. 403)*

Full-disclosure principle Principle that prescribes financial statements (including notes) to report all relevant information about an entity's operations and financial condition. *(p. 366)*

GAAP (See *generally accepted accounting principles.*) *(p. 9)*

General accounting system Accounting system for manufacturing activities based on the *periodic* inventory system. *(p. 762)*

General and administrative expenses Expenses that support the operating activities of a business. *(p. 191)*

General and administrative expense budget Plan that shows predicted operating expenses not included in the selling expenses budget. *(p. 924)*

General journal All-purpose journal for recording the debits and credits of transactions and events. *(pp. 54 & 270)*

General ledger (See *ledger.*) *(p. 49)*

General partner Partner who assumes unlimited liability for the debts of the partnership; responsible for partnership management. *(p. 473)*

General partnership Partnership in which all partners have mutual agency and unlimited liability for partnership debts. *(p. 473)*

Generally accepted accounting principles (GAAP) Rules that specify acceptable accounting practices. *(p. 9)*

Generally accepted auditing standards (GAAS) Rules that specify acceptable auditing practices.

General-purpose financial statements Statements published periodically for use by a variety of interested parties; includes the income statement, balance sheet, statement of owner's equity (or statement of retained earnings for a corporation), statement of cash flows, and notes to these statements. *(p. 675)*

Going-concern principle Principle that prescribes financial statements to reflect the assumption that the business will continue operating. *(p. 10)*

Goods in process inventory Account in which costs are accumulated for products that are in the process of being produced but are not yet complete; also called *work in process inventory*. *(pp. 729 & 764)*

Goodwill Amount by which a company's (or a segment's) value exceeds the value of its individual assets less its liabilities. *(p. 403)*

Gross margin (See *gross profit.*) *(p. 179)*

Gross margin ratio Gross margin (net sales minus cost of goods sold) divided by net sales; also called *gross profit ratio*. *(p. 193)*

Gross method Method of recording purchases at the full invoice price without deducting any cash discounts. *(p. 335)*

Gross pay Total compensation earned by an employee. *(p. 433)*

Gross profit Net sales minus cost of goods sold; also called *gross margin*. *(p. 179)*

Gross profit method Procedure to estimate inventory when the past gross profit rate is used to estimate cost of goods sold, which is then subtracted from the cost of goods available for sale. *(p. 246)*

Held-to-maturity (HTM) securities Debt securities that a company has the intent and ability to hold until they mature. *(p. 590)*

High-low method Procedure that yields an estimated line of cost behavior by graphically connecting costs associated with the highest and lowest sales volume. *(p. 886)*

Horizontal analysis Comparison of a company's financial condition and performance across time. *(p. 676)*

Hurdle rate Minimum acceptable rate of return (set by management) for an investment. *(p. 1006)*

Impairment Diminishment of an asset value. *(p. 401)*

Imprest system Method to account for petty cash; maintains a constant balance in the fund, which equals cash plus petty cash receipts. *(p. 321)*

Inadequacy Condition in which the capacity of plant assets is too small to meet the company's production demands. *(p. 389)*

Income (See *net income.*) *(p. 13)*

Income statement Financial statement that subtracts expenses from revenues to yield a net income or loss over a specified period of time; also includes any gains or losses. *(p. 17)*

Income Summary Temporary account used only in the closing process to which the balances of revenue and expense accounts (including any gains or losses) are transferred; its balance is transferred to the capital account (or retained earnings for a corporation). *(p. 141)*

Incremental cost Additional cost incurred only if a company pursues a specific course of action. *(p. 1010)*

Indefinite useful life Asset life that is not limited by legal, regulatory, contractual, competitive, economic, or other factors. *(p. 401)*

Indirect costs Costs incurred for the benefit of more than one cost object. *(p. 725)*

Indirect expenses Expenses incurred for the joint benefit of more than one department (or cost object). *(p. 849)*

Indirect labor Efforts of production employees who do not work specifically on converting direct materials into finished products and who are not clearly identified with specific units or batches of product. *(p. 731)*

Indirect labor costs Labor costs that cannot be physically traced to production of a product or service; included as part of overhead. *(p. 731)*

Indirect material Material used to support the production process but not clearly identified with products or batches of product. *(p. 728)*

Indirect method Presentation that reports net income and then adjusts it by adding and subtracting items to yield net cash from operating activities on the statement of cash flows. *(p. 628)*

Information processor Component of an accounting system that interprets, transforms, and summarizes information for use in analysis and reporting. *(p. 268)*

Information storage Component of an accounting system that keeps data in a form accessible to information processors. *(p. 268)*

Infrequent gain or loss Gain or loss not expected to recur given the operating environment of the business. *(p. 697)*

Input device Means of capturing information from source documents that enables its transfer to information processors. *(p. 268)*

Installment note Liability requiring a series of periodic payments to the lender. *(p. 554)*

Intangible assets Long-term assets (resources) used to produce or sell products or services; usually lack physical form and have uncertain benefits. *(pp. 147 & 401)*

Interest Charge for using money (or other assets) loaned from one entity to another. *(p. 364)*

Interim financial statements Financial statements covering periods of less than one year; usually based on one-, three-, or six-month periods. *(pp. 93 & 245)*

Internal controls or **Internal control system** All policies and procedures used to protect assets, ensure reliable accounting, promote efficient operations, and urge adherence to company policies. *(pp. 266 & 312)*

Internal rate of return (IRR) Rate used to evaluate the acceptability of an investment; equals the rate that yields a net present value of zero for an investment. *(p. 1005)*

Internal transactions Activities within an organization that can affect the accounting equation. *(p. 13)*

Internal users Persons using accounting information who are directly involved in managing the organization. *(p. 6)*

International Accounting Standards Board (IASB) Group that identifies preferred accounting practices and encourages global acceptance; issues International Financial Reporting Standards (IFRS). *(p. 9)*

Inventory Goods a company owns and expects to sell in its normal operations. *(p. 179)*

Inventory turnover Number of times a company's average inventory is sold during a period; computed by dividing cost of goods sold by average inventory; also called *merchandise turnover*. *(p. 236)*

Investing activities Transactions that involve purchasing and selling of long-term assets, includes making and collecting notes receivable and investments in other than cash equivalents. *(p. 624)*

Investment center Center of which a manager is responsible for revenues, costs, and asset investments. *(p. 858)*

Investment center return on total assets Center net income divided by average total assets for the center. *(p. 858)*

Invoice Itemized record of goods prepared by the vendor that lists the customer's name, items sold, sales prices, and terms of sale. *(p. 332)*

Invoice approval Document containing a checklist of steps necessary for approving the recording and payment of an invoice; also called *check authorization*. *(p. 333)*

Job Production of a customized product or service. *(p. 762)*

Job cost sheet Separate record maintained for each job. *(p. 764)*

Job lot Production of more than one unit of a customized product or service. *(p. 763)*

Job order cost accounting system Cost accounting system to determine the cost of producing each job or job lot. *(pp. 764 & 801)*

Job order production Production of special-order products; also called *customized production*. *(p. 762)*

Joint cost Cost incurred to produce or purchase two or more products at the same time. *(p. 861)*

Journal Record in which transactions are entered before they are posted to ledger accounts; also called *book of original entry*. *(p. 54)*

Journalizing Process of recording transactions in a journal. *(p. 54)*

Just-in-time (JIT) manufacturing Process of acquiring or producing inventory only when needed. *(p. 724)*

Known liabilities Obligations of a company with little uncertainty; set by agreements, contracts, or laws; also called *definitely determinable liabilities*. *(p. 430)*

Land improvements Assets that increase the benefits of land, have a limited useful life, and are depreciated. *(p. 388)*

Large stock dividend Stock dividend that is more than 25% of the previously outstanding shares. *(p. 508)*

Last-in, first-out (LIFO) Method to assign cost to inventory that assumes costs for the most recent items purchased are sold first and charged to cost of goods sold. *(p. 229)*

Lean business model Practice of eliminating waste while meeting customer needs and yielding positive company returns. *(p. 724)*

Lease Contract specifying the rental of property. *(pp. 402 & 567)*

Leasehold Rights the lessor grants to the lessee under the terms of a lease. *(p. 402)*

Leasehold improvements Alterations or improvements to leased property such as partitions and storefronts. *(p. 403)*

Least-squares regression Statistical method for deriving an estimated line of cost behavior that is more precise than the high-low method and the scatter diagram. *(p. 887)*

Ledger Record containing all accounts (with amounts) for a business; also called *general ledger*. *(p. 49)*

Lessee Party to a lease who secures the right to possess and use the property from another party (the lessor). *(p. 402)*

Lessor Party to a lease who grants another party (the lessee) the right to possess and use its property. *(p. 402)*

Liabilities Creditors' claims on an organization's assets; involves a probable future payment of assets, products, or services that a company is obligated to make due to past transactions or events. *(p. 12)*

Licenses (See *franchises*.) *(p. 403)*

Limited liability Owner can lose no more than the amount invested. *(p. 11)*

Limited liability company Organization form that combines select features of a corporation and a limited partnership; provides limited liability to its members (owners), is free of business tax, and allows members to actively participate in management. *(p. 474)*

Limited liability partnership Partnership in which a partner is not personally liable for malpractice or negligence unless that partner is responsible for providing the service that resulted in the claim. *(p. 473)*

Limited partners Partners who have no personal liability for partnership debts beyond the amounts they invested in the partnership. *(p. 473)*

Limited partnership Partnership that has two classes of partners, limited partners and general partners. *(p. 473)*

Liquid assets Resources such as cash that are easily converted into other assets or used to pay for goods, services, or liabilities. *(p. 317)*

Liquidating cash dividend Distribution of assets that returns part of the original investment to stockholders; deducted from contributed capital accounts. *(p. 508)*

Liquidation Process of going out of business; involves selling assets, paying liabilities, and distributing remainder to owners.

Liquidity Availability of resources to meet short-term cash requirements. *(pp. 317 & 675)*

List price Catalog (full) price of an item before any trade discount is deducted. *(p. 180)*

Long-term investments Long-term assets not used in operating activities such as notes receivable and investments in stocks and bonds. *(pp. 147 & 586)*

Long-term liabilities Obligations not due to be paid within one year or the operating cycle, whichever is longer. *(pp. 147 & 429)*

Lower of cost or market (LCM) Required method to report inventory at market replacement cost when that market cost is lower than recorded cost. *(p. 233)*

Maker of the note Entity who signs a note and promises to pay it at maturity. *(p. 364)*

Management by exception Management process to focus on significant variances and give less attention to areas where performance is close to the standard. *(p. 970)*

Managerial accounting Area of accounting mainly aimed at serving the decision-making needs of internal users; also called *management accounting.* *(pp. 6 & 720)*

Manufacturer Company that uses labor and operating assets to convert raw materials to finished goods. *(p. 13)*

Manufacturing budget Plan that shows the predicted costs for direct materials, direct labor, and overhead to be incurred in manufacturing units in the production budget. *(p. 935)*

Manufacturing statement Report that summarizes the types and amounts of costs incurred in a company's production process for a period; also called *cost of goods manufacturing statement.* *(p. 733)*

Margin of safety Excess of expected sales over the level of break-even sales. *(p. 893)*

Market prospects Expectations (both good and bad) about a company's future performance as assessed by users and other interested parties. *(p. 675)*

Market rate Interest rate that borrowers are willing to pay and lenders are willing to accept for a specific lending agreement given the borrowers' risk level. *(p. 547)*

Market value per share Price at which stock is bought or sold. *(p. 503)*

Master budget Comprehensive business plan that includes specific plans for expected sales, product units to be produced, merchandise (or materials) to be purchased, expenses to be incurred, plant assets to be purchased, and amounts of cash to be borrowed or loans to be repaid, as well as a budgeted income statement and balance sheet. *(p. 920)*

Matching principle Prescribes expenses to be reported in the same period as the revenues that were earned as a result of the expenses. *(pp. 94 & 358)*

Materiality principal Prescribes that accounting for items that significantly impact financial statement and any inferences from them adhere strictly to GAAP. *(p. 358)*

Materials consumption report Document that summarizes the materials a department uses during a reporting period; replaces materials requisitions. *(p. 802)*

Materials ledger card Perpetual record updated each time units are purchased or issued for production use. *(p. 765)*

Materials requisition Source document production managers use to request materials for production; used to assign materials costs to specific jobs or overhead. *(p. 767)*

Maturity date of a note Date when a note's principal and interest are due. *(p. 364)*

Merchandise (See *merchandise inventory.*) *(p. 178)*

Merchandise inventory Goods that a company owns and expects to sell to customers; also called *merchandise* or *inventory.* *(p. 179)*

Merchandise purchases budget Plan that shows the units or costs of merchandise to be purchased by a merchandising company during the budget period. *(p. 923)*

Merchandiser Entity that earns net income by buying and selling merchandise. *(p. 178)*

Merit rating Rating assigned to an employer by a state based on the employer's record of employment. *(p. 436)*

Minimum legal capital Amount of assets defined by law that stockholders must (potentially) invest in a corporation; usually defined as par value of the stock; intended to protect creditors. *(p. 503)*

Mixed cost Cost that behaves like a combination of fixed and variable costs. *(p. 883)*

Modified Accelerated Cost Recovery System (MACRS) Depreciation system required by federal income tax law. *(p. 394)*

Monetary unit principle Principle that assumes transactions and events can be expressed in money units. *(p. 10)*

Mortgage Legal loan agreement that protects a lender by giving the lender the right to be paid from the cash proceeds from the sale of a borrower's assets identified in the mortgage. *(p. 556)*

Multinational Company that operates in several countries. *(p. 599)*

Multiple-step income statement Income statement format that shows subtotals between sales and net income, categorizes expenses, and often reports the details of net sales and expenses. *(p. 191)*

Mutual agency Legal relationship among partners whereby each partner is an agent of the partnership and is able to bind the partnership to contracts within the scope of the partnership's business. *(p. 473)*

Natural business year Twelve-month period that ends when a company's sales activities are at their lowest point. *(p. 93)*

Natural resources Assets physically consumed when used; examples are timber, mineral deposits, and oil and gas fields; also called *wasting assets.* *(p. 400)*

Net assets (See *equity.*) *(p. 12)*

Net income Amount earned after subtracting all expenses necessary for and matched with sales for a period; also called *income, profit,* or *earnings.* *(p. 13)*

Net loss Excess of expenses over revenues for a period. *(p. 18)*

Net method Method of recording purchases at the full invoice price less any cash discounts. *(p. 335)*

Net pay Gross pay less all deductions; also called *take-home pay.* *(p. 433)*

Net present value (NPV) Dollar estimate of an asset's value that is used to evaluate the acceptability of an investment; computed by discounting future cash flows from the investment at a satisfactory rate and then subtracting the initial cost of the investment. *(p. 1003)*

Net realizable value Expected selling price (value) of an item minus the cost of making the sale. *(p. 224)*

Noncontrollable costs Costs that a manager does not have the power to control or strongly influence. *(p. 726)*

Noncumulative preferred stock Preferred stock on which the right to receive dividends is lost for any period when dividends are not declared. *(p. 511)*

Noninterest-bearing note Note with no stated (contract) rate of interest; interest is implicitly included in the note's face value.

Nonparticipating preferred stock Preferred stock on which dividends are limited to a maximum amount each year. *(p. 512)*

No-par value stock Stock class that has not been assigned a par (or stated) value by the corporate charter. *(p. 503)*

Nonsufficient funds (NSF) check Maker's bank account has insufficient money to pay the check; also called *hot check*. *(p. 326)*

Non-value-added time The portion of cycle time that is not directed at producing a product or service; equals the sum of inspection time, move time, and wait time. *(p. 735)*

Note (See promissory note.) *(p. 364)*

Note payable Liability expressed by a written promise to pay a definite sum of money on demand or on a specific future date(s). *(p. 364)*

Note receivable Asset consisting of a written promise to receive a definite sum of money on demand or on a specific future date(s). *(p. 49)*

Objectivity principle Principle that prescribes independent, unbiased evidence to support financial statement information. *(p. 9)*

Obsolescence Condition in which, because of new inventions and improvements, a plant asset can no longer be used to produce goods or services with a competitive advantage. *(p. 389)*

Off-balance-sheet financing Acquisition of assets by agreeing to liabilities not reported on the balance sheet. *(p. 568)*

Online processing Approach to inputting data from source documents as soon as the information is available. *(p. 281)*

Operating activities Activities that involve the production or purchase of merchandise and the sale of goods or services to customers, including expenditures related to administering the business. *(p. 623)*

Operating cycle Normal time between paying cash for merchandise or employee services and receiving cash from customers. *(p. 145)*

Operating leases Short-term (or cancelable) leases in which the lessor retains risks and rewards of ownership. *(p. 567)*

Operating leverage Extent, or relative size, of fixed costs in the total cost structure. *(p. 896)*

Opportunity cost Potential benefit lost by choosing a specific action from two or more alternatives. *(p. 726)*

Ordinary repairs Repairs to keep a plant asset in normal, good operating condition; treated as a revenue expenditure and immediately expensed. *(p. 397)*

Organization expenses (costs) Costs such as legal fees and promoter fees to bring an entity into existence. *(pp. 501 & 506)*

Out-of-pocket cost Cost incurred or avoided as a result of management's decisions. *(p. 726)*

Output devices Means by which information is taken out of the accounting system and made available for use. *(p. 269)*

Outsourcing Manager decision to buy a product or service from another entity; part of a *make-or-buy* decision; also called *make or buy*. *(p. 997)*

Outstanding checks Checks written and recorded by the depositor but not yet paid by the bank at the bank statement date. *(p. 326)*

Outstanding stock Corporation's stock held by its shareholders.

Overapplied overhead Amount by which the overhead applied to production in a period using the predetermined overhead rate exceeds the actual overhead incurred in a period. *(p. 774)*

Overhead cost variance Difference between the total overhead cost applied to products and the total overhead cost actually incurred. *(p. 966)*

Owner, capital Account showing the owner's claim on company assets; equals owner investments plus net income (or less net losses) minus owner withdrawals since the company's inception; also referred to as *equity*. *(p. 13)*

Owner investment Assets put into the business by the owner. *(p. 12)*

Owner's equity (See *equity*.) *(p. 12)*

Owner withdrawals (See *withdrawals*.) *(p. 13)*

Paid-in capital (See *contributed capital*.) *(p. 504)*

Paid-in capital in excess of par value Amount received from issuance of stock that is in excess of the stock's par value. *(p. 505)*

Par value Value assigned a share of stock by the corporate charter when the stock is authorized. *(p. 503)*

Par value of a bond Amount the bond issuer agrees to pay at maturity and the amount on which cash interest payments are based; also called *face amount* or *face value* of a bond. *(p. 544)*

Par value stock Class of stock assigned a par value by the corporate charter. *(p. 503)*

Parent Company that owns a controlling interest in a corporation (requires more than 50% of voting stock). *(p. 593)*

Participating preferred stock Preferred stock that shares with common stockholders any dividends paid in excess of the percent stated on preferred stock. *(p. 512)*

Partner return on equity Partner net income divided by average partner equity for the period. *(p. 484)*

Partnership Unincorporated association of two or more persons to pursue a business for profit as co-owners. *(pp. 10 & 472)*

Partnership contract Agreement among partners that sets terms under which the affairs of the partnership are conducted; also called *articles of partnership*. *(p. 472)*

Partnership liquidation Dissolution of a partnership by (1) selling noncash assets and allocating any gain or loss according to partners' income-and-loss ratio, (2) paying liabilities, and (3) distributing any remaining cash according to partners' capital balances. *(p. 482)*

Patent Exclusive right granted to its owner to produce and sell an item or to use a process for 17 years. *(p. 402)*

Payback period (PBP) Time-based measurement used to evaluate the acceptability of an investment; equals the time expected to pass before an investment's net cash flows equal its initial cost. *(p. 999)*

Payee of the note Entity to whom a note is made payable. *(p. 364)*

Payroll bank account Bank account used solely for paying employees; each pay period an amount equal to the total employees' net pay is deposited in it and the payroll checks are drawn on it. *(p. 448)*

Payroll deductions Amounts withheld from an employee's gross pay; also called *withholdings*. *(p. 434)*

Payroll register Record for a pay period that shows the pay period dates, regular and overtime hours worked, gross pay, net pay, and deductions. *(p. 446)*

Pension plan Contractual agreement between an employer and its employees for the employer to provide benefits to employees after they retire; expensed when incurred. *(p. 569)*

Period costs Expenditures identified more with a time period than with finished products costs; includes selling and general administrative expenses. *(p. 726)*

Periodic inventory system Method that records the cost of inventory purchased but does not continuously track the quantity available or sold to customers; records are updated at the end of each period to reflect the physical count and costs of goods available. *(p. 180)*

Permanent accounts Accounts that reflect activities related to one or more future periods; balance sheet accounts whose balances are not closed; also called *real accounts*. *(p. 140)*

Perpetual inventory system Method that maintains continuous records of the cost of inventory available and the cost of goods sold. *(p. 179)*

Petty cash Small amount of cash in a fund to pay minor expenses; accounted for using an imprest system. *(p. 321)*

Planning Process of setting goals and preparing to achieve them. *(p. 721)*

Plant assets Tangible long-lived assets used to produce or sell products and services; also called *property, plant and equipment (PP&E)* or *fixed assets*. *(pp. 96 & 386)*

Pledged assets to secured liabilities Ratio of the book value of a company's pledged assets to the book value of its secured liabilities.

Post-closing trial balance List of permanent accounts and their balances from the ledger after all closing entries are journalized and posted. *(p. 144)*

Posting Process of transferring journal entry information to the ledger; computerized systems automate this process. *(p. 54)*

Posting reference (PR) column A column in journals in which individual ledger account numbers are entered when entries are posted to those ledger accounts. *(p. 55)*

Predetermined overhead rate Rate established prior to the beginning of a period that relates estimated overhead to another variable, such as estimated direct labor, and is used to assign overhead cost to production. *(p. 770)*

Preemptive right Stockholders' right to maintain their proportionate interest in a corporation with any additional shares issued. *(p. 502)*

Preferred stock Stock with a priority status over common stockholders in one or more ways, such as paying dividends or distributing assets. *(p. 510)*

Premium on bonds Difference between a bond's par value and its higher carrying value; occurs when the contract rate is higher than the market rate; also called *bond premium*. *(p. 550)*

Premium on stock (See *contributed capital in excess of par value*.) *(p. 505)*

Prepaid expenses Items paid for in advance of receiving their benefits; classified as assets. *(p. 95)*

Price-earnings (PE) ratio Ratio of a company's current market value per share to its earnings per share; also called *price-to-earnings*. *(p. 519)*

Price variance Difference between actual and budgeted revenue or cost caused by the difference between the actual price per unit and the budgeted price per unit. *(p. 958)*

Prime costs Expenditures directly identified with the production of finished goods; include direct materials costs and direct labor costs. *(p. 731)*

Principal of a note Amount that the signer of a note agrees to pay back when it matures, not including interest. *(p. 364)*

Principles of internal control Principles prescribing management to establish responsibility, maintain records, insure assets, separate recordkeeping from custody of assets, divide responsibility for related transactions, apply technological controls, and perform reviews. *(p. 313)*

Prior period adjustment Correction of an error in a prior year that is reported in the statement of retained earnings (or statement of stockholders' equity) net of any income tax effects. *(p. 517)*

Pro forma financial statements Statements that show the effects of proposed transactions and events as if they had occurred. *(p. 140)*

Process cost accounting system System of assigning direct materials, direct labor, and overhead to specific processes; total costs associated with each process are then divided by the number of units passing through that process to determine the cost per equivalent unit. *(p. 801)*

Process cost summary Report of costs charged to a department, its equivalent units of production achieved, and the costs assigned to its output. *(p. 809)*

Process operations Processing of products in a continuous (sequential) flow of steps; also called *process manufacturing* or *process production*. *(p. 798)*

Product costs Costs that are capitalized as inventory because they produce benefits expected to have future value; include direct materials, direct labor, and overhead. *(p. 726)*

Production budget Plan that shows the units to be produced each period. *(p. 935)*

Profit (See *net income*.) *(p. 13)*

Profit center Business unit that incurs costs and generates revenues. *(p. 848)*

Profit margin Ratio of a company's net income to its net sales; the percent of income in each dollar of revenue; also called *net profit margin*. *(p. 105)*

Profitability Company's ability to generate an adequate return on invested capital. *(p. 675)*

Promissory note (or *note*) Written promise to pay a specified amount either on demand or at a definite future date; is a *note receivable* for the lender but a *note payable* for the lendee. *(p. 364)*

Proprietorship (See *sole proprietorship*.) *(p. 10)*

Proxy Legal document giving a stockholder's agent the power to exercise the stockholder's voting rights. *(p. 502)*

Purchase discount Term used by a purchaser to describe a cash discount granted to the purchaser for paying within the discount period. *(p. 181)*

Purchase order Document used by the purchasing department to place an order with a seller (vendor). *(p. 332)*

Purchase requisition Document listing merchandise needed by a department and requesting it be purchased. *(p. 332)*

Purchases journal Journal normally used to record all purchases on credit. *(p. 277)*

Quantity variance Difference between actual and budgeted revenue or cost caused by the difference between the actual number of units and the budgeted number of units. *(p. 958)*

Ratio analysis Determination of key relations between financial statement items as reflected in numerical measures. *(p. 676)*

Raw materials inventory Goods a company acquires to use in making products. *(p. 728)*

Realizable value Expected proceeds from converting an asset into cash. *(p. 359)*

Receiving report Form used to report that ordered goods are received and to describe their quantity and condition. *(p. 333)*

Recordkeeping Part of accounting that involves recording transactions and events, either manually or electronically; also called *bookkeeping*. *(p. 5)*

Registered bonds Bonds owned by investors whose names and addresses are recorded by the issuer; interest payments are made to the registered owners. *(p. 557)*

Relevance principle Information system principle prescribing that its reports be useful, understandable, timely, and pertinent for decision making. *(p. 266)*

Relevant benefits Additional or incremental revenue generated by selecting a particular course of action over another. *(p. 1009)*

Relevant range of operations Company's normal operating range; excludes extremely high and low volumes not likely to occur. *(p. 891)*

Report form balance sheet Balance sheet that lists accounts vertically in the order of assets, liabilities, and equity. *(p. 18)*

Responsibility accounting budget Report of expected costs and expenses under a manager's control. *(p. 856)*

Responsibility accounting performance report Responsibility report that compares actual costs and expenses for a department with budgeted amounts. *(p. 856)*

Responsibility accounting system System that provides information that management can use to evaluate the performance of a department's manager. *(p. 848)*

Restricted retained earnings Retained earnings not available for dividends because of legal or contractual limitations. *(p. 516)*

Retail inventory method Method to estimate ending inventory based on the ratio of the amount of goods for sale at cost to the amount of goods for sale at retail. *(p. 245)*

Retailer Intermediary that buys products from manufacturers or wholesalers and sells them to consumers. *(p. 178)*

Retained earnings Cumulative income less cumulative losses and dividends. *(p. 504)*

Retained earnings deficit Debit (abnormal) balance in Retained Earnings; occurs when cumulative losses and dividends exceed cumulative income; also called *accumulated deficit*. *(p. 507)*

Return Monies received from an investment; often in percent form. *(p. 23)*

Return on assets (See *return on total assets*) *(p. 20)*

Return on total assets Ratio reflecting operating efficiency; defined as net income divided by average total assets for the period; also called *return on assets* or *return on investment*. *(p. 594)*

Return on equity Ratio of net income to average equity for the period.

Revenue expenditures Expenditures reported on the current income statement as an expense because they do not provide benefits in future periods. *(p. 396)*

Revenue recognition principle The principle prescribing that revenue is recognized when earned. *(p. 10)*

Revenues Gross increase in equity from a company's business activities that earn income; also called *sales*. *(p. 13)*

Reverse stock split Occurs when a corporation calls in its stock and replaces each share with less than one new share; increases both market value per share and any par or stated value per share. *(p. 510)*

Reversing entries Optional entries recorded at the beginning of a period that prepare the accounts for the usual journal entries as if adjusting entries had not occurred in the prior period. *(p. 151)*

Risk Uncertainty about an expected return. *(p. 24)*

Rolling budget New set of budgets a firm adds for the next period (with revisions) to replace the ones that have lapsed. *(p. 918)*

S corporation Corporation that meets special tax qualifications so as to be treated like a partnership for income tax purposes. *(p. 474)*

Safety stock Quantity of inventory or materials over the minimum needed to satisfy budgeted demand. *(p. 923)*

Sales (See *revenues.*) *(p. 13)*

Sales budget Plan showing the units of goods to be sold or services to be provided; the starting point in the budgeting process for most departments. *(p. 922)*

Sales discount Term used by a seller to describe a cash discount granted to buyers who pay within the discount period. *(p. 181)*

Sales journal Journal normally used to record sales of goods on credit. *(p. 271)*

Sales mix Ratio of sales volumes for the various products sold by a company. *(p. 895)*

Salvage value Estimate of amount to be recovered at the end of an asset's useful life; also called *residual value* or *scrap value*. *(p. 389)*

Sarbanes-Oxley Act Created the Public *Company Accounting Oversight Board*, regulates analyst conflicts, imposes corporate governance requirements, enhances accounting and control disclosures, impacts insider transactions and executive loans, establishes new types of criminal conduct, and expands penalties for violations of federal securities laws. *(p. 11)*

Scatter diagram Graph used to display data about past cost behavior and sales as points on a diagram. *(p. 885)*

Schedule of accounts payable List of the balances of all accounts in the accounts payable ledger and their total. *(p. 278)*

Schedule of accounts receivable List of the balances for all accounts in the accounts receivable ledger and their total. *(p. 273)*

Secured bonds Bonds that have specific assets of the issuer pledged as collateral. *(p. 557)*

Securities and Exchange Commission (SEC) Federal agency Congress has charged to set reporting rules for organizations that sell ownership shares to the public. *(p. 9)*

Segment return on assets Segment operating income divided by segment average (identifiable) assets for the period. *(p. 282)*

Selling expense budget Plan that lists the types and amounts of selling expenses expected in the budget period. *(p. 924)*

Selling expenses Expenses of promoting sales, such as displaying and advertising merchandise, making sales, and delivering goods to customers. *(p. 191)*

Serial bonds Bonds consisting of separate amounts that mature at different dates. *(p. 557)*

Service company Organization that provides services instead of tangible products. *(p. 178)*

Shareholders Owners of a corporation; also called *stockholders*. *(p. 11)*

Shares Equity of a corporation divided into ownership units; also called *stock*. *(p. 11)*

Short-term investments Debt and equity securities that management expects to convert to cash within the next 3 to 12 months (or the operating cycle if longer); also called *temporary investments* or *marketable securities*. *(p. 586)*

Short-term note payable Current obligation in the form of a written promissory note. *(p. 431)*

Shrinkage Inventory losses that occur as a result of theft or deterioration. *(p. 188)*

Signature card Includes the signatures of each person authorized to sign checks on the bank account. *(p. 323)*

Simple capital structure Capital structure that consists of only common stock and nonconvertible preferred stock; consists of no dilutive securities. *(p. 519)*

Single-step income statement Income statement format that includes cost of goods sold as an expense and shows only one subtotal for total expenses. *(p. 192)*

Sinking fund bonds Bonds that require the issuer to make deposits to a separate account; bondholders are repaid at maturity from that account. *(p. 557)*

Small stock dividend Stock dividend that is 25% or less of a corporation's previously outstanding shares. *(p. 508)*

Social responsibility Being accountable for the impact that one's actions might have on society. *(p. 8)*

Sole proprietorship Business owned by one person that is not organized as a corporation; also called *proprietorship*. *(p. 10)*

Solvency Company's long-run financial viability and its ability to cover long-term obligations. *(p. 675)*

Source documents Source of information for accounting entries that can be in either paper or electronic form; also called *business papers*. *(p. 49)*

Special journal Any journal used for recording and posting transactions of a similar type. *(p. 270)*

Specific identification Method to assign cost to inventory when the purchase cost of each item in inventory is identified and used to compute cost of inventory. *(p. 227)*

Spending variance Difference between the actual price of an item and its standard price. *(p. 966)*

Spreadsheet Computer program that organizes data by means of formulas and format; also called *electronic work sheet*. *(p. 136)*

Standard costs Costs that should be incurred under normal conditions to produce a product or component or to perform a service. *(p. 959)*

State Unemployment Taxes (SUTA) State payroll taxes on employers to support its unemployment programs. *(p. 436)*

Stated value stock No-par stock assigned a stated value per share; this amount is recorded in the stock account when the stock is issued. *(p. 504)*

Statement of cash flows A financial statement that lists cash inflows (receipts) and cash outflows (payments) during a period; arranged by operating, investing, and financing. *(pp. 17 & 622)*

Statement of owner's equity Report of changes in equity over a period; adjusted for increases (owner investment and net income) and for decreases (withdrawals and net loss). *(p. 17)*

Statement of partners' equity Financial statement that shows total capital balances at the beginning of the period, any additional investment by partners, the income or loss of the period, the partners' withdrawals, and the partners' ending capital balances; also called *statement of partners' capital*. *(p. 477)*

Statement of retained earnings Report of changes in retained earnings over a period; adjusted for increases (net income), for decreases (dividends and net loss), and for any prior period adjustment.

Statement of stockholders' equity Financial statement that lists the beginning and ending balances of each major equity account and describes all changes in those accounts. *(p. 517)*

Statements of Financial Accounting Standards (SFAS) FASB publications that establish U.S. GAAP. *(p. 9)*

Step-wise cost Cost that remains fixed over limited ranges of volumes but changes by a lump sum when volume changes occur outside these limited ranges. *(p. 884)*.

Stock (See *shares*.) *(p. 11)*

Stock dividend Corporation's distribution of its own stock to its stockholders without the receipt of any payment. *(p. 508)*

Stock options Rights to purchase common stock at a fixed price over a specified period of time. *(p. 517)*

Stock split Occurs when a corporation calls in its stock and replaces each share with more than one new share; decreases both the market value per share and any par or stated value per share. *(p. 510)*

Stock subscription Investor's contractual commitment to purchase unissued shares at future dates and prices.

Stockholders (See *shareholders*.) *(p. 11)*

Stockholders' equity A corporation's equity; also called *shareholders' equity* or *corporate capital*. *(p. 504)*

Straight-line depreciation Method that allocates an equal portion of the depreciable cost of plant asset (cost minus salvage) to each accounting period in its useful life. *(pp. 97 & 390)*

Straight-line bond amortization Method allocating an equal amount of bond interest expense to each period of the bond life. *(p. 548)*

Subsidiary Entity controlled by another entity (parent) in which the parent owns more than 50% of the subsidiary's voting stock. *(p. 593)*

Subsidiary ledger List of individual sub-accounts and amounts with a common characteristic; linked to a controlling account in the general ledger. *(p. 270)*

Sunk cost Cost already incurred and cannot be avoided or changed. *(p. 726)*

Supplementary records Information outside the usual accounting records; also called *supplemental records*. *(p. 184)*

Supply chain Linkages of services or goods extending from suppliers, to the company itself, and on to customers.

T-account Tool used to show the effects of transactions and events on individual accounts. *(p. 53)*

Target cost Maximum allowable cost for a product or service; defined as expected selling price less the desired profit. *(p. 763)*

Temporary accounts Accounts used to record revenues, expenses, and withdrawals (dividends for a corporation); they are closed at the end of each period; also called *nominal accounts*. *(p. 140)*

Term bonds Bonds scheduled for payment (maturity) at a single specified date. *(p. 557)*

Throughput time (See *cycle time*.)

Time period principle Assumption that an organization's activities can be divided into specific time periods such as months, quarters, or years. *(p. 92)*

Time ticket Source document used to report the time an employee spent working on a job or on overhead activities and then to determine the amount of direct labor to charge to the job or the amount of indirect labor to charge to overhead. *(p. 768)*

Times interest earned Ratio of income before interest expense (and any income taxes) divided by interest expense; reflects risk of covering interest commitments when income varies. *(p. 441)*

Total asset turnover Measure of a company's ability to use its assets to generate sales; computed by dividing net sales by average total assets. *(p. 404)*

Total quality management (TQM) Concept calling for all managers and employees at all stages of operations to strive toward higher standards and reduce number of defects. *(p. 724)*

Trade discount Reduction from a list or catalog price that can vary for wholesalers, retailers, and consumers. *(p. 180)*

Trademark or **Trade (Brand) name** Symbol, name, phrase, or jingle identified with a company, product, or service. *(p. 403)*

Trading on the equity (See *financial leverage*.)

Trading securities Investments in debt and equity securities that the company intends to actively trade for profit. *(p. 589)*

Transaction Exchange of economic consideration affecting an entity's financial position that can be reliably measured. *(p. 13)*

Treasury stock Corporation's own stock that it reacquired and still holds. *(p. 514)*

Trial balance List of accounts and their balances at a point in time; total debit balances equal total credit balances. *(p. 63)*

Unadjusted trial balance List of accounts and balances prepared before accounting adjustments are recorded and posted. *(p. 103)*

Unavoidable expense Expense (or cost) that is not relevant for business decisions; an expense that would continue even if a department, product, or service is eliminated. *(p. 1014)*

Unclassified balance sheet Balance sheet that broadly groups assets, liabilities, and equity accounts. *(p. 145)*

Uncontrollable costs Costs that a manager does not have the power to determine or strongly influence. *(p. 856)*

Underapplied overhead Amount by which overhead incurred in a period exceeds the overhead applied to that period's production using the predetermined overhead rate. *(p. 773)*

Unearned revenue Liability created when customers pay in advance for products or services; earned when the products or services are later delivered. *(pp. 51 & 98)*

Unfavorable variance Difference in revenues or costs, when the actual amount is compared to the budgeted amount, that contributes to a lower income. *(p. 956)*

Unit contribution margin Amount a product's unit selling price exceeds its total unit variable cost.

Units-of-production depreciation Method that charges a varying amount to depreciation expense for each period of an asset's useful life depending on its usage. *(p. 391)*

Unlimited liability Legal relationship among general partners that makes each of them responsible for partnership debts if the other partners are unable to pay their shares. *(p. 473)*

Unrealized gain (loss) Gain (loss) not yet realized by an actual transaction or event such as a sale. *(p. 589)*

Unsecured bonds Bonds backed only by the issuer's credit standing; almost always riskier than secured bonds; also called *debentures*. *(p. 557)*

Unusual gain or loss Gain or loss that is abnormal or unrelated to the company's ordinary activities and environment. *(p. 697)*

Useful life Length of time an asset will be productively used in the operations of a business; also called *service life*. *(p. 389)*

Value-added time The portion of cycle time that is directed at producing a product or service; equals process time. *(p. 735)*

Value chain Sequential activities that add value to an entity's products or services; includes design, production, marketing, distribution, and service. *(p. 732)*

Variable cost Cost that changes in proportion to changes in the activity output volume. *(p. 725)*

Variance analysis Process of examining differences between actual and budgeted revenues or costs and describing them in terms of price and quantity differences. *(p. 958)*

Vendee Buyer of goods or services. *(p. 332)*

Vendor Seller of goods or services. *(p. 332)*

Vertical analysis Evaluation of each financial statement item or group of items in terms of a specific base amount. *(p. 676)*

Volume variance Difference between two dollar amounts of fixed overhead cost; one amount is the total budgeted overhead cost, and the other is the overhead cost allocated to products using the predetermined fixed overhead rate. *(p. 967)*

Voucher Internal file used to store documents and information to control cash disbursements and to ensure that a transaction is properly authorized and recorded. *(p. 320)*

Voucher register Journal (referred to as *book of original entry*) in which all vouchers are recorded after they have been approved. *(p. 334)*

Voucher system Procedures and approvals designed to control cash disbursements and acceptance of obligations. *(p. 319)*

Wage bracket withholding table Table of the amounts of income tax withheld from employees' wages. *(p. 448)*

Warranty Agreement that obligates the seller to correct or replace a product or service when it fails to perform properly within a specified period. *(p. 438)*

Weighted average Method to assign inventory cost to sales; the cost of available-for-sale units is divided by the number of units available to determine per unit cost prior to each sale that is then multiplied by the units sold to yield the cost of that sale. *(p. 230)*

Weighted-average method (See *weighted average.*) *(p. 808)*

Wholesaler Intermediary that buys products from manufacturers or other wholesalers and sells them to retailers or other wholesalers. *(p. 178)*

Withdrawals Payment of cash or other assets from a proprietorship or partnership to its owner or owners. *(p. 13)*

Work sheet Spreadsheet used to draft an unadjusted trial balance, adjusting entries, adjusted trial balance, and financial statements. *(p. 136)*

Working capital Current assets minus current liabilities at a point in time. *(p. 685)*

Working papers Analyses and other informal reports prepared by accountants and managers when organizing information for formal reports and financial statements. *(p. 136)*

Credits

Index

Chart of Accounts

Following is a typical chart of accounts. Each company has its own unique accounts and numbering system.

Assets

Current Assets

101 Cash
102 Petty cash
103 Cash equivalents
104 Short-term investments
105 Market adjustment, _____ securities (S-T)
106 Accounts receivable
107 Allowance for doubtful accounts
108 Legal fees receivable
109 Interest receivable
110 Rent receivable
111 Notes receivable
119 Merchandise inventory
120 _____ inventory
121 _____ inventory
124 Office supplies
125 Store supplies
126 _____ supplies
128 Prepaid insurance
129 Prepaid interest
131 Prepaid rent
132 Raw materials inventory
133 Goods in process inventory, _____
134 Goods in process inventory, _____
135 Finished goods inventory

Long-Term Investments

141 Long-term investments
142 Market adjustment, _____ securities (L-T)
144 Investment in _____
145 Bond sinking fund

Plant Assets

151 Automobiles
152 Accumulated depreciation—Automobiles
153 Trucks
154 Accumulated depreciation—Trucks
155 Boats
156 Accumulated depreciation—Boats
157 Professional library
158 Accumulated depreciation—Professional library
159 Law library
160 Accumulated depreciation—Law library
161 Furniture
162 Accumulated depreciation—Furniture
163 Office equipment
164 Accumulated depreciation—Office equipment
165 Store equipment
166 Accumulated depreciation—Store equipment
167 _____ equipment
168 Accumulated depreciation—_____ equipment
169 Machinery
170 Accumulated depreciation—Machinery
173 Building _____
174 Accumulated depreciation—Building _____
175 Building _____
176 Accumulated depreciation—Building _____
179 Land improvements _____
180 Accumulated depreciation—Land improvements _____
181 Land improvements _____
182 Accumulated depreciation—Land improvements _____
183 Land

Natural Resources

185 Mineral deposit
186 Accumulated depletion—Mineral deposit

Intangible Assets

191 Patents
192 Leasehold
193 Franchise
194 Copyrights
195 Leasehold improvements
196 Licenses
197 Accumulated amortization—_____

Liabilities

Current Liabilities

201 Accounts payable
202 Insurance payable
203 Interest payable
204 Legal fees payable
207 Office salaries payable
208 Rent payable
209 Salaries payable
210 Wages payable
211 Accrued payroll payable
214 Estimated warranty liability
215 Income taxes payable
216 Common dividend payable
217 Preferred dividend payable
218 State unemployment taxes payable
219 Employee federal income taxes payable
221 Employee medical insurance payable
222 Employee retirement program payable
223 Employee union dues payable
224 Federal unemployment taxes payable
225 FICA taxes payable
226 Estimated vacation pay liability

Unearned Revenues

230 Unearned consulting fees
231 Unearned legal fees
232 Unearned property management fees
233 Unearned _____ fees
234 Unearned _____ fees
235 Unearned janitorial revenue
236 Unearned _____ revenue
238 Unearned rent

Notes Payable

240 Short-term notes payable
241 Discount on short-term notes payable
245 Notes payable
251 Long-term notes payable
252 Discount on long-term notes payable

Long-Term Liabilities

253 Long-term lease liability
255 Bonds payable
256 Discount on bonds payable
257 Premium on bonds payable
258 Deferred income tax liability

Equity

Owner's Equity

301 _____, Capital
302 _____, Withdrawals
303 _____, Capital
304 _____, Withdrawals
305 _____, Capital
306 _____, Withdrawals

Paid-In Capital

307 Common stock, $ _____ par value
308 Common stock, no-par value
309 Common stock, $ _____ stated value
310 Common stock dividend distributable
311 Paid-in capital in excess of par value, Common stock
312 Paid-in capital in excess of stated value, No-par common stock
313 Paid-in capital from retirement of common stock
314 Paid-in capital, Treasury stock
315 Preferred stock
316 Paid-in capital in excess of par value, Preferred stock

Retained Earnings

318 Retained earnings
319 Cash dividends (or Dividends)
320 Stock dividends

Other Equity Accounts

321 Treasury stock, Common
322 Unrealized gain—Equity
323 Unrealized loss—Equity

Revenues

401 _____ fees earned
402 _____ fees earned
403 _____ services revenue
404 _____ services revenue
405 Commissions earned
406 Rent revenue (or Rent earned)
407 Dividends revenue (or Dividend earned)
408 Earnings from investment in _____
409 Interest revenue (or Interest earned)
410 Sinking fund earnings
413 Sales
414 Sales returns and allowances
415 Sales discounts

Cost of Sales

Cost of Goods Sold

502 Cost of goods sold
505 Purchases
506 Purchases returns and allowances
507 Purchases discounts
508 Transportation-in

Manufacturing

520 Raw materials purchases
521 Freight-in on raw materials
530 Factory payroll
531 Direct labor
540 Factory overhead
541 Indirect materials
542 Indirect labor
543 Factory insurance expired
544 Factory supervision
545 Factory supplies used
546 Factory utilities
547 Miscellaneous production costs
548 Property taxes on factory building
549 Property taxes on factory equipment
550 Rent on factory building
551 Repairs, factory equipment
552 Small tools written off
560 Depreciation of factory equipment
561 Depreciation of factory building

Standard Cost Variance

580 Direct material quantity variance
581 Direct material price variance
582 Direct labor quantity variance
583 Direct labor price variance
584 Factory overhead volume variance
585 Factory overhead controllable variance

Expenses

Amortization, Depletion, and Depreciation

601 Amortization expense—_____
602 Amortization expense—_____
603 Depletion expense—_____
604 Depreciation expense—Boats
605 Depreciation expense—Automobiles
606 Depreciation expense—Building _____
607 Depreciation expense—Building _____
608 Depreciation expense—Land improvements _____
609 Depreciation expense—Land improvements _____
610 Depreciation expense—Law library
611 Depreciation expense—Trucks
612 Depreciation expense—_____ equipment
613 Depreciation expense—_____ equipment
614 Depreciation expense—_____
615 Depreciation expense—_____

Employee-Related Expenses

620 Office salaries expense
621 Sales salaries expense
622 Salaries expense
623 _____ wages expense
624 Employees' benefits expense
625 Payroll taxes expense

Financial Expenses

630 Cash over and short
631 Discounts lost
632 Factoring fee expense
633 Interest expense

Insurance Expenses

635 Insurance expense—Delivery equipment
636 Insurance expense—Office equipment
637 Insurance expense—_____

Rental Expenses

640 Rent expense
641 Rent expense—Office space
642 Rent expense—Selling space
643 Press rental expense
644 Truck rental expense
645 _____ rental expense

Supplies Expenses

650 Office supplies expense
651 Store supplies expense
652 _____ supplies expense
653 _____ supplies expense

Miscellaneous Expenses

655 Advertising expense
656 Bad debts expense
657 Blueprinting expense
658 Boat expense
659 Collection expense
661 Concessions expense
662 Credit card expense
663 Delivery expense
664 Dumping expense
667 Equipment expense
668 Food and drinks expense
671 Gas and oil expense
672 General and administrative expense
673 Janitorial expense
674 Legal fees expense
676 Mileage expense
677 Miscellaneous expenses
678 Mower and tools expense
679 Operating expense
680 Organization expense
681 Permits expense
682 Postage expense
683 Property taxes expense
684 Repairs expense—_____
685 Repairs expense—_____
687 Selling expense
688 Telephone expense
689 Travel and entertainment expense
690 Utilities expense
691 Warranty expense
695 Income taxes expense

Gains and Losses

701 Gain on retirement of bonds
702 Gain on sale of machinery
703 Gain on sale of investments
704 Gain on sale of trucks
705 Gain on _____
706 Foreign exchange gain or loss
801 Loss on disposal of machinery
802 Loss on exchange of equipment
803 Loss on exchange of _____
804 Loss on sale of notes
805 Loss on retirement of bonds
806 Loss on sale of investments
807 Loss on sale of machinery
808 Loss on _____
809 Unrealized gain—Income
810 Unrealized loss—Income

Clearing Accounts

901 Income summary
902 Manufacturing summary

A Rose by Any Other Name

The same financial statement sometimes receives different titles. Below are some of the more common aliases.*

Balance Sheet	Statement of Financial Position Statement of Financial Condition
Income Statement	Statement of Income Operating Statement Statement of Operations Statement of Operating Activity Earnings Statement Statement of Earnings Profit and Loss (P&L) Statement
Statement of Cash Flows	Statement of Cash Flow Cash Flows Statement Statement of Changes in Cash Position Statement of Changes in Financial Position
Statement of Owner's Equity	Statement of Changes in Owner's Equity Statement of Changes in Owner's Capital Statement of Shareholders' Equity[†] Statement of Changes in Shareholders' Equity[†] Statement of Stockholders' Equity and Comprehensive Income[†] Statement of Changes in Capital Accounts[†]

*The term **Consolidated** often precedes or follows these statement titles to reflect the combination of different entities, such as a parent company and its subsidiaries.
[†]Corporation only.

We thank Dr. Louella Moore from Arkansas State University for suggesting this listing.

Working Papers, Volume 2
Chapters 12-25

for use with

Fundamental Accounting Principles

Eighteenth Edition

John J. Wild
University of Wisconsin, Madison

Kermit D. Larson
University of Texas at Austin

Barbara Chiappetta
Nassau Community College

Prepared by
John J. Wild
University of Wisconsin, Madison

Boston   Burr Ridge, IL   Dubuque, IA   Madison, WI   New York   San Francisco   St. Louis
Bangkok   Bogotá   Caracas   Kuala Lumpur   Lisbon   London   Madrid   Mexico City
Milan   Montreal   New Delhi   Santiago   Seoul   Singapore   Sydney   Taipei   Toronto

Working Papers, Volume 2, Chapters 12-25 for use with
FUNDAMENTAL ACCOUNTING PRINCIPLES
John J. Wild, Kermit D. Larson, and Barbara Chiappetta

Published by McGraw-Hill, an imprint of The McGraw-Hill Companies, Inc., 1221 Avenue of the Americas,
New York, NY 10020. Copyright © 2007 by The McGraw-Hill Companies, Inc. All rights reserved.

1 2 3 4 5 6 7 8 9 0 CUS/CUS 0 9 8 7 6 5

ISBN 13: 978-0-07-326640-4
ISBN 10: 0-07-326640-X

Table of Contents

(a) _____
_____
_____

(b) _____
_____
_____

Quick Study 12-2

	Share to Stolton	Share to Bright	Total
Net income			
Salary allowance:			
Stolton			
Bright			
Total salary allowances			
Balance of income			
Balance allocated:			
Stolton			
Bright			
Total allocated			
Balance of income			
Shares of the partners			

Quick Study 12-3

_____
_____
_____
_____

Quick Study 12-4

_____
_____
_____
_____
_____

GENERAL JOURNAL

Date	Account Titles and Explanation	P. R.	Debit	Credit

Quick Study 12-6

GENERAL JOURNAL

Date	Account Titles and Explanation	P. R.	Debit	Credit

Quick Study 12-7

_____
_____
_____
_____
_____
_____
_____
_____
_____

Characteristic	General Partnerships
1. Life	
2. Owners' liability	
3. Legal status	
4. Tax status of income	
5. Owners' authority	
6. Ease of formation	
7. Transferability of ownership	
8. Ability to raise large amounts of capital	

Exercise 12-2
Part a

Recommended Organization: _____
_____
_____
_____
_____
_____
_____

Taxation Effects: _____
_____
_____
_____

Advantages: _____
_____
_____
_____

Recommended Organization: _____
_____
_____
_____
_____
_____

Taxation Effects: _____
_____
_____

Advantages: _____
_____
_____
_____

Part c

Recommended Organization: _____
_____
_____
_____
_____
_____

Taxation Effects: _____
_____
_____

Advantages: _____
_____
_____
_____

Chapter 12   Exercise 12-3   Name _____
(1)

GENERAL JOURNAL

Date	Account Titles and Explanation	P. R.	Debit	Credit
(a)				
(b)				
(c)				

(2)

Capital account balances:	Eckert	Kelley
Initial investment		
Withdrawals		
Share of income		
Ending balances		

	Share to Kramer	Share to Knox	Total
(1)			
(2)			
(3)			

	Share to Kramer	Share to Knox	Total
(1)			

(2)

Exercise 12-6

GENERAL JOURNAL

Date		Account Titles and Explanation	P. R.	Debit	Credit

(1)

GENERAL JOURNAL

Date		Account Titles and Explanation	P. R.	Debit	Credit

(2)

GENERAL JOURNAL

Date		Account Titles and Explanation	P. R.	Debit	Credit

(3)

GENERAL JOURNAL

Date		Account Titles and Explanation	P. R.	Debit	Credit

Chapter 12   Exercise 12-8   Name _____

(1)
GENERAL JOURNAL

Date	Account Titles and Explanation	P. R.	Debit	Credit

(2)
GENERAL JOURNAL

Date	Account Titles and Explanation	P. R.	Debit	Credit

(3)
GENERAL JOURNAL

Date	Account Titles and Explanation	P. R.	Debit	Credit

(1)

	Red	White	Blue	Total
Initial investments				
Allocation of all losses				
Capital balances				

(2)

GENERAL JOURNAL

Date	Account Titles and Explanation	P. R.	Debit	Credit

(3)

GENERAL JOURNAL

Date	Account Titles and Explanation	P. R.	Debit	Credit

(a) Loss computation from selling assets: _____

_____

_____

_____

_____

_____

_____

_____

_____

(b) Loss allocation

	Turner	Roth	Lowe	Total
Capital balance before loss liquidation......................				
Allocation of loss:				
Capital balances after loss............				

(c) Liability to be paid: _____

_____

_____

Name _____

(a) Loss computation from selling assets:

_____
_____
_____
_____
_____
_____
_____
_____

(b) Loss and deficit allocation:

	Turner	Roth	Lowe	Total
Capital balance before loss..........				
Allocation of loss:				
Capital balances after loss............				
Allocation of _____ deficit to				
Cash paid by each partner............				

(c) Liability to be paid:

_____
_____

Exercise 12-12

_____
_____
_____
_____
_____
_____
_____
_____
_____
_____
_____

GENERAL JOURNAL

Date	Account Titles and Explanation	P. R.	Debit	Credit
(1)				
(2)				
(3)				

Supporting calculations:

_____

_____

_____

_____

_____

_____

_____

_____

_____

_____

_____

_____

_____

_____

_____

_____

Inc./Loss Sharing Plan	Year 1 Calculations
(a)	
(b)	
(c)	
(d)	

Inc./Loss Sharing Plan	Year 2 Calculations
(a)	
(b)	
(c)	
(d)	

Inc./Loss Sharing Plan	Year 3	
	Calculations	
(a)		
(b)		
(c)		
(d)		

Supporting Work Space:

Inc./Loss Sharing Plan	Calculations			Total
(a)				
(b)				
(c)				

PARTNERSHIP
Statement of Partners' Equity
For Year Ended December 31

				Total
Beg. capital balances				
Plus:				
Owner investments				
Net Income:				
Salary allowances				
Interest allowances				
Balance allocated				
Total net income				
Total				
Less partners' withdrawals				
End. capital balances				

Part 3

GENERAL JOURNAL

Date	Account Titles and Explanation	P. R.	Debit	Credit

GENERAL JOURNAL

Date		Account Titles and Explanation	P. R.	Debit	Credit
(a)					
(b)					
(c)					
(d)					
(e)					

GENERAL JOURNAL

Date	Account Titles and Explanation	P. R.	Debit	Credit
(a)				
(b)				
(c)				

(1)

GENERAL JOURNAL

Date		Account Titles and Explanation	P. R.	Debit	Credit

(2)

GENERAL JOURNAL

Date	Account Titles and Explanation	P. R.	Debit	Credit

(3)

GENERAL JOURNAL

Date		Account Titles and Explanation	P. R.	Debit	Credit

(4)

GENERAL JOURNAL

Date	Account Titles and Explanation	P. R.	Debit	Credit

(1)

_____
_____
_____
_____
_____
_____
_____

(2)

_____
_____
_____
_____
_____
_____
_____
_____

(3)

_____
_____
_____
_____
_____
_____
_____

Comparative Analysis--BTN 12-2

(1)

_____
_____

(2)

_____
_____

(3)

_____
_____

(4)

_____
_____
_____
_____

(1) Income allocation per original agreement:

	Maben	Orlando	Clark	Total
Salary allowance				
Per patient charges				
Totals				

(2) Income allocation per Clark's proposal:

	Maben	Orlando	Clark	Total
Per patient charges				

(3)

_____

_____

_____

_____

_____

_____

_____

_____

_____

STUDY NOTES

Organizations with Partnership Characteristics

_____
_____
_____
_____
_____
_____
_____
_____
_____
_____
_____
_____
_____
_____
_____
_____
_____
_____
_____
_____
_____
_____
_____
_____
_____
_____
_____
_____
_____
_____
_____
_____
_____
_____
_____
_____
_____
_____
_____

(1) _____
_____
_____
_____
_____
_____

(2) _____
_____
_____
_____
_____

(3) _____
_____
_____
_____
_____
_____

Chapter 12   Teamwork in Action   Name _____
            BTN 12-6

(1)

Income/Loss Sharing Plan	Calculations	Baker	Warner	Rice	Total
(a)					
(b)					
(c)					
(d)					

(2) Team members share solutions.

(3)

(1) _____
_____
_____
_____

(2) _____
_____
_____
_____

(3) _____
_____
_____
_____

Entrepreneurial Decision--BTN 12-8

(1) _____
_____
_____
_____
_____

(2) _____
_____
_____
_____

(3) _____
_____
_____
_____

(1) _____

_____

_____

(2) _____

_____

_____

(3) _____

_____

_____

_____

_____

_____

_____

_____

True Statements: _____

_____

_____

Quick Study 13-2

	Jun Company
	Stockholders' Equity
	April 2 (after stock dividend)

Quick Study 13-3

	Jun Company
	Stockholders' Equity
	April 2 (after stock dividend)

Jun Company
Stockholders' Equity
April 2 (after stock dividend)

_____
_____
_____
_____
_____
_____
_____
_____

Quick Study 13-5

GENERAL JOURNAL

Date	Account Titles and Explanation	P. R.	Debit	Credit

Quick Study 13-6
(1)
Jun Company
Stockholders' Equity
April 2 (after stock dividend)

_____
_____
_____
_____
_____

(2)
_____
_____
_____

GENERAL JOURNAL

Date	Account Titles and Explanation	P. R.	Debit	Credit

Quick Study 13-8

Jun Company
Stockholders' Equity
April 2 (after stock dividend)

Quick Study 13-9

Cash Dividend to Common Shareholders

GENERAL JOURNAL

Date	Account Titles and Explanation	P. R.	Debit	Credit

Quick Study 13-11

(1) _____

_____

_____

_____

(2) _____

_____

_____

Quick Study 13-12

Basic Earnings Per Share _____

_____

_____

_____

Quick Study 13-13

Basic Earnings Per Share _____

_____

_____

_____

Price-Earnings Ratio _____

_____

_____

Analysis _____

_____

_____

_____

Quick Study 13-15

Dividend Yield _____

_____

_____

Analysis _____

_____

_____

_____

Quick Study 13-16

_____

_____

_____

_____

_____

_____

_____

Characteristic	Corporations
1. Owner authority & control	
2. Ease of formation	
3. Transferability of ownership	
4. Ability to raise large amounts of capital	
5. Duration of Life	
6. Owner liability	
7. Legal status	
8. Tax status of income	

Exercise 13-2

GENERAL JOURNAL

Date	Account Titles and Explanation	P. R.	Debit	Credit
(1)				
(2)				
(3)				

GENERAL JOURNAL

Date	Account Titles and Explanation	P. R.	Debit	Credit
(1)				
(2)				
(3)				
(4)				

GENERAL JOURNAL

Date		Account Titles and Explanation	P. R.	Debit	Credit

Exercise 13-5

(1) _____   (4) _____

(2) _____   (5) _____

(3) _____   (6) _____

Part 1

(a) Retained Earnings: _____

_____

_____

_____

(b) Total Stockholders' Equity: _____

_____

_____

_____

_____

_____

(c) Number of Outstanding Shares: _____

_____

_____

_____

_____

Part 2

(a) Retained Earnings: _____

_____

_____

_____

(b) Total Stockholders' Equity: _____

_____

_____

_____

_____

_____

(c) Number of Outstanding Shares: _____

_____

_____

_____

_____

Part 3

_____

_____

_____

_____

_____

Part 1

GENERAL JOURNAL

Date		Account Titles and Explanation	P. R.	Debit	Credit

Part 2

	Before	After

Part 3

	Feb. 5	Feb. 28

	Preferred	Common
2006:		
2007:		
2008:		
2009:		
Totals:		

Exercise 13-9

	Preferred	Common
2006:		
2007:		
2008:		
2009:		
Totals:		

GENERAL JOURNAL

Date	Account Titles and Explanation	P. R.	Debit	Credit

Changes to the equity section include: _____

_____

_____

_____

_____

_____

_____

_____

_____

_____

_____

_____

_____

_____

_____

_____

_____

_____

_____

_____

_____

_____

Revised Stockholders' Equity Section (for support of your part 2 solution):

AMOS COMPANY
Statement of Retained Earnings
For Year Ended December 31, 2008

(1) Net Income Available to Common Stockholders: _____

_____

_____

_____

_____

_____

(2) Net Income Available to Common Stockholders: _____

_____

_____

_____

_____

_____

Exercise 13-13

(1) Net Income Available to Common Stockholders: _____

_____

_____

_____

_____

_____

(2) Net Income Available to Common Stockholders: _____

_____

_____

_____

_____

_____

Price-Earnings Ratio:

(1) _____

_____

(2) _____

_____

(3) _____

_____

(4) _____

_____

Analysis: _____

_____

Exercise 13-15
Dividend Yield:

(1) _____

_____

(2) _____

_____

(3) _____

_____

(4) _____

_____

Analysis: _____

_____

Exercise 13-16

(1) _____

_____

_____

_____

_____

_____

_____

_____

(2) _____

_____

_____

_____

_____

_____

_____

_____

Part 1

(a) _____

_____

(b) _____

_____

(c) _____

_____

(d) _____

_____

Part 2
Number of Outstanding Shares: _____

_____

_____

_____

_____

_____

Part 3
Minimum Legal Capital: _____

_____

Part 4
Total Paid-In Capital from Common Stockholders: _____

_____

_____

_____

_____

_____

Part 5
Book Value Per Common Share: _____

_____

_____

_____

GENERAL JOURNAL

Date	Account Titles and Explanation	P. R.	Debit	Credit

_____

CORPORATION

Statement of Retained Earnings

For Year Ended December 31, 2009

_____
_____
_____
_____
_____
_____
_____
_____
_____
_____

Part 3

_____

CORPORATION

Stockholders' Equity Section of the Balance Sheet

December 31, 2009

_____
_____
_____
_____
_____
_____
_____
_____
_____

Chapter 13   Problem 13-3A or 13-3B   Name _____
Part 1

Explanations for each of the entries:
_____
Oct. 2 (Jan.17)* _____
_____
Oct 25 (Feb. 5)* _____
_____
Oct. 31 (Feb. 28)* _____
_____
Nov. 5 (Mar. 14)* _____
_____
Dec. 1(Mar. 25)* _____
_____
Dec. 31 (Mar. 31)* _____
_____
_____

* Dates for Problem 13-3B are in parentheses.

Part 2

	Oct. 2 (Jan. 17)*	Oct. 25 (Feb. 5)*	Oct. 31 (Feb. 28)*	Nov. 5 (Mar. 14)*	Dec. 1 (Mar. 25)*	Dec. 31 (Mar. 31)*
Common stock...............						
Common stock dividend distributable...						
Paid-In capital in excess of par.............						
Retained earnings........						
Total equity..................						

*Dates for Problem 13-3B are in parentheses.

Problem 13-4A or 13-4B
Part 1

Outstanding Common Shares
_____
_____
_____
_____
_____
_____
_____

Cash Dividend Amounts: _____

_____
_____
_____
_____
_____

Part 3

Capitalization of Retained Earnings: _____

_____
_____
_____
_____
_____

Part 4

Cost Per Share of Treasury Stock: _____

_____
_____
_____
_____
_____

Part 5

Net Income Computation: _____

_____
_____
_____
_____
_____
_____
_____
_____
_____

(1) Market Price Per Share: _____

_____

(2) Computation of Stock Par Values: _____

_____

_____

_____

(3) Book Value Per Preferred Share: _____

_____

_____

Book Value Per Common Share: _____

_____

_____

_____

(4) Book Value Per Preferred Share: _____

_____

_____

_____

_____

Book Value Per Common Share: _____

_____

_____

_____

_____

_____

_____

(5) Book Value Per Preferred Share: _____

_____

_____

_____

_____

_____

Book Value Per Common Share: _____

_____

_____

_____

_____

_____

_____

(6) _____

_____

_____

_____

_____

_____

_____

(7) _____

_____

_____

_____

_____

_____

(1a)   GENERAL JOURNAL

Date		Account Titles and Explanation	P. R.	Debit	Credit

(1b)   GENERAL JOURNAL

Date		Account Titles and Explanation	P. R.	Debit	Credit

(1c)   GENERAL JOURNAL

Date		Account Titles and Explanation	P. R.	Debit	Credit

(2)   (a) _____

_____

_____

_____

_____

_____

_____

(b) _____

_____

_____

_____

_____

_____

(c) _____

_____

_____

_____

_____

(3) _____

_____

_____

_____

_____

_____

(1) _____

_____

_____

_____

_____

_____

_____

_____

_____

(2) _____

_____

_____

_____

_____

(3) _____

_____

_____

_____

(4) _____

_____

_____

_____

(5) _____

_____

_____

(6) Fast Forward: _____

_____

_____

_____

(1)
Best Buy Book Value Per Common Share: _____

_____

_____

Circuit City Book Value Per Common Share: _____

_____

_____

(2)
Best Buy Earnings Per Share: _____

_____

_____

Circuit City Earnings per Share: _____

_____

_____

_____

_____

(3)
Best Buy Dividend Yield: _____

_____

_____

Circuit City Dividend Yield: _____

_____

_____

Analysis: _____

_____

_____

(4)
Best Buy Price-Earnings Ratio: _____

_____

_____

Circuit City Price-Earnings Ratio: _____

_____

_____

Analysis & Interpretation: _____

_____

_____

_____

_____

_____

_____

_____

_____

_____

_____

_____

_____

_____

_____

_____

_____

_____

_____

_____

_____

_____

_____

_____

_____

_____

_____

_____

_____

_____

_____

_____

_____

_____

_____

_____

MEMORANDUM

TO:

FROM:

DATE:

SUBJECT:

Company	Earnings Per Share	Market Price of Stock	Price-Earnings Ratio

Industry Norm:

Meaning of Price-Earnings Ratio:

Comparison Across Companies:

Concluding Analysis:

Part 2

Part 3

Part 4

Part 1

(a) Impact on Financial Position due to Stock Buyback: _____

_____

_____

_____

_____

_____

_____

_____

(b) Reasons for Stock Buyback: _____

_____

_____

_____

_____

_____

_____

_____

_____

GENERAL JOURNAL

Date	Account Titles and Explanation	P. R.	Debit	Credit
Reacquisition entry				
(a)				
(b)				
(c)				
(d)				
(e)				

Part 3

Similarities: _____

_____

_____

Differences: _____

_____

_____

(1) _____

_____

_____

_____

_____

(2) _____

_____

_____

_____

_____

(3) _____

_____

_____

_____

_____

_____

	Plan A	Plan B

Part 2

	Plan A	Plan B

Part 3

_____
_____
_____
_____
_____
_____
_____
_____

Global Decision--BTN 13-10

(1) Book Value per Common Share _____

_____
_____
_____
_____

(2) Earnings per Share _____

_____
_____
_____
_____

(3) Analysis

_____
_____
_____
_____

(1) Cash Proceeds: _____

_____

(2) Total Bond Interest Expense: _____

_____

_____

_____

_____

(3) Bond Interest Expense on 1st Payment Date: _____

_____

_____

Quick Study 14-2[B]

(1) Cash Proceeds: _____

_____

(2) Total Bond Interest Expense: _____

_____

_____

_____

_____

(3) Bond Interest Expense on 1st Payment Date: _____

_____

_____

GENERAL JOURNAL

Date		Account Titles and Explanation	P. R.	Debit	Credit

Quick Study 14-4

(a) _____

_____

_____

_____

_____

_____

_____

_____

(b) _____

_____

_____

_____

_____

_____

GENERAL JOURNAL

Date	Account Titles and Explanation	P. R.	Debit	Credit

Quick Study 14-6

GENERAL JOURNAL

Date	Account Titles and Explanation	P. R.	Debit	Credit

Chapter 14 Quick Study 14-7   Name _____

(a) _____
_____
_____

(b) _____
_____
_____

(c) _____
_____
_____

Quick Study 14-8

1. _____ Registered bond   5. _____ Convertible bond
2. _____ Serial bond   6. _____ Bond indenture
3. _____ Secured bond   7. _____ Sinking fund bond
4. _____ Bearer bond   8. _____ Debenture

Quick Study 14-9

Ratio Computations: _____
_____
_____
_____
_____
_____
_____

Analysis and Interpretation: _____
_____
_____
_____

GENERAL JOURNAL

Date		Account Titles and Explanation	P. R.	Debit	Credit

Quick Study 14-11^D

GENERAL JOURNAL

Date		Account Titles and Explanation	P. R.	Debit	Credit

Quick Study 14-12^D

GENERAL JOURNAL

Date		Account Titles and Explanation	P. R.	Debit	Credit

Chapter 14   Exercise 14-1   Name _____

(1) _____
_____
_____
_____

(2)
GENERAL JOURNAL

	Date	Account Titles and Explanation	P. R.	Debit	Credit
(a)					
(b)					
(c)					

(3)
GENERAL JOURNAL

	Date	Account Titles and Explanation	P. R.	Debit	Credit
(a)					
(b)					

(1) _____

_____

_____

_____

(2) **Total Bond Interest Expense:**

_____

_____

_____

_____

_____

_____

_____

_____

_____

(3)

Semiannual Period-End	Unamortized Discount	Carrying Value
1/01/2008		
6/30/2008		
12/31/2008		
6/30/2009		
12/31/2009		
6/30/2010		
12/31/2010		

(1) _____
_____
_____
_____

(2) Total Bond Interest Expense:
_____
_____
_____
_____
_____
_____
_____
_____
_____

(3)

Semiannual Interest Period-End	(A) Cash Interest Paid (4.5% x $500,000)	(B) Bond Interest Expense [6% x Prior (E)]	(C) Discount Amortization [(B) - (A)]	(D) Unamortized Discount [Prior (D) - (C)]	(E) Carrying Value [$500,000-(D)]
1/01/2008					
6/30/2008					
12/31/2008					
6/30/2009					
12/31/2009					
6/30/2010					
12/31/2010					

(1)
_____
_____
_____

(2) Total Bond Interest Expense:
_____
_____
_____
_____
_____
_____
_____
_____

(3)

Semiannual Period-End	Unamortized Premium	Carrying Value
1/01/2008		
6/30/2008		
12/31/2008		
6/30/2009		
12/31/2009		
6/30/2010		
12/31/2010		

(1) _____

_____

_____

(2) Total Bond Interest Expense: _____

_____

_____

_____

_____

_____

_____

_____

_____

_____

(3)

Semiannual Interest Period-End	(A) Cash Interest Paid [6.5% x $400,000]	(B) Bond Interest Expense [6% x Prior (E)]	(C) Premium Amortization [(A) - (B)]	(D) Unamortized Premium [Prior (D) - (C)]	(E) Carrying Value [$400,000+(D)]
1/01/2008					
6/30/2008					
12/31/2008					
6/30/2009					
12/31/2009					
6/30/2010					
12/31/2010					

Chapter 14   Exercise 14-6   Name _____

<u>(1) Semiannual Cash Interest Payment:</u> _____

_____

_____

(2) Number of Payments: _____

_____

_____

(3) _____

_____

(4) Market Price Computation: _____

_____

_____

_____

_____

_____

_____

(5)

GENERAL JOURNAL

Date	Account Titles and Explanation	P. R.	Debit	Credit

(1) Semiannual Cash Interest Payment:

_____

_____

_____

(2) Number of Payments:

_____

_____

_____

(3) _____

_____

_____

(4) Market Price Computation:

_____

_____

_____

_____

_____

_____

_____

(5)

GENERAL JOURNAL

Date	Account Titles and Explanation	P. R.	Debit	Credit

Chapter 14   Exercise 14-8   Name _____

(1) Cash proceeds from sale:

_____
_____
_____

(2) Discount at issuance:

_____
_____
_____
_____

(3) Total Amortization for First 6 Years:

_____
_____
_____
_____

(4) Carrying value of the bonds at 12/31/2012:

_____
_____
_____
_____
_____
_____
_____

(5) Purchase price:

_____
_____

(6) Loss on retirement:

_____
_____
_____
_____

(7)   GENERAL JOURNAL

Date	Account Titles and Explanation	P. R.	Debit	Credit

Exercise 14-9[c]

(1) _____

_____

_____

_____

_____

(2)   GENERAL JOURNAL

Date	Account Titles and Explanation	P. R.	Debit	Credit

(1)

Semiannual Period-End	Unamortized Discount	Carrying Value
6/01/2007		
11/30/2007		
5/31/2008		
11/30/2008		
5/31/2009		
11/30/2009		
5/31/2010		
11/30/2010		
5/31/2011		

Supporting computations: _____

_____

_____

_____

_____

_____

_____

_____

_____

(2)   GENERAL JOURNAL

Date	Account Titles and Explanation	P. R.	Debit	Credit

(1) Amount of Each Payment: _____

_____

_____

_____

(2)

| Period Ending Date | (A) Beginning Balance [Prior (E)] | Payments | | | (E) Ending Balance [(A) - (C)] |
		(B) Debit Interest Expense [7% x (A)] +	(C) Debit Notes Payable [(D) - (B)] =	(D) Credit Cash [computed]	
2008					
2009					
2010					
2011					

GENERAL JOURNAL

Date	Account Titles and Explanation	P. R.	Debit	Credit

(1)(a)

_____

_____

_____

_____

    (b)

_____

_____

_____

(2)

_____

_____

_____

_____

_____

_____

_____

_____

(1) _____

(2) _____

(3) _____

Exercise 14-15^D

GENERAL JOURNAL

	Date	Account Titles and Explanation	P. R.	Debit	Credit
(1)					
(2)					

Exercise 14-16^D

_____

_____

_____

_____

_____

_____

_____

_____

_____

_____

_____

_____

_____

Part 1

(a)

Cash Flow	PV Table Value	Amount	Present Value

(b)

GENERAL JOURNAL

Date	Account Titles and Explanation	P. R.	Debit	Credit

Part 2

(a)

Cash Flow	PV Table Value	Amount	Present Value

(b)

GENERAL JOURNAL

Date	Account Titles and Explanation	P. R.	Debit	Credit

(a)

Cash Flow	PV Table Value	Amount	Present Value

(b)

GENERAL JOURNAL

Date	Account Titles and Explanation	P. R.	Debit	Credit

Problem 14-2A or 14-2B
Part 1

GENERAL JOURNAL

Date	Account Titles and Explanation	P. R.	Debit	Credit

(a) Cash Payment:
_____
_____

(b) Semiannual Amortization:
_____
_____
_____

(c) Bond Interest Expense:
_____
_____

Part 3

Total Bond Interest Expense: _____
_____
_____
_____
_____
_____
_____
_____
_____
_____
_____

Part 4

Semiannual Period-End	Unamortized Discount	Carrying Value
1/01/2007		
6/30/2007		
12/31/2007		
6/30/2008		
12/31/2008		

GENERAL JOURNAL

Date	Account Titles and Explanation	P. R.	Debit	Credit

Part 6--Requirements 1 through 5 are repeated assuming a bond premium

Requirement 1

GENERAL JOURNAL

Date	Account Titles and Explanation	P. R.	Debit	Credit

Requirement 2

(a) Cash Payment: _____

_____

(b) Semiannual Amortization: _____

_____

_____

(c) Bond Interest Expense: _____

_____

_____

Requirement 3

Total Bond Interest Expense: _____

_____
_____
_____
_____
_____
_____
_____
_____
_____

Requirement 4

Semiannual Period-End	Unamortized Premium	Carrying Value
1/01/2007		
6/30/2007		
12/31/2007		
6/30/2008		
12/31/2008		

Requirement 5

GENERAL JOURNAL

Date	Account Titles and Explanation	P. R.	Debit	Credit

Chapter 14   Problem 14-3A or 14-3B   Name _____
Part 1

Total Bond Interest Expense: _____

_____
_____
_____
_____
_____
_____
_____
_____

Part 2

Semiannual Interest Period-End	Unamortized Premium	Carrying Value
1/01/2007		
6/30/2007		
12/31/2007		
6/30/2008		
12/31/2008		
6/30/2009		
12/31/2009		
6/30/2010		
12/31/2010		
6/30/2011		
12/31/2011		

GENERAL JOURNAL

Date	Account Titles and Explanation	P. R.	Debit	Credit

Chapter 14 Problem 14-4A^B or 14-4B^B   Name _____

Part 1

Total Bond Interest Expense: _____
_____
_____
_____
_____
_____
_____
_____
_____
_____
_____

Part 2

Semiannual Interest Period-End	(A) Cash Interest Paid [% x $]	(B) Bond Interest Expense [% x Prior (E)]	(C) Premium Amortization [(A) - (B)]	(D) Unamortized Premium [Prior (D) - (C)]	(E) Carrying Value [$____ + (D)]
1/01/2007					
6/30/2007					
12/31/2007					
6/30/2008					
12/31/2008					
6/30/2009					
12/31/2009					
6/30/2010					
12/31/2010					
6/30/2011					
12/31/2011					

GENERAL JOURNAL

Date			P. R.	Debit	Credit

Part 4

Cash Flow	PT Table	PV Table Value	Amount	Present Value

Comparison to Part 2 Table:

GENERAL JOURNAL

Date	Account Titles and Explanation	P. R.	Debit	Credit

Part 2

Total Bond Interest Expense:

_____

_____

_____

_____

_____

_____

_____

_____

_____

_____

Part 3

Semiannual Interest Period-End	Unamortized Discount	Carrying Value
1/01/2007		
6/30/2007		
12/31/2007		
6/30/2008		
12/31/2008		

Part 4

GENERAL JOURNAL

Date	Account Titles and Explanation	P. R.	Debit	Credit

Part 5 (for Problem 14-5A only)

Chapter 14   Problem 14-6A^B or 14-6B^B   Name _____
Part 1

GENERAL JOURNAL

Date	Account Titles and Explanation	P. R.	Debit	Credit

Part 2

Total Bond Interest Expense: _____

_____
_____
_____
_____
_____
_____
_____
_____
_____
_____

Part 3

Semiannual Interest Period-End	(A) Cash Interest Paid [% x $]	(B) Bond Interest Expense [% x Prior (E)]	(C) Discount Amortization [(B) - (A)]	(D) Unamortized Discount [Prior (D) - (C)]	(E) Carrying Value [$___ - (D)]
1/01/2007					
6/30/2007					
12/31/2007					
6/30/2008					
12/31/2008					

GENERAL JOURNAL

Date	Account Titles and Explanation	P. R.	Debit	Credit

Chapter 14   Problem 14-7A^B or 14-7B^B   Name _____
Part 1

GENERAL JOURNAL

Date	Account Titles and Explanation	P. R.	Debit	Credit

Part 2

Total Bond Interest Expense: _____
_____
_____
_____
_____
_____
_____
_____
_____
_____
_____
_____

Part 3

Semiannual Interest Period-End	(A) Cash Interest Paid [_% x $ _]	(B) Bond Interest Expense [_% x Prior (E)]	(C) Premium Amortization [(A) - (B)]	(D) Unamortized Premium [Prior (D) - (C)]	(E) Carrying Value [$ _ + (D)]
1/01/2007					
6/30/2007					
12/31/2007					
6/30/2008					
12/31/2008					

Part 4

GENERAL JOURNAL

Date	Account Titles and Explanation	P. R.	Debit	Credit

Part 5

GENERAL JOURNAL

Date	Account Titles and Explanation	P. R.	Debit	Credit

Part 6

_____

_____

_____

_____

_____

_____

_____

_____

_____

_____

_____

_____

_____

Chapter 14   Problem 14-8A or 14-8B   Name _____
Part 1

Amount of Each Payment:
_____
_____
_____
_____
_____
_____
_____
_____
_____

Part 2

Period Ending Date	(A) Beginning Balance [Prior (E)]	(B) Debit Interest Expense [__% x (A)]	(C) Debit Notes Payable [(D) - (B)]	(D) Credit Cash [computed]	(E) Ending Balance [(A) - (C)]

Payments: (B), (C), (D) columns

GENERAL JOURNAL

Date	Account Titles and Explanation	P. R.	Debit	Credit

101

_____ **Company Ratio:** _____

_____

_____

_____

_____

_____

_____ **Company Ratio:** _____

_____

_____

_____

_____

_____

Part 2

Analysis and Interpretation: _____

_____

_____

_____

_____

_____

_____

_____

_____

_____

Chapter 14   Problem 14-10A^D or 14-10B^D Name _____
Part 1

Present Value of the Lease Payments: _____
_____
_____
_____

Part 2

GENERAL JOURNAL

Date		Account Titles and Explanation	P. R.	Debit	Credit

Part 3

Capital Lease Liability Payment (Amortization) Schedule:

Period Ending Date	Beginning Balance of Lease Liability	Interest on Lease Liability (__%)	Reduction of Lease Liability	Cash Lease Payment	Ending Balance of Lease Liability
Year 1					
Year 2					
Year 3					
Year 4					
Year 5					

Part 4

GENERAL JOURNAL

Date		Account Titles and Explanation	Ref.	Debit	Credit

Part 1

Maximum Loan Allowed: _____

_____

_____

_____

_____

_____

_____

_____

_____

_____

_____

Part 2

(a) Percent of Assets Financed by Debt

_____

_____

_____

(b) Percent of Assets Financed by Equity

_____

_____

_____

_____

Part 3

_____

_____

_____

_____

_____

_____

(1) _____

_____

_____

_____

_____

_____

_____

_____

(2) _____

_____

_____

(3) _____

_____

_____

(4) Fast Forward: _____

_____

_____

_____

_____

_____

_____

_____

_____

(1) Best Buy

Current Year: _____

_____

_____

_____

Prior Year: _____

_____

_____

_____

Circuit City

Current Year: _____

_____

_____

_____

Prior Year: _____

_____

_____

_____

(2) _____

_____

_____

_____

_____

_____

Chapter 14   Ethics Challenge
         BTN 14-3

Name _____

(1) _____
_____
_____
_____
_____
_____
_____
_____
_____
_____
_____

(2) _____
_____
_____
_____
_____
_____
_____
_____
_____

MEMORANDUM

TO:
FROM:
DATE:
SUBJECT:

(1) Long Term Liabilities: _____

_____

_____

_____

_____

_____

_____

(2a) _____

_____

_____

_____

_____

_____

_____

(2b) _____

_____

_____

_____

_____

_____

_____

_____
_____
_____
_____
_____
_____
_____
_____
_____
_____
_____
_____
_____
_____
_____
_____
_____
_____
_____

Part 3

_____
_____
_____
_____
_____
_____
_____
_____

Part 4

_____
_____
_____
_____
_____

Similarities	Differences

_____

_____

_____

_____

_____

_____

Part 2

_____

_____

_____

_____

_____

Part 3

_____

_____

_____

_____

_____

Part 4

_____

_____

_____

_____

_____

_____

	Current	Alternative Notes for Expansion				
		10% Note	15% Note	16% Note	17% Note	20% Note
Income before interest............						
interest............						
Net income.......						
Equity..............						
Return on equity..						

Work Space:

_____

_____

_____

Part 2

_____

_____

_____

_____

_____

_____

_____

_____

_____

_____
_____
_____
_____
_____
_____
_____
_____
_____
_____
_____

Global Decision--BTN 14-14

(1) Dixon's Current Year Ratio: _____
_____
_____

  Dixon's Prior Year Ratio: _____
_____
_____
_____
_____

(2) _____
_____
_____
_____
_____

GENERAL JOURNAL

Date	Account Titles and Explanation	P. R.	Debit	Credit

Quick Study 15-2

(1)   GENERAL JOURNAL

Date	Account Titles and Explanation	P. R.	Debit	Credit

(2) _____

_____

_____

_____

_____

(3)   GENERAL JOURNAL

Date	Account Titles and Explanation	P. R.	Debit	Credit

GENERAL JOURNAL

Date	Account Titles and Explanation	P. R.	Debit	Credit

Quick Study 15-4

GENERAL JOURNAL

Date	Account Titles and Explanation	P. R.	Debit	Credit

True: _____

_____

_____

Quick Study 15-6

(1) _____   (4) _____

(2) _____   (5) _____

(3) _____

Quick Study 15-7

GENERAL JOURNAL

Date	Account Titles and Explanation	P. R.	Debit	Credit

Quick Study 15-8

GENERAL JOURNAL

Date	Account Titles and Explanation	P. R.	Debit	Credit

GENERAL JOURNAL

Date	Account Titles and Explanation	P. R.	Debit	Credit

Quick Study 15-10

(1)

GENERAL JOURNAL

Date	Account Titles and Explanation	P. R.	Debit	Credit

(2) _____

_____

_____

_____

_____

_____

_____
_____
_____
_____
_____
_____

Quick Study 15-12

_____
_____
_____
_____
_____
_____
_____
_____

Chapter 15   Quick Study 15-13A   Name _____

GENERAL JOURNAL

Date	Account Titles and Explanation	P. R.	Debit	Credit
	Date of Sale:			
	Date of Payment:			

Quick Study 15-14A

GENERAL JOURNAL

Date	Account Titles and Explanation	P. R.	Debit	Credit

GENERAL JOURNAL

Date	Account Titles and Explanation	P. R.	Debit	Credit

(1)

GENERAL JOURNAL

Date	Account Titles and Explanation	P. R.	Debit	Credit

(2) _____

_____

_____

_____

_____

(3)

GENERAL JOURNAL

Date	Account Titles and Explanation	P. R.	Debit	Credit

Exercise 15-3

Available-for-Sale Portfolio	Cost	Market	Unrealized Gain (Loss)

GENERAL JOURNAL

Date	Account Titles and Explanation	P. R.	Debit	Credit

GENERAL JOURNAL

Date	Account Titles and Explanation	P. R.	Debit	Credit

GENERAL JOURNAL

Date		Account Titles and Explanation	P. R.	Debit	Credit

Computation of Market Adjustment:

Securities	Cost	Market	Unrealized Gain (Loss)

Exercise 15-6

GENERAL JOURNAL

Date		Account Titles and Explanation	P. R.	Debit	Credit

Computation of Market Adjustment:

	12/31/2007	12/31/2008
Cost		
Market		
Gain (Loss)		

GENERAL JOURNAL

Date	Account Titles and Explanation	P. R.	Debit	Credit
2006:				
2007:				
2008:				
2009:				

Supporting Computations:

(1) Classification of Investment

(a)

(b)

(c)

(d)

(e)

(2)   GENERAL JOURNAL

Date	Account Titles and Explanation	P. R.	Debit	Credit

Computation of Market Adjustment:

Long-Term AFS Securities	Cost	Market

GENERAL JOURNAL

Date	Account Titles and Explanation	P. R.	Debit	Credit
2008:				
2009:				

2008 Return on Total Assets: _____
_____
_____

2009 Return on Total Assets: _____
_____
_____
_____

Analysis and Interpretation: _____
_____
_____
_____
_____
_____
_____
_____

GENERAL JOURNAL

Date	Account Titles and Explanation	P. R.	Debit	Credit
2008:				
2009:				

Reported on Quarterly Statement Ended June 30, 2008:

_____
_____
_____
_____
_____

Reported on Quarterly Statement Ended September 30, 2008:

_____
_____
_____
_____
_____
_____

Reported on Quarterly Statement Ended December 31, 2008:

_____
_____
_____
_____
_____
_____

Reported on Quarterly Statement Ended March 31, 2009:

_____
_____
_____
_____
_____
_____

GENERAL JOURNAL

Date	Account Titles and Explanation	P. R.	Debit	Credit
2008:				
2009:				

GENERAL JOURNAL

Date	Account Titles and Explanation	P. R.	Debit	Credit
2010:				

Part 2

Date	Account Titles and Explanation	P. R.	Debit	Credit
2010:				

Date	Account Titles and Explanation	P. R.	Debit	Credit

Comparison of Cost and Market Values for AFS Portfolio				
Security	Computations	Cost	Market	Unrealized Gain (Loss)

Part 3

GENERAL JOURNAL

Date	Account Titles and Explanation	P. R.	Debit	Credit

Part 4

_____
_____
_____
_____
_____
_____

Part 5
Income Statement: _____
_____
_____
_____

Balance Sheet (Equity Section): _____
_____
_____
_____

GENERAL JOURNAL

Date	Account Titles and Explanation	P. R.	Debit	Credit
2008:				

Supporting work:

GENERAL JOURNAL

Date	Account Titles and Explanation	P. R.	Debit	Credit
2009:				

Supporting work:

GENERAL JOURNAL

Date	Account Titles and Explanation	P. R.	Debit	Credit
2010:				

Supporting work:

	12/31/2008	12/31/2009	12/31/2010
Long-Term AFS Securities (cost)			
Market Adjustment			
Long-Term AFS Securities (market)			

Part 3

	2008	2009	2010
Realized Gains (Losses)			
Unrealized Gains (Losses) at year-end*			

Problem 15-4A or 15-4B
Part 1
Balance sheet disclosure:

_____

_____

_____

Supporting work:

AFS Securities on Dec. 31, 2008	Cost	Market

GENERAL JOURNAL

Date	Account Titles and Explanation	P. R.	Debit	Credit

Supporting Computations:

AFS Securities	Cost	Market

Part 3
Disclosures:

Stock Sold	Cost	Sale Price	Realized Gain (Loss)

Chapter 15   Problem 15-5A or 15-5B   Name _____
Part 1

GENERAL JOURNAL

Date	Account Titles and Explanation	P. R.	Debit	Credit
2008:				
2009:				
2010:				

(2) Carrying Value Per Share: _____

_____

_____

_____

_____

(3) Change in Equity: _____

_____

_____

_____

_____

_____

_____

(1)

GENERAL JOURNAL

Date	Account Titles and Explanation	P. R.	Debit	Credit
2008:				
2009:				
2010:				

(2) Investment Cost Per Share: _____

_____

_____

_____

_____

(3) Change in Equity: _____

_____

_____

_____

_____

_____

_____

GENERAL JOURNAL

Date	Account Titles and Explanation	P. R.	Debit	Credit
2008:				

GENERAL JOURNAL

Date	Account Titles and Explanation	P. R.	Debit	Credit
2009:				

Part 2

_____

Foreign Exchange Gain (Loss) Reported: _____

_____

_____

_____

_____

_____

Part 3

_____

_____

_____

_____

_____

_____

_____

_____

_____

_____

Part 1

GENERAL JOURNAL

Date		Account Titles and Explanation	P. R.	Debit	Credit

Part 2

GENERAL JOURNAL

Date		Account Titles and Explanation	P. R.	Debit	Credit

(1) _____

_____

(2) _____

_____

_____

_____

(3) _____

_____

_____

(4) _____

_____

_____

_____

(5) Fast Forward: _____

_____

_____

_____

_____

_____

_____

_____

_____

(1) Best Buy's Return on Total Assets:

       Current Year

_____

_____

       Prior Year

_____

_____

   Circuit City's Return on Total Assets:

       Current Year

_____

_____

       Prior Year

_____

_____

(2) Best Buy's Component Analysis of Return on Total Assets:

       Current Year

_____

_____

       Prior Year

_____

_____

   Circuit City's Component Analysis of Return on Total Assets:

       Current Year

_____

_____

       Prior Year

_____

_____

(3) Current Year Analysis:

_____

_____

   Prior Year Analysis::

_____

_____

_____

(1) _____

_____

_____

_____

_____

_____

_____

(2) _____

_____

_____

_____

_____

_____

_____

_____

_____

_____

(3) _____

_____

_____

_____

MEMORANDUM

TO:
FROM:
DATE:
SUBJECT:

_____

_____

_____

_____

_____

_____

_____

_____

_____

_____

_____

_____

_____

_____

_____

_____

_____

_____

_____

_____

_____

_____

_____

_____

_____

(1) _____
_____
_____
_____
_____
_____
_____

(2) _____
_____
_____
_____
_____
_____
_____
_____

(3) _____
_____
_____
_____
_____
_____

(4) _____
_____
_____
_____

(1) _____

_____

_____

_____

(2) _____

_____

_____

_____

_____

(3) (a) _____

   (b) _____

   (c) _____

(4) _____

_____

_____

_____

_____

(5) _____

_____

_____

_____

(1)

GENERAL JOURNAL

Date	Account Titles and Explanation	P. R.	Debit	Credit

(2)

GENERAL JOURNAL

Date	Account Titles and Explanation	P. R.	Debit	Credit

(3) _____

_____

_____

_____

Hitting the Road--BTN 15-9[A]

(1) _____

(2) _____

(3) _____

_____

(1)   Return on Total Assets:

        Current Year

        Prior Year

Component Analysis of Return on Total Assets:

        Current Year

        Prior Year

(2) Current Year Analysis:

  Prior Year Analysis:

  Overall:

(1) _____

_____

_____

_____

(2) _____

_____

_____

_____

(3) _____

_____

_____

_____

(4) _____

_____

_____

_____

Quick Study 16-2

(1) _____	(6) _____
(2) _____	(7) _____
(3) _____	(8) _____
(4) _____	(9) _____
(5) _____	(10) _____

Quick Study 16-3

_____

_____

_____

_____

_____

_____

_____

_____

_____

_____
_____
_____
_____
_____
_____
_____
_____
_____

Quick Study 16-5

(1) _____
_____
_____

(2) _____
_____
_____
_____
_____
_____
_____

Quick Study 16-6

Cash Flow from Operating Activities _____
_____
_____
_____
_____
_____
_____
_____
_____

Cash Inflow from Asset Sale: _____

_____

_____

_____

_____

_____

_____

_____

Quick Study 16-8

(1) Cash Paid for Dividends _____

_____

_____

_____

_____

(1) Cash Payments toward Notes: _____

_____

_____

_____

_____

_____

Quick Study 16-9[B]

(1) Cash Received from Customer Sales: _____

_____

_____

_____

(2) Net Increase or Decrease in Cash: _____

_____

_____

_____

_____

(1) Cash Paid for Merchandise: _____

_____

_____

_____

(2) Cash Paid for Operating Expenses: _____

_____

_____

_____

Quick Study 16-11^B

Cash Flow from Operating Activities _____

_____

_____

_____

_____

_____

_____

_____

_____

_____

Quick Study 16-12

(1) _____

_____

_____

_____

_____

_____

(2) _____

_____

_____

_____

_____

_____

_____

_____

_____

_____

_____

_____

Exercise 16-1

Cash Flow from Operating Activities

_____

_____

_____

_____

_____

_____

_____

_____

_____

_____

_____

| | Statement of Cash Flows | | | Noncash Investing & Financing Activities | Not Reported on Statement or in Note |
	Operating Activities	Investing Activities	Financing Activities		
a. Paid cash to purchase inventory.					
b. Purchased land by issuing stock.					
c. Accounts receivable decreased this year.					
d. Sold equipment for cash, yielding a loss.					
e. Recorded depreciation expense.					
f. Income taxes payable increased this year.					
g. Declared and paid a cash dividend.					
h. Accounts payable decreased this year.					
i. Paid cash to settle bond payable.					
j. Prepaid expenses increased this year.					

| | | Statement of Cash Flows | | Noncash | Not Reported |
		Operating Activities	Investing Activities	Financing Activities	Investing & Financing Activities	on Statement or in Note
a.	Retired long-term bonds payable by issuing stock.					
b.	Depreciation expense recorded.					
c.	Paid cash dividend that was declared in a prior period					
d.	Sold inventory for cash.					
e.	Borrowed cash from bank by signing a 9-month note payable.					
f.	Paid cash to purchase patent.					
g.	Accepted six-month note receivable is in exchange for plant assets.					
h.	Paid cash toward accounts payable.					
i.	Collected cash from sales.					
j.	Paid cash to acquire treasury stock.					

Cash Flows from Operating Activities

_____
_____
_____
_____
_____
_____
_____
_____
_____
_____
_____

Exercise 16-5B

Case A

_____
_____
_____
_____
_____
_____
_____

Case B

_____
_____
_____
_____
_____

Case C

_____
_____
_____
_____
_____
_____
_____
_____

Cash Flows from Operating Activities

_____
_____
_____
_____
_____
_____
_____
_____
_____
_____

Supporting computations:

Exercise 16-7[B]

Cash Flows from Operating Activities

_____
_____
_____
_____
_____
_____
_____
_____

Supporting computations:

Cash Flows from Investing Activities

_____
_____
_____
_____
_____
_____
_____
_____

Exercise 16-9

Cash Flows from Investing Activities

_____
_____
_____
_____
_____
_____
_____
_____

Chapter 16   Exercise 16-10   Name _____

Ikiban, Inc.
Statement of Cash Flows (Indirect Method)
For Year Ended June 30, 2008

_____
_____
_____
_____
_____
_____
_____
_____
_____
_____
_____
_____
_____
_____
_____
_____
_____
_____
_____
_____
_____
_____
_____
_____
_____
_____
_____
_____
_____
_____

Supporting Computations for:

(1) Cash received from sale of equipment:
_____
_____
_____
_____
_____

Cash paid for new equipment:
_____
_____
_____
_____

(2) Cash paid to retire notes: _____

_____

_____

(3) Cash paid for dividends: _____

_____

_____

_____

Part 2

Cash Flow on Total Assets Ratio: _____

_____

_____

Interpretation: _____

_____

_____

Ikiban, Inc.
Statement of Cash Flows (Direct Method)
For Year Ended June 30, 2008

_____

_____

_____

_____

_____

_____

_____

_____

_____

_____

_____

_____

_____

_____

_____

_____

_____

_____

_____

_____

_____

_____

_____

_____

_____

_____

_____

Supporting Computations for:
(1) Cash received from customers:

_____

_____

_____

(2) Cash paid for merchandise inventory:

_____

_____

_____

_____

_____

(3) Cash paid for other operating expenses: _____

_____

_____

_____

_____

(4) Cash paid for income taxes: _____

_____

_____

(5) Cash received from sale of equipment: _____

_____

_____

_____

_____

Cash paid for new equipment: _____

_____

_____

_____

(6) Cash paid to retire notes: _____

_____

_____

(7) Cash paid for dividends: _____

_____

_____

_____

FERRON COMPANY
Statement of Cash Flows
For Year Ended December 31, 2008

Footnotes:

THOMAS CORPORATION
Statement of Cash Flows
For Year Ended December 31, 2008

Part 2

(a)

(b)

(c)

(d)

Statement of Cash Flows	
For Year Ended December 31, 2008	

(blank ruled lines)

Footnotes:

(blank ruled lines)

Supporting calculations:

_____
_____
_____
_____
_____
_____
_____
_____
_____

Spreadsheet for Statement of Cash Flows					
For Year Ended December 31, 2008					

		Analysis of changes		
	Dec. 31, 2007	*Debit*	*Credit*	*Dec. 31, 2008*

Balance sheet-debits:
Cash...................................
Accounts receivable......................
Merchandise inventory...................
Prepaid expenses.........................
Equipment....................................

Balance sheet-credits:
Accum. depreciation-Equip.......
Accounts payable....................
Short-term notes payable.........
Long-term notes payable..........
Common Stock, $___par value...
Paid-in capital in excess of
    par value, common stock.......
Retained earnings..................

Statement of cash flows:
Operating activities
    Net income...............................
    _____ in accts. receivable...
    _____ in merch. inventory...
    _____ in prepaid expenses...
    _____ in accounts payable...
    Depreciation expense...............
    _____ on sale of equipment..
Investing activities
    Receipt from sale of equipment...
    Payment to purchase equipment..
Financing activities
    Borrowed on short-term note....
    Payment on long-term note......
    Issued common stock for cash..
    Payments of cash dividends.....

**Noncash investing and financing
activities**
    Purchase of equip. financed
    by long-term note payable.....

Statement of Cash Flows
For Year Ended December 31, 2008

Footnotes:

Supporting calculations:

Statement of Cash Flows
For Year Ended December 31, 2008

_____
_____
_____
_____
_____
_____
_____
_____
_____
_____
_____
_____
_____
_____
_____
_____
_____
_____
_____
_____
_____
_____
_____
_____
_____

Supporting calculations:

	Spreadsheet for Statement of Cash Flows			
	For Year Ended December 31, 2008			
		Analysis of changes		
	Dec. 31, 2007	Debit	Credit	Dec. 31, 2008

Balance sheet-debits:
Cash...
Accounts receivable...........................
Merchandise inventory......................
Equipment.......................................

Balance sheet-credits:
Accum. depreciation-Equip................
Accounts payable.............................
Income taxes payable.......................
Common stock, $___par value...........
Paid-in capital in excess of
  par value, common stock............
Retained earnings.. ....

Statement of cash flows:
Operating activities
Net income.......................................
_____ in accts. receivable...........
_____ in merch. inventory...........
_____ in accounts payable..........
_____ in income taxes payable...
Depreciation expense.....................

Investing activities
Payment for equipment.....................

Financing activities
Issued common stock for cash..........
Paid cash dividends..........................

Statement of Cash Flows
For Year Ended December 31, 2008

Supporting calculations:

| SUCCESS SYSTEMS |
| Statement of Cash Flows |
| For Three Months Ended March 31, 2008 |

_____

Supporting calculations:

(1) _____
_____

(2) _____
_____
_____
_____

(3) _____
_____
_____
_____
_____
_____
_____
_____

(4) _____
_____
_____
_____
_____
_____
_____
_____
_____

(5) Fast Forward: _____
_____
_____
_____
_____
_____
_____
_____
_____

(1)   Best Buy's Cash Flow on Total Assets Ratio:

          Current Year

_____

_____

_____

          Prior Year

_____

_____

        Circuit City's Cash Flow on Total Assets Ratio:

          Current Year

_____

_____

_____

          Prior Year

_____

_____

_____

(2) _____

_____

_____

_____

_____

_____

_____

(3) _____

_____

_____

_____

_____

_____

_____

(4) _____

_____

_____

_____

_____

_____

_____

(1) (a) _____
_____
_____
_____

(b) _____
_____
_____
_____
_____
_____
_____

(2) _____
_____
_____
_____
_____
_____
_____
_____
_____
_____
_____
_____
_____
_____
_____

MEMORANDUM

TO:

FROM:

DATE:

SUBJECT:

Chapter 16   Taking It to the Net   Name _____
            BTN 16-5

(1) _____
    _____
    _____

(2) _____
    _____
    _____

(3)	2005	2004	2003
Net income (net loss)			
Cash flow from operations			
Analysis:			

    _____
    _____
    _____

(4) _____
    _____
    _____
    _____

(5) _____
    _____
    _____

(6) _____
    _____
    _____
    _____

Teamwork in Action--BTN 16-6
Part 1

(a) _____
    _____
    _____
    _____
    _____
    _____

(b)   **Similarities**   **Differences**

_____
_____
_____
_____
_____
_____
_____
_____
_____

(c) _____

_____
_____
_____
_____
_____
_____
_____
_____
_____
_____

(d) _____

_____
_____
_____
_____
_____
_____
_____
_____
_____

Part 2

Adjusting Net Income to Cash Flow from Operating Activities	
Items to Add	**Items to Subtract**
a.	
b.	
c.	
d.	

(a)

_____
_____
_____
_____
_____
_____
_____
_____

(b)

_____
_____
_____
_____
_____
_____
_____
_____
_____
_____
_____
_____
_____

(c)

_____
_____
_____
_____
_____
_____
_____
_____
_____
_____

(d)

_____
_____
_____
_____
_____
_____
_____
_____

(1)

_____

_____

_____

_____

_____

_____

(2)

_____

_____

_____

_____

_____

(3)

_____

_____

_____

_____

_____

(1) _____
_____
_____
_____
_____
_____
_____
_____
_____

(2) _____
_____
_____
_____
_____
_____
_____
_____
_____

MEMORANDUM

TO:

FROM:

DATE:

SUBJECT:

(1) _____
_____

(2) _____
_____
_____
_____
_____
_____

(3) _____
_____
_____
_____
_____

Global Decision--BTN 16-11

(1) Cash Flow on Total Assets Ratio
   Current Year: _____
_____
_____

   Prior Year: _____
_____
_____

(2) Comparative Analysis: _____
_____
_____
_____
_____

_____
_____
_____
_____
_____

Quick Study 17-2

_____
_____
_____
_____
_____
_____
_____
_____
_____
_____
_____
_____
_____
_____
_____
_____
_____
_____

Quick Study 17-3
(1) Common-Size Percents
_____
           2008
_____
           2007
_____

(2) Trend Percents
_____
           2008
_____
           2007
_____

	2008	2007	Dollar Change	Percent Change

Quick Study 17-5

(1)		(6)	
(2)		(7)	
(3)		(8)	
(4)		(9)	
(5)		(10)	

Quick Study 17-6

(1)

(2)

(3)

Quick Study 17-7

Ratio	2008	2007	Change
1. Profit Margin Ratio	9%	8%	
2. Debt Ratio	47%	42%	
3. Gross Margin Ratio	34%	46%	
4. Acid-Test Ratio	1.00	1.15	
5. Accounts Receivable Turnover	5.5	6.7	
6. Basic Earnings Per Share	$1.25	$1.10	
7. Inventory Turnover	3.6	3.4	
8. Dividend Yield	2.0%	1.2%	

Quick Study 17-8[A]

	2010	2009	2008	2007	2006

Analysis:

Exercise 17-2

Name _____

	2008	2007

Analysis:

Exercise 17-4

COMPARATIVE ANALYSIS REPORT

COMPARATIVE ANALYSIS REPORT

Simeon Company Common-Size Comparative Balance Sheets December 31, 2007-2009			
	2009	2008	2007
_____	_____	_____	_____
_____	_____	_____	_____
_____	_____	_____	_____
_____	_____	_____	_____
_____	_____	_____	_____
_____	_____	_____	_____
_____	_____	_____	_____
_____	_____	_____	_____
_____	_____	_____	_____
_____	_____	_____	_____
_____	_____	_____	_____
_____	_____	_____	_____
_____	_____	_____	_____
_____	_____	_____	_____
_____	_____	_____	_____
_____	_____	_____	_____
_____	_____	_____	_____
_____	_____	_____	_____
_____	_____	_____	_____
_____	_____	_____	_____

Analysis and interpretation:

_____
_____
_____
_____
_____
_____
_____
_____
_____
_____

(1) Current Ratio:
2009: _____
_____
_____

2008: _____
_____
_____

2007: _____
_____
_____

(2) Acid-test ratio
2009: _____
_____

2008: _____
_____

2007: _____
_____

Analysis and interpretation:
_____
_____
_____
_____
_____
_____

Chapter 17   Exercise 17-8   Name _____

1. Days' sales uncollected:
2009: _____
_____
_____
2008: _____
_____
_____

2. Accounts receivable turnover:
2009: _____
_____
_____
2008: _____
_____
_____

3. Inventory turnover:
2009: _____
_____
_____
2008: _____
_____
_____

4. Days' sales in inventory:
2009: _____
_____
2008: _____
_____
_____

Analysis and interpretation:
_____
_____
_____
_____
_____
_____
_____

(1)

_____

_____

_____

_____

_____

_____

_____

_____

(2)

_____

_____

_____

_____

_____

_____

(3)

_____

_____

_____

_____

_____

_____

_____

Analysis and interpretation:

_____

_____

_____

_____

_____

_____

_____

(1) Profit margin:
2009: _____
_____
_____

2008: _____
_____
_____
_____

(2) Total asset turnover:
2009: _____
_____
_____

2008: _____
_____
_____
_____

(3) Return on total assets:
2009: _____
_____
_____

2008: _____
_____
_____
_____

Analysis and interpretation:
_____
_____
_____
_____
_____
_____
_____
_____

(1) Return on common stockholders' equity:

2009:

_____

_____

_____

2008:

_____

_____

_____

(2) Price-earnings ratio, December 31:

2009:

_____

_____

_____

2008:

_____

_____

_____

(3) Dividend yield:

2009:

_____

_____

_____

2008:

_____

_____

_____

Analysis and interpretation:

_____

_____

_____

_____

_____

_____

_____

(1) _____	(6) _____
(2) _____	(7) _____
(3) _____	(8) _____
(4) _____	(9) _____

Exercise 17-13

Randa Merchandising
Income Statement
for year ended December 31, 2008

2009: _____

_____

2008: _____

_____

2007: _____

_____

_____

Part 2

Common-Size Comparative Income Statements For Years Ended December 31, 2009, 2008, and 2007	2009	2008	2007

Balance Sheet Data in Trend Percents December 31, 2009, 2008, and 2007	2009	2008	2007

Part 4

Significant relations revealed:

_____
_____
_____
_____
_____
_____
_____
_____
_____
_____
_____
_____
_____
_____
_____
_____
_____
_____
_____

| Income Statement Trends For Years Ended December 31, 2009-2003 | | | | | | |
2009	2008	2007	2006	2005	2004	2003

| Balance Sheet Trends December 31, 2009-2003 | | | | | | |
2009	2008	2007	2006	2005	2004	2003

Analysis and interpretation:

_____

_____

_____

_____

_____

_____

_____

_____

_____

_____

_____

_____

_____

_____

_____

_____

_____

Transaction	Current Assets	Quick Assets	Current Liabilities	Current Ratio	Acid-Test Ratio	Working Capital
Beg. Bal.						

Supporting computations:

(1) Current ratio:
_____
_____
_____

(2) Acid-test ratio:
_____
_____
_____

(3) Days' sales uncollected:
_____
_____
_____

(4) Inventory turnover:
_____
_____
_____

(5) Days' sales in inventory:
_____
_____
_____

(6) Debt-to-equity Ratio:
_____
_____
_____

(7) Times interest earned:
_____
_____
_____

(8) Profit margin ratio:
_____
_____
_____
_____

(9) Total asset turnover:

_____
_____
_____
_____

(10) Return on total assets:

_____
_____
_____
_____

(11) Return on common stockholders' equity:

_____
_____
_____
_____
_____

	Company	Company
a. Current ratio:		

b. Acid-test ratio:

c. Accounts (incl. notes) receivable turnover:

d. Inventory turnover:

e. Days' sales in inventory:

f. Days' sales uncollected:

Short-term credit risk analysis:

	Company	Company
a. Profit margin ratio:		

b. Total asset turnover:

c. Return on total assets:

d. Return on common stockholders' equity:

e. Price-earnings ratio:

f. Dividend yield:

Investment analysis:

Chapter 17   Problem 17-6A^A or 17-6B^A Name _____

Part 1   Effect of Income Taxes:

Items	Pre-Tax	___% Tax Effect	After-Tax

Part 2 Income from Continuing Operations and its Components:

_____
_____
_____
_____
_____
_____
_____
_____
_____
_____
_____
_____
_____
_____
_____
_____
_____
_____

Part 3 Income from Discontinued Segment:

_____
_____
_____
_____
_____
_____

Part 4 Income before Extraordinary Items:

_____
_____
_____
_____
_____

Part 5 Net Income:

_____
_____
_____
_____
_____
_____

(1) Gross Margin Ratio (with services revenue):

_____
_____
_____
_____

   Gross Margin Ratio (without services revenue):

_____
_____
_____
_____

   Profit Margin Ratio:

_____
_____
_____
_____

(2) Current Ratio:

_____
_____
_____
_____

   Acid-Test Ratio:

_____
_____
_____
_____

(3) Debt Ratio:

_____
_____
_____

   Equity Ratio:

_____
_____
_____

(4) Current Assets as % of Total Assets:

_____
_____
_____

   Long-Term Assets as % of Total Assets:

_____
_____
_____
_____

(1) Trend Percents for selected income statement accounts:

	2005	2004	2003
Revenues			
Cost of Goods Sold			
Selling general and admin. expenses			
Income taxes			
Net income			

(2) Common-size percents for asset categories and accounts:

	2005	2004
Total current assets		
Property and equipment, net		
Intangible assets		

(3) Analysis and Interpretation: _____

_____
_____
_____
_____
_____
_____
_____
_____
_____
_____
_____
_____
_____
_____

(4) Fast Forward _____

_____
_____
_____
_____
_____
_____
_____
_____

(1)

Key figures	Best Buy	Circuit City
Cash and cash equivalents		
Accounts receivable, net		
Inventories		
Retained earnings		
Cost of Goods Sold*		
Revenues		
Total Assets		

* Circuit City's cost of goods sold is titled cost of sales.

(2) _____
_____
_____
_____
_____
_____

(3) _____
_____
_____
_____
_____
_____

(4) _____
_____
_____
_____
_____
_____
_____
_____

(1) _____

_____

_____

_____

_____

_____

_____

_____

_____

(2) _____

_____

_____

_____

_____

_____

_____

_____

_____

_____

_____

_____

_____

_____

MEMORANDUM

TO:
FROM:
DATE:
SUBJECT:

	2004	2003
1. Profit margin ratio		
2. Gross profit ratio		
3. Return on total assets		
4. Return on common stockholders' equity		
5. Basic earnings per share		
Analysis and Interpretation:		

Part 1

_____

_____

_____

_____

_____

_____

_____

_____

_____

_____

_____

_____

_____

_____

_____

_____

_____

Part 2

_____

_____

_____

_____

_____

_____

_____

_____

_____

_____

_____

_____

_____

_____

_____

Part 3

_____

(1) _____
_____
_____

(2) _____
_____

(3) _____
_____

(4) _____
_____
_____

(1) _____

_____

_____

_____

(2) _____

_____

_____

(3) _____

_____

_____

_____

(4) _____

_____

_____

_____

(5) _____

_____

_____

_____

(6) _____

_____

_____

_____

Hitting the Road--BTN 17-9

_____

_____

_____

_____

_____

_____

_____

Identification of Differences (more than five exist):

(1) _____

_____

(2) _____

_____

(3) _____

_____

(4) _____

_____

(5) _____

_____

Answer: _____

_____

Quick Study 18-2

(1) _____   (4) _____
(2) _____   (5) _____
(3) _____

Quick Study 18-3

(1) _____   (3) _____
(2) _____   (4) _____

Quick Study 18-4

Answer: _____

_____

Quick Study 18-5

(1) _____   (4) _____
(2) _____   (5) _____
(3) _____

Quick Study 18-6

Answer: _____

_____

Quick Study 18-7

Usual Sequence: _____

_____

_____

Name _____

Quick Study 18-9

Quick Study 18-10

Briton Company
Manufacturing Statement
For Year Ended December 31, 2008

(a) _____

_____

_____

_____

_____

(b) _____

_____

_____

Quick Study 18-12

_____

_____

_____

_____

_____

_____

_____

_____

_____

Chapter 18   Exercise 18-1   Name _____

Business Decision	Primary Information Source	
	Managerial	Financial
Report financial performance to board of directors		
Estimate product cost for new line of shoes...		
Plan the budget for next quarter...................................		
Measure profitability of all individual stores..................		
Prepare financial reports according to GAAP................		
Determine amount of dividends to pay stockholders......		
Determine location and size for a new plant.................		
Evaluate a purchasing department's performance.........		

Exercise 18-2

(1) _____ is the process of setting goals and making plans to achieve them.

(2) _____ is the process of monitoring planning decisions and evaluating the organization's activities and employees.

(3) _____ usually covers a period of 5 to 10 years.

(4) _____ usually covers a period of one year.

Name _____

	Financial Accounting	Managerial Accounting
1. Users and decision makers		
2. Purpose of information		
3. Flexibility of practice		
4. Timeliness of information		
5. Time dimension		
6. Focus of information		
7. Nature of information		

Chapter 18   Exercise 18-4   *Name* _____

(a) _____

(1) _____   (3) _____

(2) _____   (4) _____

(b) _____
_____
_____
_____
_____
_____

Exercise 18-5

(1) _____

(2) _____

(3) _____

Exercise 18-6

	Product Cost		Period Cost	Direct Cost	Indirect Cost
	Prime	Conversion			
Direct materials used................					
State and federal income taxes					
Payroll taxes for production supervisor...............................					
Amortization of patents on factory machine......................					
Accident insurance on factory workers................................					
Wages to assembly workers.......					
Factory utilities.........................					
Small tools used.......................					
Bad debts expense....................					
Depreciation--Factory building....					
Advertising..............................					
Office supplies used..................					

Chapter 18   Exercise 18-7   *Name* _____

(1) Cost classifications:

(a) _____   (d) _____
(b) _____   (e) _____
(c) _____

(2) Purpose:

_____
_____
_____
_____
_____
_____
_____
_____
_____
_____
_____
_____

(1)

Product Costs	Cost by Behavior		Cost by Traceability	
	Variable	Fixed	Direct	Indirect
Annual flat fee paid for office security..				
Leather cover for soccer balls...........				
Lace to hold the leather together......				
Wages of assembly workers.............				
Taxes on factory.............................				
Coolants for machinery...................				
Machinery depreciation...................				

(2) _____

_____

_____

_____

_____

_____

_____

_____

_____

Chapter 18   Exercise 18-9   *Name* _____

(1) Identification: _____

_____

_____

_____

_____

(2)

Company 1
Sun Fresh Foods
Current Asset Section
December 31, 2008

_____

_____

_____

_____

_____

_____

_____

_____

Company 2
Salomon Skis Mfg.
Current Asset Section
December 31, 2008

_____

_____

_____

_____

_____

_____

_____

_____

_____

Discussion: _____

_____

_____

_____

_____

Merchandising Business

Viking Retail
Partial Income Statement
For Year Ended December 31, 2008

Manufacturing Business

Log Homes Manufacturing
Partial Income Statement
For Year Ended December 31, 2008

	Garcia Company	Culpepper Company
(1) COST OF GOODS MANUFACTURED		
(2) COST OF GOODS SOLD		

Account	Balance Sheet	Income Statement	Manufacturing Statement	Overhead Report
Accounts receivable.............				
Computer supplies used in office...............................				
Beginning finished goods inventory............................				
Beginning goods in process inventory............................				
Beginning raw materials inventory............................				
Cash....................................				
Depreciation expense-Factory building............................				
Depreciation expense-Factory equipment..........................				
Depreciation expense-Office building............................				
Depreciation expense-Office equipment..........................				
Direct labor..........................				
Ending finished goods inventory............................				
Ending goods in process inventory............................				
Ending raw materials inventory............................				
Factory maintenance wages..				
Computer supplies used in factory...............................				
Income taxes......................				
Insurance on factory building				
Rent cost on office building...				
Office supplies used..............				
Property taxes on factory building............................				
Raw materials purchases........				
Sales..................................				

| Shanta Company |
| Manufacturing Statement |
| For Year Ended December 31, 2008 |

| Shanta Company |
| Income Statement |
| For Year Ended December 31, 2008 |

_____

_____

_____

_____

_____

_____

_____

_____

_____

_____

_____

_____

_____

_____

_____

_____

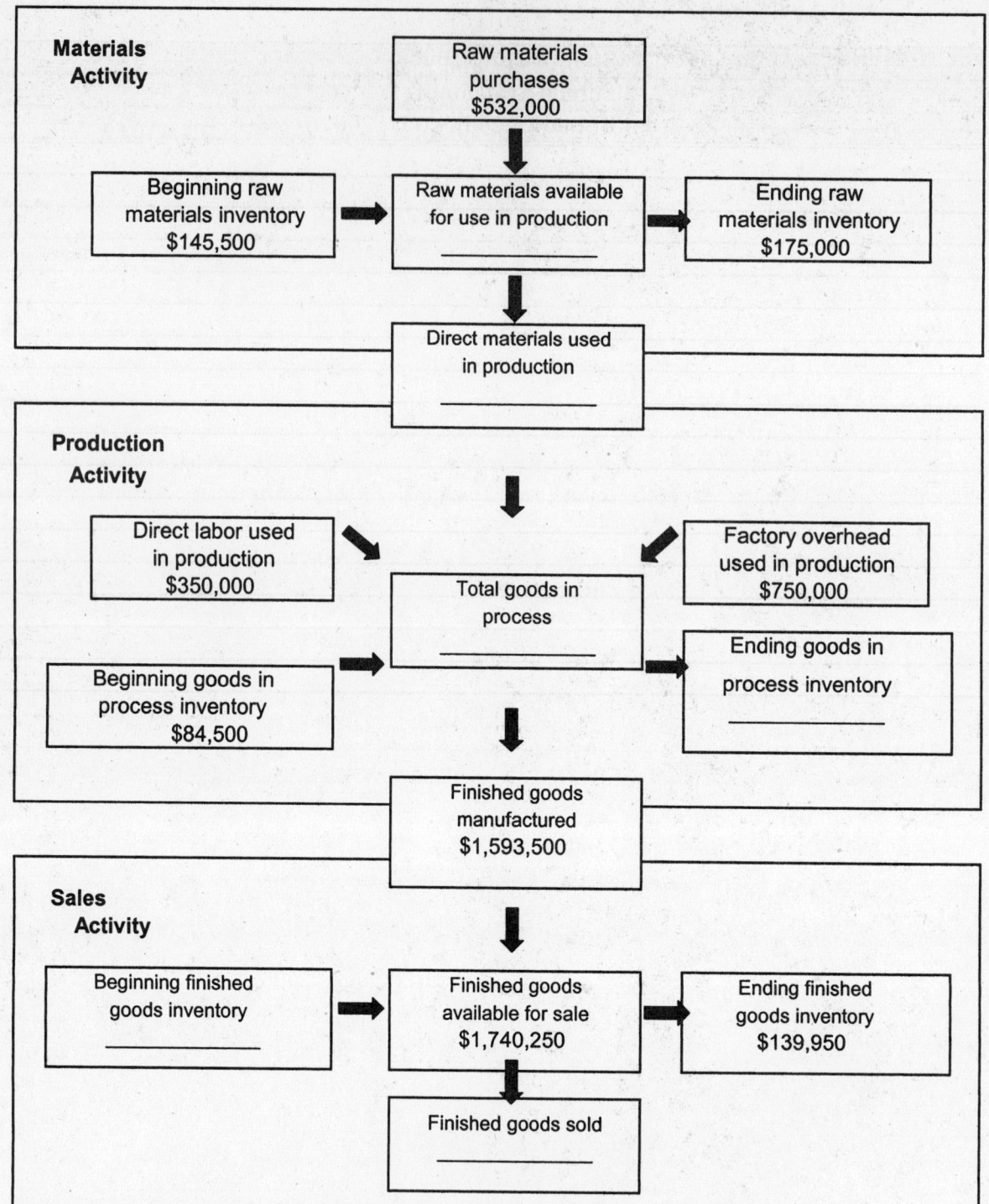

Managerial accounting contributions and responsibilities: _____

_____

_____

_____

_____

_____

_____

_____

_____

_____

_____

_____

_____

_____

_____

_____

_____

Problem 18-2A or 18-2B

(1) _____	(6) _____
(2) _____	(7) _____
(3) _____	(8) _____
(4) _____	(9) _____
(5) _____	(10) _____

Part 1

Costs	Cost by Behavior		Cost by Function	
	Variable	Fixed	Product	Period

Part 2

Computation of Manufacturing Cost per		
For Year Ended December 31, 2008		
	Total Cost	Per Unit Cost
Variable costs		
Fixed Costs		

Part 3

_____
_____
_____
_____
_____

Part 4

_____
_____
_____
_____

MEMORANDUM

TO:

FROM:

DATE:

SUBJECT: Cost classification and explanation

Cost Estimation (including opportunity costs):

(blank lined answer space)

Units and Dollar Amounts for Raw Materials Inventory

_____
_____
_____
_____
_____
_____
_____
_____
_____

Part 2

MEMORANDUM

TO:
FROM:
DATE:
SUBJECT: Consideration of JIT inventory system

_____
_____
_____
_____
_____
_____
_____
_____
_____
_____
_____
_____
_____
_____
_____
_____
_____
_____
_____

Merchandising Business

Partial Income Statement
For Year Ended December 31, 2008

Manufacturing Business

Partial Income Statement
For Year Ended December 31, 2008

MEMORANDUM

TO:

FROM:

DATE:

SUBJECT: Identifying and reporting inventory accounts

| Manufacturing Statement |
| For Year Ended December 31, 2008 |

	Income Statement
	For Year Ended December 31, 2008

Inventory Ratios	Raw Materials	Finished Goods

Analysis and discussion:

_____
_____
_____
_____
_____
_____
_____
_____
_____
_____
_____
_____
_____

Part 1 _____

_____

_____

_____

_____

_____

_____

_____

Part 2 _____

_____

_____

_____

_____

_____

_____

_____

Part 3 _____

_____

_____

_____

_____

_____

_____

_____

_____

_____

(1)

Product Costs	Cost by Behavior		Cost by Traceability	
	Variable	Fixed	Direct	Indirect
Glue to assemble workstation component parts......................				
Laminate coverings for desktops....				
Wages of desk assembler..............				
Taxes on assembly workshop........				
Depreciation on tools...................				
Electricity for workshop................				
Monthly flat fee to clean workshop.				

(2)

Success Systems
Manufacturing Statement
For Month Ended January 31, 2009

_____
_____
_____
_____
_____
_____
_____
_____
_____
_____
_____
_____

(3)

Success Systems
Partial Income Statement
For Month Ended January 31, 2009

Cost of goods sold

_____
_____
_____
_____
_____
_____
_____
_____

(1)

Estimate	Effects if Actual Results differ from Assumptions

(2)

(3) Fast Forward:

(1)

Best Buy

_____

_____

_____

_____

_____

_____

_____

Circuit City

_____

_____

_____

_____

_____

_____

(2)

_____

_____

_____

_____

_____

_____

_____

_____

Ethics Challenge BTN 18-3

(1) Account Identification _____

_____

_____

_____

_____

_____

_____

_____

(2) CFO Response _____

_____

_____

_____

_____

_____

_____

_____

_____

_____

_____

_____

MEMORANDUM

TO:
FROM:
DATE:
SUBJECT: Business student salary expectations

Summary of Ethical Standards: _____

_____

_____

_____

_____

_____

_____

_____

_____

_____

_____

_____

Attach printout of IMA Ethical Standards

_____

_____

_____

_____

_____

_____

_____

_____

_____

_____

_____

_____

_____

_____

_____

_____

_____

_____

_____

_____

_____

_____

_____

_____

_____

_____

_____

_____

_____

_____

_____

_____

_____

_____

_____

_____

_____

_____

_____

_____

_____

_____

_____

_____

_____

_____

_____

(1) _____

_____

_____

_____

_____

_____

_____

_____

_____

(2) _____

_____

_____

_____

_____

_____

_____

_____

_____

(1) Manufacturing Cost Categories

_____
_____
_____
_____
_____
_____
_____
_____
_____
_____

(2) Managerial Measures

_____
_____
_____
_____
_____
_____
_____
_____
_____
_____

(1) Customer Business Activities (from arrival through departure)

_____
_____
_____
_____
_____

(2) Costs of Customer Business Activities from Part 1

_____
_____
_____
_____
_____
_____
_____

(3) Cost Classification and Explanation

_____
_____
_____
_____
_____
_____
_____
_____

(1) Responsibilities

_____
_____
_____
_____
_____
_____
_____
_____
_____

(2) Involvement

_____
_____
_____
_____
_____
_____
_____
_____
_____
_____
_____

(1) Overhead as Percent of Direct Labor _____

_____

_____

(2) Overhead as Percent of Direct Materials _____

_____

_____

Quick Study 19-2

Job: _____

_____

Job lot: _____

_____

Quick Study 19-3

Job Cost Sheet

_____

_____

_____

_____

_____

_____

_____

_____

_____

_____

GENERAL JOURNAL

Date	Account Titles and Explanation	P. R.	Debit	Credit

Quick Study 19-5

GENERAL JOURNAL

Date	Account Titles and Explanation	P. R.	Debit	Credit

Quick Study 19-6

GENERAL JOURNAL

Date	Account Titles and Explanation	P. R.	Debit	Credit

GENERAL JOURNAL

Date	Account Titles and Explanation	P. R.	Debit	Credit

Computations: _____

_____

_____

_____

_____

(1) _____   (5) _____
(2) _____   (6) _____
(3) _____   (7) _____
(4) _____

Exercise 19-2

(1) _____
_____
_____
_____
_____
_____
_____
_____

(2) _____
_____
_____
_____
_____
_____
_____
_____

(3) _____
_____
_____
_____
_____
_____
_____
_____

(4) _____

_____

_____

_____

_____

_____

_____

Exercise 19-3

(1) Predetermined Overhead Rate _____

_____

_____

(2) _____

_____

_____

_____

_____

Exercise 19-4

(1) Predetermined Overhead Rate _____

_____

_____

(2) _____

_____

_____

_____

_____

Name _____

(1) Cost of Direct Materials Used

(2) Cost of Direct Labor Used

(3) Cost of Goods Manufactured

(4) Cost of Goods Sold

Name _____

(5) Gross Profit _____

_____

_____

_____

_____

_____

(6) Overapplied or Underapplied Overhead _____

_____

_____

_____

_____

_____

_____

Name _____

GENERAL JOURNAL

	Date	Account Titles and Explanation	P. R.	Debit	Credit
(1)					
(2)					
(3)					
(4)					
(5)					
(6)					
(7)					

GENERAL JOURNAL

Date	Account Titles and Explanation	P. R.	Debit	Credit
(8)				
(9)				
(10)				
(11)				

Exercise 19-7

(1) Predetermined Overhead Rate

_____

_____

_____

_____

_____

_____

(2 & 3) _____

_____
_____
_____
_____
_____
_____
_____
_____
_____

(4)

GENERAL JOURNAL

Date		Account Titles and Explanation	P. R.	Debit	Credit

Exercise 19-8

(1) Predetermined Overhead Rate _____

_____
_____
_____
_____
_____

(2 & 3) _____

_____
_____
_____
_____
_____
_____
_____
_____
_____

(4)

GENERAL JOURNAL

Date	Account Titles and Explanation	P. R.	Debit	Credit

(5)

GENERAL JOURNAL

Date	Account Titles and Explanation	P. R.	Debit	Credit

Supporting Computations _____

_____

_____

_____

Name _____

(1) Predetermined Overhead Rate

_____
_____
_____

(2) Direct Materials Costs

_____
_____
_____
_____
_____
_____

(3) Direct Labor Costs and Overhead Costs

_____
_____
_____
_____
_____
_____
_____
_____
_____
_____

Exercise 19-10

(1) Predetermined Overhead Rate

_____
_____
_____
_____
_____

(2)

	Goods in Process			Finished Goods		
	Cost per Unit	Units	Total Cost	Cost per Unit	Units	Total Cost
Direct materials						
Direct labor						
Overhead						
Total						

(3) _____

_____

_____

_____

_____

_____

_____

_____

_____

_____

_____

_____

_____

_____

_____

_____

_____

_____

_____

_____

_____

(1) Estimated Cost of the Architectural Job

(2) Suggested Bid Price

Total Manufacturing Costs and Costs Assigned to Each Job

Costs	Job _____	Job _____	Job _____	Total for Month

GENERAL JOURNAL

Date	Account Titles and Explanation	P. R.	Debit	Credit
(a)				
(b)				

GENERAL JOURNAL

Date	Account Titles and Explanation	P. R.	Debit	Credit
(c)				
(d)				
(e)				
(f)				

| Manufacturing Statement |
| For Month Ended _____ |

Gross Profit Computation

_____

_____

_____

_____

_____

_____

Presentation of Inventories on Balance Sheet

_____

_____

_____

_____

_____

_____

_____

Part 5

Impacts of Over- or Underapplied Overhead

_____

_____

_____

_____

_____

GENERAL JOURNAL

Date		Account Titles and Explanation	P. R.	Debit	Credit
(a)					
(b)					
(c)					
(d)					
(e)					

GENERAL JOURNAL

Date	Account Titles and Explanation	P. R.	Debit	Credit

Overhead computations:

_____
_____
_____
_____
_____
_____
_____
_____
_____
_____

Part 3

Trial Balance
December 31, 2008

	Debit	Credit

_____
_____
_____
_____
_____
_____
_____
_____
_____
_____
_____
_____
_____
_____
_____
_____
_____
_____
_____

_____

Income Statement
For Year Ended December 31, 2008

_____
_____
_____
_____
_____
_____
_____
_____

_____

Balance Sheet
December 31, 2008

_____
_____
_____
_____
_____
_____
_____
_____
_____
_____
_____
_____
_____
_____
_____
_____
_____
_____

Part 5

Error Analysis for Financial Statements

_____
_____
_____
_____
_____
_____
_____

JOB COST SHEETS

Job No. _____	
Materials...........	_____
Labor...............	_____
Overhead.........	_____
Total Cost.........	_____

Job No. _____	
Materials.........	_____
Labor...............	_____
Overhead.........	_____
Total Cost.........	_____

Job No. _____	
Materials.........	_____
Labor...............	_____
Overhead.........	_____
Total Cost.........	_____

Job No. _____	
Materials.........	_____
Labor...............	_____
Overhead.........	_____
Total Cost.........	_____

Job No. _____	
Materials.........	_____
Labor...............	_____
Overhead.........	_____
Total Cost.........	_____

GENERAL JOURNAL

Date	Account Titles and Explanation	P. R.	Debit	Credit
(a)				
(b)				
(c)				
(d)				
(e)				
(f)				
(g)				

GENERAL JOURNAL

Date	Account Titles and Explanation	P. R.	Debit	Credit
(h)				
(i)				
(j)				

Part 3

GENERAL LEDGER ACCOUNTS

Raw Materials Inventory	Factory Payroll

Goods in Process Inventory	Factory Overhead

Finished Goods Inventory	Cost of Goods Sold

Reports of Job Costs

Goods in Process Inventory:

_____
_____
_____
_____

Finished Goods Inventory:

_____
_____
_____
_____
_____

Cost of Goods Sold:

_____
_____
_____
_____
_____

Problem 19-4A or 19-4B
Part 1

(a) Predetermined Overhead Rate _____

_____
_____
_____
_____
_____

(b) Overhead Costs Applied to Jobs

Job No.	Direct Labor	Applied Overhead
_____		
_____		
_____		
_____		
_____		
Totals..................		

(c) Overapplied or Underapplied Overhead _____

_____

_____

_____

_____

_____

_____

Part 2

GENERAL JOURNAL

Date	Account Titles and Explanation	P. R.	Debit	Credit

JOB COST SHEET

Customer's Name _____ Company _____ Job No. _____

	Direct Materials			Direct Labor			Overhead Costs Applied	
Date	Requisition Number	Amount	Date	Time Ticket Number	Amount	Date	Rate	Amount
						SUMMARY OF COSTS		
						Dir. Materials..		_____
						Dir. Labor......		_____
						Overhead......		_____
Total			Total			Total Cost of the Job.........		_____

JOB COST SHEET

Customer's Name _____ Company _____ Job No. _____

	Direct Materials			Direct Labor			Overhead Costs Applied	
Date	Requisition Number	Amount	Date	Time Ticket Number	Amount	Date	Rate	Amount
						SUMMARY OF COSTS		
						Dir. Materials..		_____
						Dir. Labor......		_____
						Overhead......		_____
Total			Total			Total Cost of the Job.........		_____

MATERIALS LEDGER CARD

Item _____

	Received				Issued				Balance		
Date	Receiving Report	Units	Unit Price	Total Price	Requi-sition	Units	Unit Price	Total Price	Units	Unit Price	Total Price

MATERIALS LEDGER CARD

Item _____

	Received				Issued				Balance		
Date	Receiving Report	Units	Unit Price	Total Price	Requi-sition	Units	Unit Price	Total Price	Units	Unit Price	Total Price

MATERIALS LEDGER CARD

Item _____

	Received				Issued				Balance		
Date	Receiving Report	Units	Unit Price	Total Price	Requi-sition	Units	Unit Price	Total Price	Units	Unit Price	Total Price

GENERAL JOURNAL

Date		Account Titles and Explanation	P. R.	Debit	Credit

GENERAL LEDGER

Cash

Accounts Receivable

Sales

Cost of Goods Sold

Finished Goods Inventory

Accounts Payable

Raw Materials Inventory

Goods in Process Inventory

Factory Overhead

Factory Payroll

FACTORY OVERHEAD LEDGER

Indirect Materials

Indirect Labor

Miscellaneous Overhead

(1) Cost of Direct Materials Used Period for each Job and its Total

_____

_____

_____

_____

_____

_____

_____

_____

(2) Cost of Direct Labor Incurred Period

_____

_____

_____

_____

_____

_____

_____

_____

(3) Predetermined Overhead Rate Period

_____

_____

_____

_____

_____

_____

_____

_____

(4) Cost Transferred to Finished Goods Inventory Period

_____

_____

_____

_____

_____

_____

_____

(1) Costs that will Predictably Increase as a Percent of Sales

_____
_____
_____
_____
_____
_____
_____
_____
_____

(2) Explanation and Performance Assessment of the Costs in Part 1

_____
_____
_____
_____
_____
_____
_____
_____
_____
_____
_____
_____

(3) Roll On:

_____
_____
_____
_____
_____
_____
_____
_____
_____
_____
_____
_____
_____
_____

Chapter 19   Comparative Analysis   *Name* _____
Part 1   BTN 19-2

Best Buy	Current Year	One Year Prior	Two Years Prior
Inventory change...........			
Operating cash flow effect from inventory change....			

Circuit City	Current Year	One Year Prior	Two Years Prior
Inventory change...........			
Operating cash flow effect from inventory change....			

Part 2

Impacts of JIT Inventory System _____
_____
_____
_____
_____
_____
_____
_____
_____

Part 3

Operating Cash Flow Impacts of JIT Inventory System _____
_____
_____
_____
_____
_____
_____
_____

MEMORANDUM

TO:

FROM:

DATE:

SUBJECT: Review of Overhead Allocations

---

(1) Cost Accounting System Recommendation and Explanation

_____
_____
_____
_____
_____
_____
_____
_____
_____
_____
_____
_____
_____

(2) Document Description for Proposed Cost Accounting System

_____
_____
_____
_____
_____
_____
_____
_____
_____
_____
_____
_____

(3) Document Facilitation of Cost Accounting System

_____
_____
_____
_____
_____
_____
_____
_____
_____
_____
_____
_____
_____

MEMORANDUM

TO:
FROM:
DATE:
SUBJECT: Explanation and recommendation of job order costing software

_____
_____
_____
_____
_____
_____
_____
_____
_____
_____
_____
_____
_____
_____
_____
_____
_____
_____
_____
_____
_____
_____
_____
_____
_____
_____
_____
_____
_____
_____
_____
_____
_____

(1) Appropriateness of Job Order Cost Accounting System

_____

_____

_____

_____

_____

_____

_____

_____

_____

_____

_____

(2) Factors Indicative of Job Order System

_____

_____

_____

_____

_____

_____

_____

_____

_____

_____

_____

_____

Cost Structure Rationale

_____

_____

_____

_____

_____

_____

_____

_____

_____

_____

_____

_____

_____

_____

_____

_____

(1) _____
_____
_____
_____
_____
_____
_____
_____

(2) _____
_____
_____
_____
_____
_____
_____
_____
_____
_____
_____
_____
_____

(1)

JOB COST SHEET

Customer's Name _____ Company _____ Job No. _____

	Direct Materials			Direct Labor			Overhead Costs Applied		
Date	Requisition Number	Amount	Date	Time Ticket Number	Amount	Date	Rate	Amount	
						SUMMARY OF COSTS			
						Dir. Materials _____			
						Dir. Labor..... _____			
						Overhead..... _____			
Total			Total			Total Cost of the Job........ _____			

Explanation for Overhead Applied: _____

_____

_____

_____

(2) Report Actual Job Cost Sheet and Compare to Your Own in Part 1

(1) | Dixons | Current Year | One Year Prior |

Inventory change...

Operating cash flow effect from inventory change..

(2) Implications of JIT Inventory Systems _____

_____
_____
_____
_____
_____
_____
_____

| Best Buy | Current Year | One Year Prior | Two Years Prior |

Inventory change............

Operating cash flow effect from inventory change..

| Circuit City | Current Year | One Year Prior | Two Years Prior |

Inventory change............

Operating cash flow effect from inventory change..

(1) _____	(6) _____
(2) _____	(7) _____
(3) _____	(8) _____
(4) _____	(9) _____
(5) _____	(10) _____

Quick Study 20-2

GENERAL JOURNAL

Date	Account Titles and Explanation	P. R.	Debit	Credit

Quick Study 20-3

GENERAL JOURNAL

Date	Account Titles and Explanation	P. R.	Debit	Credit

GENERAL JOURNAL

Date		Account Titles and Explanation	P. R.	Debit	Credit

Quick Study 20-5

GENERAL JOURNAL

Date		Account Titles and Explanation	P. R.	Debit	Credit

Quick Study 20-6

EUP for Labor	Equivalent Units

Name _____

The cost of beginning inventory plus the costs added during the period should equal the
cost of units_____plus the cost of _____.

Quick Study 20-8

Explanation of Hybrid Costing System _____

_____

_____

Product or Service Identification for Hybrid Costing System _____

_____

_____

_____

Quick Study 20-9

EUP for Labor (Weighted Avg.)	Units of Product	Percent of Labor Added	Equivalent Units

Quick Study 20-9[A]

EUP for Labor	Equivalent Units

(1) _____	(5) _____
(2) _____	(6) _____
(3) _____	(7) _____
(4) _____	

Exercise 20-2

GENERAL JOURNAL

Date		Account Titles and Explanation	P. R.	Debit	Credit
1.					
2.					
3.					
4.					
5.					
6.					

GENERAL JOURNAL

Date	Account Titles and Explanation	P. R.	Debit	Credit
7.				
8.				
9.				
10.				

(a) _____

_____

(b) _____

_____

(c) _____

_____

(d) _____

_____

(e) _____

_____

(f) _____

_____

(g) _____

_____

(h) _____

_____

(i) _____

_____

(j) _____

_____

GENERAL JOURNAL

Date	Account Titles and Explanation	P. R.	Debit	Credit
1.				
2.				
3.				
4.				
5.				

Name _____

(1) Units Transferred to Finished Goods

_____

_____

_____

_____

_____

_____

(2)

Equivalent units of production	Direct Materials	Direct Labor

Name _____

1.

Cost per equivalent unit	Direct Materials	Direct Labor

2. Cost Assignment and Reconciliation

Cost per equivalent unit	Direct Materials	Direct Labor

Exercise 20-8^A

1. Cost per equivalent unit of direct materials and direct labor

	Direct Materials	Direct Labor

2. Assignment of costs to output of department

_____
_____
_____
_____
_____
_____
_____
_____
_____
_____
_____
_____
_____
_____
_____
_____
_____
_____
_____

Exercise 20-9

(1)

EUP for Materials

_____
_____
_____
_____

(2)

EUP for Materials

_____
_____
_____
_____

(3)

EUP for Materials

Exercise 20-10[A]

(1)

EUP for Materials

(2)

EUP for Materials

(3)

EUP for Materials

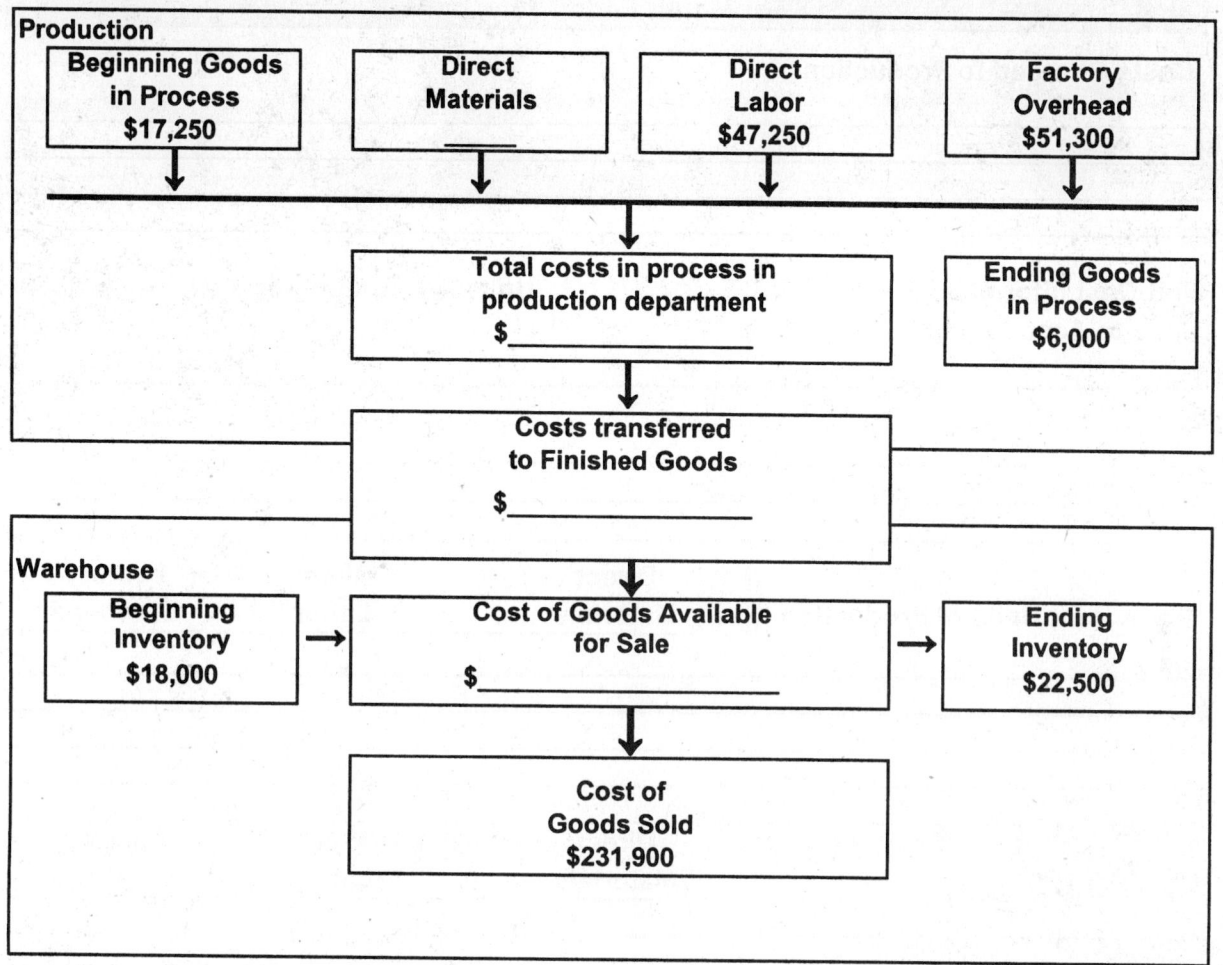

Production

| Beginning Goods in Process $17,250 | Direct Materials _____ | Direct Labor $47,250 | Factory Overhead $51,300 |

Total costs in process in production department
$_____

Ending Goods in Process $6,000

Costs transferred to Finished Goods
$_____

Warehouse

Beginning Inventory $18,000

Cost of Goods Available for Sale
$_____

Ending Inventory $22,500

Cost of Goods Sold $231,900

ASHAD COMPANY
Process Cost Summary
For Month Ended July 31

Costs Charged to Production

_____

_____

_____

_____

Unit Cost Information   **Units Accounted For**
Units to Account For

_____

_____

_____

_____

_____

Equivalent Units of Production (EUP)	Direct Materials	Direct Labor	Factory Overhead

Cost Per EUP	Direct Materials	*Direct Labor*	Factory Overhead

Cost Assignment and Reconciliation

_____

_____

_____

_____

_____

_____

_____

_____

_____

_____

_____

_____

_____

HI-TEST COMPANY
Process Cost Summary
For Month Ended September 30

Costs Charged to Production
Costs of Beginning work in process

Direct materials...	$45,000	
Direct Labor...	25,600	
Factory Overhead...	30,720	$101,320
Costs incurred this period..		
Direct materials...	375,000	
Direct Labor...	155,000	
Factory Overhead ($155,000 x 120%) .... (a) _____	(b) _____	
Total costs to account for..	(c) _____	

Unit Cost Information

Units to Account For		Units Accounted For	
Beginning goods in process...	2,000	Completed & transferred out.......	23,000
Units started this period........	28,000	Ending goods in process.............	(d) _____
Total units to account for..... (e) _____		Total units accounted for............	(f) _____

Equivalent Units of Production (EUP)	Direct Materials	Direct Labor	Factory Overhead
Units completed and transferred out...	(g)_____EUP	(h)_____EUP	(I)_____EUP
Units of ending goods in process........			
Direct materials [(j)_____ x 100%]......	(k)_____EUP		
Direct labor [(l)_____ x 40%].............		(m)_____EUP	
Factory overhead [(n)_____ x 40%]....			(o)_____EUP
Equivalent units of production...........	(p)_____EUP	(q)_____EUP	(r)_____EUP

Cost per EUP	Direct Materials	Direct Labor	Factory Overhead
Costs of beginning goods in process...	$45,000	$25,600	$30,720
Costs incurred this period...................	375,000	155,000	(s)_____
Total costs...	$420,000	$180,600	(t) $_____
/ Equivalent units of production.............	(u)_____	(v)_____	(w)_____
Cost per equivalent unit of production..	(x) $_____/EU	(y) $____/EUP	(z) $____/EUP

(continued on next page)

Cost Assignment and Reconciliation

Costs transferred out

Direct materials [(aa)$_____ x (bb)_____].................... (cc)$_____

Direct labor [(__)$7.00 x (ee)_____]............................ (ff) _____

Factory overhead [(gg)$____ x (hh)_____].................... (ii) _____

  Total transferred out.. (jj) $_____

Cost of ending good in process

Direct materials [(kk)$_____ x (ll)_____]..................... (mm)_____

Direct labor [(nn)$____ x (oo)_____].......................... (pp)_____

Factory overhead [(qq)$____ x (rr)_____]..................... (ss)_____

  Total ending goods in process... (tt)_____

Total costs accounted for...(uu)$_____

Cost of goods transferred and cost of goods sold

_____
_____
_____
_____
_____
_____
_____
_____
_____
_____
_____
_____
_____
_____
_____

Part 2

GENERAL JOURNAL

Date	Account Titles and Explanation	P. R.	Debit	Credit
a.				
b.				
c.				
d.				

GENERAL JOURNAL

Date	Account Titles and Explanation	P. R.	Debit	Credit
e.				
f.				
g.				
h.				
i.				
j.				

(a and b)

Equivalent units of production	Direct Materials	Direct Labor

Part 2

Costs per equivalent unit	Direct Materials	Direct Labor

Assignment of product costs to units

_____
_____
_____
_____
_____
_____
_____
_____
_____
_____
_____

MEMORANDUM

TO:

FROM:

DATE:

SUBJECT: Percentage of completion error analysis

Chapter 20 Problem 20-3A or 20-3B Name _____
Part 1

GENERAL JOURNAL

Date	Account Titles and Explanation	P. R.	Debit	Credit
a.				
b.				
c.				
d.				
e.				
f.				
g.				
h.				
i.				
j.				

Process Cost Summary
For Month Ended _____

Costs Charged to Production

_____
_____
_____
_____
_____
_____
_____
_____
_____

Unit Cost Information
Units to Account For   **Units Accounted For**

_____
_____
_____
_____

Equivalent Units of Production (EUP)	Direct Materials	Direct Labor	Factory Overhead

Cost per EUP	Direct Materials	Direct Labor	Factory Overhead

Cost Assignment and Reconciliation

_____
_____
_____
_____
_____
_____
_____
_____
_____
_____
_____

_____

_____

_____

_____

_____

_____

_____

_____

_____

_____

Process Cost Summary
For Month Ended _____

Costs Charged to Production

Unit Cost Information
Units to Account For   **Units Accounted For**

Equivalent Units of Production (EUP)	Direct Materials	Direct Labor	Factory Overhead

Cost per EUP	Direct Materials	Direct Labor	Factory Overhead

Cost Assignment and Reconciliation

GENERAL JOURNAL

Date		Account Titles and Explanation	P. R.	Debit	Credit

Name _____

Process Cost Summary
For Month Ended _____

Costs Charged to Production

_____
_____
_____
_____
_____
_____
_____
_____
_____

Unit Cost Information
Units to Account For   **Units Accounted For**

_____
_____
_____
_____

Equivalent Units of Production (EUP)	Direct Materials	Direct Labor	Factory Overhead

Cost per EUP	Direct Materials	Direct Labor	Factory Overhead

Cost Assignment and Reconciliation

_____
_____
_____
_____
_____
_____
_____
_____
_____
_____
_____

Part 2

GENERAL JOURNAL

Date		Account Titles and Explanation	P. R.	Debit	Credit

Part 3

(a) _____
_____
_____
_____

(b) _____
_____
_____
_____
_____
_____
_____

Process Cost Summary

For Month Ended _____

Costs Charged to Production

_____

_____

_____

_____

_____

_____

_____

_____

_____

_____

Unit Cost Information

Units to Account For	Units Accounted For
_____	_____
_____	_____
_____	_____
_____	_____
_____	_____

Equivalent Units of Production (EUP)	Direct Materials	Direct Labor	Factory Overhead

Cost per EUP	Direct Materials	Direct Labor	Factory Overhead

Cost Assignment and Reconciliation

_____
_____
_____
_____
_____
_____
_____
_____
_____
_____
_____
_____
_____
_____
_____
_____
_____

Part 2

GENERAL JOURNAL

Date		Account Titles and Explanation	P. R.	Debit	Credit

Chapter 20   Serial Problem, SP 20   *Name* _____

Part 1

Job Order Costing	Process Cosing

Part 2

_____
_____
_____
_____
_____
_____

[Note: General Ledger accounts shown in Part 4.]

GENERAL JOURNAL

Date		Account Titles and Explanation	P. R.	Debit	Credit
(a)					
(b)					
(c)					
(d)					
(e)					
(f)					

Process Cost Summary
For Month Ended _____

Costs Charged to Production

_____
_____
_____
_____
_____
_____
_____
_____
_____
_____

Unit Cost Information

Units to Account For   **Units Accounted For**

_____
_____
_____
_____

Equivalent Units of Production (EUP)	**Direct Materials**	**Direct Labor**	**Factory Overhead**

Cost per EUP	**Direct Materials**	**Direct Labor**	**Factory Overhead**

_____
_____
_____
_____
_____
_____
_____
_____
_____
_____
_____

Part 3

GENERAL JOURNAL

Date	Account Titles and Explanation	P. R.	Debit	Credit
(g)				
(h)				

General Ledger accounts:

	Raw Materials Inventory				ACCOUNT NO. 132
Date	Explanation	P.R.	DEBIT	CREDIT	BALANCE
June 30	Balance				50,000

	Goods in Process Inventory				ACCOUNT NO. 133
Date	Explanation	P.R.	DEBIT	CREDIT	BALANCE
June 30	Balance				16,270

Finished Goods Inventory   ACCOUNT NO. 135

Date	Explanation	P.R.	DEBIT	CREDIT	BALANCE
June 30	Balance				220,000

Sales   ACCOUNT NO. 413

Date	Explanation	P.R.	DEBIT	CREDIT	BALANCE

Cost of Goods Sold   ACCOUNT NO. 502

Date	Explanation	P.R.	DEBIT	CREDIT	BALANCE

Factory Payroll   ACCOUNT NO. 530

Date	Explanation	P.R.	DEBIT	CREDIT	BALANCE

Factory Overhead   ACCOUNT NO. 540

Date	Explanation	P.R.	DEBIT	CREDIT	BALANCE

Part 5
Computation of gross profit for July:

_____

_____

_____

_____

_____

_____

_____

_____

_____

_____

_____

_____

_____

Part 2

_____

_____

_____

_____

_____

_____

_____

Part 3 - Fast Forward:

_____

_____

_____

_____

_____

_____

_____

_____

_____

_____

_____

	Best Buy		Circuit City	
	Current Year	Prior Year	Current Year	Prior Year
COGS/ Total expenses				

Part 2

Analysis and Comparison of Cost Structures: _____

_____

_____

_____

_____

_____

_____

_____

MEMORANDUM

TO:

FROM:

DATE:

SUBJECT: Action plan to understand business processes

MEMORANDUM

TO:
FROM:
DATE:
SUBJECT: Explanation of cost classifications

_____

_____

_____

_____

_____

_____

_____

_____

_____

_____

_____

_____

_____

GENERAL JOURNAL

Date	Account Titles and Explanation	P. R.	Debit	Credit

(1) _____
_____
_____
_____
_____
_____

(2) _____
_____
_____
_____
_____
_____

(3) _____
_____
_____
_____
_____
_____

Entrepreneurial Decision BTN 20-8

_____
_____
_____
_____
_____
_____
_____
_____
_____
_____
_____
_____
_____

Cost description	Direct Materials	Direct Labor	Overhead	Variable cost	Fixed cost

Overhead allocation suggestions:

1. **Ratio of Cost of Goods Sold to Total Expenses**

	Current Year	Prior Year
Dixons............		

	Current Year	Prior Year
Best Buy................		

	Current Year	Prior Year
Circuit City.......................		

2. **Similarities or Differences Across Years and Companies:** _____
_____
_____
_____
_____
_____
_____
_____

Name _____

(1) _____   (5) _____
(2) _____   (6) _____
(3) _____   (7) _____
(4) _____

Quick Study 21-2

(1) _____

_____

(2) _____

_____

(3) _____

_____

(4) _____

_____

_____

Quick Study 21-3

Total Overhead Allocated to Operating Department 1: _____

_____
_____
_____
_____
_____
_____
_____
_____
_____
_____
_____
_____

Contribution to Overhead (dollars):

Dept. A

Dept. B

Dept. C

Contribution to Overhead (percent of sales):

Dept. A

Dept. B

Dept. C

Highest Contribution (Dollar & Percent)

_____

_____

Quick Study 21-5

Center	Net Income	Average Assets	Return on Assets
Basketball	$ 4,500,000	$ 20,000,000	
Soccer	1,500,000	12,500,000	
Cross-trainer	800,000	10,000,000	

Center Performance Evaluation:

_____

_____

_____

_____

Quick Study 21-6[A]

Joint Cost Assigned to Unit B Using the Value Basis of Allocation

Chapter 21   Exercise 21-1   Name _____

(1) Allocation of Indirect Expenses to Operating Departments

Supervision:

	Employees	% of Total	Cost
Materials			
Personnel			
Manufacturing			
Packaging			
Totals			

Utilities:

	Square Feet	% of Total	Cost
Materials			
Personnel			
Manufacturing			
Packaging			
Totals			

Insurance:

	Assets Value	% of Total	Cost
Materials			
Personnel			
Manufacturing			
Packaging			
Totals			

(2) Total indirect expenses assigned to operating departments:

	Supervision	Utilities	Insurance	Totals
Materials				
Personnel				
Manufacturing				
Packaging				
Totals				

Preliminary Computations (predetermined overhead rates)

Overhead Cost Pool	Total Cost	Amount of Cost Driver	Predetermined Overhead Rate
Supervision			
Depreciation			
Line Preparation			

(1) Assignment of overhead costs to the two products using ABC

Rounded edge:

	Cost Driver	Cost per Driver Unit	Allocated Cost
Supervision			
Machinery depreciation			
Line preparation			
Total overhead assigned			

Squared edge:

	Cost Driver	Cost per Driver Unit	Allocated Cost
Supervision			
Machinery depreciation			
Line preparation			
Total overhead assigned			

(2) Average cost per unit of the two products

	Rounded Edge	Squared Edge
Direct materials		
Direct labor		
Overhead (using ABC)		
Total Cost		
Quantity produced		
Average cost per foot		

(3) Comparison of Cost Allocation Methods _____

_____
_____
_____
_____
_____
_____

Exercise 21-3

	Amount Allocated	% of Total	Cost
First floor			
Second floor			
Totals			

First Floor	Sq. Feet	% of Total	Cost
Paint Dept.			
Engine Dept.			
Totals			

Second Floor	Sq. Feet	% of Total	Cost
Window Dept.			
Electrical Dept.			
Accessory Dept.			
Totals			

OVERLAND CYCLE SHOP
Department Expense Allocation Spreadsheet
For Year Ended December 31, 2008

	Allocation Base	Account Balance	Allocation of Expenses to Departments			
			Adver-tising	Admin-istrative	Cycles	Clothing
Direct expenses						
Indirect utilities expense						
Total dept. expense						
Service dept. expenses:						
Advertising						
Administrative						
Total expenses allocated to operating depts.						

Supplemental expense allocation calculation:

Utilities expense:

	Square Feet	% of Total	Cost
Advertising			
Administrative			
Cycles			
Clothing			
Total			

Advertising expense:

	Ads Placed	% of Total	Cost
Cycles			
Clothing			
Total			

Administrative expense:

	Sales	% of Total	Cost
Cycles			
Clothing			
Total			

	Allocation Base	Expense Account Balance	Allocation of Expenses to Departments				
			Adver-tising Dept.	Purchas-ing Dept.	Books Dept.	Magazine Dept.	News-paper Dept.
Total dept. expenses							
Service dept. expenses:							
Advertising........	Sales						
Purchasing......	Purchase Orders						
Total expenses allocated to operating depts................							

COZY BOOKSTORE
Departmental Expense Allocation Spreadsheet
For Period Ended _____

Allocations of service department costs to operating departments

Advertising: _____

	Sales	% of Total	Cost
Books Dept.			
Magazines Dept.			
Newspapers Dept.			
Totals			

Purchasing: _____

	Purchase Orders	% of Total	Cost
Books Dept.			
Magazines Dept.			
Newspapers Dept.			
Totals			

Name _____

Allocation of annual wages between two departments

	Hours Worked*	% of Total	Cost
Jewelry Dept.			
Hosiery Dept.			
Totals			

* Computation of hours worked in the two selling departments:

Jewelry department:

    Selling................................

    Arranging and stocking...........

Hosiery department:

    Selling................................

    Arranging and stocking...........

Total hours..............................

Name _____

Definitely Included:

_____

_____

_____

_____

_____

_____

Definitely Excluded:

_____

_____

_____

_____

_____

_____

Neither Definitely Included nor Definitely Excluded:

_____

_____

_____

_____

_____

_____

_____

(1)

Location	Net Income	Average Assets	Return on Assets
Location A			
Location B			

(2)

<table>
<tr><td colspan="2" align="center">MEMORANDUM</td></tr>
<tr><td colspan="2">TO:</td></tr>
<tr><td colspan="2">FROM:</td></tr>
<tr><td colspan="2">DATE:</td></tr>
<tr><td colspan="2">SUBJECT: Investment analysis and recommendation</td></tr>
<tr><td colspan="2"></td></tr>
</table>

Preliminary calculations

    Land Cost......................

    Improvements...............

    Total cost of lots............

Lots	Quantity	Price	Total
Canyon			
Hilltop			
Total Market value			

Allocated cost--value basis of allocation: _____

	Market Value	% of Total	Allocated Cost	Average Lot Cost
Canyon section				
Hilltop section				
Totals				

Preliminary calculations

Parts	Quantity	Price	Total
Lobster Tails			
Lobster Flakes			
Total market value			

_____

_____

_____

Allocated cost (value basis allocation): _____

Parts	Market Value	% of Total	Allocated Cost	Cost per lb.
Lobster Tails				
Lobster Flakes				
Total				

(1) Cost of goods sold

Parts	Quantity	Cost	Total
Lobster Tails			
Lobster Flakes			
Total cost of goods sold			

(2) Cost of ending inventory

Parts	Quantity	Cost	Total
Lobster Tails			
Lobster Flakes			
Total inventory cost			

Average occupancy cost = _____

These costs are assigned to departments as follows:

Department	Square Footage	Rate	Total
_____ Dept.			
_____ Dept.			

Part 2

Value-based costs are allocated to departments in two steps:

(i) Compute market value for each floor space.

Floor	Square Footage	Value per Sq. Ft.	Total
_____floor			
_____floor			
_____floor			
Total market value			

(ii) Allocate $_____to each floor based on its percent of market value.

	Market Value	% of Total	Allocated Cost	Cost per Sq. Ft.
_____floor				
_____floor				
_____floor				
Totals				

Usage-based costs allocation rate = _____

(i) Compute total allocation rates for the floors

Floor	Value	Usage	Total
_____floor			
_____floor			
_____floor			

(ii) Rates are applied to allocate occupancy costs to department(s).

Department	Square Footage	Rate	Total
_____ Department			
_____ Department			
_____ Department			

Part 3

Preferred Allocation Method _____

_____

_____

_____

_____

_____

_____

_____

Chapter 21   Problem 21-2A or 21-2B   Name _____

Part 1

Cost Center	Cost	Driver	Cost per Driver
Professional salaries			
Patient services and supplies*			
Building cost			

*Patient Services and Supplies will be Customer Supplies for P21-2B

Part 2 _____ **Service**

Activity	Cost Driver	Cost per Driver Unit	Allocated Cost
Professional salaries	Hours		
Patient services and supplies*			
Building cost	Sq. ft.		
Total			
Average cost per patient (or customer for 21-2B)			

*Patient Services and Supplies will be Customer Supplies for P21-2B

_____ **Service**

Activity	Cost Driver	Cost per Driver Unit	Allocated Cost
Professional salaries	Hours		
Patient services and supplies*			
Building cost	Sq. ft.		
Total			
Average cost per patient (or customer for 21-2B)			

*Patient Services and Supplies will be Customer Supplies for P21-2B

Analysis of Alternative Cost Allocation

_____

_____

_____

_____

_____

_____

_____

Problem 21-3A or 21-3B

				Combined
Forecasted Departmental Income Statements				
For Year Ended December 31, 2009				

Supporting computations:

(a)

RESPONSIBILITY ACCOUNTING PERFORMANCE REPORT			
Manager, _____ Department			
For the _____			
	Budgeted Amount	*Actual Amount*	*Over (Under) Budget*
CONTROLLABLE COSTS			
Raw materials			
Employee wages			
Supplies used			
Depreciation--Equipment			
Totals			

(b)

RESPONSIBILITY ACCOUNTING PERFORMANCE REPORT			
Manager, _____ Department			
For the _____			
	Budgeted Amount	*Actual Amount*	*Over (Under) Budget*
CONTROLLABLE COSTS			
Raw materials			
Employee wages			
Supplies used			
Depreciation--Equipment			
Totals			

(c)

RESPONSIBILITY ACCOUNTING PERFORMANCE REPORT			
Manager, _____ Department			
For the _____			
	Budgeted Amount	*Actual Amount*	*Over (Under) Budget*
CONTROLLABLE COSTS			
Dept. manager salaries			
Utilities			
Building rent			
Other office salaries			
Other office costs			
_____department			
_____department			
Totals			

Comparative Analysis of Manager Performance _____

_____
_____
_____
_____
_____
_____
_____

Problem 21-5A^A or 21-5B^A

Part 1

Allocation of joint costs on the basis of sales value

Cost Activity: _____

Grade	Sales Value	Percent of Total	Allocated Cost
No. 1			
No. 2			
No. 3			
Total			

Cost Activity: _____

Grade	Sales Value	Percent of Total	Allocated Cost
No. 1			
No. 2			
No. 3			
Total			

Cost Activity: _____

Grade	Sales Value	Percent of Total	Allocated Cost
No. 1			
No. 2			
No. 3			
Total			

Income Statement
For Year Ended December 31, 2008

	No. 1	No. 2	No. 3	Combined

Part 3

Analysis of Joint Cost

_____

_____

_____

_____

_____

_____

_____

_____

_____

_____

	Fiscal 2005	Fiscal 2004
Total Revenue		
Home Office		
Entertainment Software		
Consumer Electronics		
Appliances		

Part 2

_____
_____
_____
_____
_____
_____
_____

Part 3

Fast Forward

Total Revenue		
Home Office		
Entertainment Software		
Consumer Electronics		
Appliances		

Part 2

Importance of Comparable Responsibility Accounting Reports

_____

_____

_____

_____

_____

_____

_____

_____

_____

(1) Identification of any Ethical Concern(s) _____

_____
_____
_____
_____
_____
_____
_____
_____
_____
_____

(2) Action Plan to Eliminate or Reduce any Ethical Concern(s) _____

_____
_____
_____
_____
_____
_____
_____
_____
_____
_____

(3) Identification of Senior Security's Ethical Responsibility(ies) _____

_____
_____
_____
_____
_____
_____
_____
_____
_____
_____
_____

MEMORANDUM

TO:
FROM:
SUBJECT: Explanation of Home Office Expense in performance report
DATE:

_____
_____
_____
_____
_____
_____
_____
_____
_____
_____
_____
_____
_____
_____
_____
_____
_____
_____
_____
_____
_____
_____
_____
_____
_____

<u>Tutorial</u>   <u>Notes about Tutorial</u>

(i) _____

_____

_____

(ii) _____

_____

_____

_____

(iii) _____

_____

_____

_____

_____

MEMORANDUM

TO:

FROM:

SUBJECT: Applications useful in business and managerial decision making

DATE:

_____
_____
_____
_____
_____
_____
_____
_____
_____
_____
_____
_____
_____
_____
_____
_____
_____
_____
_____

Reasons for Increased Use of Activity-Based Costing

Chapter 21 *BusinessWeek Activity* Name _____
BTN 21-7

(1) _____
_____
_____
_____
_____

(2) _____
_____
_____
_____
_____
_____

(3) _____
_____
_____
_____
_____

(1) _____
_____
_____
_____
_____
_____
_____
_____
_____

(2) _____
_____
_____
_____
_____
_____
_____
_____
_____
_____
_____
_____
_____

Hitting the Road--BTN 21-9

(1) Recommendation to the Segment Departments for Responsibility Reporting
_____
_____
_____
_____
_____
_____

(2) Proposal for an Expense Allocation System

Expense	Allocation Base
Heat..........................	
Rent..........................	
Insurance..................	
Maintenance...............	

1. & 2.

Net sales growth (in percent) [non-percents in millions of pounds]

Segment	Net sales percent change from 2003 to 2004
UK Retail........................	
International Retail..............	
Total..........................	

_____

3. Identification of Fast-Growth Segment _____
_____
_____

4. Identification of Most Profitable Segment _____
_____
_____

5. Explanation of Management Use of Segment Information _____
_____
_____
_____
_____
_____
_____
_____
_____
_____

(1) _____   (5) _____

(2) _____   (6) _____

(3) _____   (7) _____

(4) _____

Quick Study 22-2

Series	Cost behavior
(1)	
(2)	
(3)	
(4)	

Quick Study 22-3

(1) Estimated line of cost behavior:

(2) Estimated cost components _____

   Fixed costs: _____

   Variable costs: _____

_____

_____

Variable Costs: _____
_____
_____

Fixed Costs: _____
_____
_____
_____
_____
_____

Quick Study 22-5
Contribution margin: _____
_____

Contribution margin ratio: _____
_____

Interpretation: _____
_____
_____

Name _____

(1)   Contribution margin per unit:

_____
_____
_____

(2)   Break-even point in units:

_____
_____
_____
_____

Quick Study 22-7

(1)   Contribution margin ratio:

_____
_____
_____

(2)   Break-even point in dollars:

_____
_____
_____
_____

Quick Study 22-8

Units to be Sold to Yield Targeted Net Income

_____
_____
_____
_____
_____
_____
_____

Quick Study 22-9

_____
_____

Identification of Company with Higher DOL: _____

Explanation: _____

_____

_____

_____

_____

_____

_____

Quick Study 22-11

Number and Type of Beepers Sold at Break-even _____

_____

_____

_____

_____

_____

_____

_____

_____

Exercise 22-1
Scatter diagram and estimated line of cost behavior.

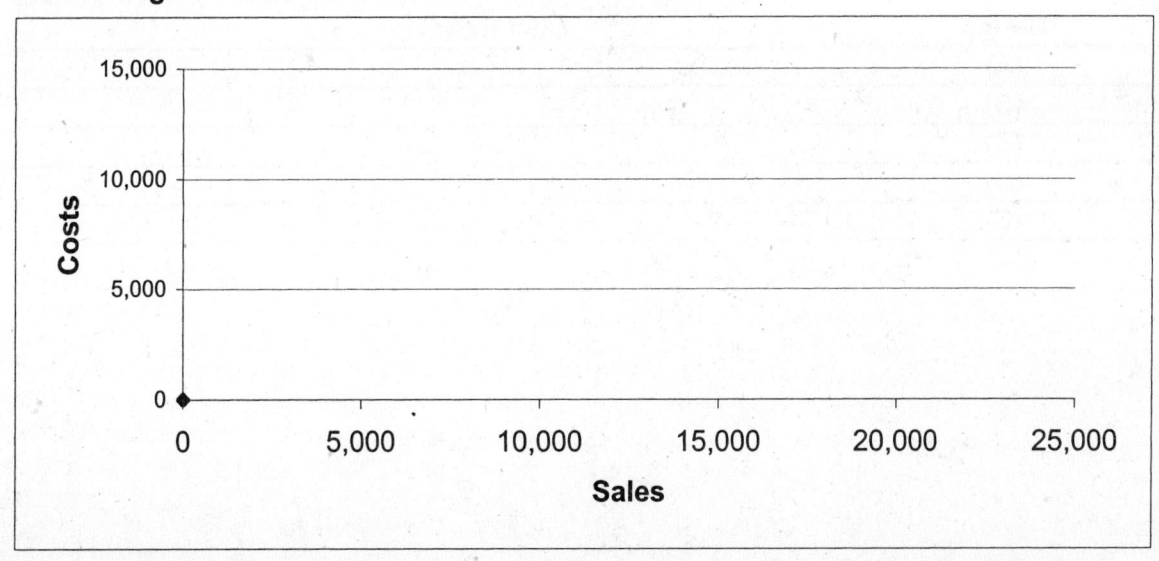

Cost behavior: _____

_____

Chapter 22   Exercise 22-2   *Name* _____

(1)

Graph	Cost Behavior
(1)	
(2)	
(3)	
(4)	
(5)	

(2)

Cost Item	Graph
(a)	
(b)	
(c)	
(d)	
(e)	

Exercise 22-3

(1)	(4)
(2)	(5)
(3)	(6)

Exercise 22-4

Series	Cost Behavior
(A)	
(B)	
(C)	
(D)	
(E)	

Chapter 22   Exercise 22-5

Name _____

(1) Dollar Sales _____
_____
_____
_____
_____
_____

(2) Total Variable Costs _____
_____
_____
_____
_____
_____

Exercise 22-6

Scatter diagram and estimated line of cost behavior.

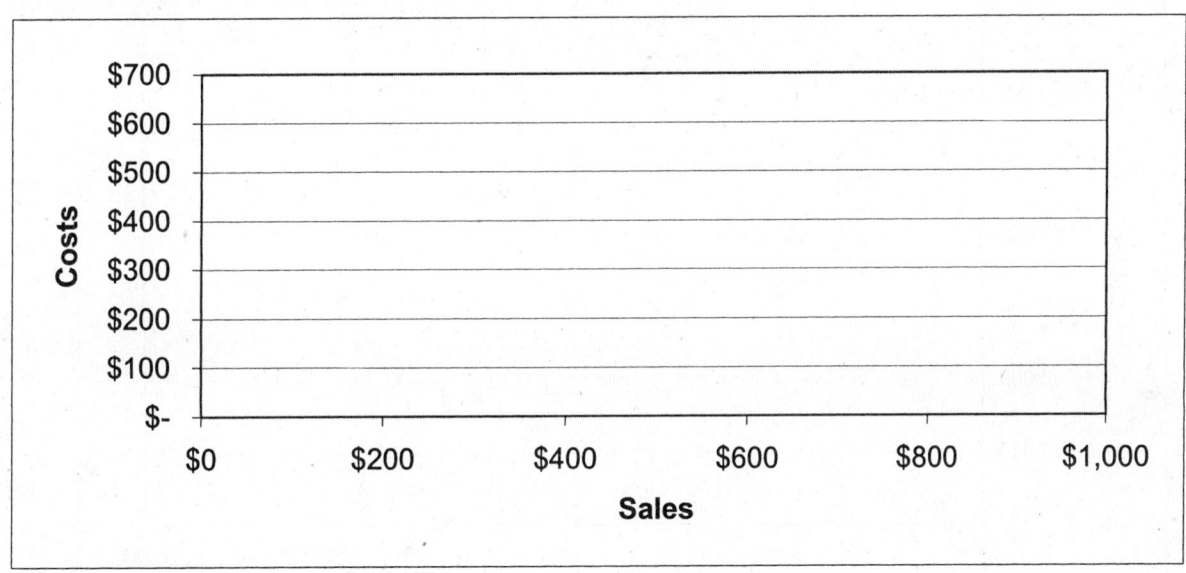

Cost behavior: _____
_____

(1)

(a)   **Contribution margin per unit:**

_____

_____

(b)   **Contribution margin ratio:**

_____

_____

(c)   **Break-even point in units:**

_____

_____

(d)   **Break-even point in dollars:**

_____

_____

(2) CVP chart:

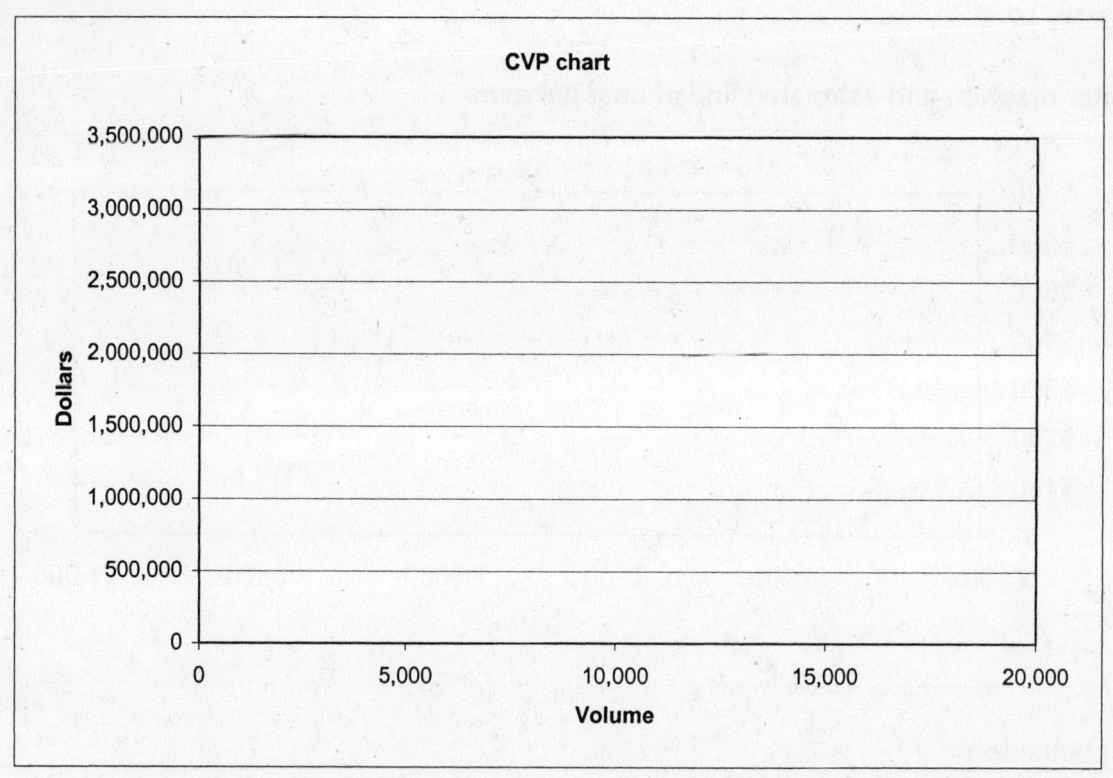

(1)

BLOOM COMPANY

Contribution Margin Income Statement (at Break-Even)

(2)

Sales (in dollars) to break even with increased fixed costs:

(1)   Unit sales at target income

_____

_____

_____

_____

_____

_____

_____

_____

_____

_____

_____

_____

(2)   Dollar sales at target income

_____

_____

_____

_____

_____

_____

_____

_____

_____

_____

Exercise 22-10

BLOOM COMPANY
Forecasted Contribution Margin Income Statement

_____

_____

_____

_____

_____

_____

_____

_____

(1) _____

_____

_____

_____

_____

_____

(2) _____

_____

_____

_____

_____

_____

_____

_____

Exercise 22-12

1(a) Next Year's Total Expected Variable Costs _____

_____

_____

_____

_____

_____

_____

_____

_____

1(b) Next Year's Total Expected Fixed Costs _____

_____

_____

_____

_____

_____

(2) CVP Chart

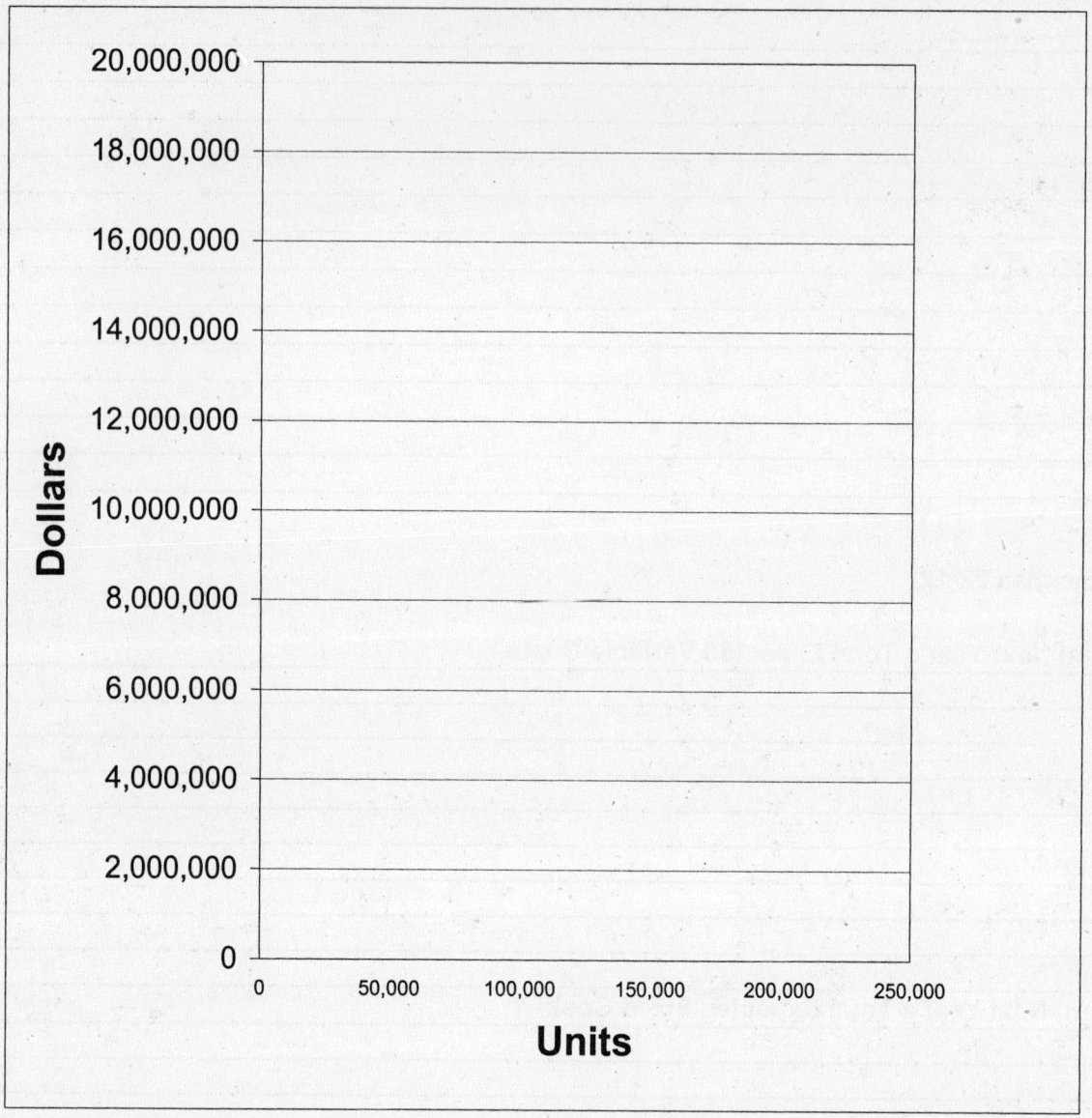

Company A's DOL: _____

_____

_____

_____

_____

_____

_____

_____

_____

_____

_____

Company B's DOL: _____

_____

_____

_____

_____

_____

_____

_____

_____

_____

_____

_____

_____

Interpretation: _____

_____

_____

_____

_____

_____

_____

(1) Selling price per composite unit:

_____
_____
_____
_____
_____
_____

(2) Variable costs per composite unit:

_____
_____
_____
_____
_____
_____
_____

(3) Break-even point in composite units:

_____
_____
_____
_____
_____
_____
_____
_____

(4) Unit sales of windows and doors at break-even point:

_____
_____
_____
_____

_____ Company Contribution Margin Income Statement For Year Ended_____	(_____ units)	Per unit	% of sales
Sales..			
Variable costs			
Contribution margin....................................			
Fixed costs			
Pretax Income...			
Income tax...			
Net Income...			

Part 3
Analysis _____

(a) Break-even point in unit sales: _____

_____

_____

_____

_____

_____

_____

_____

(b) Break-even point in dollar sales: _____

_____

_____

_____

_____

_____

_____

_____

_____

_____

Part 2
Graph for P22-2A

Graph for P22-2B

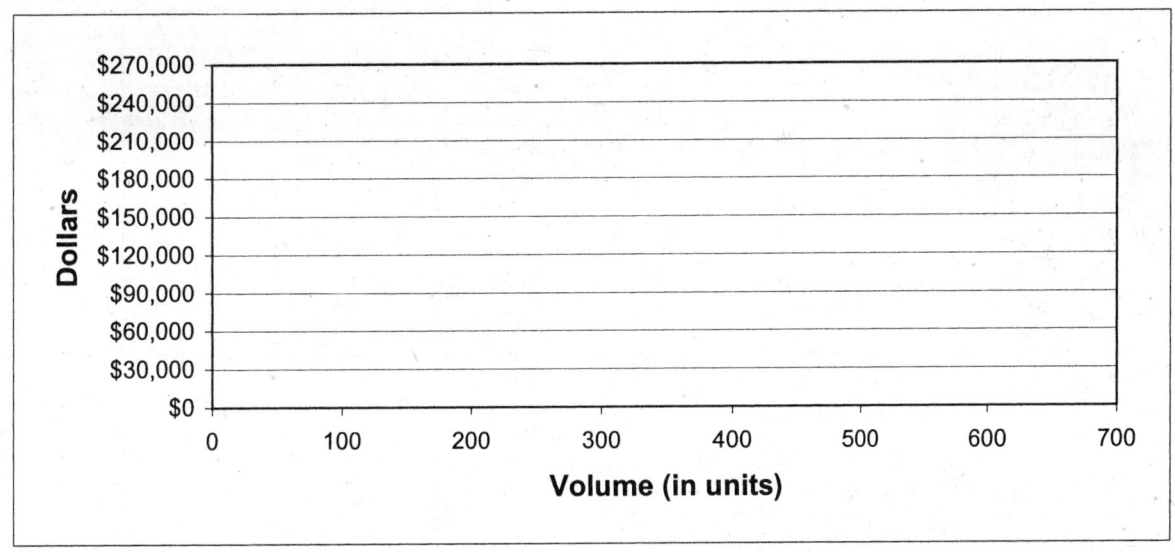

Part 3

_____

_____

Contribution Margin Income Statement (at Break-Even)

Product_____

_____

_____

_____

_____

_____

_____

_____

_____

Graph for P22-3A

Graph for P22-3B

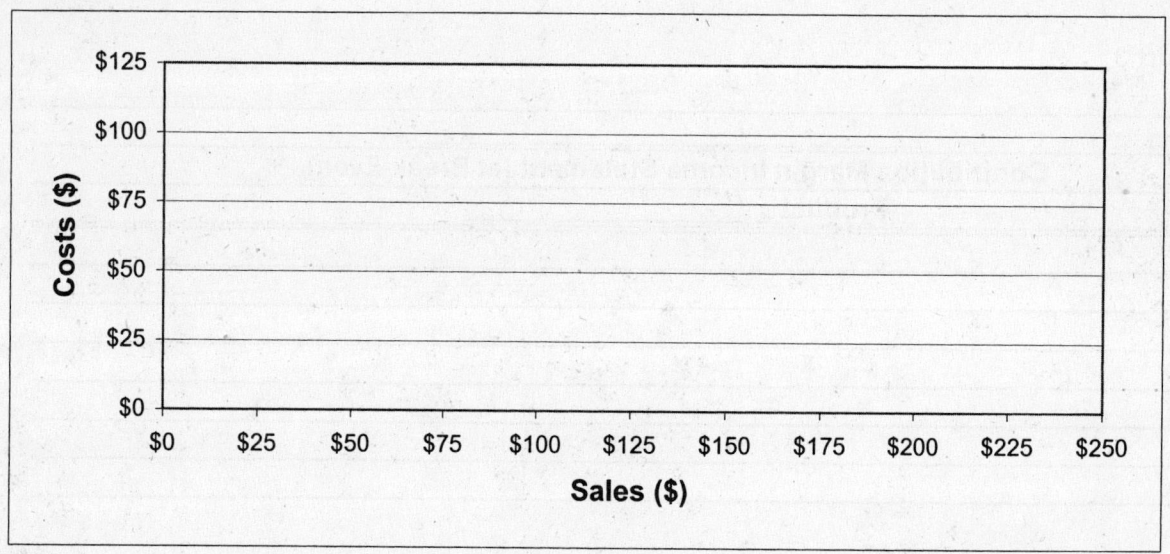

Variable costs per sales dollar: _____

_____

_____

Fixed costs: _____

_____

_____

_____

Part 3

	Predictions	
Sales (given)	$	$
Fixed costs (from part 2)		
Variable costs (from part 2)		
Total costs		

Year 2008 break-even in dollar sales:

_____

_____

_____

_____

_____

_____

_____

_____

_____

_____

Part 2

Year 2009 break-even in dollar sales:

_____

_____

_____

_____

_____

_____

_____

_____

_____

_____

_____

Part 3

_____

Forecasted Contribution Margin Income Statement
For Year Ended December 31, 2009

_____

_____

_____

_____

_____

_____

_____

Required sales in dollars:

_____
_____
_____
_____
_____
_____
_____
_____

Required sales in units:

_____
_____
_____
_____
_____
_____
_____
_____
_____
_____

Part 5

_____

Forecasted Contribution Margin Income Statement
For Year Ended December 31, 2009

_____
_____
_____
_____
_____
_____
_____
_____
_____

Part 1

Break-even in dollar sales:

   Product_____:

_____

_____

_____

_____

_____

_____

   Product_____:

_____

_____

_____

_____

_____

_____

_____

_____

Part 2

_____ COMPANY		
Forecasted Contribution Margin Income Statement		
	Product_____	Product_____

	_____COMPANY	
Forecasted Contribution Margin Income Statement		
	Product _____	Product _____

Part 4

Identification and Explanation of Greatest Change in Product Income (Loss) _____

_____
_____
_____
_____
_____
_____
_____

Part 5

Description of Potential Factors Yielding Different Product Cost Structures _____

_____
_____
_____
_____
_____
_____
_____

(a) Plan 1's (Existing Strategy for 22-6B) break-even in dollar sales:

_____
_____
_____
_____
_____
_____
_____
_____
_____

(b) Plan 2's (New Strategy for 22-6B) break-even in dollar sales:

_____
_____
_____
_____
_____
_____
_____
_____
_____
_____

Part 2

| _____COMPANY | | |
| Forecasted Contribution Margin Income Statement | | |
	Plan 1 (Existing Strategy)	*Plan 2 (New Strategy)*

Break-even analysis assuming use of <u>same</u> materials:

    Step 1: Compute break-even in composite units

_____

_____

_____

_____

_____

_____

_____

_____

_____

_____

_____

    Step 2: Compute break-even in individual product units sales

_____

_____

_____

_____

_____

_____

_____

_____

    Step 3: Compute break-even in individual product dollar sales

_____

_____

_____

_____

_____

_____

_____

Chapter 22   Problem 22-7A or 22-7B   Name _____
Part 2   (Continued)

Break-even analysis assuming use of <u>new</u> materials:

Step 1: Compute break-even in composite units

_____
_____
_____
_____
_____
_____
_____
_____
_____
_____
_____
_____

Step 2: Compute break-even in individual product unit sales

_____
_____
_____
_____
_____
_____
_____
_____
_____

Step 3: Compute break-even in individual product dollar sales

_____
_____
_____
_____
_____
_____
_____

Part 3

Management Insight for Long-Term Planning

_____
_____
_____
_____
_____

Name _____

1. Selling price per composite unit
_____
_____
_____
_____
_____

2. Variable costs per composite unit
_____
_____
_____
_____
_____

3. Break-even point in composite units
_____
_____
_____
_____
_____

4. Unit sales of desk units and chairs at break-even point
_____
_____
_____
_____
_____

(1) Identification of Costs

_____
_____
_____
_____
_____
_____
_____
_____
_____
_____
_____

(2) _____
_____
_____
_____
_____
_____
_____
_____
_____
_____
_____
_____

(3) _____
_____
_____
_____
_____
_____
_____
_____
_____
_____
_____
_____

(1)

	Best Buy	Circuit City

(2) _____

_____

_____

_____

_____

_____

_____

_____

_____

_____

MEMORANDUM

To: "Mechanics" and "Owners"
From:
Re: Analysis of labor costs from survey data
Date:

REPORT ON REVENUE & COST ASSUMPTIONS

Revenue Assumptions:

Cost Assumptions:

Information and Resources Available for Entrepreneurs

_____
_____
_____
_____
_____
_____
_____
_____
_____
_____
_____
_____
_____
_____
_____
_____
_____
_____
_____
_____
_____

Questions for Completion of CVP Analysis

For School Administration:

_____
_____
_____
_____
_____
_____
_____
_____
_____
_____
_____
_____
_____
_____
_____

For Business Owner:

_____
_____
_____
_____
_____
_____
_____
_____
_____
_____
_____
_____
_____
_____

_____
_____
_____
_____
_____

Part 2

_____
_____
_____
_____

Part 3

_____
_____
_____
_____
_____
_____
_____

(1) Types of information needed: _____

_____

_____

_____

_____

_____

_____

_____

_____

_____

_____

_____

_____

_____

_____

_____

_____

_____

_____

_____

_____

(2) Useful tool(s) for analysis: _____

_____

_____

_____

_____

_____

_____

_____

_____

_____

(1) Potential Framework for Analysis

Product	Estimated Selling Price per unit	Estimated CM ratio	Estimated CM per unit	Estimated Sales Mix	Estimated CM for each component in composite unit

Total contribution margin (CM) per composite unit..................

Estimated fixed costs per year: $_____

Break-even point in composite unit sales: $_____/$CM per composite unit =

Unit sales of individual products per year required to break-even:

(2) Report on Results of Analysis from Part 1 (including break-even analysis)

_____

_____

_____

_____

_____

_____

_____

_____

_____

_____

_____

_____

_____

_____

_____

_____

_____

_____

_____

_____

_____

_____

Name _____

(1) Identification and Explanation of CVP Analysis _____

_____

_____

_____

_____

_____

_____

(2) Products Impact for CVP Analysis

_____

_____

_____

_____

_____

_____

_____

_____

_____

_____

(3) Store Impact for CVP Analysis _____

_____

_____

_____

_____

_____

_____

Necessary Component of Master Budget: _____

_____

Quick Study 23-2

(1) _____

(2) _____

(3) _____

Quick Study 23-3

_____ Company
Computation of Budgeted Cost of Purchases
For Month Ended July 31

_____
_____
_____
_____
_____
_____

Quick Study 23-4

(1) Comparative Analysis of Budgeting Approaches: _____

_____
_____

(2) Examples of Bottom-Up Budgeting: _____

_____
_____
_____

Computation of Budgeted Accounts Receivable Balance: _____

_____

_____

_____

_____

_____

_____

_____

_____

Quick Study 23-6

_____ Company
Cash Budget
For Month Ended March 31

_____

_____

_____

_____

_____

_____

_____

_____

_____

_____

_____

_____

_____

Quick Study 23-7

(1) Description of Activity-Based Budgeting <u>and</u> Explanation of Budget Preparation

_____

_____

_____

_____

(2) Explanation of Differences between Activity-Based and Traditional Budgeting

_____

_____

_____

_____ Company
Production Budget
For Month Ended November 30

_____
_____
_____
_____
_____
_____
_____
_____

_____ Company			
Merchandise Purchases Budget			
For July, August and September			
	July	**August**	**September**

Supporting calculations:

_____

_____

_____

_____

_____

_____

_____

_____

_____

_____

_____

_____

_____

_____

_____

_____

(2) Ratio of Ending Inventory to Next Month's Sales for Each Budget Period

_____

_____

(3) Units Budgeted for Sale in October

_____

_____

_____

_____ Company			
Cash Budget			
For January, February, and March			
	January	February	March

| _____ Company |
| Cash Budget |
| For Month Ended July 31 |

_____

_____

_____

_____

_____

_____

_____

_____

_____

_____

_____

_____

_____

_____

Supporting calculations:

_____

_____

_____

_____

_____

_____

_____

_____

_____

_____

_____

_____

_____

_____

Name _____

_____ Company
Budgeted Income Statement
For Month Ended July 31

Supporting calculations:

_____ Company
Budgeted Balance Sheet
July 31

Merchandise purchases budgets

	August	September	October

Cash payments for purchases (on accounts) in October

	Dollars	Percent	Paid

Name _____

(1) Budgeted merchandise purchases:

	June	July	August

(2) Budgeted cost of goods sold:

	June	July	August

Exercise 23-7

(1) Budgeted merchandise purchases:

	July	August	September	October

Supporting calculations:

Name _____

(2) Budgeted payments on accounts payable in September:

	Purchases	Percent Paid	Dollars Paid

Budgeted payments on accounts payable in October:

	Purchases	Percent Paid	Dollars Paid

(3) Budgeted balance of accounts payable at the end of September:

	Purchases	Percent Unpaid	Dollars Unpaid

Budgeted balance of accounts payable at the end of October:

	Purchases	Percent Unpaid	Dollars Unpaid

_____ Company		
Production Budget		
Second and Third Quarters		
	Second Quarter	**Third Quarter**

Merchandise Purchases Budgets For Months of _____	Month of	Month of	Month of
Product: _____			
Product: _____			
Product: _____			

Identification and Explanation of Factors Yielding Fewer Purchases
_____

_____

_____

_____

_____

_____

_____

_____

_____

_____

_____

_____

_____

_____

_____

_____

_____

_____

Name _____

		Cash Budgets		
For Months of _____				
		Month of _____	Month of _____	Month of _____
_____				
_____				
_____				
_____				
_____				
_____				
_____				
_____				
_____				
_____				
_____				
_____				
_____				
_____				
_____				
_____				
_____				
_____				

Supporting computations: _____

_____

_____

_____

_____

_____

_____

_____

_____

_____

_____

_____

_____

_____

_____

_____

Cash collections of credit sales (accounts receivable)

From sales in month of:	*Total*	*% Collected*	Month of	Month of

Part 2
Budgeted ending inventories (in units)

	Month of	Month of	Month of	Month of

_____Company
Merchandise Purchases Budgets
For Months of_____

	Month of _____	Month of _____	Month of _____

Part 4
Cash payments on product purchases

From purchases in month of:	Total	% Paid	Month of _____	Month of _____

Cash Budgets For Months of _____	Month of _____	Month of _____

Part 6
Benefits to Management from Accurate Cash Budget Numbers _____

_____
_____
_____
_____
_____
_____
_____
_____
_____
_____
_____
_____
_____

Part 1

| | Budgeted Income Statements For Months of _____ | | |
	Month of _____	Month of _____	Month of _____

Part 2: Recommendation on Implementation of Proposed Changes _____

Part 1

Sales Budgets

Month	Budgeted Units	Budgeted Unit Price	Budgeted Total Dollars

Part 2

Merchandise Purchases Budgets

	Month of	Month of	Month of	Total

Part 3

Selling Expense Budgets

	Month of	Month of	Month of	Total

	General and Administrative Expense Budgets			
	Month of	Month of	Month of	
				Total

Supporting calculations:

Part 5

	Capital Expenditures Budgets		
	Month of	Month of	Month of

Chapter 23   Problem 23-5A or 23-5B   Name _____
Part 6   (Continued)

| | Cash Budgets | | |
	Month of	Month of	Month of

_____

Budgeted Income Statement

For Three Months Ended _____

_____
_____
_____
_____
_____
_____
_____
_____
_____
_____
_____
_____
_____
_____
_____
_____

Budgeted Balance sheet

Production Budget (in units)
_____ Quarter

_____
_____
_____
_____
_____
_____
_____
_____

Part 2

Direct Materials Budget (in lbs., except where noted)
_____ Quarter

_____
_____
_____
_____
_____
_____
_____
_____
_____
_____
_____

SUCCESS SYSTEMS Budgeted Income Statements For Months of April, May and June			
	April	May	June

Part 2: Recommendation on Implementation of Proposed Changes _____

_____

_____

_____

_____

_____

_____

_____

_____

_____

_____

_____

(a) _____

_____

_____

_____

_____

(b) _____

_____

_____

_____

_____

_____

_____

_____

Part 2

(a) _____

_____

_____

_____

(b) _____

_____

_____

_____

Part 3

Fast Forward: _____

_____

_____

_____

_____

_____

_____

_____

_____

Computation of inventory reduction under new distribution system	
Amount of ending inventory required at the 40% rule....	$
Amount of ending inventory required at the 10% rule....	_____
Difference (inventory reduction)................................	$ _____

Implication of Distribution System for Inventory Level: _____

_____

_____

_____

_____

Part 2

Explanation and Justification of JIT Inventory System _____

_____

_____

_____

_____

_____

_____

_____

_____

_____

_____

_____

_____

_____

_____

Report on "Use It or Lose It" Budgeting

MEMORANDUM

TO: _____

FROM: _____

DATE: _____

SUBJECT: Concerns with sales staff input for the sales budget

Benefits of Using e-Budgets

_____
_____
_____
_____
_____
_____
_____
_____
_____
_____
_____
_____
_____
_____
_____
_____

Part 2

Concerns with the Concept and Application of e-Budgets

_____
_____
_____
_____
_____
_____
_____
_____
_____
_____
_____
_____
_____
_____

College Costs Budget

_____

_____

_____

_____

_____

_____

_____

_____

_____

Part 1
Business Plan Elements _____
_____
_____
_____
_____
_____
_____
_____

Part 2
Benefits of Budgeting _____
_____
_____
_____
_____
_____
_____

Hitting the Road--BTN 23-9

Part 1
Identification of External Factors When Setting Budgets _____
_____
_____
_____
_____

Part 2
Identification of Potential Factors Explaining Price Differences _____
_____
_____
_____

Part 1
Importance of Administrative Expense Budget in Its Master Budgeting Process

_____
_____
_____
_____
_____
_____
_____
_____

Part 2
Identification of Administrative Expenses

_____
_____
_____
_____

Part 3
Identification and Explanation of Person Responsible for Administrative Expense Budget

_____
_____
_____
_____
_____

_____ Company		
Flexible Budget Performance Report		
For Month Ended May 31		
Flexible	*Actual*	
Budget	*Results*	*Variances*

Quick Study 24-2

Actual Total Direct Labor Cost

Quick Study 24-3

Actual Total Direct Materials Cost

Actual Pounds of Materials Used _____

_____
_____
_____
_____
_____
_____
_____
_____
_____
_____
_____
_____
_____
_____

Quick Study 24-5

(1) Description of Management by Exception Concept _____

_____
_____
_____
_____

(2) Explanation of How Standard Costs Aid Management by Exception _____

_____
_____
_____
_____
_____

Quick Study 24-6

Actual Total Overhead Cost _____

_____
_____
_____
_____
_____
_____

GENERAL JOURNAL

Date		Account Titles and Explanation	P. R.	Debit	Credit

Quick Study 24-8

Sales	Actual	Flexible Budget	Fixed Budget
Units			
Price per unit			
Total dollars			

| | Company |
| Flexible Budgets |
| For Quarter Ended March 31, 2008 |

Flexible Budget		Flexible Budget for Unit Sales of _____	Flexible Budget for Unit Sales of _____	Flexible Budget for Unit Sales of _____
Variable Amount per Unit	Total Fixed Cost			

Name _____

Item	Cost behavior
a. Depreciation on tools	
b. Pension cost	
c. Bike frames	
d. Screws for assembly	
e. Management salaries	
f. Incoming shipping expenses	
g. Office supplies	
h. Taxes on property	
i. Gas used for heating	
j. Direct labor	
k. Repair expense for tools	

		_____ Company				
		Flexible Budget Performance Report				
		For Month Ended June 30				
		Flexible		*Actual*		
		Budget		*Results*		*Variances*

_____
_____
_____
_____
_____
_____
_____
_____
_____
_____

Supporting calculations:

_____
_____
_____
_____
_____
_____
_____
_____
_____
_____
_____
_____
_____
_____

_____ Company Flexible Budget Performance Report For Month Ended July 31			
	Flexible *Budget*	*Actual* *Results*	*Variances*

Supporting calculations:

Chapter 24   Exercise 24-5   Name _____

Part 1

October variances:

_____
_____
_____
_____
_____
_____
_____
_____
_____
_____
_____
_____
_____
_____
_____
_____

November variances:

_____
_____
_____
_____
_____
_____
_____
_____
_____
_____
_____
_____
_____
_____
_____
_____
_____

Interpretation of October Direct labor Variances

_____
_____
_____
_____
_____
_____
_____
_____

Exercise 24-6
Part 1
Predetermined overhead rate computations
_____
_____
_____
_____
_____
_____
_____
_____
_____

Part 2
Variable overhead spending and efficiency variances:
    Computations:
_____
_____
_____
_____
_____
_____
_____
_____
_____

Interpretations: _____

_____

_____

_____

_____

_____

_____

Part 3
Fixed overhead spending and volume variances _____

Computations: _____

_____

_____

_____

_____

_____

_____

_____

_____

_____

_____

_____

_____

_____

_____

_____

_____

_____

Interpretation: _____

_____

_____

_____

_____

_____

_____

_____

Computation of Direct Materials Variances:

_____
_____
_____
_____
_____
_____
_____
_____
_____
_____
_____
_____
_____
_____
_____
_____
_____
_____
_____
_____
_____
_____
_____
_____
_____
_____
_____
_____

Part 2

Interpretation of Direct Materials Variances:

_____
_____
_____
_____

GENERAL JOURNAL

Date	Account Titles and Explanation	P. R.	Debit	Credit

Part 2

GENERAL JOURNAL

Date	Account Titles and Explanation	P. R.	Debit	Credit

Part 3

Identification of Variance Investigated if Applying Management by Exception

_____

_____

_____

_____

_____

_____

Computation of Total Overhead Variance

_____
_____
_____
_____
_____
_____
_____
_____
_____
_____
_____
_____
_____
_____
_____
_____

Part 2
Computation of Overhead Volume Variance

_____
_____
_____
_____
_____
_____
_____
_____
_____
_____
_____
_____
_____
_____
_____
_____
_____

Computation of Overhead Controllable Variance

_____

_____

_____

_____

_____

_____

_____

_____

_____

_____

_____

_____

_____

_____

_____

_____

_____

(1) Computation of Sales Price and Sales Volume Variances

_____
_____
_____
_____
_____
_____
_____
_____
_____
_____
_____
_____
_____
_____
_____
_____
_____
_____
_____
_____
_____
_____

(2) Interpretation of Variances from Part 1

_____
_____
_____
_____
_____
_____

Direct Materials Cost Variances

_____

_____
_____
_____
_____
_____
_____
_____
_____
_____
_____
_____
_____
_____
_____
_____
_____
_____
_____
_____
_____
_____
_____
_____
_____

Direct Labor Cost Variances

_____
_____
_____
_____
_____
_____
_____
_____
_____
_____
_____
_____
_____
_____
_____
_____
_____
_____
_____
_____
_____
_____
_____
_____
_____
_____

(a) Variable Overhead Spending and Efficiency Variances

(b) Fixed Overhead Spending and Volume Variances

_____

_____

_____

_____

_____

_____

_____

_____

_____

_____

_____

_____

_____

_____

_____

_____

_____

_____

_____

_____

_____

_____

_____

_____

_____

_____

(c) Total Overhead Controllable Variance

_____

_____

_____

_____

_____

_____

_____

_____

Variable or Fixed Classification	Amount

	Flexible Budget		Flexible Budget for Unit Sales of _____	Flexible Budget for Unit Sales of _____
_____Company Flexible Budgets For Year Ended December 31, _____	Variable Amount per Unit	Total Fixed Cost		

_____
_____
_____
_____
_____
_____
_____
_____
_____
_____
_____
_____
_____
_____
_____
_____
_____
_____
_____
_____
_____
_____
_____
_____

Part 3
Operating income increase for a _____ to _____ unit sales increase:

_____
_____
_____
_____
_____
_____
_____
_____

Operating income (loss) at _____ units:

_____
_____
_____
_____
_____
_____
_____
_____
_____

Problem 24-3A or 24-3B

Part 1

_____Company Flexible Budget Performance Report For Year Ended December 31, _____	Flexible Budget	Actual Results	Variances

(a) Analysis of sales variance

	Total	Per Unit

Interpretation:

(b) Analysis of direct materials variance

	Total	Per Unit

Interpretation:

Part 1

Variable or Fixed Classification	Amount
Variable costs (per unit):	
Fixed costs (per month):	

Part 2

_____ Company
Flexible Overhead Budgets
For Month Ended _____

Flexible Budget Variable Amount per Unit	Total Fixed Cost	Flexible Budget for Unit Sales of _____	Flexible Budget for Unit Sales of _____	Flexible Budget for Unit Sales of _____

Direct Materials Cost Variances

_____

_____

_____

_____

_____

_____

_____

_____

_____

_____

_____

_____

_____

_____

_____

_____

_____

_____

_____

_____

_____

_____

_____

_____

_____

_____

_____

Direct Labor Cost Variances

(a) Variable Overhead Spending and Efficiency Variances _____

_____

_____

_____

_____

_____

_____

_____

_____

_____

_____

_____

_____

_____

_____

_____

_____

_____

_____

_____

_____

_____

_____

_____

_____

_____

_____

_____

_____

_____

(b) Fixed Overhead Spending and Volume Variances

_____

_____

_____

_____

_____

_____

_____

_____

_____

_____

_____

_____

_____

_____

_____

_____

_____

_____

_____

_____

_____

_____

_____

_____

_____

_____

_____

_____

_____

(c) Total Overhead Controllable Variance

_____

_____

_____

_____

_____

_____

_____

_____

_____Company
Overhead Variance Report
For Month Ended _____

Volume Variance

_____

_____

_____

_____

_____

_____

Controllable Variance	Flexible Budget	Actual Results	Variances

Direct Materials Cost Variances

Direct Labor Cost Variances

(a) Variable Overhead Spending and Efficiency Variances _____

_____

_____

_____

_____

_____

_____

_____

_____

_____

_____

_____

_____

_____

_____

_____

_____

_____

_____

_____

_____

_____

_____

_____

_____

_____

_____

_____

_____

_____

(b) Fixed Overhead Spending and Volume Variances _____

_____

_____

_____

_____

_____

_____

_____

_____

_____

_____

_____

_____

_____

_____

_____

_____

_____

_____

_____

_____

_____

_____

_____

_____

_____

_____

_____

(c) Total Overhead Controllable Variance _____

_____

_____

_____

_____

_____

_____

_____

_____

_____ Company
Overhead Variance Report
For Month Ended _____

Volume Variance

_____

_____

_____

_____

_____

Controllable Variance	Flexible Budget	Actual Results	Variances

GENERAL JOURNAL

Date		Account Titles and Explanation	P. R.	Debit	Credit

Part 2

Identification of Areas and Actions when Applying Management by Exception

_____
_____
_____
_____
_____
_____
_____
_____
_____
_____
_____
_____
_____
_____

SUCCESS SYSTEMS Flexible Budget Performance Report For Quarter Ended June 30			
	Flexible Budget	Actual Results	Variances

Desk Sales...........................

Chair Sales...........................

Variable expenses.................

Contribution margin..............

Fixed expenses....................

Income from operations.........

Supporting computations:

Identification of Foreign Currency Translation (FTC) Information

_____

_____

_____

_____

_____

Part 2

Fiscal Year-End	F.C.T. Adjustment	F.C.T. Ending Balance
March 1, 2003		
February 28, 2004		
February 26, 2005		

Part 3--Fast Forward

(a) _____

_____

_____

_____

(b) _____

_____

_____

_____

_____

_____

	2 Years Prior	1 Year Prior	Current year	1 Year Ahead	2 Years Ahead
Best Buy					
Circuit City					

Part 2

Explanation of Sales Predictions _____

_____
_____
_____
_____

Ethics Challenge--BTN 24-3

Specialty	Information Input and Explanation

Name _____

MEMORANDUM

TO: _____

FROM: _____

DATE: _____

SUBJECT: Explanation and Implications of Favorable and Unfavorable Variances

_____
_____
_____
_____
_____
_____
_____
_____
_____
_____
_____
_____
_____
_____
_____
_____
_____
_____
_____
_____
_____
_____
_____
_____
_____
_____
_____
_____
_____

Explanation of Benchmarking

_____
_____
_____
_____
_____
_____
_____
_____
_____
_____
_____

Part 2

Relation between Standard Costing and Benchmarking

_____
_____
_____
_____
_____
_____
_____
_____
_____

Identification and Description of Time Elements Used for Competitive Advantage

_____

_____

_____

_____

_____

_____

_____

_____

_____

_____

_____

_____

_____

_____

_____

_____

_____

_____

_____

_____

_____

_____

_____

_____

_____

Labor Variance Impacts from Worker Productivity _____

_____

_____

_____

_____

_____

Part 2

Labor Variance Impacts from Labor Costs _____

_____

_____

_____

_____

_____

Part 3

Joint Impact from Worker Productivity and Labor Costs _____

_____

_____

_____

_____

_____

MEMORANDUM
TO: _____
FROM: _____
DATE: _____
SUBJECT: Explanation of Standard Costing and Variance Comments

(1) Observe and Record the Number and Application of Raw Materials to Pizza

_____

_____

_____

_____

_____

(2) Identify and Record Differences Across the Two Businesses in Part 1

_____

_____

_____

_____

_____

_____

(3) Estimate and Explain which Business is More Profitable

_____

_____

_____

_____

_____

_____

_____

_____

Global Decision--BTN 24-10

(1)

Dixons	One Year Prior	Current Year	One Year Ahead	Two Years Ahead
Sales				

(2) Estimation and Explanation of Sales Predictions

_____

_____

_____

_____

_____

(1) Identification of Preferred Investment

_____
_____
_____

(2) Explanation of Why Investment B might be Preferred to Investment A

_____
_____
_____
_____
_____
_____
_____

Quick Study 25-2

Payback Period

_____
_____
_____
_____
_____
_____
_____

Quick Study 25-3

Net Present Value

_____
_____
_____
_____
_____
_____
_____
_____
_____
_____
_____

Accounting Rate of Return

_____

_____
_____
_____
_____
_____

Quick Study 25-5

Most Profitable Sales Mix

_____

_____
_____
_____
_____
_____
_____
_____
_____
_____

Quick Study 25-6

Incremental Cost Analysis

_____

_____
_____
_____
_____
_____
_____
_____
_____
_____

Year	Cash Flows	Present Value of 1 at 10%	Present value of cash flows	Cumulative present value of cash flows
0				
1				
2				
3				
4				
5				

Break-Even Time

Exercise 25-1

(a) Payback Period

(b) Payback Period

	Annual Net Cash flows	Cumulative Cash Flows
Year 1		
Year 2		
Year 3		
Year 4		
Year 5		

Payback Period

_____
_____
_____
_____

Exercise 25-3

	Net Income	Depreciation	Net Cash Flow	Cumulative Cash Flow
Year 1				
Year 2				
Year 3				
Year 4				
Year 5				

Payback Period

_____
_____
_____
_____
_____
_____
_____
_____
_____

Accounting Rate of Return

_____
_____
_____
_____
_____
_____
_____
_____

Exercise 25-5

	Net Income	Cash Flows
Sales		
Materials, labor & overhead		
Depreciation		
Selling and administrative		
Pretax income		
Income taxes		
Net income		
Net cash flows		

(1) Payback Period

_____
_____
_____
_____
_____
_____

(1) Accounting Rate of Return

_____
_____
_____
_____
_____
_____
_____
_____

	Annual Net Cash Flows	Present Value of Annuity at 8%	Present Value of Net Cash Flows
Years 1 through 12			
Amount invested			
Net present value of investment			

Acceptability of Investment _____

_____

_____

_____

Exercise 25-7

1.

Project C1

	Net Cash Flows	Present Value of 1 at 12%	Present Value of Net Cash Flows
Year 1			
Year 2			
Year 3			
Totals			
Amount invested			
Net present value			

Project C2

	Net Cash Flows	Present Value of 1 at 12%	Present Value of Net Cash Flows
Year 1			
Year 2			
Year 3			
Totals			
Amount invested			
Net present value			

1.   (Continued)
Project C3

	Net Cash Flows	Present Value of 1 at 12%	Present Value of Net Cash Flows
Year 1			
Year 2			
Year 3			
Totals			
Amount invested			
Net present value			

Analysis and interpretation:

_____
_____
_____
_____

2. Internal Rate of Return vs. 12% Net Present Value

_____
_____
_____
_____

3. Internal Rate of Return for C2

_____
_____
_____
_____
_____
_____

Exercise 25-8

	Normal Volume	Additional Volume	Combined Total
Sales			
Costs and expenses			
Direct materials			
Direct labor			
Overhead			
Selling expenses			
Administrative expenses			
Total costs and expenses			
Net income			

                (Continued)

Management Recommendation: _____

_____
_____
_____

Exercise 25-9

Incremental Cost of Making the Part: _____

_____
_____
_____
_____
_____
_____
_____
_____

Incremental Cost of Buying the Part: _____

_____
_____
_____
_____
_____
_____
_____
_____
_____

Management Recommendation: _____

_____
_____
_____
_____
_____

Incremental Cost and Revenue of Additional Processing:

_____
_____
_____
_____
_____
_____
_____
_____
_____
_____
_____
_____
_____
_____

Management Recommendation:

_____
_____
_____

Exercise 25-11

(1) No Departments Eliminated:

	Total	M	N	O	P	T
Sales						
Expenses						
Avoidable						
Unavoidable						
Total expenses						
Net Income (loss)						

_____
_____
_____
_____
_____

(2) Departments with Expected Net Losses Eliminated:

	Total	M	N	O	P	T
Sales						
Expenses						
Avoidable						
Unavoidable						
Total expenses						
Net Income (loss)						

(3) Departments with Less Sales than Avoidable Expenses Eliminated:

	Total	M	N	O	P	T
Sales						
Expenses						
Avoidable						
Unavoidable						
Total expenses						
Net Income (loss)						

(1) Sales Mix Computations and Recommendation: _____

_____
_____
_____
_____
_____
_____
_____
_____
_____
_____
_____
_____
_____
_____

(2) Contribution Margin from the Recommended Sales Mix: _____

_____
_____
_____
_____
_____
_____
_____
_____

Name _____

(1) Recovery time for:
      Payback Period _____

_____

_____

      Break-even Time _____

_____

_____

_____

(2) Advantages of Break-Even time _____

_____

_____

_____

_____

_____

(3) Conditions Yielding Similar Results for Payback Period and Break-Even Time ____

_____

_____

_____

_____

_____

Part 1

Annual Straight-Line Depreciation _____

_____

_____

_____

_____

_____

Part 2

	Net Income	Net Cash Flow
Expected annual sales of new product		
Expected annual costs of new product		
Direct materials		
Direct labor		
Overhead excluding depr. on new asset		
Depreciation on new asset		
Selling and administrative expenses		
Income before taxes		
Income taxes		
Net income		
Net cash flow		

Computations: _____

_____

_____

_____

Part 3

Payback period _____

_____

_____

_____

_____

_____

Accounting rate of return _____

_____
_____
_____
_____
_____
_____
_____
_____
_____

Part 5

	Net Cash Flows	Present Value of 1 at ____%	Present Value of Net Cash Flows
Year 1			
Year 2			
Year 3			
Year 4			
Totals			
Amount invested			
Net present value			

_____
_____
_____
_____
_____

Project _____ **Net Cash Flow** _____

_____
_____
_____
_____
_____
_____

Project _____ **Net Cash Flow** _____

_____
_____
_____
_____
_____
_____

Part 2

Project _____ **Payback Period** _____

_____
_____
_____
_____
_____

Project _____ **Payback Period** _____

_____
_____
_____
_____
_____

Project _____ Accounting Rate of Return

_____

_____

_____

_____

_____

Project _____ Accounting Rate of Return

_____

_____

_____

_____

_____

Part 4

Project _____ Present Value of Net Cash Flows

	Net Cash Flows	Present Value of Annuity of 1 at ____ %	Present Value of Net Cash Flows

Project _____ Present Value of Net Cash Flows

	Net Cash Flows	Present Value of Annuity of 1 at ____ %	Present Value of Net Cash Flows

Management Recommendation: _____

_____

_____

_____

_____

_____

_____

_____

_____

Problem 25-3A or 25-3B

Part 1 Results Using Straight-Line

	(a) Income Before Deprec.	(b) Straight-Line Deprec.	(c) Taxable Income (a) - (b)	(d) __% Income Taxes	(e) Net Cash Flows (a) - (d)
Year 1					
Year 2					
Year 3					
Year 4					
Year 5					
Year 6					

Part 2 Results Using MACRS

	(a) Income Before Deprec.	(b) MACRS Deprec.	(c) Taxable Income (a) - (b)	(d) __% Income Taxes	(e) Net Cash Flows (a) - (d)
Year 1					
Year 2					
Year 3					
Year 4					
Year 5					
Year 6					

Part 3 NPV Using Straight-Line

	Net Cash Flows	Present Value of 1 at ____ %	Present Value of Net Cash Flows
Year 1			
Year 2			
Year 3			
Year 4			
Year 5			
Year 6			
Totals			
Amount invested			
Net present value			

Part 4 NPV Using MACRS

	Net Cash Flows	Present Value of 1 at ____ %	Present Value of Net Cash Flows
Year 1			
Year 2			
Year 3			
Year 4			
Year 5			
Year 6			
Totals			
Amount invested			
Net present value			

Part 5

Explanation of MACRS Implications for NPV _____

_____

_____

_____

_____

_____

_____

_____

_____

	(1) Normal Volume	(2) New Business	(3) Combined
Sales			
Costs and expenses			
Direct materials			
Direct labor			
Overhead			
Selling expenses			
Administrative expenses			
Total costs & expenses			
Operating income			

Supporting calculations:

	Product ____	*Product* ____
Selling price per unit		
Variable costs per unit		
Contribution margin per unit		
Machine hours to produce 1 unit		
Contribution per machine hour (or contribution/[hours per unit])		

Part 2

Sales Mix Recommendation: _____

_____
_____
_____
_____
_____
_____
_____
_____

Contribution Margin at Recommended Sales Mix: _____

_____
_____
_____
_____
_____

Sales Mix Recommendation:

_____

_____

_____

_____

_____

_____

_____

_____

_____

_____

_____

_____

_____

_____

_____

Contribution Margin at Recommended Sales Mix:

_____

_____

_____

_____

_____

_____

_____

_____

_____

_____

_____

Management Decision:

_____

_____

_____

_____

_____

_____

_____

_____

Sales Mix Recommendation with Second Shift:

_____
_____
_____
_____
_____
_____
_____
_____
_____
_____
_____
_____
_____
_____
_____

Contribution Margin at Recommended Sales Mix:

_____
_____
_____
_____
_____
_____
_____
_____
_____

Management Decision:

_____
_____
_____
_____
_____
_____
_____

_____Company Analysis of Expenses under Elimination of Department_____	Total Expenses	Eliminated Expenses	Continuing Expenses
Cost of goods sold			
Direct expenses			
Advertising expense			
Store supplies used			
Depreciation of store equipment			
Allocated expenses			
Sales salaries			
Rent expense			
Bad debts expense			
Office salary expense			
Insurance expense			
Miscellaneous office expense			
Total expenses			

Supporting Computations: _____

_____

_____

_____

_____

_____

_____

_____

_____Company
Forecasted Annual Income Statement
Under Plan to Eliminate Department_____

_____
_____
_____
_____
_____
_____
_____
_____
_____
_____
_____
_____
_____
_____
_____
_____
_____
_____
_____
_____
_____
_____
_____
_____

Part 3

_____Company
Reconciliation of Combined Income with Forecasted Income

Combined net income	$
Forecasted net income	$

Analysis and Recommendation: _____
_____
_____
_____

Name _____

COMPUTING NET CASH FLOWS FROM NET INCOME

	Net income	Cash flows
Sales...	$ 300,000	$
Materials, labor, & overhead................................	(160,000)	
Depreciation...	(40,000)	
Selling and administrative...................................	(30,000)	
Pretax income..	70,000	
Income taxes (30%)..	(21,000)	
Net income..	$ 49,000	
Net cash flows...		$

1. Payback period

_____
_____
_____
_____
_____
_____
_____
_____

2. Accounting rate of return

_____
_____
_____
_____
_____
_____
_____
_____

_____
_____
_____
_____
_____
_____
_____
_____
_____
_____
_____

Part 2--Fast Forward _____
_____
_____
_____
_____
_____
_____

Identification and Cost of Advertising Space

_____
_____
_____
_____
_____

Part 2
Estimation of Additional Product Sales to Cover Advertising Cost

_____
_____
_____
_____
_____
_____
_____
_____

Part 3

MEMORANDUM

TO:
FROM:
SUBJECT: Effective Advertising for Product Mix Decisions
DATE:

_____
_____
_____
_____
_____
_____
_____
_____
_____
_____
_____
_____
_____
_____

Part 1

Present Value Computation _____

_____

_____

_____

_____

_____

_____

_____

Part 2

Estimation Errors and Investment Project Evaluation _____

_____

_____

_____

_____

_____

_____

_____

_____

_____

_____

MEMORANDUM

TO:
FROM:
DATE:
SUBJECT: Evaluating Capital Investment Opportunities

_____

_____

_____

_____

_____

_____

_____

_____

_____

Part 2

_____

_____

_____

_____

_____

_____

_____

_____

_____

Project Identification

_____
_____
_____
_____
_____
_____

Qualitative Factors in Management's Decision

_____
_____
_____
_____
_____
_____
_____
_____
_____
_____
_____
_____
_____
_____
_____
_____
_____

(1) _____

_____

_____

_____

_____

_____

_____

(2) _____

_____

_____

_____

_____

_____

_____

_____

(1) Incremental Analysis:

	Model XR	Model CT

(2) Incremental Analysis:

	Model XR	Model CT

(3) Analysis and Recommendation:

_____
_____
_____

Hitting the Road--BTN 25-9
(1) Lease vs. Buy Decision:

_____
_____
_____
_____
_____
_____
_____
_____
_____
_____
_____
_____

(2) Management Recommendation to Lease or Buy

_____
_____
_____
_____
_____
_____

(1) Explanation of "Cost Activities" _____

_____

_____

_____

_____

_____

_____

(2) Rationale of "Recycled Appliances" Program _____

_____

_____

_____

_____

_____

_____

Appendix B   Quick Study B-1   *Name* _____

(1) _____

(2) _____

(3) _____

(4) _____

Quick Study B-2

Annual Rate of Interest _____

_____

_____

_____

Quick Study B-3

Years of Investment _____

_____

_____

_____

Quick Study B-4

Value of Investment _____

_____

_____

_____

Quick Study B-5

Cash Proceeds at Liquidation _____

_____

_____

_____

Quick Study B-6

Amount Willing to Pay for Project _____

_____

_____

_____

Name _____

Future Value of Retirement Program

_____
_____
_____

Exercise B-1

Years Until Payment

_____
_____
_____

Exercise B-2

Rate of Interest to be Earned

_____
_____
_____

Exercise B-3

Rate of Interest to be Earned

_____
_____
_____

Exercise B-4

Number of Annual Payments to be Received

_____
_____
_____

Exercise B-5

Rate of Interest to be Earned

_____
_____
_____

Number of Annual Investments
_____
_____
_____
_____

Exercise B-7

Cost (Present Value) of Automobile
_____
_____
_____
_____
_____
_____

Exercise B-8

Cash Proceeds from Bond
_____
_____
_____
_____
_____
_____
_____
_____

Exercise B-9

Present Value of Investment
_____
_____
_____
_____

Name _____

(1) _____
_____
_____

(2) _____
_____
_____

Exercise B-11

Amount Borrowed _____
_____
_____
_____
_____

Exercise B-12

	Single Future Payment	Number of Periods	Interest Rate	Table B.1 Value	Amount Borrowed
(a)					
(b)					
(c)					
(d)					
(e)					
(f)					

(1) First Annuity:

_____

_____

_____

_____

_____

_____

_____

_____

Second Annuity:

_____

_____

_____

_____

_____

_____

_____

(2) First Annuity:

_____

_____

_____

_____

Second Annuity:

_____

_____

_____

_____

_____

Exercise B-14

(1) Present Value of Annuity

_____

_____

_____

_____

(2) Present Value of Annuity

_____

_____

_____

(3) Present Value of Annuity

_____

_____

_____

_____

Name _____

Total Accumulated in the Account _____

_____
_____
_____
_____
_____

Exercise B-16

Total Accumulated in the Account _____

_____
_____
_____
_____
_____

Exercise B-17

Future Value of the Fund _____

_____
_____
_____

Exercise B-18

Future Value of Investment _____

_____
_____
_____

Exercise B-19

	Present or Future Value	Single Amount or Annuity	Relevant Table	Interest Rate	Number of Periods
(a)					
(b)					
(c)					
(d)					

NOTES

NOTES

NOTES

NOTES

NOTES

NOTES